U.S. House of Representatives

Telephone Directory
2019

Compiled by
CHERYL L. JOHNSON
Clerk of the House of Representatives
http://clerk.house.gov

Under Direction of the
COMMITTEE ON HOUSE ADMINISTRATION
Suite 1309 Longworth HOB
Washington, DC 20515-6157

ONE HUNDRED SIXTEENTH CONGRESS

Zoe Lofgren, CA, Chairperson
Jamie Raskin, MD, Vice Chairperson
Susan A. Davis, CA
G. K. Butterfield, NC
Marcia L. Fudge, OH
Pete Aguilar, CA

Rodney Davis, IL, Ranking Minority Member
Mark Walker, NC
Barry Loudermilk, GA

Jamie Fleet, Staff Director
Jennifer Daulby, Minority Staff Director

PRINTED ON RECYCLED PAPER

CONTENTS

House Legislative Bell Signals*

Signal	Meaning
1 long ring and a pause, followed by **3** rings	Signals the start or continuation of a notice quorum call. This call is terminated if and when 100 Members appear.
1 long ring	Termination of a notice quorum call.
2 rings	Electronically recorded vote.
2 rings and a pause, followed by **2** rings	Manual roll call vote. The bells will ring again when the Clerk reaches the R's.
2 rings and a pause, followed by **5** rings	First vote under suspension of the rules or on clustered votes. There will be **2** more rings after five minutes. The first vote will take 15 minutes, with successive votes at intervals no shorter than five minutes.
3 rings	Quorum call (possibly converted from a notice quorum call). The bells will ring again in five minutes. Members have 15 minutes to be recorded.
3 rings and a pause, followed by **3** rings	Manual quorum call. The bells will ring again when the Clerk reaches the R's.
3 rings and a pause, followed by **5** rings	Quorum call in the Committee of the Whole. This may be followed by a five-minute recorded vote.
4 rings	Adjournment of the House.
5 rings	Five-minute electronically recorded vote.
6 rings	Recess of the House.
12 rings at two-second intervals	Civil defense warning.

* LIGHTS (WHERE THEY EXIST) WILL CORRESPOND WITH RINGS.

UNITED STATES HOUSE OF REPRESENTATIVES

HOUSE LEADERSHIP

Title	Name	Phone	Room and Bldg.
Speaker	Nancy Pelosi	**225-0100**	**H232 Capitol**
Majority Leader	Steny H. Hoyer	**225-3130**	**H107 Capitol**
Majority Whip	James E. Clyburn	**226-3210**	**H329 Capitol**
Assistant Speaker	Ben Ray Luján	**225-2020**	**H132 Capitol**
Senior Chief Deputy Majority Whip	John Lewis	**225-3801**	**300 CHOB**
Senior Chief Deputy Majority Whip	Janice D. Schakowsky	**225-2111**	**2367 RHOB**
Minority Leader	Kevin McCarthy	**225-4000**	**H204 Capitol**
Minority Whip	Steve Scalise	**225-0197**	**H148 Capitol**

OFFICERS OF THE HOUSE

Title	Name	Phone	Room and Bldg.
Clerk of the House	Cheryl L. Johnson	**225-7000**	**H154 Capitol**
Sergeant at Arms	Paul D. Irving	**225-2456**	**H124 Capitol**
Chief Administrative Officer	Philip G. Kiko	**225-5555**	**HB28 Capitol**
Chaplain of the House	Rev. Patrick J. Conroy	**225-2509**	**HB25 Capitol**

PARTY OFFICERS

Title	Name	Phone	Room and Bldg.
House Democratic Caucus	Hakeem S. Jeffries (Chairman)	**225-1400**	**B245 LHOB**
House Democratic Policy and Communications Committee	David N. Cicilline (Chairman)	**226-8468**	**HB18 Capitol**
House Democratic Steering and Policy Committee	Nancy Pelosi (Chair)	**225-0100**	**H232 Capitol**
House Republican Conference	Liz Cheney (Chair)	**225-5107**	**1420 LHOB**
House Republican Policy Committee	Gary J. Palmer (Chairman)	**225-4921**	**207 CHOB**

CAPITOL OFFICIALS

Title	Name	Phone	Room and Bldg.
Architect of the Capitol (Acting)	Christine Merdon	**228-1793**	**SB16 Capitol**
Attending Physician	Dr. Brian Monahan	**225-5421**	**H166 Capitol**

REPRESENTATIVES

Three-digit room numbers are in the Cannon HOB, four-digit room numbers beginning with 1 are in the Longworth HOB, and four-digit room numbers beginning with 2 are in the Rayburn HOB.

Calls from outside the Capitol complex can be made by dialing (202) 22 plus the five-digit number listed in this directory.

Democrats in roman; Republicans in *italic*; Resident Commissioner and Delegates in **boldface**.

Death or resignation of Member indicated by bold brackets **[ ]**.

Name, State, and District	Phone	Room
OFFICE OF THE NINTH CONGRESSIONAL DISTRICT OF NORTH CAROLINA (NC, 9th)	**51976**	**132**
Abraham, Ralph Lee (LA, 5th)	**58490**	**417**
Adams, Alma S. (NC, 12th)	**51510**	**2436**
Aderholt, Robert B. (AL, 4th)	**54876**	**1203**
Aguilar, Pete (CA, 31st)	**53201**	**109**
Allen, Rick W. (GA, 12th)	**52823**	**2400**
Allred, Colin Z. (TX, 32d)	**52231**	**328**
Amash, Justin (MI, 3d)	**53831**	**106**
Amodei, Mark E. (NV, 2d)	**56155**	**104**
Armstrong, Kelly (ND, al)	**52611**	**1004**
Arrington, Jodey C. (TX, 19th)	**54005**	**1029**
Axne, Cynthia (IA, 3d)	**55476**	**330**
Babin, Brian (TX, 36th)	**51555**	**2236**
Bacon, Don (NE, 2d)	**54155**	**1024**
Baird, James R. (IN, 4th)	**55037**	**532**
Balderson, Troy (OH, 12th)	**55355**	**1221**
Banks, Jim (IN, 3d)	**54436**	**1713**
Barr, Andy (KY, 6th)	**54706**	**2430**
Barragán, Nanette Diaz (CA, 44th)	**58220**	**1030**
Bass, Karen (CA, 37th)	**57084**	**2059**
Beatty, Joyce (OH, 3d)	**54324**	**2303**
Bera, Ami (CA, 7th)	**55716**	**1727**
Bergman, Jack (MI, 1st)	**54735**	**414**
Beyer, Donald S., Jr. (VA, 8th)	**54376**	**1119**
Biggs, Andy (AZ, 5th)	**52635**	**1318**
Bilirakis, Gus M. (FL, 12th)	**55755**	**2227**
Bishop, Rob (UT, 1st)	**50453**	**123**
Bishop, Sanford D., Jr. (GA, 2d)	**53631**	**2407**
Blumenauer, Earl (OR, 3d)	**54811**	**1111**
Blunt Rochester, Lisa (DE, al)	**54165**	**1519**
Bonamici, Suzanne (OR, 1st)	**50855**	**2231**
Bost, Mike (IL, 12th)	**55661**	**1440**
Boyle, Brendan F. (PA, 2d)	**56111**	**1133**
Brady, Kevin (TX, 8th)	**54901**	**1011**
Brindisi, Anthony (NY, 22d)	**53665**	**329**
Brooks, Mo (AL, 5th)	**54801**	**2246**
Brooks, Susan W. (IN, 5th)	**52276**	**2211**
Brown, Anthony G. (MD, 4th)	**58699**	**1323**
Brownley, Julia (CA, 26th)	**55811**	**2262**
Buchanan, Vern (FL, 16th)	**55015**	**2427**
Buck, Ken (CO, 4th)	**54676**	**2455**
Bucshon, Larry (IN, 8th)	**54636**	**2313**
Budd, Ted (NC, 13th)	**54531**	**118**
Burchett, Tim (TN, 2d)	**55435**	**1122**
Burgess, Michael C. (TX, 26th)	**57772**	**2161**
Bustos, Cheri (IL, 17th)	**55905**	**1233**
Butterfield, G. K. (NC, 1st)	**53101**	**2080**
Byrne, Bradley (AL, 1st)	**54931**	**119**
Calvert, Ken (CA, 42d)	**51986**	**2205**
Carbajal, Salud O. (CA, 24th)	**53601**	**1431**
Cárdenas, Tony (CA, 29th)	**56131**	**2438**
Carson, André (IN, 7th)	**54011**	**2135**
Carter, Earl L. "Buddy" (GA, 1st)	**55831**	**2432**
Carter, John R. (TX, 31st)	**53864**	**2110**
Cartwright, Matt (PA, 8th)	**55546**	**1034**
Case, Ed (HI, 1st)	**52726**	**2443**
Casten, Sean (IL, 6th)	**54561**	**429**
Castor, Kathy (FL, 14th)	**53376**	**2052**
Castro, Joaquin (TX, 20th)	**53236**	**2241**
Chabot, Steve (OH, 1st)	**52216**	**2408**
Cheney, Liz (WY, al)	**52311**	**416**
Chu, Judy (CA, 27th)	**55464**	**2423**
Cicilline, David N. (RI, 1st)	**54911**	**2233**
Cisneros, Gilbert Ray, Jr. (CA, 39th)	**54111**	**431**
Clark, Katherine M. (MA, 5th)	**52836**	**2448**
Clarke, Yvette D. (NY, 9th)	**56231**	**2058**
Clay, Wm. Lacy (MO, 1st)	**52406**	**2428**
Cleaver, Emanuel (MO, 5th)	**54535**	**2335**
Cline, Ben (VA, 6th)	**55431**	**1009**
Cloud, Michael (TX, 27th)	**57742**	**1314**
Clyburn, James E. (SC, 6th)	**53315**	**200**
Cohen, Steve (TN, 9th)	**53265**	**2104**
Cole, Tom (OK, 4th)	**56165**	**2207**
Collins, Chris (NY, 27th)	**55265**	**2243**
Collins, Doug (GA, 9th)	**59893**	**1504**
Comer, James (KY, 1st)	**53115**	**1037**
Conaway, K. Michael (TX, 11th)	**53605**	**2469**
Connolly, Gerald E. (VA, 11th)	**51492**	**2238**
Cook, Paul (CA, 8th)	**55861**	**1027**
Cooper, Jim (TN, 5th)	**54311**	**1536**
Correa, J. Luis (CA, 46th)	**52965**	**1039**
Costa, Jim (CA, 16th)	**53341**	**2081**

REPRESENTATIVES

Name, State, and District	Phone	Room
Courtney, Joe (CT, 2d)	**52076**	**2332**
Cox, TJ (CA, 21st)	**54695**	**1728**
Craig, Angie (MN, 2d)	**52271**	**1523**
Crawford, Eric A. "Rick" (AR, 1st)	**54076**	**2422**
Crenshaw, Dan (TX, 2d)	**56565**	**413**
Crist, Charlie (FL, 13th)	**55961**	**215**
Crow, Jason (CO, 6th)	**57882**	**1229**
Cuellar, Henry (TX, 28th)	**51640**	**2372**
Cummings, Elijah E. (MD, 7th)	**54741**	**2163**
Cunningham, Joe (SC, 1st)	**53176**	**423**
Curtis, John R. (UT, 3d)	**57751**	**125**
Davids, Sharice (KS, 3d)	**52865**	**1541**
Davidson, Warren (OH, 8th)	**56205**	**1107**
Davis, Danny K. (IL, 7th)	**55006**	**2159**
Davis, Rodney (IL, 13th)	**52371**	**1740**
Davis, Susan A. (CA, 53d)	**52040**	**1214**
Dean, Madeleine (PA, 4th)	**54731**	**129**
DeFazio, Peter A. (OR, 4th)	**56416**	**2134**
DeGette, Diana (CO, 1st)	**54431**	**2111**
DeLauro, Rosa L. (CT, 3d)	**53661**	**2413**
DelBene, Suzan K. (WA, 1st)	**56311**	**2330**
Delgado, Antonio (NY, 19th)	**55614**	**1007**
Demings, Val Butler (FL, 10th)	**52176**	**217**
DeSaulnier, Mark (CA, 11th)	**52095**	**503**
DesJarlais, Scott (TN, 4th)	**56831**	**2301**
Deutch, Theodore E. (FL, 22d)	**53001**	**2447**
Diaz-Balart, Mario (FL, 25th)	**54211**	**404**
Dingell, Debbie (MI, 12th)	**54071**	**116**
Doggett, Lloyd (TX, 35th)	**54865**	**2307**
Doyle, Michael F. (PA, 18th)	**52135**	**306**
Duffy, Sean P. (WI, 7th)	**53365**	**1714**
Duncan, Jeff (SC, 3d)	**55301**	**2229**
Dunn, Neal P. (FL, 2d)	**55235**	**316**
Emmer, Tom (MN, 6th)	**52331**	**315**
Engel, Eliot L. (NY, 16th)	**52464**	**2426**
Escobar, Veronica (TX, 16th)	**54831**	**1505**
Eshoo, Anna G. (CA, 18th)	**58104**	**202**
Espaillat, Adriano (NY, 13th)	**54365**	**1630**
Estes, Ron (KS, 4th)	**56216**	**1524**
Evans, Dwight (PA, 3d)	**54001**	**1105**
Ferguson, A. Drew, IV (GA, 3d)	**55901**	**1032**
Finkenauer, Abby (IA, 1st)	**52911**	**124**
Fitzpatrick, Brian K. (PA, 1st)	**54276**	**1722**
Fleischmann, Charles J. "Chuck" (TN, 3d)	**53271**	**2410**
Fletcher, Lizzie (TX, 7th)	**52571**	**1429**
Flores, Bill (TX, 17th)	**56105**	**2228**
Fortenberry, Jeff (NE, 1st)	**54806**	**1514**
Foster, Bill (IL, 11th)	**53515**	**2366**
Foxx, Virginia (NC, 5th)	**52071**	**2462**
Frankel, Lois (FL, 21st)	**59890**	**2305**
Fudge, Marcia L. (OH, 11th)	**57032**	**2344**
Fulcher, Russ (ID, 1st)	**56611**	**1520**
Gabbard, Tulsi (HI, 2d)	**54906**	**1433**
Gaetz, Matt (FL, 1st)	**54136**	**1721**
Gallagher, Mike (WI, 8th)	**55665**	**1230**
Gallego, Ruben (AZ, 7th)	**54065**	**1131**
Garamendi, John (CA, 3d)	**51880**	**2368**
García, Jesús G. "Chuy" (IL, 4th)	**58203**	**530**
Garcia, Sylvia R. (TX, 29th)	**51688**	**1620**
Gianforte, Greg (MT, al)	**53211**	**1222**
Gibbs, Bob (OH, 7th)	**56265**	**2446**
Gohmert, Louie (TX, 1st)	**53035**	**2267**
Golden, Jared F. (ME, 2d)	**56306**	**1223**
Gomez, Jimmy (CA, 34th)	**56235**	**1530**
Gonzalez, Anthony (OH, 16th)	**53876**	**1023**
Gonzalez, Vicente (TX, 15th)	**52531**	**113**
González-Colón, Jenniffer (PR, res com)	**52615**	**1609**
Gooden, Lance (TX, 5th)	**53484**	**425**
Gosar, Paul A. (AZ, 4th)	**52315**	**2057**
Gottheimer, Josh (NJ, 5th)	**54465**	**213**
Granger, Kay (TX, 12th)	**55071**	**1026**
Graves, Garret (LA, 6th)	**53901**	**2402**
Graves, Sam (MO, 6th)	**57041**	**1135**
Graves, Tom (GA, 14th)	**55211**	**2078**
Green, Al (TX, 9th)	**57508**	**2347**
Green, Mark E. (TN, 7th)	**52811**	**533**
Griffith, H. Morgan (VA, 9th)	**53861**	**2202**
Grijalva, Raúl M. (AZ, 3d)	**52435**	**1511**
Grothman, Glenn (WI, 6th)	**52476**	**1427**
Guest, Michael (MS, 3d)	**55031**	**230**
Guthrie, Brett (KY, 2d)	**53501**	**2434**
Haaland, Debra A. (NM, 1st)	**56316**	**1237**
Hagedorn, Jim (MN, 1st)	**52472**	**325**
Harder, Josh (CA, 10th)	**54540**	**131**
Harris, Andy (MD, 1st)	**55311**	**2334**
Hartzler, Vicky (MO, 4th)	**52876**	**2235**
Hastings, Alcee L. (FL, 20th)	**51313**	**2353**
Hayes, Jahana (CT, 5th)	**54476**	**1415**
Heck, Denny (WA, 10th)	**59740**	**2452**
Hern, Kevin (OK, 1st)	**52211**	**1019**
Herrera Beutler, Jaime (WA, 3d)	**53536**	**2352**
Hice, Jody B. (GA, 10th)	**54101**	**409**
Higgins, Brian (NY, 26th)	**53306**	**2459**
Higgins, Clay (LA, 3d)	**52031**	**424**
Hill, J. French (AR, 2d)	**52506**	**1533**
Hill, Katie (CA, 25th)	**51956**	**1130**
Himes, James A. (CT, 4th)	**55541**	**1227**
Holding, George (NC, 2d)	**53032**	**1110**
Hollingsworth, Trey (IN, 9th)	**55315**	**1641**
Horn, Kendra S. (OK, 5th)	**52132**	**415**
Horsford, Steven (NV, 4th)	**59894**	**1330**
Houlahan, Chrissy (PA, 6th)	**54315**	**1218**
Hoyer, Steny H. (MD, 5th)	**54131**	**1705**
Hudson, Richard (NC, 8th)	**53715**	**2112**
Huffman, Jared (CA, 2d)	**55161**	**1527**
Huizenga, Bill (MI, 2d)	**54401**	**2232**
Hunter, Duncan (CA, 50th)	**55672**	**2429**
Hurd, Will (TX, 23d)	**54511**	**317**
Jackson Lee, Sheila (TX, 18th)	**53816**	**2079**
Jayapal, Pramila (WA, 7th)	**53106**	**1510**
Jeffries, Hakeem S. (NY, 8th)	**55936**	**2433**
Johnson, Bill (OH, 6th)	**55705**	**2336**

U.S. HOUSE OF REPRESENTATIVES

Name, State, and District	Phone	Room
Johnson, Dusty (SD, al)	**52801**	**1508**
Johnson, Eddie Bernice (TX, 30th)	**58885**	**2306**
Johnson, Henry C. "Hank", Jr. (GA, 4th)	**51605**	**2240**
Johnson, Mike (LA, 4th)	**52777**	**418**
[*Jones, Walter B.*] (NC, 3d)	**53415**	**2333**
Jordan, Jim (OH, 4th)	**52676**	**2056**
Joyce, David P. (OH, 14th)	**55731**	**1124**
Joyce, John (PA, 13th)	**52431**	**1337**
Kaptur, Marcy (OH, 9th)	**54146**	**2186**
Katko, John (NY, 24th)	**53701**	**2457**
Keating, William R. (MA, 9th)	**53111**	**2351**
Keller, Fred (PA, 12th)	**53731**	**1717**
Kelly, Mike (PA, 16th)	**55406**	**1707**
Kelly, Robin L. (IL, 2d)	**50773**	**2416**
Kelly, Trent (MS, 1st)	**54306**	**1005**
Kennedy, Joseph P., III (MA, 4th)	**55931**	**304**
Khanna, Ro (CA, 17th)	**52631**	**221**
Kildee, Daniel T. (MI, 5th)	**53611**	**203**
Kilmer, Derek (WA, 6th)	**55916**	**1410**
Kim, Andy (NJ, 3d)	**54765**	**1516**
Kind, Ron (WI, 3d)	**55506**	**1502**
King, Peter T. (NY, 2d)	**57896**	**302**
King, Steve (IA, 4th)	**54426**	**2210**
Kinzinger, Adam (IL, 16th)	**53635**	**2245**
Kirkpatrick, Ann (AZ, 2d)	**52542**	**309**
Krishnamoorthi, Raja (IL, 8th)	**53711**	**115**
Kuster, Ann M. (NH, 2d)	**55206**	**320**
Kustoff, David (TN, 8th)	**54714**	**523**
LaHood, Darin (IL, 18th)	**56201**	**1424**
LaMalfa, Doug (CA, 1st)	**53076**	**322**
Lamb, Conor (PA, 17th)	**52301**	**1224**
Lamborn, Doug (CO, 5th)	**54422**	**2371**
Langevin, James R. (RI, 2d)	**52735**	**2077**
Larsen, Rick (WA, 2d)	**52605**	**2113**
Larson, John B. (CT, 1st)	**52265**	**1501**
Latta, Robert E. (OH, 5th)	**56405**	**2467**
Lawrence, Brenda L. (MI, 14th)	**55802**	**2463**
Lawson, Al, Jr. (FL, 5th)	**50123**	**1406**
Lee, Barbara (CA, 13th)	**52661**	**2470**
Lee, Susie (NV, 3d)	**53252**	**522**
Lesko, Debbie (AZ, 8th)	**54576**	**1113**
Levin, Andy (MI, 9th)	**54961**	**228**
Levin, Mike (CA, 49th)	**53906**	**1626**
Lewis, John (GA, 5th)	**53801**	**300**
Lieu, Ted (CA, 33d)	**53976**	**403**
Lipinski, Daniel (IL, 3d)	**55701**	**2346**
Loebsack, David (IA, 2d)	**56576**	**1211**
Lofgren, Zoe (CA, 19th)	**53072**	**1401**
Long, Billy (MO, 7th)	**56536**	**2454**
Loudermilk, Barry (GA, 11th)	**52931**	**422**
Lowenthal, Alan S. (CA, 47th)	**57924**	**108**
Lowey, Nita M. (NY, 17th)	**56506**	**2365**
Lucas, Frank D. (OK, 3d)	**55565**	**2405**
Luetkemeyer, Blaine (MO, 3d)	**52956**	**2230**
Luján, Ben Ray (NM, 3d)	**56190**	**2323**
Luria, Elaine G. (VA, 2d)	**54215**	**534**
Lynch, Stephen F. (MA, 8th)	**58273**	**2109**
Malinowski, Tom (NJ, 7th)	**55361**	**426**
Maloney, Carolyn B. (NY, 12th)	**57944**	**2308**
Maloney, Sean Patrick (NY, 18th)	**55441**	**2331**
Marchant, Kenny (TX, 24th)	**56605**	**2304**
Marshall, Roger W. (KS, 1st)	**52715**	**312**
Massie, Thomas (KY, 4th)	**53465**	**2453**
Mast, Brian J. (FL, 18th)	**53026**	**2182**
Matsui, Doris O. (CA, 6th)	**57163**	**2311**
McAdams, Ben (UT, 4th)	**53011**	**130**
McBath, Lucy (GA, 6th)	**54501**	**1513**
McCarthy, Kevin (CA, 23d)	**52915**	**2468**
McCaul, Michael T. (TX, 10th)	**52401**	**2001**
McClintock, Tom (CA, 4th)	**52511**	**2312**
McCollum, Betty (MN, 4th)	**56631**	**2256**
McEachin, A. Donald (VA, 4th)	**56365**	**314**
McGovern, James P. (MA, 2d)	**56101**	**408**
McHenry, Patrick T. (NC, 10th)	**52576**	**2004**
McKinley, David B. (WV, 1st)	**54172**	**2239**
McNerney, Jerry (CA, 9th)	**51947**	**2265**
Meadows, Mark (NC, 11th)	**56401**	**2160**
Meeks, Gregory W. (NY, 5th)	**53461**	**2310**
Meng, Grace (NY, 6th)	**52601**	**2209**
Meuser, Daniel (PA, 9th)	**56511**	**326**
Miller, Carol D. (WV, 3d)	**53452**	**1605**
Mitchell, Paul (MI, 10th)	**52106**	**211**
Moolenaar, John R. (MI, 4th)	**53561**	**117**
Mooney, Alexander X. (WV, 2d)	**52711**	**2440**
Moore, Gwen (WI, 4th)	**54572**	**2252**
Morelle, Joseph D. (NY, 25th)	**53615**	**1317**
Moulton, Seth (MA, 6th)	**58020**	**1127**
Mucarsel-Powell, Debbie (FL, 26th)	**52778**	**114**
Mullin, Markwayne (OK, 2d)	**52701**	**2421**
Murphy, Stephanie N. (FL, 7th)	**54035**	**1710**
Nadler, Jerrold (NY, 10th)	**55635**	**2132**
Napolitano, Grace F. (CA, 32d)	**55256**	**1610**
Neal, Richard E. (MA, 1st)	**55601**	**2309**
Neguse, Joe (CO, 2d)	**52161**	**1419**
Newhouse, Dan (WA, 4th)	**55816**	**1414**
Norcross, Donald (NJ, 1st)	**56501**	**2437**
Norman, Ralph (SC, 5th)	**55501**	**319**
Norton, Eleanor Holmes (DC, dl)	**58050**	**2136**
Nunes, Devin (CA, 22d)	**52523**	**1013**
Ocasio-Cortez, Alexandria (NY, 14th)	**53965**	**229**
O'Halleran, Tom (AZ, 1st)	**53361**	**324**
Olson, Pete (TX, 22d)	**55951**	**2133**
Omar, Ilhan (MN, 5th)	**54755**	**1517**
Palazzo, Steven M. (MS, 4th)	**55772**	**2349**
Pallone, Frank, Jr. (NJ, 6th)	**54671**	**2107**
Palmer, Gary J. (AL, 6th)	**54921**	**207**
Panetta, Jimmy (CA, 20th)	**52861**	**212**
Pappas, Chris (NH, 1st)	**55456**	**323**
Pascrell, Bill, Jr. (NJ, 9th)	**55751**	**2409**
Payne, Donald M., Jr. (NJ, 10th)	**53436**	**103**
Pelosi, Nancy (CA, 12th)	**54965**	**1236**
Pence, Greg (IN, 6th)	**53021**	**222**

REPRESENTATIVES

Name, State, and District	Phone	Room
Perlmutter, Ed (CO, 7th)	**52645**	**1226**
Perry, Scott (PA, 10th)	**55836**	**1207**
Peters, Scott H. (CA, 52d)	**50508**	**2338**
Peterson, Collin C. (MN, 7th)	**52165**	**2204**
Phillips, Dean (MN, 3d)	**52871**	**1305**
Pingree, Chellie (ME, 1st)	**56116**	**2162**
Plaskett, Stacey E. (VI, dl)	**51790**	**2404**
Pocan, Mark (WI, 2d)	**52906**	**1421**
Porter, Katie (CA, 45th)	**55611**	**1117**
Posey, Bill (FL, 8th)	**53671**	**2150**
Pressley, Ayanna (MA, 7th)	**55111**	**1108**
Price, David E. (NC, 4th)	**51784**	**2108**
Quigley, Mike (IL, 5th)	**54061**	**2458**
Radewagen, Aumua Amata Coleman (AS, dl)	**58577**	**1339**
Raskin, Jamie (MD, 8th)	**55341**	**412**
Ratcliffe, John (TX, 4th)	**56673**	**223**
Reed, Tom (NY, 23d)	**53161**	**2263**
Reschenthaler, Guy (PA, 14th)	**52065**	**531**
Rice, Kathleen M. (NY, 4th)	**55516**	**2435**
Rice, Tom (SC, 7th)	**59895**	**512**
Richmond, Cedric L. (LA, 2d)	**56636**	**506**
Riggleman, Denver (VA, 5th)	**54711**	**1022**
Roby, Martha (AL, 2d)	**52901**	**504**
Rodgers, Cathy McMorris (WA, 5th)	**52006**	**1035**
Roe, David P. (TN, 1st)	**56356**	**102**
Rogers, Harold (KY, 5th)	**54601**	**2406**
Rogers, Mike (AL, 3d)	**53261**	**2184**
Rooney, Francis (FL, 19th)	**52536**	**120**
Rose, John W. (TN, 6th)	**54231**	**1232**
Rose, Max (NY, 11th)	**53371**	**1529**
Rouda, Harley (CA, 48th)	**52415**	**2300**
Rouzer, David (NC, 7th)	**52731**	**2439**
Roy, Chip (TX, 21st)	**54236**	**1319**
Roybal-Allard, Lucille (CA, 40th)	**51766**	**2083**
Ruiz, Raul (CA, 36th)	**55330**	**2342**
Ruppersberger, C. A. Dutch (MD, 2d)	**53061**	**2206**
Rush, Bobby L. (IL, 1st)	**54372**	**2188**
Rutherford, John H. (FL, 4th)	**52501**	**1711**
Ryan, Tim (OH, 13th)	**55261**	**1126**
Sablan, Gregorio Kilili Camacho (MP, dl)	**52646**	**2411**
Sánchez, Linda T. (CA, 38th)	**56676**	**2329**
San Nicolas, Michael F. Q. (GU, dl)	**51188**	**1632**
Sarbanes, John P. (MD, 3d)	**54016**	**2370**
Scalise, Steve (LA, 1st)	**53015**	**2049**
Scanlon, Mary Gay (PA, 5th)	**52011**	**1535**
Schakowsky, Janice D. (IL, 9th)	**52111**	**2367**
Schiff, Adam B. (CA, 28th)	**54176**	**2269**
Schneider, Bradley Scott (IL, 10th)	**54835**	**1432**
Schrader, Kurt (OR, 5th)	**55711**	**2431**
Schrier, Kim (WA, 8th)	**57761**	**1123**
Schweikert, David (AZ, 6th)	**52190**	**1526**
Scott, Austin (GA, 8th)	**56531**	**2417**
Scott, David (GA, 13th)	**52939**	**225**
Scott, Robert C. “Bobby” (VA, 3d)	**58351**	**1201**
Sensenbrenner, F. James, Jr. (WI, 5th)	**55101**	**2449**
Serrano, José E. (NY, 15th)	**54361**	**2354**
Sewell, Terri A. (AL, 7th)	**52665**	**2201**
Shalala, Donna E. (FL, 27th)	**53931**	**1320**
Sherman, Brad (CA, 30th)	**55911**	**2181**
Sherrill, Mikie (NJ, 11th)	**55034**	**1208**
Shimkus, John (IL, 15th)	**55271**	**2217**
Simpson, Michael K. (ID, 2d)	**55531**	**2084**
Sires, Albio (NJ, 8th)	**57919**	**2268**
Slotkin, Elissa (MI, 8th)	**54872**	**1531**
Smith, Adam (WA, 9th)	**58901**	**2264**
Smith, Adrian (NE, 3d)	**56435**	**502**
Smith, Christopher H. (NJ, 4th)	**53765**	**2373**
Smith, Jason (MO, 8th)	**54404**	**2418**
Smucker, Lloyd (PA, 11th)	**52411**	**127**
Soto, Darren (FL, 9th)	**59889**	**1507**
Spanberger, Abigail Davis (VA, 7th)	**52815**	**1239**
Spano, Ross (FL, 15th)	**51252**	**224**
Speier, Jackie (CA, 14th)	**53531**	**2465**
Stanton, Greg (AZ, 9th)	**59888**	**128**
Stauber, Pete (MN, 8th)	**56211**	**126**
Stefanik, Elise M. (NY, 21st)	**54611**	**318**
Steil, Bryan (WI, 1st)	**53031**	**1408**
Steube, W. Gregory (FL, 17th)	**55792**	**521**
Stevens, Haley M. (MI, 11th)	**58171**	**227**
Stewart, Chris (UT, 2d)	**59730**	**2242**
Stivers, Steve (OH, 15th)	**52015**	**2234**
Suozzi, Thomas R. (NY, 3d)	**53335**	**214**
Swalwell, Eric (CA, 15th)	**55065**	**407**
Takano, Mark (CA, 41st)	**52305**	**420**
Taylor, Van (TX, 3d)	**54201**	**1404**
Thompson, Bennie G. (MS, 2d)	**55876**	**2466**
Thompson, Glenn (PA, 15th)	**55121**	**400**
Thompson, Mike (CA, 5th)	**53311**	**406**
Thornberry, Mac (TX, 13th)	**53706**	**2208**
Timmons, William R., IV (SC, 4th)	**56030**	**313**
Tipton, Scott R. (CO, 3d)	**54761**	**218**
Titus, Dina (NV, 1st)	**55965**	**2464**
Tlaib, Rashida (MI, 13th)	**55126**	**1628**
Tonko, Paul (NY, 20th)	**55076**	**2369**
Torres, Norma J. (CA, 35th)	**56161**	**2444**
Torres Small, Xochitl (NM, 2d)	**52365**	**430**
Trahan, Lori (MA, 3d)	**53411**	**1616**
Trone, David J. (MD, 6th)	**52721**	**1213**
Turner, Michael R. (OH, 10th)	**56465**	**2082**
Underwood, Lauren (IL, 14th)	**52976**	**1118**
Upton, Fred (MI, 6th)	**53761**	**2183**
Van Drew, Jefferson (NJ, 2d)	**56572**	**331**
Vargas, Juan (CA, 51st)	**58045**	**2244**
Veasey, Marc A. (TX, 33d)	**59897**	**2348**
Vela, Filemon (TX, 34th)	**59901**	**307**
Velázquez, Nydia M. (NY, 7th)	**52361**	**2302**
Visclosky, Peter J. (IN, 1st)	**52461**	**2328**
Wagner, Ann (MO, 2d)	**51621**	**2350**
Walberg, Tim (MI, 7th)	**56276**	**2266**
Walden, Greg (OR, 2d)	**56730**	**2185**
Walker, Mark (NC, 6th)	**53065**	**1725**

U.S. HOUSE OF REPRESENTATIVES

Name, State, and District	Phone	Room
Walorski, Jackie (IN, 2d)	**53915**	**419**
Waltz, Michael (FL, 6th)	**52706**	**216**
Wasserman Schultz, Debbie (FL, 23d)	**57931**	**1114**
Waters, Maxine (CA, 43d)	**52201**	**2221**
Watkins, Steve (KS, 2d)	**56601**	**1205**
Watson Coleman, Bonnie (NJ, 12th)	**55801**	**2442**
Weber, Randy K., Sr. (TX, 14th)	**52831**	**107**
Webster, Daniel (FL, 11th)	**51002**	**1210**
Welch, Peter (VT, al)	**54115**	**2187**
Wenstrup, Brad R. (OH, 2d)	**53164**	**2419**
Westerman, Bruce (AR, 4th)	**53772**	**209**
Wexton, Jennifer (VA, 10th)	**55136**	**1217**
Wild, Susan (PA, 7th)	**56411**	**1607**
Williams, Roger (TX, 25th)	**59896**	**1708**
Wilson, Frederica S. (FL, 24th)	**54506**	**2445**
Wilson, Joe (SC, 2d)	**52452**	**1436**
Wittman, Robert J. (VA, 1st)	**54261**	**2055**
Womack, Steve (AR, 3d)	**54301**	**2412**
Woodall, Rob (GA, 7th)	**54272**	**1724**
Wright, Ron (TX, 6th)	**52002**	**428**
Yarmuth, John A. (KY, 3d)	**55401**	**402**
Yoho, Ted S. (FL, 3d)	**55744**	**1730**
Young, Don (AK, al)	**55765**	**2314**
Zeldin, Lee M. (NY, 1st)	**53826**	**2441**

HOUSE COMMITTEES

Three-digit room numbers are in the Cannon HOB or the Ford HOB, as indicated. Four-digit room numbers beginning with 1 are in the Longworth HOB; with 2, the Rayburn HOB; and with 3, 4, 5, or 6, the O'Neill HOB. Capitol room numbers begin with SB, ST, HB, HC, and HT or with H or S, followed by three digits. Room numbers beginning with CVC, HVC, or SVC are in the Capitol Visitor Center. Room numbers beginning with SD are in the Dirksen SOB, room numbers beginning with SH are in the Hart SOB, and room numbers beginning with SR are in the Russell SOB.

Calls from outside the Capitol complex can be made by dialing (202) 22 plus the five-digit number listed in this directory.

Standing Committees

	Phone	Room
Agriculture	**52171**	**1301**
Biotechnology, Horticulture, and Research	**52171**	**1301**
Commodity Exchanges, Energy, and Credit	**52171**	**1301**
Conservation and Forestry	**52171**	**1301**
General Farm Commodities and Risk Management	**52171**	**1301**
Livestock and Foreign Agriculture	**52171**	**1301**
Nutrition, Oversight, and Department Operations	**52171**	**1301**
Appropriations	**52771**	**H307**
Agriculture, Rural Development, Food and Drug Administration, and Related Agencies	**52638**	**2362A**
Commerce, Justice, Science, and Related Agencies	**53351**	**H310**
Defense	**52847**	**H405**
Energy and Water Development, and Related Agencies	**53421**	**2362B**
Financial Services and General Government	**57245**	**2000**
Homeland Security	**55834**	**2006**
Interior, Environment, and Related Agencies	**53081**	**2007**
Labor, Health and Human Services, Education, and Related Agencies	**53508**	**2358B**
Legislative Branch	**67252**	**H306**
Military Construction, Veterans Affairs, and Related Agencies	**53047**	**HT2**
State, Foreign Operations, and Related Programs	**52041**	**HT2**
Transportation, and Housing and Urban Development, and Related Agencies	**52141**	**2358A**
Armed Services	**54151**	**2216**
Intelligence and Emerging Threats and Capabilities	**62843**	**2340**
Military Personnel	**57560**	**2340**
Readiness	**68979**	**2340**
Seapower and Projection Forces	**62211**	**2340**
Strategic Forces	**51967**	**2340**
Tactical Air and Land Forces	**54440**	**2340**
Budget (CHOB)	**67200**	**204E**
Education and Labor	**53725**	**2176**
Civil Rights and Human Services	**53725**	**2176**
Early Childhood, Elementary, and Secondary Education	**53725**	**2176**
Health, Employment, Labor, and Pensions	**53725**	**2176**
Higher Education and Workforce Investment	**53725**	**2176**
Workforce Protections	**53725**	**2176**

HOUSE COMMITTEES

	Phone	Room
Energy and Commerce	**52927**	**2125**
Communications and Technology	**52927**	**2125**
Consumer Protection and Commerce	**52927**	**2125**
Energy	**52927**	**2125**
Environment and Climate Change	**52927**	**2125**
Health	**52927**	**2125**
Oversight and Investigations	**52927**	**2125**
Ethics	**57103**	**1015**
Financial Services	**54247**	**2129**
Consumer Protection and Financial Institutions	**54247**	**2129**
Diversity and Inclusion	**54247**	**2129**
Housing, Community Development, and Insurance	**54247**	**2129**
Investor Protection, Entrepreneurship, and Capital Markets	**54247**	**2129**
National Security, International Development, and Monetary Policy	**54247**	**2129**
Oversight and Investigations	**54247**	**2129**
Foreign Affairs	**55021**	**2170**
Africa, Global Health, Global Human Rights, and International Organizations	**61500**	**2170**
Asia, the Pacific, and Nonproliferation	**66434**	**2170**
Europe, Eurasia, Energy, and the Environment	**55021**	**2170**
Middle East, North Africa, and International Terrorism	**67812**	**2170**
Oversight and Investigations	**55021**	**2170**
Western Hemisphere, Civilian Security, and Trade	**53345**	**2170**
Homeland Security (FHOB)	**62616**	**176**
Border Security, Facilitation, and Operations (FHOB)	**62616**	**176**
Cybersecurity, Infrastructure Protection, and Innovation (FHOB)	**62616**	**176**
Emergency Preparedness, Response, and Recovery (FHOB)	**62616**	**176**
Intelligence and Counterterrorism (FHOB)	**62616**	**176**
Oversight, Management, and Accountability (FHOB)	**62616**	**176**
Transportation and Maritime Security (FHOB)	**62616**	**176**
House Administration	**52061**	**1309**
Elections	**52061**	**1309**
Judiciary	**53951**	**2138**
Antitrust, Commercial, and Administrative Law	**67680**	**6240**
Courts, Intellectual Property, and the Internet	**55741**	**6310**
Crime, Terrorism and Homeland Security	**55727**	**6340**
Immigration and Citizenship	**53926**	**6320**
The Constitution, Civil Rights, and Civil Liberties	**53951**	**2138**
Natural Resources	**56065**	**1324**
Energy and Mineral Resources	**56065**	**1522**
For Indigenous Peoples of the United States	**56065**	**1331**
National Parks, Forests, and Public Lands	**56065**	**1328**
Oversight and Investigations (FHOB)	**56065**	**186**
Water, Oceans, and Wildlife	**56065**	**1332**
Oversight and Reform	**55051**	**2157**
Civil Rights and Civil Liberties	**55051**	**6440**
Economic and Consumer Policy	**55051**	**6430**

	Phone	Room
Environment	**55051**	**6440**
Government Operations	**55051**	**6460**
National Security	**55051**	**6470**
Rules	**59091**	**H312**
Expedited Procedures	**59091**	**H312**
Legislative and Budget Process	**59091**	**H312**
Rules and Organization of the House	**59091**	**H312**
Science, Space, and Technology	**56375**	**2321**
Energy	**56375**	**2321**
Environment	**56375**	**2321**
Investigations and Oversight	**56375**	**2321**
Research and Technology	**56375**	**2321**
Space and Aeronautics	**56375**	**2321**
Small Business	**54038**	**2361**
Contracting and Infrastructure	**54038**	**2361**
Economic Growth, Tax and Capital Access	**54038**	**2361**
Innovation and Workforce Development	**54038**	**2361**
Investigations, Oversight and Regulations	**54038**	**2361**
Rural Development, Agriculture, Trade and Entrepreneurship	**54038**	**2361**
Transportation and Infrastructure	**54472**	**2165**
Aviation	**54472**	**2165**
Coast Guard and Maritime Transportation	**54472**	**2165**
Economic Development, Public Buildings, and Emergency Management	**54472**	**2165**
Highways and Transit	**54472**	**2165**
Railroads, Pipelines, and Hazardous Materials	**54472**	**2165**
Water Resources and Environment	**54472**	**2165**
Veterans' Affairs (LHOB)	**59756**	**B234**
Disability Assistance and Memorial Affairs (LHOB)	**59756**	**B234**
Economic Opportunity (LHOB)	**59756**	**B234**
Health (LHOB)	**59756**	**B234**
Oversight and Investigations (LHOB)	**59756**	**B234**
Technology Modernization (LHOB)	**59756**	**B234**
Ways and Means	**53625**	**1102**
Health	**53943**	**1104**
Oversight	**53625**	**2018**
Select Revenue Measures	**55522**	**1136**
Social Security	**59263**	**2018**
Trade	**56649**	**1103**
Worker and Family Support	**59263**	**1129**

Select Committees

Permanent Select Committee on Intelligence	**57690**	**HVC304**
Counterterrorism, Counterintelligence, and Counterproliferation	**57690**	**HVC304**
Defense Intelligence and Warfighter Support	**57690**	**HVC304**
Intelligence Modernization and Readiness	**57690**	**HVC304**
Strategic Technologies and Advanced Research	**57690**	**HVC304**
Select Committee on the Climate Crisis (FHOB)	**51106**	**359**

HOUSE COMMITTEES

	Phone	Room
Select Committee on the Modernization of Congress (CHOB)	**51530**	**226**

Joint Committees

	Phone	Room
Economic	**45171**	**SD-G01**
Library	**46352**	**SR-305**
Printing	**52061**	**1309**
Taxation		
(FHOB)	**53621**	**502**
(DSOB)	**45561**	**SD-G18**

ALPHABETICAL STAFF LISTING

Three-digit room numbers are in the Cannon HOB or the Ford HOB, as indicated. Four-digit room numbers beginning with 1 are in the Longworth HOB; with 2, the Rayburn HOB; and with 3, 4, 5, or 6, the O'Neill HOB. Capitol room numbers begin with SB, ST, HB, HC, and HT or with H or S, followed by three digits. Room numbers beginning with CVC, HVC, or SVC are in the Capitol Visitor Center. Room numbers beginning with SD are in the Dirksen SOB, room numbers beginning with SH are in the Hart SOB, and room numbers beginning with SR are in the Russell SOB.

Calls from outside the Capitol complex can be made by dialing (202) 22 plus the five-digit number listed in this directory.

Abadie, Madeline (CUELLAR) SCHEDULER 2209 **51640**
Abbasi, Lana (TAKANO) PRESS SECY **951-222-0203**
Abbott, Jacob (SÁNCHEZ) LEGIS CORRES 2329 **56676**
Abbott, Jessica (CAO/OFFICE OF THE CHIEF HUMAN RESOURCES OFFICER) ANALYST 102 FHOB **65987**
Abbott, Jim (SGT AT ARMS/GARAGES & PARKING) DIRECTOR G2-28 **56749**
Abboud, Khalil (CMTE-HOUSE ADMIN) DPTY STAFF DIR 1309 **52061**
Abel, Sarah (LEE, SUSIE) COMMUNICATIONS DIR 522 CHOB **53252**
Abel, Timothy (CAO/HIR – IT CUSTOMER SOLUTIONS) SR TECH SUPPORT REP 604 FHOB **61143**
Abernathy, Pamela (ADERHOLT) CONSTIT SVCS REP **256-546-0201**
Abeyta, Juan “Buddy” (LUJÁN) STAFF ASST **505-994-0499**
Abner, Joe (CHABOT) DIST DIR **513-684-2723**
Abonyi, Clement (CMTE-FINANCIAL SVCS) COORD - MBR SVCS & OUTREACH 2129 **57141**
Abouchar, Keith (MAJ LEADER) SR POLICY ADVISOR H107 **53130**
Abraham, Katrina (WATKINS) OFFICE MGR/ DIST SCHEDULER **785-234-5966**
Abraham, Sabey (KRISHNAMOORTHI) DIST DIR **847-413-1959**
Abrahamian, Arlet (LOFGREN) COUNSEL/LEGIS STAFF 1401 **53072**
Abramowitz, David (CMTE-FINANCIAL SVCS) PARLIAMENTARIAN 2129 **54247**
Abrams, Scott (SHERMAN) DIST DIR **818-501-9200**
Abreu, Randy (OCASIO-CORTEZ) ADVISOR 229 CHOB **53965**
Abusch, Aviva
(CMTE-FOREIGN AFFAIRS) STAFF ASSOC 5211 **67812**
(DEUTCH) STAFF ASST 2447 **53001**
Acero, Maureen (MCCOLLUM) LEGIS CORRES/LEGIS ASST 2256 **56631**
Aciman, Michael (RICE, KATHLEEN M.) COMMUNICATIONS DIR 2435 **55516**
Acker, Juanita (GROTHMAN) CASEWKR **920-907-0624**
Ackerman, Bootsie (WOMACK) DIST DIR **479-464-0446**
Ackerman, Emily (RESCHENTHALER) LEGIS DIR/DPTY CHIEF OF STAFF 531 CHOB **52065**
Ackerman, Melanie (CMTE-JOINT ECON) RESEARCH ANALYST - DEM SH-804 **80189**
Ackerman, Stephen (FULCHER) LEGIS ASST 1520 **56611**
Acornley, Mark
(CISNEROS) FINANCIAL ADMIN 431 CHOB **54111**
(DUFFY) ADMIN - FINANCE & PAYROLL 1714 **53365**
(LAMALFA) FINANCIAL ADMIN 322 CHOB **53076**
(SHIMKUS) FINANCIAL ADMIN 2217 **55271**
(STAUBER) FINANCIAL ADMIN 126 CHOB **56211**
Acosta, Jose (ESPAILLAT) PRESS AIDE **212-663-3900**
Acosta, Sam (ALLRED) DIR - CONSTIT SVCS **972-972-7949**
Acton, Dana (LOWEY) LEGIS DIR 2365 **56506**
Acuesta, July (CAO/HIR – ENTERPRISE INFRASTRUCT) SR SYS ENGINEER 619 FHOB **571-921-3116**
Adaki, Oren (WILSON, JOE) LEGIS DIR 1436 **52452**
Adams, Chris (FOSTER) CONSTIT ADVOCATE **630-585-7672**
Adams, David (LANGEVIN) STAFF ASST FOR TELEPHONES **401-732-9400**
Adams, Luke (COMMIS ON CHINA) RESEARCH ASSOC 243 FHOB **63766**
Adams, Susan (CMTE-APPRO) PROF STAFF MEMB 1016 **53481**
Adams, Todd (LANGEVIN) CHIEF OF STAFF 2077 **52735**
Adams, Tyler (CLINE) DIST FIELD REP **540-432-2391**
Adamson, Diane (RASKIN) ASST LEGIS CORRES 412 CHOB **55341**
Adekunle, Dorcas (WILD) DPTY CHIEF OF STAFF/LEGIS DIR 1607 **56411**
Adelakun, Deen (CAO/HIR – IT CUSTOMER SOLUTIONS) SR TECH SOLUTIONS ENGINEER 694 FHOB **56002**
Adelstein, Lillian (NORTON) LEGIS CORRES 2136 **58050**
Adeniji, Addie (CAO/HIR – CYBERSECURITY) DIR - INFO ASSURANCE 628A FHOB **61599**
Adesina, Adeola (SWALWELL) LEGIS ASST 407 CHOB **55065**
Adesina, Kellie (CMTE-AGRIC) CHIEF COUNSEL 1301 **52171**
Adiele, Frances (CLEAVER) LEGIS FELLOW 2335 **54535**
Adjei-Koranteng, Araba (LYNCH) STAFF ASST. **617-428-2000**
Adkerson, Elizabeth (LOUDERMILK) SCHEDULER 422 CHOB **52931**
Adkerson, Robert (LOUDERMILK) CHIEF OF STAFF 422 CHOB **52931**
Adkins, Elizabeth (PRICE) STAFF ASST/LEGIS CORRES 2108 **51784**
Adkins, Rick (DUNCAN, JEFF) DIST DIR/DPTY CHIEF OF STAFF **864-224-7401**
Adkins, William (CMTE-APPRO) PROF STAFF MEMB H405 **52847**
Adler, Ann (CASTEN) CHIEF OF STAFF 429 CHOB **54561**
Adler, Jeremy (HOUSE REPUB CONF) COMMUNICATIONS DIR 1420 **55107**

Adler, Lauren (HECK) DPTY DIST DIR **253-533-8332**
Ae, Pulu (RADEWAGEN) DIST DIR **684-633-3601**
Aery, Robert (HERN) DIST DIR **918-935-3222**
Afeefy, Yomna (CLERK/LCS) INFO TECH TESTING ANALYST 2401 **51182**
Afram, Amanda (CAO/HIR – CYBERSECURITY) SR INFO SYS SECUR ANALYST 650 FHOB **66574**
Agdaian, Tigran (GARAMENDI) LEGIS ASST 2368 **51880**
Agonafer, Bethy (MCBATH) DIST OFFICE MGR/ DIST SCHEDULER **470-773-6330**
Agrella, Austin (HURD) LEGIS DIR 317 CHOB **54511**
Aguilar, Birdie (AGUILAR) STAFF ASST **909-890-4445**
Aguilera, Mike (SCHIFF) DIST REP **818-450-2900**
Ahern, Jeanne B (NEAL) AIDE **413-785-0325**
Ahern, Kara
(CHENEY) CHIEF OF STAFF 416 CHOB **52311**
(HOUSE REPUB CONF) CHIEF OF STAFF 1420 **55107**
Ahern, Nolan
(CMTE-ENERGY & COMMERCE) POLICY ADVISOR 2322A **53641**
(WALDEN) LEGIS ASST 2185 **56730**
Ahmad, Fatima (SELECT CMTE-CLIMATE CRISIS) SR COUNSEL 359 FHOB **51106**
Ahmad, Viquar (CAO/OFFICE OF THE CFO) DPTY CHIEF 3140 **64650**
Ahmadi, Jonathan (HILL, KATIE) SR FIELD REP **661-568-4855**
Ahmed, Ahdel (MCNERNEY) FIELD REP **209-476-8552**
Ahmed, Maryam (BEYER) STAFF ASST 1119 **54376**
Ahmed, Muneer (CAO/ENTERPRISE APPLICATIONS) APPLICA SYS ADMIN B65 FHOB **66234**
Ahmed, Zunera (ROSE, MAX) CASEWKR - IMMIGRATION **718-667-3313**
Ahn, Kenneth (BASS) CASEWKR **323-965-1422**
Ahn, Michael (DOGGETT) PRESS ASST/LEGIS ASST 2307 **54865**
Ahrens, Elizabeth (MCBATH) DC SCHEDULER 1513 **54501**
Ahuja, Kalpana (CAO/HIR – HOUSE WEB SVCS) DIRECTOR 636 FHOB **61488**
Aien, Nelta T (SAN NICOLAS) CASEWKR **671-475-6453**
Aiken, Hannah (STEVENS) LEGIS ASST 227 CHOB **58171**
Ainge, Caitlin (TRONE) FIELD REP **301-926-0300**
Aita, Tammy (CARTWRIGHT) DPTY DIST DIR/ DIST SCHEDULER **570-341-1050**
Aita'oto, Tafito (RADEWAGEN) DIST PRESS SECY **684-633-3601**
Aitch, Izmira (MOORE) LEGIS ASST 2252 **54572**
Akhter, Naureen (OCASIO-CORTEZ) DPTY DIST DIR **718-662-5970**
Akinyemi, Florence (MEEKS) FELLOW 2310 **53461**
Akowuah, Emmanuel (INSPECTOR GENERAL) AUDITOR - INFO SYS AUDITS 386 FHOB **61250**
Akula, Mallik (CAO/ENTERPRISE APPLICATIONS) SR SOFTWARE SPEC B71 FHOB **63365**
Alagood, Kyle (PAYNE) COMMUNICATIONS DIR 103 CHOB **53436**
Alam, Nabeel (LEE, SUSIE) LEGIS ASST 522 CHOB **53252**
Al-Asadi, Shahed (BEATTY) DIST AIDE/STAFF ASST **614-220-0003**
Alatorre, Angelica (PORTER) CASEWK DIR 1117 **55611**
Alavez, Johnny (NEWHOUSE) STAFF ASST 1414 **55816**
Alavi, Alex (LAHOOD) SCHEDULER 1424 **56201**
Alawieh, Abbas (LEVIN, ANDY) LEGIS ASST 228 CHOB **54961**
Al Baghdadi, Jawad (DAVIS, SUSAN A.) COMMUNITY REP **619-280-5353**
Albares, Mike (ROBY) CHIEF OF STAFF 504 CHOB **52901**
Albert, Helen (DAVIS, RODNEY) DIST DIR/DIST SCHEDULER **217-791-6224**
Albert, Katherine (LANGEVIN) DIST SCHEDULER **401-732-9400**
Albertine, Elizabeth (DELAURO) LEGIS DIR 2413 **53661**
Alberts, Marc (CMTE-NATURAL RESOURCES) PROF STAFF 4120 **52761**
Albertson, Julia (KHANNA) DIGITAL PRESS SECY 221 CHOB **52631**
Albrecht, Madison (BURGESS) STAFF ASST 2161 **57772**
Albright, Leslie (CMTE-APPRO) PROF STAFF MEMB 1001 **53481**
Alburger, Anna (JOYCE, DAVID P.) CHIEF OF STAFF 1124 **55731**
Alcala, Sandra (HOUSE DEM CAUCUS) DIR - MEMB SVCS B245 LHOB **51400**
Alcala, Sandra (ESPAILLAT) SHARED EMPLOYEE 1630 **54365**
Alcott, Brooklyn (PANETTA) STAFF ASST **831-424-2229**
Aldous, Julianne (MCADAMS) LEGIS CORRES 130 CHOB **53011**
Alegria, Kate (LIEU) CASEWKR **323-651-1040**
Alejandro, Kristina (ESPAILLAT) DPTY SCHEDULER 1630 **54365**
Alemu, Maron (JEFFRIES) DIST DIR **718-237-2211**
Alexander, Gordon (CAO/HIR – IT CUSTOMER SOLUTIONS) TECH SOLUTIONS ENGINEER 694 FHOB **56002**
Alexander, Kathryn (CLARK) COMMUNICATIONS DIR 2448 **52836**
Alexander, LaVerne (PAYNE) CHIEF OF STAFF/CHIEF POLICY ADVISOR 103 CHOB **53436**
Alexander, Purvis (SGT AT ARMS/POLICE SVCS) LAW ENFORCEMENT COMMUNICATIONS LIAISON COMMAND **49859**
Alexander, Whitley (ROE) PRESS SECY 102 CHOB **56356**
Alexin, Aaron (CLERK/LEGIS OPS) ASST TALLY CLERK HT13 **57347**
Alexis, Matt (CLAY) STAFF ASST 2428 **52406**
Alford, John (SHERMAN) SR FIELD REP **818-501-9200**
Alioto, Nicole (MCNERNEY) CHIEF OF STAFF 2265 **51947**
Alkiek, Ghada (KILDEE) DPTY CHIEF OF STAFF 203 CHOB **53611**
Alkinburg, Kevin (HARRIS) STAFF ASST 2334 **55311**
Allala, Lylianna (JAYAPAL) COORD - OUTREACH **206-674-0040**
Allbrooks, Steve (GREEN, MARK E.) DIST DIR **629-223-6050**
Alldridge, Susan (CLERK/REPORTERS) OFFICIAL REPORTER 1718 **52627**
Allen, Aaron
(CMTE-HOUSE ADMIN) PROF STAFF 1307 **52061**
(COMMIS ON CONG MAILING STDS) PROF STAFF 1307 **59337**
Allen, Amber
(OMAR) FINANCIAL MGR **202-302-5337**
(CMTE-APPRO) FINANCIAL ADMIN H307 **52771**
(DESJARLAIS) FINANCIAL MGR 2301 **56831**
(FOSTER) ADMIN - FINANCE & PAYROLL 2366 **53515**
(FUDGE) FINANCIAL MGR 2344 **57032**
(GRANGER) FINANCIAL MGR 1026 **55071**
Allen, Amber (WALKER) DIST STAFF ASST **336-333-5005**
Allen, Anthony (BARR) DIR - CONSTIT SVCS **859-219-1366**
Allen, Brad (CMTE-APPRO) ADMIN AIDE 2358B **53508**
Allen, Brian (GOHMERT) LEGIS ASST 2267 **53035**
Allen, David (ROBY) LEGIS DIR 504 CHOB **52901**

Allen, Elizabeth (BURGESS) LEGIS ASST 2161 **57772**
Allen, Gabbi (HORN) DIST OFFICE MGR **405-602-3074**
Allen, Justin (GRANGER) FINANCIAL MGR 1026 **55071**
Allen, Katie (KILMER) LEGIS DIR 1410 **55916**
Allen, Keith (CAO/FURNISHINGS) JOURNEYMAN CABINET MAKER WA25 RHOB **58000**
Allen, Lauren (MURPHY) DIST DIR **888-205-5421**
Allen, Leslie (NORMAN) CASEWKR **803-327-1114**
Allen, Matthew (DEGETTE) LEGIS ASST 2111 **54431**
Allen, Morris (CRAIG) SR COMMUNITY LIAISON **651-846-2120**
Allen, Pat (CAO/HIR – OPS AND CONTINUITY) DIRECTOR 629 FHOB **67742**
Allen, Rachel (CHENEY) FIELD REP **307-772-2595**
Allen, Stephanie (VARGAS) FIELD REP **619-422-5963**
Allen Shires, Debbie (KUSTOFF) CASEWKR **731-423-4848**
Alli, Tylease (CMTE-ED & WORKFORCE) CHIEF CLERK 2176 **53725**
Allison, Kevin (CAO/LOGISTICS) LOGISTICS & DIST SPEC HT19 **59474**
Allison, Terisa (CMTE-FINANCIAL SVCS) EDITOR 2129 **54247**
Ally, Kehoe (NORCROSS) COMMUNICATIONS DIR 2437 **56501**
Alpert, Matthew (SERRANO) CHIEF OF STAFF 2354 **54361**
Al Shadood, Maytham (CROW) DIST DIR **720-748-7514**
Alsina, Neysa (VELÁZQUEZ) SR POLICY ADVISOR 2302 **52361**
Alston, Mark (CAO/HIR – IT CUSTOMER SOLUTIONS) TECH SOLUTIONS ENGINEER 694 FHOB **56002**
Alston, Nadia (PRICE) CASEWKR **919-859-5999**
Alston, Thomas (SCOTT, ROBERT C. "BOBBY") CONSTIT SVCS REP **757-380-1000**
Alstork, Kim M (CLERK/SVCS GRPS) COORD - MBR & FAM RM H324 **50622**
Alter, Mike (LOWEY) DIST REP **914-428-1707**
Altman, Ryan (HAGEDORN) CONSTIT OUTREACH REP **507-323-6090**
Altounian, Denise (COSTA) DIST REP **559-495-1620**
Alva, Alisa (MCNERNEY) DIST DIR **209-476-8552**
Alvarado, August (CARTER, JOHN R.) DIST DIR **512-246-1600**
Alvarado, Brenda (DEFAZIO) DIST AIDE **541-465-6732**
Alvarado, Clelia (CMTE-APPRO) ADMIN AIDE HT2 **52041**
Alvarado, Marie (CARTER, JOHN R.) SR ADVISOR **512-246-1600**
Alvarez, Alex (KIRKPATRICK) DPTY COMMUNICATIONS DIR **520-881-3588**
Alvarez, DeAnna (STANTON) SR CASEWKR **602-956-2285**
Alvarez, Gerardo (MALONEY, SEAN PATRICK) CONSTIT SVCS **845-561-1259**
Alvarez, Jazmin (KELLY, ROBIN L.) LEGIS AIDE/ASST SCHEDULER 2416 **50773**
Alvarez, Tiffany (TAKANO) FIELD REP **951-222-0203**
Alvarez, Yovi (DIAZ-BALART) CONG ASST **305-470-8555**
Alvarez Reyes, Angelica (GRIJALVA) STAFF ASST **520-622-6788**
Alves, Mercy (VELÁZQUEZ) CASEWKR **718-599-3658**
Alvey, Lisa (CAO/FINANCIAL COUNSELING) COUNSELOR B215 LHOB **63548**
Amador, Adela (HARDER) LEGIS DIR/DPTY CHIEF OF STAFF 131 CHOB **54540**
Amador, Paola (SERRANO) COMMUNICATIONS DIR 2354 **54361**
Amason, Kim (GUEST) DPTY DIR - CONSTIT SVCS **769-241-6120**
Amason, Virginia (PALMER) COORD - COMMUNITY OUTREACH **205-968-1290**
Ambinder, Michael (LEGIS COUNSEL) ASST COUNSEL 337 FHOB **56060**
Ambriz, Josue (PELOSI) LEGIS AIDE 1236 **54965**
Ambrose, Lisa (RICHMOND) CASEWKR **504-288-3777**
Ambrose, Myles (CRAIG) LEGIS CORRES 1523 **52271**
Ames, Kenneth (CAO/CUST EXPER CTR) CUSTOMER ADVOCATE B227 LHOB **58000**
Amick, Eric (CLERK/LCS) SOFTWARE ENGINEER 2401 **51182**
Amidon, Eric (ZELDIN) CHIEF OF STAFF **631-289-1097**
Ammen, Faith (WALORSKI) SCHEDULER 419 CHOB **53915**
Amster, Liz (RICE, KATHLEEN M.) LEGIS DIR 2435 **55516**
Amundsen, Hannah (KRISHNAMOORTHI) DIR - COMMUNITY OUTREACH/CONSTIT LIAISON **847-413-1959**
Anaya, Libby (TORRES SMALL) CASEWKR **575-323-6384**
Anders, John Paul (OLSON) FIELD REP **281-494-2690**
Andersen, Frederic (CAO/HOUSE DAILY PRESS) ASST DIR H315 **53945**
Anderson, Alyssa (EMMER) DPTY SCHEDULER 315 CHOB **52331**
Anderson, Ashley W (LEGIS COUNSEL) OFC MANAGERIAL ASST 337 FHOB **56060**
Anderson, Cassie (CMTE-SCIENCE) PRESS ASST - MAJ 2321 **56375**
Anderson, Celia (PASCRELL) FIELD REP **973-472-4510**
Anderson, Craig (SCOTT, AUSTIN) LEGIS ASST 2417 **56531**
Anderson, Dale (LAMBORN) CHIEF OF STAFF 2371 **54422**
Anderson, Denine (CAO/HIR - ENTERPRISE MESSAGING AND MOBILITY) SPECIAL ASST 619C FHOB **66245**
Anderson, Dontrell (CAO/FINANCIAL COUNSELING) FINANCIAL COUNSELOR B215 LHOB **60903**
Anderson, Doug (CMTE-FOREIGN AFFAIRS) GEN COUNSEL 2066 **68467**
Anderson, Elise (MALONEY, CAROLYN B.) DPTY PRESS SECY **212-860-0606**
Anderson, Emily (SUOZZI) CASEWKR - IMMIGRATION **631-923-4100**
Anderson, Eric (LAHOOD) STAFF ASST 1424 **56201**
Anderson, Gena (ROGERS, HAROLD) CASEWKR **606-679-8346**
Anderson, Griffin (KAPTUR) COMMUNICATIONS DIR 2186 **54146**
Anderson, Hannah (CRENSHAW) LEGIS ASST 413 CHOB **56565**
Anderson, Jacki (PETERSON) ECON DEV SPEC/ OUTREACH DIR **320-235-1061**
Anderson, Jeff (LAMBORN) SR ADVISOR - POLICY & OUTREACH/CONSTIT OUTREACH REP **719-520-0055**
Anderson, Jenna (COMER) CONSTIT SVCS REP **270-487-9509**
Anderson, Karen (LEGIS COUNSEL) COUNSEL 337 FHOB **56060**
Anderson, Karen (BERGMAN) DIR - CONSTIT SVCS **906-273-2227**
Anderson, Katelynn (PRICE) COMMUNICATIONS DIR **919-859-5999**
Anderson, Kwamme (CLARKE) DPTY CHIEF OF STAFF 2058 **56231**
Anderson, Lauren (LEGIS COUNSEL) STAFF ASST/ PARALEGAL 337 FHOB **56060**
Anderson, Madison (STEFANIK) COMMUNICATIONS DIR 318 CHOB **54611**

Anderson, Margie (WALDEN) FIELD REP - VETS... **541-389-4408**
Anderson, Matthew (CMTE-APPRO) SCOREKEEPER 2005 **52718**
Anderson, Morgan (HOUSE REPUB CONF) DIGITAL DIR 1420... **55107**
Anderson, Ryan (TLAIB) CHIEF OF STAFF 1628... **55126**
Anderson, Sally (NEGUSE) DPTY CHIEF OF STAFF... **970-372-3971**
Anderson, Sam (PHILLIPS) DIST PRESS SECY... **952-656-5176**
Anderson, Sharon (KIM) CASEWKR... **856-703-2700**
Anderson, Taijah (COURTNEY) CONSTIT SVCS/ COORD - OUTREACH... **860-886-0139**
Anderson, Tiara (CAO/EMPLOYEE ASSISTANCE) EMPLOYEE ASST COUNSELOR 140 FHOB... **52400**
Anderson, Tori (CMTE-OVERSIGHT & GOVT REFORM) COUNSEL 2157... **55051**
Anderson, Wendy (DEMINGS) CHIEF OF STAFF 217 CHOB... **52176**
Anderson, Wendy (WALBERG) FIELD REP... **517-780-9075**
Andino, Jessica (ESCOBAR) SCHEDULER 1505... **68389**
Andrade, Barbara (BISHOP, ROB) SCHEDULER 123 CHOB **50453**
Andrade, Edwina (ROY) DIR - CONSTIT SVCS... **210-821-5024**
Andreae, Taylor (GALLAGHER) CHIEF OF STAFF 1230... **55665**
Andres, Don (GARCÍA, JESÚS G. "CHUY") LEGIS DIR 530 CHOB... **61717**
Andres, Gary (CMTE-WAYS & MEANS) STAFF DIR - MIN 1139... **54021**
Andrews, Jess
- (CMTE-JUDICIARY) COMMUNICATIONS DIR 2226... **56906**
- (COLLINS, DOUG) COMMUNICATIONS DIR 1504... **59893**

Andrews, Jessie (DELGADO) DC CHIEF OF STAFF/LEGIS DIR 1007... **55614**
Andrews, Ninamarie (CUELLAR) SPECIAL ASST 2372... **51640**
Andrews, Steve (COMMIS ON CHINA) COUNSEL 243 FHOB... **63832**
Andrews, Thomas (CAO/HIR – ENTERPRISE INFRASTRUCT) MGR 687A FHOB... **61350**
Androff, Blake
- (HOUSE DEM POLICY AND COMMUNICATIONS CMTE) EXEC DIR HB18... **68468**
- (SPEAKER) EXEC DIR - DEM POLICY & COMMUNICATIONS CMTE H232... **50100**

Andrus, Carly (PANETTA) STAFF ASST 212 CHOB... **52861**
Andzel, Christian (ROY) STAFF ASST 1319... **54236**
Anecito, Chrissy (LEE, BARBARA) CONG AIDE... **510-763-0370**
Anello, Russell (CMTE-OVERSIGHT & GOVT REFORM) CHIEF OVERSIGHT COUNSEL 2157... **55051**
Anfinson, Thomas (SCOTT, AUSTIN) FINANCE LIAISON 2417... **56531**
Angeles, Anna Katrina (CAO/ACCOUNTING) ACCNT TECH 3110... **54539**
Angelotti, Julia (STEFANIK) LEGIS DIR 318 CHOB... **54611**
Anglen, Michael (NC03) CASEWKR/SR POLICY ADVISOR... **252-931-1003**
Angotti, Steven (CASTOR) COORD - GRANTS/ PRESS SECY... **813-871-2817**
Angulo, Jessica (DESAULNIER) DIST SCHEDULER... **925-933-2660**
Angulo, Tiffany (SCHWEIKERT) POLICY ADVISOR/SR CAUCUS POLICY ADVISOR 1526... **52190**
Animley, Kingsley
- (ALLRED) FINANCIAL ADMIN 328 CHOB... **52231**
- (CMTE-JUDICIARY) DIR - ADMIN OPS 2035... **53951**
- (MCADAMS) FINANCIAL ADMIN 130 CHOB... **53011**
- (OCASIO-CORTEZ) ADVISOR 229 CHOB... **53965**

Anonson, Colin (PERLMUTTER) LEGIS ASST 1226... **52645**
Ansari, Arya (SHERMAN) PRESS SECY 2181... **55911**
Anthony, Anya (GABBARD) OFFICE MGR... **808-541-1986**
Anthony, Tony (CAO/HOUSE RECORDING STUDIO) BROADCAST ENGINEER/PROD SPEC 2010... **53941**
Antista, Jonathan (CMTE-BUDGET) BUDGET ANALYST 204E CHOB... **67200**
Antoskiewicz, Ashley (LAHOOD) LEGIS DIR 1424... **56201**
Anzur, Jon (KELLER) CHIEF OF STAFF 1717... **53731**
Apelbaum, Perry (CMTE-JUDICIARY) CHIEF COUNSEL/ STAFF DIR 2138... **53951**
Apodaca, Joey (LIEU) FIELD REP/CONSTIT SVCS... **323-651-1040**
Apolinario, Gloria (CONAWAY) FIELD REP... **432-331-9667**
Appel, Erika (CMTE-BUDGET) BUDGET ANALYST/COORD - COALITION & MBR SVCS 204E CHOB... **67200**
Appelbaum, Michael (LONG) STAFF ASST 2454... **56536**
Appiah, Joyce (CAO/PAYROLL & BENEFITS) COUNSELOR B215 LHOB... **50116**
Appiah-Kubi, Felix (CAO/HIR – CYBERSECURITY) SR INFO TECH ENGINEER SITE 3... **571-921-3117**
Apple, Haleigh (BISHOP, SANFORD D., JR.) DIST STAFF ASST... **478-803-2631**
Aprile, Alex (MITCHELL) COORD - CONSTIT SVCS... **586-997-5010**
Aragon, Claudia (BASS) CASEWK MGR... **323-965-1422**
Araiza, Shirley (BONAMICI) DIST REP/ OUTREACH REP... **503-469-6010**
Araya, Meseret (HOUSE DEM CAUCUS) POLICY ADVISOR B245 LHOB... **51400**
Arazi, Hadar (GOTTHEIMER) DPTY DIST DIR... **201-389-1100**
Arbeit, Jeffrey (CMTE-JOINT TAX) LEGIS COUNSEL 502 FHOB... **53621**
Arbulu, Oscar (TLAIB) CASEWKR... **313-463-6220**
Arcangeli, Paul (CMTE-ARMED SVCS) STAFF DIR - MAJ 2117... **54158**
Archer, Reyn (FORTENBERRY) CHIEF OF STAFF 1514... **54806**
Archer, Tony (LAMBORN) CASEWORK - VETS... **719-520-0055**
Archie, Tyreis (CAO/HIR – IT CUSTOMER SOLUTIONS) TECH SUPPORT REP 100 CHOB... **69313**
Arevalo, Elizabeth (LIEU) LEGIS ASST 403 CHOB... **53976**
Argall, Elise (RESCHENTHALER) COMMUNICATIONS DIR 531 CHOB... **52065**
Arguello, Hector (WALTZ) LEGIS STAFF 216 CHOB... **52706**
Arias, Hector (COMMIS ON CONG MAILING STDS) STAFF ASST 1307... **59337**
Arias, Hector (CMTE-HOUSE ADMIN) STAFF ASST 1307... **52061**
Arjev, Michael (CAO/TECHNOL GOVERN & COMPLIANCE) PROGRAM MGR 647 FHOB... **66425**
Arlantico, Pat (WILLIAMS) LEGIS DIR/DPTY CHIEF OF STAFF 1708... **59896**
Armaza, Mauricio (HIMES) STAFF ASST 1227... **55541**
Armenta, Carina (BROWNLEY) DIST DIR... **805-379-1779**

Armour, Tiana (CAO/PAYROLL & BENEFITS) COUNSELOR B215 LHOB 67870
Armstrong, Carol (HOLDING) DIST DIR 919-782-4400
Armstrong, Dodie (WEBER) CONSTIT LIAISON 979-285-0231
Armstrong, Janciera (CAO/CUST EXPER CTR) DPTY CHIEF B227 LHOB 58000
Armstrong, Levar (BISHOP, SANFORD D., JR.) MIL FELLOW 2407 53631
Armstrong, Shy (JOHNSON, HENRY C. "HANK", JR.) CASEWKR - MIL/CASEWORK - VETS/ CONSTIT SVCS 770-987-2291
Arndt, Eric (COLLINS, CHRIS) SR LEGIS ASST 2243 55265
Arnesen, Emma (CASTEN) STAFF ASST 630-520-9450
Arnold, Alex (PALLONE) DIST REP/STAFF ASST 732-571-1140
Arnold, Jon (HURD) DIR - CONSTIT SVCS 210-921-3130
Arnold Marr, Betsy (DESAULNIER) CHIEF OF STAFF 503 CHOB 52095
Arnone, Mark (CMTE-APPRO) PROF STAFF MEMB 2362B 53421
Arntz, Mike (HARRIS) COMMUNITY LIAISON 410-643-5425
Aronson, Lauren Blair (CMTE-BUDGET) COMMUNICATIONS DIR - MIN 507 CHOB 67270
Arriaga, Jack (BONAMICI) LEGIS ASST 2231 50855
Arrighi, T W (BANKS) COMMUNICATIONS DIR 1713 54436
Arrojo, David (CMTE-ETHICS) COUNSEL TO THE CHAIRMAN 1015 57103
Arteaga, Stacy (HURD) FIELD REP 210-784-5023
Artz, Cyrus (FOXX) CHIEF OF STAFF 2462 52071
Asata, Heather (CAO/BUDGET POLICY) BUDGET ANALYST 3240 61454
Ash, Alesia (KIRKPATRICK) OUTREACH DIRECTOR 520-459-3115
Ash, Earl (CLARKE) LEGIS AIDE 2058 56231
Ashe, Shae (DEAN) CASEWKR - IMMIGRATION 610-382-1250
Asher, Nita (CMTE-JOINT TAX) LEGIS COUNSEL 502 FHOB 53621
Ashford, Jeff (CMTE-APPRO) PROF STAFF MEMB H310 53351
Ashton, Gus (SPANO) LEGIS DIR 224 CHOB 51252
Ashworth, Dan
(CMTE-JUDICIARY) COUNSEL 1504 56906
(COLLINS, DOUG) COUNSEL 1504 59893
Askew, Allen (WATKINS) MIL FIELD REP 785-234-5966
Aslami, Mohammad (CMTE-ENERGY & COMMERCE) COUNSEL 2125 52927
Asprea, Joe (LOWEY) DIST STAFF ASST 914-428-1707
Assanie, Sameer (JOHNSON, EDDIE BERNICE) COMMUNICATIONS DIR 214-922-8885
Assini, John (PANETTA) LEGIS ASST 212 CHOB 52861
Atchison, Darryl (CAO/HOUSE RECORDING STUDIO) CHIEF ENGINEER 2010 53941
Atchison, Kayla (GONZALEZ, ANTHONY) COMMUNITY LIAISON/DIST SCHEDULER 330-599-7037
Athy, Susan (CMTE-WAYS & MEANS) TAX COUNSEL 1129 .. 53625
Atkins, Sallie (SMITH, ADRIAN) LIAISON - AG 308-384-3900
Attebery, Alexander (CMTE-APPRO) DPTY COMMUNICATIONS DIR 1016 53481
Atterbury, Robert (NADLER) SR ASST 212-367-7350
Attermann, Jason (DEUTCH) PRESS SECY/LEGIS ASST 2447 53001
Atwater, Courtney (YOHO) STAFF ASST 1730 55744
Atwell, Francis (CUELLAR) COORD - OUTREACH 956-725-0639
Atwood, Matthew (TIPTON) PRESS SECY 218 CHOB 54761
Audino, Ernest (WALTZ) DIST DIR 386-238-9711
Augustus, Imani (PHILLIPS) LEGIS DIR 1305 52871
Aumann, Mark (KIND) CONG AIDE 715-831-9214
Auray, Christopher (FITZPATRICK) PRESS SECY 1722 54276
Austin, Andrew (GREEN, MARK E.) LEGIS AIDE 533 CHOB. 52811
Austin, Donna (PERRY) CONSTIT SVCS REP 717-635-9504
Austin, Ender (HORSFORD) DIST REP 702-963-9360
Austin, Teresa L (CLERK/LEGIS OPS) TALLY CLERK HT13. 57347
Austin-Mackenzie, Elizabeth (CMTE-VET AFFAIRS) SUBCOMM STAFF DIR - HEALTH SUBCOMM 3470 59756
Austin Reed, Keenan (MCEACHIN) CHIEF OF STAFF 314 CHOB 56365
Austin-Shipp, Nikki (WILSON, FREDERICA S.) DIR - COMMUNITY RELATIONS 305-690-5905
Autobee-Trujillo, Andrea (DEGETTE) DPTY DIST DIR 303-844-4988
Avalos, Karla (KIRKPATRICK) CHIEF OPS OFFICER 520-881-3588
Avery, Cole (ABRAHAM) COMMUNICATIONS DIR 417 CHOB 58490
Avila, Amberlynn (LAMALFA) STAFF ASST 322 CHOB 53076
Avila, Sinnai (ROYBAL-ALLARD) FIELD DPTY 323-721-8790
Avin, Amir (WEXTON) COMMUNICATIONS DIR 1217 55136
Awan, Omar (CAO) DIR - STRATEGY B227 LHOB 58000
Ayala, Juan (OLSON) STAFF ASST 2133 55951
Ayala, Maira (THOMPSON, MIKE) DIST REP 707-226-9898
Ayala, Miguel
(GONZÁLEZ-COLÓN) DPTY DIST DIR 787-723-6333
(SCHAKOWSKY) COMMUNICATIONS DIR 2367 52111
Aydin, Andrew (LEWIS) DIGITAL DIR 300 CHOB 53801
Ayrea, Maggie
(GRAVES, GARRET) LEGIS DIR 2402 53901
(SELECT CMTE-CLIMATE CRISIS) PROF STAFF MBR - REPUB 361 FHOB 51107
Azevedo, Susie (MOONEY) DIST FIELD REP 304-925-5964
Azimpoor, Kian (JAYAPAL) STAFF ASST 1510 53106
Baack, Korry (VISCLOSKY) EXEC ASST/SYS MGR 2328 52461
Babb, Alison
(BALDERSON) ADMIN - FINANCE & PAYROLL 1221 55355
(GOODEN) FINANCIAL ADMIN 425 CHOB 53484
(HOLDING) ADMIN - FINANCE & PAYROLL 1110 53032
(HUDSON) ADMIN - FINANCE & PAYROLL 2112 53715
(JOHNSON, MIKE) FINANCIAL ADMIN 418 CHOB 52777
(LESKO) FINANCIAL ADMIN 1113 54576
(WALKER) ADMIN - FINANCE & PAYROLL 1725 53065
Babbitt, Paul (O'HALLERAN) SR ADVISOR 324 CHOB 53361
Babine, Olivia (TIPTON) LEGIS CORRES 218 CHOB 54761
Babor, Edward (MALONEY, CAROLYN B.) DIST REP 718-932-1804
Bacetty, Ada (BISHOP, SANFORD D., JR.) LEGIS FELLOW 2407 53631
Bach, Mitzi (QUIGLEY) DIST SCHEDULER 773-267-5926
Bacher, Chelsea (RICE, TOM) LEGIS ASST 512 CHOB 59895
Bacskocky, Argus T (CLERK/LRC) MGR - DOCU & REQUISITIONS B81 CHOB 65200
Badame, Meghan (HUNTER) LEGIS CORRES/DPTY PRESS SECY 2429 55672
Bader, Chris (WOMACK) CONSTIT SVCS REP 479-424-1146

Badu-Nimako, Yvette
(CMTE-OVERSIGHT & GOVT REFORM) LEGIS DIR 2157 ...... **55051**
(CUMMINGS) LEGIS DIR 2163 ...... **54741**
Baessler, Sarah (BONAMICI) DIST DIR **503-469-6010**
Bagby, David (POCAN) DPTY CHIEF OF STAFF 1421 ...... **52906**
Bagi, Jennifer (BROOKS, SUSAN W.) DIST SCHEDULER **317-848-0201**
Bagwell, Eric (CLINE) SR LEGIS ASST 1009 ...... **55431**
Baham, Todd (CAO/HOUSE RECORDING STUDIO) BROADCAST PROD TECH 2010 ...... **53941**
Baig, Shahryar (ESPAILLAT) STAFF ASST 1630 ...... **54365**
Bailey, Ashley (BOST) LEGIS ASST 1440 ...... **55661**
Bailey, Benjamin (SCOTT, ROBERT C. "BOBBY") CONSTIT SVCS REP **757-380-1000**
Bailey, Dave (CAO/HIR – IT CUSTOMER SOLUTIONS) SR TECH SUPPORT REP 100 CHOB **66242**
Bailey, Don (UPTON) FINANCIAL ADMIN 2183 ...... **53761**
Bailey, Jennifer
(CLOUD) FINANCIAL ADMIN 1314 ...... **57742**
(RATCLIFFE) FINANCIAL ADMIN 223 CHOB **56673**
Bailey, Joel (PANETTA) CHIEF OF STAFF 212 CHOB **52861**
Bailey, Mariel (FORTENBERRY) CONG AIDE 1514 ...... **54806**
Bainer, Brandon (TIPTON) CASEWKR **970-241-2499**
Bair, Mimi (STIVERS) LEGIS ASST 2234 ...... **52015**
Baird, Katherine (KINZINGER) SCHEDULER 2245 ...... **53635**
Baird, Kevin (GRIFFITH) COMMUNICATIONS DIR 2202 ...... **53861**
Baker, Barb (LAHOOD) CONSTIT SVCS SPEC **217-245-1431**
Baker, Cole (SPANBERGER) LEGIS CORRES 1239 ...... **52815**
Baker, Darrell (CAO/HIR – NETWORKING ENGINEERING AND OPS) SR NETWK COMMUNICATIONS SPEC 663 FHOB **64244**
Baker, Dawn (JOHNSON, BILL) CASEWKR 2336 ...... **55705**
Baker, Eliza (CRENSHAW) CHIEF OF STAFF 413 CHOB **56565**
Baker, Greg (ESTES) LEGIS ASST 1524 ...... **56216**
Baker, James (RATCLIFFE) POLICY DIR **903-816-5270**
Baker, Jessica (CMTE-ETHICS) COUNSEL 1015 ...... **57103**
Baker, Michael (RUPPERSBERGER) OUTREACH DIR **410-628-2701**
Baker, Samantha (GROTHMAN) LEGIS ASST 1427 ...... **52476**
Baker, Stacy
(CMTE-FINANCIAL SVCS) SYS ADMIN 4340 ...... **57502**
(CMTE-JUDICIARY) DIR - INFO TECH 1504 ...... **56906**
(CMTE-OVERSIGHT & GOVT REFORM) DIR - INFO TECH 2105 ...... **55074**
Baker, Tim (ALLEN) CHIEF OF STAFF 2400 ...... **52823**
Baldwin, Amanda (BURGESS) DPTY CHIEF OF STAFF 2161 ...... **57772**
Baldwin, Jennifer (DAVIS, RODNEY) CONSTIT SVCS REP **217-403-4690**
Baldwin, Wilson (KRISHNAMOORTHI) COMMUNICATIONS DIR 115 CHOB **53711**
Balidemaj, Egzon (COURTNEY) DIST STAFF ASST **860-886-0139**
Balis, Ellen (CMTE-BUDGET) STAFF DIR - MAJ 204E CHOB. **67200**
Ball, Alex (CROW) CHIEF OF STAFF 1229 ...... **57882**
Ball, Bill (CMTE-NATURAL RESOURCES) SUBCOMM STAFF DIR 4120 ...... **52761**
Ball, Luke (GAETZ) PRESS SECY 1721 ...... **54136**
Ballard, Jimmy (DAVIS, RODNEY) LEGIS DIR 1740 ...... **52371**
Ballenger, Courtney (HERN) EXEC ASST 1019 ...... **52211**
Ballinger, Adrian (SCHRADER) STAFF ASST 2431 ...... **55711**
Ballinger, Bobby (WESTERMAN) DIST FIELD REP **479-667-0075**
Ballou, Wade (LEGIS COUNSEL) HOUSE LEGISLATIVE COUNSEL 337 FHOB **56060**
Balser, James (COOPER) ATTORNEY 1536 ...... **54311**
Balzano, Paul (CMTE-AGRIC) SR PROF STAFF 1010 ...... **50317**
Bandy, Patricia (FOXX) OFFICE MGR **336-778-0211**
Banez, Joe (CMTE-ENERGY & COMMERCE) PROF STAFF 2125 ...... **52927**
Banfield, Kelli (CAO/HOUSE RECORDING STUDIO) BROADCAST ENGINEER/PROD SPEC 2010 ...... **53941**
Banfield, Paige (MALONEY, SEAN PATRICK) DIR - OPS **845-561-1259**
Banik, Disha (JEFFRIES) LEGIS ASST 2433 ...... **55936**
Banjac, Srdan (LARSON) LEGIS ASST 1501 ...... **52265**
Bankman-Fried, Gabe (CASTEN) LEGIS CORRES 429 CHOB **54561**
Bankole, Yasmeen (KRISHNAMOORTHI) LIAISON - CONSTIT SVCS **847-413-1959**
Banks, Alan (KELLY, ROBIN L.) DIST REP **708-679-0078**
Banks, Bianca (CAO/OFFICE SUPPLY/GIFT SHOP) MGR B217 LHOB **53321**
Banks, David (CAO/HOUSE CREATIVE SVCS) SR MULTIMEDIA DEVELOPER 2002 ...... **52700**
Banks, George David (SELECT CMTE-CLIMATE CRISIS) CHIEF STRATEGIST - REPUB 361 FHOB **51107**
Banks, Linda
(CRIST) FINANCIAL MGR **703-619-5919**
(DELBENE) FINANCIAL ADMIN 2330 ...... **56311**
(HIMES) FINANCIAL ADMIN 1227 ...... **55541**
(LARSEN) FINANCIAL ADMIN 2113 ...... **52605**
(PETERS) FINANCIAL ADMIN 2338 ...... **50508**
Barab, Jordan (CMTE-ED & WORKFORCE) SR LABOR POLICY ADVISOR 230 FHOB **53725**
Barajas, Jocelyne (ADAMS) STAFF ASST 2436 ...... **51510**
Barbee, Donell (CAO/OFFICE SUPPLY/GIFT SHOP) RETAIL INVENTORY SPEC B217 LHOB **53321**
Barbee, Glenn (CAO/HIR – NETWORKING ENGINEERING AND OPS) NETWK TECH 652C FHOB **64101**
Barber, Beth (BABIN) SCHEDULER/LEGIS AIDE 2236 ...... **51555**
Barber, Craig (CMTE-ETHICS) SYS ADMIN 1015 ...... **57103**
Barber, Danelle (THORNBERRY) CONSTIT SVCS REP **806-371-8844**
Barber, Ron (KIRKPATRICK) DIST DIR **520-881-3588**
Barber, Sara (CMTE-SCIENCE) PROF STAFF - MAJ 2321 ...... **56375**
Barbera, Austin (SCOTT, ROBERT C. "BOBBY") PRESS SECY 1201 ...... **58351**
Barbero, Megan (GEN COUNSEL) ASSOC COUNSEL 219 CHOB **59700**
Barblan, Jennifer (CMTE-ENERGY & COMMERCE) CHIEF COUNSEL 2322A **53641**
Barbour, June (CAO/HOUSE RECORDING STUDIO) BROADCAST PROD TECH 2010 ...... **53941**
Barcena, Gladys (CMTE-APPRO) ADMIN ASST 2358A **52141**
Barciniak, Dana (CAO/HOUSE CREATIVE SVCS) OFFICE MGR 2002 ...... **52700**
Barczak, Liz (GONZALEZ, ANTHONY) LEGIS ASST 1023 ...... **53876**
Barefoot, Jeffrey (CAO/HOUSE RECORDING STUDIO) BROADCAST ENGINEER/PROD SPEC 2010 ...... **53941**

Barfield, Sherry (LAWSON) CASEWKR 904-354-1652
Barger, Noah (BOST) LEGIS ASST 1440 55661
Barich, Lauren (ROUDA) CONSTIT SVCS REP 714-960-6483
Barile, Ariann (JOYCE, DAVID P.) DIST OUTREACH REP 440-352-3939
Barker, Billy (ROUZER) FIELD DIR 919-938-3040
Barker, Brooke (BROWNLEY) PRESS ASST 2262 55811
Barker, Erica
(CMTE-JUDICIARY) CHIEF LEGIS CLERK 1504 56906
(COLLINS, DOUG) SR LEGIS AIDE 1504 59893
Barker, Nathan (HICE) LEGIS CORRES/COORD - INTERN & FELLOW 409 CHOB 54101
Barksdale, Marshall W (LEGIS COUNSEL) COUNSEL 337 FHOB 56060
Barnabae, Monica (CAO/CHILD CARE CENTER) ADMIN DIR 147 FHOB 69320
Barnes, Anthony (WEXTON) COORD - CONSTIT SVCS 1217 55136
Barnes, Cheryl (CMTE-ETHICS) STAFF ASST 1015 57103
Barnes, Kenneth (CLYBURN) CASEWK MGR 843-355-1211
Barnes, Lyndsey (HIGGINS, BRIAN) LEGIS ASST 2459 53306
Barnes, Shaynah (LYNCH) DIST REP 508-586-5555
Barnes, Sonia (PRICE) DIST LIAISON 919-859-5999
Barnes, William (MULLIN) CASEWKR/FIELD REP 918-687-2533
Barnes, Zaak (AXNE) LEGIS ASST 330 CHOB 55476
Baron, Dena (CMTE-APPRO) PROF STAFF MEMB 1016 53481
Baron, Zachary (CMTE-WAYS & MEANS) COUNSEL - OVERSIGHT 1129 53625
Barr, Delia (CMTE-SMALL BUSINESS) PROF STAFF 2069 55821
Barr, Jacob (CASTOR) LEGIS ASST 2052 53376
Barr, Paul (CAO/LOGISTICS) SUPERVISOR RSBC4 55057
Barranca, Alexis (ROGERS, MIKE) SCHEDULER 2184 53261
Barrett, Dennis (PRESSLEY) LEGIS CORRES 1108 55111
Barrett, Murphie (CMTE-TRANSP & INFRA) STAFF DIR 593 FHOB 54472
Barrett, Robert (CAO/ENTERPRISE APPLICATIONS) DIRECTOR B70B FHOB 66223
Barrett, Walker (WALTZ) LEGIS DIR/DPTY CHIEF 216 CHOB 52706
Barrie, Elizabeth (CORREA) LEGIS ASST/COORD - INTERN & FELLOW/LEGIS CORRES 1039 52965
Barrineau, Sara (CAO/HIR – OPS AND CONTINUITY) MGR 634 FHOB 67202
Barry, Joseph (KING, STEVE) LEGIS AIDE 2210 54426
Barry, Matthew (GRAVES, SAM) FIELD REP 816-749-0800
Barry, Will (MCHENRY) STAFF ASST 2004 52576
Barsa, Richard (SIRES) CONG AIDE 201-558-0800
Barstow, Kevin (CMTE-ENERGY & COMMERCE) CHIEF OVERSIGHT COUNSEL 2125 52927
Bart, Jackie (TRAHAN) DPTY CHIEF OF STAFF 978-459-0101
Barth, Abigail (GOTTHEIMER) LIAISON - CONSTIT SVCS 201-389-1100
Barth, Zack (WILLIAMS) LEGIS ASST 1708 59896
Barthold, Thomas A (CMTE-JOINT TAX) CHIEF OF STAFF 502 FHOB 53621
Bartlett, Claire (LOUDERMILK) FIELD DIR 770-429-1776
Bartlett, Joe (ROONEY) LEGIS ASST 120 CHOB 52536
Bartley, Tracey (GRAVES, TOM) DIR - CONSTIT SVCS 706-226-5320
Barton, Carter (FOXX) LEGIS AIDE 2462 52071
Barton, Hannah (MCADAMS) CONSTIT LIAISON 801-999-9801
Barton, Liz (RESCHENTHALER) SCHEDULER 531 CHOB 52065
Barton, Stacy (CHABOT) CHIEF OF STAFF 2408 52216
Barton, Tisha (CAO/HIR – IT CUSTOMER SOLUTIONS) SPECIAL ASST 608 FHOB 66155
Bascumbe, Andres (WATERS) LEGIS COUNSEL 2221 52201
Bashford, Janice (BASS) LEGIS DIR 2059 57084
Basilio, Tyrone (CAO/HIR – IT CUSTOMER SOLUTIONS) TECH SUPPORT REP 2067 65761
Baskin, Steve (KRISHNAMOORTHI) DIST SCHEDULER 847-413-1959
Bass, Jared (CMTE-APPRO) PROF STAFF MEMB 2358B 53508
Bass, Robbin (RATCLIFFE) DPTY DIST DIR 903-823-3173
Batchelor, Jack (GARAMENDI) SR FIELD REP 707-438-1822
Bates, Alicia (CLERK/ART & ARCHIVES) ARCHIVAL ASST JEFFERSON BUILDING, ATTIC 61300
Bates, Brian (GIBBS) LEGIS AIDE 2446 56265
Bates, Deborah (CAO/HOUSE RECORDING STUDIO) PROD/ENGINEERING SPEC 2010 53941
Batey, Laura (WILSON, JOE) DIR - CONSTIT SVCS 803-939-0041
Bath, George (CAO) SR ADVISOR 217 FHOB 64315
Batista, Aneiry (ESPAILLAT) CHIEF OF STAFF 1630 54365
Batista, Michael (CRIST) CONSTIT SVCS REP 727-318-6770
Batmanglidj, Kiyalan (CMTE-APPRO) PROF STAFF MEMB 1040A 53481
Batson, Denise (CAO/PAYROLL & BENEFITS) COUNSELOR B215 LHOB 56454
Battaglia, Jacqueline
(MIN WHIP) SCHEDULER H148 50197
(SCALISE) SCHEDULER 2049 53015
Batti, Jenna (LAMALFA) CASEWKR 530-343-1000
Bauduy, Michael (BEATTY) LEGIS AIDE/LEGIS CORRES 2303 54324
Bauerle, Brent (CICILLINE) CONSTIT SVCS REP 401-729-5600
Baugh, Patrick
(CMTE-BUDGET) FINANCIAL ADMIN 204E CHOB 67200
(CMTE-JUDICIARY) FINANCIAL ADMIN 2138 53951
Baum, Ben (MALONEY, SEAN PATRICK) SPECIAL ASST 2331 55441
Baum, Kristina (CMTE-NATURAL RESOURCES) COMMUNICATIONS DIR 1329 52761
Bauman, Brian (LATTA) DIST REP 419-422-7791
Bauman, Rachel (COMMIS ON SECUR & COOP IN EUR) POLICY ADVISOR 234 FHOB 51901
Baumgart-Turner, Kirsten (GABBARD) CONSTIT OUTREACH REP 808-541-1986
Bauserman, Trent (MAJ LEADER) SR POLICY ADVISOR H107 53130
Bautista, Rufino (LOWENTHAL) DIST SCHEDULER 714-243-4088
Bautista, Victoria (HORN) LEGIS AIDE 415 CHOB 52132
Bautista, Yamilette (CAO/CONGRESSIONAL STAFF ACAD) PROGRAM MGR B241 LHOB 63800
Bayer, Clifford (FULCHER) CHIEF OF STAFF 1520 56611
Bayer, Jake (MAJ LEADER) EXEC ASST/OFFICE MGR H107 53130
Bayles, Chris (PALMER) LEGIS ASST 207 CHOB 54921
Baylor, Christopher
(KINZINGER) SYS ADMIN 2245 53635
(MCEACHIN) SYS ADMIN 314 CHOB 56365

Bazemore, Bruce (CARTER, EARL L. "BUDDY") CASEWKR ... 912-352-0101
Bazydlo, Emily (KATKO) SCHEDULER 2457 ... 53701
Beal, Mary Dee (FERGUSON) LEGIS DIR 1032 ... 55901
Beal, Owen (PELOSI) STAFF ASST 1236 ... 54965
Beale, Ashley (THOMPSON, BENNIE G.) CASEWKR/FIELD REP ... 662-335-9003
Beamer, Nicole (CLOUD) CASEWK DIR ... 361-894-6446
Bean, David (BUCSHON) LEGIS CORRES 2313 ... 54636
Beard, Bennett (LUCAS) DIST FIELD REP ... 405-373-1958
Beard, Hillary (SEWELL) SR POLICY ADVISOR 2201 ... 52665
Bearden, Lalique (RUSH) OFFICE COORD ... 773-779-2400
Beattie, Nancy (LANGEVIN) DIR - CONSTIT SVCS ... 401-732-9400
Beatty, Paige (CAO/CHILD CARE CENTER) DIRECTOR 1100 ... 69321
Beaudreau, Helen (MENG) LEGIS DIR 2209 ... 52601
Beausang, Bethany (PINGREE) CASEWKR/ COUNSEL/CONSTIT OUTREACH REP ... 207-774-5019
Bebout, Tammie (GRIFFITH) SR CONSTIT SVCS REP ... 276-525-1405
Becerra, Cassandra (GRIJALVA) DIST SCHEDULER ... 520-622-6788
Becht, Andrew (KRISHNAMOORTHI) COORD - OPS 115 CHOB ... 53711
Beckelman, Yuri
(CMTE-VET AFFAIRS) SR ADVISOR B234 LHOB ... 59756
(TAKANO) DPTY CHIEF OF STAFF 420 CHOB ... 52305
Becker, Breanna (CAO/EMPLOYEE ASSISTANCE) EMPLOYEE ASST COUNSELOR 140 FHOB ... 52400
Becker, Matthew (RIGGLEMAN) OUTREACH DIR ... 434-791-2596
Becker, Nicholas (DELGADO) LIAISON - MIL & VET ... 845-443-2930
Beckerle, Hana (SGT AT ARMS/EMERGENCY MGMT) PROGRAM MGR 192 FHOB ... 60950
Becker-Pollet, Jennifer (LOWEY) LEGIS ASST/COUNSEL 2365 ... 56506
Beckmann, Alexander (LIPINSKI) LEGIS ASST 2346 ... 55701
Bednar, Mark (DUFFY) COMMUNICATIONS DIR 1714 ... 53365
Bedrosian, Scott (SPANO) DPTY CHIEF OF STAFF 224 CHOB ... 51252
Beebe, Erin (ARMSTRONG) LEGIS CORRES 1004 ... 52611
Beechler, Tracie (FOXX) CONSTIT LIAISON ... 828-265-0240
Begley, Andrea (ROGERS, HAROLD) FIELD REP ... 606-439-0794
Behnke, Derek (AXNE) DIST FIELD REP/ CASEWKR ... 515-400-8180
Behringer, Jenna (HARDER) PRESS SECY 131 CHOB ... 54540
Behuniak, Allison (HOLLINGSWORTH) LEGIS ASST 1641 ... 55315
Beil, Jennifer (GUTHRIE) OFFICE MGR 2434 ... 53501
Belair, Brendan
(CMTE-JUDICIARY) STAFF DIR - MIN 2142 ... 56906
(COLLINS, DOUG) STAFF DIR 1504 ... 59893
Belcher, Robert E (LAW REV COUNSEL) PRINTING EDITOR 308 FHOB ... 62411
Belchior, Isabela (JACKSON LEE) LEGIS COUNSEL 2079 ... 53816
Bell, Andrew (BUDD) CHIEF OF STAFF 118 CHOB ... 54531
Bell, Auburn (CMTE-NATURAL RESOURCES) SUBCOMM CLERK 186 FHOB ... 56065
Bell, Beth (CMTE-WAYS & MEANS) TAX COUNSEL 1136 ... 53625
Bell, Brian (CMTE-TRANSP & INFRA) COUNSEL 2165 ... 54472
Bell, Chris (CMTE-TRANSP & INFRA) LEGIS ASST 2165 ... 54472
Bell, Frank (CAO/HIR – ESCALATIONS AND OPS) MGR 608B FHOB ... 66199
Bell, Jennifer (MALONEY, CAROLYN B.) COMMUNICATIONS DIR 2308 ... 57944
Bell, Josh (ESTES) CHIEF OF STAFF 1524 ... 56216
Bell, Lyssa (CONAWAY) STAFF ASST 2469 ... 53605
Bell, Megan (ROGERS, HAROLD) CHIEF OF STAFF 2406 ... 54601
Bell, Michael (JEFFRIES) DIST STAFF ASST ... 718-237-2211
Bell, Morgan (MOULTON) DIST REP ... 978-531-1669
Bell, Patrick (RODGERS) DPTY DIST DIR ... 509-353-2374
Bell, Preston (HUDSON) LEGIS DIR 2112 ... 53715
Bellamy, Raven (CMTE-FOREIGN AFFAIRS) STAFF ASSOC 2171 ... 55021
Bellmon, Anthony (BOYLE) CONSTIT SVCS REP ... 267-335-5643
Belmonte, Paula (LIPINSKI) CONG ASST ... 773-948-6223
Belon, Reginald (MEEKS) SCHEDULER/DIR - OPS 2310 ... 53461
Belt, Camelia (SGT AT ARMS/APPOINTMENT) ASST - APPTS DESK CAPITOL ... 52551
Beltran, Elizabeth (SPEAKER) STAFF ASST H232 ... 50100
Beltran, Nate (VELA) STAFF ASST 307 CHOB ... 59901
Benavides, Sophia (CLERK/LRC) SR EXEC COMMUNICATIONS CLERK B81 CHOB ... 65200
Bender, Evan (CARTER, JOHN R.) LEGIS ASST 2110 ... 53864
Benedict, Kaleigh (MORELLE) DIR - COMMUNITY AFFAIRS ... 585-232-4850
Benettieri, Hugo (LARSON) DIST AIDE ... 860-278-8888
Benitez, Reimy (SHALALA) CONG AIDE ... 305-668-2285
Benjamin, Darren (CMTE-APPRO) PROF STAFF MEMB 1001 ... 53481
Benjamin, William
(CMTE-ENERGY & COMMERCE) SYS ADMIN 2125 ... 52927
(CMTE-OVERSIGHT & GOVT REFORM) SYS ADMIN 2157 ... 55051
Benn, Phillip (CAO/HOUSE RECORDING STUDIO) ELECTRONICS TECH 2010 ... 53941
Bennett, A Brooke (HILL, J. FRENCH) CHIEF OF STAFF 1533 ... 52506
Bennett, Cheryl (ROE) CONSTIT SVCS REP ... 423-254-1400
Bennett, Christopher (CMTE-VET AFFAIRS) PROF STAFF MEMB - ECONOMIC OPPORTUNITY SUBCOMM 3470 ... 59756
Bennett, Diana (TONKO) DIST COORD ... 518-465-0700
Bennett, Jacob (KILDEE) DPTY DIST DIR ... 810-238-8627
Bennett, McArn (CMTE-FINANCIAL SVCS) LEGIS ASST - MIN 4340 ... 57502
Bennett, Nathan (CARSON) LEGIS DIR/DPTY CHIEF 2135 ... 54011
Bennett, Parker (KELLY, MIKE) LEGIS CORRES 1707 ... 55406
Bennett, Philip (BLUMENAUER) STAFF ASST/LEGIS CORRES 1111 ... 54811
Bennett, Wells (CMTE-INTELLIGENCE) DPTY GEN COUNSEL HVC304 ... 57690
Bennigson, Daneen (BERA) CASEWK DIR ... 916-635-0505
Bennitt, Ian (CMTE-TRANSP & INFRA) STAFF DIR 585 FHOB ... 54472
Benson, Carla M (CLERK/LEGIS OPS) ASST ENROLLING CLERK HT13 ... 53153
Bensur, William (KATKO) POLICY ASST/PRESS ASST 2457 53701
Bentham, Nate (THOMPSON, MIKE) LEGIS ASST 406 CHOB ... 53311
Benton, Charles (HOUSE DEM CONG CMPGN CMTE) DIR - MBR SVCS ... 202-863-1500

Bentsen, Louise (GONZALEZ, VICENTE) LEGIS DIR 113 CHOB **52531**
Benzine, Mitchell (CMTE-OVERSIGHT & GOVT REFORM) COUNSEL 2105 .... **55074**
Beran, Lynn (CLERK/LCS) SR IT SECUR ANALYST 2401 .... **51182**
Berardi, Chris (ROONEY) COMMUNICATIONS DIR 120 CHOB **52536**
Bercovitch, Jason (PETERS) FIELD REP **858-455-5550**
Berdin, Leandra (NAPOLITANO) DIST SCHEDULER **626-350-0150**
Berg, Adam (CMTE-APPRO) CHIEF COUNSEL H307 .... **52771**
Berger, Benjamin (CMTE-SCIENCE) RESEARCH ASST - MAJ 2321 .... **56375**
Berger, Donald W (CAO/HOUSE RECORDING STUDIO) TECH DIR 2010 .... **53941**
Berger, Katie (CMTE-ED & WORKFORCE) PROF STAFF 2257 .... **53725**
Bergin, Moira (CMTE-HOMELAND SECUR) SUBCOMM STAFF DIR - CYBERSECURITY, INFRASTRUCTURE PROTECTION, AND INNOVATION SUBCOMM/COUNSEL - CYBERSECURITY, INFRASTRUCTURE PROTECTION, AND INNOVATION SUBCOMM 176 FHOB **62616**
Bergin, Robert (MORELLE) COUNSEL **585-232-4850**
Bergles, Jay (LAHOOD) CONSTIT REP **217-670-1653**
Bergman, Faith (BRINDISI) DIST FIELD REP **607-242-0200**
Bergquist, Ralene (ESTES) OFFICE MGR **316-262-8992**
Bergreen, Timothy (CMTE-INTELLIGENCE) STAFF DIR HVC304 .... **57690**
Bergren, Eric (GUTHRIE) CHIEF OF STAFF 2434 .... **53501**
Bergstad, Dillon (BLUMENAUER) CASEWK MGR **503-231-2300**
Bergwin, Diana (CMTE-HOMELAND SECUR) SUBCOMM STAFF DIR - EMERGENCY PREPAREDNESS, RESPONSE, AND RECOVERY SUBCOMM 117 FHOB **68417**
Berkson, Rachel (JAYAPAL) DIST DIR **206-674-0040**
Berman, Mia (PHILLIPS) DIST STAFF ASST 1305 .... **52871**
Berman, Rosie (COMMIS TOM LANTOS HUMAN RIGHTS) STAFF ASSOC 5100 .... **65285**
Bermudes-Castro, Paula (SABLAN) DIST MGR/ SCHEDULER **670-323-2647**
Bermudez, Navis (CMTE-TRANSP & INFRA) PROF STAFF 2165 .... **54472**
Bernacke, Michael (CUELLAR) LEGIS FELLOW 2372 .... **51640**
Bernal, Dan (PELOSI) DIST CHIEF OF STAFF **415-556-4862**
Berner, Alaina (FLETCHER) COMMUNICATIONS DIR 1429 .... **52571**
Berner, Hannah (GOTTHEIMER) LEGIS DIR 213 CHOB **54465**
Bernhard, James (RICHMOND) SPECIAL PROJ DIR **504-288-3777**
Bernhard, Sasha (DELBENE) SR POLICY ADVISOR 2330 .... **56311**
Bernstein, Eric (LEGIS COUNSEL) ASST COUNSEL 337 FHOB **56060**
Bernton, Jessica (SCHNEIDER) LEGIS DIR 1432 .... **54835**
Berret, Emily (SPEAKER) DIR - OPS H232 .... **50100**
Berríos-Vázquez, Ana (NORTON) COORD - COMMUNITY OUTREACH/CONSTIT LIAISON **202-408-9041**
Berry, Gregory (JACKSON LEE) CHIEF COUNSEL 2079 .... **53816**
Berry, Rodney (RICE, TOM) DIR - ECON DEV **843-679-9781**
Berstell, Daria (CMTE-VET AFFAIRS) STAFF ASST B234 LHOB **59756**
Bertocci, Tim (PHILLIPS) DC CHIEF OF STAFF 1305 .... **52871**
Bertram, Mary (PETERSON) STAFF ASST **320-235-1061**
Bervar, Lyndall (SMITH, ADAM) DIST REP **425-793-5180**
Besonen, Mark (FOXX) LEGIS CORRES 2462 .... **52071**
Bessaha, Nabil (CAO/HIR – CYBERSECURITY) SR INFO SYS SECUR ANALYST 650 FHOB **63868**
Best, Catherine (GOTTHEIMER) DIST DIR **201-389-1100**
Best, Charlene (CAO/ASSET MANAGEMENT) MGR 6110 .... **50090**
Best, Rae Ellen (CLERK/LRC) MGR - LIBRARY SVCS B81 CHOB **65200**
Beste, Megan (WILD) DIST DIR **484-781-6000**
Bethea, Deborah (CMTE-ETHICS) SR FINANCIAL DISCLOSURE MGR 508 FHOB **57103**
Betz, Kim (CMTE-FINANCIAL SVCS) GEN COUNSEL 4340 .... **57502**
Beyer, Ashley (TORRES SMALL) FIELD REP **575-323-6384**
Bezruki, Steffanie (BUSTOS) SR POLICY ADVISOR 1233 .... **55905**
Bhalla, Ratina (SUOZZI) CASEWK MGR **631-923-4100**
Bhambhani, Ariana (ALLEN) LEGIS CORRES 2400 .... **52823**
Bhargava, Jay (SUOZZI) PRESS SECY 214 CHOB **53335**
Bhatti, Saira (WEXTON) CONSTIT SVCS REP **703-234-3800**
Bianco, Lisa (NEGUSE) CHIEF OF STAFF 1419 .... **52161**
Bias, Gregory (CLERK) MGR - OPS H154 .... **57000**
Biba, Tim (MOULTON) COMMUNICATIONS DIR 1127 .... **58020**
Bice, Victoria (PENCE) LEGIS AIDE 222 CHOB **53021**
Bick, Caroline (JORDAN) DPTY DIST DIR **419-663-1426**
Bickel, Heather (THOMPSON, GLENN) CASEWKR **814-353-0215**
Bickham, Andrew (CAO/HIR – IT CUSTOMER SOLUTIONS) ANALYST 608C FHOB **66288**
Bickley, Theo (MALONEY, SEAN PATRICK) SPECIAL ASST **845-561-1259**
Bidelman, Kiley (CMTE-OVERSIGHT & GOVT REFORM) CLERK 2105 .... **55074**
Bieber, Matt (DEAN) COMMUNICATIONS DIR **610-382-1250**
Bien, Christopher (MIN LEADER) DPTY FLOOR DIR H204 .... **54000**
Bieniek, Kristine (HUDSON) DC SCHEDULER 2112 .... **53715**
Bieret, Stefan (SGT AT ARMS/POLICE SVCS) SR ASST HT8 **51000**
Bigelow, Christopher (CMTE-APPRO) DPTY STAFF DIR H307 .... **52771**
Biggs, Lora (BUCSHON) DIR - CONSTIT SVCS **812-465-6484**
Bilinski, John (CAO/ENTERPRISE APPLICATIONS) SR BUSINESS PROCESS APPLICA SPEC B77 FHOB **66280**
Bill, Aaron (ROE) LEGIS DIR 102 CHOB **56356**
Billard, Michael (CAO/HIR – NETWORKING ENGINEERING AND OPS) COMMUNICATIONS SPEC 681 FHOB **64215**
Billerbeck, Peter (CMTE-FOREIGN AFFAIRS) POLICY ANALYST 2420 .... **55021**
Billman, Jeffrey (HERN) DPTY CHIEF OF STAFF 1019 .... **52211**
Billman, Lauren (MILLER) LEGIS DIR 1605 .... **53452**
Billman, Tucker (WALDEN) FIELD REP **541-624-2400**
Billups, Brian (CAO/HIR – NETWORKING ENGINEERING AND OPS) NETWK TECH 681 FHOB **66357**
Billy, Kelley (ROUZER) EXEC ASST 2439 .... **52731**
Bina, Betsy (CMTE-APPRO) PROF STAFF MEMB 1001 .... **53481**
Binger, Will (AXNE) LEGIS ASST 330 CHOB **55476**
Bingham, Elizabeth S (CLERK/REPORTERS) OFFICIAL REPORTER HT59 .... **55621**
Binsted, Anne (CAO) CHIEF OF STAFF HB28 .... **55555**
Bionat, Christian (OLSON) DIST DIR **281-494-2690**
Birch, Debby (LEGIS COUNSEL) ASST OFC ADMIN 337 FHOB **56060**

Birch, Joseph (LEGIS COUNSEL) STAFF ASST 337 FHOB.... **56060**
Bird, Jessica (RUTHERFORD) LEGIS CORRES 1711.... **52501**
Birleson, Megan (SLOTKIN) DC SCHEDULER 1531.... **54872**
Biron, Christine (SOTO) CHIEF OF STAFF 1507.... **59889**
Bisenius, Matt (SENSENBRENNER) CHIEF OF STAFF 2449. **55101**
Bishop, Audrey (FOXX) CONSTIT LIAISON.... **828-265-0240**
Bishop, Jeff (STAUBER) LEGIS DIR 126 CHOB.... **56211**
Bishop, Mary (CLARKE) DIST REP.... **718-287-1142**
Bishop, Matthew (BYRNE) STAFF ASST 119 CHOB.... **54931**
Bishop, Tony (JEFFRIES) LEGIS FELLOW 2433.... **55936**
Bissonnette, Alicia (SCHRIER) LEGIS CORRES 1123.... **57761**
Bitar, Maher (CMTE-INTELLIGENCE) GEN COUNSEL HVC304.... **57690**
Bivens, Bobby (GREEN, AL) STAFF ASST 2347.... **57508**
Bivins, Samantha (HORSFORD) DIST REP.... **702-963-9360**
Bivona, John (DELGADO) CHIEF OF STAFF 1007.... **55614**
Bizzacco, Chris (CICILLINE) DIST DIR.... **401-729-5600**
Black, Dan (KENNEDY) PRESS SECY 304 CHOB.... **55931**
Black, Daniel (RADEWAGEN) LEGIS ASST/ASST COMMUNICATIONS DIR 1339.... **58577**
Black, Jon (BISHOP, SANFORD D., JR.) SR POLICY ADVISOR 2407.... **53631**
Black, Justin (CAO/OFFICE OF THE CHIEF INFORMATION OFFICER - HIR) CHIEF TECH OFFICER 630A FHOB.... **66011**
Black, Kristi (SPANBERGER) DIST COORD.... **540-321-6130**
Black, Rachel (GRAVES, TOM) STAFF ASST/LEGIS CORRES 2078.... **55211**
Blackburn, Paige (RODGERS) CONSTIT RELATIONS REP.... **509-353-2374**
Blackburn, Sara (BUDD) CONSTIT SVCS REP.... **336-998-1313**
Blackerby, Bruce (CAO/HIR – CYBERSECURITY) INFO SYS SECUR ANALYST 613 FHOB.... **68769**
Blackley, Hope (TIMMONS) DIST DIR.... **864-241-0175**
Blackman, Wade (CLARK) LEGAL COUNSEL/ CONSTIT SVCS.... **508-319-9757**
Blackmore, Taylor (BERGMAN) DIR - CONSTIT SVCS.... **231-944-7633**
Blackney, Mark (NUNES) DIST FIELD REP.... **559-323-5235**
Blacksberg, Aaron (CMTE-OVERSIGHT & GOVT REFORM) COUNSEL 2157.... **55051**
Blacksher, Sarah (BABIN) CONSTIT SVCS REP.... **409-331-8066**
Blackwell, Matt (DUNN) LEGIS DIR 316 CHOB.... **55235**
Blaine, Jarilyn (SMITH, JASON) DIGITAL DIR 2418.... **54404**
Blair, Alex (STEUBE) CHIEF OF STAFF 521 CHOB.... **55792**
Blake, Carly (CMTE-INTELLIGENCE) DPTY STAFF DIR HVC304.... **57690**
Blakely, John (GREEN, MARK E.) FIELD REP.... **629-223-6050**
Blakley, Jeff (CAO/HOUSE CREATIVE SVCS) DIRECTOR 2002.... **52700**
Blakney, Harold (CAO/HIR - ENTERPRISE MESSAGING AND MOBILITY) SR SYS ENGINEER 622 FHOB.... **66181**
Blalock, Nora (PRICE) SR LEGIS ASST 2108.... **51784**
Blanco, Jennifer (DIAZ-BALART) CONG AIDE.... **305-470-8555**
Bland, Megan (CMTE-VET AFFAIRS) PROF STAFF MEMB - HEALTH SUBCOMM 3470.... **59756**
Blanford, Meredith (DAVIS, RODNEY) PRESS SECY 1740... **52371**
Blanford, Thomas (CMTE-HOUSE ADMIN) STAFF ASST - MIN 1216.... **58281**
Blankenship, Allison (MCBATH) LEGIS AIDE 1513.... **54501**
Blankenship, April
(CMTE-ED & WORKFORCE) FINANCIAL ADMIN/SHARED EMPLOYEE 2101.... **54527**
(CMTE-TRANSP & INFRA) ADMIN - FINANCE & PAYROLL 2165.... **54472**
(CMTE-WAYS & MEANS) FINANCIAL ADMIN 1139.... **54021**
(TAYLOR) FINANCIAL ADMIN 1404.... **54201**
(YOHO) FINANCIAL ADMIN 1730.... **55744**
Blanton, Seth (TIMMONS) DIR - CONSTIT SVCS.... **864-583-3264**
Blatnik, Lauren (MITCHELL) DIST STAFF ASST.... **586-997-5010**
Blatt, Hannah (MATSUI) COMMUNICATIONS DIR 2311.... **57163**
Blaydes, Carolyn (CMTE-VET AFFAIRS) SUBCOMM STAFF DIR - DISABILITY ASSISTANCE AND MEMORIAL AFFAIRS SUBCOMM B234 LHOB.... **59756**
Blazek, Kelliann (PINGREE) LEGIS ASST 2162.... **56116**
Blazey, James (WALORSKI) DIST FIELD REP.... **574-204-2645**
Bleiberg, Daniel (FRANKEL) LEGIS ASST 2305.... **59890**
Blevins, Brent (CMTE-SCIENCE) SR POLICY ADVISOR - REPUB 394 FHOB.... **56371**
Block, Kevin (WATSON COLEMAN) LEGIS DIR 2442.... **55801**
Block-Levin, Natalie (RICE, KATHLEEN M.) COMMUNITY REP.... **516-739-3008**
Blodgett, Tim (SGT AT ARMS) DPTY SGT AT ARMS H124.... **52456**
Bloomquist, Mike (CMTE-ENERGY & COMMERCE) STAFF DIR 2322A.... **53641**
Blount, Willie (LEGIS COUNSEL) INFO SYS ANALYST 337 FHOB.... **56060**
Blum, Erika (NEGUSE) CONSTIT ADVOCATE.... **303-335-1045**
Blumenthal, Jordan
(CMTE-OVERSIGHT & GOVT REFORM) COUNSEL/POLICY ADVISOR 2157.... **55051**
(CUMMINGS) POLICY COUNSEL 2163.... **54741**
Blum-Evitts, Lyron (CMTE-AGRIC) MEMB RELATIONS COORD 1301.... **52171**
Blyden, Chidi (CMTE-ARMED SVCS) PROF STAFF 2117.... **67164**
Bodey, Mikayla (CRAIG) SR LEGIS ASST 1523.... **52271**
Boehmer, Ron (POCAN) COMMUNICATIONS DIR 1421.... **52906**
Boffelli, Claudio (SHALALA) STAFF ASST 1320.... **53931**
Boffelli, Gabriella (GONZÁLEZ-COLÓN) CHIEF OF STAFF 1609.... **52615**
Bogan, David (CAO/OFFICE SUPPLY/GIFT SHOP) SUPERVISOR B217 LHOB.... **53321**
Bogeljic, Tia (PERLMUTTER) STAFF ASST 1226.... **52645**
Boger, Kelly (CAO/ASSET MANAGEMENT) SUPERVISOR 6110.... **50090**
Boggs, Bethany (DUNN) CONSTIT SVCS SPEC.... **850-785-0812**
Boggs, Clay (TORRES) LEGIS DIR 2444.... **56161**
Boggs, Galen (KHANNA) FIELD REP.... **408-436-2720**
Boggs, Madison (ESHOO) LEGIS CORRES 202 CHOB.... **58104**
Bogner, Michael (SMITH, ADRIAN) CONSTIT SVCS REP.... **308-384-3900**
Bogorowski, Hanna (MIN LEADER) COMMUNICATIONS AIDE H204.... **54000**
Bohannon, Zach (DAVIDSON) FIELD REP.... **513-779-5400**
Bohlmann, Leah (KINZINGER) SPECIAL ASST.... **815-431-9271**
Boies, Lilia (ABRAHAM) OFFICE MGR/CASEWKR.... **318-322-3500**
Boileau, Ryan (WOODALL) STAFF ASST 1724.... **54272**
Boisseau, Anne-Marie (SPEIER) LEGIS CORRES 2465.... **53531**
Bojorquez-Gomez, Maria (DAVIS, SUSAN A.) STAFF ASST.... **619-280-5353**

Boland, Patrick
(CMTE-INTELLIGENCE) COMMUNICATIONS DIR HVC304.... **57690**
(SCHIFF) COMMUNICATIONS DIR/SR ADVISOR/DPTY CHIEF OF STAFF 2269 **54176**
Boldebuck, Calvin (POCAN) FIELD REP **608-258-9800**
Bolden, Charles (KELLY, ROBIN L.) LEGIS CORRES 2416... **50773**
Boldig, Christopher (CAO/ADMIN COUNSEL) ASSOC COUNSEL 217 FHOB **56969**
Bolen, Jacquelyn (CMTE-ENERGY & COMMERCE) PROF STAFF 2125 **54407**
Boley, Bonnie (FLEISCHMANN) STAFF ASST **423-756-2342**
Bolles, Libby (STEUBE) DPTY DIST DIR **941-575-9101**
Boman, Josiah (LUETKEMEYER) LEGIS ASST 2230 **52956**
Bombard, Jeff (DELAURO) OFFICE MGR **203-562-3718**
Bonaccorsi, Matt (MCGOVERN) COMMUNICATIONS DIR 408 CHOB **56101**
Bond, Pat (GARCIA, SYLVIA R.) LEGIS DIR 1620 **51688**
Bond, Patrick (LUCAS) COMMUNICATIONS DIR 2405 **55565**
Bond, Slade (CMTE-JUDICIARY) CHIEF COUNSEL 6240 **67680**
Bondi, Emily (CMTE-HOMELAND SECUR) PRESS ASST/ STAFF ASST 117 FHOB **68417**
Bonifacio, Noelani (HOUSE REPUB STUDY CMTE) POLICY STAFF 418 CHOB **52777**
Bonifati, Avery (ADAMS) DIST STAFF ASST/ PRESS ASST **704-344-9950**
Bonilla, Gerardo (CMTE-SMALL BUSINESS) SR ECON ADVISOR 2361 **54038**
Bonilla, Veronica (TORRES) PRESS SECY 2444 **56161**
Bonnaure, Aaron (RESCHENTHALER) CHIEF OF STAFF 531 CHOB **52065**
Bonner, Jazmine (NADLER) STAFF ASST 2132 **55635**
Bonner, Lee (MIN LEADER) DPTY SCHEDULER H204 **54000**
Bonner, Robert (CMTE-APPRO) CLERK H310 **53351**
Bonney, Victoria (PINGREE) COMMUNICATIONS DIR **207-774-5019**
Bonomo, Joe (LIPINSKI) DPTY DIST DIR **773-948-6223**
Bonthius, Daniel (OCASIO-CORTEZ) SCHEDULER 229 CHOB **53965**
Bonville, Diaz (BLUNT ROCHESTER) CONSTIT OUTREACH REP **302-858-4773**
Boogaard, Paige (RATCLIFFE) STAFF ASST 223 CHOB **56673**
Booker, Carlos (CAO/OFFICE SUPPLY/GIFT SHOP) SALES SPEC B217 LHOB **53321**
Booker, Michelle (ESPAILLAT) DPTY DIST DIR **212-663-3900**
Booker, Stephanie (THOMPSON, BENNIE G.) CASEWKR/FIELD REP **601-866-9003**
Boomhower, Amanda (DELGADO) DIST DIR **845-443-2930**
Boone, Demontre (SCOTT, ROBERT C. "BOBBY") DIR - CONSTIT SVCS **757-380-1000**
Boone, Portia (NORTON) LEGIS ASST 2136 **58050**
Boone, Russell (CAO/HIR – IT CUSTOMER SOLUTIONS) TECH SUPPORT REP 2067 **66345**
Booth, Teri (MILLER) REGIONAL REP/DIST OFFICE MGR **304-522-2201**
Booth, Whitney (CURTIS) DIST COMMUNICATIONS DIR **801-922-5400**
Boothe, Caroline (HOUSE REPUB CONF) DIR - MBR SVCS 1420 **55107**
Bope, Heath (CMTE-ARMED SVCS) PROF STAFF 2340 **53040**
Borja, Anais (PETERS) SR LEGIS ASST 2338 **50508**
Borjon, Jose (GONZALEZ, VICENTE) CHIEF OF STAFF 113 CHOB **52531**
Bormann, Sarah (BRINDISI) DIST DIR **315-732-0713**
Borne, Adele (SELECT CMTE-CLIMATE CRISIS) STAFF ASST - REPUB 361 FHOB **51107**
Bornstein, Jake (CURTIS) LEGIS DIR 125 CHOB **57751**
Bornstein, Rachael (BONAMICI) CHIEF OF STAFF 2231 **50855**
Borovsky, Joel (HOUSE EMPLOYMENT COUNSEL) ASSOC COUNSEL 4300 **57075**
Borquez-Smith, Ernestina (SCHWEIKERT) DIR - CONSTIT AFFAIRS/OFFICE MGR **480-946-2411**
Bortnick, David (CMTE-APPRO) PROF STAFF MEMB H405.. **52847**
Bortz, Ashton (MOOLENAAR) DIST CHIEF OF STAFF **989-631-2552**
Borzner, Claire (DOYLE) LEGIS ASST 306 CHOB **52135**
Bos, Amy (SENSENBRENNER) LEGIS DIR 2449 **55101**
Boshears, Cindy (FLEISCHMANN) DIST FIELD REP **865-576-1976**
Bosman, Jared (AGUILAR) LIAISON - MIL & VET **909-890-4445**
Boss, Naomi (GRAVES, SAM) FIELD REP **816-749-0800**
Bossart, Betsy (HOYER) DIST CHIEF OF STAFF **301-843-1577**
Bosworth, Jon (BLUMENAUER) LEGIS ASST 1111 **54811**
Bottoms, Bradley (GARAMENDI) CHIEF OF STAFF 2368 **51880**
Boucher, Taylor (STEFANIK) CONSTIT LIAISON **518-743-0964**
Bouchot, Enrique (CAO/ENTERPRISE APPLICATIONS) SR BUSINESS PROCESS APPLICA SPEC B73 FHOB **66208**
Boughton, Marty (CMTE-ED & WORKFORCE) PRESS SECY 2178 **69440**
Bounds, Jazmine (CAO/OFFICE SUPPLY/GIFT SHOP) SALES SPEC B217 LHOB **53321**
Bounds, Lorissa
(CMTE-ENERGY & COMMERCE) POLICY COORD 2322A **53641**
(WALDEN) CHIEF OF STAFF 2185 **56730**
Bourbon, Christy (COSTA) DIST SCHEDULER **559-495-1620**
Bourdon, Sue (WALBERG) CONSTIT RELATIONS REP **517-780-9075**
Bourk, Heather (CLERK/ART & ARCHIVES) MGR - ARCHIVES JEFFERSON BUILDING, ATTIC **61300**
Bourke, Jaron (CMTE-OVERSIGHT & GOVT REFORM) ADMIN DIR 2157 **55051**
Bourn, Anita (PALAZZO) CASEWK DIR **601-582-3246**
Bourn, Grady (CARTER, JOHN R.) LEGIS DIR 2110 **53864**
Boutwell, Debra (GUEST) DIR - SCHEDULING **769-241-6120**
Bovair, Caroline (ROUDA) ADMIN DIR/SCHEDULER 2300 **52415**
Bowden, Jamitress (CMTE-OVERSIGHT & GOVT REFORM) PRESS SECY 2157 **55051**
Bowen, Jessica (BONAMICI) LEGIS ASST 2231 **50855**
Bowen, Lindsey (BUTTERFIELD) EXEC ASST/SCHEDULER 2080 **53101**
Bowen, S K (CARTER, EARL L. "BUDDY") PRESS ASST/ STAFF ASST 2432 **55831**
Bowen, Will (MCHENRY) REGIONAL REP **704-833-0096**
Bower, Andrew (LOWENTHAL) LEGIS ASST 108 CHOB **57924**
Bower, Matthew (CMTE-APPRO) PROF STAFF MEMB H405 **52847**
Bower, Sue (WALTZ) CONSTIT SVCS **386-238-9711**
Bowers, Mandy (CMTE-HOMELAND SECUR) SUBCOMM STAFF DIR - INTELLIGENCE AND COUNTERTERRORISM SUBCOMM 117 FHOB **68417**

Bowie, Maria (COLE) LEGIS DIR/DPTY CHIEF OF STAFF 2207 56165
Bowlding, Sonia (CAO/ASSET MANAGEMENT) REC & WAREHOUSE SPEC 161 FHOB 60538
Bowlen, Joshua (NC03) CHIEF OF STAFF 2333 53415
Bowles, Maureen (WASSERMAN SCHULTZ) FINANCIAL ADMIN 1114 57931
Bowling, Michelle (COMER) PRESS SECY/LEGIS ASST 2184 53115
Bowling-Stokes, Chaunette (CAO/PAYROLL & BENEFITS) MGMT ANALYST B215 LHOB 64518
Bowman, Bryan (GONZALEZ, ANTHONY) VET ADVOCATE 330-599-7037
Bowman, Casey (HERRERA BEUTLER) CHIEF OF STAFF 360-695-6292
Bowman, Chris (LAMB) LEGIS DIR 1224 52301
Bowman, David (LEWIS) SCHEDULER 300 CHOB 53801
Bowman, Shelia (CAO/FINANCIAL COUNSELING) COUNSELOR B215 LHOB 62819
Bowyer, Kathrin (DEMINGS) STAFF ASST 321-388-9808
Boyd, Clayton (DAVIS, DANNY K.) STAFF ASST 773-533-7520
Boyd, Heather (SCANLON) DIST DIR 610-626-1913
Boyd, Krista (CMTE-OVERSIGHT & GOVT REFORM) GEN COUNSEL 2157 55051
Boyd, Kristie (CAO/HOUSE CREATIVE SVCS) PHOTOGRAPHER 2002 52700
Boyd, Petrina (CAO/OFFICE SUPPLY/GIFT SHOP) SALES SPEC B217 LHOB 53321
Boyer, Brooke (CMTE-APPRO) PROF STAFF MEMB H405 52847
Boyer, Davis (SHIMKUS) LEGIS CORRES 2217 55271
Boyer, Francis (FITZPATRICK) DIR - OPS 1722 54276
Boyer, Jesseca (CMTE-ENERGY & COMMERCE) PROF STAFF 2125 52927
Boyer, Melinda (WESTERMAN) FIELD REP 870-864-8946
Boyett, Brooke (FLETCHER) DIST DIR 713-353-8680
Boyington, Will (NEWHOUSE) COMMUNICATIONS DIR 1414 55816
Boyken, Lori (LUETKEMEYER) CONG LIAISON 573-635-7232
Boyle, Kevin (CAO/ENTERPRISE APPLICATIONS) SR BUSINESS PROCESS APPLICA SPEC B70 FHOB 64223
Boyle, Margaret (NEAL) AIDE 413-785-0325
Boysen, Dan (HOUSE DEM CONG CMPGN CMTE) NATIONAL FINANCE DIR 202-863-1500
Boztepe, Dilara (WATSON COLEMAN) DIST REP 609-883-0026
Brace, Gordon S (CLERK/LCS) SR HARDWARE ENGINEER 2401 51182
Brackens, Robert (CAO/HOUSE RECORDING STUDIO) BROADCAST PROD TECH 2010 53941
Bracy, Bobby Joe (MUCARSEL-POWELL) CONSTIT SVCS ASST 305-222-0160
Braden, Ansley (BUCK) SCHEDULER 2455 54676
Braden, Parish (CMTE-NATURAL RESOURCES) STAFF DIR 1329 52761
Bradford, Aryele (CMTE-OVERSIGHT & GOVT REFORM) COMMUNICATIONS DIR 2157 55051
Bradley, Katelynn (CMTE-FINANCIAL SVCS) DIRECTOR 3320 60736
Bradley, Katie (LOWENTHAL) STAFF ASST 108 CHOB 57924
Bradley, Nathaniel (CAO/HOUSE CREATIVE SVCS) DIR - SVC DESK & QUALITY ASSURANCE 607B FHOB 66107
Bradley, Philippa (MCKINLEY) LEGIS AIDE/LEGIS CORRES 2239 54172
Bradley, Shannon (LEVIN, MIKE) FIELD REP 760-599-5000
Brady, Daryl (ROE) FIELD REP 423-254-1400
Brady, Haley (RIGGLEMAN) DIR - OPS 1022 54711
Brady, John (CAO/FURNISHINGS) APPRENTICE UPHOLSTERER WA33 RHOB 58000
Brady, Kevin (CLERK/LEGIS OPS) ADMIN ASST HT13 57925
Brady, Michael (ESHOO) PRESS SECY 202 CHOB 58104
Brady, Sean (BUCHANAN) DPTY CHIEF 2427 55015
Bragato, Brandon (CMTE-NATURAL RESOURCES) SUBCOMM STAFF DIR 1328 56065
Bragdon, Stephanie (SARBANES) LEGIS CORRES 2370 54016
Bragg, Erica (MOONEY) STAFF ASST 304-925-5964
Bragin, Gideon (HOUSE DEM CAUCUS) EXEC DIR B245 LHOB 51400
Brahimi, Samia (CMTE-FOREIGN AFFAIRS) SR PROF STAFF 4150 68467
Brain, Michael (CMTE-APPRO) PROF STAFF MEMB 2362B 53421
Brainard, Colin (WATKINS) CHIEF OF STAFF 1205 56601
Branch, Doug (DAVIDSON) DPTY CHIEF OF STAFF 1107 56205
Branch, Ora (CLERK/LRC) SR REFERENCE LIBRARIAN B81 CHOB 65200
Branch, Roderick V (CLERK/REPORTERS) PROD ASST 193 CHOB 57187
Branche, Laveeta (JOHNSON, HENRY C. "HANK", JR.) DIST SCHEDULER 770-987-2291
Brand, Norman (CMTE-JOINT TAX) SR COUNSEL IRS-3565 202-317-4463
Brandenburg, Christopher (HOLDING) SR CONSTIT SVCS REP 919-782-4400
Brandenburg, Kirby (JORDAN) FIELD REP 419-999-6455
Brandenburg, Rachel (SLOTKIN) LEGIS ASST - MIL 1531 54872
Brandolini, Gillie (WOMACK) CONSTIT SVCS REP 479-464-0446
Brannock, Phoebe (BURCHETT) LEGIS CORRES 1122 55435
Bratcher, Brandon (DESAULNIER) DIST REP 925-933-2660
Bratton, Tyrone (LURIA) LEGIS DIR 534 CHOB 54215
Braun, Andrew (LAMBORN) LEGIS ASST - MIL 2371 54422
Bravo, Bobby (LESKO) LEGIS AIDE 1113 54576
Bravo, Sandra (BROWNLEY) CASEWKR/DIST SCHEDULER 805-379-1779
Bravo Liranza, Gabriel (GONZÁLEZ-COLÓN) LEGIS ASST 1609 52615
Braxton, Brandon (CAO/LOGISTICS) REC & WAREHOUSE SPEC RSBC4 55057
Bray, Austin (BRADY) LEGIS COUNSEL 1011 54901
Brazelton, Hallet (LEGIS COUNSEL) COUNSEL 337 FHOB 56060
Breaux, Kris (CMTE-INTELLIGENCE) SUBCOMM STAFF DIR HVC304 57690
Brebbia, Sean (CMTE-OVERSIGHT & GOVT REFORM) SR COUNSEL 2105 55074
Breck, Catey (RYAN) ECON DEV REP 330-630-7311
Breen, Anna (HERRERA BEUTLER) SR LEGIS ASST 2352 53536
Breene, Samuel (KELLY, MIKE) FIELD REP 814-454-8190
Breidenbach, Carrie (CMTE-WAYS & MEANS) CLERK 1102 53625
Breisblatt, Joshua (CMTE-JUDICIARY) COUNSEL 6320 53926
Breitenbach, Ryan (CMTE-JUDICIARY) CHIEF COUNSEL 362 FHOB 56906

Brekhus, Keith (O'HALLERAN) DIST OFFICE MGR 928-286-5338
Brennan, Andrew (ARRINGTON) COMMUNICATIONS ASST 1029 54005
Brennan, Bridget (MAJ LEADER) DIR - SCHEDULING H107. 53130
Brennan, Kevin (SGT AT ARMS/EMERGENCY MGMT) DPTY ASST SGT AT ARMS – EMERGENCY MGMT 192 FHOB 60950
Brennan, Matthew (THOMPSON, GLENN) CHIEF OF STAFF 400 CHOB 55121
Brennan, Ross (CICILLINE) LEGIS ASST 2233 54911
Brenner, Steve (LOWEY) LEGIS CORRES 2365 56506
Breslin, William (MUCARSEL-POWELL) STAFF ASST 114 CHOB 52778
Bresnahan, Brian (KUSTER) CONSTIT SVCS 603-444-7700
Bress, Matilda (ROUDA) STAFF ASST 2300 52415
Brewer, David (CMTE-OVERSIGHT & GOVT REFORM) DPTY STAFF DIR 2105 55074
Brewster, Christopher (CAO/ADMIN COUNSEL) ADMIN COUNSEL 217 FHOB 56969
Brewster, James (CAO/LOGISTICS) LOGISTICS & DIST SPEC WA16 RHOB 59474
Bridgeforth, Carlton (CMTE-AGRIC) PROF STAFF 1301 52171
Bridgeforth, Toinetta (CAO/ACQUIS MGMT) SR CONTRACTS SPEC 5110 52921
Brier, Theresa (DEUTCH) DPTY DIST DIR 954-255-8336
Briere, Kayla (HAYES) CASEWKR 860-223-8412
Briggs, Alex (GIBBS) LEGIS DIR 2446 56265
Briggs, Laura (PALLONE) STAFF ASST/DIST SCHEDULER 732-571-1140
Brill, Sophia (CMTE-JUDICIARY) COUNSEL 2035 53951
Brinson, Chris (ROGERS, MIKE) CHIEF OF STAFF 2184 53261
Briscoe, Kevin (CAO/LOGISTICS) LOGISTICS & DIST SPEC WA16 RHOB 59474
Brissette, Kelly (MCGOVERN) DIST SCHEDULER/DPTY DIST DIR 508-831-7356
Brito, Yokasta (MUCARSEL-POWELL) DIST STAFF ASST 305-222-0160
Britt, Clinton (TONKO) CHIEF OF STAFF 2369 55076
Britton, Cammie (BUTTERFIELD) DPTY DIR - CONSTIT SVCS 252-237-9816
Broady, Marc
(CMTE-OVERSIGHT & GOVT REFORM) POLICY ADVISOR 2157 55051
(CUMMINGS) POLICY COUNSEL 2163 54741
Brockwehl, Alexander (CMTE-FOREIGN AFFAIRS) PROF STAFF MEMB 5220 53345
Brodtke, John (SHERMAN) FIELD REP 818-501-9200
Brody, Perry (VELA) CHIEF OF STAFF 307 CHOB 59901
Brody, Rachel (CMTE-JOINT ECON) SOCIAL MEDIA MGR - DEM SH-804 40379
Brogan, Kelsi (JOYCE, DAVID P.) SCHEDULER 1124 55731
Bronson, Karen A (CHAPLAIN) MBR OFFICE LIAISON & PROGRAM COORD HC2 64835
Brooke, Kenneth (AMODEI) LEGIS ASST 104 CHOB 56155
Brooker, David (GALLAGHER) FIELD REP 920-301-4500
Brooks, Greg (WENSTRUP) LEGIS DIR/DPTY CHIEF OF STAFF 2419 53164
Brooks, Kyle (GIBBS) CASEWKR 419-207-0650
Brooks, Lavontae (HORSFORD) LEGIS ASST 1330 59894
Brooks, Michael (MARSHALL) LEGIS DIR 312 CHOB 52715
Brooks, Sarah (MOOLENAAR) DIR - EXTERNAL AFFAIRS 989-631-2552
Brooks, Tracy (SOTO) FIELD REP 407-452-1171
Brooks, William (KELLY, TRENT) FIELD REP - VETS 662-841-8808
Brookshire, Emma (GOHMERT) LEGIS AIDE 2267 53035
Brotman, Michelle (JEFFRIES) CONSTIT SVCS REP 718-237-2211
Brotzman, Lenora (SMITH, ADRIAN) OFFICE COORD 308-633-6333
Broughton, Christine (CLINE) DIST REP 540-857-2672
Broussard, Kristie (HIGGINS, CLAY) CASEWKR 337-703-6105
Brower, Justin (RUPPERSBERGER) LEGIS ASST - MIL 2206 53061
Brown, A J (CMTE-ENERGY & COMMERCE) COUNSEL 2125 52927
Brown, Anne (SLOTKIN) FIELD REP 517-993-0510
Brown, Baillee (PETERS) SR LEGIS ASST 2338 50508
Brown, Brandy (PERRY) COMMUNICATIONS DIR 1207 55836
Brown, Carlee (CMTE-NATURAL RESOURCES) PROF STAFF - MAJ 1332 56065
Brown, Chelsea (ARRINGTON) CHIEF OF STAFF 1029 54005
Brown, Chris (CMTE-FINANCIAL SVCS) SR PROF STAFF 4340 57502
Brown, Christopher (SGT AT ARMS/GARAGES & PARKING) SUPERVISOR G2-28 56749
Brown, Cindy (WEBSTER) COMMUNITY RELATIONS SPEC 352-383-3552
Brown, Dan (TIMMONS) LEGIS CORRES 313 CHOB 56030
Brown, Danielle (CMTE-WAYS & MEANS) GEN COUNSEL/ PARLIAMENTARIAN 1102 53625
Brown, Demetrice (CAO/HOUSE CREATIVE SVCS) SR TECH SUPPORT REP 605 FHOB 66149
Brown, Dominique (JOHNSON, EDDIE BERNICE) DIR - OPS 214-922-8885
Brown, Ebony (LEGIS COUNSEL) ASST COUNSEL 337 FHOB 56060
Brown, Elizabeth (CASTOR) LEGIS DIR 2052 53376
Brown, Erica (GAETZ) DIST AIDE 850-479-1183
Brown, Janet (CORREA) DIST FIELD REP 714-559-6190
Brown, Janet (WEBER) CASEWKR 409-835-0108
Brown, Jason (CAO/HOUSE RECORDING STUDIO) TECH DIR 2010 53941
Brown, Jenell (DAVIS, DANNY K.) FINANCIAL & ADMIN OFFICER/OFFICE MGR 2159 55006
Brown, Jennifer (COLLINS, CHRIS) PRESS ASST 2243 55265
Brown, Jessica (DAVIS, SUSAN A.) FIELD REP - VETS 619-280-5353
Brown, Joanna (WALBERG) LEGIS DIR 2266 56276
Brown, Joey (SMITH, JASON) COMMUNICATIONS DIR 2418 54404
Brown, Kaitlin (NORTON) CONSTIT LIAISON 202-408-9041
Brown, Kaitlin (MCKINLEY) EXEC ASST 2239 54172
Brown, Keith (CAO/FURNISHINGS) APPRENTICE CABINET MAKER WA39 RHOB 58000
Brown, Keith (ABRAHAM) DIST OUTREACH REP 318-322-3500
Brown, Kendra (BUTTERFIELD) CHIEF OF STAFF 2080 53101
Brown, Lanie (BABIN) REGIONAL DIR 409-883-8075
Brown, Lavell (DAVIS, DANNY K.) LEGIS ASST 2159 55006

Brown, Lawrence (CAO/HOUSE RECORDING STUDIO) BROADCAST ENGINEER/PROD SPEC 2010 **53941**
Brown, Mason (ABRAHAM) STAFF ASST 417 CHOB **58490**
Brown, Matthew (STEIL) DIR - OPS & PLANNING 1408 **53031**
Brown, Melissa (GOSAR) DIGITAL DIR 2057 **52315**
Brown, Michelle (NEAL) DIST AIDE **413-785-0325**
Brown, Nekea (CMTE-ED & WORKFORCE) DPTY CLERK 2176 **53725**
Brown, Nick (HICE) SR LEGIS ASST 409 CHOB **54101**
Brown, Nick (KUSTER) COMMUNICATIONS DIR 320 CHOB **55206**
Brown, Norchelle (BARRAGÁN) POLICY ASST **310-831-1799**
Brown, Pamela (CAO/FIRST CALL) CUSTOMER SOLUTIONS REP B227 LHOB **58000**
Brown, Ryan (DEGETTE) COMMUNICATIONS DIR 2111 **54431**
Brown, Ryan-Thomas (DESAULNIER) DIST REP **925-933-2660**
Brown, Samantha (RASKIN) DPTY COMMUNICATIONS DIR 412 CHOB **55341**
Brown, Samara (REED) LEGIS ASST 2263 **53161**
Brown, Sandra (ADAMS) SCHEDULER/DIR - OPS **704-344-9950**
Brown, Sarah (ROGERS, HAROLD) SCHEDULER 2406 **54601**
Brown, Sheba (HUFFMAN) FIELD REP **707-962-0933**
Brown, Taryn (LEVIN, ANDY) SCHEDULER 228 CHOB **54961**
Brown, Taylor (WILD) COMMUNITY & OUTREACH LIAISON **484-781-6000**
Brown, Tom (GRAVES, SAM) DIST DIR/CHIEF OF STAFF **816-792-3976**
Brown, Tommy (SCHNEIDER) LEGIS ASST 1432 **54835**
Brown, Trevor (ROONEY) CASEWKR 120 CHOB **52536**
Brown, Zack (YOUNG) PRESS SECY 2314 **55765**
Browne, Emily (KENNEDY) COMMUNICATIONS DIR **617-332-3333**
Browne, Tessa (GARAMENDI) SCHEDULER 2368 **51880**
Browning, Geoff (CLARK) LEGIS ASST 2448 **52836**
Brownlee, Matthew (MULLIN) LEGIS AIDE 2421 **52701**
Broyles, Lauren (MCHENRY) LEGIS CORRES 2004 **52576**
Brubaker, Marcus (LAMBORN) DIST DIR **719-520-0055**
Bruce, Emma (BERA) SCHEDULER/LEGIS AIDE 1727 **55716**
Bruell, Leo (LIEU) STAFF ASST 403 CHOB **53976**
Bruley, Callie (DINGELL) DIST DIR **313-278-2936**
Brumfield, Liv (BLUMENAUER) DIST FIELD REP **503-231-2300**
Brumfield, Renard (MAJ WHIP) FLOOR ASST H329 **63210**
Bruner, Charles (CLERK/LCS) AUDIO TECH 2401 **51182**
Brunet, Yanet (DEUTCH) CASEWKR **561-470-5440**
Brunink, Tarin (MOOLENAAR) DIR - CONSTIT SVCS **989-631-2552**
Brunner, Ilana (CMTE-ED & WORKFORCE) GEN COUNSEL 2176 **53725**
Bruno, Richard
(CMTE-SMALL BUSINESS) DC SCHEDULER 2361 **54038**
(VELÁZQUEZ) DC SCHEDULER 2302 **52361**
Bruns, Benjamin (HERRERA BEUTLER) LEGIS ASST 2352 **53536**
Bryan, Robyn (KILDEE) COMMUNICATIONS DIR 203 CHOB **53611**
Bryant, Arthur (WAGNER) COMMUNICATIONS DIR 2350 **51621**
Bryant, Heather (BISHOP, SANFORD D., JR.) FINANCIAL ADMIN 2407 **53631**
Bryant, Janine (VARGAS) DIST DIR **619-422-5963**
Bryant, Lakeisha (KHANNA) FIELD REP **408-436-2720**
Bryant, Madeline (WESTERMAN) SCHEDULER 209 CHOB **53772**
Bryant, Michael (BISHOP, SANFORD D., JR.) FIELD REP **229-439-8067**
Bryant, Rebecca (SMITH, ADAM) COMMUNICATIONS DIR 2264 **58901**
Bryant, Rick (KELLY, ROBIN L.) SR ADVISOR **708-679-0078**
Bryant, Sherry (CLERK/REPORTERS) OFFICIAL REPORTER 1718 **52627**
Bryant, Tabetha (FOXX) OFFICE MGR 2462 **52071**
Buchanan, Natalie (MIN LEADER) DIR - MEMB SVCS H204 **54000**
Bucheli, Daniel (SPANO) COMMUNICATIONS DIR 224 CHOB **51252**
Buchman, MarDee (BUCHANAN) CASEWKR **941-747-9081**
Buckalew, Adam "Buck" (CMTE-ENERGY & COMMERCE) DIR - COALITIONS/DPTY CHIEF COUNSEL 2322A **53641**
Buckler, Ricky (CAO/ENTERPRISE APPLICATIONS) BUSINESS PROCESS APPLICA SPEC B70 FHOB **53230**
Buckler, Troy (CAO/ACQUIS MGMT) PURCHASING AGENT 5110 **61080**
Buckley, Christopher (ZELDIN) SPECIAL ASST **631-289-1097**
Buckner, Ann Hilton (GUEST) EXEC ASST 230 CHOB **55031**
Buddharaju, Deep (CMTE-OVERSIGHT & GOVT REFORM) COUNSEL 2105 **55074**
Bueno, Jacqueline (GARCÍA, JESÚS G. "CHUY") DIGITAL ASST/STAFF ASST **510-965-3304**
Buentello, Luis (CLOUD) FIELD REP **361-884-2222**
Bugger, Doug (SHIMKUS) DPTY PRESS SECY **618-288-7190**
Buhl, Cindy (MCGOVERN) LEGIS DIR 408 CHOB **56101**
Buhr, Patrick (PERLMUTTER) LEGIS CORRES 1226 **52645**
Buish, Jordan (GOHMERT) RESEARCH ASST 2267 **53035**
Buki, Christopher (MCKINLEY) LEGIS DIR 2239 **54172**
Bull, Leasha (MULLIN) CASEWKR **918-423-5951**
Bull, Nick (CMTE-JOINT TAX) SR ECONOMIST 595 FHOB **67575**
Bunn, Ashley (CAO/CONGRESSIONAL STAFF ACAD) SR INSTRUCTIONAL DESIGNER B241 LHOB **63800**
Bunshaft, Zachary (DAVIS, SUSAN A.) COMMUNITY REP **619-280-5353**
Bunting, Luke (MARCHANT) COMMUNICATIONS DIR 2304 **56605**
Buono, Elizabeth (DELGADO) CONSTIT SVCS REP **845-443-2930**
Burack, Bryan (CMTE-FOREIGN AFFAIRS) PROF STAFF - MIN 4150 **68467**
Burch, Kenneth (CAO/ENTERPRISE APPLICATIONS) BUSINESS PROCESS APPLICA SPEC B75 FHOB **51513**
Burchick, Jeb (DUFFY) PRESS ASST 1714 **53365**
Burdick, Cliff (MOOLENAAR) LEGIS CORRES 117 CHOB **53561**
Burge, Carissa (NEGUSE) LEGIS ASST 1419 **52161**
Burger, Katie (JOYCE, DAVID P.) DIST OUTREACH REP **440-352-3939**
Burgess, Abbi (CRAWFORD) LEGIS ASST/ CASEWKR **870-203-0540**
Burgess, Amy
(BONAMICI) OFFICE MGR 2231 **50855**
(CASE) OFFICE MGR 2443 **52726**
(MCBATH) FINANCIAL ADMIN 1513 **54501**
(ROSE, MAX) FINANCIAL ADMIN 1529 **53371**
Burgess, Jami (HECK) CHIEF OF STAFF 2452 **59740**
Burgett, Don (HUNTER) COMMUNITY REP **619-448-5201**
Burgin, Charlie (O'HALLERAN) SCHEDULER 324 CHOB **53361**
Burian, David (BROOKS, SUSAN W.) CONSTIT SVCS REP **317-848-0201**

Burke, Jill (KELLY, MIKE) DIR - CONSTIT SVCS........ **724-342-7170**
Burke, Molly (WAGNER) LEGIS ASST 2350.......... **51621**
Burke, Robby
(MCCARTHY) STAFF ASST 2468.......... **52915**
(MIN LEADER) STAFF ASST H204.......... **54000**
Burke, Rory (GOSAR) LEGIS ANALYST 2057.......... **52315**
Burke, Sarah (SMITH, JASON) DIST DIR/DPTY CHIEF OF STAFF 2418.......... **54404**
Burke, Warren (LEGIS COUNSEL) COUNSEL 337 FHOB....... **56060**
Burkot, Gregory (GUTHRIE) FIELD REP.......... **270-842-9896**
Burleson, Marisa (ARRINGTON) SCHEDULING DIR 1029..... **54005**
Burnell, Jessica (HIGGINS, BRIAN) LEGIS ASST 2459.......... **53306**
Burnett, Bradie (WEBER) DIST SCHEDULER.......... **281-316-0231**
Burnette, Antonio (LEE, BARBARA) DIST STAFF ASST.......... **510-763-0370**
Burnham, Elizabeth (CAO/MBR SVCS) MBR SVCS COORD B235 LHOB.......... **53644**
Burns, Amelia (BERGMAN) SCHEDULER 414 CHOB.......... **54735**
Burns, Andrew (SGT AT ARMS/CHAMBER SECUR) MGR - CHAMBER SUPPORT SVCS HB6.......... **50067**
Burns, Daniel (CMTE-JOINT ECON) DPTY DIR - REPUB SD-G01.......... **40647**
Burns, Emily (HILL, KATIE) CHIEF OF STAFF 1130.......... **51956**
Burns, Jackie (SHERRILL) COMMUNICATIONS DIR 1208...... **55034**
Burns, Michael (CMTE-APPRO) DPTY COMMUNICATIONS DIR H307.......... **52771**
Burns, Mike (TIMMONS) SR ADVISOR.......... **864-241-0175**
Burns, Stuart (POSEY) CHIEF OF STAFF 2150.......... **53671**
Burns, Sydney (CMTE-HOUSE ADMIN) STAFF ASST 1309... **52061**
Burns-Sulltrop, Judy (O'HALLERAN) CASEWK MGR.......... **928-286-5338**
Burris, Kevin (CMTE-FINANCIAL SVCS) CHIEF OVERSIGHT COUNSEL 2129.......... **54247**
Burroughs, Mary (MCEACHIN) DIST REP.......... **757-942-6050**
Burroughs, Nicholas (CONNOLLY) STAFF ASST 2238......... **51492**
Burroughs, Nikole (CMTE-FOREIGN AFFAIRS) STAFF DIR 5102.......... **62754**
Bursey, Evan (CMTE-FOREIGN AFFAIRS) STAFF ASSOC 2170.......... **55021**
Burtis, Christina (KATKO) CONSTIT SVCS REP........ **315-423-5657**
Burton, Christa (RASKIN) OUTREACH DIR.......... **301-354-1000**
Burton, Willie (DAVIS, DANNY K.) STAFF ASST 2159.......... **55006**
Burton-Jones, Elizabeth (CHABOT) PRESS AIDE 2408....... **52216**
Burwell, Dollie (BUTTERFIELD) DIR - CONSTIT SVCS.......... **919-908-0164**
Busby, Francine (LEVIN, MIKE) DIST DIR.......... **760-599-5000**
Bush, Andy (FERGUSON) DIST DIR.......... **770-683-2033**
Bush, Anthony (CUMMINGS) STAFF ASST 2163.......... **54741**
Bush, Douglas (CMTE-ARMED SVCS) DPTY STAFF DIR 2117.......... **61645**
Bush, Jed (HECK) STAFF ASST/DIGITAL ASST 2452.......... **59740**
Bush, Nick (STIVERS) LEGIS DIR/DPTY CHIEF OF STAFF 2234.......... **52015**
Bushen, Quinn (HIGGINS, BRIAN) CASEWKR.......... **716-852-3501**
Bushnell, Jenna (LIEU) COMMUNICATIONS DIR 403 CHOB **53976**
Bushue, Riley (WALDEN) LEGIS DIR 2185.......... **56730**
Busick, Chelsea (LOFGREN) STAFF ASST 1401.......... **53072**
Busovsky, John (THOMPSON, GLENN) LEGIS DIR 400 CHOB.......... **55121**
Bussa, Biftu (OMAR) DIST STAFF ASST.......... **612-333-1272**
Butcher, Courtney (CMTE-ED & WORKFORCE) DIR - COALITIONS & MBR SVCS 6150.......... **54527**
Butherus, Danny (BUCK) LEGIS CORRES 2455.......... **54676**
Butler, Courtney (ROY) EXEC SCHEDULER 1319.......... **54236**
Butler, Elizabeth (SMUCKER) ADMIN DIR 127 CHOB.......... **52411**
Butler, James (CAO/PAYROLL & BENEFITS) DIRECTOR B215 LHOB.......... **54599**
Butler, Jeff (MCHENRY) CHIEF OF STAFF 2004.......... **52576**
Butler, Morgan (MAJ WHIP) DIGITAL DIR H329.......... **63210**
Butler, Robin (CMTE-OVERSIGHT & GOVT REFORM) FINANCIAL ADMIN 2157.......... **55051**
Butler, Tanya T (CMTE-JOINT TAX) STATISTICAL ANALYST 595 FHOB.......... **67575**
Butler, Timothy (KELLY, MIKE) DIST DIR.......... **814-454-8190**
Butler, Tuere (LEWIS) DIST DIR.......... **404-659-0116**
Buttke, Emma (GALLAGHER) DPTY DIST DIR.......... **920-301-4500**
Butts, Peter, Jr (JOHNSON, HENRY C. "HANK", JR.) SYS ADMIN/CONSTIT SVCS REP.......... **770-987-2291**
Buwalda, Dale (PENCE) DIST FIELD REP/ CONSTIT SVCS.......... **812-799-5230**
Buyak, Caroline (ROBY) LEGIS ASST 504 CHOB.......... **52901**
Byer, Jenny (LEVIN, ANDY) FIELD REP/ CASEWKR.......... **586-498-7122**
Byers, Chuck (LESKO) CONSTIT REP.......... **623-776-7911**
Byers, John (HURD) CHIEF OF STAFF 317 CHOB.......... **54511**
Byon, Fiona (HOUSE DEM CAUCUS) DIGITAL ASST B245 LHOB.......... **51400**
Byrd, Beau (JOHNSON, DUSTY) CONSTIT SVCS REP.......... **605-646-6454**
Byrd, Susannah (ESCOBAR) DIST DIR.......... **915-541-1400**
Byrne, Emily (TRAHAN) DIST DIR.......... **978-459-0101**
Caal Skonos, Francesca (SLOTKIN) STAFF ASST 1531..... **54872**
Cabral, Ramon (SERRANO) DPTY DIST DIR.......... **718-620-0084**
Caceres, Christa (CARTWRIGHT) CASEWKR.......... **570-371-0317**
Caddock, John (MOONEY) LEGIS ASST 2440.......... **52711**
Cade, Sanya (CAO/OFFICE OF THE CFO) DPTY CHIEF 3140.......... **64650**
Cadena, Jaran (CLOUD) STAFF ASST.......... **361-884-2222**
Cafritz, Zachary (BEYER) DPTY CHIEF OF STAFF/LEGIS DIR 1119.......... **54376**
Cahan, Jaclyn (CMTE-FOREIGN AFFAIRS) COUNSEL 2173. **55021**
Cahill, James (CMTE-APPRO) EDITOR HB13A.......... **52851**
Cain, Hunter (TITUS) DIR - COMMUNITY OUTREACH/DIST REP.......... **702-220-9823**
Cairns, Becky (CMTE-NATURAL RESOURCES) PROF STAFF - MAJ 1522.......... **56065**
Calanni, Rachel (CMTE-JUDICIARY) PROF STAFF 6320....... **53926**
Calcagni, Michael (TURNER) LEGIS ASST - MIL 2082.......... **56465**
Calder, Vanessa Brown (CMTE-JOINT ECON) SR POLICY ADVISOR - REPUB SD-G01.......... **43922**
Calderon, Tatiana (MOORE) LEGIS ASST 2252.......... **54572**
Caldwell, Marcel (CMTE-APPRO) ADMIN ASST 2362B.......... **53421**
Caldwell, Witt (JOHNSON, MIKE) LEGIS CORRES 418 CHOB.......... **52777**
Calhoun, Larry (YOHO) CHIEF OF STAFF 1730.......... **55744**
Calixtro, Mariajose (ESCOBAR) DIST REP.......... **915-541-1400**
Callaghan, Molly (HAALAND) DIST STAFF ASST/ DIST SCHEDULER.......... **505-288-2529**
Callahan, Abbie (NEGUSE) LEGIS CORRES 1419.......... **52161**

Callaway, Jenny (HUFFMAN) DIST DIR.................... 415-258-9657
Callaway, Libby (JOYCE, JOHN) SR LEGIS ASST 1337........ 52431
Callaway, Robert (CAO/HOUSE RECORDING STUDIO) SR BROADCAST ENGINEER 2010........ 53941
Callejas, Courtney (WEXTON) SR POLICY ADVISOR 1217.. 55136
Callen, Ashley (CMTE-JUDICIARY) SR ADVISOR/COUNSEL 189 FHOB........ 56906
Callen, Paul (LEGIS COUNSEL) SR COUNSEL 337 FHOB..... 56060
Callen, Will (WATKINS) CASEWKR........ 620-231-5966
Callwood, Kyza (PLASKETT) STAFF ASST........ 340-774-4408
Calvo, Thomas Jerome, Jr (SAN NICOLAS) EXEC ASST........ 671-475-6453
Cama, Jennifer (CMTE-APPRO) PROF STAFF MEMB 2358B........ 53508
Camacho, Antoinette (SABLAN) STAFF ASST........ 670-323-2647
Camacho, Patricia (BARRAGÁN) SR CASEWKR........ 310-831-1799
Camara, Hatou (SERRANO) COMMUNITY LIAISON 2354..... 54361
Cambio, Kaaren (CRENSHAW) FIELD REP........ 713-860-1330
Cambon, Allen (ABRAHAM) SR LEGIS ASST 417 CHOB....... 58490
Cambon, Emily (WALKER) SCHEDULER 1725........ 53065
Cameron, Breanna (CLEAVER) LIAISON - MIL & VET........ 816-833-4545
Cameron, Carlos (ROGERS, HAROLD) FIELD REP........ 606-679-8346
Cameron, Charles (BURCHETT) FIELD REP........ 865-984-5464
Cameron, Christina (MIN LEADER) DPTY PRESS SECY H204........ 54000
Cameron, Michael (RODGERS) STAFF ASST 1035........ 52006
Cammack, Kat (YOHO) DPTY CHIEF OF STAFF........ 352-505-0838
Cammauf, Nick (SMUCKER) CASEWKR........ 717-393-0667
Camp, Abigail (CMTE-TRANSP & INFRA) DIR - COALITIONS 2164........ 59446
Camp, Terry (CMTE-NATURAL RESOURCES) PROF STAFF 4170........ 52761
Campbell, Annie (CISNEROS) SCHEDULER 431 CHOB........ 54111
Campbell, Ashley (DAVIS, SUSAN A.) DIST SCHEDULER/SR COMMUNITY REP........ 619-280-5353
Campbell, Brigid (NADLER) SCHEDULER 2132........ 55635
Campbell, Caroline (CMTE-FOREIGN AFFAIRS) PRESS SECY - MIN 2066........ 68467
Campbell, Doug (CMTE-FOREIGN AFFAIRS) DPTY STAFF DIR 2152........ 55021
Campbell, Jay (CRAWFORD) LEGIS ASST 2422........ 54076
Campbell, Kyle (MCCLINTOCK) LEGIS CORRES 2312........ 52511
Campbell, Travis (BISHOP, ROB) CONSTIT LIAISON........ 801-625-0107
Canchola, Aissa (PRESSLEY) LEGIS DIR 1108........ 55111
Canini, Lisa (CMTE-HOMELAND SECUR) SUBCOMM STAFF DIR - OVERSIGHT, MANAGEMENT, AND ACCOUNTABILITY SUBCOMM 176 FHOB........ 62616
Cannon, Drew (HARTZLER) FIELD REP........ 417-532-5582
Cannon, Nikki (MCNERNEY) COMMUNICATIONS DIR 2265. 51947
Cannon, Sarah (SIMPSON) LEGIS DIR 2084........ 55531
Cantrell, Samantha (MILLER) ASST PRESS SECY 1605...... 53452
Capece, Sonny (GIANFORTE) FIELD REP........ 406-502-1435
Caplan, Josh (ROYBAL-ALLARD) LEGIS DIR 2083........ 51766
Cappetto, Richard (CAO/CUST EXPER CTR) CHIEF B227 LHOB........ 66769
Capron, Margaret (SPEAKER) SR POLICY ADVISOR - POLICY & COMMUNICATIONS H232........ 50100
Capuzzi, Nina (SLOTKIN) DIST SCHEDULER........ 517-993-0510
Caraballo, Madeline (CAO/HIR – HOUSE WEB SVCS) INTERNET SYS SPEC 636 FHOB........ 61633
Carcamo, Alicia (CAO/ACCOUNTING) STAFF ACCOUNTANT 3110........ 61792
Card, Becky (BROOKS, SUSAN W.) PRESS SECY 2211........ 52276
Cardenas, Natalia (GARCÍA, JESÚS G. "CHUY") LIAISON - CONSTIT SVCS........ 773-342-0774
Care, Terry (TITUS) CASEWKR........ 702-220-9823
Carey, Laura (CMTE-FOREIGN AFFAIRS) SR PROF STAFF 2471........ 55021
Carey, Leah (TORRES) DC SCHEDULER/OFFICE MGR 2444........ 56161
Carey, Molly (MALONEY, SEAN PATRICK) LEGIS DIR 2331.. 55441
Carey-Barone, Stefanie (HOYER) DIR - CONSTIT SVCS........ 301-843-1577
Cariaso, Vanessa Ann Sanchez (SAN NICOLAS) EXEC ASST........ 671-475-6453
Carithers, Charles (CMTE-HOMELAND SECUR) PROF STAFF 176 FHOB........ 62616
Carl, Emma (SPANBERGER) SCHEDULER 1239........ 52815
Carlin, Emily (GONZALEZ, ANTHONY) COMMUNICATIONS DIR 1023........ 53876
Carlos, Colleen (DEAN) LEGIS DIR 129 CHOB........ 54731
Carlos, Maddie (CASTEN) COMMUNICATIONS DIR 429 CHOB........ 54561
Carlough, Chad (BYRNE) CHIEF OF STAFF 119 CHOB........ 54931
Carlson, Johnna (MCCAUL) CHIEF OF STAFF 2001........ 52401
Carlson, Libby (SCHRIER) COMMUNICATIONS DIR 1123..... 57761
Carlson, Steven (PAPPAS) LEGIS DIR 323 CHOB........ 55456
Carlstrom, Peter (RUIZ) FIELD REP........ 760-424-8888
Carlton, Ron (TRAHAN) LEGIS DIR 1616........ 53411
Carmack, Dustin (RATCLIFFE) CHIEF OF STAFF 223 CHOB........ 56673
Carman, Jonathan (STEFANIK) CONSTIT LIAISON........ 518-561-2324
Carman, MeKenna (DESJARLAIS) EXEC ASST 2301........ 56831
Carmichael, Grace (KRISHNAMOORTHI) LEGIS CORRES 115 CHOB........ 53711
Carnahan, David (HILL, J. FRENCH) LIAISON - MIL & VET/SR DIST REP........ 501-324-5941
Carnes, Alexandra (CMTE-HOMELAND SECUR) SUBCOMM STAFF DIR - BORDER SECURITY, FACILITATION, AND OPERATIONS SUBCOMM 176 FHOB.... 62616
Carnes, Thomas (HASTINGS) LEGIS DIR/SR COUNSEL 2353........ 51313
Carney, Conor (ROSE, JOHN W.) SR LEGIS ASST 1232....... 54231
Carney, Michael (CAO/ASSET MANAGEMENT) MGR 6110.. 50090
Carney, Ryan (STEIL) CHIEF OF STAFF 1408........ 53031
Carnnia, Casey (CAO/HIR – HOUSE WEB SVCS) INTERNET SYS ENGINEER 636 FHOB........ 63846
Caron, Hillary (KRISHNAMOORTHI) LEGIS COUNSEL 115 CHOB........ 53711
Carpenter, Christopher (CAO/HOUSE RADIO-TV GALLERY) COORD - DIGITAL MEDIA H320........ 55214
Carpenter, Glenn (SMITH, ADAM) DIST REP........ 425-793-5180
Carpenter, Kylie (JAYAPAL) DIGITAL STRATEGIST 1510..... 53106
Carpenter, Mary (CARTER, EARL L. "BUDDY") DPTY CHIEF OF STAFF/COMMUNICATIONS DIR 2432........ 55831
Carr, Christina (GALLEGO) COMMUNICATIONS DIR 1131.... 54065

Carr, Colin (LOUDERMILK) LEGIS DIR 422 CHOB **52931**
Carr, Josh (CAO/HIR – ENTERPRISE INFRASTRUCT) SR SYS ENGINEER 619 FHOB **571-921-3121**
Carr, Julie (YARMUTH) CHIEF OF STAFF 402 CHOB **55401**
Carr, Machalagh
(CMTE-WAYS & MEANS) PARLIAMENTARIAN/GEN COUNSEL 1139 .... **54021**
(MIN LEADER) GEN COUNSEL H204 .... **54000**
Carr, Melissa
(HAGEDORN) HR SPEC 325 CHOB **52472**
(WALTZ) FINANCIAL MGR 216 CHOB **52706**
Carr, Nick (ROONEY) DIR - DIGITAL MEDIA 120 CHOB **52536**
Carraco, Will (GIANFORTE) LEGIS DIR 1222 .... **53211**
Carray, Mariah (TORRES) LEGIS ASST 2444 .... **56161**
Carreiro, David (CLERK/LRC) DOCU CLERK B81 CHOB **65200**
Carrico, Ron (CAO/ENTERPRISE APPLICATIONS) SR BUSINESS PROCESS APPLICA SPEC B77 FHOB **64601**
Carrillo, Francisco (BARRAGÁN) DIST DIR **310-831-1799**
Carrillo, Manuel Joe (HOUSE DEM CAUCUS) DIR - OPS B245 LHOB **51400**
Carrillo, Paulina (GONZALEZ, VICENTE) EXEC ASST/ SCHEDULER 113 CHOB **52531**
Carroll, Chris (LURIA) COMMUNICATIONS DIR 534 CHOB **54215**
Carroll, Jeff (CMTE-ENERGY & COMMERCE) STAFF DIR 2125 .... **52927**
Carroll, Jessica (CMTE-ARMED SVCS) PROF STAFF 2340 .... **54440**
Carroll, Patricia (GREEN, MARK E.) FIELD REP **629-223-6050**
Carroll, Patrick (PAPPAS) DIR - CONSTIT SVCS/ OUTREACH DIRECTOR **603-285-4300**
Carson, Lawrence (CAO/OFFICE SUPPLY/GIFT SHOP) SALES SPEC B217 LHOB **53321**
Carstensen, Zachary (JAYAPAL) OUTREACH DIR **206-674-0040**
Cartagena, George (CLERK/REPORTERS) ASST CHIEF CLERK - DEBATES HT59 .... **55621**
Carter, Abigail (WEXTON) CHIEF OF STAFF 1217 .... **55136**
Carter, Barbara (ADAMS) DIR - CONSTIT SVCS **704-344-9950**
Carter, Cephas (CLERK/LCS) SR AUDIO TECH 2401 .... **51182**
Carter, Chris (HUDSON) CHIEF OF STAFF 2112 .... **53715**
Carter, D'Andre (MALINOWSKI) EXEC SCHEDULER 426 CHOB **55361**
Carter, D'Andrea (WILSON, FREDERICA S.) COMMUNICATIONS AIDE **305-690-5905**
Carter, Delisa (CAO/ENTERPRISE APPLICATIONS) SR SOFTWARE SPEC B75 FHOB **51832**
Carter, Erin (LURIA) COORD - DIST OUTREACH **757-364-7650**
Carter, Jessica (ROONEY) CHIEF OF STAFF 120 CHOB **52536**
Carter, Mickeala (CMTE-AGRIC) COORD - OUTREACH 1301 .... **52171**
Carter, Slayten (SCOTT, AUSTIN) FIELD REP/ DIST OFFICE MGR **478-971-1776**
Carter, Tiffany (CAO/OFFICE OF THE CHIEF HUMAN RESOURCES OFFICER) ADMIN SPEC 102 FHOB **52926**
Carter, Will (BABIN) CONSTIT SVCS REP **832-780-0966**
Carton, Jennifer (MURPHY) POLICY ADVISOR 1710 .... **54035**
Carton, Katie (LOEBSACK) CASEWKR **563-323-5988**
Cartwright, Makenzie (BACON) DIST STAFF ASST **402-938-0300**
Cary, Steven (CRIST) DIST DIR **727-318-6770**
Casados, Joseph (LUJÁN) CONSTIT SVCS OFFICER **505-994-0499**
Casanova, Anna (ROY) CONSTIT SVCS **210-821-5024**
Case, Michael (BARR) LEGIS CORRES 2430 .... **54706**
Casey, Brandon (CMTE-WAYS & MEANS) STAFF DIR - DEM 1102 .... **53625**
Casey, Jose (CUNNINGHAM) FIELD REP **843-521-2530**
Casey, Shannon (PAYNE) SCHEDULER 103 CHOB **53436**
Cash, Caroline (COMER) CHIEF OF STAFF 2184 .... **53115**
Cash, Jennifer (SCHRIER) LEGIS ASST 1123 .... **57761**
Caskey, Aurora (CLERK/LRC) ASST REGISTRATION & COMPLIANCE CLERK B81 CHOB **65200**
Casman, Ryan (LAWRENCE) STAFF ASST 2463 .... **55802**
Cassady, Alison (SELECT CMTE-CLIMATE CRISIS) DPTY STAFF DIR - DEM 359 FHOB **51106**
Cassano, Daniella (MCCLINTOCK) STAFF ASST **916-786-5560**
Cassidy, Erin (LATTA) SCHEDULER 2467 .... **56405**
Cassidy, Patrick (COURTNEY) COMMUNICATIONS DIR 2332 .... **52076**
Cassidy, Thomas (LEGIS COUNSEL) COUNSEL 337 FHOB **56060**
Castagna, Charles (JOYCE, DAVID P.) SR LEGIS ASST 1124 .... **55731**
Castagnola, Michael (CMTE-OVERSIGHT & GOVT REFORM) PROF STAFF MEMB 2157 .... **55051**
Castaneda, Anton (HURD) LEGIS ASST 317 CHOB **54511**
Castano, Paola (SCHAKOWSKY) CONSTIT ADVOCATE **773-506-7100**
Castella, Francesco (CMTE-FINANCIAL SVCS) LEGIS ASST - MIN 4340 .... **57502**
Castillo, Lisa (LEGIS COUNSEL) ASST COUNSEL 337 FHOB **56060**
Castillo, Valentin (SERRANO) LEGIS ASST/PRESS ASST 2354 .... **54361**
Castillo, Victor G (ROYBAL-ALLARD) CHIEF OF STAFF 2083 .... **51766**
Castle, Colleen (HARTZLER) LEGIS CORRES 2235 .... **52876**
Castor, Stephen (CMTE-OVERSIGHT & GOVT REFORM) GEN COUNSEL 2105 .... **55074**
Castro, Adrienne (TAKANO) LEGIS ASST 420 CHOB **52305**
Castro, Andre (FLORES) COMMUNICATIONS DIR 2228 .... **56105**
Castro, Antonio (PRICE) SYS ADMIN 2108 .... **51784**
Castro, Daniel (VEASEY) FIELD REP **214-741-1387**
Castro, Elba (ESPAILLAT) COUNSEL 1630 .... **54365**
Castro, Evelyn (SERRANO) STAFF ASST **718-620-0084**
Castro, Fred (GONZALEZ, VICENTE) COUNSEL 113 CHOB **52531**
Castro, Luz (ROYBAL-ALLARD) FIELD DPTY **323-721-8790**
Casturo, Robert (LEGIS COUNSEL) ASST COUNSEL 337 FHOB **56060**
Catalfamo, John (CMTE-WAYS & MEANS) CLERK/LEGIS ASST 1103 .... **53625**
Catarata, Karl Joseph (LEE, SUSIE) DIST REP **702-963-9336**
Cathcart, Kenna (CLERK/LRC) CATALOG LIBRARIAN B81 CHOB **65200**
Catto, Gregor (ADERHOLT) LEGIS CORRES 1203 .... **54876**
Cavanaugh, Margaret (STAUBER) DIR - CONSTIT SVCS **218-481-6396**
Cavanaugh, Micah (WRIGHT) DPTY CHIEF OF STAFF 428 CHOB **52002**
Cavell, David (GRAVES, GARRET) DIST DIR **985-448-4103**
Cawood, Marge (GRIFFITH) STAFF ASST **276-525-1405**

Ceasar, Jenny (FRANKEL) COORD - DIST OUTREACH ... 561-998-9045
Cecala, George (POSEY) COMMUNICATIONS DIR/DPTY CHIEF OF STAFF 2150 ... 53671
Ceccato, Matthew (BERA) DIST DIR ... 916-635-0505
Ceja, Hannah (VARGAS) LEGIS CORRES 2244 ... 58045
Ceja, Matthew (TAKANO) LEGIS CORRES 420 CHOB ... 52305
Celeste, Raymond (NC03) LEGIS ASST - MIL 2333 ... 53415
Centeno, Crystal (SÁNCHEZ) DIST SCHEDULER ... 562-860-5050
Cep, Melinda (CMTE-AGRIC) LEGIS POLICY DIR 1301 ... 52171
Cerga, Vlad (CMTE-FOREIGN AFFAIRS) INFO RESOURCE MGR 2170 ... 57575
Cervenak, Jason (CMTE-JUDICIARY) CHIEF COUNSEL - MIN 362 FHOB ... 56906
Cesaro, Victoria (HARRIS) SCHEDULER 2334 ... 55311
Cespedes Baez, Rolando (ESPAILLAT) DPTY DIST DIR ... 718-450-8241
Cevasco, Marc (LIEU) CHIEF OF STAFF 403 CHOB ... 53976
Chace, Karen (CAO/PAYROLL & BENEFITS) COUNSELOR B215 LHOB ... 57119
Chafin, Claude (CMTE-ARMED SVCS) COMMUNICATIONS DIR - MIN 2340 ... 63988
Chakerian, Mary (SHERMAN) STAFF ASST ... 818-501-9200
Chakmak, Kathryn (SMITH, JASON) LEGIS ASST 2418 ... 54404
Chakrabarti, Saikat (OCASIO-CORTEZ) CHIEF OF STAFF 229 CHOB ... 51830
Chaletzky, Ana (CAO/ACCOUNTING) MGR 3110 ... 54539
Chalhoub, Theresa
(CMTE-OVERSIGHT & GOVT REFORM) COUNSEL 2157 ... 55051
(CUMMINGS) POLICY COUNSEL 2163 ... 54741
Chalkley, Regina (SCOTT, AUSTIN) CONSTIT SVCS REP ... 478-971-1776
Chalmers, Eric (STANTON) SR DIST REP ... 602-956-2285
Chambliss, Kevin
(MUCARSEL-POWELL) DIST OUTREACH REP ... 305-222-0160
(SHALALA) OUTREACH REP ... 305-668-2285
Chamness, Charlie (HORN) LEGIS AIDE 415 CHOB ... 52132
Chan, Jennifer (JAYAPAL) SR LEGIS ASST 1510 ... 53106
Chance, Scott (COLE) FIELD REP ... 580-357-2131
Chandler, Danny
(BROOKS, SUSAN W.) SYS ADMIN 2211 ... 52276
(SERRANO) SYS ADMIN 2354 ... 54361
(WASSERMAN SCHULTZ) SYS ADMIN 1114 ... 57931
Chandler, Dylan (DUFFY) LEGIS ASST 1714 ... 53365
Chandler, Jennifer (MCGOVERN) CHIEF OF STAFF 408 CHOB ... 56101
Chandler, Shana (SMITH, ADAM) CHIEF OF STAFF 2264 ... 68453
Chandrasekhar, Vivek (CMTE-JOINT TAX) LEGIS COUNSEL 502 FHOB ... 53621
Chang, Anthony (CMTE-FINANCIAL SVCS) SR PROF STAFF 4340 ... 57502
Chang, Claris (HARDER) DIR - OPS/SCHEDULING DIR 131 CHOB ... 54540
Chang, Lena (CMTE-OVERSIGHT & GOVT REFORM) SR COUNSEL 2157 ... 55051
Chang, Shao (THOMPSON, MIKE) CONSTIT SVCS REP ... 707-226-9898
Chang, Winnie (CMTE-APPRO) PROF STAFF MEMB 2358A 52141
Chao, Daniel (NAPOLITANO) CHIEF OF STAFF 1610 ... 55256
Chao, Ken-Ben (CASE) LEGIS CORRES 2443 ... 52726
Chapman, Jayne (DEUTCH) COMMUNITY LIAISON ... 561-470-5440
Chapman, Karen (ESHOO) CHIEF OF STAFF ... 650-323-2984
Chapman, Parker (CMTE-VET AFFAIRS) LEGIS AIDE 3460. 53527
Chappell, Perry (ROUZER) LEGIS ASST 2439 ... 52731
Charara, Robert (LEVIN, ANDY) DIST STAFF ASST ... 586-498-7122
Chargualaf, Jesse (CAO/HOUSE RECORDING STUDIO) BROADCAST ENGINEER/PROD SPEC 2010 ... 53941
Charnick, Kendra (BIGGS) CONSTIT SVCS ... 480-699-8239
Charon, Justyn (LANGEVIN) CONSTIT SVCS REP ... 401-732-9400
Chartrand, Jennifer (CMTE-APPRO) PROF STAFF MEMB H405 ... 52847
Chasick, Alex (CMTE-ENERGY & COMMERCE) COUNSEL 2125 ... 52927
Chasnoff, Megan L (LEGIS COUNSEL) COUNSEL 337 FHOB ... 56060
Chaudhary, Sahil (ENGEL) SR ADVISOR - HEALTH 2426 ... 52464
Chautin, John (HIGGINS, CLAY) FIELD REP ... 337-703-6105
Chaves, Erika (BUCK) DIST REP ... 720-639-9165
Chavez, Carina (PANETTA) DPTY DIST DIR ... 831-424-2229
Chavez, Eric (LUJÁN) CONSTIT LIAISON ... 505-984-8950
Chavez Carranza, Rolando (GOMEZ) STAFF ASST ... 213-481-1425
Chelak, Joseph (RIGGLEMAN) COMMUNICATIONS DIR 1022 ... 54711
Chen, Alice (GREEN, AL) COMMUNITY & OUTREACH LIAISON ... 713-383-9234
Chen, Mingzhi (COMMIS ON CHINA) RESEARCH ASSOC 243 FHOB ... 63795
Chenault, Randy (CHABOT) CONSTIT LIAISON ... 513-684-2723
Cheng, Becky (CHU) DIST DIR ... 626-304-0110
Chernin, Michael (LIEU) LEGIS ASST 403 CHOB ... 53976
Cherry, Arnez (BISHOP, SANFORD D., JR.) CONSTIT SVCS ... 706-320-9477
Cherry, Stephanie (SPEAKER) DIR - MEDIA AFFAIRS H232 50100
Chertow, Elazar (QUIGLEY) STAFF ASST 2458 ... 54061
Chess, Daarina (SIRES) DIR - CONSTIT SVCS ... 201-309-0301
Chevalier Mosely, Jacque (CMTE-ED & WORKFORCE) DIR - EDUC POLICY 2257 ... 53725
Chhem, Steven (CLERK/LCS) SOFTWARE ENGINEER 2401 ... 51182
Chiappardi, Frances (CLERK/LEGIS OPS) CHIEF HT13 ... 57925
Chiba, Koh (DEAN) CHIEF OF STAFF 129 CHOB ... 54731
Childers, Brooke (CARTER, EARL L. "BUDDY") DIST DIR ... 912-352-0101
Childress, Allison (GALLEGO) SCHEDULER 1131 ... 54065
Childress, Taylor (FLEISCHMANN) LEGIS CORRES 2410 ... 53271
Ching, Anthony (CASE) POLICY ADVISOR 2443 ... 52726
Chintamani, Sameer (CASTEN) SCHEDULER 429 CHOB ... 54561
Chippendale, Jenna (MALONEY, SEAN PATRICK) CONSTIT ADVOCATE ... 845-561-1259
Chirico, Michael (MILLER) DPTY CHIEF OF STAFF/DIST DIR 1605 ... 53452
Chiu, Jimmy (CAO/ENTERPRISE APPLICATIONS) HRIS - APPLICA SYS ANALYST B73 FHOB ... 62189
Chiucchini, Kate (RICE, KATHLEEN M.) LEGIS COUNSEL 2435 ... 55516

Cho, Austin (CLERK/LRC) OPS ASST B81 CHOB **65200**
Cho, James (TORRES) CHIEF OF STAFF 2444 **56161**
Cho, Wonjun (CLERK/LCS) APPLICA SUPPORT ANALYST 2401 **51182**
Chong, Peter (FITZPATRICK) VET ADVOCATE/ MIL ADVOCATE **215-579-8102**
Chotvacs, Anne Marie (CMTE-APPRO) STAFF DIR 1016 **53481**
Chougule, Akash (CMTE-ED & WORKFORCE) PROF STAFF MEMB 6150 **57101**
Chovil, Andres (GABBARD) LEGIS ASST 1433 **54906**
Chow, Steven (GOMEZ) FIELD DPTY **213-481-1425**
Christ, Billy (ROUZER) FIELD REP **910-395-0202**
Christel, Jared (RADEWAGEN) LEGIS ASST/CASEWKR 1339 **58577**
Christensen, Eric (CLERK/COMMUNICA) SR CONTENT DEVELOPER 293 CHOB **51908**
Christensen, Nick (CMTE-TRANSP & INFRA) DIR - COALITIONS & MBR SVCS 2164 **59446**
Christesen, Michael (SUOZZI) STAFF ASST 214 CHOB **53335**
Christian, "Bill" (WEBER) LEGIS DIR 107 CHOB **52831**
Christian, Jordan (DUNCAN, JEFF) CONSTIT LIAISON/DIST SCHEDULER/FIELD REP **864-224-7401**
Christian, Taylor (JOHNSON, BILL) DIST STAFF ASST **330-337-6951**
Christiana, Linda (LARSON) DIST SCHEDULER/ EXEC ASST **860-278-8888**
Christiansen, Jenna (GOTTHEIMER) SCHEDULER 213 CHOB **54465**
Christianson, Andrew (JOHNSON, DUSTY) CHIEF OF STAFF 1508 **52801**
Christianson, Mike (CUMMINGS) SPECIAL ASST **410-685-9199**
Christie, Brett (CURTIS) INFO TECH ASST **801-922-5400**
Christie, John (ADAMS) LEGIS DIR 2436 **51510**
Christ-Miller, Cynthia (WALTZ) CONSTIT SVCS **386-302-0442**
Christophel, Sharon (WALORSKI) CONSTIT LIAISON **574-204-2645**
Christopherson, Collin (GRANGER) ADVISOR - DEFENSE 1026 **55071**
Christrup, Henry (LEGIS COUNSEL) COUNSEL 337 FHOB **56060**
Christy, Mary (ARMSTRONG) DIR - CONSTIT SVCS **701-353-6665**
Chrobak, Catherine (TITUS) LEGIS CORRES 2464 **55965**
Chukwu, Chioma (CMTE-OVERSIGHT & GOVT REFORM) SR EXEC COUNSELOR 2157 **55051**
Chulak, Daniel (PALLONE) DIST REP/STAFF ASST **732-571-1140**
Chun, Dave (GABBARD) DPTY LEGIS DIR 1433 **54906**
Chuprik, Sergey (JEFFRIES) FIELD REP **718-373-0033**
Church, Lee (JEFFRIES) DIST FIELD REP **718-237-2211**
Churchill, Tim (WATKINS) LEGIS ASST 1205 **56601**
Churchwell, Leslie (PALAZZO) DIST OFFICE MGR **228-864-7670**
Ciampa, Deane (SUOZZI) LEGIS CORRES 214 CHOB **53335**
Cianciotti, Tyler (BOST) SCHEDULER 1440 **55661**
Ciango, Jacob (CAO/ENTERPRISE APPLICATIONS) APPLICA SYS ADMIN B75 FHOB **62230**
Ciapciak, Elle (MEUSER) SR LEGIS ASST 326 CHOB **56511**
Ciarlante, Nick (CMTE-INTELLIGENCE) REPUB BUDGET DIR & INVESTIGATION COORD HVC304 **54121**
Cicale, Michael (CAO/CAPITOL SVC CTR) SR CAPITOL SVC REP HT3 **58000**
Cicchella, Jamie (YOHO) LEGIS ASST 1730 **55744**
Ciccone, Joseph (NAPOLITANO) LEGIS ASST/ SCHEDULER 1610 **55256**
Cid, Gabriela (BARRAGÁN) FIELD REP **310-831-1799**
Cilke, James M (CMTE-JOINT TAX) SR ECONOMIST 595 FHOB **57575**
Cimino, Pietro (KINZINGER) FIELD REP **815-708-8032**
Cincotta, Sam (CAO/CUST EXPER CTR) ANALYST B227 LHOB **58000**
Cinquegrani, Julia (WILD) LEGIS ASST 1607 **56411**
Ciofani, Nick (JOYCE, DAVID P.) DIST DIR/DPTY CHIEF OF STAFF **330-425-9291**
Ciotti, Nick (MAST) DIST DIR **561-530-7778**
Ciotto, Billy (LARSON) SR DIST REP **860-278-8888**
Cirenza, Gabrielle (STEUBE) SCHEDULER 521 CHOB **55792**
Cisneros, Alex (GONZALEZ, ANTHONY) LEGIS ASST 1023 **53876**
Cissell, Afton (DOGGETT) COUNSEL 2307 **54865**
Citron, Lauren (RUSH) LEGIS ASST 2188 **54372**
Clanahan, Chase (SHIMKUS) SR LEGIS ASST 2217 **55271**
Clancy, Tom (SCANLON) LEGIS ASST/RULES ASSOC 1535 **52011**
Clark, Alex (JOYCE, JOHN) PERSONAL ASST 1337 **52431**
Clark, Allison (BYRNE) CONSTIT SVCS REP **251-989-2664**
Clark, Annie (LESKO) LEGIS ASST 1113 **54576**
Clark, Carson (ADERHOLT) FIELD REP/PRESS SECY **256-734-6043**
Clark, Cynthia (NEAL) AIDE **413-442-0946**
Clark, Elena (STEUBE) LEGIS CORRES 521 CHOB **55792**
Clark, Jon (CMTE-VET AFFAIRS) SUBCOMM STAFF DIR - ECONOMIC OPPORTUNITY SUBCOMM 3460 **65491**
Clark, Jonathan (DAVIS, SUSAN A.) SR COMMUNITY REP **619-280-5353**
Clark, Kyle (BACON) CONSTIT OUTREACH REP **402-938-0300**
Clark, Lisa (BERA) CASEWKR **916-635-0505**
Clark, Marion (CAO/HOUSE CREATIVE SVCS) SR TELECOMMUNICATIONS ADMIN 692 FHOB **52700**
Clark, Raymel
(DINGELL) INFO TECH MGR 116 CHOB **54071**
(YARMUTH) INFO TECH MGR 402 CHOB **55401**
Clark, Robert (MATSUI) LEGIS CORRES 2311 **57163**
Clark-Donald, Onaray (PAYNE) STAFF ASST **973-645-3213**
Clarke, John (CAO/ASSET MANAGEMENT) SUPERVISOR WA23 RHOB **58214**
Clarke, John (MIN WHIP) SPECIAL ASST H148 **50197**
Clarke, Philipp (RICE, TOM) LEGIS CORRES 512 CHOB **59895**
Clason, Tiffany (MCADAMS) DIST DIR **801-999-9801**
Class, Facia (MENG) COMMUNITY OUTREACH SPEC **718-358-6364**
Claude, Ronald (PRESSLEY) FIELD REP **617-850-0040**
Claus, Greg (SCHNEIDER) DPTY DIST DIR **847-383-4870**
Clauson, Ilene (CMTE-NATURAL RESOURCES) DIR - OPS 1327A **56065**
Clay, Gerietta (CUMMINGS) STAFF ASST **410-685-9199**
Clay, Gordon M (CMTE-JOINT TAX) SR LEGIS COUNSEL SD-G18 **45561**
Clay, Regina (CUMMINGS) AREA DIR **410-465-8259**
Clayton, Ashley (UNDERWOOD) SCHEDULER/DIST SCHEDULER 1118 **52976**

Clayton, Janice (BOST) CASEWKR.......... 618-457-5787
Clayton-Bullock, Latoya (CAO/ACQUIS MGMT) SR PROCUREMENT SPEC 5110.......... 52921
Clement, Mary Kate (SCANLON) DPTY CHIEF OF STAFF/ SCHEDULER 1535.......... 52011
Clemons, Nick (KENNEDY) DIST DIR.......... 617-332-3333
Clemonts-James, Corliss (CLERK/LRC) DPTY CHIEF B81 CHOB.......... 65200
Clendinen, Cletis (PLASKETT) DIST DIR.......... 340-774-4408
Clerinx, Wendy (CMTE-HOMELAND SECUR) PROF STAFF 176 FHOB.......... 62616
Cleveland, Christina (BIGGS) CONSTIT RELATIONS REP.......... 480-699-8239
Clifford, Ken (ROONEY) LEGIS ASST 120 CHOB.......... 52536
Cline, Eva (MOOLENAAR) LEGIS ASST 117 CHOB.......... 53561
Clinton, James (ROSE, MAX) CASEWKR.......... 718-667-3313
Cloch, Adam (FORTENBERRY) PRESS ASST/STAFF ASST 1514.......... 54806
Clocker, John (CAO) DEPUTY CAO HB28.......... 55555
Cloud, Carter (COLE) LEGIS ASST 2207.......... 56165
Cloud, Hamilton (WATERS) SPECIAL PROJ DIR.......... 323-757-8900
Cloud, Sam (HUDSON) STAFF ASST/STAFF ASST - COMMUNICATIONS 2112.......... 53715
Clouse, Sarah "Sally" (GEN COUNSEL) ATTORNEY 219 CHOB.......... 59700
Cloutier, Kathy (GOLDEN) DIST REP.......... 207-241-6767
Coakley, Kristen (CAO/HIR – ENTERPRISE INFRASTRUCT) TELEPHONE SYS CONSULT 692 FHOB.......... 56002
Coates, Carson (HERRERA BEUTLER) DIST STAFF ASST.......... 360-695-6292
Cobb, Brittany (CLERK/LRC) ASST REGISTRATION & COMPLIANCE CLERK B81 CHOB.......... 65200
Cobb, Everett (SGT AT ARMS/APPOINTMENT) ASST - APPTS DESK CANNON.......... 52551
Cobb, Faye (CMTE-APPRO) PROF STAFF MEMB H306.......... 67252
Cobb, Nate (SENSENBRENNER) DC SCHEDULER/OFFICE MGR/SYS ADMIN 2449.......... 55101
Coburn, Try (NORTON) SCHEDULER/EXEC ASST 2136.......... 58050
Cochran, Cameron (DOYLE) CASEWKR - IMMIGRATION.......... 412-390-1499
Cochran, Courtney (WATSON COLEMAN) DPTY CHIEF OF STAFF 2442.......... 55801
Cockerham, Brandon (LOUDERMILK) COMMUNICATIONS DIR 422 CHOB.......... 52931
Cockerill, Jason (HOLLINGSWORTH) FIELD REP.......... 812-288-3999
Coe, Holly (HECK) STAFF ASST.......... 360-459-8514
Coe, Nicholas (CRAIG) DIST DIR.......... 651-846-2120
Coe, Tyler (CMTE-APPRO) ADMIN ASST 2007.......... 53081
Coffey, Jim (BURGESS) DIST OUTREACH REP.......... 940-497-5031
Coffey, Stephen (CARTWRIGHT) LEGIS DIR 1034.......... 55546
Coffield, Mark (STEWART) EXEC ASST/SCHEDULER 2242.......... 59730
Coffman, Sarah (COMER) LEGIS ASST/COORD - GRANTS & SPEC PROJ 2184.......... 53115
Coghlan, Aisling (BLUMENAUER) DIST DIR.......... 503-231-2300
Cohen, Andrew (ESHOO) STAFF ASST 202 CHOB.......... 58104
Cohen, Audra (POCAN) CASEWKR/CASEWK MGR.......... 608-258-9800
Cohen, Chelsea (GOHMERT) SCHEDULER/OFFICE MGR 2267.......... 53035
Cohen, Danielle (DEGETTE) PRESS ASST/COORD - DIGITAL MEDIA 2111.......... 54431
Cohen, Ira (DAVIS, DANNY K.) COMMUNICATIONS DIR.......... 773-533-7520
Cohen, Jacqueline (CMTE-ENERGY & COMMERCE) CHIEF ENVIRON COUNSEL 2125.......... 54407
Cohen, Joseph (LAW REV COUNSEL) ASST COUNSEL 308 FHOB.......... 62411
Cohen, Linda (CMTE-INTELLIGENCE) PROF STAFF - MAJ HVC304.......... 57690
Cohen, Lisa B (DEGETTE) CHIEF OF STAFF 2111.......... 54431
Cohen, Nicole (CMTE-APPRO) PROF STAFF MEMB HT2.......... 53047
Cohen, Noah (GOMEZ) STAFF ASST 1530.......... 56235
Cohen, Quincy (WILSON, FREDERICA S.) DIR - FIELD OPS.......... 305-690-5905
Cohen, Rosaline (CMTE-HOMELAND SECUR) CHIEF COUNSEL 176 FHOB.......... 62616
Cohn, Karen (PORTER) SR FIELD REP 1117.......... 55611
Cohn, Maya (WELCH) STAFF ASST 2187.......... 54115
Coker, Max (NEGUSE) STAFF ASST 1419.......... 52161
Colaccio, Joe (DAVIDSON) STAFF ASST 1107.......... 56205
Colbert, Ray (CAO/HOUSE RECORDING STUDIO) SR BROADCAST ENGINEER/PROD SPEC 2010.......... 53941
Cole, Caitlyn (SMITH, ADAM) DIST SCHEDULER/ DIST OFFICE MGR.......... 425-793-5180
Cole, Molly (CONNOLLY) LEGIS ASST 2238.......... 51492
Cole, Sally (SENSENBRENNER) SR CASEWKR.......... 262-784-1111
Cole, Susan (CLERK/LEGIS OPS) READING CLERK HT13.......... 57925
Cole, Susan (CLERK/LRC) INTEGRATED RESOURCES LIBRARIAN B81 CHOB.......... 65200
Coleman, Cheryl (SGT AT ARMS/APPOINTMENT) ASST - APPTS DESK CVC.......... 52551
Coleman, Emanuel (SGT AT ARMS/GARAGES & PARKING) ASST SUPERVISOR G2-28.......... 56749
Coleman, Everett (CMTE-ARMED SVCS) PROF STAFF G2L2.......... 50883
Coleman, Joycelyn (CMTE-NATURAL RESOURCES) CALENDAR CLERK 1324.......... 56065
Coleman-Jones, Sable (TAYLOR) DIST DIR.......... 972-202-4150
Collier, William (LOEBSACK) SR LEGIS ASST 1211.......... 56576
Collins, Casey (GIANFORTE) FIELD REP.......... 406-502-1435
Collins, Elle (RICE, TOM) TAX COUNSEL/LEGIS ASST 512 CHOB.......... 59895
Collins, Erin (BALDERSON) COMMUNICATIONS DIR 1221.......... 55355
Collins, John (CAO/HOUSE RECORDING STUDIO) BROADCAST PROD TECH 2010.......... 53941
Collins, Kathleen (LOFGREN) CONG ASST.......... 408-271-8700
Collins, Michael (SR CHF DPTY MAJ WHIP – LEWIS) CHIEF OF STAFF 343 CHOB.......... 53801
Collins, Michael (LEWIS) CHIEF OF STAFF 300 CHOB.......... 53801
Collins-Mandeville, Aimee (DEMINGS) LEGIS DIR 217 CHOB.......... 52176
Collinsworth, Mel (BERGMAN) CONSTIT SVCS.......... 231-944-7633
Collis, Lystra (CLARKE) DIST REP.......... 718-287-1142
Colom, Belane (CAO/ACCOUNTING) ACCNT TECH 3110.......... 60432
Colombo, Erina (PRESSLEY) CIVIC ENGAGEMENT MANAGER.......... 617-850-0040
Colon, Hector (ROSE, MAX) LEGIS ASST 1529.......... 53371
Colon, Kimberly (DIAZ-BALART) STAFF ASST.......... 305-470-8555
Colona, Zac (ROSE, JOHN W.) STAFF ASST 1232.......... 54231

Colton, Kimber (PINGREE) COUNSEL 2162 56116
Colvett, Jacqueline (CMTE-FOREIGN AFFAIRS) DIGITAL MGR 2152 55021
Colwell, Robin (CMTE-ENERGY & COMMERCE) CHIEF COUNSEL 2322A 53641
Combelic, Alexa (COURTNEY) LEGIS DIR 2332 52076
Combs, Bobbie (SGT AT ARMS/APPOINTMENT) ASST - APPTS DESK RAYBURN 52551
Combs, Leslie (SCHAKOWSKY) DIST DIR 773-506-7100
Comeau, Julia (BACON) LEGIS ASST 1024 54155
Comer, Jonathan (SGT AT ARMS/POLICE SVCS) DIST SECUR SPECIALIST 173 FHOB 53380
Comer, Michael (MIN WHIP) DIGITAL STRATEGIST H148 50197
Comis, Adam (CMTE-HOMELAND SECUR) COMMUNICATIONS DIR 176 FHOB 62616
Commins, Zac (ROUDA) SR LEGIS ASST 2300 52415
Commodore, Lakeisha (SGT AT ARMS) EXEC ASST H124 52456
Como, Peter (CMTE-TRANSP & INFRA) STAFF ASST 2164 59446
Compton, Megan (MEADOWS) LEGIS ASST 2160 56401
Conaghan, Sean P (CLERK/LCS) SOFTWARE ENGINEER 2401 51182
Conant, Jacqueline (CASE) DIST DIR 808-650-6688
Conaway, Ashleigh (HUNTER) FIELD REP 619-448-5201
Conboy, Chloe (BUCHANAN) CASEWKR 941-951-6643
Concepcion, Marilyn (DELAURO) CASEWKR 203-562-3718
Condarco-Quesada, Carlos (SHALALA) CONG AIDE 305-668-2285
Condon, Katherine (AMASH) DIST DIR 616-451-8383
Coney, Lillie (JACKSON LEE) POLICY DIR 2079 53816
Conklin, Caralee (GOHMERT) LEGIS DIR 2267 53035
Conley, Sarah (ARRINGTON) CONSTIT SVCS REP 325-675-9779
Connally, Tom (CMTE-SCIENCE) COUNSEL 394 FHOB 56371
Conn-Catechis, Jennifer (LUJÁN) DIST DIR 505-984-8950
Connelly, Chris (HARTZLER) CHIEF OF STAFF 2235 52876
Connelly, Erin (RICE, KATHLEEN M.) DIST STAFF ASST 516-739-3008
Connelly, Henry (SPEAKER) DPTY COMMUNICATIONS DIR H232 50100
Connolly, Brenda (MENG) EXEC ASST 2209 52601
Connolly, Jesse (PINGREE) CHIEF OF STAFF 207-774-5019
Connolly, Josh (SPEIER) CHIEF OF STAFF 2465 53531
Connolly, Kathlyn (LOWEY) DIST SCHEDULER 914-428-1707
Connolly, Katie (MCCOLLUM) DIST SCHEDULER 651-224-9191
Connolly, Melissa (NADLER) LEGIS DIR 2132 55635
Connor, Crozer (THOMPSON, MIKE) LEGIS ASST 406 CHOB 53311
Connor, Evelyn (BOST) CASEWKR 618-457-5787
Connor, Justin (SUOZZI) FIELD REP/DPTY DIST DIR 718-631-0400
Connor, Kathleen (RASKIN) DIST DIR 301-354-1000
Connor, Meredith (CMTE-HOUSE ADMIN) PROF STAFF 1309 52061
Conover, Marla (MOOLENAAR) CONSTIT RELATIONS REP 989-631-2552
Conroy, Chris (DEFAZIO) DIST FIELD REP 541-440-3523
Conroy, Patrick J (CHAPLAIN) CHAPLAIN OF THE HOUSE HB25 52509
Conru, Paula (YOUNG) EXEC ASST/SCHEDULER 2314 55765
Constance, Erica (WEXTON) DIST DIR 703-234-3800
Constangy, Billy (HUDSON) DIST DIR 704-786-1612
Conway, James (LYNCH) STAFF ASST 2109 58273
Coogle, Christine (GEN COUNSEL) LAW CLERK 219 CHOB 59700
Cook, Bennie (SMITH, JASON) FIELD REP 573-364-2455
Cook, Eric (CAO/HIR – NETWORKING ENGINEERING AND OPS) NETWK TECH 680 FHOB 64435
Cook, Jordan (ROY) FIELD REP 512-871-5959
Cook, Julia (PARLIAMENTARIAN) ASST PARLIAMENTARIAN H209 57373
Cook, Kris (WAGNER) DIST REP 636-779-5449
Cooke, Catherine (CLERK/COMMUNICA) CHIEF 293 CHOB 51908
Cooke, Corey (CMTE-TRANSP & INFRA) DPTY GEN COUNSEL 2164 59446
Cooke, Hannah (MCCLINTOCK) EXEC ASST 2312 52511
Cooke, Jason (ROUZER) LEGIS DIR 2439 52731
Cooke, Marylou (ROUZER) STAFF ASST 2439 52731
Cooke-Cooper, Teresa (SCOTT, DAVID) CONSTIT SVCS REP/FIELD REP 770-210-5073
Cooper, Chris (JOYCE, DAVID P.) CHIEF COUNSEL 1124 55731
Cooper, Hannah (BROWN) LEGIS CORRES 1323 58699
Cooper, Kadeem (CMTE-OVERSIGHT & GOVT REFORM) COUNSEL 2157 55051
Cooper, Richard (CAO/ACCOUNTING) STAFF ACCOUNTANT 3110 56525
Cooper, Valerie (DEAN) CASEWKR 610-382-1250
Cooper-Wall, Samuel (KUSTER) LEGIS CORRES 320 CHOB 55206
Cope, Stephanie (MAST) LEGIS CORRES 2182 53026
Copeland, Laney (WOODALL) LEGIS ASST 1724 54272
Copland, Lori (ENGEL) DIST MGR 718-796-9700
Copps-Peters, Norma (BISHOP, ROB) OFFICE MGR 801-625-0107
Coran, Robin (BUCK) DPTY DIST DIR 720-639-9165
Corbet, Drew (CLERK/LCS) HELP DESK TECH 2401 51182
Corbett, Derick (WOODALL) CHIEF OF STAFF 770-232-3005
Corbett-Rizzutto, Megan (HIGGINS, BRIAN) DIST DIR 716-852-3501
Corbin, Kim (CMTE-RULES) SR HEALTH POLICY ADVISOR H312 59091
Corcoran, Glenda (MATSUI) DIST DIR 916-498-5600
Corcoran, Kathleen (COURTNEY) SCHEDULER 2332 52076
Cordero, Ginamarie (NORCROSS) CASEWK DIR 856-427-7000
Cordonnier, David (BALDERSON) DIST FIELD REP 614-523-2555
Cordova, Andre (GONZALEZ, VICENTE) STAFF ASST 113 CHOB 52531
Corley, Sarah
(CMTE-RULES) COMMUNICATIONS DIR 1116 59191
(COLE) COMMUNICATIONS DIR 2207 56165
Cormier, Ward (HIGGINS, CLAY) LEGIS DIR 424 CHOB 52031
Cornejo, Luis (CAO/HIR – ENTERPRISE INFRASTRUCT) SR SYS ENGINEER 617 FHOB 66522
Cornell, Becky (AGUILAR) CHIEF OF STAFF 109 CHOB 53201
Cornell, Kevin (INSPECTOR GENERAL) MGMT ANALYST 386 FHOB 61250
Cornett, Chelsea (PETERSON) STAFF ASST 2204 52165
Cornibert, Agnes (SABLAN) OFFICE MGR/EXEC ASST 2411 52646

Cornwall, Vanessa (DEFAZIO) DIST AIDE 541-465-6732
Correll, Charles (MIN LEADER) SPEECHWRITER H204 54000
Corrigan, Dave (DEAN) DIST FIELD REP 215-884-4300
Cortez, Marcella (GOMEZ) DIST DIR 213-481-1425
Cortez, Marisela (VELA) DIST DIR 956-544-8352
Cosci, Emily (STEFANIK) SCHEDULING DIR 318 CHOB 54611
Cosgrove, Kat (PAPPAS) SR LEGIS ASST 323 CHOB 55456
Costa, Janie (DAVIS, RODNEY) LEGIS ASST 1740 52371
Costakos, Catherine (LUETKEMEYER) COMMUNICATIONS DIR 2230 52956
Costas, Tyler (HOLLINGSWORTH) LEGIS CORRES/STAFF ASST 1641 55315
Costigan, Maria (COURTNEY) LEGIS ASST 2332 52076
Cote, Steve (CMTE-FINANCIAL SVCS) STAFF DIR - MIN 4340 57502
Cotner, Kelly (MCCAUL) DIR - OPS 2001 52401
Cotton, Erin (KUSTER) COORD - CONSTIT SVCS/COORD - OUTREACH 603-226-1002
Coufal, Teresa (CLERK/LEGIS OPS) BILL CLERK HT13 57598
Couhig, Ben (BABIN) CHIEF OF STAFF 2236 51555
Coulbourn, Betsey (BLUNT ROCHESTER) LEGIS ASST 1519 54165
Courchene, Brien (TAKANO) LEGIS AIDE 420 CHOB 52305
Couri, Jerry (CMTE-ENERGY & COMMERCE) DPTY CHIEF COUNSEL 564 FHOB 53641
Courtney, Jennifer
(SMITH, CHRISTOPHER H.) SR CASEWKR 609-585-7878
(SMITH, CHRISTOPHER H.) SR CASEWKR 732-350-2300
Courtney, Will (KUSTOFF) STAFF ASST 523 CHOB 54714
Cousimano, Jonathan (BROWNLEY) OUTREACH DIR/SCHEDULER 2262 55811
Cousins, Weldon (JOHNSON, MIKE) STAFF ASST 418 CHOB 52777
Couture, R J (KILDEE) LEGIS CORRES 203 CHOB 53611
Couture, Traci (RODGERS) DIST DIR 509-353-2374
Couture, Whitney (DEFAZIO) DIST AIDE 541-465-6732
Coverton, Antoinette (CLERK/REPORTERS) SR LEGIS DATA ANALYST HT59 55621
Covey-Brandt, Alexis (MAJ LEADER) CHIEF OF STAFF H107 53130
Covington, Lauren (CONNOLLY) SCHEDULER 2238 51492
Cowan, Tonia (THOMPSON, BENNIE G.) EXEC ASST 601-866-9003
Cowles, Charlotte (CHENEY) LEGIS ASST 416 CHOB 52311
Cox, Brandon (LEE, SUSIE) CHIEF OF STAFF 522 CHOB 53252
Cox, Bridget (CAO/ENTERPRISE APPLICATIONS) SR SYS ANALYST B77 FHOB 66041
Cox, Caitlin (CARBAJAL) CASEWKR/DIST REP 805-546-8348
Cox, Ken (LEGIS COUNSEL) ASST COUNSEL 337 FHOB 56060
Cox, Lindsey (BROWN) DIR - OPS 1323 58699
Cox, Olivia (FLETCHER) SCHEDULER 1429 52571
Cox, William M (CLERK/REPORTERS) ADMIN AND TECH SUPPORT SPEC 1718 52627
Coyle, Sarah (MIN LEADER) ASST MGR - CLOAKRM H204 54000
Coyle, Steven (RICE, KATHLEEN M.) LEGIS ASST 2435 55516
Coyne, Thomas (CAO/OFFICE OF THE CHIEF LOGISTICS OFFICER) CHIEF LOGISTICS OFFICER WA35 RHOB 51896
Crabtree, Chris (BANKS) SR ADVISOR 260-702-4750
Crabtree, Katy (KILMER) DIST REP 360-373-9725
Craddock, Jessica (FERGUSON) CONSTIT SVCS 770-683-2033
Craddock, Reed (KELLY, TRENT) SCHEDULER 1005 54306
Crain, Megan (DESAULNIER) STAFF ASST 925-933-2660
Cramer, Martha (BLUMENAUER) LEGIS ASST 1111 54811
Crane, Katie (WILLIAMS) STAFF ASST 1708 59896
Crane, Mark (GREEN, MARK E.) FIELD REP 931-266-4483
Cranston, Seana (MASSIE) LEGIS DIR/DPTY CHIEF OF STAFF 2453 53465
Cravens, Tyler (DAVIS, RODNEY) DPTY DIST DIR 309-252-8834
Cravins, Yvette (CLAY) CHIEF OF STAFF 2428 52406
Crawford, Chris (CARTER, EARL L. "BUDDY") CHIEF OF STAFF 2432 55831
Crawford, Todd (FORTENBERRY) CASEWKR 402-438-1598
Crerand, Emily (ROUDA) CHIEF OF STAFF 2300 52415
Cressy, Jennifer (MCCLINTOCK) COMMUNICATIONS DIR 2312 52511
Cretsinger, Wiltsie (KING, STEVE) DIST DIR 2210 54426
Crews, Judith (FLORES) LEGIS CORRES 2228 56105
Crisostomo, Jose A (SAN NICOLAS) RECEPTIONIST 671-475-6453
Crisp, Shannon (GOHMERT) CASEWKR 903-561-6349
Crisp, Timia (SARBANES) LEGIS ASST 2370 54016
Crittenden, Allison (CRAWFORD) SR LEGIS ASST 2422 54076
Crocker, Nicholas (CMTE-HOUSE ADMIN) PROF STAFF - MIN 1216 58281
Crockett, Gene (RYAN) LIAISON - CONSTIT SVCS 330-373-0074
Croft, Ryan (GROTHMAN) LEGIS DIR 1427 52476
Crofts, Natalie (BONAMICI) PRESS SECY 2231 50855
Croke, Kjersten (CLINE) DIST REP 540-857-2672
Crombie, Louis (STAUBER) FIELD REP 218-355-0862
Cronin, Maggie (DUFFY) DIST SCHEDULER 715-298-9344
Cronin, Sarah (KUSTER) DIGITAL MGR 320 CHOB 55206
Crosby, Katy (CMTE-FOREIGN AFFAIRS) SR PROF STAFF MBR 2471 55201
Crosby, Olivia (DUNN) REGIONAL DIR 850-785-0812
Crosley, Kemorley (YOUNG) LEGIS CORRES 2314 55765
Cross, Harold (GUEST) LIAISON - MIL & VET 769-241-6120
Cross, Tracy (WESTERMAN) DIST FIELD REP/CASEWK DIR 479-667-0075
Crosswhite, Caleb (CMTE-AGRIC) DPTY CHIEF COUNSEL/PROF STAFF 1010 50317
Crotts, Jamie (CAO/HIR – CYBERSECURITY) MGR - OUTREACH & COMMUNICATIONS 642A FHOB 66207
Crotty, Jim (FORTENBERRY) COMMUNICATIONS DIR 402-438-1598
Crotty, Mairead (LEGIS COUNSEL) STAFF ASST/PARALEGAL 337 FHOB 56060
Crouch, Sarah
(BALDERSON) ADMIN - FINANCE & PAYROLL 1221 55355
(GOODEN) FINANCIAL ADMIN 425 CHOB 53484
Crowell, Heather (CMTE-HOMELAND SECUR) GPO DETAILEE 176 FHOB 62616
Crowley, Connor (ARMSTRONG) LEGIS AIDE 1004 52611
Crowley, Danielle (MCCLINTOCK) DIR - CONSTIT SVCS 916-786-5560
Cruickshanks, Brian (CLOUD) COMMUNICATIONS DIR 361-894-6446

Crumley, Luke (BALDERSON) ASST DIST DIR......... 614-523-2555
Cruz, Anthony (BUCHANAN) COMMUNICATIONS DIR 2427. 55015
Cruz, Evelyn (VELÁZQUEZ) DIST DIR......................... 718-599-3658
Cruz, Gabriel (MURPHY) MIL FELLOW 1710............................ 54035
Cruz, Isabel (PAYNE) COORD - CONSTIT SVCS...... 973-645-3213
Cruz, Jose (HORN) COMMUNITY OUTREACH SPEC.. 405-602-3074
Cruz, Mary (NORCROSS) DIST DIR.......................... 856-427-7000
Cruz, Ruben (GREEN, AL) STAFF ASST.................. 713-383-9234
Cruz-De Jesus, Victoria (CMTE-WAYS & MEANS) STAFF ASST 1102.. 53625
Cruz Munoz, Mariana (CMTE-FOREIGN AFFAIRS) STAFF ASSOC 5222.. 53345
Cruz-Olivari, John (GONZÁLEZ-COLÓN) DIST STAFF ASST 1609.. 52615
Crystal, Howard (CLERK/REPORTERS) EDITOR - COMMITTEES 1718.. 52627
Cubbedge Redd, Kim (NEGUSE) CONSTIT ADVOCATE.. 970-372-3971
Cuellar, Chelsea (JOHNSON, DUSTY) MGR - OPS.. 605-275-2868
Cuevas, Stephanie (AGUILAR) LEGIS DIR 109 CHOB......... 53201
Cuff, Loren (CAO/HIR – HOUSE WEB SVCS) INTERNET SYS SPEC 627 FHOB.. 58035
Cuffee, Danielle (CAO/ASSET MANAGEMENT) ACCNT MGMT COUNSELOR 6110.. 50090
Cuffey, Lawrence (CAO/ASSET MANAGEMENT) SR REC & WAREHOUSE SPEC WA23 RHOB... 58214
Cullen, Cate (OLSON) COMMUNICATIONS DIR 2133............. 55951
Cullum, Rebekah (STEIL) CONSTIT SVCS.............. 608-752-4050
Culp, Rita (CMTE-APPRO) CLERK 2007....................................... 53081
Culver, Jared (PERRY) LEGIS DIR 1207...................................... 55836
Culver, Linda (SIMPSON) AREA DIR......................... 208-734-7219
Cummings, Tim (ARRINGTON) DPTY CHIEF 1029................. 54005
Cummins, Annie (WENSTRUP) CASEWKR............ 513-474-7777
Cummins, Emily (JAYAPAL) SCHEDULER 1510...................... 53106
Cunningham, Candace (CAO/OFFICE OF THE CHIEF HUMAN RESOURCES OFFICER) GENERALIST 102 FHOB... 61426
Cunningham, Chris (MCADAMS) LEGIS ASST 130 CHOB... 53011
Cunningham, Quincy (BAIRD) DIST CHIEF OF STAFF.. 317-563-5567
Cunningham, Scott (MARCHANT) DPTY CHIEF 2304........... 56605
Cunningham, William (CMTE-OVERSIGHT & GOVT REFORM) COUNSEL/SR POLICY ADVISOR 6430.................. 55051
Cunnington, Michael (FULCHER) DIST DIR............ 208-888-3188
Cunnington, Mike (GONZALEZ, ANTHONY) CONSTIT SVCS REP.. 440-783-3696
Cuprill, Carlos (CAO/HOUSE CREATIVE SVCS) SUPERVISOR 100 CHOB.. 69314
Cureton, Laura (BRADY) SCHEDULING DIR 1011.................. 54901
Curran, Pat (BURGESS) LEGIS CORRES 2161......................... 57772
Curran, Susan (PAPPAS) PRESS SECY 323 CHOB............... 55456
Curran Horrell, Abby (KUSTER) CHIEF OF STAFF 320 CHOB.. 55206
Curry, Cat (WILLIAMS) SCHEDULER 1708................................ 59896
Curry, Tom (RICE, KATHLEEN M.) DIR - CONSTIT AFFAIRS.. 516-739-3008
Curtis, Katherine (CMTE-FOREIGN AFFAIRS) SPECIAL ASST TO THE STAFF DIR 2066.. 68467
Curtis, Ryan (LANGEVIN) CONSTIT SVCS REP...... 401-732-9400
Curtis, Sarah (KENNEDY) DPTY CHIEF OF STAFF/LEGIS DIR 304 CHOB.. 55931
Cutrona, Dante (MEUSER) CHIEF OF STAFF 326 CHOB....... 56511
Cutts, Kenneth (BISHOP, SANFORD D., JR.) DIST DIR.. 229-439-8067
Cybulski, Greg (FOSTER) PRESS SECY................... 630-585-7672
Cylke, Laura (CMTE-APPRO) PROF STAFF MEMB 2000........ 57245
Czarnecki, Chris (SENSENBRENNER) STAFF ASST 2449.... 55101
Czufin, Sarah (BAIRD) LEGIS DIR 532 CHOB.......................... 55037
Dabney, Miranda (HERN) PRESS SECY 1019........................ 52211
Dacey, Ted (MOONEY) DPTY CHIEF OF STAFF/ COMMUNICATIONS DIR 2440... 52711
Dadlani, Priya (CAO/OFC OF EMPLOYEE ADVOCACY) ASSOC COUNSEL 301 FHOB... 58800
Dahl, Ryan (CAO/HOUSE RADIO-TV GALLERY) MEDIA LOGISTICS COORD H320.. 55214
Dahlstrom, Darren (CAO/FURNISHINGS) MGR WA25 RHOB.. 58000
Dailey, David (SCOTT, ROBERT C. "BOBBY") CHIEF OF STAFF 1201.. 58351
Dailey Jones, Nicole (KAPTUR) PRESS ASST........ 216-767-5933
Dakheel, Lina (SUOZZI) LEGIS ASST/ADVISOR - FOREIGN POLICY 214 CHOB.. 53335
Dale, Evan (GARCIA, SYLVIA R.) SCHEDULER 1620.............. 51688
Dale, Tatum (BARR) DPTY DIST DIR.......................... 859-219-1366
D'Alesandro, Paul (DOYLE) DIST DIR....................... 412-390-1499
Dalfonso, J D (LAHOOD) COMMUNICATIONS DIR.. 309-671-7027
Dallas, Carolyn (HICE) FIELD REP/CONSTIT SVCS.. 770-207-1776
Dallman, Alex (GROTHMAN) CONSTIT OUTREACH REP/DIST FIELD REP............................. 920-907-0624
Daly, Cecilia (CAO/ADMIN COUNSEL) ADMIN COUNSEL 217 FHOB.. 56969
Daly, Lisa (LEGIS COUNSEL) SR COUNSEL 337 FHOB.......... 56060
Daly, Madeline (HAYES) LEGIS ASST 1415............................ 54476
Damato, Alex (MATSUI) SR LEGIS ASST/TECH ADVISOR 2311.. 57163
Damron, David (WASSERMAN SCHULTZ) COMMUNICATIONS DIR 1114... 57931
Damschen, Robert (CMTE-WAYS & MEANS) COMMUNICATIONS DIR 1139... 54021
Danaher, Joseph (GREEN, MARK E.) LEGIS ASST 533 CHOB.. 52811
Dangers, Jamie (LAMBORN) SR LEGIS ASST 2371................ 54422
Daniel, Clinton (FULCHER) REGIONAL DIR............. 208-743-1388
Daniel, George (CAO/OFFICE OF THE CHIEF LOGISTICS OFFICER) ASST CLO WA29 RHOB.. 66645
Daniel, Jada (CAO/OFFICE DESIGN AND MOVE SVCS) MGR B216 LHOB.. 64742
Daniel, Ted (SGT AT ARMS/CHAMBER SECUR) ASST SGT AT ARMS HB6.. 50067
Daniels, Bryant (ENGEL) COMMUNICATIONS DIR/DPTY DIST DIR.. 718-796-9700
Daniels, David (KENNEDY) STAFF ASST 304 CHOB............. 55931
Daniels, Jamie (NEWHOUSE) DIST DIR..................... 509-452-3243
Daniels, John (BEYER) CONSTIT LIAISON................ 703-658-5403
Daniels, Ryan (MAJ WHIP) DPTY COMMUNICATIONS DIR H329.. 63210

Daniels, Timothy (HARRIS) LEGIS DIR/COUNSEL 2334........ **55311**
Dankler, Mike (WALORSKI) CHIEF OF STAFF 419 CHOB...... **53915**
Darby, Reginald (STEUBE) LEGIS DIR 521 CHOB................. **55792**
Darden, Bill (ROE) DIST DIR.. **423-247-8161**
Das, Tanya (CMTE-SCIENCE) PROF STAFF - MAJ 2321........ **56375**
Dash, Carl (BOYLE) CONSTIT SVCS REP................... **267-335-5643**
Dashow, Jordan (CMTE-JUDICIARY) PROF STAFF 2138...... **53951**
Daugherty, Abbey (REED) COMMUNICATIONS ADVISOR 2263.. **53161**
Daughtrey, Erica (SIRES) COMMUNICATIONS DIR.. **201-309-0301**
Daulby, Jennifer (CMTE-HOUSE ADMIN) STAFF DIR - MIN 1316.. **58281**
Davenport, Collin (CONNOLLY) LEGIS DIR 2238.................... **51492**
Davenport, Tammy (CRAWFORD) SR CASEWKR.. **870-203-0540**
Davey, Sarah (PANETTA) PRESS SECY 212 CHOB............... **52861**
David, Andrew (HIGGINS, CLAY) COMMUNICATIONS DIR 424 CHOB.. **52031**
Davidman, Karyn (SCHNEIDER) CASEWK DIR....... **847-383-4870**
Davidson, Alex (MITCHELL) COMMUNICATIONS DIR 211 CHOB.. **52106**
Davidson, Betsy (SUOZZI) PRESS ASST................ **631-923-4100**
Davidson, Dustin
(GRAVES, GARRET) LEGIS ASST 2402.................................... **53901**
(SELECT CMTE-CLIMATE CRISIS) PROF STAFF MBR - REPUB 361 FHOB.. **51107**
Davidson, Philip (LIPINSKI) COMMUNICATIONS DIR.. **773-948-6223**
Davila, Kitty (SERRANO) HOUSING SPEC/DIR - INTAKE.. **718-620-0084**
Davin, Mike (LATTA) LEGIS ASST 2467.................................... **56405**
Davis, Aaron (CMTE-TRANSP & INFRA) STAFF DIR 2165..... **54472**
Davis, Alec (CMTE-APPRO) PROF STAFF MEMB 1016.......... **53481**
Davis, Alysa (LAMBORN) LEGIS ASST 2371............................ **54422**
Davis, Annaliese (HOYER) PRESS SECY 1705...................... **54131**
Davis, Ben (RATCLIFFE) LEGIS FELLOW 223 CHOB.............. **56673**
Davis, Carlton (CMTE-JUDICIARY) CHIEF OVERSIGHT COUNSEL 2226.. **56906**
Davis, Charlotte (STEIL) LEGIS ASST 1408............................ **53031**
Davis, Chip (O'HALLERAN) DIST DIR........................ **928-286-5338**
Davis, David (BRADY) CHIEF OF STAFF 1011........................ **54901**
Davis, Dylan (JOHNSON, MIKE) COMMUNITY LIAISON.. **318-840-0309**
Davis, Eric (CMTE-BUDGET) POLICY ADVISOR 507 CHOB... **67270**
Davis, Ernie (BEATTY) DIST DIR................................ **614-220-0003**
Davis, Fred (DAVIS, DANNY K.) STAFF ASST............. **773-533-7520**
Davis, Gaetan (GOLDEN) SCHEDULER 1223........................ **56306**
Davis, Jael (PALLONE) DIST FIELD REP................... **732-249-8892**
Davis, Jodi (GRANGER) STAFF ASST 1026............................ **55071**
Davis, John J (CAO/HOUSE RECORDING STUDIO) BROADCAST PROD TECH 2010.. **53941**
Davis, Jordan (CMTE-ENERGY & COMMERCE) SR ADVISOR 2322A.. **53641**
Davis, Lester (LAHOOD) CONSTIT SVCS REP/ DIST OFFICE MGR.. **309-671-7027**
Davis, Lynne (DESJARLAIS) FIELD REP................... **615-896-1986**
Davis, Marcee (BROWNLEY) DIST REP.................... **805-379-1779**
Davis, Mary (OLSON) CASEWK DIR............................ **281-494-2690**
Davis, Melanie
(BUCSHON) SYS ADMIN 2313.. **54636**
(CLINE) SYS ADMIN 1009.. **55431**
(KING, STEVE) SYS ADMIN 2210.. **54426**
(SIMPSON) SYS ADMIN 2084.. **55531**
(WAGNER) SYS ADMIN 2350.. **51621**
Davis, Rachel (LEGIS COUNSEL) STAFF ASST 337 FHOB... **56060**
Davis, Scott (CAO/PAYROLL & BENEFITS) GENERALIST B215 LHOB.. **54550**
Davis, Sharon (CMTE-ENERGY & COMMERCE) CHIEF CLERK 2125.. **52927**
Davis, Sheila (SCOTT, DAVID) CONSTIT SVCS REP/FIELD REP.. **770-432-5405**
Davis, Stachia (CAO/OFFICE DESIGN AND MOVE SVCS) DIRECTOR B216 LHOB.. **64742**
Davis, Susan (BUCSHON) LEGIS ASST 2313............................ **54636**
Davis, Tami (WEXTON) SR OUTREACH DIR............ **703-234-3800**
Davis Johnson, Chonya (BEATTY) SR LEGIS ASST 2303.. **54324**
Davison, Casey (LOFGREN) LEGIS CORRES 1401............... **53072**
Davison, Ollie (SEWELL) DPTY DIST DIR................ **205-254-1960**
Dawson, Billie (WALBERG) CONSTIT RELATIONS REP.. **517-780-9075**
Dawson, Demitri (DEUTCH) PRESS ASST RAYBURN........... **53001**
Dawson, Earnestine (HOUSE DEM CAUCUS) DIGITAL DIR B245 LHOB.. **51400**
Dawson, Kevin (KELLY, MIKE) LEGIS ASST 1707.................. **55406**
Dawson, Mark (ADERHOLT) LEGIS DIR 1203.......................... **54876**
Day, Jonathan (WILSON, JOE) CHIEF OF STAFF 1436.......... **52452**
Day, Pamela (YOUNG) CHIEF OF STAFF 2314........................ **55765**
Deal, Rocky (MCCLINTOCK) CHIEF OF STAFF...... **916-786-5560**
Dean, Joseph (CAO/FURNISHINGS) LEAD UPHOLSTERER WA33 RHOB.. **58000**
Dean, Melissa (GIANFORTE) FIELD REP................ **406-969-1736**
Dean, Penny M (CLERK/REPORTERS) OFFICIAL REPORTER 1718.. **52627**
Dean, Sarah (CMTE-VET AFFAIRS) PROF STAFF MEMB - HEALTH SUBCOMM 3470.. **59756**
Dean, Tanner (BAIRD) STAFF ASST 532 CHOB........................ **55037**
Deangelo, Anthony (KIM) COMMUNICATIONS DIR 1516...... **54765**
Deatherage, Craig (DUNN) LIAISON - MIL & VET... **850-891-8610**
Deatherage, Zach (WOMACK) STAFF ASST 2412................. **54301**
Deatley, James (BROWN) LEGIS ASST 1323.......................... **58699**
Deboer, Rebecca (AMASH) DIST REP.................... **616-451-8383**
DeBrosse, Frank (TURNER) DIST DIR...................... **937-225-2843**
DeCant, Kyle (CMTE-ED & WORKFORCE) COUNSEL - LABOR POLICY 2051C.. **53725**
DeCesaro, Anne (CMTE-WAYS & MEANS) SUBCOMM STAFF DIR 1139.. **54021**
Decker, Bradford (BROOKS, MO) LEGIS CORRES 2246....... **54801**
Decker, James (BURGESS) CHIEF OF STAFF 2161.............. **57772**
Decker, Paige (CMTE-WAYS & MEANS) DIR - COALITIONS & MBR SVCS 1139.. **54021**
Dedrick, Katherine W (CMTE-TRANSP & INFRA) STAFF DIR 2165.. **54472**
Deery, Katherina (GABBARD) STAFF ASST/OFFICE COORD 1433.. **54906**
Dees-Hollis, Misty (PENCE) CONSTIT SVCS REP.. **812-799-5230**
Defensor, Sahara (SAN NICOLAS) COUNSEL/CHIEF POLICY ADVISOR 1632.. **51188**

DeFilippo, Katarina (ESTES) LEGIS CORRES 1524 ..... **56216**
DeFreitas, Matt
(CMTE-HOUSE ADMIN) DIR - FRANKING COMMISSION 1307 ..... **52061**
(COMMIS ON CONG MAILING STDS) STAFF DIR 1307 ..... **59337**
Degenfelder, Ken (CMTE-NATURAL RESOURCES) PROF STAFF 4450 ..... **52761**
Degou, Lisa (TRAHAN) SCHEDULER 1616 ..... **53411**
DeGraff, Kenneth (SPEAKER) SR POLICY ADVISOR H232 ..... **50100**
DeGrasse, Alexander (STEFANIK) DIR - STRATEGIC COMMUNICATIONS 318 CHOB **54611**
DeGregorio, Nick (SHERRILL) CASEWKR **973-526-5668**
DeGroot, Elliot (SLOTKIN) LEGIS ASST 1531 ..... **54872**
DeHart, Bridgette (PAYNE) LEGIS DIR 103 CHOB **53436**
Dehlinger, Nancy (RADEWAGEN) EXEC ASST/EXEC SCHEDULER/OFFICE MGR 1339 ..... **58577**
Dehnel, Kendall (RODGERS) LEGIS CORRES 1035 ..... **52006**
DeJesus, James (DEUTCH) OUTREACH ADVISOR **561-470-5440**
DeJonghe, Nina (BASS) STAFF ASST 2059 ..... **57084**
DeLandro, Veronica (HAYES) DIST DIR **860-223-8412**
Delaney, Eric (CMTE-RULES) PROF STAFF - MAJ H312 ..... **59091**
Delaney, Patrick (CMTE-AGRIC) COMMUNICATIONS DIR 1301 ..... **52171**
Delano, Gwen (LONG) CASEWKR **417-781-1041**
De Lara, Pablo (CÁRDENAS) CASEWKR **818-221-3718**
DeLauro, Mallory (SWALWELL) DIST DIR/ ADVISOR - FOREIGN POLICY **510-370-3322**
Delisle, Kaldon (CAO/FURNISHINGS) JOURNEYMAN - FURN SPEC WA22 RHOB **58000**
Dell'Oliver, Max (O'HALLERAN) CONSTIT SVCS REP **928-304-0131**
Del Monico, Tim (RUIZ) CHIEF OF STAFF 2342 ..... **55330**
Deloatch-Everett, Nancy (PASCRELL) CASEWKR **973-523-5152**
Deloma, Jill (DELAURO) CASEWKR **203-562-3718**
De Los Santos, Karen (VELA) DPTY CHIEF 307 CHOB **59901**
Del Rosario, John (SABLAN) STAFF ASST 2411 ..... **52646**
Deluca, Alan (CAO/HIR – ENTERPRISE INFRASTRUCT) MGR - OPS 679 FHOB **66452**
DeLuca, Andrew (LOFGREN) SCHEDULER 1401 ..... **53072**
De Luca, Sebastian (KINZINGER) LEGIS ASST 2245 ..... **53635**
Delury, Kevin (KING, PETER T.) DIST REP **516-541-4225**
Del Valle Ortiz, Melissa (VELÁZQUEZ) COMMUNITY & HOUSING COORD **718-599-3658**
Demakos, Michael (RICE, KATHLEEN M.) LEGIS ASST 2435 ..... **55516**
DeMarco, David (CMTE-NATURAL RESOURCES) DIR - INFO TECH 1322 ..... **56065**
DeMarco, David (INSPECTOR GENERAL) MGMT ANALYST 386 FHOB **61250**
DeMarco, Stephanie (UPTON) LEGIS ASST 2183 ..... **53761**
Demicheli, Nick (DOYLE) CASEWKR - MIL **412-283-4451**
Deming, Jefferson (WESTERMAN) LEGIS DIR 209 CHOB **53772**
Dempsey, Eddy (MULLIN) FIELD REP **918-423-5951**
Dempsey, Sean (LOEBSACK) STAFF ASST 1211 ..... **56576**
Denboer, Stephen (AMASH) DIST REP **616-451-8383**
Denegri, Andre (CAO/ASSET MANAGEMENT) FINANCIAL ANALYST 6110 ..... **50090**
Denis, Lydia (MEUSER) LEGIS CORRES 326 CHOB **56511**
Denison, Rick (COOK) FIELD REP **760-247-1815**
Denk, Hilary (FOSTER) DIST DIR **630-585-7672**
Dennis, Amy (DESJARLAIS) FIELD REP **931-962-3180**
Dennis-Morial, Kemah (RICHMOND) SR ADVISOR 506 CHOB **56636**
Dennison, Brianna (LOEBSACK) DIST REP **319-351-0789**
Denny, Leah Grace (WILSON, JOE) LEGIS ASST 1436 ..... **52452**
Denoyer, Casey (STEVENS) LEGIS ASST 227 CHOB **58171**
Dent, Richard (CAO/FURNISHINGS) MASTER CARPET MECHANIC WA32 RHOB **58000**
Deoudes, John (MARCHANT) LEGIS DIR 2304 ..... **56605**
DePadua, Carmen (PASCRELL) CASEWKR **973-523-5152**
DePew, Kenneth (CRENSHAW) LEGIS ASST 413 CHOB **56565**
DePina, Gloria (HIMES) CONSTIT SVCS REP **203-353-9400**
Derby, Elena (CMTE-JOINT TAX) ANALYST 595 FHOB **67575**
Derheim, Luke (MOOLENAAR) DIST REP **989-631-2552**
Derr, April (CUNNINGHAM) DIR - CONSTIT SVCS **843-352-7572**
Derrick, Hope (MAJ WHIP) COMMUNICATIONS DIR H329 ..... **63210**
Derrick, Scott (CAO/HOUSE CREATIVE SVCS) GRAPHIC DESIGNER 2002 ..... **52700**
DeSai, Sonali (CHU) LEGIS DIR 2423 ..... **55464**
Descamps, Nicholas (GIANFORTE) LEGIS CORRES 1222 ..... **53211**
Deshler, Andrew (SCHRADER) STAFF ASST 2431 ..... **55711**
Deshmukh, Harsh (MCGOVERN) LEGIS ASST 408 CHOB **56101**
DeSousa, Sierra (SCHIFF) DIST REP **818-450-2900**
Dessauer, Liz (PENCE) DPTY DIST DIR **812-799-5230**
DeStefano, Gabriella (WILD) STAFF ASST 1607 ..... **56411**
Detrick, Alissa (DAVIDSON) DIST OFFICE MGR/ CASEWKR **937-339-1524**
Detter, Laura (PERRY) LEGIS ASST 1207 ..... **55836**
Detweiler, Bethany (CAO/CHILD CARE CENTER) ADMIN SPEC 147 FHOB **69320**
Dever, Tyler (SPANO) STAFF ASST 224 CHOB **51252**
Devin, Michael (MOULTON) DIST REP **978-531-1669**
Devine, Julie (GRAVES, SAM) LEGIS DIR 1135 ..... **57041**
Devine, Rachel (CMTE-TRANSP & INFRA) STAFF DIR/SR COUNSEL 2251 ..... **54472**
Devivo, Brianna (COURTNEY) FIELD REP **860-741-6011**
Devlin, Kathleen (LAMALFA) LEGIS CORRES 322 CHOB **53076**
DeVooght, Joseph (VISCLOSKY) DPTY CHIEF OF STAFF 2328 ..... **52461**
Devora, Damaris (GARCÍA, JESÚS G. "CHUY") SR CONSTIT SVCS REP **773-342-0774**
Devougas, Hope (MOORE) OUTREACH SPEC **414-297-1140**
Dewhirst, Diane (SPEAKER) DPTY CHIEF OF STAFF H232 ..... **50100**
Dewillis-Marcano, Alyson (CROW) CONSTIT ADVOCATE **720-748-7514**
DeWitt, Cynthia (KELLY, ROBIN L.) DIR - CONSTIT SVCS/DIST DIR **708-679-0078**
DeWitt, Kolby (KING, STEVE) DIST REP **712-224-4692**
DeWitte, Jon (HUIZENGA) CHIEF OF STAFF 2232 ..... **54401**
Dews, Elizabeth (BUDD) DIR - SCHED/ADMIN 118 CHOB **54531**
Dexter, Barry (CMTE-JOINT ECON) SYS ADMIN SD-G01 ..... **40374**
Dey, Jodi (PETERSON) STAFF ASST **218-847-5056**
Dhar, Sreyashe (LEE, SUSIE) SCHEDULER 522 CHOB **53252**
Dhyne, Noel (VAN DREW) EXEC ASST **609-625-5008**
Diallo, Leila (BEATTY) EXEC ASST/SCHEDULER 2303 ..... **54324**
Diamond, Rena (JEFFRIES) CONSTIT SVCS REP **718-373-0033**
Diaz, Cristina (CRAIG) CONSTIT ADVOCATE **651-846-2120**

Diaz, Frances (SABLAN) SR LEGIS ASST 2411 ... **52646**
Diaz Marrero, Jose (GONZÁLEZ-COLÓN) SR POLICY ADVISOR 1609 ... **52615**
Dibblee, Christian (LUCAS) LEGIS ASST 2405 ... **55565**
Diblasio, Carla (CMTE-WAYS & MEANS) HEALTH COUNSEL 1139 ... **54021**
Dicio, Erica (YARMUTH) LEGIS ASST 402 CHOB ... **55401**
Dickerson, Barbara (NAPOLITANO) CONG LIAISON ... **626-350-0150**
Dickerson, Jasmine (CMTE-AGRIC) SUBCOMM STAFF DIR 1301 ... **52171**
Dickerson, Matt (HOUSE REPUB STUDY CMTE) POLICY DIR 418 CHOB ... **52777**
Dickie, James (CAO/HOUSE RECORDING STUDIO) MGR - ENGINEERING OPS 2010 ... **53941**
Dickinson, Jordan (KILDEE) SR LEGIS ASST 203 CHOB ... **53611**
Didiuk, Monica (SMITH, ADRIAN) CHIEF OF STAFF 502 CHOB ... **56435**
Diederich, Anna (STANTON) LEGIS ASST 128 CHOB ... **59888**
Dieffenderfer, Gary (CAO/ENTERPRISE APPLICATIONS) APPLICA DATABASE SPEC/SR BUSINESS PROCESS APPLICA SPEC 638 FHOB ... **66246**
Diehl, Glen (CMTE-ARMED SVCS) PROF STAFF MEMB 2340 ... **66504**
Dieringer, Brett (WOMACK) LEGIS CORRES 2412 ... **54301**
Dierker, Ryan (WENSTRUP) SR LEGIS ASST 2419 ... **53164**
Dierkes, Joan (MATSUI) DIST SCHEDULER/DIST EXEC ASST ... **916-498-5600**
Dietrich, Ross (GONZÁLEZ-COLÓN) LEGIS DIR 1609 ... **52615**
Dietz, Lonnie (TAYLOR) CHIEF OF STAFF 1404 ... **54201**
Diffley, Ryan (GRAVES, TOM) LEGIS ASST 2078 ... **55211**
DiFranco, Sam (LIPINSKI) SPECIAL PROJ ASST ... **773-948-6223**
DiFulvio, Brandon (KELLY, ROBIN L.) STAFF ASST 2416 ... **50773**
Diggins, Megan (BLUNT ROCHESTER) LEGIS CORRES 1519 ... **54165**
DiGiacomo, Anthony (KELLY, MIKE) LIAISON - MIL & VET ... **814-454-8190**
DiGnan, Mariah Caitlin (SUOZZI) DIST SCHEDULER/LEGIS AIDE ... **631-923-4100**
DiGregorio, Zack (GOTTHEIMER) PRESS SECY ... **201-389-1100**
Dilan, Tess (YOHO) ADMIN ASST ... **352-505-0838**
DiLeone, Maria (MENG) DIST SCHEDULER ... **718-358-6364**
Diller, Matthew (CMTE-RULES) POLICY DIR 1116 ... **59191**
Dilley, Jared (JORDAN) DPTY CHIEF OF STAFF 2056 ... **52676**
Dillihay, Marilyn (COHEN) CHIEF OF STAFF 2104 ... **53265**
Dillon, Althea (MCBATH) PRESS ASST/STAFF ASST 1513 ... **54501**
Dillon, Chad (UPTON) CONSTIT SVCS REP ... **269-385-0039**
Dillon, Joe (WALORSKI) STAFF ASST 419 CHOB ... **53915**
Dillon, Ryan (BARRAGÁN) EXEC ASST/SCHEDULER 1030 ... **58220**
Dillon, Sean (GRANGER) DPTY CHIEF OF STAFF 1026 ... **55071**
Dillon, Thomas (LEGIS COUNSEL) HUMAN RESOURCES ADMIN 337 FHOB ... **56060**
Dilworth, Ryan (GIBBS) LEGIS AIDE 2446 ... **56265**
Dimenstein, Katherina (SCHWEIKERT) CHIEF OF STAFF 1526 ... **52190**
Dimitroff, Kallen (GARCIA, SYLVIA R.) SPECIAL ASST/ ADVISOR - HEALTH POLICY 1620 ... **51688**
Dinakar, Aditi (MENG) LEGIS CORRES 2209 ... **52601**
Dinkel, Matt (DOYLE) COMMUNICATIONS DIR 306 CHOB ... **52135**
Diohep, Elizabeth (ESTES) LEGIS ASST 1524 ... **56216**
Di Palma, Mason (TURNER) STAFF & PRESS ASST 2082 ... **56465**
Discigil, Justin (WALDEN) COMMUNICATIONS DIR 2185 ... **56730**
Disrud, Douglas (CMTE-APPRO) PROF STAFF MEMB 1001 **53481**
Diver, Joe (AXNE) CHIEF OF STAFF 330 CHOB ... **55476**
Dixon, Chad (GUEST) FIELD REP ... **769-241-6120**
Dixon, Kelly (CMTE-RULES) STAFF DIR H152 ... **59191**
Dixon-Tymus, Vivian (SGT AT ARMS/APPOINTMENT) ASST - APPTS DESK RAYBURN ... **52551**
Dmeza, Gilbert (ROUZER) CASEWORK - VETS ... **910-395-0202**
Doan, Phoebe (CLERK/COMMUNICA) GRAPHIC DESIGNER 293 CHOB ... **51908**
Dobbins, Halee (BANKS) PRESS ASST 1713 ... **54436**
Dobbins, Mark (CAO/ACQUIS MGMT) PURCHASING MGR 5110 ... **52921**
Dobkowski, Natasha (WEBSTER) DIST STAFF ASST ... **352-241-9220**
Dobo, David (GONZALEZ, ANTHONY) SR DIST REP ... **440-783-3696**
Dobson, Waynna (BLUNT ROCHESTER) CONSTIT SVCS REP ... **302-830-2330**
Dodd, Owen (BISHOP, SANFORD D., JR.) SR POLICY ADVISOR 2407 ... **53631**
Dodd, Wayne (LOUDERMILK) DIST DIR ... **770-429-1776**
Dodge, Allison (DELAURO) CASEWKR/ COMMUNITY OUTREACH SPEC ... **203-562-3718**
Dodge, Barbara (STIVERS) FINANCIAL ADMIN 2234 ... **52015**
Dodge, Suzanne (THOMPSON, MIKE) FELLOW 406 CHOB. **53311**
Dodoo, Isaac (SCOTT, DAVID) DPTY DIST DIR ... **770-432-5405**
Doggett, Patrick (KINZINGER) DPTY DIST DIR ... **815-432-0580**
Doherty, CeCe (VAN DREW) DIR - CONSTIT SVCS ... **609-625-5008**
Doherty, Katie (HARTZLER) EXEC DIR - VALUES ACTION TEAM 2235 ... **52876**
Doherty, Ryan (CMTE-FOREIGN AFFAIRS) PROF STAFF MEMB 5211 ... **67812**
Dohr, Bob (SGT AT ARMS) CHIEF OPERATING OFFICER H124 ... **52456**
Dolan, Tom (DUNN) STAFF ASST 316 CHOB ... **55235**
Dolberg, Andrew (WASSERMAN SCHULTZ) COORD - DIST OUTREACH 1114 ... **57931**
Dolin, Rachel (CMTE-WAYS & MEANS) PROF STAFF 1104 ... **53943**
Dollhopf, Kevin (DINGELL) LEGIS ASST 116 CHOB ... **54071**
Dolton, Scott (BACON) CONSTIT LIAISON ... **402-938-0300**
Domenech, Emily (CMTE-SCIENCE) SR POLICY ADVISOR - REPUB 394 FHOB ... **56371**
Dominguez, Raphael (ESPAILLAT) SCHEDULER 1630 ... **54365**
Dominguez, Rebecca (STANTON) STAFF ASST ... **602-956-2285**
Dominguez De Marty, Idalia (SERRANO) EXEC ADMIN 2354 ... **54361**
Domino, Karen (RICHMOND) DPTY DIST DIR ... **504-288-3777**
Dominy, Janet (GUEST) DIR - CONSTIT SVCS ... **769-241-6120**
Donachie, Robert (ROY) COMMUNICATIONS DIR 1319 ... **54236**
Donahue, Kathryn (CMTE-ETHICS) SR COUNSEL 1015 ... **57103**
Donahue, Kristen (PARLIAMENTARIAN) ASST CLERK TO THE PARLIAMENTARIAN H209 ... **57373**
Donahue, Kyle F (CLERK/LCS) DIR - APPLICA DEVELOPMENT 2401 ... **51182**
Donat, Joseph (MALONEY, SEAN PATRICK) DIST DIR ... **845-561-1259**
Donches, Michelle (TURNER) MGR - BUDGET 2082 ... **56465**

Donesa, Chris (CMTE-ETHICS) COUNSEL TO THE RANKING MEMBER 1015 **57103**
Doney, Lauren (RASKIN) COMMUNICATIONS DIR/DPTY CHIEF OF STAFF 412 CHOB **55341**
Donlon, Andrew (TRONE) FIELD REP **301-926-0300**
Donlon, Sara (STIVERS) SCHEDULER/DIR - OPS **614-771-4968**
Donnellan, Matt (MILLER) CHIEF OF STAFF 1605 **53452**
Donnelly, Andrew (BLUNT ROCHESTER) LEGIS ASST 1519 **54165**
Donnelly, John (GRAVES, TOM) CHIEF OF STAFF 2078 **55211**
Donoghue, Taylor (TRONE) SR FIELD REP **301-926-0300**
Donovan, Garrett (KEATING) CHIEF OF STAFF 2351 **53111**
Doocy, Mary (MEADOWS) LEGIS COUNSEL 2160 **56401**
Dooley, Debbie (MULLIN) FIELD REP **918-283-6262**
Dooley, Geneva (CAO/ENTERPRISE APPLICATIONS) SR SOFTWARE ENGINEER B70 FHOB **51835**
Dooley, Zach (BURCHETT) LEGIS DIR 1122 **55435**
Doomes, Elliot (CMTE-APPRO) PROF STAFF MEMB 2000 **57245**
Dopkeen, Bess (CMTE-ARMED SVCS) PROF STAFF 2340 **56710**
D'Orazio, Mike (RESCHENTHALER) LEGIS AIDE 531 CHOB **52065**
Dorfman, Clara (NADLER) OFC ASST **212-367-7350**
Dorfman, David (CLARKE) LEGIS DIR 2058 **56231**
Dorn, Sam (JEFFRIES) PRESS ASST/DIGITAL DIR 2433 **55936**
Dorner, Evan (AGUILAR) LEGIS ASST 109 CHOB **53201**
Dorney, Tom (LEWIS) SR LEGIS ASST 300 CHOB **53801**
Dorothy, Michelle (HOULAHAN) CHIEF OF STAFF 1218 **54315**
Dorrien, Eric (MOOLENAAR) CONSTIT RELATIONS REP **989-631-2552**
Dorrough, Parker (AGUILAR) COMMUNICATIONS DIR 109 CHOB **53201**
Dorsey, Rykia (WATERS) PRESS SECY 2221 **52201**
Doss, Darrell (CLAY) POLICY ADVISOR 2428 **52406**
Doss, Jade (CARTER, JOHN R.) CASEWKR **512-246-1600**
Dos Santos, Elizabeth (DIAZ-BALART) EXEC ASST/LEGIS AIDE 404 CHOB **54211**
Dos Santos, Jordan (HOLLINGSWORTH) CASEWKR **812-288-3999**
Doster, Curtis (DELGADO) SR LEGIS ASST 1007 **55614**
Dotson, Bernadine (CMTE-VET AFFAIRS) FINANCIAL ADMIN/OFFICE MGR 3470 **59756**
Doty, Brian (ROSE, MAX) STAFF ASST 1529 **53371**
Doty, Erin (RUIZ) LEGIS DIR 2342 **55330**
Doty, John
(CMTE-JUDICIARY) SR ADVISOR 2138 **53951**
(NADLER) DIRECTOR 2132 **55635**
Dotzler, Doreen (CLERK/REPORTERS) SR OFFICIAL REPORTER HT59 **55621**
Doucette, Kellie (SHERRILL) DIST DIR **973-526-5668**
Dougall, Troy (CURTIS) STAFF ASST 125 CHOB **57751**
Dougherty, Matthew (DINGELL) SCHEDULING DIR 116 CHOB **54071**
Dougherty, Robert (BRINDISI) LEGIS DIR 329 CHOB **53665**
Dougherty, Shannon (COLLINS, CHRIS) LIAISON - CONSTIT SVCS **585-519-4002**
Douglas, Daniel (TURNER) DIST STAFF ASST **937-225-2843**
Douglas, Errin (PRESSLEY) STAFF ASST 1108 **55111**
Douglas, Jane (ALLEN) STAFF ASST 2400 **52823**
Douglas, Madeline (NEGUSE) SCHEDULER 1419 **52161**
Douglas, Victori (COHEN) STAFF ASST **901-544-4131**
Douthitt, Lily (COMER) STAFF ASST 1037 **53115**
Doux, Jules (FLEISCHMANN) CASEWKR **423-756-2342**
Dowd, Brian (CARTWRIGHT) DIST STAFF ASST **570-341-1050**
Dowd, Timothy A (CMTE-JOINT TAX) SR ECONOMIST 595 FHOB **67575**
Dowdell, Emily (CARTER, JOHN R.) COMMUNICATIONS DIR **512-246-1600**
Dowdy, Tracy (CARTER, EARL L. "BUDDY") STAFF ASST **912-352-0101**
Dowling, Kevin (ZELDIN) LEGIS DIR 2441 **53826**
Downs, Jordan (GUEST) CHIEF OF STAFF 230 CHOB **55031**
Downs, Taylor (CMTE-WAYS & MEANS) SUBCOMM CLERK/LEGIS ASST 2018 **59263**
Doyle, William (ZELDIN) DIR - CONSTIT AFFAIRS **631-289-1097**
Dozier, Brian (CAO/ASSET MANAGEMENT) SR REC & WAREHOUSE SPEC 161 FHOB **60538**
Dragano, Garrett (WILSON, JOE) SPECIAL ASST/CASEWKR **803-642-6416**
Drago, Rebecca (CUNNINGHAM) COMMUNICATIONS DIR 423 CHOB **53176**
Drake, Seth (YARMUTH) CONG AIDE **502-582-5129**
Dreiling, Mark (BACON) CHIEF OF STAFF 1024 **54155**
Driscoll, John (HUFFMAN) DIST REP **707-407-3585**
Driscoll, Laura (DELGADO) SR LEGIS ASST 1007 **55614**
Droog, Anita (BERGMAN) DIST AIDE **231-944-7633**
Druckman, Emily (KRISHNAMOORTHI) PRESS SECY 115 CHOB **53711**
Drulis, Mitchelle (MALINOWSKI) DIST DIR **908-547-3307**
Drummond, Elizabeth (CMTE-ARMED SVCS) PROF STAFF 2340 **67171**
Drummond, LaDedra (JACKSON LEE) SCHEDULER 2079 **53816**
Drzewicki, John (HOUSE REPUB CONF) POLICY DIR 1420 **55107**
Dubad, Arwa (TLAIB) STAFF ASST 1628 **55126**
Dubbs, Andrea (THOMPSON, GLENN) SR CASEWKR/DIST OFFICE MGR **814-353-0215**
Dube, Luke (VEASEY) STAFF ASST 2348 **59897**
Dubose, Jihan (KELLY, ROBIN L.) DIST REP **708-679-0078**
Dubuisson, Marlon (CONNOLLY) OUTREACH REP 2241-D TACKETT'S MILL DR **571-408-4407**
Duby, Sarah (SCHNEIDER) CONSTIT SVCS REP **847-383-4870**
Ducksworth, Monique (LEGIS COUNSEL) STAFF ASST 337 FHOB **56060**
Duckworth, Brian (ALLRED) LEGIS ASST 328 CHOB **52231**
Duckworth, Jill (PALAZZO) COMMUNICATIONS DIR **601-582-3246**
Duclos, Leslie (KENNEDY) DPTY DIST REP **508-431-1110**
Dudley, Betsy (COHEN) SR LEGIS ASST 2104 **53265**
Dudley, Lauren (CMTE-TRANSP & INFRA) COUNSEL - INVESTIGATIONS & OVERSIGHT 2165 **54472**
Dudziak, Peter (JOHNSON, DUSTY) LEGIS CORRES 1508 **52801**
Duenas, Joseph (CAO/HIR – ESCALATIONS AND OPS) SR SYS SUPPORT ENGINEER 604 FHOB **69470**
Duggins, Cori (RUPPERSBERGER) DIST DIR/ CASEWK SUPERVISOR **410-628-2701**
Dugue, Monalisa (CMTE-JUDICIARY) DPTY CHIEF COUNSEL 6340 **55727**
Dulaney, Emmalynn (CMTE-OVERSIGHT & GOVT REFORM) DPTY PRESS SECY 2157 **55051**
Dumler, Ambler (GRIFFITH) CONSTIT SVCS REP **276-525-1405**

Dunbar, Avis (ROGERS, MIKE) CASEWKR ... 334-745-6221
Dunbar, MaCherie (HOULAHAN) CASEWKR ... 610-295-0815
Duncan, Chris (MCCARTHY) DIST SCHEDULER ... 661-327-3611
Duncan, Kerry (LOFGREN) CONG ASST ... 408-271-8700
Dunham, Oscar (HORSFORD) SCHEDULING DIR 1330 ... 59894
Dunham, Will (MIN LEADER) POLICY DIR H204 ... 54000
Dunklin, Kelda (CAO/HIR – IT CUSTOMER SOLUTIONS) SR TECH SUPPORT REP 604 FHOB ... 66179
Dunn, Andrew (BONAMICI) STAFF ASST/LEGIS CORRES 2231 ... 50855
Dunn, Joe (HAYES) CHIEF OF STAFF 1415 ... 54476
Dunn, Jordan (GALLAGHER) PRESS SECY 1230 ... 55665
Dunn, Katie (TONKO) FIELD REP ... 518-465-0700
Dunn, Kyle (HORN) DIR - SCHEDULING & ADVANCE 415 CHOB ... 52132
Dunn, McKayla (RICE, TOM) SCHEDULER 512 CHOB ... 59895
Dunn, Mike (LARSON) LEGIS CORRES 1501 ... 52265
Dunn, Nichole (MCADAMS) CHIEF OF STAFF 130 CHOB ... 53011
Dunn, Randy (CLEAVER) COMMUNITY AFFAIRS LIAISON ... 816-842-4545
Dunstan, Lynn (GRAVES, GARRET) CONSTIT SVCS REP ... 225-442-1731
Dupont, Zach (NEAL) LEGIS ASST/LEGIS CORRES 2309 ... 55601
Duque, Carolina (SCHNEIDER) DIST AIDE ... 847-383-4870
Duran, Patrick (LUJÁN) FIELD REP ... 505-994-0499
Duran, Rolando (CAO/HOUSE RECORDING STUDIO) ELECTRONICS TECH 2010 ... 53941
Durand, Adam (PETERSON) DPTY CHIEF OF STAFF/ LEGIS DIR 2204 ... 52165
Durkin, Kate (SCHAKOWSKY) LEGIS ASST 2367 ... 52111
Durrer, Austin (CRIST) CHIEF OF STAFF 215 CHOB ... 55961
Durst, Jacob (THOMPSON, GLENN) STAFF ASST 400 CHOB ... 55121
Dusenbury, Rhett (MOONEY) DIST REP 2440 ... 52711
Duthler, Jennifer (HUIZENGA) DIST REP ... 616-570-0917
Dutton, John (HARRIS) CHIEF OF STAFF 2334 ... 55311
Duval, Claire (CMTE-FOREIGN AFFAIRS) DIR - MBR SVCS & COALITIONS 2066 ... 68467
Duval, Jhostyn (SIRES) LEGIS ASST 2268 ... 57919
Duvall, Zellie (ALLEN) LEGIS ASST 2400 ... 52823
Duveneck, Katherine (SCHWEIKERT) LEGIS DIR 1526 ... 52190
Dwyer, Billy (KELLY, ROBIN L.) DIST REP ... 708-679-0078
Dwyer, Matthew (CMTE-TRANSP & INFRA) PROF STAFF 2165 ... 54472
Dwyer, Steve
(HOYER) DIGITAL DIR 1705 ... 54131
(MAJ LEADER) SR POLICY ADVISOR/DIGITAL DIR H107 ... 53130
Dybas, Samantha (LAHOOD) LEGIS ASST 1424 ... 56201
Dye, Jon (BARR) DIST STAFF ASST ... 859-219-1366
Dye, Russell (CMTE-OVERSIGHT & GOVT REFORM) COMMUNICATIONS COUNSEL 2105 ... 55074
Dyer, Cindy (COLLINS, DOUG) DIR - CONSTIT SVCS ... 770-297-3388
Dyer, Jacqueline (FITZPATRICK) CONSTIT ADVOCATE ... 215-579-8102
Dyke, Bobby (MCCAUL) STAFF ASST ... 512-473-2357
Dyson, Laura (CAO/HIR – ENTERPRISE ARCHITECT) SR ENTERPRISE ARCHITECT 645 FHOB ... 60592
Dyson, Nzinga (CMTE-HOMELAND SECUR) COUNSEL 176 FHOB ... 62616
Dziadon, Daniel (CMTE-SCIENCE) PROF STAFF MBR - REPUB 394 FHOB ... 56371
Eager, Thomas (CMTE-INTELLIGENCE) PROF STAFF - MAJ HVC304 ... 57690
Eagleburger, Jason (RIGGLEMAN) SR ADVISOR - FOREIGN POLICY 1022 ... 54711
Eaglin, Hope (CAO/HIR – CYBERSECURITY) SR INFO SYS SECUR ANALYST 650 FHOB ... 61586
Early, Ryan (MCGOVERN) LEGIS CORRES 408 CHOB ... 56101
Earwood, Elizabeth (PALMER) LEGIS CORRES 207 CHOB. 54921
Easter, Abbi (MCEACHIN) SR ADVISOR ... 804-486-1840
Easter, Andrea (KING, STEVE) DIST REP ... 712-580-7754
Eatman, Emma (CMTE-ED & WORKFORCE) PRESS AIDE 2176 ... 53725
Eaton, Chuck (HIGGINS, BRIAN) CHIEF OF STAFF ... 716-852-3501
Ebadi, Jesse (CARBAJAL) DIST REP/CASEWKR ... 805-730-1710
Eberhart, Aaron (HAGEDORN) CONSTIT OUTREACH REP ... 507-323-6090
Eberle, Jonathan (BIGGS) STAFF ASST 1318 ... 52635
Ebner, Casey (LEGIS COUNSEL) ASST COUNSEL 337 FHOB ... 56060
Echols, Deborah (BROOKS, MO) CASEWKR ... 256-551-0190
Eckblad, Ariel (OCASIO-CORTEZ) LEGIS DIR 229 CHOB ... 53965
Eckert, Josephine (CMTE-APPRO) PROF STAFF MEMB 2358A ... 52141
Eckstein, Mathew (LEGIS COUNSEL) SR COUNSEL 337 FHOB ... 56060
Eckstein, Zachary (GOTTHEIMER) LEGIS ASST 213 CHOB 54465
Edari, Nialah (MAJ WHIP) STAFF ASST H329 ... 63210
Eddowes, Chris (SMUCKER) LEGIS ASST 127 CHOB ... 52411
Edelson, Brandey (DEUTCH) DIR - COMMUNITY OUTREACH ... 561-470-5440
Edelson, Oliver (PAPPAS) LEGIS CORRES 323 CHOB ... 55456
Edge, James (FLORES) REGIONAL DIR ... 979-703-4037
Edmiston, Suanne (KING, STEVE) LEGIS DIR 2210 ... 54426
Edmonson, Catherine (CUELLAR) DPTY CHIEF OF STAFF 2372 ... 51640
Edmonson, Robert (PELOSI) CHIEF OF STAFF 1236 ... 54965
Edmonson, Robert (SPEAKER) POLICY ADVISOR H232 ... 50100
Edward, Ryley (CAO/LOGISTICS) REC & WAREHOUSE SPEC RSBC4 ... 55057
Edwards, Catherine (CMTE-APPRO) ADMIN AIDE HB13A ... 52851
Edwards, Imani (FUDGE) SCHEDULER/OFFICE MGR 2344. 57032
Edwards, Jasi (WATSON COLEMAN) SPECIAL ASST ... 609-883-0026
Edwards, Joe (MEEKS) EXEC DIR ... 718-725-6000
Edwards, Yul (DAVIS, DANNY K.) CHIEF OF STAFF 2159 ... 55006
Edwards-Jenks, Jonas (ROSE, MAX) COMMUNICATIONS DIR 1529 ... 53371
Effingham, Damon (PHILLIPS) LEGIS COUNSEL 1305 ... 52871
Egekeze, Ijeoma (SCOTT, DAVID) LEGIS ASST 225 CHOB. 52939
Egerson, Troy (CAO/FURNISHINGS) MASTER UPHOLSTERER WA33 RHOB ... 58000
Eglin, Jessika (LAWSON) STAFF ASST 1406 ... 50123
Egorin, Melanie (CMTE-WAYS & MEANS) DPTY STAFF DIR - SUBCOMM 1104 ... 53943
Ehlich, Bethany (BRINDISI) SCHEDULER 329 CHOB ... 53665
Ehly, Ryan (NORCROSS) LEGIS DIR 2437 ... 56501
Ehrenberg, Mia (SPEAKER) PRESS ASST H232 ... 50100

Ehrendreich, Cooper (HIGGINS, BRIAN) SCHEDULER/ PRESS ASST 2459 53306
Ehrenkrantz, Joseph (CMTE-JUDICIARY) PROF STAFF 6240 67680
Eichar, Andrew
(CMTE-OVERSIGHT & GOVT REFORM) PRESS SECY 2157 55051
(CUMMINGS) PRESS SECY 2163 54741
Eichinger, Kevin (JORDAN) CHIEF OF STAFF 2056 52676
Eichmann, Rebecca (SPANBERGER) STAFF ASST 1239 52815
Einterz, Frannie (CLARK) LEGIS ASST 2448 52836
Eisenberger, Andrew (KELLY, MIKE) COMMUNICATIONS DIR 1707 55406
El, Olga (NORCROSS) DIST REP/CASEWKR 856-427-7000
Eleftherion, Anthony (CAO/BUDGET POLICY) BUDGET ANALYST 3240 61457
Elias, Andrew (CAO/HOUSE RADIO-TV GALLERY) DPTY DIR H320 55214
Elias, Christina (SHALALA) CONG AIDE 305-668-2285
Elias, Minna (MALONEY, CAROLYN B.) DIST CHIEF OF STAFF 212-860-0606
Eligan, Veronica (CMTE-JUDICIARY) PROF STAFF 6340 55727
Elizalde, Hector (NAPOLITANO) DPTY DIST DIR 626-350-0150
Elizalde, Rafael (TAKANO) DIST DIR 951-222-0203
Elizandro, John (MEUSER) COMMUNICATIONS DIR 326 CHOB 56511
Elkins, Kevin (ROSE, MAX) DIST DIR 718-667-3313
Elkins, Olivia (SWALWELL) SCHEDULER 407 CHOB 55065
Ellard, Angela (CMTE-WAYS & MEANS) CHIEF COUNSEL - TRADE/STAFF DIR - MIN 1139 54021
Ellertson, Larry (CURTIS) CASEWKR 801-922-5400
Elleson, Benjamin (LONG) LEGIS DIR 2454 56536
Ellin, James (CAO/HIR – NETWORKING ENGINEERING AND OPS) NETWK SYS ENGINEER 664 FHOB 62833
Elliott, Beverly (MEADOWS) FIELD REP 828-452-6022
Elliott, Claire (YARMUTH) EXEC ASST 402 CHOB 55401
Elliott, Farar P (CLERK/ART & ARCHIVES) CHIEF JEFFERSON BUILDING, ATTIC 61300
Elliott, Jacqueline (LAWRENCE) PRESS AIDE/ STAFF ASST 248-356-2052
Elliott, Joel (FINKENAUER) CHIEF OF STAFF 124 CHOB 52911
Elliott, Ronald (CAO/HIR – CYBERSECURITY) SR INFO SYS SECUR ANALYST 612 FHOB 65575
Ellis, Franklin (CAO/HIR – ESCALATIONS AND OPS) SR SYS SUPPORT ENGINEER 601 FHOB 62723
Ellis, Rebecca (WELCH) STATE DIR 802-652-2450
Ellis, Shirley (MOORE) SR ADVISOR/DIST DIR 414-297-1140
Ellis-Gregg, Sharon (CAO/PAYROLL & BENEFITS) ASST B215 LHOB 55089
Ellis-Jones, Deborah (CAO/MBR SVCS) PAYROLL ADMIN B235 LHOB 53644
Ellison, Amber (STANTON) LEGIS CORRES 128 CHOB 59888
Ellison, Carol (BILIRAKIS) CASEWK MGR 727-232-2921
Ellison, Greg (HIGGINS, CLAY) SPECIAL PROJ 337-703-6105
Ellison, Matthew (MAJ WHIP) DPTY POLICY DIR H329 63210
Eloranta, John (STAUBER) DIR - GRANTS 218-481-6396
Elul, Gabrielle (CMTE-BUDGET) ECONOMIST 204E CHOB 67200
Emamali, Nicole (CAO/HIR – IT CUSTOMER SOLUTIONS) SR TECH SUPPORT REP 608B FHOB 66411
Emerick Clerkin, Amy (GRIJALVA) CHIEF OF STAFF 1511. 52435
Emery, Ciara (HUFFMAN) FIELD REP 707-407-3585
Emery, Micelle (CAO) ADMIN SPEC HB28 55555
Emfield, Josh (CURTIS) DPTY STATE DIR 801-922-5400
Emhof, Jaryn (WEBSTER) CHIEF OF STAFF/ COMMUNICATIONS DIR 1210 51002
Emmendorfer, Nicholas (BERGMAN) DIST AIDE 906-273-2227
Emmer, Jack (DUFFY) LEGIS CORRES 1714 53365
Emmons, Julie (WALKER) DIST DIR 336-229-0159
Emmons, William (CMTE-JUDICIARY) PROF STAFF 2035 53951
Eng, Marvin (SMITH, ADAM) DIST REP 425-793-5180
Engdahl, Seth (VISCLOSKY) SR LEGIS ASST 2328 52461
Engelhardt, Steven (CLAY) COMMUNICATIONS DIR 314-669-9393
Engelking, Madison (BROOKS, MO) SCHEDULER/OFFICE MGR 2246 54801
Engell, David Jr (RODGERS) REGIONAL REP 509-684-3481
Enggasser, Harry (BOYLE) CONSTIT SVCS REP 215-426-4616
England, Richard (OLSON) LEGIS DIR 2133 55951
Engling, Maximilian (MIN LEADER) DPTY DIR - OUTREACH/MBR SVCS ADVISOR H204 54000
English, Brystol (CMTE-SCIENCE) PROF STAFF - MAJ 2321 56375
English, Cachavious (SEWELL) CHIEF OF STAFF 2201 52665
English, Joseph (CAO/HIR – OPS AND CONTINUITY) COMMUNICATIONS SPEC 648 FHOB 60069
English, Josh (CAO/FURNISHINGS) MASTER CABINET MAKER WA25 RHOB 58000
Englund, Mary Sue (CMTE-HOUSE ADMIN) DIR - ADMIN OPS 1216 58281
Engquist, Laura (BALDERSON) DPTY CHIEF OF STAFF 1221 55355
Enlow, Alex (KELLY, TRENT) STAFF ASST 1005 54306
Enmeier, Grace (LUCAS) FIELD REP 405-373-1958
Ennesser, Tracy (CMTE-SMALL BUSINESS) STAFF ASST 2361 54038
Enochs, Chase (STIVERS) STAFF ASST/FIELD REP 740-654-2654
Enos, Ben (DESAULNIER) DIST REP 503 CHOB 52095
Enz, Daniel (TORRES) DIST DIR 909-481-6474
Epstein, Laura (DELGADO) COMMUNICATIONS DIR 1007 55614
Erb, Chris (CMTE-RULES) DIR - INFO TECH/DIR - ADMIN OPS 1116 59191
Erb, Logan (ZELDIN) PRESS ASST 631-289-1097
Erickson, Janet (CMTE-APPRO) PROF STAFF MEMB 2007 53081
Erickson, Kathy (DEFAZIO) DIST FIELD REP 541-269-2609
Erickson, Kristofor (CMTE-FINANCIAL SVCS) DPTY STAFF DIR 2129 54247
Erickson, Roger (ESTES) FIELD REP 316-262-8992
Erkel, Richard (VELÁZQUEZ) FINANCIAL SVCS COUNSEL 2302 52361
Ernst, Max (FINKENAUER) LEGIS ASST 124 CHOB 52911
Erste, Mark (CHABOT) LEGIS ASST 2408 52216
Ertel, Elizabeth
(CMTE-ENERGY & COMMERCE) OFFICE MGR 2125 52927
(PALLONE) ADMIN - FINANCE & PAYROLL 2107 54671
Ervin, Dana (CMTE-APPRO) PROF STAFF MEMB 283 FHOB 53881
Erving, James (CAO/HIR – ENTERPRISE INFRASTRUCT) COMMUNICATIONS SPEC 677 FHOB 571-921-3333
Erwin, Alex (GRAVES, GARRET) LEGIS CORRES 2402 53901

Esau, Allie (STAUBER) LEGIS ASST 126 CHOB 56211
Escalante, Clarissa (VISCLOSKY) STAFF ASST. 219-795-1844
Escubio, John (CAO/HIR – OPS AND CONTINUITY) TECH SUPPORT REP 648 FHOB 66141
Eskandani, Rebekah (CMTE-SCIENCE) COMMUNICATIONS DIR 2321 56375
Eskridge, Robert (CMTE-ETHICS) COUNSEL 1015 57103
Espaillat, Edili (SERRANO) CONG ASST 718-620-0084
Espinosa, Christopher (CMTE-NATURAL RESOURCES) DIR - COMMUNITY RELATIONS 1324 56065
Espinosa, Kimberly (LUJÁN) LEGIS DIR 2323 56190
Espinoza, Sol (CMTE-JOINT ECON) SR POLICY ANALYST - DEM SH-804 80188
Esser, Carley (HARTZLER) LEGIS ASST 2235 52876
Estelle, Beth (BALDERSON) CASEWKR/CONSTIT SVCS REP 614-523-2555
Estep, Nana (ROGERS, HAROLD) RECEPTIONIST 606-439-0794
Estes, Maia (BROWN) CHIEF OF STAFF 1323 58699
Estes-Petty, Randi-Joanne A
(CMTE-ED & WORKFORCE) SPECIAL ASST TO THE CHAIRMAN/SHARED EMPLOYEE 1201 58351
(SCOTT, ROBERT C. "BOBBY") DPTY CHIEF OF STAFF 1201 58351
Estevez Perez, Ashley (NORCROSS) DIST REP 856-427-7000
Etchison, Cheryl (CAO/PAYROLL & BENEFITS) MGR - PAYROLL & BENEFITS B215 LHOB 64611
Ethier, Virginia (HOUSE HISTORIAN) RESEARCH ASST JEFFERSON BUILDING, ATTIC 61300
Ethington, Ryan (GOODEN) LEGIS DIR 425 CHOB 53484
Etienne, Ashley (SPEAKER) COMMUNICATIONS DIR/SR ADVISOR H232 50100
Etienne, Christopher (RICHMOND) LEGIS AIDE 506 CHOB 56636
Etka, Patrick (WELCH) SCHEDULER/EXEC ASST/OFFICE MGR 2187 54115
Etue, John (WILLIAMS) CHIEF OF STAFF 512-473-8910
Etzkorn, Edward (CMTE-BUDGET) BUDGET ANALYST 204E CHOB 67200
Eubanks, Courtney (ROE) SCHEDULER/OFFICE MGR/EXEC ASST 102 CHOB 56356
Eubanks, Sydney (CRENSHAW) STAFF ASST 413 CHOB 56565
Eusebio, Abbey (SCHAKOWSKY) CONSTIT ADVOCATE 847-328-3409
Evans, Kyle (CLERK/LRC) PUBLIC INFO SPEC B81 CHOB 65200
Evans, Melissa
(BOST) ADMIN - FINANCE & PAYROLL 1440 55661
(JORDAN) FINANCIAL ADMIN 2056 52676
(MEADOWS) ADMIN - FINANCE & PAYROLL 2160 56401
(RESCHENTHALER) ADMIN - FINANCE & PAYROLL 531 CHOB 52065
Evans, Michelle (LAW REV COUNSEL) ASST COUNSEL 308 FHOB 62411
Evans, Rodney (CMTE-JOINT ECON) POLICY ADVISOR - REPUB SD-G01 81195
Evans, Tom (CAO/HIR – CYBERSECURITY) INFO SYS SECUR ANALYST 612 FHOB 62231
Evans, Tricia (CALVERT) DPTY CHIEF OF STAFF/EXEC ASST 2205 51986
Evans, Vincent (LAWSON) SCHEDULER/SPECIAL ASST 1406 50123
Evans, William (CMTE-INTELLIGENCE) COUNSEL - OVERSIGHT HVC304 57690
Evans, William R, Jr (CAO/HOUSE RECORDING STUDIO) ELECTRONICS TECH 2010 53941
Evans Morrison, Danielle (SCALISE) FIELD REP 985-893-9064
Eveland, Alex (KIND) LEGIS DIR 1502 55506
Everett, Gabriela (LEE, SUSIE) DIST REP/SCHEDULER 702-963-9336
Everett, Julie (JOHNSON, MIKE) COMMUNITY LIAISON 318-840-0309
Everton, Alli (MURPHY) SCHEDULER 1710 54035
Evich, Jordan (HERRERA BEUTLER) LEGIS DIR/DPTY CHIEF OF STAFF 2352 53536
Ewers, Gretchen (CAO/FINANCIAL COUNSELING) MGR B215 LHOB 52220
Ewing, John (CAO/ASSET MANAGEMENT) ACCNT MGMT COUNSELOR 6110 56792
Ewing, Maria (KUSTER) SCHEDULER 320 CHOB 55206
Eyong, Joseph (RASKIN) FIELD REP 301-354-1000
Eyster, Lisa (FLEISCHMANN) DIST DIR 2410 53271
Facchiano, Greg (SMUCKER) CHIEF OF STAFF 127 CHOB. 52411
Facchiano, Kathee (HIGGINS, CLAY) CHIEF OF STAFF 424 CHOB 52031
Fagen, Hannah (HOLLINGSWORTH) FIELD REP 317-851-8241
Fahey, Chris (HIGGINS, BRIAN) SR POLICY ADVISOR 716-852-3501
Fairhurst, Deborah (LAWSON) DIST DIR 850-558-9450
Faison, Shawna (CAO/HOUSE CREATIVE SVCS) GRAPHIC DESIGNER 2002 52700
Faker, Janet (WALORSKI) CONSTIT LIAISON 574-223-4373
Falcon, Luis (GRIJALVA) DIST AIDE 623-536-3388
Falcone, Anthony (PORTER) CASEWKR 1117 55611
Falencki, Michael (CMTE-TRANSP & INFRA) STAFF DIR 2165 54472
Falk, Aaron (MCCARTHY) FIELD REP 661-327-3611
Fall, Yvette (ROSE, MAX) CASEWKR 718-667-3313
Falvey, Sean (CMTE-ARMED SVCS) CLERK 2216 54151
Fann, Chelsea (HAYES) STAFF ASST 860-223-8412
Fansler, Debra (SHIMKUS) DIST DIR 618-288-7190
Fansler, Sarah (BURCHETT) DIR - COMMUNITY OUTREACH 865-523-3772
Faraco-Hadlock, Amelia (WEXTON) STAFF ASST 1217 55136
Farel, James M (CLERK/LRC) DOCU PROD CLERK B81 CHOB 65200
Farewell, Robbie (LEVIN, MIKE) SR LEGIS ASST 1626 53906
Farias, Jahaira (LEE, SUSIE) DIST REP 702-963-9336
Farina, Adam (MOULTON) SPEECHWRITER 1127 58020
Farley, Joann (CAO/FINANCIAL COUNSELING) FINANCIAL COUNSELOR B215 LHOB 50189
Farmer, Zach (DAVIDSON) LEGIS CORRES 1107 56205
Farnin, Scott (BEATTY) FINANCIAL SVCS COUNSEL 2303 54324
Farnsworth, Brandon (STEIL) DIR - OPS & PLANNING 608-752-4050
Farray, Susy (TITUS) STAFF ASST 702-220-9823
Farry, Margaret (O'HALLERAN) LEGIS ASST 324 CHOB 53361
Farvour, Beth (VARGAS) SCHEDULER 2244 58045
Fashola, Kevin (MEEKS) FELLOW 2310 53461
Faulkner, Gershom (CRIST) DPTY DIST DIR 727-318-6770

Faulkner, Jennifer (CLINE) DIST SCHEDULER **540-857-2672**
Fay, Samantha (RYAN) LEGIS ASST 1126 ..... **55261**
Fears, Jordan (WAGNER) DIST FIELD REP **636-779-5449**
Featherson, Wendy (DEMINGS) SCHEDULER/EXEC ASST 217 CHOB **52176**
Febro, Patti (POSEY) LIAISON - CONSTIT SVCS **321-632-1776**
Febus, Diana (VELÁZQUEZ) CASEWKR **718-599-3658**
Fedderman, Richard (ENGEL) DIR - CONSTIT SVCS **718-796-9700**
Feeney, Annamarie (BOYLE) SR CONSTIT SVCS REP **215-335-3355**
Feeney, Sarah (CMTE-OVERSIGHT & GOVT REFORM) STAFF ASST 2105 ..... **55074**
Feeney, William (LEWIS) LEGIS CORRES/POLICY ADVISOR 300 CHOB **53801**
Fegley, Kate (LURIA) SCHEDULER 534 CHOB **54215**
Feinswog, Alison (LEVIN, MIKE) LEGIS CORRES 1626 ..... **53906**
Feizi, Farima (GARAMENDI) DIST AIDE 2368 ..... **51880**
Feldblum, Bryan (PARLIAMENTARIAN) INFO TECH MGR HT52 ..... **51122**
Felder, Cole (CMTE-HOUSE ADMIN) GEN COUNSEL 1216 ..... **58281**
Feldgus, Steve (CMTE-NATURAL RESOURCES) DPTY STAFF DIR - MAJ STAFF/SUBCOMM STAFF DIR 1522 ..... **56065**
Feldhaus, Katie (COOPER) DIST SCHEDULER **615-736-5295**
Feldman, Anne (CROW) COMMUNICATIONS DIR 1229 ..... **57882**
Feldman, Jared (COSTA) LEGIS DIR/LEGIS COUNSEL 2081 ..... **53341**
Feldman, Lisa (CHABOT) SCHEDULER 2408 ..... **52216**
Feldman, Vanessa (HOULAHAN) SCHEDULER 1218 ..... **54315**
Feldpausch, Sarah (MITCHELL) LEGIS ASST 211 CHOB **52106**
Felix, Gilbert (COX) DIST DIR **661-864-7736**
Felix, Melvin (CARTWRIGHT) PRESS SECY 1034 ..... **55546**
Fellows, Courtney Webb (SMITH, CHRISTOPHER H.) SR LEGIS ASST 2373 ..... **53765**
Felmlee, Brenda (TIPTON) FIELD REP **719-587-5105**
Felt, Nicholas (SUOZZI) FIELD REP **631-923-4100**
Fendrick, Josh (GOTTHEIMER) ADVISOR - ECON POLICY 213 CHOB **54465**
Ferguson, Betsy (CMTE-OVERSIGHT & GOVT REFORM) COUNSEL 2105 ..... **55074**
Ferguson, Beverly (BABIN) REGIONAL DIR **832-780-0966**
Ferguson, Carolyn (ROE) CONSTIT SVCS REP **423-247-8161**
Fergusson, Patrick (WATERS) LEGIS DIR 2221 ..... **52201**
Ferland, John (MASSIE) CHIEF OF STAFF 2453 ..... **53465**
Fernandez, Bruce
(CMTE-OVERSIGHT & GOVT REFORM) PROF STAFF MEMB 6470 ..... **55051**
(LYNCH) LEGIS DIR/DPTY CHIEF OF STAFF 2109 ..... **58273**
Fernandez, Chris (PERRY) LEGIS CORRES 1207 ..... **55836**
Fernandez, Denise (DAVIS, SUSAN A.) LEGIS CORRES 1214 ..... **52040**
Fernandez, Tania (CASTOR) CONSTIT SVCS **813-871-2817**
Ferniza, Sandra (GALLEGO) INTERGOVT LIAISON **602-256-0551**
Ferraiuoli Hornedo, Veronica (GONZÁLEZ-COLÓN) LEGAL COUNSEL 1609 ..... **52615**
Ferrance, Brandon (JOYCE, JOHN) STAFF ASST 1337 ..... **52431**
Ferrara, Anna (CMTE-SCIENCE) STAFF ASST - REPUB 394 FHOB **56371**
Ferrari, Jake (WITTMAN) MIL FELLOW 2055 ..... **54261**
Ferree, Logan (HUFFMAN) DPTY CHIEF OF STAFF/LEGIS DIR 1527 ..... **55161**
Ferro, Jon
(CMTE-JUDICIARY) PARLIAMENTARIAN/COUNSEL 2142 ..... **56906**
(COLLINS, DOUG) PARLIAMENTARIAN 1504 ..... **59893**
Fertitta, Ella (WALORSKI) PRESS ASST 419 CHOB **53915**
Fery, Matthew (HIGGINS, BRIAN) DC CHIEF OF STAFF 2459 ..... **53306**
Fetterman, Kris (DELAURO) SPEECHWRITER 2413 ..... **53661**
Fetzer, Kelsey (BERGMAN) LEGIS ASST 414 CHOB **54735**
Feyerherm, Alan (FORTENBERRY) LEGIS DIR/DPTY CHIEF OF STAFF 1514 ..... **54806**
Ficenec, Samuel (BACON) STAFF ASST 1024 ..... **54155**
Fidler, Joshua (MEUSER) CONSTIT SVCS REP **570-871-6370**
Fields, Cassandra (CMTE-OVERSIGHT & GOVT REFORM) COUNSEL 2157 ..... **55051**
Fields, Darlene (RICHMOND) DPTY DIST DIR **225-636-5600**
Fields, Jay (HOUSE REPUB STUDY CMTE) POLICY STAFF 418 CHOB **52777**
Fields, McKenzie (PELOSI) STAFF ASST 1236 ..... **54965**
Fields, Peggy (CLERK/LEGIS OPS) ASST BILL CLERK HT13 ..... **57598**
Fields, Shayna (AMASH) DIST REP **616-451-8383**
Fierro, Alia (CMTE-FINANCIAL SVCS) PROF STAFF - MAJ 2129 ..... **54247**
Figel, Claire
(CMTE-FOREIGN AFFAIRS) STAFF ASSOC 2066STAFF ASSOC 2066 ..... **68467**
(CMTE-FOREIGN AFFAIRS) STAFF ASSOC 2066STAFF ASSOC 2066 ..... **68467**
Figueredo, Cristian (HUNTER) STAFF ASST 2429 ..... **55672**
Figueroa, Ana (ROYBAL-ALLARD) DIST CHIEF OF STAFF **323-721-8790**
Figueroa, Blanca (CARBAJAL) CASEWKR/DIST REP **805-730-1710**
Figueroa, Kevin (LEE, BARBARA) LEGIS CORRES 2470 ..... **52661**
Figueroa, Marie (JEFFRIES) DIST SCHEDULER/ COORD - COMMUNITY OUTREACH **718-237-2211**
Fike, Cari (PALMER) LEGIS DIR 207 CHOB **54921**
Fike, Hugh (CLOUD) LEGIS DIR 1314 ..... **57742**
Fillingim, Kristin (GRAVES, TOM) SCHEDULER 2078 ..... **55211**
Fillion, Jane (MORELLE) LEGIS CORRES 1317 ..... **53615**
Fine, Lauren (MIN WHIP) COMMUNICATIONS DIR H148 ..... **50197**
Fine, Sarah (CAO) ANALYST B227 LHOB **58000**
Finkel, Matthew (CMTE-FOREIGN AFFAIRS) STAFF ASSOC 2170 ..... **55021**
Finks, Lauren (CMTE-SMALL BUSINESS) CLERK 2361 ..... **54038**
Finn, Colin (GABBARD) LEGIS CORRES 1433 ..... **54906**
Finn, Kaulana (GABBARD) CONSTIT OUTREACH REP **808-541-1986**
Finnegan, Richard (HIGGINS, BRIAN) DIST FIELD REP **716-852-3501**
Fins, Eric (KENNEDY) SR LEGIS ASST 304 CHOB **55931**
Fischer, Adam (CMTE-ENERGY & COMMERCE) POLICY ANALYST 2125 ..... **54407**
Fischer, Amanda (PORTER) CHIEF OF STAFF 1117 ..... **55611**
Fischer, Bart (CMTE-AGRIC) DPTY STAFF DIR/CHIEF ECONOMIST 1010 ..... **50317**
Fischer, Jordan (CHENEY) FIELD REP **307-414-1677**

Fischer, Robert, Jr (DEM CLOAKRM) ASST FLOOR CHIEF H222 57330
Fisher, Chris (CRIST) LEGIS DIR 215 CHOB 55961
Fisher, Jerome (CAO/HIR – IT CUSTOMER SOLUTIONS) SR TECH SOLUTIONS ENGINEER 694 FHOB 56002
Fishman, Molly (SPEIER) LEGIS DIR 2465 53531
Fitzella, James (CMTE-RULES) SR PROF STAFF H152 59191
Fitzgerald, Doug (TIPTON) CASEWKR/DIST FIELD REP/REGIONAL DIR 719-542-1073
Fitzgerald, Frances (COHEN) STAFF ASST 2104 53265
Fitzgerald, Jonna (GOHMERT) DIST DIR 903-561-6349
Fitzmaurice, Paul A (CLERK/LCS) HELP DESK TECH 2401. 51182
Fitzpatrick, Caitlin (SGT AT ARMS/HOUSE SECURITY) STAFF ASST HVC301 62044
Fitzpatrick, Casey (ARMSTRONG) DPTY CHIEF OF STAFF - POLICY 1004 52611
Fitzpatrick, Erica (LARSON) STAFF ASST 860-278-8888
Fitzpatrick, Felicity (CARSON) DIST EXEC ASST ... 317-283-6516
Fitzpatrick, Kevin (CMTE-SMALL BUSINESS) STAFF DIR 2069 55821
Fitzpatrick, Mike (SMUCKER) STAFF ASST 717-393-0667
Fitzpatrick, Mitzi (UPTON) CONSTIT SVCS REP.. ... 269-385-0039
Fitzpatrick, Paul (MEADOWS) CHIEF OF STAFF 2160 56401
Fitzpatrick, Robert (SGT AT ARMS/POLICE SVCS) DPTY ASST SGT AT ARMS - POLICE SVCS/LAW ENFORCEMENT HT8 51000
Fitzsimmons, Liam (PALLONE) CHIEF OF STAFF 2107 54671
Flaherty, Eddie (CMTE-HOUSE ADMIN) CHIEF CLERK 1313 55172
Flaim, Sarah (CMTE-APPRO) COMMUNICATIONS DIR 1016 53481
Flanigan, Bill (CMTE-INTELLIGENCE) PROF STAFF - MIN HVC304 54121
Fleege, Rob (BILIRAKIS) FIELD REP - VETS 727-232-2921
Fleet, Jamie (CMTE-HOUSE ADMIN) STAFF DIR 1309 52061
Fleischman, Julian (MAST) LEGIS AIDE 2182 53026
Fleishman, Susan (LEGIS COUNSEL) SR COUNSEL 337 FHOB 56060
Fleming, Brooke (HOLDING) CONSTIT SVCS REP 919-782-4400
Fleming, Denise (AXNE) LEGIS DIR 330 CHOB 55476
Fleming, Joyce (BONAMICI) CASEWKR/ OUTREACH REP/DIST SCHEDULER 503-469-6010
Fleming, Katherine (GUTHRIE) LEGIS ASST 2434 53501
Flenar, Chelsea (SIRES) LEGIS ASST 2268 57919
Fletcher, Gloria (NC03) DIST STAFF ASST 252-931-1003
Fletcher, John (ROY) LEGIS CORRES 1319 54236
Fletcher, Letitia (CMTE-FOREIGN AFFAIRS) PRINTING MGR 5190 51045
Flick, Andy (TRONE) CHIEF OF STAFF 1213 52721
Flink, Laurie (WASSERMAN SCHULTZ) DPTY DIST DIR 305-936-5724
Flint, Derek (NEWHOUSE) DIST REP 509-452-3243
Flipse, Scott (COMMIS ON CHINA) COMMUNICATIONS DIR 243 FHOB 63777
Flood, Pat (BACON) NATIONAL SECUR ADVISOR 1024 54155
Flores, Chris (KILDEE) DIST DIR 810-238-8627
Flores, Daniel (CMTE-JUDICIARY) CHIEF COUNSEL 189 FHOB 56906
Flores, Erika (CISNEROS) SR FIELD REP 714-459-4575
Flores, Josie (GRANGER) CASEWK DIR 817-338-0909
Flores, Tony (CORREA) STAFF ASST 1039 52965
Florio, Drew (MIN LEADER) DIR - STRATEGIC COMMUNICATIONS H204 54000
Florio, Michael (SUOZZI) CHIEF OF STAFF 631-923-4100
Flory, Fiona (LAMB) LEGIS AIDE 1224 52301
Flowers, Darien (ALLRED) STAFF ASST 328 CHOB 52231
Floyd-Buggs, Kathy (COOPER) OFFICE DIR/DIR - COMMUNITY OUTREACH 615-736-5295
Fluellen, Ian (COSTA) LEGIS ASST 2081 53341
Fluhr, Chris (CMTE-NATURAL RESOURCES) SUBCOMM STAFF DIR/PROF STAFF - MIN 4450 52761
Fluker, Megan (COMMIS ON CHINA) RESEARCH ASSOC 243 FHOB 63831
Flynn, Anthony
(GALLEGO) CASEWORK - VETS 1131 54065
(SCANLON) CHIEF OF STAFF 1535 52011
Flynn, George (PRESSLEY) PRESS ASST 1108 55111
Flynn, Kathleen (CMTE-HOMELAND SECUR) SUBCOMM STAFF DIR - OVERSIGHT, MANAGEMENT, AND ACCOUNTABILITY SUBCOMM 117 FHOB 68417
Focht, Louis (KUSTOFF) STAFF ASST 901-682-4422
Fogarty, Kevin (KING, PETER T.) CHIEF OF STAFF/PRESS SECY/SCHEDULER 302 CHOB 57896
Fogarty, Margaret Tucker (CMTE-ENERGY & COMMERCE) STAFF ASST 2322A 53641
Fogwell, Courtney (MUCARSEL-POWELL) LEGIS DIR/ DPTY CHIEF OF STAFF 114 CHOB 52778
Foley, Libby (MCCOLLUM) LEGIS ASST 2256 56631
Foley, Mark (LEVIN, MIKE) DIR - ADMIN OPS/SCHEDULER 1626 53906
Foley, Martha (CMTE-APPRO) CLERK 2362A 52638
Fontana, Daniel (DEUTCH) LEGIS CORRES 2447 53001
Fonte, Yvonne (HOULAHAN) CASEWKR 610-295-0815
Fontneau, Bruce (CAO/HIR - ENTERPRISE MESSAGING AND MOBILITY) SR SYS ENGINEER 624 FHOB 61522
Foont, Jennie (RASKIN) SR CASEWKR 301-354-1000
Foradori, Lisa (CLERK/REPORTERS) OFFICIAL REPORTER 1718 52627
Forbes, Stacy (CUELLAR) LEGIS FELLOW 2372 51640
Ford, Betty (MULLIN) FIELD REP 918-423-5951
Ford, Darin (CAO/HIR – IT CUSTOMER SOLUTIONS) SR TECH SUPPORT REP 2067 64043
Ford, Janet (PALLONE) STAFF ASST 732-249-8892
Ford, Molly (BUCK) DIST REP 970-702-2136
Ford, Taylor (HICE) DIR - OPS/SCHEDULING DIR 409 CHOB 54101
Fordyce, Joseph (ENGEL) STAFF ASST 718-796-9700
Foreman, Lorraine (SGT AT ARMS) SPECIAL ASST H124... 52456
Forero, Laura (MUCARSEL-POWELL) DC SCHEDULER/ LEGIS CORRES 114 CHOB 52778
Forgione, John (CAO/FIRST CALL) SR CUSTOMER SOLUTIONS REP B227 LHOB 58000
Forlini, Tony (MITCHELL) DIST DIR 586-997-5010
Forman, Alfred (CMTE-FINANCIAL SVCS) SYS ADMIN 2129 54247
Forrest, Jennifer (WALDEN) SCHEDULER 2185 56730
Forrester, Scott (HAALAND) DIST DIR 505-288-4816
Forte-Mackay, Jackie (HOUSE DEM CONG CMPGN CMTE) CHIEF FINANCIAL OFFICER 202-863-1500
Fortson, Rene (SCOTT, AUSTIN) DIST REP 229-396-5175
Fosina, Andrew (CHENEY) LEGIS CORRES 416 CHOB 52311
Foster, Cameron (HERN) CHIEF OF STAFF 1019 52211

Foster, Charles (CAO/PAYROLL & BENEFITS) ASST B215 LHOB ... 54579
Foster, Daniel (CMTE-ED & WORKFORCE) COUNSEL - HEALTH & LABOR 2257 ... 53725
Foster, Ellen (BRINDISI) CHIEF OF STAFF 329 CHOB ... 53665
Foster, Janet (WOMACK) MGR - CONSTIT SVCS ... 479-464-0446
Foster, Janet (CMTE-ETHICS) COUNSEL 1015 ... 57103
Foster, Michael (SGT AT ARMS/HOUSE SECURITY) SECUR OFFICER HVC301 ... 62044
Foster, Ola (RADEWAGEN) OFFICE MGR/ SCHEDULER/DIST EXEC ASST ... 684-633-3601
Foster, Olivia (CMTE-OVERSIGHT & GOVT REFORM) EXEC ASST 2157 ... 55051
Foster, Rebecca (ROSE, JOHN W.) DIST DIR ... 931-854-9430
Foster, Robin Lake (MCCARTHY) DIST ADMIN ... 661-327-3611
Foster Stickney, Lakecia (HOUSE DEM CAUCUS) POLICY DIR B245 LHOB ... 51400
Foti, Leslie (GOSAR) ADMIN DIR 2057 ... 52315
Fountain, Anika (CAO/HIR – IT CUSTOMER SOLUTIONS) TECH SOLUTIONS TECH 694 FHOB ... 56002
Fountain, Melvin (RUSH) DIST AIDE ... 773-779-2400
Foushee, Kylie (GUTHRIE) FIELD REP ... 270-842-9896
Fowkes, Robert (LYNCH) DIST DIR ... 617-428-2000
Fowler, Clayton (MCCARTHY) FIELD REP ... 661-327-3611
Fowler, Kendra (NUNES) DIR - CONSTIT SVCS ... 559-733-3861
Fowler, Mark (WELCH) SR LEGIS ASST 2187 ... 54115
Fowler, Nathaniel (CRAIG) CONSTIT LIAISON ... 651-846-2120
Fowler, Zach (WILD) SR LEGIS COUNSEL 1607 ... 56411
Fowlke, Lorie (CURTIS) STATE DIR ... 801-922-5400
Fox, Alexa (COSTA) LEGIS ASST 2081 ... 53341
Fox, Jen (MCBATH) COMMUNICATIONS DIR 1513 ... 54501
Fox, Kevin (KHANNA) LEGIS ASST 221 CHOB ... 52631
Fox, Sally (STEIL) COMMUNICATIONS DIR 1408 ... 53031
Foxx, Rhonda (ADAMS) CHIEF OF STAFF 2436 ... 51510
Foy Alberto, Valerie (BACON) LEGIS COUNSEL 1024 ... 54155
Frame, Carly (BOYLE) LEGIS ASST 1133 ... 56111
Francis, Lina (PRESSLEY) COMMUNICATIONS DIR 1108 ... 55111
Franco, Miguel (CÁRDENAS) CHIEF OF STAFF 2438 ... 56131
Franco, Sam (CMTE-VET AFFAIRS) PROF STAFF MEMB - DISABILITY ASSISTANCE AND MEMORIAL AFFAIRS SUBCOMM B234 LHOB ... 59756
Francois, Conrad (PLASKETT) STAFF ASST 2404 ... 51790
Franger, Melissa (SGT AT ARMS/POLICE SVCS) LEC PROGRAM ADMIN 173 FHOB ... 53380
Frank, Florence (PORTER) STAFF ASST 1117 ... 55611
Frankel, Max (QUIGLEY) SR LEGIS ASST 2458 ... 54061
Franklin, Margaret (LAWSON) LEGIS DIR 1406 ... 50123
Frappoli, Amelia (CLERK/LEGIS OPS) ASST TALLY CLERK HT13 ... 57925
Frasier, Savannah (CLOUD) SR COMMUNICATIONS STRATEGIST/SR COMMUNICATIONS ADVISOR 1314 ... 57742
Frauman, Caroline (MOORE) TAX COUNSEL 2252 ... 54572
Fravel, Don (CAO/HIR – IT CUSTOMER SOLUTIONS) TECH SOLUTIONS TECH 694 FHOB ... 56002
Frazee, James (BACON) CONSTIT LIAISON ... 402-938-0300
Frazee, Skeek (PINGREE) CASEWKR ... 207-774-5019
Frazer, Caitlin (HOULAHAN) LEGIS DIR 1218 ... 54315
Frazier, Janae (WALKER) PRESS SECY 1725 ... 53065
Frech, Jason (CAO/HIR – IDENTITY GOV AND ADMIN) SR SYS ENGINEER 01W60ACF ... 64455
Frederick, Theresa (LAWSON) CASEWKR ... 850-558-9450
Freebairn, Spencer (GRANGER) CHIEF OF STAFF 1026 ... 55071
Freed, Jake (PALLONE) STAFF ASST 2107 ... 54671
Freedman, Ben (KILMER) STAFF ASST 1410 ... 55916
Freeman, Antoinette (CAO/HOUSE CREATIVE SVCS) ADMIN SPEC 2002 ... 52840
Freeman, Mishawn (CMTE-ED & WORKFORCE) STAFF ASST 2176 ... 53725
Freeney, Malcolm (CAO/HIR – HOUSE WEB SVCS) PROJ MGR 637 FHOB ... 66197
Freimark, Zachary (EMMER) DIST REP ... 763-241-6848
French, Charles (CAO/HIR – NETWORKING ENGINEERING AND OPS) SR NETWK TECH 652C FHOB ... 66430
French, Courtney (CMTE-OVERSIGHT & GOVT REFORM) SR COUNSEL 2157 ... 55051
French, Lauren (LUJÁN) COMMUNICATIONS DIR 2323 ... 56190
French, Miranda (BUSTOS) DIR - CONSTIT SVCS ... 309-786-3406
Fresquez, Michael (COOK) COMMUNICATIONS DIR 1027 ... 55861
Freyre, Karla (MOONEY) STAFF ASST 2440 ... 52711
Frias, Carmen (KIRKPATRICK) CHIEF OF STAFF 309 CHOB ... 52542
Frias, Marcus (CMTE-TRANSP & INFRA) DIGITAL DIR 2029 ... 54472
Fried, Matt (GOTTHEIMER) COMMUNICATIONS DIR 213 CHOB ... 54465
Friedfeld-Gebaide, Sophie (KIM) STAFF ASST 1516 ... 54765
Friedman, Aharon (CMTE-WAYS & MEANS) TAX COUNSEL 1139 ... 54021
Friedman, Aurelia (LIEU) FIELD REP ... 323-651-1040
Friedman, Jake (GOTTHEIMER) DPTY DIR - OPS ... 201-389-1100
Friedman, Julia (CMTE-WAYS & MEANS) COUNSEL 1103 ... 56649
Friedman, Sarah (GEN COUNSEL) LAW CLERK 219 CHOB ... 59700
Frierson, Heather (CLEAVER) COMMUNICATIONS DIR ... 816-842-4545
Frischknecht, Jessica (FINKENAUER) COMMUNICATIONS DIR/SR ADVISOR 124 CHOB ... 52911
Fritcke, Emily (HIMES) SCHEDULER 1227 ... 55541
Fritschner, Aaron (BEYER) COMMUNICATIONS DIR 1119 ... 54376
Fritz, Eric (CAO/HIR – ENTERPRISE INFRASTRUCT) OPS TEAM LEAD 618 FHOB ... 63840
Froelich, Melissa (CMTE-ENERGY & COMMERCE) CHIEF COUNSEL 2322A ... 53641
Fromm, Molly (CMTE-WAYS & MEANS) PARLIAMENTARIAN/GEN COUNSEL 1139 ... 54021
Frost, Dylan (HILL, J. FRENCH) LEGIS DIR 1533 ... 52506
Frost, Whitney (CLEAVER) DIST DIR ... 816-842-4545
Fruci, Jean (CMTE-ENERGY & COMMERCE) ENERGY & ENVIRON POLICY ADVISOR 2125 ... 54407
Fry, Courtney (MAJ LEADER) DPTY DIR - OUTREACH/MBR SVCS ADVISOR H107 ... 53130
Fry, Lance (CAO/FURNISHINGS) DIRECTOR WA29A RHOB ... 66886
Fry, Miriam (BYRNE) SR LEGIS ASST 119 CHOB ... 54931
Fryer, Paul (BISHOP, SANFORD D., JR.) DIST FIELD REP ... 229-439-8067
Fuatagavi, Fua (RADEWAGEN) COORD - HEALTH POLICY/CASEWKR/CASEWKR - IMMIGRATION ... 684-633-3601
Fuellbier, Ken (LESKO) OUTREACH DIR ... 623-776-7911
Fuentes, Joe (CALVERT) LEGIS ASST 2205 ... 51986

Fuentes, Leonardo (PASCRELL) CASEWKR/ FIELD REP 201-935-2248
Fuller, Hannah (RICE, KATHLEEN M.) STAFF ASST 516-739-3008
Fuller, Katrina (REED) CASEWKR 716-708-6369
Fuller, Kim
(FLETCHER) FINANCIAL ADMIN 1429 52571
(GALLEGO) ADMIN - FINANCE & PAYROLL 1131 54065
Fullerton, Laura (CMTE-FOREIGN AFFAIRS) DPTY STAFF DIR - MIN STAFF 2066 68467
Fulmer, Brendan (KELLY, MIKE) SR LEGIS ASST 1707 55406
Fulton, Austin (CURTIS) LEGIS CORRES 125 CHOB 57751
Fultz, Garrett (JOHNSON, MIKE) LEGIS COUNSEL 418 CHOB 52777
Fultz, Rosalind (CHABOT) CONSTIT LIAISON 513-684-2723
Funches, Brenda (THOMPSON, BENNIE G.) CASEWKR/FIELD REP 601-866-9003
Furman, Andrew (FLORES) LEGIS ASST 2228 56105
Furnari, Shannon (WELCH) DPTY STATE DIR 802-652-2450
Fury, Ian (JORDAN) COMMUNICATIONS DIR 2056 52676
Fybel, Rachel (ESHOO) SR HEALTH POLICY ADVISOR 202 CHOB 58104
Fyock, Bradley (CAO/HIR – ENTERPRISE INFRASTRUCT) MGR SITE 3 571-921-3105
Gabriel, Nick (MCEACHIN) CASEWKR 757-942-6050
Gabrielson, Carly (DEFAZIO) OUTREACH DIR 541-465-6732
Gabrysh, Elena (WOODALL) CONSTIT SVCS REP 770-232-3005
Gadbois, Stephanie (CMTE-APPRO) PROF STAFF MEMB 1001 53481
Gage, Austin (ROGERS, HAROLD) LEGIS ASST 2406 54601
Gage, Paul (SCHRADER) CHIEF OF STAFF 2431 55711
Gagliardi, Shala (SHERRILL) CASEWKR - IMMIGRATION 973-526-5668
Gagne, Sally (MCCOLLUM) STAFF ASST 651-224-9191
Gagnon, Jason (CALVERT) COMMUNICATIONS DIR 951-277-0042
Gaillard, Phillip (RICE, TOM) COORD - COMMUNITY OUTREACH 843-445-6459
Gaines, Julia (CAO/OFFICE OF THE CHIEF LOGISTICS OFFICER) SPECIAL ASST WB2 RHOB 61985
Galanski, John (KELLY, MIKE) LIAISON - MIL & VET 724-342-7170
Galante, Amy (MAST) CONSTIT SVCS REP 772-403-0900
Gale, Madeline (MARSHALL) EXEC ASST 312 CHOB 52715
Gale, Stephen (THOMPSON, MIKE) DIST REP 707-542-7182
Galindo, Jorge (GONZALEZ, VICENTE) LEGIS ASST 113 CHOB 52531
Galisewski, Ryan (SPEIER) LEGIS ASST 2465 53531
Gallagher, Bettyanne (WASSERMAN SCHULTZ) CASEWK DIR 954-845-1179
Gallagher, Brendan J (LEGIS COUNSEL) ASST COUNSEL 337 FHOB 56060
Gallagher, Meaghan (TRAHAN) DIST STAFF ASST 978-459-0101
Gallagher, Megan (CMTE-FINANCIAL SVCS) STAFF ASST 4340 57502
Gallagher, Meghan (CMTE-FOREIGN AFFAIRS) PROF STAFF - MIN 2066 68467
Gallagher, Peter (CMTE-NATURAL RESOURCES) PROF STAFF - MAJ 1522 56065
Gallagher, Renee (CAO/HIR – CYBERSECURITY) SR INFO SYS SECUR ANALYST 612 FHOB 67296
Gallagher, Tom (CAO/HIR – ESCALATIONS AND OPS) MGR 608C FHOB 66172
Gallagher Main, Katherine (BOST) CASEWKR 618-622-0766
Gallegos, Alexis (CUELLAR) CONSTIT SVCS REP 956-424-3942
Gallegos, Claudio (CORREA) DIST DIR 714-559-6190
Galloway, Kaylee (DELBENE) CONSTIT OUTREACH REP 360-416-7879
Galloway, Kiera (PETERS) DIR - CONSTIT SVCS 858-455-5550
Galloway, Meghann (CÁRDENAS) LEGIS COUNSEL 2438 56131
Galvis-Delgado, Felipe (TORRES SMALL) LEGIS ASST 430 CHOB 52365
Gama, Krystal (LEE, SUSIE) DIST STAFF ASST 702-963-9336
Gama, Roberto (GOMEZ) SR FIELD REP 213-481-1425
Gamalski, Eleanor (LEVIN, ANDY) FIELD REP/ CASEWKR 586-498-7122
Gambo, Theresa (CMTE-ENERGY & COMMERCE) HR SPEC/OFFICE ADMIN 2322A 53641
Gamboa, Javier (VAN DREW) LEGIS DIR 331 CHOB 56572
Gambrel, Diana (DEGETTE) SCHEDULER/EXEC ASST 2111 54431
Gamel, Sherri (LUCAS) DIST DIR 405-373-1958
Gamela, Renee (THOMPSON, GLENN) COMMUNICATIONS DIR 400 CHOB 55121
Gandhi, Ricky (CMTE-JOINT ECON) ECONOMIST - DEM 244 FHOB 56024
Gandhi, Sajit (CMTE-FOREIGN AFFAIRS) SR PROF STAFF 2064 55021
Gandia, Natalia (GONZÁLEZ-COLÓN) LEGIS ASST 1609 52615
Gannon, Kevin (COLLINS, CHRIS) LEGIS ASST 2243 55265
Gansman, Dana
(GOTTHEIMER) DIST SCHEDULER 213 CHOB 54465
(SELECT CMTE-CLIMATE CRISIS) CLERK 359 FHOB 51106
Gao, Greta (CMTE-OVERSIGHT & GOVT REFORM) COUNSEL 2157 55051
Garand, Brian (MCKINLEY) LEGIS ASST 2239 54172
Garay, German (CAO/HOUSE RECORDING STUDIO) BROADCAST PROD TECH 2010 53941
Garay, Monica (VELÁZQUEZ) STAFF & PRESS ASST 2302 52361
Garber, Lindsey
(CMTE-RULES) PROF STAFF - MAJ H312 59091
(HASTINGS) RULES ASSOC/COUNSEL 2353 51313
Garcia, Alexis (CUELLAR) LEGIS FELLOW 2372 51640
Garcia, Christopher (HAALAND) SCHEDULER 1237 55737
Garcia, David (GARCÍA, JESÚS G. "CHUY") LIAISON - CONSTIT SVCS 773-342-0774
Garcia, Eddie (KELLY, TRENT) MIL FELLOW 1005 54306
Garcia, Emmanuel (PANETTA) CONG AIDE 831-429-1976
Garcia, Jessica (CARSON) CASEWKR 317-283-6516
Garcia, John (CAO/FURNISHINGS) MASTER FINISHER WA22 RHOB 58000
Garcia, Lanette (GARCÍA, JESÚS G. "CHUY") LEGIS ASST 530 CHOB 55087
Garcia, Martha (GRIJALVA) DIST AIDE 928-343-7933
Garcia, Melissa (CMTE-APPRO) PROF STAFF MEMB 283 FHOB 53881

Garcia, Mory
(CMTE-SMALL BUSINESS) OFFICE MGR 2361 **54038**
(VELÁZQUEZ) OFFICE MGR 2302 **52361**
Garcia, Natasha (CMTE-APPRO) PROF STAFF MEMB 283 FHOB **53881**
Garcia, Nestor (CASE) COMMUNICATIONS DIR **808-650-6688**
Garcia, Pamela (LUJÁN) CONSTIT LIAISON **505-454-3038**
García, Patty (GARCÍA, JESÚS G. "CHUY") DIST DIR **773-342-0774**
Garcia, Sandra (COSTA) DIST REP **559-495-1620**
Garcia, Sarah (CMTE-VET AFFAIRS) SUBCOMM STAFF DIR - TECHNOLOGY MODERNIZATION SUBCOMM B234 LHOB **59756**
Garcia, Vikki (SARBANES) COMMUNITY OUTREACH SPEC **410-832-8890**
Garcilazo, Michelle (HUFFMAN) FIELD REP **415-258-9657**
Gard, Sean (MOORE) CHIEF OF STAFF 2252 **54572**
Gardenhour, Benjamin (CMTE-BUDGET) EXEC ASST 507 CHOB **67270**
Gardner, Ashanee (SIRES) STAFF ASST 2268 **57919**
Gardner, Keri (HICE) COORD - GRANTS/ CONSTIT SVCS ASST **770-207-1776**
Gardner, Phil (HECK) DIST DIR **360-459-8514**
Gargiulo, Michele (PALAZZO) DIST DIR **228-864-7670**
Garlock, Emily (CHABOT) CONSTIT LIAISON **513-684-2723**
Garner, Shelby (MALONEY, CAROLYN B.) DIST REP **212-860-0606**
Garrett, Brian (CMTE-ARMED SVCS) PROF STAFF 2340 **53439**
Garrett, Debbie (CLINE) DIST DIR **540-885-3861**
Garrett, Emerald (MAJ WHIP) SR STAFF ASST H329 **63210**
Garrett, Teri (WOMACK) FIELD REP **870-741-6900**
Garrison, Samuel (CARTER, JOHN R.) STAFF ASST/DPTY PRESS SECY 2110 **53864**
Garry, Corey (KUSTER) DIST DIR **603-226-1002**
Garten, Alicia (LARSON) LEGIS ASST 1501 **52265**
Gartin, Randy (CMTE-WAYS & MEANS) CHIEF TAX COUNSEL 1139 **54021**
Gartland, Patricia (KING, PETER T.) DIST REP **516-541-4225**
Garza, Alejandra (DEGETTE) SR CONG AIDE **303-844-4988**
Garza, Jesse (DUFFY) DIST DIR **715-808-8160**
Garza, Johnathan (CMTE-NATURAL RESOURCES) COORD - OUTREACH 186 FHOB **56065**
Garza, Marcus (SERRANO) LEGIS ASST 2354 **54361**
Garza, Rosa (KIRKPATRICK) CONSTIT SVCS SPEC **520-881-3588**
Garzon, Arturo (AMODEI) CONSTIT SVCS REP **775-686-5760**
Gaskins, James (CAO/HIR - ENTERPRISE MESSAGING AND MOBILITY) TEAM LEAD 616 FHOB **66259**
Gaskins, Petra (WATSON COLEMAN) DIR - COMMUNITY OUTREACH **609-883-0026**
Gaspar, Jennifer (CMTE-OVERSIGHT & GOVT REFORM) COUNSEL 2157 **55051**
Gastonguay, Robert (AMODEI) STAFF ASST **775-686-5760**
Gaston Simon, Susan (FITZPATRICK) DIST DIR **215-579-8102**
Gates, Corey (CAO/FURNISHINGS) MASTER UPHOLSTERER WA33 RHOB **58000**
Gates, Jen (CRAIG) COMMUNICATIONS DIR **651-846-2120**
Gates, Thomas (CAO/HIR – ENTERPRISE INFRASTRUCT) SR SYS ENGINEER 617 FHOB **66167**
Gates, Trena (CAO/FINANCIAL COUNSELING) COUNSELOR B215 LHOB **62088**
Gates, Zach (WAGNER) SR LEGIS ASST 2350 **51621**
Gault, Freddie (TIMMONS) DIR - OUTREACH & MEMB SVCS **864-583-3264**
Gause, Nkili (CLYBURN) LEGIS CORRES 200 CHOB **53315**
Gavin, Patrick (POSEY) DIST DIR/DIST SCHEDULER **321-632-1776**
Gavin, Stephen (THOMPSON, BENNIE G.) SR CASEWKR **601-946-9003**
Gavin-Parks, Ingrid (RUSH) DPTY DIR 2188 **54372**
Gaydos, Lauren (GUTHRIE) COMMUNICATIONS DIR 2434 **53501**
Gayle, Charles (CMTE-JUDICIARY) COUNSEL - OVERSIGHT 2035 **53951**
Gayle, Kathleen (WITTMAN) COMMUNICATIONS DIR/ LEGIS ASST 2055 **54261**
Gbadamosi, Akolade (OMAR) COMMUNITY REP **612-333-1272**
Gearhart, Chloe (AXNE) DIST FIELD REP/ CASEWKR **515-400-8180**
Gebbia, Jack (SHERRILL) LEGIS CORRES 1208 **55034**
Gee, James (WATSON COLEMAN) CHIEF OF STAFF 2442 **55801**
Geiger, Teri (BALDERSON) CHIEF OF STAFF **614-523-2555**
Geiselhart, Mike (SMUCKER) LEGIS CORRES 127 CHOB **52411**
Geiser, Lauren (NADLER) CASEWKR **212-367-7350**
Geller, Jamie (CASTRO) COMMUNICATIONS DIR 2241 **53236**
Geller, Matt (SUOZZI) CASEWORK - VETS **631-923-4100**
Gelman, Peter (SARBANES) LEGIS ASST 2370 **54016**
Gelwicks, Laura (LARSEN) COMMUNITY LIAISON **360-733-4500**
Genard, Francois (COX) CHIEF OF STAFF 1728 **54695**
Gentile, Rachel (CMTE-NATURAL RESOURCES) PROF STAFF - MAJ 1332 **56065**
Gentry, Elizabeth (HICE) PRESS ASST/LEGIS ASST 409 CHOB **54101**
Gentry, Jonathan (LIEU) INFO TECH MGR 403 CHOB **53976**
George, Bill (MCCLINTOCK) PRESS SECY **916-786-5560**
George, Daniel (YOUNG) STATE DIR **907-271-5978**
George, Kevin (LYNCH) SR POLICY ADVISOR 2109 **58273**
George, Natalie (CMTE-JOINT ECON) POLICY ANALYST - DEM SH-804 **81377**
George, Scott (SCOTT, ROBERT C. "BOBBY") SR CONSTIT SVCS REP **757-380-1000**
George-Winkler, Nkechi (SCOTT, ROBERT C. "BOBBY") SR ADVISOR **757-380-1000**
Gepert, Darla (CAO/ASSET MANAGEMENT) SPECIAL ASST 6110 **50090**
Gerace, Nathan (MEUSER) DIST STAFF ASST **570-871-6370**
Gerarden, Paul (CAO/CUST EXPER CTR) CUSTOMER ADVOCATE B227 LHOB **58000**
Gerber, Dallas (GIBBS) COMMUNICATIONS DIR/DPTY CHIEF OF STAFF 2446 **56265**
Gerbo, George (CLERK/LRC) PUBLIC INFO SPEC B81 CHOB **65200**
Germain, Naomie (HAALAND) STAFF ASST 1237 **56318**
German, Emily (CMTE-AGRIC) LEGIS ASST 1301 **52171**
German, Justin (STEVENS) CHIEF OF STAFF 227 CHOB **58171**
Germansky, Nancy (FRANKEL) CONSTIT SVCS **561-998-9045**
Germany, Ebony (DAVIDS) STAFF ASST 1541 **64407**

Gerrity, Colleen (CARTWRIGHT) COMMUNICATIONS DIR 570-341-1050
Gerson, Julian (CMTE-JUDICIARY) STAFF ASST 2138 53951
Gerson, Kevin
(TITUS) COMMUNICATIONS DIR 2464 55965
(WASSERMAN SCHULTZ) DIGITAL DIR/PRESS SECY 1114 57931
Gerson, Matthew (DELGADO) JR LEGIS ASST 1007 55614
Gerstell, Jonathan (LURIA) LEGIS ASST 534 CHOB 54215
Gertsema, Jay (TITUS) CHIEF OF STAFF 2464 55965
Gerzof, Devin (CMTE-WAYS & MEANS) PROF STAFF - MIN 1139 54021
Getz, Kara
(CMTE-WAYS & MEANS) COUN TO THE CHAIRMAN 1102 53625
(NEAL) COUN TO THE CHAIRMAN 2309 55601
Geurink, Jenni (CMTE-VET AFFAIRS) PRESS ASST B234 LHOB 59756
Ghaffari, Lisa (DELAURO) STAFF ASST 2413 53661
Ghani, Richard (KEATING) POLICY ADVISOR 2351 53111
Giacchetti, Angela (HILL, KATIE) DIST DIR 661-568-4855
Giachetti, David (CMTE-ARMED SVCS) PROF STAFF 2340 66162
Giammarella, Alyssa (CHU) SCHEDULER 2423 55464
Giancarlo, Angie (CMTE-APPRO) PROF STAFF MEMB 1001 53481
Giancola, Tom (KUSTER) COORD - CONSTIT SVCS/COORD - OUTREACH 603-595-2006
Gianni, Sarah (LARSON) SCHEDULER/EXEC ASST 1501 52265
Gibbons, Mary Pat (MCGOVERN) DIST REP 508-831-7356
Gibbs, Debbi (GARAMENDI) DIST DIR 530-753-5301
Gibson, Brandon (GONZALEZ, ANTHONY) DIST STAFF ASST 440-783-3696
Gibson, Chase (CMTE-JOINT TAX) COUNSEL IRS-3565 202-317-4463
Gibson, Chris (WEXTON) LEGIS CORRES 1217 55136
Gibson, Danica (JOHNSON, DUSTY) CONSTIT SVCS REP 605-646-6454
Gibson, Diana (CUMMINGS) STAFF ASST 410-685-9199
Gibson, Dylan (SPEAKER) DIGITAL DIR H232 50100
Gibson, Kristen (MCCOLLUM) MIL FELLOW 2256 56631
Gibson, Pat (BURCHETT) FIELD REP - VETS/ CASEWKR 865-523-3772
Gibson, Tatum (HUDSON) COMMUNICATIONS DIR 2112 53715
Giesemann, Evan (SEWELL) ADVISOR - ECON POLICY 2201 52665
Giesige, Nicole (LATTA) DIST REP 419-354-8700
Giffin, Ty (JOHNSON, BILL) CASEWKR 740-376-0868
Gilbert, Crystal (LOUDERMILK) DIR - CONSTIT SVCS 770-429-1776
Gilbert, Evan (CMTE-ENERGY & COMMERCE) DPTY PRESS SECY 2125 52927
Gilbert, Jocilyn (LEWIS) STAFF ASST 404-659-0116
Gilbert, Jonathan (LEVIN, MIKE) LEGIS DIR 1626 53906
Gilbert, Sarah (HOLDING) LEGIS ASST 1110 53032
Gilbride, Mark (STIVERS) LEGIS ASST/DPTY LEGIS DIR 2234 52015
Gilchrist, Caleb (DAVIS, DANNY K.) DPTY CHIEF OF STAFF 2159 55006
Gildner, Leigh Anna (HILL, J. FRENCH) DIST REP 501-324-5941
Gill, Hannah (CMTE-RULES) PROF STAFF 1116 59191
Gill, Kelly (COSTA) DIR - CONSTIT SVCS 559-495-1620
Gillespie, James (MIN LEADER) ASST MGR - CLOAKRM H204 54000
Gillespie, Lauren (YOHO) LEGIS CORRES 1730 55744
Gillespie, Maura (KINZINGER) COMMUNICATIONS DIR 2245 53635
Gilley, Allison (LEGIS COUNSEL) ASST COUNSEL 337 FHOB 56060
Gillis, Daniel (CAO/OFFICE OF THE CHIEF HUMAN RESOURCES OFFICER) ADA AIDE 102 FHOB 52926
Gillispie, Elaine (BISHOP, SANFORD D., JR.) FIELD REP 706-320-9477
Gilmartin, Jaimee (WATSON COLEMAN) SCHEDULER 609-883-0026
Gilmore, Joan (CAO/FINANCIAL COUNSELING) ANALYST B215 LHOB 61174
Gilmore, Michael (LAHOOD) CONSTIT SVCS SPEC 309-671-7027
Gilpin, Austin (ESTES) SPECIAL PROJ COORD 316-262-8992
Gilroy, Rachel (HARTZLER) DIST FIELD REP 816-884-3411
Gingrich, Amy (CMTE-WAYS & MEANS) STAFF DIR 1139 54021
Ginis, Alex (HAYES) LEGIS DIR 1415 54476
Ginsberg, Wendy (CMTE-OVERSIGHT & GOVT REFORM) SUBCOMM STAFF DIR 6460 55051
Ginsburg, Andrew (SWALWELL) LEGIS DIR 407 CHOB 55065
Ginsburg, Bob (GARCÍA, JESÚS G. "CHUY") SR POLICY ADVISOR 530 CHOB 61496
Gionson, Ilihia (GABBARD) CONSTIT OUTREACH REP 808-541-1986
Giordano, David (CMTE-WAYS & MEANS) PROF STAFF 1139 54021
Giosa, Chris (CMTE-JOINT TAX) SR ECONOMIST 595 FHOB 67575
Giovine, Ben (KIM) DIST DIR 732-504-0490
Girelli, Austin (SLOTKIN) LEGIS CORRES 1531 54872
Girmscheid, Jake (UNDERWOOD) DIST STAFF ASST 630-549-2190
Gitter, Cynthia (LEVIN, MIKE) FIELD REP 949-281-2449
Giulino, Danielle (AGUILAR) SCHEDULER/DIR - OPS 109 CHOB 53201
Givand, Diana (CAO/OFC OF EMPLOYEE ADVOCACY) ASSOC COUNSEL 301 FHOB 58800
Givens, Patricia (CASTOR) DIST OFFICE MGR 813-871-2817
Gizara, Michael (CAO/HIR – CYBERSECURITY) OPS TEAM LEAD 612 FHOB 66577
Glaser, Karen (BROOKS, SUSAN W.) DIST DIR/ DPTY CHIEF OF STAFF 317-848-0201
Glaser, Megan (TRONE) STAFF ASST 301-926-0300
Glasgow, Savannah (BILIRAKIS) STAFF ASST 2227 55755
Glass, Indira (LAWRENCE) DPTY DIST DIR/ OFFICE MGR 248-356-2052
Glass, Talia (OMAR) COMMUNITY REP 612-333-1272
Glasscock, Stacey (LUCAS) CHIEF OF STAFF 405-373-1958
Gleason, John (CMTE-FOREIGN AFFAIRS) FINANCIAL OFFICER 5190 54291
Gleick, Daniel (DEMINGS) COMMUNICATIONS DIR 217 CHOB 52176
Glenn, Courtney (SPANBERGER) DIST COORD 804-401-4110
Glenn, William (HOLDING) COMMUNICATIONS DIR 919-782-4400
Glezer, Claire (SCHNEIDER) DIR - OPS 1432 54835

Gloor, Jackie (CLOUD) SPECIAL PROJ.... **361-894-6446**
Glosson, Janice L (CLERK/LRC) REGISTRATION & COMPLIANCE CLERK B81 CHOB.... **65200**
Glover, Chester (DEMINGS) CASEWKR.... **321-388-9808**
Glynn, Chelsea (AGUILAR) LEGIS AIDE 109 CHOB.... **53201**
Goczkowski, Andrew (SCHAKOWSKY) COORD - GRANTS/CONSTIT ADVOCATE.... **847-328-3409**
Goddard, Ruben (PAYNE) LEGIS CORRES 103 CHOB.... **53436**
Goddeeris, Andrew (TLAIB) COUNSEL.... **313-463-6220**
Godfrey, Ian (PASCRELL) FIELD REP.... **973-523-5152**
Godinez, Christine (TITUS) LEGIS ASST 2464.... **55965**
Godinich, Drew (COX) COMMUNICATIONS DIR 1728.... **54695**
Goedke, Jennifer (THOMPSON, MIKE) DPTY CHIEF OF STAFF/LEGIS DIR 406 CHOB.... **53311**
Goel, Purva (CRAIG) STAFF ASST 1523.... **52271**
Goessler, Maggie (RATCLIFFE) LEGIS AIDE 223 CHOB.... **56673**
Goetz, Vic (SCHNEIDER) SR POLICY ADVISOR 1432.... **54835**
Goff, Hans (ASST SPEAKER) DIR - MEMB SVCS H132.... **52020**
Goff, Shuwanza (MAJ LEADER) DIR - FLOOR H107.... **53130**
Goggin, Kelly (CMTE-ARMED SVCS) PROF STAFF 2340.... **63229**
Goggins, James (CAO/HIR – NETWORKING ENGINEERING AND OPS) NETWK COMMUNICATIONS SPEC 685 FHOB.... **64214**
Gogolin, Sean (BEYER) PRESS SECY 1119.... **54376**
Goharioon, Laila (MCBATH) LEGIS ASST 1513.... **54501**
Gohringer, Jeff (CMTE-RULES) COMMUNICATIONS DIR H312.... **59091**
Goins, Hope (CMTE-HOMELAND SECUR) STAFF DIR 176 FHOB.... **62616**
Gokcigdem, Murat (JOHNSON, EDDIE BERNICE) CHIEF OF STAFF/EXEC SCHEDULER/LEGIS STAFF 2306.... **58885**
Gold, Jeffrey E (CLERK/LCS) DIR - SYS AND OPS 2401.... **51182**
Goldberg, Lewis (HASTINGS) CONG ASST.... **954-733-2800**
Goldberger, Justin (MCEACHIN) LEGIS ASST 314 CHOB.... **56365**
Goldeen, Ben (COSTA) SR POLICY ADVISOR 2081.... **53341**
Golden, Alexandra (CMTE-OVERSIGHT & GOVT REFORM) CHIEF HEALTH COUNSEL 2157.... **55051**
Golden, J Z (LARSEN) SR LEGIS ASST 2113.... **52605**
Golden, Kevin (MALONEY, SEAN PATRICK) DIR - SCHEDULING & ADVANCE 2331.... **55441**
Golden, Matthew (MCBATH) STAFF ASST/LEGIS CORRES 1513.... **54501**
Golden, Priscilla (DOGGETT) CONSTIT SVCS.... **210-704-1080**
Goldenberg, Rachael (HARDER) CHIEF OF STAFF 131 CHOB.... **54540**
Goldenstein, Jim (COMER) LEGIS DIR 2184.... **53115**
Goldes, Jordan (MENG) COMMUNICATIONS DIR.... **718-358-6364**
Goldfarb, David (STEIL) LEGIS DIR 1408.... **53031**
Goldie, Monica (CMTE-APPRO) PROF STAFF MEMB 283 FHOB.... **53881**
Golding, Ishaan (THOMPSON, MIKE) SCHEDULER 406 CHOB.... **53311**
Goldman, Daniel (CMTE-INTELLIGENCE) SR ADVISOR & DIR OF INVESTIGATIONS HVC304.... **57690**
Goldman, Julia (HIMES) DIGITAL ASST 1227.... **55541**
Goldman, Lisa (CMTE-ENERGY & COMMERCE) SR COUNSEL 2125.... **52927**
Goldsborough-Lee, Angel (CAO/HIR – IT CUSTOMER SOLUTIONS) DIR - IT CUSTOMER SOLUTIONS 607A FHOB **65108**
Goldson, Chris (MOORE) LEGIS DIR 2252.... **54572**
Goldstein, Andrea (CMTE-VET AFFAIRS) POLICY ADVISOR - HEALTH SUBCOMM 3470.... **59756**
Goldstein, Felicia (FRANKEL) DIST DIR.... **561-998-9045**
Gomes, Nick (COSTA) DIST REP.... **209-384-1620**
Gomez, Diana (DOGGETT) FIELD REP.... **512-916-5921**
Gomez, Matthew (CMTE-SMALL BUSINESS) COUNSEL 2361.... **54038**
Gomez, Nancy (SMITH, CHRISTOPHER H.) STAFF ASST.... **609-585-7878**
Gonin, Jon (KUSTER) STAFF ASST 320 CHOB.... **55206**
Gonnelli, Lauren (GOTTHEIMER) CONSTIT OUTREACH REP.... **201-389-1100**
Gonzales, Walter (RUPPERSBERGER) LEGIS DIR/DPTY CHIEF OF STAFF 2206.... **53061**
Gonzalez, Briana (HARDER) DIST REP/MGR - GRANTS.... **209-579-5458**
Gonzalez, Cesar (DIAZ-BALART) CHIEF OF STAFF 404 CHOB.... **54211**
Gonzalez, Damaris (CASTOR) CONSTIT SVCS.... **813-871-2817**
Gonzalez, Elizabeth (CLERK/LRC) PUBLIC INFO SPEC B81 CHOB.... **65200**
Gonzalez, Lea Margarita (CÁRDENAS) FIELD REP.... **818-221-3718**
Gonzalez, Leilani (WASSERMAN SCHULTZ) STAFF ASST 1114.... **57931**
Gonzalez, Pablo (CAO/HIR – OPS AND CONTINUITY) COMMUNICATIONS SPEC 632A FHOB.... **571-921-3339**
Gonzalez, Rosario (CAO/FIRST CALL) SR CUSTOMER SOLUTIONS REP B227 LHOB.... **58000**
Gonzalez, Samantha (CMTE-VET AFFAIRS) SR PROF STAFF - HEALTH SUBCOMM 3460.... **59154**
Gonzalez, Santiago (CROW) POLICY ADVISOR 1229.... **57882**
Gonzalez, Sergio
(BARRAGÁN) INFO TECH SYS ANALYST 1030.... **58220**
(CÁRDENAS) SHARED EMPLOYEE 2438.... **56131**
(CISNEROS) TECH SUPPORT REP 431 CHOB.... **54111**
(CORREA) SYS ADMIN 1039.... **52965**
(RUIZ) SYS ADMIN 2342.... **55330**
Gonzalez, Steve (CMTE-BUDGET) POLICY ADVISOR 507 CHOB.... **67270**
Gonzalez-Thompson, Amanda (COLLINS, DOUG) COMMUNICATIONS DIR.... **770-297-3388**
Gooch, Anne (PARLIAMENTARIAN) ASST PARLIAMENTARIAN H209.... **57373**
Good, Mackenzie L (CLERK/ART & ARCHIVES) COLLECTIONS SPEC JEFFERSON BUILDING, ATTIC.... **61300**
Goodlow, Lisa (CAO/HIR – CYBERSECURITY) SR COMMUNICATIONS SECUR ANALYST 602 FHOB.... **64551**
Goodman, Betsy (GALLAGHER) EXEC ASST.... **920-301-4500**
Goodman, Eliana (KUSTOFF) LEGIS ASST 523 CHOB.... **54714**
Goodman, Ted (PENCE) COMMUNICATIONS DIR 222 CHOB.... **53021**
Goodridge, Ann (PINGREE) CASEWKR/ CASEWK MGR.... **207-774-5019**
Goodwin, Amber (SCOTT, AUSTIN) MIL FELLOW 2417.... **56531**
Goodwin, Joshua (TIMMONS) COMMUNICATIONS DIR 313 CHOB.... **56030**
Goodwin, Natalie (BROOKS, SUSAN W.) DC SCHEDULER 2211.... **52276**

Goolsby, Beth (HICE) DIR - CONSTIT SVCS ... 706-969-1461
Gorczynski, John (GARCIA, SYLVIA R.) ADVISOR - DEFENSE/ADVISOR - FOREIGN POLICY/CHIEF OF STAFF 1620 ... 51688
Gordon, Greta Hebert (LYNCH) FINANCIAL ADMIN 2109 ... 58273
Gordon, Harrison (GOTTHEIMER) STAFF ASST 213 CHOB. 54465
Gordon, Waverly (CMTE-ENERGY & COMMERCE) DPTY CHIEF COUNSEL 2125 ... 52927
Gore, Russell (HOUSE EMPLOYMENT COUNSEL) SR ASSOC COUNSEL 4300 ... 57075
Gorrocino, Irma (SÁNCHEZ) FIELD REP ... 562-860-5050
Gorski, Jennifer (CMTE-FOREIGN AFFAIRS) DIR - OPS 2066 ... 68467
Gorud, Chris (LOWENTHAL) LEGIS DIR 108 CHOB ... 57924
Gosnell, Ellen
(MIN WHIP) DIR - OPS H148 ... 50197
(SCALISE) DIR - OPS 2049 ... 53015
Goss, Trinity (CMTE-OVERSIGHT & GOVT REFORM) STAFF ASST 2157 ... 55051
Gosselin, Geoffrey (CMTE-HOMELAND SECUR) DPTY STAFF DIR 117 FHOB ... 68417
Gossum, Michael (COMER) COMMUNICATIONS DIR ... 270-487-9509
Gottheim, Robert (NADLER) DIST DIR ... 212-367-7350
Gotwald, Robert (CMTE-JOINT TAX) COUNSEL IRS-3565 ... 202-317-4463
Gould, Alexandra (COLLINS, CHRIS) DIR - CONSTIT SVCS ... 716-634-2324
Gould, Gabrielle
(CMTE-FOREIGN AFFAIRS) STAFF DIR 5193 ... 53111
(KEATING) LEGIS DIR 2351 ... 53111
Gould, Kate (KHANNA) CONG FELLOW 221 CHOB ... 52631
Gould, Melissa (CAO/HIR – HOUSE WEB SVCS) PROD ANALYST 646 FHOB ... 66196
Gould, Michael (CAO/ENTERPRISE APPLICATIONS) MGR B74 FHOB ... 60811
Goulding, Matthew (SMITH, ADRIAN) COMMUNICATIONS DIR 502 CHOB ... 56435
Goulet, Dana (ROONEY) DIR - CONSTIT SVCS ... 239-599-6033
Gourdikian, Alexandra
(MCCARTHY) SCHEDULER 2468 ... 52915
(MIN LEADER) SCHEDULING DIR H204 ... 54000
Gower, John (MEUSER) DPTY DIST DIR ... 570-871-6370
Goyzueta, Annie (VARGAS) PRESS AIDE 2244 ... 58045
Graben, Beverly (ROGERS, MIKE) CASEWKR ... 256-236-5655
Grace, Abigail (CMTE-INTELLIGENCE) PROF STAFF - MAJ HVC304 ... 57690
Grace, Andrea (ZELDIN) EXEC ASST/SCHEDULER 2441 ... 53826
Gradison, Andrew (SMITH, JASON) ADVISOR - HEALTH POLICY 2418 ... 54404
Grady, Caitlin (PHILLIPS) DIST SCHEDULER ... 952-656-5176
Graeter, Luke (WENSTRUP) LEGIS ASST/LEGIS CORRES 2419 ... 53164
Graeub, Andrew (CAO/HIR – NETWORKING ENGINEERING AND OPS) MGR 663 FHOB ... 66291
Graff, Caleb (CMTE-ENERGY & COMMERCE) PROF STAFF MEMB 2322A ... 53641
Graff, Jessica (BUCSHON) SCHEDULER 2313 ... 54636
Gragg, Jordan (ROGERS, HAROLD) RECEPTIONIST ... 606-679-8346
Graham, AnnMarie (STIVERS) COMMUNICATIONS ASST/ PRESS ASST 2234 ... 52015
Graham, Chloe (MCCARTHY) STAFF ASST ... 661-327-3611
Graham, Timothy (BUTTERFIELD) LEGIS AIDE 2080 ... 53101
Graham, Victoria (RUPPERSBERGER) DIGITAL ASST/ STAFF ASST 2206 ... 53061
Grajeda, Claudio (SGT AT ARMS/HOUSE SECURITY) SYS ADMIN HVC301 ... 62044
Grandwilliams, Harrison (WASSERMAN SCHULTZ) DPTY DIST DIR ... 954-845-1179
Grange, Robyn (RUSH) DIST DIR ... 773-779-2400
Granger, Karen (CLERK/LRC) MGR - PUBLIC INFO B81 CHOB ... 65200
Grano, Jill (NEGUSE) DIR - COMMUNITY AFFAIRS ... 303-335-1045
Grant, Ayanti (COURTNEY) DIST DIR ... 860-886-0139
Grant, Joshua (WILSON, JOE) STAFF ASST/LEGIS CORRES 1436 ... 52452
Grant, Katie (MAJ LEADER) COMMUNICATIONS DIR H107 ... 53130
Grant, Lisa (CAO/ACQUIS MGMT) CHIEF 5110 ... 52921
Gras, Pam (JOHNSON, MIKE) COMMUNITY LIAISON/CASEWKR ... 318-840-0309
Graupensperger, Joe (CMTE-JUDICIARY) CHIEF COUNSEL 6340 ... 55727
Gravitt, Blaine (SPANO) DIST DIR ... 863-644-8215
Grawien, Christopher (GROTHMAN) SR LEGIS ASST 1427 52476
Gray, Betty (CMTE-ARMED SVCS) EXEC ASST 2117 ... 54158
Gray, Jason (CMTE-APPRO) PROF STAFF MEMB H307 ... 52771
Gray, Lauren (HIMES) DIGITAL ASST ... 203-333-6600
Gray, Lisa (LESKO) DIST DIR ... 623-776-7911
Gray, Michael (PAYNE) DIST DIR ... 973-645-3213
Grechko, Maxwell (MOONEY) LEGIS CORRES 2440 ... 52711
Greco, Ashley (TIPTON) DIST FIELD REP ... 970-259-1490
Greco, Jackie (CAO/FINANCIAL COUNSELING) COUNSELOR B215 LHOB ... 60537
Greco, Kristie (DEFAZIO) CHIEF OF STAFF 2134 ... 56416
Green, Caroline (CAO/HIR – ESCALATIONS AND OPS) TECH SUPPORT REP 601 FHOB ... 63001
Green, Courtney (MAJ WHIP) PRESS ASST H329 ... 63210
Green, Geoffrey (SCALISE) LEGIS DIR 2049 ... 53015
Green, Jon (CROW) LEGIS ASST - MIL 1229 ... 57882
Green, Joshua (TIPTON) CHIEF OF STAFF 218 CHOB ... 54761
Green, Kathie (BANKS) CONSTIT SVCS SPEC ... 260-702-4750
Green, Meghan (CMTE-INTELLIGENCE) COUNSEL HVC304 ... 54121
Green, Mitchell (CAO/ACQUIS MGMT) CONTRACT SUPPORT ADMIN 5110 ... 52921
Green, Robert (CMTE-ED & WORKFORCE) DIR - WORKFORCE POLICY 6150 ... 54527
Green, Samuel (WEBSTER) CONSTIT SVCS ... 352-241-9220
Green, Shannon (CMTE-INTELLIGENCE) SR COUNSEL FOR INVESTIGATIONS HVC304 ... 57690
Greenbaum, Mark (PASCRELL) COMMUNICATIONS DIR 2409 ... 55751
Greenberg, Hana (KIND) CHIEF OF STAFF 1502 ... 55506
Greenberg, Jake (CMTE-JUDICIARY) COUNSEL - OVERSIGHT 2226 ... 56906
Greenberg, Katie (TONKO) LEGIS CORRES 2369 ... 55076
Green Bishop, Joseph (JOHNSON, EDDIE BERNICE) COMMUNICATIONS AIDE ... 214-922-8885

Greene, Chelsea (POSEY) CASEWKR 321-632-1776
Greene, Craig (CMTE-ARMED SVCS) PROF STAFF 2340 55540
Greene, Emily (JORDAN) LEGIS ASST 2056 52676
Greene, Kaia (SEWELL) COORD - GRANTS/ CONSTIT SVCS REP 205-254-1960
Greene, Samantha (BROWNLEY) COMMUNICATIONS DIR 2262 55811
Greener, April (SPEAKER) RESEARCH DIR H232 50100
Greenfield, George
(CLARKE) INFO TECH SYS ANALYST 2058 56231
(CLEAVER) SYS ADMIN 2335 54535
(DEMINGS) SYS ADMIN 217 CHOB 52176
(ESPAILLAT) DIR - TECH 1630 54365
(GREEN, AL) SYS ADMIN 2347 57508
(LAWRENCE) DIR - INFO SYS 2463 55802
(PETERS) SYS ADMIN 2338 50508
Greengrass, David (CMTE-JUDICIARY) SR COUNSEL 2138 53951
Greenhalgh, Michelle (DEGETTE) POLICY DIR - HEALTH 2111 54431
Greenlee, Brendan (STEVENS) STAFF ASST 227 CHOB 58171
Green-Newton, King (DEFAZIO) LEGIS CORRES 2134 56416
Greenwood, Alexandra (GARCIA, SYLVIA R.) LEGIS CLERK 1620 51688
Greer, Brian (CMTE-ARMED SVCS) PROF STAFF 2340 68454
Greer, Jacqueline (DAVIS, DANNY K.) STAFF ASST 773-533-7520
Greeson, Autum (LAHOOD) CONSTIT SVCS REP 309-671-7027
Greeves, Trina (MULLIN) CASEWKR 918-283-6262
Gregory, Sean (KIM) DIST FIELD REP 856-703-2700
Grenelle, James (BILIRAKIS) CASEWKR 727-232-2921
Gressard, Lindsay (CMTE-NATURAL RESOURCES) PROF STAFF 186 FHOB 56065
Gretsky, Gavin (KATKO) FIELD REP 315-423-5657
Grey, Chelsea (JOHNSON, HENRY C. "HANK", JR.) LEGIS ASST 2240 51605
Grider, Michael (BURCHETT) CHIEF OF STAFF 1122 55435
Griego-Schneider, Mary Jane (GARAMENDI) SR FIELD REP 2368 51880
Griffeth, Carlee (SCHRADER) COMMUNICATIONS DIR 2431 55711
Griffin, Deborah (SMITH, JASON) CONSTIT SVCS SPEC 573-335-0101
Griffin, Drew (LATTA) COMMUNICATIONS DIR 2467 56405
Griffin, Kristin (SMITH, CHRISTOPHER H.) FINANCIAL ADMIN 2373 53765
Griffin, Sean (GOHMERT) COUNSEL 2267 53035
Griffin, Taylor (SPEAKER) PRESS SECY H232 50100
Griffith, Albert (ROONEY) CASEWKR 239-599-6033
Griffith, Brian (CHABOT) COMMUNICATIONS DIR 513-684-2723
Griffiths, Luci (STEWART) LEGIS ASST 2242 59730
Grimes, Benjamin (YARMUTH) LEGIS CORRES 402 CHOB. 55401
Grimes, Chris (KIRKPATRICK) LEGIS FELLOW 309 CHOB... 52542
Grimes, Ron (RYAN) CHIEF OF STAFF 1126 55261
Grimm, David (JORDAN) DIST AIDE 419-999-6455
Grimm, Tyler (CMTE-OVERSIGHT & GOVT REFORM) CHIEF ADVISOR FOR POLICY, STRATEGY & COMMUNICATIONS 2105 55074
Grisafi, Jen (SHERRILL) DIST SCHEDULER 973-526-5668
Gristina, Alexander (PALLONE) STAFF ASST/SCHEDULER 2107 54671
Griswold, Kelsey (SMITH, CHRISTOPHER H.) LEGIS DIR 2373 53765
Groce, Aaron (CROW) STAFF ASST 1229 57882
Grogis, Joshua (COLE) CHIEF OF STAFF 2207 56165
Groh, Sarah (PRESSLEY) CHIEF OF STAFF 1108 55111
Groneman, Belinda (ZELDIN) CONG AIDE/ CASEWKR - IMMIGRATION/IMMIGRATION SPEC ... 631-289-1097
Gronski, Robert (CAO/ENTERPRISE APPLICATIONS) SR BUSINESS PROCESS APPLICA SPEC B73 FHOB 51411
Grooms, Susanne (CMTE-OVERSIGHT & GOVT REFORM) DPTY STAFF DIR/CHIEF COUNSEL 2157 55051
Gropper, Adam (CMTE-JOINT TAX) LEGIS COUNSEL SD-G18 45561
Gros, Lauren (LARSEN) DC SCHEDULER 2113 52605
Grosky, Gretchen (TRAHAN) PRESS SECY 978-459-0101
Gross, Casey (KINZINGER) CASEWKR 815-431-9271
Gross, Charles (NORMAN) CONG AIDE 803-327-1114
Gross, Hillary (GIBBS) CHIEF OF STAFF 2446 56265
Gross, Joshua (DUNCAN, JEFF) LEGIS DIR 2229 55301
Gross, Justin (LEGIS COUNSEL) COUNSEL 337 FHOB 56060
Grossman, Andrew (CMTE-WAYS & MEANS) CHIEF TAX COUNSEL 1136 55522
Grossman, James D (LEGIS COUNSEL) SR COUNSEL 337 FHOB 56060
Grossman, Zachary (ENGEL) LEGIS AIDE 2426 52464
Grubar, Francis (CICILLINE) SCHEDULER 2233 54911
Grubbs, Adam (KELLY, TRENT) LEGIS ASST/LIAISON - AG 1005 54306
Grubbs, Kevin (SGT AT ARMS/POLICE SVCS) DPTY ASST SGT AT ARMS - POLICE SVCS/LAW ENFORCEMENT HT8... 51000
Gruber, Hali (MEUSER) DIR - OPS 326 CHOB 56511
Gruda, Matthew (FITZPATRICK) DIST OFFICE MGR 215-579-8102
Gruters, Sydney (STEUBE) DIST DIR 941-575-9101
Guaglianone, Paul (HOUSE REPUB CONF) DIR - COALITIONS 1420 55107
Guajardo, Anissa (VELA) CASEWKR 956-520-8273
Guarascio, Tiffany (CMTE-ENERGY & COMMERCE) DPTY STAFF DIR 2125 52927
Guduru, Pratap (CAO/HIR – ENTERPRISE INFRASTRUCT) OPS TEAM LEAD 639 FHOB 62048
Guerra, Liana (SOTO) DPTY CHIEF OF STAFF 1507 59889
Guerra, Marisol (TORRES) DPTY DIST DIR 909-481-6474
Guerrero, Bertha (GOMEZ) CHIEF OF STAFF 1530 56235
Guerrero, Lolita (GARCIA, SYLVIA R.) FIELD REP 832-325-3150
Guerrero, Luis (DOGGETT) STAFF ASST 2307 54865
Guerrero, Miguel Louis (PELOSI) FIELD REP/ CASEWKR 415-556-4862
Guevara, Jose (CORREA) FIELD REP - VETS/ DIST FIELD REP 714-559-6190
Guffin, Elliott (HUDSON) LEGIS CORRES 2112 53715
Gugliotta, Norman (CAO/FINANCIAL COUNSELING) COUNSELOR B215 LHOB 63549
Guilbeau, Morgan (STANTON) STAFF ASST 128 CHOB 59888
Guild, Sara (DUFFY) OUTREACH DIR 715-298-9348
Guillen, José (CMTE-BUDGET) SYS ADMIN 204E CHOB 67200

Gullickson, Kirsten (CLERK/LCS) PRINCIPAL LEGIS ANALYST 2401 51182
Gulsehn, Jay (CARTER, EARL L. "BUDDY") ADVISOR - HEALTH POLICY 2432 55831
Gulvas, Greg (VISCLOSKY) DIR - CONSTIT SVCS 219-795-1844
Gum, Rhett (MARCHANT) COORD - DIST OUTREACH 972-556-0162
Gumbiner, Caleigh (CRAIG) CONSTIT ADVOCATE 651-846-2120
Gumina, Grace (AMASH) EXEC ASST 106 CHOB 53831
Gunderson-Schwarz, Abby (LESKO) CHIEF OF STAFF 1113 54576
Gunn, Robert (CLERK/LRC) EXEC COMMUNICATIONS CLERK B81 CHOB 65200
Gunn, Sylvester (CMTE-JOINT TAX) STAFF ASST 502 FHOB 53621
Gurak, Erin (DOGGETT) DIST DIR 512-916-5921
Gural, Harry (CMTE-JOINT ECON) STAFF DIR - DEM SH-804 45171
Gurnak, Mary (VISCLOSKY) CASEWKR 219-795-1844
Gustafson, Eric (FLORES) LEGIS DIR 2228 56105
Gustave, Peggy (DEMINGS) CASEWKR 321-388-9808
Gutierrez, Carmen (HURD) FIELD REP 830-422-2040
Gutierrez, Jailene (COSTA) DIST REP 209-384-1620
Gutierrez, Margarita (SCHIFF) CASEWKR 818-450-2900
Gutrick, Patrice (SGT AT ARMS/APPOINTMENT) ASST - APPTS DESK CANNON 52551
Guzman, Paola (VARGAS) FIELD REP 619-422-5963
Guzman Bortolotti, Luis (BACON) CONSTIT LIAISON 402-938-0300
Guzman-Toro, Omar (DEMINGS) LEGIS ASST 217 CHOB 52176
Gwozdz, Isabelle (BRADY) DIGITAL PRESS SECY 1011 54901
Gwyn, Katherine (JOHNSON, BILL) SCHEDULER 2336 55705
Gye, Raymond (DAVIS, DANNY K.) CONSTIT SVCS REP 773-533-7520
Haag, Thomas (KATKO) DPTY DIST DIR 315-423-5657
Haaga, Owen (CMTE-JOINT ECON) SR ECONOMIST - DEM 244 FHOB 52223
Haas, Greg (CARBAJAL) DIST REP/CASEWKR 805-546-8348
Haberly, Kelsey (WALTZ) CORRES ASST 216 CHOB 52706
Haberman, Caitlin (CMTE-ENERGY & COMMERCE) PROF STAFF 2125 54407
Habib, Phillip (WILSON, JOE) ADMIN ASST/ SPECIAL ASST 803-939-0041
Habib, Sameh (CMTE-JOINT TAX) ECONOMIST 595 FHOB 67575
Hackbarth, Andy (SCHRADER) LEGIS CORRES 2431 55711
Hacker, Austin (CMTE-NATURAL RESOURCES) DPTY PRESS SECY 1329 52761
Hacker, Michael (MAJ WHIP) SR ADVISOR H329 63210
Hadad, Christopher (PASCRELL) STAFF ASST 2409 55751
Haddad, Mannal (CMTE-HOUSE ADMIN) PRESS SECY 1313 52061
Haddad, Raaed (HUIZENGA) SR LEGIS ASST 2232 54401
Haddeland, Connie (MCCOLLUM) CONSTIT SVCS REP 651-224-9191
Hadden, Emily (DUNN) LEGIS CORRES 316 CHOB 55235
Haddox, John (MAST) FIELD REP 772-403-0900
Hadro, Matthew (SMITH, CHRISTOPHER H.) PRESS SECY 2373 53765
Haedtler, Jordan (GARCÍA, JESÚS G. "CHUY") LEGIS ASST 530 CHOB 58203
Hagan, Anne (VEASEY) DIST DIR 817-920-9086
Hagenbuch, Stephen (LEGIS COUNSEL) ASST COUNSEL 337 FHOB 56060
Hagens-Jordan, Jessica (HIMES) ADVISOR - FOREIGN POLICY/ADVISOR - DEFENSE 1227 55541
Hager, Nicole (CMTE-HOMELAND SECUR) PRESS SECY 117 FHOB 68417
Hagerott, Virginia (LURIA) LEGIS CORRES 534 CHOB 54215
Hagerup, Loni (SENSENBRENNER) CHIEF OF STAFF 262-784-1111
Haggerty, Phylicia (BONAMICI) DIST REP/ CASEWKR/OUTREACH REP 503-469-6010
Haglin, Marilyn (STAUBER) CASEWKR/OFFICE MGR 218-481-6396
Haglund, Gary (CMTE-BUDGET) POLICY ADVISOR 507 CHOB 67270
Hagnauer, Karl (LEGIS COUNSEL) ASST COUNSEL 337 FHOB 56060
Hague, Danny (BROWNLEY) LEGIS ASST 2262 55811
Hague, Sarah (MALONEY, CAROLYN B.) DIST REP 212-860-0606
Hahn, Carolyn (CMTE-FINANCIAL SVCS) SR COUNSEL - MAJ 2129 54247
Hahn, Jim (HAGEDORN) COMMUNICATIONS DIR 325 52472
Haigler, Monique (CAO/PAYROLL & BENEFITS) COUNSELOR B215 LHOB 60073
Hailstone, Mitchell (GREEN, MARK E.) COMMUNICATIONS DIR 533 CHOB 52811
Haines, Christian (CMTE-ED & WORKFORCE) GEN COUNSEL 2257 53725
Hair, Connie (GOHMERT) CHIEF OF STAFF 2267 53035
Hair, John (DUFFY) POLICY ADVISOR 1714 53365
Hair, Robert (CAO/HIR – ENTERPRISE INFRASTRUCT) DIRECTOR 686B FHOB 62359
Hajinazarian, Ike (CMTE-HOMELAND SECUR) DPTY PRESS SECY 176 FHOB 62616
Halcrow, Stephanie (CMTE-ARMED SVCS) PROF STAFF 2340 66164
Hale, Keenan (GREEN, AL) LEGIS AIDE 2347 57508
Hall, Amy (CMTE-APPRO) PROF STAFF MEMB 283 FHOB 53881
Hall, Amy (CMTE-WAYS & MEANS) SUBCOMM STAFF DIR 1104 53943
Hall, Angie (GRIFFITH) CONSTIT SVCS REP 540-381-5671
Hall, Ashley (DINGELL) FIELD REP 313-278-2936
Hall, Daniel (CLERK/REPORTERS) CHIEF CLERK - COMMITTEES 1718 52627
Hall, Dottie (RUSH) SR CONSTIT SVCS REP 773-779-2400
Hall, Hunter (CARTER, EARL L. "BUDDY") DIST FIELD REP 912-352-0101
Hall, Jordan (PENCE) FIELD REP 812-799-5230
Hall, Katrina (LAW REV COUNSEL) ASST COUNSEL 308 FHOB 62411
Hall, Marty (SELECT CMTE-CLIMATE CRISIS) STAFF DIR – REPUB 361 FHOB 51107
Hall, Mike (SHIMKUS) REGIONAL DIR 217-347-7947
Hall, Morgan (CAO/HIR – ENTERPRISE INFRASTRUCT) FACILITIES MGMT SPEC SITE 3 571-921-3125
Hall, Rosemary (RUSH) SECY/EXEC ASST 773-779-2400

Hall, Travis (GIANFORTE) COMMUNICATIONS DIR 1222 53211
Halpern, Jonathan (BISHOP, SANFORD D., JR.) LEGIS DIR 2407 53631
Halter, Kim (GUTHRIE) DIR - CONSTIT SVCS 270-842-9896
Hamada, Jimmy (GABBARD) CONSTIT OUTREACH REP 808-541-1986
Hamedi, Kayla (NADLER) LEGIS ASST/PRESS ASST 2132 55635
Hamel, Ryan (CAO/HOUSE PERIODICAL PRESS) THIRD ASST H304 52941
Hamilton, Ellen (CHU) SR LEGIS ASST 2423 55464
Hamilton, Emma (BROOKS, SUSAN W.) LEGIS CORRES 2211 52276
Hamilton, Eric (MALINOWSKI) FIELD REP 908-547-3307
Hamilton, Erik (DAVIS, RODNEY) STAFF ASST 217-791-6224
Hamilton, Jacqueline (BASS) CONSTIT SVCS REP 323-965-1422
Hamilton, Mark (CMTE-ETHICS) INVESTIGATIVE CLERK 1015 57103
Hamilton, Mike (MCKINLEY) CHIEF OF STAFF 2239 54172
Hamilton, Perry (SEWELL) SCHEDULER/LEGIS AIDE 2201 52665
Hamilton, Ryan (TRAHAN) CASEWKR 1616 53411
Hamilton, Ryan (MARCHANT) LEGIS CORRES 2304 56605
Hamlett, Joyce (SGT AT ARMS/CHAMBER SECUR) ASST TO THE SGT AT ARMS - FLOOR SECUR HB6 50067
Hamlin, Robert (HOLDING) DIR - LEGIS CORRES 1110 53032
Hamlin Bias, Lori (CMTE-APPRO) SCOREKEEPER 2005 52718
Hamm, Kimberly (GEN COUNSEL) ASSOC COUNSEL 219 CHOB 59700
Hammill, Andrew (SPEAKER) DPTY CHIEF OF STAFF H232 50100
Hammon, Beth
(CMTE-OVERSIGHT & GOVT REFORM) PROF STAFF MEMB 6440 55051
(ROUDA) LEGIS ASST 2300 52415
Hammond, Jackson (BAIRD) LEGIS ASST 532 CHOB 55037
Hammond, Kimberly (NORMAN) OFFICE MGR/PRESS ASST 319 CHOB 55501
Hammond, Ron (DAVIDSON) LEGIS ASST 1107 56205
Hammond, Tom (CMTE-SCIENCE) SR POLICY ADVISOR - REPUB 394 FHOB 56371
Hammonds, McKenzie (ARRINGTON) CONSTIT SVCS REP 806-763-1611
Hamner, Caryn (BROOKS, MO) LEGIS ASST - MIL 2246 54801
Hamner, Philip (CAO/ACCOUNTING) DIRECTOR 3110 56551
Hampson, James (BUCK) LEGIS DIR 2455 54676
Han, Minsu (FLEISCHMANN) SR POLICY ADVISOR 2410 53271
Hance, Elizabeth (PALMER) PRESS SECY 207 CHOB 54921
Hancock, Hannah (STIVERS) COMMUNICATIONS ASST 2234 52015
Hancock, Sabrina (ROY) LEGIS ASST 1319 54236
Hancotte, Marian (BERGMAN) CASEWKR 231-944-7633
Hand, Joe (LOEBSACK) PRESS SECY/DPTY CHIEF OF STAFF 1211 56576
Hand, Robert (COMMIS ON SECUR & COOP IN EUR) POLICY ADVISOR 234 FHOB 51901
Hand, Shane (COLE) LEGIS ASST 2207 56165
Handal, Megan (CMTE-ARMED SVCS) CLERK 2340 68979
Handau, Megan (HAYES) LEGIS CORRES 1415 54476
Handey, Courtney (CRAWFORD) SCHEDULER 2422 54076
Handy, Bridget (CMTE-ED & WORKFORCE) LEGIS ASST 6140 54527
Haney, Winston (CAO/ASSET MANAGEMENT) ACCNT MGMT COUNSELOR 6110 50090
Hanger, Lillian (CLERK/LRC) REGISTRATION & COMPLIANCE CLERK B81 CHOB 65200
Hankerson, Derek (MAST) CONSTIT RELATIONS REP 772-336-2877
Hanley, William (CARTWRIGHT) ECON DEV REP 570-371-0317
Hanlon, Sandy (KING, STEVE) DIST REP 712-224-4692
Hanna, Mena (FORTENBERRY) SR POLICY ADVISOR 1514 54806
Hannahs, Joel (RADEWAGEN) COMMUNICATIONS DIR 1339 58577
Hannan, Virginia (RATCLIFFE) CONSTIT SVCS REP 972-771-0100
Hanner, Brooks (GEN COUNSEL) ASST COUNSEL 219 CHOB 59700
Hannon, Tiffany (BROWN) CONSTIT SVCS 301-458-2600
Hanrahan, Matthew (CLINE) LEGIS CORRES 1009 55431
Hansell, Christopher (SMITH, CHRISTOPHER H.) LEGIS CORRES 2373 53765
Hansen, Andrew (BUCSHON) COMMUNICATIONS DIR 2313 54636
Hansen, Anna (CMTE-APPRO) ADMIN ASST H307 52771
Hansen, Corey (UPTON) CONSTIT SVCS REP 269-982-1986
Hansen, Deborah (WALTZ) OFFICE ADMIN 216 CHOB 52706
Hansen, Joni (BUCHANAN) CONSTIT SVCS REP 941-951-6643
Hanson, Marc (CISNEROS) DIST DIR 714-459-4575
Hanson, Sarah (CRIST) SR LEGIS ASST 215 CHOB 55961
Hanson, Tanner
(CMTE-NATURAL RESOURCES) SR ADVISOR 4170 52761
(GOSAR) LEGIS ANALYST 2057 52315
Hantz, Chuck (SHIMKUS) DIST AIDE 217-446-0664
Haq, Rabia (CAO/ENTERPRISE APPLICATIONS) BUSINESS PROCESS APPLICA SPEC B70 FHOB 63838
Harclerode, Justin (CMTE-TRANSP & INFRA) COMMUNICATIONS DIR 2164 59446
Hard, Alison (CMTE-ED & WORKFORCE) PROF STAFF 2257 53725
Hardaway, Eric (EVANS) DIR - CONSTIT SVCS 215-276-0340
Hardaway, Michael (HOUSE DEM CAUCUS) COMMUNICATIONS DIR/SR ADVISOR B245 LHOB 51400
Hardecke, Laura (LUETKEMEYER) OFFICE MGR 573-635-7232
Harden, Blake (CMTE-WAYS & MEANS) TRADE COUNSEL 1139 54021
Hardie, Gary (BARRAGÁN) POLICY ASST 310-831-1799
Hardimon, Madison (WRIGHT) LEGIS AIDE 428 CHOB 52002
Hardin, Elizabeth (MCEACHIN) CASEWKR 804-486-1840
Hardy, Johanna (CMTE-TRANSP & INFRA) STAFF DIR 505 FHOB 54472
Hare, Dan (TURNER) SR LEGIS ASST 2082 56465
Hargadon, Laural (CAO/HIR – CYBERSECURITY) MGR - INFO ASSURANCE 650 FHOB 63807
Hargrove, Brian (CAO/LOGISTICS) BLDG SUPERVISOR WA16 RHOB 59474
Hariharan, Arya (CMTE-JUDICIARY) COUNSEL - OVERSIGHT 2138 53951
Harley, Derek (WENSTRUP) CHIEF OF STAFF 2419 53164

Harlin, Andrea (AGUILAR) SR FIELD REP ... 909-890-4445
Harman, Heather (CMTE-JOINT TAX) LEGIS TAX ACCOUNTANT 502 FHOB ... 53621
Harman, Jan (DUNCAN, JEFF) FIELD REP ... 864-681-1028
Harmann, Jean (LEGIS COUNSEL) SR COUNSEL 337 FHOB ... 56060
Harmon, Tess (BARRAGÁN) CASEWKR ... 310-831-1799
Harney, Benjamin (MALONEY, CAROLYN B.) COUNSEL 2308 ... 57944
Harold, Meryl (HIMES) ADVISOR - HEALTH POLICY/STAFF ASST 1227 ... 55541
Haro-Perez, Khenia (SCOTT, ROBERT C. "BOBBY") SPECIAL ASST ... 757-380-1000
Harper, Barbara (EMMER) SR CASEWKR ... 763-241-6848
Harper, Bill (MCCOLLUM) CHIEF OF STAFF 2256 ... 56631
Harrah, Angie (TURNER) CASEWKR ... 937-225-2843
Harrell, Ewo (NEGUSE) CONSTIT ADVOCATE ... 970-372-3971
Harrell, James (CMTE-TRANSP & INFRA) ADMIN 2165 ... 54472
Harrell, Maggie (ROY) LEGIS DIR 1319 ... 54236
Harrell, Vickie (CAO/HIR – NETWORKING ENGINEERING AND OPS) SR NETWK COMMUNICATIONS SPEC 685 FHOB ... 60260
Harrelson, Jill (CMTE-TRANSP & INFRA) BUDGET DIR - MAJ/DPTY COUNSEL 2165 ... 54472
Harriford, Scott (CUNNINGHAM) SR FIELD REP ... 843-352-7572
Harrington, Ellen (CMTE-SMALL BUSINESS) SR PROF STAFF MBR 2361 ... 54038
Harrington, Julia (PERLMUTTER) LEGIS ASST 1226 ... 52645
Harrington, Keith (CAO/FINANCIAL COUNSELING) COUNSELOR B215 LHOB ... 61538
Harrington, Molly (MITCHELL) DIR - OPS 211 CHOB ... 52106
Harris, Aaron (GOODEN) CHIEF OF STAFF 425 CHOB ... 53484
Harris, Andrea (UNDERWOOD) CHIEF OF STAFF 1118 ... 52976
Harris, Camren (FUDGE) CONG LIAISON ... 216-522-4900
Harris, Chandra (SCOTT, DAVID) DIST DIR ... 770-210-5073
Harris, Charlotte (KUSTER) COORD - CONSTIT SVCS/COORD - OUTREACH ... 603-595-2006
Harris, Clifford A, Jr (CLERK) OPS ASST H154 ... 57000
Harris, Darryn (BASS) DIST DIR ... 323-965-1422
Harris, Donald (CAO/HIR – NETWORKING ENGINEERING AND OPS) SUPERVISOR 663A FHOB ... 63854
Harris, Eric (GOMEZ) COMMUNICATIONS DIR 1530 ... 56235
Harris, Erick (CHABOT) LEGIS COUNSEL 2408 ... 52216
Harris, Jocelyn (CMTE-BUDGET) COUNSEL/BUDGET ANALYST 204E CHOB ... 67200
Harris, Karen (KAPTUR) CONG ASST ... 419-259-7500
Harris, Kevin (CAO/FURNISHINGS) MASTER FINISHER WA22 RHOB ... 58000
Harris, Kimberly (LARSON) DIST AIDE ... 860-278-8888
Harris, Melanie (CMTE-ARMED SVCS) PROF STAFF 2340 ... 66120
Harris, Meryl (LOWEY) DIR - CONSTIT SVCS ... 914-428-1707
Harris, Michael (WASSERMAN SCHULTZ) LEGIS ASST 1114 ... 57931
Harris, Molly (SHIMKUS) DIR - OPS/EXEC ASST 2217 ... 55271
Harris, Rafael (CAO/HIR – ENTERPRISE INFRASTRUCT) OPS TEAM LEAD 618 FHOB ... 61243
Harris, Scott (SEWELL) LEGIS CORRES 2201 ... 52665
Harris, Yuroba (GARCIA, SYLVIA R.) SPECIAL EVENTS DIR/DIR - DIST PROJ ... 832-325-3150

Harrison, Amy (CRENSHAW) CASEWK MGR ... 713-860-1330
Harrison, Benjamin (ESCOBAR) LEGIS AIDE 1505 ... 68334
Harrison, Jessica (FLORES) SCHEDULER 2228 ... 56105
Harrison, Mike (HUNTER) COMMUNICATIONS DIR/DIST CHIEF OF STAFF ... 619-448-5201
Harry, John (CMTE-VET AFFAIRS) PROF STAFF MEMB - TECHNOLOGY MODERNIZATION SUBCOMM B234 LHOB ... 59756
Hart, Arline (MEEKS) STAFF ASST 2310 ... 53461
Hart, Beverly (MALONEY, SEAN PATRICK) LEGIS CORRES 2331 ... 55441
Hart, Hailey (LUETKEMEYER) LEGIS DIR 2230 ... 52956
Hart, Iain (GARAMENDI) SR POLICY ADVISOR 2368 ... 51880
Hart, Meaghan (PENCE) LEGIS CORRES 222 CHOB ... 53021
Hart, Sean (MORELLE) COMMUNICATIONS DIR ... 585-232-4850
Hart, Tosha (DUNCAN, JEFF) CASEWKR ... 864-681-1028
Hartl, Kellie
(COOK) EXEC ASST 1027 ... 55861
(GABBARD) FINANCIAL ADMIN 1433 ... 54906
(GRAVES, SAM) FINANCIAL ADMIN 1135 ... 57041
(NORMAN) FINANCIAL ADMIN 319 CHOB ... 55501
Hartley, Kevin (OLSON) LEGIS ASST 2133 ... 55951
Hartley, Mia (MCCOLLUM) SCHEDULER 2256 ... 56631
Hartman, David (DELAURO) CONG AIDE ... 203-562-3718
Hartman, Kirsten (UNDERWOOD) DPTY CHIEF OF STAFF - COMMUNICATIONS 1118 ... 52976
Hartsough, Jacqueline (GARAMENDI) CONSTIT SVCS REP ... 530-753-5301
Hartwich, Alison (LEGIS COUNSEL) COUNSEL 337 FHOB ... 56060
Hartz, Joe (CMTE-SMALL BUSINESS) POLICY DIR 2069 ... 55821
Harvey, Christopher (FLETCHER) LEGIS ASST 1429 ... 52571
Harvey, Derek (CMTE-INTELLIGENCE) SR ADVISOR FOR ANALYSIS HVC304 ... 54121
Harvey, Heather (CARSON) CASEWORK - VETS ... 317-283-6516
Harvey, Jamie (CAO/HIR – IT CUSTOMER SOLUTIONS) SR TELECOMMUNICATIONS ADMIN 692 FHOB ... 56002
Harvey, Jason (FOXX) LEGIS ASST 2462 ... 52071
Harvey, Judy (CMTE-ENERGY & COMMERCE) COUNSEL 2125 ... 52927
Harvey, Kinsey (CAO/HOUSE RADIO-TV GALLERY) MEDIA LOGISTICS COORD H320 ... 55214
Harvey, Nicole (DAVIS, DANNY K.) DIR - CONSTIT SVCS ... 773-533-7520
Harvey, Robert P (CMTE-JOINT TAX) DPTY CHIEF OF STAFF 595 FHOB ... 67575
Harvey, Stephen (RIGGLEMAN) OUTREACH DIR ... 434-973-9631
Harvey, Tom (WEBER) LEGIS AIDE 107 CHOB ... 52831
Hasan, Rasheedah (CMTE-VET AFFAIRS) CHIEF CLERK - COMMITTEES B234 LHOB ... 59756
Hasenberg, Amy (CMTE-JUDICIARY) PRESS SECY 2226 ... 56906
Haskell, Elizabeth (WELCH) STAFF ASST ... 802-652-2450
Haskell, Will (HIMES) SCHEDULER/STAFF ASST ... 203-333-6600
Haskins, Selena (CLERK/ART & ARCHIVES) ADMIN ASST JEFFERSON BUILDING, ATTIC ... 61300
Haslett, Brighton (CMTE-FINANCIAL SVCS) COUNSEL 4340 ... 57502
Hassell, Fred (SARBANES) DIR - CONSTIT SVCS ... 410-832-8890
Hassmann, Cheryl (CARTER, JOHN R.) DIST FIELD REP ... 254-933-1392

Hatch, Erin (CMTE-WAYS & MEANS) PRESS SECY - DEM 1102 ... 53625
Hatfield, Bob (BILIRAKIS) COORD - COMMUNITY OUTREACH ... 727-232-2921
Hatter, Drew (STIVERS) LEGIS CORRES/LEGIS AIDE 2234 ... 52015
Hatter, John (PENCE) CONSTIT SVCS ... 812-799-5230
Hattori, Harriet (MATSUI) DIST STAFF ASST ... 916-498-5600
Hauff, Kevin (LEGIS COUNSEL) STAFF ASST/PARALEGAL 337 FHOB ... 56060
Haurek, Alex
(CMTE-SMALL BUSINESS) SR ADVISOR 2361 ... 54038
(VELÁZQUEZ) COMMUNICATIONS DIR 2302 ... 52361
Havenner, Sheila
(CMTE-ED & WORKFORCE) DIR - INFO TECH 2051A ... 53725
(HICE) LEAD SYS ADMIN 409 CHOB ... 54101
(NAPOLITANO) SYS ADMIN 1610 ... 55256
Havens, Brittany (CMTE-ENERGY & COMMERCE) PROF STAFF MEMB 564 FHOB ... 53641
Haverly, Jordan (SHIMKUS) COMMUNICATIONS DIR 2217 ... 55271
Hawkins, Ben (HIMES) STAFF ASST ... 203-333-6600
Hawkins, Jazzelynn (COOPER) LEGIS CORRES 1536 ... 54311
Hawkins, Johanna (CAO/WORKFLOW MGMT) COORD WA35 RHOB ... 65888
Hawkins, Megan (LEGIS COUNSEL) ASST COUNSEL 337 FHOB ... 56060
Hawkins-Green, Margot (CAO/EMPLOYEE ASSISTANCE) EMPLOYEE ASSISTANCE SPEC 140 FHOB ... 52400
Hawley, Tom (CMTE-ARMED SVCS) PROF STAFF MEMB 2340 ... 65688
Hayden, Kathy (CLINE) DIST REP ... 540-857-2672
Hayden, Matt (LATTA) STAFF ASST 2467 ... 56405
Hayes, Colin (CMTE-BUDGET) POLICY ADVISOR 507 CHOB ... 67270
Hayes, Debra (RYAN) DIST SCHEDULER/EXEC ASST ... 330-373-0074
Hayes, Jessica (HICE) DPTY CHIEF OF STAFF/ DIST DIR ... 770-207-1776
Hayes, John (MARCHANT) LIAISON - MIL ... 972-556-0162
Hayes, Kathleen (CAO/FIRST CALL) CUSTOMER SOLUTIONS REP B227 LHOB ... 58000
Hayes, Kendall (CUELLAR) CONSTIT SVCS REP ... 210-271-2851
Hayes, Mark (HOUSE EMPLOYMENT COUNSEL) SR ASSOC COUNSEL 4300 ... 57075
Hayes, Mecole (MALONEY, SEAN PATRICK) LEGIS ASST 2331 ... 55441
Hayes, Michelle (CAO/TECHNOL GOVERN & COMPLIANCE) SR SYS ENGINEER 647 FHOB ... 66108
Hayes, Molly (PAPPAS) CONSTIT SVCS REP ... 603-285-4300
Hayes, Renaldo (CLERK/LRC) LIBRARY ASST B81 CHOB ... 65200
Haymore, Tyler (BUDD) LEGIS ASST 118 CHOB ... 54531
Haynes, Brenda (LAMALFA) DIST REP ... 530-223-5898
Haynes, Hayden (JOHNSON, MIKE) CHIEF OF STAFF 418 CHOB ... 52777
Haynes, Wilfred
(PELOSI) DIR - INFO TECH 1236 ... 54965
(SPEAKER) DIR - INFO TECH H232 ... 50100
Haynes, Yutiva Michelle (CLERK/COMMUNICA) ADMIN ASST 293 CHOB ... 51908
Hayslett, Barbara (GOLDEN) DIST REP/SR CASEWKR ... 207-492-6009
Head, Lisa (COLE) CASEWKR/OFFICE MGR ... 405-329-6500
Headrick, Terrie (NUNES) CONSTIT LIAISON ... 559-733-3861
Healton, Kelly (LOWEY) DPTY CHIEF OF STAFF/ SCHEDULER 2365 ... 56506
Healy, Christian (RESCHENTHALER) SR LEGIS ASST 531 CHOB ... 52065
Healy, Colleen (CMTE-JOINT ECON) FINANCIAL DIR SD-G01 ... 40370
Healy, Laura (MITCHELL) LEGIS CORRES 211 CHOB ... 52106
Heard, Clayton (LOWENTHAL) FIELD REP ... 562-436-3828
Heard, Jenna (FERGUSON) SCHEDULER 1032 ... 55901
Hearin, Colleen (TITUS) SCHEDULER/EXEC ASST 2464 ... 55965
Hearn, Bri (BALDERSON) LEGIS ASST 1221 ... 55355
Hearne, Walter (CMTE-APPRO) PROF STAFF MEMB H405 ... 52847
Heasley, Lauren (RUIZ) SCHEDULER 2342 ... 55330
Heckscher, Fiona (LEGIS COUNSEL) ASST COUNSEL 337 FHOB ... 56060
Hedgepeth, Ryan (LAWRENCE) CHIEF OF STAFF 2463 ... 55802
Hedlund, Darren (JOHNSON, DUSTY) LEGIS DIR 1508 ... 52801
Heeb, John (CAO/ENTERPRISE APPLICATIONS) SR BUSINESS PROCESS APPLICA SPEC B69 FHOB ... 62187
Heffernan, Katie (RUTHERFORD) LEGIS ASST 1711 ... 52501
Heffley, Joe (DOYLE) COMMUNITY & OUTREACH LIAISON ... 412-390-1499
Heflin, Jena (CONAWAY) COORD - DIGITAL MEDIA 2469 ... 53605
Hegarty, Katie (BALDERSON) DIST STAFF ASST ... 614-523-2555
Hegeman, Joe (GRAVES, SAM) FIELD REP ... 816-792-3976
Heggem, Christine (GIANFORTE) CHIEF OF STAFF 1222 ... 53211
Heide, Marty (TURNER) SPECIAL EVENTS DIR/ CONSTIT OUTREACH REP ... 937-225-2843
Heidegger, Ken (MURPHY) LEGIS CORRES 1710 ... 54035
Heidenreich, Mitch (CASE) STAFF ASST 2443 ... 52726
Heineman, Andrew (NADLER) LEGIS ASST 2132 ... 55635
Heinemann, John (CMTE-FINANCIAL SVCS) COUNSEL 2129 ... 54247
Heinrich, Stephanie
(CURTIS) DC SCHEDULER 125 CHOB ... 57751
(NEWHOUSE) STAFF ASST 1414 ... 55816
Heinsohn, Madison (BURCHETT) CASEWKR ... 865-523-3772
Heisten, Jake (LONG) FIELD REP ... 417-781-1041
Heitkamp, Courtney (JOHNSON, DUSTY) DIST DIR/COMMUNICATIONS ADVISOR ... 605-275-2868
Heitlinger, David (RUPPERSBERGER) LEGIS ASST 2206 ... 53061
Helder, Zach (ROUDA) COMMUNICATIONS DIR 2300 ... 52415
Helfant, Matt (CLEAVER) DIR - DIGITAL MEDIA/LEGIS AIDE 2335 ... 54535
Heller, Alexandra (HIMES) CONSTIT SVCS REP ... 203-333-6600
Heller, Austin (WENSTRUP) FELLOW ... 513-474-7777
Heller, Jessica (CMTE-OVERSIGHT & GOVT REFORM) COUNSEL 2157 ... 55051
Hellwig, Charles (HOLDING) FIELD REP ... 919-782-4400
Helms, Emily (CLOUD) SCHEDULER 1314 ... 57742
Helton, Aaron (WILLIAMS) DIST FIELD REP/ DPTY DIST DIR ... 512-473-8910
Helton, Flo (GOODEN) CASEWKR ... 214-765-6789
Helwig, Janice (COMMIS ON SECUR & COOP IN EUR) POLICY ADVISOR 234 FHOB ... 51901
Hembree, Debra (PALAZZO) CONSTIT LIAISON ... 228-202-8104
Hempelmann, Goeff (WOMACK) LEGIS DIR 2412 ... 54301

Hemphill, Maurice (CAO) MGR HB28 55555
Henderson, Andrew (MCCAUL) LEGIS FELLOW 2001 52401
Henderson, Clarissa (NUNES) SPECIAL PROJ COORD 559-733-3861
Henderson, Claytrice (THOMPSON, BENNIE G.) LEGIS ASST 2466 55876
Henderson, Gerard (SCOTT, DAVID) OFFICE MGR/ SCHEDULER 225 CHOB 52939
Henderson, Jared (COX) LEGIS DIR 1728 54695
Henderson, Matthew (DAVIDSON) COMMUNICATIONS DIR 1107 56205
Henderson, Miranda (FLORES) CASEWKR/ COORD - GRANTS 979-703-4037
Henderson, Stanley (BASS) STAFF 323-965-1422
Henderson, William
(CHENEY) SPECIAL ASST TO THE CHAIR 416 CHOB 52311
(HOUSE REPUB CONF) SPECIAL ASST TO THE CHAIR 1420 55107
Hendrix, Holly (FLEISCHMANN) LEGIS ASST/SCHEDULER 2410 53271
Hendrix, Kemba (CMTE-HOUSE ADMIN) PROF STAFF 1306A 52061
Hendrixson-White, Jennifer (CMTE-FOREIGN AFFAIRS) SR PROF STAFF 2170 55021
Henline, Robert (CMTE-HOUSE ADMIN) DIR - MBR SVCS 1309 52061
Hennessy, Kelly (MALONEY, CAROLYN B.) POLICY ADVISOR 2308 57944
Henniger, Christian (SMITH, CHRISTOPHER H.) STAFF ASST 2373 53765
Henriquez, Alejandra (EMMER) CASEWKR 763-241-6848
Henry, Charles (SCALISE) DIST CHIEF OF STAFF 504-837-1259
Henry, Wiley (COHEN) CONSTIT SVCS REP 901-544-4131
Henry, Willie (COHEN) DPTY DIST DIR 901-544-4131
Henry-Bryant, Heather
(GARAMENDI) ADMIN - FINANCE & PAYROLL 2368 51880
(GRIJALVA) FINANCIAL ADVISOR 1511 52435
(HECK) FINANCE LIAISON 2452 59740
(LEVIN, MIKE) FINANCIAL ADMIN 1626 53906
(LOFGREN) SHARED EMPLOYEE/BUDGET OFFICER 1401 53072
(MCNERNEY) FINANCIAL ADMIN 2265 51947
Henschel, Nate (UPTON) DIST REP 269-385-0039
Henshall, Eric (ESHOO) LEGIS ASST 202 CHOB 58104
Henshaw, Emilee (SIMPSON) SCHEDULER 2084 55531
Henson, Chris (CARBAJAL) DIST CHIEF OF STAFF 805-730-1710
Henson, Mark (HIMES) CHIEF OF STAFF 1227 55541
Heppard, Scott (BOYLE) DIST DIR 215-426-4616
Herbaugh, Cheryl (BISHOP, SANFORD D., JR.) LEGIS FELLOW 2407 53631
Herbert, Chad (GROTHMAN) SR CONSTIT SVCS REP 920-907-0624
Herbert, Donna (CMTE-ETHICS) DIR - ADMIN STAFF 1015 57103
Herbert, Gregory (CAO/ASSET MANAGEMENT) REC & WAREHOUSE SPEC WA23 RHOB 58214
Herbert, Jacob (PENCE) STAFF ASST 222 CHOB 53021
Herbin, Jaylon (ADAMS) DIST LIAISON 704-344-9950
Herbst, Leslie (SMITH, JASON) CONSTIT SVCS SPEC/OFFICE MGR 573-335-0101
Heredia, Luis (GALLEGO) DIST DIR 602-256-0551
Herfindahl, Grant (PETERSON) ADVISOR 320-235-1061
Herman, Jenny (QUIGLEY) OUTREACH COORD 773-267-5926
Herman, Leah (CAO/HOUSE CREATIVE SVCS) PHOTOGRAPHER 2002 52700
Herman, Mary (KILDEE) DIST STAFF ASST 810-238-8627
Herman, Michael (CMTE-APPRO) PROF STAFF MEMB 2006 55834
Herman, Monica (SMITH, CHRISTOPHER H.) LEGIS ASST 2373 53765
Hermann, Michael (CMTE-ARMED SVCS) PROF STAFF 2117 68971
Hermosillo, Rebecca (THOMPSON, MIKE) SR FIELD REP 707-542-7182
Hernandez, Antonia (JOHNSON, EDDIE BERNICE) CONSTIT SVCS 214-922-8885
Hernandez, Jessica (CUELLAR) DIST DIR 956-725-0639
Hernandez, Jose (LEE, BARBARA) DPTY DIST DIR 510-763-0370
Hernandez, Laura (DIAZ-BALART) PRESS SECY 404 CHOB 54211
Hernandez, Marina (DOGGETT) CONG AIDE 512-916-5921
Hernandez, Martha (JACKSON LEE) OFC ASST 713-655-0050
Hernandez, Melany (ROONEY) DIST REP 239-599-6033
Hernandez, Michelle (OCASIO-CORTEZ) CASEWKR 718-662-5970
Hernandez, Nichole
(CUELLAR) COORD - OUTREACH /CONSTIT SVCS REP 956-424-3942
(CUELLAR) COORD - OUTREACH /CONSTIT SVCS REP 956-487-5603
Hernandez Rivera, Maribel (OCASIO-CORTEZ) DIST DIR 718-662-5970
Hernandez-Serna, Antonietta (CASTRO) DIST DIR 210-348-8216
Hernandez-Stern, Benjamin (CMTE-JUDICIARY) COUNSEL 6340 55727
Hernandez-Torres, Zaida (GONZÁLEZ-COLÓN) STAFF 1609 52615
Hernandez Trumkul, Perla (NAPOLITANO) DIST DIR 626-350-0150
Herrador, Samantha (HILL, KATIE) FIELD REP/ CONSTIT SVCS REP 661-839-0532
Herrbach, Joe (FUDGE) LEGIS ASST 2344 57032
Herrera, Bobby (GONZALEZ, VICENTE) CONSTIT REP 956-682-5545
Herrera, Gabriela (MATSUI) CASEWKR 916-498-5600
Herring, Lindley (ARRINGTON) DIST DIR 806-763-1611
Herrock, Emma (ABRAHAM) SCHEDULER/OFFICE MGR 417 CHOB 58490
Herron, Angela (UPTON) LEGIS CORRES/PRESS ASST 2183 53761
Herron, Kayla (WATKINS) EXEC ASST/SCHEDULER 1205 56601
Hersey, Eric (CMTE-FINANCIAL SVCS) COMMUNICATIONS DIR 2129 54247
Hershberger, Jared (LOEBSACK) DIST REP 319-351-0789
Hervig, Angela (CUNNINGHAM) STAFF ASST/PRESS ASST 423 CHOB 53176
Hervig, Mary Beth (BOYLE) STAFF ASST 1133 56111
Herzig, Walt (LEVIN, ANDY) DIST DIR 586-498-7122

Hessel, Stacey (DUFFY) CONSTIT SVCS REP......... 715-392-3984
Hester, Patrick (STEFANIK) DPTY LEGIS DIR 318 CHOB...... 54611
Hester, Thomas (MCCAUL) LEGIS DIR 2001........................... 52401
Hetherington Cunfer, Katherine (MEUSER) DPTY DIST DIR.. 570-871-6370
Hettervig, Ross (CMTE-AGRIC) DIGITAL OUTREACH SPEC 1301... 52171
Heussner, Holly (CHENEY) LEGIS ASST 416 CHOB.............. 52311
Hewitt, Adam (DAVIDSON) CHIEF OF STAFF.......... 937-339-1524
Heyrend, Alyson (MCADAMS) COMMUNICATIONS DIR.................................... 801-999-9801
Hezekiah, Nathaniel (MEEKS) COMMUNITY LIAISON... 718-725-6000
Hguyen, Andy (WRIGHT) DIST DIR.......................... 817-077-5037
Hibbs, Cynthia (CAO/HIR – NETWORKING ENGINEERING AND OPS) NETWK COORD 679 FHOB.. 66410
Hickenlooper, Audrey (CMTE-ETHICS) CLERK - ADVICE AND EDUC 1015.. 57103
Hicklin, Cathy Rose (NORMAN) CASEWK DIR...... 803-327-1114
Hickman, Donna (SMITH, JASON) DIST OFFICE MGR... 573-756-9755
Hickman, Samuel (KELLY, TRENT) LEGIS ASST 1005.......... 54306
Hickner, Alex (BAIRD) STAFF ASST.......................... 317-563-5567
Hicks, Allison (CRAWFORD) OFFICE MGR/ CASEWKR... 870-203-0540
Hicks, Michael (COLLINS, CHRIS) LIAISON - CONSTIT SVCS... 716-634-2324
Hicks, Rob (BROOKS, SUSAN W.) LEGIS DIR 2211................ 52276
Hidalgo, Adriana
(PELOSI) DIST SCHEDULER/EXEC ASST.................. 415-556-4862
(SPEAKER) SCHEDULER H232... 50100
Higginbotham, Keith (LOWENTHAL) COMMUNICATIONS DIR/SR POLICY ADVISOR 108 CHOB.. 57924
Higgins, Craig (CMTE-APPRO) PROF STAFF MEMB HT2...... 52041
Higgins, Dakota (COOK) DPTY DIST DIR................. 760-247-1815
Higgins, Haydn (SGT AT ARMS/EMERGENCY MGMT) EMERGENCY MGMT SPEC 192 FHOB.. 60950
Higgins, Jay (CLARK) CONSTIT SVCS REP.............. 617-354-0292
Higgins, Sean (HIMES) LEGIS CORRES 1227.......................... 55541
Higgins, Sean (BUSTOS) COMMUNICATIONS DIR 1233........ 55905
High, Mark R (CMTE-JOINT TAX) INFO TECH SYS ANALYST 595 FHOB.. 67575
Hildebrand, Asher (PRICE) DIST DIR/CHIEF OF STAFF... 919-859-5999
Hilkin, Jacob (NORMAN) LEGIS DIR 319 CHOB........................ 55501
Hill, Antonia (HOYER) LEGIS CORRES 1705............................ 54131
Hill, Bernard, Jr (SGT AT ARMS/INFO SVCS) SYS ADMIN H124.. 52456
Hill, Christine (CMTE-VET AFFAIRS) SUBCOMM STAFF DIR - HEALTH SUBCOMM 3460.. 59154
Hill, Dave (YOHO) CASEWKR.. 352-505-0838
Hill, Elizabeth (CMTE-TRANSP & INFRA) STAFF DIR 2251.... 54472
Hill, Katherine (PENCE) EXEC ASST/OFFICE MGR 222 CHOB... 53021
Hill, Kyle (DELBENE) LEGIS DIR 2330.. 56311
Hill, Lesley (HILL, J. FRENCH) LEGIS ASST 1533..................... 52506
Hill, Preston (MIN LEADER) POLICY ADVISOR H204.............. 54000
Hill, Shavonda (BISHOP, SANFORD D., JR.) DPTY DIST DIR... 478-803-2631

Hill, Tony (LAWSON) FIELD REP................................ 904-354-1652
Hilleary, Van (ROSE, JOHN W.) CHIEF OF STAFF 1232......... 54231
Hillebrands, Joan (UPTON) CHIEF OF STAFF 2183.............. 53761
Hiller, Aaron (CMTE-JUDICIARY) DPTY CHIEF COUNSEL - OVERSIGHT 2138.. 53951
Hilliard, Grace (WALKER) DIR - OPS 1725............................ 53065
Hilton, Naomi (SPANO) SCHEDULER 224 CHOB..................... 51252
Hines, Kalila (BLUNT ROCHESTER) SCHEDULER 1519......... 54165
Hinkle, Scott (VARGAS) LEGIS DIR/DPTY CHIEF OF STAFF 2244.. 58045
Hinman, Alyssa (CMTE-APPRO) MBR SVCS ASST 1016....... 53481
Hinojosa, Juan (QUIGLEY) CHIEF OF STAFF 2458................ 54061
Hinojosa, Karen (GONZALEZ, VICENTE) CONSTIT REP.. 956-682-5545
Hinson, Mark (DEMINGS) COORD - COMMUNITY OUTREACH.. 321-388-9808
Hipp, David (BISHOP, ROB) CONSTIT LIAISON......... 801-625-0107
Hippe, Jim (FLEISCHMANN) CHIEF OF STAFF/COUNSEL 2410.. 53271
Hira, Elizabeth (CMTE-HOUSE ADMIN) COUNSEL - ELECTIONS 1309.. 52061
Hirsch, Harold E (CMTE-JOINT TAX) SR LEGIS COUNSEL 502 FHOB.. 53621
Hirsch, Jill (SHERRILL) DIST DIR.............................. 973-526-5668
Hirsch, Patrick (CAO/HOUSE RECORDING STUDIO) DIR - HOUSE RECORDING STUDIO 2010............................ 53941
Hite, Chase (GRAVES, SAM) STAFF ASST 1135..................... 57041
Hittle, Taylor (MULLIN) LEGIS DIR 2421................................ 52701
Hittos, Elizabeth (BILIRAKIS) CHIEF OF STAFF 2227............ 55755
Hixon, Christopher (CMTE-OVERSIGHT & GOVT REFORM) STAFF DIR 2105... 55074
Hixson, Jana (FLORES) REGIONAL DIR.................. 254-732-0748
Hnat, Olivia (RODGERS) DPTY CHIEF OF STAFF 1035.......... 52006
Hobart, Hunter (PALMER) LEGIS ASST 207 CHOB................ 54921
Hobbs, Tyler (LONG) DIST DIR................................. 417-889-1800
Hochberg, Jacob (VELÁZQUEZ) LEGIS ASST 2302.............. 52361
Hochberg, Mitchel (SPEIER) LEGIS ASST 2465..................... 53531
Hochschild, Keenan (MIN LEADER) COORD - DIGITAL MEDIA H204.. 54000
Hodge, Lauren (ALLEN) DPTY CHIEF OF STAFF 2400.......... 52823
Hodge, Matthew (CRENSHAW) LEGIS DIR 413 CHOB.......... 56565
Hodge, Olivia (FRANKEL) PRESS SECY 2305........................ 59890
Hodges, Hayley (SCHWEIKERT) CASEWKR........... 480-946-2411
Hodges, John (CAO/OFFICE SUPPLY/GIFT SHOP) DIRECTOR B217 LHOB... 53321
Hodgkins, Caitlin (CMTE-RULES) POLICY DIR H312............. 59091
Hodgkins, Holly (MCGOVERN) DIST REP.............. 508-831-7356
Hodgkins, Sarah (DIAZ-BALART) LEGIS ASST 404 CHOB.... 54211
Hodgkins, Shelby (DUNN) COMMUNICATIONS DIR 316 CHOB... 55235
Hodson, Nathan (RODGERS) CHIEF OF STAFF 1035............ 52006
Hoeck, Matthew (LUJÁN) DC SCHEDULER 2323.................... 56190
Hoehne, Jena (SMITH, ADRIAN) DIST DIR............... 308-384-3900
Hoehn-Saric, Alex (CMTE-ENERGY & COMMERCE) CHIEF COUN COMMUNICATIONS & CONSUMER PROTECTION 2125.. 52927
Hofer, Brian (SMITH, ADRIAN) DIST STAFF ASST... 308-384-3900
Hoffman, Austin (MEADOWS) STAFF ASST 2160.................. 56401
Hoffman, Landon (DUNN) REGIONAL DIR............... 850-891-8610

Hoffnagle, Nick (NAT REPUB CONG CMTE) DIR - DATA ... 202-479-7000
Hofmann, Ryan (HOUSE REPUB CONF) LEGIS ASST 1420. 55107
Hofstad, Elizabeth (CLERK/REPORTERS) EDITOR - COMMITTEES 1718 ... 52627
Hogan, Jacob (FLORES) FIELD REP ... 254-732-0748
Hogan, Patrick (DELBENE) SPECIAL ASST ... 425-485-0085
Hogg, Spencer (GRAVES, TOM) SPECIAL ASST ... 706-226-5320
Hogge, James (BERGMAN) COMMUNICATIONS DIR ... 231-944-7633
Hogin, Andrew (KUSTOFF) LEGIS DIR 523 CHOB ... 54714
Hogue, Claudia (GARCIA, SYLVIA R.) DIST DIR ... 832-325-3150
Hokhold, Mark (CAO/HIR – ENTERPRISE INFRASTRUCT) SYS ENGINEER 617 FHOB ... 571-921-3109
Hokit, Max (CARBAJAL) LEGIS CORRES/LEGIS AIDE 1431... 53601
Holbert, Andrew (LEE, SUSIE) DIST REP ... 702-963-9336
Holbrook, Trent (NORTON) LEGIS ASST 2136 ... 58050
Holcomb, John (CRAWFORD) LEGIS CORRES 2422 ... 54076
Holden, Caroline (CARTER, EARL L. "BUDDY") LEGIS CORRES 2432 ... 55831
Holding, Sonny (TRONE) DIST DIR ... 301-926-0300
Holdridge, Rachelle (TORRES SMALL) LEGIS CORRES 430 CHOB ... 52365
Hollabaugh, Allison (COMMIS ON SECUR & COOP IN EUR) COUNSEL 234 FHOB ... 51901
Holland, Gregory (CAO/LOGISTICS) LOGISTICS & DIST SPEC HT19 ... 59474
Holland, Meghan (NORMAN) LEGIS COUNSEL 319 CHOB.. 55501
Holland, Micaela (GROTHMAN) DIST SCHEDULER ... 920-907-0624
Holland, Peter (GAETZ) LEGIS CORRES 1721 ... 54136
Holland, Stephen
(CMTE-ENERGY & COMMERCE) HEALTH COUNSEL 2125.. 55056
(SCHRADER) LEGIS ASST/COUNSEL 2431 ... 55711
Hollander, Emily (WAGNER) CONSTIT SVCS REP ... 636-779-5449
Hollander, Evan (CMTE-APPRO) COMMUNICATIONS DIR H307 ... 52771
Holleman-Perez, Vicki (NEWHOUSE) DIST REP ... 509-452-3243
Hollendonner, Jeffrey (SMITH, CHRISTOPHER H.) DIST DIR ... 609-585-7878
Hollerich, Cody (PETERSON) STAFF ASST 2204 ... 52165
Holley, Steven (CAO/LOGISTICS) LOGISTICS & DIST SPEC WA16 RHOB ... 59474
Holliday, Clarence (GREEN, AL) CONSTIT SVCS ... 713-383-9234
Holliday, Jayme (EVANS) LEGIS ASST 1105 ... 54001
Holliday, Tami (ROONEY) DPTY CHIEF OF STAFF ... 239-599-6033
Hollingshead, Megan (LYNCH) SCHEDULER/LEGIS ASST 2109 ... 58273
Hollis, Elizabeth "Liz" (CMTE-ED & WORKFORCE) DIR - FINANCE & PERSONNEL 2051B ... 53725
Hollis, Justin (HURD) DIST DIR ... 210-921-3130
Hollis, Kate (ROBY) SCHEDULER 504 CHOB ... 52901
Hollowell, Christian (CMTE-HOMELAND SECUR) EXEC ASST 176 FHOB ... 62616
Hollrah, Jennifer (CMTE-APPRO) PROF STAFF MEMB HT2. 53047
Holman, Ella (CAO/OFFICE OF THE CHIEF HUMAN RESOURCES OFFICER) COMMUNICATIONS STRATEGIST 102 FHOB ... 61403
Holman, Regina (TURNER) DIST REP 2082 ... 56465
Holman, Rose Anne (ALLEN) CONSTIT SVCS REP ... 912-403-3311
Holmes, Adam (CLERK/LEGIS OPS) ASST ENROLLING CLERK HT13 ... 53153
Holmes, Ethan (KIND) LEGIS ASST 1502 ... 55506
Holmes, Nathaniel (SPEAKER) DPTY DIR - SCHEDULING & ADVANCE H232 ... 50100
Holsen, Matt (SENSENBRENNER) COORD - DIST OUTREACH ... 262-784-1111
Holt, Clinton (CAO/HOUSE RECORDING STUDIO) BROADCAST ENGINEER/PROD SPEC 2010 ... 53941
Holt, Daniel (MCGOVERN) SCHEDULER/DIR - OPS 408 CHOB ... 56101
Holt, Gregory (MCCLINTOCK) CONSTIT SVCS OFFICER ... 916-786-5560
Holtmann, Thomas P (CMTE-JOINT TAX) SR ECONOMIST 595 FHOB ... 67575
Holtmeyer, Matthew (BACON) CONSTIT LIAISON ... 402-938-0300
Holyfield, Ainsley
(HOUSE REPUB STUDY CMTE) COMMUNICATIONS DIR 418 CHOB ... 52777
(JOHNSON, MIKE) COMMUNICATIONS DIR 418 CHOB ... 52777
Holzberg, Gordon (ADAMS) LEGIS CORRES 2436 ... 51510
Homer, Debe (COLE) CASEWKR ... 405-329-6500
Honard, Victoria (DELBENE) SR POLICY ADVISOR 2330 ... 56311
Honeycutt, Brandon (CMTE-AGRIC) SUBCOMM STAFF DIR 1301 ... 52171
Hood, Elizabeth (DINGELL) DIST SCHEDULER ... 313-278-2936
Hood, Kaila (DEGETTE) CONG AIDE ... 303-844-4988
Hood, Nikolai (CRENSHAW) LEGIS CORRES 413 CHOB ... 56565
Hood, Patricia (WATSON COLEMAN) DIST REP ... 609-883-0026
Hooghan, Priyanka (CMTE-SCIENCE) STAFF DIR - MAJ 2321 ... 56375
Hook, Erynn (COLLINS, CHRIS) CHIEF OF STAFF 2243 ... 55265
Hook, Michael (COLLINS, CHRIS) SR ADVISOR 2243 ... 55265
Hook, Tyler (CLINE) STAFF ASST 1009 ... 55431
Hooker, Kaitlin (O'HALLERAN) DIGITAL DIR 324 CHOB ... 53361
Hooks, David (MEEKS) COMMUNITY LIAISON 2310 ... 53461
Hooper, Blake (HUFFMAN) FIELD REP ... 415-258-9657
Hooper, Tammy (CHENEY) STATE DIR ... 307-772-2595
Hoover, Logan (REED) SR LEGIS ASST 2263 ... 53161
Hope, Karin (CMTE-WAYS & MEANS) TAX COUNSEL 1139.. 54021
Hope, Stacy (COMMIS ON SECUR & COOP IN EUR) COMMUNICATIONS DIR 234 FHOB ... 51901
Hopkins, Jenna (CMTE-HOMELAND SECUR) LEGIS ASST 176 FHOB ... 62616
Hopkins, Lara (CASTOR) SCHEDULER/DPTY CHIEF OF STAFF 2052 ... 53376
Hopkins, Rachael (DOYLE) CASEWKR ... 412-283-4451
Hopper, Blake (WEBER) DPTY DIST DIR ... 409-835-0108
Horder, Michael (CONAWAY) SR LEGIS ASST 2469 ... 53605
Horn, Joanne (SMUCKER) CASEWK DIR ... 717-393-0667
Hornberger, Danielle (HARRIS) CONSTIT LIAISON ... 410-588-5670
Hornburg, Richard (CAO/ENTERPRISE APPLICATIONS) BUSINESS PROCESS APPLICA SPEC B75 FHOB ... 66233
Horta, Christofer (SHALALA) LEGIS ASST 1320 ... 53931
Horton, Brett (MIN WHIP) CHIEF OF STAFF/COUNSEL H148 50197

Horton, Emily (PINGREE) FIELD REP ... 207-774-5019
Horton, Isiah (BROWN) CONSTIT SVCS ... 301-458-2600
Horton, Jonathan (CHU) STAFF ASST ... 626-304-0110
Horton-Diaz, Daniel (MUCARSEL-POWELL) DIST DIR ... 305-222-0160
Horwich, Lloyd (CLERK) LEGAL COUNSEL H154 ... 57000
Hosking-Young, Chantel (MCKINLEY) DIST FIELD REP ... 304-232-3801
Hoskins, Borden (RIGGLEMAN) LEGIS DIR 1022 ... 54711
Hostelley, Stephen (GONZALEZ, ANTHONY) LEGIS DIR 1023 ... 53876
Hough, Holly (HUNTER) SR LEGIS ASST 2429 ... 55672
Hough, Michael (MOONEY) CHIEF OF STAFF 2440 ... 52711
Houghton, Joseph (CAO/HIR – ENTERPRISE INFRASTRUCT) MGR 686 FHOB ... 61607
Houlihan, Ryan (PHILLIPS) LEGIS CORRES 1305 ... 52871
House, Andrew (CMTE-INTELLIGENCE) PROF STAFF - MIN HVC304 ... 54121
House, Jon (CLARK) LIAISON - MIL & VET ... 617-354-0292
House, Marc (CARSON) STAFF ASST ... 317-283-6516
Housel, Paul (ADERHOLT) FIELD DIR ... 205-221-2310
Houser, Danielle (DUNN) LEGIS ASST 316 CHOB ... 55235
Houser, Elaina (PASCRELL) LEGIS DIR 2409 ... 55751
Houser, Melani (CMTE-JOINT TAX) CHIEF STATISTICAL ANALYST 595 FHOB ... 67575
Houser, Sheila (ROE) ADMIN ASST ... 423-247-8161
Houston, Zachary (MCCARTHY) LEGIS CORRES/PRESS AIDE 2468 ... 52915
Hovagimian, Mary (SCHIFF) DIST REP ... 818-450-2900
Hoven, Christopher (SCHIFF) ADMIN ASST 2269 ... 54176
Hovhannisyan, Rozy (FLORES) CONSTIT LIAISON ... 254-732-0748
Hovland, Eli (CMTE-ED & WORKFORCE) STAFF ASST 2051C ... 53725
Howard, Adam (TURNER) CHIEF OF STAFF 2082 ... 56465
Howard, Brad (MURPHY) CHIEF OF STAFF 1710 ... 54035
Howard, Howard (RADEWAGEN) FIELD REP/ EDUC POLICY ADVISOR/COORD - GRANTS ... 684-633-3601
Howard, Jordan (BYRNE) SCHEDULER 119 CHOB ... 54931
Howard, Michael (INSPECTOR GENERAL) ASST DIR - INFO SYS AUDITS 386 FHOB ... 61250
Howard, Mike (WRIGHT) STAFF ASST 428 CHOB ... 52002
Howe, Donna (ABRAHAM) OFFICE MGR ... 318-445-0818
Howell, Kandace (HORN) COMMUNITY OUTREACH SPEC ... 405-602-3074
Howell, Paul (KELLY, TRENT) CHIEF OF STAFF 1005 ... 54306
Howell, Zach (KATKO) CHIEF OF STAFF 2457 ... 53701
Hrinkevich, Mary (ZELDIN) LEGIS CORRES/PRESS ASST 2441 ... 53826
Hromada, Erin (HOUSE HISTORIAN) DIR - HISTORIAN STAFF JEFFERSON BUILDING, ATTIC ... 61300
Hrovat, Sarah (GOHMERT) PRESS ASST 2267 ... 53035
Hruska, Courtney (KAPTUR) SCHEDULER/OFFICE MGR 2186 ... 54146
Hsia, Jacqueline (VELÁZQUEZ) COMMUNITY LIAISON ... 212-619-2606
Hsieh, Jacqueline (MENG) LEGIS ASST 2209 ... 52601
Hsu, Lily (GEN COUNSEL) LAW CLERK 219 CHOB ... 59700
Hsu, Yvonne (CLARK) SR ADVISOR 2448 ... 52836
Huang, Alex (LAWRENCE) SR LEGIS ASST 2463 ... 55802
Hubbard, Diane (BAIRD) COMMUNITY LIAISON ... 317-563-5567
Hubbard, Eric (JOHNSON, HENRY C. "HANK", JR.) FIELD REP/COMMUNITY LIAISON ... 770-987-2291
Huch, Leighton (BUSTOS) LEGIS ASST 1233 ... 55905
Huckleberry, Chris (SCHRADER) LEGIS DIR/DPTY CHIEF 2431 ... 55711
Huddleston, Catherine (SGT AT ARMS/CHAMBER SECUR) ASST SPECIAL EVENTS/PROTOCOL HB6 ... 50067
Huddleston, Charli (CMTE-OVERSIGHT & GOVT REFORM) PRESS SECY 2105 ... 55074
Huddleston, James (DEFAZIO) LEGIS ASST 2134 ... 56416
Hudson, Stone (BLUMENAUER) STAFF ASST ... 503-231-2300
Hudson, Susan (RICE, TOM) FIELD REP ... 843-445-6459
Hudspith, Michael (LARSEN) STAFF ASST 2113 ... 52605
Huebner, Tim (DINGELL) LEGIS CORRES/LEGIS AIDE 116 CHOB ... 54071
Huertas, Aaron (SELECT CMTE-CLIMATE CRISIS) COMMUNICATIONS DIR - DEM 359 FHOB ... 51106
Huff, Lee (BIGGS) FIELD REP - VETS ... 480-699-8239
Huff, Robin (DUNCAN, JEFF) CASEWKR ... 864-681-1028
Huffman, Kate (POCAN) LEGIS ASST 1421 ... 52906
Huggins, Rachel (BURGESS) LEGIS DIR 2161 ... 57772
Hughes, Carolyn "Carrie" (CMTE-ED & WORKFORCE) DIR - HEALTH & HUMAN SVCS 2257 ... 53725
Hughes, Jamal (CAO/ASSET MANAGEMENT) ACCNT MGMT COUNSELOR 6110 ... 56792
Hughes, Lauren (BISHOP, SANFORD D., JR.) OFFICE MGR/SCHEDULER 2407 ... 53631
Hughes, Michael (CAO/FINANCIAL COUNSELING) FINANCIAL COUNSELOR ... 703-490-8578
Hughes, Scott (CHENEY) DPTY CHIEF OF STAFF 416 CHOB ... 52311
Hughes, Sharon (DAVIDSON) CASEWKR/ OFFICE MGR ... 513-779-5400
Hughes, Tanya (SGT AT ARMS/ID SVCS) ASST/ID SVCS 321 CHOB ... 53820
Hughes, William (MIN WHIP) POLICY DIR H148 ... 50197
Hugman, Rachel (LAMB) SR LEGIS ASST 1224 ... 52301
Hulbert, Gabe (COSTA) DIST REP ... 209-384-1620
Hull, Cameron (FLETCHER) STAFF ASST/LEGIS CORRES 1429 ... 52571
Hull, Cordell (CMTE-INTELLIGENCE) GEN COUNSEL HVC304 ... 54121
Hull, Cynthia (HAALAND) CONSTIT SVCS REP ... 505-288-4022
Hull, Z J (LOFGREN) COUNSEL/LEGIS STAFF 1401 ... 53072
Hulme, Betsy (CMTE-INTELLIGENCE) STAFF ASST HVC304 ... 54121
Humes, Alexandra (MIN LEADER) COORD - MBR SVCS & OUTREACH H204 ... 54000
Humiston, Kellie (CLERK/REPORTERS) OFFICIAL REPORTER HT59 ... 55621
Humke, Diane (CLERK/REPORTERS) EDITOR - COMMITTEES 1718 ... 52627
Hummel, Coletta (DAVIDS) CONSTIT SVCS/ CONSTIT OUTREACH REP ... 913-621-0832
Humphrey, Cameron (YOUNG) LEGIS ASST 2314 ... 55765
Hunn, Jocelyn (CMTE-APPRO) PROF STAFF MEMB 2007 ... 53081
Hunsaker, Abigail (STEWART) DIR - CONSTIT AFFAIRS ... 801-364-5550
Hunt, Alison (REED) DIST DIR ... 607-654-7566

Hunt, Daniel (CAO/HIR – NETWORKING ENGINEERING AND OPS) SR NETWK COMMUNICATIONS SPEC 685 FHOB....... **61829**
Hunter, Aaron (DAVIS, SUSAN A.) PRESS SECY 1214....... **52040**
Hunter, Jordan (THORNBERRY) COMMUNICATIONS DIR 2208....... **53706**
Hunter, Katie (ALLEN) LEGIS DIR 2400....... **52823**
Hunter, Kirk (BANKS) CONG FELLOW 1713....... **54436**
Hunter, Peter (RICHMOND) LEGIS DIR 506 CHOB....... **56636**
Hunter, Robert (CLYBURN) FIELD REP....... **803-799-1100**
Hunter, Ryan (DINGELL) FIELD REP....... **734-481-1100**
Hunter, Steve (CAO/ASSET MANAGEMENT) ACCNT MGMT COUNSELOR 6110....... **56792**
Hunter-Williams, Jill (DAVIS, DANNY K.) DPTY CHIEF OF STAFF 2159....... **55006**
Huntley, Maxwell (WITTMAN) LEGIS ASST - MIL 2055....... **54261**
Hupper, Dani (SUOZZI) LEGIS AIDE/DC SCHEDULER 214 CHOB....... **53335**
Hurd, Nathaniel (COMMIS ON SECUR & COOP IN EUR) POLICY ADVISOR 234 FHOB....... **51901**
Hurlbert, Josh (GRAVES, SAM) DIST MGR....... **816-792-3976**
Hurley, Lindsay (MARCHANT) LEGIS ASST 2304....... **56605**
Hurrell, Mary (JAYAPAL) PRESS SECY 1510....... **53106**
Hurwitz, Ross (SPEAKER) DPTY DIR - SPEECHWRITING H232....... **50100**
Husbands, Patrick (SCOTT, DAVID) CONSTIT SVCS REP....... **770-432-5405**
Hussain, Zeenath (LEVIN, ANDY) DIR - CONSTIT SVCS....... **586-498-7122**
Hutchinson, Myeisha (SEWELL) COORD - OUTREACH....... **205-254-1960**
Hutchinson, Paige (ALLRED) CHIEF OF STAFF 328 CHOB. **52231**
Huthsing, Colton (LONG) SCHEDULER 2454....... **56536**
Hutterer, Ben (KIND) LEGIS ASST 1502....... **55506**
Huxley-Cohen, Rachel (FRANKEL) COMMUNICATIONS DIR 2305....... **59890**
Huyen, Thanh (UPTON) APPLICA SYS ADMIN 2183....... **53761**
Hyland, Thomas (REED) STAFF ASST 2263....... **53161**
Hyman, Amanda (MCKINLEY) COMMUNICATIONS DIR 2239....... **54172**
Hyppolite, Marven (MOULTON) CASEWKR....... **978-531-1669**
Hysom, Tim (LOWENTHAL) CHIEF OF STAFF 108 CHOB....... **57924**
Hytha, Emily (CONAWAY) COMMUNICATIONS DIR 2469....... **53605**
Iacobellis, Samuel (SPEAKER) MBR SVCS STAFF ASST H232....... **50100**
Ibarra, Jay (WILSON, JOE) DPTY PRESS SECY 1436....... **52452**
Ibarra, Marcos (LEE, SUSIE) LEGIS ASST 522 CHOB....... **53252**
Ibrahim, Aya (PRESSLEY) LEGIS ASST 1108....... **55111**
Idelson, Holly (RASKIN) CHIEF COUNSEL 412 CHOB....... **55341**
Iger, Michael (MALONEY, CAROLYN B.) CHIEF OF STAFF 2308....... **57944**
Igleheart, Alex (ROSE, JOHN W.) LEGIS DIR 1232....... **54231**
Iglesias, Rachel (BABIN) REGIONAL DIR....... **409-331-8066**
Igo, Spencer (STAUBER) FIELD REP....... **218-355-0726**
Ikene, Eunice (CMTE-ED & WORKFORCE) LABOR POLICY ADVISOR 2051C....... **53725**
Ikoku, Robert (GALLEGO) SR POLICY ADVISOR 1131....... **54065**
Ilaria, Jessica (HARDER) LEGIS ASST 131 CHOB....... **54540**
Ilog, Angela (CAO/ACQUIS MGMT) RESOURCE MGR 5110... **52921**
Ince, Cara (COOPER) COMMUNICATIONS DIR....... **615-736-5295**
Incerto, Jacquelyn (MILLER) LEGIS ASST 1605....... **53452**
Inderfurth, Alison (PERLMUTTER) CHIEF OPERATING OFFICER 1226....... **52645**
Infanzon, Hollis (CUNNINGHAM) DIST DIR....... **843-352-7572**
Ingram, Christina (SCOTT, ROBERT C. "BOBBY") LEGIS ASST 1201....... **58351**
Ingram, Kara (CLERK/LCS) SOFTWARE ENGINEER 2401....... **51182**
Ingrassia, Maria (MALONEY, SEAN PATRICK) CONSTIT ADVOCATE....... **845-561-1259**
Innis, Alyssa (EVANS) COORD - DIGITAL MEDIA/LEGIS AIDE 1105....... **54001**
Iodice, Carolyn (AMASH) LEGIS DIR 106 CHOB....... **53831**
Iozzi, Mark (CMTE-FOREIGN AFFAIRS) DPTY CHIEF COUNSEL 2173....... **55021**
Irving, Paul D (SGT AT ARMS) SERGEANT AT ARMS H124.. **52456**
Irwin, Kate (KILMER) DIST REP....... **360-373-9725**
Isaguirre, Eli (STEVENS) DPTY DIST DIR....... **734-853-3040**
Ischiropoulos, Dean (SCANLON) LEGIS CORRES 1535....... **52011**
Isenberg, Erin (RYAN) DPTY CHIEF OF STAFF 1126....... **55261**
Islam, Nadia (CUELLAR) CONSTIT SVCS REP....... **210-271-2851**
Ismail, Lori (CMTE-RULES) PROF STAFF - MAJ H312....... **59091**
Ismail, Seth (CLYBURN) LEGIS CORRES 200 CHOB....... **53315**
Isse, Ali (OMAR) DPTY DIST DIR....... **612-333-1272**
Istel, Sarah (CMTE-JUDICIARY) COUNSEL - OVERSIGHT 2035....... **53951**
Italiano, Christopher (CLERK/REPORTERS) EDITOR HT59 **55621**
Itnyre, Timothy (COOK) DIST DIR....... **760-247-1815**
Iverson, Andrew (STEIL) SPECIAL ASST....... **608-752-4050**
Iverson, George (LESKO) SCHEDULER 1113....... **54576**
Ives, Barbara (THOMPSON, GLENN) SR CASEWKR....... **814-670-0432**
Ives, Christina (DELGADO) SCHEDULER 1007....... **55614**
Iwu, Nnamdi (BASS) CONSTIT SVCS REP....... **323-965-1422**
Izaguirre, Glenda (KEATING) DIST REP....... **508-999-6462**
Jaarda, Christopher (BUCK) COUNSEL 2455....... **54676**
Jabbar, Angeline (PLASKETT) LEGIS DIR 2404....... **51790**
Jablonski, Jordan (MORELLE) DIST STAFF ASST....... **585-232-4850**
Jackelen, Karrie (KIND) DIST DIR....... **608-782-2558**
Jackman, Michael (KEATING) DIST DIR....... **508-746-9000**
Jackson, Audra (DEM CLOAKRM) ASST MGR - CLOAKRM H222....... **57330**
Jackson, Ben (FLETCHER) LEGIS DIR 1429....... **52571**
Jackson, Brandi (COOPER) SCHEDULER 1536....... **54311**
Jackson, Brandy (BYRNE) CONSTIT SVCS REP/ COORD - GRANTS....... **251-690-2811**
Jackson, Damien C (CLERK/REPORTERS) DPTY CHIEF 1718....... **52627**
Jackson, Darryl (JACKSON LEE) DIST DIR 2079....... **53816**
Jackson, David (POSEY) DIR - COMMUNITY RELATIONS....... **772-226-1701**
Jackson, Edward, III (KUSTOFF) REGIONAL DIR....... **731-423-4848**
Jackson, Eric (CMTE-APPRO) SYS ADMIN 2005....... **52718**
Jackson, Jack (O'HALLERAN) DIST DIR....... **520-316-0839**
Jackson, Jake (TORRES SMALL) LEGIS ASST 430 CHOB.... **52365**
Jackson, Jamie (CMTE-ARMED SVCS) DPTY GEN COUNSEL 2117....... **53432**
Jackson, Joicelynne (CASTOR) LEGIS ASST 2052....... **53376**

Jackson, Jonathan (JOHNSON, EDDIE BERNICE) LEGIS ASST 2306 ... 58885
Jackson, Joshua (SMITH, ADRIAN) LEGIS DIR 502 CHOB ... 56435
Jackson, Joshua (COLE) LEGIS ASST 2207 ... 56165
Jackson, Kyle (BUCSHON) CHIEF OF STAFF 2313 ... 54636
Jackson, Matt (ROUDA) LEGIS CORRES 2300 ... 52415
Jackson, Matt (BARR) STAFF ASST 2430 ... 54706
Jackson, Paul (FOXX) CONSTIT LIAISON ... 336-778-0211
Jackson, Reggie (CAO/HIR – IT CUSTOMER SOLUTIONS) SR TECH SUPPORT REP 606 FHOB ... 66979
Jackson, Rosalind (CMTE-JUDICIARY) PROF STAFF 6310. 55741
Jackson, Ryan (SCOTT, ROBERT C. "BOBBY") CONSTIT SVCS REP ... 757-380-1000
Jackson, Sandra (BEATTY) CASEWK MGR ... 614-220-0003
Jackson, Sarah (CAO/BUDGET POLICY) DIRECTOR 3240 ... 56792
Jackson, Sarah (DESAULNIER) LEGIS DIR 503 CHOB ... 52095
Jackson, Sarah (PELOSI) POLICY ASSOC 1236 ... 54965
Jackson, Tasia (JEFFRIES) CHIEF OF STAFF 2433 ... 55936
Jackson, Timothy (BROOKS, MO) CASEWKR ... 256-551-0190
Jackson, Wanda (CAO/HIR – IT CUSTOMER SOLUTIONS) MGR 678 FHOB ... 60416
Jacobs, Brandon (CMTE-OVERSIGHT & GOVT REFORM) STAFF ASST 2157 ... 55051
Jacobs, Daniel (SARBANES) COMMUNICATIONS DIR 2370. 54016
Jacobs, James (SPANO) CONSTIT RELATIONS ... 863-644-8215
Jacobs, Kyle (ROE) LEGIS ASST 102 CHOB ... 56356
Jacobs, Lauren (CHU) CONSTIT SVCS REP ... 626-304-0110
Jacobs, Mike (GALLAGHER) LEGIS ASST 1230 ... 55665
Jacobs, Rachel (HOLLINGSWORTH) DIST CHIEF OF STAFF ... 812-288-3999
Jacobson, Bradley (CAO/HIR - ENTERPRISE MESSAGING AND MOBILITY) BRANCH MGR 619 FHOB ... 63841
Jacobson, Corey (LIEU) LEGIS DIR 403 CHOB ... 53976
Jacobstein, Eric (CMTE-FOREIGN AFFAIRS) SR POLICY ADVISOR 2170 ... 55021
Jadallah, Diala (LEE, BARBARA) SR POLICY ADVISOR 2470 ... 52661
Jaffe, Jenna (NADLER) CASEWKR ... 212-367-7350
Jakious, Rick (MOULTON) DIST DIR ... 978-531-1669
James, Capre (CLERK/LRC) ASST RECORDS MGMT SPEC B81 CHOB ... 65200
James, Deirdre A (CMTE-JOINT TAX) SR LEGIS COUNSEL 502 FHOB ... 53621
James, Lee (REED) REGIONAL DIR/CONSTIT SVCS SPEC ... 716-379-8434
James, Melissa (GEN COUNSEL) ADMIN DIR 219 CHOB ... 59700
James, Ty (THOMPSON, BENNIE G.) PRESS SECY/LEGIS ASST 2466 ... 55876
James, Tyler (DUNCAN, JEFF) FIELD REP ... 864-224-7401
James, Wyndess (WALDEN) FIELD REP - VETS. ... 541-776-4646
Jamieson, Ainsley (GOLDEN) STAFF ASST 1223 ... 56306
Jamison, Reno (SHIMKUS) DIST AIDE ... 217-446-0664
Jamison, Sandra (THOMPSON, BENNIE G.) FIELD REP/CASEWKR ... 662-326-9003
Janani, Maryam (SPANBERGER) LEGIS DIR 1239 ... 52815
Janis, Evan (SGT AT ARMS/EMERGENCY MGMT) PROGRAM MGR 192 FHOB ... 60950
Jankiewicz, Joe (SCHIFF) LEGIS DIR 2269 ... 54176
Janoson, Meghan (DEAN) DIST SCHEDULER ... 215-884-4300
Jansen, Dave (CMTE-TRANSP & INFRA) STAFF DIR 507 FHOB ... 54472
Janssen, Julian Christopher (SAN NICOLAS) CASEWKR ... 671-475-6453
Janssen, Miranda (STAUBER) FIELD REP ... 763-552-3359
Janushkowsky, Stephen (BABIN) LEGIS DIR 2236 ... 51555
Jarmula, Ryan (PENCE) DPTY CHIEF OF STAFF/DIST DIR ... 812-799-5230
Jarnagin, Angie (ROE) CONSTIT SVCS REP ... 423-254-1400
Jarnot, Brittany (LARSEN) COMMUNITY LIAISON ... 425-252-3188
Jaroch, Jessica (LIPINSKI) CONG AIDE ... 773-948-6223
Jaross, Maria (VELA) SR CASEWKR ... 956-544-8352
Jarrell, Dan (CAO/CUST EXPER CTR) COORD - OPS B227 LHOB ... 58000
Jarrett, Chelsea (ROGERS, HAROLD) OFFICE MGR/SYS ADMIN 2406 ... 54601
Jarus, Allison (QUIGLEY) SR POLICY ADVISOR 2458 ... 54061
Jarvis, Michele (FULCHER) STAFF ASST/DIST SCHEDULER ... 208-888-3188
Jaslow, Allison (HOUSE DEM CONG CMPGN CMTE) EXEC DIR ... 202-863-1500
Javier, Maximo (ESPAILLAT) DIST OFFICE MGR ... 718-450-8241
Jaycox, Katie (HARDER) DIST REP ... 209-579-5458
Jazayeri, Naveed (CMTE-HOMELAND SECUR) PROF STAFF 176 FHOB ... 62616
Jecko, Brittany (CAO/OFFICE OF THE CHIEF HUMAN RESOURCES OFFICER) MGR 102 FHOB ... 67472
Jedlicka, Damion (CMTE-JOINT TAX) DIR - INFO TECH 595 FHOB ... 67575
Jeffers, Connor (BRINDISI) LEGIS ASST - MIL 329 CHOB ... 53665
Jefferson, Kenyatta (CAO/HIR - ENTERPRISE MESSAGING AND MOBILITY) TECH SOLUTIONS ENGINEER 621 FHOB ... 66057
Jefferson, Lynwood (CAO/LOGISTICS) LOGISTICS & DIST SPEC WA16 RHOB ... 59474
Jefferson, Shawn (CAO/HIR – HOUSE WEB SVCS) INTERNET SYS SPEC 644C FHOB ... 66165
Jeffery, Maureen (JOYCE, DAVID P.) DPTY DIST DIR ... 440-352-3939
Jehl, Russ (BANKS) DPTY DIST DIR ... 260-702-4750
Jelnicky, Michelle (BERGMAN) LEGIS DIR/DPTY CHIEF 414 CHOB ... 54735
Jenkins, Britteny (CMTE-OVERSIGHT & GOVT REFORM) SUBCOMM STAFF DIR 6440 ... 55051
Jenkins, Dan (GOLDEN) LEGIS ASST 1223 ... 56306
Jenkins, James (CAO/LOGISTICS) PROGRAM MGR WA26 RHOB ... 66643
Jenkins, Jenelle (CAO/ADMIN COUNSEL) PARALEGAL 217 FHOB ... 56969
Jenkins, Lloyd (PARLIAMENTARIAN) CLERK TO THE PARLIAMENTARIAN H209 ... 57373
Jenkins, Michelle (GRIFFITH) DIST DIR ... 276-525-1405
Jenkins, Molly (CMTE-VET AFFAIRS) PRESS SECY 3460 ... 53527
Jenkins, Rachel (RYAN) LEGIS ASST 1126 ... 55261
Jenks, Peter (BISHOP, ROB) DIST DIR ... 801-625-0107
Jennings, Alyssa (BAIRD) SCHEDULER 532 CHOB ... 55037
Jennings, Araceli (CAO/FINANCIAL COUNSELING) FINANCIAL ASST B215 LHOB ... 63560
Jennings, Chase (BUDD) COMMUNICATIONS DIR 118 CHOB ... 54531

Jennings, Kate (BUSTOS) DIST DIR ... **309-786-3406**
Jennings, Solomon (CAO/WOUNDED WARRIOR) PROGRAM MGR 354 FHOB ... **61944**
Jensen, Danielle (BACON) COMMUNICATIONS DIR ... **402-938-0300**
Jensen, Susan (CMTE-JUDICIARY) SR COUNSEL/ PARLIAMENTARIAN 2138 ... **53951**
Jeppson, Chelsie (CMTE-BUDGET) DIGITAL DIR 204E CHOB ... **67200**
Jepson, Kristin (CMTE-INTELLIGENCE) DIR - SECUR HVC304 ... **57690**
Jernigan, Jacob (GARAMENDI) LEGIS ASST 2368 ... **51880**
Jesaitis, Katie (DINGELL) DIST FIELD REP ... **313-278-2936**
Jessup, Debbie (ROYBAL-ALLARD) ADVISOR - HEALTH POLICY 2083 ... **51766**
Jester, Shawn (HARRIS) CONSTIT LIAISON ... **443-944-8624**
Jeter, Kristina
(INTERPARLMN AFFAIRS) DPTY DIR/SPECIAL EVENTS/ PROTOCOL HC4 ... **64576**
(SPEAKER) DPTY DIR/SPECIAL EVENTS/PROTOCOL H232 **50100**
Jevning, Marshal (BONAMICI) CASEWKR/ OUTREACH REP/DIST REP ... **503-469-6010**
Jewell, Matthew (SCALISE) FIELD REP ... **504-837-1259**
Jimenez, Blanca (WATERS) DIST DIR ... **323-757-8900**
Jin, Sophie (COMMIS ON CHINA) RESEARCH ASSOC 243 FHOB ... **63778**
Joachim, Robert (CMTE-APPRO) PROF STAFF MEMB 2006 ... **55834**
Jochem, Julie (SHERRILL) DC SCHEDULER 1208 ... **55034**
Johann, Derek (CAO/ASSET MANAGEMENT) SUPERVISOR WA23 RHOB ... **58214**
Johannes, Sigrid (SPANBERGER) PRESS ASST 1239 ... **52815**
Johnsen, Jakob (ROGERS, HAROLD) LEGIS DIR 2406 ... **54601**
Johnson, Alex (COMMIS ON SECUR & COOP IN EUR) CHIEF OF STAFF 234 FHOB ... **51901**
Johnson, Alice (SCOTT, AUSTIN) COORD - DIST OUTREACH ... **229-396-5175**
Johnson, Andre (CAO/HIR – NETWORKING ENGINEERING AND OPS) SR NETWK TECH 652C FHOB ... **66430**
Johnson, Benjamin (WILLIAMS) LEGIS ASST 1708 ... **59896**
Johnson, Blake (CMTE-ED & WORKFORCE) STAFF ASST 2101 ... **54527**
Johnson, Blake (PAYNE) COORD - COMMUNITY OUTREACH ... **862-229-2994**
Johnson, Bruce (CMTE-FINANCIAL SVCS) DPTY CHIEF COUNSEL 2129 ... **54247**
Johnson, Camisha (CMTE-HOMELAND SECUR) LEGIS ASST 176 FHOB ... **62616**
Johnson, Candace (RASKIN) SCHEDULER 412 CHOB ... **55341**
Johnson, Cate (CMTE-SCIENCE) PROF STAFF MBR - REPUB 394 FHOB ... **56371**
Johnson, Chelbi (GRAVES, GARRET) COMMUNITY LIAISON ... **225-442-1731**
Johnson, Cheryl L (CLERK) CLERK OF THE HOUSE H154 .. **57000**
Johnson, Cilicia (NORTON) CONSTIT LIAISON ... **202-408-9041**
Johnson, Cleveland (ZELDIN) CONG AIDE/ CASEWORK - VETS/COORD - VETS OUTREACH ... **631-289-1097**
Johnson, Crystal (RATCLIFFE) SCHEDULER 223 CHOB ... **56673**
Johnson, Daniel (CMTE-JUDICIARY) INVESTIGATIVE COUNSEL 189 FHOB ... **56906**
Johnson, Dianna (SEWELL) CONSTIT SVCS REP ... **334-877-4414**
Johnson, Dillon (LUCAS) LEGIS ASST 2405 ... **55565**
Johnson, Dusty (BUCK) DIST REP ... **970-702-2136**
Johnson, Dwayne (CAO/OFFICE SUPPLY/GIFT SHOP) RETAIL INVENTORY SPEC B217 LHOB ... **53321**
Johnson, Elizabeth (VISCLOSKY) DIR - PROJ ... **219-795-1844**
Johnson, Ellen (CMTE-OVERSIGHT & GOVT REFORM) SR PROF STAFF MBR 2105 ... **55074**
Johnson, Emily (ROBY) COMMUNICATIONS DIR 504 CHOB **52901**
Johnson, Eric (CAO/WORKFLOW MGMT) COORD WA35 RHOB ... **65888**
Johnson, Eric (DEUTCH) ADVISOR ... **561-470-5440**
Johnson, Eric (LOUDERMILK) LEGIS ASST 422 CHOB ... **52931**
Johnson, Franklin (HASTINGS) CONG ASST ... **954-733-2800**
Johnson, Ingrid (UPTON) STAFF ASST/DIST SCHEDULER 2183 ... **53761**
Johnson, James (PALLONE) LEGIS AIDE 2107 ... **54671**
Johnson, John (CMTE-ARMED SVCS) STAFF ASST 2216 ... **54151**
Johnson, Kathleen M (HOUSE HISTORIAN) MGR - ORAL HISTORY JEFFERSON BUILDING, ATTIC ... **61300**
Johnson, Keith (CLERK/REPORTERS) OFFICIAL REPORTER 1718 ... **52627**
Johnson, Ken (CMTE-ETHICS) COUNSEL 1015 ... **57103**
Johnson, Kendra (KIRKPATRICK) DIR - CONSTIT SVCS ... **520-881-3588**
Johnson, Kevin (KUSTOFF) FIELD REP ... **901-682-4422**
Johnson, Kris (HUDSON) CONSTIT LIAISON ... **910-997-2070**
Johnson, Kristen (BROOKS, SUSAN W.) SPEECHWRITER 2211 ... **52276**
Johnson, Kwasi (CAO/LOGISTICS) LOGISTICS & DIST SPEC WA16 RHOB ... **59474**
Johnson, Lonnie (CMTE-APPRO) SYS ADMIN 2005 ... **52718**
Johnson, Marc (CMTE-HOMELAND SECUR) CLERK 176 FHOB ... **62616**
Johnson, Margaret (CAO/OFFICE DESIGN AND MOVE SVCS) SR PROJ SPECIALIST B216 LHOB ... **64742**
Johnson, Meaghan (WEXTON) SCHEDULER 1217 ... **55136**
Johnson, Natalie (HOUSE REPUB CONF) DPTY PRESS SECY 1420 ... **55107**
Johnson, Nicholas (CMTE-HOMELAND SECUR) CLERK 176 FHOB ... **62616**
Johnson, Paul (BISHOP, ROB) LEGIS ASST 123 CHOB ... **50453**
Johnson, Robert (CAO/CAPITOL SVC CTR) CAPITOL SVC REP HT3 ... **58000**
Johnson, Robert (CAO/HIR – IDENTITY GOV AND ADMIN) SR SYS ENGINEER 615 FHOB ... **51329**
Johnson, Ryan (RUSH) COMMUNICATIONS DIR 2188 ... **54372**
Johnson, Sean (GOSAR) LIAISON - MIL & VET ... **480-882-2697**
Johnson, Sharon (GUEST) DPTY CHIEF OF STAFF 230 CHOB ... **55031**
Johnson, Spencer (CMTE-ARMED SVCS) GEN COUNSEL 2117 ... **54224**
Johnson, Stanton (CMTE-SCIENCE) DPTY CHIEF COUNSEL 2321 ... **56375**
Johnson, Steven L (INSPECTOR GENERAL) ASST DIR 386 FHOB ... **61250**
Johnson, Tallman (CMTE-FINANCIAL SVCS) SR PROF STAFF 4340 ... **57502**

Johnson, Teresa (SGT AT ARMS/APPOINTMENT) MGR – APPTS DESK HB6 50067
Johnson, Tina (HECK) CASEWKR 360-459-8514
Johnson, Tommy (BOYLE) CONSTIT SVCS REP 215-426-4616
Johnson, Tucker (PINGREE) STAFF ASST/LEGIS ASST 2162 56116
Johnson, Will (CMTE-ARMED SVCS) PROF STAFF MEMB 2216 51977
Johnston, Allison (BUCSHON) FIELD REP 812-465-6484
Johnston, Ashton (CMTE-AGRIC) PROF STAFF 1010 50317
Johnston, Evan (PINGREE) LEGIS DIR 2162 56116
Johnston, Glen (CAO/CUST EXPER CTR) DIRECTOR B227 LHOB 58000
Johnston, Kimberly (LARSEN) CHIEF OF STAFF 2113 52605
Johnston, Susannah (LOUDERMILK) LEGIS ASST 422 CHOB 52931
Joice, Jim (WATKINS) COMMUNICATIONS DIR 1205 56601
Jolly, Ernie (MEEKS) LEGIS DIR/POLICY ADVISOR - FINANCIAL SVCS/DPTY CHIEF OF STAFF 2310 53461
Jolly, Lisa V (HOUSE EMPLOYMENT COUNSEL) SR SECY 4300 57075
Jona, Ariel (CMTE-ED & WORKFORCE) STAFF ASST 2257 53725
Jones, Adam (HERN) FIELD REP 918-935-3222
Jones, Allen (SCOTT, ROBERT C. "BOBBY") STAFF ASST 1201 58351
Jones, Amy Raaf (CMTE-ED & WORKFORCE) DIR - EDUC & HUMAN SVCS POLICY 6140 54527
Jones, Asha (HORSFORD) CHIEF OF STAFF 1330 59894
Jones, Ashley (ASST SPEAKER) SR ADVISOR H132 52020
Jones, Brenda (LEWIS) COMMUNICATIONS DIR 300 CHOB 53801
Jones, Carol (BUCSHON) DIST DIR 812-465-6484
Jones, Caroline (CMTE-WAYS & MEANS) CLERK 1139 54021
Jones, Charles (CAO/HIR – NETWORKING ENGINEERING AND OPS) SR NETWK COMMUNICATIONS SPEC 685 FHOB 63521
Jones, Chris (BILIRAKIS) LEGIS ASST 2227 55755
Jones, Chris (WITTMAN) DIST REP/DPTY DIST DIR 804-443-0668
Jones, Christina (DAVIDS) DIR - OPS/SCHEDULER 1541 67208
Jones, Clarence (CAO/HIR – NETWORKING ENGINEERING AND OPS) SR NETWK TECH 652C FHOB 66430
Jones, Clinton (CMTE-FINANCIAL SVCS) SR PROF STAFF 4340 57502
Jones, Davita (CLERK) EXEC ADMIN H154 57000
Jones, Deborah (CAO/FINANCIAL COUNSELING) FINANCIAL COUNSELOR B215 LHOB 50160
Jones, Deborah E (INSPECTOR GENERAL) ADMIN ASST 386 FHOB 61250
Jones, Diem-Linh (CMTE-APPRO) PROF STAFF MEMB 2362A 52638
Jones, Dona (HASTINGS) CONG ASST 561-676-7911
Jones, Dylan (WATKINS) STAFF ASST 1205 56601
Jones, Gary (KILDEE) CONSTIT SVCS REP 810-238-8627
Jones, Jediah (MCEACHIN) DIR - OPS/SCHEDULER/ PRESS ASST 314 CHOB 56365
Jones, John (DOYLE) CASEWKR 412-664-4049
Jones, Joyce (WILSON, FREDERICA S.) COMMUNICATIONS DIR 2445 54506
Jones, Keith (CMTE-AGRIC) SR PROF STAFF 1301 52171
Jones, Kelly (PORTER) DIST DIR 1117 55611
Jones, Kimberly (BLUNT ROCHESTER) DIST SCHEDULER 1519 54165
Jones, Kyle (PARLIAMENTARIAN) ASST PARLIAMENTARIAN H209 57373
Jones, Lenzie (BISHOP, SANFORD D., JR.) CASEWORK - VETS 706-320-9477
Jones, Lindley (NC03) STAFF ASST 2333 53415
Jones, Pamela (WEBSTER) COMMUNITY RELATIONS SPEC 352-241-9220
Jones, Robert (NC03) CASEWKR 252-931-1003
Jones, Rodney (CAO/HIR – IT CUSTOMER SOLUTIONS) SR TECH SUPPORT REP 2067 66419
Jones, Roscoe (SPANBERGER) CHIEF OF STAFF 1239 52815
Jones, Sean (CMTE-HOUSE ADMIN) LEGIS CLERK 1309 52061
Jones, Sophie (CMTE-FOREIGN AFFAIRS) STAFF ASSOC 2152 55021
Jones, Stephanie (BROWNLEY) FELLOW 2262 55811
Jones, Stephen (CAO/HIR - ENTERPRISE MESSAGING AND MOBILITY) TEAM LEAD 621 FHOB 69919
Jones, Sydney (KAPTUR) LEGIS CORRES/STAFF ASST 2186 54146
Jones, Tammye (BISHOP, SANFORD D., JR.) DIST FIELD REP 229-439-8067
Jones, Taylor (CMTE-HOMELAND SECUR) SUBCOMM CLERK 176 FHOB 62616
Jones, Trevor (MCNERNEY) LEGIS AIDE/DC SCHEDULER 2265 51947
Jones, Valerie (GRAVES, TOM) CONSTIT SVCS REP 706-226-5320
Jones, Yolanda (CAO/PAYROLL & BENEFITS) GENERALIST B215 LHOB 50674
Jones-Johnson, Tammy (COSTA) PRESS SECY 559-495-1620
Jonnala, Jay (CAO/ENTERPRISE APPLICATIONS) SR BUSINESS PROCESS APPLICA SPEC B70 FHOB 60892
Jordan, Anthony (SERRANO) DIST DIR 718-620-0084
Jordan, Ashley (CAO/OFFICE DESIGN AND MOVE SVCS) ADMIN SPEC B216 LHOB 64742
Jordan, Catherine (NC03) SR ADVISOR 252-931-1003
Jordan, Charles (RATCLIFFE) LIAISON - CONSTIT SVCS 903-823-3173
Jordan, Chelsa (CAO/HIR - ENTERPRISE MESSAGING AND MOBILITY) SYS ENGINEER 624 FHOB 66529
Jordan, Christopher (CAO/OFFICE OF THE CHIEF INFORMATION OFFICER - HIR) CHIEF OPS OFFICER 631 FHOB 62082
Jordan, James (CAO/LOGISTICS) LOGISTICS & DIST SPEC HT19 59474
Jordan, Jeremy (COHEN) CONSTIT SVCS REP 901-544-4131
Jordan, Kyle (GUEST) DPTY DIST DIR 662-324-0007
Jordan, Nicholas (CISNEROS) CHIEF OF STAFF 431 CHOB 54111
Jordan, Yong (CAO/HIR – IT CUSTOMER SOLUTIONS) SR TECH SOLUTIONS ENGINEER 694 FHOB 56002
Jorgensen, Rebekah (WESTERMAN) COMMUNICATIONS DIR 209 CHOB 53772
Jorgenson, Mariel (GALLEGO) LEGIS CORRES/POLICY AIDE 1131 54065
Joseph, Connor (SPANBERGER) PRESS SECY 1239 52815
Joseph, Davidson (MEEKS) DIST AIDE 718-725-6000
Joseph, Elizabeth (GUEST) POLICY DIR 230 CHOB 55031

Joseph, Kristen (GONZALEZ, ANTHONY) STAFF ASST 1023 53876
Joseph, Laverne (PLASKETT) CASEWKR 340-778-5900
Joy, Adam (CAO/ASSET MANAGEMENT) ACCNT MGMT COUNSELOR 6110 56792
Joyce, Annetta (TLAIB) CASEWKR 313-463-6220
Joyce, Kathleen (DEAN) DIST DIR 215-884-4300
Joyce, Kathleen (SGT AT ARMS) ASST SGT AT ARMS H124 52456
Joyner, Alex (GREEN, MARK E.) DIST STAFF ASST 931-266-4483
Joyner, Miekl (LEGIS COUNSEL) STAFF ASST 337 FHOB 56060
Juarez, Nancy (CARBAJAL) LEGIS DIR/DPTY CHIEF OF STAFF 1431 53601
Jucha, Catherine (DESAULNIER) STAFF ASST/LEGIS CORRES 503 CHOB 52095
Judd, Derek (MITCHELL) LEGIS ASST 211 CHOB 52106
Judge, Dien (LOEBSACK) DIST REP 319-351-0789
Judge, Nancy (CAO/CAPITOL SVC CTR) CAPITOL SVC REP HT3 58000
Judkins, Gianna (HAYES) SCHEDULER/EXEC ASST 1415 54476
Jufiar, Dolores (LOFGREN) OFFICE MGR/SR CASEWKR 408-271-8700
Juliano, Robin (CMTE-APPRO) PROF STAFF MEMB 2358B 53508
Julien, Robert (MAJ WHIP) STAFF ASST H329 63210
Julius, Nicole (BUTTERFIELD) COMMUNICATIONS DIR/ POLICY ADVISOR 2080 53101
Jumde, Anushree (HILL, J. FRENCH) DIST DIR 501-358-3481
Jung, Melissa (CMTE-SMALL BUSINESS) DPTY STAFF DIR/CHIEF COUNSEL 2361 54038
Justice, Steve (BANKS) CONSTIT RELATIONS 260-702-4750
Jønler, Simon (NORMAN) PRESS SECY/LEGIS CORRES 319 CHOB 55501
Kaai, Krystal (CHU) EXEC DIR 2423 55464
Ka'Aikala, Shanise (CASE) SCHEDULER 2443 52726
Kaardal, Sam (STAUBER) STAFF ASST 126 CHOB 56211
Kaberle, Jonni (CMTE-APPRO) DPTY STAFF DIR 1016 53481
Kachinske, Edward (CAO/HOUSE DAILY PRESS) ASST DIR H315 53945
Kaczmarek, Beth (CLINE) SCHEDULER 1009 55431
Kaczmarski, Edward (VAN DREW) DPTY CHIEF OF STAFF 331 CHOB 56572
Kadri, Jannie (DINGELL) CASEWKR/CASEWKR - IMMIGRATION 313-278-2936
Kaelin, Jim (SGT AT ARMS/INFO SVCS) CHIEF INFO OFFICER H124 52456
Kaelin, Tommy (BRINDISI) PRESS ASST 329 CHOB 53665
Kagey, Hannah (JOHNSON, DUSTY) LEGIS ASST 1508 52801
Kaguyutan, Janice (CMTE-FOREIGN AFFAIRS) CHIEF COUNSEL 2173 55021
Kahan, Zach (CMTE-ENERGY & COMMERCE) OUTREACH & MBR SVCS COORD 2125 52927
Kahler, Kent (CAO/HIR – ENTERPRISE INFRASTRUCT) SYS ENGINEER 622 FHOB 61259
Kahn, Rebecca (HILL, KATIE) SCHEDULER/LEGIS AIDE 1130 51956
Kahng, Esther (CMTE-FINANCIAL SVCS) DIR - HOUSING POLICY 2129 54247
Kaighin, Kevin (CUELLAR) MIL FELLOW 2372 51640
Kaiser, Heinz (ABRAHAM) LEGIS ASST - MIL 417 CHOB 58490
Kaiser, Khaula (BASS) LEGIS AIDE 2059 57084
Kaissi, Brian (KRISHNAMOORTHI) LEGIS DIR 115 CHOB 53711
Kalagher, Kendall (JOYCE, DAVID P.) LEGIS DIR 1124 55731
Kalam, Nuriddin (GONZALEZ, VICENTE) CONSTIT REP 956-682-5545
Kaldahl, Rachel (CMTE-WAYS & MEANS) SUBCOMM STAFF DIR 1139 54021
Kale, Rahul (HOULAHAN) COMMUNICATIONS DIR 1218 54315
Kalinga, Tatyana (LEE, BARBARA) DIST DIR 510-763-0370
Kalinich, Gail (CASTEN) SR POLICY ADVISOR 630-520-9450
Kalka, Melissa (THORNBERRY) CONSTIT SVCS REP 806-371-8844
Kalyanam, Aruna (CMTE-WAYS & MEANS) SUBCOMM STAFF DIR/DPTY CHIEF COUNSEL 1136 55522
Kamp, Aimee (JOHNSON, DUSTY) REGIONAL DIR 605-622-1060
Kanakis, Marcie (CLERK/LRC) EDITOR B81 CHOB 65200
Kaniewska, Joanna (FITZPATRICK) DIST STAFF ASST 215-579-8102
Kannan, Valadi (CAO/HIR – ENTERPRISE INFRASTRUCT) SR SYS ENGINEER 639 FHOB 66181
Kannenberg, Loren (KIND) DIST CHIEF OF STAFF 608-782-2558
Kanter, Eric (GOLDEN) LEGIS DIR 1223 56306
Kanter, Jason (CMTE-WAYS & MEANS) PROF STAFF 2018 59263
Kaplan, Emma (SPEAKER) FLOOR ASST H232 50100
Kaplan, Jake (SCHNEIDER) DIST AIDE 847-383-4870
Kaplan, Matthew (KAPTUR) APPRO ASSOC/COUNSEL 2186 54146
Kaplan Feinmann, Sarah (FLETCHER) CHIEF OF STAFF 1429 52571
Kappler, Jacqui (JOHNSON, HENRY C. "HANK", JR.) LEGIS DIR 2240 51605
Karabatsos, Alex (TRAHAN) LEGIS CORRES 1616 53411
Karafotas, Peter (CICILLINE) CHIEF OF STAFF 2233 54911
Karapetyan, Elina (COSTA) SCHEDULER 2081 53341
Karbowsky, Jared (BROWN) CONSTIT SVCS 301-458-2600
Karim, Fatima (MEEKS) SPECIAL PROJ COORD 2310 53461
Karlen, Ashley (JOHNSON, BILL) DIR - CONSTIT SVCS 740-432-2366
Karr, Elizabeth (MIN LEADER) CHIEF OF STAFF H204 54000
Karstens, Elise (BIGGS) STAFF ASST 480-699-8239
Kartye, Melinda (GOHMERT) CONSTIT SVCS REP 903-561-6349
Karve, Chai (CLARK) CONSTIT OUTREACH REP 2448 52836
Karvelas, David (BUCHANAN) CHIEF OF STAFF 2427 55015
Karvelas, Matthew (HILL, J. FRENCH) LEGIS ASST 1533 52506
Kashat, Delia (LAWRENCE) LEGIS CORRES 2463 55802
Kastning, Timothy (FULCHER) REGIONAL DIR 208-667-1027
Katich, Steve (KAPTUR) CHIEF OF STAFF ONE 57702
Katikanani, Shivajyothi (CLERK/LCS) DEVELOPER/SR ANALYST 2401 51182
Kato, Ken (HOUSE HISTORIAN) ASSOC HISTORIAN JEFFERSON BUILDING, ATTIC 61300
Katsnelson, Sara (GOTTHEIMER) LIAISON - CONSTIT SVCS 201-389-1100
Katz, Joel (COLLINS, DOUG) CHIEF OF STAFF 770-297-3388
Katz, Rachel (HERRERA BEUTLER) CASEWK MGR 360-695-6292

Kaumo, Christopher (CMTE-NATURAL RESOURCES) SUBCOMM STAFF DIR/DPTY STAFF DIR 1413A 56065
Kaushal, Natasha (ROUDA) FIELD REP 714-960-6483
Kavanaugh, Lindsay (CMTE-ARMED SVCS) PROF STAFF 2340 55416
Kaveney, Brian (YOHO) COMMUNICATIONS DIR 1730 55744
Kay, Jessie (MALONEY, CAROLYN B.) DIST REP 212-860-0606
Kaye, Amanda (TLAIB) DIST SCHEDULER 313-463-6220
Kazin, Danny (HOUSE DEM CONG CMPGN CMTE) DPTY EXEC DIR/DIR - CAMPAIGNS 202-863-1500
Kazvini-Gore, Nick (KAPTUR) LEGIS ASST 2186 54146
Keady, Jimmy (RIGGLEMAN) SR ADVISOR 1022 54711
Kean, Chandra (CLERK/REPORTERS) OFFICIAL REPORTER HT59 55621
Keane, Michael (CAO/WORKFLOW MGMT) MGR WA35 RHOB 65888
Keating, Rosemary (DEM CLOAKRM) ASST FLOOR MGR H222 57330
Keating, Ryan (RYAN) SR ADVISOR/DPTY CHIEF OF STAFF/LEGIS DIR 1126 55261
Keating, Sean (SGT AT ARMS/POLICE SVCS) SR ASST FOR POLICE SVCS/LAW ENFORCEMENT HT8 51000
Keegan, Patricia (LOWEY) DIST DIR 914-428-1707
Keegan, Tom (RICE, TOM) FIELD REP 843-445-6459
Keeler, Ben (JOHNSON, BILL) COMMUNICATIONS DIR 330-337-6951
Keeler, Sarah (JOHNSON, BILL) DIST DIR 330-337-6951
Keenan, Matthew (FULCHER) LEGIS CORRES 1520 56611
Keene, Sarah (TRAHAN) REGIONAL DIR 978-459-0101
Keesling, Nicole (BANKS) SCHEDULER 1713 54436
Keeter, Brett (MCHENRY) DIST DIR 704-833-0096
Keeys, Mia (KELLY, ROBIN L.) LEGIS ASST 2416 50773
Kehrli, Caroline (CMTE-ARMED SVCS) CLERK 2340 62843
Keib, James (KATKO) DIST DIR 315-423-5657
Keightley, Rebecca (CALVERT) LEGIS DIR/DPTY CHIEF OF STAFF 2205 51986
Keita, Kamilah
(INTERPARLMN AFFAIRS) DPTY DIR - INFO TECH HC4 61766
(SPEAKER) DPTY DIR/INFO TECH MGR H232 50100
Keith, Steve (CMTE-INTELLIGENCE) PROF STAFF - MIN HVC304 54121
Kellaher, Anthony (CAO/HOUSE RADIO-TV GALLERY) MEDIA LOGISTICS COORD H320 55214
Kellaher, Don (SGT AT ARMS) SR ADVISOR TO THE SGT AT ARMS H124 52456
Kelland, Jonathan (LYNCH) DIST REP 617-428-2000
Keller, Charlie (WAGNER) CHIEF OF STAFF 2350 51621
Keller, David (BANKS) CHIEF OF STAFF 1713 54436
Keller, Keenan (CMTE-JUDICIARY) SR COUNSEL 2138 53951
Kelley, Kevin (CAO/FIRST CALL) CUSTOMER SOLUTIONS REP B227 LHOB 58000
Kelley, Raymond (CMTE-VET AFFAIRS) STAFF DIR - MAJ B234 LHOB 59756
Kelley, Tara (CAO/HIR – ENTERPRISE INFRASTRUCT) COMMUNICATIONS SPEC 01GG48 61356
Kelly, Graham (HILL, KATIE) LEGIS DIR 1130 51956
Kelly, Karen (ROGERS, HAROLD) DIR - DIST AFFAIRS 606-679-8346
Kelly, Kate (KUSTOFF) COMMUNICATIONS DIR 523 CHOB 54714
Kelly, Lindy (MAJ WHIP) SR ADVISOR H329 63210
Kelly, Melissa (OLSON) CHIEF OF STAFF 2133 55951
Kelly, Mike (POCAN) CASEWKR 608-258-9800
Kelly, Rachel (KILMER) CHIEF OF STAFF 1410 55916
Kelly, Ryan (JOYCE, DAVID P.) DIST STAFF ASST 440-352-3939
Kelsaw, Capreece (HAYES) STAFF ASST 1415 54476
Kelsch, Esther (FUDGE) DIST FIELD REP 216-522-4900
Kemp, Jazmine (JOHNSON, DUSTY) PRESS SECY 1508 52801
Kempler, Jeff (BANKS) SPECIAL ASST 1713 54436
Kendrick, Will (DUNN) DIST DIR 850-891-8610
Keniry, Dan (CMTE-BUDGET) STAFF DIR - MIN 507 CHOB 67270
Kennedy, Brendan (DOGGETT) FIELD REP 210-704-1080
Kennedy, Colleen (PALAZZO) PRESS SECY 2349 55772
Kennedy, Drew (WILSON, JOE) SR LEGIS ASST/LEGIS ASST - MIL 1436 52452
Kennedy, James (BOYLE) SPECIAL PROJ DIR 215-335-3355
Kennedy, J D (CLOUD) DIST DIR 361-884-2222
Kennedy, John (KING, STEVE) COMMUNICATIONS DIR 2210 54426
Kennedy, Kreg (ADERHOLT) FIELD REP 256-381-3450
Kennedy, Nicholas (FORTENBERRY) CASEWKR 1514 54806
Kennedy, Theresa (HIGGINS, BRIAN) DIST SCHEDULER/COMMUNICATIONS DIR 716-852-3501
Kennett, Dave (CALVERT) CHIEF OF STAFF 2205 51986
Kenny, Peter (CMTE-OVERSIGHT & GOVT REFORM) CHIEF INVESTIGATIVE COUNSEL 2157 55051
Keosian, Chris (SWALWELL) ASST LEGIS CORRES 407 CHOB 55065
Keplinger, Patrick (RUIZ) DIST FIELD REP 951-765-2304
Keralis, Joel (SMITH, ADRIAN) LEGIS ASST 502 CHOB 56435
Kerman, Allison (WAGNER) STAFF ASST 2350 51621
Kermott, Julia (CORREA) SCHEDULER 1039 52965
Kerr, Kim (CMTE-INTELLIGENCE) DIR - INFORMATION MANAGEMENT HVC304 57690
Kerr, Liam (MCKINLEY) STAFF ASST 2239 54172
Kerr, Robert (FLEISCHMANN) LEGIS ASST 2410 53271
Kessler, Rick (CMTE-ENERGY & COMMERCE) SR ADVISOR/STAFF DIR - ENERGY & ENVIRON 2125 54407
Kessock, Chloe (CRIST) PRESS ASST/COORD - CONSTIT SVCS 727-318-6770
Ketchel, Micah (WALTZ) CHIEF OF STAFF 216 CHOB 52706
Kettelkamp, Meg (DAVIS, RODNEY) CONSTIT SVCS REP 217-824-5117
Ketterer, Jeremy (LUETKEMEYER) DPTY CHIEF OF STAFF 573-635-7232
Key, Matthew (CARTER, JOHN R.) CONSTIT LIAISON 254-933-1392
Key-Shinard, Jean (THOMPSON, BENNIE G.) DIST SCHEDULER 601-866-9003
Khalifa, Kyle (CURTIS) INFO TECH ASST 125 CHOB 57751
Khan, Lina (CMTE-JUDICIARY) COUNSEL 6240 67680
Khan, Sadaf (CMTE-FOREIGN AFFAIRS) STAFF DIR 5222 53345
Khan, Sheresh (CORREA) PRESS ASST/LEGIS ASST 1039. 52965
Khan, Sophia (BEYER) LEGIS AIDE 1119 54376
Khanna, Raman (JAYAPAL) COORD - CONSTIT SVCS 206-674-0040
Khaterzai, Saha (CMTE-ENERGY & COMMERCE) PROF STAFF 2125 55056
Khau, Dennis (CLERK/LCS) SR SOFTWARE ENGINEER 2401 51182

Khun Leng, Sara (TRAHAN) DIR - CONSTIT SVCS 978-459-0101
Kibodya, Abdul-Kareem (NEAL) AIDE 413-785-0325
Kiedrowicz, Melissa (SÁNCHEZ) LEGIS DIR 2329 56676
Kiefhaber, Peter (CMTE-APPRO) PROF STAFF MEMB 2007 53081
Kielty, Peter (CMTE-ENERGY & COMMERCE) GEN COUNSEL 2322A 53641
Kiko, Jennifer (GIBBS) FIELD REP 419-207-0650
Kiko, Philip G (CAO) CHIEF ADMINISTRATIVE OFFICER HB28 55555
Kilayko, Michael Manejero (SAN NICOLAS) EXEC ASST 671-475-6453
Kilbride, Paul (CMTE-APPRO) PROF STAFF MEMB H405 52847
Kiles, Keith (CMTE-OVERSIGHT & GOVT REFORM) COUNSEL 2157 55051
Kiley, Will (GRANGER) LEGIS CORRES 1026 55071
Kilgore, Carly (HOLDING) STAFF ASST 1110 53032
Killeen, Sarah (BUCSHON) DPTY CHIEF OF STAFF/LEGIS DIR 2313 54636
Killian, Abbie (ALLRED) LEGIS CORRES 328 CHOB 52231
Killin, Jessica (SHALALA) CHIEF OF STAFF 1320 53931
Kilroy, Jaclyn (CMTE-APPRO) PROF STAFF MEMB 2358B 53508
Kilson, Franklin (CAO/HIR – NETWORKING ENGINEERING AND OPS) NETWK TECH 652C FHOB 66430
Kim, Gina (CMTE-OVERSIGHT & GOVT REFORM) COUNSEL 2157 55051
Kim, Janet (CMTE-OVERSIGHT & GOVT REFORM) CHIEF COUNSEL - INVESTIGATIONS 2157 55051
Kim, Jonah (LURIA) STAFF ASST 534 CHOB 54215
Kim, Patty (ESHOO) DPTY CHIEF OF STAFF/ COUNSEL 650-323-2984
Kim, Priscilla (LOFGREN) LEGIS ASST 1401 53072
Kim, Scott (CLERK/LCS) CHIEF 2401 51182
Kimball, Cheryl (WITTMAN) CASEWKR 540-659-2734
Kimball, Mark (CAO/HIR – IT CUSTOMER SOLUTIONS) SR TECH SUPPORT REP 605 FHOB 64437
Kimber, Taylor (DESAULNIER) DIST REP 503 CHOB 52095
Kimbrough, Jhamene (CAO/HIR - VENDOR MGMT) SYS ANALYST 643C FHOB 63734
Kimelman, David (ESPAILLAT) STAFF ASST 1630 54365
Kim-Hummel, Justin (STEUBE) LEGIS AIDE 521 CHOB 55792
Kimosh, Michael (CAO/ASSET MANAGEMENT) ANALYST 6110 50090
King, Brady (HORN) CHIEF OF STAFF 415 CHOB 52132
King, Carolyn (WITTMAN) CHIEF OF STAFF 2055 54261
King, Christina (CMTE-JOINT ECON) SR ECONOMIST - REPUB SD-G01 40367
King, Emily (CMTE-BUDGET) BUDGET ANALYST 204E CHOB 67200
King, Emily (RODGERS) DIR - OPS 1035 52006
King, Emma (COURTNEY) DPTY DIST DIR 2332 52076
King, Jackie (CHENEY) FIELD REP 307-261-6595
King, Kassie (HILL, KATIE) COMMUNICATIONS DIR 1130 51956
King, Kathryn (CRAWFORD) RESEARCH ASST 2422 54076
King, Kyle (BLUMENAUER) SCHEDULER 1111 54811
King, Luke (COMER) DIR - CONSTIT SVCS 270-487-9509
King, Shanna (SEWELL) CONSTIT SVCS REP 334-262-1919
King, Wayne (MEADOWS) DPTY CHIEF OF STAFF/DIST DIR 828-693-5660
King, Wells (CMTE-JOINT ECON) POLICY ADVISOR - REPUB SD-G01 45426
Kingery, Rachel (MCEACHIN) COORD - DIST OUTREACH 314 CHOB 56365
Kinner, Mily (MILLER) SCHEDULER 1605 53452
Kinney, Erik (SENSENBRENNER) LEGIS ASST 2449 55101
Kinney, Ryann (DELAURO) SCHEDULER/EXEC ASST 2413 53661
Kiple, Carol (HARRIS) CONSTIT LIAISON 410-588-5670
Kirby, Max (FERGUSON) FIELD REP 770-683-2033
Kirchberg, Olivia (KIND) LEGIS CORRES/LEGIS ASST 1502 55506
Kirk, John (VAN DREW) DIST DIR 609-625-5008
Kirkwood, Michael (JACKSON LEE) DIST AIDE 2079 53816
Kirkwood, Rebekah (WILD) SCHEDULER 1607 56411
Kirlin, Michael (CMTE-HOMELAND SECUR) DPTY STAFF DIR 117 FHOB 68417
Kirsch, Isabel (SLOTKIN) LEGIS FELLOW 1531 54872
Kirsch, Steven (SCHNEIDER) COMMUNICATIONS DIR 1432 54835
Kirschke-Schwartz, Evie (CARTWRIGHT) SCHEDULER/ LEGIS CORRES 1034 55546
Kirsh, Ari (SHIMKUS) LEGIS ASST 2217 55271
Kisner, Chelsea (CUNNINGHAM) CASEWKR 843-521-2530
Kissel, Rainer (MOONEY) FIELD REP 304-264-8810
Kizzier, Kyle (MITCHELL) CHIEF OF STAFF 211 CHOB 52106
Klaiman, Seth (LANGEVIN) DIST CHIEF OF STAFF 401-732-9400
Klein, Dana (NAT REPUB CONG CMTE) DIR - FINANCE 202-479-7000
Klein, Kyle (CMTE-HOMELAND SECUR) SUBCOMM STAFF DIR - TRANSPORTATION AND MARITIME SECURITY SUBCOMM 117 FHOB 68417
Klein, Lee (FORTENBERRY) FIELD REP 402-379-2064
Klein, Lexi (RIGGLEMAN) STAFF ASST 1022 54711
Klein, Michael (SCHRADER) CASEWORK - VETS 503-557-1324
Kleitsch, Jessica (AMODEI) LEGIS CORRES 104 CHOB 56155
Klemp, Kyle (DAVIDS) MGR - CONSTIT SVCS 913-621-0832
Kline, Rachel (MURPHY) STAFF ASST 1710 54035
Klotz, Karen (WITTMAN) COORD - OUTREACH 540-659-2734
Klump, Allen (DUNCAN, JEFF) CHIEF OF STAFF 2229 55301
Knackstedt, Kimberly (CMTE-ED & WORKFORCE) DISABILITY POLICY ADVISOR 230 FHOB 53725
Knapp, Daneen (JORDAN) STAFF ASST/ CASEWKR 419-663-1426
Knapp, Evelyn (JOHNSON, HENRY C. "HANK", JR.) STAFF ASST/LEGIS CORRES 2240 51605
Knauer, Chris (CMTE-ENERGY & COMMERCE) STAFF DIR FOR OVERSIGHT 2125 52927
Knell, Katherine (CAO/ENTERPRISE APPLICATIONS) MGR B73 FHOB 68496
Knight, Alissa (CMTE-ETHICS) STAFF ASST 1015 57103
Knight, Jaclyn (BUCHANAN) SCHEDULER 2427 55015
Knight, Kevin (SCHWEIKERT) DPTY CHIEF OF STAFF/DIST DIR 480-946-2411
Knight, Natali (WEBSTER) SCHEDULER 352-241-9220
Knight, Natalie (MCBATH) LEGIS COUNSEL 1513 54501
Knight, Travis (CUELLAR) SR LEGIS AIDE/COUNSEL 2372 51640
Knott, Tucker (HOLDING) CHIEF OF STAFF 1110 53032
Knowles, Catherine (BROOKS, SUSAN W.) DPTY CHIEF OF STAFF 2211 52276

Knowles, Joseph (FITZPATRICK) DPTY CHIEF OF STAFF/ LEGIS DIR 1722 54276
Knudson, Kate
(INTERPARLMN AFFAIRS) DIRECTOR HC4 61437
(SPEAKER) DIRECTOR/SPECIAL EVENTS H232 50100
Kobayashi, Asami (CASE) DIST STAFF ASST 808-650-6688
Koch, Mary Margaret (FOSTER) DIST SCHEDULER/DIST STAFF ASST 630-585-7672
Koch, Walt (HIGGINS, BRIAN) SR CASEWKR/ CASEWKR - MIL/CASEWORK - VETS 716-852-3501
Koerner, Nissa (LEE, BARBARA) PRESS ASST 2470 52661
Koetzle, Desiree (STAUBER) CHIEF OF STAFF 126 CHOB 56211
Koetzle, Patrick (GABBARD) LEGIS ASST 1433 54906
Kohler, John (BALDERSON) LEGIS CORRES 1221 55355
Kohlrieser, Andrew (HUIZENGA) LEGIS ASST 2232 54401
Kokaly, Bill (COLLINS, DOUG) FIELD REP 770-297-3388
Kolano, Emily (HECK) LEGIS ASST/PRESS SECY 2452 59740
Kolar, Jacob (KUSTOFF) SPECIAL ASST 901-682-4422
Kolb, Devin (CÁRDENAS) SCHEDULER 2438 56131
Kollmeier, Bob (LONG) LIAISON - AG 417-889-1800
Kolodjeski, Erin (CMTE-APPRO) PROF STAFF MEMB HT2 52041
Komisarjevsky, Stephen (RICE, KATHLEEN M.) COMMUNITY REP 516-739-3008
Koncar, Steve (MCCLINTOCK) DPTY CHIEF OF STAFF/ LEGIS DIR 2312 52511
Konolige, Rebecca (CMTE-NATURAL RESOURCES) PROF STAFF 4120 52761
Konrath, Patrick (GROTHMAN) LEGIS AIDE 1427 52476
Konya, John (CMTE-AGRIC) DIR - INFO TECH 1301 52171
Koohmaraie, Bijan (CMTE-ENERGY & COMMERCE) COUNSEL 564 FHOB 53641
Kooiman, Matthew (HUIZENGA) DIST REP 616-570-0917
Koontz, Cara (CMTE-WAYS & MEANS) DIGITAL DIR 1102 53625
Kopec, Rachel (RODGERS) DIR - COALITIONS 1035 52006
Koppula, Sujit (BROWNLEY) STAFF ASST 2262 55811
Kopshever, Kristin (CMTE-SCIENCE) ADMIN DIR/DIR OF MBR SVCS – MAJ 2321 56375
Koren, Michael (CMTE-OVERSIGHT & GOVT REFORM) PROF STAFF MEMB 2105 55074
Korn, Simon (HARDER) LEGIS CORRES/STAFF ASST 131 CHOB 54540
Korst, Andrew (CARTER, JOHN R.) LEGIS CORRES 2110 53864
Korten, Bradley (WATSON COLEMAN) LEGIS ASST 2442 55801
Koski, Amanda (GABBARD) SCHEDULER 1433 54906
Kosova, Elly (TRONE) STAFF ASST 1213 52721
Kostelic, Luanne (POCAN) DIST OFFICE MGR/ CASEWKR 608-258-9800
Koszela, Kaylan (CUNNINGHAM) DIR - COMMUNITY OUTREACH 843-352-7572
Kotman, Dan (WALBERG) COMMUNICATIONS DIR 2266 56276
Kotschwar, Nichole (CMTE-JOINT LIBRARY) PROF STAFF SR-305 46352
Kotschwar, Nichole (CMTE-JOINT PRINTING) PROF STAFF SR-305 46352
Kotsovos, Michael (LONG) STAFF ASST 2454 56536
Koulouris, Dean (CMTE-APPRO) PROF STAFF MEMB HT2 52041
Kouri, Joey (LAHOOD) LEGIS CORRES 1424 56201
Kovach, Ron (WATKINS) CASEWKR 785-234-5966
Kovacs, Billy (KIRKPATRICK) OUTREACH DIRECTOR 520-881-3588
Kovalovich, Aria (CMTE-SCIENCE) RESEARCH ASST - MAJ 2321 56375
Kowalewski, Albin (HOUSE HISTORIAN) HISTORICAL PUBLICATIONS SPEC JEFFERSON BUILDING, ATTIC 61300
Kowalewski, Matthew (PARLIAMENTARIAN) ASST CLERK TO THE PARLIAMENTARIAN H209 57373
Kozloski, Kory (HOUSE DEM CONG CMPGN CMTE) NATIONAL POLITICAL DIR - FRONTLINE 202-863-1500
Koztoski, Douglas (CAO/HOUSE RECORDING STUDIO) BROADCAST PROD TECH 2010 53941
Kozubski, Susan (INSPECTOR GENERAL) ASST DIR 386 FHOB 61250
Krahel, Kyle (LEVIN, MIKE) DPTY DIST DIR 760-599-5000
Krall, Matthew (JOHNSON, DUSTY) SPECIAL ASST 1508 52801
Kraly, Elizabeth (CAO/OFFICE OF THE CHIEF HUMAN RESOURCES OFFICER) DPTY CHIEF 102 FHOB 66138
Kramer, Austin (HARTZLER) DIST DIR 2235 52876
Kramer, Brian (LOEBSACK) DIST REP 563-323-5988
Krantz, Josh (CMTE-ENERGY & COMMERCE) POLICY ANALYST 2125 52927
Kranz, Daniel (KATKO) STAFF ASST 2457 53701
Kranz, Jeannie (BABIN) ADVISOR - SCIENCE 832-780-0966
Krasny, Dustin (WALBERG) DIST DIR/DIR - OPS 517-780-9075
Kratz, Jeff (BACON) LEGIS DIR 1024 54155
Krause, Andrew (ALLRED) STAFF ASST 972-972-7949
Krawiec, Carolina (SHERMAN) DIR - CONSTIT SVCS 818-501-9200
Krebs, Robert (AXNE) LEGIS CORRES 330 CHOB 55476
Kreft, Kevin (MASSIE) DIST STAFF ASST 2453 53465
Kreitzer, Tom (CAO/HIR – OPS AND CONTINUITY) MGR - OPS 632A FHOB 60302
Krekorian, Elise (DUNCAN, JEFF) LEGIS ASST 2229 55301
Kremer, Marnie (CMTE-NATURAL RESOURCES) PROF STAFF - MAJ 1332 56065
Kremkau, Rebecca (CAO/PAYROLL & BENEFITS) SYS ANALYST B215 LHOB 61473
Krenz, Bonnie (SPANBERGER) LEGIS ASST 1239 52815
Krepich, Christopher (SENSENBRENNER) COMMUNICATIONS DIR 2449 55101
Kresse, Carol (GONZALEZ, ANTHONY) SCHEDULER 1023 53876
Kretzschmar, Natalie (JOHNSON, BILL) PRESS SECY/ LEGIS CORRES 2336 55705
Krieger, Robyn (MIN WHIP) STAFF ASST H148 50197
Kringer, Elizabeth (BISHOP, SANFORD D., JR.) CASEWKR 478-803-2631
Krivsky, Andrew (FOXX) CONSTIT LIAISON 336-778-0211
Krogman, Travis (KUSTER) LEGIS DIR 320 CHOB 55206
Kroitor, Jason (ROSE, JOHN W.) LEGIS CORRES 1232 54231
Krongaus, McKinley (MATSUI) EXEC ASST/SCHEDULER 2311 57163
Kronzer, Jay (GREEN, MARK E.) LEGIS DIR 533 CHOB 52811
Krovi, Varun (LAWRENCE) LEGIS DIR 2463 55802
Krueger, Christian (CASTRO) LEGIS CORRES 2241 53236
Krupnick, Alexander (NORCROSS) LEGIS ASST 2437 56501
Kubicki, Paul (LEGIS COUNSEL) ASST COUNSEL 337 FHOB 56060
Kubon, Tom (VISCLOSKY) CASEWKR 219-795-1844
Kuckuck, Jeffrey (BIGGS) SR POLICY ADVISOR 1318 52635
Kuebler, Sam (KINZINGER) LEGIS CORRES 2245 53635

Kuehn, Dillon (SMITH, ADRIAN) STAFF ASST 502 CHOB...... 56435
Kuerbitz, Catherine (SCOTT, DAVID) LEGIS ASST 225 CHOB...... 52939
Kugler, Rebecca (NUNES) PRESS AIDE 1013...... 52523
Kugler, Sara (WASSERMAN SCHULTZ) DIGITAL PRESS SECY 1114...... 57931
Kuhn, Elena (SPEAKER) PRESS/ADVISOR H232...... 50100
Kuhns, Colby (COOK) LEGIS ASST - MIL/LEGIS DIR 1027...... 55861
Kulig, Liz (PAPPAS) SCHEDULER 323 CHOB...... 55456
Kum, Courtney (STEFANIK) LEGIS ASST - MIL 318 CHOB...... 54611
Kumpf, Roger (MCHENRY) REGIONAL DIR...... 828-669-0600
Kundanis, George (SPEAKER) DPTY CHIEF OF STAFF H232...... 50100
Kunes, Cindy (THOMPSON, GLENN) DIST SCHEDULER...... 814-353-0215
Kunin, Tamara (CRAIG) CHIEF OF STAFF 1523...... 52271
Kunse, Suzanne (SCHRADER) DIST DIR...... 503-557-1324
Kupe, Laura (CMTE-HOMELAND SECUR) COUNSEL 176 FHOB...... 62616
Kuper, Karen (CAO/HIR – ENTERPRISE INFRASTRUCT) MGR - OPS/SPECIAL ASST 677 FHOB...... 571-921-3321
Kupperman, Jonathan (HUNTER) LEGIS ASST 2429...... 55672
Kuppuri, Manjula (CAO/ENTERPRISE APPLICATIONS) SR BUSINESS PROCESS APPLICA SPEC B70 FHOB...... 59915
Kurspahic, Vesna (WOODALL) CONSTIT SVCS REP...... 770-232-3005
Kurth, Tim (CMTE-ENERGY & COMMERCE) DPTY CHIEF COUNSEL 564 FHOB...... 53641
Kurtz, Kelley
(KING, STEVE) FINANCIAL & ADMIN OFFICER 2210...... 54426
(WOODALL) ADMIN ASST/SCHEDULER 1724...... 54272
Kustin, Casey
(CMTE-FOREIGN AFFAIRS) STAFF DIR 5211...... 67812
(DEUTCH) SR POLICY ADVISOR/SUBCOMM STAFF DIR 2447...... 53001
Kwak, Sally (CMTE-JOINT TAX) ECONOMIST SD-G18...... 45561
Kwapnioski, Kimberly (FORTENBERRY) DIST AIDE...... 402-438-1598
Kwiecinski, Craig (LAMB) CHIEF OF STAFF 1224...... 52301
Kwon, Jean (CMTE-APPRO) PROF STAFF MEMB HT2...... 52041
La, Alisa (SPEAKER) SPECIAL ASST TO THE SPEAKER H232...... 50100
LaBorde, Kate (BIGGS) LEGIS DIR 1318...... 52635
Labotte, Ellie (BUSTOS) CONSTIT ADVOCATE...... 309-786-3406
Labovick, Hannah (FRANKEL) STAFF ASST 2305...... 59890
Laboy, Elsie (WILD) CONSTIT ADVOCATE...... 484-781-6000
Labrake, Andre (CAO/LOGISTICS) REC & WAREHOUSE SPEC RSBC4...... 55057
Lacapa, Rochelle (O'HALLERAN) CONSTIT SVCS REP...... 928-286-5338
LaCapra, Quin (PETERS) DIR - DIGITAL MEDIA...... 858-455-5550
LaCava, Julia (CLERK/REPORTERS) OFFICIAL REPORTER HT59...... 55621
Lackey, Jennifer (CMTE-RULES) SR PROF STAFF H152...... 59191
Ladak, Nawaid (JOHNSON, EDDIE BERNICE) LEGIS ASST 2306...... 58885
Ladet, Janae (CMTE-FINANCIAL SVCS) PROF STAFF - MAJ 2129...... 54247
Lafargue, Sophia (MEEKS) CHIEF OF STAFF 2310...... 53461
Lafleur, Shirlee (WILSON, FREDERICA S.) DIR - FIELD OPS...... 305-690-5905
Lafountain, Charity (CHENEY) FIELD REP...... 307-261-6595
La Fountain, Peter (LANGEVIN) LEGIS ASST 2077...... 52735
Lafuente, Gilbert (CUELLAR) COORD - OUTREACH...... 210-271-2851
Lainez, Julio (MOULTON) LEGIS DIR 1127...... 58020
Lake, Naomi (GARCÍA, JESÚS G. "CHUY") LEGIS CORRES 530 CHOB...... 55096
Lalle, Stephanie (CMTE-ED & WORKFORCE) DPTY COMMUNICATIONS DIR 2176...... 53725
Lam, Carrie (NAPOLITANO) CASEWKR...... 626-350-0150
Lam, Kristine
(CMTE-OVERSIGHT & GOVT REFORM) DPTY STAFF DIR 6460...... 55051
(CONNOLLY) LEGIS ASST 2238...... 51492
Laman, Denise (TAYLOR) SR CONSTIT SVCS REP...... 972-202-4150
Lamb, Jennifer (DELAURO) DIST DIR...... 203-562-3718
Lambert, Denise (BURCHETT) SCHEDULER/DIR - FINANCE...... 865-523-3772
Lambert, Jimmy (CLERK/LCS) SR SOFTWARE ENGINEER 2401...... 51182
Lambert, Stephanie (LAWSON) COMMUNICATIONS DIR 1406...... 50123
Lambeth, Chance (ROUZER) DIST DIR...... 910-253-6111
Lammers, Emily (LATTA) LEGIS CORRES 2467...... 56405
LaMonica, Tracey (HILL, KATIE) CONSTIT SVCS REP/FIELD REP...... 661-839-0532
Lampman, Zachary (BUCHANAN) STAFF ASST 2427...... 55015
Lancheros, Maria (JOHNSON, HENRY C. "HANK", JR.) IMMIGRATION LIAISON...... 770-987-2291
Lanctin, Jonathan (DUFFY) CONSTIT SVCS REP...... 715-298-9344
Landa, Mackenzie (SELECT CMTE-CLIMATE CRISIS) COUNSEL 359 FHOB...... 51106
Landefeld, Paul (CMTE-JOINT TAX) ECONOMIST 595 FHOB...... 67575
Landis, NormaJean (GRIFFITH) DIST SCHEDULER...... 540-381-5671
Landrum, Charles (CRAWFORD) FIELD REP...... 870-203-0540
Lane, Carey (CAO/HOUSE RECORDING STUDIO) AUDIO SPEC 2010...... 53941
Lane, Katherine (LAW REV COUNSEL) ASST COUNSEL 308 FHOB...... 62411
Lane, Philisha (CUMMINGS) SPECIAL PROJ/ RESOURCE MGR...... 410-685-9199
Lane, Will (DUNCAN, JEFF) LEGIS CORRES 2229...... 55301
Lane-Wyant, Jillian (GAETZ) CHIEF OF STAFF 1721...... 54136
Lanfranconi, Alex (RUTHERFORD) PRESS SECY 1711...... 52501
Lange, Katherine (GRIFFITH) LEGIS CORRES 2202...... 53861
Langenderfer, James (MAST) CHIEF OF STAFF 2182...... 53026
Langer, Cass (KHANNA) OFFICE MGR/ COMMUNITY LIAISON...... 408-436-2720
Langer, Jack
(CMTE-INTELLIGENCE) COMMUNICATIONS DIR - MIN HVC304...... 54121
(NUNES) COMMUNICATIONS DIR 1013...... 52523
Langley, William (CAO/ENTERPRISE APPLICATIONS) BUSINESS PROCESS APPLICA SPEC B77 FHOB...... 66061

Langnes, James (STEIL) STAFF ASST 1408 53031
LaNier, Elisa (CMTE-OVERSIGHT & GOVT REFORM) DIR - OPS/CHIEF CLERK 2157 55051
Lansing, Jackie (CALVERT) CASEWKR 951-277-0042
Lantz, Ashley (GOTTHEIMER) CHIEF OF STAFF 213 CHOB. 54465
Lara, Sally (VELA) CASEWKR 956-276-4497
Large, Alex (CMTE-VET AFFAIRS) PROF STAFF MEMB 3460 53527
Large, Patrick (PALAZZO) DPTY CHIEF OF STAFF 2349 55772
Larkin, Brendan
(CMTE-ENERGY & COMMERCE) POLICY COORD 2125 52927
(TONKO) SR POLICY ADVISOR 2369 55076
Larkin, Brenna (MULLIN) STAFF ASST 2421 52701
Larkin, Kellie (CMTE-OVERSIGHT & GOVT REFORM) PARLIAMENTARIAN/SR COUNSEL 2157 55051
Larkins, William (HASTINGS) DIST STAFF ASST. 954-733-2800
Larochelle, Scott (CMTE-WAYS & MEANS) STAFF ASST 1102 53625
LaRosa, Michael (HOUSE DEM POLICY AND COMMUNICATIONS CMTE) COMMUNICATIONS DIR HB18 67204
Larsen, Chris (LARSEN) COMMUNITY LIAISON 425-252-3188
Larsen, Nicholas (HIMES) LEGIS ASST 1227 55541
Larson, Sally Rose
(CMTE-JUDICIARY) POLICY ADVISOR 1504 56906
(COLLINS, DOUG) DPTY CHIEF OF STAFF 1504 59893
LaSalle, Kenny (CÁRDENAS) LEGIS AIDE 2438 56131
Laska, Alex (FINKENAUER) LEGIS ASST 124 CHOB 52911
Lasseigne, Philip (DAVIS, RODNEY) COORD - GRANTS & SPEC PROJ 918-205-8660
Lassiter, Hillary (PENCE) LEGIS DIR 222 CHOB 53021
LaSure, Aaron (CMTE-HOUSE ADMIN) PROF STAFF 1309 52061
Latt, Zay (PELOSI) CASEWKR - IMMIGRATION 415-556-4862
Latta, Dave (ROGERS, MIKE) FELLOW 2184 53261
Latu, Dan (SIRES) LEGIS CORRES 2268 57919
Lau, David (CAO/HIR – CYBERSECURITY) ENTERPRISE COMPLIANCE LEAD 650 FHOB 63826
Lau, Sam (CMTE-BUDGET) COMMUNICATIONS DIR 204E CHOB 67200
Laubon, Ashlee (CLERK/COMMUNICA) SR GRAPHIC DESIGNER 293 CHOB 51908
Laudick, Courtney (LEVIN, ANDY) LEGIS CORRES 228 CHOB 54961
Laufer, John (MURPHY) DPTY CHIEF OF STAFF/LEGIS DIR 1710 54035
Laufersweiler, Austin (LEVIN, ANDY) COMMUNICATIONS DIR 228 CHOB 54961
Laughlin, Rose (CMTE-RULES) PROF STAFF - MAJ H312 59091
Laukitis, R J (WALBERG) CHIEF OF STAFF 2266 56276
Lauren, Osborne (BARR) SCHEDULER 2430 54706
Laurie, Paul (KINZINGER) LEGIS AIDE 2245 53635
Lauritzen, Anne (WILD) CONSTIT ADVOCATE 610-333-1170
Lauron, Antonio (CLERK/LCS) SR SOFTWARE ENGINEER 2401 51182
Lauterbach, Jennifer (LESKO) SR LEGIS ASST 1113 54576
Laven, Zack (SCHWEIKERT) LEGIS ASST 1526 52190
Laven Jones, Sarah (DOGGETT) LEGIS ASST 2307 54865
Laverdiere, Maria (TONKO) EXEC DIR 2369 55076
Law, Marianne (CLERK/LCS) OPS ASST 2401 51182
Lawler, Will (SENSENBRENNER) LEGIS ASST 2449 55101
Lawrence, Amy (MULLIN) COMMUNICATIONS DIR 2421 52701
Lawrence, Betsy (CMTE-JUDICIARY) COUNSEL 6320 53926
Lawrence, Erik (CLOUD) SPECIAL PROJ/FED LIAISON 361-884-2222
Lawrence, Jason (SCOTT, AUSTIN) CHIEF OF STAFF 2417 56531
Lawson, Chris (ADERHOLT) ADMIN DIR/SCHEDULER/SYS ADMIN 1203 54876
Lawson, Dion
(ADAMS) FINANCIAL ADMIN 2436 51510
(BEATTY) SHARED EMPLOYEE 2303 54324
(DEMINGS) FINANCIAL ADMIN 217 CHOB 52176
(GREEN, AL) FINANCIAL ADMIN 2347 57508
(LAWRENCE) FINANCIAL ADVISOR 2463 55802
Lawson, Dion (ESPAILLAT) ADMIN - FINANCE & PAYROLL 1630 54365
Lax, Kelsey (CMTE-ETHICS) STAFF ASST 1015 57103
Layden, William (WESTERMAN) LEGIS ASST 209 CHOB 53772
Layman, Joseph (CMTE-APPRO) PROF STAFF MEMB 2362A 52638
Layman-Wood, January (CLERK/COMMUNICA) DPTY CHIEF 293 CHOB 51908
Layton, Chip (JOHNSON, MIKE) DPTY CHIEF OF STAFF/DIST DIR 318-840-0309
Layton, Elise (WALBERG) SR CASEWKR 517-780-9075
Le, Catherine (GREEN, AL) CONSTIT SVCS 713-383-9234
Le, Christy (CORREA) DIST FIELD REP 714-559-6190
Lea, Robyn (PELOSI) MGR - CORRES 1236 54965
Lea, Sam (CAO/HIR – CYBERSECURITY) SR SYS SECUR ENGINEER 612 FHOB 64151
Leach, Cindy S (CLERK/LCS) DIR - SYS ANALYSIS AND QA 2401 51182
Leahy, Terry (INSPECTOR GENERAL) MGMT ANALYST 386 FHOB 61250
Lear, Madeline (DAVIS, RODNEY) STAFF ASST 1740 52371
Leasure, Matt (DEFAZIO) EXEC ASST/SYS ADMIN 2134 56416
Leatherbury, Michelle (CAO/HIR – ENTERPRISE INFRASTRUCT) COMMUNICATIONS SPEC 687 FHOB 60200
Leathersich, Joseph (MORELLE) COMMUNICATIONS AIDE 585-232-4850
Leavandosky, Stacey (LOFGREN) CHIEF OF STAFF 1401 53072
Leblanc, Cody (BUCK) DIST REP 970-702-2136
LeBlanc, Madison (HIGGINS, CLAY) STAFF ASST 424 CHOB 52031
Leboeuf, Beila (CMTE-JOINT ECON) SR ECONOMIST - REPUB SD-G01 47578
LeCates, Joseph (CMTE-JOINT TAX) ECONOMIST 595 FHOB 67575
Leck, Kelsey (CAO/ENTERPRISE APPLICATIONS) BUSINESS PROCESS APPLICA SPEC B77 FHOB 66043
Ledbetter, Rachel (SCOTT, AUSTIN) PRESS SECY 2417 56531
Ledoux, Jerrie (JOHNSON, MIKE) COMMUNITY LIAISON 337-392-3146
Ledoux, Leroy (RADEWAGEN) FIELD DIR 684-633-3601
Lee, Andrea (THOMPSON, BENNIE G.) CHIEF OF STAFF/ SCHEDULER 2466 55876
Lee, Bertram (CMTE-ED & WORKFORCE) POLICY COUNSEL 230 FHOB 53725
Lee, Brian (LUJÁN) CONSTIT SVCS 505-863-0582
Lee, Carianne (WATSON COLEMAN) LEGIS CORRES 2442 55801
Lee, Chao (MCCOLLUM) SR DIST REP 651-224-9191
Lee, Chris (WALORSKI) DIST DIR 574-204-2645

Lee, Christine (HARTZLER) LEGIS DIR 2235 **52876**
Lee, Cindy (CHU) CONSTIT SVCS REP **626-304-0110**
Lee, Daniel (PORTER) FIELD REP 1117 **55611**
Lee, Darnell (CAO/OFFICE OF THE CHIEF HUMAN RESOURCES OFFICER) DPTY CHIEF 102 FHOB **66451**
Lee, Doug (QUIGLEY) LEGIS DIR/DPTY CHIEF OF STAFF 2458 **54061**
Lee, Ian (MALONEY, SEAN PATRICK) COMMUNICATIONS DIR 2331 **55441**
Lee, Jenn (TORRES SMALL) PRESS SECY/DIGITAL DIR 430 CHOB **52365**
Lee, Joy (CMTE-HOUSE ADMIN) COUNSEL - MIN 1216 **58281**
Lee, Kaozouapa (WATSON COLEMAN) SR POLICY ADVISOR 2442 **55801**
Lee, Kathleen (PANETTA) DIST DIR **831-424-2229**
Lee, Katie (LANGEVIN) LEGIS ASST 2077 **52735**
Lee, Keonte (CLYBURN) STAFF ASST 200 CHOB **53315**
Lee, Luther (O'HALLERAN) CONSTIT SVCS REP **928-286-5338**
Lee, Matt (PAPPAS) CHIEF OF STAFF 323 CHOB **55456**
Lee, Myra (LAWRENCE) COORD - COMMUNITY OUTREACH **248-356-2052**
Lee, Nga (CAO/ACCOUNTING) STAFF ACCOUNTANT 3110 **54538**
Lee, Rachel (ROSE, JOHN W.) COMMUNICATIONS DIR 1232 **54231**
Lee, Richard (PETERSON) LEGIS ASST 2204 **52165**
Lee, Sarah (CMTE-BUDGET) BUDGET ANALYST 204E CHOB **67200**
Lee, Seryeung (SPEAKER) DPTY PRESS SECY H232 **50100**
Lee, Una (CMTE-ENERGY & COMMERCE) CHIEF HEALTH COUNSEL 2125 **55056**
Lee, Vanessa (LEE, BARBARA) CONG AIDE **510-763-0370**
Lee, Yujin (KIM) LEGIS DIR 1516 **54765**
Leech, Katie (SGT AT ARMS/HOUSE SECURITY) STAFF ASST HVC301 **62044**
Leeds, David (MALONEY, CAROLYN B.) DIST REP **212-860-0606**
Lefaive, Erica (WEBER) LEGIS AIDE 107 CHOB **52831**
Lefevers, Sara (GAETZ) COORD - COMMUNITY OUTREACH **850-479-1183**
Leffler, Matthew (GUTHRIE) CONSTIT SVCS ASST **270-842-9896**
Leganski, John (MIN LEADER) DIR - FLOOR OPS H204 **54000**
Legg, Mike (CMTE-TRANSP & INFRA) DIR - TRAVEL, SECUR, & FACILITIES 2165 **54472**
Leggieri, Rebecca (CMTE-APPRO) CLERK H405 **52847**
Leggiero, Brandon (AMODEI) LEGIS ASST 104 CHOB **56155**
Legrand, Nadine (SGT AT ARMS/APPOINTMENT) ASST - APPTS DESK CAPITOL **52551**
Legrand-Wittich, Anika (OCASIO-CORTEZ) PRESS ASST 229 CHOB **53965**
Le Grant, Carlyn (CMTE-NATURAL RESOURCES) STAFF ASST 1324 **56065**
Lehman, Ryan (MALONEY, SEAN PATRICK) DPTY CHIEF OF STAFF 2331 **55441**
Lehn, Kim (CMTE-ARMED SVCS) PROF STAFF MEMB 2340 **62923**
Leibell, Zach (HOUSE DEM CAUCUS) DPTY PRESS SECY B245 LHOB **51400**
Leibowitz, Liz (LOWEY) LEGIS ASST 2365 **56506**
Leiby, Frederick (CAO/CUST EXPER CTR) SR CONTRACT ADMIN B227 LHOB **58000**
Leighton, Roz (ARMSTRONG) CHIEF OF STAFF 1004 **52611**
Leighton, Stephen (MAST) DPTY CHIEF OF STAFF **772-403-0900**
Leingang, Nicky (OMAR) SR COMMUNITY REP **612-333-1272**
Leininger, Maria (SCHRIER) DIST DIR **425-657-1001**
Leisemann, John (SENSENBRENNER) STAFF ASST **262-784-1111**
Leiserson, Nicholas (LANGEVIN) LEGIS DIR/SYS ADMIN 2077 **52735**
Leja, Jan (COOK) FIELD REP **760-247-1815**
Lemieux, Adam (LARSEN) DIST DIR **425-252-3188**
Lemire, Daniel (MORELLE) SCHEDULER 1317 **53615**
Lemma, Anthony (MENG) DIST DIR **718-358-6364**
LeNard, Dennis (SGT AT ARMS/EMERGENCY MGMT) EMERGENCY MGMT SPEC 192 FHOB **60950**
Lenderman, Lyudmila (JEFFRIES) CONSTIT SVCS REP **718-373-0033**
Lennon, Jaime (RUPPERSBERGER) COMMUNICATIONS DIR **410-628-2701**
Lenoir, Jeanette (MOORE) PRESS SECY 2252 **54572**
Lents, Deborah (GRAVES, TOM) STAFF ASST **706-226-5320**
Lentz, Connor (HOLLINGSWORTH) LEGIS DIR 1641 **66853**
Lentz, Daniel (HICE) FIELD REP **478-457-0007**
Leonard, Morgan (NAPOLITANO) LEGIS ASST 1610 **55256**
Leonard, Rick (RYAN) DIST DIR **330-373-0074**
Leonard, Shelley (CMTE-JOINT TAX) LEGIS COUNSEL 502 FHOB **53621**
Leon Guerrero, Kenneth W B (SAN NICOLAS) CASEWKR - MIL/CASEWORK - VETS **671-475-6453**
Leonova, Sofya (LIPINSKI) LEGIS DIR 2346 **55701**
Leou, Ryan (LIEU) STAFF ASST **323-651-1040**
Lepire, Cami (BRADY) SR HEALTH POLICY ADVISOR 1011 **54901**
Lerma, Eduardo (ESCOBAR) CHIEF OF STAFF 1505 **68330**
Leshtz, David (LOEBSACK) DIST REP **319-351-0789**
Lesinski, James (CMTE-OVERSIGHT & GOVT REFORM) COUNSEL 2105 **55074**
Leslie, Matt (WEXTON) LEGIS ASST 1217 **55136**
Lesnewsky, Erik (CAO/OFFICE OF THE CHIEF HUMAN RESOURCES OFFICER) ADA AIDE 102 FHOB **52926**
Lespinasse, Marie (MEEKS) COMMUNITY LIAISON **718-725-6000**
Lessley, Lucinda (CMTE-OVERSIGHT & GOVT REFORM) POLICY DIR 2157 **55051**
Lester, Dean
(BUCSHON) OFFICE ADMIN 2313 **54636**
(CUELLAR) ADMIN - FINANCE & PAYROLL 2372 **51640**
(FULCHER) OFFICE ADMIN 1520 **56611**
(HERN) FINANCIAL ADMIN 1019 **52211**
(MOONEY) OFFICE ADMIN 2440 **52711**
(ROBY) OFFICE ADMIN 504 CHOB **52901**
(STEUBE) ADMIN - FINANCE & PAYROLL 521 CHOB **55792**
Letlow, Luke (ABRAHAM) CHIEF OF STAFF 417 CHOB **58490**
Lett, Chelsea (LESKO) DPTY DIST DIR **623-776-7911**
Lett, Gloria J (CLERK) DPTY CLERK H154 **57000**
Letter, Douglas N (GEN COUNSEL) HOUSE GENERAL COUNSEL 219 CHOB **59700**
Letz, Deborah (LAW REV COUNSEL) ASST COUNSEL 308 FHOB **62411**
Leuschen, James (MAJ LEADER) SR POLICY ADVISOR H107 **53130**

Lev, Mark (CAO/ENTERPRISE APPLICATIONS) SR BUSINESS PROCESS APPLICA SPEC B77 FHOB 51420
Levar, Mary Ann (QUIGLEY) DIST DIR 773-267-5926
Leverich, Gerald (CMTE-ENERGY & COMMERCE) SR COUNSEL 2125 52927
Levin, Sarah (CMTE-WAYS & MEANS) PROF STAFF 1104 53943
Levine, Doug (GOSAR) STAFF ASST 2057 52315
Levine, Noah (HOULAHAN) DIST SCHEDULER 610-883-5050
Levinson, Tyler (BEATTY) PRESS ASST/LEGIS CORRES 2303 54324
Levitan, Rachel (CMTE-FOREIGN AFFAIRS) DPTY COMMUNICATIONS DIR/POLICY ADVISOR 2152 55021
Lewis, Alvin (ROGERS, MIKE) FIELD REP/ SPECIAL PROJ DIR 334-745-6221
Lewis, Amy (MATSUI) COMMUNICATIONS DIR 916-498-5600
Lewis, Chanan (CUMMINGS) SPECIAL ASST 410-685-9199
Lewis, Charity (FRANKEL) COORD - DIST OUTREACH 561-998-9045
Lewis, Chasseny (WILSON, FREDERICA S.) CHIEF OF STAFF 2445 54506
Lewis, Curt (AGUILAR) DIR - GRANTS 909-890-4445
Lewis, Dale (HERRERA BEUTLER) DPTY DIST DIR 360-695-6292
Lewis, Jim (KELLY, ROBIN L.) COMMUNICATIONS DIR 2416 50773
Lewis, Jordan (WATSON COLEMAN) DIST REP 609-883-0026
Lewis, Jourdan (CMTE-ENERGY & COMMERCE) POLICY ANALYST 2125 52927
Lewis, Katherine (NUNES) LEGIS AIDE 1013 52523
Lewis, Kendrick (CRIST) COORD - DIST OUTREACH/DIST PRESS SECY 727-318-6770
Lewis, Teresa (WENSTRUP) REGIONAL DIR 513-605-1380
Lewis, Thomas (COLE) FIELD REP 405-329-6500
Leyba, Julie (TORRES) FIELD REP 909-481-6474
Li, Leah (KILMER) LEGIS CORRES 1410 55916
Li, Sydney (MENG) COMMUNITY LIAISON 718-358-6364
Lichtman, Miles (CMTE-OVERSIGHT & GOVT REFORM) PROF STAFF MEMB 2157 55051
Liebenson, Justine (SMITH, ADAM) LEGIS CORRES 2264 58901
Lieteau, Karim (CAO/WOUNDED WARRIOR) PROJ SPEC 354 FHOB 61954
Lifhits, Jenna (HOUSE REPUB CONF) DPTY POLICY DIR 1420 55107
Liftman, Daniel (HASTINGS) CONG ASST 561-676-7911
Light, Barbara (ROBY) CONSTIT SVCS REP 334-794-9680
Liles, Linda (GRAVES, TOM) CONSTIT SVCS REP 706-290-1776
Lillis, Joe (LONG) CHIEF OF STAFF 2454 56536
Lim, Chau (CAO/ACCOUNTING) SR ACCOUNTANT 3110 61019
Lim, Sarah (CMTE-NATURAL RESOURCES) CHIEF COUNSEL 1324 56065
Lim, Woo (TRAHAN) LEGIS ASST 1616 53411
Limbach, Shannon (ROUDA) CONSTIT SVCS REP 714-960-6483
Limjoco, Marie (SCHAKOWSKY) DIR - COMMUNITY AFFAIRS 847-328-3409
Lin, Alice (CMTE-WAYS & MEANS) POLICY ADVISOR 1136 55522
Lin, Kakuti (LEGIS COUNSEL) COUNSEL 337 FHOB 56060
Lincoln, Amanda (HOUSE REPUB STUDY CMTE) POLICY STAFF 418 CHOB 52777
Lincoln, Jack (LAMALFA) LEGIS ASST 322 CHOB 53076
Lindblom, John (COMMIS ON CHINA) RESEARCH ASSOC 243 FHOB 63766
Lindgren, Paige (ABRAHAM) PRESS ASST/LEGIS CORRES 417 CHOB 58490
Lindholm, Danielle (CMTE-FINANCIAL SVCS) NATIONAL SECUR ADVISOR 2129 54247
Lindow, Hannah (SLOTKIN) PRESS SECY 1531 54872
Lindow, Michaila (BROOKS, MO) LEGIS AIDE 2246 54801
Lindsay, Andre (CMTE-ED & WORKFORCE) STAFF ASST 2257 53725
Lindsey, Brian (LAW REV COUNSEL) SR COUNSEL 308 FHOB 62411
Line, Nelson M (CLERK/REPORTERS) SYS ANALYST HT59 55621
Linehan, Solara (SIMPSON) LEGIS ASST 208-334-1953
Ling, Melanie (TAKANO) CONSTIT SVCS REP 951-222-0203
Ling, Taylor (GROTHMAN) DIST STAFF ASST 920-907-0624
Ling, Vivian (CMTE-SMALL BUSINESS) COUNSEL 2069 55821
Linginfelter, Jennifer (BURCHETT) DIST DIR/ COMMUNICATIONS DIR 865-523-3772
Lington, Laura (MASSIE) COMMUNICATIONS DIR 2453 53465
Link, Adam (THORNBERRY) MIL FELLOW 2208 53706
Link, Craig (MAJ WHIP) DPTY FLOOR DIR H329 63210
Linn, Lindy (CHENEY) FIELD REP 307-277-9701
Linnehan Oursler, Tara (RUPPERSBERGER) CHIEF OF STAFF 2206 53061
Linsk, Reed (HUNTER) DPTY CHIEF OF STAFF 2429 55672
Linskey, Kevin (CMTE-APPRO) DIR - INVESTIGATIONS H307 53881
Linsmayer, Lauren (CMTE-SCIENCE) PROF STAFF - MAJ 2321 56375
Linville, Ray (CAO/HIR – ENTERPRISE INFRASTRUCT) SR SYS ENGINEER 622 FHOB 59276
Liotta, Christina (HERN) LEGIS AIDE 1019 52211
Lipe, Jon (BRINDISI) LEGIS ASST 329 CHOB 53665
Lipkowitz, Dan (PRICE) LEGIS ASST 2108 51784
Lipman, Joshua (DEUTCH) LEGIS DIR/COUNSEL 2447 53001
Lipow, Alex (COHEN) STAFF ASST/SCHEDULER 2104 53265
Lipscomb, Hunter (PALAZZO) CHIEF OF STAFF 2349 55772
Lipsich, Wendi (DEUTCH) DIST DIR 561-470-5440
Liquerman, Michael (WASSERMAN SCHULTZ) COORD - OUTREACH /PRESS ASST 954-845-1179
Lira, Nancy (ROYBAL-ALLARD) CASEWK MGR 323-721-8790
Lis, Jakub (CICILLINE) DIST SCHEDULER 401-729-5600
Lis, Tony (BERGMAN) CHIEF OF STAFF 414 CHOB 54735
Lisman, Sarah (HUIZENGA) DIST REP 616-570-0917
Lisowski, Nick (WESTERMAN) LEGIS AIDE 209 CHOB 53772
Litten, Josh (HOUSE HISTORIAN) SR RESEARCH ASST JEFFERSON BUILDING, ATTIC 6130
Litterell, Allison (LUCAS) CASEWKR 405-373-195
Little, Andreal (CAO/HIR – ESCALATIONS AND OPS) ASST PROJ MGR 607 FHOB 698
Little, Cathy (CMTE-APPRO) DIR - INFO TECH 2005 527
Little, Harold (CAO/HIR – IT CUSTOMER SOLUTIONS) SR TECH SOLUTIONS ENGINEER 694 FHOB 56
Little, Jason (BLUMENAUER) DIST SCHEDULER/ FIELD REP 503-231-
Little, Luke (GUEST) LEGIS ASST 230 CHOB 5
Littler, Lisa (ROUZER) DPTY DIST DIR 919-938
Littrell, Avery (BABIN) LEGIS ASST 2236 ....

Lively, Brock (GOODEN) LEGIS AIDE 425 CHOB 53484
Livingston, Austin (NORMAN) COMMUNICATIONS DIR 803-327-1114
Livingston, Chris (LEE, BARBARA) SCHEDULER/EXEC ASST 2470 52661
Lizarraga, Jaime (SPEAKER) SR ADVISOR H232 50100
Lloyd, Brandon (LOWEY) DIST REP 914-428-1707
Lloyd, Elizabeth (SMUCKER) STAFF ASST 127 CHOB 52411
Lloyd, William (STIVERS) FIELD REP 740-654-2654
Loach, Eric M (LAW REV COUNSEL) SR SYS ENGINEER 308 FHOB 62411
Lobel, Zack (JEFFRIES) LEGIS COUNSEL 2433 55936
Lobrano, Wyatt (ABRAHAM) DIST DIR 318-322-3500
Locke, James (DESJARLAIS) LEGIS COUNSEL 2301 56831
Locke, Nancy (CMTE-NATURAL RESOURCES) CHIEF CLERK 1324 56065
Lockerby, Justine (LOWENTHAL) CONSTIT SVCS REP 562-436-3828
Lockman, Michele (BOYLE) CONSTIT SVCS REP 215-335-3355
Lockwood, Bonnie (HIGGINS, BRIAN) SPECIAL PROJ DIR 716-852-3501
Loden, Kathleen (CMTE-HOMELAND SECUR) DPTY STAFF DIR 117 FHOB 68417
Loeb, Isaac (WELCH) SR LEGIS ASST 2187 54115
Loera-Martinez, Monica (ROYBAL-ALLARD) EXEC ASST/SCHEDULER 323-721-8790
Loewe, Erica (CMTE-FINANCIAL SVCS) PRESS SECY 2129 54247
Lofquist, Kurt (RIGGLEMAN) SPECIAL ASST 434-973-9631
Lofton, Lane (CUNNINGHAM) CHIEF OF STAFF 423 CHOB 53176
Logan, Cherita (DAVIS, DANNY K.) DIST DIR 773-533-7520
Loggie, Matthew (LEGIS COUNSEL) STAFF ASST 337 FHOB 56060
Lohr, Mitch (SCHAKOWSKY) LEGIS CORRES/STAFF ASST 2367 52111
Lolli, Tim (GONZALEZ, ANTHONY) CHIEF OF STAFF 1023 53876
Lombardi, Kyle
(MCCARTHY) LEGIS DIR 2468 52915
(MIN LEADER) LEGIS DIR H204 54000
Lomis, Alana (RESCHENTHALER) EXEC ASST 531 CHOB 52065
London, Claire (BACON) EXEC ASST 1024 54155
Lonergan, Vincent (SGT AT ARMS/ID SVCS) ASST/ID SVCS 321 CHOB 53820
Long, Holly (CLEAVER) EXEC ASST/ SCHEDULER 816-842-4545
Long, John (CAO/CAPITOL SVC CTR) DIR - CAPITOL SVC CENTER HT3 58000
Long, Karyn (CLAY) EXEC ASST/SCHEDULER 2428 52406
Long, Michael (SPEAKER) SR ADVISOR/DIR - MEMB SVCS H232 50100
Long, Ryan (CMTE-ENERGY & COMMERCE) DPTY STAFF DIR 2322A 53641
Longoria, Mark (CLOUD) DPTY DIST DIR/DIST FIELD REP 361-894-6446
Lonsberry, Lee (BISHOP, ROB) COMMUNICATIONS DIR/ PRESS SECY 123 CHOB 50453
Look, Judy (YARMUTH) CONG AIDE 502-582-5129
Loomis, Casaday (KING, STEVE) POLICY ADVISOR/DIST SCHEDULER 712-224-4692
Loomis, Jane (BURGESS) CONSTIT LIAISON 940-497-5031
Looney, Jack (SGT AT ARMS/ID SVCS) DIRECTOR/ID SVCS 321 CHOB 53820
Loope, Emilee (CLINE) DIST REP/ COMMUNICATIONS ASST 540-432-2391
Looser, Brian (SHIMKUS) LEGIS DIR 2217 55271
Lopez, Baltazar (ESHOO) SR FIELD REP 650-323-2984
Lopez, Francisco (BARRAGÁN) STAFF ASST 310-831-1799
Lopez, Jacqueline (RUIZ) DIST DIR 760-424-8888
Lopez, Janessa (BUCK) LEGIS AIDE 2455 54676
Lopez, Joseph (COX) DIST REP 559-460-6070
López, Juan (COSTA) CHIEF OF STAFF 2081 53341
Lopez, Mark (VISCLOSKY) CHIEF OF STAFF 219-795-1844
Lopez, Radhames (ESPAILLAT) SPECIAL ASST 212-663-3900
Lopez, Sonya (LUJÁN) CONSTIT LIAISON 505-984-8950
Lopez-Campillo, Juan (CAO/OFC OF EMPLOYEE ADVOCACY) SR ASSOC COUNSEL 301 FHOB 58800
Lopez-Sandoval, Elizabeth (ESCOBAR) COMMUNICATIONS DIR 1505 68331
Loraine, Jennifer (MIN LEADER) SR POLICY ADVISOR H204 54000
Lord, Jonathan (CMTE-ARMED SVCS) PROF STAFF 2117 66235
Lord, Mark (GUTHRIE) DIST DIR 270-842-9896
Lorenzo, Elizabeth (PAYNE) CONSTIT SVCS ASST 201-369-0392
Lorenzo, Vanessa (CAO/FINANCIAL COUNSELING) FINANCIAL COUNSELOR B215 LHOB 61197
Lothian, Lainey (WATKINS) SR LEGIS ASST 1205 56601
Lou, Theresa (CMTE-FOREIGN AFFAIRS) POLICY ANALYST 2064 55021
Loudermilk, Travis (GRAVES, TOM) FIELD REP 706-226-5320
Louis-Charles, Nadgey (HICE) COMMUNICATIONS DIR 409 CHOB 54101
Lounsbury, Connor (HOULAHAN) PRESS SECY 1218 54315
Loutsenhizer, Nicole (INSPECTOR GENERAL) AUDITOR 386 FHOB 61250
Louwagie, Meg (PETERSON) STAFF ASST 507-537-2299
Love, Randy (EVANS) SCHEDULER/EXEC ASST 1105 54001
Love, Reba (SEWELL) CASEWK MGR 205-752-5380
Lovell, Christian (DELAURO) LEGIS ASST 2413 53661
Lovett, Kasey (FLEISCHMANN) COMMUNICATIONS DIR 2410 53271
Lovett, Tracy (PRICE) DIST LIAISON 919-967-7924
Loving, Andrea (CMTE-JUDICIARY) CHIEF COUNSEL 189 FHOB 56906
Loving, Anthony (CAO/ENTERPRISE APPLICATIONS) APPLICA DATABASE SPEC 638 FHOB 66214
Lovinger, Dvora (SARBANES) CHIEF OF STAFF 2370 54016
Lowdermilk, T J (CMTE-APPRO) PROF STAFF MEMB H310 53351
Lowe, Jonathan (CHABOT) LEGIS DIR 2408 52216
Lowe, Molly (AMODEI) LEGIS DIR 104 CHOB 56155
Lowe, Sean (RYAN) STAFF ASST 1126 55261
Lowe, Susan G (SGT AT ARMS/ID SVCS) ASST/ID SVCS 321 CHOB 53820
Lowenstein, Jeffrey (SCHIFF) CHIEF OF STAFF 2269 54176
Lowes, Sue (GOHMERT) DIST STAFF ASST 903-561-6349
Lowrance, Conley (GRANGER) ADMIN ASST 1026 55071
Lowry, Joe (SGT AT ARMS/EMERGENCY MGMT) DIR - PREPAREDNESS 192 FHOB 60950
Lowry, Michael (DUNN) CHIEF OF STAFF 316 CHOB 55235

Lowry, Zachary (MARSHALL) LEGIS ASST 312 CHOB **52715**
Lozano, Josh (NEWHOUSE) DPTY DIST DIR **509-713-7374**
Lozier, Georgia (HUDSON) DPTY DIST DIR **704-786-1612**
Lu, Diem-Mi (FOSTER) SR POLICY ADVISOR/LEGIS COUNSEL 2366 .... **53515**
Lubas, Genevieve (MALINOWSKI) DIST STAFF ASST **908-547-3307**
Lubisich, Matt (KIRKPATRICK) SCHEDULER 309 CHOB **52542**
Lucas, David (DOYLE) CHIEF OF STAFF 306 CHOB **52135**
Lucas, Erin (BUCSHON) SPECIAL PROJ DIR **812-232-0523**
Lucas, Mackenzie (VAN DREW) COMMUNICATIONS DIR 331 CHOB **56572**
Lucero, Kimberly (CLERK/LCS) DPTY CHIEF 2401 .... **51182**
Luchette, Richard (CICILLINE) COMMUNICATIONS DIR 2233 .... **54911**
Lucier, Mike (WEXTON) LEGIS DIR 1217 .... **55136**
Ludwig, Karen (MEUSER) CONSTIT SVCS REP **717-603-1459**
Lue, Bert (CMTE-JOINT TAX) ECONOMIST 502 FHOB **53621**
Lueders, Mary (BROOKS, SUSAN W.) DIR - CONSTIT SVCS **317-848-0201**
Lueken, Paige (CAO/OFFICE OF THE CHIEF HUMAN RESOURCES OFFICER) GENERALIST 102 FHOB **60247**
Luffman, Bunky (HARRIS) COMMUNITY LIAISON **443-944-8624**
Luginbill, Scott (WALKER) CHIEF OF STAFF 1725 .... **53065**
Lukken, Garrett (PERLMUTTER) CONSTIT SVCS REP **303-274-7944**
Lum, Kelvin (BERA) LEGIS DIR 1727 .... **55716**
Lumia, Jason (COOPER) LEGIS DIR/DPTY CHIEF OF STAFF 1536 .... **54311**
Luna, Eli (TORRES SMALL) CASEWKR **575-323-6384**
Luna, Linoshka (GONZÁLEZ-COLÓN) LEGIS CORRES 1609 **52615**
Lundberg, Brittany (CMTE-TRANSP & INFRA) POLICY ANALYST 2251 .... **54472**
Lundmark, Joseph (SGT AT ARMS/POLICE SVCS) DIST SECUR SPECIALIST 173 FHOB **53380**
Lundy, Chris (JEFFRIES) CONSTIT SVCS REP **718-237-2211**
Lunneborg, Nick (EMMER) SR LEGIS ASST 315 CHOB **52331**
Luper, Debbie (ESTES) DIST DIR **316-262-8992**
Lustig, Joseph (RICHMOND) LEGIS ASST 506 CHOB **56636**
Ly, Phong (LOWENTHAL) SR FIELD REP **714-243-4088**
Lyles, Willie (CLYBURN) LEGIS DIR 200 CHOB **53315**
Lyman, April (CAO/CUST EXPER CTR) CUSTOMER ADVOCATE B227 LHOB **58000**
Lynch, Brittany (CMTE-HOMELAND SECUR) PROF STAFF MEMB 176 FHOB **62616**
Lynch, Daniel (LARSON) DIST AIDE **860-278-8888**
Lynch, Daniel (LYNCH) SR DIST REP **617-428-2000**
Lynch, Justin (CMTE-ARMED SVCS) CLERK 2117 .... **63297**
Lynch, Liza (VELA) SCHEDULER/OFFICE MGR 307 CHOB **59901**
Lynch, Paul (ALLEN) CONSTIT SVCS REP **706-228-1980**
Lynn, Hans (WELCH) LEGIS CORRES 2187 .... **54115**
Lynskey, Elizabeth (HARRIS) DIR - CONSTIT SVCS/DIR - DIST AFFAIRS 2334 .... **55311**
Lyon, Laura (TAYLOR) SR LEGIS ASST 1404 .... **54201**
Lyons, Cullen (MALONEY, SEAN PATRICK) LIAISON - MIL & VET **845-561-1259**
Lyons, Holly Woodruff (CMTE-TRANSP & INFRA) STAFF DIR/SR COUNSEL 592 FHOB **54472**
Lytle, Michael (THORNBERRY) CONSTIT SVCS REP **940-692-1700**

Maaiki, Sara (TLAIB) SCHEDULER/OFFICE MGR 1628 .... **55126**
Maas, Jennifer (CAO/HIR – HOUSE WEB SVCS) MGR 645A FHOB **66156**
MacArthur, Chris (MOOLENAAR) SR LEGIS ASST 117 CHOB **53561**
MacDonald, Asher (MOULTON) SPECIAL ASST 1127 .... **58020**
MacDonald, Don
(CMTE-FOREIGN AFFAIRS) PROF STAFF - MIN 5212 .... **66434**
(SHERMAN) CHIEF OF STAFF 2181 .... **55911**
MacDonald, Liam (ROE) LEGIS CORRES 102 CHOB **56356**
Mace, Emily (WESTERMAN) LEGIS COUNSEL 209 CHOB **53772**
MacFarlan, Tori (OLSON) SR FIELD REP **281-494-2690**
MacFarlane, Alex (THOMPSON, MIKE) COMMUNICATIONS DIR 406 CHOB **53311**
Macheledt, Marshall (JORDAN) LEGIS CORRES 2056 .... **52676**
Mack, Jonathan (MEUSER) STAFF ASST 326 CHOB **56511**
Mack, Tim (DEAN) PRESS AIDE 129 CHOB **54731**
MacKenzie, Matthew (CMTE-AGRIC) SR COUNSEL 1301 .... **52171**
Mackey, Alex (ROE) LEGIS FELLOW 102 CHOB **56356**
Mackie, Kathleen T (CMTE-JOINT TAX) SR ECONOMIST 595 FHOB **67575**
Mackney, Kim (LONG) CASEWKR **417-781-1041**
MacLean, Casey (CMTE-NATURAL RESOURCES) SUBCOMM CLERK 1332 .... **56065**
MacLeod, Carter (KIND) STAFF ASST 1502 .... **55506**
MacMann, Julie (STIVERS) STAFF ASST 2234 .... **52015**
MacNaughton, John (CMTE-ARMED SVCS) PROF STAFF 2340 .... **64532**
Macri, Suzanne (HIGGINS, BRIAN) DIST OFFICE MGR/CASEWKR - IMMIGRATION **716-252-1274**
Maddatu, Patricia (CLERK/LRC) OUTREACH LIBRARIAN B81 CHOB **65200**
Madden, Wendy (MCKINLEY) FIELD REP **304-284-8506**
Maddock, Ryan (KEATING) DIST REP **508-771-6868**
Maddux, David (CAO/CONGRESSIONAL STAFF ACAD) DIRECTOR B241 LHOB **63800**
Madni, Brittany (BALDERSON) LEGIS DIR 1221 .... **55355**
Madrid, Max (CORREA) DIST REP **714-559-6190**
Madrigal, Lindsey (COX) DIST SCHEDULER **559-460-6070**
Madrigal-Hooper, Iliana (HUFFMAN) DIST SCHEDULER **415-258-9657**
Madsen, Cam (STEWART) LEGIS DIR 2242 .... **59730**
Magary, Adam (CLOUD) CHIEF OF STAFF 1314 .... **57742**
Magee, Erin (PETERS) DIST SCHEDULER/FIELD REP **858-455-5550**
Maghamfar, Dustin (CMTE-ENERGY & COMMERCE) AIR & CLIMATE COUNSEL 2125 .... **54407**
Magruder, Timothy (CAO/FURNISHINGS) MASTER FINISHER WA22 RHOB **58000**
Mahan, Kathy (COSTA) DPTY CHIEF OF STAFF/ DIST DIR **559-495-1620**
Mahar-Piersma, Auke (CMTE-TRANSP & INFRA) PROF STAFF 2251 .... **54472**
Maher, Dan (BOYLE) SCHEDULER/SPECIAL ASST 1133 .... **56111**
Mahfood, Maggie (CAO) EXEC ASST HB28 .... **55555**
Mahler, Sam (GRAVES, TOM) SR LEGIS ASST 2078 .... **55211**
Mahmood, Saman (ROSE, MAX) AREA DIR **718-667-3313**
Mahoney, Christina (CLEAVER) LEGIS DIR 2335 .... **54535**
Mahr, Tom (MAJ LEADER) POLICY DIR H107 .... **53130**

Maiale, Mike (PERRY) STAFF ASST 1207 **55836**
Maiden, Leigh (LANGEVIN) LEGIS ASST - MIL 2077 **52735**
Maiden, Lewis (CAO/LOGISTICS) LOGISTICS & DIST SPEC B23 FHOB **59474**
Maillet, Patrick (MCCOLLUM) LEGIS ASST 2256 **56631**
Maiman, Seth (SABLAN) LEGIS DIR 2411 **52646**
Maitland, Michael (NORCROSS) CHIEF OF STAFF 2437 **56501**
Majette, Ebony (MORELLE) STAFF ASST 1317 **53615**
Major, Lisa (CMTE-INTELLIGENCE) PROF STAFF - MIN HVC304 **54121**
Maldonado, Alexandra (PALLONE) DIST REP **732-249-8892**
Maldonado, Jenn (VARGAS) FIELD REP **619-422-5963**
Maldonado, Rose Ann (CASTRO) DIR - CONSTIT SVCS **210-348-8216**
Malec, Nicole (CONNOLLY) CONSTIT SVCS REP **703-256-3071**
Malec, Stuart (LANGEVIN) CONSTIT SVCS REP **401-732-9400**
Maleczkowicz, Nicholas (FITZPATRICK) CONSTIT ADVOCATE **215-579-8102**
Malen, Christopher (HURD) SR LEGIS ASST 317 CHOB **54511**
Malicdem, Aaron-John (BUTTERFIELD) STAFF ASST/DIR - OPS 2080 **53101**
Malik, Mariam (CMTE-HOUSE ADMIN) STAFF ASST 1309 **52061**
Mallard, Kris (CMTE-APPRO) PROF STAFF MEMB 2006 **55834**
Mallik, Avy (CMTE-FINANCIAL SVCS) SR COUNSEL - MAJ 2129 **54247**
Mallison, Bill (CMTE-VET AFFAIRS) SUBCOMM STAFF DIR - TECHNOLOGY MODERNIZATION SUBCOMM 3460 **51900**
Mallon, Michael (CAO/LOGISTICS) MGR - LOGISTICS WA23 RHOB **51637**
Mallory, DeWayne (CASTOR) OUTREACH DIR **813-871-2817**
Malloy, Deon (CAO/HIR – IT CUSTOMER SOLUTIONS) SUPERVISOR 2067 **64796**
Malloy, Jerome (WALKER) CONSTIT LIAISON **336-333-5005**
Malloy, Terri (ZELDIN) STAFF ASST **631-289-1097**
Malmberg, Alice (ESHOO) STAFF ASST **650-323-2984**
Malone, Eboni (LAWRENCE) EXEC SCHEDULER 2463 **55802**
Malone, Katie (CUMMINGS) SPECIAL ASST **410-719-8777**
Malone, Patrick (HIMES) COMMUNICATIONS DIR 1227 **55541**
Maloof, Michael (BURCHETT) LEGIS ASST 1122 **55435**
Malowitz, Jesse (LOWEY) DIST REP **845-639-3485**
Maloy, Celeste (STEWART) COUNSEL 2242 **59730**
Maloy, Rudolph (LAWSON) FIELD REP **850-558-9450**
Malspeis, Momi (RUTHERFORD) DIR - CONSTIT SVCS **904-831-5205**
Manasco, James (ADERHOLT) FIELD REP **256-546-0201**
Mancilla, Beatriz (HUIZENGA) DIST REP **616-570-0917**
Mandalika, Swapanthi (KHANNA) FIELD REP **408-436-2720**
Manecke, Dominic (BEATTY) COMMUNICATIONS DIR 2303 **54324**
Maneval, Chris (EMMER) CHIEF OF STAFF 315 CHOB **52331**
Manganello, Jennifer (CARTWRIGHT) CASEWKR/SPEECHWRITER **570-341-1050**
Mangano, Jennifer (GOTTHEIMER) LEGIS CORRES 213 CHOB **54465**
Mangini, Louis (DELAURO) LABOR LIAISON **203-562-3718**
Mangrum, Pearl
(INTERPARLMN AFFAIRS) FINANCIAL ADMIN HC4 **61766**
(PELOSI) FINANCIAL ADMIN 1236 **54965**
(SPEAKER) FINANCIAL DIR H232 **50100**

Mankiewicz, Lisa (MITCHELL) COORD - CONSTIT SVCS **586-997-5010**
Manley, Bret (DAVIS, RODNEY) CHIEF OF STAFF 1740 **52371**
Manley, Dominique (BOST) DIST STAFF ASST **618-622-0766**
Manley, Nicole (CLINE) LEGIS DIR 1009 **55431**
Mann, Liz (CURTIS) ASST COUNSEL 125 CHOB **57751**
Mann, Nikita (TURNER) LEGIS ASST - MIL 2082 **56465**
Manning, Matt (PANETTA) LEGIS DIR 212 CHOB **52861**
Manosalvas, Marcos (CMTE-FINANCIAL SVCS) DIGITAL DIR 2129 **54247**
Mansbach, Hannah (QUIGLEY) LEGIS AIDE 2458 **54061**
Mansbach, Shana (SPEAKER) DIR - SPEECHWRITING H232 **50100**
Mansour, Michael (KINZINGER) LEGIS DIR 2245 **53635**
Manter, Emily (GOLDEN) CONSTIT SVCS REP **207-241-6767**
Mantor, Karin (HAGEDORN) SCHEDULER **507-323-6090**
Manwaring, Lucetia (KILDEE) SR CONSTIT SVCS REP **810-238-8627**
Manzer, Tracy (SPEIER) COMMUNICATIONS DIR 2465 **53531**
Manzo, Maria (FOSTER) OUTREACH DIR **630-585-7672**
Maple, Kaala (CLYBURN) CASEWKR **803-799-1100**
Maples, Chris (HUDSON) CONSTIT RELATIONS REP **910-997-2070**
Maples, Chris (HUDSON) CASEWKR **910-246-5374**
Mara, Lisa (LAMALFA) REGIONAL DIR **530-878-5035**
Marable, Eugene (CAO/ASSET MANAGEMENT) ACCNT MGMT COUNSELOR 6110 **56792**
Marc, Shelly (LEE, BARBARA) DPTY CHIEF OF STAFF 2470 **52661**
Marca, Danny (CMTE-FOREIGN AFFAIRS) ASST SYS ADMIN 2170 **66592**
Marcel-Keyes, Andrew (MCCLINTOCK) SR LEGIS ASST 2312 **52511**
Marcello, Pamela (SCHIFF) DIST REP **818-450-2900**
Marceny, Veronica (CROW) CONSTIT ADVOCATE **720-748-7514**
Marchese, Nino (MASSIE) LEGIS ASST 2453 **53465**
Marchese, Steve (CMTE-APPRO) CLERK HT2 **52041**
Marciano, Tina (FRANKEL) CONSTIT SVCS **561-998-9045**
Marcus, Jeremy (CARTWRIGHT) DPTY CHIEF OF STAFF 1034 **55546**
Marcus, Ralph (CAO/HOUSE RECORDING STUDIO) TECH DIR 2010 **53941**
Marcus, Robert (SCHAKOWSKY) CHIEF OF STAFF 2367 **52111**
Marder, Paul (BANKS) MIL FELLOW 1713 **54436**
Mardik, Thomas (BRADY) DPTY DIST DIR **936-441-5700**
Marek, Natalie (MALINOWSKI) STAFF ASST 426 CHOB **55361**
Margolis, Sara (HOULAHAN) LEGIS ASST 1218 **54315**
Mariam, Salem (SMITH, ADAM) SCHEDULING DIR 2264 **58901**
Mariani, Ian (CMTE-APPRO) COMMUNICATIONS ASST H307 **52771**
Marin, Mark (CMTE-OVERSIGHT & GOVT REFORM) DIR - OVERSIGHT 2105 **55074**
Markgraf, Teresa (SCHRADER) DIST SCHEDULER **503-557-1324**
Markiewicz, Graham (HECK) LEGIS COUNSEL 2452 **59740**
Markle, Lindsay (BANKS) LEGIS ASST - MIL 1713 **54436**
Markley, Sarah (CMTE-FOREIGN AFFAIRS) STAFF ASSOC 2066 **68467**
Markman, Clio (ROSE, MAX) AREA DIR **718-667-3313**

Markowitz, Jessica (AMODEI) EXEC ASST 104 CHOB.......... 56155
Marks, Shana (ESPAILLAT) COMMUNITY LIAISON.......... 212-663-3900
Marlin, John Tepper (CMTE-JOINT ECON) SR ECONOMIST - DEM 368 FHOB.......... 63228
Marlow, Joel (CAO/HIR - ENTERPRISE MESSAGING AND MOBILITY) SR SYS ENGINEER 623 FHOB.......... 64040
Marm, Deborah (NC03) CASEWKR.......... 252-931-1003
Marphis, Pamela (SCALISE) LIAISON - CONSTIT SVCS.......... 504-837-1259
Marquardt, Kelly (DELBENE) CONG LIAISON.......... 425-485-0085
Marquez, Angel (VARGAS) FIELD REP.......... 619-422-5963
Marquez, Denise (TORRES) DIST SCHEDULER.......... 909-481-6474
Marquez, Gabriela (CÁRDENAS) DIST DIR.......... 818-221-3718
Marquez, Nicole (SHALALA) DC SCHEDULER 1320.......... 53931
Marquez, Tommy (HUNTER) CASEWK DIR.......... 619-448-5201
Marquez-Paz, Natasha (GONZÁLEZ-COLÓN) SCHEDULER 1609.......... 52615
Marquis, Nivia (UPTON) CONSTIT SVCS REP.......... 269-385-0039
Marron, Brenna (HOUSE DEM CONG CMPGN CMTE) DIR - MBR ENGAGEMENT & POLITICAL STRATEGY.......... 202-863-1500
Marroquin, Dixie (CLERK/SVCS GRPS) HOUSE FLOOR OPS CLERK H222.......... 57330
Marrow, Dan (GOTTHEIMER) SR LEGIS ASST 213 CHOB.......... 54465
Marsh, James (KELLY, MIKE) EXEC ASST 1707.......... 55406
Marsh, Patti (COHEN) EXEC ASST/DIST SCHEDULER.......... 901-544-4131
Marsh, Steve (CAO/ACCOUNTING) MGR 3110.......... 62292
Marshall, John
(CMTE-ENERGY & COMMERCE) POLICY COORD 2125.......... 52927
(RUSH) SR POLICY ADVISOR 2188.......... 54372
Marshall, John (MALINOWSKI) COORD - GRANTS & SPEC PROJ.......... 908-547-3307
Marsico, Jodi (PERRY) CONSTIT SVCS REP.......... 717-603-4980
Marston, Alexander (CMTE-HOMELAND SECUR) SUBCOMM STAFF DIR - TRANSPORTATION AND MARITIME SECURITY SUBCOMM 176 FHOB.......... 62616
Martell, Katrina (HASTINGS) LEGIS ASST 2353.......... 51313
Martens, John (CMTE-APPRO) PROF STAFF MEMB 1016.......... 53481
Marter, Jean (CMTE-FINANCIAL SVCS) CLERK 2129.......... 54247
Marticorena, Brieana (PORTER) LEGIS DIR 1117.......... 55611
Martin, Amanda (SWALWELL) CONSTIT SVCS REP.......... 510-370-3322
Martin, Andrea (CARSON) LEGAL COUNSEL/SR POLICY ADVISOR 2135.......... 54011
Martin, Bryan (NC03) LEGIS ASST 2333.......... 53415
Martin, Christopher (CAO/FURNISHINGS) MASTER CABINET MAKER WA25 RHOB.......... 58000
Martin, Christopher (HOUSE REPUB CONF) DIR - RAPID RESPONSE 1420.......... 55107
Martin, Daniel (ESTES) LEGIS ASST 1524.......... 56216
Martin, Donyale (DINGELL) CASEWKR.......... 313-278-2936
Martin, Eric (PASCRELL) SCHEDULER.......... 973-523-5152
Martin, Gail (CLERK/REPORTERS) EDITOR HT59.......... 55621
Martin, Jaria (CMTE-ED & WORKFORCE) STAFF ASST 2176.......... 53725
Martin, John (CMTE-ED & WORKFORCE) COUNSEL - WORKFORCE POLICY 6150.......... 57101
Martin, John (STEVENS) SCHEDULER 227 CHOB.......... 58171
Martin, Josh (THORNBERRY) CHIEF OF STAFF 2208.......... 53706
Martin, Mary (CMTE-ENERGY & COMMERCE) CHIEF COUNSEL 2322A.......... 53641
Martin, Michael (HERN) LEGIS ASST/COUNSEL 1019.......... 52211
Martin, Monica (MCCARTHY) CONSTIT SVCS.......... 661-327-3611
Martin, Prescott (CMTE-AGRIC) SR COUNSEL 1301.......... 52171
Martin, Robin (JOYCE, DAVID P.) CASEWKR.......... 440-352-3939
Martin, Sarah (CMTE-ED & WORKFORCE) PROF STAFF MEMB 6150.......... 57101
Martin, Theresa (HIGGINS, CLAY) CASEWKR.......... 337-656-2833
Martin, Todd (MARCHANT) DIR - DIST AFFAIRS.......... 972-556-0162
Martin, Will (GOODEN) COMMUNICATIONS DIR 425 CHOB.......... 53484
Martin, Zach (PETERSON) LEGIS ASST 2204.......... 52165
Martinez, Albert
(GONZALEZ, VICENTE) DIST DIR.......... 361-209-3027
(GONZALEZ, VICENTE) DIST DIR.......... 361-279-3341
Martinez, Alex (GRIJALVA) CONSTIT SVCS.......... 520-622-6788
Martinez, Ana (CMTE-RULES) STAFF ASST H312.......... 59091
Martinez, Austin (CASTRO) CONSTIT SVCS REP.......... 210-348-8216
Martinez, Brittany
(MCCARTHY) PRESS SECY 2468.......... 52915
(MIN LEADER) DPTY PRESS SECY H204.......... 54000
Martinez, Eimy (HAYES) OUTREACH REP.......... 860-223-8412
Martinez, Jonathan (VELÁZQUEZ) SR LEGIS ASST 2302.......... 52361
Martinez, Laura (CORREA) CASEWKR.......... 714-559-6190
Martinez, Leslie (CUELLAR) DIST PRESS SECY.......... 956-725-0639
Martinez, Michelle (SOTO) DIST DIR.......... 407-452-1171
Martinez, Natalie (CRAIG) LEGIS ASST 1523.......... 52271
Martinez, Raul (SHALALA) DIST DIR.......... 305-668-2285
Martinez, Teresa (GOSAR) DIR - OUTREACH & COALITIONS.......... 480-882-2697
Martinez, Travis (NEWHOUSE) LEGIS ASST 1414.......... 55816
Martinez, Vanessa (ROYBAL-ALLARD) DIST OFFICE MGR/SPECIAL ASST.......... 323-721-8790
Martinez-Cartagena, Charles (CASTOR) PRESS ASST/OUTREACH ASST.......... 813-871-2817
Martins, Richard (CAO/HIR – NETWORKING ENGINEERING AND OPS) MGR 687 FHOB.......... 66268
Martirosyan, Maria (GOMEZ) LEGIS CORRES 1530.......... 56235
Martorony, Gene (SIRES) CHIEF OF STAFF 2268.......... 57919
Marvel, Toby (BAIRD) LEGIS ASST 532 CHOB.......... 55037
Masga, Harry James (SABLAN) STAFF ASST.......... 670-532-2647
Mash, Kim (ROSE, JOHN W.) CASEWKR.......... 615-206-8204
Masheter, Frederick (CAO/ACQUIS MGMT) PURCHASING AGENT 5112.......... 61080
Masiya, Shingayi (GABBARD) CONSTIT OUTREACH REP.......... 808-541-1986
Mask, Karen (SPANBERGER) DIST DIR.......... 804-401-4110
Mason, Chandler (EVANS) LEGIS CORRES/STAFF ASST 1105.......... 54001
Mason, Graham (LUJÁN) DPTY CHIEF OF STAFF 2323.......... 56190
Mason, Tamika (MAJ WHIP) TECH DIR H329.......... 63210
Mason, Tron (CAO/HIR – NETWORKING ENGINEERING AND OPS) SR NETWK COMMUNICATIONS SPEC 663 FHOB.......... 60482
Mason, William (GREEN, MARK E.) DEVELOPMENT DIR 533 CHOB.......... 52811
Massaro, A Paul, III (COMMIS ON SECUR & COOP IN EUR) POLICY ADVISOR 234 FHOB.......... 51901

Massarolo, Charles (KAPTUR) STAFF ASST 216-767-5933
Massengale, Doug (CAO/HOUSE RECORDING STUDIO) CHIEF ENGINEER 2010 53941
Massey, Edwilla (CLAY) DIR - CONSTIT SVCS 314-367-1970
Mastrangelo, David
(LURIA) FINANCIAL ADMIN 534 CHOB 54215
(TONKO) DIR - OPS 2369 55076
Masucci, Justin (CMTE-APPRO) PROF STAFF MEMB 2362A 52638
Matambo, Mutale (CUMMINGS) SPECIAL ASST 410-685-9199
Matar, Sara (ZELDIN) SR LEGIS AIDE 2441 53826
Matesic, Hannah (CMTE-ED & WORKFORCE) DIR - OPS 2101 54527
Mathews, Ella (COOPER) STAFF ASST 1536 54311
Mathieu, Herline (CLEAVER) DC SCHEDULER/LEGIS AIDE 2335 54535
Mathis, Josh
(CMTE-SCIENCE) STAFF DIR 394 FHOB 56371
(LUCAS) STAFF DIR 2405 55565
Mathis, Marc (CAO/HIR – NETWORKING ENGINEERING AND OPS) NETWK TECH 652C FHOB 66430
Mathisen, Dean (BACON) SR CONSTIT LIAISON 402-938-0300
Mathur, Rricha (CHU) LEGIS COUNSEL 2423 55464
Matlaga, Michael (CMTE-FOREIGN AFFAIRS) POLICY ANALYST 2420 55021
Matos-Moran, Robert (WATSON COLEMAN) CONSTIT SVCS 609-883-0026
Matoush, Monica (CMTE-ARMED SVCS) COMMUNICATIONS DIR 2117 65048
Matt, Svetlana (MCNERNEY) LEGIS ASST 2265 51947
Matteson, Nate (KENNEDY) STAFF ASST 304 CHOB 55931
Matthews, Christopher (KEATING) COORD - OUTREACH 508-746-9000
Matthews, Heidi (GONZALEZ, ANTHONY) DIST DIR 330-599-7037
Matthews, Jonathan, III (MCCAUL) DPTY COMMUNICATIONS DIR 2001 52401
Matthews, Linda (FUDGE) SCHEDULER/DIST OFFICE MGR 216-522-4900
Matthews, Macey (BRINDISI) COMMUNICATIONS DIR 329 CHOB 53665
Matthews, Michael (BROWN) LEGIS ASST 1323 58699
Matthews, Sarah (CMTE-ENERGY & COMMERCE) PRESS SECY 2322A 53641
Matthews, Stacey (ROGERS, HAROLD) CASEWKR 606-679-8346
Matthews-Storey, Angie (SCOTT, DAVID) CONSTIT SVCS/FIELD REP/OFFICE MGR 770-432-5405
Mattina, Bobby (HECK) COMMUNICATIONS DIR 2452 59740
Mattocks, Tom (CMTE-AGRIC) PRESS SECY 1301 52171
Matty, Paloma (GRIJALVA) DIST AIDE 1511 52435
Maturo, Justin (TAKANO) LEGIS DIR 420 CHOB 52305
Mauldin, Evan (CAO/FINANCIAL COUNSELING) MGR B215 LHOB 61186
Mautz, James (STEFANIK) STAFF ASST 318 CHOB 54611
Maxwell, Ana (CLYBURN) STAFF ASST 803-799-1100
Maxwell, Bryanta (CLYBURN) DIST EXEC ASST 803-799-1100
Maxwell, Chloe (HILL, J. FRENCH) DIST REP/ COORD - GRANTS & SPEC PROJ 501-324-5941
Maxwell, Josh (CMTE-AGRIC) SR PROF STAFF 1010 50317
Maxwell, Richard (HILL, J. FRENCH) DIST REP/ LIAISON - MIL & VET 501-324-5941
Maxwell, Sean (PRICE) LEGIS DIR 2108 51784
May, Eric (MCADAMS) LEGIS DIR 130 CHOB 53011
Mayayeva, Yana (FRANKEL) LEGIS ASST 2305 59890
Maybin, Jenny (MEADOWS) FIELD REP 828-693-5660
Mayeda, Ali (BONAMICI) DIST REP/OUTREACH REP/PRESS ASST 503-469-6010
Mayer, Jesse (CUNNINGHAM) DIR - OPS 423 CHOB 53176
Mayes, Nina (FLETCHER) OUTREACH DIRECTOR 713-353-8680
May-Gillespie, Sarita (CAO/HIR – ENTERPRISE INFRASTRUCT) SR TELECOMMUNICATIONS ADMIN 680 FHOB 56677
Maynard, Rick (COHEN) CONSTIT SVCS REP 901-544-4131
Mazol, Deborah (BIGGS) CHIEF OF STAFF 1318 52635
Mazyck, Veleter (FUDGE) CHIEF OF STAFF 2344 57032
Mazzola, Katherine (WITTMAN) LEGIS CORRES 2055 54261
Mbongo, Eyole (CASTRO) LEGIS CORRES/STAFF ASST 2241 53236
McAdams, Callie (CMTE-AGRIC) DEPUTY CHIEF ECONOMIST 1010 50317
McAfee, Andrew (WENSTRUP) FIELD REP 513-474-7777
McAfee, Karen (CMTE-WAYS & MEANS) STAFF DIR FOR OVERSIGHT 1129 51025
McAllister, Thomas (DUNCAN, JEFF) SCHEDULER/ OFFICE MGR 2229 55301
McAloon, Kevin (CMTE-ENERGY & COMMERCE) PROF STAFF MEMB 2125 52927
McAndrews, Sean (MEADOWS) LEGIS CORRES 2160 56401
McArdle, Dawn (GAETZ) DIST DIR 850-479-1183
McAuliffe, Emily (CMTE-SCIENCE) STAFF ASST - MAJ 2321 56375
McBeth, Agnes (ROSE, MAX) ECON DEV REP 718-667-3313
McBrayer, Thomas (FOXX) STAFF ASST 828-265-0240
McBride, Debby (ROGERS, MIKE) OFFICE MGR/ CASEWKR 2184 53261
McBride, Erin (ROUZER) LEGIS CORRES 2439 52731
McBride, Lauren (SGT AT ARMS/EMERGENCY MGMT) EMERGENCY MGMT SPEC 192 FHOB 60950
McBride-Chambers, Liz (CAO/EMPLOYEE ASSISTANCE) DIRECTOR 140 FHOB 52400
McCabe, Conor (POCAN) DIGITAL DIR/PRESS SECY 1421. 52906
McCabe, Michael, Jr (FITZPATRICK) LEGIS ASST 1722 54276
McCabe, Sean (WALKER) SR LEGIS ASST 1725 53065
McCaffrey, Barbara (CLERK/SVCS GRPS) COORD - CONGRESSWOMN STE H235 54196
McCain, Brian (TIPTON) DIST DIR 719-542-1073
McCain, Ed (GOODEN) DIST DIR 214-765-6789
McCall, Ronda (CLERK/SVCS GRPS) CLOAKRM FOOD MGR - MAJ H222 61154
McCampbell, Denzel (TLAIB) COMMUNICATIONS DIR 313-463-6220
McCandless, David (CHABOT) DIST REP 513-421-8704
McCane, Chris (MASSIE) DIST DIR 859-426-0080
McCann, Chris (DEAN) LEGIS ASST 129 CHOB 54731
McCann, Kristin (MORELLE) DIST DIR 585-232-4850
McCarren, Blake (STEVENS) PRESS SECY 227 CHOB 58171
McCarthy, Jessica (NEWHOUSE) DIST REP 509-452-3243

McCarthy, John (SCALISE) FELLOW 2049 53015
McCarthy, John (BOYLE) CHIEF OF STAFF 1133 56111
McCarthy, Kyle (O'HALLERAN) STAFF ASST 520-316-0839
McCarty, Cody (TORRES SMALL) DIST FIELD REP/CASEWKR 575-323-6384
McCarty, Molly (CMTE-ETHICS) INVESTIGATOR 1015 57103
McCauley, Erica (CAO/FINANCIAL COUNSELING) FINANCIAL COUNSELOR B215 LHOB 65082
McClain, Lauren (CMTE-HOMELAND SECUR) SUBCOMM STAFF DIR - EMERGENCY PREPAREDNESS, RESPONSE, AND RECOVERY SUBCOMM 176 FHOB 62616
McCleaf, Colin (SARBANES) CONSTIT SVCS REP 410-832-8890
McClelland, Cody (MCEACHIN) DIR - SR POLICY 314 CHOB 56365
McClelland, Ethan (CMTE-HOMELAND SECUR) PARLIAMENTARIAN 176 FHOB 62616
McClelland, Katherine (CMTE-ED & WORKFORCE) PROF STAFF 230 FHOB 50868
McClure, Janelle (ALLRED) LEGIS DIR 328 CHOB 52231
McClure, Randy (BERGMAN) CASEWORK - VETS 231-944-7633
McCollum, Kelly Lungren (GRIFFITH) CHIEF OF STAFF 2202 53861
McCollum, Sandra (RUSH) RECEPTIONIST 773-779-2400
McCone, Kelly (POCAN) OFFICE MGR/SCHEDULER 1421 52906
McConnell, Forrest (CMTE-HOMELAND SECUR) GEN COUNSEL 117 FHOB 68417
McConnell, Karen (CLERK/REPORTERS) OFFICIAL REPORTER HT59 55621
McConnell, Meghan (SÁNCHEZ) LEGIS AIDE 2329 56676
McCormack, Ryan (DUFFY) LEGIS DIR 1714 53365
McCormick, James (CMTE-APPRO) PROF STAFF MEMB 1040A 53481
McCormick-Torres, Melanie (BURGESS) CASEWK DIR 940-497-5031
McCoy, Moyer (CMTE-WAYS & MEANS) CLERK/LEGIS ASST 1129 51025
McCoy, Raymond (PELOSI) CONG AIDE 415-556-4862
McCrary, David (MCHENRY) DIR - CONSTIT SVCS 828-327-6100
McCreary, Clay (MEADOWS) FIELD REP 828-426-8701
McCrea-Wood, Artrice (CAO/OFFICE OF THE CHIEF HUMAN RESOURCES OFFICER) HUMAN RESOURCES COORD 102 FHOB 60266
McCullough, Mary (SPEAKER) CHIEF OF STAFF H232 50100
McCullough, Matt (BOST) CHIEF OF STAFF 1440 55661
McCullough, Tom (POSEY) LEGIS CORRES/STAFF ASST 2150 53671
McCully, Shannon (CMTE-APPRO) PROF STAFF MEMB H310 53351
McCumber, Kevin (CLERK/LEGIS OPS) DPTY CHIEF HT13 51454
McCune, Collin (CMTE-FINANCIAL SVCS) DIR - MBR SVCS & COALITIONS 4340 57502
McDaniel, Nathan (ROY) DIST DIR 210-821-5024
McDaniels, Virginia (AXNE) STAFF ASST 330 CHOB 55476
McDermott, Kevin (CMTE-ED & WORKFORCE) SR LABOR POLICY ADVISOR 2051C 53725
McDermott, Lauren (KEATING) COUNSEL/ COMMUNICATIONS DIR 2351 53111
McDevitt, Mark (TRAHAN) COMMUNICATIONS DIR 1616 53411
McDonald, Bradley (CAO/ENTERPRISE APPLICATIONS) MGR B70A FHOB 66437
McDonald, David (COLLINS, DOUG) FIELD REP 770-297-3388
McDonald, Diamond (VARGAS) STAFF ASST 2244 58045
McDonald, Therese (SCANLON) MGR - CONSTIT SVCS 610-626-1913
McDonough, Aisling (CMTE-ENERGY & COMMERCE) POLICY COORD 2125 52927
McDowell, Addison (BUDD) CONSTIT SVCS REP 336-998-1313
McDowell, Sheila (CMTE-BUDGET) OFFICE MGR 204E CHOB 67200
McDuffie, Bennetta (CLERK/LRC) ADMIN ASST B81 CHOB 65200
McDuffie, Damion (NORTON) CONSTIT LIAISON 202-408-9041
McElvein, Elizabeth (CMTE-JUDICIARY) PROF STAFF MEMB 2138 53951
McEvoy, Daniel (SGT AT ARMS/EMERGENCY MGMT) EMERGENCY MGMT SPEC 192 FHOB 60950
McFadden, Miranda (CAO/BUDGET POLICY) FINANCIAL ANALYST 3240 61474
McFadden, Saint Juan (CAO/PAYROLL & BENEFITS) SR GENERALIST B215 LHOB 56456
McFall, Morgan (ROY) CONSTIT LIAISON 512-871-5959
McFarland, Kyle (CMTE-HOMELAND SECUR) DIR - SECUR 176 FHOB 62616
McFarland, William (SGT AT ARMS/HOUSE SECURITY) DIRECTOR HVC301 62044
McGarry, Daniel (CMTE-APPRO) PROF STAFF MEMB 283 FHOB 53881
McGarry, Thomas (CAO/FURNISHINGS) LEAD CABINET MAKER WA25 RHOB 58000
McGarvey, Carla (SHALALA) LEGIS DIR 1320 53931
McGavran, Kathleen (CALVERT) CASEWKR 951-277-0042
McGee, Ashanti (LEE, SUSIE) DIST REP 702-963-9336
McGee, Mike (CLERK/LRC) SR REQUISITIONS & PRINTING CLERK B81 CHOB 65200
McGehee, J D (WESTERMAN) DIST DIR 501-609-9796
McGinn, Matthew (CICILLINE) LEGIS ASST 2233 54911
McGinnis, Michael (CMTE-SMALL BUSINESS) DPTY PRESS SECY/DIGITAL STRATEGIST 2361 54038
McGlinch, Peg (CMTE-WAYS & MEANS) SR COUNSEL 1136 55522
McGlinchey, Daniel (CMTE-FINANCIAL SVCS) DIR - INTERNATIONAL AFFAIRS 2129 54247
McGlone, Edward (CMTE-TRANSP & INFRA) PROF STAFF 2165 54472
McGovern, Sarah (ADAMS) COMMUNICATIONS DIR 2436 51510
McGowan, Colleen (LAMALFA) LEGIS DIR 322 CHOB 53076
McGregor, Courtney (BLUNT ROCHESTER) STATE DIR 302-830-2330
McGuinness, Jackie (SEWELL) COMMUNICATIONS DIR 2201 52665
McGuinness, Michael (LAWRENCE) COMMUNITY OUTREACH SPEC 248-356-2052
McGuire, Caitlyn (LIPINSKI) LEGIS ASST 2346 55701
McGuire, James C (CMTE-JOINT TAX) ECONOMIST 595 FHOB 67575
McGuire, Kevin (RUPPERSBERGER) STAFF ASST 410-628-2701

McGuire, Ryan (CRIST) LEGIS ASST 215 CHOB 55961
McHale, Sterling (PETERS) LEGIS DIR 2338 50508
McHan, Abby (CLOUD) LEGIS ASST/LEGIS CORRES 1314 57742
McIlvaine, Lauren (GABBARD) PRESS SECY 1433 54906
McInnis, Margaret (KAPTUR) LEGIS ASST 2186 54146
McIntosh, Tina (LOUDERMILK) CASE MGR 770-429-1776
McKay, Kyle (WALKER) STAFF ASST 1725 53065
McKee, Scott (CMTE-APPRO) PROF STAFF MEMB 2362B 53421
McKelvey, Will (KHANNA) LEGIS CORRES/LEGIS ASST 221 CHOB 52631
McKemey, Tripp (GIANFORTE) SR LEGIS ASST 1222 53211
McKenna, Brenda (HAALAND) FIELD REP 505-288-6224
McKeogh, Katie
(MIN WHIP) PRESS ASST H148 50197
(SCALISE) PRESS ASST 2049 53015
McKeon, Seamus (LARSEN) LEGIS CORRES 2113 52605
McKeown, Kati (MCCARTHY) CONSTIT SVCS 661-327-3611
McKibben, Megan (SCHRADER) FIELD REP 503-557-1324
McKiernan, Neil (COURTNEY) CHIEF OF STAFF 2332 52076
McKinley, Jared (LEWIS) COORD - OUTREACH 404-659-0116
McKinney, Patrick (KATKO) CONSTIT SVCS REP 315-423-5657
McKinney, Paula (BOYLE) CONSTIT SVCS REP. 267-335-5643
McKinney, Tamel (MURPHY) DIST FIELD REP 888-205-5421
McKinstry, Karen (CLERK/ART & ARCHIVES) DPTY CHIEF JEFFERSON BUILDING, ATTIC 61300
McKittrick, David (CAO/ENTERPRISE APPLICATIONS) SR BUSINESS PROCESS APPLICA SPEC B69 FHOB 61053
McKittrick, Kerry (LANGEVIN) LEGIS ASST 2077 52735
McKnight, Luke (ROBY) STAFF ASST 504 CHOB 52901
McLain-Snipes, Amanda (HORN) DIST DIR 405-602-3074
McLaren, Ellen (DEUTCH) DPTY CHIEF OF STAFF 2447 53001
McLaren, Moutray (TIMMONS) CHIEF OF STAFF 313 CHOB 56030
McLaren, Nicole (SOTO) LEGIS COUNSEL 1507 59889
McLaren, Ryan (WELCH) OUTREACH REP 802-652-2450
McLaughlin, Lawrence P (CLERK/LEGIS OPS) JOURNAL CLERK HT13 55558
McLaughlin, Paul (CMTE-JOINT TAX) LEGIS COUNSEL 502 FHOB 53621
McLaughlin, Sabrina (WILD) SR CONSTIT ADVOCATE 484-781-6000
McLean, Mikkyla (CAO/OFFICE OF THE CHIEF HUMAN RESOURCES OFFICER) GENERALIST 102 FHOB 60274
McLerran, Elissa (ADERHOLT) LEGIS ASST 1203 54876
McMahon, Amelia (ROBY) CONSTIT SVCS REP 334-428-1129
McManus, Marliss (HUIZENGA) DPTY CHIEF OF STAFF 2232 54401
McMenamin, Erin (BROOKS, SUSAN W.) LEGIS ASST 2211 52276
McMichael, Chara (WEBER) CHIEF OF STAFF 107 CHOB 52831
McMillan, Katie (GABBARD) CONSTIT OUTREACH REP 808-541-1986
McMillion, Kim (MILLER) DPTY DIST DIR 304-250-6177
McMullen, Debra (CMTE-JOINT TAX) SR STAFF ASST 502 FHOB 53621
McMurray, Matt (ESHOO) CHIEF OF STAFF 202 CHOB 58104
McMurray, Matthew (KELLY, ROBIN L.) SR LEGIS ASST 2416 50773
McNabb, Kelley (CMTE-ED & WORKFORCE) COMMUNICATIONS DIR 2178 69440
McNamara, Ellen (SGT AT ARMS/EMERGENCY MGMT) EXEC ASST 192 FHOB 60950
McNamee, Cait (SWALWELL) PRESS SECY 407 CHOB 55065
McNamee, Christopher (CMTE-VET AFFAIRS) DPTY STAFF DIR - MIN STAFF/SUBCOMM STAFF DIR/GEN COUNSEL 3460 53569
McNamee, James (ZELDIN) STAFF ASST 2441 53826
McNeil, Rebecca (MALINOWSKI) CONSTIT SVCS REP 908-547-3307
McNeill, Rachel (KENNEDY) MIL FELLOW 617-332-3333
McNeillie, Nancy (LEGIS COUNSEL) OFFICE ADMIN 337 FHOB 56060
McNerney, George (COLLINS, CHRIS) FIELD DIR 716-634-2324
McNichols, Jim (LUETKEMEYER) DIST DIR 636-239-2276
McNutt, Connor (OMAR) CHIEF OF STAFF 1517 54755
McPherson, William (COLE) DIST DIR 405-329-6500
McPike, Richard (TAKANO) CHIEF OF STAFF 420 CHOB 52305
McQueen, Darby (BROOKS, MO) STAFF ASST 2246 54801
McQuerry, Michael (PLASKETT) COMMUNICATIONS DIR 2404 51790
McReynolds, Allyson (CALVERT) LEGIS ASST 2205 51986
McSwain, Jennifer
(CAO/HIR – CYBERSECURITY) SPECIAL ASST 630A FHOB. 61116
(CAO/HIR – OPS AND CONTINUITY) SPECIAL ASST 630A FHOB 61116
McTague, Mary Kate (DELBENE) DC SCHEDULER 2330 56311
McVae, Bryan (HARTZLER) SR LEGIS ASST 2235 52876
McWherter, Mary (COOPER) LEGIS ASST 1536 54311
McWilliams, Jennifer (GIBBS) STAFF ASST 419-207-0650
Meachum, Pete (DUFFY) CHIEF OF STAFF 1714 53365
Meadows, Carrie (NEWHOUSE) CHIEF OF STAFF 1414 55816
Meadows, Sonya (SGT AT ARMS/GARAGES & PARKING) ADMIN SPEC G2-28 56749
Meads, Karen (LONG) DIST SCHEDULER 417-889-1800
Meagher, Nikki (MARSHALL) DIST EXEC ASST/ CASEWKR 785-829-9000
Means, Jade (SCHNEIDER) STAFF ASST 1432 54835
Means, Kristine M (CMTE-JOINT TAX) EXEC ASST 502 FHOB 53621
Mecadon, Christa (CARTWRIGHT) CASEWKR 570-341-1050
Mecher, David (RICE, KATHLEEN M.) LEGIS CORRES 2435 55516
Mecher, Greg (KENNEDY) CHIEF OF STAFF 304 CHOB 55931
Mederos, Leticia (DELAURO) CHIEF OF STAFF 2413 53661
Medina, Josie (GRIJALVA) DIR - CONSTIT SVCS 520-622-6788
Medina, Rob (POSEY) DIR - MIL & COMMUNITY RELATIONS 321-632-1776
Medley, Megan (ADERHOLT) DPTY LEGIS DIR 1203 54876
Medrano, Martin (CISNEROS) DPTY DIST DIR 714-459-4575
Medzhibovsky, Boris (AGUILAR) CHIEF OF STAFF 909-890-4445
Mee, Eric (LEVIN, MIKE) COMMUNICATIONS DIR 1626 53906
Meegan, Erin (ROSE, MAX) LEGIS DIR 1529 53371
Meehan, Colin (CMTE-HOMELAND SECUR) RESEARCH ASST 117 FHOB 68417
Meek, Nancy (MCHENRY) SR DIST REP 828-327-6100
Meek, Robert (FOXX) DIST DIR 828-265-0240

Meeker, Anne (MOULTON) CASEWKR 978-531-1669
Meeker, Autumn (BROOKS, SUSAN W.) CONSTIT SVCS REP 765-640-5115
Mehdi, Yazmin (JAYAPAL) COORD - OUTREACH 206-674-0040
Mehlman, Beth (RICE, KATHLEEN M.) COMMUNITY LIAISON 516-739-3008
Mehrabi, Emma (LEE, BARBARA) LEGIS DIR 2470 52661
Mehta, Aalok (CMTE-APPRO) PROF STAFF MEMB 2000 57245
Meicher, Sherrie (MCCAUL) CASEWKR 281-255-8372
Meinert, Kimberly (CMTE-WAYS & MEANS) PROF STAFF 2018 59263
Meininger, Lauren (HECK) SCHEDULER 2452 59740
Meister, Darlene (CAO/OFFICE OF THE CHIEF HUMAN RESOURCES OFFICER) DIRECTOR 102 FHOB 52926
Mejia, Marcia (CASTOR) DIST DIR 813-871-2817
Melander, Kyle (FITZPATRICK) DIR - CONSTIT SVCS 215-579-8102
Melara, Alvaro (SCHNEIDER) CONSTIT SVCS REP 847-383-4870
Melbye, Linnea (STAUBER) SCHEDULER 126 CHOB 56211
Melcher, Eloise (PINGREE) LEGIS CORRES 2162 56116
Melcher, Harold (MCCOLLUM) COMMUNITY OUTREACH SPEC 651-224-9191
Melick, Ray (PALMER) DIST DIR 205-968-1290
Melton, Chyna (RICHMOND) LEGIS AIDE 506 CHOB 56636
Meltzer, Richard (SPEAKER) POLICY DIR H232 50100
Melvin, Justin (KUSTOFF) DPTY CHIEF OF STAFF 523 CHOB 54714
Menardy, Alexandra (LARSEN) LEGIS ASST 2113 52605
Menchel, Samuel (COURTNEY) LEGIS CORRES 2332 52076
Mendez, Emilio (CORREA) LEGIS DIR 1039 52965
Mendive, Dirk (FULCHER) REGIONAL DIR 208-888-3188
Mendoza, Brandon (DAVIS, SUSAN A.) SR LEGIS AIDE 1214 52040
Mendoza, Joanna (O'HALLERAN) FIELD REP - VETS 520-316-0839
Mendoza, Lydia (CAO/PAYROLL & BENEFITS) COUNSELOR B215 LHOB 58051
Menefee-Libey, Nell (CHU) STAFF ASST 2423 55464
Meneses, Manuel (COURTNEY) CASEWORK - VETS 860-886-0139
Menon, Vijay (CMTE-JOINT ECON) POLICY ADVISOR - REPUB SD-G01 40377
Menorca, Diane (GRAVES, TOM) FINANCIAL ADMIN 2078 55211
Menorca, Doug (BILIRAKIS) SPECIAL ASST 2227 55755
Menos, Frieda (JEFFRIES) DIR - CONSTIT SVCS 718-373-0033
Mensie, Alyssa (MCEACHIN) SPECIAL ASST 314 CHOB 56365
Merberg, Julie (VELA) SR POLICY ADVISOR 307 CHOB 59901
Mercado, Gladys (LARSON) DIST AIDE 860-278-8888
Mercer, Ian (CHABOT) LEGIS CORRES 2408 52216
Merchant, Elaine A (CLERK/REPORTERS) OFFICIAL REPORTER HT59 55621
Merchant, Kusai (CMTE-APPRO) PROF STAFF MEMB 2007 53081
Merchant, Sam (GREEN, AL) CONSTIT SVCS 713-383-9234
Meredith, Diana (CMTE-BUDGET) DPTY STAFF DIR - MAJ STAFF 204E CHOB 67200
Meredith, Dwaine (CAO/LOGISTICS) LOGISTICS & DIST SPEC WA16 RHOB 59474
Merrill, Leslie (PINGREE) CASEWKR 207-774-5019
Merritt, Jessica (QUIGLEY) CONG AIDE 773-267-5926
Merritt, Tammy (FLEISCHMANN) DIST FIELD REP 865-576-1976
Mertens, Traci (CLERK/REPORTERS) OFFICIAL REPORTER 1718 52627
Meryweather, Kelly (LEGIS COUNSEL) STAFF ASST/ PARALEGAL 337 FHOB 56060
Meryweather, Tom (LEGIS COUNSEL) STAFF ASST/ PARALEGAL 337 FHOB 56060
Merz, Julie (MAJ LEADER) SR ADVISOR H107 53130
Messen, Kimberly (COOK) OFC ASST 760-247-1815
Messer, Lizzie (PALAZZO) LEGIS CORRES 2349 55772
Metzler, Franmarie (CAO/HOUSE CREATIVE SVCS) PHOTOGRAPHER 2002 52700
Meuse, Justin (CROW) LEGIS DIR 1229 57882
Meyer, Andrew (CLERK/SVCS GRPS) HOUSE FLOOR OPS CLERK H223 57350
Meyer, Ashley (RUPPERSBERGER) COORD - BUSINESS & STATE/LOCAL GOVT COALITIONS/ DIR - GOVT & BUSINESS RELATIONS 410-628-2701
Meyer, Branden (STIVERS) LIAISON - MIL 740-654-2654
Meyer, Eddie (VARGAS) LEGIS ASST 2244 58045
Meyer, Jesse (MALONEY, SEAN PATRICK) COORD - GRANTS & SPEC PROJ 845-561-1259
Meyer, Katherine (MIN LEADER) SR POLICY ADVISOR H204 54000
Meyer, Matthew
(CMTE-VET AFFAIRS) MBR - SVCS ASSOC 3460 53527
(ROE) CHIEF OF STAFF 102 CHOB 56356
Meyer, Pauline (GALLAGHER) FIELD REP 920-301-4500
Meyer, Theresa (EMMER) LEGIS CORRES 315 CHOB 52331
Meza, Danny (CASTRO) CHIEF OF STAFF 2241 53236
Michael, Emily (GRIFFITH) SR POLICY ADVISOR 2202 53861
Michalek, E H Ned (ENGEL) ADMIN ASST 2426 52464
Michalek, William (CAO/HIR – ENTERPRISE INFRASTRUCT) ADMIN - BILLING 686 FHOB 69785
Michalson, Kristine (CAO/HOUSE DAILY PRESS) ASST DIR H315 53945
Middlebrooks, Jake (CMTE-ED & WORKFORCE) PROF STAFF MEMB 6140 56558
Middleton, Carson (FOXX) LEGIS DIR/DPTY CHIEF OF STAFF 2462 52071
Middleton, Joeana (DEGETTE) DIST DIR 303-844-4988
Middleton, John (SMITH, JASON) LEGIS CORRES 573-335-0101
Mier, Jessica (DAVIS, SUSAN A.) DIST DIR 619-280-5353
Migdail, Rhonda (CMTE-JOINT TAX) LEGIS COUNSEL 502 FHOB 53621
Mignone, Laurie (CMTE-APPRO) PROF STAFF MEMB 2358B 53508
Miguel, Naomi (CMTE-NATURAL RESOURCES) PROF STAFF - MAJ 1331 56065
Mikeska, Bri (MCCAUL) LEGIS CORRES 2001 52401
Mikeska, Marita (MCCAUL) CASEWKR 979-830-8497
Mikhanjian, Lucine (COX) STAFF ASST 1728 54695
Milam, Marcus (LESKO) CONSTIT SVCS REP 623-776-7911
Milasi, Francesco (CAO/HIR – NETWORKING ENGINEERING AND OPS) SR NETWK TECH 652C FHOB 66430
Milberg, Hayden (CMTE-APPRO) PROF STAFF MEMB H405 52847

Milbut, Anthony (CAO/HIR – NETWORKING ENGINEERING AND OPS) SR NETWK COMMUNICATIONS SPEC 687 FHOB ... 571-921-3167
Milenkevich, Amber (LAWSON) LEGIS CORRES 1406 ... 50123
Miles, Erica (CMTE-FINANCIAL SVCS) DIRECTOR 2129 ... 54247
Miles, Steven (SGT AT ARMS/APPOINTMENT) ASST - APPTS DESK CVC ... 52551
Miles, Suzanne (GUTHRIE) FIELD REP ... 270-842-9896
Miles, Yana (CMTE-FINANCIAL SVCS) SR COUNSEL - MAJ 2129 ... 54247
Milla, Danny (AGUILAR) CONSTIT SVCS REP ... 909-890-4445
Millard, Rachel (CMTE-AGRIC) COMMUNICATIONS DIR 1010 ... 50317
Miller, Annick (CMTE-NATURAL RESOURCES) PROF STAFF - MIN 4120 ... 52761
Miller, Ben (HUFFMAN) CHIEF OF STAFF 1527 ... 55161
Miller, Brandon (CMTE-NATURAL RESOURCES) PROF STAFF 4170 ... 52761
Miller, Brooke (CARTER, EARL L. "BUDDY") EXEC ASST 2432 ... 55831
Miller, Brooke (AXNE) DIST FIELD REP/ CASEWKR ... 515-400-8180
Miller, Bruce (AMODEI) CHIEF OF STAFF 104 CHOB ... 56155
Miller, Carolyn (LAWRENCE) CASEWK MGR ... 248-356-2052
Miller, Chris (RUTHERFORD) DIST DIR ... 904-831-5205
Miller, Collin (MEADOWS) STAFF ASST ... 828-693-5660
Miller, Dan (CMTE-ENERGY & COMMERCE) POLICY ANALYST 2125 ... 52927
Miller, Debbie (MCBATH) CASEWK MGR 1513 ... 54501
Miller, Deborah (SGT AT ARMS/APPOINTMENT) ASST - APPTS DESK CAPITOL ... 52551
Miller, Diane (HIGGINS, CLAY) CASEWKR ... 337-703-6105
Miller, Elise (KELLY, ROBIN L.) DIST REP ... 708-679-0078
Miller, Fred (CMTE-TRANSP & INFRA) GEN COUNSEL 2164. 59446
Miller, Gabrielle (BUSTOS) OUTREACH & MBR SVCS ASST 1233 ... 55905
Miller, Glenn
(CMTE-NATURAL RESOURCES) SR POLICY ADVISOR 1511 ... 56065
(GRIJALVA) SR POLICY ADVISOR 1511 ... 52435
Miller, Jack (NORTON) COMMUNICATIONS DIR 2136 ... 58050
Miller, Jacob (BYRNE) STAFF ASST - COMMUNICATIONS 119 CHOB ... 54931
Miller, James (DEFAZIO) DIST AIDE ... 541-465-6732
Miller, James (DUFFY) OUTREACH REP ... 715-392-3984
Miller, Jonas (CARTER, JOHN R.) CHIEF OF STAFF ... 512-246-1600
Miller, Jonathan (SWALWELL) LEGIS ASST 407 CHOB ... 55065
Miller, Kathryn (BYRNE) CONSTIT SVCS REP ... 251-690-2811
Miller, Kayla (RODGERS) STAFF ASST 1035 ... 52006
Miller, Keisha (RICE, KATHLEEN M.) CONG LIAISON ... 516-739-3008
Miller, Kelly (AMASH) LEGIS ASST 106 CHOB ... 53831
Miller, Kirby (KELLY, TRENT) LEGIS DIR 1005 ... 54306
Miller, Leila (CARBAJAL) PRESS ASST/STAFF ASST 1431 ... 53601
Miller, Louis, III (CAO/OFFICE SUPPLY/GIFT SHOP) RETAIL INVENTORY SPEC B217 LHOB ... 53321
Miller, MacKenzie (SPANBERGER) DIST COORD ... 804-401-4110
Miller, Matt (CLINE) CHIEF OF STAFF 1009 ... 55431
Miller, Megan Bel (SCALISE) DC CHIEF OF STAFF 2049 ... 53015
Miller, Michael (CAO/HIR – HOUSE WEB SVCS) MGR 626 FHOB ... 66279
Miller, Morna (CMTE-WAYS & MEANS) SUBCOMM STAFF DIR 2018 ... 59263
Miller, Patrick (YOHO) CONSTIT ADVOCATE ... 352-390-6413
Miller, Richard D (CMTE-ED & WORKFORCE) DIR - LABOR POLICY 2051C ... 53725
Miller, Rikki (HOUSE DEM CAUCUS) PRESS ASST B245 LHOB ... 51400
Miller, Rose (CAO/PAYROLL & BENEFITS) SR COUNSELOR B215 LHOB ... 54578
Miller, Sarah (MAST) LEGIS ASST 2182 ... 53026
Miller, Scott
(SWALWELL) CONSTIT SVCS REP ... 510-370-3322
(CMTE-INTELLIGENCE) CONG FELLOW HVC304 ... 57690
Miller, Shanley (SCHRIER) SCHEDULER 1123 ... 57761
Miller, Shawn (CAO/CONGRESSIONAL STAFF ACAD) OPS ASST B241 LHOB ... 63800
Miller, Shea (ROGERS, MIKE) PRESS SECY 2184 ... 53261
Miller, Susie (MARCHANT) DPTY CHIEF/DIR - DIST AFFAIRS ... 972-556-0162
Miller, Wade (ROY) CHIEF OF STAFF 1319 ... 54236
Miller-Lamill, Eloise (CAO/HOUSE RECORDING STUDIO) BROADCAST PROD TECH 2010 ... 53941
Milli, Josette (GONZALEZ, ANTHONY) SR OUTREACH DIR ... 440-783-3696
Millord, Betsy (MEEKS) COMMUNITY LIAISON ... 347-230-4032
Mills, Clay (BROOKS, MO) COMMUNICATIONS DIR 2246 ... 54801
Mills, Michael (CLERK/LCS) SR SOFTWARE ENGINEER 2401 ... 51182
Milner, Katie (LOUDERMILK) STAFF ASST 422 CHOB ... 52931
Milnes, Lauren (JEFFRIES) LEGIS CORRES/DIR - SCHEDULING 2433 ... 55936
Milon, Colin (DEAN) LEGIS ASST 129 CHOB ... 54731
Milton, Ashton (SGT AT ARMS/ID SVCS) ASST/ID SVCS 116 FHOB ... 53820
Mims, Amanda (CMTE-HOMELAND SECUR) OFFICE MGR 176 FHOB ... 62616
Mims, Andrew (RICE, TOM) DIR - DIST AFFAIRS ... 843-445-6459
Mims, Derrick (LOWENTHAL) SR ADVISOR ... 562-436-3828
Min, James
(MCCARTHY) CHIEF OF STAFF 2468 ... 52915
(MIN LEADER) DPTY CHIEF OF STAFF H204 ... 54000
Minehardt, Adam
(CMTE-SMALL BUSINESS) STAFF DIR 2361 ... 54038
(VELÁZQUEZ) CHIEF OF STAFF 2302 ... 52361
Mineiro, Sarah (CMTE-ARMED SVCS) PROF STAFF MEMB 2340 ... 60120
Minges, Joe (PERLMUTTER) LEGIS ASST 1226 ... 52645
Minkler, Ann (MIN WHIP) DPTY FLOOR DIR H148 ... 50197
Minor, Jack (WALKER) COMMUNICATIONS DIR ... 336-333-5005
Minor, Leslie (CAO/FINANCIAL COUNSELING) COUNSELOR B215 LHOB ... 61194
Minturn, John (CAO/HIR – CYBERSECURITY) ACTING DIR - INFO SECUR 612A FHOB ... 64554
Mion, Steven (HUFFMAN) DC SCHEDULER 1527 ... 55161
Miranda, Jose (ROYBAL-ALLARD) LEGIS ASST 2083 ... 51766
Miranda-Gallardo, Norma (GONZÁLEZ-COLÓN) CASEWORK - VETS ... 787-723-6333

Mirviss, Sophie (PHILLIPS) DC SCHEDULER 1305 52871
Mirza, Sana (HOYER) CONSTIT LIAISON 301-474-0119
Mishkin, Kelsey (GRIJALVA) DPTY CHIEF OF STAFF 1511 52435
Misselwitz, Kelly (OMAR) LEGIS DIR 1517 54755
Miszcak, Joe (LAWRENCE) COORD - CONSTIT SVCS 2463 55802
Mitcham, Bart (LOUDERMILK) FIELD REP 770-429-1776
Mitchell, Charlotte (COLE) DIST SCHEDULER 405-329-6500
Mitchell, Kendall (CLARKE) STAFF ASST 2058 56231
Mitchell, Maggie (CAO/HIR – ENTERPRISE INFRASTRUCT) ADMIN - BILLING 678A FHOB 66415
Mitchell, Nicolas (CMTE-INTELLIGENCE) INVESTIGATIVE COUNSEL HVC304 57690
Mitchell, Rashawn (CUNNINGHAM) LEGIS DIR 423 CHOB 53176
Mitchell, Sherrie (CRAWFORD) CASEWKR 870-203-0540
Mitchell, Will (CRAIG) LEGIS DIR 1523 52271
Mitchem, Luke (WALKER) CONSTIT LIAISON 336-626-3060
Mitchiner, Zachary (JOHNSON, EDDIE BERNICE) STAFF ASST 2306 58885
Mix, Kelsey (STAUBER) COMMUNICATIONS DIR 126 CHOB 56211
Mizrahi, Celine (NADLER) DIR - COMMUNITY RELATIONS 212-367-7350
Mizutani, Kota (CMTE-ED & WORKFORCE) STAFF WRITER 2176 53725
Mlinar, Alyene (CMTE-WAYS & MEANS) PROF STAFF 1139 54021
Moberly, Matthew (BOST) DPTY DIST DIR 618-457-5787
Modeste, Brian (CMTE-NATURAL RESOURCES) SUBCOMM STAFF DIR 186 FHOB 56065
Modica, Michael (CAO/HIR - VENDOR MGMT) MGR 642 FHOB 64232
Moe, Kari (GARCÍA, JESÚS G. "CHUY") CHIEF OF STAFF 530 CHOB 55092
Moeglein, Vivian (WESTERMAN) CHIEF OF STAFF 209 CHOB 53772
Moelk, Carter (WENSTRUP) DPTY COMMUNICATIONS DIR 2419 53164
Moeller, Lea (MUCARSEL-POWELL) DIR - COMMUNITY OUTREACH 305-292-4485
Moeny, Kitra (DEFAZIO) STAFF ASST 2134 56416
Moffitt, Katherine (UPTON) SR LEGIS ASST 2183 53761
Moffitt, Melissa (SGT AT ARMS) TACTICAL COMMUNICATIONS SPEC H124 52456
Mohamed, Hamdi (JAYAPAL) COORD - CONSTIT SVCS 206-674-0040
Mohamed, Mohamed (CLARKE) DPTY DIST REP 718-287-1142
Molina, Amanda (LEGIS COUNSEL) ASST COUNSEL 337 FHOB 56060
Molina, David (SAN NICOLAS) LEGIS ASST 1632 51188
Molina, James (TURNER) LEGIS CORRES 2082 56465
Molina, Sayanna (GRIJALVA) LEGIS AIDE 1511 52435
Moll, Andrew (CAO/HIR – HOUSE WEB SVCS) SR INTERNET SYS SPEC 640 FHOB 66054
Moll, Pam (ARMSTRONG) DIST OFFICE MGR 701-353-6665
Molnar, Wendy (CLERK/REPORTERS) OFFICIAL REPORTER 1718 52627
Molof, Doug (DOGGETT) SR LEGIS ASST 2307 54865
Molter, Meagan (GRAVES, GARRET) STAFF ASST 2402 53901
Molt-West, Alicia (TRAHAN) CHIEF OF STAFF 1616 53411
Molyneux, Lisa (CMTE-APPRO) CLERK 2000 57245
Molz, Bonnie (MARSHALL) OFFICE MGR 620-765-7800
Monachino, Benedict (ZELDIN) CONG AIDE/ SOCIAL WKR 631-289-1097
Monahan, Timothy
(CMTE-HOUSE ADMIN) DIR - OVERSIGHT 1216 58281
(CMTE-JOINT LIBRARY) DIR - OVERSIGHT 1216 58281
(CMTE-JOINT PRINTING) DIR - OVERSIGHT 1216 58281
Monge, Katherine (SPEAKER) SR COUNSEL H232 50100
Monger, Jon (CMTE-ENERGY & COMMERCE) COUNSEL 2125 52927
Monje, Carlos (CMTE-FOREIGN AFFAIRS) PROF STAFF 2066 68467
Monks, Dylan (DESJARLAIS) LEGIS ASST 2301 56831
Montalbano, Nick (HIGGINS, BRIAN) LEGIS CORRES 2459 53306
Montan, Kaitlyn (CASTRO) LEGIS ASST 2241 53236
Montano, Lisa (SHERMAN) CONSTIT SVCS OFFICER 818-501-9200
Montes, David (GALLEGO) CHIEF OF STAFF 1131 54065
Montesinos, Victor (MALONEY, CAROLYN B.) DIR - CONSTIT SVCS 212-860-0606
Montfort, Elysa (CMTE-ENERGY & COMMERCE) PRESS SECY 2125 52927
Montgomery, Billy (CONNOLLY) CONSTIT SVCS REP 703-256-3071
Montgomery, Christa (LUETKEMEYER) DIST DIR 636-327-7055
Montgomery, Kelli (CLEAVER) POLICY COORD 816-842-4545
Montgomery, Meg (PHILLIPS) CASEWKR 952-656-5176
Montgomery, Robert (MOORE) SCHEDULER 2252 54572
Monticello, Ben (BERGMAN) LEGIS CORRES 414 CHOB 54735
Montiel, Johanna (CARBAJAL) LEGIS ASST 1431 53601
Montoya-Picazo, Ricardo (BUSTOS) CONSTIT ADVOCATE/FIELD REP 815-968-8011
Moomau, Pamela H (CMTE-JOINT TAX) SR ECONOMIST 595 FHOB 67575
Moon, Becky (DESJARLAIS) CASEWKR/FIELD REP 931-381-9920
Moon, Danielle (CASTRO) SCHEDULER/LEGIS AIDE 2241 53236
Moon, Katharine (PANETTA) CONG AIDE 212 CHOB 52861
Mooney, Brandon (CMTE-ENERGY & COMMERCE) DPTY CHIEF COUNSEL 564 FHOB 53641
Mooney, Jackie (GRAVES, TOM) CONSTIT SVCS REP 706-290-1776
Moore, Brad (THOMPSON, GLENN) DIST DIR 814-670-0432
Moore, Cartwright (NORTON) SR CONSTIT LIAISON 202-408-9041
Moore, Cheryl (POSEY) DIR - COMMUNITY RELATIONS 321-383-6090
Moore, Cole (TAYLOR) FIELD REP 972-202-4150
Moore, Dylan (BUCSHON) SR LEGIS ASST 2313 54636
Moore, Edwarda (CAO/FINANCIAL COUNSELING) FINANCIAL COUNSELOR B215 LHOB 50137
Moore, Garrett (SMITH, ADAM) DIST REP 425-793-5180
Moore, Gary (CAO/HIR – NETWORKING ENGINEERING AND OPS) SR NETWK TECH 652C FHOB 66430
Moore, Jarrett (RASKIN) CONSTIT SVCS 301-354-1000
Moore, Jon (HAALAND) MGR - CONSTIT SVCS 505-288-4602
Moore, Katie (MARSHALL) SR LEGIS ASST 312 CHOB 52715
Moore, Marimac (DUNCAN, JEFF) LEGIS ASST/PRESS ASST 2229 55301

Moore, Max (CMTE-ED & WORKFORCE) OFFICE AIDE 230 FHOB 53725
Moore, Rachel (CMTE-JOINT TAX) ECONOMIST 595 FHOB. 67575
Moore, Reginald (THOMPSON, BENNIE G.) FIELD REP/CASEWKR 662-455-9003
Moore, Shane
(BARRAGÁN) ADMIN - FINANCE & PAYROLL 1030 58220
(BASS) FINANCIAL ADVISOR 2059 57084
(CORREA) FINANCIAL ADMIN 1039 52965
(SUOZZI) MGR - PAYROLL & BENEFITS 214 CHOB 53335
Moore, Stephen (PALAZZO) FIELD DIR 601-582-3246
Moore, Stephon (YARMUTH) CONG AIDE 502-582-5129
Moore, William (NC03) DIST DIR 252-931-1003
Moorer, Gerard (DAVIS, DANNY K.) DPTY DIST DIR 773-533-7520
Moorman, Miranda (MULLIN) SR LEGIS ASST 2421 52701
Mora, Edward (SWALWELL) CONSTIT SVCS REP 510-370-3322
Mora, Margarita (HORSFORD) DIST REP 702-963-9360
Mora, Teresa (STEIL) DIR - OUTREACH & MEMB SVCS 608-752-4050
Mora-Castrellon, Christian (LOFGREN) CONG ASST 408-271-8700
Morales, Aaron (GONZALEZ, VICENTE) PRESS SECY 113 CHOB 52531
Morales, Andrea (DIAZ-BALART) CONG AIDE 305-470-8555
Morales, Claudia (FLETCHER) CASEWKR 713-353-8680
Morales, Jill (SMITH, CHRISTOPHER H.) SR CASEWKR 732-780-3035
Morales, MacKenzie (GOODEN) SCHEDULER 425 CHOB.. 53484
Moralez-Diaz, Ritzy (PASCRELL) DIST DIR 973-523-5152
Moran, Catherine (PARLIAMENTARIAN) PRECEDENT DIGITAL EDITOR 4470 51122
Moran, Kelsey (FRANKEL) CHIEF OF STAFF 2305 59890
Moran, Ryan (CAO/ACQUIS MGMT) SR CONTRACTS SPEC 5110 52921
Moran, Tom (MILLER) COMMUNICATIONS DIR 1605 53452
Moran, Yanira (SGT AT ARMS/APPOINTMENT) ASST - APPTS DESK HVC 52551
Morcelo, Lucy (VELÁZQUEZ) EXEC ASST/DIST SCHEDULER 718-599-3658
More, Isabella (CMTE-WAYS & MEANS) COUNSEL - OVERSIGHT 1129 51025
Morehouse, Mark (CMTE-ARMED SVCS) PROF STAFF 2340 52340
Morell, Ada (SIRES) DPTY CHIEF OF STAFF 908-820-0692
Moretti, Scott (CAO/HIR – NETWORKING ENGINEERING AND OPS) NETWK TECH 652C FHOB 66430
Morgan, Bob (CARTWRIGHT) DPTY CHIEF OF STAFF/DIST DIR 570-341-1050
Morgan, Cody (CAO/FURNISHINGS) MASTER CARPET MECHANIC WA32 RHOB 58000
Morgan, David (LAMALFA) DIST REP 530-878-5035
Morgan, Diane (ALLEN) EXEC ASST 706-228-1980
Morgan, Jeff (TONKO) LEGIS DIR 2369 55076
Morgan, Kate (LAMBORN) SCHEDULER 2371 54422
Morgan, Martina (GREEN, AL) OFFICE MGR/ SCHEDULER 202-510-3047
Morgan, Matthew (CMTE-JUDICIARY) COUNSEL 2138 53951
Morgan, Ryan (OMAR) LEGIS ASST 1517 54755
Morgan, Teri (CMTE-HOUSE ADMIN) DPTY STAFF DIR 1309 52061
Morgante, Samuel (LEE, SUSIE) DPTY CHIEF OF STAFF/ LEGIS DIR 522 CHOB 53252
Mori, T'Nelta (SAN NICOLAS) EXEC ASST/FINANCIAL & ADMIN OFFICER 1632 51188
Moriarty, Maureen (LARSON) CHIEF OF STAFF 860-278-8888
Morley, Andrew (STAUBER) LEGIS ASST 126 CHOB 56211
Morley, Autumn (DIAZ-BALART) COUNSEL/SR POLICY ADVISOR 404 CHOB 54211
Morley, Katie (WOMACK) STAFF ASST 2412 54301
Morris, Alex (WILSON, JOE) CASEWKR - MIL/ DPTY DIST DIR 803-939-0041
Morris, Alexandra (WELCH) LEGIS AIDE 2187 54115
Morris, Bo (NEGUSE) LEGIS DIR 1419 52161
Morris, Booker (JACKSON LEE) DIST AIDE 713-655-0050
Morris, Brad (JOHNSON, MIKE) LEGIS DIR 418 CHOB 52777
Morris, Elizabeth (WELCH) CONSTIT SVCS REP 802-652-2450
Morris, Kevin (CAO/ACQUIS MGMT) ADMIN - CONTRACTS 5110 52921
Morris, Maddy (GIANFORTE) SCHEDULING DIR 1222 53211
Morris, Nicole (CAO) DIRECTOR 217 FHOB 61045
Morris, Susan (CLERK/REPORTERS) ASST CHIEF CLERK - DEBATES HT59 55621
Morris, Theresa K (KAPTUR) CONG ASST 419-259-7500
Morrison, Chas (GALLAGHER) LEGIS DIR 1230 55665
Morrison, Lale (HASTINGS) CHIEF OF STAFF 2353 51313
Morrison, Samuel (CAO/FURNISHINGS) JOURNEYMAN - TEXT SPEC WA33 RHOB 58000
Morrissette, Eric (CLEAVER) SR POLICY ADVISOR 2335 54535
Morrissey, John (WALORSKI) COMMUNICATIONS DIR 419 CHOB 53915
Morrow, Jennifer (NUNES) OFFICE MGR/SCHEDULER/ EXEC ASST 1013 52523
Morrow, Madeline (GIBBS) LEGIS CORRES 2446 56265
Morrow, Seth (BYRNE) DPTY CHIEF OF STAFF/DIR - PRESS & COMMUNICATIONS 119 CHOB 54931
Morse, Kyle (BLUNT ROCHESTER) PRESS SECY 1519 54165
Morse, Rachel (HORN) COMMUNITY OUTREACH SPEC 405-602-3074
Morse, Stacy (EMMER) DIST DIR 763-241-6848
Morton, Lisette
(CMTE-JUDICIARY) POLICY DIR/DIR - MBR SVCS 2138 53951
(NADLER) POLICY DIR 2132 55635
Mosca, Tina (HIGGINS, CLAY) CASEWKR 337-656-2833
Moses, Sarah (ARRINGTON) CONSTIT SVCS REP 806-763-1611
Moses, Zachary (JOYCE, DAVID P.) LEGIS ASST 1124 55731
Mosley, Joseph (CAO/HOUSE RECORDING STUDIO) TECH DIR 2010 53941
Most, Danielle (SLOTKIN) LEGIS DIR 1531 54872
Motley, Essence (RUSH) ASST TO THE CONGRESSMAN/ STAFF ASST 2188 54372
Motta, Art (SWALWELL) LEGIS ASST 407 CHOB 55065
Motta, Ashley (PAPPAS) SR CONSTIT SVCS REP 603-285-4300
Motta, Wendy (CARBAJAL) DIST REP/CASEWKR 805-730-1710
Moura, Kelly (SARBANES) SCHEDULER 2370 54016
Mower, Christian (MCADAMS) FIELD REP 801-999-9801

Moxley, Richard (BUDD) CONSTIT SVCS REP........ 336-998-1313
Moxley, Sarah (CMTE-HOMELAND SECUR) SUBCOMM STAFF DIR - CYBERSECURITY, INFRASTRUCTURE PROTECTION, AND INNOVATION SUBCOMM 117 FHOB...... 68417
Moxley, Steven (CAO/HIR – CYBERSECURITY) SR INFO SYS SECUR ANALYST 612 FHOB........ 65562
Moya, David (CAO/HIR - ENTERPRISE MESSAGING AND MOBILITY) SYS ENGINEER 619 FHOB........ 571-921-3255
Moye, Frankie (NC03) OUTREACH REP........ 252-931-1003
Moye, Imani (RICE, KATHLEEN M.) COMMUNITY REP........ 516-739-3008
Moyer, Jonathan (HERN) SR ADVISOR........ 918-935-3222
Moylan, Ana (JOHNSON, HENRY C. "HANK", JR.) STAFF ASST........ 770-987-2291
Mucchetti, Michael (DOGGETT) CHIEF OF STAFF 2307....... 54865
Mueller, Lauren (CMTE-RULES) PRESS ASST H312........ 59091
Muglia, Lauren (PERRY) CHIEF OF STAFF 1207........ 55836
Muhammad, Jacqui (UNDERWOOD) DIST MGR.... 630-549-2190
Muhammad, Sabir (ROUDA) STAFF ASST 2300........ 52415
Muir, Linda (CMTE-APPRO) SCOREKEEPER 2005........ 52718
Mujkanovic, Nermina (DEGETTE) CONG AIDE...... 303-844-4988
Mulcahey, Chris (THOMPSON, GLENN) LEGIS CORRES 400 CHOB........ 55121
Muldavin, Hannah (TRONE) COMMUNICATIONS DIR 1213. 52721
Mulder, Matt (CMTE-FINANCIAL SVCS) DPTY STAFF DIR 4340........ 57502
Mule, Alex (KING, PETER T.) DIST STAFF ASST...... 516-541-4225
Mulero, Sarah (BOYLE) CONSTIT SVCS REP........ 267-335-5643
Mulieri, Daniel (HASTINGS) DIST STAFF ASST........ 954-733-2800
Mulka, Stephanie (PANETTA) EXEC ASST/SCHEDULER 212 CHOB........ 52861
Mulkerrin, Margaret (MAJ LEADER) DPTY PRESS SECY H107........ 53130
Mull, Keigan (CMTE-WAYS & MEANS) TRADE COUNSEL 1103........ 56649
Mullany, Ben (RIGGLEMAN) STAFF ASST 1022........ 54711
Mullen, Hannah (PERLMUTTER) SPECIAL EVENTS/DIR - CONSTIT SVCS........ 303-274-7944
Mullen, Kelly (CAO/HIR – ESCALATIONS AND OPS) SR SYS SUPPORT ENGINEER 601 FHOB........ 67090
Mullen, Marissa (DUNN) SCHEDULER 316 CHOB........ 55235
Mullendore, Jared (FINKENAUER) DIST DIR........ 319-364-2288
Mullendore, Wyatt (GRAVES, SAM) JR LEGIS ASST/ CASEWKR 1135........ 57041
Muller, Cheryl (CLERK) PERSONNEL DIR H154........ 57000
Mulligan, Edward T (LAW REV COUNSEL) ASST COUNSEL 308 FHOB........ 62411
Mulligan, Jessica (JAYAPAL) LEGIS ASST 1510........ 53106
Mullinax, Cooper (COLLINS, DOUG) SPECIAL ASST 1504... 59893
Mullins, Grant (CMTE-FOREIGN AFFAIRS) SR COUNSEL - MIN 2066........ 68467
Mullins, Maggie (CONAWAY) SCHEDULER 2469........ 53605
Mullon, Meghan (CMTE-ENERGY & COMMERCE) STAFF ASST 2125........ 52927
Multani, Dalvinder (CLERK/LCS) DIR - PROJ 2401........ 51182
Mulvey, Aaron (DAVIS, RODNEY) LEGIS CORRES 1740........ 52371
Mulvey, Timothy (CMTE-FOREIGN AFFAIRS) COMMUNICATIONS DIR - DEM 2170........ 55021
Mulvihill, Jerry (LIPINSKI) CHIEF CASEWKR........ 773-948-6223
Mumpower, Cody (GRIFFITH) FIELD REP........ 276-525-1405
Mun, Andrey V (CLERK/LCS) SR SOFTWARE ENGINEER 2401........ 51182
Muncy, James (CAO/HIR – NETWORKING ENGINEERING AND OPS) SR NETWK TECH 680 FHOB........ 66034
Munday, J (CMTE-JOINT TAX) DIR - SECUR 595 FHOB........ 67575
Munger, Amanda (LARSEN) COMMUNICATIONS DIR 2113. 52605
Munoz, Bertha (PANETTA) CONG AIDE........ 831-424-2229
Munoz, Cassandra (TITUS) CASEWKR........ 702-220-9823
Munoz, Chantell (KILMER) CONSTIT SVCS REP.... 360-373-9725
Munoz, Rene (TORRES SMALL) CHIEF OF STAFF 430 CHOB........ 52365
Munoz Lopez, Laura (STANTON) LEGIS ASST 128 CHOB.. 59888
Muns, Jenni (KUSTER) PRESS SECY........ 603-226-1002
Munschauer, Lyman (NAT REPUB CONG CMTE) DIGITAL DIR........ 202-479-7000
Munson, Mary Grace (HILL, J. FRENCH) EXEC ASST/ SCHEDULER 1533........ 52506
Murillo Villasenor, Carlos (ESCOBAR) STAFF ASST 1505. 68328
Muro, Cindy (GOMEZ) CASEWKR 1530........ 56235
Murphy, Abby (LAMB) SR ADVISOR 1224........ 52301
Murphy, Allison (VAN DREW) CHIEF OF STAFF 331 CHOB.. 56572
Murphy, Braden
(MCCARTHY) LEGIS ASST 2468........ 52915
(MIN LEADER) LEGIS ASST H204........ 54000
Murphy, Chastity (TLAIB) LEGIS ASST 1628........ 55126
Murphy, Cullen (MIN LEADER) AIDE H204........ 54000
Murphy, Devin (GAETZ) LEGIS DIR 1721........ 54136
Murphy, Devon (BISHOP, ROB) LEGIS ASST 123 CHOB........ 50453
Murphy, Elaina (GUTHRIE) LEGIS AIDE 2434........ 53501
Murphy, Jason (GRAVES, TOM) LEGIS DIR 2078........ 55211
Murphy, Johannah (REED) SCHEDULER 2263........ 53161
Murphy, Jolyn (CALVERT) DIST DIR........ 951-277-0042
Murphy, Jon (HURD) STAFF ASST 317 CHOB........ 54511
Murphy, Kelly
(CHENEY) FINANCIAL ADMIN 416 CHOB........ 52311
(DELGADO) FINANCIAL DIR 1007........ 55614
(JACKSON LEE) SHARED EMPLOYEE 2079........ 53816
(TORRES) FINANCIAL ADMIN 2444........ 56161
Murphy, Larrisa (CAO/FIRST CALL) CUSTOMER SOLUTIONS REP B227 LHOB........ 58000
Murphy, Laura (SLOTKIN) DIST LIAISON........ 517-993-0510
Murphy, Lori (CAO/PAYROLL & BENEFITS) COUNSELOR B215 LHOB........ 69377
Murphy, Melissa (ROUZER) CHIEF OF STAFF 2439........ 52731
Murphy, Michael (HOUSE HISTORIAN) HISTORICAL PUBLICATIONS SPEC JEFFERSON BUILDING, ATTIC........ 61300
Murphy, Morgan (WALDEN) LEGIS CORRES 2185........ 56730
Murphy, Phil
(CMTE-ENERGY & COMMERCE) POLICY COORD 2125........ 52927
(DOYLE) LEGIS DIR 306 CHOB........ 52135
Murphy, Rita (CICILLINE) DIR - CONSTIT AFFAIRS........ 401-729-5600
Murphy, Robert (CAO/HIR – IDENTITY GOV AND ADMIN) DIRECTOR 620B FHOB........ 61709
Murphy, Sharon (REED) EXEC ASST........ 607-654-7566
Murphy, Sylvia (MCEACHIN) DIST REP........ 757-942-6050
Murphy, Victoria F (CLERK) SPECIAL ASST TO THE CLERK H154........ 57000

Murray, Alexis (CMTE-ED & WORKFORCE) PROF STAFF MEMB 6150 57101
Murray, Amber (OLSON) STAFF ASST 281-494-2690
Murray, Camille (GOTTHEIMER) MGR - CONSTIT SVCS 201-389-1100
Murray, Carol (CMTE-VET AFFAIRS) OFFICE MGR B234 LHOB 59756
Murray, Darlene (ENGEL) OFFICE MGR/SCHEDULER 2426 52464
Murray, Elizabeth (PORTER) DIR - OPS 1117 55611
Murray, Kathryn (BROOKS, MO) DIST FIELD REP 256-551-0190
Murray, Katie (LOEBSACK) SCHEDULER/ADVISOR - HEALTH POLICY 1211 56576
Murray, Katie (JOHNSON, DUSTY) REGIONAL DIR 605-646-6454
Murray, Kristin (BUCSHON) STAFF ASST 812-232-0523
Murry, Luke (MIN LEADER) NATIONAL SECUR ADVISOR H204 54000
Murthy, Veena (CMTE-JOINT TAX) LEGIS COUNSEL 502 FHOB 53621
Muscolini, John (CMTE-APPRO) ADMIN ASST 1016 53481
Musser, Alexandria (SPEIER) LEGIS ASST 2465 53531
Mustello, Marci (KELLY, MIKE) DIST SCHEDULER 724-282-2557
Mutschall, Sarah (CMTE-ETHICS) COUNSEL 1015 57103
Muzeroll, Kim (SCHAKOWSKY) DPTY CHIEF OF STAFF/ EXEC ASST 2367 52111
Myers, Anthony (CAO/HIR – NETWORKING ENGINEERING AND OPS) NETWK COMMUNICATIONS SPEC 685 FHOB 66412
Myers, Cailey (JOHNSON, BILL) STAFF ASST 2336 55705
Myers, Katherine (SIMPSON) LEGIS ASST 2084 55531
Myers, Lenette (RUSH) DIR - ADMIN STAFF 2188 54372
Myers, Lewis (PLASKETT) DIR - ADMIN OPS 2404 51790
Myers, Mike (SGT AT ARMS/APPOINTMENT) ASST - APPTS DESK CVC 52551
Myhill, Don (CLERK) SPECIAL ASST TO THE CLERK H154 57000
Myhill, Meghan (DUNN) REGIONAL DIR 850-891-8610
Mylott, Lauren (WASSERMAN SCHULTZ) SCHEDULING DIR/SPECIAL ASST 1114 57931
Nabity, Caroline (CMTE-OVERSIGHT & GOVT REFORM) COUNSEL 2105 55074
Nadeau, Seth (MCGOVERN) DIST REP 508-831-7356
Nadherny, Taylor (RASKIN) STAFF ASST 412 CHOB 55341
Naft, Jeff (WOODALL) COMMUNICATIONS DIR 1724 54272
Nagales, Mark (SPEIER) DIR - CONSTIT SVCS 650-342-0300
Nagaraj, Renuka (CICILLINE) LEGIS COUNSEL 2233 54911
Nagle, Brianna (DAVIS, RODNEY) SCHEDULER 1740 52371
Nagy, Steven (SÁNCHEZ) FIELD REP 562-860-5050
Nail, Mitchell (CRAWFORD) FIELD REP 870-203-0540
Nail, Sarah-Hope (CLOUD) LEGIS ASST/LEGIS CORRES 1314 57742
Najieb-Locke, Halimah (CMTE-ARMED SVCS) PROF STAFF 2117 61055
Nalivkina, Olena (HUNTER) SCHEDULER/SYS ADMIN 2429 55672
Nall, Phyllis (LOUDERMILK) DIST OFFICE MGR 770-429-1776
Nalls, Dennis (MIN WHIP) FLOOR ASST H148 50197
Nance, Robert (CLYBURN) DIST DIR 803-799-1100
Napier, Benjamin (MIN WHIP) DIR - FLOOR OPS H148 50197
Napoliello, David (CMTE-TRANSP & INFRA) SR POLICY ADVISOR 2251 54472
Napuri, Alyssa (ROUDA) FIELD DIR 714-960-6483
Narayan, Rishaun (PORTER) DIST STAFF ASST 1117 55611
Nash, Madison (WOMACK) SCHEDULER 2412 54301
Nash, Michael (CAO/TECHNOL GOVERN & COMPLIANCE) MGR 643 FHOB 66418
Nasielski, Katharine (MENG) LEGIS ASST 2209 52601
Nasr, Haitham (CAO/HOUSE RECORDING STUDIO) SR BROADCAST ENGINEER/PROD SPEC 2010 53941
Nassif, Marybeth (CMTE-APPRO) PROF STAFF MEMB 2000 57245
Nasta, Sarah (CMTE-HOUSE ADMIN) COUNSEL - ELECTIONS 1309 52061
Nation, Doug (MCHENRY) LEGIS DIR 2004 52576
Natonski, David (RIGGLEMAN) CHIEF OF STAFF 1022 54711
Natonski, Liz (CROW) CHIEF OPS OFFICER 1229 57882
Naughton, Alex (OLSON) DPTY PRESS SECY 2133 55951
Naughton, Christopher (CAO/FIRST CALL) PROGRAM MGR B227 LHOB 58000
Navarro, Cindy (HAYES) DIGITAL ASST/PRESS ASST 860-223-8412
Nave, Lou (ROSE, JOHN W.) FIELD REP 931-854-9430
Navin, Liz (CMTE-WAYS & MEANS) LEGIS ASST 1139 54021
Navratil, Eileen (NEWHOUSE) DIST REP 509-452-3243
Nawrocki Bradley, Jenifer (RUTHERFORD) LEGIS DIR 1711 52501
Naylor, Brandon (DAVIDS) LEGIS DIR 1541 67212
Nayowith, Hannah (HILL, KATIE) DIR - OPS 1130 51956
Nazaretova, Katy (LARSEN) LEGIS ASST 2113 52605
Ndikum, Alex (CLEAVER) LEGIS AIDE 2335 54535
Neal, Andrew (PARLIAMENTARIAN) PRECEDENT EDITOR 4470 51122
Nealy, Kenneth (JOHNSON, EDDIE BERNICE) LEGIS DIR 2306 58885
Nedzar, Tamar (CMTE-ETHICS) SR COUNSEL 1015 57103
Neece, Michael (NORMAN) DIST OUTREACH REP 803-327-1114
Needham, Chris (RICE, TOM) CONSTIT SVCS REP 843-445-6459
Neeley, Madison (MOONEY) CONSTIT SVCS REP 304-925-5964
Neff, Daniel (MOONEY) DIST REP 304-264-8810
Negatu, Samuel (GOMEZ) LEGIS DIR 1530 56235
Neighbors, Matt (RODGERS) LEGIS COUNSEL 1035 52006
Neill, Andrew (FULCHER) LEGIS DIR 1520 56611
Neill, James (SIMPSON) SR LEGIS ASST 2084 55531
Neitzel, William (STEIL) LEGIS CORRES 1408 53031
Nelson, Andrew (KEATING) POLICY ADVISOR 508-771-0666
Nelson, Becky (DEFAZIO) DIST SCHEDULER 541-465-6732
Nelson, Jacob (HOUSE DEM CAUCUS) POLICY ASSOC B245 LHOB 51400
Nelson, Jonathan
(EVANS) FINANCIAL ADMIN 1105 54001
(GOTTHEIMER) MGR - PAYROLL & BENEFITS 213 CHOB 54465
(MAST) FINANCIAL ADMIN 2182 53026
(MCEACHIN) FINANCIAL ADMIN 314 CHOB 56365
(YARMUTH) ACCOUNTANT 402 CHOB 55401
Nelson, Juan (CAO/ACCOUNTING) STAFF ACCOUNTANT 3110 61573
Nelson, Lisa (KENNEDY) SR DIST REP 508-431-1110

Nelson, Merrick (CMTE-ED & WORKFORCE) DIGITAL MGR 2176 ... 53725
Nelson, Nate (GAETZ) DIR - MIL & COMMUNITY RELATIONS ... 850-479-1183
Nelson, Poppy (AMASH) CHIEF OF STAFF 106 CHOB ... 53831
Nelson, Scott (HOULAHAN) CASEWKR ... 610-883-5050
Nelson, Timothy (CASE) CHIEF OF STAFF/LEGIS DIR 2443 52726
Nentwich, Nicole (RIGGLEMAN) LEGIS CORRES 1022 ... 54711
Nepomuceno, Rachel (HERRERA BEUTLER) EXEC ASST 2352 ... 53536
Nerad, Jason (CASTEN) CASEWKR ... 630-520-9450
Neralla, Ven (LEVIN, ANDY) CHIEF OF STAFF 228 CHOB ... 54961
Nerantzis, Anthony (JORDAN) STAFF ASST 2056 ... 52676
Ness, Robert (PETERSON) STAFF ASST ... 320-235-1061
Neuman, Jaclyn (MAST) SCHEDULER 2182 ... 53026
Neville, Pam (ROUZER) DIST OFFICE MGR ... 910-253-6111
Newbold, Patrick (BISHOP, SANFORD D., JR.) MIL FELLOW 2407 ... 53631
Newby, Darek (CMTE-APPRO) CLERK 2006 ... 55834
Newell, Ashley (BUCSHON) CONSTIT SVCS REP/STAFF ASST ... 812-465-6484
Newell, Martha (YOUNG) LEGIS ASST 2314 ... 55765
Newgaard, Luke
(EMMER) LEGIS ASST 315 CHOB ... 52331
(WEBSTER) LEGIS ASST 1210 ... 51002
Newman, Bruce (YOUNG) SPECIAL ASST 2314 ... 55765
Newman, Jacqui (HOUSE DEM CONG CMPGN CMTE) CHIEF OPERATING OFFICER ... 202-863-1500
Newman, John (KUSTOFF) LEGIS CORRES/PRESS ASST 523 CHOB ... 54714
Newman, Joseph (ESPAILLAT) ASST COMMUNICATIONS DIR 1630 ... 54365
Newton, Jason (HAYES) COMMUNICATIONS DIR 1415 ... 54476
Newton, John (RADEWAGEN) WEB ADMIN/INFO TECH MGR ... 684-633-3601
Newton, Jonathan (CMTE-JOINT TAX) INFO TECH SYS ANALYST 595 FHOB ... 67575
Neyman, Lisa (DEFAZIO) DIST STAFF ASST ... 541-465-6732
Ng, Lauri (CMTE-FINANCIAL SVCS) COUNSEL - MAJ 2129 ... 54247
Nghiem, Hieu (CAO/ENTERPRISE APPLICATIONS) SR BUSINESS PROCESS APPLICA SPEC B73 FHOB ... 61153
Nguyen, Alexander (SÁNCHEZ) COMMUNICATIONS DIR 2329 ... 56676
Nguyen, Angela (LOFGREN) DIST SCHEDULER/ CONG ASST ... 408-271-8700
Nguyen, Anna (BLUMENAUER) DIST PRESS SECY ... 503-231-2300
Nguyen, Anthony (PETERS) DIST DIR ... 858-455-5550
Nguyen, Colleen (BERA) SR POLICY ADVISOR 1727 ... 55716
Nguyen, Dao (MURPHY) SR POLICY ADVISOR 1710 ... 54035
Nguyen, Hiep (KHANNA) SR FIELD REP ... 408-436-2720
Nguyen, Ngoc (LOWENTHAL) LEGIS ASST 108 CHOB ... 57924
Nguyen, Nho (CAO/HIR – IDENTITY GOV AND ADMIN) SR SYS ENGINEER 615 FHOB ... 63094
Nguyen, Phi (CAO/HOUSE CREATIVE SVCS) PHOTOGRAPHER 2002 ... 52700
Nguyen, Van (CAO/HIR – HOUSE WEB SVCS) SR SOFTWARE ENGINEER 644B FHOB ... 65685
Nichola, Mike (SOTO) LEGIS DIR 1507 ... 59889
Nicholas, Caroline (SCHIFF) STAFF ASST 2269 ... 54176
Nicholas, Donald (WILLIAMS) DIST FIELD REP/ MIL FIELD REP ... 512-473-8910
Nicholas, Paul (HOYER) STAFF ASST 1705 ... 54131
Nichols, Ashley (CMTE-NATURAL RESOURCES) PROF STAFF 4120 ... 52761
Nichols, Bryan (GRAVES, SAM) DIST FIELD REP/COMMUNICATIONS DIR ... 573-221-3400
Nichols, Jimmie (GUEST) FIELD REP ... 769-241-6120
Nicholson, Nikki (BYRNE) CONSTIT SVCS REP/ SPECIAL EVENTS ... 251-690-2811
Nicholson, Terry (WATERS) RECEPTIONIST ... 323-757-8900
Nickson, Julie (LEE, BARBARA) CHIEF OF STAFF 2470 ... 52661
Nickson, Michael
(BERA) FINANCIAL ADMIN 1727 ... 55716
(CHU) FINANCIAL ADMIN 2423 ... 55464
(KRISHNAMOORTHI) FINANCIAL ADVISOR 115 CHOB ... 53711
(LEE, BARBARA) FINANCIAL COUNSELOR 2470 ... 52661
(LIEU) ADMIN - FINANCE & PAYROLL 403 CHOB ... 53976
(WATSON COLEMAN) FINANCIAL ADMIN 2442 ... 55801
Nicoletti, John (GARAMENDI) SR FIELD REP 2368 ... 51880
Niedzielski, Jonathan (MCGOVERN) DIST DIR ... 508-831-7356
Nielsen, Allison (SMUCKER) COMMUNICATIONS DIR 127 CHOB ... 52411
Nielsen, Michael (GOMEZ) DIST OFFICE MGR ... 213-481-1425
Niemasik, Kaylee (PORTER) LEGIS COUNSEL 1117 ... 55611
Nienberg, Troy (KILDEE) LEGIS DIR 203 CHOB ... 53611
Nigaglioni, Angel (SERRANO) LEGIS COUNSEL/LEGIS DIR 2354 ... 54361
Nirenberg, Andrew (HOLDING) AIDE 1110 ... 53032
Nista, Julia (HARRIS) PRESS SECY 2334 ... 55311
Nitschke, Darrell (ARMSTRONG) REGIONAL DIR ... 702-354-6700
Niver, April (CARTWRIGHT) ECON DEV SPEC ... 570-371-0317
Nixon, Andrew (ROONEY) LEGIS CORRES 120 CHOB ... 52536
Nixon, Keith
(ENGEL) SHARED EMPLOYEE 2426 ... 52464
(PALLONE) ASST FOR TECH SUPPORT 2107 ... 54671
Nixon, Molly (AMASH) LEGIS COUNSEL 106 CHOB ... 53831
Nixon, Natalie (CMTE-HOMELAND SECUR) CHIEF ADMIN OFFICER 176 FHOB ... 62616
Nkollo, Taylor (LEWIS) STAFF ASST 300 CHOB ... 53801
Nlewedim, Gloria (PRICE) PRESS SECY 2108 ... 51784
Noble, Daniel (CMTE-INTELLIGENCE) SR COUNSEL FOR INVESTIGATIONS HVC304 ... 57690
Nodvin, Leah
(CMTE-FOREIGN AFFAIRS) STAFF ASSOC 5212 ... 66434
(SHERMAN) LEGIS AIDE 2181 ... 55911
Noel, Tiffany (BROOKS, MO) DIST DIR ... 256-551-0190
Nogis, Janine (SABLAN) STAFF ASST ... 670-323-2647
Noguera, Stephanie (KENNEDY) OUTREACH DIR ... 617-332-3333
Noh, Andrew (ROUDA) LEGIS DIR/DPTY CHIEF OF STAFF 2300 ... 52415
Nolan, Emmitt (CARTER, EARL L. "BUDDY") FIELD REP ... 912-265-9010
Nolan, Geoffrey (GRIJALVA) COMMUNICATIONS DIR 1511. 52435
Noland-Dennis, Meleah (RUTHERFORD) DIST OFFICE MGR ... 904-831-5205
Nolin, Sarah (ROONEY) PRESS AIDE 120 CHOB ... 52536
Nong, Eric (ROUDA) DIST FIELD REP ... 714-960-6483

Noonan, Mary McDermott (SMITH, CHRISTOPHER H.) CHIEF OF STAFF 2373 **53765**
Nora, Myrtle (CAO/FURNISHINGS) MASTER DRAPERY MANUFACTURER WA32 RHOB **58000**
Nordquist, Jeremy (O'HALLERAN) CHIEF OF STAFF 324 CHOB **53361**
Norfleet, Jessica (YOHO) DIST DIR **352-505-0838**
Norman, Corey (CURTIS) CHIEF OF STAFF 125 CHOB **57751**
Norman, Mela Lousie (SLOTKIN) CHIEF OF STAFF 1531 **54872**
Norman, Sherry (WALTZ) CONSTIT SVCS **386-238-9711**
Norris, Matthew (CAO/HIR – CYBERSECURITY) ACTING MGR - INFO SECUR 612 FHOB **65561**
Northcott, Kylie (LUCAS) CASEWKR **405-373-1958**
Northern, Jayne E (CMTE-JOINT TAX) EXEC ASST SD-G18 **45561**
Northrop, Alison (CMTE-HOMELAND SECUR) DIR - OVERSIGHT 176 FHOB **62616**
Northrop, Michael (FERGUSON) LEGIS AIDE 1032 **55901**
Norton, Philip (BERA) FIELD REP **916-635-0505**
Norvell, Emma (CISNEROS) LEGIS DIR 431 CHOB **54111**
Norwood, Carlton (ALLEN) PRESS SECY 2400 **52823**
Notter, Jim (HOYER) CHIEF OF STAFF 1705 **54131**
Novotny, Josef (CLERK/LEGIS OPS) READING CLERK HT13 **57584**
Nowak, Jason (CAO/ENTERPRISE APPLICATIONS) SR SOFTWARE SPEC B75 FHOB **69414**
Nowill, Jeffrey (PLASKETT) SR COUNSEL 2404 **51790**
Noyes, Kyle (CMTE-HOMELAND SECUR) PROF STAFF MEMB 117 FHOB **68417**
Nsiah, Kwabena (RICHMOND) CHIEF OF STAFF 506 CHOB **56636**
Nuce, Kai (HERRERA BEUTLER) CASEWKR **360-695-6292**
Nullet, Dominic (HIGGINS, CLAY) LEGIS CORRES 424 CHOB **52031**
Nulty, Scott (THOMPSON, GLENN) SR LEGIS ASST 400 CHOB **55121**
Nunez, Christina (DOGGETT) LEGIS AIDE 2307 **54865**
Nurse, Courtney (CAO/HIR – IT CUSTOMER SOLUTIONS) SR TECH SUPPORT REP 100 CHOB **61849**
Nurse, Dylan (SCOTT, DAVID) CONSTIT SVCS REP **770-210-5073**
Nusinzon, Igor (CAO/HIR – ENTERPRISE INFRASTRUCT) SR SYS ENGINEER 622 FHOB **63720**
Nuttall, Robert (SEWELL) LEGIS ASST 2201 **52665**
Nyce, Benjamin (STEFANIK) LEGIS CORRES 318 CHOB **54611**
Nystrom, Katy (MUCARSEL-POWELL) DIGITAL PRESS SECY 114 CHOB **52778**
Oates, Kimberly (CAO/HOUSE RADIO-TV GALLERY) SR MEDIA LOGISTICS COORD H320 **55214**
Oatman, Laura (ROUDA) DIST DIR **714-960-6483**
Ober, Jed (WILD) CHIEF OF STAFF 1607 **56411**
Oberhelman, Jim (KING, STEVE) DIST REP **515-573-2738**
Obermann, Richard (CMTE-SCIENCE) CHIEF OF STAFF - MAJ 2321 **56375**
Obermiller, Chad (BERA) CHIEF OF STAFF 1727 **55716**
O'Boyle, David (CAO/CUST EXPER CTR) MGR - COMMUNICATIONS 217 FHOB **66660**
O'Boyle, Nicholas (ESTES) LEGIS DIR 1524 **56216**
O'Brien, Abigail (KIRKPATRICK) COMMUNICATIONS DIR 309 CHOB **52542**
O'Brien, Hillary (CMTE-SCIENCE) PROF STAFF MBR - REPUB 394 FHOB **56371**
O'Brien, Kristine (CMTE-TRANSP & INFRA) DIR - OUTREACH & MEMB SVCS 2165 **54472**
O'Brien, Mary (CAO/OFFICE SUPPLY/GIFT SHOP) SALES SPEC B217 LHOB **53321**
O'Brien, Melissa A (CMTE-JOINT TAX) TAX RESOURCE SPEC SD-462 **40494**
O'Brien, Sean (NEWHOUSE) LEGIS DIR 1414 **55816**
O'Brien, Tom (CMTE-APPRO) PROF STAFF MEMB 1001 **53481**
O'Brien, Tucker (BILIRAKIS) DIST AIDE/DIST OFFICE MGR **727-940-5860**
Obscura, Julio (SPEAKER) CREATIVE DIR H232 **50100**
Ochoa, Christine (ROYBAL-ALLARD) EXEC ASST/OFFICE MGR 2083 **51766**
Ochoa, Cindy (HURD) FIELD REP **210-921-3130**
O'Connell, Molly (DAVIDSON) SCHEDULER 1107 **56205**
O'Connell, Richie (CALVERT) SR LEGIS ASST 2205 **51986**
O'Connor, Erin (KATKO) COMMUNICATIONS DIR/COUNSEL **315-423-5657**
O'Connor, George (BOST) COMMUNICATIONS DIR 1440 **55661**
O'Connor, Jennifer (CMTE-WAYS & MEANS) ADMIN - COMMITTEE 1102 **53625**
O'Connor, Mary
(BILIRAKIS) FINANCIAL ADMIN 2227 **55755**
(HIGGINS, CLAY) FINANCIAL ADMIN 424 CHOB **52031**
(MEUSER) FINANCIAL ADMIN 326 CHOB **56511**
(MILLER) SHARED EMPLOYEE 1605 **53452**
(SMUCKER) ADMIN - FINANCE & PAYROLL 127 CHOB **52411**
(WAGNER) SHARED EMPLOYEE/FINANCIAL ADMIN 2350 **51621**
O'Connor, Patrick (NEAL) LEGIS ASST 2309 **55601**
O'Connor, Patrick (CUELLAR) STAFF ASST/LEGIS CORRES 2209 **51640**
O'Connor, Shaun (NORCROSS) CONSTIT OUTREACH REP **856-427-7000**
O'Dell-Gernert, Maxine (FLEISCHMANN) DIST FIELD REP **423-745-4671**
Odomirok, Mary (MALONEY, CAROLYN B.) DIST REP **212-860-0606**
O'Donnell, Jerry (NAPOLITANO) DIR - PRESS & COMMUNICATIONS/LEGIS ASST 1610 **55256**
Oehmen, Jon (FLORES) CHIEF OF STAFF 2228 **56105**
Ogbeifun, Matthew (OMAR) COMMUNITY REP **612-333-1272**
Ogle, David (CUNNINGHAM) LEGIS ASST - MIL 423 CHOB **53176**
Ogra, Alexis (COLLINS, CHRIS) LIAISON - CONSTIT SVCS **585-519-4002**
O'Grady, Jamie (DOYLE) DIST SCHEDULER **412-390-1499**
O'Grady, Patrick (MASSIE) LEGIS ASST 2453 **53465**
Oh, Paul (WOODALL) FIELD REP **770-232-3005**
O'Hanlon, Ann (BEYER) CHIEF OF STAFF 1119 **54376**
O'Hara, Brian (HERN) DPTY DIST DIR **918-935-3222**
O'Hara, Elizabeth
(CMTE-WAYS & MEANS) DPTY STAFF DIR 1102 **53625**
(NEAL) DPTY CHIEF OF STAFF 2309 **55601**
O'Hara, Kelsey (HILL, KATIE) PROGRAM DIR/ RESEARCH DIR **661-802-0244**
O'Hara, Laura T (HOUSE HISTORIAN) SR HISTORICAL WEB EDITOR JEFFERSON BUILDING, ATTIC **61300**
O'Hara, Tracie (ROE) CONSTIT SVCS REP **423-247-8161**

...ISE APPLICATIONS) SR ...ENGINEER B69 FHOB 66273
...ngela (CMTE-APPRO) PROF STAFF MEMB 2358A 52141
Oinuma, Colleen (SCHIFF) DPTY DIST DIR 818-450-2900
Ojeda-Tiru, Doris (ENGEL) CASEWKR 718-796-9700
Okhlopkov, Sergei (CLERK/LCS) SYS ENGINEER 2401 51182
Okolo, Osaremen (SCHAKOWSKY) LEGIS ASST 2367 52111
Okolosi, Nailah (SCANLON) MGR - CONSTIT SVCS 610-626-1913
Okoniewski, Anderson (KUSTOFF) SCHEDULER 523 CHOB 54714
Okula, Victoria (SCHWEIKERT) STAFF ASST/ CASEWKR 480-946-2411
Olchyk, Ross (LONG) LEGIS ASST 2454 56536
Old Crow, Alexa (CMTE-TRANSP & INFRA) LEGIS ASST 2165 54472
Oldham, Lindsay (CAO/PAYROLL & BENEFITS) FINANCIAL ANALYST B215 LHOB 53793
O'Leary, Justin (VAN DREW) DPTY CHIEF OF STAFF 331 CHOB 56572
Oleksak, David (KEATING) SCHEDULER/PRESS ASST 2351 53111
Oliva, Tomas (VARGAS) SR FIELD REP 760-312-9900
Olivares, Shazia (MATSUI) STAFF ASST 2311 57163
Olivari, Renzo (LEE, SUSIE) PRESS SECY 522 CHOB 53252
Olivas, Celia (SWALWELL) STAFF ASST 407 CHOB 55065
Oliver, Brooke (RODGERS) ADMIN - FINANCE & PAYROLL 1035 52006
Oliver, Charlane (COOPER) DIST FIELD REP 615-736-5295
Oliver, Ebbony (CAO/OFFICE OF THE CHIEF HUMAN RESOURCES OFFICER) HUMAN RESOURCES COORD 102 FHOB 60272
Oliver, Jan (CMTE-SMALL BUSINESS) CHIEF COUNSEL/ DPTY STAFF DIR 2069 55821
Oliveros, Gloria (DIAZ-BALART) DIST DIR 305-470-8555
Olsen, Eric (GARAMENDI) COMMUNICATIONS DIR 2368 51880
Olson, Kathryn (CMTE-WAYS & MEANS) SUBCOMM STAFF DIR 2018 59263
Olson, Mark (MENG) LEGIS AIDE/PRESS SECY 2209 52601
Olson, Rollie (PHILLIPS) DIST STAFF ASST 952-656-5176
Olson, Sarah (GRAVES, SAM) FIELD REP/ CASEWK MGR 816-792-3976
O'Mara, Raymond (SARBANES) DPTY CHIEF OF STAFF/ LEGIS DIR 2370 54016
Ombres, Devon (RASKIN) SR COUNSEL 412 CHOB 55341
Oms, Alejandro (HAALAND) LEGIS CORRES 1237 56302
O'Neal, David (NORMAN) DIST DIR 803-327-1114
O'Neal, Whitley (TAKANO) SR LEGIS ASST 420 CHOB 52305
O'Neil, Jeff (PERLMUTTER) LEGIS DIR 1226 52645
O'Neil, Rachelle (LEWIS) CONSTIT SVCS REP 404-659-0116
O'Neill, Andrew (POCAN) LEGIS ASST 1421 52906
Onorato, Brad (THOMPSON, MIKE) DPTY CHIEF OF STAFF 707-226-9898
Onwubiko, Udochi (CMTE-ED & WORKFORCE) COUNSEL - LABOR POLICY 2051C 53725
Oo, Olivia (CÁRDENAS) LEGIS ASST 2438 56131
Opachan, Mark (CMTE-ETHICS) COUNSEL 1015 57103
Oparil, Marie (MORELLE) LEGIS ASST 1317 53615
Ophaso, Farouk (CMTE-APPRO) PROF STAFF MEMB 2362B 53421
O'Quinn, Erin (SCHRIER) CHIEF OF STAFF 1123 57761
Orama, Valerie (SOTO) FIELD REP 407-452-1171
Ordaz, Azabel (YOUNG) SPECIAL ASST 907-271-5978
Oreck, Zoe (JEFFRIES) LEGIS DIR/COUNSEL 2433 55936
Orgel, Cheri (BROWNLEY) DPTY DIST DIR 805-379-1779
Oria, Yma (LOWEY) DIST REP 914-428-1707
Orlando, Joe (CMTE-ENERGY & COMMERCE) STAFF ASST 2125 52927
Ornelas, Chiakis (MCNERNEY) DPTY DIST DIR 209-476-8552
Ornstein, Nick (THOMPSON, MIKE) LEGIS CORRES 406 CHOB 53311
Orozco, Ashley (BROWNLEY) DIST REP 805-379-1779
Orozco Valencia, Esmeralda (CISNEROS) STAFF ASST 714-459-4575
Orpilla, Mel (THOMPSON, MIKE) SR DIST REP 707-645-1888
Orrick, Michael (CAO/FIRST CALL) CUSTOMER SOLUTIONS REP B227 LHOB 58000
Ortega, Dennis (CMTE-JOINT TAX) HELP DESK TECH 595 FHOB 67575
Ortega, Kimberly (BARRAGÁN) PRESS ASST 310-831-1799
Ortegon, Catherine (HIMES) CONSTIT SVCS REP 203-333-6600
Ortiz, Alexander (YOUNG) LEGIS DIR/DPTY CHIEF OF STAFF 2314 55765
Ortiz, Griselda (SÁNCHEZ) FIELD REP 562-860-5050
Ortiz, Sammy (VELÁZQUEZ) CONG AIDE 718-599-3658
Osborn, Claire (BARR) LEGIS ASST 2430 54706
Osborne, Amanda (MALINOWSKI) COMMUNICATIONS DIR 426 CHOB 55361
Osborne, Christopher (LEGIS COUNSEL) COUNSEL 337 FHOB 56060
Osborne, Janine (WALKER) DIR - CONSTIT SVCS 336-229-0159
Osborne, Tucker (HUDSON) CONSTIT SVCS REP/MGR - OUTREACH 704-786-1612
O'Shea, Casey (SCHNEIDER) CHIEF OF STAFF 1432 54835
Osheroff, Benjamin (PARLIAMENTARIAN) ASST PARLIAMENTARIAN H209 57373
Osmond, Kari (WATSON COLEMAN) DPTY CHIEF OF STAFF 609-883-0026
Osorio, Mariana (LYNCH) SR LEGIS ASST 2109 58273
Ostrander, Michael (STEFANIK) DIST DIR 518-743-0964
Ostrich, Jay (PERRY) DIST DIR 717-603-4980
Ostro, Zachary (KELLY, ROBIN L.) LEGIS DIR 2416 50773
O'Sullivan, Meghan (COURTNEY) LEGIS ASST 2332 52076
O'Sullivan, Ryan (DELGADO) LIAISON - VETS 845-443-2930
Oswald, Justin (MENG) CHIEF OF STAFF 2209 52601
Oszakiewski, Brian (LIPINSKI) CHIEF OF STAFF 773-948-6223
Otero, Miguel (DIAZ-BALART) DPTY CHIEF OF STAFF 305-470-8555
Otero, Simon (TORRES SMALL) CASEWKR 575-323-6384
O'Toole, Ryan (MIN LEADER) CLOAKROOM DIR H204 54000
O'Toole, Ryan (REPUB CLOAKRM) CLOAKROOM DIR H223 57350
Ott, Alan (GROTHMAN) DIST DIR 920-907-0624
Ou, Howard (CISNEROS) POLICY ADVISOR 431 CHOB 54111
Ouertatani, Charla (CMTE-FINANCIAL SVCS) STAFF DIR 2129 54247
Oulahyane, Melissia (CAO/ACCOUNTING) ACCNT TECH 3110 65063

Ours, Nick (OLSON) CASEWKR 281-494-2690
Overbeek, Kimberly (CMTE-BUDGET) BUDGET ANALYST 204E CHOB 67200
Overby, Anne (ROY) LIAISON - MIL 830-896-0154
Overby, Frank (CAO/FURNISHINGS) MASTER CARPET MECHANIC WA32 RHOB 58000
Overend, Christopher J (CMTE-JOINT TAX) SR ECONOMIST 585 FHOB 67575
Overton, Crystal (DAVIS, DANNY K.) PERSONAL ASST 773-533-7520
Owen, Emily (MCNERNEY) STAFF ASST/DIST SCHEDULER 925-754-0716
Owen, James (KELLY, TRENT) FIELD REP 662-841-8808
Owen, Joshua (MULLIN) FIELD REP 918-687-2533
Owen, Nekia (THOMPSON, BENNIE G.) EXEC SECY/FINANCIAL ADMIN 601-866-9003
Owens, Ben (KIRKPATRICK) STAFF ASST/LEGIS CORRES 309 CHOB 52542
Owens, Karen (NORTON) DIST DIR 202-408-9041
Owens, Kibwe (CLERK) ADMIN ASST H154 57000
Owens, Lindsay (JAYAPAL) DPTY CHIEF OF STAFF/LEGIS DIR 1510 53106
Owens, Michael (CAO/HOUSE RECORDING STUDIO) BROADCAST PROD TECH 2010 53941
Owens, Tonya (ROGERS, HAROLD) CASEWKR/ RECEPTIONIST 606-886-0844
Owusu-Mensah, Kwasi (CLERK/LCS) NETWK ADMIN 2401 51182
Paasch, Dan (BILIRAKIS) DIST AIDE/DIST SCHEDULER 727-232-2921
Pa'au, Ina (RADEWAGEN) CASEWKR 684-633-3601
Pace, Angie (HARRIS) COMMUNITY RELATIONS ASST 443-944-8624
Pace, Davis (RATCLIFFE) LEGIS DIR 223 CHOB 56673
Pacheco, Ricardo (BARRAGÁN) STAFF ASST/LEGIS CORRES 1030 58220
Pacilio, Anna (VEASEY) COMMUNICATIONS DIR 2348 59897
Paciorek, Josh (UPTON) COMMUNICATIONS DIR 2183 53761
Pack, Chris (NAT REPUB CONG CMTE) COMMUNICATIONS DIR 202-479-7000
Pack, Nancy (HURD) SCHEDULER/DPTY CHIEF OF STAFF 317 CHOB 54511
Padavic, Samantha (CICILLINE) LEGIS CORRES 2233 54911
Padgett, Ashleigh (LOUDERMILK) LEGIS CORRES 422 CHOB 52931
Padilla, Ashleigh (LEVIN, MIKE) STAFF ASST 760-599-5000
Padilla, Corbette (CONAWAY) REGIONAL DIR 432-687-2390
Padro, Enrique (DIAZ-BALART) CONG AIDE 239-348-1620
Padro-Raldiris, Marieli (GONZÁLEZ-COLÓN) COMMUNICATIONS DIR 787-723-6333
Page, Esther (RIGGLEMAN) DIR - CONSTIT SVCS 434-973-9631
Page, Laura (LAMALFA) REGIONAL DIR 530-343-1000
Pagon Marchena, Claudia (OCASIO-CORTEZ) STAFF ASST/LEGIS CORRES 229 CHOB 53965
Paik, Aurora (LIEU) LEGIS ASST/PRESS SECY 403 CHOB 53976
Paikowsky, Steven (WASSERMAN SCHULTZ) SR ADVISOR 1114 57931
Painter, Heather (LAMB) LEGIS ASST 1224 52301
Painter, Stetson (CRAWFORD) FIELD REP 870-424-2075

Pakledinaz, Adam (WEBSTER) STAF
Palacios, Stephanie (MURPHY) CONSTIT ADVOCATE 888-2
Palasits, Sara (CMTE-SCIENCE) PROF STAFF - MAJ 2321 5637
Palencia, Stephanie (AGUILAR) LEGIS CORRES/STAFF ASST 109 CHOB 53201
Paleologos, Mary (KELLY, ROBIN L.) DIST PRESS SECY 708-679-0078
Palermo, Trish (MCCOLLUM) STAFF ASST/LEGIS CORRES 2256 56631
Palmer, Ashli (MAJ WHIP) DIR - FLOOR H329 63210
Palmer, Jonathan (WENSTRUP) STAFF ASST/LEGIS CORRES 2419 53164
Palmer, Mark (NORMAN) FIELD REP/CASEWKR 803-327-1114
Palmer, William (ADERHOLT) LEGIS ASST 1203 54876
Palumbo, Samantha (DELAURO) SCHEDULER 203-562-3718
Paluskiewicz, J P (CMTE-ENERGY & COMMERCE) CHIEF COUNSEL 2322A 53641
Pampati, Shivani (SPEAKER) STAFF ASST H232 50100
Pancrazio, Nick (HOUSE DEM CONG CMPGN CMTE) DPTY EXEC DIR - ADMINISTRATION & PLANNING 202-863-1500
Pandya, Nishith (RUSH) LEGIS DIR 2188 54372
Paniagua-Uribe, Daisy (LIEU) FIELD REP 323-651-1040
Panone, Jenny (CMTE-APPRO) PROF STAFF MEMB 1001 53481
Panos, Peter (NEAL) AIDE 413-785-0325
Pansius, Susan (KIM) DIR - CONSTIT SVCS 856-703-2700
Pany, Christopher (CAO/CUST EXPER CTR) CONTRACT SUPPORT ADMIN B227 LHOB 58000
Papa, Katie
(BUSTOS) OFFICE MGR 1233 55905
(KILDEE) FINANCIAL ADMIN 203 CHOB 53611
(LOWEY) OFFICE MGR 2365 56506
Pappas, George (CMTE-INTELLIGENCE) SR ADVISOR - MBR SVCS HVC304 54121
Pappas, Kathy (FERGUSON) CONSTIT SVCS REP 770-683-2033
Parafiniuk, Sadie (GROTHMAN) DPTY DIST DIR 920-907-0624
Pardal, Agustina (TIPTON) SCHEDULER/FINANCIAL ADMIN 218 CHOB 54761
Pardieck, Karrie (PENCE) CONSTIT SVCS 812-799-5230
Pardo, Ali (HOUSE REPUB CONF) NATIONAL PRESS SECY 1420 55107
Pardue, Liz (CMTE-RULES) DPTY STAFF DIR H312 59091
Parella, Courtney (CMTE-HOUSE ADMIN) COMMUNICATIONS DIR - MIN 1216 58281
Parent, Charyssa (MARSHALL) COMMUNICATIONS DIR 312 CHOB 52715
Paretzky, Kenneth I (LAW REV COUNSEL) SR COUNSEL 308 FHOB 62411
Paris, Martin (AMODEI) CONSTIT RELATIONS REP 775-777-7705
Paris-Behr, Caroline (UNDERWOOD) SR POLICY ADVISOR 1118 52976
Parisi, Christina (MALONEY, CAROLYN B.) LEGIS DIR 2308 57944
Park, James (CMTE-JUDICIARY) CHIEF COUNSEL 2138 53951
Parker, Allison (COMMIS ON SECUR & COOP IN EUR) COUNSEL 234 FHOB 51901
Parker, Arden (DEGETTE) OFFICE COORD 303-844-4988
Parker, Kevina (CAO/ACCOUNTING) ACCNT TECH 3110 59909

Parker, Kyle (COMMIS ON SECUR & COOP IN EUR) SR SENATE STAFF REP 234 FHOB **51901**
Parker, Kyle (BUTTERFIELD) SR POLICY ADVISOR 2080 .... **53101**
Parker, Larkin (SCHRADER) EXEC ASST 2431 .... **55711**
Parker, Leslie (GRAVES, SAM) LEGIS ASST 1135 .... **57041**
Parker, Robyn (WILLIAMS) DIST DIR **817-774-2575**
Parker, Sabrina (COLE) EXEC ASST 2207 .... **56165**
Parker, Susan (KELLY, TRENT) COMMUNICATIONS DIR **662-841-8808**
Parker, Sydney (TRONE) STAFF ASST 1213 .... **52721**
Parker, Woody (GREEN, MARK E.) SR CASEWKR **931-266-4483**
Parker, Wyndee (SPEAKER) NATIONAL SECUR ADVISOR H232 .... **50100**
Parker-Cox, Felicia (EVANS) CONG AIDE/EXEC ASST **215-276-0340**
Parkinson, Rachel (STEWART) CONSTIT SVCS 2242 .... **59730**
Parks, Stephanie (CMTE-WAYS & MEANS) SUBCOMM STAFF DIR 1139 .... **54021**
Parlapiano, Amanda (JORDAN) STAFF ASST/ CASEWKR **419-999-6455**
Parmar, Naveen (CMTE-SMALL BUSINESS) POLICY DIR/ GEN COUNSEL 2361 .... **54038**
Parmiter, Robert (CMTE-JUDICIARY) DPTY STAFF DIR - MIN STAFF 2142 .... **56906**
Parnell, Mack (LOUDERMILK) FIELD REP **770-429-1776**
Parnes, Jonathan (CMTE-HOMELAND SECUR) COUNSEL 176 FHOB **62616**
Parobek, Stacy (AMODEI) DIST DIR **775-686-5760**
Parr, Diana (LIEU) LEGIS FELLOW 403 CHOB **53976**
Parrish, Hannah (YOHO) EXEC ASST **352-505-0838**
Parsons, Ben (WALORSKI) CONSTIT LIAISON **574-204-2645**
Parthasarathy, Kalyani (LEGIS COUNSEL) ASST COUNSEL 337 FHOB **56060**
Partin, John (TIMMONS) LEGIS ASST 313 CHOB **56030**
Partridge, Willard (CAO/OFFICE DESIGN AND MOVE SVCS) SR PROJ SPECIALIST B216 LHOB **64742**
Pascarella, David (SCOTT, AUSTIN) CONSTIT SVCS REP **478-971-1776**
Pasternak, Douglas (CMTE-TRANSP & INFRA) DIR - INVESTIGATIONS 587 FHOB **54472**
Pasteur, Nicole (STANTON) COMMUNICATIONS DIR/ POLICY ADVISOR 128 CHOB **59888**
Pastore, Matt (LOWEY) SCHEDULER/EXEC ASST 2365 .... **56506**
Pastran, Rafael (CAO/FURNISHINGS) JOURNEYMAN - FURN SPEC WA22 RHOB **58000**
Patchett, Kaity (AXNE) DIST DIR **515-400-8180**
Pate, Cynthia (ROBY) FIELD REP **334-262-7718**
Pate, Gabriella (TAYLOR) DIR - COMMUNITY OUTREACH **972-202-4150**
Patel, Dhaval (CAO/HIR – ENTERPRISE INFRASTRUCT) MGR SITE 3 .... **571-921-3307**
Patel, Kamal (THORNBERRY) LEGIS ASST 2208 .... **53706**
Patel, Miya (NEGUSE) LEGIS ASST 1419 .... **52161**
Patel, Nina (SCOTT, ROBERT C. "BOBBY") LEGIS COUNSEL 1201 .... **58351**
Patel, Rina (DEAN) LEGIS CORRES 129 CHOB **54731**
Patel, Saad (INSPECTOR GENERAL) DIR - INFO SYS 386 FHOB **61250**
Patel, Twinkle (STEUBE) SR LEGIS ASST 521 CHOB **55792**
Patel, Vedant (JAYAPAL) COMMUNICATIONS DIR 1510 .... **53106**
Patil, Neil (CMTE-WAYS & MEANS) SUBCOMM CLERK/ LEGIS ASST 1104 .... **53943**
Patrick, Brian (HUIZENGA) COMMUNICATIONS DIR **616-570-0917**
Patrida, Deyssi (RUIZ) CASEWKR **760-424-8888**
Patterson, Addie (DUNCAN, JEFF) COMMUNICATIONS DIR 2229 .... **55301**
Patterson, Brandon (LEE, BARBARA) DIST PRESS SECY **510-763-0370**
Patterson, Levi (LUJÁN) LEGIS ASST 2323 .... **56190**
Patterson, Michael (KELLY, TRENT) CASEWKR/ CASEWKR - MIL/CASEWORK - VETS **662-841-8808**
Patterson, Robyn (HORSFORD) COMMUNICATIONS DIR 1330 .... **59894**
Patton, Cynthia (DAVIS, SUSAN A.) DPTY CHIEF OF STAFF/SCHEDULER 1214 .... **52040**
Paulk, Elaine (SCOTT, AUSTIN) CONSTIT SVCS REP **229-396-5175**
Pauls, Michael (NORCROSS) LEGIS CORRES 2437 .... **56501**
Paulsen, Megan (COLLINS, CHRIS) EXEC ASST 2243 .... **55265**
Paulson, Katie (SHALALA) LEGIS CORRES 1320 .... **53931**
Pavlak, Michael (CMTE-JOINT TAX) RESEARCH ASST 595 FHOB **67575**
Pavlock, Cara (HIMES) DIST DIR **203-333-6600**
Pavlovich, Natasha M (MATSUI) CASEWKR **916-498-5600**
Pawlow, Jonathan (CMTE-TRANSP & INFRA) SR COUNSEL 585 FHOB **54472**
Pawlow, Jonathan (SMITH, ADAM) LEGIS DIR/DPTY CHIEF OF STAFF 2264 .... **58901**
Pay, Katelyn (WALDEN) DIST FIELD REP **541-776-4646**
Payette, Andrew (KRISHNAMOORTHI) STAFF ASST **847-413-1959**
Payne, Alex (SCHRIER) LEGIS DIR 1123 .... **57761**
Payne, Chelsea (MARCHANT) CONSTIT SVCS **972-556-0162**
Payne, Frazier (BYRNE) DPTY DIST DIR/FIELD REP **251-690-2811**
Payne, Liz (TIPTON) LEGIS DIR 218 CHOB **54761**
Payton, Rayshon (HORN) LEGIS DIR 415 CHOB **52132**
Payton, Sheila (MOORE) OUTREACH SPEC **414-297-1140**
Paz, Carlos (ESPAILLAT) SHARED EMPLOYEE 1630 .... **54365**
Paz, Julio (LANGEVIN) CONSTIT SVCS REP **401-732-9400**
Pazik, Meghan (CASTEN) STAFF ASST 429 CHOB **54561**
Pearce, Rachel (BACON) LEGIS ASST 1024 .... **54155**
Pearson, Christa (WEBSTER) DIST DIR **352-241-9230**
Pearson, Michael (CMTE-JOINT ECON) RESEARCH ASST - DEM SH-804 .... **40364**
Pearson, Stephen (CAO/HIR – NETWORKING ENGINEERING AND OPS) SR NETWK SYS ENGINEER 664 FHOB **63544**
Pearson, Tim (CMTE-JUDICIARY) PUBLICATIONS CLERK 367 FHOB **53951**
Pease, Annie (CICILLINE) CONSTIT SVCS REP **401-729-5600**
Peavey, Laura (CMTE-FINANCIAL SVCS) PRESS SECY 4340 .... **57502**
Pecoraro, Brandon (CMTE-JOINT TAX) ECONOMIST 595 FHOB **67575**
Pedone, Jeanette (CLERK/REPORTERS) ASST CHIEF CLERK - DEBATES HT59 .... **55621**
Pedramrazi, Armita (SCANLON) LEGIS DIR 1535 .... **52011**

Pedrotti, Max (MILLER) LEGIS CORRES 1605 53452
Peek, Lincoln (WELCH) COMMUNICATIONS DIR 2187 54115
Peek, Tracy (MCHENRY) STAFF ASST 828-327-6100
Peel, Kaitlyn (CMTE-ENERGY & COMMERCE) DIGITAL DIR 2125 52927
Peele, Nancy (GRAVES, GARRET) ASST CHIEF OF STAFF 2402 53901
Pegues, Robin (SGT AT ARMS/ID SVCS) ASST/ID SVCS 321 CHOB 53820
Peifer, Ann (SCHIFF) DIST DIR 818-450-2900
Peiper, Pamela (HERRERA BEUTLER) DIST DIR 360-695-6292
Peirson, Zach (SMUCKER) DIST DIR 717-393-0667
Pekkala, Jonathan (CRIST) SCHEDULER/OFFICE MGR/ CHIEF OPS OFFICER 215 CHOB 55961
Pelkyi, Tenzin (GREEN, AL) LEGIS ASST 2347 57508
Pelletier, Justin
(CMTE-SMALL BUSINESS) SR ADVISOR 2361 54038
(VELÁZQUEZ) LEGIS DIR 2302 52361
Pelletier, Pat (MITCHELL) LEGIS DIR/DPTY CHIEF OF STAFF 211 CHOB 52106
Pellito, John (MORELLE) COMMUNITY LIAISON/ DIST LIAISON 585-232-4850
Pena, Nancy (CARTER, JOHN R.) LIAISON - CONSTIT SVCS 512-246-1600
Penaloza, Virginia (COX) DIR - CONSTIT SVCS 559-460-6070
Penaroza, Kainoa (GABBARD) CHIEF OF STAFF 808-541-1986
Pence, Hallie (CLINE) SR LEGIS ASST 1009 55431
Pence, Robert (NAPOLITANO) FIELD REP/ CASEWKR 626-350-0150
Pendarvis, Stephanie (WILSON, JOE) SCHEDULER/EXEC ASST 1436 52452
Pender, Melissa (HILL, KATIE) CONSTIT SVCS REP 661-802-0244
Penharlow, Kevin (CAO/OFFICE OF THE CHIEF HUMAN RESOURCES OFFICER) SAFETY & OCCUPATIONAL HEALTH SPEC 643A FHOB 60295
Pennington, Daryl (HOYER) SR CONSTIT LIAISON 301-474-0119
Pennington, Nicholas (LANGEVIN) STAFF ASST 2077 52735
Peoples, Amber (NORMAN) SCHEDULER 319 CHOB 55501
Pepen, Enrique (KENNEDY) DIST STAFF ASST 617-332-3333
Perdichizzi, Gabriela (TAYLOR) LEGIS ASST 1404 54201
Pereida, Jose (VELA) DIST DIR 361-230-9776
Perelmuter, Stuart (YARMUTH) SPEECHWRITER 402 CHOB 55401
Perepelyuk, Marina (PANETTA) CONG AIDE 212 CHOB 52861
Perera, Stephanie (BERA) LEGIS CORRES 1727 55716
Perez, Benjie H. (SAN NICOLAS) EXEC ASST 671-475-6453
Perez, Cassandra (CORREA) DIST SCHEDULER 714-559-6190
Perez, David (KHANNA) STAFF ASST 221 CHOB 52631
Perez, Gabriel (GONZALEZ, VICENTE) DIST STAFF ASST 956-682-5545
Perez, Michael (DAVIS, SUSAN A.) LEGIS ASST/ COMMUNICATIONS ASST 1214 52040
Perez, Robert (SCHNEIDER) STAFF ASST 847-383-4870
Perez, Stephanie (VARGAS) DIST AIDE 619-422-5963
Perez-Acosta, Mehgan (JOYCE, JOHN) DPTY CHIEF OF STAFF 1337 52431
Perkes, Rhonda (STEWART) FIELD REP 801-364-5550
Perkins, Bailey (HORN) LEGIS ASST 415 CHOB 52132
Perkins, Brian (SPEIER) DIR - DIST AFFAIRS 650-342-0300
Perkins, Janet (CAO/HIR – IT CUSTOMER SOLUTIONS) TECH SOLUTIONS ENGINEER 694 FHOB 56002
Perkins, Kelsey (CLARK) DIST DIR 617-354-0292
Perkins, Nate (CMTE-RULES) DIR - LEGIS OPS H312 59091
Perkins, Olga (WALKER) CONSTIT LIAISON 336-333-5005
Perkins, Tommy (CAO/FURNISHINGS) APPRENTICE UPHOLSTERER WA33 RHOB 58000
Perkins, Trudy (CUMMINGS) DPTY CHIEF OF STAFF/COMMUNICATIONS DIR 410-685-9199
Perkins, Wuan (CMTE-WAYS & MEANS) SYS ADMIN 1102 53625
Perlmutter, Ari (SCHRIER) STAFF ASST 1123 57761
Perlstein, Andrew (DESAULNIER) LEGIS ASST 503 CHOB 52095
Perrino, Jenny (KAPTUR) LEGIS DIR/DPTY CHIEF 2186 54146
Perrone, Lisa (LARSON) DIST AIDE/SR ADVISOR 860-278-8888
Perry, Anne (LARSON) SR POLICY ADVISOR 1501 52265
Perry, Deborah (CUMMINGS) SPECIAL ASST 410-685-9199
Perry, Jill (FLORES) STAFF ASST 254-732-0748
Perry, John (CAO/FURNISHINGS) MASTER CABINET MAKER WA25 RHOB 58000
Perry, Victoria (DELGADO) DPTY DIR 845-443-2930
Persaud, Clifton (INSPECTOR GENERAL) ASST DIR - INFO SYS AUDITS 386 FHOB 61250
Persico, Tim (MALONEY, SEAN PATRICK) CHIEF OF STAFF 2331 55441
Person, Candace (ESPAILLAT) COMMUNICATIONS DIR 1630 54365
Pertierra, Ericka (CRENSHAW) SPECIAL PROJ 713-860-1330
Peruccio, Caitlin (DELAURO) LEGIS ASST 2413 53661
Pescatore, Brittney (CMTE-ETHICS) DIR - INVESTIGATIONS 1015 57103
Peters, Jamiyl (PAYNE) SR LEGIS ASST 103 CHOB 53436
Peters, Joseph (DAVIS, DANNY K.) LEGIS CORRES 2159 55006
Peters, Robert (RATCLIFFE) LEGIS ASST 223 CHOB 56673
Petersen, Barbara (PLASKETT) SPECIAL PROJ 2404 51790
Petersen, Steven (CMTE-NATURAL RESOURCES) SUBCOMM STAFF DIR 4120 52761
Peterson, Andrea (FLETCHER) COMMUNICATIONS ASST 713-353-8680
Peterson, Ben (MCCOLLUM) LEGIS DIR 2256 56631
Peterson, Carol (CAO/OFFICE OF THE CFO) FINANCE LIAISON 3140 50665
Peterson, Elly (ARMSTRONG) SCHEDULING DIR 1004 52611
Peterson, Martha (MEADOWS) FIELD REP 828-765-0573
Peterson, Michael (VISCLOSKY) LEGIS ASST 2328 52461
Peterson, Miranda (PALLONE) LEGIS ASST 2107 54671
Peterson, Sage (CMTE-BUDGET) ADVISOR - MBR SVCS/ OUTREACH ADVISOR 507 CHOB 67270
Peterson, Savanna (CRAIG) SCHEDULER 1523 52271
Peterson, Vincent (RYAN) COMMUNITY AFFAIRS LIAISON 330-373-0074
Peterson-Wood, Emily (YOUNG) SPECIAL ASST 907-456-0210
Petit, Cody (JOHNSON, BILL) STAFF ASST 2336 55705
Peto, Lisa (CMTE-FINANCIAL SVCS) CHIEF COUNSEL/ LEGIS DIR 2129 54247
Petrick, David (COMMIS ON CHINA) RESEARCH ASSOC 243 FHOB 63766

Pettit, Matthew (NEWHOUSE) LEGIS CORRES/LEGIS AIDE 1414 55816
Pettit, Sydney (MCKINLEY) LEGIS ASST 2239 54172
Pettitt, Mark (BROOKS, MO) CHIEF OF STAFF 2246 54801
Petty, Catherine (YOUNG) DPTY STATE DIR 907-271-5978
Pew, Penny (GOSAR) DIST DIR/DIR - GOVT, BUSINESS, & COMMUNITY AFFAIRS 480-882-2697
Peyton, Russell (KIRKPATRICK) LEGIS FELLOW 309 CHOB 52542
Pfeiffer, Amy (KIM) CHIEF OF STAFF 1516 54765
Pfeiffer, Connor (HURD) LEGIS ASST 317 CHOB 54511
Pflieger, Charles (TAYLOR) STAFF ASST 1404 54201
Pfrang, Steve (LAHOOD) CHIEF OF STAFF 1424 56201
Phalen, Luke (KINZINGER) FIELD REP 815-431-9271
Pham, Anthony (LOWENTHAL) STAFF ASST 108 CHOB 57924
Pham, Vincent (LOFGREN) CONG AIDE 408-271-8700
Phan, Dean (CAO/HIR – NETWORKING ENGINEERING AND OPS) SUPERVISOR 663A FHOB 66307
Phaup, Elliott (RUPPERSBERGER) SCHEDULER/POLICY ADVISOR/EXEC ASST 2206 53061
Phelan, Andy (JOHNSON, HENRY C. "HANK", JR.) COMMUNICATIONS DIR 770-987-2291
Phelps, Ashley (DAVIS, RODNEY) COMMUNICATIONS DIR 1740 52371
Phelps, David (BRINDISI) DIST FIELD REP 315-732-0713
Phenix, Lucy (GONZALEZ, VICENTE) RECEPTIONIST 956-682-5545
Philips, Mariah (KENNEDY) SCHEDULER 304 CHOB 55931
Phillips, Ashleigh
(HOYER) CONSTIT LIAISON 301-843-1577
(CAO/CUST EXPER CTR) CUSTOMER ADVOCATE B227 LHOB 58000
Phillips, Brian, Jr (DELGADO) PRESS ASST/STAFF ASST 1007 55614
Phillips, Clay (CASTOR) CHIEF OF STAFF 2052 53376
Phillips, Jackie (FULCHER) STAFF ASST/ CONSTIT SVCS REP 208-888-3188
Phillips, Jamali (CAO/HIR - ENTERPRISE MESSAGING AND MOBILITY) SR SYS ENGINEER 621 FHOB 60010
Phillips, Lisa (CAO/ACCOUNTING) STAFF ACCOUNTANT 3110 69350
Phillips, Troy (CMTE-AGRIC) DPTY STAFF DIR 1301 52171
Phipps, Jane (VEASEY) EXEC ASST 2348 59897
Phoenix, Candyce (CMTE-OVERSIGHT & GOVT REFORM) SUBCOMM STAFF DIR 6440 55051
Piard, Christina (BUTTERFIELD) DIR - COMMUNITY OUTREACH 919-908-0164
Piatt, Austin (BALDERSON) STAFF ASST/LEGIS AIDE 1221 55355
Piazza, John (CMTE-SCIENCE) CHIEF COUNSEL - MAJ 2321 56375
Piazza, Richard (CAO/PAYROLL & BENEFITS) MGMT ANALYST B215 LHOB 52562
Pic, Jordan
(CMTE-ED & WORKFORCE) SHARED EMPLOYEE 2462 52071
(FOXX) SCHEDULER 2462 52071
Piccioli, Laura (BUSTOS) SCHEDULER 1233 55905
Pickel, Toni (BISHOP, SANFORD D., JR.) CONSTIT SVCS/OFFICE MGR 229-439-8067
Pickett, Krystal (BISHOP, SANFORD D., JR.) DIST STAFF ASST 229-439-8067
Picolla, Joseph (INSPECTOR GENERAL) DPTY INSPECTOR GENERAL 386 FHOB 61250
Piepho, Judah (CLARK) SCHEDULER 2448 52836
Pierce, Hannah (KIND) SCHEDULER 1502 55506
Piereschi, Vivian (WASSERMAN SCHULTZ) SR CONSTIT ADVOCATE 954-845-1179
Pierre-Canel, Christian (LAWSON) LEGIS ASST 1406 50123
Pierson, Crawford (SCOTT, AUSTIN) SCHEDULER/OFFICE MGR 2417 56531
Pietkiewicz, Kate (TURNER) SCHEDULER 2082 56465
Piland, Mark (NORMAN) CHIEF OF STAFF 319 CHOB 55501
Pileggi, Anthony (STEFANIK) CHIEF OF STAFF 318 CHOB 54611
Pilipenko, Diana (CMTE-INTELLIGENCE) PROF STAFF - MAJ HVC304 57690
Pilkerton, Sandra (CAO/HOUSE RECORDING STUDIO) OFFICE MGR 2010 53941
Pillie, Derek (BANKS) DIR - CONSTIT SVCS 260-702-4750
Pillis, Maggie (SHERMAN) SCHEDULING DIR 2181 55911
Pillow, Rob (GUEST) COMMUNICATIONS DIR 230 CHOB 55031
Pillsbury, Naomi (WOODALL) CONSTIT SVCS REP 770-232-3005
Pina, Oriana (SOTO) COMMUNICATIONS DIR 1507 59889
Pincilotti, Ivanna (BERA) CASEWKR 916-635-0505
Pinckney, Janna
(CMTE-JUDICIARY) DIR - INFO TECH 2451 53951
(HUFFMAN) SYS ADMIN 1527 55161
(LAWSON) SYS ADMIN 1406 50123
(MCNERNEY) SYS ADMIN 2265 51947
(NADLER) SYS ADMIN 2132 55635
(TORRES) SHARED EMPLOYEE 2444 56161
Pineda, Charlotte (MARSHALL) ADVISOR - HEALTH POLICY 312 CHOB 52715
Pinegar, Hilary (SMITH, JASON) LEGIS ASST 2418 54404
Pineiro, Eli (SAN NICOLAS) EXEC ASST 1632 51188
Pingeton, Stephen E (CLERK/LRC) MGR - RECORDS & REGISTRATION B81 CHOB 65200
Pinkett, Durwood (VAN DREW) CASEWK DIR 609-625-5008
Pinson, Alex (ROGERS, HAROLD) LEGIS ASST 2406 54601
Pinson, Stephen (CAO/HIR – CYBERSECURITY) SR INFO SYS SECUR ANALYST 612 FHOB 66579
Pintar, Maryanne (PETERS) CHIEF OF STAFF 858-455-5550
Piper, Brian (FERGUSON) STAFF ASST 1032 55901
Pirc, Austin (CHABOT) STAFF ASST 2408 52216
Pirron, Kyle (HAGEDORN) LEGIS ASST/LEGIS ASST - MIL 325 52472
Pisano, Will (KUSTER) LEGIS ASST 320 CHOB 55206
Pitifer, Mark (REED) CASEWKR 315-759-5229
Pittman, Anthony (NORCROSS) ASST 856-427-7000
Pittman, Lisa (CMTE-NATURAL RESOURCES) CHIEF COUNSEL 1329 52761
Pitts, Julia (EVANS) CONG AIDE 215-276-0340
Pizer, Jonathan (QUIGLEY) COMMUNITY & OUTREACH LIAISON 773-267-5926
Plake, Lindsay (CHU) SCHEDULER 626-304-0110
Plan, Maile (CHU) FIELD REP/CASEWKR 626-304-0110
Plank, Jilian (NUNES) CHIEF OF STAFF 1013 52523
Planning, David (CMTE-FINANCIAL SVCS) MBR SVCS & COALITIONS ASST 4340 57502
Plasencia, Suzi (GRANGER) LEGIS DIR 1026 55071

Plasky, Naomi (QUIGLEY) LEGIS FELLOW 2458 **54061**
Plassche, Clare (SIRES) LEGIS DIR 2268 **57919**
Plaster, Will (CLERK) ASST TO THE CLERK H154 **57000**
Plater, Angelina (LEGIS COUNSEL) STAFF ASST 337 FHOB **56060**
Platt, Anna (BROWN) LEGIS DIR 1323 **58699**
Plaugher, Joe (THOMPSON, MIKE) FIELD REP **707-542-7182**
Plaut, Brian (HOUSE REPUB CONF) DIR - OPS 1420 **55107**
Pleasant, LaTriece (BROWN) STAFF ASST **301-458-2600**
Pleasant-Jones, P J (RUPPERSBERGER) COMMUNITY AFFAIRS LIAISON **410-628-2701**
Pledger, Xeron (JOHNSON, HENRY C. "HANK", JR.) CONSTIT SVCS **770-987-2291**
Plinski, Brian (BONAMICI) CASEWKR/ OUTREACH REP/DIST REP **503-469-6010**
Plowden, Vincent (CAO/FURNISHINGS) LEAD FINISHER WA22 RHOB **58000**
Plunto, Larissa (MCCAUL) REGIONAL DIR **281-398-1247**
Plush, Lewis (BUCHANAN) LEGIS CORRES 2427 **55015**
Pluviose, Veronique (CMTE-ED & WORKFORCE) STAFF DIR 2176 **53725**
Pobur, Colleen (STEVENS) DIST DIR **734-853-3040**
Podkolzina, Alexandra (LOFGREN) CONG ASST **408-271-8700**
Podliska, Rick (POSEY) SR POLICY ADVISOR 2150 **53671**
Poe, Phil (CMTE-FINANCIAL SVCS) POLICY ASST 4340 **57502**
Poe, Virginia (CRIST) LEGIS ASST 215 CHOB **55961**
Pohl, Remy (ENGEL) STAFF ASST **914-699-4100**
Pointer, Katherine (CMTE-HOMELAND SECUR) DIR - MBR SVCS 117 FHOB **68417**
Poirot, Debra (WOODALL) DIST DIR **770-232-3005**
Poitevien, Erika (CMTE-WAYS & MEANS) ASST TO THE STAFF DIR 1102 **53625**
Polanowicz, Kathleen (MCGOVERN) SR ADVISOR **508-831-7356**
Polefka, Emma (WEBER) COMMUNICATIONS DIR 107 CHOB **52831**
Policastro, Marie (HOLLINGSWORTH) DIST SCHEDULER 1641 **55315**
Poling, Parker (NAT REPUB CONG CMTE) EXEC DIR **202-479-7000**
Polisar, Evan (HASTINGS) PRESS SECY/LEGIS ASST 2353 **51313**
Pollack, Daniel (MENG) COMMUNITY LIAISON **718-358-6364**
Pollack, George (KING, PETER T.) LEGIS ASST 302 CHOB **57896**
Pollas, Yardly (RUSH) SR COUNSEL/CHIEF OF STAFF 2188 **54372**
Pollet, Kyle (LEVIN, ANDY) FIELD REP/ CASEWKR **586-498-7122**
Pollinger, Dawn (KUSTER) DIR - CONSTIT SVCS **603-226-1002**
Pollock, Samuel (BUCSHON) FIELD REP **812-232-0523**
Polzin, Savannah (SPEAKER) DPTY DIR - SCHEDULING H232 **50100**
Pomeroy, James (RIGGLEMAN) CONSTIT SVCS REP **434-973-9631**
Pomeroy, Julia (BLUMENAUER) SR ADVISOR **503-231-2300**
Pond, Shirley (DESJARLAIS) CONSTIT SVCS REP **423-472-7500**
Pontzer, Deborah (THOMPSON, GLENN) ECON DEV SPEC **814-670-0432**
Pool, Caleb (THORNBERRY) DIST REP **806-371-8844**
Pool, Leigh (GOODEN) OUTREACH COORD **214-765-6789**
Poole, Jennifer (LOUDERMILK) CASE MGR **770-429-1776**
Poole, Julie (INSPECTOR GENERAL) ASST DIR 386 FHOB **61250**
Poole, Todd (BUDD) DIST DIR **336-998-1313**
Popadiuk, Mary (CMTE-BUDGET) GEN COUNSEL 507 CHOB **67270**
Porroa, Ivelisse (RUIZ) LEGIS ASST 2342 **55330**
Porter, Bob (MASSIE) SR CONSTIT SVCS REP **859-426-0080**
Porter, Carrie (MASSIE) CONSTIT LIAISON/DIST STAFF ASST/ASST SCHEDULER **859-426-0080**
Porter, Christopher (COOK) FIELD REP 1027 **55861**
Porter, Jalina (RICHMOND) COMMUNICATIONS DIR 506 CHOB **56636**
Porter, John (BRADY) DPTY CHIEF OF STAFF - POLICY 1011 **54901**
Porter, Megan (HOUSE REPUB CONF) MBR SVCS ASST 1420 **55107**
Portillo, Deborah (VELA) SR ADVISOR 307 CHOB **59901**
Posey, DeBorah (HASTINGS) OFFICE DIR 2353 **51313**
Postell, Joyce (WILSON, FREDERICA S.) DIST DIR **305-690-5905**
Pottle Urquhart, Morgan (GOLDEN) DIST REP **207-249-7400**
Pough, Tracie (WASSERMAN SCHULTZ) CHIEF OF STAFF 1114 **57931**
Poulios, Allison (LATTA) CHIEF OF STAFF 2467 **56405**
Poursoltan, Cameron (MCCAUL) LEGIS ASST 2001 **52401**
Powell, Erica (CLAY) LEGIS DIR 2428 **52406**
Powell, Jared (RODGERS) PRESS SECY 1035 **52006**
Powell, Jason (CMTE-OVERSIGHT & GOVT REFORM) DPTY GEN COUNSEL 2157 **55051**
Powell, Jessica (WOMACK) LEGIS ASST 2412 **54301**
Powell, Jo Anne (CONAWAY) REGIONAL DIR **325-659-4010**
Powell, Latrice (SPEAKER) DPTY FLOOR DIR H232 **50100**
Powell, Lee Ann (CARTER, EARL L. "BUDDY") DIST STAFF ASST **912-352-0101**
Powell, Millie (WILSON, JOE) EXEC ASST/DIST OFFICE MGR **803-939-0041**
Power, Thomas (BILIRAKIS) LEGIS DIR/DPTY CHIEF OF STAFF 2227 **55755**
Powers, William (NEAL) LEGAL COUNSEL **413-785-0325**
Powerz, Darius (CAO/HIR – IT CUSTOMER SOLUTIONS) SR TECH SUPPORT REP 100 CHOB **62299**
Prabhu, Sruthi (WALKER) LEGIS ASST 1725 **53065**
Prasanna, Sandeep (CMTE-HOMELAND SECUR) COUNSEL 176 FHOB **62616**
Prater, Lori (KELLY, MIKE) TAX COUNSEL 1707 **55406**
Pratt, Kris (DEFAZIO) LEGIS DIR 2134 **56416**
Pratt, Michael (CAO/LOGISTICS) LOGISTICS & DIST SPEC HT19 **59474**
Presley, Jessica (CMTE-JUDICIARY) DIR - DIGITAL COMMUNICATIONS 2035 **53951**
Presta, Tony (KELLY, ROBIN L.) SCHEDULER/ DPTY DIST DIR **708-679-0078**
Presti, Hunter (CMTE-TRANSP & INFRA) PROF STAFF 592 FHOB **54472**
Preston, Emma (KHANNA) SCHEDULER/EXEC ASST 221 CHOB **52631**
Price, Everett (COMMIS ON SECUR & COOP IN EUR) POLICY ADVISOR 234 FHOB **51901**
Price, Larry (INSPECTOR GENERAL) DIRECTOR 386 FHOB **61250**

Price, Reva (SPEAKER) OUTREACH DIRECTOR/SR ADVISOR H232 50100
Prichard, Ji (CMTE-WAYS & MEANS) TAX COUNSEL 1136 55522
Priehs, Kayla (MULLIN) DPTY CHIEF OF STAFF 2421 52701
Prieur L'Heureux, Alexis (MOULTON) CHIEF OF STAFF 1127 58020
Prime, Max (TONKO) CONG AIDE 518-465-0700
Primes, Kayla (HOULAHAN) LEGIS CORRES 1218 54315
Primus, Robert (BARRAGÁN) CHIEF OF STAFF 1030 58220
Primus, Wendell (SPEAKER) SR HEALTH & BUDGET POLICY ADVISOR H232 50100
Prince, Erik (PLASKETT) CHIEF 2404 51790
Pritschau, Mary (CAO/CUST EXPER CTR) CUSTOMER ADVOCATE B227 LHOB 58000
Probst, Scott (LEGIS COUNSEL) COUNSEL 337 FHOB 56060
Proby, Tera (OMAR) OFFICE MGR 1517 54755
Procaccino, Gabriel (ROSE, MAX) DIST SCHEDULER 718-667-3313
Proferes, Jerrica (GREEN, MARK E.) SCHEDULER 533 CHOB 52811
Proffitt, Gavin (HOUSE REPUB STUDY CMTE) POLICY STAFF 418 CHOB 52777
Propst, Johan (SHERMAN) LEGIS AIDE 2181 55911
Prost, Gary (MCNERNEY) SR FIELD REP 209-476-8552
Pruett, Jeremy (LONG) FIELD REP 417-889-1800
Pruett, Kimberly (MCCLINTOCK) DIR - COMMUNITY OUTREACH 916-786-5560
Prus, Julia (WENSTRUP) LEGIS ASST 2419 53164
Ptasienski, Michael (INSPECTOR GENERAL) INSPECTOR GENERAL OF THE HOUSE 386 FHOB 61250
Puckett, Bobby (DEFAZIO) LEGIS ASST 2134 56416
Puente, Joseph (SHALALA) COMMUNICATIONS DIR 1320 53931
Pugh, Glen (ARRINGTON) REGIONAL DIR 325-675-9779
Pugh, Kim (CAO/ENTERPRISE APPLICATIONS) SR BUSINESS PROCESS APPLICA SPEC B73 FHOB 66294
Pujadas, Irantzu (LOWENTHAL) DPTY DIST DIR 562-436-3828
Pulido, Mark (LOWENTHAL) DPTY CHIEF OF STAFF 562-436-3828
Pulis, Jenelle (CLERK/LEGIS OPS) ASST JOURNAL CLERK HT13 55558
Pulitzer, Mina (ALLRED) SCHEDULER 328 CHOB 52231
Pump, Barry (CLERK/REPORTERS) CHIEF CLERK - DEBATES HT59 55621
Pun, Arlene (PETERS) STAFF ASST/LEGIS AIDE 2338 50508
Purcell, Heather (KHANNA) COMMUNICATIONS DIR 221 CHOB 52631
Purcell, Marianne (KUSTOFF) DIST DIR 901-682-4422
Purdy, Julian (SMITH, ADAM) OFFICE MGR/LEGIS ASST 2264 58901
Puro, Sarah (CMTE-APPRO) PROF STAFF MEMB 2358A 52141
Putnam, Gabi (PALAZZO) DIST STAFF ASST 228-864-7670
Putz, Scott (CMTE-TRANSP & INFRA) ASST SYS ADMIN 2253 54472
Puzzuoli, Len (CAO/OFFICE OF THE CFO) CHIEF 3140 64616
Pyatt, Jon (BUSTOS) CHIEF OF STAFF 1233 55905
Pyke, Tom (KHANNA) DIST DIR 408-436-2720
Quantius, Sue (CMTE-APPRO) PROF STAFF MEMB H306 67252
Quarterman, Craig (SIMPSON) REGIONAL DIR 208-334-1953
Quartz, Evelyn (CMTE-SMALL BUSINESS) PRESS SECY 2361 54038
Quattrone, John (SGT AT ARMS/POLICE SVCS) ASST SGT AT ARMS - POLICE SVCS/LAW ENFORCEMENT HT8 51000
Queen, Michael (CLERK/LRC) DIGITAL LIBRARIAN B81 CHOB 65200
Quesada Andrade, America (BISHOP, ROB) LEGIS CORRES 123 CHOB 50453
Quezada, Jose (COSTA) DIST STAFF ASST 559-495-1620
Quibuyen, Michael (CISNEROS) PRESS SECY 431 CHOB 54111
Quigley, Elizabeth (NEAL) AIDE 413-785-0325
Quigley, Lisa (COOPER) CHIEF OF STAFF 615-736-5295
Quinn, Conor (LARSON) DPTY CHIEF OF STAFF 860-278-8888
Quinn, Katherine (CMTE-ARMED SVCS) PROF STAFF 2340 62167
Quinn, Leslie (JOHNSON, MIKE) COORD - GRANTS & SPEC PROJ 318-840-0309
Quinones, Iris (VELÁZQUEZ) COMMUNITY LIAISON 212-619-2606
Quintanilla, Ana (TITUS) DIR - CONSTIT AFFAIRS/DIST REP 702-220-9823
Quintanilla, Iliana (CAO/CUST EXPER CTR) GRAPHIC DESIGNER 217 FHOB 58000
Quintas, Hernan (RUIZ) PRESS SECY 760-424-8888
Quintyne, Chris (JEFFRIES) LEGIS COUNSEL 2433 55936
Quiroa, David (MCGOVERN) DIST REP 508-831-7356
Quist-Demars, Kelly (TONKO) CONSTIT REP 518-843-3400
Qureshi, Janet (BRADY) CASEWK DIR 936-441-5700
Rackard, N'Dea (BISHOP, SANFORD D., JR.) LEGIS CORRES/MGR - OUTREACH & COMMUNICATIONS 2407 53631
Radding, Elena (BERA) STAFF ASST 1727 55716
Radice, Lauren (BASS) EXEC SCHEDULER 2059 57084
Radovich Piper, Danielle (PERLMUTTER) CHIEF OF STAFF 303-274-7944
Raducci, Jen (DEUTCH) CASEWKR 561-470-5440
Raelea, Taylor (BROWN) STAFF ASST 1323 58699
Rafferty, Caitriona (WALTZ) LEGIS CORRES 216 CHOB 52706
Rafferty, Palmer (HUIZENGA) LEGIS DIR 2232 54401
Ragan, Crystal (NUNES) DIST DIR 559-733-3861
Rager, Jessica (CLERK/LEGIS OPS) CLERK - CMTE DIGEST HT13 57925
Raghavan, Gautam (JAYAPAL) CHIEF OF STAFF 1510 53106
Ragsdale, Chris (WITTMAN) MIL FELLOW 2055 54261
Rahn, Samuel (CRAIG) DIST SCHEDULER 651-846-2120
Rains, Brannon (CMTE-ENERGY & COMMERCE) STAFF ASST 2322A 53641
Raj, Ravi (HOULAHAN) STAFF ASST 1218 54315
Rajzer, Stephen (WALBERG) DIST DIR/DIR - ADMIN OPS 517-780-9075
Rakhimov, Mukhsimjon (CAO/HIR – HOUSE WEB SVCS) SR INTERNET SYS ENGINEER 627 FHOB 62140
Rako, Morgan (TURNER) PRESS SECY 2082 56465
Ramadan, Ahmad (DINGELL) FIELD REP 313-278-2936
Rambosk, Kevin (DINGELL) LEGIS DIR 116 CHOB 54071
Rambough, Janean (ARMSTRONG) DIST OFFICE MGR 702-354-6700
Rambow, Andrea (CMTE-APPRO) PROF STAFF MEMB 283 FHOB 53881
Ramey, Chad (LUETKEMEYER) CHIEF OF STAFF 2230 52956
Ramirez, Angela (ASST SPEAKER) CHIEF H132 52020
Ramirez, Angela (LUJÁN) CHIEF OF STAFF 2323 56190
Ramirez, Chris (GOODEN) STAFF ASST 214-765-6789

Ramirez, Dayanara (TAKANO) COMMUNICATIONS DIR 420 CHOB 52305
Ramirez, Eliza (MALINOWSKI) LEGIS DIR 426 CHOB 55361
Ramirez, Matthew (SPEAKER) OUTREACH ADVISOR H232 50100
Ramirez, Osvaldo (CÁRDENAS) CASEWKR 818-221-3718
Ramirez, Samantha (CRIST) ASST PRESS SECY 215 CHOB 55961
Ramirez Kornacki, Olga (CAO/HOUSE RADIO-TV GALLERY) DIRECTOR H320 55214
Ramirez Quintero, Samantha (CRIST) PRESS ASST 215 CHOB 55961
Ramos, Caroline (MCBATH) CONSTIT SVCS REP/CASEWKR/FIELD REP 470-773-6330
Ramos, Diana (ESCOBAR) DIR - CONSTIT SVCS 915-541-1400
Ramos, Humberto (GALLEGO) DIST STAFF ASST 602-256-0551
Ramos, Jacqueline (CMTE-FOREIGN AFFAIRS) SR PROF STAFF 2420 55021
Ramos, Mario (TORRES) FIELD REP/CASEWKR 909-481-6474
Ramos, Melissa (HORSFORD) DIST STAFF ASST 702-963-9360
Ramos, Tito (MCNERNEY) CONSTIT REP 925-754-0716
Rampey, Dominick (CAO/HOUSE RECORDING STUDIO) PROD SPEC/SR BROADCAST ENGINEER 2010 53941
Ramsey, Logan (AMODEI) COMMUNICATIONS DIR 104 CHOB 56155
Ramzanali, Asad (ESHOO) SR TECH POLICY ADVISOR 202 CHOB 58104
Randaccio, James (ROYBAL-ALLARD) STAFF ASST/ LEGIS CORRES 2083 51766
Randall, Brittany (CMTE-HOUSE ADMIN) DIR - MEMB SVCS 1316 58281
Randall, Robin (CAO/PAYROLL & BENEFITS) GENERALIST B215 LHOB 52275
Range, Cheyenne (WILSON, FREDERICA S.) SPECIAL ASST 2445 54506
Rangel, Brenda (VELA) CASEWKR/PRESS AIDE 956-544-8352
Rangel, Juan (SÁNCHEZ) LEGIS AIDE 2329 56676
Ranieri, Hilary (TIMMONS) LEGIS DIR 313 CHOB 56030
Rank, Ethan (BONAMICI) SCHEDULER 2231 50855
Rankin, Christina (KENNEDY) LEGIS CORRES 304 CHOB 55931
Ranstrom, Tim (NEAL) SCHEDULER/LEGIS ASST 2309 55601
Rapallo, David (CMTE-OVERSIGHT & GOVT REFORM) STAFF DIR 2157 55051
Rapoport, Sylvia (COOPER) FELLOW 615-736-5295
Rapp, Jeffrey (MURPHY) SR LEGIS ASST 1710 54035
Rardin, David (JOHNSON, BILL) LEGIS DIR 2336 55705
Rasch, Terry (BROWNLEY) FELLOW 805-379-1779
Rascher, Mallory (MEADOWS) SCHEDULER 2160 56401
Rasmussen, Reid (JOHNSON, DUSTY) SPECIAL ASST 605-275-2868
Ratliff, Kim (ADAMS) EVENTS MGR 704-344-9950
Ratliffe, Pam (RICE, TOM) DIST STAFF ASST/ CONSTIT SVCS REP 843-679-9781
Ratner, Mark
(CMTE-ENERGY & COMMERCE) POLICY COORD 2322A 53641
(UPTON) LEGIS DIR/DPTY CHIEF OF STAFF 2183 53761
Ratterree, Trent (HORN) COMMUNITY OUTREACH SPEC 405-602-3074
Ratto, Mark (BOST) LEGIS DIR 1440 55661
Rauber, John (LAHOOD) DPTY COMMUNICATIONS DIR 1424 56201
Rauch, Laura (CMTE-ARMED SVCS) PROF STAFF MEMB 2119 66712
Rausch, Scott (MOONEY) LEGIS DIR 2440 52711
Ravas, Joslyn (SGT AT ARMS/HOUSE SECURITY) SECUR OFFICER HVC301 62044
Rawat, Vinod (CAO/HIR – HOUSE WEB SVCS) INTERNET SYS SPEC 646 FHOB 66283
Rawlins, Genevieve (CURTIS) DIST OFFICE MGR 801-922-5400
Ray, Rebecca (WALDEN) LEGIS ASST 2185 56730
Ray, Trevor (HARTZLER) STAFF ASST 2235 52876
Rayfield, John (CMTE-TRANSP & INFRA) STAFF DIR 505 FHOB 54472
Raymond, Chrissy (MOULTON) POLICY ADVISOR 1127 58020
Rayner, Jonathan (BROWN) LEGIS ASST - MIL 1323 58699
Rayzor, Ronda (HUNTER) OFFICE MGR 619-448-5201
Rea, Ryan (WALDEN) STAFF ASST 2185 56730
Read, Jennifer (CMTE-FINANCIAL SVCS) COUNSEL 2129 54247
Ream, Anne (ESHOO) SR ADVISOR - HEALTH 650-323-2984
Reardon, Brian (CMTE-INTELLIGENCE) CONG FELLOW HVC304 57690
Reardon, Erica (QUIGLEY) POLICY ADVISOR 773-267-5926
Reasbeck, Libby (MCKINLEY) DIST DIR 304-232-3801
Reasco, Kayla (HAYES) OUTREACH DIR 860-223-8412
Reasor, Christiana (WATKINS) LEGIS AIDE 1205 56601
Reath, Eric (SMUCKER) OUTREACH REP 717-393-0667
Rebnord, Daniel (CMTE-OVERSIGHT & GOVT REFORM) SUBCOMM STAFF DIR 6470 55051
Rebold, Liza (MUCARSEL-POWELL) LEGIS CORRES 114 CHOB 52778
Rebscher, Dawn (PALLONE) DIST FIELD REP 732-571-1140
Reckling, Anna (HILL, J. FRENCH) STAFF ASST 501-324-5941
Rector, Ren'Ee (JOHNSON, BILL) FIELD REP - VETS 740-376-0868
Reddick-Smith, Shadawn (CMTE-JUDICIARY) COMMUNICATIONS DIR 2138 53951
Reddish, Bill (HARRIS) COMMUNITY LIAISON 443-944-8624
Reddy, Sanjay (STEVENS) LEGIS CORRES 227 CHOB 58171
Redick, Taylor (CMTE-FOREIGN AFFAIRS) POLICY ANALYST 2471 55021
Reed, Dawn (VISCLOSKY) SCHEDULER/ CONSTIT RELATIONS LIAISON 219-795-1844
Reed, J R (MASSIE) FIELD REP 606-324-9898
Reed, Krystie (VISCLOSKY) CASEWKR 219-795-1844
Reed, Mary (DAVIS, DANNY K.) CONSTIT SVCS 773-533-7520
Reed, Matthew (MCCLINTOCK) OFFICE DIR 916-786-5560
Reed, Michael (SWALWELL) CHIEF OF STAFF 407 CHOB 55065
Reed, Michael (BISHOP, SANFORD D., JR.) CHIEF OF STAFF 2407 53631
Reed, Truman (YOUNG) LEGIS ASST 2314 55765
Reeder, Raven (NORTON) CHIEF OF STAFF 2136 58050
Reel, Matt (CMTE-VET AFFAIRS) DPTY STAFF DIR 3470 59756
Reese, Kristi (CMTE-WAYS & MEANS) DIGITAL DIR 1139 54021
Reese, Sarah (BABIN) PRESS SECY 2236 51555
Reeves, Octavian (CAO/ENTERPRISE APPLICATIONS) RESOURCE ANALYST 630A FHOB 66539

Reeves, Robert (CLERK) DPTY CLERK H154 **57000**
Reeves-Martin, Tara (MOONEY) CONSTIT SVCS REP **304-264-8810**
Regan, Kate (FRANKEL) SCHEDULER 2305 **59890**
Regan, Timothy (CLERK/LEGIS OPS) ASST TALLY CLERK HT13 **57347**
Reger, Amy (COMMIS ON CHINA) RESEARCH ASSOC 243 FHOB **63769**
Register, Kathy (JOHNSON, HENRY C. "HANK", JR.) DIST DIR **770-987-2291**
Reibach, Stacey (RESCHENTHALER) DIST DIR **724-206-4800**
Reich, David (CMTE-APPRO) CLERK H306 **67252**
Reid, Colston (MALINOWSKI) CHIEF OF STAFF 426 CHOB **55361**
Reid, Edward (CAO/HOUSE RECORDING STUDIO) BROADCAST PROD TECH 2010 **53941**
Reid, Karen (CAO/OFFICE SUPPLY/GIFT SHOP) SUPPLY ACCNT SPEC B217 LHOB **53321**
Reilingh, Eddie (DELBENE) LEGIS CORRES 2330 **56311**
Reilly, Nell (RICE, KATHLEEN M.) CHIEF OF STAFF 2435 **55516**
Reimers, Jackson (CAO/FINANCIAL COUNSELING) MGR B215 LHOB **61531**
Reimers, Jerad (SMITH, ADRIAN) COMMUNITY LIAISON **308-384-3900**
Reinecke, Griffin (CMTE-SCIENCE) RESEARCH ASST - MAJ 2321 **56375**
Reinert, Will (REED) COMMUNICATIONS DIR 2263 **53161**
Reingold, Sarah (STEVENS) LEGIS DIR 227 CHOB **58171**
Reinshuttle, Michelle (CMTE-APPRO) MBR SVCS ASST 1016 **53481**
Reis, Leslie (KRISHNAMOORTHI) DIR - CONSTIT SVCS **847-413-1959**
Reiser, Martin (MIN WHIP) DPTY POLICY DIR H148 **50197**
Reising, John (MIN WHIP) DIR - OPS & MBR SVCS H148 **50197**
Reitz, Tim (HICE) LEGIS DIR 409 CHOB **54101**
Relfe, Mitch (BYRNE) LEGIS DIR/LEGIS COUNSEL 119 CHOB **54931**
Relic, Becky (CMTE-BUDGET) DPTY STAFF DIR - MIN STAFF 507 CHOB **67270**
Rell, Brian (ADERHOLT) CHIEF OF STAFF 1203 **54876**
Remal, Colin (PRESSLEY) MGR - CONSTIT SVCS **617-850-0040**
Remke, Matthew (CAO/HIR - ENTERPRISE MESSAGING AND MOBILITY) SR SYS ENGINEER 623 FHOB **56153**
Render, Ray (ROSE, JOHN W.) DPTY DIST DIR **615-206-8204**
Renken, Courtney (GRANGER) CASEWKR **817-338-0909**
Rens, Sarah (LEGIS COUNSEL) ASST COUNSEL 337 FHOB **56060**
Renteria, Alejandro (UNDERWOOD) LEGIS DIR 1118 **52976**
Renteria, Andrew (FITZPATRICK) CHIEF OF STAFF 1722 **54276**
Renz, Brandon (CMTE-ED & WORKFORCE) STAFF DIR 2101 **54527**
Reslen, Carmen (SIRES) FIELD REP **201-558-0800**
Resnick, Mira (CMTE-FOREIGN AFFAIRS) SR PROF STAFF 2170 **55021**
Resnikoff, Brendan (KILMER) DIST SCHEDULER **253-272-3515**
Reteguis, Karla (MEEKS) CONG LIAISON **718-725-6000**
Reuschel, Trevor (BUSTOS) DPTY CHIEF OF STAFF 1233 **55905**
Reutter, Matthew (COURTNEY) CONSTIT SVCS **860-741-6011**
Reyes, Arturo (PRICE) DIST STAFF ASST **919-859-5999**
Reyes, Dilenny (SOTO) DIST STAFF ASST **407-452-1171**
Reyes, Elsy (SGT AT ARMS/APPOINTMENT) ASST - APPTS DESK CANNON **52551**
Reyes, Erica (CARBAJAL) DIST REP/CASEWKR **805-546-8348**
Reyes, Gil (YARMUTH) LEGIS ASST 402 CHOB **55401**
Reyes, Juanita (MALONEY, CAROLYN B.) DIST MGR **212-860-0606**
Reyes, Ruben (GRIJALVA) DIST DIR **520-622-6788**
Reyes, Shayra (SERRANO) COMMUNITY LIAISON **718-620-0084**
Reyes-Palma, Nicole (MURPHY) COORD - OUTREACH **888-205-5421**
Reyna, Luz (BLUMENAUER) FIELD REP **503-231-2300**
Reynolds, Gisselle (DIAZ-BALART) LEGIS ASST/DIR - CONSTIT SVCS 404 CHOB **54211**
Reynolds, Margaret (GOLDEN) DIST DIR **207-241-6767**
Reynolds, Sarnata (CMTE-JUDICIARY) COUNSEL 6320 **53926**
Reynolds, Thomas (WOODALL) LEGIS ASST 1724 **54272**
Reynoso, Klarissa (OCASIO-CORTEZ) LEGIS CORRES 229 CHOB **51823**
Rezaee-Rod, Paniz (CUNNINGHAM) LEGIS ASST 423 CHOB **53176**
Rhinehart Van Tassell, Melanie (THOMPSON, MIKE) CHIEF OF STAFF 406 CHOB **53311**
Rhoades, Matthew (CMTE-ARMED SVCS) PROF STAFF 2117 **62583**
Rhoden, Steven (CASTOR) STAFF ASST 2052 **53376**
Rhodes, Christine (ALLEN) CONSTIT SVCS REP **706-228-1980**
Rhodes, Mashell (CAO/HIR – IT CUSTOMER SOLUTIONS) SR TELECOMMUNICATIONS ADMIN 692 FHOB **56002**
Rhones, Sherman (CAO/LOGISTICS) LOGISTICS & DIST SPEC WA16 RHOB **59474**
Rhue, Phanalphie (ADAMS) DIST DIR **704-344-9950**
Rhyne, Curtis (HOLDING) LEGIS DIR/DPTY CHIEF OF STAFF 1110 **53032**
Ricchetti, Tiger (DINGELL) STAFF ASST 116 CHOB **54071**
Ricci, Alex (CMTE-ED & WORKFORCE) PROF STAFF MEMB 6140 **56558**
Rice, Adam (ROGERS, HAROLD) FIELD REP **606-886-0844**
Rice, Edmund B (CMTE-FOREIGN AFFAIRS) SR PROF STAFF 2170 **55021**
Rice, Kelicia (CARTER, JOHN R.) DPTY CHIEF OF STAFF 2110 **53864**
Rice, Lawrence (CAO/ENTERPRISE APPLICATIONS) SR BUSINESS PROCESS APPLICA SPEC B70 FHOB **59925**
Rice, Matt (SHIMKUS) DIST AIDE **618-288-7190**
Rice, Rose (SCANLON) STAFF ASST **610-626-1913**
Rice, Thomas
(CMTE-FOREIGN AFFAIRS) PROF STAFF 2066 **68467**
(MCCAUL) SR LEGIS ASST 2001 **52401**
Rice-Davis, Chelsey (SCHNEIDER) LEGIS CORRES 1432 **54835**
Rich, Benjamin (PASCRELL) CHIEF OF STAFF 2409 **55751**
Rich, Elonda (LEGIS COUNSEL) STAFF ASST/PARALEGAL 337 FHOB **56060**
Rich, Matt (GOLDEN) LEGIS ASST 1223 **56306**
Rich, Zach (STEVENS) CASEWKR **734-853-3040**
Richard, Joel (DEUTCH) SR COUNSEL 2447 **53001**
Richards, Gabby (SCANLON) COMMUNICATIONS DIR 1535 **52011**
Richards, John (CAO/HIR – HOUSE WEB SVCS) INTERNET SYS SPEC 626 FHOB **60581**

Richards, Justin (NAT REPUB CONG CMTE) POLITICAL DIR 202-479-7000
Richards, Mary Jo (STEFANIK) REGIONAL DIR 315-782-3150
Richards, Michael (OLSON) SR LEGIS ASST 2133 55951
Richards, Robert (KILMER) CONSTIT SVCS REP 253-272-3515
Richards, Zachary (CMTE-JOINT TAX) ECONOMIST 595 FHOB 67575
Richardson, Anne (CMTE-JUDICIARY) DIGITAL DIR 2226 56906
Richardson, Dorothy (YOHO) CASEWK MGR 904-276-9626
Richardson, Emily (MATSUI) SR LEGIS ASST 2311 57163
Richardson, Larissa (TLAIB) DIST DIR 313-463-6220
Richardson, Mary Ellen (LAHOOD) LEGIS ASST 1424 56201
Richman, Josh (SWALWELL) COMMUNICATIONS DIR 510-370-3322
Richman, Karyn (CMTE-APPRO) PROF STAFF MEMB 2006 55834
Richmond, Kristin (CMTE-APPRO) ADMIN AIDE 2007 53081
Richter, Jane (LOWEY) STAFF ASST 2365 56506
Richter, Robin (CAO/HIR – IT CUSTOMER SOLUTIONS) TELEPHONE SYS CONSULT 692 FHOB 56002
Richter, Shannon (CMTE-APPRO) PROF STAFF MEMB H405 52847
Rickenbacker, John (CLYBURN) FIELD DIR 803-799-1100
Ricks, Rosena (BUTTERFIELD) CONSTIT SVCS REP 252-237-9816
Rico, Catalina (MCNERNEY) CONSTIT REP 209-476-8552
Ridder, Benjamin (CMTE-ED & WORKFORCE) LEGIS ASST 6150 57101
Riddle, Donald (CAO/ENTERPRISE APPLICATIONS) SR BUSINESS PROCESS APPLICA SPEC B73 FHOB 66236
Ridenour, Greg (KINZINGER) FIELD REP 815-431-9271
Rider, Verne (FITZPATRICK) VET ADVOCATE 215-579-8102
Ridgell, William (CAO/LOGISTICS) LOGISTICS & DIST SPEC WA16 RHOB 59474
Ridgway, Hunter (CARTWRIGHT) CHIEF OF STAFF 1034 55546
Riding, Ally (CURTIS) COMMUNICATIONS DIR 125 CHOB 57751
Riegel, Jenni (SMITH, JASON) MGR - CONSTIT SVCS 573-364-2455
Riemenschneider, John (AXNE) CASEWKR/DIST FIELD REP 208 55476
Rierson, Megumi (CRAIG) PRESS ASST 1523 52271
Riesterer, Angeline (HERRERA BEUTLER) COMMUNICATIONS DIR 2352 53536
Riffle, Daniel (OCASIO-CORTEZ) POLICY ADVISOR - FINANCIAL SVCS 229 CHOB 53965
Riggins, Nathan (KIM) LEGIS CORRES 1516 54765
Riggs, Ezra (TIPTON) STAFF ASST 218 CHOB 54761
Riley, Carmelitta (SGT AT ARMS) ADMIN SPEC H124 52456
Riley, Daniel (CROW) CONSTIT ADVOCATE 720-748-7514
Riley, Regan (TRONE) FIELD REP 301-926-0300
Riley, Ruth (LEWIS) EXEC ASST/SCHEDULER 404-659-0116
Riley, Tena (COLLINS, DOUG) DIST STAFF ASST 770-297-3388
Rill, Katrina (SPEIER) DIST PRESS SECY/DPTY DIST DIR 650-342-0300
Rime, Abby (EMMER) PRESS SECY 763-241-6848
Rimke, Shawna (CALVERT) CASEWKR/DIST REP 951-277-0042
Rindels, Emma
(MCCARTHY) LEGIS ASST 2468 52915
(MIN LEADER) LEGIS ASST H204 54000
Ringer, Chris (DUNCAN, JEFF) STAFF ASST 2229 55301
Ringhand, Derek (HAGEDORN) CONSTIT OUTREACH REP 507-323-6090
Riordan, Erica (TITUS) LEGIS ASST 2464 55965
Rios, Brandon Ricardo (CMTE-OVERSIGHT & GOVT REFORM) COUNSEL 2157 55051
Rios, Diana (GOMEZ) LEGIS ASST 1530 56235
Ripke, Jackie (CMTE-APPRO) PROF STAFF MEMB H405 52847
Ripp, Kelli (JOHNSON, BILL) LEGIS ASST 2336 55705
Rippeteau, Judy (ROYBAL-ALLARD) RECEPTIONIST 2083 51766
Risinger, Tara (YOUNG) SPECIAL ASST 907-271-5978
Ritchey, George (CMTE-FOREIGN AFFAIRS) PROF STAFF/ SECUR OFFICER G324 55021
Ritchie, Ryan (COLLINS, CHRIS) STAFF ASST 2243 55265
Ritner, Molly (HOUSE DEM CONG CMPGN CMTE) NATIONAL POLITICAL DIR - CAMPAIGNS & RECRUITMENT 202-863-1500
Rivard, Mitchell (KILDEE) CHIEF OF STAFF 203 CHOB 53611
Rivas, Edgar (O'HALLERAN) LEGIS ASST 324 CHOB 53361
Rivas, Victoria (ROYBAL-ALLARD) LEGIS ASST 2083 51766
Rivera, Awilda (SERRANO) SR STAFF ASST 718-620-0084
Rivera, Irene (CMTE-SMALL BUSINESS) PROCUREMENT COUN 2361 54038
Rivera, Karina (HURD) FIELD REP 915-235-6421
Rivera, Keanu (SCANLON) LEGIS ASST 1535 52011
Rivera, Kevin (LARSON) DIST AIDE/PRESS ASST 860-278-8888
Rivera, Martin (SOTO) LEGIS ASST 1507 59889
Rivera Romero, Thomas (CISNEROS) LEGIS CORRES 431 CHOB 54111
Rivers, Marlian (CAO/LOGISTICS) BLDG SUPERVISOR B23 FHOB 59474
Riviezzo, Domenick (HICE) CONSTIT SVCS REP 478-457-0007
Roach, Bob (CMTE-FINANCIAL SVCS) INVESTIGATOR 2129 54247
Roach, Kevin (CAO/HIR - ENTERPRISE MESSAGING AND MOBILITY) TEAM LEAD 624 FHOB 66229
Robayo, Maria (CASTOR) LEGIS CORRES 2052 53376
Robb, Brian (FOSTER) COORD - OUTREACH 815-280-5876
Robb, Priya (NEGUSE) CONSTIT ADVOCATE 303-335-1045
Robbins, Alex (CONNOLLY) CONSTIT OUTREACH REP 703-256-3071
Roberts, Alivia (CMTE-ENERGY & COMMERCE) PRESS ASST 2125 52927
Roberts, Angie (RADEWAGEN) STAFF ASST 1339 58577
Roberts, Becca (THOMPSON, MIKE) CONSTIT SVCS REP 707-645-1888
Roberts, Carl (LIPINSKI) LEGIS CORRES 2346 55701
Roberts, Connor (BUCSHON) STAFF ASST 2313 54636
Roberts, Craig (SHIMKUS) CHIEF OF STAFF 2217 55271
Roberts, Dallas (HECK) CONSTIT OUTREACH REP 360-459-8514
Roberts, Drew (CMTE-RULES) RESEARCH ASST 1116 59191
Roberts, Jesse (CMTE-HOUSE ADMIN) COUNSEL - MIN 1216 58281
Roberts, Kaitlyn (BRADY) DPTY SCHEDULER 1011 54901
Roberts, Madeline (CROW) STAFF ASST 720-748-7514
Roberts, Patrick (GONZALEZ, VICENTE) OUTREACH LIAISON - WOUNDED WARRIOR 956-682-5545

Roberts, Sarah (DELGADO) CONSTIT SVCS REP 845-443-2930
Roberts, Zach (SCOTT, AUSTIN) LEGIS CORRES 2417 56531
Robertson, Angel (MAST) SR OUTREACH DIR/ COORD - OUTREACH 772-336-2877
Robertson, Brent (MARSHALL) CHIEF OF STAFF 312 CHOB 52715
Robertson, Deborah (CAO/ACCOUNTING) SR ACCOUNTANT 3110 55028
Robertson, James (SGT AT ARMS/APPOINTMENT) ASST - APPTS DESK CVC 52551
Robertson, Kyle (PENCE) CHIEF OF STAFF 222 CHOB 53021
Robertson, Ritika (BUCK) CHIEF OF STAFF 2455 54676
Robertson, Sara (CRAWFORD) PRESS SECY 2422 54076
Robertson, Summer (BILIRAKIS) DPTY CHIEF OF STAFF 727-232-2921
Robertson, Whitney (JOHNSON, MIKE) DPTY PRESS SECY 418 CHOB 52777
Robie, Gina (CURTIS) DIST SCHEDULER/EXEC ASST 801-922-5400
Robinette, Jamie (SPANO) CHIEF OF STAFF 224 CHOB 51252
Robins, Heath (SMITH, JASON) DIST REP 573-335-0101
Robins, Mary Jane (KILMER) DIST REP 360-797-3623
Robinson, Brent (WITTMAN) DPTY CHIEF OF STAFF 2055 54261
Robinson, Brittan (DEMINGS) LEGIS CORRES 217 CHOB 52176
Robinson, Danielle (DAVIDS) DIST DIR 913-621-0832
Robinson, Hannah (SHERRILL) LEGIS CORRES 1208 55034
Robinson, Kalvin (CMTE-FINANCIAL SVCS) STAFF ASST 2129 54247
Robinson, Lesley (GIANFORTE) STATE DIR 406-969-1736
Robinson, Miller (FERGUSON) LEGIS CORRES 1032 55901
Robinson, Nicole (WATERS) EXEC ASST 323-757-8900
Robinson, Taesha (SGT AT ARMS/APPOINTMENT) ASST - APPTS DESK CVC 52551
Robinson, Timothy (CMTE-ENERGY & COMMERCE) CHIEF COUNSEL 2125 52927
Robinson, Walker (YARMUTH) LEGIS CORRES 402 CHOB 55401
Robles, Elena (NAPOLITANO) CASEWKR/SR FIELD REP 626-350-0150
Robles, Enrique
(CHU) DPTY DIST DIR 626-304-0110
(CHU) DPTY DIST DIR 909-625-5394
Robles, Martha (SIRES) CONG AIDE 201-558-0800
Robles, Ruby (CISNEROS) STAFF ASST 431 CHOB 54111
Robles, Sergio (BERA) FIELD REP 916-635-0505
Robreno, Andrew (SMUCKER) LEGIS DIR 127 CHOB 52411
Rocha, Alex (DEUTCH) EXEC ASST/EXEC SCHEDULER 561-470-5440
Roche, Kevin (CAO/ENTERPRISE APPLICATIONS) APPLICA DATABASE SPEC 638 FHOB 66136
Rock, Cecily W (CMTE-JOINT TAX) SR LEGIS COUNSEL 502 FHOB 53621
Rockaway, Stacie (MASSIE) FIELD REP 502-265-9119
Rockwell, Nick (THOMPSON, GLENN) LEGIS ASST 400 CHOB 55121
Rockwood, Bill (SOTO) LEGIS ASST 1507 59889
Roday, Zack (CMTE-ENERGY & COMMERCE) COMMUNICATIONS DIR 2322A 53641
Rodden, Grace (CMTE-VET AFFAIRS) GEN COUNSEL B234 LHOB 59756
Rodgers, Kevin (WALBERG) LEGIS CORRES 2266 56276
Rodman, Nicholas (HOUSE REPUB STUDY CMTE) POLICY STAFF 418 CHOB 52777
Rodriguez, Angelica (HUNTER) COMMUNITY REP 619-448-5201
Rodriguez, Christina (CÁRDENAS) CONG AIDE 818-221-3718
Rodriguez, Cynthia (ESPAILLAT) DIR - CONSTIT SVCS 212-663-3900
Rodriguez, Diana (SGT AT ARMS/GARAGES & PARKING) SPECIAL PROJ ASST G2-28 56749
Rodriguez, Edgar (TORRES) DPTY PRESS SECY 2444 56161
Rodriguez, Fabiola (COX) LEGIS ASST/PRESS SECY 1728 54695
Rodriguez, Jasmine (CASTRO) CONSTIT SVCS REP 210-348-8216
Rodriguez, Jason (HORSFORD) DPTY CHIEF 1330 59894
Rodriguez, Jeremy (PERLMUTTER) CONSTIT SVCS REP 303-274-7944
Rodriguez, Joanna (WALTZ) COMMUNICATIONS DIR 216 CHOB 52706
Rodriguez, Josh (HIMES) CONSTIT RELATIONS REP 203-333-6600
Rodriguez, Laura (MUCARSEL-POWELL) CHIEF OF STAFF 114 CHOB 52778
Rodriguez, Leonardo (SCOTT, DAVID) LEGIS CORRES 225 CHOB 52939
Rodriguez, Luis (KELLY, ROBIN L.) DIST REP 773-321-2001
Rodriguez, Nathan (CALVERT) STAFF ASST 951-277-0042
Rodriguez, Rachael (GREEN, AL) DIST DIR 713-383-9234
Rodriguez, Roman (ESTES) DIST PRESS SECY 316-262-8992
Rodriguez, Taina (SCHAKOWSKY) CONSTIT ADVOCATE 773-506-7100
Rodriguez, Vivian (SOTO) OUTREACH DIR 407-452-1171
Rodriguez Arroyo, Allison (GONZÁLEZ-COLÓN) DIST MGR 787-723-6333
Rodriguez-Beamud, Janille (GONZÁLEZ-COLÓN) DPTY CHIEF OF STAFF/LEGIS COUNSEL 1609 52615
Rodriguez-Ciampoli, Fabiola (GARCÍA, JESÚS G. "CHUY") COMMUNICATIONS DIR 530 CHOB 61497
Rodriguez-Parker, Gladys (MCGOVERN) DIST REP 508-831-7356
Rodriquez, Chloe (CMTE-ENERGY & COMMERCE) POLICY ANALYST 2125 52927
Rodriquez, Nicolas (LIEU) DIST DIR 323-651-1040
Rodvold, Zach (PHILLIPS) DIST CHIEF OF STAFF 952-656-5176
Roe, Austin (LESKO) STAFF ASST 623-776-7911
Roe, Bill (WATKINS) DPTY CHIEF OF STAFF 785-234-5966
Roe, Exodie, III (MCNERNEY) SR LEGIS ASST 2265 51947
Roeder, Debby (WALTZ) CONSTIT SVCS 386-279-0707
Rogan, Bob (WELCH) CHIEF OF STAFF 2187 54115
Rogers, Ann (HOUSE EMPLOYMENT COUNSEL) COUNSEL 4300 57075
Rogers, Carol (BARR) COMMUNICATIONS ADVISOR/OFFICE MGR 859-219-1366
Rogers, Casey (ROBY) FIELD REP 334-262-7718
Rogers, Cindy (SUOZZI) DIST DIR 631-923-4100
Rogers, Doris (CLERK/SVCS GRPS) ASST CLOAKRM FOOD MGR - MIN H223 63637
Rogers, Ivy (KUSTOFF) FIELD REP 731-412-1037
Rogers, Jacob (COLLINS, DOUG) STAFF ASST 1504 59893

Rogers, Jason (BIGGS) GEN COUNSEL 1318 52635
Rogers, Justin (CAO/FURNISHINGS) DRAPERY INSTALLER WA32 RHOB 58000
Rogers, Lucia J (CMTE-JOINT TAX) EXEC ASST 502 FHOB 53621
Rogers, Merrilee (COHEN) LEGIS CORRES 2104 53265
Rogerson, Randy (CAO/FURNISHINGS) APPRENTICE CABINET MAKER WA25 RHOB 58000
Rogers Thorpe, Amanda (CMTE-INTELLIGENCE) PROF STAFF - MAJ HVC304 57690
Rogge, Alexah (FULCHER) COMMUNICATIONS DIR 1520 56611
Rogin, Joshua (DEUTCH) CHIEF OF STAFF 2447 53001
Rogness, Becky (HAGEDORN) SR COMMUNICATIONS ADVISOR 325 CHOB 52472
Rohan, Mariah (KELLY, MIKE) CONSTIT SVCS REP 814-454-8190
Rohn, Kim (GOLDEN) CONSTIT SVCS REP 207-492-6009
Rohr, Jessica (SMITH, CHRISTOPHER H.) STAFF ASST/CASEWKR 732-780-3035
Rohr, Kate (DAVIDS) LEGIS ASST 1541 67210
Rohrschneider, Sarah (BEYER) CONSTIT OUTREACH REP 703-658-5403
Roig, Kevin (GRAVES, GARRET) DPTY CHIEF OF STAFF - COMMUNICATIONS 2402 53901
Rokus, Phil (HUIZENGA) STAFF ASST 2232 54401
Rollins, Deborah (WRIGHT) CASEWKR 817-077-5037
Rollins, Sheri (ROGERS, MIKE) DIST DIR 256-236-5655
Rolnicki, Rachel (CORREA) DIST FIELD REP 714-559-6190
Rom, Kerry (CRENSHAW) COMMUNICATIONS DIR 413 CHOB 56565
Roman, Mark (SMITH, JASON) CHIEF OF STAFF 2418 54404
Romano, Karli (CAO/HIR – NETWORKING ENGINEERING AND OPS) SPECIAL ASST SITE 63983
Romeo, Andrew (JOYCE, JOHN) COMMUNICATIONS DIR 1337 52431
Romero, Cristian (MENG) CONSTIT LIAISON/ COMMUNITY LIAISON 718-358-6364
Romero, Ignacio (TAKANO) CASEWK MGR 951-222-0203
Romero, Tumia (DAVIS, DANNY K.) SR ADVISOR 773-533-7520
Romero-Rodriguez, Eladia (MCGOVERN) REGIONAL REP 978-466-3552
Romick, Brian (MAJ LEADER) DPTY CHIEF OF STAFF H107 53130
Ronan, Wyatt (PAPPAS) COMMUNICATIONS DIR 603-285-4300
Roney, Elizabeth (BYRNE) DIST DIR 251-690-2811
Ronis, Carolyn (CMTE-ED & WORKFORCE) COUNSEL - CIVIL RIGHTS 230 FHOB 53725
Ronk, Joshua (CMTE-HOMELAND SECUR) PROF STAFF MEMB 117 FHOB 68417
Rooney, Patrick (MEUSER) LEGIS DIR 326 CHOB 56511
Roopchand, Fern (WILD) CONSTIT ADVOCATE 484-781-6000
Roos, Amber
(BROOKS, SUSAN W.) FINANCIAL ASST 2211 52276
(RODGERS) ADMIN - FINANCE & PAYROLL 1035 52006
Roper, Andrea (KILMER) DIST DIR 253-272-3515
Rorick, Lisa (RUIZ) DIR - CONSTIT SVCS 760-424-8888
Rorke, Michael (WALBERG) STAFF ASST 2266 56276
Rosado, Mary (BARR) CHIEF OF STAFF 2430 54706
Rosales, Lauren (DOGGETT) CONSTIT SVCS REP 512-916-5921
Rosario, Maritza (VELÁZQUEZ) STAFF ASST 718-599-3658
Rose, Ashley (BUCHANAN) SR COUNSEL 2427 55015
Rose, Stu (LANGEVIN) OFFICE MGR/SCHEDULER 2077 52735
Rose, Thomas (CAO/LOGISTICS) SUPERVISOR - LOGISTICS & DIST WA16 RHOB 59474
Rosebrock, Rachel (HARRIS) CONSTIT LIAISON 410-643-5425
Roseme, Jean (WILSON, FREDERICA S.) DPTY CHIEF OF STAFF 2445 54506
Rosemond, John (MIN LEADER) SPECIAL ASST H204 54000
Rosen, Kenneth (CLERK/REPORTERS) EDITOR - COMMITTEES 1718 52627
Rosen, Talia (MOORE) LEGIS ASST 2252 54572
Rosenbaum, Ben (TITUS) LEGIS DIR/DPTY CHIEF OF STAFF 2464 55965
Rosenberg, Adam (CMTE-SCIENCE) STAFF DIR - MAJ 2321 56375
Rosenfeld, Anne (KING, PETER T.) DIST DIR 516-541-4225
Rosenfeld, Jan (CMTE-WAYS & MEANS) SYS ADMIN 1139 54021
Rosenthal, Andrea (HILL, KATIE) DPTY DIST DIR 661-839-0532
Roshan, Qais (KENNEDY) LEGIS ASST 304 CHOB 55931
Rosner, Lara (CMTE-WAYS & MEANS) PROF STAFF 1139 54021
Ross, Amena (GREEN, AL) CHIEF OF STAFF 2347 57508
Ross, David (DAVIS, RODNEY) LEGIS ASST 1740 52371
Ross, Donna (MOORE) DIST OFFICE MGR 414-297-1140
Ross, Gavin (BROWNLEY) LEGIS ASST 2262 55811
Ross, Hadley (LEGIS COUNSEL) SR COUNSEL 337 FHOB 56060
Ross, Jason (RATCLIFFE) DIST CHIEF OF STAFF 972-771-0100
Ross, Kimberly (BEATTY) CHIEF OF STAFF/CHIEF COUNSEL 2303 54324
Ross, Patricia
(PELOSI) SR POLICY ADVISOR 1236 54965
(SPEAKER) SR POLICY ADVISOR H232 50100
Ross, Rebecca (CMTE-ARMED SVCS) PROF STAFF 2216 54100
Ross, Robert (MALINOWSKI) ADMIN - FINANCE & PAYROLL 426 CHOB 55361
Ross, Sandra (THORNBERRY) DIST DIR 940-692-1700
Ross, Susan (CMTE-APPRO) PROF STAFF MEMB 1016 53481
Ross, Tim (GIBBS) DIST DIR 419-207-0650
Ross, Zeke (CMTE-ETHICS) COUNSEL 1015 57103
Rossi, Janet (WOODALL) LEGIS DIR 1724 54272
Rossi, Karmen (CHENEY) FIELD REP 307-772-2595
Rossi, Rachel (CMTE-JUDICIARY) COUNSEL 6340 55727
Rossi, Sabrina (KING, PETER T.) DIST STAFF ASST 516-541-4225
Rossiter, Paul (CAO/FURNISHINGS) JOURNEYMAN LOCKSMITH WA15 RHOB 64185
Rossman, George (TIPTON) FIELD REP 970-241-2499
Rota, Robert V, Jr (CLERK/LEGIS OPS) ENROLLING CLERK HT13 53153
Rotert, Blair (WRIGHT) LEGIS DIR 428 CHOB 52002
Roth, Alexander (JOYCE, DAVID P.) DIST OUTREACH REP 440-352-3939
Roth, David (CMTE-APPRO) ADMIN AIDE 2006 55834
Roth, Kristine (CMTE-JOINT TAX) SR LEGIS COUNSEL SD-G18 45561
Roth, Sarah (TRONE) STAFF ASST 301-926-0300

Rother, Katy (CMTE-OVERSIGHT & GOVT REFORM) POLICY DIR 2105 55074
Rountree, Tara (MCEACHIN) DPTY CHIEF OF STAFF 757-942-6050
Rouse, Patricia (CAO/HOUSE RECORDING STUDIO) AUDIO SPEC 2010 53941
Rousseau, Maggie (DINGELL) COMMUNICATIONS DIR 116 CHOB 54071
Row, Matt (BAIRD) DIR - CONSTIT SVCS 317-563-5567
Rowe, Deborah (MAJ LEADER) FLOOR ASST H107 53130
Rowe, Joanna (MCHENRY) CONSTIT RELATIONS LIAISON 828-327-6100
Rowe, Sue (KAPTUR) CASEWK MGR/ SCHEDULER 419-259-7500
Rowe, Teresa (CAO/HOUSE CREATIVE SVCS) DIRECTOR 2002 52700
Rowland, Catherine (LEVIN, ANDY) LEGIS DIR 228 CHOB. 54961
Rowland, Lindsey (KELLY, TRENT) LIAISON - MIL 1005 54306
Rowland, Matt (GREEN, AL) LEGIS ASST 2347 57508
Rowley, Kalene (MAST) DIR - CONSTIT SVCS 772-336-2877
Rowley, Katy (YARMUTH) LEGIS DIR 402 CHOB 55401
Roy, Nikki
(CMTE-ENERGY & COMMERCE) POLICY COORD 2125 52927
(DEGETTE) ENERGY & ENVIRON POLICY ADVISOR 2111 54431
Royce, Zak (GALLEGO) DIR - CONSTIT SVCS 602-256-0551
Ruane, Megan (DEAN) STAFF ASST 129 CHOB 54731
Rubin, Dan (CMTE-WAYS & MEANS) COMMUNICATIONS DIR - DEM 1102 53625
Rubin, Isaac (RUIZ) LEGIS CORRES/PRESS ASST 2342 55330
Rubinger, Grace (BEYER) LEGIS CORRES 1119 54376
Rubio, Sophia (BEYER) SCHEDULER 1119 54376
Rubio, Tina (PELOSI) DIST OFFICE MGR 415-556-4862
Rucker, Terrance (HOUSE HISTORIAN) HISTORICAL PUBLICATIONS SPEC JEFFERSON BUILDING, ATTIC 61300
Rudd, Diana (HOUSE DEM CAUCUS) VICE CHAIR COUN/ VICE CHAIR DIR - MEMB SVCS B245 LHOB 51400
Ruddy, Jack (CMTE-TRANSP & INFRA) DPTY STAFF DIR 2164 59446
Rude, Laura (BUSTOS) CONSTIT ADVOCATE 309-966-1813
Rudolph, Kim (CARSON) CHIEF OF STAFF 2135 54011
Rueff, Glenn (CLERK/LCS) SR SOFTWARE ENGINEER 2401 51182
Ruhlen, Mary Ellen
(CRENSHAW) ADMIN - FINANCE & PAYROLL 413 CHOB 56565
(HUIZENGA) FINANCIAL OFFICER 2232 54401
(WALORSKI) FINANCIAL ADMIN 419 CHOB 53915
(WESTERMAN) ADMIN - FINANCE & PAYROLL 209 CHOB 53772
Ruiz, Fernando (SMITH, ADAM) LEGIS ASST 2264 58901
Ruiz, Xenia (HOUSE DEM CAUCUS) VICE CHAIR DIR - OUTREACH B245 LHOB 51400
Rumley, Matthew (SÁNCHEZ) CASEWK MGR 562-860-5050
Runkel, Nick (WOMACK) LEGIS CORRES 2412 54301
Running, Rich (FINKENAUER) DIST REP 319-364-2288
Rupert, Gerald (CAO/HOUSE PERIODICAL PRESS) FIRST ASST H304 52941
Rupert-Shropshire, Saundrea (MCGOVERN) SR LEGIS ASST 408 CHOB 56101
Rupnow, Colton (CLERK/LEGIS OPS) ASST BILL CLERK HT13 57925
Rush, Laura (CMTE-OVERSIGHT & GOVT REFORM) DPTY CHIEF CLERK/SECUR OFFICER 2157 55051
Rushing, Glenn (JACKSON LEE) CHIEF OF STAFF 2079 53816
Ruskowsky, Dianna (CMTE-ED & WORKFORCE) FINANCE & PERSONNEL ADVISOR 2051B 53725
Russak, Maddy (AXNE) COMMUNICATIONS DIR/DPTY CHIEF OF STAFF 330 CHOB 55476
Russel, Steve (BOST) COORD - VETS OUTREACH 618-622-0766
Russell, Chance (ROE) STAFF ASST 102 CHOB 56356
Russell, Dave (PRICE) DIST LIAISON 919-967-7924
Russell, David (CLERK/LRC) PUBLIC INFO SPEC B81 CHOB 65200
Russell, David (MOOLENAAR) COMMUNICATIONS DIR 117 CHOB 53561
Russell, DeShannon (RICHMOND) CASEWKR/ DPTY DIST DIR 504-365-0390
Russell, George (CAO/FURNISHINGS) JOURNEYMAN - TEXT SPEC WA33 RHOB 58000
Russell, Gisele (SCOTT, ROBERT C. "BOBBY") DIST DIR 757-380-1000
Russell, Hannah (DESJARLAIS) LEGIS ASST 2301 56831
Russell, Kayley (FLEISCHMANN) CASEWKR 423-756-2342
Russell, Matthew (CONAWAY) LEGIS DIR 2469 53605
Russell, Morgan (CLERK/ART & ARCHIVES) CURATORIAL RESEARCH ASST JEFFERSON BUILDING, ATTIC 61300
Russell, Nina (LUJÁN) LEGIS CORRES 2323 56190
Russell, Sam (CMTE-RULES) STAFF ASST H312 59091
Russell, Scott R (CMTE-BUDGET) BUDGET ANALYST 204E CHOB 67200
Russell, Tracey (CMTE-APPRO) ADMIN AIDE 283 FHOB 53881
Russett, Matthew (NEAL) DIST AIDE 413-442-0946
Rust, Thomas (CMTE-ETHICS) CHIEF COUNSEL/STAFF DIR 1015 57103
Rusthoven, Mark (BANKS) SR LEGIS ASST 1713 54436
Rustvang, Jeff (ARMSTRONG) STATE DIR 701-353-6665
Ruth, Karen (MOOLENAAR) CONSTIT RELATIONS REP 989-631-2552
Ruthven, Martha (WILSON, JOE) SPECIAL ASST/CASEWKR 803-642-6416
Rutkin, Amy
(NADLER) CHIEF OF STAFF 212-367-7350
(CMTE-JUDICIARY) CHIEF OF STAFF 2138 53951
Rutzen, Linda (LAMBORN) STAFF ASST/ CONSTIT SVCS SPEC 719-520-0055
Ruvolo, Jane (KAPTUR) CONG ASST/GRANTS SPEC 419-259-7500
Ryan, Angela (SMITH, CHRISTOPHER H.) EXEC SCHEDULER/OFFICE MGR 2373 53765
Ryan, Dj (LAMB) SCHEDULER 1224 52301
Ryan, Erin (LAMALFA) REGIONAL DIR 530-223-5898
Ryan, Katie (CAO) DIRECTOR B227 LHOB 65174
Ryan, Kimberly (CASE) DIST STAFF ASST 808-650-6688
Ryan, Lindsay (MOOLENAAR) CHIEF OF STAFF 117 CHOB 53561
Ryan, Magen (SCHNEIDER) DIST DIR 847-383-4870
Ryan, Michael (UPTON) DIST REP 269-982-1986
Ryan, R Kevin (LYNCH) CHIEF OF STAFF 2109 58273
Ryan, Sean (BLUMENAUER) PRESS SECY 1111 54811
Ryan, Shelia (KELLY, TRENT) CASEWKR/ SPECIAL ASST 662-841-8808

Ryon, Bradley (NC03) LEGIS DIR 2333 53415
Rzepski, Peg (BOYLE) CONSTIT SVCS REP 215-426-4616
Saba, Geo (KHANNA) NATIONAL SECUR ADVISOR 221 CHOB 52631
Sabag, Terra (LARSEN) LEGIS DIR/DPTY CHIEF OF STAFF 2113 52605
Sabater, Alexandra (ESCOBAR) LEGIS ASST - MIL 1505 68336
Sablan, Tina (SABLAN) COORD - OUTREACH 670-323-2647
Sabol, Samantha (SCHWEIKERT) LEGIS CORRES 1526 52190
Saccardi, Adam (ZELDIN) CONG AIDE/FIELD REP 631-289-1097
Sachartoff, Noah (SHERMAN) STAFF ASST 818-501-9200
Sachse, Andrew (HOUSE DEM CAUCUS) DPTY DIR - MBR SVCS B245 LHOB 51400
Sada, Roberto
(CMTE-ENERGY & COMMERCE) POLICY COORD 2125 52927
(PALLONE) LEGIS AIDE 2107 54671
Sadler, Alex (CMTE-FOREIGN AFFAIRS) POLICY ANALYST 2064 55021
Sadler, Brooke (CAO/ACQUIS MGMT) PURCHASING AGENT 5110 61080
Sadler, Hailey (WENSTRUP) COMMUNICATIONS AIDE 2419 53164
Sadlosky, Daniel (MIN WHIP) POLICY ADVISOR H148 50197
Saegesser, Jodi (WRIGHT) CASEWKR 817-077-5037
Saez, Mariel (MAJ LEADER) DPTY COMMUNICATIONS DIR H107 53130
Safley, Cam (BUDD) CONSTIT SVCS REP 336-858-5013
Safo, Edward (CLERK/LRC) ASST REGISTRATION & COMPLIANCE CLERK B81 CHOB 65200
Safreed, Molly (REED) CASEWKR 607-654-7566
Safsten, Greg (BIGGS) DPTY CHIEF OF STAFF/ DIST DIR 480-699-8239
Sagul, Peggy (BISHOP, SANFORD D., JR.) CONSTIT SVCS 706-320-9477
Saheb, Zahraa (VEASEY) LEGIS ASST 2348 59897
Sahgal, Rishi (MCNERNEY) LEGIS DIR 2265 51947
Said, Hadeel (CARSON) STAFF ASST 2135 54011
Saiyady, Ishtar (HARDER) CASEWK MGR 209-579-5458
Saji, Stancy (MENG) DIR - CONSTIT SVCS 718-358-6364
Salamone, John (CAO/OFFICE OF THE CHIEF HUMAN RESOURCES OFFICER) CHIEF 102 FHOB 50012
Salas, Damien (CLERK/COMMUNICA) MULTIMEDIA DEVELOPER 293 CHOB 51908
Salas, Stephen (LUJÁN) CONSTIT LIAISON 505-454-3038
Salas-Abarca, Manny (CLEAVER) COMMUNITY LIAISON 816-842-4545
Salay, Rebecca (CMTE-APPRO) PROF STAFF MEMB 2358A 52141
Salazar, Adrienne (TLAIB) PRESS SECY 1628 55126
Salazar, Catalina (COURTNEY) STAFF ASST - COMMUNICATIONS 2332 52076
Salazar, Felicia (HAALAND) COMMUNICATIONS DIR 1237 64207
Salazar, Julio (VELÁZQUEZ) COMMUNITY LIAISON 718-599-3658
Salazar, Miguel (CMTE-VET AFFAIRS) COMMUNICATIONS DIR B234 LHOB 59756
Salazar, Norma (GRIJALVA) LEGIS AIDE 1511 52435
Salazar, Ray (MAJ LEADER) DPTY FLOOR DIR H107 53130
Salberg, Wendy (FOSTER) CASEWKR 630-585-7672
Saldana, Vladimir (TRAHAN) REGIONAL DIR 978-459-0101
Saleeby, Emily
(GIANFORTE) ADMIN - FINANCE & PAYROLL 1222 53211
(WILSON, JOE) LEGIS ASST/OFFICE MGR 1436 52452
Saleme, Emily (MITCHELL) STAFF ASST 211 CHOB 52106
Salen, Jen (COMMIS ON CHINA) SR RESEARCH ASSOC 243 FHOB 63766
Salerno, Francis (LIPINSKI) CONG AIDE 773-948-6223
Salmon, Kathryn (CMTE-APPRO) PROF STAFF MEMB 1001 53481
Salrin, Megan (VISCLOSKY) STAFF ASST 2328 52461
Salter, Rebecca (SMITH, ADRIAN) SCHEDULER 502 CHOB 56435
Sammis, Coby (HIGGINS, CLAY) FIELD REP 337-656-2833
Sample, John (HAGEDORN) DIR - DIGITAL MEDIA 325 52472
Samuel, Asha (PAPPAS) FELLOW 323 CHOB 55456
Samuel, Twaun (WATERS) CHIEF OF STAFF 2221 52201
Samuels, Michael (CAO/ENTERPRISE APPLICATIONS) MGR - SUPPORT SYS B74B FHOB 62186
Sanchez, Carlos (ASST SPEAKER) SR ADVISOR H132 52020
Sanchez, David (DEMINGS) CASEWKR 321-388-9808
Sanchez, Jaclyn (SHALALA) STAFF ASST 305-668-2285
Sanchez, Jacqueline (BLUNT ROCHESTER) CHIEF OF STAFF 1519 54165
Sanchez, Jacqueline (ESCOBAR) LEGIS DIR 1505 68332
Sanchez, Maritza (ESPAILLAT) IMMIGRATION SPEC 212-663-3900
Sanchez, Martha (RASKIN) LEGIS ASST 412 CHOB 55341
Sanchez, Monica (CMTE-NATURAL RESOURCES) DPTY PRESS SECY 1334 56065
Sanchez, Sofia (HAALAND) SR FIELD REP 505-288-0378
Sanchez, Tery (CASTOR) CONSTIT SVCS 813-871-2817
Sandberg, Heather (HUIZENGA) DPTY CHIEF OF STAFF 616-414-5516
Sanders, Mark (SCOTT, AUSTIN) LEGIS ASST 2417 56531
Sanders, Rita (FORTENBERRY) DIST AIDE 402-438-1598
Sanderson, Tyler (CMTE-OVERSIGHT & GOVT REFORM) COUNSEL 2105 55074
Sandigo, Larry (STANTON) POLICY ADVISOR 602-956-2285
Sandlin, Erin (CARBAJAL) EXEC ASST/LEGIS ASST 1431 53601
Sandman, Dana (CMTE-AGRIC) CHIEF CLERK/DIR - SCHEDULING 1301 52171
Sandoval, Maria (MOORE) CASEWKR/ COMMUNITY OUTREACH SPEC 414-297-1140
Sandschafer, Monica (GALLEGO) SR OUTREACH DIR 602-256-0551
Sandy, Bayley (CMTE-TRANSP & INFRA) DPTY COMMUNICATIONS DIR 2029 54472
Sans, Nate (VISCLOSKY) LEGIS ASST 2328 52461
Santa, Leidy (CAO/HIR – ENTERPRISE INFRASTRUCT) SYS ENGINEER 620 FHOB 66024
Santa Cruz, Daniel (GOMEZ) DIGITAL ASST 213-481-1425
Santino, Tony (CHENEY) MIL FELLOW 416 CHOB 52311
Santos, Laura (CMTE-BUDGET) STAFF ASST 204E CHOB 67200
Santos, Lucas (MOULTON) DIST REP 978-531-1669
Santos, Melissa (HARDER) DIST REP 209-579-5458
Santoy, Julissa (GARCÍA, JESÚS G. "CHUY") DIR - OPS/ SCHEDULER 530 CHOB 53575
Sanusi-Hopes, Zainab (CAO/ENTERPRISE APPLICATIONS) SR BUSINESS PROCESS APPLICA SPEC B70 FHOB 60172

Saparow, Bobby (FERGUSON) CHIEF OF STAFF 1032 55901
Sarar, Ariana (CMTE-APPRO) PROF STAFF MEMB H405 52847
Sarasohn, Peter (KRISHNAMOORTHI) LEGIS AIDE 115 CHOB 53711
Sarkesian, Lauren (BEYER) LEGIS COUNSEL 1119 54376
Sarmiento, Victor (CMTE-TRANSP & INFRA) RESEARCH ASST 2164 59446
Sarnowski, Angelisa (CAO/OFFICE OF THE CHIEF HUMAN RESOURCES OFFICER) MGR 102 FHOB 67472
Saroff, Laurie (CORREA) CHIEF OF STAFF 1039 52965
Sarubbi, Vincent (NORCROSS) LEGIS ASST 2437 56501
Sarvana, Adam (CMTE-NATURAL RESOURCES) COMMUNICATIONS DIR 1334 56065
Sass, Paul
(CMTE-TRANSP & INFRA) STAFF DIR 2164 59446
(GRAVES, SAM) CHIEF OF STAFF 1135 57041
Sasso, Sean (DOYLE) CASEWORK - VETS 412-664-4049
Satalin, Patrick (WELCH) LEGIS DIR/DPTY CHIEF OF STAFF 2187 54115
Satchell, Samantha (CMTE-ENERGY & COMMERCE) PROF STAFF 2125 54407
Satterthwaite, Sean (MIN WHIP) SPEECHWRITER H148 50197
Saunders, Eugene (TURNER) DIST STAFF ASST 937-225-2843
Saunders, William (CLYBURN) FIELD REP - VETS 803-799-1100
Sauvage, Charles (CONAWAY) LEGIS CORRES 2469 53605
Savage, Amber (COLE) FIELD REP 580-436-5375
Savage, Megan (BROOKS, SUSAN W.) CHIEF OF STAFF 2211 52276
Savaria, Nicholas (DELAURO) CASEWKR 203-562-3718
Sawyer, Decontee (PHILLIPS) CASEWKR 952-656-5176
Sawyer, Katie (MARSHALL) STATE DIR 785-829-9000
Sawyer, Paul (GRAVES, GARRET) CHIEF OF STAFF 2402 ... 53901
Sawyers, Marcus (LEWIS) SPECIAL ASST 300 CHOB 53801
Saxon, Ethan (SHERRILL) CHIEF OF STAFF 1208 55034
Sayed, Rona (PINGREE) DIST STAFF ASST 207-774-5019
Saylor, Lisa (LONG) CASEWKR 417-889-1800
Saylor, Ryan (CLINE) COMMUNICATIONS DIR 1009 55431
Scaer, John (BANKS) STAFF ASST 260-702-4750
Scaggs, Janice (WOMACK) FIELD REP 479-424-1146
Scala, David (CMTE-OVERSIGHT & GOVT REFORM) PROF STAFF MEMB 2105 55074
Scala, Robert (HIGGINS, BRIAN) STAFF ASST 2459 53306
Scales, Bret (CAO/HIR – OPS AND CONTINUITY) COMMUNICATIONS SPEC 633 FHOB 63020
Scales-Preston, Shanelle (DESAULNIER) DIST DIR 925-933-2660
Scanlon, Emily (SGT AT ARMS/EMERGENCY MGMT) DIR - CONTINUITY PLANS & OPS 192 FHOB 60950
Scannell, Brooke (CLARK) CHIEF OF STAFF 2448 52836
Schaefer, Sonja (VISCLOSKY) LEGIS ASST 2328 52461
Schafer, Katie (CMTE-NATURAL RESOURCES) PRESS ASST 1324 56065
Schaffer, Jeff (DOYLE) ECON DEV REP 412-283-4451
Scharfetter, Alex (WENSTRUP) DIST DIR 513-474-7777
Schauerte, Mark (KRISHNAMOORTHI) CHIEF OF STAFF 115 CHOB 53711
Schaufler, Lisa (SMITH, CHRISTOPHER H.) STAFF ASST/CASEWKR 732-780-3035
Schaumburg, Mandy (CMTE-ED & WORKFORCE) DPTY DIR - EDUC & HUMAN SVCS POLICY/CHIEF COUNSEL 6140 56558
Scheenstra, Hannah (CMTE-ARMED SVCS) EXEC ASST 2340 68980
Schein, Michelle (SHERMAN) STAFF ASSOC 2181 55911
Schelble, Nathan (GALLEGO) LEGIS DIR 1131 54065
Schellhaas, Melissa (CAO/ENTERPRISE APPLICATIONS) BUSINESS PROCESS APPLICA SPEC B69 FHOB 66717
Schellin, Meredith (CMTE-ED & WORKFORCE) DPTY PRESS SECY/DIGITAL MGR 2178 69440
Schemm, Cari (CAO/HOUSE CREATIVE SVCS) GRAPHIC DESIGNER 2002 52700
Schemmel, Nick (CARTER, EARL L. "BUDDY") LEGIS DIR 2432 55831
Scherling, Grant (CAO/HOUSE RECORDING STUDIO) PRINCIPAL ENGINEER 2010 53941
Schertz, Matt (CMTE-AGRIC) STAFF DIR 1010 50317
Scheuer, Alex (HOUSE DEM CAUCUS) CAUCUS ASST B245 LHOB 51400
Schifrin, Samantha (PRICE) NATIONAL SECUR ADVISOR 2108 51784
Schilling, Patrick (PERRY) LEGIS ASST 1207 55836
Schilling, Sophia (MCCOLLUM) LEGIS CORRES/LEGIS ASST 2256 56631
Schilt, Adam (LEGIS COUNSEL) ASST COUNSEL 337 FHOB 56060
Schimmenti, Jayson (MOOLENAAR) LEGIS DIR 117 CHOB 53561
Schinazi, Yann (WILD) LEGIS AIDE/SPEECHWRITER 1607.. 56411
Schindler, Linda (BRADY) CASEWKR 936-439-9532
Schisler, Katherine (BEYER) SR LEGIS ASST 1119 54376
Schlabach, Shanna (GIBBS) CASEWK MGR/ OFFICE MGR 419-207-0650
Schlager, Erika (COMMIS ON SECUR & COOP IN EUR) COUNSEL 234 FHOB 51901
Schlesinger, Julian (VEASEY) COORD - OUTREACH 817-920-9086
Schliewe, Stacy (GRAVES, GARRET) DPTY COMMUNICATIONS DIR/COMMUNITY LIAISON 225-442-1731
Schloeder, Jo (SMITH, CHRISTOPHER H.) DPTY CHIEF OF STAFF/DIST DIR 732-780-3035
Schloesser, Chris (KHANNA) LEGIS DIR 221 CHOB 52631
Schlueter, Erik (POCAN) FIELD REP 608-258-9800
Schmid, Jason (CMTE-ARMED SVCS) PROF STAFF 2340 64952
Schmidt, Aaron (DELBENE) CHIEF OF STAFF 2330 56311
Schmidt, Derrick (CAO/HIR – CYBERSECURITY) FORENSIC LEAD 613 FHOB 68773
Schmidt, Hannah (CMTE-SMALL BUSINESS) PROF STAFF 2069 55821
Schmidt, Maggie (FOSTER) SCHEDULER 2366 53515
Schmidtlein, Meghan (GRAVES, SAM) SR LEGIS ASST 1135 57041
Schmitt, Karen (HERN) OFFICE MGR 1019 52211
Schmitt, Michelle (MCADAMS) DIGITAL DIR 801-999-9801
Schmitt, Regina (CAO/HOUSE RECORDING STUDIO) MGR - PROD OPS 2010 53941
Schmitz, Doc (REED) LIAISON - MIL & VET 607-654-7566
Schmucker, Lauren (PALAZZO) STAFF ASST 2349 55772
Schneider, Grant (CMTE-ARMED SVCS) PROF STAFF 2340 57150

Schneider, Joshua (CMTE-SCIENCE) PROF STAFF - MAJ 2321 .... **56375**
Schneider, Katherine (CASTRO) PRESS SECY 2241 .... **53236**
Schneider, Lindsay (LAMBORN) LEGIS ASST 2371 .... **54422**
Schneider, Timothy (BALDERSON) STAFF ASST **614-523-2555**
Schnell, Erin (LOEBSACK) LEGIS ASST 1211 .... **56576**
Schnelle, Alex (COHEN) LEGIS ASST 2104 .... **53265**
Schoelhamer, Mike (SMITH, JASON) DIST FIELD REP **573-756-9755**
Schoenbach, Beth (DEFAZIO) COMMUNICATIONS DIR 2134 .... **56416**
Schooler, Sherri (CAO/HIR – NETWORKING ENGINEERING AND OPS) NETWK COMMUNICATIONS SPEC 677 FHOB **571-921-3303**
Schoultz, Nichelle (BROWN) DIST DIR **301-458-2600**
Schramm, Heidi (CMTE-JOINT TAX) ECONOMIST 595 FHOB **67575**
Schreiber, Charlie (CMTE-FINANCIAL SVCS) COUNSEL 4340 .... **57502**
Schreiner, Julie (GOSAR) OFFICE MGR **928-445-1683**
Schrodt, Corey (ROONEY) LEGIS DIR 120 CHOB **52536**
Schroeder, Amy (HUFFMAN) FIELD REP **415-258-9657**
Schroeder, Ricki (CMTE-AGRIC) LEGIS ASST/MBR SVCS COORD 1010 .... **50317**
Schroeder, Robert (CARTER, JOHN R.) CONG FELLOW/ NATIONAL SECUR ADVISOR 2110 .... **53864**
Schroeter, Cora (TONKO) DIR - CONSTIT SVCS/ DIST OFFICE MGR **518-374-4547**
Schubert, Jason (CAO/HIR – ENTERPRISE INFRASTRUCT) SR SYS ENGINEER 619 FHOB **571-921-3434**
Schueler, Jacob (COSTA) LEGIS CORRES/PRESS ASST 2081 .... **53341**
Schuessler, Leslie (LAMALFA) CASEWKR **530-343-1000**
Schuler, Christopher (YARMUTH) PRESS SECY 402 CHOB **55401**
Schuler, Robert (WALTZ) STAFF ASST 216 CHOB **52706**
Schulte, Natalie (HILL, J. FRENCH) PRESS ASST 1533 .... **52506**
Schulte, Victoria (PORTER) DIST SCHEDULER 1117 .... **55611**
Schultz, Isaac (STAUBER) DIST DIR **218-481-6396**
Schultz, Marty (WALORSKI) LEGIS DIR 419 CHOB **53915**
Schultz, Steven (PAYNE) LEGIS ASST 103 CHOB **53436**
Schultz, Thomas (GIANFORTE) PRESS SECY **406-502-1435**
Schumacher, Joe (WITTMAN) DIST DIR/ OUTREACH DIR **804-730-6595**
Schuneman, William (KINZINGER) STAFF ASST 2245 .... **53635**
Schutte, Corinna (HOUSE REPUB STUDY CMTE) DIGITAL ASST 418 CHOB **52777**
Schutte, Tanner (LAHOOD) STAFF ASST **309-671-7027**
Schwalb, Janet (CMTE-HOUSE ADMIN) PROF STAFF - MIN 1216 .... **58281**
Schwalbach, Bob (SABLAN) CHIEF OF STAFF 2411 .... **52646**
Schwartz, Benji (MALINOWSKI) LEGIS ASST/LEGIS CORRES 426 CHOB **55361**
Schwartz, Brooke (HILL, KATIE) CONSTIT SVCS REP **661-568-4855**
Schwartz, Mona (BLUMENAUER) FIELD REP **503-231-2300**
Schwartz, Paige (SCOTT, ROBERT C. "BOBBY") SR LEGIS ASST 1201 .... **58351**
Schwarz, Daniel
(CMTE-JUDICIARY) DIR - STRATEGIC COMMUNICATIONS 2138 .... **53951**
(NADLER) COMMUNICATIONS DIR 2132 .... **55635**
Schwegman, Rachel (LATTA) SR LEGIS ASST 2467 .... **56405**
Sciascia, Anthony (LEGIS COUNSEL) COUNSEL 337 FHOB **56060**
Sciascia, Jordan (HUFFMAN) LEGIS AIDE 1527 .... **55161**
Scibetta, Andrew (CORREA) COMMUNICATIONS DIR 1039 **52965**
Scordato, Tory (KILMER) SCHEDULER 1410 .... **55916**
Scott, Andrea (CARSON) CASEWKR/COORD - COMMUNITY OUTREACH **317-283-6516**
Scott, Charles (WILSON, FREDERICA S.) DPTY DIR - OUTREACH/MBR SVCS ADVISOR **305-690-5905**
Scott, Denise (CMTE-FINANCIAL SVCS) FINANCIAL & ADMIN OFFICER 2129 .... **54247**
Scott, Hugh Jay (CLERK/LCS) AUDIO TECH 2401 .... **51182**
Scott, Nicole (LUCAS) SR ADVISOR 2405 .... **55565**
Scott, Seth (STANTON) CHIEF OF STAFF/GEN COUNSEL **602-956-2285**
Scott, Stephanie (GREEN, MARK E.) SR CASEWKR **629-223-6050**
Scott, Sydney (POCAN) LEGIS CORRES/STAFF ASST 1421 **52906**
Scott Martin, Cecily (KIM) SCHEDULER 1516 .... **54765**
Scoufaras, Nicholas (WOODALL) LEGIS ASST 1724 .... **54272**
Scribner, Tory (GIANFORTE) CASEWKR **406-952-1280**
Scruggs, Suzanne (UPTON) SCHEDULER 2183 .... **53761**
Scully, Timothy (NEAL) STAFF ASST 2309 .... **55601**
Seabrook, William (DAVIS, SUSAN A.) LEGIS ASST 1214 .... **52040**
Seago, Katelyn (CHENEY) SCHEDULER 416 CHOB **52311**
Seal, Matt (CLERK/REPORTERS) PROD ASST 193 CHOB **57187**
Seal, Robert (CAO/HIR – IT CUSTOMER SOLUTIONS) SR TELECOMMUNICATIONS ADMIN 692 FHOB **56002**
Seales, Donnell (SGT AT ARMS/GARAGES & PARKING) ASST DIR G2-28 .... **56749**
Seaman, Tom (KILMER) LEGIS FELLOW 1410 .... **55916**
Sears, Glen (CMTE-FINANCIAL SVCS) DIR - POLICY 2129 .... **54247**
Sears, Katherine (JOYCE, DAVID P.) COMMUNICATIONS DIR 1124 .... **55731**
Sears, Sandra (WILSON, FREDERICA S.) ADVISOR - HEALTH POLICY **305-690-5905**
Seasholtz, Christian (PAPPAS) CONSTIT SVCS REP **603-285-4300**
Sebastian, Cassandra (LAMBORN) COMMUNICATIONS DIR **719-520-0055**
Sebright, Taunia (SPANO) CONSTIT SVCS **863-644-8215**
Secada, Irene (SHALALA) OUTREACH REP **305-668-2285**
Seckman, Cristina L (CLERK/REPORTERS) EDITOR - COMMITTEES 1718 .... **52627**
Seda, Megan (ALLEN) CONSTIT SVCS REP **706-228-1980**
Sedano, Cody (COX) DIST REP **661-864-7736**
Seddighi, Andrew (CMTE-WAYS & MEANS) SUBCOMM CLERK 2018 .... **59263**
Seed, Ryan (BONAMICI) DIST STAFF ASST **503-469-6010**
Seeds, Michael (THORNBERRY) LEGIS DIR/DPTY CHIEF OF STAFF 2208 .... **53706**
Seeley, Greg (HAALAND) FIELD REP **505-288-4199**
Seep, Ralph V (LAW REV COUNSEL) HOUSE LAW REVISION COUNSEL 308 FHOB **62411**

Sege, Aaron (GOLDEN) LEGIS CORRES 1223 .... **56306**
Segmen, Cortney (TRONE) LEGIS ASST 1213 .... **52721**
Segovia, Francine (DAVIS, SUSAN A.) MIL FELLOW 1214 .... **52040**
Segovia, Sylvia (CUELLAR) CONSTIT SVCS REP **956-725-0639**
Sehgal, Tanya (CMTE-HOUSE ADMIN) SR ELECTIONS COUNSEL 1309 .... **52061**
Sehr, Gabriel (COURTNEY) LEGIS ASST - MIL 2332 .... **52076**
Seid, Sophica (RICE, TOM) PRESS SECY 512 CHOB **59895**
Seidel, Aly (CAO/CUST EXPER CTR) COMMUNICATIONS ANALYST 217 FHOB **58000**
Seideman, Tina (BIGGS) SCHEDULER 1318 .... **52635**
Seidl, Zachary (BASS) DPTY PRESS SECY 2059 .... **57084**
Seidman, Marla (ESHOO) CASEWKR **650-323-2984**
Seidman, Pearl (CLEAVER) LEGIS FELLOW 2335 .... **54535**
Seifers, Brantley (HOLLINGSWORTH) LEGIS ASST 1641 .... **66871**
Seiger, Ryan (CMTE-TRANSP & INFRA) STAFF DIR/SR COUNSEL 505 FHOB **54472**
Self, Beanie (COHEN) DPTY DIST DIR **901-544-4131**
Self, Jason (MULLIN) CASEWKR **918-687-2533**
Self, Joan (BURGESS) DIST AIDE **940-497-5031**
Sellas, Kristen (BILIRAKIS) LIAISON - MIL & VET/ CASEWK DIR **727-232-2921**
Sellers, Joshua (PANETTA) CONG AIDE **831-429-1976**
Selvey, David (CRAWFORD) FIELD REP 2422 .... **54076**
Semachko, Jessica (TRONE) LEGIS ASST 1213 .... **52721**
Semanko, Nicholas (BEATTY) LEGIS DIR/COUNSEL 2303 .... **54324**
Semoes, Melissa (NUNES) DIR - CONSTIT SVCS **559-733-3861**
Senft, Lea (FITZPATRICK) CONSTIT ADVOCATE **215-579-8102**
Sengstock, Kathleen (WATERS) LEGIS ASST 2221 .... **52201**
Sennott, Daniel (CMTE-ARMED SVCS) PROF STAFF MEMB 2340 .... **57192**
Sense, Rick (GALLAGHER) DIST DIR **920-301-4500**
Senseman, Davis (OMAR) DIST DIR **612-333-1272**
Sensenbrenner, Bob (SGT AT ARMS) COUNSEL H124 .... **52456**
Serio, Will (DELAURO) COMMUNICATIONS DIR 2413 .... **53661**
Serra, John (SCHRADER) DIST FIELD REP **503-557-1324**
Serrano Ruvalcaba, Jaqueline (CÁRDENAS) LEGIS ASST 2438 .... **56131**
Serstad, Garrett (BANKS) STAFF ASST 1713 .... **54436**
Servin, Sarah (SMITH, ADAM) DIST DIR **425-793-5180**
Sessoms, Shawn (CAO/FINANCIAL COUNSELING) FINANCIAL COUNSELOR B215 LHOB **68967**
Seum, Kristin (GRIFFITH) LEGIS COUNSEL/LEGIS DIR 2202 .... **53861**
Seva'aetasi, Tago (RADEWAGEN) CONSTIT REP/CASEWKR - IMMIGRATION/CASEWORK - VETS **684-633-3601**
Seward, Larry (BEATTY) OUTREACH DIR **614-220-0003**
Shabbeer, Mohammed (CAO/ENTERPRISE APPLICATIONS) LEAD SYS ADMIN B75 FHOB **66231**
Shaben, Zach (KRISHNAMOORTHI) STAFF ASST 115 CHOB **53711**
Shackelford, Lindsey (CMTE-FINANCIAL SVCS) DIR - OPS 4340 .... **57502**
Shaffer, Alexandra (HUFFMAN) COMMUNICATIONS DIR 1527 .... **55161**
Shaffer, Shasta (SOTO) CASEWK DIR **407-452-1171**
Shah, Amish (CMTE-OVERSIGHT & GOVT REFORM) COUNSEL 2157 .... **55051**
Shah, Kirat (CAO/OFFICE OF THE CHIEF LOGISTICS OFFICER) RESOURCE MGR WA26 RHOB **54057**
Shah, Noor (ESHOO) SCHEDULER 202 CHOB **58104**
Shahbaz, Donna (CMTE-APPRO) PROF STAFF MEMB 2007 .... **53081**
Shahinian, Yvette (SÁNCHEZ) DIST DIR **562-860-5050**
Shahoulian, David
(CMTE-JUDICIARY) CHIEF COUNSEL 6320 .... **53926**
(LOFGREN) CHIEF COUNSEL/IMMIGRATION SPEC/ SHARED EMPLOYEE 189 FHOB **56906**
Shalhoub, Fadlou (CAO/HIR - VENDOR MGMT) SR SYS ANALYST 643C FHOB **60477**
Shalia, Amol (KRISHNAMOORTHI) DC SCHEDULER 115 CHOB **53711**
Sham, Julian (LIEU) LEGIS AIDE 403 CHOB **53976**
Shanahan, Michael (WATSON COLEMAN) PRESS SECY 2442 .... **55801**
Shand, Mona (SLOTKIN) DIST REP **517-993-0510**
Shankar, Murthy (CAO/HIR – CYBERSECURITY) SYS SECUR ENGINEER 650 FHOB **66252**
Shapiro, Calli (CASTEN) LEGIS DIR 429 CHOB **54561**
Shapiro, Jennifer (CLEAVER) CHIEF OF STAFF 2335 .... **54535**
Shapiro, Jessica (LEGIS COUNSEL) COUNSEL 337 FHOB **56060**
Shapiro, Kristin (GEN COUNSEL) ASST COUNSEL 219 CHOB **59700**
Shapiro, Larry (DAVIS, DANNY K.) CONSTIT OUTREACH REP **773-533-7520**
Share, Alison (KILDEE) LEGIS COUNSEL 203 CHOB **53611**
Sharifian, Julie (CARTER, JOHN R.) CONSTIT REP **512-246-1600**
Sharma, Moh (CMTE-JUDICIARY) ADVISOR - MBR SVCS/ OUTREACH ADVISOR 2035 .... **53951**
Sharma, Sapna (CMTE-ARMED SVCS) PROF STAFF 2117 .... **55050**
Sharp, Kyle (HORSFORD) LEGIS AIDE 1330 .... **59894**
Sharp, Raegan (WESTERMAN) DIST SCHEDULER/FIELD REP **501-609-9796**
Shatynski, Kristen (CMTE-ENERGY & COMMERCE) PROF STAFF MEMB 2322A **53641**
Shaver, Jacob (STEFANIK) STAFF ASST **315-782-3150**
Shaver, Kathy (LATTA) DPTY DIST DIR **419-782-1996**
Shaw, April (MCCOLLUM) CONSTIT SVCS REP **651-224-9191**
Shaw, Diana (GUTHRIE) STAFF ASST 2434 .... **53501**
Shaw, Don (GARCIA, SYLVIA R.) COMMUNICATIONS DIR/ TAX ADVISOR/ADVISOR - SCIENCE 1620 .... **51688**
Shaw, Elliot (GRIFFITH) DPTY COMMUNICATIONS DIR/ EXEC ASST 2202 .... **53861**
Shaw, Jacqui (THOMPSON, GLENN) STAFF ASST 400 CHOB **55121**
Shaw, Lucy (RASKIN) LEGIS CORRES 412 CHOB **55341**
Shaw, Mindy (GRIFFITH) LEGIS ASST 2202 .... **53861**
Shaw, Rebecca (HOLLINGSWORTH) CHIEF OF STAFF 1641 .... **66858**
Shay, Michael (MEUSER) MGR - CONSTIT SVCS/GRANTS SPEC **570-871-6370**
Shea, Mitch (SCALISE) STAFF ASST 2049 .... **53015**
Sheedy, Rich (HOLDING) LEGIS CORRES 1110 .... **53032**
Sheehan, Leo (CARSON) LEGIS ASST 2135 .... **54011**
Sheehan, Patrick (GOTTHEIMER) CONSTIT OUTREACH REP **973-940-1117**
Sheehy, Joe (NAPOLITANO) LEGIS DIR 1610 .... **55256**

Shefchik, Cheryl (STEFANIK) MIL FELLOW 318 CHOB 54611
Shefelman, Will (RICE, KATHLEEN M.) STAFF ASST 2435 55516
Sheff, Samara (DELBENE) STAFF & PRESS ASST 2330 56311
Sheffield, Rachel (CMTE-JOINT ECON) SR POLICY ADVISOR - REPUB SD-G01 45171
Sheils, Hope (CMTE-JOINT ECON) RESEARCH ASST - DEM SH-804 81341
Shelor, Edward (HICE) SPECIAL ASST 478-457-0007
Shelton, Ashley (CRAWFORD) LEGIS DIR 2422 54076
Shelton, John (POSEY) LEGIS ASST/LEGIS CORRES 2150 53671
Shelton, Lisa (CMTE-AGRIC) SR PROF STAFF 1301 52171
Shen, David (CMTE-NATURAL RESOURCES) CONTENT & MULTIMEDIA PRODUCER 1334 56065
Shen, Valerie (CMTE-OVERSIGHT & GOVT REFORM) CHIEF COUNSEL/SR POLICY ADVISOR 6440 55051
Shepard, Eric (CMTE-RULES) PROF STAFF 1116 59191
Shepherd, Amanda (AXNE) SCHEDULER 330 CHOB 55476
Sheppard, Abigail (VELA) STAFF ASST 307 CHOB 59901
Shepperson, Baxter (CAO/HIR – ENTERPRISE INFRASTRUCT) SR SYS ENGINEER 619 FHOB 571-921-3108
Sherman, Lisa (DAVIS, SUSAN A.) CHIEF OF STAFF 1214 52040
Sherrill, Savanna (BUDD) CONSTIT SVCS REP 336-998-1313
Sherrod, Jay (CRAWFORD) FIELD REP 501-843-3043
Shewcraft, Scott (FOSTER) CHIEF OF STAFF 2366 53515
Shewmaker, Robert (HIGGINS, CLAY) LEGIS ASST 424 CHOB 52031
Shields, Brendan (CMTE-FOREIGN AFFAIRS) STAFF DIR - MIN 2066 68467
Shim, Linda (CHU) CHIEF OF STAFF 2423 55464
Shim, Wonyong (BUTTERFIELD) LEGIS CORRES 2080 53101
Shima, Frank J (CMTE-JOINT TAX) ADMIN SPEC 502 FHOB 53621
Shimek, Jaime (CMTE-APPRO) CLERK 2362B 53421
Shireman, Gina (SLOTKIN) CASEWKR 517-993-0510
Shivener, Kellie (WENSTRUP) CASEWKR 513-605-1380
Shockey, Tori (FULCHER) CASEWK DIR 208-888-3188
Shoemaker, Airlie (CAO/FINANCIAL COUNSELING) FINANCIAL COUNSELOR B215 LHOB 50180
Shoemaker, Jeremy (JOYCE, JOHN) CHIEF OF STAFF 1337 52431
Shorter, Quincy (CAO/ASSET MANAGEMENT) MGR 6110 56792
Shoulders, Meco (THOMPSON, BENNIE G.) LEGIS CORRES/STAFF ASST 2466 55876
Shpak, Anna (LEGIS COUNSEL) COUNSEL 337 FHOB 56060
Shuart, Amy (CMTE-WAYS & MEANS) SUBCOMM STAFF DIR 1139 54021
Shull, Kristen (SHIMKUS) DIST AIDE 618-252-8271
Shuman, Nichole (CLERK/LEGIS OPS) ASST JOURNAL CLERK HT13 52868
Shumate, Jonah (CRAWFORD) CHIEF OF STAFF 2422 54076
Shumate, Nicholas (CLERK/LRC) REFERENCE ASST B81 CHOB 65200
Shumate, Sam (BUDD) LEGIS CORRES 118 CHOB 54531
Shupe, Madi (STEWART) COMMUNICATIONS DIR 2242 59730
Shust, Diane (SUOZZI) DPTY CHIEF OF STAFF/LEGIS DIR 214 CHOB 53335
Shylkofski, Stephen (WEBSTER) DIR - CONSTIT SVCS 352-241-9220
Siao, Stephen (GREEN, MARK E.) CHIEF OF STAFF 533 CHOB 52811
Sibley, Sean (BUSTOS) DPTY PRESS SECY/STAFF ASST 1233 55905
Sibulo, Cody (RYAN) PRESS SECY/DIGITAL DIR 1126 55261
Siddiqui, Faisal
(BERA) SYS ADMIN 1727 55716
(CMTE-AGRIC) SYS ADMIN 1301 52171
(CMTE-JUDICIARY) DPTY DIR - INFO TECH 2451 53951
(CONAWAY) SYS ADMIN 2469 53605
(FOSTER) SYS ADMIN 2366 53515
(GARAMENDI) TECH SOLUTIONS TECH 2368 51880
(HECK) SYS ADMIN 2452 59740
(QUIGLEY) SYS ADMIN 2458 54061
Siddle, Clark (BALDERSON) DPTY COMMUNICATIONS DIR 614-523-2555
Sidle, Logan (GARAMENDI) DIST AIDE 2368 51880
Sidney, Arthur (JOHNSON, HENRY C. "HANK", JR.) CHIEF OF STAFF 2240 51605
Siebenaler, Michael (CRAIG) SR ADVISOR 651-846-2120
Siegel, Janice (NADLER) DIR - OPS 2132 55635
Siegel, Shira (LOWEY) SR LEGIS ASST 2365 56506
Siegrist, Sally (BAIRD) COMMUNITY LIAISON 317-563-5567
Sienicki, David (CMTE-ARMED SVCS) PROF STAFF 2340 54469
Sierra, David (CAO/HIR – IT CUSTOMER SOLUTIONS) TECH SUPPORT REP 100 CHOB 66274
Sievers, Samantha (LANGEVIN) STAFF ASST 401-732-9400
Sigal, Nate (GRIJALVA) DIST AIDE 520-622-6788
Sigala, Daphne (CISNEROS) DIST SCHEDULER 714-459-4575
Sikora, Alexia (WOMACK) COMMUNICATIONS DIR 2412 54301
Sikorskyj, Lucian (CMTE-INTELLIGENCE) SUBCOMM STAFF DIR HVC304 57690
Silberberg, David (CHU) LEGIS AIDE 2423 55464
Silberman, Zachary (CMTE-FOREIGN AFFAIRS) SR PROF STAFF 4150 68467
Sills, Dennis (BUTTERFIELD) LEGIS DIR 2080 53101
Silva, Ed (YOHO) CONSTIT ADVOCATE 904-276-9626
Silva, Max (CICILLINE) LIAISON - MIL & VET/ CONSTIT SVCS REP 401-729-5600
Silva, Natasha (LYNCH) SR LEGIS ASST 2109 58273
Silva, Pifas (ESCOBAR) DIST REP 915-541-1400
Silva, Sebastian (MUCARSEL-POWELL) COMMUNICATIONS DIR 114 CHOB 52778
Silver, Aaron (DESAULNIER) DIST REP 503 CHOB 52095
Silver, Matthew (DAVIDSON) LEGIS DIR 1107 56205
Silverberg, Daniel (MAJ LEADER) SR POLICY ADVISOR H107 53130
Silverberg, Emily (TONKO) SR LEGIS ASST 2369 55076
Silverman, David (PELOSI) MGR - CORRES 1236 54965
Silverton-Peel, Oliver (SÁNCHEZ) SCHEDULER 2329 56676
Simeon, Jessica (RICHMOND) STAFF ASST 504-288-3777
Simmons, Anne (CMTE-AGRIC) STAFF DIR 1301 52171
Simmons, Chris (CMTE-JOINT TAX) DOCU PROD SPEC 502 FHOB 53621
Simmons, Jermaine (WATSON COLEMAN) SPECIAL ASST 2442 55801
Simmons, Robert (MEEKS) DIST CHIEF OF STAFF 718-725-6000
Simmons, Ronald (CAO/LOGISTICS) SUPERVISOR - LOGISTICS & DIST WA16 RHOB 59474
Simms, Alexis (FUDGE) PRESS ASST/COORD - DIGITAL MEDIA 216-522-4900

Simms, Cecilia (SARBANES) CONSTIT SVCS REP **410-832-8890**
Simms, Vernon (CUMMINGS) CHIEF OF STAFF 2163 ..... **54741**
Simon, David (WILSON, FREDERICA S.) SR LEGIS ASST 2445 ..... **54506**
Simon, David (PHILLIPS) SPECIAL PROJ DIR 1305 ..... **52871**
Simon, Matthew (LESKO) DPTY CHIEF OF STAFF/LEGIS DIR 1113 ..... **54576**
Simon, Nicholas (PALLONE) DIST REP/STAFF ASST **732-249-8892**
Simon, Noah (BEYER) DIST DIR **703-658-5403**
Simonetti, Stephen (WALORSKI) LEGIS ASST 419 CHOB **53915**
Simons, Brett (GIANFORTE) FIELD REP **406-502-1435**
Simons, David (BARR) SR LEGIS ASST 2430 ..... **54706**
Simons, Emily (SCHIFF) COMMUNICATIONS DIR 2269 ..... **54176**
Simpkins, Damon (CAO/LOGISTICS) LOGISTICS & DIST SPEC B23 FHOB **59474**
Simpson, Jamie (CMTE-JUDICIARY) CHIEF COUNSEL 6310 ..... **55741**
Simpson, Kelly (RUTHERFORD) CHIEF OF STAFF 1711 ..... **52501**
Simpson, Kyle (CMTE-FINANCIAL SVCS) STAFF ASST - MIN 4340 ..... **57502**
Simpson, Paul (THORNBERRY) DPTY DIST DIR **806-371-8844**
Simpson, Sandy (COMER) DIST DIR **270-487-9509**
Simpson, Susan (CAO/RISK MGMT) CHIEF 217 FHOB **66766**
Simpson, Teresa (SCHIFF) DIST REP **818-450-2900**
Sims, Aislan (CAO/CUST EXPER CTR) EXEC ASST B227 LHOB **58000**
Sims, Carolyn (CAO/ACQUIS MGMT) PURCHASING AGENT 5110 ..... **61080**
Sims, Megan (CARSON) DIST DIR **317-283-6516**
Singh, Gagan (CAO/HIR – HOUSE WEB SVCS) MGR 636 FHOB **67128**
Singletary, Raymond (MEEKS) COMMUNITY LIAISON **347-230-4032**
Sinkfield, Jessica (WILSON, FREDERICA S.) DPTY POLICY DIR **305-690-5905**
Sinoff, Benjamin (CMTE-ED & WORKFORCE) DIR - EDUC OVERSIGHT 230 FHOB **53725**
Sippel, Kristin (MOORE) OUTREACH SPEC **414-297-1140**
Sisson, Donald (CMTE-RULES) STAFF DIR H312 ..... **59091**
Sivak, Amanda (CLERK/LRC) EXEC COMMUNICATIONS CLERK B81 CHOB **65200**
Sivalingam, Yuvaraj (CISNEROS) NATIONAL SECUR ADVISOR 431 CHOB **54111**
Siwik, Max (GONZALEZ, ANTHONY) LEGIS CORRES 1023 ..... **53876**
Skaggs, Marissa (CMTE-INTELLIGENCE) PROF STAFF - MIN HVC304 ..... **54121**
Skala, Ed (CMTE-FINANCIAL SVCS) SR PROF STAFF 4340 ..... **57502**
Skaleski, Kerry (GALLAGHER) CONSTIT SVCS REP **920-301-4500**
Skarvelis, Michele (LAW REV COUNSEL) ASST COUNSEL 308 FHOB **62411**
Skillman, David (BLUMENAUER) LEGIS COUNSEL/DPTY CHIEF OF STAFF 1111 ..... **54811**
Skladany, Jon (CMTE-FINANCIAL SVCS) CHIEF OVERSIGHT COUNSEL 4340 ..... **57502**
Skolky, Ashley (CAO/OFC OF EMPLOYEE ADVOCACY) PARALEGAL 301 FHOB **58800**
Skoog, Kaitlynn (GIANFORTE) LEGIS ASST 1222 ..... **53211**
Skouras, Lindsey (LAW REV COUNSEL) ASST COUNSEL 308 FHOB **62411**
Skretny, Brian
(CMTE-FOREIGN AFFAIRS) PROF STAFF - MAJ 2426 ..... **52464**
(ENGEL) LEGIS DIR 2426 ..... **52464**
Slagell, Alison (LUCAS) LEGIS ASST 2405 ..... **55565**
Slane, Adam (STIVERS) SR CASEWKR **614-771-4968**
Slater, Lee (CMTE-WAYS & MEANS) DIR - OUTREACH & MEMB SVCS 1102 ..... **53625**
Slater, Lindsay (SIMPSON) CHIEF OF STAFF 2084 ..... **55531**
Slattery, Amy (KUSTER) DIR - COMMUNITY OUTREACH **603-226-1002**
Slaughter, James (LAWRENCE) OUTREACH COORD **248-356-2052**
Slavin, Eli (CLARKE) DIST REP **718-287-1142**
Slaybaugh, Haley (LAMALFA) SCHEDULER 322 CHOB **53076**
Slevin, Jeremy (OMAR) COMMUNICATIONS DIR 1517 ..... **54755**
Slifko, Brian (CAO/HIR – NETWORKING ENGINEERING AND OPS) NETWK TECH 680 FHOB **62831**
Sloans, Tonya (CMTE-ETHICS) SR COUNSEL 508 FHOB **57103**
Slobodin, Alan (CMTE-ENERGY & COMMERCE) SR INVESTIGATIVE COUNSEL 564 FHOB **53641**
Sloves, Todd (ESPAILLAT) LEGIS DIR - VICE CHAIR 1630 ..... **54365**
Slusser, Hannah (GIANFORTE) DIST STAFF ASST **406-502-1435**
Small, Bobby (CAO/LOGISTICS) MGR - LOGISTICS WA16 RHOB **59474**
Small, Emily (SPEIER) STAFF ASST 2465 ..... **53531**
Small, Jeff (GOSAR) EXEC DIR 2057 ..... **52315**
Small, Leslie (BARR) DIST DIR **859-219-1366**
Smalls, Cherrie (SCOTT, DAVID) CONSTIT SVCS REP **770-210-5073**
Smethers, Will (GALLAGHER) LEGIS ASST 1230 ..... **55665**
Smith, Alicia (CMTE-HOMELAND SECUR) COUNSEL 176 FHOB **62616**
Smith, Allison (BONAMICI) LEGIS DIR/DPTY CHIEF OF STAFF 2231 ..... **50855**
Smith, Amanda (MCCAUL) COMMUNICATIONS DIR 2001 ..... **52401**
Smith, Angela (FINKENAUER) SCHEDULER/EXEC ASST 124 CHOB **52911**
Smith, Ashley (CMTE-AGRIC) SUBCOMM STAFF DIR 1301 ..... **52171**
Smith, Barry (MAST) LEGIS DIR 2182 ..... **53026**
Smith, Brandon (CMTE-INTELLIGENCE) DIR - OPS HVC304 ..... **57690**
Smith, Brandon (ESTES) STAFF ASST 1524 ..... **56216**
Smith, Brett (FERGUSON) FIELD REP **770-683-2033**
Smith, Brian (GUTHRIE) DIR - ECON DEV **270-842-9896**
Smith, Brigid (SARBANES) DIR - GOVT, BUSINESS, & COMMUNITY AFFAIRS **410-832-8890**
Smith, Caleb (MIN LEADER) DIR - DIGITAL COMMUNICATIONS H204 ..... **54000**
Smith, Caleb (LURIA) CASEWKR **757-364-7650**
Smith, Cameron (HOUSE REPUB POLICY CMTE) EXEC DIR 207 CHOB **54921**
Smith, Cameron (TIMMONS) LEGIS CORRES 313 CHOB **56030**
Smith, Camille (PALMER) SCHEDULER 207 CHOB **54921**
Smith, Carissa (CMTE-OVERSIGHT & GOVT REFORM) DIGITAL PRESS SECY 2157 ..... **55051**
Smith, Chandler (CALVERT) STAFF ASST 2205 ..... **51986**

Smith, Chandler (GONZALEZ, VICENTE) LEGIS ASST 113 CHOB.......... 52531
Smith, Charles (CAO/OFFICE DESIGN AND MOVE SVCS) PROJ SPEC B216 LHOB.......... 64742
Smith, Christina A (CLERK/REPORTERS) OFFICIAL REPORTER HT59.......... 55621
Smith, Ciera (LAWSON) STAFF ASST.......... 904-354-1652
Smith, Connor (CMTE-APPRO) ADMIN ASST 283 FHOB.......... 53881
Smith, Cynthia (CAO/HIR – ENTERPRISE INFRASTRUCT) ADMIN SPEC 686 FHOB.......... 69785
Smith, Danny (FLORES) STAFF ASST 2228.......... 56105
Smith, Ed (MITCHELL) COORD - OUTREACH.......... 586-997-5010
Smith, Emily Ann (WAGNER) SCHEDULER 2350.......... 51621
Smith, Enix (RICHMOND) DPTY CHIEF OF STAFF.......... 504-288-3777
Smith, Evan (DESAULNIER) LEGIS ASST 503 CHOB.......... 52095
Smith, Evan (KILMER) DIST REP.......... 253-272-3515
Smith, Hannah (LONG) PRESS SECY 2454.......... 56536
Smith, Heather (LESKO) COMMUNICATIONS DIR 1113.......... 54576
Smith, Jackie (RUTHERFORD) DIR - DIST PROJ.......... 904-831-5205
Smith, Jackson (TIPTON) LEGIS ASST 218 CHOB.......... 54761
Smith, Jacob (KAPTUR) CASEWORK - VETS.......... 216-767-5933
Smith, Jamie (CONNOLLY) COMMUNICATIONS DIR 2238.......... 51492
Smith, Jared (HOUSE DEM CONG CMPGN CMTE) COMMUNICATIONS DIR.......... 202-863-1500
Smith, Jason (PARLIAMENTARIAN) DPTY PARLIAMENTARIAN H209.......... 57373
Smith, Jayna (SMITH, ADAM) CASEWKR.......... 425-793-5180
Smith, Jonathan (GRAVES, GARRET) STAFF ASST.......... 225-442-1731
Smith, Joshua (JOHNSON, HENRY C. "HANK", JR.) CONSTIT SVCS.......... 770-987-2291
Smith, Judd (ROBY) SR COUNSEL 504 CHOB.......... 52901
Smith, Kana (CASE) LEGIS ASST 2443.......... 52726
Smith, Katherine (CMTE-VET AFFAIRS) LEGIS AIDE - DISABILITY ASSISTANCE AND MEMORIAL AFFAIRS SUBCOMM 3460.......... 53527
Smith, Kathy (GRIFFITH) STAFF ASST.......... 540-381-5671
Smith, Katie (HOLDING) SCHEDULER 1110.......... 53032
Smith, Kelsey (SPEAKER) DIR - SCHEDULER & ADVANCE H232.......... 50100
Smith, Kirby (LUCAS) DIST FIELD REP.......... 405-373-1958
Smith, Mackenzie (KENNEDY) LEGIS CORRES 304 CHOB. 55931
Smith, Maggie (TAYLOR) SR CONSTIT SVCS REP.......... 972-202-4150
Smith, Marilyn (TONKO) ECON DEV REP.......... 518-465-0700
Smith, Marissa (OLSON) LEGIS AIDE 2133.......... 55951
Smith, Marquetta (DAVIS, DANNY K.) SPECIAL PROJ/ASST DIST DIR.......... 773-533-7520
Smith, Mary Ann (SCHRADER) CASEWKR.......... 503-588-9100
Smith, Matthew (CMTE-APPRO) PROF STAFF MEMB H310. 53351
Smith, Matthew (CLERK/LRC) PUBLIC INFO SPEC B81 CHOB.......... 65200
Smith, Megan (PORTER) DIR - OUTREACH & MEMB SVCS 1117.......... 55611
Smith, Mike (HOUSE DEM CONG CMPGN CMTE) DPTY EXEC DIR - FINANCE & MBR ENGAGEMENT.......... 202-863-1500
Smith, Nicholas (MARCHANT) LEGIS ASST 2304.......... 56605
Smith, Nicole (DUNN) DIR - CONSTIT SVCS.......... 850-785-0812
Smith, Patricia (CLERK/SVCS GRPS) CLOAKRM FOOD MGR - MIN H223.......... 63637
Smith, Rebekah (ROGERS, HAROLD) LEGIS CORRES 2406.......... 54601
Smith, Robby (ROY) SR LEGIS ASST 1319.......... 54236
Smith, Robert (KELLY, TRENT) FIELD REP.......... 662-327-0748
Smith, Sawyer (COHEN) PRESS ASST 2104.......... 53265
Smith, Sean (BILIRAKIS) SCHEDULER 2227.......... 55755
Smith, Shane (SPEAKER) SCHEDULE & ADVANCE COORD H232.......... 50100
Smith, Shonna (DAVIS, DANNY K.) RECEPTIONIST.......... 773-533-7520
Smith, Steven (HILL, J. FRENCH) COMMUNICATIONS DIR 1533.......... 52506
Smith, Symonne (WATERS) SCHEDULER 2221.......... 52201
Smith, Thomas (KIM) LEGIS ASST 1516.......... 54765
Smith, Tom (MOOLENAAR) CONSTIT RELATIONS REP.......... 989-631-2552
Smith, Tonia (CMTE-ETHICS) DIRECTOR 1015.......... 57103
Smith, Travonne (KIRKPATRICK) CONSTIT SVCS REP.......... 520-881-3588
Smith, Trevor
(MCCARTHY) SR LEGIS ASST 2468.......... 52915
(MIN LEADER) SR LEGIS ASST H204.......... 54000
Smith, Veneice G (CLERK/LCS) INFO TECH SYS ANALYST 2401.......... 51182
Smith, Vernetta (CLEAVER) EXEC ASST.......... 816-842-4545
Smith, William (PALMER) CHIEF OF STAFF 207 CHOB.......... 54921
Smith, William (CAO/HOUSE RECORDING STUDIO) BROADCAST PROD TECH 2010.......... 53941
Smith, William (COLLINS, DOUG) LEGIS AIDE 1504.......... 59893
Smith, William (JOYCE, DAVID P.) STAFF ASST/LEGIS AIDE 1124.......... 55731
Smith, Willie (BLUMENAUER) CHIEF OF STAFF.......... 503-231-2300
Smith-Baker, Margaret (ROGERS, MIKE) ADMIN ASST/CASEWKR.......... 256-236-5655
Smith RuBoss, Daniel (DOGGETT) SR POLICY ADVISOR 2307.......... 54865
Smithwick, Kyle (CMTE-OVERSIGHT & GOVT REFORM) COUNSEL 2105.......... 55074
Smolinsky, Curran (WITTMAN) STAFF ASST 2055.......... 54261
Smoloski, Walter (HARRIS) LEGIS CORRES 2334.......... 55311
Smoot, Danielle (ROGERS, HAROLD) DIR - PRESS & COMMUNICATIONS.......... 606-679-8346
Smotkin, Danielle (ROUZER) DIR - PRESS & COMMUNICATIONS 2439.......... 52731
Smullen, Mike (JOHNSON, BILL) CHIEF OF STAFF 2336.......... 55705
Snead, Josh (CMTE-WAYS & MEANS) COUNSEL 1139.......... 54021
Sneden, Susan (CAO/WORKFLOW MGMT) COORD WA35 RHOB.......... 65888
Snelgrove, Eric (CMTE-ARMED SVCS) PROF STAFF 2340.......... 66064
Snorton, Clifton (CARSON) DIST EXEC ASST.......... 317-283-6516
Snow, Adam (STEWART) DPTY DIST DIR.......... 435-627-1500
Snyder, Alexis (WILSON, FREDERICA S.) DIST CHIEF OF STAFF.......... 305-690-5905
Snyder, Ari (GRIFFITH) STAFF ASST 2202.......... 53861
Snyder, Les (CAO/HIR – ENTERPRISE INFRASTRUCT) SR SYS ENGINEER SITE 3.......... 571-921-3325
Snyder, Lora (CMTE-NATURAL RESOURCES) SUBCOMM STAFF DIR 1332.......... 56065

Snyder, Mark (HIMES) LEGIS DIR 1227 **55541**
Snyder, Nathaniel (PALAZZO) CONG FELLOW 2349 **55772**
Snyder, Rachael (LOEBSACK) CASEWKR **319-351-0789**
Snyder, Rachel (HOYER) POLICY ADVISOR 1705 **54131**
Snyder, Rebecca (HECK) CHIEF CASEWKR **360-459-8514**
Sobel, John (COOK) CHIEF OF STAFF 1027 **55861**
Sodaro, Dylan (PASCRELL) SR LEGIS ASST 2409 **55751**
Soenksen, Amy (ASST SPEAKER) OUTREACH DIR H132 **52020**
Soffen, Kim (BOYLE) COMMUNICATIONS ASST 1133 **56111**
Sohn, Natalie (CMTE-ENERGY & COMMERCE) COUNSEL 564 FHOB **53641**
Sokolov, Anne (ROSE, MAX) CHIEF OF STAFF 1529 **53371**
Sokolov, Dahlia (CMTE-SCIENCE) STAFF DIR - MAJ 2321 **56375**
Solem, Rebekah (PETERSON) SR LEGIS ASST/ SCHEDULER 2204 **52165**
Solis, Cesar (PETERS) FIELD REP **858-455-5550**
Solis, Jesse (CMTE-WAYS & MEANS) PRESS SECY 1139 **54021**
Sollazzo, Amanda (GRAVES, SAM) EXEC ASST 1135 **57041**
Sollers, Danielle (CAO/PAYROLL & BENEFITS) COUNSELOR B215 LHOB **60048**
Solock, Mark (QUIGLEY) LEGAL COUNSEL **773-267-5926**
Solomon, Feven (HORSFORD) LEGIS CORRES 1330 **59894**
Solomon, Katie (FINKENAUER) STAFF ASST 124 CHOB **52911**
Solomon, William (CAO/ENTERPRISE APPLICATIONS) BUSINESS PROCESS APPLICA SPEC B62 FHOB **66263**
Solorzano, Willis (CAO/FURNISHINGS) APPRENTICE CABINET MAKER WA25 RHOB **58000**
Solow, Corey (MCEACHIN) LEGIS DIR 314 CHOB **56365**
Solyan, Bradley (FRANKEL) LEGIS ASST 2305 **59890**
Somani, Zahra (SCHAKOWSKY) STAFF ASST **773-506-7100**
Somasundaram, Nita (BEYER) CASEWK MGR **703-658-5403**
Song, Elli (QUIGLEY) CONG AIDE **773-267-5926**
Songer, Michael (YOUNG) LEGIS ASST - MIL 2314 **55765**
Sonneborn, Matt (TONKO) COMMUNICATIONS DIR 2369 **55076**
Sorensen, Amy (SIMPSON) DIST FIELD REP **208-523-6701**
Sorensen, Joshua (SIMPSON) FIELD REP **208-523-6701**
Sorensen, Rachel (KRISHNAMOORTHI) LEGIS ASST 115 CHOB **53711**
Sorenson, Kathryn (LURIA) CHIEF OF STAFF 534 CHOB **54215**
Sorenson, Zach (SCHIFF) LEGIS AIDE 2269 **54176**
Sorour, Mahyar (OMAR) SR LEGIS ASST 1517 **54755**
Sorrendino, Abbie (MORELLE) LEGIS DIR 1317 **53615**
Soskin, Benjamin (ROYBAL-ALLARD) COMMUNICATIONS DIR 2083 **51766**
Soto, Sandra (LOFGREN) DIST CHIEF OF STAFF **408-271-8700**
Sottnick, Fred (JOYCE, JOHN) LEGIS ASST 1337 **52431**
Souchet-Moura, Kathy (CARSON) COORD - OUTREACH /IMMIGRATION LIAISON **317-283-6516**
Soults, Daniel (CAO/ASSET MANAGEMENT) REC & WAREHOUSE SPEC WA23 RHOB **58214**
Sours, David (HICE) CHIEF OF STAFF 409 CHOB **54101**
South, John (MAST) CONSTIT SVCS REP **561-530-7778**
Southard, Tristan (KATKO) LEGIS ASST 2457 **53701**
Souvall, Andrew (CMTE-ENERGY & COMMERCE) COMMUNICATIONS DIR/OUTREACH DIR/DIR - MBR SVCS 2125 **52927**
Souvandara, Sinthasone (CAO/HIR – ENTERPRISE INFRASTRUCT) ADMIN 620 FHOB **66270**
Souza, Allen (CMTE-INTELLIGENCE) STAFF DIR - MIN HVC304 **54121**
Sowell, Tucker (GRANGER) STAFF ASST **817-338-0909**
Sowyrda, Brian (TORRES SMALL) DPTY CHIEF/ COMMUNICATIONS DIR 430 CHOB **52365**
Space, Melissa (CAO/OFFICE OF THE CHIEF HUMAN RESOURCES OFFICER) DIRECTOR 102 FHOB **64078**
Spadavecchia, Dominique (ARRINGTON) SR LEGIS ASST 1029 **54005**
Spak, Michael (MAJ LEADER) STAFF ASST H107 **53130**
Spannagel, Mark (LAMALFA) CHIEF OF STAFF 322 CHOB **53076**
Sparkman, Walter (RUSH) DIST AIDE **773-779-2400**
Sparks, Matthew
(MCCARTHY) COMMUNICATIONS DIR 2468 **52915**
(MIN LEADER) COMMUNICATIONS DIR H204 **54000**
Sparling, Jeri (TRONE) DIR - OPS 1213 **52721**
Spasiano, Jack (DELAURO) SR LEGIS ASST 2413 **53661**
Spaulding, Brian (WALORSKI) DPTY CHIEF OF STAFF **574-204-2645**
Spaulding, Stephen (CMTE-HOUSE ADMIN) COUNSEL - ELECTIONS 1309 **52061**
Spaun, Lydia (GOODEN) OUTREACH COORD **214-765-6789**
Spealman, Jennafer (CMTE-BUDGET) POLICY DIR 507 CHOB **67270**
Spears, Ian (MCBATH) LEGIS DIR 1513 **54501**
Spears, Tracy (AMODEI) CONSTIT SVCS REP **775-686-5760**
Specht, Brittan (MIN LEADER) SR POLICY ADVISOR H204 **54000**
Speed, Chris (MCBATH) CONSTIT SVCS/FIELD REP/CASEWKR **470-773-6330**
Speight, Reginald (BUTTERFIELD) DIST DIR **252-237-9816**
Spencer, Christian (BUCHANAN) LEGIS ASST 2427 **55015**
Spencer, Harden (CLEAVER) STAFF ASST 2335 **54535**
Spencer, Jacy (SMITH, ADRIAN) LIAISON - AG/ COMMUNITY LIAISON **308-384-3900**
Spencer, Peter (CMTE-ENERGY & COMMERCE) SR PROF STAFF MBR 564 FHOB **53641**
Spencer, Raquel (CMTE-BUDGET) GEN COUNSEL 204E CHOB **67200**
Spencer, Tanner (BANKS) LEGIS ASST 1713 **54436**
Speranza, Erik (SGT AT ARMS/EMERGENCY MGMT) ASST SGT AT ARMS - EMERGENCY MGMT 192 FHOB **60950**
Sperling, Erik (KHANNA) SR POLICY ADVISOR/COUNSEL 221 CHOB **52631**
Spicer, Kevin (VISCLOSKY) COMMUNICATIONS DIR 2328 **52461**
Spiegelman, Abby (FLORES) FIELD REP **512-373-3378**
Spieker, Martha (PETERS) PRESS SECY 2338 **50508**
Spikes, Harry (CUMMINGS) DIR - DIST AFFAIRS **410-685-9199**
Spinozzi, Isabella (QUIGLEY) SCHEDULER/DIR - OPS 2458 **54061**
Spiro, Pete (KHANNA) CHIEF OF STAFF 221 CHOB **52631**
Spitzer, Max (PARLIAMENTARIAN) PRECEDENT EDITOR 4470 **51122**
Splinter, David (CMTE-JOINT TAX) ECONOMIST 595 FHOB **67575**
Spohn, Carole Anne (RUTHERFORD) SCHEDULING DIR 1711 **52501**
Spolarich, Gillian (FRANKEL) PRESS SECY 2305 **59890**
Spotleson, Vinny (TITUS) DIST DIR **702-220-9823**
Spratt, Shelley (YARMUTH) SR CONG AIDE **502-933-5863**
Spriggs, Brandon (SGT AT ARMS/POLICE SVCS) ASST FOR TECH SUPPORT 173 FHOB **53380**
Springfield, Clyde (CAO/ACCOUNTING) SR ACCOUNTANT 3110 **61540**

Srinivasa, Veena (LEGIS COUNSEL) COUNSEL 337 FHOB. 56060
Sroka, Will (GIBBS) STAFF ASST 2446 56265
St. Dennis, Monica (CLERK/LRC) REFERENCE LIBRARIAN B81 CHOB 65200
St. Hubert, Zacharie (DELGADO) CONSTIT SVCS REP 845-443-2930
St. Louis, Numa (EVANS) DIST REP 215-276-0340
Stacey, Royal (CAO/HIR – OPS AND CONTINUITY) INFO TECH MGR 634A FHOB 63360
Stafford, Barbara (GRIFFITH) CONSTIT SVCS REP 540-381-5671
Stafford, Dillion (CRIST) CONSTIT SVCS REP 727-318-6770
Stafford, Julia (SCHRADER) LEGIS ASST 2431 55711
Stafford, Krista (MCHENRY) SR LEGIS ASST 2004 52576
Stagno, Laura (THORNBERRY) STAFF ASST 2208 53706
Stahl, Mike (TIMMONS) SR ADVISOR 864-241-0175
Stalcup-Gutierrez, Alexus (FITZPATRICK) STAFF ASST 1722 54276
Stallings, Bernadine (FUDGE) COMMUNICATIONS DIR 2344 57032
Stallings, Marshall (SMITH, JASON) STAFF ASST 2418 54404
Stallings, Tria (CLARKE) SCHEDULER 2058 56231
Stamps, Nathan (BILIRAKIS) LEGIS CORRES 2227 55755
Stanard, Alexa (SLOTKIN) DPTY CHIEF OF STAFF 517-993-0510
Stanberry, Charlyn (CLARKE) CHIEF OF STAFF 2058 56231
Stankiewicz, Claudia (BRINDISI) STAFF ASST 329 CHOB 53665
Stanley, Angel (CAO/ACCOUNTING) STAFF ACCOUNTANT 3110 59902
Stanley, Elizabeth (NORCROSS) STAFF ASST 2437 56501
Stanley, Elizabeth (LOWEY) CHIEF OF STAFF 2365 56506
Stanley, Mathew (POSEY) FELLOW 2150 53671
Stanley, Nick (GRANGER) COORD - OUTREACH 817-338-0909
Stansberry, Jennifer (BURCHETT) SR CASEWKR 865-523-3772
Stanton, Danice (KIND) CONG AIDE 608-782-2558
Stanton, Kimberly (CMTE-FOREIGN AFFAIRS) SR PROF STAFF MBR 5100 53599
Stanton, Kimberly (COMMIS TOM LANTOS HUMAN RIGHTS) SR PROF STAFF 5100 58097
Stanton, Rich (RADEWAGEN) LEGIS DIR 1339 58577
Stanwood, Jenna (DELAURO) LEGIS CORRES/LEGIS ASST 2413 53661
Stapleford, Randy (WALTZ) MIL FIELD REP 386-302-0442
Staples, Ian (DAVIS, SUSAN A.) LEGIS DIR 1214 52040
Staples, Randall (CMTE-APPRO) ADMIN ASST 2362A 52638
Stapleton, John (CMTE-FOREIGN AFFAIRS) SR PROF STAFF 4150 68467
Starace, Mario (DUNCAN, JEFF) DIST SCHEDULER/CONSTIT LIAISON 864-224-7401
Stark, Sharon (CONNOLLY) DIST DIR 703-256-3071
Starkey, Charles (CAO/HIR – OPS AND CONTINUITY) MGR 634 FHOB 66131
Starr, Shane (LAMALFA) DIST REP 530-343-1000
Starr, Walt (KELLY, TRENT) FIELD REP/CASEWKR 662-449-3090
Staudt, Cole (FITZPATRICK) COMMUNICATIONS DIR 1722 54276
Stayton, Amanda (COX) LEGIS AIDE 1728 54695
Steacy, Zachary (CMTE-ARMED SVCS) DIR - LEGIS OPS 2117 68634
Steadman, Liam (BUSTOS) LEGIS CORRES 1233 [illegible]
Stechschulte, Alissa (THOMPSON, GLENN) SCHEDULER/OFFICE MGR 400 CHOB 55121
Stechschulte, Will (GOSAR) LEGIS CORRES 2057 52315
Steck, Joe (HAGEDORN) FIELD REP - VETS 507-323-6090
Stecklow, Eric (BERA) OUTREACH DIR 1727 55716
Steel, Sabrina (LEVIN, ANDY) LEGIS ASST 228 CHOB 54961
Steele, Danielle (CMTE-ENERGY & COMMERCE) COUNSEL 2322A 53641
Steele, Gregory
(ESTES) COMMUNICATIONS DIR 1524 56216
(HUDSON) STAFF ASST/PRESS ASST 2112 53715
Steele, Lakeisha (CMTE-ED & WORKFORCE) PROF STAFF 2257 53725
Steele, Sophia (HUDSON) LEGIS CORRES 2112 53715
Steelman, Carson (WALKER) LEGIS CORRES 1725 53065
Steenekamp, Thomas (MURPHY) CONSTIT SVCS SPEC 888-205-5421
Stefanski, Daniel (BIGGS) COMMUNICATIONS DIR 1318 52635
Steffen, Richard (SPEIER) SR ADVISOR 650-342-0300
Steffens, Jessica (CMTE-FOREIGN AFFAIRS) SR PROF STAFF 4150 68467
Stegemoller, Hilary (CONAWAY) REGIONAL DIR 325-646-1950
Steger, Michael (SENSENBRENNER) LEGIS ASST 2449 55101
Steigleder, Stephen (CMTE-APPRO) CLERK 2358B 53508
Stein, Christopher (CAO/FURNISHINGS) JOURNEYMAN CABINET MAKER WA25 RHOB 58000
Stein, Elizah (AMASH) LEGIS AIDE 106 CHOB 53831
Stein, Maribeth (SCHAKOWSKY) CONSTIT ADVOCATE 773-506-7100
Stein, Marin (CMTE-APPRO) PROF STAFF MEMB HT2 52041
Stein, Todd (PINGREE) LEGIS ASST 2162 56116
Steinbaum, Jason (CMTE-FOREIGN AFFAIRS) STAFF DIR - MAJ 2152 55021
Steinberg, Ted (BOYLE) LEGIS ASST 1133 56111
Steinberger, Ben (HILL, KATIE) SR ADVISOR 1130 51956
Steiner, Matthew (CMTE-ETHICS) FINANCIAL DISCLOSURE CLERK 1015 57103
Steinhafel, Ben (SENSENBRENNER) LEGIS ASST/LEGIS CORRES 2449 55101
Steinmetz, Adam (CMTE-BUDGET) POLICY ADVISOR 507 CHOB 67270
Steinmuller, April (CAO/HOUSE RECORDING STUDIO) ADMIN SPEC 2010 53941
Steitz, Danielle (CMTE-ARMED SVCS) CLERK 2340 57560
Stemen, John (BRINDISI) DIST FIELD REP 315-732-0713
Stenberg, Rachel (DELBENE) CASEWKR 425-485-0085
Stephanou, Scott (LARSON) CHIEF OF STAFF 1501 52265
Stephens, Harper (ROBY) LEGIS CORRES/PRESS ASST 504 CHOB 52901
Stephens, Juli (JOHNSON, BILL) FIELD REP 740-534-9431
Stephens, Rachel (RATCLIFFE) PRESS SECY/COMMUNICATIONS DIR 223 CHOB 56673
Stephenson, Christiana (HOUSE DEM CAUCUS) PRESS SECY B245 LHOB 51400
Stephenson, Mark (CMTE-OVERSIGHT & GOVT REFORM) LEGIS DIR 2157 55051
Stepney, Eric (CAO/HOUSE RECORDING STUDIO) AUDIO SPEC 2010 53941

Sterkx, Craig (LEGIS COUNSEL) COORD - PUBLICATIONS 337 FHOB 56060
Stern, Hannah (PETERS) SCHEDULER/LEGIS AIDE 2338 50508
Stern, Keith (SPEAKER) DIR - FLOOR OPS H232 50100
Stern, Richard (HOUSE REPUB STUDY CMTE) POLICY STAFF 418 CHOB 52777
Stevens, Anais (DOGGETT) CONG AIDE 210-704-1080
Stevens, Chris (KING, STEVE) EXEC DIR 2210 54426
Stevens, Courtney (PALAZZO) SR LEGIS ASST 2349 55772
Stevens, Kim
(CÁRDENAS) FINANCIAL ADMIN 2438 56131
(JOHNSON, HENRY C. "HANK", JR.) ACCOUNTANT 2240 51605
(LAWSON) ADMIN - FINANCE & PAYROLL 1406 50123
(THOMPSON, MIKE) FINANCIAL ADMIN 406 CHOB 53311
(WILD) FINANCIAL ADMIN 1607 56411
Stevens, Sarah (KING, STEVE) CHIEF OF STAFF 2210 54426
Stevenson, Carol (HAGEDORN) DIST DIR 507-323-6090
Stevenson, Christen Janell (INSPECTOR GENERAL) ASST DIR 386 FHOB 61250
Stevenson, Marisa (SGT AT ARMS/INFO SVCS) SYS ADMIN H124 52456
Stevenson, Stephanie (KELLY, MIKE) SPECIAL PROJ DIR 724-282-2557
Steward, Lindsay (CMTE-WAYS & MEANS) PROF STAFF 1139 54021
Stewart, Adam (BISHOP, ROB) LEGIS DIR 123 CHOB 50453
Stewart, Brad (MAST) COMMUNICATIONS DIR/DPTY CHIEF OF STAFF 2182 53026
Stewart, Bradford (GUEST) DIST DIR 769-241-6120
Stewart, Christine (CAO/ACQUIS MGMT) DIRECTOR 5110 52921
Stewart, Danielle (GRAVES, TOM) COMMUNICATIONS DIR 2078 55211
Stewart, Jennifer (CMTE-ARMED SVCS) STAFF DIR - MIN 2340 68980
Stewart, Josh (ALLRED) COMMUNICATIONS DIR 328 CHOB 52231
Stewart, Katherine (ADAMS) LEGIS ASST 2436 51510
Stewart, Robert (SEWELL) COORD - COMMUNITY OUTREACH 334-877-4414
Stewart, Tom (SHERRILL) LEGIS DIR 1208 55034
Stiefel, Joshua (CMTE-ARMED SVCS) PROF STAFF 2340 66339
Stiles, Jo (MORELLE) LEGIS ASST 1317 53615
Stiles, Meaghan (MATSUI) CASEWKR 916-498-5600
Stiles, Melissa (WALDEN) DIST FIELD REP 541-776-4646
Stiles, Samantha (CMTE-FOREIGN AFFAIRS) DIR - OPS 2171 55021
Stivers, Jon (COMMIS ON CHINA) STAFF DIR 243 FHOB 63766
Stiverson, Brittany (STIVERS) CASEWORK - VETS 740-654-2654
Stock, Allison (PETERSON) CHIEF OF STAFF 218-847-5056
Stockert, Kevin (BLUMENAUER) LEGIS ASST 1111 54811
Stockwell, Scott (LOEBSACK) LEGIS DIR/DPTY CHIEF OF STAFF 1211 56576
Stoever, Michael (MCNERNEY) LEGIS ASST 2265 51947
Stokes, Zach (ALLEN) DIST FIELD REP 912-243-9452
Stokes, Zachary (SCHRADER) LEGIS ASST 2431 55711
Stolitzka, Anna (MOULTON) SCHEDULER 1127 58020
Stoll, Thomas (CMTE-JUDICIARY) COUNSEL 189 FHOB 56906
Stonebraker, Austin M (CMTE-BUDGET) DIGITAL DIR 507 CHOB 67270
Stonebraker, Miriam (WAGNER) DIST DIR 636-779-5449
Stoner, Hunter (TAYLOR) SCHEDULER 1404 54201
Stookey, Megan (CMTE-NATURAL RESOURCES) CLERK 1329 52761
Stooksbury, Melissa (COLE) STAFF ASST 2207 56165
Stopp, Mike (MULLIN) CHIEF OF STAFF 918-687-2533
Story, Chad (MOONEY) DIST DIR 2440 52711
Stosz, Conrad (CMTE-INTELLIGENCE) RESEARCH ASST HVC304 57690
Stotesbery, Katherine (DOGGETT) LEGIS ASST/ COMMUNICATIONS DIR 2307 54865
Stotler, Brad (LAHOOD) DIST DIR 309-671-7027
Stout, Ben (HICE) SR FIELD REP 770-207-1776
Stout, Doug (SMITH, ADRIAN) LEGIS ASST 502 CHOB 56435
Stovall, Shannon (BIGGS) LEGIS CORRES 1318 52635
Stover, Braden (ROSE, JOHN W.) SCHEDULER 1232 54231
Straatmann, Alex (SMITH, ADRIAN) DIR - CONSTIT SVCS 308-384-3900
Strader, Nick (WALDEN) DIST FIELD REP 541-389-4408
Stradford, Kierstin (CUMMINGS) LEGIS CORRES/SYS ADMIN 2163 54741
Straka, Joshua (MCCOLLUM) DIST DIR 651-224-9191
Stranz, Mike (CMTE-AGRIC) SUBCOMM STAFF DIR 1301 52171
Strasser, Madeline (CMTE-JUDICIARY) CHIEF CLERK 2138 53951
Stratton, Amy (CMTE-OVERSIGHT & GOVT REFORM) CLERK 2157 55051
Straughn, Patricia (CMTE-AGRIC) CHIEF COUNSEL 1010 50317
Street, Caren (BASS) CHIEF OF STAFF 2059 57084
Strickland, Kelle (SGT AT ARMS) CHIEF OF STAFF H124 52456
Stricklen, Elizabeth (CAO/OFFICE OF THE CFO) OFFICE MGR 3140 54391
Stringer, Mary Elizabeth (WALBERG) SCHEDULER 2266 56276
Stringfield, Joyce (CLERK) ADMIN - BUDGET & PROJ H154 57000
Strizak, Alexander (RUIZ) STAFF ASST 760-424-8888
Strizever, Michelle H (CLERK/ART & ARCHIVES) PHOTOGRAPHY & DIGITAL CONTENT SPECIALIST JEFFERSON BUILDING, ATTIC 61300
Strock, Callie (HURD) PRESS SECY 317 CHOB 54511
Strodel, Allison (CLERK/LEGIS OPS) ASST JOURNAL CLERK HT13 57925
Strohmaier, Kathryn (CMTE-FINANCIAL SVCS) COUNSEL - MAJ 2129 54247
Stroia, Matthew (KELLY, MIKE) CHIEF OF STAFF 1707 55406
Strom, John (CMTE-NATURAL RESOURCES) SR COUNSEL 4170 52761
Strombom, Emily (LOWENTHAL) LEGIS ASST 108 CHOB 57924
Strong, Kendall (RUPPERSBERGER) LEGIS CORRES/ LEGIS ASST 2206 53061
Stross, Matthew (HOLDING) LEGIS COUNSEL 1110 53032
Strother, Will (BURCHETT) LEGIS ASST 1122 55435
Strott, Carol (CAO/HIR – IT CUSTOMER SOLUTIONS) TECH SUPPORT REP 2067 64044
Stroud, Ceason (PERRY) STAFF ASST 717-635-9504
Strub, Hannah (BYRNE) LEGIS ASST - MIL 119 CHOB 54931
Struble, Matthias (BERGMAN) LEGIS CORRES 414 CHOB 54735
Stuart, Jasmine (RUPPERSBERGER) CONSTIT LIAISON 410-628-2701
Stuart, Keri (LUETKEMEYER) DIR - CONSTIT SVCS 573-635-7232

Stubbs, Connor (SMITH, ADAM) LEGIS ASST 2264 58901
Stuber, Aubrey (HOULAHAN) OPS ASST 1218 54315
Stuckert, Sherry (STIVERS) CASEWKR 937-283-7049
Stuckey, John (FERGUSON) CONSTIT SVCS REP 770-683-2033
Studley, Ben (DELBENE) LIAISON - VETS 425-485-0085
Stuedell, Brooke (TORRES SMALL) LEGIS DIR 430 CHOB 52365
Stukes, Gail (CLYBURN) CASEWKR 803-799-1100
Stumpf, LeRoy (PETERSON) STAFF ASST 218-847-5056
Styron, Stuart (DEMINGS) SR LEGIS ASST 217 CHOB 52176
Su, Peter (HAGEDORN) CHIEF OF STAFF 325 CHOB 52472
Suarato, Ben (CHU) COMMUNICATIONS DIR 2423 55464
Suarez, Neesha (MOULTON) CASEWKR 978-531-1669
Suber, Kathy (CMTE-INTELLIGENCE) SUBCOMM STAFF DIR HVC304 57690
Subich, Brian (THOMPSON, GLENN) FIELD REP 814-419-8583
Suchite, Rogelio (CICILLINE) CASEWKR 401-729-5600
Sudbay, Karen (PINGREE) SCHEDULER 207-774-5019
Sueppel, Rob (LOEBSACK) DIST DIR 563-323-5988
Sugarman, Elise (PETERS) LEGIS CORRES 2338 50508
Sugarman, Maxine (BONAMICI) LEGIS ASST 2231 50855
Suggs-Brigety, Naomia (CMTE-FOREIGN AFFAIRS) STAFF ASSOC 5190 61500
Suh, Jessica (CMTE-RULES) DPTY CLERK H312 59091
Suh, Joon (MCBATH) CHIEF OF STAFF 1513 54501
Sukol, Robert M (LAW REV COUNSEL) DPTY COUNSEL 308 FHOB 62411
Sulc, Kevin (BROOKS, SUSAN W.) DPTY DIST DIR 765-640-5115
Sulkala, Lea (SÁNCHEZ) CHIEF OF STAFF 2329 56676
Sullenberger, Keith A (INSPECTOR GENERAL) ASST DIR 386 FHOB 61250
Sullivan, Bart (COHEN) COMMUNICATIONS DIR 2104 53265
Sullivan, Chris (HIGGINS, CLAY) FIELD REP 337-703-6105
Sullivan, Mary-Margaret (FULCHER) STAFF ASST 1520 56611
Sullivan, Maxine (ENGEL) CASEWKR 718-320-2314
Sullivan, Michael (HOUSE REPUB CONF) POLICY COORD 1420 55107
Sullivan, Tim
(CMTE-HOUSE ADMIN) DIR - FRANKING COMMISSION 1216 58281
(COMMIS ON CONG MAILING STDS) STAFF DIR - MIN 1216 60647
Sumbrum, Abbie (WENSTRUP) SCHEDULER/OFFICE MGR 2419 53164
Summers, Brennan (SIMPSON) FIELD REP 208-523-6701
Summers, Damon (CAO/LOGISTICS) REC & WAREHOUSE SPEC RSBC4 59474
Summers, Emma (JORDAN) EXEC ASST/SCHEDULER/ LEGIS AIDE 2056 52676
Sumner, Danielle (MALONEY, CAROLYN B.) STAFF ASST 2308 57944
Sumner, Nancy (CAO/HIR – NETWORKING ENGINEERING AND OPS) SR NETWK TECH 652C FHOB 66430
Sumner, Rebecca (ROGERS, HAROLD) CASEWKR 606-679-8346
Sun, Kevin (HOUSE REPUB CONF) STAFF ASST 1420 55107
Sundahl, Alan
(ABRAHAM) ADMIN - FINANCE & PAYROLL 417 CHOB 58490
(CLARKE) ADMIN - FINANCE & PAYROLL 2058 56231
Sunday, Jessica (THORNBERRY) EXEC ASST 2208 53706
Sundby, Janet (KIND) CONG AIDE 715-831-9214
Sunderhaus, Jessica (ABRAHAM) CASEWKR 318-445-0818
Sunn, Meagan (CMTE-SMALL BUSINESS) PROF STAFF MEMB 2361 54038
Sunstrum, Greg (DINGELL) CHIEF OF STAFF 116 CHOB 54071
Suplee, Andrew (CAO/HIR – NETWORKING ENGINEERING AND OPS) SR NETWK SYS ENGINEER 664 FHOB 61827
Supon, Justin (CAO/HOUSE DAILY PRESS) DPTY DIR H315 53945
Sur, Christine (HUFFMAN) LEGIS ASST 1527 55161
Surber, Amy (BANKS) DPTY CHIEF OF STAFF/LEGIS DIR 1713 54436
Surdin, Samantha (SPANO) FIELD REP 863-644-8215
Suruma, Askia (VEASEY) CHIEF OF STAFF 2348 59897
Susalla, Michael (SGT AT ARMS/POLICE SVCS) LAW ENFORCEMENT COMMUNICATIONS LIAISON COMMAND 49859
Sutcliffe, T J (CMTE-WAYS & MEANS) PROF STAFF 2018 59263
Sutey, William (CMTE-ARMED SVCS) PROF STAFF 2340 62099
Sutphin, Holly (PERRY) FIELD REP 717-635-9504
Sutton, Tracee (STANTON) LEGIS DIR/DPTY CHIEF OF STAFF 128 CHOB 59888
Suydam, Marcus (CAO/ACQUIS MGMT) ADMIN - CONTRACTS 5110 52921
Svoboda, Timothy (GROTHMAN) COMMUNICATIONS DIR 1427 52476
Swan, Carol (CAO/FURNISHINGS) MGR - FURNISHINGS WA32 RHOB 58000
Swanson, Fran (FINKENAUER) LEGIS AIDE/PRESS SECY 124 CHOB 52911
Swarers, Vita (BRADY) CASEWK MGR 936-439-9532
Swartz, Emily
(CAO/EMPLOYEE ASSISTANCE) COORD 140 FHOB 66312
(CAO/HOUSE WELLNESS CTR) PROGRAM COORD 140 FHOB 52400
Swartzendruber, Douglas (CAO/HOUSE RECORDING STUDIO) BROADCAST ENGINEER/PROD SPEC 2010 53941
Sweeney, Catherine (HORN) COMMUNICATIONS DIR 415 CHOB 52132
Sweet, Chris (DIAZ-BALART) LEGIS DIR 404 CHOB 54211
Swender, Becca (MARSHALL) DPTY DIST DIR 620-765-7800
Swick, Anna (HARTZLER) COMMUNICATIONS DIR 2235 52876
Swift, Afton (HERRERA BEUTLER) POLICY ADVISOR 360-695-6292
Swig, Sarah (PELOSI) LEGIS CORRES 1236 54965
Swindle, Alex (LEGIS COUNSEL) LEGIS RESEARCH ANALYST 337 FHOB 56060
Swindle, Bessie (GREEN, AL) COMMUNITY LIAISON 713-383-9234
Swiss, Kathryn (LEGIS COUNSEL) ASST COUNSEL 337 FHOB 56060
Switzer, Kenneth (ENGEL) DPTY DIR - CONSTIT SVCS 718-796-9700
Swope, Carrie (PASCRELL) ADVISOR - HEALTH POLICY 2409 55751
Swope, Clayton (KILMER) LEGIS ASST - MIL 1410 55916
Swords, John (MCGOVERN) LEGIS ASST 408 CHOB 56101
Syed, Mohsin (CMTE-TRANSP & INFRA) GEN COUNSEL 2165 54472
Sylvester, Ashley (SCHWEIKERT) OFFICE MGR/ SCHEDULER 1526 52190

Synnes, Mark (LEGIS COUNSEL) SR COUNSEL 337 FHOB.. 56060
Sypolt, Jennifer (LIPINSKI) ADMIN ASST/SCHEDULER/SYS ADMIN 2346 55701
Szabo, John (CMTE-ETHICS) COUNSEL 1015 57103
Szajner, Karsten (SLOTKIN) CASEWKR 517-993-0510
Szczesniewski, Linda (NORCROSS) DIST REP 856-427-7000
Szpindor, Catherine (CAO/OFFICE OF THE CHIEF INFORMATION OFFICER - HIR) CIO 631 FHOB 69788
Szwec, Peter (LEGIS COUNSEL) SR SYS ANALYST 337 FHOB 56060
Tabalba, Angelyn (HORSFORD) DIST STAFF ASST 702-963-9360
Tabarzadi, Shahla (CAO/HIR – NETWORKING ENGINEERING AND OPS) SR NETWK COMMUNICATIONS SPEC 688 FHOB 66266
Tachiki-Chin, Kimberlee (ROYBAL-ALLARD) SR FIELD REP 323-721-8790
Taft, Janee (EVANS) CONG AIDE 215-276-0340
Taft, Tammy E (CLERK/REPORTERS) OFFICE AND PROD ASST 1718 52627
Tagen, Julie (RASKIN) CHIEF OF STAFF 412 CHOB 55341
Taggart, Michael (RODGERS) LEGIS DIR 1035 52006
Tagoilelagi, Uta (RADEWAGEN) SR POLICY ADVISOR 684-633-3601
Taheri, Kevin (GALLAGHER) LEGIS CORRES 1230 55665
Tahirkheli, Sylvia (LAW REV COUNSEL) STAFF ASST 308 FHOB 62411
Tai, Katherine (CMTE-WAYS & MEANS) CHIEF COUNSEL - TRADE 1103 56649
Talmage, Sarah (ZELDIN) LEGIS AIDE 2441 53826
Talus, Ben (SHALALA) SR LEGIS ASST 1320 53931
Talvitie, Travis (CMTE-JOINT LIBRARY) DPTY STAFF DIR - DEM SR-481 46352
Talvitie, Travis (CMTE-JOINT PRINTING) DPTY STAFF DIR - DEM SR-481 46352
Tam, Catalina (PORTER) STAFF ASST 1117 55611
Tamayo, Justin (STEUBE) LEGIS COUNSEL 521 CHOB 55792
Tammadge, James (CAO/HIR – ENTERPRISE INFRASTRUCT) SR SYS ENGINEER 617 FHOB 69826
Tanga, Adam (SABLAN) SR ADVISOR 2411 52646
Tankel, Judith (ALLRED) DIST DIR 972-972-7949
Tannenbaum, Lisa (ENGEL) DIR - COMMUNITY OUTREACH 718-796-9700
Tanner, Ashley (JOHNSON, DUSTY) FIELD REP 605-622-1060
Tanner, John (GOHMERT) DIST FIELD REP 903-561-6349
Tanzyus, David (BOST) DIST DIR 618-622-0766
Tapia, Edna (TORRES SMALL) SCHEDULER 430 CHOB 52365
Tapia, Elizabeth (LAMBORN) SR CASEWKR 719-520-0055
Tarango-Chavez, Emily (CASTRO) CONSTIT SVCS REP 210-348-8216
Tarpey, Molly Rose (LYNCH) COMMUNICATIONS DIR 617-428-2000
Tarwid, Caroline (STAUBER) LEGIS CORRES 126 CHOB 56211
Tash, Michael (STEVENS) CASEWK MGR 734-853-3040
Tata, Shantanu (DELBENE) SR POLICY ADVISOR 2330 56311
Tatarian, Lisa
(CASTEN) FINANCIAL ADMIN 429 CHOB 54561
(CICILLINE) LEGIS COUNSEL/DIR - FINANCE 2233 54911
(CLARK) ADMIN - FINANCE & PAYROLL 2448 52836
(SCANLON) FINANCIAL ADMIN/OFFICE MGR 1535 52011
Tatelman, Todd (GEN COUNSEL) DPTY COUNSEL 219 CHOB 59700
Tatupu, Jeremiah (RADEWAGEN) SR CASEWKR 684-633-3601
Tauster, Deena (KING, PETER T.) LEGIS DIR 302 CHOB 57896
Taylor, Andrew (CMTE-FOREIGN AFFAIRS) SR ECON ADVISOR 4150 68467
Taylor, Anita (CLARKE) DIST DIR 718-287-1142
Taylor, Anita (SGT AT ARMS/EMERGENCY MGMT) EMERGENCY MGMT SPEC 192 FHOB 60950
Taylor, Barbara (JORDAN) DPTY DIST DIR 419-999-6455
Taylor, Ben (BABIN) LEGIS CORRES 2236 51555
Taylor, Carissa (NORMAN) DIST SCHEDULER/ DIST OFFICE MGR 803-327-1114
Taylor, Christopher (FLORES) LEGIS ASST 2228 56105
Taylor, Daniel
(CMTE-HOUSE ADMIN) CHIEF COUNSEL 1309 52061
(DEUTCH) LEGIS CORRES 2447 53001
Taylor, Gloria (WITTMAN) DPTY PRESS SECY 2055 54261
Taylor, Heath (FLEISCHMANN) STAFF ASST 2410 53271
Taylor, Jake (SMUCKER) FIELD REP 717-969-6133
Taylor, Jennifer (ADERHOLT) DIR - CONSTIT SVCS 256-734-6043
Taylor, Joelle (BRINDISI) DIST SCHEDULER 315-732-0713
Taylor, Kim (FINKENAUER) CASEWKR 319-364-2288
Taylor, Paul (CMTE-JUDICIARY) CHIEF COUNSEL 362 FHOB 56906
Taylor, Rebecca (MCCOLLUM) SR LEGIS ASST 2256 56631
Taylor, Ronald, Sr (CAO/HIR – ENTERPRISE INFRASTRUCT) SYS ENGINEER 641 FHOB 66333
Taylor, Shaun (HUDSON) LEGIS ASST 2112 53715
Taylor, Terrance (HOYER) DPTY DIST DIR 301-474-0119
Taylor, Zachary (CMTE-ARMED SVCS) CLERK 2340 51967
Teague, James (RUSH) CONSTIT SVCS ASSOC 773-779-2400
Teasley, Richard (CAO/HIR – CYBERSECURITY) SYS SECUR ENGINEER 612 FHOB 64111
Tecklenburg, Michael (SPEAKER) COUNSEL H232 50100
Teclu, Yonathan (OMAR) LEGIS CORRES 1517 54755
Teebi, Noor (TONKO) LEGIS ASST 2369 55076
Teehan, Shana (BRADY) COMMUNICATIONS DIR/SR ADVISOR 1011 54901
Tehrani, Michael (SCOTT, AUSTIN) LEGIS ASST - MIL/ LEGIS DIR 2417 56531
Teicher, Ethan (BROWN) DPTY PRESS SECY 1323 58699
Teixeira, Allison (DAVIDS) CHIEF OF STAFF 1541 56027
Tell, Regina (CLERK/REPORTERS) OFFICIAL REPORTER 1718 52627
Tellez, Daniel (FULCHER) SCHEDULER/PRESS ASST 1520 56611
Tembo, Kay (ADAMS) SR DIST REP 704-344-9950
Tempel, Whitney (WATKINS) DIST REP 785-234-5966
Tenbrink, Trevor (HUIZENGA) LEGIS ASST 2232 54401
Tencer, Lisa (TLAIB) CASEWKR 313-463-6220
Tener, William (ROGERS, HAROLD) STAFF ASST 2406 54601
Tenney, Keeley (OLSON) EXEC ASST 2133 55951
Tenorio, Peter Michael (SABLAN) DIST DIR 670-323-2647
Tensen, Julie (SIMPSON) SCHEDULER/OFFICE MGR 208-334-1953
Teppala, Harshitha (LIEU) SCHEDULER 403 CHOB 53976
Tercek, Margo (DESAULNIER) LEGIS ASST 503 CHOB 52095
Terrazas, Rick (HUNTER) CHIEF OF STAFF 2429 55672

Terrell, Myra J (HOUSE EMPLOYMENT COUNSEL) SR SECY 4300 57075
Terrillion, Kathleen (KING, PETER T.) DIST REP 516-541-4225
Terry, Ella (CLERK/SVCS GRPS) ASST CLOAKRM FOOD MGR - MAJ H222 61154
Terry, Ellisha (JOHNSON, EDDIE BERNICE) CONSTIT SVCS 214-922-8885
Terry, Syd
(CMTE-ENERGY & COMMERCE) POLICY COORD 2125 52927
(SCHAKOWSKY) LEGIS DIR 2367 52111
(SR CHF DPTY MAJ WHIP – SCHAKOWSKY) LEGIS DIR 2367 52111
Tertullien, Vernita (HIMES) DIR - COMMUNITY OUTREACH 203-333-6600
Teska, Rebecca (GROTHMAN) LEGIS AIDE/EXEC SCHEDULER 1427 52476
Tetlow, Faith (LIEU) CASEWKR 323-651-1040
Teves-Roda, Elizabeth (KEATING) DIST REP 508-999-6462
Tew, Sophia (CLERK/LRC) ASST EDITOR B81 CHOB 65200
Tewelde, Yodit (DEAN) DIR - OPS/SCHEDULING DIR 129 CHOB 54731
Tewksbury, Gene (COURTNEY) CONSTIT SVCS 860-886-0139
Tewksbury, Paul (CAO/EMPLOYEE ASSISTANCE) SR EMPLOYEE ASSISTANCE COUNSELOR 140 FHOB 52400
Tewoldeberhan, Alem (JOHNSON, HENRY C. "HANK", JR.) SCHEDULER/OFFICE MGR 2240 51605
Thacker, Jeff (WOMACK) FIELD REP 479-464-0446
Thaeler, Ben (DAVIDSON) DIST DIR 937-339-1524
Thames, Madison (MULLIN) SCHEDULER 2421 52701
Thapa, Jain (LEE, BARBARA) CONG AIDE 510-763-0370
Thatte, Tejasi (CÁRDENAS) DPTY CHIEF OF STAFF/LEGIS DIR 2438 56131
Theissen, Anthony (SCHIFF) LEGIS ASST 2269 54176
Theodossiou, Taylor (MCHENRY) PRESS SECY 2004 52576
Theriot, Luke (VELA) SR ADVISOR - POLICY & OUTREACH 307 CHOB 59901
Thibodeau, Joe (TRAHAN) REGIONAL DIR 978-459-0101
Thiessen, Gary (CAO/FIRST CALL) MGR B227 LHOB 58000
Thigpen, Brinsley (ALLEN) DIST DIR 706-228-1980
Thigpen, Christine (WEBER) CASEWKR - IMMIGRATION 979-285-0231
Thomas, Aaron (HOULAHAN) CASEWKR 610-883-5050
Thomas, Alison (GAETZ) SCHEDULER 1721 54136
Thomas, Ben (CASTRO) LEGIS DIR 2241 53236
Thomas, Brad (CMTE-ED & WORKFORCE) SR POLICY ADVISOR - EDUC 6140 56558
Thomas, Brendan (DESJARLAIS) COMMUNICATIONS DIR 2301 56831
Thomas, Brian (MARCHANT) CHIEF OF STAFF 2304 56605
Thomas, Byron (WILSON, JOE) SPECIAL ASST/ CASEWKR 803-939-0041
Thomas, Cam (HERN) CONSTIT SVCS REP 918-935-3222
Thomas, Delvin (WILSON, FREDERICA S.) COORD - OPS 305-690-5905
Thomas, Denise (CAO/LOGISTICS) REC & WAREHOUSE SPEC RSBC4 55057
Thomas, Evan (CONAWAY) DIST DIR 432-687-2390
Thomas, Faye (CMTE-AGRIC) ADMIN - COMMITTEE 1301 52171
Thomas, James (LAMBORN) DPTY CHIEF OF STAFF/ LEGIS DIR 2371 54422
Thomas, Jason (CAO/LOGISTICS) LOGISTICS & DIST SPEC WA16 RHOB 59474
Thomas, Kenneth (LAW REV COUNSEL) SYS ADMIN 308 FHOB 62411
Thomas, Marzie (COHEN) DIST DIR 901-544-4131
Thomas, Melissa (LAWSON) STAFF ASST 850-558-9450
Thomas, Nia (NORTON) STAFF ASST 202-408-9041
Thomas, Petrina (CMTE-FINANCIAL SVCS) STAFF ASST - MAJ 2129 54247
Thomas, Ronald (CLERK/LRC) CHIEF B81 CHOB 65200
Thomas, Shea (GOHMERT) CASEWKR 903-561-6349
Thomas, Tiana (PLASKETT) LEGIS ASST 2404 51790
Thomas, Vincent (CLERK/REPORTERS) PROD ASST 193 CHOB 57187
Thomas-Wright, Patricia (SGT AT ARMS/ID SVCS) ASST/ ID SVCS 321 CHOB 53820
Thompson, Adam (CAO/ACCOUNTING) STAFF ACCOUNTANT 3110 57922
Thompson, Cora
(ADAMS) INFO TECH MGR 2436 51510
(BONAMICI) TECH SUPPORT REP 2231 50855
(CASE) INFO SYS SECUR MGR 2443 52726
(CUNNINGHAM) SHARED EMPLOYEE 423 CHOB 53176
(FUDGE) INFO TECH MGR 2344 57032
(HORN) INFO TECH MGR 415 CHOB 52132
(PAYNE) SYS ADMIN 103 CHOB 53436
Thompson, David (CRIST) LEGIS CORRES 215 CHOB 55961
Thompson, Elizabeth (GARAMENDI) SR POLICY ADVISOR 2368 51880
Thompson, Hart (CARTER, EARL L. "BUDDY") LEGIS ASST 2432 55831
Thompson, Jacqueline (YARMUTH) CONG AIDE 502-582-5129
Thompson, Jamila (LEWIS) LEGIS DIR 300 CHOB 53801
Thompson, Jessica (WEBSTER) LEGIS CORRES 1210 51002
Thompson, Jett (TAYLOR) LEGIS DIR 1404 54201
Thompson, Katie (CMTE-ARMED SVCS) DIR - SECUR 2337 55733
Thompson, Katie (HURD) COMMUNICATIONS DIR 317 CHOB 54511
Thompson, Mark (CAO/HIR – ENTERPRISE INFRASTRUCT) MGR 620C FHOB 66264
Thompson, Maryah (MOORE) STAFF ASST/LEGIS CORRES 2252 54572
Thompson, Matthew (LUETKEMEYER) SPECIAL ASST 573-635-7232
Thompson, Mischa (COMMIS ON SECUR & COOP IN EUR) POLICY ADVISOR 234 FHOB 51901
Thompson, Monica (LAW REV COUNSEL) STAFF ASST 308 FHOB 62411
Thompson, Phillip (CAO/HIR - ENTERPRISE MESSAGING AND MOBILITY) SR SYS ENGINEER 623 FHOB 68483
Thompson, Rachel (HURD) LEGIS CORRES 317 CHOB 54511
Thompson, Ryan (HOUSE DEM CONG CMPGN CMTE) CHIEF DIGITAL OFFICER 202-863-1500
Thompson, Ryan (WRIGHT) CHIEF OF STAFF 428 CHOB 52002
Thompson, Scott (CMTE-INTELLIGENCE) TREASURY DETAILEE HVC304 57690
Thompson, Stacy (HOULAHAN) LEGIS ASST 1218 54315

Thompson, Stephen (CAO/ASSET MANAGEMENT) REC & WAREHOUSE SPEC WA23 RHOB 50090
Thompson, Teneisha (CLERK) ADMIN - CONTRACTS H154 57000
Thompson, Tola (LAWSON) CHIEF OF STAFF 1406 50123
Thompson, Una (CAO/PAYROLL & BENEFITS) GENERALIST B215 LHOB 54595
Thomson, Emma (BURGESS) COMMUNICATIONS DIR 2161 57772
Thomson, Shestin
(CMTE-FOREIGN AFFAIRS) STAFF ASSOC 5193 53111
(KEATING) LEGIS CORRES 2351 53111
Thorne, Dray
(HOUSE REPUB CONF) DIR - INFO TECH 1420 55107
(RODGERS) DIR - INFO TECH 1035 52006
Thornton, Steve (CLARK) LEGIS DIR 2448 52836
Thorp, Kyle (MURPHY) CONSTIT ADVOCATE 888-205-5421
Thorpe, Katelynn (LOWEY) COMMUNICATIONS DIR 2365 56506
Threadgill, Tyler (KUSTOFF) CHIEF OF STAFF 523 CHOB 54714
Thrift, Laura (BLUMENAUER) LEGIS DIR 1111 54811
Thurman, Aaron (CMTE-INTELLIGENCE) SUBCOMM STAFF DIR HVC304 57690
Thurman, Kari (PAPPAS) DIST DIR 603-285-4300
Thurman, Mary (BOST) DIST STAFF ASST 618-622-0766
Tiani, James (CAO/ACQUIS MGMT) SR CONTRACTS SPEC 5110 52921
Tibbetts, Gary (BUCHANAN) FIELD REP 941-747-9081
Tibbetts, Sally (BUCHANAN) DIST DIR 941-951-6643
Tidwell, Daniel (FLEISCHMANN) LEGIS DIR/LEGIS COUNSEL 2410 53271
Tien, Michael (CMTE-TRANSP & INFRA) SR COUNSEL 2251 54472
Tiersky, Alex (COMMIS ON SECUR & COOP IN EUR) POLICY ADVISOR 234 FHOB 51901
Tighe, Stephen (PASCRELL) PRESS ASST 973-523-5152
Tilghman, Anna (PRICE) SR ADVISOR 919-859-5999
Tiller, Jennifer (CMTE-AGRIC) SR PROF STAFF 1010 50317
Tillman, Arrica (CAO/PAYROLL & BENEFITS) MGR B215 LHOB 54581
Tilson, Daniel (CAO/HOUSE RECORDING STUDIO) BROADCAST PROD TECH 2010 53941
Timm, Jeff (GOSAR) VET ADVOCATE 928-445-1683
Timmerman, Adam (HARTZLER) FIELD REP 816-884-3411
Timmerman, Amy (FERGUSON) COMMUNICATIONS DIR 1032 55901
Timmins, Gary (FOSTER) SR POLICY ADVISOR 2366 53515
Tin, Yadana (CAO/HOUSE DAILY PRESS) DIRECTOR H315. 53945
Tirella, Maxie (ROY) COORD - DIST OUTREACH 830-896-0154
Tisdale, Nicole (CMTE-HOMELAND SECUR) SUBCOMM STAFF DIR - INTELLIGENCE AND COUNTERTERRORISM SUBCOMM/COUNSEL - INTELLIGENCE AND COUNTERTERRORISM SUBCOMM 176 FHOB 62616
Tittle, Jeremy (CARBAJAL) CHIEF OF STAFF 1431 53601
Titus, Alison (CMTE-AGRIC) LEGIS ASST 1301 52171
Titus, Tony (SGT AT ARMS/ID SVCS) ASST/ID SVCS 321 CHOB 53820
Tizzani, Philip (CMTE-APPRO) PROF STAFF MEMB 2358B 53508
Tjelmeland, Brenan (GRANGER) EXEC ASST 1026 55071
Tobias, Teona (CAO/HIR – ENTERPRISE INFRASTRUCT) SR TELECOMMUNICATIONS ADMIN 692 FHOB 56002
Tobias-Cohen, Laurie (ESPAILLAT) CONSTIT LIAISON 212-663-3900
Tobin, Kim (BRINDISI) DIST STAFF ASST 315-732-0713
Tobin, Sean (BOYLE) COMMUNICATIONS DIR 1133 56111
Todacheene, Heidi (HAALAND) LEGIS ASST 1237 56143
Todd, McKinzii (BARR) CONSTIT SVCS OFFICER 859-219-1366
Tolar, Mac (CAO/WOUNDED WARRIOR) DIRECTOR 355 FHOB 61915
Tolba, Willy (SHERRILL) CASEWORK - VETS/ CASEWKR - MIL 973-526-5668
Tollefson, Elise (REED) LEGIS DIR 2263 53161
Tolleson, Jesse (CMTE-ARMED SVCS) PROF STAFF 2340 68774
Tomero, Leonor (CMTE-ARMED SVCS) COUNSEL 2340 52526
Toner, Mark (COMMIS ON SECUR & COOP IN EUR) SR ADVISOR 234 FHOB 51901
Toney, Fred (CAO/HIR – OPS AND CONTINUITY) SR SYS ENGINEER 634A FHOB 64573
Tonizzo, David (CAO/HIR – HOUSE WEB SVCS) SR INTERNET SYS SPEC 642A FHOB 571-921-3205
Topper, David (LEGIS COUNSEL) ASST SYS ADMIN 337 FHOB 56060
Topping, Brandon (SGT AT ARMS/APPOINTMENT) ASST - APPTS DESK CAPITOL 52551
Topping, Kristen (DESJARLAIS) CASEWKR 615-896-1986
Toretto, Courtney (DOGGETT) DPTY DIST DIR 512-916-5921
Torina, Gabrielle (BUSTOS) CONSTIT ADVOCATE/FIELD REP 815-968-8011
Torrence, Jamari (LEVIN, ANDY) STAFF ASST 228 CHOB 54961
Torres, Andrew (HASTINGS) CONG ASST 954-733-2800
Torres, Benito (ESCOBAR) DIST REP 915-541-1400
Torres, Rosario (INSPECTOR GENERAL) AUDITOR 386 FHOB 61250
Torres-Colón, Narel (GONZÁLEZ-COLÓN) DIST DIR 787-723-6333
Tortorici, Nick (ARMSTRONG) SR LEGIS AIDE 1004 52611
Toscano, Stephanie (GONZALEZ, VICENTE) DIST DIR 956-682-5545
Toufanian, Melissa (DELGADO) CHIEF COMMUNICATIONS ADVISOR 1007 55614
Touton, Camille (CMTE-TRANSP & INFRA) PROF STAFF 585 FHOB 54472
Towers, Jon (CMTE-VET AFFAIRS) STAFF DIR - MIN 3460 53527
Townsend, Digna (NORCROSS) COORD - OUTREACH 856-427-7000
Toy, Lauren (LEE, SUSIE) STAFF ASST 522 CHOB 53252
Tozzi, Piero
(COMMIS TOM LANTOS HUMAN RIGHTS) SR PROF STAFF 5100 53765
(SMITH, CHRISTOPHER H.) COUNSEL 2373 53765
Tracy, Collin (RODGERS) DIST SCHEDULER 509-353-2374
Tragni, Lina (SWALWELL) DIST OFFICE MGR/ DIST SCHEDULER 510-370-3322
Trainor, Sophie (GUTHRIE) LEGIS DIR 2434 53501
Tranghese, William (NEAL) PRESS SECY/CHIEF OF STAFF 2309 55601
Trapani, Emily (CMTE-HOMELAND SECUR) SUBCOMM STAFF DIR - BORDER SECURITY, FACILITATION, AND OPERATIONS SUBCOMM 117 FHOB 68417
Trauberman, Jacob (MAJ LEADER) SPECIAL ASST H107 53130

Traylor, Katrice (CROW) DIR - CONSTIT SVCS........ **720-748-7514**
Traynham, Benjamin (CMTE-SCIENCE) COUNSEL/SR POLICY ADVISOR - REPUB 394 FHOB........ **56371**
Traynham, Eleanor (DUFFY) SCHEDULER 1714........ **53365**
Treadway, Jenn (LARSEN) DIST SCHEDULER........ **425-252-3188**
Treasure, Kyle (CMTE-JOINT ECON) DIGITAL MEDIA DIR - REPUB SD-G01........ **46419**
Trees, Candice (DAVIS, RODNEY) COMMUNITY OUTREACH SPEC........ **217-791-6224**
Trejo, Travis (HARRIS) LEGIS ASST........ **410-643-5425**
Tremblay, Robert (NEAL) STAFF ASST 2309........ **55601**
Trent, Brian (OCASIO-CORTEZ) COMMUNICATIONS DIR 229 CHOB........ **53965**
Trent, Julia (EMMER) STAFF ASST 315 CHOB........ **52331**
Tresvant, Dalton (CLYBURN) DIRECTOR........ **803-799-1100**
Tricomi, Grace (MCHENRY) SCHEDULER 2004........ **52576**
Trigg, H Brenton (CMTE-JOINT TAX) SR ECONOMIST 595 FHOB........ **67575**
Trimmer, Shane (LOWENTHAL) SR LEGIS ASST 108 CHOB........ **57924**
Trinward, Pam (PINGREE) DIST OUTREACH REP........ **207-873-5713**
Tripplaar, Maria (CMTE-VET AFFAIRS) SUBCOMM STAFF DIR - DISABILITY ASSISTANCE AND MEMORIAL AFFAIRS SUBCOMM 3460........ **59164**
Trister, Sarah (CICILLINE) LEGIS DIR/DPTY CHIEF OF STAFF 2233........ **54911**
Trokey, Claire (SCALISE) LEGIS ASST 2049........ **53015**
Trombetta, Joseph (CAO/FURNISHINGS) MASTER CARPET MECHANIC WA32 RHOB........ **58000**
Trombly, Ian (KEATING) DIST REP........ **508-999-6462**
Troutman, Mary (MASSIE) ADMIN DIR/DIST SCHEDULER........ **859-426-0080**
Trowbridge, Fred (SCALISE) DIR - PROJ 2049........ **53015**
Truding, Bradley
(CMTE-OVERSIGHT & GOVT REFORM) COUNSEL 2157........ **55051**
(NORTON) CHIEF COUNSEL/LEGIS DIR 2136........ **58050**
Trujillo, Rafael (TORRES) CASE MGR........ **909-481-6474**
Trulock, Alison (CLERK/ART & ARCHIVES) ASSOC ARCHIVIST JEFFERSON BUILDING, ATTIC........ **61300**
Truluck, Walker (RICE, TOM) LEGIS DIR 512 CHOB........ **59895**
Trumka, Richard (CMTE-OVERSIGHT & GOVT REFORM) SUBCOMM STAFF DIR 6430........ **55051**
Trumpetto, Brynna (MALONEY, SEAN PATRICK) OUTREACH DIR........ **845-561-1259**
Truong, Mike (CAO/HIR – NETWORKING ENGINEERING AND OPS) SR NETWK COMMUNICATIONS SPEC 680 FHOB........ **202-765-9238**
Truxal, Charlie (GAETZ) LEGIS ASST - MIL 1721........ **54136**
Trzeciak, Kimberlee (CMTE-ENERGY & COMMERCE) CHIEF HEALTH ADVISOR 2125........ **55056**
Tsafoulias, Christina (TRONE) LEGIS DIR 1213........ **52721**
Tsai, Sabrina (COMMIS ON CHINA) RESEARCH ASSOC 243 FHOB........ **63833**
Tuck, Emily (CAO/OFFICE OF THE CHIEF HUMAN RESOURCES OFFICER) DIR - PRIVACY 102 FHOB........ **50668**
Tucker, Cheryle (CMTE-TRANSP & INFRA) SR PROF STAFF 2165........ **54472**
Tucker, Copeland (CARSON) COMMUNICATIONS DIR 2135........ **54011**
Tucker, David (CMTE-HOUSE ADMIN) PARLIAMENTARIAN 1309........ **52061**
Tucker, Mark (MURPHY) DIST SCHEDULER........ **888-205-5421**
Tucker, Matt (JOYCE, JOHN) LEGIS DIR 1337........ **52431**
Tucker, Mike (DEAN) CASEWK MGR........ **610-382-1250**
Tucker, Natalie
(CUNNINGHAM) CASEWKR........ **843-352-7572**
(CMTE-JOINT TAX) LEGIS TAX ACCOUNTANT 502 FHOB........ **53621**
Tucker, Phil (SWALWELL) FIELD REP/CASEWKR........ **510-370-3322**
Tucker, Sally (NEGUSE) COMMUNICATIONS DIR 1419........ **52161**
Tucker, Tom (CMTE-APPRO) DIR - OPS H307........ **52771**
Tudor, Chris (MCCLINTOCK) DC CHIEF OF STAFF 2312........ **52511**
Tulloch, Rebecca (MALONEY, CAROLYN B.) SCHEDULER 2308........ **57944**
Tumolo, Ann (WENSTRUP) COMMUNICATIONS DIR 2419........ **53164**
Turbyfill, Brian (WASSERMAN SCHULTZ) DIR - APPRO 1114........ **57931**
Turek, Stanley (CAO/FINANCIAL COUNSELING) FINANCIAL COUNSELOR B215 LHOB........ **69451**
Turk, Allison (YOHO) SCHEDULER 1730........ **55744**
Turner, Ben (EVANS) COMMUNICATIONS DIR 1105........ **54001**
Turner, Janet (LIEU) FIELD REP/CONSTIT SVCS........ **323-651-1040**
Turner, Johnny (BROOKS, MO) DIST FIELD REP........ **256-355-9400**
Turner, Joi (MCCARTHY) CONSTIT SVCS........ **661-327-3611**
Turner, Julie (CMTE-VET AFFAIRS) COUNSEL - DISABILITY ASSISTANCE AND MEMORIAL AFFAIRS SUBCOMM B234 LHOB........ **59756**
Turner, Kam (TIMMONS) COORD - GRANTS........ **864-241-0175**
Turner, Lee (JOHNSON, MIKE) REGIONAL REP........ **337-392-3146**
Turner, Mary (TLAIB) CASEWKR........ **313-203-7540**
Turner, Naia (GABBARD) STAFF ASST........ **808-541-1986**
Turner, Richard (SIRES) DIST DIR........ **201-558-0800**
Turner, Shawnda (LUETKEMEYER) STAFF ASST 2230........ **52956**
Turner, Will (ADERHOLT) LEGIS AIDE 1203........ **54876**
Turner-Dixon, Kimberly (EVANS) CHIEF OF STAFF........ **215-276-0340**
Turney, Bob (CAO/HIR – IT CUSTOMER SOLUTIONS) SR TECH SUPPORT REP 100 CHOB........ **66099**
Twinchek, Michael (CMTE-TRANSP & INFRA) CLERK 588 FHOB........ **55082**
Tylee, Dustin (CAO/FURNISHINGS) MASTER CARPET MECHANIC WA32 RHOB........ **58000**
Tyree-Edwards, Cynthia (CAO/HIR – IT CUSTOMER SOLUTIONS) TECH SUPPORT REP 2067........ **60550**
Tyson, Antrell (MCBATH) DIST DIR........ **470-773-6330**
Ubezonu, Nd (MAJ WHIP) FLOOR ASST H329........ **63210**
Uhing, Cody (O'HALLERAN) COMMUNICATIONS DIR 324 CHOB........ **53361**
Umanos, Krista (HUIZENGA) DIST REP........ **616-570-0917**
Underwood, Ricardo (CAO/HIR - ENTERPRISE MESSAGING AND MOBILITY) SR TECH SUPPORT REP 621 FHOB........ **67112**
Ung, Sandra (MENG) CASEWKR/SPECIAL ASST........ **718-358-6364**
Ungerman, Felix (BACON) DPTY CHIEF OF STAFF........ **402-938-0300**
Ungrey, Jennifer (AMASH) SR DIST REP........ **616-451-8383**
Unruh Cohen, Ana (SELECT CMTE-CLIMATE CRISIS) STAFF DIR - DEM 359 FHOB........ **51106**
Unseth, Drew (ADERHOLT) STAFF ASST 1203........ **54876**

Upshur, R Terry (INSPECTOR GENERAL) ADMIN DIR 386 FHOB 61250
Urbina, Luis (CMTE-NATURAL RESOURCES) DPTY COUNSEL 1324 56065
Ureno, Fatima (HARDER) CONSTIT SVCS ASSOC 209-579-5458
Uriarte, Jonathan (MURPHY) COMMUNICATIONS DIR 1710 54035
Uribe, Anthony (BERA) STAFF ASST 916-635-0505
Urman, John (CAO/HOUSE RECORDING STUDIO) BROADCAST PROD TECH 2010 53941
Urrabazo, Claudia (MAJ LEADER) OUTREACH ADVISOR H107 53130
Ursprung, Timothy (KING, PETER T.) LEGIS ASST 302 CHOB 57896
Ussery, Mike (LONG) DIR - CONSTIT SVCS/ SPECIAL PROJ DIR 417-889-1800
Uyehara, Ryan
(CMTE-FOREIGN AFFAIRS) PROF STAFF MEMB 5102 55716
(BERA) LEGIS ASST 1727 55716
Vadas, Matt (RYAN) CONSTIT LIAISON 330-373-0074
Vaiau, Steve (RADEWAGEN) DIST FIELD REP 684-633-3601
Vakharia, Shivani (GRAVES, TOM) LEGIS ASST/PRESS ASST 2078 55211
Valdez, Craig (TITUS) OUTREACH SPEC/STAFF ASST 702-220-9823
Valdez, Elizabeth (LEE, BARBARA) DIST SCHEDULER/DIST OFFICE MGR 510-763-0370
Valdez, Nayomi (TORRES SMALL) DIST DIR 575-323-6384
Valdez, Teresa (AGUILAR) DIST DIR 909-890-4445
Valega, Ellie (GARCIA, SYLVIA R.) STAFF ASST 1620 51688
Valenta, Valentina (POSEY) LEGIS DIR 2150 53671
Valentine, Natalie (SCOTT, ROBERT C. "BOBBY") LEGIS CORRES 1201 58351
Valerio, Ilissa (GARCÍA, JESÚS G. "CHUY") LIAISON - CONSTIT SVCS 773-342-0774
Valerio, Victor (RODGERS) REGIONAL REP 509-529-9358
Vallandingham, George (CAO/FURNISHINGS) LEAD CARPET MECHANIC WA32 RHOB 58000
Valle, Katherine (CMTE-ED & WORKFORCE) SR EDUC POLICY ADVISOR 2257 53725
Vallejo, Jessica (MAJ WHIP) FLOOR ASST H329 63210
Vallejo, Jose (VEASEY) FIELD REP 817-920-9086
Valle-Riestra, Jenna (MCNERNEY) STAFF ASST 2265 51947
Valverde, Andrea (MCADAMS) DIR - OPS 130 CHOB 53011
Van Allen, Aaron (CLINE) DIST REP 434-845-8306
Van Blaricom, Justin (FOSTER) LEGIS CORRES/STAFF ASST 2366 53515
Van Buren, Jon (PENCE) SR LEGIS ASST 222 CHOB 53021
Van Buren, Rick (CMTE-ENERGY & COMMERCE) HEALTH COUNSEL 2125 52927
Vanbuskirk, Victoria (GIBBS) FIELD REP 330-737-1631
Vance, Nicholas (RUTHERFORD) SR LEGIS ASST 1711 52501
Vance, Sarah (CMTE-OVERSIGHT & GOVT REFORM) SR PROF STAFF MBR/OUTREACH DIR 2105 55074
Vandergriff, Kristen (GRANGER) DIST DIR 817-338-0909
Van der Heide, Jennifer (HAALAND) CHIEF OF STAFF 1237 55275
Van Der Lugt, Roel (HECK) CONSTIT OUTREACH REP 360-459-8514
VanderToll, Hunt (BARR) LEGIS ASST - MIL 2430 54706
Vanderveen, Ben (AMASH) SR ADVISOR 616-451-8383
Van De Water, Parker (CMTE-APPRO) ADMIN ASST 2000. 57245
Vanegas, Natalia (MUCARSEL-POWELL) DPTY DIST DIR 305-222-0160
Vanek, Michelle (LEGIS COUNSEL) COUNSEL 337 FHOB 56060
Van Flein, Tom (GOSAR) CHIEF OF STAFF/CHIEF COUNSEL 2057 52315
Vangrow, Ali (WEXTON) LEGIS ASST 1217 55136
Vanhecke, Lucie (BUSTOS) DIST SCHEDULER/ DPTY DIST DIR 309-786-3406
Van Mersbergen, Rachael (GIBBS) SCHEDULER 2446 56265
Van Ness, Ethan (DESAULNIER) LEGIS ASST 503 CHOB 52095
Vannozzi, Michael (LEE, SUSIE) DIST DIR 522 CHOB 53252
Vanoy, Lee (ROGERS, MIKE) CONSTIT SVCS REP 334-745-6221
Van Sickle, Ben (WRIGHT) LEGIS CORRES 428 CHOB 52002
Van Stralen, Kara (LEVIN, MIKE) CHIEF OF STAFF 1626 53906
Van Valkenburg, Denise (RIGGLEMAN) DIST DIR 434-791-2596
Van Wye, Joseph (CMTE-JUDICIARY) PROF STAFF 6240 67680
VanZandt, Julie (HAGEDORN) CASEWKR 507-323-6090
Varandani, Rajinder (CLERK/LCS) SR NETWORK ADMIN 2401 51182
Varela, Blanca (O'HALLERAN) DIST DIR 520-316-0839
Varela Rosa, Margarita (CMTE-NATURAL RESOURCES) OUTREACH COORD 186 FHOB 56065
Varese, Dane (POCAN) DIST DIR 608-258-9800
Vargas, Jazmin (VEASEY) DIGITAL PRESS SECY 2348 59897
Vargas, Jose (CAO/HIR – ESCALATIONS AND OPS) NETWK TECH 601 FHOB 66430
Vargas, Kevin (CROW) CONSTIT ADVOCATE 720-748-7514
Vargish, Nick (HECK) LEGIS CORRES/LEGIS AIDE 2452 59740
Vargo, Alex (BUDD) LEGIS DIR 118 CHOB 54531
Varner, Nicole (VEASEY) LEGIS DIR 2348 59897
Vasilescu, Dikran (MEEKS) COMMUNICATIONS DIR 2310 53461
Vasquez, Daniel (GARCIA, SYLVIA R.) FIELD REP/DIGITAL ASST 832-325-3150
Vassar, Banyon (CMTE-ED & WORKFORCE) DPTY DIR - INFO TECH 2051A 53725
Vasser, Don (HURD) FIELD REP 210-921-3130
Vastola, Maria (CMTE-ARMED SVCS) PROF STAFF MEMB 2340 54252
Vaughan, Alan (CAO/FURNISHINGS) MGR - FURNISHINGS WA32 RHOB 58000
Vaughan, Heather (CMTE-SCIENCE) COMMUNICATIONS DIR - REPUB 394 FHOB 56371
Vaughan, Nicole (CAO/HOUSE RECORDING STUDIO) ADMIN SPEC 2010 53941
Vaughan, Robin (BURGESS) DPTY DIST DIR 940-497-5031
Vaughn, Bill (TURNER) DIST FIELD REP 937-225-2843
Vaughn, Emma (JOYCE, DAVID P.) PRESS ASST/LEGIS CORRES 1124 55731
Vaughn, Jim (CLEAVER) SPECIAL PROJ COORD 816-842-4545
Vaughn, Richard (DESJARLAIS) CHIEF OF STAFF 2301 56831
Vaughn, Wesley (BEATTY) LEGIS CORRES/STAFF ASST 2303 54324
Vaughns, Thomas (CAO/HIR – IT CUSTOMER SOLUTIONS) SR TELECOMMUNICATIONS ADMIN 692 FHOB 56002
Vazquez, Alma (JACKSON LEE) DIST AIDE 2079 53816

Vazquez, Maru (TORRES) STAFF ASST 2444 56161
Vazquez, Ruth (BROWNLEY) STAFF ASST 805-379-1779
Veale, John (LAMALFA) LEGIS ASST 322 CHOB 53076
Veatch, Courtney (DUNN) LEGIS ASST/COUNSEL 316 CHOB 55235
Vecchi, Jonathan (BILIRAKIS) LEGIS COUNSEL 2227 55755
Vega, Emmanuel (CMTE-HOMELAND SECUR) DIGITAL COORD 176 FHOB 62616
Velasquez, Melvin (CAO/HIR – ENTERPRISE INFRASTRUCT) SYS ENGINEER SITE 3 571-921-3157
Veliz, MaryEllen (DOGGETT) DPTY CHIEF OF STAFF 210-704-1080
Vemuri, Kumar (CAO/HIR – CYBERSECURITY) SR SYS ENGINEER 612 FHOB 61254
Venable, Tommy (CAO/HIR – HOUSE WEB SVCS) MGR 644C FHOB 63362
Venegas, Jazmine (ESCOBAR) DIST OFFICE MGR 915-541-1400
Ventre, James (CAO/HIR – NETWORKING ENGINEERING AND OPS) SR NETWK SYS ENGINEER SITE 3 571-921-3113
Verett, Whitney (ROGERS, MIKE) LEGIS DIR 2184 53261
Verghese, Matthew (BROWN) DPTY CHIEF OF STAFF/ COMMUNICATIONS DIR 1323 58699
Verhelst, Noelle (SMUCKER) LEGIS ASST 127 CHOB 52411
Vernetti, Dana (MORELLE) PRESS SECY 585-232-4850
Vernon, Lauren (CMTE-NATURAL RESOURCES) SUBCOMM CLERK 1332 56065
Verobish, Andrea (THOMPSON, GLENN) DIST STAFF ASST 814-419-8583
Verrill, Ted (ABRAHAM) DPTY CHIEF OF STAFF/LEGIS DIR 417 CHOB 58490
VerVelde, Brandon (ARMSTRONG) COMMUNICATIONS DIR 1004 52611
Ver Velde, Rachel (GROTHMAN) CHIEF OF STAFF 1427 52476
Verville, Ashley (PERLMUTTER) COMMUNICATIONS DIR/PRESS SECY 303-274-7944
Vesey, Gabi (BLUNT ROCHESTER) STAFF ASST 1519 54165
Vetrano, Mary Lynn (CLERK/REPORTERS) EDITOR - COMMITTEES HT59 55621
Vetter, Anna (TAYLOR) COMMUNICATIONS DIR 1404 54201
Vey, Madeline (LATTA) LEGIS COUNSEL/LEGIS DIR 2467 56405
Viall, Claire (CMTE-ED & WORKFORCE) PROF STAFF 2257 53725
Viau, Evan (WALBERG) LEGIS ASST 2266 56276
Vice, Ethan (PALMER) FIELD DIR/DPTY DIST DIR 205-968-1290
Vickers, Randal (CAO/OFFICE OF THE CHIEF INFORMATION OFFICER - HIR) CHIEF INFO SECUR OFFICER 630A FHOB 66205
Victor, Kyle (MATSUI) CHIEF OF STAFF 2311 57163
Victorin, Liz (SIRES) CONG AIDE 201-309-0301
Vidor, Kelly (WEBER) EXEC SCHEDULER 107 CHOB 52831
Vient, Darla (STEUBE) CASEWKR 941-575-9101
Vierday, Darren (SOTO) FIELD REP 202-600-0843
Vieson, Christopher (CMTE-HOMELAND SECUR) STAFF DIR 117 FHOB 68417
Vig, Jasleen (OMAR) STAFF ASST 1517 54755
Viggiano, Michael (WASSERMAN SCHULTZ) JR LEGIS ASST 1114 57931
Vijayaraghavan, Rukmani (KILMER) LEGIS FELLOW 1410 55916
Villa, Cristina
(CMTE-NATURAL RESOURCES) SCHEDULER 1511 56065
(GRIJALVA) SCHEDULER 1511 52435
Villa, Rick (SGT AT ARMS/CHAMBER SECUR) ASST TO THE SGT AT ARMS - FLOOR SECUR HB6 50067
Villaca, Naomi (GALLAGHER) DIR - OPS/SCHEDULER 1230 55665
Villagomez, Candy G (CLERK/LRC) RECORDS MGMT SPEC B81 CHOB 65200
Villagomez, Macarena (PERLMUTTER) DIST STAFF ASST 303-274-7944
Villagomez, Walter F (CLERK/LRC) DOCU PROD CLERK B81 CHOB 65200
Villalvazo, Jose (TRAHAN) LEGIS ASST 1616 53411
Villano, Peter (CMTE-ARMED SVCS) PROF STAFF 2340 60080
Villanueva, Diana (CARBAJAL) DIST SCHEDULER 805-730-1710
Villanueva, Josie (HORSFORD) LEGIS DIR 1330 59894
Villar, Luz (PRESSLEY) DIST EXEC ASST 617-850-0040
Villers, Robert (MCKINLEY) CASEWKR/CONSTIT SVCS 304-422-5972
Vincentz, Kathleen (ZELDIN) COMMUNICATIONS DIR 2441 53826
Vinesett, Molly (POSEY) DC SCHEDULER/EXEC ASST/ COORD - INTERN & FELLOW 2150 53671
Vinyard, Ashlee (BAIRD) CHIEF OF STAFF 532 CHOB 55037
Virga, Elizabeth (KILDEE) SCHEDULER/EXEC ASST 203 CHOB 53611
Viskovich, Bronti (MILLER) STAFF ASST 1605 53452
Vitale, Austin (PANETTA) LEGIS CORRES 212 CHOB 52861
Viterbi, Samantha (DAVIS, SUSAN A.) STAFF ASST/LEGIS CORRES 1214 52040
Viterise, Michele (KILMER) LEGIS COUNSEL 1410 55916
Vo, Quoc-An (CAO/ENTERPRISE APPLICATIONS) BUSINESS PROCESS APPLICA SPEC B77 FHOB 69830
Vogel, Ann (LUETKEMEYER) SCHEDULER 2230 52956
Vogel Philbrick, Alexis (SERRANO) LEGIS AIDE/ SCHEDULER 2354 54361
Vogl, Jillian (HARTZLER) SCHEDULER 2235 52876
Vogt, Lori (GOHMERT) STAFF ASST 2267 53035
Vonende, Kyle (MAST) PRESS SECY 2182 53026
Von Harders, Kimberly (CAO/TECHNOL GOVERN & COMPLIANCE) SVC MGR 644A FHOB 66048
Von Stein, Jesse (YOUNG) LEGIS ASST 2314 55765
Voorman, David (FOXX) LEGIS ASST 2462 52071
Voytovich, Olya (CUELLAR) PRESS SECY 2372 51640
Vruwink, Amy Sue (KIND) CONG AIDE 608-782-2558
Vuna, Elizabeth (SCHIFF) DIST REP 818-450-2900
Waaraniemi, Aaron (EMMER) OUTREACH DIR 763-241-6848
Wacker, Lillian (ROSE, MAX) SCHEDULER 1529 53371
Wade, Christopher (CISNEROS) FIELD REP 714-459-4575
Wade, Hal (WILSON, JOE) SPECIAL ASST/ CASEWKR 803-939-0041
Wade, Landy (RICE, KATHLEEN M.) SCHEDULER 2435 55516
Wadsworth, William (MASSIE) DC SCHEDULER 2453 53465
Wadyka, Heather (CMTE-ED & WORKFORCE) STAFF ASST 2101 54527
Wagener, Sharon (BROWNLEY) LEGIS DIR 2262 55811
Wagley, Rachel (WAGNER) LEGIS DIR 2350 51621

Wagner, Christy (MOULTON) SR ADVISOR - FOREIGN POLICY 1127 58020
Wagner, John F, Jr (LAW REV COUNSEL) SR COUNSEL 308 FHOB 62411
Wagner, Mattheus (NUNES) LEGIS AIDE 1013 52523
Wagner, Megan (LUCAS) SCHEDULER 2405 55565
Wagner, Zachary (RUTHERFORD) STAFF ASST 1711 52501
Wagner-Anderson, Clara (SERRANO) SCHEDULER/EXEC SECY 718-620-0084
Wagoner, Phyllis (DEFAZIO) DIR - CONSTIT SVCS 541-465-6732
Wainright, Abby (SCOTT, AUSTIN) STAFF ASST 2417 56531
Wajda, Sara (BACON) DIST EXEC ASST 402-938-0300
Wakeman, Raffaela (CMTE-INTELLIGENCE) PROF STAFF - MAJ/COUNSEL HVC304 57690
Walden, Daniel (CRENSHAW) ADMIN DIR 413 CHOB 56565
Walden, Susan (CRENSHAW) DIST DIR 713-860-1330
Waldron, Erin (DEMINGS) COORD - COMMUNITY DEV 321-388-9808
Walecki, Jack (JOHNSON, MIKE) LEGIS ASST 418 CHOB 52777
Wali-Johnson, Abdur (DELAURO) CASEWKR 203-562-3718
Walker, Adrienne (GRANGER) LEGIS ASST 1026 55071
Walker, Alexa (HOUSE REPUB STUDY CMTE) DIR - OUTREACH & COALITIONS 418 CHOB 52777
Walker, Amanda
(COMER) FINANCIAL ADMIN 2184 53115
(CURTIS) CHIEF FINANCIAL OFFICER 125 CHOB 57751
(WATKINS) FINANCIAL ADMIN 1205 56601
Walker, Amy (HUNTER) COMMUNITY REP 619-448-5201
Walker, Antoine (CMTE-WAYS & MEANS) TECH DIR 1102 53625
Walker, Beau (WOMACK) CHIEF OF STAFF 2412 54301
Walker, Christian (KIRKPATRICK) LEGIS DIR 309 CHOB 52542
Walker, Edward
(CMTE-ENERGY & COMMERCE) TECH DIR 2125 52927
(CMTE-OVERSIGHT & GOVT REFORM) TECH DIR 2157 55051
Walker, Elisa (CMTE-WAYS & MEANS) PROF STAFF 2018 59263
Walker, Jacob (CMTE-WAYS & MEANS) STAFF ASST 1139 54021
Walker, Jeanne (FORTENBERRY) CONSTIT REP 402-438-1598
Walker, Katelyn (CMTE-ED & WORKFORCE) COUNSEL 2176 53725
Walker, Lisa (KIRKPATRICK) LEGIS ASST 309 CHOB 52542
Walker, Melinda (CLERK/REPORTERS) CHIEF HT59 52627
Walker, Quristin (UNDERWOOD) STAFF ASST 1118 52976
Walker, Ryan (WALKER) LEGIS DIR 1725 53065
Walker, Sally (LEGIS COUNSEL) COUNSEL 337 FHOB 56060
Walker, Steven (MIN WHIP) SR STAFF ASST H148 50197
Walker, Sue (HOULAHAN) DIST DIR 610-883-5050
Walker, Tommy (DEGETTE) DPTY CHIEF OF STAFF 2111 54431
Walkinshaw, James (CONNOLLY) CHIEF OF STAFF 2238 51492
Wall, Aimee (DESAULNIER) PRESS SECY 503 CHOB 52095
Wall, Erin (COLLINS, DOUG) EXEC ASST 1504 59893
Wall, Kelsey (HOUSE REPUB POLICY CMTE) SR POLICY ADVISOR 207 CHOB 54921
Wall, Matt (NAT REPUB CONG CMTE) RESEARCH DIR 202-479-7000
Wallace, Alfonzo (CAO/LOGISTICS) BLDG SUPERVISOR WA16 RHOB 59474
Wallace, Amanda (RUTHERFORD) CONSTIT SVCS REP 904-831-5205
Wallace, Butch (WILSON, JOE) DIST DIR 803-939-0041
Wallace, Huston (HORN) STAFF ASST 415 CHOB 52132
Wallace, John (LOUDERMILK) FIELD REP 770-429-1776
Wallace, Katie (NEGUSE) LEGIS ASST 1419 52161
Wallace, Lacey (NEWHOUSE) EXEC ASST/SCHEDULER 1414 55816
Wallace, Lynese (PRESSLEY) POLICY ADVISOR 1108 55111
Wallace, Nikki (SIMPSON) COMMUNICATIONS DIR 208-334-1953
Wallace, Sharon (CAO/HIR – HOUSE WEB SVCS) INTERNET SYS SPEC 627 FHOB 63809
Wallace, Tyra (PERRY) DIR - CONSTIT SVCS 717-603-4980
Waller, Caroline (WRIGHT) SCHEDULER 428 CHOB 52002
Walsh, Amanda (RICE, KATHLEEN M.) DIST DIR 516-739-3008
Walsh, Bonnie (KINZINGER) DIST DIR 815-431-9271
Walsh, Conor (SUOZZI) LEGIS ASST 214 CHOB 53335
Walsh, James (YOHO) LEGIS DIR 1730 55744
Walsh, Joel (CMTE-HOMELAND SECUR) PROF STAFF 176 FHOB 62616
Walsh, Steve (HARTZLER) PRESS SECY/FIELD REP 573-442-9311
Walsh, Tim (VARGAS) CHIEF OF STAFF 2244 58045
Walters, Jennifer (CAO/HOUSE PERIODICAL PRESS) SECOND ASST H304 52941
Walters, Tristan (GOODEN) LEGIS AIDE 425 CHOB 53484
Walton, Austin (WITTMAN) SR LEGIS ASST 2055 54261
Walvort, Bradley (SGT AT ARMS/EMERGENCY MGMT) EMERGENCY MGMT SPEC 192 FHOB 60950
Wambold, Adam (CMTE-ETHICS) PROF STAFF 1015 57103
Wang, Gary (CAO/HIR – IDENTITY GOV AND ADMIN) SR ADVISOR 647 FHOB 60574
Wang, George (LARSON) STAFF ASST 1501 52265
Wang, Jackii (WASSERMAN SCHULTZ) LEGIS ASST 1114 57931
Wang, Lily (CMTE-NATURAL RESOURCES) CLERK 1328 56065
Wang, Tim (KATKO) LEGIS ASST 2457 53701
Warbinton, Tanner (LONG) SR LEGIS ASST 2454 56536
Ward, Cheraisse (CAO/PAYROLL & BENEFITS) GENERALIST B215 LHOB 50667
Ward, Edwina (HASTINGS) DIST SCHEDULER 954-733-2800
Ward, James (CAO/RISK MGMT) SR ANALYST 217 FHOB 67257
Ward, Jennifer (VEASEY) DIR - CONSTIT SVCS 817-920-9086
Ward, Larry (CLYBURN) DIST AIDE 803-799-1100
Ward, Ruth (JOHNSON, MIKE) SCHEDULER/DIR - OPS/ POLICY ADVISOR 418 CHOB 52777
Ward, Sam (LOEBSACK) LEGIS CORRES 1211 56576
Wardell, Dominque (LURIA) LEGIS ASST 534 CHOB 54215
Ward Williams, Lori (ROBY) DIST DIR 334-262-7718
Ware, Calvin (CAO/LOGISTICS) LOGISTICS & DIST SPEC WA33A RHOB 59474
Ware, Fannie (THOMPSON, BENNIE G.) DIST DIR 601-866-9003
Ware, Josie (DAVIS, DANNY K.) DIST OFFICE MGR 773-533-7520
Warfield, Tazmyah (CAO/FINANCIAL COUNSELING) FINANCIAL COUNSELOR B215 LHOB 60913
Warlick, Jordan (COMMIS ON SECUR & COOP IN EUR) OFFICE DIR 234 FHOB 51901
Warner, Cameron (JORDAN) DIST DIR 419-999-6455
Warner, Karen (HARDER) DIST DIR 209-579-5458

Warner, Lesley (CMTE-FOREIGN AFFAIRS) PROF STAFF MEMB 2471 **55021**
Warren, Bonny (ROSE, JOHN W.) CASEWKR **931-854-9430**
Warren, Debra (WEBSTER) CONSTIT SVCS **352-241-9220**
Warren, Dominique (TLAIB) LEGIS DIR 1628 **55126**
Warren, Gregory (CMTE-WAYS & MEANS) ASST CLERK 1139 **54021**
Warren, Samantha (FOSTER) LEGIS DIR 2366 **53515**
Warshaw, Johanna (DAVIDS) PRESS SECY 1541 **67209**
Washburn, Heather (BRADY) DIST DIR **936-441-5700**
Washington, ArRone (CUNNINGHAM) STAFF ASST **843-352-7572**
Washington, Crystal (CUMMINGS) SPECIAL ASST **410-685-9199**
Washington, David (LEWIS) STAFF ASST **404-659-0116**
Washington, Gerald (BISHOP, SANFORD D., JR.) STAFF ASST **706-320-9477**
Washington, Jason (CAO/FINANCIAL COUNSELING) FINANCIAL COUNSELOR B215 LHOB **61582**
Washington, Matthew (CMTE-APPRO) CLERK HT2 **53047**
Washington, Samantha (PAYNE) STAFF ASST **973-645-3213**
Washington, Terrence (CAO/LOGISTICS) LOGISTICS & DIST SPEC RAYBURN **59474**
Washington, Timla (THOMPSON, BENNIE G.) COORD - COMMUNITY OUTREACH **662-335-9003**
Washington, Velmon C (CLERK/LRC) ASST REQUISITIONS & PRINTING CLERK B81 CHOB **65200**
Washington, Venetia (DAVIDS) CONSTIT SVCS **913-621-0832**
Wasielewski, Karen (KEATING) DPTY DIST DIR **508-746-9000**
Waskiewicz, Steve (CMTE-RULES) SR PROF STAFF H152 **59191**
Waskow, Jean (CUMMINGS) SCHEDULER 2163 **54741**
Waskowsky, Kim (BALDERSON) SCHEDULER 1221 **55355**
Wasniewski, Matthew A (HOUSE HISTORIAN) HOUSE HISTORIAN JEFFERSON BUILDING, ATTIC **61300**
Wasson, Lou (DELBENE) COMMUNICATIONS DIR 2330 **56311**
Waterman, Kelly (BABIN) DIST DIR **832-780-0966**
Waters, Laura (CMTE-OVERSIGHT & GOVT REFORM) COUNSEL 2157 **55051**
Waters, Michael (GIANFORTE) MIL FIELD REP **406-969-1736**
Watkins, Cedric (THOMPSON, BENNIE G.) CASEWKR/FIELD REP **662-741-9003**
Watkins, David (CMTE-NATURAL RESOURCES) STAFF DIR FOR NAT RESCS CMTE 1324 **56065**
Watkins, Sarah (CAO/ENTERPRISE APPLICATIONS) SR BUSINESS PROCESS APPLICA SPEC B70 FHOB **62346**
Watkins, Shelly (HOLLINGSWORTH) CASEWK MGR **812-288-3999**
Watkins, Yelberton
(CLYBURN) CHIEF OF STAFF 200 CHOB **53315**
(MAJ WHIP) CHIEF OF STAFF H329 **63210**
Watson, Brad (CMTE-BUDGET) SR POLICY ADVISOR 507 CHOB **67270**
Watson, Greg (SCALISE) LEGIS ASST 2049 **53015**
Watson, Jackie (SCOTT, AUSTIN) DIR - CONSTIT SVCS **229-396-5175**
Watson, Nancy (CONAWAY) REGIONAL DIR **325-247-2826**
Watt, Pamela (GAETZ) DIST AIDE **850-479-1183**
Watts, Lona (PRESSLEY) SCHEDULING DIR 1108 **55111**
Wavrunek, Glenn (POCAN) CHIEF OF STAFF 1421 **52906**
Way, Kashi M (CMTE-JOINT TAX) SR LEGIS COUNSEL SD-G18 **45561**
Wayne, Drew (REED) CHIEF OF STAFF 2263 **53161**
Weadon, Andrea (CAO/HIR – IT CUSTOMER SOLUTIONS) BRANCH MGR 608B FHOB **66352**
Weast, Maddy (CHENEY) PRESS SECY 416 CHOB **52311**
Weatherbee, Nicholas (MORELLE) CHIEF OF STAFF 1317 **53615**
Weatherford, Austin (KINZINGER) CHIEF OF STAFF 2245 **53635**
Weaver, Denise (PALMER) CASEWKR **205-968-1290**
Weaver, Denise (MEUSER) CONSTIT SVCS REP **570-871-6370**
Weaver, Kyle (WOMACK) DIR - PROJ **479-464-0446**
Weaver, Maura (KIM) DIST FIELD REP **732-504-0490**
Weaver, Trenton (BEATTY) DIST LIAISON **614-220-0003**
Webb, Brandon (KELLY, ROBIN L.) CHIEF OF STAFF 2416 **50773**
Webb, Glennis (CLERK/LEGIS OPS) DAILY DIGEST CLERK HT13 **51501**
Webb, Jed (WEBER) DIST DIR **281-316-0231**
Webb, Lindsey (LARSEN) DIST OUTREACH REP **425-252-3188**
Webb Smith, Laura (BROOKS, MO) DIST FIELD REP **256-718-5155**
Weber, Amy (SHIMKUS) DIST AIDE **618-288-7190**
Weber, J C (ALLRED) DIGITAL ASST **972-972-7949**
Weber, John (JOHNSON, DUSTY) SR POLICY ADVISOR 1508 **52801**
Weber, Zachary (LAWRENCE) LEGIS ASST 2463 **55802**
Webster, Crystal (GREEN, AL) DIST ADMIN/DIST MGR **713-383-9234**
Webster, Gary (STEWART) DIST DIR **801-364-5550**
Webster, Katie (HOLLINGSWORTH) COMMUNICATIONS DIR 1641 **66854**
Webster, Kichelle (ADAMS) LEGIS ASST 2436 **51510**
Weddle, Willy (KELLY, TRENT) FIELD REP **662-258-7240**
Weed, Krista (BLUNT ROCHESTER) CASEWKR **302-830-2330**
Weglein, Michael (MAST) LEGIS ASST 2182 **53026**
Wehr, Aron (BACON) PRESS SECY 1024 **54155**
Weigelt, Tinisha (BANKS) DIST DIR **260-702-4750**
Wein, Justin (PRICE) DPTY CHIEF OF STAFF 2108 **51784**
Weiner, Jessica (ARRINGTON) STAFF ASST 1029 **54005**
Weiner, Matt (LOFGREN) SR POLICY ADVISOR 1401 **53072**
Weinerman, Hannah (NADLER) COMMUNITY LIAISON **212-367-7350**
Weinhagen, Robert F, Jr (LEGIS COUNSEL) SR COUNSEL 337 FHOB **56060**
Weinhart, Jennifer (HOUSE REPUB STUDY CMTE) POLICY STAFF 418 CHOB **52777**
Weinroth, Alexandra (CMTE-BUDGET) PRESS SECY 204E CHOB **67200**
Weinstein, Lara (NORCROSS) DIR - OPS/SCHEDULER 2437 **56501**
Weintraub, Josh (PENCE) STAFF ASST 222 CHOB **53021**
Weisbroth, Nina (RASKIN) CONSTIT SVCS **301-354-1000**
Weiser, Daniel (CAO/CUST EXPER CTR) COMMUNICATIONS DIR 217 FHOB **61091**
Weisman, Matthew (COHEN) LEGIS DIR/COUNSEL 2104 **53265**
Weiss, Adam (EVANS) LEGIS ASST 1105 **54001**
Weiss, Bettina (SPANBERGER) MGR - OPS 1239 **52815**
Weiss, Bryan
(CAO/EMPLOYEE ASSISTANCE) PROGRAM MGR 140 FHOB **61997**
(CAO/HOUSE WELLNESS CTR) PROGRAM MGR 140 FHOB **61997**

Weiss, Guido (GABBARD) LEGIS DIR 1433 **54906**
Weiss, Harris (BRINDISI) DIST FIELD REP **607-242-0200**
Weiss, Sarina (CMTE-NATURAL RESOURCES) SUBCOMM CLERK 1522 **56065**
Weissmann, Adam (MAJ LEADER) SPEECHWRITER H107. **53130**
Weisz, Joshua (CMTE-ED & WORKFORCE) COMMUNICATIONS DIR 2176 **53725**
Weitz, Bill (ENGEL) CHIEF OF STAFF **718-796-9700**
Welch, Brendan (PHILLIPS) COMMUNICATIONS DIR 1305.. **52871**
Welch, Haydn (SPEAKER) STAFF ASST H232 **50100**
Weldon, Scott (GRANGER) COMMUNICATIONS DIR 1026 **55071**
Wellen, Sophie (TORRES) LEGIS CORRES 2444 **56161**
Wells, Ashley (HERN) CONSTIT SVCS REP **918-935-3222**
Wells, Royale (CAO/FINANCIAL COUNSELING) FINANCIAL COUNSELOR B215 LHOB **60901**
Welsh, James (WALORSKI) LEGIS ASST 419 CHOB **53915**
Weltge, Jessica (JOHNSON, BILL) LEGIS ASST 2336 **55705**
Wemple, Brian (GIANFORTE) STAFF ASST 1222 **53211**
Wemple, Douglas (WELCH) PRESS ASST/STAFF ASST 2187 **54115**
Wendt, Jonah (ROY) STAFF ASST 1319 **54236**
Wengloski, Laura (SGT AT ARMS/EMERGENCY MGMT) PROGRAM MGR 192 FHOB **60950**
Wennerstrom, Thomas (DESJARLAIS) CASEWKR **615-896-1986**
Wentworth, Kathleen (SPEIER) CASEWKR **650-342-0300**
Wentz, Blaise (SCHWEIKERT) CASEWKR **480-946-2411**
Wentzel, Josh (MEADOWS) LEGIS ASST 2160 **56401**
Wenzel, Kenneth (CAO/HIR – ENTERPRISE INFRASTRUCT) OPS TEAM LEAD 618 FHOB **60124**
Wera, Eric (HAALAND) LEGIS DIR 1237 **55853**
Werden, Mary (FOSTER) COMMUNICATIONS DIR 2366 **53515**
Werley, Kate (DOYLE) ADVISOR - HEALTH POLICY 306 CHOB **52135**
Werner, Sara (FOXX) PRESS SECY 2462 **52071**
Wertheimer, Michael (KEATING) SR POLICY ADVISOR 2351 **53111**
Weseliza, Karen (COURTNEY) CONSTIT SVCS **860-741-6011**
Wesley, Kortney (LAWSON) DIST DIR **904-354-1652**
Wesley, Shanel (CAO/HIR – IT CUSTOMER SOLUTIONS) SR TELECOMMUNICATIONS ADMIN 677 FHOB **56002**
Wessells, Jackson (LEE, SUSIE) LEGIS CORRES 522 CHOB **53252**
West, Daniel (HAGEDORN) LEGIS CORRES 325 **52472**
West, Julius (SPEAKER) SR ADVISOR H232 **50100**
West, Leah (SOTO) FIELD REP **202-615-1308**
West, Lucas (LUETKEMEYER) SR POLICY ADVISOR 2230 **52956**
West, Rachel (CMTE-ED & WORKFORCE) SR ECON & ENERGY POLICY ADVISOR 230 FHOB **50868**
Westfall, Lana (WEXTON) CONSTIT SVCS REP 1217 **55136**
Westmoreland, Grayson (CMTE-VET AFFAIRS) LEGIS ASST 3460 **53527**
Wetherald, Margaret
(CHENEY) FINANCIAL ADMIN 416 CHOB **52311**
(CMTE-AGRIC) ADMIN DIR 1301 **52171**
(CONAWAY) FINANCIAL ADMIN 2469 **53605**
(DAVIS, RODNEY) FINANCIAL ADMIN 1740 **52371**
(HOLLINGSWORTH) ADMIN - FINANCE & PAYROLL/ SHARED EMPLOYEE 1641 **55315**
Whalen, Mitch (HILL, J. FRENCH) STAFF ASST 1533 **52506**
Whalen, Sarah (DEGETTE) DIST SCHEDULER **303-844-4988**
Whatley, Pierre (CMTE-FINANCIAL SVCS) PROF STAFF MEMB 2129 **54247**
Wheat, Heath (ALLEN) SCHEDULER/DIR - OPS 2400 **52823**
Wheatley, Miriam (THOMPSON, MIKE) SR COUNSEL 406 CHOB **53311**
Wheeler, Craig (HERRERA BEUTLER) STAFF ASST 2352 **53536**
Wheeler, Jillian (CMTE-JOINT ECON) COMMUNICATIONS DIR - REPUB SD-G01 **43616**
Wheelock, Jason (CMTE-APPRO) PROF STAFF MEMB HT2 **52041**
Wheelock, Jennifer (CMTE-BUDGET) BUDGET ANALYST 204E CHOB **67200**
Whelan, Dan (DEFAZIO) DIST DIR **541-465-6732**
Whetstone, Courtney (STIVERS) CHIEF OF STAFF 2234 **52015**
Whippy, Peter
(CMTE-HOUSE ADMIN) COMMUNICATIONS DIR 1313 **52061**
(LOFGREN) DIR - PRESS & COMMUNICATIONS 1401 **53072**
Whisnant, Jordan (MEADOWS) FIELD REP **828-432-2699**
Whitaker, Jason (CAO/HIR – NETWORKING ENGINEERING AND OPS) NETWK SYS ENGINEER 681 FHOB **61669**
Whitaker, Jodi (BARR) COMMUNICATIONS DIR **859-219-1366**
Whitaker, Laura (CAO/HIR – IT CUSTOMER SOLUTIONS) TECH SUPPORT REP 2067 **62208**
Whitcomb, Maxwell (MALONEY, CAROLYN B.) SR POLICY ADVISOR 2308 **57944**
White, Aaron (KIND) COMMUNICATIONS DIR 1502 **55506**
White, Allie (FERGUSON) LEGIS ASST 1032 **55901**
White, Bob (FLEISCHMANN) DPTY CHIEF OF STAFF **423-756-2342**
White, Bubba (GUEST) LEGIS ASST 230 CHOB **55031**
White, Byron (CAO/FINANCIAL COUNSELING) FINANCIAL COUNSELOR B215 LHOB **61133**
White, Clay (STEWART) CHIEF OF STAFF 2242 **59730**
White, Connor (DAVIDSON) LEGIS ASST 1107 **56205**
White, Daniel (CAO/HIR – ENTERPRISE INFRASTRUCT) SR SYS ENGINEER SITE 3 **571-921-3198**
White, Elizabeth (KATKO) LEGIS CORRES 2457 **53701**
White, Eric (PRESSLEY) DIST DIR **617-850-0040**
White, Frances (GUEST) CONSTIT SVCS **601-693-6681**
White, Frankie (CLERK/LRC) PUBLIC INFO SPEC B81 CHOB **65200**
White, Grace (SCHWEIKERT) PRESS SECY 1526 **52190**
White, Gregg (CAO/HIR – IT CUSTOMER SOLUTIONS) SR TECH SUPPORT REP 100 CHOB **66077**
White, Janssen (PRICE) SCHEDULER/EXEC ASST 2108 **51784**
White, Katie (CMTE-WAYS & MEANS) TRADE COUNSEL 1103 **56649**
White, Logan (CLOUD) STAFF ASST 1314 **57742**
White, Shenita (CMTE-ARMED SVCS) CLERK 2216 **54151**
White, Sonja (DEMINGS) DIST DIR **321-388-9808**
White, Stephanie (LAMALFA) CONSTIT SVCS REP **530-223-5898**
White, Trevor (CMTE-AGRIC) PROF STAFF 1010 **50317**
White, Victoria (WEBSTER) COMMUNITY RELATIONS ASST **352-241-9204**
White, Wendell (AGUILAR) SR POLICY ADVISOR/LEGIS ASST - MIL 109 CHOB **53201**

Whited, Melinda (KELLY, TRENT) FIELD REP/ CASEWKR - IMMIGRATION 662-687-1525
Whitehead, Benjamin (CASTRO) COORD - GRANTS & SPEC PROJ 210-348-8216
Whitehouse, Christina (WITTMAN) DIST REP 804-730-6595
Whitehouse, Lin (MAJ WHIP) ADVISOR - MBR SVCS H329 63210
Whiteman, Lynette (KIM) OUTREACH ADVISOR 732-504-0490
Whiteside, Donovan (BURCHETT) EXEC ASST 1122 55435
Whiting, Zach (KING, STEVE) POLICY ADVISOR 712-580-7754
Whitlock, Angelia (GUTHRIE) CONSTIT SVCS REP 270-842-9896
Whitmire, Bud (GRAVES, TOM) DIST DIR/DPTY CHIEF OF STAFF 706-290-1776
Whitmyer, John (CAO/HIR – IT CUSTOMER SOLUTIONS) SR TECH SUPPORT REP 694 FHOB 56002
Whitney, Jim (CMTE-JOINT ECON) SR POLICY ADVISOR - DEM 246 FHOB 53923
Whitney, Pam (CMTE-SCIENCE) STAFF DIR - MAJ 2321 56375
Whitson, Ian (ROUZER) LEGIS ASST 2439 52731
Whittaker, Alexandra (CMTE-WAYS & MEANS) TRADE COUNSEL 1103 56649
Whittaker, Larry
(CMTE-SCIENCE) SYS ADMIN 2321 56375
(CMTE-TRANSP & INFRA) SYS ADMIN 2253 54472
(TONKO) SYS ADMIN 2369 55076
Whittaker, Leigh (PRICE) LEGIS ASST 2108 51784
Whittlesey, Tess (CARBAJAL) COMMUNICATIONS DIR 1431 53601
Wicht, Emily (CLINE) DIST REP 540-432-2391
Wick, Anne (CASTEN) DIST DIR 630-520-9450
Wick, Chloe (ROONEY) SCHEDULER 120 CHOB 52536
Wickersham, Dave (LURIA) DIST DIR 757-364-7650
Wickes, Bill (KILDEE) CASEWKR 810-238-8627
Wickham, Thomas J, Jr (PARLIAMENTARIAN) PARLIAMENTARIAN H209 57373
Wickre, Jenn (CMTE-SCIENCE) SR POLICY ADVISOR - REPUB 394 FHOB 56371
Widenhouse, Olivia (TIMMONS) SCHEDULER 313 CHOB 56030
Wieand, Jeffrey (MIN WHIP) COUNSEL H148 50197
Wiese, Karl (CAO/FURNISHINGS) JOURNEYMAN CABINET MAKER WA25 RHOB 58000
Wiest, Carol (PERRY) SCHEDULER 717-603-4980
Wigley, Pearlette (RYAN) COORD - COMMUNITY DEV/CONSTIT ADVOCATE 330-740-0193
Wilbourn, Anna (HILL, J. FRENCH) LEGIS ASST/LEGIS CORRES 1533 52506
Wilbourn, Jeffrey (CAO/FURNISHINGS) MASTER FINISHER WA22 RHOB 58000
Wilcox, Faith (SCANLON) STAFF ASST 1535 52011
Wilcox, Libbie (MALONEY, SEAN PATRICK) DIGITAL PRESS SECY 2331 55441
Wilder, Donald (CAO/HIR – ENTERPRISE INFRASTRUCT) OPS TEAM LEAD SITE 3 571-921-3123
Wiles, Martie (COMER) SR FIELD REP 270-408-1865
Wiley, Daniel (VELÁZQUEZ) DIST DIR 718-599-3658
Wilhite, L (CAO/OFC OF EMPLOYEE ADVOCACY) DIRECTOR 301 FHOB 58800
Wilkens, Kyle (CLEAVER) DIR - RURAL POLICY 660-584-7373
Wilkerson, Emanuel (DEAN) LEGIS ASST 215-884-4300
Wilkes, Christina (SPEAKER) SR PRESS ASST H232 50100
Wilkins, Richard (DESJARLAIS) LEGIS DIR 2301 56831
Wilkinson, Mitchell (LUCAS) LEGIS CORRES 2405 55565
Wilkinson, Zachery (CARSON) LEGIS ASST 2135 54011
Williams, Alexa (MOOLENAAR) EXEC ASST 117 CHOB 53561
Williams, Bradley (CAO/FURNISHINGS) JOURNEYMAN CABINET MAKER WA25 RHOB 58000
Williams, Cheri (KILMER) DIR - CONSTIT SVCS 360-373-9725
Williams, Clifton (FUDGE) DIST DIR 216-522-4900
Williams, Colleen (TONKO) DIST DIR 518-465-0700
Williams, Diane (CONAWAY) REGIONAL DIR 682-936-2577
Williams, Evan (TIPTON) LEGIS ASST 218 CHOB 54761
Williams, Evelyn (HIGGINS, BRIAN) DIST OFFICE MGR 716-852-3501
Williams, Jakaria (WILSON, FREDERICA S.) CONG AIDE 305-690-5905
Williams, James (CAO/HIR – NETWORKING ENGINEERING AND OPS) SR NETWK COMMUNICATIONS SPEC 685A FHOB 69339
Williams, Jay (HORN) DIR - CONSTIT SVCS 405-602-3074
Williams, Jerome (CAO/ENTERPRISE APPLICATIONS) SVC MGR B62 FHOB 66029
Williams, Joan (FUDGE) COORD - DIST OUTREACH 330-835-4758
Williams, Juanita (LURIA) CASEWKR 757-364-7650
Williams, Kayla (HIGGINS, BRIAN) LEGIS DIR 2459 53306
Williams, Kimberly Carey (HOUSE EMPLOYMENT COUNSEL) SR ASSOC COUNSEL 4300 57075
Williams, Kwentoria A (GREEN, AL) STAFF ASST 713-383-9234
Williams, Lauren (CMTE-ED & WORKFORCE) PROF STAFF MEMB 6150 57101
Williams, Lauren (WOODALL) LEGIS CORRES 1724 54272
Williams, Louis, Jr (CAO/HIR – NETWORKING ENGINEERING AND OPS) NETWK SYS ENGINEER 664 FHOB 66267
Williams, Maisha (HASTINGS) CONG ASST 954-733-2800
Williams, Mark (CONAWAY) CHIEF OF STAFF 2469 53605
Williams, Melinda (SEWELL) DIST DIR 334-262-1921
Williams, Ola (CMTE-FINANCIAL SVCS) SR PROF STAFF MBR 2129 54247
Williams, Pamela (CMTE-JOINT TAX) OFFICE ADMIN 502 FHOB 53621
Williams, Parker (LAMALFA) COMMUNICATIONS DIR 322 CHOB 53076
Williams, Patricia (HASTINGS) CHIEF OF STAFF 954-733-2800
Williams, Samantha (CLAY) DIST AIDE 314-367-1970
Williams, Shelby (BARR) DIR - DIST PROJ 859-219-1366
Williams, Shenette (CAO/PAYROLL & BENEFITS) COUNSELOR B215 LHOB 61495
Williams, Stami (WILSON, JOE) COMMUNICATIONS DIR 1436 52452
Williams, Tommy (CAO/PAYROLL & BENEFITS) COUNSELOR B215 LHOB 60036
Williams, Waverly (CAO/HIR – NETWORKING ENGINEERING AND OPS) SR NETWK COMMUNICATIONS SPEC 688 FHOB 66498
Williams-Luster, April (KELLY, ROBIN L.) DIST REP 773-321-2001
Williamson, Ben (MEADOWS) COMMUNICATIONS DIR 2160 56401

Williamson, Ramona (SCALISE) FIELD REP.......... 504-837-1259
Willingham, Kimberly (GOHMERT) COMMUNICATIONS DIR 2267.......... 53035
Willis, Michael (ABRAHAM) FIELD REP.......... 318-445-0818
Willming, Cody (SÁNCHEZ) LEGIS AIDE 2329.......... 56676
Wilson, Amelia (COMER) FIELD REP.......... 270-487-9509
Wilson, Catherine (JOYCE, DAVID P.) LEGIS ASST 1124.......... 55731
Wilson, Diane (CAO/HIR – IT CUSTOMER SOLUTIONS) SUPERVISOR 694 FHOB.......... 56002
Wilson, Haley (ROGERS, MIKE) LEGIS ASST 2184.......... 53261
Wilson, James (CAO/HIR – IT CUSTOMER SOLUTIONS) TECH SOLUTIONS ENGINEER 694 FHOB.......... 56002
Wilson, Jeffrey (TURNER) LEGIS DIR 2082.......... 56465
Wilson, Jennifer (RICE, TOM) CHIEF OF STAFF 512 CHOB. 59895
Wilson, Jordan (WITTMAN) SCHEDULER/OFFICE MGR 2055.......... 54261
Wilson, Kellie (CAO/FINANCIAL COUNSELING) FINANCIAL COUNSELOR B215 LHOB.......... 60245
Wilson, Laura (JOHNSON, BILL) SR POLICY ADVISOR 2336 55705
Wilson, Reed (KINZINGER) DPTY DIST DIR.......... 815-431-9271
Wilson, Ricky (SGT AT ARMS/HOUSE SECURITY) ASST DIR HVC301.......... 62044
Wilson, Tyler (FINKENAUER) LEGIS DIR/DPTY CHIEF OF STAFF 124 CHOB.......... 52911
Wilson-Meyer, Zoe (WILD) COMMUNICATIONS DIR 1607.......... 56411
Wimberly, DeShun (CAO/FURNISHINGS) JOURNEYMAN - FURN SPEC WA25 RHOB.......... 58000
Wimbush, Tameka (BISHOP, SANFORD D., JR.) CONSTIT SVCS.......... 229-439-8067
Winchester, Selina (WILD) CONSTIT ADVOCATE.......... 610-333-1170
Windham, Troy (ALLEN) CONSTIT SVCS REP.......... 478-272-4030
Windheim, Taryn (REED) REGIONAL DIR.......... 315-759-5229
Winfrey, David (GRANGER) LEGIS ASST 1026.......... 55071
Winkelman, Chris (NAT REPUB CONG CMTE) GEN COUNSEL.......... 202-479-7000
Winn, Jennifer (SAN NICOLAS) DIST DIR.......... 671-475-6453
Winneberger, Robyn (PRICE) CASEWK MGR.......... 919-859-5999
Winnick, Daniel (CMTE-WAYS & MEANS) TAX COUNSEL 1136.......... 55522
Winnick, Everett
(CMTE-ED & WORKFORCE) SYS ADMIN/SHARED EMPLOYEE 2051A.......... 53725
(CMTE-ENERGY & COMMERCE) DIR - INFO TECH 2322A.......... 53641
(CMTE-NATURAL RESOURCES) DPTY DIR - INFO TECH 1322.......... 56065
Winship, Jacqueline (WAGNER) FIELD REP.......... 636-779-5449
Winship, Scott (CMTE-JOINT ECON) EXEC DIR SD-G01.......... 45171
Winter, Samuel (HOUSE HISTORIAN) RESEARCH ASST JEFFERSON BUILDING, ATTIC.......... 61300
Winters, Adam (QUIGLEY) DIST STAFF ASST.......... 773-267-5926
Wirkkala, Rheanne (CMTE-INTELLIGENCE) PROF STAFF HVC304.......... 57690
Wirt, David (LATTA) DIST DIR.......... 419-354-8700
Wiser, Devin (BISHOP, ROB) CHIEF OF STAFF 123 CHOB.......... 50453
Wisniewski, Kathleen (SMITH, CHRISTOPHER H.) STAFF ASST.......... 609-585-7878
Wissmann, Yvette (NAT REPUB CONG CMTE) POLICY DIR.......... 202-479-7000
With, Erik (BURGESS) DIST DIR.......... 940-497-5031
Withers, Stephanie (MCADAMS) EXEC ASST.......... 801-999-9801
Witherspoon, John (ROE) SR LEGIS ASST 102 CHOB.......... 56356
Witte, David (WESTERMAN) DPTY DIST DIR/MIL FIELD REP.......... 501-609-9796
Witte, Eric (LOEBSACK) CHIEF OF STAFF 1211.......... 56576
Witte, Jeremy (CMTE-AGRIC) PROF STAFF 1010.......... 50317
Witte, Sydney (ARRINGTON) CONSTIT RELATIONS REP.......... 806-763-1611
Wittebort, Marisa (YARMUTH) SR LEGIS ASST.......... 502-582-5129
Wivchar, Felicia (CLERK/ART & ARCHIVES) ASSOC CURATOR JEFFERSON BUILDING, ATTIC.......... 61300
Woerpel, Eli (RIGGLEMAN) LEGIS ASST 1022.......... 54711
Wofsy, Noah (LEGIS COUNSEL) DPTY LEGIS COUNSEL 337 FHOB.......... 56060
Wohleber, Andrea (CMTE-TRANSP & INFRA) PROF STAFF 2251.......... 54472
Woiton, Sonia (DOGGETT) CONG AIDE.......... 512-916-5921
Wojcicki, Sam (CASTEN) LEGIS ASST 429 CHOB.......... 54561
Wojciechowski, Ed (SGT AT ARMS/POLICE SVCS) SR LAW ENFORCEMENT LIAISON HT8.......... 51000
Woldemariam, Wintta (MAJ WHIP) POLICY DIR H329.......... 63210
Wolf, Ian (FRANKEL) LEGIS DIR 2305.......... 59890
Wolfe, Jaxon (HECK) LEGIS ASST 2452.......... 59740
Wolfe, Jordan (SARBANES) LEGIS AIDE 2370.......... 54016
Wolfe, Kaity (COMER) DIR - OPS 2184.......... 53115
Wolff, Ben (BROWN) DPTY DIST DIR.......... 301-458-2600
Wolfgang, Donna K (INSPECTOR GENERAL) ASST DIR 386 FHOB.......... 61250
Wolfgram, Kelsey (HIGGINS, CLAY) SR LEGIS ASST 424 CHOB.......... 52031
Wolf-Johnson, Maximilian (WILSON, FREDERICA S.) PRESS SECY 2445.......... 54506
Wolford, Judith (SIRES) ADMIN DIR/SCHEDULER 2268.......... 57919
Wolgast, Keisha (MOOLENAAR) DIST STAFF ASST.......... 989-631-2552
Wolke, Chad (CASE) DIST STAFF ASST.......... 808-650-6688
Woll, Samantha (SLOTKIN) DPTY DIST DIR.......... 517-993-0510
Wolman, Lauren (SHERMAN) LEGIS DIR/DPTY CHIEF 2181.......... 55911
Woltornist, Alexei (HOUSE REPUB STUDY CMTE) COMMUNICATIONS DIR 418 CHOB.......... 52777
Womble, Jeanine (CMTE-ARMED SVCS) PROF STAFF 2340.......... 62336
Wong, Andy (COMMIS ON CHINA) COUNSEL 243 FHOB.......... 63791
Wong, Jordan (PORTER) COMMUNICATIONS DIR 1117.......... 55611
Wong, Stephanie (SPEAKER) SPECIAL ASST TO THE EXEC OFFICE H232.......... 50100
Wonsyld, Risa (WALDEN) DIST FIELD REP.......... 541-308-0300
Wood, Caroline (VAN DREW) LEGIS ASST 331 CHOB.......... 56572
Wood, Jennifer (KATKO) LEGIS DIR 2457.......... 53701
Wood, Joel (STEFANIK) REGIONAL DIR.......... 518-561-2324
Wood, John (COOPER) IMMIGRATION LIAISON/ SR CONSTIT LIAISON.......... 615-736-5295
Wood, Jordan (LUETKEMEYER) LEGIS CORRES 2230.......... 52956
Wood, Kendra (CMTE-SCIENCE) CLERK 2321.......... 56375
Wood, Kevin (CAO/FURNISHINGS) MASTER CARPET MECHANIC WA32 RHOB.......... 58000
Wood, Natasha (HUFFMAN) STAFF ASST/LEGIS CORRES 1527.......... 55161

Wood, Salley (CAO/OFFICE OF THE CHIEF HUMAN RESOURCES OFFICER) SPECIAL PROJ DIR 217 FHOB........ **65116**
Wood, Zachary (CLERK/LRC) PUBLIC INFO SPEC B81 CHOB........ **65200**
Woodard, Andrea (CMTE-JUDICIARY) CLERK 189 FHOB.... **56906**
Woodburn, Charles (CAO/LOGISTICS) DIR - LOGISTICS WA27 RHOB........ **59474**
Woodburn, Thomas (DEGETTE) SR LEGIS ASST 2111........ **54431**
Woodbury, Brendan (HECK) LEGIS DIR 2452........ **59740**
Woodhead, Marie (FORTENBERRY) DIST DIR........ **402-438-1598**
Woodie, Darrell (BUCHANAN) FIELD REP........ **941-951-6643**
Woodin, Maggie (GALLAGHER) LEGIS ASST 1230........ **55665**
Woodrow, Jean (CAO/HIR – ESCALATIONS AND OPS) PROJ MGR 601 FHOB........ **66256**
Woods, Charles (KELLY, TRENT) LEGIS ASST - MIL 1005... **54306**
Woods, Marquis (NORTON) STAFF ASST 2136........ **58050**
Woods, Randy (CMTE-JOINT ECON) COMMUNICATIONS DIR - DEM SD-G01........ **42599**
Woods, Shayne (BILIRAKIS) LEGIS ASST 2227........ **55755**
Woodson-Samuels, Tyrae (ENGEL) DIR - CONSTIT SVCS........ **914-699-4100**
Woodward, Aisha (GOLDEN) CHIEF OF STAFF 1223........ **56306**
Woodward, Canon (BURCHETT) STAFF ASST 1122........ **55435**
Woodward, Gary (SCOTT, DAVID) CHIEF OF STAFF 225 CHOB........ **52939**
Woodward, Josh (YOHO) LEGIS ASST 1730........ **55744**
Woodward, Nathaniel (WATERS) AIDE........ **323-757-8900**
Woodward, Ryan (KING, PETER T.) SR LEGIS ASST 302 CHOB........ **57896**
Woody, Thaddeus (VEASEY) SR LEGIS ASST 2348........ **59897**
Wooldridge, Linda (MCKINLEY) CONSTIT REP/ CASEWK DIR........ **304-284-8506**
Woolley, Mark (ZELDIN) DIST DIR........ **631-289-1097**
Woolley, Michelle (ZELDIN) CONG AIDE........ **631-209-4235**
Worley, Katie (CLARK) CONSTIT SVCS REP........ **617-354-0292**
Worrell, Christopher (MCHENRY) LEGIS ASST 2004........ **52576**
Worsham, Janna (HARTZLER) CASEWKR........ **573-442-9311**
Woytcke, Holly (CARSON) EXEC ASST 2135........ **54011**
Wray, Sherrye (CAO/HIR – ENTERPRISE INFRASTRUCT) SYS ENGINEER 639 FHOB........ **63794**
Wright, Andrew (KILMER) COMMUNICATIONS DIR 1410...... **55916**
Wright, B G (CMTE-APPRO) PROF STAFF MEMB H310........ **53351**
Wright, Gina (COMMIS ON CONG MAILING STDS) PROF STAFF 1307........ **59337**
Wright, Gina (CMTE-HOUSE ADMIN) PROF STAFF 1309....... **52061**
Wright, Grace (SPANO) LEGIS CORRES 224 CHOB........ **51252**
Wright, James (BACON) DPTY DIST DIR........ **402-938-0300**
Wright, Jincy (ADERHOLT) CONSTIT SVCS REP..... **205-221-2310**
Wright, Judy (COMMIS ON CHINA) ADMIN DIR 243 FHOB..... **63767**
Wright, Lawrence (CAO/ENTERPRISE APPLICATIONS) BUSINESS PROCESS APPLICA SPEC B77 FHOB........ **53285**
Wright, Logan (SPANO) GEN COUNSEL/LEGIS ASST 224 CHOB........ **51252**
Wright, Monique (WILLIAMS) CONSTIT LIAISON 1708........ **59896**
Wright, Richard (CAO/ASSET MANAGEMENT) SR REC & WAREHOUSE SPEC WA23 RHOB........ **58214**
Wright, Sangina (CMTE-SCIENCE) RESEARCH ASST - MAJ 2321........ **56375**
Wright, Timothy (CAO/HIR – OPS AND CONTINUITY) SR COMMUNICATIONS SPEC 632A FHOB........ **60195**
Wright, Tuley (CMTE-ENERGY & COMMERCE) ENERGY & ENVIRON POLICY ADVISOR 2125........ **54407**
Wright, Wayne (RICHMOND) LIAISON - SMALL BUSINESS........ **504-288-3777**
Wriston, Blair (MCEACHIN) LEGIS AIDE 314 CHOB........ **56365**
Wroten, Desiree (TAKANO) SCHEDULER/EXEC ASST 420 CHOB........ **52305**
Wu, Tonia (JOHNSON, EDDIE BERNICE) LEGIS ASST 2306. **58885**
Wu, William (CMTE-INTELLIGENCE) BUDGET DIR - MAJ HVC304........ **57690**
Wulfing, Rina (DEFAZIO) SR LEGIS ASST 2134........ **56416**
Wunsche, Krista (CUNNINGHAM) LEGIS CORRES/STAFF ASST 423 CHOB........ **53176**
Wurzburg, Thea (WELCH) CONSTIT SVCS REP..... **802-652-2450**
Wykowski, Henry (CMTE-NATURAL RESOURCES) PROF STAFF - MAJ 1328........ **56065**
Wynn, Keifer (WALKER) FIELD REP........ **336-333-5005**
Wysocky, Jess (THOMPSON, MIKE) STAFF ASST 406 CHOB........ **53311**
Wyszynski, Whitney (CLERK/COMMUNICA) CONTENT DEVELOPER 293 CHOB........ **51908**
Xu, Lin (CMTE-JOINT TAX) ECONOMIST 595 FHOB........ **67575**
Yackel, Rick (REED) LEGIS CORRES 2263........ **53161**
Yager, Austin (RUIZ) LEGIS ASST 2342........ **55330**
Yahn, Ina (RADEWAGEN) CHIEF OF STAFF 1339........ **58577**
Yahner, Kelly (CLERK/LEGIS OPS) ASST BILL CLERK HT13 **57598**
Yamada, Herbert (SABLAN) LEGIS ASST 2411........ **52646**
Yamakawa, Leeann (WALBERG) OFFICE MGR..... **517-780-9075**
Yancey, Michael (BURGESS) LEGIS ASST 2161........ **57772**
Yanchury, Amanda (MCCOLLUM) COMMUNICATIONS DIR 2256........ **56631**
Yang, Jena (SMITH, ADAM) CASEWKR........ **425-793-5180**
Yang, Rosemary (COOK) PRESS ASST 1027........ **55861**
Yanick, Brittany (BUCK) COMMUNICATIONS DIR 2455........ **54676**
Yantis, Noah (MOOLENAAR) STAFF ASST 117 CHOB........ **53561**
Yarborough, Joe, III (RICE, TOM) FIELD REP........ **843-679-9781**
Yarwood, Janette
(CMTE-FOREIGN AFFAIRS) STAFF DIR 5190........ **61500**
(BASS) SUBCOMM STAFF DIR 2059........ **57084**
Yates, Ella
(CMTE-JUDICIARY) DIR - MBR SVCS & COALITIONS 2142... **56906**
(COLLINS, DOUG) COORD - MBR SVCS & OUTREACH 1504........ **59893**
Yates, Lynn (RUPPERSBERGER) LIAISON - CONSTIT SVCS........ **410-628-2701**
Yates, Malcolm (SCANLON) DIR - CONSTIT SVCS........ **610-626-1913**
Yates, Marshall (BROOKS, MO) LEGIS COUNSEL/LEGIS DIR 2246........ **54801**
Yates, Nicole (YARMUTH) DIST DIR........ **502-582-5129**
Yates, Perry (CMTE-APPRO) PROF STAFF MEMB 2362A...... **52638**
Yatrousis, Mary (LARSON) COMMUNICATIONS DIR 1501.... **52265**
Yauger, Patricia (RESCHENTHALER) DIR - CONSTIT SVCS........ **724-219-4200**
Yavor, Robert (CMTE-SMALL BUSINESS) SR PROF STAFF 2069........ **55821**
Yazdani-Zonoz, Ebrahim (RATCLIFFE) LEGIS COUNSEL 223 CHOB........ **56673**
Ybarra, Cesar (BIGGS) LEGIS ASST 1318........ **52635**
Yea, Annie (CARBAJAL) LEGIS ASST - MIL 1431........ **53601**

Yelinski, Chad (MEADOWS) LEGIS DIR 2160 **56401**
Yerbey, Lindsey (PALMER) STAFF ASST 207 CHOB **54921**
Yerge, James (CAO/LOGISTICS) REC & WAREHOUSE SPEC RSBC4 **55057**
Yezak, Jennifer (CMTE-AGRIC) DPTY CLERK 1301 **52171**
Yi, Sang (CMTE-NATURAL RESOURCES) SUBCOMM STAFF DIR 4170 **52761**
Yim, Daniel (MUCARSEL-POWELL) LEGIS ASST 114 CHOB **52778**
Yin, Jocelyn (CMTE-ARMED SVCS) GAO DETAILEE 2117 **65610**
Yingst, Bambi (DESAULNIER) SCHEDULER/EXEC ASST 503 CHOB **52095**
Yoakum, Linda (DAVIS, RODNEY) CONG AIDE **217-403-4690**
York, Adam (WATKINS) LEGIS DIR 1205 **56601**
York, Jemma
(HOUSE DEM POLICY AND COMMUNICATIONS CMTE) DPTY DIR HB18 **50251**
(SPEAKER) DPTY DIR H232 **50100**
Yost, Eric (CARTER, JOHN R.) MIL FELLOW 2110 **53864**
Youmans, Donald (CAO/HIR - ENTERPRISE MESSAGING AND MOBILITY) SR SYS ENGINEER 624 FHOB **66361**
Young, Anna (ROUZER) CASEWORK - VETS **910-395-0202**
Young, Anna (POCAN) STAFF ASST **608-258-9800**
Young, Brady (LEGIS COUNSEL) SR COUNSEL 337 FHOB **56060**
Young, C J (CMTE-ENERGY & COMMERCE) PRESS SECY 2125 **52927**
Young, Cora (THOMPSON, MIKE) DIST FIELD REP/LIAISON - VETS **707-645-1888**
Young, Dana (BABIN) CONSTIT SVCS **409-883-8075**
Young, Ellen (DOYLE) EXEC ASST 306 CHOB **52135**
Young, James (CAO/HIR – IDENTITY GOV AND ADMIN) TEAM LEAD 616 FHOB **571-921-3114**
Young, Jensen (ABRAHAM) DIST OUTREACH REP **318-445-0818**
Young, Lenny (BROWNLEY) CHIEF OF STAFF 2262 **55811**
Young, Natalie (DOYLE) COMMUNICATIONS ASST 306 CHOB **52135**
Young, Sarah (CMTE-APPRO) PROF STAFF MEMB HT2 **53047**
Young, Shalanda (CMTE-APPRO) STAFF DIR H307 **52771**
Young, Sherry (CMTE-APPRO) ADMIN AIDE H405 **52847**
Youngblood, Suzanne (CMTE-TRANSP & INFRA) DPTY COMMUNICATIONS DIR 2164 **59446**
Youngdahl, Sarah (RESCHENTHALER) CONSTIT SVCS REP **724-206-4800**
Youngquist, Emma (PHILLIPS) CASEWK SUPERVISOR **952-656-5176**
Youngsmith, Barron (CMTE-ARMED SVCS) PROF STAFF 2117 **65662**
Youpel, Mary (CMTE-NATURAL RESOURCES) PROF STAFF 4120 **52761**
Yow, Jocelyn (CISNEROS) CASEWK MGR **714-459-4575**
Yu, Cathy (CMTE-ED & WORKFORCE) DIR - LABOR OVERSIGHT 230 FHOB **53725**
Yu, Crystal (ESHOO) FIELD REP **650-323-2984**
Yurik, Karl (CARTER, JOHN R.) MIL FELLOW 2110 **53864**
Zach, Gabriella (CMTE-FOREIGN AFFAIRS) SR PROF STAFF 4150 **68467**
Zachary, Ruth (WILLIAMS) CASEWKR/DPTY DIR - CONSTIT SVCS **817-774-2575**
Zafaranlou, Ashley (STANTON) EXEC ASST/MEDIA ASST 128 CHOB **59888**
Zaferakis, Nicholas, Jr (LYNCH) SR DIST REP **617-428-2000**
Zahran, Tariq (CMTE-NATURAL RESOURCES) COORD - MBR SVCS & OUTREACH 186 FHOB **56065**
Zaidi, Syed (GOMEZ) PRESS ASST 1530 **56235**
Zajac, Emily (HUIZENGA) SCHEDULER 2232 **54401**
Zakarauskaite, Akvile (KRISHNAMOORTHI) DIST STAFF ASST **847-413-1959**
Zamar, Yves (HAALAND) SR LEGIS ASST 1237 **65047**
Zamora, Katy (CLERK/REPORTERS) OFFICIAL REPORTER 1718 **52627**
Zamora, Raquel (CLERK/REPORTERS) EDITOR - COMMITTEES 1718 **52627**
Zams, Kelly
(BROOKS, MO) FINANCIAL & ADMIN OFFICER 2246 **54801**
(HORN) FINANCIAL ADMIN 415 CHOB **52132**
(HOULAHAN) FINANCIAL ADMIN 1218 **54315**
(ROUDA) ADMIN - FINANCE & PAYROLL 2300 **52415**
Zaragoza, Patricia (CÁRDENAS) STAFF ASST 2438 **56131**
Zatkowski, Robert (CAO/HOUSE PERIODICAL PRESS) DIRECTOR H304 **52941**
Zavac, David (KAPTUR) CONG ASST **419-259-7500**
Zavala, Eddie (CUELLAR) PRESS ASST **956-725-0639**
Zavala, S J (GONZALEZ, VICENTE) CONSTIT REP **956-682-5545**
Zawitoski, Daniel (PETERS) DC CHIEF OF STAFF 2338 **50508**
Zeb, Sue (JOHNSON, EDDIE BERNICE) SPECIAL PROJ COORD **214-922-8885**
Zegers, Ted (CMTE-BUDGET) BUDGET ANALYST 204E CHOB **67200**
Zelenko, Leslie (POCAN) SR LEGIS ASST 1421 **52906**
Zeller, Nick (GOLDEN) COMMUNICATIONS DIR 1223 **56306**
Zenk, Katie (CMTE-AGRIC) SUBCOMM STAFF DIR/ ECONOMIST 1301 **52171**
Zenone, Heather (BASS) SR POLICY ADVISOR 2059 **57084**
Zepeda, Marilyn (GRIJALVA) LEGIS CORRES 1511 **52435**
Zeppieri, Carla (CMTE-ARMED SVCS) PROF STAFF 2340 **56703**
Zetts, Michael (RYAN) COMMUNICATIONS DIR 1126 **55261**
Zhu, Jen (CMTE-WAYS & MEANS) PROF STAFF 1104 **53943**
Ziegler, Daniel (HOUSE REPUB STUDY CMTE) EXEC DIR 418 CHOB **52777**
Ziegler, Lauren (BABIN) SR LEGIS ASST 2236 **51555**
Zieh, Joy (CLARK) STAFF ASST/LEGIS CORRES 2448 **52836**
Zielke, Janet (UPTON) SR CONSTIT SVCS REP **269-982-1986**
Zimpher, Nate (BALDERSON) SR LEGIS ASST 1221 **55355**
Zinda, Landon (EMMER) LEGIS DIR 315 CHOB **52331**
Zinkle, Taylor (HAGEDORN) CASEWKR **507-323-6090**
Zipperer, Richard (STEIL) CHIEF OF STAFF **608-752-4050**
Zirngibl, Wendy (THOMPSON, MIKE) FELLOW 406 CHOB **53311**
Zlotnik, Asher (ROSE, MAX) LEGIS ASST 1529 **53371**
Zook, Michelle (RATCLIFFE) MGR - CONSTIT SVCS **972-771-0100**
Zubkoff, Jordana (CAO/PAYROLL & BENEFITS) MGMT ANALYST B215 LHOB **60788**
Zucker, Joshua (CMTE-OVERSIGHT & GOVT REFORM) ASST CLERK 2157 **55051**
Zukrow, Leslie (DAVIDS) DIST STAFF ASST **913-621-0832**
Zwaanstra, Johnny (LESKO) LEGIS CORRES 1113 **54576**
Zyblikewycz, Helena (CMTE-TRANSP & INFRA) SUBCOMM STAFF DIR 2251 **54472**

REPRESENTATIVES AND STAFF

Three-digit room numbers are in the Cannon HOB or the Ford HOB, as indicated. Four-digit room numbers beginning with 1 are in the Longworth HOB; with 2, the Rayburn HOB; and with 3, 4, 5, or 6, the O'Neill HOB.

Calls from outside the Capitol complex can be made by dialing (202) 22 plus the five-digit number listed in this directory.

Death or resignation of Member indicated by bold brackets **[ ]**.

[Representative]

North Carolina, 9th

132 CANNON HOB (ZIP: 20515-3309) **225-1976**

Representative Ralph Lee Abraham

Louisiana, 5th

417 CANNON HOB (ZIP: 20515-1805) **225-8490**
Avery, Cole COMMUNICATIONS DIR 417 CHOB **58490**
Brown, Mason STAFF ASST 417 CHOB **58490**
Cambon, Allen SR LEGIS ASST 417 CHOB **58490**
Herrock, Emma SCHEDULER/OFFICE MGR 417 CHOB **58490**
Kaiser, Heinz LEGIS ASST - MIL 417 CHOB **58490**
Letlow, Luke CHIEF OF STAFF 417 CHOB **58490**
Lindgren, Paige PRESS ASST/LEGIS CORRES 417 CHOB **58490**
Sundahl, Alan ADMIN - FINANCE & PAYROLL 417 CHOB **58490**
Verrill, Ted DPTY CHIEF OF STAFF/LEGIS DIR 417 CHOB **58490**

DISTRICT OFFICES

CENTRAL LOUISIANA—2003 MACARTHUR DR, BLDG 5, ALEXANDRIA, LA 71301
Howe, Donna OFFICE MGR **318-445-0818**
Sunderhaus, Jessica CASEWKR **318-445-0818**
Willis, Michael FIELD REP **318-445-0818**
Young, Jensen DIST OUTREACH REP **318-445-0818**

NORTH LOUISIANA—426 DESIARD ST, MONROE, LA 71201
Boies, Lilia OFFICE MGR/CASEWKR **318-322-3500**
Brown, Keith DIST OUTREACH REP **318-322-3500**
Lobrano, Wyatt DIST DIR **318-322-3500**

Representative Alma S. Adams

North Carolina, 12th

2436 RAYBURN HOB (ZIP: 20515-3312) **225-1510**
Barajas, Jocelyne STAFF ASST 2436 .... **51510**
Christie, John LEGIS DIR 2436 .... **51510**
Foxx, Rhonda CHIEF OF STAFF 2436 .... **51510**
Holzberg, Gordon LEGIS CORRES 2436 .... **51510**
Lawson, Dion FINANCIAL ADMIN 2436 .... **51510**
McGovern, Sarah COMMUNICATIONS DIR 2436 .... **51510**
Stewart, Katherine LEGIS ASST 2436 .... **51510**
Thompson, Cora INFO TECH MGR 2436 .... **51510**
Webster, Kichelle LEGIS ASST 2436 .... **51510**

DISTRICT OFFICE

CHARLOTTE—801 E MOREHEAD ST, CHARLOTTE, NC 28202
Bonifati, Avery DIST STAFF ASST/PRESS ASST **704-344-9950**
Brown, Sandra SCHEDULER/DIR - OPS **704-344-9950**
Carter, Barbara DIR - CONSTIT SVCS **704-344-9950**
Herbin, Jaylon DIST LIAISON **704-344-9950**
Ratliff, Kim EVENTS MGR **704-344-9950**
Rhue, Phanalphie DIST DIR **704-344-9950**
Tembo, Kay SR DIST REP **704-344-9950**

Representative Robert B. Aderholt

Alabama, 4th

1203 LONGWORTH HOB (ZIP: 20515-0104) **225-4876**
Catto, Gregor LEGIS CORRES 1203 .... **54876**
Dawson, Mark LEGIS DIR 1203 .... **54876**
Lawson, Chris ADMIN DIR/SCHEDULER/SYS ADMIN 1203 .... **54876**
McLerran, Elissa LEGIS ASST 1203 .... **54876**
Medley, Megan DPTY LEGIS DIR 1203 .... **54876**
Palmer, William LEGIS ASST 1203 .... **54876**
Rell, Brian CHIEF OF STAFF 1203 .... **54876**
Turner, Will LEGIS AIDE 1203 .... **54876**
Unseth, Drew STAFF ASST 1203 .... **54876**

DISTRICT OFFICES

CULLMAN—205 FOURTH AVE NE, SUITE 104, CULLMAN, AL 35055
Clark, Carson FIELD REP/PRESS SECY **256-734-6043**
Taylor, Jennifer DIR - CONSTIT SVCS **256-734-6043**

GADSDEN—600 BROAD ST, SUITE 107, GADSDEN, AL 35901
Abernathy, Pamela CONSTIT SVCS REP **256-546-0201**
Manasco, James FIELD REP **256-546-0201**

JASPER—1710 ALABAMA AVE, 247 CARL ELLIOTT BLDG, JASPER, AL 35501-5400
Housel, Paul FIELD DIR **205-221-2310**
Wright, Jincy CONSTIT SVCS REP **205-221-2310**

TUSCUMBIA—1011 GEORGE WALLACE BLVD, SUITE 146, TUSCUMBIA, AL 35674
Kennedy, Kreg FIELD REP **256-381-3450**

Representative Pete Aguilar

California, 31st

109 CANNON HOB (ZIP: 20515-0531) **225-3201**
Cornell, Becky CHIEF OF STAFF 109 CHOB **53201**
Cuevas, Stephanie LEGIS DIR 109 CHOB **53201**
Dorner, Evan LEGIS ASST 109 CHOB **53201**
Dorrough, Parker COMMUNICATIONS DIR 109 CHOB **53201**
Giulino, Danielle SCHEDULER/DIR - OPS 109 CHOB **53201**
Glynn, Chelsea LEGIS AIDE 109 CHOB **53201**

Palencia, Stephanie LEGIS CORRES/STAFF ASST 109 CHOB .. 53201
White, Wendell SR POLICY ADVISOR/LEGIS ASST - MIL 109 CHOB 53201

DISTRICT OFFICE

SAN BERNARDINO—685 E CARNEGIE DR, SUITE 100, SAN BERNARDINO, CA 92408

Aguilar, Birdie STAFF ASST 909-890-4445
Bosman, Jared LIAISON - MIL & VET 909-890-4445
Harlin, Andrea SR FIELD REP 909-890-4445
Lewis, Curt DIR - GRANTS 909-890-4445
Medzhibovsky, Boris CHIEF OF STAFF 909-890-4445
Milla, Danny CONSTIT SVCS REP 909-890-4445
Valdez, Teresa DIST DIR 909-890-4445

Representative Rick W. Allen

Georgia, 12th

2400 RAYBURN HOB (ZIP: 20515-1012) **225-2823**
Baker, Tim CHIEF OF STAFF 2400 52823
Bhambhani, Ariana LEGIS CORRES 2400 52823
Douglas, Jane STAFF ASST 2400 52823
Duvall, Zellie LEGIS ASST 2400 52823
Hodge, Lauren DPTY CHIEF OF STAFF 2400 52823
Hunter, Katie LEGIS DIR 2400 52823
Norwood, Carlton PRESS SECY 2400 52823
Wheat, Heath SCHEDULER/DIR - OPS 2400 52823

DISTRICT OFFICES

AUGUSTA—2743 PERIMETER PKWY, BLDG 200, SUITE 105, AUGUSTA, GA 30909

Lynch, Paul CONSTIT SVCS REP 706-228-1980
Morgan, Diane EXEC ASST 706-228-1980
Rhodes, Christine CONSTIT SVCS REP 706-228-1980
Seda, Megan CONSTIT SVCS REP 706-228-1980
Thigpen, Brinsley DIST DIR 706-228-1980

DUBLIN—100 S CHURCH ST, DUBLIN, GA 31021

Windham, Troy CONSTIT SVCS REP 478-272-4030

STATESBORO—50 E MAIN ST, STATESBORO, GA 30458

Stokes, Zach DIST FIELD REP 912-243-9452

VIDALIA—107 OLD AIRPORT RD, SUITE A, VIDALIA, GA 30475

Holman, Rose Anne CONSTIT SVCS REP 912-403-3311

Representative Colin Z. Allred

Texas, 32d

328 CANNON HOB (ZIP: 20515-4332) **225-2231**
Animely, Kingsley FINANCIAL ADMIN 328 CHOB 52231
Duckworth, Brian LEGIS ASST 328 CHOB 52231
Flowers, Darien STAFF ASST 328 CHOB 52231
Hutchinson, Paige CHIEF OF STAFF 328 CHOB 52231
Killian, Abbie LEGIS CORRES 328 CHOB 52231
McClure, Janelle LEGIS DIR 328 CHOB 52231
Pulitzer, Mina SCHEDULER 328 CHOB 52231
Stewart, Josh COMMUNICATIONS DIR 328 CHOB 52231

DISTRICT OFFICE

RICHARDSON—100 N CENTRAL EXPRESSWAY, SUITE 602, RICHARDSON, TX 75080

Acosta, Sam DIR - CONSTIT SVCS 972-972-7949
Krause, Andrew STAFF ASST 972-972-7949
Tankel, Judith DIST DIR 972-972-7949
Weber, J C DIGITAL ASST 972-972-7949

Representative Justin Amash

Michigan, 3d

106 CANNON HOB (ZIP: 20515-2203) **225-3831**
Gumina, Grace EXEC ASST 106 CHOB 53831
Iodice, Carolyn LEGIS DIR 106 CHOB 53831
Miller, Kelly LEGIS ASST 106 CHOB 53831
Nelson, Poppy CHIEF OF STAFF 106 CHOB 53831
Nixon, Molly LEGIS COUNSEL 106 CHOB 53831
Stein, Elizah LEGIS AIDE 106 CHOB 53831

DISTRICT OFFICES

BATTLE CREEK—70 W MICHIGAN AVE, SUITE 212, BATTLE CREEK, MI 49017........ 269-205-3823

GRAND RAPIDS—110 MICHIGAN ST NW, SUITE 460, FED BLDG, GRAND RAPIDS, MI 49503-2313

Condon, Katherine DIST DIR 616-451-8383
Deboer, Rebecca DIST REP 616-451-8383
Denboer, Stephen DIST REP 616-451-8383
Fields, Shayna DIST REP 616-451-8383
Ungrey, Jennifer SR DIST REP 616-451-8383
Vanderveen, Ben SR ADVISOR 616-451-8383

Representative Mark E. Amodei

Nevada, 2d

104 CANNON HOB (ZIP: 20515-2802) **225-6155**
Brooke, Kenneth LEGIS ASST 104 CHOB 56155
Kleitsch, Jessica LEGIS CORRES 104 CHOB 56155
Leggiero, Brandon LEGIS ASST 104 CHOB 56155
Lowe, Molly LEGIS DIR 104 CHOB 56155
Markowitz, Jessica EXEC ASST 104 CHOB 56155
Miller, Bruce CHIEF OF STAFF 104 CHOB 56155
Ramsey, Logan COMMUNICATIONS DIR 104 CHOB 56155

DISTRICT OFFICES

ELKO—905 RAILROAD ST, SUITE 104D, ELKO, NV 89801

Paris, Martin CONSTIT RELATIONS REP 775-777-7705

RENO—5310 KIETZKE LANE, SUITE 103, RENO, NV 89511

Garzon, Arturo CONSTIT SVCS REP 775-686-5760
Gastonguay, Robert STAFF ASST 775-686-5760
Parobek, Stacy DIST DIR 775-686-5760
Spears, Tracy CONSTIT SVCS REP 775-686-5760

Representative Kelly Armstrong

North Dakota, At Large

1004 LONGWORTH HOB (ZIP: 20515-3400) **225-2611**
Beebe, Erin LEGIS CORRES 1004 52611
Crowley, Connor LEGIS AIDE 1004 52611
Fitzpatrick, Casey DPTY CHIEF OF STAFF - POLICY 1004 52611
Leighton, Roz CHIEF OF STAFF 1004 52611
Peterson, Elly SCHEDULING DIR 1004 52611
Tortorici, Nick SR LEGIS AIDE 1004 52611
VerVelde, Brandon COMMUNICATIONS DIR 1004 52611

DISTRICT OFFICES

BISMARCK—220 E ROSSER AVE, ROOM 228, BISMARCK, ND 58501

Nitschke, Darrell REGIONAL DIR 702-354-6700
Rambough, Janean DIST OFFICE MGR 702-354-6700

FARGO—3217 FIECHTNER DR, SUITE B, FARGO, ND 58103

Christy, Mary DIR - CONSTIT SVCS 701-353-6665
Moll, Pam DIST OFFICE MGR 701-353-6665
Rustvang, Jeff STATE DIR 701-353-6665

Representative Jodey C. Arrington

Texas, 19th

1029 LONGWORTH HOB (ZIP: 20515-4319) 225-4005
Brennan, Andrew COMMUNICATIONS ASST 1029 .... **54005**
Brown, Chelsea CHIEF OF STAFF 1029 .... **54005**
Burleson, Marisa SCHEDULING DIR 1029 .... **54005**
Cummings, Tim DPTY CHIEF 1029 .... **54005**
Spadavecchia, Dominique SR LEGIS ASST 1029 .... **54005**
Weiner, Jessica STAFF ASST 1029 .... **54005**

DISTRICT OFFICES

ABILENE—500 CHESTNUT ST, UNIT 819, ABILENE, TX 79602
Conley, Sarah CONSTIT SVCS REP **325-675-9779**
Pugh, Glen REGIONAL DIR **325-675-9779**

LUBBOCK—1312 TEXAS AVE, LUBBOCK, TX 79401
Hammonds, McKenzie CONSTIT SVCS REP **806-763-1611**
Herring, Lindley DIST DIR **806-763-1611**
Moses, Sarah CONSTIT SVCS REP **806-763-1611**
Witte, Sydney CONSTIT RELATIONS REP **806-763-1611**

Representative Cynthia Axne

Iowa, 3d

330 CANNON HOB (ZIP: 20515-1503) 225-5476
Barnes, Zaak LEGIS ASST 330 CHOB **55476**
Binger, Will LEGIS ASST 330 CHOB **55476**
Diver, Joe CHIEF OF STAFF 330 CHOB **55476**
Fleming, Denise LEGIS DIR 330 CHOB **55476**
Krebs, Robert LEGIS CORRES 330 CHOB **55476**
McDaniels, Virginia STAFF ASST 330 CHOB **55476**
Russak, Maddy COMMUNICATIONS DIR/DPTY CHIEF OF STAFF 330 CHOB **55476**
Shepherd, Amanda SCHEDULER 330 CHOB **55476**

DISTRICT OFFICES

COUNCIL BLUFFS—501 5TH AVE, COUNCIL BLUFFS, IA 51503 712-890-3117

CRESTON—208 W TAYLOR, CRESTON, IA 50801
Riemenschneider, John CASEWKR/DIST FIELD REP **225-5476**

DES MOINES—400 E COURT AVE, SUITE 346, DES MOINES, IA 50309
Behnke, Derek DIST FIELD REP/CASEWKR **515-400-8180**
Gearhart, Chloe DIST FIELD REP/CASEWKR **515-400-8180**
Miller, Brooke DIST FIELD REP/CASEWKR **515-400-8180**
Patchett, Kaity DIST DIR **515-400-8180**

Representative Brian Babin

Texas, 36th

2236 RAYBURN HOB (ZIP: 20515-4336) 225-1555
Barber, Beth SCHEDULER/LEGIS AIDE 2236 .... **51555**
Couhig, Ben CHIEF OF STAFF 2236 .... **51555**
Janushkowsky, Stephen LEGIS DIR 2236 .... **51555**
Littrell, Avery LEGIS ASST 2236 .... **51555**
Reese, Sarah PRESS SECY 2236 .... **51555**
Taylor, Ben LEGIS CORRES 2236 .... **51555**
Ziegler, Lauren SR LEGIS ASST 2236 .... **51555**

DISTRICT OFFICES

DEER PARK—203 IVY AVE, SUITE 600, DEER PARK, TX 77536
Carter, Will CONSTIT SVCS REP **832-780-0966**
Ferguson, Beverly REGIONAL DIR **832-780-0966**
Kranz, Jeannie ADVISOR - SCIENCE **832-780-0966**
Waterman, Kelly DIST DIR **832-780-0966**

ORANGE—1201 S CHILDERS RD, ORANGE, TX 77630
Brown, Lanie REGIONAL DIR **409-883-8075**
Young, Dana CONSTIT SVCS **409-883-8075**

WOODVILLE—100 W BLUFF DR, WOODVILLE, TX 75979
Blacksher, Sarah CONSTIT SVCS REP **409-331-8066**
Iglesias, Rachel REGIONAL DIR **409-331-8066**

Representative Don Bacon

Nebraska, 2d

1024 LONGWORTH HOB (ZIP: 20515-2702) 225-4155
TOLL-FREE NO. 1-888-221-7452
Comeau, Julia LEGIS ASST 1024 .... **54155**
Dreiling, Mark CHIEF OF STAFF 1024 .... **54155**
Ficenec, Samuel STAFF ASST 1024 .... **54155**
Flood, Pat NATIONAL SECUR ADVISOR 1024 .... **54155**
Foy Alberto, Valerie LEGIS COUNSEL 1024 .... **54155**
Kratz, Jeff LEGIS DIR 1024 .... **54155**
London, Claire EXEC ASST 1024 .... **54155**
Pearce, Rachel LEGIS ASST 1024 .... **54155**
Wehr, Aron PRESS SECY 1024 .... **54155**

DISTRICT OFFICE

OMAHA—13906 GOLD CIRCLE, SUITE 101, OMAHA, NE 68144
Cartwright, Makenzie DIST STAFF ASST **402-938-0300**
Clark, Kyle CONSTIT OUTREACH REP **402-938-0300**
Dolton, Scott CONSTIT LIAISON **402-938-0300**
Frazee, James CONSTIT LIAISON **402-938-0300**
Guzman Bortolotti, Luis CONSTIT LIAISON **402-938-0300**
Holtmeyer, Matthew CONSTIT LIAISON **402-938-0300**
Jensen, Danielle COMMUNICATIONS DIR **402-938-0300**
Mathisen, Dean SR CONSTIT LIAISON **402-938-0300**
Ungerman, Felix DPTY CHIEF OF STAFF **402-938-0300**
Wajda, Sara DIST EXEC ASST **402-938-0300**
Wright, James DPTY DIST DIR **402-938-0300**

Representative James R. Baird

Indiana, 4th

532 CANNON HOB (ZIP: 20515-1404) 225-5037
Czufin, Sarah LEGIS DIR 532 CHOB **55037**
Dean, Tanner STAFF ASST 532 CHOB **55037**
Hammond, Jackson LEGIS ASST 532 CHOB **55037**
Jennings, Alyssa SCHEDULER 532 CHOB **55037**
Marvel, Toby LEGIS ASST 532 CHOB **55037**
Vinyard, Ashlee CHIEF OF STAFF 532 CHOB **55037**

DISTRICT OFFICE

DANVILLE—355 S WASHINGTON ST, SUITE 210, DANVILLE, IN 46122
Cunningham, Quincy DIST CHIEF OF STAFF **317-563-5567**
Hickner, Alex STAFF ASST **317-563-5567**
Hubbard, Diane COMMUNITY LIAISON **317-563-5567**
Row, Matt DIR - CONSTIT SVCS **317-563-5567**
Siegrist, Sally COMMUNITY LIAISON **317-563-5567**

Representative Troy Balderson

Ohio, 12th

1221 LONGWORTH HOB (ZIP: 20515-3512) 225-5355
TOLL-FREE NO. 1-855-728-6412
Babb, Alison ADMIN - FINANCE & PAYROLL 1221 .... **55355**

Collins, Erin COMMUNICATIONS DIR 1221 55355
Crouch, Sarah ADMIN - FINANCE & PAYROLL 1221 55355
Engquist, Laura DPTY CHIEF OF STAFF 1221 55355
Hearn, Bri LEGIS ASST 1221 55355
Kohler, John LEGIS CORRES 1221 55355
Madni, Brittany LEGIS DIR 1221 55355
Piatt, Austin STAFF ASST/LEGIS AIDE 1221 55355
Waskowsky, Kim SCHEDULER 1221 55355
Zimpher, Nate SR LEGIS ASST 1221 55355

DISTRICT OFFICE

CENTRAL OHIO—250 E WILSON BRIDGE RD, SUITE 100, WORTHINGTON, OH 43085
TOLL-FREE NUMBER 1-855-728-6412
Cordonnier, David DIST FIELD REP 614-523-2555
Crumley, Luke ASST DIST DIR 614-523-2555
Estelle, Beth CASEWKR/CONSTIT SVCS REP 614-523-2555
Geiger, Teri CHIEF OF STAFF 614-523-2555
Hegarty, Katie DIST STAFF ASST 614-523-2555
Schneider, Timothy STAFF ASST 614-523-2555
Siddle, Clark DPTY COMMUNICATIONS DIR 614-523-2555

Representative Jim Banks

Indiana, 3d

1713 LONGWORTH HOB (ZIP: 20515-1403) **225-4436**
Arrighi, T W COMMUNICATIONS DIR 1713 54436
Dobbins, Halee PRESS ASST 1713 54436
Hunter, Kirk CONG FELLOW 1713 54436
Keesling, Nicole SCHEDULER 1713 54436
Keller, David CHIEF OF STAFF 1713 54436
Kempler, Jeff SPECIAL ASST 1713 54436
Marder, Paul MIL FELLOW 1713 54436
Markle, Lindsay LEGIS ASST - MIL 1713 54436
Rusthoven, Mark SR LEGIS ASST 1713 54436
Serstad, Garrett STAFF ASST 1713 54436
Spencer, Tanner LEGIS ASST 1713 54436
Surber, Amy DPTY CHIEF OF STAFF/LEGIS DIR 1713 54436

DISTRICT OFFICE

FORT WAYNE—1300 S HARRISON ST, FORT WAYNE, IN 46802
Crabtree, Chris SR ADVISOR 260-702-4750
Green, Kathie CONSTIT SVCS SPEC 260-702-4750
Jehl, Russ DPTY DIST DIR 260-702-4750
Justice, Steve CONSTIT RELATIONS 260-702-4750
Pillie, Derek DIR - CONSTIT SVCS 260-702-4750
Scaer, John STAFF ASST 260-702-4750
Weigelt, Tinisha DIST DIR 260-702-4750

Representative Andy Barr

Kentucky, 6th

2430 RAYBURN HOB (ZIP: 20515-1706) **225-4706**
Case, Michael LEGIS CORRES 2430 54706
Jackson, Matt STAFF ASST 2430 54706
Lauren, Osborne SCHEDULER 2430 54706
Osborn, Claire LEGIS ASST 2430 54706
Rosado, Mary CHIEF OF STAFF 2430 54706
Simons, David SR LEGIS ASST 2430 54706
VanderToll, Hunt LEGIS ASST - MIL 2430 54706

DISTRICT OFFICE

LEXINGTON—2709 OLD ROSEBUD RD, SUITE 100, LEXINGTON, KY 40509
Allen, Anthony DIR - CONSTIT SVCS 859-219-1366
Dale, Tatum DPTY DIST DIR 859-219-1366
Dye, Jon DIST STAFF ASST 859-219-1366
Rogers, Carol COMMUNICATIONS ADVISOR/OFFICE MGR 859-219-1366
Small, Leslie DIST DIR 859-219-1366
Todd, McKinzii CONSTIT SVCS OFFICER 859-219-1366
Whitaker, Jodi COMMUNICATIONS DIR 859-219-1366
Williams, Shelby DIR - DIST PROJ 859-219-1366

Representative Nanette Diaz Barragán

California, 44th

1030 LONGWORTH HOB (ZIP: 20515-0544) **225-8220**
Dillon, Ryan EXEC ASST/SCHEDULER 1030 58220
Gonzalez, Sergio INFO TECH SYS ANALYST 1030 58220
Moore, Shane ADMIN - FINANCE & PAYROLL 1030 58220
Pacheco, Ricardo STAFF ASST/LEGIS CORRES 1030 58220
Primus, Robert CHIEF OF STAFF 1030 58220

DISTRICT OFFICES

CARSON—701 E CARSON ST, CARSON, CA 90745 310-233-4811

SAN PEDRO FLAGSHIP—302 W FIFTH ST, SUITE 201, SAN PEDRO, CA 90731
Brown, Norchelle POLICY ASST 310-831-1799
Camacho, Patricia SR CASEWKR 310-831-1799
Carrillo, Francisco DIST DIR 310-831-1799
Cid, Gabriela FIELD REP 310-831-1799
Hardie, Gary POLICY ASST 310-831-1799
Harmon, Tess CASEWKR 310-831-1799
Lopez, Francisco STAFF ASST 310-831-1799
Ortega, Kimberly PRESS ASST 310-831-1799

SOUTH GATE—8650 CALIFORNIA AVE, SOUTH GATE, CA 90280 323-563-9562

Representative Karen Bass

California, 37th

2059 RAYBURN HOB (ZIP: 20515-0537) **225-7084**
Bashford, Janice LEGIS DIR 2059 57084
DeJonghe, Nina STAFF ASST 2059 57084
Kaiser, Khaula LEGIS AIDE 2059 57084
Moore, Shane FINANCIAL ADVISOR 2059 57084
Radice, Lauren EXEC SCHEDULER 2059 57084
Seidl, Zachary DPTY PRESS SECY 2059 57084
Street, Caren CHIEF OF STAFF 2059 57084
Yarwood, Janette SUBCOMM STAFF DIR 2059 57084
Zenone, Heather SR POLICY ADVISOR 2059 57084

DISTRICT OFFICE

LOS ANGELES—4929 WILSHIRE BLVD, SUITE 650, LOS ANGELES, CA 90010
Ahn, Kenneth CASEWKR 323-965-1422
Aragon, Claudia CASEWK MGR 323-965-1422
Hamilton, Jacqueline CONSTIT SVCS REP 323-965-1422
Harris, Darryn DIST DIR 323-965-1422
Henderson, Stanley STAFF 323-965-1422
Iwu, Nnamdi CONSTIT SVCS REP 323-965-1422

Representative Joyce Beatty

Ohio, 3d

2303 RAYBURN HOB (ZIP: 20515-3503) **225-4324**
Bauduy, Michael LEGIS AIDE/LEGIS CORRES 2303 54324

Davis Johnson, Chonya SR LEGIS ASST 2303 54324
Diallo, Leila EXEC ASST/SCHEDULER 2303 54324
Farnin, Scott FINANCIAL SVCS COUNSEL 2303 54324
Lawson, Dion SHARED EMPLOYEE 2303 54324
Levinson, Tyler PRESS ASST/LEGIS CORRES 2303 54324
Manecke, Dominic COMMUNICATIONS DIR 2303 54324
Ross, Kimberly CHIEF OF STAFF/CHIEF COUNSEL 2303 54324
Semanko, Nicholas LEGIS DIR/COUNSEL 2303 54324
Vaughn, Wesley LEGIS CORRES/STAFF ASST 2303 54324

DISTRICT OFFICE

COLUMBUS—471 E BROAD ST, SUITE 1100, COLUMBUS, OH 43215

Al-Asadi, Shahed DIST AIDE/STAFF ASST 614-220-0003
Davis, Ernie DIST DIR 614-220-0003
Jackson, Sandra CASEWK MGR 614-220-0003
Seward, Larry OUTREACH DIR 614-220-0003
Weaver, Trenton DIST LIAISON 614-220-0003

Representative Ami Bera

California, 7th

1727 LONGWORTH HOB (ZIP: 20515-0507) 225-5716

Bruce, Emma SCHEDULER/LEGIS AIDE 1727 55716
Lum, Kelvin LEGIS DIR 1727 55716
Nguyen, Colleen SR POLICY ADVISOR 1727 55716
Nickson, Michael FINANCIAL ADMIN 1727 55716
Obermiller, Chad CHIEF OF STAFF 1727 55716
Perera, Stephanie LEGIS CORRES 1727 55716
Radding, Elena STAFF ASST 1727 55716
Siddiqui, Faisal SYS ADMIN 1727 55716
Stecklow, Eric OUTREACH DIR 1727 55716
Uyehara, Ryan LEGIS ASST 1727 55716

DISTRICT OFFICE

RANCHO CORDOVA—8950 CAL CENTER DR, BLDG 3, SUITE 100, SACRAMENTO, CA 95826

Bennigson, Daneen CASEWK DIR 916-635-0505
Ceccato, Matthew DIST DIR 916-635-0505
Clark, Lisa CASEWKR 916-635-0505
Norton, Philip FIELD REP 916-635-0505
Pincilotti, Ivanna CASEWKR 916-635-0505
Robles, Sergio FIELD REP 916-635-0505
Uribe, Anthony STAFF ASST 916-635-0505

Representative Jack Bergman

Michigan, 1st

414 CANNON HOB (ZIP: 20515-2201) 225-4735

Burns, Amelia SCHEDULER 414 CHOB 54735
Fetzer, Kelsey LEGIS ASST 414 CHOB 54735
Jelnicky, Michelle LEGIS DIR/DPTY CHIEF 414 CHOB 54735
Lis, Tony CHIEF OF STAFF 414 CHOB 54735
Monticello, Ben LEGIS CORRES 414 CHOB 54735
Struble, Matthias LEGIS CORRES 414 CHOB 54735

DISTRICT OFFICES

MARQUETTE—1500 W WASHINGTON ST, SUITE 2, MARQUETTE, MI 49855

Anderson, Karen DIR - CONSTIT SVCS 906-273-2227
Emmendorfer, Nicholas DIST AIDE 906-273-2227

TRAVERSE CITY—1396 DOUGLAS DR, SUITE 101, TRAVERSE CITY, MI 49696

Blackmore, Taylor DIR - CONSTIT SVCS 231-944-7633
Collinsworth, Mel CONSTIT SVCS 231-944-7633
Droog, Anita DIST AIDE 231-944-7633
Hancotte, Marian CASEWKR 231-944-7633
Hogge, James COMMUNICATIONS DIR 231-944-7633
McClure, Randy CASEWORK - VETS 231-944-7633

Representative Donald S. Beyer, Jr.

Virginia, 8th

1119 LONGWORTH HOB (ZIP: 20515-4608) 225-4376

Ahmed, Maryam STAFF ASST 1119 54376
Cafritz, Zachary DPTY CHIEF OF STAFF/LEGIS DIR 1119 54376
Fritschner, Aaron COMMUNICATIONS DIR 1119 54376
Gogolin, Sean PRESS SECY 1119 54376
Khan, Sophia LEGIS AIDE 1119 54376
O'Hanlon, Ann CHIEF OF STAFF 1119 54376
Rubinger, Grace LEGIS CORRES 1119 54376
Rubio, Sophia SCHEDULER 1119 54376
Sarkesian, Lauren LEGIS COUNSEL 1119 54376
Schisler, Katherine SR LEGIS ASST 1119 54376

DISTRICT OFFICE

ARLINGTON—1901 N MOORE ST, SUITE 1108, ARLINGTON, VA 22209

Daniels, John CONSTIT LIAISON 703-658-5403
Rohrschneider, Sarah CONSTIT OUTREACH REP 703-658-5403
Simon, Noah DIST DIR 703-658-5403
Somasundaram, Nita CASEWK MGR 703-658-5403

Representative Andy Biggs

Arizona, 5th

1318 LONGWORTH HOB (ZIP: 20515-0305) 225-2635

Eberle, Jonathan STAFF ASST 1318 52635
Kuckuck, Jeffrey SR POLICY ADVISOR 1318 52635
LaBorde, Kate LEGIS DIR 1318 52635
Mazol, Deborah CHIEF OF STAFF 1318 52635
Rogers, Jason GEN COUNSEL 1318 52635
Seideman, Tina SCHEDULER 1318 52635
Stefanski, Daniel COMMUNICATIONS DIR 1318 52635
Stovall, Shannon LEGIS CORRES 1318 52635
Ybarra, Cesar LEGIS ASST 1318 52635

DISTRICT OFFICE

MESA—2509 S POWER RD, SUITE 204, MESA, AZ 85209

Charnick, Kendra CONSTIT SVCS 480-699-8239
Cleveland, Christina CONSTIT RELATIONS REP 480-699-8239
Huff, Lee FIELD REP - VETS 480-699-8239
Karstens, Elise STAFF ASST 480-699-8239
Safsten, Greg DPTY CHIEF OF STAFF/DIST DIR 480-699-8239

Representative Gus M. Bilirakis

Florida, 12th

2227 RAYBURN HOB (ZIP: 20515-0912) 225-5755

Glasgow, Savannah STAFF ASST 2227 55755
Hittos, Elizabeth CHIEF OF STAFF 2227 55755
Jones, Chris LEGIS ASST 2227 55755
Menorca, Doug SPECIAL ASST 2227 55755
O'Connor, Mary FINANCIAL ADMIN 2227 55755
Power, Thomas LEGIS DIR/DPTY CHIEF OF STAFF 2227 55755
Smith, Sean SCHEDULER 2227 55755

Stamps, Nathan LEGIS CORRES 2227 55755
Vecchi, Jonathan LEGIS COUNSEL 2227 55755
Woods, Shayne LEGIS ASST 2227 55755

DISTRICT OFFICES

NEW PORT RICHEY—7132 LITTLE RD, NEW PORT RICHEY, FL 34654
TOLL-FREE NUMBER **1-866-773-2871**
Ellison, Carol CASEWK MGR 727-232-2921
Fleege, Rob FIELD REP - VETS 727-232-2921
Grenelle, James CASEWKR 727-232-2921
Hatfield, Bob COORD - COMMUNITY OUTREACH 727-232-2921
Paasch, Dan DIST AIDE/DIST SCHEDULER 727-232-2921
Robertson, Summer DPTY CHIEF OF STAFF 727-232-2921
Sellas, Kristen LIAISON - MIL & VET/CASEWK DIR 727-232-2921

TARPON SPRINGS—600 KLOSTERMAN RD, ROOM BB-038, TARPON SPRINGS, FL 34689
O'Brien, Tucker DIST AIDE/DIST OFFICE MGR 727-940-5860

Representative Rob Bishop

Utah, 1st

123 CANNON HOB (ZIP: 20515-4401) **225-0453**
Andrade, Barbara SCHEDULER 123 CHOB 50453
Johnson, Paul LEGIS ASST 123 CHOB 50453
Lonsberry, Lee COMMUNICATIONS DIR/PRESS SECY 123 CHOB 50453
Murphy, Devon LEGIS ASST 123 CHOB 50453
Quesada Andrade, America LEGIS CORRES 123 CHOB 50453
Stewart, Adam LEGIS DIR 123 CHOB 50453
Wiser, Devin CHIEF OF STAFF 123 CHOB 50453

DISTRICT OFFICES

BRIGHAM CITY—6 N MAIN ST, BRIGHAM CITY, UT 84302 .... **801-625-0107**

OGDEN—1017 FED BLDG, 324 25TH ST, OGDEN, UT 84401
Campbell, Travis CONSTIT LIAISON 801-625-0107
Copps-Peters, Norma OFFICE MGR 801-625-0107
Hipp, David CONSTIT LIAISON 801-625-0107
Jenks, Peter DIST DIR 801-625-0107

VERNAL—152 E 100 NORTH, VERNAL, UT 84078 .... **435-781-5302**

Representative Sanford D. Bishop, Jr.

Georgia, 2d

2407 RAYBURN HOB (ZIP: 20515-1002) **225-3631**
Armstrong, Levar MIL FELLOW 2407 53631
Bacetty, Ada LEGIS FELLOW 2407 53631
Black, Jon SR POLICY ADVISOR 2407 53631
Bryant, Heather FINANCIAL ADMIN 2407 53631
Dodd, Owen SR POLICY ADVISOR 2407 53631
Halpern, Jonathan LEGIS DIR 2407 53631
Herbaugh, Cheryl LEGIS FELLOW 2407 53631
Hughes, Lauren OFFICE MGR/SCHEDULER 2407 53631
Newbold, Patrick MIL FELLOW 2407 53631
Rackard, N'Dea LEGIS CORRES/MGR - OUTREACH & COMMUNICATIONS 2407 53631
Reed, Michael CHIEF OF STAFF 2407 53631

DISTRICT OFFICES

ALBANY—323 PINE ST, SUITE 400, ALBANY, GA 31701
Bryant, Michael FIELD REP 229-439-8067
Cutts, Kenneth DIST DIR 229-439-8067
Fryer, Paul DIST FIELD REP 229-439-8067
Jones, Tammye DIST FIELD REP 229-439-8067
Pickel, Toni CONSTIT SVCS/OFFICE MGR 229-439-8067
Pickett, Krystal DIST STAFF ASST 229-439-8067
Wimbush, Tameka CONSTIT SVCS 229-439-8067

COLUMBUS—18 NINTH ST, SUITE 201, COLUMBUS, GA 31901
Cherry, Arnez CONSTIT SVCS 706-320-9477
Gillispie, Elaine FIELD REP 706-320-9477
Jones, Lenzie CASEWORK - VETS 706-320-9477
Sagul, Peggy CONSTIT SVCS 706-320-9477
Washington, Gerald STAFF ASST 706-320-9477

MACON—300 MULBERRY ST, SUITE 502, MACON, GA 31201
Apple, Haleigh DIST STAFF ASST 478-803-2631
Hill, Shavonda DPTY DIST DIR 478-803-2631
Kringer, Elizabeth CASEWKR 478-803-2631

Representative Earl Blumenauer

Oregon, 3d

1111 LONGWORTH HOB (ZIP: 20515-3703) **225-4811**
Bennett, Philip STAFF ASST/LEGIS CORRES 1111 54811
Bosworth, Jon LEGIS ASST 1111 54811
Cramer, Martha LEGIS ASST 1111 54811
King, Kyle SCHEDULER 1111 54811
Ryan, Sean PRESS SECY 1111 54811
Skillman, David LEGIS COUNSEL/DPTY CHIEF OF STAFF 1111 54811
Stockert, Kevin LEGIS ASST 1111 54811
Thrift, Laura LEGIS DIR 1111 54811

DISTRICT OFFICE

PORTLAND—911 NE 11TH AVE, SUITE 200, PORTLAND, OR 97232
Bergstad, Dillon CASEWK MGR 503-231-2300
Brumfield, Liv DIST FIELD REP 503-231-2300
Coghlan, Aisling DIST DIR 503-231-2300
Hudson, Stone STAFF ASST 503-231-2300
Little, Jason DIST SCHEDULER/FIELD REP 503-231-2300
Nguyen, Anna DIST PRESS SECY 503-231-2300
Pomeroy, Julia SR ADVISOR 503-231-2300
Reyna, Luz FIELD REP 503-231-2300
Schwartz, Mona FIELD REP 503-231-2300
Smith, Willie CHIEF OF STAFF 503-231-2300

Representative Lisa Blunt Rochester

Delaware, At Large

1519 LONGWORTH HOB (ZIP: 20515-0800) **225-4165**
Coulbourn, Betsey LEGIS ASST 1519 54165
Diggins, Megan LEGIS CORRES 1519 54165
Donnelly, Andrew LEGIS ASST 1519 54165
Hines, Kalila SCHEDULER 1519 54165
Jones, Kimberly DIST SCHEDULER 1519 54165
Morse, Kyle PRESS SECY 1519 54165
Sanchez, Jacqueline CHIEF OF STAFF 1519 54165
Vesey, Gabi STAFF ASST 1519 54165

DISTRICT OFFICES

GEORGETOWN—28 THE CIRCLE, SUITE 2, GEORGETOWN, DE 19947
Bonville, Diaz CONSTIT OUTREACH REP 302-858-4773

WILMINGTON—1105 N MARKET ST, SUITE 400, WILMINGTON, DE 19801
Dobson, Waynna CONSTIT SVCS REP 302-830-2330
McGregor, Courtney STATE DIR 302-830-2330
Weed, Krista CASEWKR 302-830-2330

Representative Suzanne Bonamici

Oregon, 1st

2231 RAYBURN HOB (ZIP: 20515-3701) **225-0855**
Arriaga, Jack LEGIS ASST 2231 ..... **50855**
Bornstein, Rachael CHIEF OF STAFF 2231 ..... **50855**
Bowen, Jessica LEGIS ASST 2231 ..... **50855**
Burgess, Amy OFFICE MGR 2231 ..... **50855**
Crofts, Natalie PRESS SECY 2231 ..... **50855**
Dunn, Andrew STAFF ASST/LEGIS CORRES 2231 ..... **50855**
Rank, Ethan SCHEDULER 2231 ..... **50855**
Smith, Allison LEGIS DIR/DPTY CHIEF OF STAFF 2231 ..... **50855**
Sugarman, Maxine LEGIS ASST 2231 ..... **50855**
Thompson, Cora TECH SUPPORT REP 2231 ..... **50855**

DISTRICT OFFICE

BEAVERTON—12725 SW MILLIKAN WAY, SUITE 220, BEAVERTON, OR 97005
TOLL-FREE NUMBER 1-800-422-4003
Araiza, Shirley DIST REP/OUTREACH REP **503-469-6010**
Baessler, Sarah DIST DIR **503-469-6010**
Fleming, Joyce CASEWKR/OUTREACH REP/DIST SCHEDULER **503-469-6010**
Haggerty, Phylicia DIST REP/CASEWKR/OUTREACH REP **503-469-6010**
Jevning, Marshal CASEWKR/OUTREACH REP/DIST REP **503-469-6010**
Mayeda, Ali DIST REP/OUTREACH REP/PRESS ASST . **503-469-6010**
Plinski, Brian CASEWKR/OUTREACH REP/DIST REP ... **503-469-6010**
Seed, Ryan DIST STAFF ASST **503-469-6010**

Representative Mike Bost

Illinois, 12th

1440 LONGWORTH HOB (ZIP: 20515-1312) **225-5661**
Bailey, Ashley LEGIS ASST 1440 ..... **55661**
Barger, Noah LEGIS ASST 1440 ..... **55661**
Cianciotti, Tyler SCHEDULER 1440 ..... **55661**
Evans, Melissa ADMIN - FINANCE & PAYROLL 1440 ..... **55661**
McCullough, Matt CHIEF OF STAFF 1440 ..... **55661**
O'Connor, George COMMUNICATIONS DIR 1440 ..... **55661**
Ratto, Mark LEGIS DIR 1440 ..... **55661**

DISTRICT OFFICES

CARBONDALE—300 E MAIN ST, CARBONDALE, IL 62901
Clayton, Janice CASEWKR **618-457-5787**
Connor, Evelyn CASEWKR **618-457-5787**
Moberly, Matthew DPTY DIST DIR **618-457-5787**

MT. VERNON—MT. VERNON CITY HALL, 1100 MAIN ST, MT. VERNON, IL 62864 618-513-5294

O'FALLON—302 W STATE ST, O'FALLON, IL 62269
Gallagher Main, Katherine CASEWKR **618-622-0766**
Manley, Dominique DIST STAFF ASST **618-622-0766**
Russel, Steve COORD - VETS OUTREACH **618-622-0766**
Tanzyus, David DIST DIR **618-622-0766**
Thurman, Mary DIST STAFF ASST **618-622-0766**

Representative Brendan F. Boyle

Pennsylvania, 2d

1133 LONGWORTH HOB (ZIP: 20515-3802) **225-6111**
Frame, Carly LEGIS ASST 1133 ..... **56111**
Hervig, Mary Beth STAFF ASST 1133 ..... **56111**
Maher, Dan SCHEDULER/SPECIAL ASST 1133 ..... **56111**
McCarthy, John CHIEF OF STAFF 1133 ..... **56111**
Soffen, Kim COMMUNICATIONS ASST 1133 ..... **56111**
Steinberg, Ted LEGIS ASST 1133 ..... **56111**
Tobin, Sean COMMUNICATIONS DIR 1133 ..... **56111**

DISTRICT OFFICES

FISHTOWN—2630 MEMPHIS ST, PHILADELPHIA, PA 19125
Enggasser, Harry CONSTIT SVCS REP **215-426-4616**
Heppard, Scott DIST DIR **215-426-4616**
Johnson, Tommy CONSTIT SVCS REP **215-426-4616**
Rzepski, Peg CONSTIT SVCS REP **215-426-4616**

NORTHEAST PHILADELPHIA—8572 BUSTLETON AVE, PHILADELPHIA, PA 19152
Feeney, Annamarie SR CONSTIT SVCS REP **215-335-3355**
Kennedy, James SPECIAL PROJ DIR **215-335-3355**
Lockman, Michele CONSTIT SVCS REP **215-335-3355**

OLNEY OFFICE—5675 NORTH FRONT ST, SUITE 180, PHILADELPHIA, PA 19120
Bellmon, Anthony CONSTIT SVCS REP **267-335-5643**
Dash, Carl CONSTIT SVCS REP **267-335-5643**
McKinney, Paula CONSTIT SVCS REP **267-335-5643**
Mulero, Sarah CONSTIT SVCS REP **267-335-5643**

Representative Kevin Brady

Texas, 8th

1011 LONGWORTH HOB (ZIP: 20515-4308) **225-4901**
Bray, Austin LEGIS COUNSEL 1011 ..... **54901**
Cureton, Laura SCHEDULING DIR 1011 ..... **54901**
Davis, David CHIEF OF STAFF 1011 ..... **54901**
Gwozdz, Isabelle DIGITAL PRESS SECY 1011 ..... **54901**
Lepire, Cami SR HEALTH POLICY ADVISOR 1011 ..... **54901**
Porter, John DPTY CHIEF OF STAFF - POLICY 1011 ..... **54901**
Roberts, Kaitlyn DPTY SCHEDULER 1011 ..... **54901**
Teehan, Shana COMMUNICATIONS DIR/SR ADVISOR 1011 ..... **54901**

DISTRICT OFFICES

CONROE—200 RIVER POINTE DR, SUITE 304, CONROE, TX 77304
Mardik, Thomas DPTY DIST DIR **936-441-5700**
Qureshi, Janet CASEWK DIR **936-441-5700**
Washburn, Heather DIST DIR **936-441-5700**

HUNTSVILLE—1300 11TH ST, SUITE 400, HUNTSVILLE, TX 77340
Schindler, Linda CASEWKR **936-439-9532**
Swarers, Vita CASEWK MGR **936-439-9532**

Representative Anthony Brindisi

New York, 22d

329 CANNON HOB (ZIP: 20515-3222) **225-3665**
Dougherty, Robert LEGIS DIR 329 CHOB **53665**
Ehlich, Bethany SCHEDULER 329 CHOB **53665**
Foster, Ellen CHIEF OF STAFF 329 CHOB **53665**
Jeffers, Connor LEGIS ASST - MIL 329 CHOB **53665**
Kaelin, Tommy PRESS ASST 329 CHOB **53665**
Lipe, Jon LEGIS ASST 329 CHOB **53665**
Matthews, Macey COMMUNICATIONS DIR 329 CHOB **53665**
Stankiewicz, Claudia STAFF ASST 329 CHOB **53665**

DISTRICT OFFICES

BINGHAMTON—49 COURT ST, SUITE 210, BINGHAMTON, NY 13901
Bergman, Faith DIST FIELD REP **607-242-0200**
Weiss, Harris DIST FIELD REP **607-242-0200**

UTICA—430 COURT ST, SUITE 102, UTICA, NY 13502
Bormann, Sarah DIST DIR **315-732-0713**
Phelps, David DIST FIELD REP **315-732-0713**
Stemen, John DIST FIELD REP **315-732-0713**

Taylor, Joelle DIST SCHEDULER 315-732-0713
Tobin, Kim DIST STAFF ASST 315-732-0713

Representative Mo Brooks

Alabama, 5th

2246 RAYBURN HOB (ZIP: 20515-0105) 225-4801
Decker, Bradford LEGIS CORRES 2246 54801
Engelking, Madison SCHEDULER/OFFICE MGR 2246 54801
Hamner, Caryn LEGIS ASST - MIL 2246 54801
Lindow, Michaila LEGIS AIDE 2246 54801
McQueen, Darby STAFF ASST 2246 54801
Mills, Clay COMMUNICATIONS DIR 2246 54801
Pettitt, Mark CHIEF OF STAFF 2246 54801
Yates, Marshall LEGIS COUNSEL/LEGIS DIR 2246 54801
Zams, Kelly FINANCIAL & ADMIN OFFICER 2246 54801

DISTRICT OFFICES

DECATUR—302 LEE ST, ROOM 86, DECATUR, AL 35601
Turner, Johnny DIST FIELD REP 256-355-9400

FLORENCE—102 S COURT ST, SUITE 310, FLORENCE, AL 35630
Webb Smith, Laura DIST FIELD REP 256-718-5155

HUNTSVILLE—2101 CLINTON AVE W, SUITE 302, HUNTSVILLE, AL 35805
Echols, Deborah CASEWKR 256-551-0190
Jackson, Timothy CASEWKR 256-551-0190
Murray, Kathryn DIST FIELD REP 256-551-0190
Noel, Tiffany DIST DIR 256-551-0190

Representative Susan W. Brooks

Indiana, 5th

2211 RAYBURN HOB (ZIP: 20515-1405) 225-2276
Card, Becky PRESS SECY 2211 52276
Chandler, Danny SYS ADMIN 2211 52276
Goodwin, Natalie DC SCHEDULER 2211 52276
Hamilton, Emma LEGIS CORRES 2211 52276
Hicks, Rob LEGIS DIR 2211 52276
Johnson, Kristen SPEECHWRITER 2211 52276
Knowles, Catherine DPTY CHIEF OF STAFF 2211 52276
McMenamin, Erin LEGIS ASST 2211 52276
Roos, Amber FINANCIAL ASST 2211 52276
Savage, Megan CHIEF OF STAFF 2211 52276

DISTRICT OFFICES

ANDERSON—120 E 8TH ST, SUITE 101, ANDERSON, IN 46016
Meeker, Autumn CONSTIT SVCS REP 765-640-5115
Sulc, Kevin DPTY DIST DIR 765-640-5115

CARMEL—11611 N MERIDIAN ST, SUITE 415, CARMEL, IN 46032
TOLL-FREE NUMBER 1-800-382-6020
Bagi, Jennifer DIST SCHEDULER 317-848-0201
Burian, David CONSTIT SVCS REP 317-848-0201
Glaser, Karen DIST DIR/DPTY CHIEF OF STAFF 317-848-0201
Lueders, Mary DIR - CONSTIT SVCS 317-848-0201

Representative Anthony G. Brown

Maryland, 4th

1323 LONGWORTH HOB (ZIP: 20515-2004) 225-8699
Cooper, Hannah LEGIS CORRES 1323 58699
Cox, Lindsey DIR - OPS 1323 58699
Deatley, James LEGIS ASST 1323 58699
Estes, Maia CHIEF OF STAFF 1323 58699
Matthews, Michael LEGIS ASST 1323 58699
Platt, Anna LEGIS DIR 1323 58699
Raelea, Taylor STAFF ASST 1323 58699
Rayner, Jonathan LEGIS ASST - MIL 1323 58699
Teicher, Ethan DPTY PRESS SECY 1323 58699
Verghese, Matthew DPTY CHIEF OF STAFF/COMMUNICATIONS DIR 1323 58699

DISTRICT OFFICES

ANNE ARUNDEL—2666 RIVA RD, SUITE 120, ANNAPOLIS, MD 21401 410-266-3249

PRINCE GEORGE'S COUNTY—9701 APOLLO DR, SUITE 103, UPPER MARLBORO, MD 20774
Hannon, Tiffany CONSTIT SVCS 301-458-2600
Horton, Isiah CONSTIT SVCS 301-458-2600
Karbowsky, Jared CONSTIT SVCS 301-458-2600
Pleasant, LaTriece STAFF ASST 301-458-2600
Schoultz, Nichelle DIST DIR 301-458-2600
Wolff, Ben DPTY DIST DIR 301-458-2600

Representative Julia Brownley

California, 26th

2262 RAYBURN HOB (ZIP: 20515-0526) 225-5811
Barker, Brooke PRESS ASST 2262 55811
Cousimano, Jonathan OUTREACH DIR/SCHEDULER 2262 55811
Greene, Samantha COMMUNICATIONS DIR 2262 55811
Hague, Danny LEGIS ASST 2262 55811
Jones, Stephanie FELLOW 2262 55811
Koppula, Sujit STAFF ASST 2262 55811
Ross, Gavin LEGIS ASST 2262 55811
Wagener, Sharon LEGIS DIR 2262 55811
Young, Lenny CHIEF OF STAFF 2262 55811

DISTRICT OFFICES

OXNARD—201 E 4TH ST, SUITE 209B, OXNARD, CA 93030
Bravo, Sandra CASEWKR/DIST SCHEDULER 805-379-1779

THOUSAND OAKS—223 E THOUSAND OAKS BLVD, SUITE 220, THOUSAND OAKS, CA 91360
Armenta, Carina DIST DIR 805-379-1779
Davis, Marcee DIST REP 805-379-1779
Orgel, Cheri DPTY DIST DIR 805-379-1779
Orozco, Ashley DIST REP 805-379-1779
Rasch, Terry FELLOW 805-379-1779
Vazquez, Ruth STAFF ASST 805-379-1779

Representative Vern Buchanan

Florida, 16th

2427 RAYBURN HOB (ZIP: 20515-0916) 225-5015
Brady, Sean DPTY CHIEF 2427 55015
Cruz, Anthony COMMUNICATIONS DIR 2427 55015
Karvelas, David CHIEF OF STAFF 2427 55015
Knight, Jaclyn SCHEDULER 2427 55015
Lampman, Zachary STAFF ASST 2427 55015
Plush, Lewis LEGIS CORRES 2427 55015
Rose, Ashley SR COUNSEL 2427 55015
Spencer, Christian LEGIS ASST 2427 55015

DISTRICT OFFICES

BRADENTON—1051 MANATEE AVE W, SUITE 305, BRADENTON, FL 34205
Buchman, MarDee CASEWKR 941-747-9081
Tibbetts, Gary FIELD REP 941-747-9081

SARASOTA—111 S ORANGE AVE, SUITE 202W, SARASOTA, FL 34236
Conboy, Chloe CASEWKR 941-951-6643

Hansen, Joni CONSTIT SVCS REP 941-951-6643
Tibbetts, Sally DIST DIR 941-951-6643
Woodie, Darrell FIELD REP 941-951-6643

Representative Ken Buck

Colorado, 4th

2455 RAYBURN HOB (ZIP: 20515-0604) 225-4676
Braden, Ansley SCHEDULER 2455 54676
Butherus, Danny LEGIS CORRES 2455 54676
Hampson, James LEGIS DIR 2455 54676
Jaarda, Christopher COUNSEL 2455 54676
Lopez, Janessa LEGIS AIDE 2455 54676
Robertson, Ritika CHIEF OF STAFF 2455 54676
Yanick, Brittany COMMUNICATIONS DIR 2455 54676

DISTRICT OFFICES

CASTLE ROCK—900 CASTLETON RD, SUITE 112, CASTLE ROCK, CO 80109
Chaves, Erika DIST REP 720-639-9165
Coran, Robin DPTY DIST DIR 720-639-9165

GREELEY—1023 39TH AVE, UNIT B, GREELEY, CO 80634
Ford, Molly DIST REP 970-702-2136
Johnson, Dusty DIST REP 970-702-2136
Leblanc, Cody DIST REP 970-702-2136

Representative Larry Bucshon

Indiana, 8th

2313 RAYBURN HOB (ZIP: 20515-1408) 225-4636
TOLL-FREE NO. 1-866-567-0227
Bean, David LEGIS CORRES 2313 54636
Davis, Melanie SYS ADMIN 2313 54636
Davis, Susan LEGIS ASST 2313 54636
Graff, Jessica SCHEDULER 2313 54636
Hansen, Andrew COMMUNICATIONS DIR 2313 54636
Jackson, Kyle CHIEF OF STAFF 2313 54636
Killeen, Sarah DPTY CHIEF OF STAFF/LEGIS DIR 2313 54636
Lester, Dean OFFICE ADMIN 2313 54636
Moore, Dylan SR LEGIS ASST 2313 54636
Roberts, Connor STAFF ASST 2313 54636

DISTRICT OFFICES

EVANSVILLE—420 MAIN ST, SUITE 1402, EVANSVILLE, IN 47708
Biggs, Lora DIR - CONSTIT SVCS 812-465-6484
Johnston, Allison FIELD REP 812-465-6484
Jones, Carol DIST DIR 812-465-6484
Newell, Ashley CONSTIT SVCS REP/STAFF ASST 812-465-6484

TERRE HAUTE—901 WABASH AVE, SUITE 140, TERRE HAUTE, IN 47807
Lucas, Erin SPECIAL PROJ DIR 812-232-0523
Murray, Kristin STAFF ASST 812-232-0523
Pollock, Samuel FIELD REP 812-232-0523

Representative Ted Budd

North Carolina, 13th

118 CANNON HOB (ZIP: 20515-3313) 225-4531
Bell, Andrew CHIEF OF STAFF 118 CHOB 54531
Dews, Elizabeth DIR - SCHED/ADMIN 118 CHOB 54531
Haymore, Tyler LEGIS ASST 118 CHOB 54531
Jennings, Chase COMMUNICATIONS DIR 118 CHOB 54531
Shumate, Sam LEGIS CORRES 118 CHOB 54531
Vargo, Alex LEGIS DIR 118 CHOB 54531

DISTRICT OFFICES

ADVANCE—128 PEACHTREE LANE, SUITE A, ADVANCE, NC 27006
Blackburn, Sara CONSTIT SVCS REP 336-998-1313
McDowell, Addison CONSTIT SVCS REP 336-998-1313
Moxley, Richard CONSTIT SVCS REP 336-998-1313
Poole, Todd DIST DIR 336-998-1313
Sherrill, Savanna CONSTIT SVCS REP 336-998-1313

HIGH POINT—1208 EASTCHESTER DR, SUITE 203, HIGH POINT, NC 27265
Safley, Cam CONSTIT SVCS REP 336-858-5013

Representative Tim Burchett

Tennessee, 2d

1122 LONGWORTH HOB (ZIP: 20515-4202) 225-5435
Brannock, Phoebe LEGIS CORRES 1122 55435
Dooley, Zach LEGIS DIR 1122 55435
Grider, Michael CHIEF OF STAFF 1122 55435
Maloof, Michael LEGIS ASST 1122 55435
Strother, Will LEGIS ASST 1122 55435
Whiteside, Donovan EXEC ASST 1122 55435
Woodward, Canon STAFF ASST 1122 55435

DISTRICT OFFICES

KNOXVILLE—800 MARKET ST, SUITE 110, KNOXVILLE, TN 37902
Fansler, Sarah DIR - COMMUNITY OUTREACH 865-523-3772
Gibson, Pat FIELD REP - VETS/CASEWKR 865-523-3772
Heinsohn, Madison CASEWKR 865-523-3772
Lambert, Denise SCHEDULER/DIR - FINANCE 865-523-3772
Linginfelter, Jennifer DIST DIR/COMMUNICATIONS DIR 865-523-3772
Stansberry, Jennifer SR CASEWKR 865-523-3772

MARYVILLE—331 COURT ST, MARYVILLE, TN 37804
Cameron, Charles FIELD REP 865-984-5464

Representative Michael C. Burgess

Texas, 26th

2161 RAYBURN HOB (ZIP: 20515-4326) 225-7772
Albrecht, Madison STAFF ASST 2161 57772
Allen, Elizabeth LEGIS ASST 2161 57772
Baldwin, Amanda DPTY CHIEF OF STAFF 2161 57772
Curran, Pat LEGIS CORRES 2161 57772
Decker, James CHIEF OF STAFF 2161 57772
Huggins, Rachel LEGIS DIR 2161 57772
Thomson, Emma COMMUNICATIONS DIR 2161 57772
Yancey, Michael LEGIS ASST 2161 57772

DISTRICT OFFICE

LAKE DALLAS—2000 S STEMMONS FWY, SUITE 200, LAKE DALLAS, TX 75065
Coffey, Jim DIST OUTREACH REP 940-497-5031
Loomis, Jane CONSTIT LIAISON 940-497-5031
McCormick-Torres, Melanie CASEWK DIR 940-497-5031
Self, Joan DIST AIDE 940-497-5031
Vaughan, Robin DPTY DIST DIR 940-497-5031
With, Erik DIST DIR 940-497-5031

Representative Cheri Bustos

Illinois, 17th

1233 LONGWORTH HOB (ZIP: 20515-1317) **225-5905**
Bezruki, Steffanie SR POLICY ADVISOR 1233 .... **55905**
Higgins, Sean COMMUNICATIONS DIR 1233 .... **55905**
Huch, Leighton LEGIS ASST 1233 .... **55905**
Miller, Gabrielle OUTREACH & MBR SVCS ASST 1233 .... **55905**
Papa, Katie OFFICE MGR 1233 .... **55905**
Piccioli, Laura SCHEDULER 1233 .... **55905**
Pyatt, Jon CHIEF OF STAFF 1233 .... **55905**
Reuschel, Trevor DPTY CHIEF OF STAFF 1233 .... **55905**
Sibley, Sean DPTY PRESS SECY/STAFF ASST 1233 .... **55905**
Steadman, Liam LEGIS CORRES 1233 .... **55905**

DISTRICT OFFICES

PEORIA—820 SW ADAMS ST, PEORIA, IL 61602
Rude, Laura CONSTIT ADVOCATE **309-966-1813**

ROCKFORD—119 N CHURCH ST, SUITE 101, ROCKFORD, IL 61101
Montoya-Picazo, Ricardo CONSTIT ADVOCATE/FIELD REP **815-968-8011**
Torina, Gabrielle CONSTIT ADVOCATE/FIELD REP **815-968-8011**

ROCK ISLAND—2401 4TH AVE, ROCK ISLAND, IL 61201
French, Miranda DIR - CONSTIT SVCS **309-786-3406**
Jennings, Kate DIST DIR **309-786-3406**
Labotte, Ellie CONSTIT ADVOCATE **309-786-3406**
Vanhecke, Lucie DIST SCHEDULER/DPTY DIST DIR ... **309-786-3406**

Representative G. K. Butterfield

North Carolina, 1st

2080 RAYBURN HOB (ZIP: 20515-3301) **225-3101**
Bowen, Lindsey EXEC ASST/SCHEDULER 2080 .... **53101**
Brown, Kendra CHIEF OF STAFF 2080 .... **53101**
Graham, Timothy LEGIS AIDE 2080 .... **53101**
Julius, Nicole COMMUNICATIONS DIR/POLICY ADVISOR 2080 .. **53101**
Malicdem, Aaron-John STAFF ASST/DIR - OPS 2080 .... **53101**
Parker, Kyle SR POLICY ADVISOR 2080 .... **53101**
Shim, Wonyong LEGIS CORRES 2080 .... **53101**
Sills, Dennis LEGIS DIR 2080 .... **53101**

DISTRICT OFFICES

DURHAM—2741 CAMPUS WALK AVE, BLDG 400, SUITE 300, DURHAM, NC 27705
Burwell, Dollie DIR - CONSTIT SVCS **919-908-0164**
Piard, Christina DIR - COMMUNITY OUTREACH **919-908-0164**

WILSON—216 NE NASH ST, SUITE B, WILSON, NC 27893
Britton, Cammie DPTY DIR - CONSTIT SVCS **252-237-9816**
Ricks, Rosena CONSTIT SVCS REP **252-237-9816**
Speight, Reginald DIST DIR **252-237-9816**

Representative Bradley Byrne

Alabama, 1st

119 CANNON HOB (ZIP: 20515-0101) **225-4931**
Bishop, Matthew STAFF ASST 119 CHOB **54931**
Carlough, Chad CHIEF OF STAFF 119 CHOB **54931**
Fry, Miriam SR LEGIS ASST 119 CHOB **54931**
Howard, Jordan SCHEDULER 119 CHOB **54931**
Miller, Jacob STAFF ASST - COMMUNICATIONS 119 CHOB **54931**
Morrow, Seth DPTY CHIEF OF STAFF/DIR - PRESS & COMMUNICATIONS 119 CHOB **54931**
Relfe, Mitch LEGIS DIR/LEGIS COUNSEL 119 CHOB **54931**
Strub, Hannah LEGIS ASST - MIL 119 CHOB **54931**

DISTRICT OFFICES

BALDWIN COUNTY—502 W LEE AVE, SUMMERDALE, AL 36580
Clark, Allison CONSTIT SVCS REP **251-989-2664**

MOBILE—11 N WATER ST, SUITE 15290, MOBILE, AL 36602
TOLL-FREE NUMBER **1-800-288-USA1**
Jackson, Brandy CONSTIT SVCS REP/COORD - GRANTS **251-690-2811**
Miller, Kathryn CONSTIT SVCS REP **251-690-2811**
Nicholson, Nikki CONSTIT SVCS REP/SPECIAL EVENTS **251-690-2811**
Payne, Frazier DPTY DIST DIR/FIELD REP **251-690-2811**
Roney, Elizabeth DIST DIR **251-690-2811**

Representative Ken Calvert

California, 42d

2205 RAYBURN HOB (ZIP: 20515-0542) **225-1986**
Evans, Tricia DPTY CHIEF OF STAFF/EXEC ASST 2205 .... **51986**
Fuentes, Joe LEGIS ASST 2205 .... **51986**
Keightley, Rebecca LEGIS DIR/DPTY CHIEF OF STAFF 2205 .... **51986**
Kennett, Dave CHIEF OF STAFF 2205 .... **51986**
McReynolds, Allyson LEGIS ASST 2205 .... **51986**
O'Connell, Richie SR LEGIS ASST 2205 .... **51986**
Smith, Chandler STAFF ASST 2205 .... **51986**

DISTRICT OFFICE

CORONA CITY HALL—400 S VICENTIA AVE, SUITE 125, CORONA, CA 92882
Gagnon, Jason COMMUNICATIONS DIR **951-277-0042**
Lansing, Jackie CASEWKR **951-277-0042**
McGavran, Kathleen CASEWKR **951-277-0042**
Murphy, Jolyn DIST DIR **951-277-0042**
Rimke, Shawna CASEWKR/DIST REP **951-277-0042**
Rodriguez, Nathan STAFF ASST **951-277-0042**

Representative Salud O. Carbajal

California, 24th

1431 LONGWORTH HOB (ZIP: 20515-0524) **225-3601**
Hokit, Max LEGIS CORRES/LEGIS AIDE 1431 .... **53601**
Juarez, Nancy LEGIS DIR/DPTY CHIEF OF STAFF 1431 .... **53601**
Miller, Leila PRESS ASST/STAFF ASST 1431 .... **53601**
Montiel, Johanna LEGIS ASST 1431 .... **53601**
Sandlin, Erin EXEC ASST/LEGIS ASST 1431 .... **53601**
Tittle, Jeremy CHIEF OF STAFF 1431 .... **53601**
Whittlesey, Tess COMMUNICATIONS DIR 1431 .... **53601**
Yea, Annie LEGIS ASST - MIL 1431 .... **53601**

DISTRICT OFFICES

SAN LUIS OBISPO —1411 MARSH ST, SUITE 205, SAN LUIS OBISPO, CA 93401
Cox, Caitlin CASEWKR/DIST REP **805-546-8348**
Haas, Greg DIST REP/CASEWKR **805-546-8348**
Reyes, Erica DIST REP/CASEWKR **805-546-8348**

SANTA BARBARA —360 S HOPE AVE, C-301, SANTA BARBARA, CA 93105
Ebadi, Jesse DIST REP/CASEWKR **805-730-1710**
Figueroa, Blanca CASEWKR/DIST REP **805-730-1710**
Henson, Chris DIST CHIEF OF STAFF **805-730-1710**
Motta, Wendy DIST REP/CASEWKR **805-730-1710**
Villanueva, Diana DIST SCHEDULER **805-730-1710**

SANTA MARIA—1619 S THORNBURG ST, SANTA MARIA, CA 93458 805-730-1710

Representative Tony Cárdenas

California, 29th

2438 RAYBURN HOB (ZIP: 20515-0529) **225-6131**
Franco, Miguel CHIEF OF STAFF 2438 .... **56131**
Galloway, Meghann LEGIS COUNSEL 2438 .... **56131**
Gonzalez, Sergio SHARED EMPLOYEE 2438 .... **56131**
Kolb, Devin SCHEDULER 2438 .... **56131**
LaSalle, Kenny LEGIS AIDE 2438 .... **56131**
Oo, Olivia LEGIS ASST 2438 .... **56131**
Serrano Ruvalcaba, Jaqueline LEGIS ASST 2438 .... **56131**
Stevens, Kimberly FINANCIAL ADMIN 2438 .... **56131**
Thatte, Tejasi DPTY CHIEF OF STAFF/LEGIS DIR 2438 .... **56131**
Zaragoza, Patricia STAFF ASST 2438 .... **56131**

DISTRICT OFFICE

PANORAMA CITY—9612 VAN NUYS BLVD, SUITE 201, PANORAMA CITY, CA 91402
De Lara, Pablo CASEWKR **818-221-3718**
Gonzalez, Lea Margarita FIELD REP **818-221-3718**
Marquez, Gabriela DIST DIR **818-221-3718**
Ramirez, Osvaldo CASEWKR **818-221-3718**
Rodriguez, Christina CONG AIDE **818-221-3718**

Representative André Carson

Indiana, 7th

2135 RAYBURN HOB (ZIP: 20515-1407) **225-4011**
Bennett, Nathan LEGIS DIR/DPTY CHIEF 2135 .... **54011**
Martin, Andrea LEGAL COUNSEL/SR POLICY ADVISOR 2135 .... **54011**
Rudolph, Kim CHIEF OF STAFF 2135 .... **54011**
Said, Hadeel STAFF ASST 2135 .... **54011**
Sheehan, Leo LEGIS ASST 2135 .... **54011**
Tucker, Copeland COMMUNICATIONS DIR 2135 .... **54011**
Wilkinson, Zachery LEGIS ASST 2135 .... **54011**
Woytcke, Holly EXEC ASST 2135 .... **54011**

DISTRICT OFFICE

INDIANAPOLIS—300 E FALL CREEK PKWY N DR, SUITE 300, INDIANAPOLIS, IN 46205
Fitzpatrick, Felicity DIST EXEC ASST **317-283-6516**
Garcia, Jessica CASEWKR **317-283-6516**
Harvey, Heather CASEWORK - VETS **317-283-6516**
House, Marc STAFF ASST **317-283-6516**
Scott, Andrea CASEWKR/COORD - COMMUNITY OUTREACH **317-283-6516**
Sims, Megan DIST DIR **317-283-6516**
Snorton, Clifton DIST EXEC ASST **317-283-6516**
Souchet-Moura, Kathy COORD - OUTREACH /IMMIGRATION LIAISON **317-283-6516**

Representative Earl L. "Buddy" Carter

Georgia, 1st

2432 RAYBURN HOB (ZIP: 20515-1001) **225-5831**
Bowen, S K PRESS ASST/STAFF ASST 2432 .... **55831**
Carpenter, Mary DPTY CHIEF OF STAFF/COMMUNICATIONS DIR 2432 .... **55831**
Crawford, Chris CHIEF OF STAFF 2432 .... **55831**
Gulsehn, Jay ADVISOR - HEALTH POLICY 2432 .... **55831**
Holden, Caroline LEGIS CORRES 2432 .... **55831**
Miller, Brooke EXEC ASST 2432 .... **55831**
Schemmel, Nick LEGIS DIR 2432 .... **55831**
Thompson, Hart LEGIS ASST 2432 .... **55831**

DISTRICT OFFICES

BRUNSWICK—1510 NEWCASTLE ST, SUITE 200, BRUNSWICK, GA 31520
Nolan, Emmitt FIELD REP **912-265-9010**

SAVANNAH—6602 ABERCORN ST, SAVANNAH, GA 31405
Bazemore, Bruce CASEWKR **912-352-0101**
Childers, Brooke DIST DIR **912-352-0101**
Dowdy, Tracy STAFF ASST **912-352-0101**
Hall, Hunter DIST FIELD REP **912-352-0101**
Powell, Lee Ann DIST STAFF ASST **912-352-0101**

Representative John R. Carter

Texas, 31st

2110 RAYBURN HOB (ZIP: 20515-4331) **225-3864**
Bender, Evan LEGIS ASST 2110 .... **53864**
Bourn, Grady LEGIS DIR 2110 .... **53864**
Garrison, Samuel STAFF ASST/DPTY PRESS SECY 2110 .... **53864**
Korst, Andrew LEGIS CORRES 2110 .... **53864**
Rice, Kelicia DPTY CHIEF OF STAFF 2110 .... **53864**
Schroeder, Robert CONG FELLOW/NATIONAL SECUR ADVISOR 2110 .... **53864**
Yost, Eric MIL FELLOW 2110 .... **53864**
Yurik, Karl MIL FELLOW 2110 .... **53864**

DISTRICT OFFICES

BELL COUNTY—6544B S GENERAL BRUCE DR, TEMPLE, TX 76502
Hassmann, Cheryl DIST FIELD REP **254-933-1392**
Key, Matthew CONSTIT LIAISON **254-933-1392**

ROUND ROCK—1717 N INTERSTATE HWY 35, SUITE 303, ROUND ROCK, TX 78664
Alvarado, August DIST DIR **512-246-1600**
Alvarado, Marie SR ADVISOR **512-246-1600**
Doss, Jade CASEWKR **512-246-1600**
Dowdell, Emily COMMUNICATIONS DIR **512-246-1600**
Miller, Jonas CHIEF OF STAFF **512-246-1600**
Pena, Nancy LIAISON - CONSTIT SVCS **512-246-1600**
Sharifian, Julie CONSTIT REP **512-246-1600**

Representative Matt Cartwright

Pennsylvania, 8th

1034 LONGWORTH HOB (ZIP: 20515-3808) **225-5546**
Coffey, Stephen LEGIS DIR 1034 .... **55546**
Felix, Melvin PRESS SECY 1034 .... **55546**
Kirschke-Schwartz, Evie SCHEDULER/LEGIS CORRES 1034 .... **55546**
Marcus, Jeremy DPTY CHIEF OF STAFF 1034 .... **55546**
Ridgway, Hunter CHIEF OF STAFF 1034 .... **55546**

DISTRICT OFFICES

SCRANTON—226 WYOMING AVE, SCRANTON, PA 18503
Aita, Tammy DPTY DIST DIR/DIST SCHEDULER **570-341-1050**
Dowd, Brian DIST STAFF ASST **570-341-1050**
Gerrity, Colleen COMMUNICATIONS DIR **570-341-1050**
Manganello, Jennifer CASEWKR/SPEECHWRITER **570-341-1050**
Mecadon, Christa CASEWKR **570-341-1050**
Morgan, Bob DPTY CHIEF OF STAFF/DIST DIR **570-341-1050**

WILKES-BARRE—20 N PENNSYLVANIA AVE, SUITE 201, WILKES-BARRE, PA 18711
Caceres, Christa CASEWKR **570-371-0317**
Hanley, William ECON DEV REP **570-371-0317**
Niver, April ECON DEV SPEC **570-371-0317**

Representative Ed Case

Hawaii, 1st

2443 RAYBURN HOB (ZIP: 20515-1101) 225-2726
Burgess, Amy OFFICE MGR 2443 52726
Chao, Ken-Ben LEGIS CORRES 2443 52726
Ching, Anthony POLICY ADVISOR 2443 52726
Heidenreich, Mitch STAFF ASST 2443 52726
Ka'Aikala, Shanise SCHEDULER 2443 52726
Nelson, Timothy CHIEF OF STAFF/LEGIS DIR 2443 52726
Smith, Kana LEGIS ASST 2443 52726
Thompson, Cora INFO SYS SECUR MGR 2443 52726

DISTRICT OFFICE

HONOLULU—1132 BISHOP ST, SUITE 1910, HONOLULU, HI 96813
Conant, Jacqueline DIST DIR 808-650-6688
Garcia, Nestor COMMUNICATIONS DIR 808-650-6688
Kobayashi, Asami DIST STAFF ASST 808-650-6688
Ryan, Kimberly DIST STAFF ASST 808-650-6688
Wolke, Chad DIST STAFF ASST 808-650-6688

Representative Sean Casten

Illinois, 6th

429 CANNON HOB (ZIP: 20515-1306) 225-4561
Adler, Ann CHIEF OF STAFF 429 CHOB 54561
Bankman-Fried, Gabe LEGIS CORRES 429 CHOB 54561
Carlos, Maddie COMMUNICATIONS DIR 429 CHOB 54561
Chintamani, Sameer SCHEDULER 429 CHOB 54561
Pazik, Meghan STAFF ASST 429 CHOB 54561
Shapiro, Calli LEGIS DIR 429 CHOB 54561
Tatarian, Lisa FINANCIAL ADMIN 429 CHOB 54561
Wojcicki, Sam LEGIS ASST 429 CHOB 54561

DISTRICT OFFICE

DISTRICT OFFICE—2700 INTERNATIONAL DR, SUITE 304, WEST CHICAGO, IL 60185
Arnesen, Emma STAFF ASST 630-520-9450
Kalinich, Gail SR POLICY ADVISOR 630-520-9450
Nerad, Jason CASEWKR 630-520-9450
Wick, Anne DIST DIR 630-520-9450

Representative Kathy Castor

Florida, 14th

2052 RAYBURN HOB (ZIP: 20515-0914) 225-3376
Barr, Jacob LEGIS ASST 2052 53376
Brown, Elizabeth LEGIS DIR 2052 53376
Hopkins, Lara SCHEDULER/DPTY CHIEF OF STAFF 2052 53376
Jackson, Joicelynne LEGIS ASST 2052 53376
Phillips, Clay CHIEF OF STAFF 2052 53376
Rhoden, Steven STAFF ASST 2052 53376
Robayo, Maria LEGIS CORRES 2052 53376

DISTRICT OFFICE

TAMPA—4144 N ARMENIA AVE, SUITE 300, TAMPA, FL 33607
TOLL-FREE NUMBER 1-888-266-0205
Angotti, Steven COORD - GRANTS/PRESS SECY 813-871-2817
Fernandez, Tania CONSTIT SVCS 813-871-2817
Givens, Patricia DIST OFFICE MGR 813-871-2817
Gonzalez, Damaris CONSTIT SVCS 813-871-2817
Mallory, DeWayne OUTREACH DIR 813-871-2817
Martinez-Cartagena, Charles PRESS ASST/OUTREACH ASST 813-871-2817
Mejia, Marcia DIST DIR 813-871-2817
Sanchez, Tery CONSTIT SVCS 813-871-2817

Representative Joaquin Castro

Texas, 20th

2241 RAYBURN HOB (ZIP: 20515-4320) 225-3236
Geller, Jamie COMMUNICATIONS DIR 2241 53236
Krueger, Christian LEGIS CORRES 2241 53236
Mbongo, Eyole LEGIS CORRES/STAFF ASST 2241 53236
Meza, Danny CHIEF OF STAFF 2241 53236
Montan, Kaitlyn LEGIS ASST 2241 53236
Moon, Danielle SCHEDULER/LEGIS AIDE 2241 53236
Schneider, Katherine PRESS SECY 2241 53236
Thomas, Ben LEGIS DIR 2241 53236

DISTRICT OFFICE

SAN ANTONIO—727 E CESAR E CHAVEZ BLVD, SUITE B-128, SAN ANTONIO, TX 78206
Hernandez-Serna, Antonietta DIST DIR 210-348-8216
Maldonado, Rose Ann DIR - CONSTIT SVCS 210-348-8216
Martinez, Austin CONSTIT SVCS REP 210-348-8216
Rodriguez, Jasmine CONSTIT SVCS REP 210-348-8216
Tarango-Chavez, Emily CONSTIT SVCS REP 210-348-8216
Whitehead, Benjamin COORD - GRANTS & SPEC PROJ 210-348-8216

Representative Steve Chabot

Ohio, 1st

2408 RAYBURN HOB (ZIP: 20515-3501) 225-2216
Barton, Stacy CHIEF OF STAFF 2408 52216
Burton-Jones, Elizabeth PRESS AIDE 2408 52216
Erste, Mark LEGIS ASST 2408 52216
Feldman, Lisa SCHEDULER 2408 52216
Harris, Erick LEGIS COUNSEL 2408 52216
Lowe, Jonathan LEGIS DIR 2408 52216
Mercer, Ian LEGIS CORRES 2408 52216
Pirc, Austin STAFF ASST 2408 52216

DISTRICT OFFICES

CINCINNATI—441 VINE ST, SUITE 3003, CINCINNATI, OH 45202
Abner, Joe DIST DIR 513-684-2723
Chenault, Randy CONSTIT LIAISON 513-684-2723
Fultz, Rosalind CONSTIT LIAISON 513-684-2723
Garlock, Emily CONSTIT LIAISON 513-684-2723
Griffith, Brian COMMUNICATIONS DIR 513-684-2723

WARREN COUNTY—11 S BROADWAY ST, LEBANON, OH 45036
McCandless, David DIST REP 513-421-8704

Representative Liz Cheney

Wyoming, At Large

416 CANNON HOB (ZIP: 20515-5000) 225-2311
TOLL-FREE NO. 1-888-879-3599
Ahern, Kara CHIEF OF STAFF 416 CHOB 52311
Cowles, Charlotte LEGIS ASST 416 CHOB 52311
Fosina, Andrew LEGIS CORRES 416 CHOB 52311
Henderson, Will SPECIAL ASST TO THE CHAIR 416 CHOB 52311
Heussner, Holly LEGIS ASST 416 CHOB 52311
Hughes, Scott DPTY CHIEF OF STAFF 416 CHOB 52311
Murphy, Kelly FINANCIAL ADMIN 416 CHOB 52311
Santino, Tony MIL FELLOW 416 CHOB 52311
Seago, Katelyn SCHEDULER 416 CHOB 52311

Weast, Maddy PRESS SECY 416 CHOB 52311
Wetherald, Margaret FINANCIAL ADMIN 416 CHOB 52311

DISTRICT OFFICES

CASPER—100 EAST B ST, ROOM 4003, CASPER, WY 82602
King, Jackie FIELD REP 307-261-6595
Lafountain, Charity FIELD REP 307-261-6595

CHEYENNE—2120 CAPITOL AVE, SUITE 8005, CHEYENNE, WY 82001
Allen, Rachel FIELD REP 307-772-2595
Hooper, Tammy STATE DIR 307-772-2595
Rossi, Karmen FIELD REP 307-772-2595

GILLETTE—300 S GILLETTE AVE, SUITE 2000, GILLETTE, WY 82716
Fischer, Jordan FIELD REP 307-414-1677

RIVERTON—325 W MAIN ST, UNIT B, RIVERTON, WY 82501
Linn, Lindy FIELD REP 307-277-9701

Representative Judy Chu

California, 27th

2423 RAYBURN HOB (ZIP: 20515-0527) 225-5464
DeSai, Sonali LEGIS DIR 2423 55464
Giammarella, Alyssa SCHEDULER 2423 55464
Hamilton, Ellen SR LEGIS ASST 2423 55464
Kaai, Krystal EXEC DIR 2423 55464
Mathur, Rricha LEGIS COUNSEL 2423 55464
Menefee-Libey, Nell STAFF ASST 2423 55464
Nickson, Michael FINANCIAL ADMIN 2423 55464
Shim, Linda CHIEF OF STAFF 2423 55464
Silberberg, David LEGIS AIDE 2423 55464
Suarato, Ben COMMUNICATIONS DIR 2423 55464

DISTRICT OFFICES

CLAREMONT—415 FOOTHILL BLVD, SUITE 122, CLAREMONT, CA 91711
Robles, Enrique DPTY DIST DIR 909-625-5394

PASADENA—527 S LAKE AVE, SUITE 250, PASADENA, CA 91101
Cheng, Becky DIST DIR 626-304-0110
Horton, Jonathan STAFF ASST 626-304-0110
Jacobs, Lauren CONSTIT SVCS REP 626-304-0110
Lee, Cindy CONSTIT SVCS REP 626-304-0110
Plake, Lindsay SCHEDULER 626-304-0110
Plan, Maile FIELD REP/CASEWKR 626-304-0110
Robles, Enrique DPTY DIST DIR 626-304-0110

Representative David N. Cicilline

Rhode Island, 1st

2233 RAYBURN HOB (ZIP: 20515-3901) 225-4911
Brennan, Ross LEGIS ASST 2233 54911
Grubar, Francis SCHEDULER 2233 54911
Karafotas, Peter CHIEF OF STAFF 2233 54911
Luchette, Richard COMMUNICATIONS DIR 2233 54911
McGinn, Matthew LEGIS ASST 2233 54911
Nagaraj, Renuka LEGIS COUNSEL 2233 54911
Padavic, Samantha LEGIS CORRES 2233 54911
Sarkisian Tatarian, Alisa LEGIS COUNSEL/DIR - FINANCE 2233 54911
Trister, Sarah LEGIS DIR/DPTY CHIEF OF STAFF 2233 54911

DISTRICT OFFICE

PAWTUCKET—1070 MAIN ST, SUITE 300, PAWTUCKET, RI 02860
Bauerle, Brent CONSTIT SVCS REP 401-729-5600
Bizzacco, Chris DIST DIR 401-729-5600
Lis, Jakub DIST SCHEDULER 401-729-5600
Murphy, Rita DIR - CONSTIT AFFAIRS 401-729-5600
Pease, Annie CONSTIT SVCS REP 401-729-5600
Silva, Max LIAISON - MIL & VET/CONSTIT SVCS REP 401-729-5600
Suchite, Rogelio CASEWKR 401-729-5600

Representative Gilbert Ray Cisneros, Jr.

California, 39th

431 CANNON HOB (ZIP: 20515-0539) 225-4111
Acornley, Mark FINANCIAL ADMIN 431 CHOB 54111
Campbell, Annie SCHEDULER 431 CHOB 54111
Gonzalez, Sergio TECH SUPPORT REP 431 CHOB 54111
Jordan, Nicholas CHIEF OF STAFF 431 CHOB 54111
Norvell, Emma LEGIS DIR 431 CHOB 54111
Ou, Howard POLICY ADVISOR 431 CHOB 54111
Quibuyen, Michael PRESS SECY 431 CHOB 54111
Rivera Romero, Thomas LEGIS CORRES 431 CHOB 54111
Robles, Ruby STAFF ASST 431 CHOB 54111
Sivalingam, Yuvaraj NATIONAL SECUR ADVISOR 431 CHOB 54111

DISTRICT OFFICE

FULLERTON—1440 N HARBOR BLVD, SUITE 601, FULLERTON, CA 92835
Flores, Erika SR FIELD REP 714-459-4575
Hanson, Marc DIST DIR 714-459-4575
Medrano, Martin DPTY DIST DIR 714-459-4575
Orozco Valencia, Esmeralda STAFF ASST 714-459-4575
Sigala, Daphne DIST SCHEDULER 714-459-4575
Wade, Christopher FIELD REP 714-459-4575
Yow, Jocelyn CASEWK MGR 714-459-4575

Representative Katherine M. Clark

Massachusetts, 5th

2448 RAYBURN HOB (ZIP: 20515-2105) 225-2836
Alexander, Kathryn COMMUNICATIONS DIR 2448 52836
Browning, Geoff LEGIS ASST 2448 52836
Einterz, Frannie LEGIS ASST 2448 52836
Hsu, Yvonne SR ADVISOR 2448 52836
Karve, Chai CONSTIT OUTREACH REP 2448 52836
Piepho, Judah SCHEDULER 2448 52836
Scannell, Brooke CHIEF OF STAFF 2448 52836
Tatarian, Alisa ADMIN - FINANCE & PAYROLL 2448 52836
Thornton, Steve LEGIS DIR 2448 52836
Zieh, Joy STAFF ASST/LEGIS CORRES 2448 52836

DISTRICT OFFICES

CAMBRIDGE—701 CONCORD AVE, SUITE 101, CAMBRIDGE, MA 02138
Higgins, Jay CONSTIT SVCS REP 617-354-0292
House, Jon LIAISON - MIL & VET 617-354-0292
Perkins, Kelsey DIST DIR 617-354-0292
Worley, Katie CONSTIT SVCS REP 617-354-0292

METROWEST REGIONAL—116 CONCORD ST, SUITE 1, FRAMINGHAM, MA 01702
Blackman, Wade LEGAL COUNSEL/CONSTIT SVCS 508-319-9757

Representative Yvette D. Clarke

New York, 9th

2058 RAYBURN HOB (ZIP: 20515-3209) 225-6231
Anderson, Kwamme DPTY CHIEF OF STAFF 2058 56231
Ash, Earl LEGIS AIDE 2058 56231

Dorfman, David LEGIS DIR 2058 56231
Greenfield, George INFO TECH SYS ANALYST 2058 56231
Mitchell, Kendall STAFF ASST 2058 56231
Stallings, Tria SCHEDULER 2058 56231
Stanberry, Charlyn CHIEF OF STAFF 2058 56231
Sundahl, Alan ADMIN - FINANCE & PAYROLL 2058 56231

DISTRICT OFFICE

BROOKLYN—222 LENOX RD, SUITES 1 & 2, BROOKLYN, NY 11226
Bishop, Mary DIST REP 718-287-1142
Collis, Lystra DIST REP 718-287-1142
Mohamed, Mohamed DPTY DIST REP 718-287-1142
Slavin, Eli DIST REP 718-287-1142
Taylor, Anita DIST DIR 718-287-1142

Representative Wm. Lacy Clay

Missouri, 1st

2428 RAYBURN HOB (ZIP: 20515-2501) 225-2406
Alexis, Matt STAFF ASST 2428 52406
Cravins, Yvette CHIEF OF STAFF 2428 52406
Doss, Darrell POLICY ADVISOR 2428 52406
Long, Karyn EXEC ASST/SCHEDULER 2428 52406
Powell, Erica LEGIS DIR 2428 52406

DISTRICT OFFICES

EAGLETON —111 S 10TH ST, SUITE 24.344, SAINT LOUIS, MO 63102
Massey, Edwilla DIR - CONSTIT SVCS 314-367-1970
Williams, Samantha DIST AIDE 314-367-1970

FIRST BANK BUILDING—1281 GRAHAM RD, SUITE 202, SAINT LOUIS, MO 63031 314-383-5240

GRAVOIS—6830 GRAVOIS AVE, SAINT LOUIS, MO 63116
Engelhardt, Steven COMMUNICATIONS DIR 314-669-9393

Representative Emanuel Cleaver

Missouri, 5th

2335 RAYBURN HOB (ZIP: 20515-2505) 225-4535
Adiele, Frances LEGIS FELLOW 2335 54535
Greenfield, George SYS ADMIN 2335 54535
Helfant, Matt DIR - DIGITAL MEDIA/LEGIS AIDE 2335 54535
Mahoney, Christina LEGIS DIR 2335 54535
Mathieu, Herline DC SCHEDULER/LEGIS AIDE 2335 54535
Morrissette, Eric SR POLICY ADVISOR 2335 54535
Ndikum, Alex LEGIS AIDE 2335 54535
Seidman, Pearl LEGIS FELLOW 2335 54535
Shapiro, Jennifer CHIEF OF STAFF 2335 54535
Spencer, Harden STAFF ASST 2335 54535

DISTRICT OFFICES

HIGGINSVILLE—1923 MAIN ST, HIGGINSVILLE, MO 64037
Wilkens, Kyle DIR - RURAL POLICY 660-584-7373

INDEPENDENCE—411 MAPLE AVE, SUITE F, INDEPENDENCE, MO 64050
Cameron, Breanna LIAISON - MIL & VET 816-833-4545

KANSAS CITY—101 W 31ST ST, KANSAS CITY, MO 64108
Dunn, Randy COMMUNITY AFFAIRS LIAISON 816-842-4545
Frierson, Heather COMMUNICATIONS DIR 816-842-4545
Frost, Whitney DIST DIR 816-842-4545
Long, Holly EXEC ASST/SCHEDULER 816-842-4545
Montgomery, Kelli POLICY COORD 816-842-4545
Salas-Abarca, Manny COMMUNITY LIAISON 816-842-4545
Smith, Vernetta EXEC ASST 816-842-4545
Vaughn, Jim SPECIAL PROJ COORD 816-842-4545

Representative Ben Cline

Virginia, 6th

1009 LONGWORTH HOB (ZIP: 20515-4606) 225-5431
Bagwell, Eric SR LEGIS ASST 1009 55431
Davis, Melanie SYS ADMIN 1009 55431
Hanrahan, Matthew LEGIS CORRES 1009 55431
Hook, Tyler STAFF ASST 1009 55431
Kaczmarek, Beth SCHEDULER 1009 55431
Manley, Nicole LEGIS DIR 1009 55431
Miller, Matt CHIEF OF STAFF 1009 55431
Pence, Hallie SR LEGIS ASST 1009 55431
Saylor, Ryan COMMUNICATIONS DIR 1009 55431

DISTRICT OFFICES

HARRISONBURG—70 N MASON ST, SUITE 110, HARRISONBURG, VA 22802
Adams, Tyler DIST FIELD REP 540-432-2391
Loope, Emilee DIST REP/COMMUNICATIONS ASST 540-432-2391
Wicht, Emily DIST REP 540-432-2391

LYNCHBURG—916 MAIN ST, SUITE 300, LYNCHBURG, VA 24504
Van Allen, Aaron DIST REP 434-845-8306

ROANOKE—10 FRANKLIN RD, SUITE 510, ROANOKE, VA 54011
Broughton, Christine DIST REP 540-857-2672
Croke, Kjersten DIST REP 540-857-2672
Faulkner, Jennifer DIST SCHEDULER 540-857-2672
Hayden, Kathy DIST REP 540-857-2672

STAUNTON—117 S LEWIS ST, SUITE 215, STAUNTON, VA 24401
Garrett, Debbie DIST DIR 540-885-3861

Representative Michael Cloud

Texas, 27th

1314 LONGWORTH HOB (ZIP: 20515-4327) 225-7742
Bailey, Jennifer FINANCIAL ADMIN 1314 57742
Fike, Hugh LEGIS DIR 1314 57742
Frasier, Savannah SR COMMUNICATIONS STRATEGIST/SR COMMUNICATIONS ADVISOR 1314 57742
Helms, Emily SCHEDULER 1314 57742
Magary, Adam CHIEF OF STAFF 1314 57742
McHan, Abby LEGIS ASST/LEGIS CORRES 1314 57742
Nail, Sarah-Hope LEGIS ASST/LEGIS CORRES 1314 57742
White, Logan STAFF ASST 1314 57742

DISTRICT OFFICES

CORPUS CHRISTI—101 N SHORELINE BLVD, SUITE 305, CORPUS CHRISTI, TX 78401
Buentello, Luis FIELD REP 361-884-2222
Cadena, Jaran STAFF ASST 361-884-2222
Kennedy, J D DIST DIR 361-884-2222
Lawrence, Erik SPECIAL PROJ/FED LIAISON 361-884-2222

VICTORIA—111 N GLASS ST, VICTORIA, TX 77901
Beamer, Nicole CASEWK DIR 361-894-6446
Cruickshanks, Brian COMMUNICATIONS DIR 361-894-6446
Gloor, Jackie SPECIAL PROJ 361-894-6446
Longoria, Mark DPTY DIST DIR/DIST FIELD REP 361-894-6446

Representative James E. Clyburn

South Carolina, 6th

200 CANNON HOB (ZIP: 20515-4006) 225-3315
Gause, Nkili LEGIS CORRES 200 CHOB 53315
Ismail, Seth LEGIS CORRES 200 CHOB 53315
Lee, Keonte STAFF ASST 200 CHOB 53315

Lyles, Willie LEGIS DIR 200 CHOB 53315
Watkins, Yelberton R CHIEF OF STAFF 200 CHOB 53315

DISTRICT OFFICES

COLUMBIA—1225 LADY ST, SUITE 200, COLUMBIA, SC 29201

Hunter, Robert FIELD REP 803-799-1100
Maple, Kaala CASEWKR 803-799-1100
Maxwell, Ana STAFF ASST 803-799-1100
Maxwell, Bryanta DIST EXEC ASST 803-799-1100
Nance, Robert DIST DIR 803-799-1100
Rickenbacker, John FIELD DIR 803-799-1100
Saunders, William FIELD REP - VETS 803-799-1100
Stukes, Gail CASEWKR 803-799-1100
Tresvant, Dalton DIRECTOR 803-799-1100
Ward, Larry DIST AIDE 803-799-1100

KINGSTREE—130 W MAIN ST, KINGSTREE, SC 29556

Barnes, Kenneth CASEWK MGR 843-355-1211

Representative Steve Cohen

Tennessee, 9th

2104 RAYBURN HOB (ZIP: 20515-4209) 225-3265

Dillihay, Marilyn CHIEF OF STAFF 2104 53265
Dudley, Betsy SR LEGIS ASST 2104 53265
Fitzgerald, Frances STAFF ASST 2104 53265
Lipow, Alex STAFF ASST/SCHEDULER 2104 53265
Rogers, Merrilee LEGIS CORRES 2104 53265
Schnelle, Alex LEGIS ASST 2104 53265
Smith, Sawyer PRESS ASST 2104 53265
Sullivan, Bart COMMUNICATIONS DIR 2104 53265
Weisman, Matthew LEGIS DIR/COUNSEL 2104 53265

DISTRICT OFFICE

MEMPHIS—167 N MAIN ST, SUITE 369, MEMPHIS, TN 38103

Douglas, Victori STAFF ASST 901-544-4131
Henry, Wiley CONSTIT SVCS REP 901-544-4131
Henry, Willie DPTY DIST DIR 901-544-4131
Jordan, Jeremy CONSTIT SVCS REP 901-544-4131
Marsh, Patti EXEC ASST/DIST SCHEDULER 901-544-4131
Maynard, Rick CONSTIT SVCS REP 901-544-4131
Self, Beanie DPTY DIST DIR 901-544-4131
Thomas, Marzie DIST DIR 901-544-4131

Representative Tom Cole

Oklahoma, 4th

2207 RAYBURN HOB (ZIP: 20515-3604) 225-6165

Bowie, Maria LEGIS DIR/DPTY CHIEF OF STAFF 2207 56165
Cloud, Carter LEGIS ASST 2207 56165
Corley, Sarah COMMUNICATIONS DIR 2207 56165
Grogis, Joshua CHIEF OF STAFF 2207 56165
Hand, Shane LEGIS ASST 2207 56165
Jackson, Joshua LEGIS ASST 2207 56165
Parker, Sabrina EXEC ASST 2207 56165
Stooksbury, Melissa STAFF ASST 2207 56165

DISTRICT OFFICES

ADA—100 E 13TH ST, SUITE 213, ADA, OK 74820

Savage, Amber FIELD REP 580-436-5375

LAWTON—711 SW D AVE, SUITE 201, LAWTON, OK 73501

Chance, Scott FIELD REP 580-357-2131

NORMAN—2424 SPRINGER DR, SUITE 201, NORMAN, OK 73069

Head, Lisa CASEWKR/OFFICE MGR 405-329-6500
Homer, Debe CASEWKR 405-329-6500
Lewis, Thomas FIELD REP 405-329-6500
McPherson, William DIST DIR 405-329-6500
Mitchell, Charlotte DIST SCHEDULER 405-329-6500

Representative Chris Collins

New York, 27th

2243 RAYBURN HOB (ZIP: 20515-3227) 225-5265

Arndt, Eric SR LEGIS ASST 2243 55265
Brown, Jennifer PRESS ASST 2243 55265
Gannon, Kevin LEGIS ASST 2243 55265
Hook, Erynn CHIEF OF STAFF 2243 55265
Hook, Michael SR ADVISOR 2243 55265
Paulsen, Megan EXEC ASST 2243 55265
Ritchie, Ryan STAFF ASST 2243 55265

DISTRICT OFFICES

CLARENCE—8203 MAIN ST, SUITE 2, CLARENCE, NY 14221

Gould, Alexandra DIR - CONSTIT SVCS 716-634-2324
Hicks, Michael LIAISON - CONSTIT SVCS 716-634-2324
McNerney, George FIELD DIR 716-634-2324

GENESEO—128 MAIN ST, SUITE 3, GENESEO, NY 14454

Dougherty, Shannon LIAISON - CONSTIT SVCS 585-519-4002
Ogra, Alexis LIAISON - CONSTIT SVCS 585-519-4002

Representative Doug Collins

Georgia, 9th

1504 LONGWORTH HOB (ZIP: 20515-1009) 225-9893

Andrews, Jess COMMUNICATIONS DIR 1504 59893
Ashworth, Dan COUNSEL 1504 59893
Barker, Erica SR LEGIS AIDE 1504 59893
Belair, Brendan STAFF DIR 1504 59893
Ferro, Jon PARLIAMENTARIAN 1504 59893
Larson, Sally Rose DPTY CHIEF OF STAFF 1504 59893
Mullinax, Cooper SPECIAL ASST 1504 59893
Rogers, Jacob STAFF ASST 1504 59893
Smith, William LEGIS AIDE 1504 59893
Wall, Erin EXEC ASST 1504 59893
Yates, Ella COORD - MBR SVCS & OUTREACH 1504 59893

DISTRICT OFFICE

GAINESVILLE—210 WASHINGTON ST NW, SUITE 202, GAINESVILLE, GA 30501

Dyer, Cindy DIR - CONSTIT SVCS 770-297-3388
Gonzalez-Thompson, Amanda COMMUNICATIONS DIR 770-297-3388
Katz, Joel CHIEF OF STAFF 770-297-3388
Kokaly, Bill FIELD REP 770-297-3388
McDonald, David FIELD REP 770-297-3388
Riley, Tena DIST STAFF ASST 770-297-3388

Representative James Comer

Kentucky, 1st

1037 LONGWORTH HOB (ZIP: 20515-1701) 225-3115

Bowling, Michelle PRESS SECY/LEGIS ASST 2184 53115
Cash, Caroline CHIEF OF STAFF 2184 53115
Coffman, Sarah LEGIS ASST/COORD - GRANTS & SPEC PROJ 2184 53115
Douthitt, Lily STAFF ASST 1037 53115
Goldenstein, Jim LEGIS DIR 2184 53115

Walker, Amanda FINANCIAL ADMIN 2184 53115
Wolfe, Katy DIR - OPS 2184 53115

DISTRICT OFFICES

MADISONVILLE—67 N MAIN ST, MADISONVILLE, KY 42431
Wilson, Amelia FIELD REP 270-487-9509

PADUCAH—300 S 3RD ST, PADUCAH, KY 42003
Wiles, Martie SR FIELD REP 270-408-1865

TOMPKINSVILLE—200 N MAIN ST, SUITE F, TOMPKINSVILLE, KY 42167
TOLL-FREE NUMBER 1-180-032-8562 X9
Anderson, Jenna CONSTIT SVCS REP 270-487-9509
Gossum, Michael COMMUNICATIONS DIR 270-487-9509
King, Luke DIR - CONSTIT SVCS 270-487-9509
Simpson, Sandy DIST DIR 270-487-9509

Representative K. Michael Conaway

Texas, 11th

2469 RAYBURN HOB (ZIP: 20515-4311) 225-3605
Bell, Lyssa STAFF ASST 2469 53605
Heflin, Jena COORD - DIGITAL MEDIA 2469 53605
Horder, Michael SR LEGIS ASST 2469 53605
Hytha, Emily COMMUNICATIONS DIR 2469 53605
Mullins, Maggie SCHEDULER 2469 53605
Russell, Matthew LEGIS DIR 2469 53605
Sauvage, Charles LEGIS CORRES 2469 53605
Siddiqui, Faisal SYS ADMIN 2469 53605
Wetherald, Margaret FINANCIAL ADMIN 2469 53605
Williams, Mark CHIEF OF STAFF 2469 53605

DISTRICT OFFICES

BROWNWOOD—CITY HALL, 501 CENTER AVE, BROWNWOOD, TX 76801
Stegemoller, Hilary REGIONAL DIR 325-646-1950

GRANBURY—132 N HOUSTON ST, GRANBURY, TX 76048
Williams, Diane REGIONAL DIR 682-936-2577

LLANO—CO ANNEX, 104 W SANDSTONE ST, LLANO, TX 78643
Watson, Nancy REGIONAL DIR 325-247-2826

MIDLAND—6 DESTA DR, SUITE 2000, MIDLAND, TX 79705
TOLL-FREE NUMBER 1-866-882-3811
Padilla, Corbette REGIONAL DIR 432-687-2390
Thomas, Evan DIST DIR 432-687-2390

ODESSA—411 W 8TH ST, 5TH FLOOR, CITY MANAGER'S OFFICE, ODESSA, TX 79761
Apolinario, Gloria FIELD REP 432-331-9667

SAN ANGELO—O C FISHER FED BLDG, 33 E TWOHIG AVE, SUITE 307, SAN ANGELO, TX 76903
Powell, Jo Anne REGIONAL DIR 325-659-4010

Representative Gerald E. Connolly

Virginia, 11th

2238 RAYBURN HOB (ZIP: 20515-4611) 225-1492
Burroughs, Nicholas STAFF ASST 2238 51492
Cole, Molly LEGIS ASST 2238 51492
Covington, Lauren SCHEDULER 2238 51492
Davenport, Collin LEGIS DIR 2238 51492
Lam, Kristine LEGIS ASST 2238 51492
Smith, Jamie COMMUNICATIONS DIR 2238 51492
Walkinshaw, James CHIEF OF STAFF 2238 51492

DISTRICT OFFICES

ANNANDALE—4115 ANNANDALE RD, SUITE 103, ANNANDALE, VA 22003
Malec, Nicole CONSTIT SVCS REP 703-256-3071
Montgomery, Billy CONSTIT SVCS REP 703-256-3071
Robbins, Alex CONSTIT OUTREACH REP 703-256-3071
Stark, Sharon DIST DIR 703-256-3071

WOODBRIDGE—2241-D TACKETT'S MILL DR, WOODBRIDGE, VA 22192
Dubuisson, Marlon OUTREACH REP 571-408-4407

Representative Paul Cook

California, 8th

1027 LONGWORTH HOB (ZIP: 20515-0508) 225-5861
Fresquez, Michael COMMUNICATIONS DIR 1027 55861
Hartl, Kellie EXEC ASST 1027 55861
Kuhns, Colby LEGIS ASST - MIL/LEGIS DIR 1027 55861
Porter, Christopher FIELD REP 1027 55861
Sobel, John CHIEF OF STAFF 1027 55861
Yang, Rosemary PRESS ASST 1027 55861

DISTRICT OFFICE

APPLE VALLEY—14955 DALE EVANS PKWY, APPLE VALLEY, CA 92307
Denison, Rick FIELD REP 760-247-1815
Higgins, Dakota DPTY DIST DIR 760-247-1815
Itnyre, Timothy DIST DIR 760-247-1815
Leja, Jan FIELD REP 760-247-1815
Messen, Kimberly OFC ASST 760-247-1815

Representative Jim Cooper

Tennessee, 5th

1536 LONGWORTH HOB (ZIP: 20515-4205) 225-4311
Balser, James ATTORNEY 1536 54311
Hawkins, Jazzelynn LEGIS CORRES 1536 54311
Jackson, Brandi SCHEDULER 1536 54311
Lumia, Jason LEGIS DIR/DPTY CHIEF OF STAFF 1536 54311
Mathews, Ella STAFF ASST 1536 54311
McWherter, Mary LEGIS ASST 1536 54311

DISTRICT OFFICE

NASHVILLE—605 CHURCH ST, NASHVILLE, TN 37219
Feldhaus, Katie DIST SCHEDULER 615-736-5295
Floyd-Buggs, Kathy OFFICE DIR/DIR - COMMUNITY OUTREACH 615-736-5295
Ince, Cara COMMUNICATIONS DIR 615-736-5295
Oliver, Charlane DIST FIELD REP 615-736-5295
Quigley, Lisa CHIEF OF STAFF 615-736-5295
Rapoport, Sylvia FELLOW 615-736-5295
Wood, John IMMIGRATION LIAISON/SR CONSTIT LIAISON 615-736-5295

Representative J. Luis Correa

California, 46th

1039 LONGWORTH HOB (ZIP: 20515-0546) 225-2965
Barrie, Elizabeth LEGIS ASST/COORD - INTERN & FELLOW/LEGIS CORRES 1039 52965
Flores, Tony STAFF ASST 1039 52965
Gonzalez, Sergio SYS ADMIN 1039 52965
Kermott, Julia SCHEDULER 1039 52965
Khan, Sheresh PRESS ASST/LEGIS ASST 1039 52965
Mendez, Emilio LEGIS DIR 1039 52965
Moore, Shane FINANCIAL ADMIN 1039 52965

Saroff, Laurie CHIEF OF STAFF 1039 52965
Scibetta, Andrew COMMUNICATIONS DIR 1039 52965

DISTRICT OFFICE

SANTA ANA—2323 N BROADWAY, SUITE 319, SANTA ANA, CA 92706

Brown, Janet DIST FIELD REP 714-559-6190
Gallegos, Claudio DIST DIR 714-559-6190
Guevara, Jose FIELD REP - VETS/DIST FIELD REP 714-559-6190
Le, Christy DIST FIELD REP 714-559-6190
Madrid, Max DIST REP 714-559-6190
Martinez, Laura CASEWKR 714-559-6190
Perez, Cassandra DIST SCHEDULER 714-559-6190
Rolnicki, Rachel DIST FIELD REP 714-559-6190

Representative Jim Costa

California, 16th

2081 RAYBURN HOB (ZIP: 20515-0516) 225-3341
Feldman, Jared LEGIS DIR/LEGIS COUNSEL 2081 53341
Fluellen, Ian LEGIS ASST 2081 53341
Fox, Alexa LEGIS ASST 2081 53341
Goldeen, Ben SR POLICY ADVISOR 2081 53341
Karapetyan, Elina SCHEDULER 2081 53341
López, Juan CHIEF OF STAFF 2081 53341
Schueler, Jacob LEGIS CORRES/PRESS ASST 2081 53341

DISTRICT OFFICES

FRESNO—855 M ST, SUITE 940, FRESNO, CA 93721

Altounian, Denise DIST REP 559-495-1620
Bourbon, Christy DIST SCHEDULER 559-495-1620
Garcia, Sandra DIST REP 559-495-1620
Gill, Kelly DIR - CONSTIT SVCS 559-495-1620
Jones-Johnson, Tammy PRESS SECY 559-495-1620
Mahan, Kathy DPTY CHIEF OF STAFF/DIST DIR 559-495-1620
Quezada, Jose DIST STAFF ASST 559-495-1620

MERCED—2222 M ST, SUITE 305, MERCED, CA 95340

Gomes, Nick DIST REP 209-384-1620
Gutierrez, Jailene DIST REP 209-384-1620
Hulbert, Gabe DIST REP 209-384-1620

Representative Joe Courtney

Connecticut, 2d

2332 RAYBURN HOB (ZIP: 20515-0702) 225-2076
Cassidy, Patrick COMMUNICATIONS DIR 2332 52076
Combelic, Alexa LEGIS DIR 2332 52076
Corcoran, Kathleen SCHEDULER 2332 52076
Costigan, Maria LEGIS ASST 2332 52076
King, Emma DPTY DIST DIR 2332 52076
McKiernan, Neil CHIEF OF STAFF 2332 52076
Menchel, Samuel LEGIS CORRES 2332 52076
O'Sullivan, Meghan LEGIS ASST 2332 52076
Salazar, Catalina STAFF ASST - COMMUNICATIONS 2332 52076
Sehr, Gabriel LEGIS ASST - MIL 2332 52076

DISTRICT OFFICES

ENFIELD—77 HAZARD AVE, UNIT J, ENFIELD, CT 06082

Devivo, Brianna FIELD REP 860-741-6011
Reutter, Matthew CONSTIT SVCS 860-741-6011
Weseliza, Karen CONSTIT SVCS 860-741-6011

NORWICH—55 MAIN ST, SUITE 250, NORWICH, CT 06360

Anderson, Taijah CONSTIT SVCS/COORD - OUTREACH 860-886-0139
Balidemaj, Egzon DIST STAFF ASST 860-886-0139
Grant, Ayanti DIST DIR 860-886-0139
Meneses, Manuel CASEWORK - VETS 860-886-0139
Tewksbury, Gene CONSTIT SVCS 860-886-0139

Representative TJ Cox

California, 21st

1728 LONGWORTH HOB (ZIP: 20515-0521) 225-4695
Genard, Francois CHIEF OF STAFF 1728 54695
Godinich, Drew COMMUNICATIONS DIR 1728 54695
Henderson, Jared LEGIS DIR 1728 54695
Mikhanjian, Lucine STAFF ASST 1728 54695
Rodriguez, Fabiola LEGIS ASST/PRESS SECY 1728 54695
Stayton, Amanda LEGIS AIDE 1728 54695

DISTRICT OFFICES

BAKERSFIELD—2700 M ST, SUITE 250B, BAKERSFIELD, CA 93301

Felix, Gilbert DIST DIR 661-864-7736
Sedano, Cody DIST REP 661-864-7736

SELMA—2117 SELMA ST, SELMA, CA 93662

Lopez, Joseph DIST REP 559-460-6070
Madrigal, Lindsey DIST SCHEDULER 559-460-6070
Penaloza, Virginia DIR - CONSTIT SVCS 559-460-6070

Representative Angie Craig

Minnesota, 2d

1523 LONGWORTH HOB (ZIP: 20515-2302) 225-2271
Ambrose, Myles LEGIS CORRES 1523 52271
Bodey, Mikayla SR LEGIS ASST 1523 52271
Goel, Purva STAFF ASST 1523 52271
Kunin, Tamara CHIEF OF STAFF 1523 52271
Martinez, Natalie LEGIS ASST 1523 52271
Mitchell, Will LEGIS DIR 1523 52271
Peterson, Savanna SCHEDULER 1523 52271
Rierson, Megumi PRESS ASST 1523 52271

DISTRICT OFFICE

BURNSVILLE—12940 HARRIET AVE S, BURNSVILLE, MN 55337

Allen, Morris SR COMMUNITY LIAISON 651-846-2120
Coe, Nicholas DIST DIR 651-846-2120
Diaz, Cristina CONSTIT ADVOCATE 651-846-2120
Fowler, Nathaniel CONSTIT LIAISON 651-846-2120
Gates, Jen COMMUNICATIONS DIR 651-846-2120
Gumbiner, Caleigh CONSTIT ADVOCATE 651-846-2120
Rahn, Samuel DIST SCHEDULER 651-846-2120
Siebenaler, Michael SR ADVISOR 651-846-2120

Representative Eric A. "Rick" Crawford

Arkansas, 1st

2422 RAYBURN HOB (ZIP: 20515-0401) 225-4076
Campbell, Jay LEGIS ASST 2422 54076
Crittenden, Allison SR LEGIS ASST 2422 54076
Handey, Courtney SCHEDULER 2422 54076
Holcomb, John LEGIS CORRES 2422 54076
King, Kathryn RESEARCH ASST 2422 54076
Robertson, Sara PRESS SECY 2422 54076
Selvey, David FIELD REP 2422 54076
Shelton, Ashley LEGIS DIR 2422 54076
Shumate, Jonah CHIEF OF STAFF 2422 54076

DISTRICT OFFICES

CABOT—112 S FIRST ST, CABOT, AR 72023

Sherrod, Jay FIELD REP 501-843-3043

DUMAS—101 E WATERMAN ST, DUMAS, AR 71639..... 870-377-5571

JONESBORO—2400 E HIGHLAND DR, SUITE 300, JONESBORO, AR 72401

Burgess, Abbi LEGIS ASST/CASEWKR 870-203-0540
Davenport, Tammy SR CASEWKR 870-203-0540
Hicks, Allison OFFICE MGR/CASEWKR 870-203-0540
Landrum, Charles FIELD REP 870-203-0540
Mitchell, Sherrie CASEWKR 870-203-0540
Nail, Mitchell FIELD REP 870-203-0540

MOUNTAIN HOME—1001 HWY 62 E, SUITE 9, MOUNTAIN HOME, AR 72653

Painter, Stetson FIELD REP 870-424-2075

Representative Dan Crenshaw

Texas, 2d

413 CANNON HOB (ZIP: 20515-4302) 225-6565
TOLL-FREE NO. 1-866-425-6565

Anderson, Hannah LEGIS ASST 413 CHOB 56565
Baker, Eliza CHIEF OF STAFF 413 CHOB 56565
DePew, Kenneth LEGIS ASST 413 CHOB 56565
Eubanks, Sydney STAFF ASST 413 CHOB 56565
Hodge, Matthew LEGIS DIR 413 CHOB 56565
Hood, Nikolai LEGIS CORRES 413 CHOB 56565
Rom, Kerry COMMUNICATIONS DIR 413 CHOB 56565
Ruhlen, Mary ADMIN - FINANCE & PAYROLL 413 CHOB 56565
Walden, Daniel ADMIN DIR 413 CHOB 56565

DISTRICT OFFICE

KINGWOOD—1801 KINGWOOD DR, SUITE 240, KINGWOOD, TX 77339

Cambio, Kaaren FIELD REP 713-860-1330
Harrison, Amy CASEWK MGR 713-860-1330
Pertierra, Ericka SPECIAL PROJ 713-860-1330
Walden, Susan DIST DIR 713-860-1330

Representative Charlie Crist

Florida, 13th

215 CANNON HOB (ZIP: 20515-0913) 225-5961

Banks, Linda FINANCIAL MGR 215 CHOB 703-619-5919
Durrer, Austin CHIEF OF STAFF 215 CHOB 55961
Fisher, Chris LEGIS DIR 215 CHOB 55961
Hanson, Sarah SR LEGIS ASST 215 CHOB 55961
McGuire, Ryan LEGIS ASST 215 CHOB 55961
Pekkala, Jonathan SCHEDULER/OFFICE MGR/CHIEF OPS OFFICER 215 CHOB 55961
Poe, Virginia LEGIS ASST 215 CHOB 55961
Ramirez, Samantha ASST PRESS SECY 215 CHOB 55961
Ramirez Quintero, Samantha PRESS ASST 215 CHOB 55961
Thompson, David LEGIS CORRES 215 CHOB 55961

DISTRICT OFFICE

DOWNTOWN ST. PETE—696 1ST AVE N, SUITE 203, ST. PETERSBURG, FL 33701

Batista, Michael CONSTIT SVCS REP 727-318-6770
Cary, Steven DIST DIR 727-318-6770
Faulkner, Gershom DPTY DIST DIR 727-318-6770
Kessock, Chloe PRESS ASST/COORD - CONSTIT SVCS 727-318-6770
Lewis, Kendrick COORD - DIST OUTREACH/DIST PRESS SECY 727-318-6770
Stafford, Dillion CONSTIT SVCS REP 727-318-6770

Representative Jason Crow

Colorado, 6th

1229 LONGWORTH HOB (ZIP: 20515-0606) 225-7882

Ball, Alex CHIEF OF STAFF 1229 57882
Feldman, Anne COMMUNICATIONS DIR 1229 57882
Gonzalez, Santiago POLICY ADVISOR 1229 57882
Green, Jon LEGIS ASST - MIL 1229 57882
Groce, Aaron STAFF ASST 1229 57882
Meuse, Justin LEGIS DIR 1229 57882
Natonski, Liz CHIEF OPS OFFICER 1229 57882

DISTRICT OFFICE

AURORA—3300 S PARKER RD, SUITE 100, AURORA, CO 80014

Al Shadood, Maytham DIST DIR 720-748-7514
Dewillis-Marcano, Alyson CONSTIT ADVOCATE 720-748-7514
Marceny, Veronica CONSTIT ADVOCATE 720-748-7514
Riley, Daniel CONSTIT ADVOCATE 720-748-7514
Roberts, Madeline STAFF ASST 720-748-7514
Traylor, Katrice DIR - CONSTIT SVCS 720-748-7514
Vargas, Kevin CONSTIT ADVOCATE 720-748-7514

Representative Henry Cuellar

Texas, 28th

2372 RAYBURN HOB (ZIP: 20515-4328) 225-1640

Abadie, Madeline SCHEDULER 2209 51640
Andrews, Ninamarie SPECIAL ASST 2372 51640
Bernacke, Michael LEGIS FELLOW 2372 51640
Edmonson, Catherine DPTY CHIEF OF STAFF 2372 51640
Forbes, Stacy LEGIS FELLOW 2372 51640
Garcia, Alexis LEGIS FELLOW 2372 51640
Kaighin, Kevin MIL FELLOW 2372 51640
Knight, Travis SR LEGIS AIDE/COUNSEL 2372 51640
Lester, Dean ADMIN - FINANCE & PAYROLL 2372 51640
O'Connor, Patrick STAFF ASST/LEGIS CORRES 2209 51640
Voytovich, Olya PRESS SECY 2372 51640

DISTRICT OFFICES

LAREDO—602 E CALTON RD, SUITE 2, LAREDO, TX 78041

Atwell, Francis COORD - OUTREACH 956-725-0639
Hernandez, Jessica DIST DIR 956-725-0639
Martinez, Leslie DIST PRESS SECY 956-725-0639
Segovia, Sylvia CONSTIT SVCS REP 956-725-0639
Zavala, Eddie PRESS ASST 956-725-0639

MISSION—117 E TOM LANDRY ST, MISSION, TX 78572

Gallegos, Alexis CONSTIT SVCS REP 956-424-3942
Hernandez, Nichole COORD - OUTREACH /CONSTIT SVCS REP 956-424-3942

RIO GRANDE CITY—100 NORTH FM 3167, SUITE 208, RIO GRANDE CITY, TX 78582

Hernandez, Nichole COORD - OUTREACH /CONSTIT SVCS REP 956-487-5603

SAN ANTONIO—615 E HOUSTON ST, SUITE 563, SAN ANTONIO, TX 78205
TOLL-FREE NUMBER.......... 1-877-780-0028

Hayes, Kendall CONSTIT SVCS REP 210-271-2851
Islam, Nadia CONSTIT SVCS REP 210-271-2851
Lafuente, Gilbert COORD - OUTREACH 210-271-2851

Representative Elijah E. Cummings

Maryland, 7th

2163 RAYBURN HOB (ZIP: 20515-2007) **225-4741**
Badu-Nimako, Yvette LEGIS DIR 2163 .... **54741**
Blumenthal, Jordan POLICY COUNSEL 2163 .... **54741**
Broady, Marc POLICY COUNSEL 2163 .... **54741**
Bush, Anthony STAFF ASST 2163 .... **54741**
Chalhoub, Theresa POLICY COUNSEL 2163 .... **54741**
Eichar, Andrew PRESS SECY 2163 .... **54741**
Simms, Vernon CHIEF OF STAFF 2163 .... **54741**
Stradford, Kierstin LEGIS CORRES/SYS ADMIN 2163 .... **54741**
Waskow, Jean SCHEDULER 2163 .... **54741**

DISTRICT OFFICES

BALTIMORE—1010 PARK AVE, SUITE 105, BALTIMORE, MD 21201
Christianson, Mike SPECIAL ASST **410-685-9199**
Clay, Gerietta STAFF ASST **410-685-9199**
Gibson, Diana STAFF ASST **410-685-9199**
Lane, Philisha SPECIAL PROJ/RESOURCE MGR **410-685-9199**
Lewis, Chanan SPECIAL ASST **410-685-9199**
Matambo, Mutale SPECIAL ASST **410-685-9199**
Perkins, Trudy DPTY CHIEF OF STAFF/COMMUNICATIONS DIR **410-685-9199**
Perry, Deborah SPECIAL ASST **410-685-9199**
Spikes, Harry DIR - DIST AFFAIRS **410-685-9199**
Washington, Crystal SPECIAL ASST **410-685-9199**

CATONSVILLE—754 FREDERICK RD, CATONSVILLE, MD 21228
Malone, Katie SPECIAL ASST **410-719-8777**

ELLICOTT CITY—8267 MAIN ST, ROOM 102, ELLICOTT CITY, MD 21043
Clay, Regina AREA DIR **410-465-8259**

Representative Joe Cunningham

South Carolina, 1st

423 CANNON HOB (ZIP: 20515-4001) **225-3176**
Drago, Rebecca COMMUNICATIONS DIR 423 CHOB **53176**
Hervig, Angela STAFF ASST/PRESS ASST 423 CHOB **53176**
Lofton, Lane CHIEF OF STAFF 423 CHOB **53176**
Mayer, Jesse DIR - OPS 423 CHOB **53176**
Mitchell, Rashawn LEGIS DIR 423 CHOB **53176**
Ogle, David LEGIS ASST - MIL 423 CHOB **53176**
Rezaee-Rod, Paniz LEGIS ASST 423 CHOB **53176**
Thompson, Cora SHARED EMPLOYEE 423 CHOB **53176**
Wunsche, Krista LEGIS CORRES/STAFF ASST 423 CHOB **53176**

DISTRICT OFFICES

BEAUFORT—710 BOUNDARY ST, NO. 1D, BEAUFORT, SC 29902
Casey, Jose FIELD REP **843-521-2530**
Kisner, Chelsea CASEWKR **843-521-2530**

MT. PLEASANT—530 JOHNNIE DODDS BLVD, SUITE 201, MT. PLEASANT, SC 29464
Derr, April DIR - CONSTIT SVCS **843-352-7572**
Harriford, Scott SR FIELD REP **843-352-7572**
Infanzon, Hollis DIST DIR **843-352-7572**
Koszela, Kaylan DIR - COMMUNITY OUTREACH **843-352-7572**
Tucker, Natalie CASEWKR **843-352-7572**
Washington, ArRone STAFF ASST **843-352-7572**

Representative John R. Curtis

Utah, 3d

125 CANNON HOB (ZIP: 20515-4403) **225-7751**
Bornstein, Jake LEGIS DIR 125 CHOB **57751**
Dougall, Troy STAFF ASST 125 CHOB **57751**
Fulton, Austin LEGIS CORRES 125 CHOB **57751**
Heinrich, Stephanie DC SCHEDULER 125 CHOB **57751**
Khalifa, Kyle INFO TECH ASST 125 CHOB **57751**
Mann, Liz ASST COUNSEL 125 CHOB **57751**
Norman, Corey CHIEF OF STAFF 125 CHOB **57751**
Riding, Ally COMMUNICATIONS DIR 125 CHOB **57751**
Walker, Amanda CHIEF FINANCIAL OFFICER 125 CHOB **57751**

DISTRICT OFFICE

PROVO—3549 N UNIVERSITY AVE, PROVO, UT 84604
Booth, Whitney DIST COMMUNICATIONS DIR **801-922-5400**
Christie, Brett INFO TECH ASST **801-922-5400**
Ellertson, Larry CASEWKR **801-922-5400**
Emfield, Josh DPTY STATE DIR **801-922-5400**
Fowlke, Lorie STATE DIR **801-922-5400**
Rawlins, Genevieve DIST OFFICE MGR **801-922-5400**
Robie, Gina DIST SCHEDULER/EXEC ASST **801-922-5400**

Representative Sharice Davids

Kansas, 3d

1541 LONGWORTH HOB (ZIP: 20515-1603) **225-2865**
Germany, Ebony STAFF ASST 1541 .... **64407**
Jones, Christina DIR - OPS/SCHEDULER 1541 .... **67208**
Naylor, Brandon LEGIS DIR 1541 .... **67212**
Rohr, Kate LEGIS ASST 1541 .... **67210**
Teixeira, Allison CHIEF OF STAFF 1541 .... **56027**
Warshaw, Johanna PRESS SECY 1541 .... **67209**

DISTRICT OFFICES

OVERLAND PARK—7325 W 79TH ST, OVERLAND PARK, KS 66204
Hummel, Coletta CONSTIT SVCS/CONSTIT OUTREACH REP **913-621-0832**
Klemp, Kyle MGR - CONSTIT SVCS **913-621-0832**
Robinson, Danielle DIST DIR **913-621-0832**
Washington, Venetia CONSTIT SVCS **913-621-0832**
Zukrow, Leslie DIST STAFF ASST **913-621-0832**

WYANDOTTE COUNTY—753 STATE AVE, SUITE 460, KANSAS CITY, KS 66101 913-766-3993

Representative Warren Davidson

Ohio, 8th

1107 LONGWORTH HOB (ZIP: 20515-3508) **225-6205**
Branch, Doug DPTY CHIEF OF STAFF 1107 .... **56205**
Colaccio, Joe STAFF ASST 1107 .... **56205**
Farmer, Zach LEGIS CORRES 1107 .... **56205**
Hammond, Ron LEGIS ASST 1107 .... **56205**
Henderson, Matthew COMMUNICATIONS DIR 1107 .... **56205**
O'Connell, Molly SCHEDULER 1107 .... **56205**
Silver, Matthew LEGIS DIR 1107 .... **56205**
White, Connor LEGIS ASST 1107 .... **56205**

DISTRICT OFFICES

BUTLER COUNTY—8857 CINCINNATI-DAYTON RD, NO. 102, WEST CHESTER, OH 45069
Bohannon, Zach FIELD REP **513-779-5400**
Hughes, Sharon CASEWKR/OFFICE MGR **513-779-5400**

SPRINGFIELD—76 E HIGH ST, 3RD FLOOR, SPRINGFIELD, OH 45502 937-322-1120

TROY—20 DOTCOM DR, TROY, OH 45373
Detrick, Alissa DIST OFFICE MGR/CASEWKR **937-339-1524**

Hewitt, Adam CHIEF OF STAFF ... 937-339-1524
Thaeler, Ben DIST DIR ... 937-339-1524

Representative Danny K. Davis

Illinois, 7th

2159 RAYBURN HOB (ZIP: 20515-1307) ... 225-5006
Brown, Jenell FINANCIAL & ADMIN OFFICER/OFFICE MGR 2159 ... 55006
Brown, Lavell LEGIS ASST 2159 ... 55006
Burton, Willie STAFF ASST 2159 ... 55006
Edwards, Yul CHIEF OF STAFF 2159 ... 55006
Gilchrist, Caleb DPTY CHIEF OF STAFF 2159 ... 55006
Hunter-Williams, Jill DPTY CHIEF OF STAFF 2159 ... 55006
Peters, Joseph LEGIS CORRES 2159 ... 55006

DISTRICT OFFICE

CHICAGO—2813-15 W FIFTH AVE, CHICAGO, IL 60612
Boyd, Clayton STAFF ASST ... 773-533-7520
Cohen, Ira COMMUNICATIONS DIR ... 773-533-7520
Davis, Fred STAFF ASST ... 773-533-7520
Greer, Jacqueline STAFF ASST ... 773-533-7520
Gye, Raymond CONSTIT SVCS REP ... 773-533-7520
Harvey, Nicole DIR - CONSTIT SVCS ... 773-533-7520
Logan, Cherita DIST DIR ... 773-533-7520
Moorer, Gerard DPTY DIST DIR ... 773-533-7520
Overton, Crystal PERSONAL ASST ... 773-533-7520
Reed, Mary CONSTIT SVCS ... 773-533-7520
Romero, Tumia SR ADVISOR ... 773-533-7520
Shapiro, Larry CONSTIT OUTREACH REP ... 773-533-7520
Smith, Marquetta SPECIAL PROJ/ASST DIST DIR ... 773-533-7520
Smith, Shonna RECEPTIONIST ... 773-533-7520
Ware, Josie DIST OFFICE MGR ... 773-533-7520

Representative Rodney Davis

Illinois, 13th

1740 LONGWORTH HOB (ZIP: 20515-1313) ... 225-2371
Ballard, Jimmy LEGIS DIR 1740 ... 52371
Blanford, Meredith PRESS SECY 1740 ... 52371
Costa, Janie LEGIS ASST 1740 ... 52371
Lear, Madeline STAFF ASST 1740 ... 52371
Manley, Bret CHIEF OF STAFF 1740 ... 52371
Mulvey, Aaron LEGIS CORRES 1740 ... 52371
Nagle, Brianna SCHEDULER 1740 ... 52371
Phelps, Ashley COMMUNICATIONS DIR 1740 ... 52371
Ross, David LEGIS ASST 1740 ... 52371
Wetherald, Margaret FINANCIAL ADMIN 1740 ... 52371

DISTRICT OFFICES

CHAMPAIGN—2004 FOX DR, CHAMPAIGN, IL 61820
Baldwin, Jennifer CONSTIT SVCS REP ... 217-403-4690
Yoakum, Linda CONG AIDE ... 217-403-4690

DECATUR—243 S WATER ST, SUITE 100, DECATUR, IL 62523
Albert, Helen DIST DIR/DIST SCHEDULER ... 217-791-6224
Hamilton, Erik STAFF ASST ... 217-791-6224

MARYVILLE—15 PROFESSIONAL PARK DR, MARYVILLE, IL 62062
Lasseigne, Philip COORD - GRANTS & SPEC PROJ ... 918-205-8660

NORMAL—104 W NORTH ST, NORMAL, IL 61761
Cravens, Tyler DPTY DIST DIR ... 309-252-8834

SPRINGFIELD—2833 S GRAND AVE EAST, SPRINGFIELD, IL 62703
Trees, Candice COMMUNITY OUTREACH SPEC ... 217-791-6224

TAYLORVILLE—108 W MARKET ST, TAYLORVILLE, IL 62568
Kettelkamp, Meg CONSTIT SVCS REP ... 217-824-5117

Representative Susan A. Davis

California, 53d

1214 LONGWORTH HOB (ZIP: 20515-0553) ... 225-2040
Fernandez, Denise LEGIS CORRES 1214 ... 52040
Hunter, Aaron PRESS SECY 1214 ... 52040
Mendoza, Brandon SR LEGIS AIDE 1214 ... 52040
Patton, Cynthia DPTY CHIEF OF STAFF/SCHEDULER 1214 ... 52040
Perez, Michael LEGIS ASST/COMMUNICATIONS ASST 1214 ... 52040
Seabrook, William LEGIS ASST 1214 ... 52040
Segovia, Francine MIL FELLOW 1214 ... 52040
Sherman, Lisa CHIEF OF STAFF 1214 ... 52040
Staples, Ian LEGIS DIR 1214 ... 52040
Viterbi, Samantha STAFF ASST/LEGIS CORRES 1214 ... 52040

DISTRICT OFFICE

SAN DIEGO—2700 ADAMS AVE, SUITE 102, SAN DIEGO, CA 92116
Al Baghdadi, Jawad COMMUNITY REP ... 619-280-5353
Bojorquez-Gomez, Maria STAFF ASST ... 619-280-5353
Brown, Jessica FIELD REP - VETS ... 619-280-5353
Bunshaft, Zachary COMMUNITY REP ... 619-280-5353
Campbell, Ashley DIST SCHEDULER/SR COMMUNITY REP ... 619-280-5353
Clark, Jonathan SR COMMUNITY REP ... 619-280-5353
Mier, Jessica DIST DIR ... 619-280-5353

Representative Madeleine Dean

Pennsylvania, 4th

129 CANNON HOB (ZIP: 20515-3804) ... 225-4731
Carlos, Colleen LEGIS DIR 129 CHOB ... 54731
Chiba, Koh CHIEF OF STAFF 129 CHOB ... 54731
Mack, Tim PRESS AIDE 129 CHOB ... 54731
McCann, Chris LEGIS ASST 129 CHOB ... 54731
Milon, Colin LEGIS ASST 129 CHOB ... 54731
Patel, Rina LEGIS CORRES 129 CHOB ... 54731
Ruane, Megan STAFF ASST 129 CHOB ... 54731
Tewelde, Yodit DIR - OPS/SCHEDULING DIR 129 CHOB ... 54731

DISTRICT OFFICES

GLENSIDE—115 E GLENSIDE AVE, SUITE 1, GLENSIDE, PA 19038
Corrigan, Dave DIST FIELD REP ... 215-884-4300
Janoson, Meghan DIST SCHEDULER ... 215-884-4300
Joyce, Kathleen DIST DIR ... 215-884-4300
Wilkerson, Emanuel LEGIS ASST ... 215-884-4300

NORRISTOWN—101 E MAIN ST, SUITE A, NORRISTOWN, PA 19401
Ashe, Shae CASEWKR - IMMIGRATION ... 610-382-1250
Bieber, Matt COMMUNICATIONS DIR ... 610-382-1250
Cooper, Valerie CASEWKR ... 610-382-1250
Tucker, Mike CASEWK MGR ... 610-382-1250

Representative Peter A. DeFazio

Oregon, 4th

2134 RAYBURN HOB (ZIP: 20515-3704) ... 225-6416
Greco, Kristie CHIEF OF STAFF 2134 ... 56416
Green-Newton, King LEGIS CORRES 2134 ... 56416
Huddleston, James LEGIS ASST 2134 ... 56416
Leasure, Matt EXEC ASST/SYS ADMIN 2134 ... 56416
Moeny, Kitra STAFF ASST 2134 ... 56416
Pratt, Kris LEGIS DIR 2134 ... 56416
Puckett, Bobby LEGIS ASST 2134 ... 56416
Schoenbach, Beth COMMUNICATIONS DIR 2134 ... 56416
Wulfing, Rina SR LEGIS ASST 2134 ... 56416

DISTRICT OFFICES

COOS BAY—125 CENTRAL AVE, SUITE 350, COOS BAY, OR 97420

Erickson, Kathy DIST FIELD REP 541-269-2609

EUGENE—405 E 8TH AVE, NO. 2030, EUGENE, OR 97401

Alvarado, Brenda DIST AIDE 541-465-6732
Cornwall, Vanessa DIST AIDE 541-465-6732
Couture, Whitney DIST AIDE 541-465-6732
Gabrielson, Carly OUTREACH DIR 541-465-6732
Miller, James DIST AIDE 541-465-6732
Nelson, Becky DIST SCHEDULER 541-465-6732
Neyman, Lisa DIST STAFF ASST 541-465-6732
Wagoner, Phyllis DIR - CONSTIT SVCS 541-465-6732
Whelan, Dan DIST DIR 541-465-6732

ROSEBURG—612 SE JACKSON ST, SUITE 9, ROSEBURG, OR 97470

Conroy, Chris DIST FIELD REP 541-440-3523

Representative Diana DeGette

Colorado, 1st

2111 RAYBURN HOB (ZIP: 20515-0601) 225-4431

Allen, Matthew LEGIS ASST 2111 54431
Brown, Ryan COMMUNICATIONS DIR 2111 54431
Cohen, Danielle PRESS ASST/COORD - DIGITAL MEDIA 2111 .. 54431
Cohen, Lisa B CHIEF OF STAFF 2111 54431
Gambrel, Diana SCHEDULER/EXEC ASST 2111 54431
Greenhalgh, Michelle POLICY DIR - HEALTH 2111 54431
Roy, Nikki ENERGY & ENVIRON POLICY ADVISOR 2111 54431
Walker, Tommy DPTY CHIEF OF STAFF 2111 54431
Woodburn, Thomas SR LEGIS ASST 2111 54431

DISTRICT OFFICE

DENVER—600 GRANT ST, SUITE 202, DENVER, CO 80203

Autobee-Trujillo, Andrea DPTY DIST DIR 303-844-4988
Garza, Alejandra SR CONG AIDE 303-844-4988
Hood, Kaila CONG AIDE 303-844-4988
Middleton, Joeana DIST DIR 303-844-4988
Mujkanovic, Nermina CONG AIDE 303-844-4988
Parker, Arden OFFICE COORD 303-844-4988
Whalen, Sarah DIST SCHEDULER 303-844-4988

Representative Rosa L. DeLauro

Connecticut, 3d

2413 RAYBURN HOB (ZIP: 20515-0703) 225-3661

Albertine, Elizabeth LEGIS DIR 2413 53661
Fetterman, Kris SPEECHWRITER 2413 53661
Ghaffari, Lisa STAFF ASST 2413 53661
Kinney, Ryann SCHEDULER/EXEC ASST 2413 53661
Lovell, Christian LEGIS ASST 2413 53661
Mederos, Leticia CHIEF OF STAFF 2413 53661
Peruccio, Caitlin LEGIS ASST 2413 53661
Serio, Will COMMUNICATIONS DIR 2413 53661
Spasiano, Jack SR LEGIS ASST 2413 53661
Stanwood, Jenna LEGIS CORRES/LEGIS ASST 2413 53661

DISTRICT OFFICE

NEW HAVEN—59 ELM ST, NEW HAVEN, CT 06510

Bombard, Jeff OFFICE MGR 203-562-3718
Concepcion, Marilyn CASEWKR 203-562-3718
Deloma, Jill CASEWKR 203-562-3718
Dodge, Allison CASEWKR/COMMUNITY OUTREACH SPEC 203-562-3718
Hartman, David CONG AIDE 203-562-3718
Lamb, Jennifer DIST DIR 203-562-3718
Mangini, Louis LABOR LIAISON 203-562-3718
Palumbo, Samantha SCHEDULER 203-562-3718
Savaria, Nicholas CASEWKR 203-562-3718
Wali-Johnson, Abdur CASEWKR 203-562-3718

Representative Suzan K. DelBene

Washington, 1st

2330 RAYBURN HOB (ZIP: 20515-4701) 225-6311

Banks, Linda FINANCIAL ADMIN 2330 56311
Bernhard, Sasha SR POLICY ADVISOR 2330 56311
Hill, Kyle LEGIS DIR 2330 56311
Honard, Victoria SR POLICY ADVISOR 2330 56311
McTague, Mary Kate DC SCHEDULER 2330 56311
Reilingh, Eddie LEGIS CORRES 2330 56311
Schmidt, Aaron CHIEF OF STAFF 2330 56311
Sheff, Samara STAFF & PRESS ASST 2330 56311
Tata, Shantanu SR POLICY ADVISOR 2330 56311
Wasson, Lou COMMUNICATIONS DIR 2330 56311

DISTRICT OFFICES

BOTHELL—22121 17TH AVE SE, SUITE 220, BOTHELL, WA 98021

Hogan, Patrick SPECIAL ASST 425-485-0085
Marquardt, Kelly CONG LIAISON 425-485-0085
Stenberg, Rachel CASEWKR 425-485-0085
Studley, Ben LIAISON - VETS 425-485-0085

MOUNT VERNON—204 W MONTGOMERY ST, MOUNT VERNON, WA 98273

Galloway, Kaylee CONSTIT OUTREACH REP 360-416-7879

Representative Antonio Delgado

New York, 19th

1007 LONGWORTH HOB (ZIP: 20515-3219) 225-5614

Andrews, Jessie DC CHIEF OF STAFF/LEGIS DIR 1007 55614
Bivona, John CHIEF OF STAFF 1007 55614
Doster, Curtis SR LEGIS ASST 1007 55614
Driscoll, Laura SR LEGIS ASST 1007 55614
Epstein, Laura COMMUNICATIONS DIR 1007 55614
Gerson, Matthew JR LEGIS ASST 1007 55614
Ives, Christina SCHEDULER 1007 55614
Murphy, Kelly FINANCIAL DIR 1007 55614
Phillips, Brian, Jr PRESS ASST/STAFF ASST 1007 55614
Toufanian, Melissa CHIEF COMMUNICATIONS ADVISOR 1007 55614

DISTRICT OFFICE

KINGSTON—256 CLINTON AVE, KINGSTON, NY 12401

Becker, Nicholas LIAISON - MIL & VET 845-443-2930
Boomhower, Amanda DIST DIR 845-443-2930
Buono, Elizabeth CONSTIT SVCS REP 845-443-2930
O'Sullivan, Ryan LIAISON - VETS 845-443-2930
Perry, Victoria DPTY DIR 845-443-2930
Roberts, Sarah CONSTIT SVCS REP 845-443-2930
St. Hubert, Zacharie CONSTIT SVCS REP 845-443-2930

Representative Val Butler Demings

Florida, 10th

217 CANNON HOB (ZIP: 20515-0910) 225-2176

Anderson, Wendy CHIEF OF STAFF 217 CHOB 52176
Collins-Mandeville, Aimee LEGIS DIR 217 CHOB 52176
Featherson, Wendy SCHEDULER/EXEC ASST 217 CHOB 52176
Gleick, Daniel COMMUNICATIONS DIR 217 CHOB 52176
Greenfield, George SYS ADMIN 217 CHOB 52176

Guzman-Toro, Omar LEGIS ASST 217 CHOB 52176
Lawson, Dion FINANCIAL ADMIN 217 CHOB 52176
Robinson, Brittan LEGIS CORRES 217 CHOB 52176
Styron, Stuart SR LEGIS ASST 217 CHOB 52176

DISTRICT OFFICE

ORLANDO—2295 S HIAWASSEE RD, SUITE 301, ORLANDO, FL 32835

Bowyer, Kathrin STAFF ASST 321-388-9808
Glover, Chester CASEWKR 321-388-9808
Gustave, Peggy CASEWKR 321-388-9808
Hinson, Mark COORD - COMMUNITY OUTREACH 321-388-9808
Sanchez, David CASEWKR 321-388-9808
Waldron, Erin COORD - COMMUNITY DEV 321-388-9808
White, Sonja DIST DIR 321-388-9808

Representative Mark DeSaulnier

California, 11th

503 CANNON HOB (ZIP: 20515-0511) **225-2095**
Arnold Marr, Betsy CHIEF OF STAFF 503 CHOB 52095
Enos, Ben DIST REP 503 CHOB 52095
Jackson, Sarah LEGIS DIR 503 CHOB 52095
Jucha, Catherine STAFF ASST/LEGIS CORRES 503 CHOB 52095
Kimber, Taylor DIST REP 503 CHOB 52095
Perlstein, Andrew LEGIS ASST 503 CHOB 52095
Silver, Aaron DIST REP 503 CHOB 52095
Smith, Evan LEGIS ASST 503 CHOB 52095
Tercek, Margo LEGIS ASST 503 CHOB 52095
Van Ness, Ethan LEGIS ASST 503 CHOB 52095
Wall, Aimee PRESS SECY 503 CHOB 52095
Yingst, Bambi SCHEDULER/EXEC ASST 503 CHOB 52095

DISTRICT OFFICES

RICHMOND—440 CIVIC CENTER PLAZA, RICHMOND, CA 94804 510-620-1000

WALNUT CREEK—3100 OAK RD, SUITE 110, WALNUT CREEK, CA 94597

Angulo, Jessica DIST SCHEDULER 925-933-2660
Bratcher, Brandon DIST REP 925-933-2660
Brown, Ryan-Thomas DIST REP 925-933-2660
Crain, Megan STAFF ASST 925-933-2660
Scales-Preston, Shanelle DIST DIR 925-933-2660

Representative Scott DesJarlais

Tennessee, 4th

2301 RAYBURN HOB (ZIP: 20515-4204) **225-6831**
Allen, Amber FINANCIAL MGR 2301 56831
Carman, MeKenna EXEC ASST 2301 56831
Locke, James LEGIS COUNSEL 2301 56831
Monks, Dylan LEGIS ASST 2301 56831
Russell, Hannah LEGIS ASST 2301 56831
Thomas, Brendan COMMUNICATIONS DIR 2301 56831
Vaughn, Richard CHIEF OF STAFF 2301 56831
Wilkins, Richard LEGIS DIR 2301 56831

DISTRICT OFFICES

CLEVELAND—301 KEITH ST, SUITE 212, CLEVELAND, TN 37311

Pond, Shirley CONSTIT SVCS REP 423-472-7500

COLUMBIA—808 S GARDEN ST, 2ND FLOOR, COLUMBIA, TN 38401

Moon, Becky CASEWKR/FIELD REP 931-381-9920

MURFREESBORO—305 W MAIN ST, MURFREESBORO, TN 37130

Davis, Lynne FIELD REP 615-896-1986
Topping, Kristen CASEWKR 615-896-1986
Wennerstrom, Thomas CASEWKR 615-896-1986

WINCHESTER—200 S JEFFERSON ST, SUITE 311, WINCHESTER, TN 37398

Dennis, Amy FIELD REP 931-962-3180

Representative Theodore E. Deutch

Florida, 22d

2447 RAYBURN HOB (ZIP: 20515-0922) **225-3001**
Abusch, Aviva STAFF ASST 2447 53001
Attermann, Jason PRESS SECY/LEGIS ASST 2447 53001
Dawson, Demitri PRESS ASST RAYBURN 53001
Fontana, Daniel LEGIS CORRES 2447 53001
Kustin, Casey SR POLICY ADVISOR/SUBCOMM STAFF DIR 2447 53001
Lipman, Joshua LEGIS DIR/COUNSEL 2447 53001
McLaren, Ellen DPTY CHIEF OF STAFF 2447 53001
Richard, Joel SR COUNSEL 2447 53001
Rogin, Joshua CHIEF OF STAFF 2447 53001
Taylor, Daniel LEGIS CORRES 2447 53001

DISTRICT OFFICES

BOCA—7900 GLADES RD, SUITE 250, BOCA RATON, FL 33434

Brunet, Yanet CASEWKR 561-470-5440
Chapman, Jayne COMMUNITY LIAISON 561-470-5440
DeJesus, James OUTREACH ADVISOR 561-470-5440
Edelson, Brandey DIR - COMMUNITY OUTREACH 561-470-5440
Johnson, Eric ADVISOR 561-470-5440
Lipsich, Wendi DIST DIR 561-470-5440
Raducci, Jen CASEWKR 561-470-5440
Rocha, Alex EXEC ASST/EXEC SCHEDULER 561-470-5440

BROWARD COLLEGE—111 E LAS OLAS BLVD, FORT LAUDERDALE, FL 33301 954-255-8336

CORAL SPRINGS—1300 CORAL SPRINGS DR, CORAL SPRINGS, FL 33071

Brier, Theresa DPTY DIST DIR 954-255-8336

MARGATE—5790 MARGATE BLVD, MARGATE, FL 33063 954-972-6454

Representative Mario Diaz-Balart

Florida, 25th

404 CANNON HOB (ZIP: 20515-0925) **225-4211**
Dos Santos, Elizabeth EXEC ASST/LEGIS AIDE 404 CHOB 54211
Gonzalez, Cesar CHIEF OF STAFF 404 CHOB 54211
Hernandez, Laura PRESS SECY 404 CHOB 54211
Hodgkins, Sarah LEGIS ASST 404 CHOB 54211
Morley, Autumn COUNSEL/SR POLICY ADVISOR 404 CHOB 54211
Reynolds, Gisselle LEGIS ASST/DIR - CONSTIT SVCS 404 CHOB 54211
Sweet, Chris LEGIS DIR 404 CHOB 54211

DISTRICT OFFICES

DORAL—8669 NW 36TH ST, SUITE 100, DORAL, FL 33166

Alvarez, Yovi CONG ASST 305-470-8555
Blanco, Jennifer CONG AIDE 305-470-8555
Colon, Kimberly STAFF ASST 305-470-8555
Morales, Andrea CONG AIDE 305-470-8555
Oliveros, Gloria DIST DIR 305-470-8555
Otero, Miguel DPTY CHIEF OF STAFF 305-470-8555

NAPLES—4715 GOLDEN GATE PKWY, SUITE 1, NAPLES, FL 34116

Padro, Enrique CONG AIDE 239-348-1620

Representative Debbie Dingell

Michigan, 12th

116 CANNON HOB (ZIP: 20515-2212) **225-4071**
Clark, Raymel INFO TECH MGR 116 CHOB **54071**
Dollhopf, Kevin LEGIS ASST 116 CHOB **54071**
Dougherty, Matthew SCHEDULING DIR 116 CHOB **54071**
Huebner, Tim LEGIS CORRES/LEGIS AIDE 116 CHOB **54071**
Rambosk, Kevin LEGIS DIR 116 CHOB **54071**
Ricchetti, Tiger STAFF ASST 116 CHOB **54071**
Rousseau, Maggie COMMUNICATIONS DIR 116 CHOB **54071**
Sunstrum, Greg CHIEF OF STAFF 116 CHOB **54071**

DISTRICT OFFICES

DEARBORN—19855 W OUTER DR, 103E, DEARBORN, MI 48124
Bruley, Callie DIST DIR **313-278-2936**
Hall, Ashley FIELD REP **313-278-2936**
Hood, Elizabeth DIST SCHEDULER **313-278-2936**
Jesaitis, Katie DIST FIELD REP **313-278-2936**
Kadri, Jannie CASEWKR/CASEWKR - IMMIGRATION ... **313-278-2936**
Martin, Donyale CASEWKR **313-278-2936**
Ramadan, Ahmad FIELD REP **313-278-2936**

YPSILANTI—301 W MICHIGAN AVE, SUITE 400, YPSILANTI, MI 48197
Hunter, Ryan FIELD REP **734-481-1100**

Representative Lloyd Doggett

Texas, 35th

2307 RAYBURN HOB (ZIP: 20515-4335) **225-4865**
Ahn, Michael PRESS ASST/LEGIS ASST 2307 .... **54865**
Cissell, Afton COUNSEL 2307 .... **54865**
Guerrero, Luis STAFF ASST 2307 .... **54865**
Laven Jones, Sarah LEGIS ASST 2307 .... **54865**
Molof, Doug SR LEGIS ASST 2307 .... **54865**
Mucchetti, Michael CHIEF OF STAFF 2307 .... **54865**
Nunez, Christina LEGIS AIDE 2307 .... **54865**
Smith RuBoss, Daniel SR POLICY ADVISOR 2307 .... **54865**
Stotesbery, Katherine LEGIS ASST/COMMUNICATIONS DIR 2307 .... **54865**

DISTRICT OFFICES

AUSTIN—300 E 8TH ST, SUITE 763, AUSTIN, TX 78701-3224
Gomez, Diana FIELD REP **512-916-5921**
Gurak, Erin DIST DIR **512-916-5921**
Hernandez, Marina CONG AIDE **512-916-5921**
Rosales, Lauren CONSTIT SVCS REP **512-916-5921**
Toretto, Courtney DPTY DIST DIR **512-916-5921**
Woiton, Sonia CONG AIDE **512-916-5921**

SAN ANTONIO—217 W TRAVIS ST, SAN ANTONIO, TX 78205
Golden, Priscilla CONSTIT SVCS **210-704-1080**
Kennedy, Brendan FIELD REP **210-704-1080**
Stevens, Anais CONG AIDE **210-704-1080**
Veliz, MaryEllen DPTY CHIEF OF STAFF **210-704-1080**

Representative Michael F. Doyle

Pennsylvania, 18th

306 CANNON HOB (ZIP: 20515-3818) **225-2135**
Borzner, Claire LEGIS ASST 306 CHOB **52135**
Dinkel, Matt COMMUNICATIONS DIR 306 CHOB **52135**
Lucas, David CHIEF OF STAFF 306 CHOB **52135**
Murphy, Phil LEGIS DIR 306 CHOB **52135**
Werley, Kate ADVISOR - HEALTH POLICY 306 CHOB **52135**
Young, Ellen EXEC ASST 306 CHOB **52135**
Young, Natalie COMMUNICATIONS ASST 306 CHOB **52135**

DISTRICT OFFICES

MCKEESPORT—627 LYSLE BLVD, MCKEESPORT, PA 15132
Jones, John CASEWKR **412-664-4049**
Sasso, Sean CASEWORK - VETS **412-664-4049**

PITTSBURGH—2637 E CARSON ST, PITTSBURGH, PA 15203
Cochran, Cameron CASEWKR - IMMIGRATION **412-390-1499**
D'Alesandro, Paul DIST DIR **412-390-1499**
Heffley, Joe COMMUNITY & OUTREACH LIAISON **412-390-1499**
O'Grady, Jamie DIST SCHEDULER **412-390-1499**

SOUTH HILLS—4705 LIBRARY RD, BETHEL PARK, PA 15102
Demicheli, Nick CASEWKR - MIL **412-283-4451**
Hopkins, Rachael CASEWKR **412-283-4451**
Schaffer, Jeff ECON DEV REP **412-283-4451**

Representative Sean P. Duffy

Wisconsin, 7th

1714 LONGWORTH HOB (ZIP: 20515-4907) **225-3365**
TOLL-FREE NO. **1-855-585-4251**
Acornley, Mark ADMIN - FINANCE & PAYROLL 1714 .... **53365**
Bednar, Mark COMMUNICATIONS DIR 1714 .... **53365**
Burchick, Jeb PRESS ASST 1714 .... **53365**
Chandler, Dylan LEGIS ASST 1714 .... **53365**
Emmer, Jack LEGIS CORRES 1714 .... **53365**
Hair, John POLICY ADVISOR 1714 .... **53365**
McCormack, Ryan LEGIS DIR 1714 .... **53365**
Meachum, Pete CHIEF OF STAFF 1714 .... **53365**
Traynham, Eleanor SCHEDULER 1714 .... **53365**

DISTRICT OFFICES

HAYWARD—15569 RAILROAD ST, SUITE 302, HAYWARD, WI 54843
Hessel, Stacey CONSTIT SVCS REP **715-392-3984**
Miller, James OUTREACH REP **715-392-3984**

HUDSON—502 2ND ST, SUITE 202, HUDSON, WI 54016
Garza, Jesse DIST DIR **715-808-8160**

WAUSAU—208 GRAND AVE, WAUSAU, WI 54403
Cronin, Maggie DIST SCHEDULER **715-298-9344**
Guild, Sara OUTREACH DIR **715-298-9348**
Lanctin, Jonathan CONSTIT SVCS REP **715-298-9344**

Representative Jeff Duncan

South Carolina, 3d

2229 RAYBURN HOB (ZIP: 20515-4003) **225-5301**
Gross, Joshua LEGIS DIR 2229 .... **55301**
Klump, Allen CHIEF OF STAFF 2229 .... **55301**
Krekorian, Elise LEGIS ASST 2229 .... **55301**
Lane, Will LEGIS CORRES 2229 .... **55301**
McAllister, Thomas SCHEDULER/OFFICE MGR 2229 .... **55301**
Moore, Marimac LEGIS ASST/PRESS ASST 2229 .... **55301**
Patterson, Addie COMMUNICATIONS DIR 2229 .... **55301**
Ringer, Chris STAFF ASST 2229 .... **55301**

DISTRICT OFFICES

ANDERSON—303 W BELTLINE BLVD, ANDERSON, SC 29625
Adkins, Rick DIST DIR/DPTY CHIEF OF STAFF **864-224-7401**
Christian, Jordan CONSTIT LIAISON/DIST SCHEDULER/FIELD REP **864-224-7401**

James, Tyler FIELD REP 864-224-7401
Starace, Mario DIST SCHEDULER/CONSTIT LIAISON .. 864-224-7401

CLINTON—100 PLAZA CIRCLE, SUITE A1, CLINTON, SC 29325

Harman, Jan FIELD REP 864-681-1028
Hart, Tosha CASEWKR 864-681-1028
Huff, Robin CASEWKR 864-681-1028

Representative Neal P. Dunn

Florida, 2d

316 CANNON HOB (ZIP: 20515-0902) 225-5235

Blackwell, Matt LEGIS DIR 316 CHOB 55235
Dolan, Tom STAFF ASST 316 CHOB 55235
Hadden, Emily LEGIS CORRES 316 CHOB 55235
Hodgkins, Shelby COMMUNICATIONS DIR 316 CHOB 55235
Houser, Danielle LEGIS ASST 316 CHOB 55235
Lowry, Michael CHIEF OF STAFF 316 CHOB 55235
Mullen, Marissa SCHEDULER 316 CHOB 55235
Veatch, Courtney LEGIS ASST/COUNSEL 316 CHOB 55235

DISTRICT OFFICES

PANAMA CITY—840 W 11TH ST, SUITE 2250, PANAMA CITY, FL 32401

Boggs, Bethany CONSTIT SVCS SPEC 850-785-0812
Crosby, Olivia REGIONAL DIR 850-785-0812
Smith, Nicole DIR - CONSTIT SVCS 850-785-0812

TALLAHASSEE—300 S ADAMS ST, TALLAHASSEE, FL 32301

Deatherage, Craig LIAISON - MIL & VET 850-891-8610
Hoffman, Landon REGIONAL DIR 850-891-8610
Kendrick, Will DIST DIR 850-891-8610
Myhill, Meghan REGIONAL DIR 850-891-8610

Representative Tom Emmer

Minnesota, 6th

315 CANNON HOB (ZIP: 20515-2306) 225-2331

Anderson, Alyssa DPTY SCHEDULER 315 CHOB 52331
Lenz, Catherine LEGIS ASST 315 CHOB 52331
Lunneborg, Nick SR LEGIS ASST 315 CHOB 52331
Maneval, Chris CHIEF OF STAFF 315 CHOB 52331
Meyer, Theresa LEGIS CORRES 315 CHOB 52331
Trent, Julia STAFF ASST 315 CHOB 52331
Zinda, Landon LEGIS DIR 315 CHOB 52331

DISTRICT OFFICE

OTSEGO—9201 QUADAY AVE NE, OTSEGO, MN 55330

Freimark, Zachary DIST REP 763-241-6848
Harper, Barbara SR CASEWKR 763-241-6848
Henriquez, Alejandra CASEWKR 763-241-6848
Morse, Stacy DIST DIR 763-241-6848
Rime, Abby PRESS SECY 763-241-6848
Waaraniemi, Aaron OUTREACH DIR 763-241-6848

Representative Eliot L. Engel

New York, 16th

2426 RAYBURN HOB (ZIP: 20515-3216) 225-2464

Chaudhary, Sahil SR ADVISOR - HEALTH 2426 52464
Grossman, Zachary LEGIS AIDE 2426 52464
Michalek, E H Ned ADMIN ASST 2426 52464
Murray, Darlene OFFICE MGR/SCHEDULER 2426 52464
Nixon, Keith SHARED EMPLOYEE 2426 52464
Skretny, Brian LEGIS DIR 2426 52464

DISTRICT OFFICES

BRONX—3655 JOHNSON AVE, BRONX, NY 10463

Copland, Lori DIST MGR 718-796-9700
Daniels, Bryant COMMUNICATIONS DIR/DPTY DIST DIR 718-796-9700
Fedderman, Richard DIR - CONSTIT SVCS 718-796-9700
Fordyce, Joseph STAFF ASST 718-796-9700
Ojeda-Tiru, Doris CASEWKR 718-796-9700
Switzer, Kenneth DPTY DIR - CONSTIT SVCS 718-796-9700
Tannenbaum, Lisa DIR - COMMUNITY OUTREACH 718-796-9700
Weitz, Bill CHIEF OF STAFF 718-796-9700

CO-OP—177 DREISER LOOP, ROOM 3, BRONX, NY 10475

Sullivan, Maxine CASEWKR 718-320-2314

WESTCHESTER—6 GRAMATAN AVE, SUITE 205, MOUNT VERNON, NY 10550

Pohl, Remy STAFF ASST 914-699-4100
Woodson-Samuels, Tyrae DIR - CONSTIT SVCS 914-699-4100

Representative Veronica Escobar

Texas, 16th

1505 LONGWORTH HOB (ZIP: 20515-4316) 225-4831

Andino, Jessica SCHEDULER 1505 68389
Harrison, Benjamin LEGIS AIDE 1505 68334
Lerma, Eduardo CHIEF OF STAFF 1505 68330
Lopez-Sandoval, Elizabeth COMMUNICATIONS DIR 1505 68331
Murillo Villasenor, Carlos STAFF ASST 1505 68328
Sabater, Alexandra LEGIS ASST - MIL 1505 68336
Sanchez, Jacqueline LEGIS DIR 1505 68332

DISTRICT OFFICE

EL PASO—WELLS FARGO PLAZA, N KANSAS ST, SUITE 1500, EL PASO, TX 79901

Byrd, Susannah DIST DIR 915-541-1400
Calixtro, Mariajose DIST REP 915-541-1400
Ramos, Diana DIR - CONSTIT SVCS 915-541-1400
Silva, Pifas DIST REP 915-541-1400
Torres, Benito DIST REP 915-541-1400
Venegas, Jazmine DIST OFFICE MGR 915-541-1400

Representative Anna G. Eshoo

California, 18th

202 CANNON HOB (ZIP: 20515-0518) 225-8104

Boggs, Madison LEGIS CORRES 202 CHOB 58104
Brady, Michael PRESS SECY 202 CHOB 58104
Cohen, Andrew STAFF ASST 202 CHOB 58104
Fybel, Rachel SR HEALTH POLICY ADVISOR 202 CHOB 58104
Henshall, Eric LEGIS ASST 202 CHOB 58104
McMurray, Matt CHIEF OF STAFF 202 CHOB 58104
Ramzanali, Asad SR TECH POLICY ADVISOR 202 CHOB 58104
Shah, Noor SCHEDULER 202 CHOB 58104

DISTRICT OFFICE

PALO ALTO—698 EMERSON ST, PALO ALTO, CA 94301

Chapman, Karen CHIEF OF STAFF 650-323-2984
Kim, Patty DPTY CHIEF OF STAFF/COUNSEL 650-323-2984
Lopez, Baltazar SR FIELD REP 650-323-2984
Malmberg, Alice STAFF ASST 650-323-2984
Ream, Anne SR ADVISOR - HEALTH 650-323-2984

Seidman, Marla CASEWKR 650-323-2984
Yu, Crystal FIELD REP 650-323-2984

Representative Adriano Espaillat

New York, 13th

1630 LONGWORTH HOB (ZIP: 20515-3213) 225-4365
Alcala, Sandra SHARED EMPLOYEE 1630 54365
Alejandro, Kristina DPTY SCHEDULER 1630 54365
Baig, Shahryar STAFF ASST 1630 54365
Batista, Aneiry CHIEF OF STAFF 1630 54365
Castro, Elba COUNSEL 1630 54365
Dominguez, Raphael SCHEDULER 1630 54365
Greenfield, George DIR - TECH 1630 54365
Kimelman, David STAFF ASST 1630 54365
Lawson, Dion ADMIN - FINANCE & PAYROLL 1630 54365
Newman, Joseph ASST COMMUNICATIONS DIR 1630 54365
Paz, Carlos SHARED EMPLOYEE 1630 54365
Person, Candace COMMUNICATIONS DIR 1630 54365
Sloves, Todd LEGIS DIR - VICE CHAIR 1630 54365

DISTRICT OFFICES

BRONX—2530 GRAND CONCOURSE, BRONX, NY 10458
Cespedes Baez, Rolando DPTY DIST DIR 718-450-8241
Javier, Maximo DIST OFFICE MGR 718-450-8241

HARLEM—163 W 125TH ST, NEW YORK, NY 10027
Acosta, Jose PRESS AIDE 212-663-3900
Booker, Michelle DPTY DIST DIR 212-663-3900
Lopez, Radhames SPECIAL ASST 212-663-3900
Marks, Shana COMMUNITY LIAISON 212-663-3900
Rodriguez, Cynthia DIR - CONSTIT SVCS 212-663-3900
Sanchez, Maritza IMMIGRATION SPEC 212-663-3900
Tobias-Cohen, Laurie CONSTIT LIAISON 212-663-3900

Representative Ron Estes

Kansas, 4th

1524 LONGWORTH HOB (ZIP: 20515-1604) 225-6216
Baker, Greg LEGIS ASST 1524 56216
Bell, Josh CHIEF OF STAFF 1524 56216
DeFilippo, Katarina LEGIS CORRES 1524 56216
Diohep, Elizabeth LEGIS ASST 1524 56216
Martin, Daniel LEGIS ASST 1524 56216
O'Boyle, Nicholas LEGIS DIR 1524 56216
Smith, Brandon STAFF ASST 1524 56216
Steele, Gregory COMMUNICATIONS DIR 1524 56216

DISTRICT OFFICE

WICHITA—7701 E KELLOGG DR, SUITE 510, WICHITA, KS 67207
Bergquist, Ralene OFFICE MGR 316-262-8992
Erickson, Roger FIELD REP 316-262-8992
Gilpin, Austin SPECIAL PROJ COORD 316-262-8992
Luper, Debbie DIST DIR 316-262-8992
Rodriguez, Roman DIST PRESS SECY 316-262-8992

Representative Dwight Evans

Pennsylvania, 3d

1105 LONGWORTH HOB (ZIP: 20515-3803) 225-4001
Holliday, Jayme LEGIS ASST 1105 54001
Innis, Alyssa COORD - DIGITAL MEDIA/LEGIS AIDE 1105 54001
Love, Randy SCHEDULER/EXEC ASST 1105 54001
Mason, Chandler LEGIS CORRES/STAFF ASST 1105 54001
Nelson, Jonathan FINANCIAL ADMIN 1105 54001
Turner, Ben COMMUNICATIONS DIR 1105 54001
Weiss, Adam LEGIS ASST 1105 54001

DISTRICT OFFICE

PHILADELPHIA—7174 OGONTZ AVE, PHILADELPHIA, PA 19138
Hardaway, Eric DIR - CONSTIT SVCS 215-276-0340
Parker-Cox, Felicia CONG AIDE/EXEC ASST 215-276-0340
Pitts, Julia CONG AIDE 215-276-0340
St. Louis, Numa DIST REP 215-276-0340
Taft, Janee CONG AIDE 215-276-0340
Turner-Dixon, Kimberly CHIEF OF STAFF 215-276-0340

Representative A. Drew Ferguson IV

Georgia, 3d

1032 LONGWORTH HOB (ZIP: 20515-1003) 225-5901
Beal, Mary Dee LEGIS DIR 1032 55901
Heard, Jenna SCHEDULER 1032 55901
Northrop, Michael LEGIS AIDE 1032 55901
Piper, Brian STAFF ASST 1032 55901
Robinson, Miller LEGIS CORRES 1032 55901
Saparow, Bobby CHIEF OF STAFF 1032 55901
Timmerman, Amy COMMUNICATIONS DIR 1032 55901
White, Allie LEGIS ASST 1032 55901

DISTRICT OFFICE

NEWNAN—1601 E HWY 34, SUITE B, NEWNAN, GA 30265
Bush, Andy DIST DIR 770-683-2033
Craddock, Jessica CONSTIT SVCS 770-683-2033
Kirby, Max FIELD REP 770-683-2033
Pappas, Kathy CONSTIT SVCS REP 770-683-2033
Smith, Brett FIELD REP 770-683-2033
Stuckey, John CONSTIT SVCS REP 770-683-2033

Representative Abby Finkenauer

Iowa, 1st

124 CANNON HOB (ZIP: 20515-1501) 225-2911
Elliott, Joel CHIEF OF STAFF 124 CHOB 52911
Ernst, Max LEGIS ASST 124 CHOB 52911
Frischknecht, Jessica COMMUNICATIONS DIR/SR ADVISOR 124 CHOB 52911
Laska, Alex LEGIS ASST 124 CHOB 52911
Smith, Angela SCHEDULER/EXEC ASST 124 CHOB 52911
Solomon, Katie STAFF ASST 124 CHOB 52911
Swanson, Fran LEGIS AIDE/PRESS SECY 124 CHOB 52911
Wilson, Tyler LEGIS DIR/DPTY CHIEF OF STAFF 124 CHOB 52911

DISTRICT OFFICE

CEDAR RAPIDS—308 3RD ST SE, SUITE 200, CEDAR RAPIDS, IA 52401
Mullendore, Jared DIST DIR 319-364-2288
Running, Rich DIST REP 319-364-2288
Taylor, Kim CASEWKR 319-364-2288

Representative Brian K. Fitzpatrick

Pennsylvania, 1st

1722 LONGWORTH HOB (ZIP: 20515-3801) 225-4276
Auray, Christopher PRESS SECY 1722 54276
Boyer, Francis DIR - OPS 1722 54276

Knowles, Joseph DPTY CHIEF OF STAFF/LEGIS DIR 1722 .... **54276**
McCabe, Michael, Jr LEGIS ASST 1722 .... **54276**
Renteria, Andrew CHIEF OF STAFF 1722 .... **54276**
Stalcup-Gutierrez, Alexus STAFF ASST 1722 .... **54276**
Staudt, Cole COMMUNICATIONS DIR 1722 .... **54276**

DISTRICT OFFICE

LANGHORNE—1717 LANGHORNE NEWTOWN RD, LANGHORNE, PA 19047

Chong, Peter VET ADVOCATE/MIL ADVOCATE **215-579-8102**
Dyer, Jacqueline CONSTIT ADVOCATE **215-579-8102**
Gaston Simon, Susan DIST DIR **215-579-8102**
Gruda, Matthew DIST OFFICE MGR **215-579-8102**
Kaniewska, Joanna DIST STAFF ASST **215-579-8102**
Maleczkowicz, Nicholas CONSTIT ADVOCATE **215-579-8102**
Melander, Kyle DIR - CONSTIT SVCS **215-579-8102**
Rider, Verne VET ADVOCATE **215-579-8102**
Senft, Lea CONSTIT ADVOCATE **215-579-8102**

Representative Charles J. "Chuck" Fleischmann

Tennessee, 3d

2410 RAYBURN HOB (ZIP: 20515-4203) **225-3271**
Childress, Taylor LEGIS CORRES 2410 .... **53271**
Eyster, Lisa DIST DIR 2410 .... **53271**
Han, Minsu SR POLICY ADVISOR 2410 .... **53271**
Hendrix, Holly LEGIS ASST/SCHEDULER 2410 .... **53271**
Hippe, Jim CHIEF OF STAFF/COUNSEL 2410 .... **53271**
Kerr, Robert LEGIS ASST 2410 .... **53271**
Lovett, Kasey COMMUNICATIONS DIR 2410 .... **53271**
Taylor, Heath STAFF ASST 2410 .... **53271**
Tidwell, Daniel LEGIS DIR/LEGIS COUNSEL 2410 .... **53271**

DISTRICT OFFICES

ATHENS—6 E MADISON AVE, ATHENS, TN 37303

O'Dell-Gernert, Maxine DIST FIELD REP **423-745-4671**

CHATTANOOGA—900 GEORGIA AVE, SUITE 126, CHATTANOOGA, TN 37402

Boley, Bonnie STAFF ASST **423-756-2342**
Doux, Jules CASEWKR **423-756-2342**
Russell, Kayley CASEWKR **423-756-2342**
White, Bob DPTY CHIEF OF STAFF **423-756-2342**

OAK RIDGE—200 ADMINISTRATION RD, SUITE 100, OAK RIDGE, TN 37830

Boshears, Cindy DIST FIELD REP **865-576-1976**
Merritt, Tammy DIST FIELD REP **865-576-1976**

Representative Lizzie Fletcher

Texas, 7th

1429 LONGWORTH HOB (ZIP: 20515-4307) **225-2571**
Berner, Alaina COMMUNICATIONS DIR 1429 .... **52571**
Cox, Olivia SCHEDULER 1429 .... **52571**
Fuller, Kim FINANCIAL ADMIN 1429 .... **52571**
Harvey, Christopher LEGIS ASST 1429 .... **52571**
Hull, Cameron STAFF ASST/LEGIS CORRES 1429 .... **52571**
Jackson, Ben LEGIS DIR 1429 .... **52571**
Kaplan Feinmann, Sarah CHIEF OF STAFF 1429 .... **52571**

DISTRICT OFFICE

HOUSTON—5599 SAN FELIPE ST, SUITE 950, HOUSTON, TX 77056

Boyett, Brooke DIST DIR **713-353-8680**
Mayes, Nina OUTREACH DIRECTOR **713-353-8680**
Morales, Claudia CASEWKR **713-353-8680**
Peterson, Andrea COMMUNICATIONS ASST **713-353-8680**

Representative Bill Flores

Texas, 17th

2228 RAYBURN HOB (ZIP: 20515-4317) **225-6105**
Castro, Andre COMMUNICATIONS DIR 2228 .... **56105**
Crews, Judith LEGIS CORRES 2228 .... **56105**
Furman, Andrew LEGIS ASST 2228 .... **56105**
Gustafson, Eric LEGIS DIR 2228 .... **56105**
Harrison, Jessica SCHEDULER 2228 .... **56105**
Oehmen, Jon CHIEF OF STAFF 2228 .... **56105**
Smith, Danny STAFF ASST 2228 .... **56105**
Taylor, Christopher LEGIS ASST 2228 .... **56105**

DISTRICT OFFICES

AUSTIN—14205 BURNET RD, SUITE 230, AUSTIN, TX 78728

Spiegelman, Abby FIELD REP **512-373-3378**

BRYAN/COLLEGE STATION—3000 BRIARCREST DR, SUITE 406, BRYAN, TX 77802

Edge, James REGIONAL DIR **979-703-4037**
Henderson, Miranda CASEWKR/COORD - GRANTS **979-703-4037**

WACO—400 AUSTIN AVE, SUITE 302, WACO, TX 76701

Hixson, Jana REGIONAL DIR **254-732-0748**
Hogan, Jacob FIELD REP **254-732-0748**
Hovhannisyan, Rozy CONSTIT LIAISON **254-732-0748**
Perry, Jill STAFF ASST **254-732-0748**

Representative Jeff Fortenberry

Nebraska, 1st

1514 LONGWORTH HOB (ZIP: 20515-2701) **225-4806**
Archer, Reyn CHIEF OF STAFF 1514 .... **54806**
Bailey, Mariel CONG AIDE 1514 .... **54806**
Cloch, Adam PRESS ASST/STAFF ASST 1514 .... **54806**
Feyerherm, Alan LEGIS DIR/DPTY CHIEF OF STAFF 1514 .... **54806**
Hanna, Mena SR POLICY ADVISOR 1514 .... **54806**
Kennedy, Nicholas CASEWKR 1514 .... **54806**

DISTRICT OFFICES

FREMONT—641 N BROAD ST, FREMONT, NE 68026........ **402-727-0888**

LINCOLN—301 S 13TH ST, SUITE 100, LINCOLN, NE 68508

Crawford, Todd CASEWKR **402-438-1598**
Crotty, Jim COMMUNICATIONS DIR **402-438-1598**
Kwapnioski, Kimberly DIST AIDE **402-438-1598**
Sanders, Rita DIST AIDE **402-438-1598**
Walker, Jeanne CONSTIT REP **402-438-1598**
Woodhead, Marie DIST DIR **402-438-1598**

NORFOLK—MCMILL BLDG, 125 S 4TH ST, NORFOLK, NE 68701

Klein, Lee FIELD REP **402-379-2064**

Representative Bill Foster

Illinois, 11th

2366 RAYBURN HOB (ZIP: 20515-1311) **225-3515**
Allen, Amber ADMIN - FINANCE & PAYROLL 2366 .... **53515**
Lu, Diem-Mi SR POLICY ADVISOR/LEGIS COUNSEL 2366 .... **53515**
Schmidt, Maggie SCHEDULER 2366 .... **53515**
Shewcraft, Scott CHIEF OF STAFF 2366 .... **53515**
Siddiqui, Faisal SYS ADMIN 2366 .... **53515**
Timmins, Gary SR POLICY ADVISOR 2366 .... **53515**
Van Blaricom, Justin LEGIS CORRES/STAFF ASST 2366 .... **53515**

Warren, Samantha LEGIS DIR 2366 53515
Werden, Mary COMMUNICATIONS DIR 2366 53515

DISTRICT OFFICES

AURORA—2711 E NEW YORK ST, SUITE 204, AURORA, IL 60502
Adams, Chris CONSTIT ADVOCATE 630-585-7672
Cybulski, Greg PRESS SECY 630-585-7672
Denk, Hilary DIST DIR 630-585-7672
Koch, Mary Margaret DIST SCHEDULER/DIST STAFF ASST 630-585-7672
Manzo, Maria OUTREACH DIR 630-585-7672
Salberg, Wendy CASEWKR 630-585-7672

JOLIET—815 N LARKIN AVE, SUITE 206, JOLIET, IL 60435
Robb, Brian COORD - OUTREACH 815-280-5876

Representative Virginia Foxx

North Carolina, 5th

2462 RAYBURN HOB (ZIP: 20515-3305) 225-2071
Artz, Cyrus CHIEF OF STAFF 2462 52071
Barton, Carter LEGIS AIDE 2462 52071
Besonen, Mark LEGIS CORRES 2462 52071
Bryant, Tabetha OFFICE MGR 2462 52071
Harvey, Jason LEGIS ASST 2462 52071
Middleton, Carson LEGIS DIR/DPTY CHIEF OF STAFF 2462 52071
Pic, Jordan SCHEDULER 2462 52071
Voorman, David LEGIS ASST 2462 52071
Werner, Sara PRESS SECY 2462 52071

DISTRICT OFFICES

BOONE—400 SHADOWLINE DR, SUITE 205, BOONE, NC 28607
Beechler, Tracie CONSTIT LIAISON 828-265-0240
Bishop, Audrey CONSTIT LIAISON 828-265-0240
McBrayer, Thomas STAFF ASST 828-265-0240
Meek, Robert DIST DIR 828-265-0240

CLEMMONS—3540 CLEMMONS RD, SUITE 125, CLEMMONS, NC 27012
TOLL-FREE NUMBER 1-866-677-8968
Bandy, Patricia OFFICE MGR 336-778-0211
Jackson, Paul CONSTIT LIAISON 336-778-0211
Krivsky, Andrew CONSTIT LIAISON 336-778-0211

Representative Lois Frankel

Florida, 21st

2305 RAYBURN HOB (ZIP: 20515-0921) 225-9890
Bleiberg, Daniel LEGIS ASST 2305 59890
Hodge, Olivia PRESS SECY 2305 59890
Huxley-Cohen, Rachel COMMUNICATIONS DIR 2305 59890
Labovick, Hannah STAFF ASST 2305 59890
Mayayeva, Yana LEGIS ASST 2305 59890
Moran, Kelsey CHIEF OF STAFF 2305 59890
Regan, Kate SCHEDULER 2305 59890
Solyan, Bradley LEGIS ASST 2305 59890
Spolarich, Gillian PRESS SECY 2305 59890
Wolf, Ian LEGIS DIR 2305 59890

DISTRICT OFFICE

BOCA RATON—2500 N MILITARY TRAIL, SUITE 490, BOCA RATON, FL 33431
Ceasar, Jenny COORD - DIST OUTREACH 561-998-9045
Germansky, Nancy CONSTIT SVCS 561-998-9045
Goldstein, Felicia DIST DIR 561-998-9045
Lewis, Charity COORD - DIST OUTREACH 561-998-9045
Marciano, Tina CONSTIT SVCS 561-998-9045

Representative Marcia L. Fudge

Ohio, 11th

2344 RAYBURN HOB (ZIP: 20515-3511) 225-7032
Allen, Amber FINANCIAL MGR 2344 57032
Edwards, Imani SCHEDULER/OFFICE MGR 2344 57032
Herrbach, Joe LEGIS ASST 2344 57032
Mazyck, Veleter CHIEF OF STAFF 2344 57032
Stallings, Bernadine COMMUNICATIONS DIR 2344 57032
Thompson, Cora INFO TECH MGR 2344 57032

DISTRICT OFFICES

AKRON—1225 LAWTON ST, AKRON, OH 44320
Williams, Joan COORD - DIST OUTREACH 330-835-4758

CLEVELAND—4834 RICHMOND RD, SUITE 150, WARRENSVILLE HEIGHTS, OH 44128
Harris, Camren CONG LIAISON 216-522-4900
Kelsch, Esther DIST FIELD REP 216-522-4900
Matthews, Linda SCHEDULER/DIST OFFICE MGR 216-522-4900
Simms, Alexis PRESS ASST/COORD - DIGITAL MEDIA 216-522-4900
Williams, Clifton DIST DIR 216-522-4900

Representative Russ Fulcher

Idaho, 1st

1520 LONGWORTH HOB (ZIP: 20515-1201) 225-6611
Ackerman, Stephen LEGIS ASST 1520 56611
Bayer, Clifford CHIEF OF STAFF 1520 56611
Keenan, Matthew LEGIS CORRES 1520 56611
Lester, Dean OFFICE ADMIN 1520 56611
Neill, Andrew LEGIS DIR 1520 56611
Rogge, Alexah COMMUNICATIONS DIR 1520 56611
Sullivan, Mary-Margaret STAFF ASST 1520 56611
Tellez, Daniel SCHEDULER/PRESS ASST 1520 56611

DISTRICT OFFICES

COEUR D'ALENE—1250 IRONWOOD DR, SUITE 241, COEUR D'ALENE, ID 83814
Kastning, Timothy REGIONAL DIR 208-667-1027

LEWISTON—313 D ST, SUITE 107, LEWISTON, ID 83501
Daniel, Clinton REGIONAL DIR 208-743-1388

MERIDIAN—33 E BROADWAY AVE, SUITE 251, MERIDIAN, ID 83642
Cunnington, Michael DIST DIR 208-888-3188
Jarvis, Michele STAFF ASST/DIST SCHEDULER 208-888-3188
Mendive, Dirk REGIONAL DIR 208-888-3188
Phillips, Jackie STAFF ASST/CONSTIT SVCS REP 208-888-3188
Shockey, Tori CASEWK DIR 208-888-3188

Representative Tulsi Gabbard

Hawaii, 2d

1433 LONGWORTH HOB (ZIP: 20515-1102) 225-4906
Chovil, Andres LEGIS ASST 1433 54906
Chun, Dave DPTY LEGIS DIR 1433 54906
Deery, Katherina STAFF ASST/OFFICE COORD 1433 54906
Finn, Colin LEGIS CORRES 1433 54906
Hartl, Kellie FINANCIAL ADMIN 1433 54906
Koetzle, Patrick LEGIS ASST 1433 54906
Koski, Amanda SCHEDULER 1433 54906
McIlvaine, Lauren PRESS SECY 1433 54906
Weiss, Guido LEGIS DIR 1433 54906

DISTRICT OFFICE

HONOLULU—300 ALA MOANA BLVD, NO. 5-104, HONOLULU, HI 96850

Anthony, Anya OFFICE MGR 808-541-1986
Baumgart-Turner, Kirsten CONSTIT OUTREACH REP 808-541-1986
Finn, Kaulana CONSTIT OUTREACH REP 808-541-1986
Gionson, Ilihia CONSTIT OUTREACH REP 808-541-1986
Hamada, Jimmy CONSTIT OUTREACH REP 808-541-1986
Masiya, Shingayi CONSTIT OUTREACH REP 808-541-1986
McMillan, Katie CONSTIT OUTREACH REP 808-541-1986
Penaroza, Kainoa CHIEF OF STAFF 808-541-1986
Turner, Naia STAFF ASST 808-541-1986

Representative Matt Gaetz

Florida, 1st

1721 LONGWORTH HOB (ZIP: 20515-0901) 225-4136
Ball, Luke PRESS SECY 1721 54136
Holland, Peter LEGIS CORRES 1721 54136
Lane-Wyant, Jillian CHIEF OF STAFF 1721 54136
Murphy, Devin LEGIS DIR 1721 54136
Thomas, Alison SCHEDULER 1721 54136
Truxal, Charlie LEGIS ASST - MIL 1721 54136

DISTRICT OFFICE

PENSACOLA—226 S PALAFOX PL, PENSACOLA, FL 32503

Brown, Erica DIST AIDE 850-479-1183
Lefevers, Sara COORD - COMMUNITY OUTREACH 850-479-1183
McArdle, Dawn DIST DIR 850-479-1183
Nelson, Nate DIR - MIL & COMMUNITY RELATIONS 850-479-1183
Watt, Pamela DIST AIDE 850-479-1183

Representative Mike Gallagher

Wisconsin, 8th

1230 LONGWORTH HOB (ZIP: 20515-4908) 225-5665
Andreae, Taylor CHIEF OF STAFF 1230 55665
Dunn, Jordan PRESS SECY 1230 55665
Jacobs, Mike LEGIS ASST 1230 55665
Morrison, Chas LEGIS DIR 1230 55665
Smethers, Will LEGIS ASST 1230 55665
Taheri, Kevin LEGIS CORRES 1230 55665
Villaca, Naomi DIR - OPS/SCHEDULER 1230 55665
Woodin, Maggie LEGIS ASST 1230 55665

DISTRICT OFFICE

DE PERE—1702 SCHEURING RD, SUITE B, DE PERE, WI 54115

Brooker, David FIELD REP 920-301-4500
Buttke, Emma DPTY DIST DIR 920-301-4500
Goodman, Betsy EXEC ASST 920-301-4500
Meyer, Pauline FIELD REP 920-301-4500
Sense, Rick DIST DIR 920-301-4500
Skaleski, Kerry CONSTIT SVCS REP 920-301-4500

Representative Ruben Gallego

Arizona, 7th

1131 LONGWORTH HOB (ZIP: 20515-0307) 225-4065
Carr, Christina COMMUNICATIONS DIR 1131 54065
Childress, Allison SCHEDULER 1131 54065
Flynn, Anthony CASEWORK - VETS 1131 54065
Fuller, Kim ADMIN - FINANCE & PAYROLL 1131 54065
Ikoku, Robert SR POLICY ADVISOR 1131 54065
Jorgenson, Mariel LEGIS CORRES/POLICY AIDE 1131 54065
Montes, David CHIEF OF STAFF 1131 54065
Schelble, Nathan LEGIS DIR 1131 54065

DISTRICT OFFICE

PHOENIX—1601 NORTH 7TH ST, SUITE 310, PHOENIX, AZ 85006

Ferniza, Sandra INTERGOVT LIAISON 602-256-0551
Heredia, Luis DIST DIR 602-256-0551
Ramos, Humberto DIST STAFF ASST 602-256-0551
Royce, Zak DIR - CONSTIT SVCS 602-256-0551
Sandschafer, Monica SR OUTREACH DIR 602-256-0551

Representative John Garamendi

California, 3d

2368 RAYBURN HOB (ZIP: 20515-0503) 225-1880
Agdaian, Tigran LEGIS ASST 2368 51880
Bottoms, Bradley CHIEF OF STAFF 2368 51880
Browne, Tessa SCHEDULER 2368 51880
Feizi, Farima DIST AIDE 2368 51880
Griego-Schneider, Mary Jane SR FIELD REP 2368 51880
Hart, Iain SR POLICY ADVISOR 2368 51880
Henry-Bryant, Heather ADMIN - FINANCE & PAYROLL 2368 51880
Jernigan, Jacob LEGIS ASST 2368 51880
Nicoletti, John SR FIELD REP 2368 51880
Olsen, Eric COMMUNICATIONS DIR 2368 51880
Siddiqui, Faisal TECH SOLUTIONS TECH 2368 51880
Sidle, Logan DIST AIDE 2368 51880
Thompson, Elizabeth SR POLICY ADVISOR 2368 51880

DISTRICT OFFICES

DAVIS—412 G ST, DAVIS, CA 95616

Gibbs, Debbi DIST DIR 530-753-5301
Hartsough, Jacqueline CONSTIT SVCS REP 530-753-5301

FAIRFIELD—1261 TRAVIS BLVD, SUITE 180, FAIRFIELD, CA 94533

Batchelor, Jack SR FIELD REP 707-438-1822

Representative Jesús G. "Chuy" García

Illinois, 4th

530 CANNON HOB (ZIP: 20515-1304) 225-8203
Andres, Don LEGIS DIR 530 CHOB 61717
Bueno, Jacqueline DIGITAL ASST/STAFF ASST 530 CHOB 510-965-3304
Garcia, Lanette LEGIS ASST 530 CHOB 55087
Ginsburg, Bob SR POLICY ADVISOR 530 CHOB 61496
Haedtler, Jordan LEGIS ASST 530 CHOB 58203
Lake, Naomi LEGIS CORRES 530 CHOB 55096
Moe, Kari CHIEF OF STAFF 530 CHOB 55092
Rodriguez-Ciampoli, Fabiola COMMUNICATIONS DIR 530 CHOB 61497
Santoy, Julissa DIR - OPS/SCHEDULER 530 CHOB 53575

DISTRICT OFFICE

CHICAGO—3240 W FULLERTON AVE, CHICAGO, IL 60647

Cardenas, Natalia LIAISON - CONSTIT SVCS 773-342-0774
Devora, Damaris SR CONSTIT SVCS REP 773-342-0774
Garcia, David LIAISON - CONSTIT SVCS 773-342-0774
García, Patty DIST DIR 773-342-0774
Valerio, Ilissa LIAISON - CONSTIT SVCS 773-342-0774

Representative Sylvia R. Garcia

Texas, 29th

1620 LONGWORTH HOB (ZIP: 20515-4329) 225-1688
Bond, Pat LEGIS DIR 1620 51688

Dale, Evan SCHEDULER 1620 51688
Dimitroff, Kallen SPECIAL ASST/ADVISOR - HEALTH POLICY 1620 51688
Gorczynski, John ADVISOR - DEFENSE/ADVISOR - FOREIGN POLICY/ CHIEF OF STAFF 1620 51688
Greenwood, Alexandra LEGIS CLERK 1620 51688
Shaw, Don COMMUNICATIONS DIR/TAX ADVISOR/ADVISOR - SCIENCE 1620 51688
Valega, Ellie STAFF ASST 1620 51688

DISTRICT OFFICE

HOUSTON—11811 EAST FREEWAY, SUITE 430, HOUSTON, TX 77029

Guerrero, Lolita FIELD REP 832-325-3150
Harris, Yuroba SPECIAL EVENTS DIR/DIR - DIST PROJ 832-325-3150
Hogue, Claudia DIST DIR 832-325-3150
Vasquez, Daniel FIELD REP/DIGITAL ASST 832-325-3150

Representative Greg Gianforte

Montana, At Large

1222 LONGWORTH HOB (ZIP: 20515-2600) **225-3211**
Carraco, Will LEGIS DIR 1222 53211
Descamps, Nicholas LEGIS CORRES 1222 53211
Hall, Travis COMMUNICATIONS DIR 1222 53211
Heggem, Christine CHIEF OF STAFF 1222 53211
McKemey, Tripp SR LEGIS ASST 1222 53211
Morris, Maddy SCHEDULING DIR 1222 53211
Saleeby, Emily ADMIN - FINANCE & PAYROLL 1222 53211
Skoog, Kaitlynn LEGIS ASST 1222 53211
Wemple, Brian STAFF ASST 1222 53211

DISTRICT OFFICES

BILLINGS—222 N 32ND ST, SUITE 900, BILLINGS, MT 59101

Dean, Melissa FIELD REP 406-969-1736
Robinson, Lesley STATE DIR 406-969-1736
Waters, Michael MIL FIELD REP 406-969-1736

GREAT FALLS—710 CENTRAL AVE, GREAT FALLS, MT 59401

Scribner, Tory CASEWKR 406-952-1280

HELENA—7 WEST 6TH AVE, SUITE 3B, HELENA, MT 59601

Capece, Sonny FIELD REP 406-502-1435
Collins, Casey FIELD REP 406-502-1435
Schultz, Thomas PRESS SECY 406-502-1435
Simons, Brett FIELD REP 406-502-1435
Slusser, Hannah DIST STAFF ASST 406-502-1435

Representative Bob Gibbs

Ohio, 7th

2446 RAYBURN HOB (ZIP: 20515-3507) **225-6265**
Bates, Brian LEGIS AIDE 2446 56265
Briggs, Alex LEGIS DIR 2446 56265
Dilworth, Ryan LEGIS AIDE 2446 56265
Gerber, Dallas COMMUNICATIONS DIR/DPTY CHIEF OF STAFF 2446 56265
Gross, Hillary CHIEF OF STAFF 2446 56265
Morrow, Madeline LEGIS CORRES 2446 56265
Sroka, Will STAFF ASST 2446 56265
Van Mersbergen, Rachael SCHEDULER 2446 56265

DISTRICT OFFICES

ASHLAND—110 COTTAGE ST, ASHLAND, OH 44805

Brooks, Kyle CASEWKR 419-207-0650
Kiko, Jennifer FIELD REP 419-207-0650
McWilliams, Jennifer STAFF ASST 419-207-0650
Ross, Tim DIST DIR 419-207-0650
Schlabach, Shanna CASEWK MGR/OFFICE MGR 419-207-0650

CANTON—110 CENTRAL PLAZA S, CANTON, OH 44702

Vanbuskirk, Victoria FIELD REP 330-737-1631

Representative Louie Gohmert

Texas, 1st

2267 RAYBURN HOB (ZIP: 20515-4301) **225-3035**
Allen, Brian LEGIS ASST 2267 53035
Brookshire, Emma LEGIS AIDE 2267 53035
Buish, Jordan RESEARCH ASST 2267 53035
Cohen, Chelsea SCHEDULER/OFFICE MGR 2267 53035
Conklin, Caralee LEGIS DIR 2267 53035
Griffin, Sean COUNSEL 2267 53035
Hair, Connie CHIEF OF STAFF 2267 53035
Hrovat, Sarah PRESS ASST 2267 53035
Vogt, Lori STAFF ASST 2267 53035
Willingham, Kimberly COMMUNICATIONS DIR 2267 53035

DISTRICT OFFICES

LONGVIEW—GREGG COUNTY COURTHOUSE, 101 E METHVIN ST, SUITE 302, LONGVIEW, TX 75601 .... **903-236-8597**
TOLL-FREE NUMBER **1-866-535-6302**

LUFKIN—LUFKIN CITY HALL, 300 E SHEPHERD AVE, SUITE 210, LUFKIN, TX 75901 .... **936-632-3180**
TOLL-FREE NUMBER **1-866-535-6302**

MARSHALL—102 W HOUSTON ST, MARSHALL, TX 75670
TOLL-FREE NUMBER **1-866-535-6302**

NACOGDOCHES—101 W MAIN, SUITE 160, NACOGDOCHES, TX 75961
TOLL-FREE NUMBER **1-866-535-6302**

TYLER—1121 ESE LOOP 323, SUITE 206, TYLER, TX 75701
TOLL-FREE NUMBER **1-866-535-6302**

Crisp, Shannon CASEWKR 903-561-6349
Fitzgerald, Jonna DIST DIR 903-561-6349
Kartye, Melinda CONSTIT SVCS REP 903-561-6349
Lowes, Sue DIST STAFF ASST 903-561-6349
Tanner, John DIST FIELD REP 903-561-6349
Thomas, Shea CASEWKR 903-561-6349

Representative Jared F. Golden

Maine, 2d

1223 LONGWORTH HOB (ZIP: 20515-1902) **225-6306**
Davis, Gaetan SCHEDULER 1223 56306
Jamieson, Ainsley STAFF ASST 1223 56306
Jenkins, Dan LEGIS ASST 1223 56306
Kanter, Eric LEGIS DIR 1223 56306
Rich, Matt LEGIS ASST 1223 56306
Sege, Aaron LEGIS CORRES 1223 56306
Woodward, Aisha CHIEF OF STAFF 1223 56306
Zeller, Nick COMMUNICATIONS DIR 1223 56306

DISTRICT OFFICES

BANGOR—6 STATE ST, SUITE 101, BANGOR, ME 04401

Pottle Urquhart, Morgan DIST REP 207-249-7400

CARIBOU—7 HATCH DR, SUITE 230, CARIBOU, ME 04736

Hayslett, Barbara DIST REP/SR CASEWKR 207-492-6009
Rohn, Kim CONSTIT SVCS REP 207-492-6009

LEWISTON—179 LISBON ST, LEWISTON, ME 04240

Cloutier, Kathy DIST REP 207-241-6767

Manter, Emily CONSTIT SVCS REP 207-241-6767
Reynolds, Margaret DIST DIR 207-241-6767

Representative Jimmy Gomez

California, 34th

1530 LONGWORTH HOB (ZIP: 20515-0534) **225-6235**
Cohen, Noah STAFF ASST 1530 56235
Guerrero, Bertha CHIEF OF STAFF 1530 56235
Harris, Eric COMMUNICATIONS DIR 1530 56235
Martirosyan, Maria LEGIS CORRES 1530 56235
Muro, Cindy CASEWKR 1530 56235
Negatu, Samuel LEGIS DIR 1530 56235
Rios, Diana LEGIS ASST 1530 56235
Zaidi, Syed PRESS ASST 1530 56235

DISTRICT OFFICE

LOS ANGELES—350 S BIXEL ST, NO. 120, LOS ANGELES, CA 90017
Chavez Carranza, Rolando STAFF ASST 213-481-1425
Chow, Steven FIELD DPTY 213-481-1425
Cortez, Marcella DIST DIR 213-481-1425
Gama, Roberto SR FIELD REP 213-481-1425
Nielsen, Michael DIST OFFICE MGR 213-481-1425
Santa Cruz, Daniel DIGITAL ASST 213-481-1425

Representative Anthony Gonzalez

Ohio, 16th

1023 LONGWORTH HOB (ZIP: 20515-3516) **225-3876**
Barczak, Liz LEGIS ASST 1023 53876
Carlin, Emily COMMUNICATIONS DIR 1023 53876
Cisneros, Alex LEGIS ASST 1023 53876
Hostelley, Stephen LEGIS DIR 1023 53876
Joseph, Kristen STAFF ASST 1023 53876
Kresse, Carol SCHEDULER 1023 53876
Lolli, Tim CHIEF OF STAFF 1023 53876
Siwik, Max LEGIS CORRES 1023 53876

DISTRICT OFFICES

CANTON—4150 BELDEN VILLAGE ST, SUITE 607, CANTON, OH 44718
Atchison, Kayla COMMUNITY LIAISON/DIST SCHEDULER 330-599-7037
Bowman, Bryan VET ADVOCATE 330-599-7037
Matthews, Heidi DIST DIR 330-599-7037

STRONGSVILLE—13477 PROSPECT RD, SUITE 212, STRONGSVILLE, OH 44149
Cunnington, Mike CONSTIT SVCS REP 440-783-3696
Dobo, David SR DIST REP 440-783-3696
Gibson, Brandon DIST STAFF ASST 440-783-3696
Milli, Josette SR OUTREACH DIR 440-783-3696

Representative Vicente Gonzalez

Texas, 15th

113 CANNON HOB (ZIP: 20515-4315) **225-2531**
Bentsen, Louise LEGIS DIR 113 CHOB 52531
Borjon, Jose CHIEF OF STAFF 113 CHOB 52531
Carrillo, Paulina EXEC ASST/SCHEDULER 113 CHOB 52531
Castro, Fred COUNSEL 113 CHOB 52531
Cordova, Andre STAFF ASST 113 CHOB 52531
Galindo, Jorge LEGIS ASST 113 CHOB 52531
Morales, Aaron PRESS SECY 113 CHOB 52531
Smith, Chandler LEGIS ASST 113 CHOB 52531

DISTRICT OFFICES

BENAVIDES—131 W MAIN ST, BENAVIDES, TX 78341
Martinez, Albert DIST DIR 361-279-3341

FALFURRIAS—217 E MILLER ST, SUITE 200, FALFURRIAS, TX 78355
Martinez, Albert DIST DIR 361-209-3027

MCALLEN—1305 W HACKBERRY AVE, MCALLEN, TX 78501
Herrera, Bobby CONSTIT REP 956-682-5545
Hinojosa, Karen CONSTIT REP 956-682-5545
Kalam, Nuriddin CONSTIT REP 956-682-5545
Perez, Gabriel DIST STAFF ASST 956-682-5545
Phenix, Lucy RECEPTIONIST 956-682-5545
Roberts, Patrick OUTREACH LIAISON - WOUNDED WARRIOR 956-682-5545
Toscano, Stephanie DIST DIR 956-682-5545
Zavala, S J CONSTIT REP 956-682-5545

SAN DIEGO—404 S MIER ST, SAN DIEGO, TX 78384
Martinez, Albert DIST DIR 361-279-3341

SEGUIN—1243 CARDINAL LANE, SEGUIN, TX 78155 ... **830-358-0497**

Resident Commissioner Jenniffer González-Colón

Puerto Rico, Resident Commissioner

1609 LONGWORTH HOB (ZIP: 20515-5401) **225-2615**
Boffelli, Gabriella CHIEF OF STAFF 1609 52615
Bravo Liranza, Gabriel LEGIS ASST 1609 52615
Cruz-Olivari, John DIST STAFF ASST 1609 52615
Diaz Marrero, Jose SR POLICY ADVISOR 1609 52615
Dietrich, Ross LEGIS DIR 1609 52615
Ferraiuoli Hornedo, Veronica LEGAL COUNSEL 1609 52615
Gandia, Natalia LEGIS ASST 1609 52615
Hernandez-Torres, Zaida STAFF 1609 52615
Luna, Linoshka LEGIS CORRES 1609 52615
Marquez-Paz, Natasha SCHEDULER 1609 52615
Rodriguez-Beamud, Janille DPTY CHIEF OF STAFF/LEGIS COUNSEL 1609 52615

DISTRICT OFFICE

SAN JUAN—157 AVE DE LA CONSTITUCIÓN, ANTIGUO EDIFICIO DE MEDI, SAN JUAN, PR 00901
Ayala, Michael DPTY DIST DIR 787-723-6333
Miranda-Gallardo, Norma CASEWORK - VETS 787-723-6333
Padro-Raldiris, Marieli COMMUNICATIONS DIR 787-723-6333
Rodriguez Arroyo, Allison DIST MGR 787-723-6333
Torres-Colón, Narel DIST DIR 787-723-6333

Representative Lance Gooden

Texas, 5th

425 CANNON HOB (ZIP: 20515-4305) **225-3484**
Babb, Alison FINANCIAL ADMIN 425 CHOB 53484
Crouch, Sarah FINANCIAL ADMIN 425 CHOB 53484
Ethington, Ryan LEGIS DIR 425 CHOB 53484
Harris, Aaron CHIEF OF STAFF 425 CHOB 53484
Lively, Brock LEGIS AIDE 425 CHOB 53484

Martin, Will COMMUNICATIONS DIR 425 CHOB 53484
Morales, MacKenzie SCHEDULER 425 CHOB 53484
Walters, Tristan LEGIS AIDE 425 CHOB 53484

DISTRICT OFFICE

MESQUITE—1806 LBJ FWY, SUITE 725, MESQUITE, TX 75150
Helton, Flo CASEWKR 214-765-6789
McCain, Ed DIST DIR 214-765-6789
Pool, Leigh OUTREACH COORD 214-765-6789
Ramirez, Chris STAFF ASST 214-765-6789
Spaun, Lydia OUTREACH COORD 214-765-6789

Representative Paul A. Gosar

Arizona, 4th

2057 RAYBURN HOB (ZIP: 20515-0304) 225-2315
TOLL-FREE NO. 1-888-737-1266
Brown, Melissa DIGITAL DIR 2057 52315
Burke, Rory LEGIS ANALYST 2057 52315
Foti, Leslie ADMIN DIR 2057 52315
Hanson, Tanner LEGIS ANALYST 2057 52315
Levine, Doug STAFF ASST 2057 52315
Small, Jeff EXEC DIR 2057 52315
Stechschulte, Will LEGIS CORRES 2057 52315
Van Flein, Tom CHIEF OF STAFF/CHIEF COUNSEL 2057 52315

DISTRICT OFFICES

GOLD CANYON—6499 S KINGS RANCH RD, SUITE 4, GOLD CANYON, AZ 85118
Johnson, Sean LIAISON - MIL & VET 480-882-2697
Martinez, Teresa DIR - OUTREACH & COALITIONS 480-882-2697
Pew, Penny DIST DIR/DIR - GOVT, BUSINESS, & COMMUNITY AFFAIRS 480-882-2697

KINGMAN—220 N 4TH ST, KINGMAN, AZ 86401 928-445-1683

PRESCOTT—122 N CORTEZ ST, SUITE 104, PRESCOTT, AZ 86301
Schreiner, Julie OFFICE MGR 928-445-1683
Timm, Jeff VET ADVOCATE 928-445-1683

Representative Josh Gottheimer

New Jersey, 5th

213 CANNON HOB (ZIP: 20515-3005) 225-4465
Berner, Hannah LEGIS DIR 213 CHOB 54465
Christiansen, Jenna SCHEDULER 213 CHOB 54465
Eckstein, Zachary LEGIS ASST 213 CHOB 54465
Fendrick, Josh ADVISOR - ECON POLICY 213 CHOB 54465
Fried, Matt COMMUNICATIONS DIR 213 CHOB 54465
Gansman, Dana DIST SCHEDULER 213 CHOB 54465
Gordon, Harrison STAFF ASST 213 CHOB 54465
Lantz, Ashley CHIEF OF STAFF 213 CHOB 54465
Mangano, Jennifer LEGIS CORRES 213 CHOB 54465
Marrow, Dan SR LEGIS ASST 213 CHOB 54465
Nelson, Jonathan MGR - PAYROLL & BENEFITS 213 CHOB 54465

DISTRICT OFFICES

GLEN ROCK—65 HARRISTOWN RD, SUITE 104, GLEN ROCK, NJ 07452
Arazi, Hadar DPTY DIST DIR 201-389-1100
Barth, Abigail LIAISON - CONSTIT SVCS 201-389-1100
Best, Catherine DIST DIR 201-389-1100
DiGregorio, Zack PRESS SECY 201-389-1100
Friedman, Jake DPTY DIR - OPS 201-389-1100
Gonnelli, Lauren CONSTIT OUTREACH REP 201-389-1100
Katsnelson, Sara LIAISON - CONSTIT SVCS 201-389-1100
Murray, Camille MGR - CONSTIT SVCS 201-389-1100

HACKENSACK—65 CENTRAL AVE, HACKENSACK, NJ 07601 973-814-4076

NEWTON—93 SPRING ST, SUITE 408, NEWTON, NJ 07860
Sheehan, Patrick CONSTIT OUTREACH REP 973-940-1117

RINGWOOD—60 MARGARET KING AVE, RINGWOOD, NJ 07456 973-814-4076

VERNON—21 CHURCH ST, VERNON, NJ 07462 973-814-4076

WASHINGTON BOROUGH —100 BELVIDERE AVE, WASHINGTON, NJ 07882 973-814-4076

Representative Kay Granger

Texas, 12th

1026 LONGWORTH HOB (ZIP: 20515-4312) 225-5071
Allen, Amber FINANCIAL MGR 1026 55071
Allen, Justin FINANCIAL MGR 1026 55071
Christopherson, Collin ADVISOR - DEFENSE 1026 55071
Davis, Jodi STAFF ASST 1026 55071
Dillon, Sean DPTY CHIEF OF STAFF 1026 55071
Freebairn, Spencer CHIEF OF STAFF 1026 55071
Kiley, Will LEGIS CORRES 1026 55071
Lowrance, Conley ADMIN ASST 1026 55071
Plasencia, Suzi LEGIS DIR 1026 55071
Tjelmeland, Brenan EXEC ASST 1026 55071
Walker, Adrienne LEGIS ASST 1026 55071
Weldon, Scott COMMUNICATIONS DIR 1026 55071
Winfrey, David LEGIS ASST 1026 55071

DISTRICT OFFICE

FORT WORTH—1701 RIVER RUN RD, SUITE 407, FORT WORTH, TX 76107
Flores, Josie CASEWK DIR 817-338-0909
Renken, Courtney CASEWKR 817-338-0909
Sowell, Tucker STAFF ASST 817-338-0909
Stanley, Nick COORD - OUTREACH 817-338-0909
Vandergriff, Kristen DIST DIR 817-338-0909

Representative Garret Graves

Louisiana, 6th

2402 RAYBURN HOB (ZIP: 20515-1806) 225-3901
Ayrea, Maggie LEGIS DIR 2402 53901
Davidson, Dustin LEGIS ASST 2402 53901
Erwin, Alex LEGIS CORRES 2402 53901
Molter, Meagan STAFF ASST 2402 53901
Peele, Nancy ASST CHIEF OF STAFF 2402 53901
Roig, Kevin DPTY CHIEF OF STAFF - COMMUNICATIONS 2402 53901
Sawyer, Paul CHIEF OF STAFF 2402 53901

DISTRICT OFFICES

BATON ROUGE—2351 ENERGY DR, SUITE 1200, BATON ROUGE, LA 70808
Dunstan, Lynn CONSTIT SVCS REP 225-442-1731
Johnson, Chelbi COMMUNITY LIAISON 225-442-1731
Schliewe, Stacy DPTY COMMUNICATIONS DIR/COMMUNITY LIAISON 225-442-1731
Smith, Jonathan STAFF ASST 225-442-1731

LIVINGSTON—29261 FROST RD, 2ND FLOOR, LIVINGSTON, LA 70754 225-686-4413

THIBODAUX—908 E FIRST ST, NSU CANDIES HALL, SUITE 405, THIBODAUX, LA 70301
Cavell, David DIST DIR 985-448-4103

Representative Sam Graves

Missouri, 6th

1135 LONGWORTH HOB (ZIP: 20515-2506) 225-7041
Devine, Julie LEGIS DIR 1135 .... **57041**
Hartl, Kellie FINANCIAL ADMIN 1135 .... **57041**
Hite, Chase STAFF ASST 1135 .... **57041**
Mullendore, Wyatt JR LEGIS ASST/CASEWKR 1135 .... **57041**
Parker, Leslie LEGIS ASST 1135 .... **57041**
Sass, Paul CHIEF OF STAFF 1135 .... **57041**
Schmidtlein, Meghan SR LEGIS ASST 1135 .... **57041**
Sollazzo, Amanda EXEC ASST 1135 .... **57041**

DISTRICT OFFICES

HANNIBAL—906 BROADWAY, P.O. BOX 364, HANNIBAL, MO 63401
Nichols, Bryan DIST FIELD REP/COMMUNICATIONS DIR **573-221-3400**

KANSAS CITY—11724 NW PLAZA CIRCLE, SUITE 900, KANSAS CITY, MO 64153
Brown, Tom DIST DIR/CHIEF OF STAFF **816-792-3976**
Hegeman, Joe FIELD REP **816-792-3976**
Hurlbert, Josh DIST MGR **816-792-3976**
Olson, Sarah FIELD REP/CASEWK MGR **816-792-3976**

ST. JOSEPH—411 JULES ST, ROOM 111, ST. JOSEPH, MO 64501
Barry, Matthew FIELD REP **816-749-0800**
Boss, Naomi FIELD REP **816-749-0800**

Representative Tom Graves

Georgia, 14th

2078 RAYBURN HOB (ZIP: 20515-1014) 225-5211
Black, Rachel STAFF ASST/LEGIS CORRES 2078 .... **55211**
Diffley, Ryan LEGIS ASST 2078 .... **55211**
Donnelly, John CHIEF OF STAFF 2078 .... **55211**
Fillingim, Kristin SCHEDULER 2078 .... **55211**
Mahler, Sam SR LEGIS ASST 2078 .... **55211**
Menorca, Diane FINANCIAL ADMIN 2078 .... **55211**
Murphy, Jason LEGIS DIR 2078 .... **55211**
Stewart, Danielle COMMUNICATIONS DIR 2078 .... **55211**
Vakharia, Shivani LEGIS ASST/PRESS ASST 2078 .... **55211**

DISTRICT OFFICES

DALTON—702 S THORNTON AVE, DALTON, GA 30720
Bartley, Tracey DIR - CONSTIT SVCS **706-226-5320**
Hogg, Spencer SPECIAL ASST **706-226-5320**
Jones, Valerie CONSTIT SVCS REP **706-226-5320**
Lents, Deborah STAFF ASST **706-226-5320**
Loudermilk, Travis FIELD REP **706-226-5320**

ROME—600 FIRST ST, SUITE 301, ROME, GA 30161
Liles, Linda CONSTIT SVCS REP **706-290-1776**
Mooney, Jackie CONSTIT SVCS REP **706-290-1776**
Whitmire, Bud DIST DIR/DPTY CHIEF OF STAFF **706-290-1776**

Representative Al Green

Texas, 9th

2347 RAYBURN HOB (ZIP: 20515-4309) 225-7508
Bivens, Bobby STAFF ASST 2347 .... **57508**
Greenfield, George SYS ADMIN 2347 .... **57508**
Hale, Keenan LEGIS AIDE 2347 .... **57508**
Lawson, Dion FINANCIAL ADMIN 2347 .... **57508**
Morgan, Martina OFFICE MGR/SCHEDULER 2347 .... **510-3047**
Pelkyi, Tenzin LEGIS ASST 2347 .... **57508**
Ross, Amena CHIEF OF STAFF 2347 .... **57508**
Rowland, Matt LEGIS ASST 2347 .... **57508**

DISTRICT OFFICE

HOUSTON—3003 S LOOP WEST, SUITE 460, HOUSTON, TX 77054
Chen, Alice COMMUNITY & OUTREACH LIAISON **713-383-9234**
Cruz, Ruben STAFF ASST **713-383-9234**
Holliday, Clarence CONSTIT SVCS **713-383-9234**
Le, Catherine CONSTIT SVCS **713-383-9234**
Merchant, Sam CONSTIT SVCS **713-383-9234**
Rodriguez, Rachael DIST DIR **713-383-9234**
Swindle, Bessie COMMUNITY LIAISON **713-383-9234**
Webster, Crystal DIST ADMIN/DIST MGR **713-383-9234**
Williams, Kwentoria A STAFF ASST **713-383-9234**

Representative Mark E. Green

Tennessee, 7th

533 CANNON HOB (ZIP: 20515-4207) 225-2811
Austin, Andrew LEGIS AIDE 533 CHOB **52811**
Danaher, Joseph LEGIS ASST 533 CHOB **52811**
Hailstone, Mitchell COMMUNICATIONS DIR 533 CHOB **52811**
Kronzer, Jay LEGIS DIR 533 CHOB **52811**
Mason, William DEVELOPMENT DIR 533 CHOB **52811**
Proferes, Jerrica SCHEDULER 533 CHOB **52811**
Siao, Stephen CHIEF OF STAFF 533 CHOB **52811**

DISTRICT OFFICES

CLARKSVILLE—128 N SECOND ST, SUITE 104, CLARKSVILLE, AL 37040
Crane, Mark FIELD REP **931-266-4483**
Joyner, Alex DIST STAFF ASST **931-266-4483**
Parker, Woody SR CASEWKR **931-266-4483**

FRANKLIN—305 PUBLIC SQUARE, SUITE 212, FRANKLIN, TN 37064
Allbrooks, Steve DIST DIR **629-223-6050**
Blakely, John FIELD REP **629-223-6050**
Carroll, Patricia FIELD REP **629-223-6050**
Scott, Stephanie SR CASEWKR **629-223-6050**

Representative H. Morgan Griffith

Virginia, 9th

2202 RAYBURN HOB (ZIP: 20515-4609) 225-3861
Baird, Kevin COMMUNICATIONS DIR 2202 .... **53861**
Lange, Katherine LEGIS CORRES 2202 .... **53861**
McCollum, Kelly Lungren CHIEF OF STAFF 2202 .... **53861**
Michael, Emily SR POLICY ADVISOR 2202 .... **53861**
Seum, Kristin LEGIS COUNSEL/LEGIS DIR 2202 .... **53861**
Shaw, Elliot DPTY COMMUNICATIONS DIR/EXEC ASST 2202 .... **53861**
Shaw, Mindy LEGIS ASST 2202 .... **53861**
Snyder, Ari STAFF ASST 2202 .... **53861**

DISTRICT OFFICES

ABINGDON—323 W MAIN ST, ABINGDON, VA 24210-2841
Bebout, Tammie SR CONSTIT SVCS REP **276-525-1405**
Cawood, Marge STAFF ASST **276-525-1405**
Dumler, Ambler CONSTIT SVCS REP **276-525-1405**
Jenkins, Michelle DIST DIR **276-525-1405**
Mumpower, Cody FIELD REP **276-525-1405**

CHRISTIANSBURG—17 W MAIN ST, CHRISTIANSBURG, VA 24073
Hall, Angie CONSTIT SVCS REP **540-381-5671**
Landis, NormaJean DIST SCHEDULER **540-381-5671**

Smith, Kathy STAFF ASST 540-381-5671
Stafford, Barbara CONSTIT SVCS REP 540-381-5671

Representative Raúl M. Grijalva

Arizona, 3d

1511 LONGWORTH HOB (ZIP: 20515-0303) 225-2435
Emerick Clerkin, Amy CHIEF OF STAFF 1511 52435
Henry-Bryant, Heather FINANCIAL ADVISOR 1511 52435
Matty, Paloma DIST AIDE 1511 52435
Miller, Glenn SR POLICY ADVISOR 1511 52435
Mishkin, Kelsey DPTY CHIEF OF STAFF 1511 52435
Molina, Sayanna LEGIS AIDE 1511 52435
Nolan, Geoffrey COMMUNICATIONS DIR 1511 52435
Salazar, Norma LEGIS AIDE 1511 52435
Villa, Cristina SCHEDULER 1511 52435
Zepeda, Marilyn LEGIS CORRES 1511 52435

DISTRICT OFFICES

AVONDALE—1415 N CENTRAL AVE, SUITE B, AVONDALE, AZ 85393
Falcon, Luis DIST AIDE 623-536-3388

SOMERTON/YUMA—146 N STATE AVE, SOMERTON, AZ 85350
Garcia, Martha DIST AIDE 928-343-7933

TUCSON—101 W IRVINGTON RD, TUCSON, AZ 85714
Alvarez Reyes, Angelica STAFF ASST 520-622-6788
Becerra, Cassandra DIST SCHEDULER 520-622-6788
Martinez, Alex CONSTIT SVCS 520-622-6788
Medina, Josie DIR - CONSTIT SVCS 520-622-6788
Reyes, Ruben DIST DIR 520-622-6788
Sigal, Nate DIST AIDE 520-622-6788

Representative Glenn Grothman

Wisconsin, 6th

1427 LONGWORTH HOB (ZIP: 20515-4906) 225-2476
Baker, Samantha LEGIS ASST 1427 52476
Croft, Ryan LEGIS DIR 1427 52476
Grawien, Christopher SR LEGIS ASST 1427 52476
Konrath, Patrick LEGIS AIDE 1427 52476
Svoboda, Timothy COMMUNICATIONS DIR 1427 52476
Teska, Rebecca LEGIS AIDE/EXEC SCHEDULER 1427 52476
Ver Velde, Rachel CHIEF OF STAFF 1427 52476

DISTRICT OFFICE

FOND DU LAC—24 W PIONEER RD, FOND DU LAC, WI 54935
Acker, Juanita CASEWKR 920-907-0624
Dallman, Alex CONSTIT OUTREACH REP/DIST FIELD REP 920-907-0624
Herbert, Chad SR CONSTIT SVCS REP 920-907-0624
Holland, Micaela DIST SCHEDULER 920-907-0624
Ling, Taylor DIST STAFF ASST 920-907-0624
Ott, Alan DIST DIR 920-907-0624
Parafiniuk, Sadie DPTY DIST DIR 920-907-0624

Representative Michael Guest

Mississippi, 3d

230 CANNON HOB (ZIP: 20515-2403) 225-5031
Buckner, Ann Hilton EXEC ASST 230 CHOB 55031
Downs, Jordan CHIEF OF STAFF 230 CHOB 55031
Johnson, Sharon DPTY CHIEF OF STAFF 230 CHOB 55031
Joseph, Elizabeth POLICY DIR 230 CHOB 55031
Little, Luke LEGIS ASST 230 CHOB 55031
Pillow, Rob COMMUNICATIONS DIR 230 CHOB 55031
White, Bubba LEGIS ASST 230 CHOB 55031

DISTRICT OFFICES

BRANDON—308B E GOVERNMENT ST, BRANDON, MS 39042
Amason, Kim DPTY DIR - CONSTIT SVCS 769-241-6120
Boutwell, Debra DIR - SCHEDULING 769-241-6120
Cross, Harold LIAISON - MIL & VET 769-241-6120
Dixon, Chad FIELD REP 769-241-6120
Dominy, Janet DIR - CONSTIT SVCS 769-241-6120
Nichols, Jimmie FIELD REP 769-241-6120
Stewart, Bradford DIST DIR 769-241-6120

BROOKHAVEN—230 S WHITWORTH, BROOKHAVEN, MS 39601 601-823-3400

MERIDIAN—2214 5TH ST, SUITE 2170, MERIDIAN, MS 39301
White, Frances CONSTIT SVCS 601-693-6681

STARKVILLE—600 RUSSELL ST, SUITE 160, STARKVILLE, MS 39759
Jordan, Kyle DPTY DIST DIR 662-324-0007

Representative Brett Guthrie

Kentucky, 2d

2434 RAYBURN HOB (ZIP: 20515-1702) 225-3501
Beil, Jennifer OFFICE MGR 2434 53501
Bergren, Eric CHIEF OF STAFF 2434 53501
Fleming, Katherine LEGIS ASST 2434 53501
Gaydos, Lauren COMMUNICATIONS DIR 2434 53501
Murphy, Elaina LEGIS AIDE 2434 53501
Shaw, Diana STAFF ASST 2434 53501
Trainor, Sophie LEGIS DIR 2434 53501

DISTRICT OFFICES

BOWLING GREEN—996 WILKINSON TRACE, SUITE B2, BOWLING GREEN, KY 42103
Burkot, Gregory FIELD REP 270-842-9896
Foushee, Kylie FIELD REP 270-842-9896
Halter, Kim DIR - CONSTIT SVCS 270-842-9896
Leffler, Matthew CONSTIT SVCS ASST 270-842-9896
Lord, Mark DIST DIR 270-842-9896
Whitlock, Angelia CONSTIT SVCS REP 270-842-9896

DAVIESS COUNTY—2200 AIRPORT RD, OWENSBORO, KY 42301
Miles, Suzanne FIELD REP 270-842-9896

HARDIN COUNTY—411 W LINCOLN TRAIL BLVD, RADCLIFF, KY 40160
Smith, Brian DIR - ECON DEV 270-842-9896

Representative Debra A. Haaland

New Mexico, 1st

1237 LONGWORTH HOB (ZIP: 20515-3101) 225-6316
Garcia, Christopher SCHEDULER 1237 55737
Germain, Naomie STAFF ASST 1237 56318
Oms, Alejandro LEGIS CORRES 1237 56302
Salazar, Felicia COMMUNICATIONS DIR 1237 64207
Todacheene, Heidi LEGIS ASST 1237 56143
Van der Heide, Jennifer CHIEF OF STAFF 1237 55275
Wera, Eric LEGIS DIR 1237 55853
Zamar, Yves SR LEGIS ASST 1237 65047

DISTRICT OFFICE

ALBUQUERQUE—400 GOLD AVE SW, ALBUQUERQUE, NM 87102
Callaghan, Molly DIST STAFF ASST/DIST SCHEDULER 505-288-2529

Forrester, Scott DIST DIR 505-288-4816
Hull, Cynthia CONSTIT SVCS REP 505-288-4022
McKenna, Brenda FIELD REP 505-288-6224
Moore, Jon MGR - CONSTIT SVCS 505-288-4602
Sanchez, Sofia SR FIELD REP 505-288-0378
Seeley, Greg FIELD REP 505-288-4199

Representative Jim Hagedorn

Minnesota, 1st

325 CANNON HOB (ZIP: 20515-2301) 225-2472
Carr, Melissa HR SPEC 325 CHOB 52472
Hahn, Jim COMMUNICATIONS DIR 325 52472
Pirron, Kyle LEGIS ASST/LEGIS ASST - MIL 325 52472
Rogness, Becky SR COMMUNICATIONS ADVISOR 325 CHOB .. 52472
Sample, John DIR - DIGITAL MEDIA 325 52472
Su, Peter CHIEF OF STAFF 325 CHOB 52472
West, Daniel LEGIS CORRES 325 52472

DISTRICT OFFICES

MANKATO—11 CIVIC CENTER PLAZA, SUITE 301, MANKATO, MN 56001
Mantor, Karin SCHEDULER 507-323-6090
Ringhand, Derek CONSTIT OUTREACH REP 507-323-6090
Steck, Joe FIELD REP - VETS 507-323-6090
Stevenson, Carol DIST DIR 507-323-6090
VanZandt, Julie CASEWKR 507-323-6090
Zinkle, Taylor CASEWKR 507-323-6090

ROCHESTER—1530 GREENVIEW DR SW, SUITE 207, ROCHESTER, MN 55902
Altman, Ryan CONSTIT OUTREACH REP 507-323-6090
Eberhart, Aaron CONSTIT OUTREACH REP 507-323-6090

Representative Josh Harder

California, 10th

131 CANNON HOB (ZIP: 20515-0510) 225-4540
Amador, Adela LEGIS DIR/DPTY CHIEF OF STAFF 131 CHOB ... 54540
Behringer, Jenna PRESS SECY 131 CHOB 54540
Chang, Claris DIR - OPS/SCHEDULING DIR 131 CHOB 54540
Goldenberg, Rachael CHIEF OF STAFF 131 CHOB 54540
Ilaria, Jessica LEGIS ASST 131 CHOB 54540
Korn, Simon LEGIS CORRES/STAFF ASST 131 CHOB 54540

DISTRICT OFFICE

MODESTO—4701 SISK RD, MODESTO, CA 95356
Gonzalez, Briana DIST REP/MGR - GRANTS 209-579-5458
Jaycox, Katie DIST REP 209-579-5458
Saiyady, Ishtar CASEWK MGR 209-579-5458
Santos, Melissa DIST REP 209-579-5458
Ureno, Fatima CONSTIT SVCS ASSOC 209-579-5458
Warner, Karen DIST DIR 209-579-5458

Representative Andy Harris

Maryland, 1st

2334 RAYBURN HOB (ZIP: 20515-2001) 225-5311
Alkinburg, Kevin STAFF ASST 2334 55311
Cesaro, Victoria SCHEDULER 2334 55311
Daniels, Timothy LEGIS DIR/COUNSEL 2334 55311
Dutton, John CHIEF OF STAFF 2334 55311
Lynskey, Elizabeth DIR - CONSTIT SVCS/DIR - DIST AFFAIRS 2334 55311
Nista, Julia PRESS SECY 2334 55311
Smoloski, Walter LEGIS CORRES 2334 55311

DISTRICT OFFICES

BEL AIR—15 E CHURCHVILLE RD, SUITE 102B, BEL AIR, MD 21014
Hornberger, Danielle CONSTIT LIAISON 410-588-5670
Kiple, Carol CONSTIT LIAISON 410-588-5670

KENT ISLAND—100 OLDE POINT VILLAGE, SUITE 101, CHESTER, MD 21619
Arntz, Mike COMMUNITY LIAISON 410-643-5425
Rosebrock, Rachel CONSTIT LIAISON 410-643-5425
Trejo, Travis LEGIS ASST 410-643-5425

SALISBURY—100 E MAIN ST, SUITE 702, SALISBURY, MD 21801
Jester, Shawn CONSTIT LIAISON 443-944-8624
Luffman, Bunky COMMUNITY LIAISON 443-944-8624
Pace, Angie COMMUNITY RELATIONS ASST 443-944-8624
Reddish, Bill COMMUNITY LIAISON 443-944-8624

Representative Vicky Hartzler

Missouri, 4th

2235 RAYBURN HOB (ZIP: 20515-2504) 225-2876
Castle, Colleen LEGIS CORRES 2235 52876
Connelly, Chris CHIEF OF STAFF 2235 52876
Doherty, Katie EXEC DIR - VALUES ACTION TEAM 2235 52876
Esser, Carley LEGIS ASST 2235 52876
Kramer, Austin DIST DIR 2235 52876
Lee, Christine LEGIS DIR 2235 52876
McVae, Bryan SR LEGIS ASST 2235 52876
Ray, Trevor STAFF ASST 2235 52876
Swick, Anna COMMUNICATIONS DIR 2235 52876
Vogl, Jillian SCHEDULER 2235 52876

DISTRICT OFFICES

COLUMBIA—2415 CARTER LANE, SUITE 4, COLUMBIA, MO 65201
Walsh, Steve PRESS SECY/FIELD REP 573-442-9311
Worsham, Janna CASEWKR 573-442-9311

HARRISONVILLE—1909 N COMMERCIAL ST, HARRISONVILLE, MO 64701
Gilroy, Rachel DIST FIELD REP 816-884-3411
Timmerman, Adam FIELD REP 816-884-3411

LEBANON—219 N ADAMS ST, LEBANON, MO 65536
Cannon, Drew FIELD REP 417-532-5582

Representative Alcee L. Hastings

Florida, 20th

2353 RAYBURN HOB (ZIP: 20515-0920) 225-1313
Carnes, Thomas LEGIS DIR/SR COUNSEL 2353 51313
Garber, Lindsey RULES ASSOC/COUNSEL 2353 51313
Martell, Katrina LEGIS ASST 2353 51313
Morrison, Lale CHIEF OF STAFF 2353 51313
Polisar, Evan PRESS SECY/LEGIS ASST 2353 51313
Posey, DeBorah OFFICE DIR 2353 51313

DISTRICT OFFICES

TAMARAC—5701 NW 88TH AVE, SUITE 200, TAMARAC, FL 33311
Goldberg, Lewis CONG ASST 954-733-2800
Johnson, Franklin CONG ASST 954-733-2800
Larkins, William DIST STAFF ASST 954-733-2800
Mulieri, Daniel DIST STAFF ASST 954-733-2800
Torres, Andrew CONG ASST 954-733-2800
Ward, Edwina DIST SCHEDULER 954-733-2800

Williams, Maisha CONG ASST 954-733-2800
Williams, Patricia CHIEF OF STAFF 954-733-2800

WEST PALM BEACH—5725 CORPORATE WAY, SUITE 208, WEST PALM BEACH, FL 33407

Jones, Dona CONG ASST 561-676-7911
Liftman, Daniel CONG ASST 561-676-7911

Representative Jahana Hayes

Connecticut, 5th

1415 LONGWORTH HOB (ZIP: 20515-0705) 225-4476

Daly, Madeline LEGIS ASST 1415 54476
Dunn, Joe CHIEF OF STAFF 1415 54476
Ginis, Alex LEGIS DIR 1415 54476
Handau, Megan LEGIS CORRES 1415 54476
Judkins, Gianna SCHEDULER/EXEC ASST 1415 54476
Kelsaw, Capreece STAFF ASST 1415 54476
Newton, Jason COMMUNICATIONS DIR 1415 54476

DISTRICT OFFICE

WATERBURY—108 BANK ST, SECOND FLOOR, WATERBURY, CT 06702

Briere, Kayla CASEWKR 860-223-8412
DeLandro, Veronica DIST DIR 860-223-8412
Fann, Chelsea STAFF ASST 860-223-8412
Martinez, Eimy OUTREACH REP 860-223-8412
Navarro, Cindy DIGITAL ASST/PRESS ASST 860-223-8412
Reasco, Kayla OUTREACH DIR 860-223-8412

Representative Denny Heck

Washington, 10th

2452 RAYBURN HOB (ZIP: 20515-4710) 225-9740

Burgess, Jami CHIEF OF STAFF 2452 59740
Bush, Jed STAFF ASST/DIGITAL ASST 2452 59740
Henry-Bryant, Heather FINANCE LIAISON 2452 59740
Kolano, Emily LEGIS ASST/PRESS SECY 2452 59740
Markiewicz, Graham LEGIS COUNSEL 2452 59740
Mattina, Bobby COMMUNICATIONS DIR 2452 59740
Meininger, Lauren SCHEDULER 2452 59740
Siddiqui, Faisal SYS ADMIN 2452 59740
Vargish, Nick LEGIS CORRES/LEGIS AIDE 2452 59740
Wolfe, Jaxon LEGIS ASST 2452 59740
Woodbury, Brendan LEGIS DIR 2452 59740

DISTRICT OFFICES

LACEY—420 COLLEGE ST SE, SUITE 3000, LACEY, WA 98503

Coe, Holly STAFF ASST 360-459-8514
Gardner, Phil DIST DIR 360-459-8514
Johnson, Tina CASEWKR 360-459-8514
Roberts, Dallas CONSTIT OUTREACH REP 360-459-8514
Snyder, Rebecca CHIEF CASEWKR 360-459-8514
Van Der Lugt, Roel CONSTIT OUTREACH REP 360-459-8514

LAKEWOOD—6000 MAIN ST SW, SUITE 3B, LAKEWOOD, WA 98499

Adler, Lauren DPTY DIST DIR 253-533-8332

Representative Kevin Hern

Oklahoma, 1st

1019 LONGWORTH HOB (ZIP: 20515-3601) 225-2211

Ballenger, Courtney EXEC ASST 1019 52211
Billman, Jeffrey DPTY CHIEF OF STAFF 1019 52211
Dabney, Miranda PRESS SECY 1019 52211
Foster, Cameron CHIEF OF STAFF 1019 52211
Lester, Dean FINANCIAL ADMIN 1019 52211
Liotta, Christina LEGIS AIDE 1019 52211
Martin, Michael LEGIS ASST/COUNSEL 1019 52211
Schmitt, Karen OFFICE MGR 1019 52211

DISTRICT OFFICE

TULSA—2448 E 81ST ST, SUITE 5150, TULSA, OK 74137

Aery, Robert DIST DIR 918-935-3222
Jones, Adam FIELD REP 918-935-3222
Moyer, Jonathan SR ADVISOR 918-935-3222
O'Hara, Brian DPTY DIST DIR 918-935-3222
Thomas, Cam CONSTIT SVCS REP 918-935-3222
Wells, Ashley CONSTIT SVCS REP 918-935-3222

Representative Jaime Herrera Beutler

Washington, 3d

2352 RAYBURN HOB (ZIP: 20515-4703) 225-3536

Breen, Anna SR LEGIS ASST 2352 53536
Bruns, Benjamin LEGIS ASST 2352 53536
Evich, Jordan LEGIS DIR/DPTY CHIEF OF STAFF 2352 53536
Nepomuceno, Rachel EXEC ASST 2352 53536
Riesterer, Angeline COMMUNICATIONS DIR 2352 53536
Wheeler, Craig STAFF ASST 2352 53536

DISTRICT OFFICE

VANCOUVER—750 ANDERSON ST, SUITE B, VANCOUVER, WA 98661

Bowman, Casey CHIEF OF STAFF 360-695-6292
Coates, Carson DIST STAFF ASST 360-695-6292
Katz, Rachel CASEWK MGR 360-695-6292
Lewis, Dale DPTY DIST DIR 360-695-6292
Nuce, Kai CASEWKR 360-695-6292
Peiper, Pamela DIST DIR 360-695-6292
Swift, Afton POLICY ADVISOR 360-695-6292

Representative Jody B. Hice

Georgia, 10th

409 CANNON HOB (ZIP: 20515-1010) 225-4101

Barker, Nathan LEGIS CORRES/COORD - INTERN & FELLOW 409 CHOB 54101
Brown, Nick SR LEGIS ASST 409 CHOB 54101
Ford, Taylor DIR - OPS/SCHEDULING DIR 409 CHOB 54101
Gentry, Elizabeth PRESS ASST/LEGIS ASST 409 CHOB 54101
Havenner, Sheila LEAD SYS ADMIN 409 CHOB 54101
Louis-Charles, Nadgey COMMUNICATIONS DIR 409 CHOB 54101
Reitz, Tim LEGIS DIR 409 CHOB 54101
Sours, David CHIEF OF STAFF 409 CHOB 54101

DISTRICT OFFICES

MILLEDGEVILLE—3015 HERITAGE RD, SUITE 6, MILLEDGEVILLE, GA 31061

Lentz, Daniel FIELD REP 478-457-0007
Riviezzo, Domenick CONSTIT SVCS REP 478-457-0007
Shelor, Edward SPECIAL ASST 478-457-0007

MONROE—100 COURT ST, MONROE, GA 30655

Dallas, Carolyn FIELD REP/CONSTIT SVCS 770-207-1776
Gardner, Keri COORD - GRANTS/CONSTIT SVCS ASST 770-207-1776
Hayes, Jessica DPTY CHIEF OF STAFF/DIST DIR 770-207-1776
Stout, Ben SR FIELD REP 770-207-1776

THOMSON—210 RAILROAD ST, ROOM 2401, THOMSON, GA 30824

Goolsby, Beth DIR - CONSTIT SVCS 706-969-1461

Representative Brian Higgins

New York, 26th

2459 RAYBURN HOB (ZIP: 20515-3226) 225-3306
Barnes, Lyndsey LEGIS ASST 2459 53306
Burnell, Jessica LEGIS ASST 2459 53306
Ehrendreich, Cooper SCHEDULER/PRESS ASST 2459 53306
Fery, Matthew DC CHIEF OF STAFF 2459 53306
Montalbano, Nick LEGIS CORRES 2459 53306
Scala, Robert STAFF ASST 2459 53306
Williams, Kayla LEGIS DIR 2459 53306

DISTRICT OFFICES

BUFFALO—LARKIN AT EXCHANGE, 726 EXCHANGE ST, SUITE 601, BUFFALO, NY 14210
Bushen, Quinn CASEWKR 716-852-3501
Corbett-Rizzutto, Megan DIST DIR 716-852-3501
Eaton, Chuck CHIEF OF STAFF 716-852-3501
Fahey, Chris SR POLICY ADVISOR 716-852-3501
Finnegan, Richard DIST FIELD REP 716-852-3501
Kennedy, Theresa DIST SCHEDULER/COMMUNICATIONS DIR 716-852-3501
Koch, Walt SR CASEWKR/CASEWKR - MIL/CASEWORK - VETS 716-852-3501
Lockwood, Bonnie SPECIAL PROJ DIR 716-852-3501
Williams, Evelyn DIST OFFICE MGR 716-852-3501

NIAGARA FALLS—800 MAIN ST, SUITE 3C, NIAGARA FALLS, NY 14301
Macri, Suzanne DIST OFFICE MGR/CASEWKR - IMMIGRATION 716-252-1274

Representative Clay Higgins

Louisiana, 3d

424 CANNON HOB (ZIP: 20515-1803) 225-2031
Cormier, Ward LEGIS DIR 424 CHOB 52031
David, Andrew COMMUNICATIONS DIR 424 CHOB 52031
Facchiano, Kathee CHIEF OF STAFF 424 CHOB 52031
LeBlanc, Madison STAFF ASST 424 CHOB 52031
Nullet, Dominic LEGIS CORRES 424 CHOB 52031
O'Connor, Mary FINANCIAL ADMIN 424 CHOB 52031
Shewmaker, Robert LEGIS ASST 424 CHOB 52031
Wolfgram, Kelsey SR LEGIS ASST 424 CHOB 52031

DISTRICT OFFICES

LAFAYETTE —600 JEFFERSON ST, SUITE 808, LAFAYETTE, LA 70501
Broussard, Kristie CASEWKR 337-703-6105
Chautin, John FIELD REP 337-703-6105
Ellison, Greg SPECIAL PROJ 337-703-6105
Miller, Diane CASEWKR 337-703-6105
Sullivan, Chris FIELD REP 337-703-6105

LAKE CHARLES —1 LAKESHORE DR, SUITE 1670, LAKE CHARLES, LA 70629
Martin, Theresa CASEWKR 337-656-2833
Mosca, Tina CASEWKR 337-656-2833
Sammis, Coby FIELD REP 337-656-2833

Representative J. French Hill

Arkansas, 2d

1533 LONGWORTH HOB (ZIP: 20515-0402) 225-2506
Bennett, A Brooke CHIEF OF STAFF 1533 52506
Frost, Dylan LEGIS DIR 1533 52506
Hill, Lesley LEGIS ASST 1533 52506
Karvelas, Matthew LEGIS ASST 1533 52506
Munson, Mary Grace EXEC ASST/SCHEDULER 1533 52506
Schulte, Natalie PRESS ASST 1533 52506
Smith, Steven COMMUNICATIONS DIR 1533 52506
Whalen, Mitch STAFF ASST 1533 52506
Wilbourn, Anna LEGIS ASST/LEGIS CORRES 1533 52506

DISTRICT OFFICES

CONWAY—1105 DEER ST, SUITE 12, CONWAY, AR 72032
Jumde, Anushree DIST DIR 501-358-3481

LITTLE ROCK—1501 N UNIVERSITY AVE, SUITE 630, LITTLE ROCK, AR 72207
Carnahan, David LIAISON - MIL & VET/SR DIST REP .. 501-324-5941
Gildner, Leigh Anna DIST REP 501-324-5941
Maxwell, Chloe DIST REP/COORD - GRANTS & SPEC PROJ 501-324-5941
Maxwell, Richard DIST REP/LIAISON - MIL & VET 501-324-5941
Reckling, Anna STAFF ASST 501-324-5941

Representative Katie Hill

California, 25th

1130 LONGWORTH HOB (ZIP: 20515-0525) 225-1956
Burns, Emily CHIEF OF STAFF 1130 51956
Kahn, Rebecca SCHEDULER/LEGIS AIDE 1130 51956
Kelly, Graham LEGIS DIR 1130 51956
King, Kassie COMMUNICATIONS DIR 1130 51956
Nayowith, Hannah DIR - OPS 1130 51956
Steinberger, Ben SR ADVISOR 1130 51956

DISTRICT OFFICES

PALMDALE—1008 W AVE M14, SUITE E, PALMDALE, CA 93551
Herrador, Samantha FIELD REP/CONSTIT SVCS REP 661-839-0532
LaMonica, Tracey CONSTIT SVCS REP/FIELD REP 661-839-0532
Rosenthal, Andrea DPTY DIST DIR 661-839-0532

SANTA CLARITA—23734 VALENCIA BLVD, SUITE 206, SANTA CLARITA, CA 91355
Ahmadi, Jonathan SR FIELD REP 661-568-4855
Giacchetti, Angela DIST DIR 661-568-4855
Schwartz, Brooke CONSTIT SVCS REP 661-568-4855

SIMI VALLEY—1445 E LOS ANGELES AVE, SIMI VALLEY, CA 93065
O'Hara, Kelsey PROGRAM DIR/RESEARCH DIR 661-802-0244
Pender, Melissa CONSTIT SVCS REP 661-802-0244

Representative James A. Himes

Connecticut, 4th

1227 LONGWORTH HOB (ZIP: 20515-0704) 225-5541
Armaza, Mauricio STAFF ASST 1227 55541
Banks, Lin FINANCIAL ADMIN 1227 55541
Fritcke, Emily SCHEDULER 1227 55541
Goldman, Julia DIGITAL ASST 1227 55541
Hagens-Jordan, Jessica ADVISOR - FOREIGN POLICY/ADVISOR - DEFENSE 1227 55541
Harold, Meryl ADVISOR - HEALTH POLICY/STAFF ASST 1227 55541
Henson, Mark CHIEF OF STAFF 1227 55541
Higgins, Sean LEGIS CORRES 1227 55541
Larsen, Nicholas LEGIS ASST 1227 55541
Malone, Patrick COMMUNICATIONS DIR 1227 55541
Snyder, Mark LEGIS DIR 1227 55541

DISTRICT OFFICES

BRIDGEPORT—211 STATE ST, 2ND FLOOR, BRIDGEPORT, CT 06604-4223

TOLL-FREE NUMBER 1-866-453-0028
Gray, Lauren DIGITAL ASST 203-333-6600
Haskell, Will SCHEDULER/STAFF ASST 203-333-6600
Hawkins, Ben STAFF ASST 203-333-6600
Heller, Alexandra CONSTIT SVCS REP 203-333-6600
Ortegon, Catherine CONSTIT SVCS REP 203-333-6600
Pavlock, Cara DIST DIR 203-333-6600
Rodriguez, Josh CONSTIT RELATIONS REP 203-333-6600
Tertullien, Vernita DIR - COMMUNITY OUTREACH 203-333-6600

STAMFORD—888 WASHINGTON BLVD, FLOOR 10, STAMFORD, CT 06901-2927

DePina, Gloria CONSTIT SVCS REP 203-353-9400

Representative George Holding

North Carolina, 2d

1110 LONGWORTH HOB (ZIP: 20515-3302) 225-3032
Babb, Alison ADMIN - FINANCE & PAYROLL 1110 53032
Gilbert, Sarah LEGIS ASST 1110 53032
Hamlin, Robert DIR - LEGIS CORRES 1110 53032
Kilgore, Carly STAFF ASST 1110 53032
Knott, Tucker CHIEF OF STAFF 1110 53032
Nirenberg, Andrew AIDE 1110 53032
Rhyne, Curtis LEGIS DIR/DPTY CHIEF OF STAFF 1110 53032
Sheedy, Rich LEGIS CORRES 1110 53032
Smith, Katie SCHEDULER 1110 53032
Stross, Matthew LEGIS COUNSEL 1110 53032

DISTRICT OFFICE

RALEIGH—7200 FALLS OF NEUSE RD, SUITE 204, RALEIGH, NC 27615

Armstrong, Carol DIST DIR 919-782-4400
Brandenburg, Christopher SR CONSTIT SVCS REP .. 919-782-4400
Fleming, Brooke CONSTIT SVCS REP 919-782-4400
Glenn, William COMMUNICATIONS DIR 919-782-4400
Hellwig, Charles FIELD REP 919-782-4400

Representative Trey Hollingsworth

Indiana, 9th

1641 LONGWORTH HOB (ZIP: 20515-1409) 225-5315
Behuniak, Allison LEGIS ASST 1641 55315
Costas, Tyler LEGIS CORRES/STAFF ASST 1641 55315
Lentz, Connor LEGIS DIR 1641 66853
Policastro, Marie DIST SCHEDULER 1641 55315
Seifers, Brantley LEGIS ASST 1641 66871
Shaw, Rebecca CHIEF OF STAFF 1641 66858
Webster, Katie COMMUNICATIONS DIR 1641 66854
Wetherald, Margaret ADMIN - FINANCE & PAYROLL/SHARED EMPLOYEE 1641 55315

DISTRICT OFFICES

FRANKLIN—100 E JEFFERSON ST, FRANKLIN, IN 46131

Fagen, Hannah FIELD REP 317-851-8241

JEFFERSONVILLE—321 QUARTERMASTER CT, JEFFERSONVILLE, IN 47130

Cockerill, Jason FIELD REP 812-288-3999
Dos Santos, Jordan CASEWKR 812-288-3999
Jacobs, Rachel DIST CHIEF OF STAFF 812-288-3999
Watkins, Shelly CASEWK MGR 812-288-3999

Representative Kendra S. Horn

Oklahoma, 5th

415 CANNON HOB (ZIP: 20515-3605) 225-2132
Bautista, Victoria LEGIS AIDE 415 CHOB 52132
Chamness, Charlie LEGIS AIDE 415 CHOB 52132
Dunn, Kyle DIR - SCHEDULING & ADVANCE 415 CHOB 52132
King, Brady CHIEF OF STAFF 415 CHOB 52132
Payton, Rayshon LEGIS DIR 415 CHOB 52132
Perkins, Bailey LEGIS ASST 415 CHOB 52132
Sweeney, Catherine COMMUNICATIONS DIR 415 CHOB 52132
Thompson, Cora INFO TECH MGR 415 CHOB 52132
Wallace, Huston STAFF ASST 415 CHOB 52132
Zams, Kelly FINANCIAL ADMIN 415 CHOB 52132

DISTRICT OFFICE

OKLAHOMA CITY—400 N WALKER AVE, SUITE 210, OKLAHOMA CITY, OK 73102

Allen, Gabbi DIST OFFICE MGR 405-602-3074
Cruz, Jose COMMUNITY OUTREACH SPEC 405-602-3074
Howell, Kandace COMMUNITY OUTREACH SPEC 405-602-3074
McLain-Snipes, Amanda DIST DIR 405-602-3074
Morse, Rachel COMMUNITY OUTREACH SPEC 405-602-3074
Ratterree, Trent COMMUNITY OUTREACH SPEC 405-602-3074
Williams, Jay DIR - CONSTIT SVCS 405-602-3074

Representative Steven Horsford

Nevada, 4th

1330 LONGWORTH HOB (ZIP: 20515-2804) 225-9894
Brooks, Lavontae LEGIS ASST 1330 59894
Dunham, Oscar SCHEDULING DIR 1330 59894
Jones, Asha CHIEF OF STAFF 1330 59894
Patterson, Robyn COMMUNICATIONS DIR 1330 59894
Rodriguez, Jason DPTY CHIEF 1330 59894
Sharp, Kyle LEGIS AIDE 1330 59894
Solomon, Feven LEGIS CORRES 1330 59894
Villanueva, Josie LEGIS DIR 1330 59894

DISTRICT OFFICE

LAS VEGAS—2250 LAS VEGAS BLVD, N SUITE 500, NORTH LAS VEGAS, NV 89030

Austin, Ender DIST REP 702-963-9360
Bivins, Samantha DIST REP 702-963-9360
Mora, Margarita DIST REP 702-963-9360
Ramos, Melissa DIST STAFF ASST 702-963-9360
Tabalba, Angelyn DIST STAFF ASST 702-963-9360

Representative Chrissy Houlahan

Pennsylvania, 6th

1218 LONGWORTH HOB (ZIP: 20515-3806) 225-4315
Dorothy, Michelle CHIEF OF STAFF 1218 54315
Feldman, Vanessa SCHEDULER 1218 54315
Frazer, Caitlin LEGIS DIR 1218 54315
Kale, Rahul COMMUNICATIONS DIR 1218 54315
Lounsbury, Connor PRESS SECY 1218 54315
Margolis, Sara LEGIS ASST 1218 54315
Primes, Kayla LEGIS CORRES 1218 54315
Raj, Ravi STAFF ASST 1218 54315
Stuber, Aubrey OPS ASST 1218 54315
Thompson, Stacy LEGIS ASST 1218 54315
Zams, Kelly FINANCIAL ADMIN 1218 54315

DISTRICT OFFICES

READING—815 WASHINGTON ST, READING, PA 19601
Dunbar, MaCherie CASEWKR 610-295-0815
Fonte, Yvonne CASEWKR 610-295-0815

WEST CHESTER—709 E GAY ST, WEST CHESTER, PA 19380
Levine, Noah DIST SCHEDULER 610-883-5050
Nelson, Scott CASEWKR 610-883-5050
Thomas, Aaron CASEWKR 610-883-5050
Walker, Sue DIST DIR 610-883-5050

Representative Steny H. Hoyer

Maryland, 5th

1705 LONGWORTH HOB (ZIP: 20515-2005) 225-4131
Davis, Annaliese PRESS SECY 1705 54131
Dwyer, Steve DIGITAL DIR 1705 54131
Hill, Antonia LEGIS CORRES 1705 54131
Nicholas, Paul STAFF ASST 1705 54131
Notter, Jim CHIEF OF STAFF 1705 54131
Snyder, Rachel POLICY ADVISOR 1705 54131

DISTRICT OFFICES

GREENBELT—6500 CHERRYWOOD LANE, SUITE 310, GREENBELT, MD 20770
Mirza, Sana CONSTIT LIAISON 301-474-0119
Pennington, Daryl SR CONSTIT LIAISON 301-474-0119
Taylor, Terrance DPTY DIST DIR 301-474-0119

WHITE PLAINS—4475 REGENCY PL, SUITE 203, WHITE PLAINS, MD 20695
Bossart, Betsy DIST CHIEF OF STAFF 301-843-1577
Carey-Barone, Stefanie DIR - CONSTIT SVCS 301-843-1577
Phillips, Ashleigh CONSTIT LIAISON 301-843-1577

Representative Richard Hudson

North Carolina, 8th

2112 RAYBURN HOB (ZIP: 20515-3308) 225-3715
Babb, Alison ADMIN - FINANCE & PAYROLL 2112 53715
Bell, Preston LEGIS DIR 2112 53715
Bieniek, Kristine DC SCHEDULER 2112 53715
Carter, Chris CHIEF OF STAFF 2112 53715
Cloud, Sam STAFF ASST/STAFF ASST - COMMUNICATIONS 2112 53715
Gibson, Tatum COMMUNICATIONS DIR 2112 53715
Guffin, Elliott LEGIS CORRES 2112 53715
Steele, Greg STAFF ASST/PRESS ASST 2112 53715
Steele, Sophia LEGIS CORRES 2112 53715
Taylor, Shaun LEGIS ASST 2112 53715

DISTRICT OFFICES

CONCORD—325 MCGILL AVE NW, SUITE 500, CONCORD, NC 28027
Constangy, Billy DIST DIR 704-786-1612
Lozier, Georgia DPTY DIST DIR 704-786-1612
Osborne, Tucker CONSTIT SVCS REP/MGR - OUTREACH 704-786-1612

FAYETTEVILLE—225 GREEN ST, NO. 202, FAYETTEVILLE, NC 28301
Johnson, Kris CONSTIT LIAISON 910-997-2070
Maples, Chris CONSTIT RELATIONS REP 910-997-2070

PINEHURST—3395 AIRPORT RD, SUITE 105, PINEHURST, NC 28374
Maples, Chris CASEWKR 910-246-5374

Representative Jared Huffman

California, 2d

1527 LONGWORTH HOB (ZIP: 20515-0502) 225-5161
Ferree, Logan DPTY CHIEF OF STAFF/LEGIS DIR 1527 55161
Miller, Ben CHIEF OF STAFF 1527 55161
Mion, Steven DC SCHEDULER 1527 55161
Pinckney, Janna SYS ADMIN 1527 55161
Sciascia, Jordan LEGIS AIDE 1527 55161
Shaffer, Alexandra COMMUNICATIONS DIR 1527 55161
Sur, Christine LEGIS ASST 1527 55161
Wood, Natasha STAFF ASST/LEGIS CORRES 1527 55161

DISTRICT OFFICES

EUREKA—317 THIRD ST, SUITE 1, EUREKA, CA 95501
Driscoll, John DIST REP 707-407-3585
Emery, Ciara FIELD REP 707-407-3585

FORT BRAGG—430 N FRANKLIN ST, P.O. BOX 2208, FORT BRAGG, CA 95437
Brown, Sheba FIELD REP 707-962-0933

PETALUMA—206 G ST, UNIT NO. 3, PETALUMA, CA 94952 707-981-8967

SAN RAFAEL—999 FIFTH AVE, NO. 290, SAN RAFAEL, CA 94901
Callaway, Jenny DIST DIR 415-258-9657
Garcilazo, Michelle FIELD REP 415-258-9657
Hooper, Blake FIELD REP 415-258-9657
Madrigal-Hooper, Iliana DIST SCHEDULER 415-258-9657
Schroeder, Amy FIELD REP 415-258-9657

UKIAH—200 S SCHOOL ST, SUITE 1, UKIAH, CA 95482 707-671-7449

Representative Bill Huizenga

Michigan, 2d

2232 RAYBURN HOB (ZIP: 20515-2202) 225-4401
DeWitte, Jon CHIEF OF STAFF 2232 54401
Haddad, Raaed SR LEGIS ASST 2232 54401
Kohlrieser, Andrew LEGIS ASST 2232 54401
McManus, Marliss DPTY CHIEF OF STAFF 2232 54401
Rafferty, Palmer LEGIS DIR 2232 54401
Rokus, Phil STAFF ASST 2232 54401
Ruhlen, Mary FINANCIAL OFFICER 2232 54401
Tenbrink, Trevor LEGIS ASST 2232 54401
Zajac, Emily SCHEDULER 2232 54401

DISTRICT OFFICES

GRAND HAVEN—1 S HARBOR AVE, SUITE 6B, GRAND HAVEN, MI 49417
Sandberg, Heather DPTY CHIEF OF STAFF 616-414-5516

GRANDVILLE—4555 WILSON AVE SW, SUITE 3, GRANDVILLE, MI 49418
Duthler, Jennifer DIST REP 616-570-0917
Kooiman, Matthew DIST REP 616-570-0917
Lisman, Sarah DIST REP 616-570-0917
Mancilla, Beatriz DIST REP 616-570-0917
Patrick, Brian COMMUNICATIONS DIR 616-570-0917
Umanos, Krista DIST REP 616-570-0917

Representative Duncan Hunter

California, 50th

2429 RAYBURN HOB (ZIP: 20515-0550) 225-5672
Badame, Meghan LEGIS CORRES/DPTY PRESS SECY 2429 55672

Figueredo, Cristian STAFF ASST 2429 .... **55672**
Hough, Holly SR LEGIS ASST 2429 .... **55672**
Kupperman, Jonathan LEGIS ASST 2429 .... **55672**
Linsk, Reed DPTY CHIEF OF STAFF 2429 .... **55672**
Nalivkina, Olena SCHEDULER/SYS ADMIN 2429 .... **55672**
Terrazas, Rick CHIEF OF STAFF 2429 .... **55672**

DISTRICT OFFICE

EL CAJON—1611 N MAGNOLIA AVE, SUITE 310, EL CAJON, CA 92020
Burgett, Don COMMUNITY REP **619-448-5201**
Conaway, Ashleigh FIELD REP **619-448-5201**
Harrison, Mike COMMUNICATIONS DIR/DIST CHIEF OF STAFF **619-448-5201**
Marquez, Tommy CASEWK DIR **619-448-5201**
Rayzor, Ronda OFFICE MGR **619-448-5201**
Rodriguez, Angelica COMMUNITY REP **619-448-5201**
Walker, Amy COMMUNITY REP **619-448-5201**

Representative Will Hurd

Texas, 23d

317 CANNON HOB (ZIP: 20515-4323) 225-4511
Agrella, Austin LEGIS DIR 317 CHOB **54511**
Byers, John CHIEF OF STAFF 317 CHOB **54511**
Castaneda, Anton LEGIS ASST 317 CHOB **54511**
Malen, Christopher SR LEGIS ASST 317 CHOB **54511**
Murphy, Jon STAFF ASST 317 CHOB **54511**
Pack, Nancy SCHEDULER/DPTY CHIEF OF STAFF 317 CHOB **54511**
Pfeiffer, Connor LEGIS ASST 317 CHOB **54511**
Strock, Callie PRESS SECY 317 CHOB **54511**
Thompson, Katie COMMUNICATIONS DIR 317 CHOB **54511**
Thompson, Rachel LEGIS CORRES 317 CHOB **54511**

DISTRICT OFFICES

DEL RIO—1104 W 10TH ST, DEL RIO, TX 78840
Gutierrez, Carmen FIELD REP **830-422-2040**

EAGLE PASS—100 MONROE ST, EAGLE PASS, TX 78852
Arteaga, Stacy FIELD REP **210-784-5023**

FORT STOCKTON—PECOS CO COURTHOUSE, 1ST FLOOR, 103 WEST CALLAGHAN, FORT STOCKTON, TX 79735.... 210-620-1961

SAN ANTONIO—THE FEDERAL BLDG, 727 E CESAR E. CHAVEZ BLVD, SAN ANTONIO, TX 78206
Arnold, Jon DIR - CONSTIT SVCS **210-921-3130**
Hollis, Justin DIST DIR **210-921-3130**
Ochoa, Cindy FIELD REP **210-921-3130**
Vasser, Don FIELD REP **210-921-3130**

SOCORRO—124 S HORIZON BLVD, SOCORRO, TX 79927
Rivera, Karina FIELD REP **915-235-6421**

Representative Sheila Jackson Lee

Texas, 18th

2079 RAYBURN HOB (ZIP: 20515-4318) 225-3816
Belchior, Isabela LEGIS COUNSEL 2079 .... **53816**
Berry, Gregory CHIEF COUNSEL 2079 .... **53816**
Coney, Lillie POLICY DIR 2079 .... **53816**
Drummond, LaDedra SCHEDULER 2079 .... **53816**
Jackson, Darryl DIST DIR 2079 .... **53816**
Kirkwood, Michael DIST AIDE 2079 .... **53816**
Murphy, Kelly SHARED EMPLOYEE 2079 .... **53816**
Rushing, Glenn CHIEF OF STAFF 2079 .... **53816**
Vazquez, Alma DIST AIDE 2079 .... **53816**

DISTRICT OFFICES

ACRES HOME—6719 W MONTGOMERY RD, SUITE 204, HOUSTON, TX 77019.......... 713-691-4882

FIFTH WARD—4300 LYONS AVE, SUITE 200, HOUSTON, TX 77020.......... 713-227-7740

HEIGHTS—420 W 19TH ST, HOUSTON, TX 77008.......... 713-861-4070

HOUSTON—1919 SMITH ST, SUITE 1180, MICKEY LELAND BLDG, HOUSTON, TX 77002
Hernandez, Martha OFC ASST **713-655-0050**
Morris, Booker DIST AIDE **713-655-0050**

Representative Pramila Jayapal

Washington, 7th

1510 LONGWORTH HOB (ZIP: 20515-4707) 225-3106
Azimpoor, Kian STAFF ASST 1510 .... **53106**
Carpenter, Kylie DIGITAL STRATEGIST 1510 .... **53106**
Chan, Jennifer SR LEGIS ASST 1510 .... **53106**
Cummins, Emily SCHEDULER 1510 .... **53106**
Hurrell, Mary PRESS SECY 1510 .... **53106**
Mulligan, Jessica LEGIS ASST 1510 .... **53106**
Owens, Lindsay DPTY CHIEF OF STAFF/LEGIS DIR 1510 .... **53106**
Patel, Vedant COMMUNICATIONS DIR 1510 .... **53106**
Raghavan, Gautam CHIEF OF STAFF 1510 .... **53106**

DISTRICT OFFICE

SEATTLE—1904 3RD AVE, NO. 510, SEATTLE, WA 98101
Allala, Lylianna COORD - OUTREACH **206-674-0040**
Berkson, Rachel DIST DIR **206-674-0040**
Carstensen, Zachary OUTREACH DIR **206-674-0040**
Khanna, Raman COORD - CONSTIT SVCS **206-674-0040**
Mehdi, Yazmin COORD - OUTREACH **206-674-0040**
Mohamed, Hamdi COORD - CONSTIT SVCS **206-674-0040**

Representative Hakeem S. Jeffries

New York, 8th

2433 RAYBURN HOB (ZIP: 20515-3208) 225-5936
Banik, Disha LEGIS ASST 2433 .... **55936**
Bishop, Tony LEGIS FELLOW 2433 .... **55936**
Dorn, Sam PRESS ASST/DIGITAL DIR 2433 .... **55936**
Jackson, Tasia CHIEF OF STAFF 2433 .... **55936**
Lobel, Zack LEGIS COUNSEL 2433 .... **55936**
Milnes, Lauren LEGIS CORRES/DIR - SCHEDULING 2433 .... **55936**
Oreck, Zoe LEGIS DIR/COUNSEL 2433 .... **55936**
Quintyne, Chris LEGIS COUNSEL 2433 .... **55936**

DISTRICT OFFICES

CENTRAL BROOKLYN—55 HANSON PL, SUITE 603, BROOKLYN, NY 11217
TOLL-FREE NUMBER.......... 1-718-237-2211
Alemu, Maron DIST DIR **718-237-2211**
Bell, Michael DIST STAFF ASST **718-237-2211**
Brotman, Michelle CONSTIT SVCS REP **718-237-2211**
Church, Lee DIST FIELD REP **718-237-2211**
Figueroa, Marie DIST SCHEDULER/COORD - COMMUNITY OUTREACH **718-237-2211**
Lundy, Chris CONSTIT SVCS REP **718-237-2211**

SOUTH BROOKLYN—445 NEPTUNE AVE, FIRST FLOOR, BROOKLYN, NY 11224
TOLL-FREE NUMBER.......... 1-718-373-0033
Chuprik, Sergey FIELD REP **718-373-0033**
Diamond, Rena CONSTIT SVCS REP **718-373-0033**
Lenderman, Lyudmila CONSTIT SVCS REP **718-373-0033**
Menos, Frieda DIR - CONSTIT SVCS **718-373-0033**

Representative Bill Johnson

Ohio, 6th

2336 RAYBURN HOB (ZIP: 20515-3506) **225-5705**
Baker, Dawn CASEWKR 2336 .... **55705**
Gwyn, Katherine SCHEDULER 2336 .... **55705**
Kretzschmar, Natalie PRESS SECY/LEGIS CORRES 2336 .... **55705**
Myers, Cailey STAFF ASST 2336 .... **55705**
Petit, Cody STAFF ASST 2336 .... **55705**
Rardin, David LEGIS DIR 2336 .... **55705**
Ripp, Kelli LEGIS ASST 2336 .... **55705**
Smullen, Mike CHIEF OF STAFF 2336 .... **55705**
Weltge, Jessica LEGIS ASST 2336 .... **55705**
Wilson, Laura SR POLICY ADVISOR 2336 .... **55705**

DISTRICT OFFICES

CAMBRIDGE—116 SOUTHGATE PKWY, CAMBRIDGE, OH 43725
Karlen, Ashley DIR - CONSTIT SVCS **740-432-2366**

IRONTON—202 PARK AVE, SUITE C, IRONTON, OH 45638
Stephens, Juli FIELD REP **740-534-9431**

MARIETTA—246 FRONT ST, MARIETTA, OH 45750
Giffin, Ty CASEWKR **740-376-0868**
Rector, Ren'Ee FIELD REP - VETS **740-376-0868**

SALEM—192 E STATE ST, SALEM, OH 44460
TOLL-FREE NUMBER **1-855-376-0868**
Christian, Taylor DIST STAFF ASST **330-337-6951**
Keeler, Ben COMMUNICATIONS DIR **330-337-6951**
Keeler, Sarah DIST DIR **330-337-6951**

Representative Dusty Johnson

South Dakota, At Large

1508 LONGWORTH HOB (ZIP: 20515-4100) **225-2801**
Christianson, Andrew CHIEF OF STAFF 1508 .... **52801**
Dudziak, Peter LEGIS CORRES 1508 .... **52801**
Hedlund, Darren LEGIS DIR 1508 .... **52801**
Kagey, Hannah LEGIS ASST 1508 .... **52801**
Kemp, Jazmine PRESS SECY 1508 .... **52801**
Krall, Matthew SPECIAL ASST 1508 .... **52801**
Weber, John SR POLICY ADVISOR 1508 .... **52801**

DISTRICT OFFICES

ABERDEEN—304 6TH AVE SE, ABERDEEN, SD 57401
Kamp, Aimee REGIONAL DIR **605-622-1060**
Tanner, Ashley FIELD REP **605-622-1060**

RAPID CITY—2525 W MAIN ST, SUITE 310, RAPID CITY, SD 57702
Byrd, Beau CONSTIT SVCS REP **605-646-6454**
Gibson, Danica CONSTIT SVCS REP **605-646-6454**
Murray, Katie REGIONAL DIR **605-646-6454**

SIOUX FALLS—300 N DAKOTA AVE, SUITE 314, SIOUX FALLS, SD 57104
Cuellar, Chelsea MGR - OPS **605-275-2868**
Heitkamp, Courtney DIST DIR/COMMUNICATIONS ADVISOR **605-275-2868**
Rasmussen, Reid SPECIAL ASST **605-275-2868**

Representative Eddie Bernice Johnson

Texas, 30th

2306 RAYBURN HOB (ZIP: 20515-4330) **225-8885**
Gokcigdem, Murat CHIEF OF STAFF/EXEC SCHEDULER/LEGIS STAFF 2306 .... **58885**
Jackson, Jonathan LEGIS ASST 2306 .... **58885**
Ladak, Nawaid LEGIS ASST 2306 .... **58885**
Mitchiner, Zachary STAFF ASST 2306 .... **58885**
Nealy, Kenneth LEGIS DIR 2306 .... **58885**
Wu, Tonia LEGIS ASST 2306 .... **58885**

DISTRICT OFFICE

DALLAS—1825 MARKET CENTER BLVD, SUITE 440, DALLAS, TX 75207
Assanie, Sameer COMMUNICATIONS DIR **214-922-8885**
Brown, Dominique DIR - OPS **214-922-8885**
Green Bishop, Joseph COMMUNICATIONS AIDE **214-922-8885**
Hernandez, Antonia CONSTIT SVCS **214-922-8885**
Terry, Ellisha CONSTIT SVCS **214-922-8885**
Zeb, Sue SPECIAL PROJ COORD **214-922-8885**

Representative Henry C. "Hank" Johnson, Jr.

Georgia, 4th

2240 RAYBURN HOB (ZIP: 20515-1004) **225-1605**
Grey, Chelsea LEGIS ASST 2240 .... **51605**
Kappler, Jacqui LEGIS DIR 2240 .... **51605**
Knapp, Evelyn STAFF ASST/LEGIS CORRES 2240 .... **51605**
Sidney, Arthur CHIEF OF STAFF 2240 .... **51605**
Stevens, Kimberly ACCOUNTANT 2240 .... **51605**
Tewoldeberhan, Alem SCHEDULER/OFFICE MGR 2240 .... **51605**

DISTRICT OFFICE

DECATUR—5240 SNAPFINGER PARK DR, SUITE 140, DECATUR, GA 30035
Armstrong, Shy CASEWKR - MIL/CASEWORK - VETS/CONSTIT SVCS **770-987-2291**
Branche, Laveeta DIST SCHEDULER **770-987-2291**
Butts, Peter, Jr SYS ADMIN/CONSTIT SVCS REP **770-987-2291**
Hubbard, Eric FIELD REP/COMMUNITY LIAISON **770-987-2291**
Lancheros, Maria IMMIGRATION LIAISON **770-987-2291**
Moylan, Ana STAFF ASST **770-987-2291**
Phelan, Andy COMMUNICATIONS DIR **770-987-2291**
Pledger, Xeron CONSTIT SVCS **770-987-2291**
Register, Kathy DIST DIR **770-987-2291**
Smith, Joshua CONSTIT SVCS **770-987-2291**

Representative Mike Johnson

Louisiana, 4th

418 CANNON HOB (ZIP: 20515-1804) **225-2777**
Babb, Alison FINANCIAL ADMIN 418 CHOB **52777**
Caldwell, Witt LEGIS CORRES 418 CHOB **52777**
Cousins, Weldon STAFF ASST 418 CHOB **52777**
Fultz, Garrett LEGIS COUNSEL 418 CHOB **52777**
Haynes, Hayden CHIEF OF STAFF 418 CHOB **52777**
Holyfield, Ainsley COMMUNICATIONS DIR 418 CHOB **52777**
Morris, Brad LEGIS DIR 418 CHOB **52777**
Robertson, Whitney DPTY PRESS SECY 418 CHOB **52777**
Walecki, Jack LEGIS ASST 418 CHOB **52777**
Ward, Ruth SCHEDULER/DIR - OPS/POLICY ADVISOR 418 CHOB **52777**

DISTRICT OFFICES

BOSSIER CITY—2250 HOSPITAL DR, SUITE 248, BOSSIER CITY, LA 71111
Davis, Dylan COMMUNITY LIAISON **318-840-0309**
Everett, Julie COMMUNITY LIAISON **318-840-0309**
Gras, Pam COMMUNITY LIAISON/CASEWKR **318-840-0309**

Layton, Chip DPTY CHIEF OF STAFF/DIST DIR 318-840-0309
Quinn, Leslie COORD - GRANTS & SPEC PROJ 318-840-0309

NORTHWESTERN STATE UNIVERSITY—444 CASPARI DR, SOUTH HALL, ROOM 224, NATCHITOCHES, LA 71497 318-357-5731

NORTHWESTERN STATE UNIVERSITY - FT. POLK—3329 UNIVERSITY PKWY, BLDG 552, ROOM 24, LEESVILLE, LA 71446

Ledoux, Jerrie COMMUNITY LIAISON 337-392-3146
Turner, Lee REGIONAL REP 337-392-3146

[Representative Walter B. Jones]

North Carolina, 3d

2333 RAYBURN HOB (ZIP: 20515-3303) 225-3415

Bowlen, Joshua CHIEF OF STAFF 2333 53415
Celeste, Raymond LEGIS ASST - MIL 2333 53415
Jones, Lindley STAFF ASST 2333 53415
Martin, Bryan LEGIS ASST 2333 53415
Ryon, Bradley LEGIS DIR 2333 53415

DISTRICT OFFICE

GREENVILLE—1105-C CORPORATE DR, GREENVILLE, NC 27858

Anglen, Michael CASEWKR/SR POLICY ADVISOR 252-931-1003
Fletcher, Gloria DIST STAFF ASST 252-931-1003
Jones, Robert CASEWKR 252-931-1003
Jordan, Catherine SR ADVISOR 252-931-1003
Marm, Deborah CASEWKR 252-931-1003
Moore, William DIST DIR 252-931-1003
Moye, Frankie OUTREACH REP 252-931-1003

Representative Jim Jordan

Ohio, 4th

2056 RAYBURN HOB (ZIP: 20515-3504) 225-2676

Dilley, Jared DPTY CHIEF OF STAFF 2056 52676
Eichinger, Kevin CHIEF OF STAFF 2056 52676
Fury, Ian COMMUNICATIONS DIR 2056 52676
Greene, Emily LEGIS ASST 2056 52676
Macheledt, Marshall LEGIS CORRES 2056 52676
Nerantzis, Anthony STAFF ASST 2056 52676
Summers, Emma EXEC ASST/SCHEDULER/LEGIS AIDE 2056 .. 52676
Wade, Melissa FINANCIAL ADMIN 2056 52676

DISTRICT OFFICES

BUCYRUS—500 S SANDUSKY AVE, BUCYRUS, OH 44820 419-663-1426

LIMA—3121 W ELM PLAZA, LIMA, OH 45805-2516

Brandenburg, Kirby FIELD REP 419-999-6455
Grimm, David DIST AIDE 419-999-6455
Parlapiano, Amanda STAFF ASST/CASEWKR 419-999-6455
Taylor, Barbara DPTY DIST DIR 419-999-6455
Warner, Cameron DIST DIR 419-999-6455

NORWALK—13B E MAIN ST, NORWALK, OH 44857

Bick, Caroline DPTY DIST DIR 419-663-1426
Knapp, Daneen STAFF ASST/CASEWKR 419-663-1426

Representative David P. Joyce

Ohio, 14th

1124 LONGWORTH HOB (ZIP: 20515-3514) 225-5731

Alburger, Anna CHIEF OF STAFF 1124 55731
Brogan, Kelsi SCHEDULER 1124 55731
Castagna, Charles SR LEGIS ASST 1124 55731
Cooper, Chris CHIEF COUNSEL 1124 55731
Kalagher, Kendall LEGIS DIR 1124 55731
Moses, Zachary LEGIS ASST 1124 55731
Sears, Katherine COMMUNICATIONS DIR 1124 55731
Smith, William STAFF ASST/LEGIS AIDE 1124 55731
Vaughn, Emma PRESS ASST/LEGIS CORRES 1124 55731
Wilson, Catherine LEGIS ASST 1124 55731

DISTRICT OFFICES

MENTOR—8500 STATION ST, SUITE 390, MENTOR, OH 44060
TOLL-FREE NUMBER 1-800-447-0529

Barile, Ariann DIST OUTREACH REP 440-352-3939
Burger, Katie DIST OUTREACH REP 440-352-3939
Jeffery, Maureen DPTY DIST DIR 440-352-3939
Kelly, Ryan DIST STAFF ASST 440-352-3939
Martin, Robin CASEWKR 440-352-3939
Roth, Alexander DIST OUTREACH REP 440-352-3939

TWINSBURG—10075 RAVENNA RD, TWINSBURG, OH 44087

Ciofani, Nick DIST DIR/DPTY CHIEF OF STAFF 330-425-9291

Representative John Joyce

Pennsylvania, 13th

1337 LONGWORTH HOB (ZIP: 20515-3813) 225-2431

Callaway, Libby SR LEGIS ASST 1337 52431
Clark, Alex PERSONAL ASST 1337 52431
Ferrance, Brandon STAFF ASST 1337 52431
Perez-Acosta, Mehgan DPTY CHIEF OF STAFF 1337 52431
Romeo, Andrew COMMUNICATIONS DIR 1337 52431
Shoemaker, Jeremy CHIEF OF STAFF 1337 52431
Sottnick, Fred LEGIS ASST 1337 52431
Tucker, Matt LEGIS DIR 1337 52431

DISTRICT OFFICES

ALTOONA—5414 6TH AVE, ALTOONA, PA 16602 814-656-6081

CHAMBERSBURG—100 LINCOLN WAY E, SUITE B, CHAMBERSBURG, PA 17201 717-753-6344

SOMERSET—451 STOYSTOWN RD, SUITE 102, SOMERSET, PA 15501 814-485-6020

Representative Marcy Kaptur

Ohio, 9th

2186 RAYBURN HOB (ZIP: 20515-3509) 225-4146

Anderson, Griffin COMMUNICATIONS DIR 2186 54146
Hruska, Courtney SCHEDULER/OFFICE MGR 2186 54146
Jones, Sydney LEGIS CORRES/STAFF ASST 2186 54146
Kaplan, Matthew APPRO ASSOC/COUNSEL 2186 54146
Kazvini-Gore, Nick LEGIS ASST 2186 54146
McInnis, Margaret LEGIS ASST 2186 54146
Perrino, Jenny LEGIS DIR/DPTY CHIEF 2186 54146

DISTRICT OFFICES

CLEVELAND—17021 LORAIN AVE, CLEVELAND, OH 44111
TOLL-FREE NUMBER 1-800-964-4699

Dailey Jones, Nicole PRESS ASST 216-767-5933
Massarolo, Charles STAFF ASST 216-767-5933
Smith, Jacob CASEWORK - VETS 216-767-5933

LORAIN—200 W ERIE AVE, LORAIN, OH 44052 440-288-1500
TOLL-FREE NUMBER 1-800-964-4699

TOLEDO—ONE MARITIME PLAZA, 6TH FLOOR, TOLEDO, OH 43604
TOLL-FREE NUMBER 1-800-964-4699

Harris, Karen CONG ASST 419-259-7500
Katich, Steve CHIEF OF STAFF 225-7702
Morris, Theresa K CONG ASST 419-259-7500
Rowe, Sue CASEWK MGR/SCHEDULER 419-259-7500

Ruvolo, Jane CONG ASST/GRANTS SPEC 419-259-7500
Zavac, David CONG ASST 419-259-7500

Representative John Katko

New York, 24th

2457 RAYBURN HOB (ZIP: 20515-3224) 225-3701
Bazydlo, Emily SCHEDULER 2457 53701
Bensur, William POLICY ASST/PRESS ASST 2457 53701
Howell, Zach CHIEF OF STAFF 2457 53701
Kranz, Daniel STAFF ASST 2457 53701
Southard, Tristan LEGIS ASST 2457 53701
Wang, Tim LEGIS ASST 2457 53701
White, Elizabeth LEGIS CORRES 2457 53701
Wood, Jennifer LEGIS DIR 2457 53701

DISTRICT OFFICES

AUBURN—71 GENESEE ST, AUBURN, NY 13021 315-253-4068

SYRACUSE—440 S WARREN ST, SUITE 711, SYRACUSE, NY 13202
Burtis, Christina CONSTIT SVCS REP 315-423-5657
Gretsky, Gavin FIELD REP 315-423-5657
Haag, Thomas DPTY DIST DIR 315-423-5657
Keib, James DIST DIR 315-423-5657
McKinney, Patrick CONSTIT SVCS REP 315-423-5657
O'Connor, Erin COMMUNICATIONS DIR/COUNSEL 315-423-5657

Representative William R. Keating

Massachusetts, 9th

2351 RAYBURN HOB (ZIP: 20515-2109) 225-3111
Donovan, Garrett CHIEF OF STAFF 2351 53111
Ghani, Richard POLICY ADVISOR 2351 53111
Gould, Gabrielle LEGIS DIR 2351 53111
McDermott, Lauren COUNSEL/COMMUNICATIONS DIR 2351 ... 53111
Oleksak, David SCHEDULER/PRESS ASST 2351 53111
Thomson, Shestin LEGIS CORRES 2351 53111
Wertheimer, Michael SR POLICY ADVISOR 2351 53111

DISTRICT OFFICES

HYANNIS—297 STEVENS ST, SUITE E, HYANNIS, MA 02601
Maddock, Ryan DIST REP 508-771-6868
Nelson, Andrew POLICY ADVISOR 508-771-0666

NEW BEDFORD—128 UNION ST, SUITE 103, NEW BEDFORD, MA 02740
Izaguirre, Glenda DIST REP 508-999-6462
Teves-Roda, Elizabeth DIST REP 508-999-6462
Trombly, Ian DIST REP 508-999-6462

PLYMOUTH—170 COURT ST, PLYMOUTH, MA 02360
Jackman, Michael DIST DIR 508-746-9000
Matthews, Christopher COORD - OUTREACH 508-746-9000
Wasielewski, Karen DPTY DIST DIR 508-746-9000

Representative Fred Keller

Pennsylvania, 12th

1717 LONGWORTH HOB (ZIP: 20515-3812) 225-3731
Anzur, Jon CHIEF OF STAFF 1717 53731

DISTRICT OFFICES

SELINSGROVE—713 BRIDGE ST, ROOM 29, SELINSGROVE, PA 17870 570-374-9469

TUNKHANNOCK—181 W TIOGA ST, SUITE 2, TUNKHANNOCK, PA 18657 570-996-6550

WILLIAMSPORT—1020 COMMERCE PARK DR, SUITE 1A, WILLIAMSPORT, PA 17701 570-322-3961

Representative Mike Kelly

Pennsylvania, 16th

1707 LONGWORTH HOB (ZIP: 20515-3816) 225-5406
Bennett, Parker LEGIS CORRES 1707 55406
Dawson, Kevin LEGIS ASST 1707 55406
Eisenberger, Andrew COMMUNICATIONS DIR 1707 55406
Fulmer, Brendan SR LEGIS ASST 1707 55406
Marsh, James EXEC ASST 1707 55406
Prater, Lori TAX COUNSEL 1707 55406
Stroia, Matthew CHIEF OF STAFF 1707 55406

DISTRICT OFFICES

BUTLER—218 E DIAMOND ST, SUITE 210, BUTLER, PA 16001
Mustello, Marci DIST SCHEDULER 724-282-2557
Stevenson, Stephanie SPECIAL PROJ DIR 724-282-2557

ERIE—208 E BAYFRONT PKWY, SUITE 102, ERIE, PA 16507
Breene, Samuel FIELD REP 814-454-8190
Butler, Timothy DIST DIR 814-454-8190
DiGiacomo, Anthony LIAISON - MIL & VET 814-454-8190
Rohan, Mariah CONSTIT SVCS REP 814-454-8190

SHARON—33 CHESTNUT AVE, SHARON, PA 16146
Burke, Jill DIR - CONSTIT SVCS 724-342-7170
Galanski, John LIAISON - MIL & VET 724-342-7170

Representative Robin L. Kelly

Illinois, 2d

2416 RAYBURN HOB (ZIP: 20515-1302) 225-0773
Alvarez, Jazmin LEGIS AIDE/ASST SCHEDULER 2416 50773
Bolden, Charles LEGIS CORRES 2416 50773
DiFulvio, Brandon STAFF ASST 2416 50773
Keeys, Mia LEGIS ASST 2416 50773
Lewis, Jim COMMUNICATIONS DIR 2416 50773
McMurray, Matthew SR LEGIS ASST 2416 50773
Ostro, Zachary LEGIS DIR 2416 50773
Webb, Brandon CHIEF OF STAFF 2416 50773

DISTRICT OFFICES

CHICAGO—1000 E 111TH ST, 5TH FLOOR, CHICAGO, IL 60628
Rodriguez, Luis DIST REP 773-321-2001
Williams-Luster, April DIST REP 773-321-2001

MATTESON—600 HOLIDAY PLAZA DR, MATTESON, IL 60443
Banks, Alan DIST REP 708-679-0078
Bryant, Rick SR ADVISOR 708-679-0078
DeWitt, Cynthia DIR - CONSTIT SVCS/DIST DIR 708-679-0078
Dubose, Jihan DIST REP 708-679-0078
Dwyer, Billy DIST REP 708-679-0078
Miller, Elise DIST REP 708-679-0078
Paleologos, Mary DIST PRESS SECY 708-679-0078
Presta, Tony SCHEDULER/DPTY DIST DIR 708-679-0078

Representative Trent Kelly

Mississippi, 1st

1005 LONGWORTH HOB (ZIP: 20515-2401) 225-4306
Craddock, Reed SCHEDULER 1005 54306
Enlow, Alex STAFF ASST 1005 54306
Garcia, Eddie MIL FELLOW 1005 54306
Grubbs, Adam LEGIS ASST/LIAISON - AG 1005 54306
Hickman, Samuel LEGIS ASST 1005 54306
Howell, Paul CHIEF OF STAFF 1005 54306
Miller, Kirby LEGIS DIR 1005 54306

Rowland, Lindsey LIAISON - MIL 1005 54306
Woods, Charles LEGIS ASST - MIL 1005 54306

DISTRICT OFFICES

COLUMBUS—318 SEVENTH ST N, SUITE D, COLUMBUS, MS 39701
Smith, Robert FIELD REP 662-327-0748

COLUMBUS (MAILING)—P.O. BOX 1012, COLUMBUS, MS 39703 662-327-0748

EUPORA—855 S DUNN ST, EUPORA, MS 39744
Weddle, Willy FIELD REP 662-258-7240

FARMINGTON—4135 COUNTY RD 200, CORINTH, MS 38834
Whited, Melinda FIELD REP/CASEWKR - IMMIGRATION 662-687-1525

HERNANDO—2565 CAFFEY ST, NO. 200, HERNANDO, MS 38632
Starr, Walt FIELD REP/CASEWKR 662-449-3090

HERNANDO (MAILING)—P.O. BOX 218, HERNANDO, MS 38632 662-449-3090

TUPELO—431 W MAIN ST, SUITE 450, TUPELO, MS 38804
Brooks, William FIELD REP - VETS 662-841-8808
Owen, James FIELD REP 662-841-8808
Parker, Susan COMMUNICATIONS DIR 662-841-8808
Patterson, Michael CASEWKR/CASEWKR - MIL/CASEWORK - VETS 662-841-8808
Ryan, Shelia CASEWKR/SPECIAL ASST 662-841-8808

Representative Joseph P. Kennedy III

Massachusetts, 4th

304 CANNON HOB (ZIP: 20515-2104) 225-5931
Black, Dan PRESS SECY 304 CHOB 55931
Curtis, Sarah DPTY CHIEF OF STAFF/LEGIS DIR 304 CHOB 55931
Daniels, David STAFF ASST 304 CHOB 55931
Fins, Eric SR LEGIS ASST 304 CHOB 55931
Matteson, Nate STAFF ASST 304 CHOB 55931
Mecher, Greg CHIEF OF STAFF 304 CHOB 55931
Philips, Mariah SCHEDULER 304 CHOB 55931
Rankin, Christina LEGIS CORRES 304 CHOB 55931
Roshan, Qais LEGIS ASST 304 CHOB 55931
Smith, Mackenzie LEGIS CORRES 304 CHOB 55931

DISTRICT OFFICES

ATTLEBORO—8 N MAIN ST, SUITE 200, ATTLEBORO, MA 02703
Duclos, Leslie DPTY DIST REP 508-431-1110
Nelson, Lisa SR DIST REP 508-431-1110

NEWTON—29 CRAFTS ST, SUITE 375, NEWTON, MA 02458
Browne, Emily COMMUNICATIONS DIR 617-332-3333
Clemons, Nick DIST DIR 617-332-3333
McNeill, Rachel MIL FELLOW 617-332-3333
Noguera, Stephanie OUTREACH DIR 617-332-3333
Pepen, Enrique DIST STAFF ASST 617-332-3333

Representative Ro Khanna

California, 17th

221 CANNON HOB (ZIP: 20515-0517) 225-2631
Albertson, Julia DIGITAL PRESS SECY 221 CHOB 52631
Fox, Kevin LEGIS ASST 221 CHOB 52631
Gould, Kate CONG FELLOW 221 CHOB 52631
McKelvey, Will LEGIS CORRES/LEGIS ASST 221 CHOB 52631
Perez, David STAFF ASST 221 CHOB 52631
Preston, Emma SCHEDULER/EXEC ASST 221 CHOB 52631
Purcell, Heather COMMUNICATIONS DIR 221 CHOB 52631
Saba, Geo NATIONAL SECUR ADVISOR 221 CHOB 52631
Schloesser, Chris LEGIS DIR 221 CHOB 52631
Sperling, Erik SR POLICY ADVISOR/COUNSEL 221 CHOB 52631
Spiro, Pete CHIEF OF STAFF 221 CHOB 52631

DISTRICT OFFICE

SANTA CLARA—3150 DE LA CRUZ BLVD, NO. 240, SANTA CLARA, CA 95054
Boggs, Galen FIELD REP 408-436-2720
Bryant, Lakeisha FIELD REP 408-436-2720
Langer, Cass OFFICE MGR/COMMUNITY LIAISON 408-436-2720
Mandalika, Swapanthi FIELD REP 408-436-2720
Nguyen, Hiep SR FIELD REP 408-436-2720
Pyke, Tom DIST DIR 408-436-2720

Representative Daniel T. Kildee

Michigan, 5th

203 CANNON HOB (ZIP: 20515-2205) 225-3611
Alkiek, Ghada DPTY CHIEF OF STAFF 203 CHOB 53611
Bryan, Robyn COMMUNICATIONS DIR 203 CHOB 53611
Couture, R J LEGIS CORRES 203 CHOB 53611
Dickinson, Jordan SR LEGIS ASST 203 CHOB 53611
Nienberg, Troy LEGIS DIR 203 CHOB 53611
Papa, Katie FINANCIAL ADMIN 203 CHOB 53611
Rivard, Mitchell CHIEF OF STAFF 203 CHOB 53611
Share, Alison LEGIS COUNSEL 203 CHOB 53611
Virga, Elizabeth SCHEDULER/EXEC ASST 203 CHOB 53611

DISTRICT OFFICE

FLINT—601 S SAGINAW ST, SUITE 403, FLINT, MI 48502
Bennett, Jacob DPTY DIST DIR 810-238-8627
Flores, Chris DIST DIR 810-238-8627
Herman, Mary DIST STAFF ASST 810-238-8627
Jones, Gary CONSTIT SVCS REP 810-238-8627
Manwaring, Lucetia SR CONSTIT SVCS REP 810-238-8627
Wickes, Bill CASEWKR 810-238-8627

Representative Derek Kilmer

Washington, 6th

1410 LONGWORTH HOB (ZIP: 20515-4706) 225-5916
Allen, Katie LEGIS DIR 1410 55916
Freedman, Ben STAFF ASST 1410 55916
Kelly, Rachel CHIEF OF STAFF 1410 55916
Li, Leah LEGIS CORRES 1410 55916
Scordato, Tory SCHEDULER 1410 55916
Seaman, Tom LEGIS FELLOW 1410 55916
Swope, Clayton LEGIS ASST - MIL 1410 55916
Vijayaraghavan, Rukmani LEGIS FELLOW 1410 55916
Viterise, Michele LEGIS COUNSEL 1410 55916
Wright, Andrew COMMUNICATIONS DIR 1410 55916

DISTRICT OFFICES

BREMERTON—345 6TH ST, SUITE 500, BREMERTON, WA 98337
Crabtree, Katy DIST REP 360-373-9725
Irwin, Kate DIST REP 360-373-9725
Munoz, Chantell CONSTIT SVCS REP 360-373-9725
Williams, Cheri DIR - CONSTIT SVCS 360-373-9725

PORT ANGELES—332 E 5TH ST, PORT ANGELES, WA 98362
Robins, Mary Jane DIST REP 360-797-3623

TACOMA—950 PACIFIC AVE, SUITE 1230, TACOMA, WA 98402
Resnikoff, Brendan DIST SCHEDULER 253-272-3515
Richards, Robert CONSTIT SVCS REP 253-272-3515

Roper, Andrea DIST DIR 253-272-3515
Smith, Evan DIST REP 253-272-3515

Representative Andy Kim

New Jersey, 3d

1516 LONGWORTH HOB (ZIP: 20515-3003) 225-4765
Deangelo, Anthony COMMUNICATIONS DIR 1516 54765
Friedfeld-Gebaide, Sophie STAFF ASST 1516 54765
Lee, Yujin LEGIS DIR 1516 54765
Pfeiffer, Amy CHIEF OF STAFF 1516 54765
Riggins, Nathan LEGIS CORRES 1516 54765
Scott Martin, Cecily SCHEDULER 1516 54765
Smith, Thomas LEGIS ASST 1516 54765

DISTRICT OFFICES

TOMS RIVER—33 WASHINGTON ST, TOMS RIVER, NJ 08753
Giovine, Ben DIST DIR 732-504-0490
Weaver, Maura DIST FIELD REP 732-504-0490
Whiteman, Lynette OUTREACH ADVISOR 732-504-0490

WILLINGBORO—429 JOHN F. KENNEDY WAY, WILLINGBORO, NJ 08046
Anderson, Sharon CASEWKR 856-703-2700
Gregory, Sean DIST FIELD REP 856-703-2700
Pansius, Susan DIR - CONSTIT SVCS 856-703-2700

Representative Ron Kind

Wisconsin, 3d

1502 LONGWORTH HOB (ZIP: 20515-4903) 225-5506
Eveland, Alex LEGIS DIR 1502 55506
Greenberg, Hana CHIEF OF STAFF 1502 55506
Holmes, Ethan LEGIS ASST 1502 55506
Hutterer, Ben LEGIS ASST 1502 55506
Kirchberg, Olivia LEGIS CORRES/LEGIS ASST 1502 55506
MacLeod, Carter STAFF ASST 1502 55506
Pierce, Hannah SCHEDULER 1502 55506
White, Aaron COMMUNICATIONS DIR 1502 55506

DISTRICT OFFICES

EAU CLAIRE—131 S BARSTOW ST, NO. 301, EAU CLAIRE, WI 54701
Aumann, Mark CONG AIDE 715-831-9214
Sundby, Janet CONG AIDE 715-831-9214

LA CROSSE—205 5TH AVE S, SUITE 400, LA CROSSE, WI 54601
TOLL-FREE NUMBER 1-888-442-8040
Jackelen, Karrie DIST DIR 608-782-2558
Kannenberg, Loren DIST CHIEF OF STAFF 608-782-2558
Stanton, Danice CONG AIDE 608-782-2558
Vruwink, Amy Sue CONG AIDE 608-782-2558

Representative Peter T. King

New York, 2d

302 CANNON HOB (ZIP: 20515-3202) 225-7896
Fogarty, Kevin CHIEF OF STAFF/PRESS SECY/SCHEDULER 302 CHOB 57896
Pollack, George LEGIS ASST 302 CHOB 57896
Tauster, Deena LEGIS DIR 302 CHOB 57896
Ursprung, Timothy LEGIS ASST 302 CHOB 57896
Woodward, Ryan SR LEGIS ASST 302 CHOB 57896

DISTRICT OFFICE

MASSAPEQUA PARK—1003 PARK BLVD, MASSAPEQUA PARK, NY 11762
Delury, Kevin DIST REP 516-541-4225
Gartland, Patricia DIST REP 516-541-4225
Mule, Alex DIST STAFF ASST 516-541-4225
Rosenfeld, Anne DIST DIR 516-541-4225
Rossi, Sabrina DIST STAFF ASST 516-541-4225
Terrillion, Kathleen DIST REP 516-541-4225

Representative Steve King

Iowa, 4th

2210 RAYBURN HOB (ZIP: 20515-1504) 225-4426
Barry, Joseph LEGIS AIDE 2210 54426
Cretsinger, Wiltsie DIST DIR 2210 54426
Davis, Melanie SYS ADMIN 2210 54426
Edmiston, Suanne LEGIS DIR 2210 54426
Kennedy, John COMMUNICATIONS DIR 2210 54426
Kurtz, Kelley FINANCIAL & ADMIN OFFICER 2210 54426
Stevens, Chris EXEC DIR 2210 54426
Stevens, Sarah CHIEF OF STAFF 2210 54426

DISTRICT OFFICES

AMES—1421 S BELL AVE, SUITE 102, AMES, IA 50010 515-232-2885

FORT DODGE—723 CENTRAL AVE, FORT DODGE, IA 50501
Oberhelman, Jim DIST REP 515-573-2738

MASON CITY—202 1ST ST SE, SUITE 126, MASON CITY, IA 50401 641-201-1624

SIOUX CITY—320 6TH ST, ROOM 112, SIOUX CITY, IA 51101
DeWitt, Kolby DIST REP 712-224-4692
Hanlon, Sandy DIST REP 712-224-4692
Loomis, Casaday POLICY ADVISOR/DIST SCHEDULER 712-224-4692

SPENCER—306 GRAND AVE, P.O. BOX 650, SPENCER, IA 51301
Easter, Andrea DIST REP 712-580-7754
Whiting, Zach POLICY ADVISOR 712-580-7754

Representative Adam Kinzinger

Illinois, 16th

2245 RAYBURN HOB (ZIP: 20515-1316) 225-3635
Baird, Katherine SCHEDULER 2245 53635
Baylor, Christopher SYS ADMIN 2245 53635
De Luca, Sebastian LEGIS ASST 2245 53635
Gillespie, Maura COMMUNICATIONS DIR 2245 53635
Kuebler, Sam LEGIS CORRES 2245 53635
Laurie, Paul LEGIS AIDE 2245 53635
Mansour, Michael LEGIS DIR 2245 53635
Schuneman, William STAFF ASST 2245 53635
Weatherford, Austin CHIEF OF STAFF 2245 53635

DISTRICT OFFICES

OTTAWA—628 COLUMBUS ST, SUITE 507, OTTAWA, IL 61350
Bohlmann, Leah SPECIAL ASST 815-431-9271
Gross, Casey CASEWKR 815-431-9271
Phalen, Luke FIELD REP 815-431-9271
Ridenour, Greg FIELD REP 815-431-9271
Walsh, Bonnie DIST DIR 815-431-9271
Wilson, Reed DPTY DIST DIR 815-431-9271

ROCKFORD—725 N LYFORD RD, SUITE 3, ROCKFORD, IL 61107
Cimino, Pietro FIELD REP 815-708-8032

WATSEKA—342 W WALNUT ST, WATSEKA, IL 60970
Doggett, Patrick DPTY DIST DIR 815-432-0580

Representative Ann Kirkpatrick

Arizona, 2d

309 CANNON HOB (ZIP: 20515-0302) 225-2542
Frias, Carmen CHIEF OF STAFF 309 CHOB 52542
Grimes, Chris LEGIS FELLOW 309 CHOB 52542
Lubisich, Matt SCHEDULER 309 CHOB 52542
O'Brien, Abigail COMMUNICATIONS DIR 309 CHOB 52542
Owens, Ben STAFF ASST/LEGIS CORRES 309 CHOB 52542
Peyton, Russell LEGIS FELLOW 309 CHOB 52542
Walker, Christian LEGIS DIR 309 CHOB 52542
Walker, Lisa LEGIS ASST 309 CHOB 52542

DISTRICT OFFICES

SIERRA VISTA—77 CALLE PORTAL, SUITE B160, SIERRA VISTA, AZ 85635
Ash, Alesia OUTREACH DIRECTOR 520-459-3115

TUCSON—1636 N SWAN RD, SUITE 200, TUCSON, AZ 85712
Alvarez, Alex DPTY COMMUNICATIONS DIR 520-881-3588
Avalos, Karla CHIEF OPS OFFICER 520-881-3588
Barber, Ron DIST DIR 520-881-3588
Garza, Rosa CONSTIT SVCS SPEC 520-881-3588
Johnson, Kendra DIR - CONSTIT SVCS 520-881-3588
Kovacs, Billy OUTREACH DIRECTOR 520-881-3588
Smith, Travonne CONSTIT SVCS REP 520-881-3588

Representative Raja Krishnamoorthi

Illinois, 8th

115 CANNON HOB (ZIP: 20515-1308) 225-3711
Baldwin, Wilson COMMUNICATIONS DIR 115 CHOB 53711
Becht, Andrew COORD - OPS 115 CHOB 53711
Carmichael, Grace LEGIS CORRES 115 CHOB 53711
Caron, Hillary LEGIS COUNSEL 115 CHOB 53711
Druckman, Emily PRESS SECY 115 CHOB 53711
Kaissi, Brian LEGIS DIR 115 CHOB 53711
Nickson, Mike FINANCIAL ADVISOR 115 CHOB 53711
Sarasohn, Peter LEGIS AIDE 115 CHOB 53711
Schauerte, Mark CHIEF OF STAFF 115 CHOB 53711
Shaben, Zach STAFF ASST 115 CHOB 53711
Shalia, Amol DC SCHEDULER 115 CHOB 53711
Sorensen, Rachel LEGIS ASST 115 CHOB 53711

DISTRICT OFFICE

SCHAUMBURG—1701 E WOODFIELD RD, SUITE 704, SCHAUMBURG, IL 60173
Abraham, Sabey DIST DIR 847-413-1959
Amundsen, Hannah DIR - COMMUNITY OUTREACH/CONSTIT LIAISON 847-413-1959
Bankole, Yasmeen LIAISON - CONSTIT SVCS 847-413-1959
Baskin, Steve DIST SCHEDULER 847-413-1959
Payette, Andrew STAFF ASST 847-413-1959
Reis, Leslie DIR - CONSTIT SVCS 847-413-1959
Zakarauskaite, Akvile DIST STAFF ASST 847-413-1959

Representative Ann M. Kuster

New Hampshire, 2d

320 CANNON HOB (ZIP: 20515-2902) 225-5206
Brown, Nick COMMUNICATIONS DIR 320 CHOB 55206
Cooper-Wall, Samuel LEGIS CORRES 320 CHOB 55206
Cronin, Sarah DIGITAL MGR 320 CHOB 55206
Curran Horrell, Abby CHIEF OF STAFF 320 CHOB 55206
Ewing, Maria SCHEDULER 320 CHOB 55206
Gonin, Jon STAFF ASST 320 CHOB 55206
Krogman, Travis LEGIS DIR 320 CHOB 55206
Pisano, Will LEGIS ASST 320 CHOB 55206

DISTRICT OFFICES

CONCORD—18 N MAIN ST, 4TH FLOOR, CONCORD, NH 03301
Cotton, Erin COORD - CONSTIT SVCS/COORD - OUTREACH 603-226-1002
Garry, Corey DIST DIR 603-226-1002
Muns, Jenni PRESS SECY 603-226-1002
Pollinger, Dawn DIR - CONSTIT SVCS 603-226-1002
Slattery, Amy DIR - COMMUNITY OUTREACH 603-226-1002

NASHUA—184 MAIN ST, SUITE 222, NASHUA, NH 03060
Giancola, Tom COORD - CONSTIT SVCS/COORD - OUTREACH 603-595-2006
Harris, Charlotte COORD - CONSTIT SVCS/COORD - OUTREACH 603-595-2006

NORTH COUNTRY—33 MAIN ST, SUITE 202, LITTLETON, NH 03561
Bresnahan, Brian CONSTIT SVCS 603-444-7700

Representative David Kustoff

Tennessee, 8th

523 CANNON HOB (ZIP: 20515-4208) 225-4714
Courtney, Will STAFF ASST 523 CHOB 54714
Goodman, Eliana LEGIS ASST 523 CHOB 54714
Hogin, Andrew LEGIS DIR 523 CHOB 54714
Kelly, Kate COMMUNICATIONS DIR 523 CHOB 54714
Melvin, Justin DPTY CHIEF OF STAFF 523 CHOB 54714
Newman, John LEGIS CORRES/PRESS ASST 523 CHOB 54714
Okoniewski, Anderson SCHEDULER 523 CHOB 54714
Threadgill, Tyler CHIEF OF STAFF 523 CHOB 54714

DISTRICT OFFICES

DYERSBURG—425 W COURT ST, DYERSBURG, TN 38024
Rogers, Ivy FIELD REP 731-412-1037

JACKSON—117 N LIBERTY ST, JACKSON, TN 38301
Allen Shires, Debbie CASEWKR 731-423-4848
Jackson, Edward, III REGIONAL DIR 731-423-4848

MEMPHIS—5900 POPLAR AVE, SUITE 202, MEMPHIS, TN 38119
Focht, Louis STAFF ASST 901-682-4422
Johnson, Kevin FIELD REP 901-682-4422
Kolar, Jacob SPECIAL ASST 901-682-4422
Purcell, Marianne DIST DIR 901-682-4422

Representative Darin LaHood

Illinois, 18th

1424 LONGWORTH HOB (ZIP: 20515-1318) 225-6201
Alavi, Alex SCHEDULER 1424 56201
Anderson, Eric STAFF ASST 1424 56201
Antoskiewicz, Ashley LEGIS DIR 1424 56201
Dybas, Samantha LEGIS ASST 1424 56201
Kouri, Joey LEGIS CORRES 1424 56201
Pfrang, Steve CHIEF OF STAFF 1424 56201
Rauber, John DPTY COMMUNICATIONS DIR 1424 56201
Richardson, Mary Ellen LEGIS ASST 1424 56201

DISTRICT OFFICES

BLOOMINGTON—3004 GE RD, SUITE 1B, BLOOMINGTON, IL 61704 309-205-9556

JACKSONVILLE—201 W MORGAN ST, JACKSONVILLE, IL 62650
Baker, Barb CONSTIT SVCS SPEC 217-245-1431

PEORIA—100 NE MONROE ST, ROOM 100, PEORIA, IL 61602-1003
Dalfonso, J D COMMUNICATIONS DIR 309-671-7027

Davis, Lester CONSTIT SVCS REP/DIST OFFICE MGR 309-671-7027
Gilmore, Michael CONSTIT SVCS SPEC 309-671-7027
Greeson, Autum CONSTIT SVCS REP 309-671-7027
Schutte, Tanner STAFF ASST 309-671-7027
Stotler, Brad DIST DIR 309-671-7027

SPRINGFIELD—235 S 6TH ST, SPRINGFIELD, IL 62701

Bergles, Jay CONSTIT REP 217-670-1653

Representative Doug LaMalfa

California, 1st

322 CANNON HOB (ZIP: 20515-0501) 225-3076

Acornley, Mark FINANCIAL ADMIN 322 CHOB 53076
Avila, Amberlynn STAFF ASST 322 CHOB 53076
Devlin, Kathleen LEGIS CORRES 322 CHOB 53076
Lincoln, Jack LEGIS ASST 322 CHOB 53076
McGowan, Colleen LEGIS DIR 322 CHOB 53076
Slaybaugh, Haley SCHEDULER 322 CHOB 53076
Spannagel, Mark CHIEF OF STAFF 322 CHOB 53076
Veale, John LEGIS ASST 322 CHOB 53076
Williams, Parker COMMUNICATIONS DIR 322 CHOB 53076

DISTRICT OFFICES

AUBURN—2399 RICKENBACKER WAY, AUBURN, CA 95602

Mara, Lisa REGIONAL DIR 530-878-5035
Morgan, David DIST REP 530-878-5035

CHICO—120 INDEPENDENCE CIR, SUITE B, CHICO, CA 95973

Batti, Jenna CASEWKR 530-343-1000
Page, Laura REGIONAL DIR 530-343-1000
Schuessler, Leslie CASEWKR 530-343-1000
Starr, Shane DIST REP 530-343-1000

REDDING—2885 CHURN CREEK RD, SUITE C, REDDING, CA 96002-1147

Haynes, Brenda DIST REP 530-223-5898
Ryan, Erin REGIONAL DIR 530-223-5898
White, Stephanie CONSTIT SVCS REP 530-223-5898

Representative Conor Lamb

Pennsylvania, 17th

1224 LONGWORTH HOB (ZIP: 20515-3817) 225-2301

Bowman, Chris LEGIS DIR 1224 52301
Flory, Fiona LEGIS AIDE 1224 52301
Hugman, Rachel SR LEGIS ASST 1224 52301
Kwiecinski, Craig CHIEF OF STAFF 1224 52301
Murphy, Abby SR ADVISOR 1224 52301
Painter, Heather LEGIS ASST 1224 52301
Ryan, Dj SCHEDULER 1224 52301

Representative Doug Lamborn

Colorado, 5th

2371 RAYBURN HOB (ZIP: 20515-0605) 225-4422

Anderson, Dale CHIEF OF STAFF 2371 54422
Braun, Andrew LEGIS ASST - MIL 2371 54422
Dangers, Jamie SR LEGIS ASST 2371 54422
Davis, Alysa LEGIS ASST 2371 54422
Morgan, Kate SCHEDULER 2371 54422
Schneider, Lindsay LEGIS ASST 2371 54422
Thomas, James DPTY CHIEF OF STAFF/LEGIS DIR 2371 54422

DISTRICT OFFICE

COLORADO SPRINGS—1125 KELLY JOHNSON BLVD, SUITE 330, COLORADO SPRINGS, CO 80907

Anderson, Jeff SR ADVISOR - POLICY & OUTREACH/CONSTIT OUTREACH REP 719-520-0055
Archer, Tony CASEWORK - VETS 719-520-0055
Brubaker, Marcus DIST DIR 719-520-0055
Rutzen, Linda STAFF ASST/CONSTIT SVCS SPEC 719-520-0055
Sebastian, Cassandra COMMUNICATIONS DIR 719-520-0055
Tapia, Elizabeth SR CASEWKR 719-520-0055

Representative James R. Langevin

Rhode Island, 2d

2077 RAYBURN HOB (ZIP: 20515-3902) 225-2735

Adams, Todd CHIEF OF STAFF 2077 52735
La Fountain, Peter LEGIS ASST 2077 52735
Lee, Katie LEGIS ASST 2077 52735
Leiserson, Nicholas LEGIS DIR/SYS ADMIN 2077 52735
Maiden, Leigh LEGIS ASST - MIL 2077 52735
McKittrick, Kerry LEGIS ASST 2077 52735
Pennington, Nicholas STAFF ASST 2077 52735
Rose, Stu OFFICE MGR/SCHEDULER 2077 52735

DISTRICT OFFICE

WARWICK—SUMMIT SOUTH, 300 CENTERVILLE RD, SUITE 200, WARWICK, RI 02886

Adams, David STAFF ASST FOR TELEPHONES 401-732-9400
Albert, Katherine DIST SCHEDULER 401-732-9400
Beattie, Nancy DIR - CONSTIT SVCS 401-732-9400
Charon, Justyn CONSTIT SVCS REP 401-732-9400
Curtis, Ryan CONSTIT SVCS REP 401-732-9400
Klaiman, Seth DIST CHIEF OF STAFF 401-732-9400
Malec, Stuart CONSTIT SVCS REP 401-732-9400
Paz, Julio CONSTIT SVCS REP 401-732-9400
Sievers, Samantha STAFF ASST 401-732-9400

Representative Rick Larsen

Washington, 2d

2113 RAYBURN HOB (ZIP: 20515-4702) 225-2605

Banks, Linda FINANCIAL ADMIN 2113 52605
Golden, J Z SR LEGIS ASST 2113 52605
Gros, Lauren DC SCHEDULER 2113 52605
Hudspith, Michael STAFF ASST 2113 52605
Johnston, Kimberly CHIEF OF STAFF 2113 52605
McKeon, Seamus LEGIS CORRES 2113 52605
Menardy, Alexandra LEGIS ASST 2113 52605
Munger, Amanda COMMUNICATIONS DIR 2113 52605
Nazaretova, Katy LEGIS ASST 2113 52605
Sabag, Terra LEGIS DIR/DPTY CHIEF OF STAFF 2113 52605

DISTRICT OFFICES

BELLINGHAM—119 N COMMERCIAL ST, SUITE 275, BELLINGHAM, WA 98225

Gelwicks, Laura COMMUNITY LIAISON 360-733-4500

EVERETT—2930 WETMORE AVE, SUITE 9F, EVERETT, WA 98201-4070

TOLL-FREE NUMBER 1-800-562-1385
Jarnot, Brittany COMMUNITY LIAISON 425-252-3188
Larsen, Chris COMMUNITY LIAISON 425-252-3188
Lemieux, Adam DIST DIR 425-252-3188
Treadway, Jenn DIST SCHEDULER 425-252-3188
Webb, Lindsey DIST OUTREACH REP 425-252-3188

Representative John B. Larson

Connecticut, 1st

1501 LONGWORTH HOB (ZIP: 20515-0701) **225-2265**
Banjac, Srdan LEGIS ASST 1501 .... **52265**
Dunn, Mike LEGIS CORRES 1501 .... **52265**
Garten, Alicia LEGIS ASST 1501 .... **52265**
Gianni, Sarah SCHEDULER/EXEC ASST 1501 .... **52265**
Perry, Anne SR POLICY ADVISOR 1501 .... **52265**
Stephanou, Scott CHIEF OF STAFF 1501 .... **52265**
Wang, George STAFF ASST 1501 .... **52265**
Yatrousis, Mary COMMUNICATIONS DIR 1501 .... **52265**

DISTRICT OFFICE

HARTFORD—221 MAIN ST, 2ND FLOOR, HARTFORD, CT 06106-1864
TOLL-FREE NUMBER **1-888-716-4734**
Benettieri, Hugo DIST AIDE **860-278-8888**
Christiana, Linda DIST SCHEDULER/EXEC ASST **860-278-8888**
Ciotto, Billy SR DIST REP **860-278-8888**
Fitzpatrick, Erica STAFF ASST **860-278-8888**
Harris, Kimberly DIST AIDE **860-278-8888**
Lynch, Daniel DIST AIDE **860-278-8888**
Mercado, Gladys DIST AIDE **860-278-8888**
Moriarty, Maureen CHIEF OF STAFF **860-278-8888**
Perrone, Lisa DIST AIDE/SR ADVISOR **860-278-8888**
Quinn, Conor DPTY CHIEF OF STAFF **860-278-8888**
Rivera, Kevin DIST AIDE/PRESS ASST **860-278-8888**

Representative Robert E. Latta

Ohio, 5th

2467 RAYBURN HOB (ZIP: 20515-3505) **225-6405**
Cassidy, Erin SCHEDULER 2467 .... **56405**
Davin, Mike LEGIS ASST 2467 .... **56405**
Griffin, Drew COMMUNICATIONS DIR 2467 .... **56405**
Hayden, Matt STAFF ASST 2467 .... **56405**
Lammers, Emily LEGIS CORRES 2467 .... **56405**
Poulios, Allison CHIEF OF STAFF 2467 .... **56405**
Schwegman, Rachel SR LEGIS ASST 2467 .... **56405**
Vey, Madeline LEGIS COUNSEL/LEGIS DIR 2467 .... **56405**

DISTRICT OFFICES

BOWLING GREEN—1045 N MAIN ST, SUITE 6, BOWLING GREEN, OH 43402
TOLL-FREE NUMBER **1-800-541-6446**
Giesige, Nicole DIST REP **419-354-8700**
Wirt, David DIST DIR **419-354-8700**

DEFIANCE—101 CLINTON ST, SUITE 1200, DEFIANCE, OH 43512
Shaver, Kathy DPTY DIST DIR **419-782-1996**

FINDLAY—318 DORNEY PLAZA, ROOM 302, FINDLAY, OH 45840
Bauman, Brian DIST REP **419-422-7791**

Representative Brenda L. Lawrence

Michigan, 14th

2463 RAYBURN HOB (ZIP: 20515-2214) **225-5802**
Casman, Ryan STAFF ASST 2463 .... **55802**
Greenfield, George DIR - INFO SYS 2463 .... **55802**
Hedgepeth, Ryan CHIEF OF STAFF 2463 .... **55802**
Huang, Alex SR LEGIS ASST 2463 .... **55802**
Kashat, Delia LEGIS CORRES 2463 .... **55802**
Krovi, Varun LEGIS DIR 2463 .... **55802**
Lawson, Dion FINANCIAL ADVISOR 2463 .... **55802**
Malone, Eboni EXEC SCHEDULER 2463 .... **55802**
Miszcak, Joe COORD - CONSTIT SVCS 2463 .... **55802**
Weber, Zachary LEGIS ASST 2463 .... **55802**

DISTRICT OFFICE

SOUTHFIELD—26700 LAHSER RD, SUITE 330, SOUTHFIELD, MI 48033
Elliott, Jacqueline PRESS AIDE/STAFF ASST **248-356-2052**
Glass, Indira DPTY DIST DIR/OFFICE MGR **248-356-2052**
Lee, Myra COORD - COMMUNITY OUTREACH **248-356-2052**
McGuinness, Michael COMMUNITY OUTREACH SPEC **248-356-2052**
Miller, Carolyn CASEWK MGR **248-356-2052**
Slaughter, James OUTREACH COORD **248-356-2052**

Representative Al Lawson, Jr.

Florida, 5th

1406 LONGWORTH HOB (ZIP: 20515-0905) **225-0123**
Eglin, Jessika STAFF ASST 1406 .... **50123**
Evans, Vincent SCHEDULER/SPECIAL ASST 1406 .... **50123**
Franklin, Margaret LEGIS DIR 1406 .... **50123**
Lambert, Stephanie COMMUNICATIONS DIR 1406 .... **50123**
Milenkevich, Amber LEGIS CORRES 1406 .... **50123**
Pierre-Canel, Christian LEGIS ASST 1406 .... **50123**
Pinckney, Janna SYS ADMIN 1406 .... **50123**
Stevens, Kimberly ADMIN - FINANCE & PAYROLL 1406 .... **50123**
Thompson, Tola CHIEF OF STAFF 1406 .... **50123**

DISTRICT OFFICES

JACKSONVILLE—117 W DUVAL ST, 2ND FLOOR, JACKSONVILLE, FL 32202
Barfield, Sherry CASEWKR **904-354-1652**
Hill, Tony FIELD REP **904-354-1652**
Smith, Ciera STAFF ASST **904-354-1652**
Wesley, Kortney DIST DIR **904-354-1652**

TALLAHASSEE—435 N MACOMB ST, TALLAHASSEE, FL 32301
Fairhurst, Deborah DIST DIR **850-558-9450**
Frederick, Theresa CASEWKR **850-558-9450**
Maloy, Rudolph FIELD REP **850-558-9450**
Thomas, Melissa STAFF ASST **850-558-9450**

Representative Barbara Lee

California, 13th

2470 RAYBURN HOB (ZIP: 20515-0513) **225-2661**
Figueroa, Kevin LEGIS CORRES 2470 .... **52661**
Jadallah, Diala SR POLICY ADVISOR 2470 .... **52661**
Koerner, Nissa PRESS ASST 2470 .... **52661**
Livingston, Chris SCHEDULER/EXEC ASST 2470 .... **52661**
Marc, Shelly DPTY CHIEF OF STAFF 2470 .... **52661**
Mehrabi, Emma LEGIS DIR 2470 .... **52661**
Nickson, Julie CHIEF OF STAFF 2470 .... **52661**
Nickson, Michael FINANCIAL COUNSELOR 2470 .... **52661**

DISTRICT OFFICE

OAKLAND—1301 CLAY ST, SUITE 1000-N, OAKLAND, CA 94612
Anecito, Chrissy CONG AIDE **510-763-0370**
Burnette, Antonio DIST STAFF ASST **510-763-0370**
Hernandez, Jose DPTY DIST DIR **510-763-0370**
Kalinga, Tatyana DIST DIR **510-763-0370**
Lee, Vanessa CONG AIDE **510-763-0370**
Patterson, Brandon DIST PRESS SECY **510-763-0370**

Thapa, Jain CONG AIDE ... 510-763-0370
Valdez, Elizabeth DIST SCHEDULER/DIST OFFICE MGR ... 510-763-0370

Representative Susie Lee

Nevada, 3d

522 CANNON HOB (ZIP: 20515-2803) ... 225-3252
Abel, Sarah COMMUNICATIONS DIR 522 CHOB ... 53252
Alam, Nabeel LEGIS ASST 522 CHOB ... 53252
Cox, Brandon CHIEF OF STAFF 522 CHOB ... 53252
Dhar, Sreyashe SCHEDULER 522 CHOB ... 53252
Ibarra, Marcos LEGIS ASST 522 CHOB ... 53252
Morgante, Samuel DPTY CHIEF OF STAFF/LEGIS DIR 522 CHOB ... 53252
Olivari, Renzo PRESS SECY 522 CHOB ... 53252
Toy, Lauren STAFF ASST 522 CHOB ... 53252
Vannozzi, Michael DIST DIR 522 CHOB ... 53252
Wessells, Jackson LEGIS CORRES 522 CHOB ... 53252

DISTRICT OFFICE

LAS VEGAS—8872 S EASTERN AVE, SUITES 210 & 220, LAS VEGAS, NV 89123
Catarata, Karl Joseph DIST REP ... 702-963-9336
Everett, Gabriela DIST REP/SCHEDULER ... 702-963-9336
Farias, Jahaira DIST REP ... 702-963-9336
Gama, Krystal DIST STAFF ASST ... 702-963-9336
Holbert, Andrew DIST REP ... 702-963-9336
McGee, Ashanti DIST REP ... 702-963-9336

Representative Debbie Lesko

Arizona, 8th

1113 LONGWORTH HOB (ZIP: 20515-0308) ... 225-4576
Babb, Alison FINANCIAL ADMIN 1113 ... 54576
Bravo, Bobby LEGIS AIDE 1113 ... 54576
Clark, Annie LEGIS ASST 1113 ... 54576
Gunderson-Schwarz, Abby CHIEF OF STAFF 1113 ... 54576
Iverson, George SCHEDULER 1113 ... 54576
Lauterbach, Jennifer SR LEGIS ASST 1113 ... 54576
Simon, Matthew DPTY CHIEF OF STAFF/LEGIS DIR 1113 ... 54576
Smith, Heather COMMUNICATIONS DIR 1113 ... 54576
Zwaanstra, Johnny LEGIS CORRES 1113 ... 54576

DISTRICT OFFICE

GLENDALE—7121 W BELL RD, SUITE 200, GLENDALE, AZ 85308
Byers, Chuck CONSTIT REP ... 623-776-7911
Fuellbier, Ken OUTREACH DIR ... 623-776-7911
Gray, Lisa DIST DIR ... 623-776-7911
Lett, Chelsea DPTY DIST DIR ... 623-776-7911
Milam, Marcus CONSTIT SVCS REP ... 623-776-7911
Roe, Austin STAFF ASST ... 623-776-7911

Representative Andy Levin

Michigan, 9th

228 CANNON HOB (ZIP: 20515-2209) ... 225-4961
Alawieh, Abbas LEGIS ASST 228 CHOB ... 54961
Brown, Taryn SCHEDULER 228 CHOB ... 54961
Laudick, Courtney LEGIS CORRES 228 CHOB ... 54961
Laufersweiler, Austin COMMUNICATIONS DIR 228 CHOB ... 54961
Neralla, Ven CHIEF OF STAFF 228 CHOB ... 54961
Rowland, Catherine LEGIS DIR 228 CHOB ... 54961
Steel, Sabrina LEGIS ASST 228 CHOB ... 54961
Torrence, Jamari STAFF ASST 228 CHOB ... 54961

DISTRICT OFFICE

WARREN—30500 VAN DYKE AVE, WARREN, MI 48093
Byer, Jenny FIELD REP/CASEWKR ... 586-498-7122
Charara, Robert DIST STAFF ASST ... 586-498-7122
Gamalski, Eleanor FIELD REP/CASEWKR ... 586-498-7122
Herzig, Walt DIST DIR ... 586-498-7122
Hussain, Zeenath DIR - CONSTIT SVCS ... 586-498-7122
Pollet, Kyle FIELD REP/CASEWKR ... 586-498-7122

Representative Mike Levin

California, 49th

1626 LONGWORTH HOB (ZIP: 20515-0549) ... 225-3906
Farewell, Robbie SR LEGIS ASST 1626 ... 53906
Feinswog, Alison LEGIS CORRES 1626 ... 53906
Foley, Mark DIR - ADMIN OPS/SCHEDULER 1626 ... 53906
Gilbert, Jonathan LEGIS DIR 1626 ... 53906
Henry-Bryant, Heather FINANCIAL ADMIN 1626 ... 53906
Mee, Eric COMMUNICATIONS DIR 1626 ... 53906
Van Stralen, Kara CHIEF OF STAFF 1626 ... 53906

DISTRICT OFFICES

DANA POINT—33282 GOLDEN LANTERN, SUITE 102, DANA POINT, CA 92629
Gitter, Cynthia FIELD REP ... 949-281-2449

OCEANSIDE—2204 EL CAMINO REAL, SUITE 314, OCEANSIDE, CA 92054
Bradley, Shannon FIELD REP ... 760-599-5000
Busby, Francine DIST DIR ... 760-599-5000
Krahel, Kyle DPTY DIST DIR ... 760-599-5000
Padilla, Ashleigh STAFF ASST ... 760-599-5000

Representative John Lewis

Georgia, 5th

300 CANNON HOB (ZIP: 20515-1005) ... 225-3801
Aydin, Andrew DIGITAL DIR 300 CHOB ... 53801
Bowman, David SCHEDULER 300 CHOB ... 53801
Collins, Michael CHIEF OF STAFF 300 CHOB ... 53801
Dorney, Tom SR LEGIS ASST 300 CHOB ... 53801
Feeney, William LEGIS CORRES/POLICY ADVISOR 300 CHOB . 53801
Jones, Brenda COMMUNICATIONS DIR 300 CHOB ... 53801
Nkollo, Taylor STAFF ASST 300 CHOB ... 53801
Sawyers, Marcus SPECIAL ASST 300 CHOB ... 53801
Thompson, Jamila LEGIS DIR 300 CHOB ... 53801

DISTRICT OFFICE

ATLANTA—THE EQUITABLE BLDG, ROOM 1920, 100 PEACHTREE ST NW, ATLANTA, GA 30303
Butler, Tuere DIST DIR ... 404-659-0116
Gilbert, Jocilyn STAFF ASST ... 404-659-0116
McKinley, Jared COORD - OUTREACH ... 404-659-0116
O'Neil, Rachelle CONSTIT SVCS REP ... 404-659-0116
Riley, Ruth EXEC ASST/SCHEDULER ... 404-659-0116
Washington, David STAFF ASST ... 404-659-0116

Representative Ted Lieu

California, 33d

403 CANNON HOB (ZIP: 20515-0533) ... 225-3976
Arevalo, Elizabeth LEGIS ASST 403 CHOB ... 53976

Bruell, Leo STAFF ASST 403 CHOB 53976
Bushnell, Jenna COMMUNICATIONS DIR 403 CHOB 53976
Cevasco, Marc CHIEF OF STAFF 403 CHOB 53976
Chernin, Michael LEGIS ASST 403 CHOB 53976
Gentry, Jonathan INFO TECH MGR 403 CHOB 53976
Jacobson, Corey LEGIS DIR 403 CHOB 53976
Nickson, Michael ADMIN - FINANCE & PAYROLL 403 CHOB 53976
Paik, Aurora LEGIS ASST/PRESS SECY 403 CHOB 53976
Parr, Diana LEGIS FELLOW 403 CHOB 53976
Sham, Julian LEGIS AIDE 403 CHOB 53976
Teppala, Harshitha SCHEDULER 403 CHOB 53976

DISTRICT OFFICES

LOS ANGELES—5055 WILSHIRE BLVD, SUITE 310, LOS ANGELES, CA 90036

Alegria, Kate CASEWKR 323-651-1040
Apodaca, Joey FIELD REP/CONSTIT SVCS 323-651-1040
Friedman, Aurelia FIELD REP 323-651-1040
Leou, Ryan STAFF ASST 323-651-1040
Paniagua-Uribe, Daisy FIELD REP 323-651-1040
Rodriquez, Nicolas DIST DIR 323-651-1040
Tetlow, Faith CASEWKR 323-651-1040
Turner, Janet FIELD REP/CONSTIT SVCS 323-651-1040

MANHATTAN BEACH—1600 ROSECRANS AVE, 4TH FLOOR, MANHATTAN BEACH, CA 90266 310-321-7664

Representative Daniel Lipinski

Illinois, 3d

2346 RAYBURN HOB (ZIP: 20515-1303) **225-5701**

Beckmann, Alexander LEGIS ASST 2346 55701
Leonova, Sofya LEGIS DIR 2346 55701
McGuire, Caitlyn LEGIS ASST 2346 55701
Roberts, Carl LEGIS CORRES 2346 55701
Sypolt, Jennifer ADMIN ASST/SCHEDULER/SYS ADMIN 2346 55701

DISTRICT OFFICES

CHICAGO—6245 S ARCHER AVE, CHICAGO, IL 60638
TOLL-FREE NUMBER 1-866-822-5701

Belmonte, Paula CONG ASST 773-948-6223
Bonomo, Joe DPTY DIST DIR 773-948-6223
Davidson, Philip COMMUNICATIONS DIR 773-948-6223
DiFranco, Sam SPECIAL PROJ ASST 773-948-6223
Jaroch, Jessica CONG AIDE 773-948-6223
Mulvihill, Jerry CHIEF CASEWKR 773-948-6223
Oszakiewski, Brian CHIEF OF STAFF 773-948-6223
Salerno, Francis CONG AIDE 773-948-6223

LOCKPORT—222 E 9TH ST, NO. 109, LOCKPORT, IL 60441 815-838-1990

OAK LAWN—5210 W 95TH ST, SUITE 104, OAK LAWN, IL 60453 708-424-0853

ORLAND PARK—14700 S RAVINIA AVE, ORLAND PARK, IL 60462 708-403-4379

Representative David Loebsack

Iowa, 2d

1211 LONGWORTH HOB (ZIP: 20515-1502) **225-6576**

Collier, William SR LEGIS ASST 1211 56576
Dempsey, Sean STAFF ASST 1211 56576
Hand, Joe PRESS SECY/DPTY CHIEF OF STAFF 1211 56576
Murray, Katie SCHEDULER/ADVISOR - HEALTH POLICY 1211 56576
Schnell, Erin LEGIS ASST 1211 56576
Stockwell, Scott LEGIS DIR/DPTY CHIEF OF STAFF 1211 56576
Ward, Sam LEGIS CORRES 1211 56576
Witte, Eric CHIEF OF STAFF 1211 56576

DISTRICT OFFICES

DAVENPORT—209 W 4TH ST, NO. 104, DAVENPORT, IA 52801
TOLL-FREE NUMBER 1-866-914-IOWA

Carton, Katie CASEWKR 563-323-5988
Kramer, Brian DIST REP 563-323-5988
Sueppel, Rob DIST DIR 563-323-5988

IOWA CITY—125 S DUBUQUE ST, IOWA CITY, IA 52240-4003

Dennison, Brianna DIST REP 319-351-0789
Hershberger, Jared DIST REP 319-351-0789
Judge, Dien DIST REP 319-351-0789
Leshtz, David DIST REP 319-351-0789
Snyder, Rachael CASEWKR 319-351-0789

Representative Zoe Lofgren

California, 19th

1401 LONGWORTH HOB (ZIP: 20515-0519) **225-3072**

Abrahamian, Arlet COUNSEL/LEGIS STAFF 1401 53072
Bryant, Heather SHARED EMPLOYEE/BUDGET OFFICER 1401 . 53072
Busick, Chelsea STAFF ASST 1401 53072
Davison, Casey LEGIS CORRES 1401 53072
DeLuca, Andrew SCHEDULER 1401 53072
Hull, Z J COUNSEL/LEGIS STAFF 1401 53072
Kim, Priscilla LEGIS ASST 1401 53072
Leavandosky, Stacey CHIEF OF STAFF 1401 53072
Shahoulian, David CHIEF COUNSEL/IMMIGRATION SPEC/SHARED EMPLOYEE 189 FHOB 56906
Weiner, Matt SR POLICY ADVISOR 1401 53072
Whippy, Peter DIR - PRESS & COMMUNICATIONS 1401 53072

DISTRICT OFFICE

SAN JOSE—635 N FIRST ST, SUITE B, SAN JOSE, CA 95112

Collins, Kathleen CONG ASST 408-271-8700
Duncan, Kerry CONG ASST 408-271-8700
Jufiar, Dolores OFFICE MGR/SR CASEWKR 408-271-8700
Mora-Castrellon, Christian CONG ASST 408-271-8700
Nguyen, Angela DIST SCHEDULER/CONG ASST 408-271-8700
Pham, Vincent CONG AIDE 408-271-8700
Podkolzina, Alexandra CONG ASST 408-271-8700
Soto, Sandra DIST CHIEF OF STAFF 408-271-8700

Representative Billy Long

Missouri, 7th

2454 RAYBURN HOB (ZIP: 20515-2507) **225-6536**

Appelbaum, Michael STAFF ASST 2454 56536
Elleson, Benjamin LEGIS DIR 2454 56536
Huthsing, Colton SCHEDULER 2454 56536
Kotsovos, Michael STAFF ASST 2454 56536
Lillis, Joe CHIEF OF STAFF 2454 56536
Olchyk, Ross LEGIS ASST 2454 56536
Smith, Hannah PRESS SECY 2454 56536
Warbinton, Tanner SR LEGIS ASST 2454 56536

DISTRICT OFFICES

JOPLIN—2727 E 32ND ST, SUITE 2, JOPLIN, MO 64804

Delano, Gwen CASEWKR 417-781-1041
Heisten, Jake FIELD REP 417-781-1041
Mackney, Kim CASEWKR 417-781-1041

SPRINGFIELD—3232 E RIDGEVIEW ST, SPRINGFIELD, MO 65804

Hobbs, Tyler DIST DIR 417-889-1800

Kollmeier, Bob LIAISON - AG 417-889-1800
Meads, Karen DIST SCHEDULER 417-889-1800
Pruett, Jeremy FIELD REP 417-889-1800
Saylor, Lisa CASEWKR 417-889-1800
Ussery, Mike DIR - CONSTIT SVCS/SPECIAL PROJ DIR 417-889-1800

Representative Barry Loudermilk

Georgia, 11th

422 CANNON HOB (ZIP: 20515-1011) **225-2931**
Adkerson, Elizabeth SCHEDULER 422 CHOB 52931
Adkerson, Robert CHIEF OF STAFF 422 CHOB 52931
Carr, Colin LEGIS DIR 422 CHOB 52931
Cockerham, Brandon COMMUNICATIONS DIR 422 CHOB 52931
Johnson, Eric LEGIS ASST 422 CHOB 52931
Johnston, Susannah LEGIS ASST 422 CHOB 52931
Milner, Katie STAFF ASST 422 CHOB 52931
Padgett, Ashleigh LEGIS CORRES 422 CHOB 52931

DISTRICT OFFICES

ATLANTA—600 GALLERIA PKWY SE, SUITE 120, ATLANTA, GA 30339
Bartlett, Claire FIELD DIR 770-429-1776

BARTOW—135 CHEROKEE AVE, SUITE 251, CARTERSVILLE, GA 30120
Parnell, Mack FIELD REP 770-429-1776

WOODSTOCK—9898 HWY 92, SUITE 100, WOODSTOCK, GA 30188
Dodd, Wayne DIST DIR 770-429-1776
Gilbert, Crystal DIR - CONSTIT SVCS 770-429-1776
McIntosh, Tina CASE MGR 770-429-1776
Mitcham, Bart FIELD REP 770-429-1776
Nall, Phyllis DIST OFFICE MGR 770-429-1776
Poole, Jennifer CASE MGR 770-429-1776
Wallace, John FIELD REP 770-429-1776

Representative Alan S. Lowenthal

California, 47th

108 CANNON HOB (ZIP: 20515-0547) **225-7924**
Bower, Andrew LEGIS ASST 108 CHOB 57924
Bradley, Katie STAFF ASST 108 CHOB 57924
Gorud, Chris LEGIS DIR 108 CHOB 57924
Higginbotham, Keith COMMUNICATIONS DIR/SR POLICY ADVISOR 108 CHOB 57924
Hysom, Tim CHIEF OF STAFF 108 CHOB 57924
Nguyen, Ngoc LEGIS ASST 108 CHOB 57924
Pham, Anthony STAFF ASST 108 CHOB 57924
Strombom, Emily LEGIS ASST 108 CHOB 57924
Trimmer, Shane SR LEGIS ASST 108 CHOB 57924

DISTRICT OFFICES

GARDEN GROVE—12865 MAIN ST, SUITE 200, GARDEN GROVE, CA 92840
Bautista, Rufino DIST SCHEDULER 714-243-4088
Ly, Phong SR FIELD REP 714-243-4088

LONG BEACH—100 W BROADWAY ST, WEST TOWER, SUITE 600, LONG BEACH, CA 90802
Heard, Clayton FIELD REP 562-436-3828
Lockerby, Justine CONSTIT SVCS REP 562-436-3828
Mims, Derrick SR ADVISOR 562-436-3828
Pujadas, Irantzu DPTY DIST DIR 562-436-3828
Pulido, Mark DPTY CHIEF OF STAFF 562-436-3828

Representative Nita M. Lowey

New York, 17th

2365 RAYBURN HOB (ZIP: 20515-3217) **225-6506**
Acton, Dana LEGIS DIR 2365 56506
Becker-Pollet, Jennifer LEGIS ASST/COUNSEL 2365 56506
Brenner, Steve LEGIS CORRES 2365 56506
Healton, Kelly DPTY CHIEF OF STAFF/SCHEDULER 2365 56506
Leibowitz, Liz LEGIS ASST 2365 56506
Papa, Katie OFFICE MGR 2365 56506
Pastore, Matt SCHEDULER/EXEC ASST 2365 56506
Richter, Jane STAFF ASST 2365 56506
Siegel, Shira SR LEGIS ASST 2365 56506
Stanley, Elizabeth CHIEF OF STAFF 2365 56506
Thorpe, Katelynn COMMUNICATIONS DIR 2365 56506

DISTRICT OFFICES

NEW CITY—67 N MAIN ST, NEW CITY, NY 10956
Malowitz, Jesse DIST REP 845-639-3485

WHITE PLAINS—222 MAMARONECK AVE, SUITE 312, WHITE PLAINS, NY 10605
Alter, Mike DIST REP 914-428-1707
Asprea, Joe DIST STAFF ASST 914-428-1707
Connolly, Kathlyn DIST SCHEDULER 914-428-1707
Harris, Meryl DIR - CONSTIT SVCS 914-428-1707
Keegan, Patricia DIST DIR 914-428-1707
Lloyd, Brandon DIST REP 914-428-1707
Oria, Yma DIST REP 914-428-1707

Representative Frank D. Lucas

Oklahoma, 3d

2405 RAYBURN HOB (ZIP: 20515-3603) **225-5565**
Bond, Patrick COMMUNICATIONS DIR 2405 55565
Dibblee, Christian LEGIS ASST 2405 55565
Johnson, Dillon LEGIS ASST 2405 55565
Mathis, Josh STAFF DIR 2405 55565
Scott, Nicole SR ADVISOR 2405 55565
Slagell, Alison LEGIS ASST 2405 55565
Wagner, Megan SCHEDULER 2405 55565
Wilkinson, Mitchell LEGIS CORRES 2405 55565

DISTRICT OFFICE

CANADIAN COUNTY—10952 NW EXPRESSWAY, SUITE B, YUKON, OK 73099
Beard, Bennett DIST FIELD REP 405-373-1958
Enmeier, Grace FIELD REP 405-373-1958
Gamel, Sherri DIST DIR 405-373-1958
Glasscock, Stacey CHIEF OF STAFF 405-373-1958
Litterell, Allison CASEWKR 405-373-1958
Northcott, Kylie CASEWKR 405-373-1958
Smith, Kirby DIST FIELD REP 405-373-1958

Representative Blaine Luetkemeyer

Missouri, 3d

2230 RAYBURN HOB (ZIP: 20515-2503) **225-2956**
Boman, Josiah LEGIS ASST 2230 52956
Costakos, Catherine COMMUNICATIONS DIR 2230 52956
Hart, Hailey LEGIS DIR 2230 52956
Ramey, Chad CHIEF OF STAFF 2230 52956
Turner, Shawnda STAFF ASST 2230 52956
Vogel, Ann SCHEDULER 2230 52956

West, Lucas SR POLICY ADVISOR 2230 52956
Wood, Jordan LEGIS CORRES 2230 52956

DISTRICT OFFICES

JEFFERSON CITY—2117 MISSOURI BLVD, JEFFERSON CITY, MO 65109
Boyken, Lori CONG LIAISON 573-635-7232
Hardecke, Laura OFFICE MGR 573-635-7232
Ketterer, Jeremy DPTY CHIEF OF STAFF 573-635-7232
Stuart, Keri DIR - CONSTIT SVCS 573-635-7232
Thompson, Matthew SPECIAL ASST 573-635-7232

WASHINGTON—516 JEFFERSON ST, WASHINGTON, MO 63090
McNichols, Jim DIST DIR 636-239-2276

WENTZVILLE—113 E PEARCE BLVD, WENTZVILLE, MO 63385
Montgomery, Christa DIST DIR 636-327-7055

Representative Ben Ray Luján

New Mexico, 3d

2323 RAYBURN HOB (ZIP: 20515-3103) **225-6190**
Espinosa, Kimberly LEGIS DIR 2323 56190
French, Lauren COMMUNICATIONS DIR 2323 56190
Hoeck, Matthew DC SCHEDULER 2323 56190
Mason, Graham DPTY CHIEF OF STAFF 2323 56190
Patterson, Levi LEGIS ASST 2323 56190
Ramirez, Angela CHIEF OF STAFF 2323 56190
Russell, Nina LEGIS CORRES 2323 56190

DISTRICT OFFICES

FARMINGTON—FARMINGTON CITY HALL, 800 MUNICIPAL DR, FARMINGTON, NM 87401 505-324-1005

GALLUP—110 W AZTEC AVE, SUITE 102, GALLUP, NM 87301
Lee, Brian CONSTIT SVCS 505-863-0582

LAS VEGAS—903 UNIVERSITY AVE, P.O. BOX 1368, LAS VEGAS, NM 87701
Garcia, Pamela CONSTIT LIAISON 505-454-3038
Salas, Stephen CONSTIT LIAISON 505-454-3038

RIO RANCHO—3200 CIVIC CENTER CIRCLE NE, SUITE 330, RIO RANCHO, NM 87144
Abeyta, Juan "Buddy" STAFF ASST 505-994-0499
Casados, Joseph CONSTIT SVCS OFFICER 505-994-0499
Duran, Patrick FIELD REP 505-994-0499

SANTA FE—1611 CALLE LORCA, SUITE A, SANTA FE, NM 87505
Chavez, Eric CONSTIT LIAISON 505-984-8950
Conn-Catechis, Jennifer DIST DIR 505-984-8950
Lopez, Sonya CONSTIT LIAISON 505-984-8950

TUCUMCARI—CHAMBER OF COMMERCE, 404 W ROUTE 66 BLVD, TUCUMCARI, NM 88401 575-461-3029

Representative Elaine G. Luria

Virginia, 2d

534 CANNON HOB (ZIP: 20515-4602) **225-4215**
Bratton, Tyrone LEGIS DIR 534 CHOB 54215
Carroll, Chris COMMUNICATIONS DIR 534 CHOB 54215
Fegley, Kate SCHEDULER 534 CHOB 54215
Gerstell, Jonathan LEGIS ASST 534 CHOB 54215
Hagerott, Virginia LEGIS CORRES 534 CHOB 54215
Kim, Jonah STAFF ASST 534 CHOB 54215
Mastrangelo, David FINANCIAL ADMIN 534 CHOB 54215
Sorenson, Kathryn CHIEF OF STAFF 534 CHOB 54215
Wardell, Dominque LEGIS ASST 534 CHOB 54215

DISTRICT OFFICE

VIRGINIA BEACH—283 CONSTITUTION DR, SUITE 900, VIRGINIA BEACH, VA 23462
Carter, Erin COORD - DIST OUTREACH 757-364-7650
Smith, Caleb CASEWKR 757-364-7650
Wickersham, Dave DIST DIR 757-364-7650
Williams, Juanita CASEWKR 757-364-7650

Representative Stephen F. Lynch

Massachusetts, 8th

2109 RAYBURN HOB (ZIP: 20515-2108) **225-8273**
Conway, James STAFF ASST 2109 58273
Fernandez, Bruce LEGIS DIR/DPTY CHIEF OF STAFF 2109 58273
George, Kevin SR POLICY ADVISOR 2109 58273
Gordon, Greta Hebert FINANCIAL ADMIN 2109 58273
Hollingshead, Megan SCHEDULER/LEGIS ASST 2109 58273
Osorio, Mariana SR LEGIS ASST 2109 58273
Ryan, R Kevin CHIEF OF STAFF 2109 58273
Silva, Natasha SR LEGIS ASST 2109 58273

DISTRICT OFFICES

BOSTON—1 HARBOR ST, SUITE 304, BOSTON, MA 02210
Adjei-Koranteng, Araba STAFF ASST 617-428-2000
Fowkes, Robert DIST DIR 617-428-2000
Kelland, Jonathan DIST REP 617-428-2000
Lynch, Daniel SR DIST REP 617-428-2000
Tarpey, Molly Rose COMMUNICATIONS DIR 617-428-2000
Zaferakis, Nicholas, Jr SR DIST REP 617-428-2000

BROCKTON—37 BELMONT ST, SUITE 3, BROCKTON, MA 02301
Barnes, Shaynah DIST REP 508-586-5555

QUINCY—1245 HANCOCK ST, SUITE 41, QUINCY, MA 02169 617-657-6305

Representative Tom Malinowski

New Jersey, 7th

426 CANNON HOB (ZIP: 20515-3007) **225-5361**
Carter, D'Andre EXEC SCHEDULER 426 CHOB 55361
Marek, Natalie STAFF ASST 426 CHOB 55361
Osborne, Amanda COMMUNICATIONS DIR 426 CHOB 55361
Ramirez, Eliza LEGIS DIR 426 CHOB 55361
Reid, Colston CHIEF OF STAFF 426 CHOB 55361
Ross, Robert ADMIN - FINANCE & PAYROLL 426 CHOB 55361
Schwartz, Benji LEGIS ASST/LEGIS CORRES 426 CHOB 55361

DISTRICT OFFICE

SOMERVILLE—58 E MAIN ST, 1ST FLOOR, SOMERVILLE, NJ 08876
Drulis, Mitchelle DIST DIR 908-547-3307
Hamilton, Eric FIELD REP 908-547-3307
Lubas, Genevieve DIST STAFF ASST 908-547-3307
Marshall, John COORD - GRANTS & SPEC PROJ 908-547-3307
McNeil, Rebecca CONSTIT SVCS REP 908-547-3307

Representative Carolyn B. Maloney

New York, 12th

2308 RAYBURN HOB (ZIP: 20515-3212) **225-7944**
Bell, Jennifer COMMUNICATIONS DIR 2308 57944
Harney, Benjamin COUNSEL 2308 57944
Hennessy, Kelly POLICY ADVISOR 2308 57944

Iger, Michael CHIEF OF STAFF 2308 57944
Parisi, Christina LEGIS DIR 2308 57944
Sumner, Danielle STAFF ASST 2308 57944
Tulloch, Rebecca SCHEDULER 2308 57944
Whitcomb, Maxwell SR POLICY ADVISOR 2308 57944

DISTRICT OFFICES

ASTORIA—31-19 NEWTOWN AVE, ASTORIA, NY 11102
Babor, Edward DIST REP 718-932-1804

BROOKLYN—619 LORIMER ST, BROOKLYN, NY 11211 718-349-5972

NEW YORK—1651 THIRD AVE, SUITE 311, NEW YORK, NY 10128
Anderson, Elise DPTY PRESS SECY 212-860-0606
Elias, Minna DIST CHIEF OF STAFF 212-860-0606
Garner, Shelby DIST REP 212-860-0606
Hague, Sarah DIST REP 212-860-0606
Kay, Jessie DIST REP 212-860-0606
Leeds, David DIST REP 212-860-0606
Montesinos, Victor DIR - CONSTIT SVCS 212-860-0606
Odomirok, Mary DIST REP 212-860-0606
Reyes, Juanita DIST MGR 212-860-0606

Representative Sean Patrick Maloney

New York, 18th

2331 RAYBURN HOB (ZIP: 20515-3218) **225-5441**
Baum, Ben SPECIAL ASST 2331 55441
Carey, Molly LEGIS DIR 2331 55441
Golden, Kevin DIR - SCHEDULING & ADVANCE 2331 55441
Hart, Beverly LEGIS CORRES 2331 55441
Hayes, Mecole LEGIS ASST 2331 55441
Lee, Ian COMMUNICATIONS DIR 2331 55441
Lehman, Ryan DPTY CHIEF OF STAFF 2331 55441
Persico, Tim CHIEF OF STAFF 2331 55441
Wilcox, Libbie DIGITAL PRESS SECY 2331 55441

DISTRICT OFFICE

NEWBURGH—123 GRAND ST, 2ND FLOOR, NEWBURGH, NY 12550
Alvarez, Gerardo CONSTIT SVCS 845-561-1259
Banfield, Paige DIR - OPS 845-561-1259
Bickley, Theo SPECIAL ASST 845-561-1259
Chippendale, Jenna CONSTIT ADVOCATE 845-561-1259
Donat, Joseph DIST DIR 845-561-1259
Ingrassia, Maria CONSTIT ADVOCATE 845-561-1259
Lyons, Cullen LIAISON - MIL & VET 845-561-1259
Meyer, Jesse COORD - GRANTS & SPEC PROJ 845-561-1259
Trumpetto, Brynna OUTREACH DIR 845-561-1259

Representative Kenny Marchant

Texas, 24th

2304 RAYBURN HOB (ZIP: 20515-4324) **225-6605**
Bunting, Luke COMMUNICATIONS DIR 2304 56605
Cunningham, Scott DPTY CHIEF 2304 56605
Deoudes, John LEGIS DIR 2304 56605
Hamilton, Ryan LEGIS CORRES 2304 56605
Hurley, Lindsay LEGIS ASST 2304 56605
Smith, Nicholas LEGIS ASST 2304 56605
Thomas, Brian CHIEF OF STAFF 2304 56605

DISTRICT OFFICE

IRVING—9901 E VALLEY RANCH PKWY, SUITE 3035, IRVING, TX 75063
Gum, Rhett COORD - DIST OUTREACH 972-556-0162
Hayes, John LIAISON - MIL 972-556-0162
Martin, Todd DIR - DIST AFFAIRS 972-556-0162
Miller, Susie DPTY CHIEF/DIR - DIST AFFAIRS 972-556-0162
Payne, Chelsea CONSTIT SVCS 972-556-0162

Representative Roger W. Marshall

Kansas, 1st

312 CANNON HOB (ZIP: 20515-1601) **225-2715**
Brooks, Michael LEGIS DIR 312 CHOB 52715
Gale, Madeline EXEC ASST 312 CHOB 52715
Lowry, Zachary LEGIS ASST 312 CHOB 52715
Moore, Katie SR LEGIS ASST 312 CHOB 52715
Parent, Charyssa COMMUNICATIONS DIR 312 CHOB 52715
Pineda, Charlotte ADVISOR - HEALTH POLICY 312 CHOB 52715
Robertson, Brent CHIEF OF STAFF 312 CHOB 52715

DISTRICT OFFICES

GARDEN CITY—816 CAMPUS DR, NO. 500, GARDEN CITY, KS 67846
Molz, Bonnie OFFICE MGR 620-765-7800
Swender, Becca DPTY DIST DIR 620-765-7800

SALINA—200 E IRON ST, SALINA, KS 67401
Meagher, Nikki DIST EXEC ASST/CASEWKR 785-829-9000
Sawyer, Katie STATE DIR 785-829-9000

Representative Thomas Massie

Kentucky, 4th

2453 RAYBURN HOB (ZIP: 20515-1704) **225-3465**
Cranston, Seana LEGIS DIR/DPTY CHIEF OF STAFF 2453 53465
Ferland, John CHIEF OF STAFF 2453 53465
Kreft, Kevin DIST STAFF ASST 2453 53465
Lington, Laura COMMUNICATIONS DIR 2453 53465
Marchese, Nino LEGIS ASST 2453 53465
O'Grady, Patrick LEGIS ASST 2453 53465
Wadsworth, William DC SCHEDULER 2453 53465

DISTRICT OFFICES

ASHLAND—1700 GREENUP AVE, R-505, ASHLAND, KY 41101
Reed, J R FIELD REP 606-324-9898

NORTHERN KENTUCKY—541 BUTTERMILK PIKE, SUITE 208, CRESCENT SPRINGS, KY 41017
McCane, Chris DIST DIR 859-426-0080
Porter, Bob SR CONSTIT SVCS REP 859-426-0080
Porter, Carrie CONSTIT LIAISON/DIST STAFF ASST/ASST SCHEDULER 859-426-0080
Troutman, Mary ADMIN DIR/DIST SCHEDULER 859-426-0080

OLDHAM COUNTY—108 W JEFFERSON ST, LA GRANGE, KY 40031
Rockaway, Stacie FIELD REP 502-265-9119

Representative Brian J. Mast

Florida, 18th

2182 RAYBURN HOB (ZIP: 20515-0918) **225-3026**
Cope, Stephanie LEGIS CORRES 2182 53026
Fleischman, Julian LEGIS AIDE 2182 53026
Langenderfer, James CHIEF OF STAFF 2182 53026
Miller, Sarah LEGIS ASST 2182 53026
Nelson, Jonathan FINANCIAL ADMIN 2182 53026

Neuman, Jaclyn SCHEDULER 2182 53026
Smith, Barry LEGIS DIR 2182 53026
Stewart, Brad COMMUNICATIONS DIR/DPTY CHIEF OF STAFF 2182 53026
Vonende, Kyle PRESS SECY 2182 53026
Weglein, Michael LEGIS ASST 2182 53026

DISTRICT OFFICES

NORTH PALM BEACH—420 U.S. HWY ONE, SUITE 19, NORTH PALM BEACH, FL 33408
Ciotti, Nick DIST DIR 561-530-7778
South, John CONSTIT SVCS REP 561-530-7778

PORT ST. LUCIE—121 SW PORT ST. LUCIE BLVD, ROOM 187, PORT ST. LUCIE, FL 34984
Hankerson, Derek CONSTIT RELATIONS REP 772-336-2877
Robertson, Angel SR OUTREACH DIR/COORD - OUTREACH 772-336-2877
Rowley, Kalene DIR - CONSTIT SVCS 772-336-2877

STUART—171 SW FLAGLER AVE, STUART, FL 34994
Galante, Amy CONSTIT SVCS REP 772-403-0900
Haddox, John FIELD REP 772-403-0900
Leighton, Stephen DPTY CHIEF OF STAFF 772-403-0900

Representative Doris O. Matsui

California, 6th

2311 RAYBURN HOB (ZIP: 20515-0506) 225-7163
Blatt, Hannah COMMUNICATIONS DIR 2311 57163
Clark, Robert LEGIS CORRES 2311 57163
Damato, Alex SR LEGIS ASST/TECH ADVISOR 2311 57163
Krongaus, McKinley EXEC ASST/SCHEDULER 2311 57163
Olivares, Shazia STAFF ASST 2311 57163
Richardson, Emily SR LEGIS ASST 2311 57163
Victor, Kyle CHIEF OF STAFF 2311 57163

DISTRICT OFFICE

SACRAMENTO—12-600 ROBERT T. MATSUI U.S. COURTHOUSE, 501 I ST, SACRAMENTO, CA 95814
Corcoran, Glenda DIST DIR 916-498-5600
Dierkes, Joan DIST SCHEDULER/DIST EXEC ASST 916-498-5600
Hattori, Harriet DIST STAFF ASST 916-498-5600
Herrera, Gabriela CASEWKR 916-498-5600
Lewis, Amy COMMUNICATIONS DIR 916-498-5600
Pavlovich, Natasha M CASEWKR 916-498-5600
Stiles, Meaghan CASEWKR 916-498-5600

Representative Ben McAdams

Utah, 4th

130 CANNON HOB (ZIP: 20515-4404) 225-3011
Aldous, Julianne LEGIS CORRES 130 CHOB 53011
Animley, Kingsley FINANCIAL ADMIN 130 CHOB 53011
Cunningham, Chris LEGIS ASST 130 CHOB 53011
Dunn, Nichole CHIEF OF STAFF 130 CHOB 53011
May, Eric LEGIS DIR 130 CHOB 53011
Valverde, Andrea DIR - OPS 130 CHOB 53011

DISTRICT OFFICE

WEST JORDAN—9067 S 1300 WEST, SUITE 101, WEST JORDAN, UT 84088
Barton, Hannah CONSTIT LIAISON 801-999-9801
Clason, Tiffany DIST DIR 801-999-9801
Heyrend, Alyson COMMUNICATIONS DIR 801-999-9801
Mower, Christian FIELD REP 801-999-9801
Schmitt, Michelle DIGITAL DIR 801-999-9801
Withers, Stephanie EXEC ASST 801-999-9801

Representative Lucy McBath

Georgia, 6th

1513 LONGWORTH HOB (ZIP: 20515-1006) 225-4501
Ahrens, Elizabeth DC SCHEDULER 1513 54501
Blankenship, Allison LEGIS AIDE 1513 54501
Burgess, Amy FINANCIAL ADMIN 1513 54501
Dillon, Althea PRESS ASST/STAFF ASST 1513 54501
Fox, Jen COMMUNICATIONS DIR 1513 54501
Goharioon, Laila LEGIS ASST 1513 54501
Golden, Matthew STAFF ASST/LEGIS CORRES 1513 54501
Knight, Natalie LEGIS COUNSEL 1513 54501
Miller, Debbie CASEWK MGR 1513 54501
Spears, Ian LEGIS DIR 1513 54501
Suh, Joon CHIEF OF STAFF 1513 54501

DISTRICT OFFICE

SANDY SPRINGS—5775 GLENRIDGE DR, BLDG B, SUITE 380, ATLANTA, GA 30328
Agonafer, Bethy DIST OFFICE MGR/DIST SCHEDULER 470-773-6330
Ramos, Caroline CONSTIT SVCS REP/CASEWKR/FIELD REP 470-773-6330
Speed, Chris CONSTIT SVCS/FIELD REP/CASEWKR 470-773-6330
Tyson, Antrell DIST DIR 470-773-6330

Representative Kevin McCarthy

California, 23d

2468 RAYBURN HOB (ZIP: 20515-0523) 225-2915
Burke, Robby STAFF ASST 2468 52915
Gourdikian, Alexandra SCHEDULER 2468 52915
Houston, Zachary LEGIS CORRES/PRESS AIDE 2468 52915
Lombardi, Kyle LEGIS DIR 2468 52915
Martinez, Brittany PRESS SECY 2468 52915
Min, James CHIEF OF STAFF 2468 52915
Murphy, Braden LEGIS ASST 2468 52915
Rindels, Emma LEGIS ASST 2468 52915
Smith, Trevor SR LEGIS ASST 2468 52915
Sparks, Matthew COMMUNICATIONS DIR 2468 52915

DISTRICT OFFICE

BAKERSFIELD—4100 EMPIRE DR, SUITE 150, BAKERSFIELD, CA 93309
Duncan, Chris DIST SCHEDULER 661-327-3611
Falk, Aaron FIELD REP 661-327-3611
Foster, Robin Lake DIST ADMIN 661-327-3611
Fowler, Clayton FIELD REP 661-327-3611
Graham, Chloe STAFF ASST 661-327-3611
Martin, Monica CONSTIT SVCS 661-327-3611
McKeown, Kati CONSTIT SVCS 661-327-3611
Turner, Joi CONSTIT SVCS 661-327-3611

Representative Michael T. McCaul

Texas, 10th

2001 RAYBURN HOB (ZIP: 20515-4310) 225-2401
Carlson, Johnna CHIEF OF STAFF 2001 52401
Cotner, Kelly DIR - OPS 2001 52401
Henderson, Andrew LEGIS FELLOW 2001 52401

Hester, Thomas LEGIS DIR 2001 52401
Matthews, Jonathan, III DPTY COMMUNICATIONS DIR 2001 52401
Mikeska, Bri LEGIS CORRES 2001 52401
Poursoltan, Cameron LEGIS ASST 2001 52401
Rice, Thomas SR LEGIS ASST 2001 52401
Smith, Amanda COMMUNICATIONS DIR 2001 52401

DISTRICT OFFICES

AUSTIN—3301 NORTHLAND DR, SUITE 212, AUSTIN, TX 78731
Dyke, Bobby STAFF ASST 512-473-2357

BRENHAM—2000 S MARKET ST, SUITE 303, BRENHAM, TX 77833
Mikeska, Marita CASEWKR 979-830-8497

KATY—1773 WESTBOROUGH DR, SUITE 223, KATY, TX 77449
Plunto, Larissa REGIONAL DIR 281-398-1247

TOMBALL—990 VILLAGE SQUARE, SUITE B, TOMBALL, TX 77375
Meicher, Sherrie CASEWKR 281-255-8372

Representative Tom McClintock

California, 4th

2312 RAYBURN HOB (ZIP: 20515-0504) 225-2511
Campbell, Kyle LEGIS CORRES 2312 52511
Cooke, Hannah EXEC ASST 2312 52511
Cressy, Jennifer COMMUNICATIONS DIR 2312 52511
Koncar, Steve DPTY CHIEF OF STAFF/LEGIS DIR 2312 52511
Marcel-Keyes, Andrew SR LEGIS ASST 2312 52511
Tudor, Chris DC CHIEF OF STAFF 2312 52511

DISTRICT OFFICE

ROSEVILLE—2200A DOUGLAS BLVD, SUITE 240, ROSEVILLE, CA 95661
Cassano, Daniella STAFF ASST 916-786-5560
Crowley, Danielle DIR - CONSTIT SVCS 916-786-5560
Deal, Rocky CHIEF OF STAFF 916-786-5560
George, Bill PRESS SECY 916-786-5560
Holt, Gregory CONSTIT SVCS OFFICER 916-786-5560
Pruett, Kimberly DIR - COMMUNITY OUTREACH 916-786-5560
Reed, Matthew OFFICE DIR 916-786-5560

Representative Betty McCollum

Minnesota, 4th

2256 RAYBURN HOB (ZIP: 20515-2304) 225-6631
Acero, Maureen LEGIS CORRES/LEGIS ASST 2256 56631
Foley, Libby LEGIS ASST 2256 56631
Gibson, Kristen MIL FELLOW 2256 56631
Harper, Bill CHIEF OF STAFF 2256 56631
Hartley, Mia SCHEDULER 2256 56631
Maillet, Patrick LEGIS ASST 2256 56631
Palermo, Trish STAFF ASST/LEGIS CORRES 2256 56631
Peterson, Ben LEGIS DIR 2256 56631
Schilling, Sophia LEGIS CORRES/LEGIS ASST 2256 56631
Taylor, Rebecca SR LEGIS ASST 2256 56631
Yanchury, Amanda COMMUNICATIONS DIR 2256 56631

DISTRICT OFFICE

ST. PAUL—661 LASALLE ST, SUITE 110, ST. PAUL, MN 55114
Connolly, Katie DIST SCHEDULER 651-224-9191
Gagne, Sally STAFF ASST 651-224-9191
Haddeland, Connie CONSTIT SVCS REP 651-224-9191
Lee, Chao SR DIST REP 651-224-9191
Melcher, Harold COMMUNITY OUTREACH SPEC 651-224-9191
Shaw, April CONSTIT SVCS REP 651-224-9191
Straka, Joshua DIST DIR 651-224-9191

Representative A. Donald McEachin

Virginia, 4th

314 CANNON HOB (ZIP: 20515-4604) 225-6365
Austin Reed, Keenan CHIEF OF STAFF 314 CHOB 56365
Baylor, Chris SYS ADMIN 314 CHOB 56365
Goldberger, Justin LEGIS ASST 314 CHOB 56365
Jones, Jediah DIR - OPS/SCHEDULER/PRESS ASST 314 CHOB 56365
Kingery, Rachel COORD - DIST OUTREACH 314 CHOB 56365
McClelland, Cody DIR - SR POLICY 314 CHOB 56365
Mensie, Alyssa SPECIAL ASST 314 CHOB 56365
Nelson, Jonathan FINANCIAL ADMIN 314 CHOB 56365
Solow, Corey LEGIS DIR 314 CHOB 56365
Wriston, Blair LEGIS AIDE 314 CHOB 56365

DISTRICT OFFICES

HAMPTON ROADS—131 N SARATOGA ST, SUITE B, SUFFOLK, VA 23434
Burroughs, Mary DIST REP 757-942-6050
Gabriel, Nick CASEWKR 757-942-6050
Murphy, Sylvia DIST REP 757-942-6050
Rountree, Tara DPTY CHIEF OF STAFF 757-942-6050

RICHMOND—110 N ROBINSON ST, SUITE 403, RICHMOND, VA 23220
Easter, Abbi SR ADVISOR 804-486-1840
Hardin, Elizabeth CASEWKR 804-486-1840

Representative James P. McGovern

Massachusetts, 2d

408 CANNON HOB (ZIP: 20515-2102) 225-6101
Bonaccorsi, Matt COMMUNICATIONS DIR 408 CHOB 56101
Buhl, Cindy LEGIS DIR 408 CHOB 56101
Chandler, Jennifer CHIEF OF STAFF 408 CHOB 56101
Deshmukh, Harsh LEGIS ASST 408 CHOB 56101
Early, Ryan LEGIS CORRES 408 CHOB 56101
Holt, Daniel SCHEDULER/DIR - OPS 408 CHOB 56101
Rupert-Shropshire, Saundrea SR LEGIS ASST 408 CHOB 56101
Swords, John LEGIS ASST 408 CHOB 56101

DISTRICT OFFICES

LEOMINSTER—24 CHURCH ST, ROOM 24, LEOMINSTER, MA 01453
Romero-Rodriguez, Eladia REGIONAL REP 978-466-3552

NORTHAMPTON—94 PLEASANT ST, NORTHAMPTON, MA 01060 413-341-8700

WORCESTER—12 E WORCESTER ST, SUITE 1, WORCESTER, MA 01604
Brissette, Kelly DIST SCHEDULER/DPTY DIST DIR 508-831-7356
Gibbons, Mary Pat DIST REP 508-831-7356
Hodgkins, Holly DIST REP 508-831-7356
Nadeau, Seth DIST REP 508-831-7356
Niedzielski, Jonathan DIST DIR 508-831-7356
Polanowicz, Kathleen SR ADVISOR 508-831-7356
Quiroa, David DIST REP 508-831-7356
Rodriguez-Parker, Gladys DIST REP 508-831-7356

Representative Patrick T. McHenry

North Carolina, 10th

2004 RAYBURN HOB (ZIP: 20515-3310) 225-2576
Barry, Will STAFF ASST 2004 52576
Broyles, Lauren LEGIS CORRES 2004 52576
Butler, Jeff CHIEF OF STAFF 2004 52576
Nation, Doug LEGIS DIR 2004 52576

Stafford, Krista SR LEGIS ASST 2004 .... **52576**
Theodossiou, Taylor PRESS SECY 2004 .... **52576**
Tricomi, Grace SCHEDULER 2004 .... **52576**
Worrell, Christopher LEGIS ASST 2004 .... **52576**

DISTRICT OFFICES

BLACK MOUNTAIN—160 MIDLAND AVE, BLACK MOUNTAIN, NC 28711
Kumpf, Roger REGIONAL DIR **828-669-0600**

GASTONIA—128 W MAIN AVE, SUITE 115, GASTONIA, NC 28053
Bowen, Will REGIONAL REP **704-833-0096**
Keeter, Brett DIST DIR **704-833-0096**

HICKORY—P.O. BOX 1830, HICKORY, NC 28603
TOLL-FREE NUMBER 1-800-477-2576
McCrary, David DIR - CONSTIT SVCS **828-327-6100**
Meek, Nancy SR DIST REP **828-327-6100**
Peek, Tracy STAFF ASST **828-327-6100**
Rowe, Joanna CONSTIT RELATIONS LIAISON **828-327-6100**

Representative David B. McKinley

West Virginia, 1st

2239 RAYBURN HOB (ZIP: 20515-4801) **225-4172**
Bradley, Philippa LEGIS AIDE/LEGIS CORRES 2239 .... **54172**
Brown, Kaitlin EXEC ASST 2239 .... **54172**
Buki, Christopher LEGIS DIR 2239 .... **54172**
Garand, Brian LEGIS ASST 2239 .... **54172**
Hamilton, Mike CHIEF OF STAFF 2239 .... **54172**
Hyman, Amanda COMMUNICATIONS DIR 2239 .... **54172**
Kerr, Liam STAFF ASST 2239 .... **54172**
Pettit, Sydney LEGIS ASST 2239 .... **54172**

DISTRICT OFFICES

MORGANTOWN—709 BEECHURST AVE, SUITE 29, MORGANTOWN, WV 26505
Madden, Wendy FIELD REP **304-284-8506**
Wooldridge, Linda CONSTIT REP/CASEWK DIR **304-284-8506**

PARKERSBURG—408 MARKET ST, PARKERSBURG, WV 26101
Villers, Robert CASEWKR/CONSTIT SVCS **304-422-5972**

WHEELING—1100 MAIN ST, SUITE 101, WHEELING, WV 26003
Hosking-Young, Chantel DIST FIELD REP **304-232-3801**
Reasbeck, Libby DIST DIR **304-232-3801**

Representative Jerry McNerney

California, 9th

2265 RAYBURN HOB (ZIP: 20515-0509) **225-1947**
Alioto, Nicole CHIEF OF STAFF 2265 .... **51947**
Cannon, Nikki COMMUNICATIONS DIR 2265 .... **51947**
Henry-Bryant, Heather FINANCIAL ADMIN 2265 .... **51947**
Jones, Trevor LEGIS AIDE/DC SCHEDULER 2265 .... **51947**
Matt, Svetlana LEGIS ASST 2265 .... **51947**
Pinckney, Janna SYS ADMIN 2265 .... **51947**
Roe, Exodie, III SR LEGIS ASST 2265 .... **51947**
Sahgal, Rishi LEGIS DIR 2265 .... **51947**
Stoever, Michael LEGIS ASST 2265 .... **51947**
Valle-Riestra, Jenna STAFF ASST 2265 .... **51947**

DISTRICT OFFICES

ANTIOCH—4703 LONE TREE WAY, ANTIOCH, CA 94531
Owen, Emily STAFF ASST/DIST SCHEDULER **925-754-0716**
Ramos, Tito CONSTIT REP **925-754-0716**

STOCKTON—2222 GRAND CANAL BLVD, NO. 7, STOCKTON, CA 95207
Ahmed, Ahdel FIELD REP **209-476-8552**
Alva, Alisa DIST DIR **209-476-8552**
Ornelas, Chiakis DPTY DIST DIR **209-476-8552**
Prost, Gary SR FIELD REP **209-476-8552**
Rico, Catalina CONSTIT REP **209-476-8552**

Representative Mark Meadows

North Carolina, 11th

2160 RAYBURN HOB (ZIP: 20515-3311) **225-6401**
Compton, Megan LEGIS ASST 2160 .... **56401**
Doocy, Mary LEGIS COUNSEL 2160 .... **56401**
Fitzpatrick, Paul CHIEF OF STAFF 2160 .... **56401**
Hoffman, Austin STAFF ASST 2160 .... **56401**
McAndrews, Sean LEGIS CORRES 2160 .... **56401**
Rascher, Mallory SCHEDULER 2160 .... **56401**
Wade, Melissa ADMIN - FINANCE & PAYROLL 2160 .... **56401**
Wentzel, Josh LEGIS ASST 2160 .... **56401**
Williamson, Ben COMMUNICATIONS DIR 2160 .... **56401**
Yelinski, Chad LEGIS DIR 2160 .... **56401**

DISTRICT OFFICES

BURKE COUNTY—305 E UNION ST, SUITE A100, MORGANTON, NC 28655
Whisnant, Jordan FIELD REP **828-432-2699**

CALDWELL—HEALTH AND HUMAN SERVICES BLDG, 2345 MORGANTON BLVD, LENOIR, NC 28645
McCreary, Clay FIELD REP **828-426-8701**

HAYWOOD—285 N MAIN ST, SUITE 1300, WAYNESVILLE, NC 28786
Elliott, Beverly FIELD REP **828-452-6022**

HENDERSON—200 N GROVE ST, SUITE 90, HENDERSONVILLE, NC 28792
King, Wayne DPTY CHIEF OF STAFF/DIST DIR **828-693-5660**
Maybin, Jenny FIELD REP **828-693-5660**
Miller, Collin STAFF ASST **828-693-5660**

MCDOWELL—100 SPAULDING RD, MARION, NC 28752 828-432-2699

MITCHELL—11 CRYSTAL ST, P.O. BOX 646, SPRUCE PINE, NC 28777
Peterson, Martha FIELD REP **828-765-0573**

Representative Gregory W. Meeks

New York, 5th

2310 RAYBURN HOB (ZIP: 20515-3205) **225-3461**
Akinyemi, Florence FELLOW 2310 .... **53461**
Belon, Reginald SCHEDULER/DIR - OPS 2310 .... **53461**
Fashola, Kevin FELLOW 2310 .... **53461**
Hart, Arline STAFF ASST 2310 .... **53461**
Hooks, David COMMUNITY LIAISON 2310 .... **53461**
Jolly, Ernie LEGIS DIR/POLICY ADVISOR - FINANCIAL SVCS/DPTY CHIEF OF STAFF 2310 .... **53461**
Karim, Fatima SPECIAL PROJ COORD 2310 .... **53461**
Lafargue, Sophia CHIEF OF STAFF 2310 .... **53461**
Vasilescu, Dikran COMMUNICATIONS DIR 2310 .... **53461**

DISTRICT OFFICES

JAMAICA—153-01 JAMAICA AVE, 2ND FLOOR, JAMAICA, NY 11432-3870
Edwards, Joe EXEC DIR **718-725-6000**
Hezekiah, Nathaniel COMMUNITY LIAISON **718-725-6000**
Joseph, Davidson DIST AIDE **718-725-6000**
Lespinasse, Marie COMMUNITY LIAISON **718-725-6000**

Reteguis, Karla CONG LIAISON 718-725-6000
Simmons, Robert DIST CHIEF OF STAFF 718-725-6000

ROCKAWAY—67-12 ROCKAWAY BEACH BLVD, AVERNE, NY 11692

Millord, Betsy COMMUNITY LIAISON 347-230-4032
Singletary, Raymond COMMUNITY LIAISON 347-230-4032

Representative Grace Meng

New York, 6th

2209 RAYBURN HOB (ZIP: 20515-3206) **225-2601**

Beaudreau, Helen LEGIS DIR 2209 52601
Connolly, Brenda EXEC ASST 2209 52601
Dinakar, Aditi LEGIS CORRES 2209 52601
Hsieh, Jacqueline LEGIS ASST 2209 52601
Nasielski, Katharine LEGIS ASST 2209 52601
Olson, Mark LEGIS AIDE/PRESS SECY 2209 52601
Oswald, Justin CHIEF OF STAFF 2209 52601

DISTRICT OFFICES

FLUSHING—40-13 159TH ST, FLUSHING, NY 11358

Class, Facia COMMUNITY OUTREACH SPEC 718-358-6364
DiLeone, Maria DIST SCHEDULER 718-358-6364
Goldes, Jordan COMMUNICATIONS DIR 718-358-6364
Lemma, Anthony DIST DIR 718-358-6364
Li, Sydney COMMUNITY LIAISON 718-358-6364
Pollack, Daniel COMMUNITY LIAISON 718-358-6364
Romero, Cristian CONSTIT LIAISON/COMMUNITY LIAISON 718-358-6364
Saji, Stancy DIR - CONSTIT SVCS 718-358-6364
Ung, Sandra CASEWKR/SPECIAL ASST 718-358-6364

FOREST HILLS—118-35 QUEENS BLVD, 17TH FLOOR, FOREST HILLS, NY 11375 718-358-6364

Representative Daniel Meuser

Pennsylvania, 9th

326 CANNON HOB (ZIP: 20515-3809) **225-6511**

Ciapciak, Elle SR LEGIS ASST 326 CHOB 56511
Cutrona, Dante CHIEF OF STAFF 326 CHOB 56511
Denis, Lydia LEGIS CORRES 326 CHOB 56511
Elizandro, John COMMUNICATIONS DIR 326 CHOB 56511
Gruber, Hali DIR - OPS 326 CHOB 56511
Mack, Jonathan STAFF ASST 326 CHOB 56511
O'Connor, Mary FINANCIAL ADMIN 326 CHOB 56511
Rooney, Patrick LEGIS DIR 326 CHOB 56511

DISTRICT OFFICES

LEBANON COUNTY—1044 E MAIN ST, PALMYRA, PA 17078

Ludwig, Karen CONSTIT SVCS REP 717-603-1459

POTTSVILLE—121 PROGRESS AVE, SUITE 110, POTTSVILLE, PA 17901

Fidler, Joshua CONSTIT SVCS REP 570-871-6370
Gerace, Nathan DIST STAFF ASST 570-871-6370
Gower, John DPTY DIST DIR 570-871-6370
Hetherington Cunfer, Katherine DPTY DIST DIR 570-871-6370
Shay, Michael MGR - CONSTIT SVCS/GRANTS SPEC . 570-871-6370
Weaver, Denise CONSTIT SVCS REP 570-871-6370

Representative Carol D. Miller

West Virginia, 3d

1605 LONGWORTH HOB (ZIP: 20515-4803) **225-3452**

Billman, Lauren LEGIS DIR 1605 53452
Cantrell, Samantha ASST PRESS SECY 1605 53452
Chirico, Michael DPTY CHIEF OF STAFF/DIST DIR 1605 53452
Donnellan, Matt CHIEF OF STAFF 1605 53452
Incerto, Jacquelyn LEGIS ASST 1605 53452
Kinner, Mily SCHEDULER 1605 53452
Moran, Tom COMMUNICATIONS DIR 1605 53452
O'Connor, Mary SHARED EMPLOYEE 1605 53452
Pedrotti, Max LEGIS CORRES 1605 53452
Viskovich, Bronti STAFF ASST 1605 53452

DISTRICT OFFICES

BECKLEY—223 PRINCE ST, BECKLEY, WV 25801

McMillion, Kim DPTY DIST DIR 304-250-6177

BLUEFIELD—601 FEDERAL ST, BLUEFIELD, WV 24701 304-325-6800

HUNTINGTON—865 FIFTH ST, SUITE 152, HUNTINGTON, WV 25701

Booth, Teri REGIONAL REP/DIST OFFICE MGR 304-522-2201

Representative Paul Mitchell

Michigan, 10th

211 CANNON HOB (ZIP: 20515-2210) **225-2106**

Davidson, Alex COMMUNICATIONS DIR 211 CHOB 52106
Feldpausch, Sarah LEGIS ASST 211 CHOB 52106
Harrington, Molly DIR - OPS 211 CHOB 52106
Healy, Laura LEGIS CORRES 211 CHOB 52106
Judd, Derek LEGIS ASST 211 CHOB 52106
Kizzier, Kyle CHIEF OF STAFF 211 CHOB 52106
Pelletier, Pat LEGIS DIR/DPTY CHIEF OF STAFF 211 CHOB 52106
Saleme, Emily STAFF ASST 211 CHOB 52106

DISTRICT OFFICE

SHELBY TOWNSHIP—48701 VAN DYKE AVE, SHELBY TOWNSHIP, MI 48317

Aprile, Alex COORD - CONSTIT SVCS 586-997-5010
Blatnik, Lauren DIST STAFF ASST 586-997-5010
Forlini, Tony DIST DIR 586-997-5010
Mankiewicz, Lisa COORD - CONSTIT SVCS 586-997-5010
Smith, Ed COORD - OUTREACH 586-997-5010

Representative John R. Moolenaar

Michigan, 4th

117 CANNON HOB (ZIP: 20515-2204) **225-3561**

Burdick, Cliff LEGIS CORRES 117 CHOB 53561
Cline, Eva LEGIS ASST 117 CHOB 53561
MacArthur, Chris SR LEGIS ASST 117 CHOB 53561
Russell, David COMMUNICATIONS DIR 117 CHOB 53561
Ryan, Lindsay CHIEF OF STAFF 117 CHOB 53561
Schimmenti, Jayson LEGIS DIR 117 CHOB 53561
Williams, Alexa EXEC ASST 117 CHOB 53561
Yantis, Noah STAFF ASST 117 CHOB 53561

DISTRICT OFFICE

MIDLAND—200 E MAIN ST, SUITE 230, MIDLAND, MI 48640

Bortz, Ashton DIST CHIEF OF STAFF 989-631-2552
Brooks, Sarah DIR - EXTERNAL AFFAIRS 989-631-2552
Brunink, Tarin DIR - CONSTIT SVCS 989-631-2552
Conover, Marla CONSTIT RELATIONS REP 989-631-2552
Derheim, Luke DIST REP 989-631-2552
Dorrien, Eric CONSTIT RELATIONS REP 989-631-2552
Ruth, Karen CONSTIT RELATIONS REP 989-631-2552

Smith, Tom CONSTIT RELATIONS REP 989-631-2552
Wolgast, Keisha DIST STAFF ASST 989-631-2552

Representative Alexander X. Mooney

West Virginia, 2d

2440 RAYBURN HOB (ZIP: 20515-4802) 225-2711
Caddock, John LEGIS ASST 2440 52711
Dacey, Ted DPTY CHIEF OF STAFF/COMMUNICATIONS DIR 2440 52711
Dusenbury, Rhett DIST REP 2440 52711
Freyre, Karla STAFF ASST 2440 52711
Grechko, Maxwell LEGIS CORRES 2440 52711
Hough, Michael CHIEF OF STAFF 2440 52711
Lester, Dean OFFICE ADMIN 2440 52711
Rausch, Scott LEGIS DIR 2440 52711
Story, Chad DIST DIR 2440 52711

DISTRICT OFFICES

CHARLESTON—405 CAPITOL ST, SUITE 306, CHARLESTON, WV 25301
Azevedo, Susie DIST FIELD REP 304-925-5964
Bragg, Erica STAFF ASST 304-925-5964
Neeley, Madison CONSTIT SVCS REP 304-925-5964

MARTINSBURG—300 FOXCROFT AVE, SUITE 101, MARTINSBURG, WV 25401
Kissel, Rainer FIELD REP 304-264-8810
Neff, Daniel DIST REP 304-264-8810
Reeves-Martin, Tara CONSTIT SVCS REP 304-264-8810

Representative Gwen Moore

Wisconsin, 4th

2252 RAYBURN HOB (ZIP: 20515-4904) 225-4572
Aitch, Izmira LEGIS ASST 2252 54572
Calderon, Tatiana LEGIS ASST 2252 54572
Frauman, Caroline TAX COUNSEL 2252 54572
Gard, Sean CHIEF OF STAFF 2252 54572
Goldson, Chris LEGIS DIR 2252 54572
Lenoir, Jeanette PRESS SECY 2252 54572
Montgomery, Robert SCHEDULER 2252 54572
Rosen, Talia LEGIS ASST 2252 54572
Thompson, Maryah STAFF ASST/LEGIS CORRES 2252 54572

DISTRICT OFFICE

MILWAUKEE—250 E WISCONSIN AVE, SUITE 950, MILWAUKEE, WI 53202
Devougas, Hope OUTREACH SPEC 414-297-1140
Ellis, Shirley SR ADVISOR/DIST DIR 414-297-1140
Payton, Sheila OUTREACH SPEC 414-297-1140
Ross, Donna DIST OFFICE MGR 414-297-1140
Sandoval, Maria CASEWKR/COMMUNITY OUTREACH SPEC 414-297-1140
Sippel, Kristin OUTREACH SPEC 414-297-1140

Representative Joseph D. Morelle

New York, 25th

1317 LONGWORTH HOB (ZIP: 20515-3225) 225-3615
Fillion, Jane LEGIS CORRES 1317 53615
Lemire, Daniel SCHEDULER 1317 53615
Majette, Ebony STAFF ASST 1317 53615
Oparil, Marie LEGIS ASST 1317 53615
Sorrendino, Abbie LEGIS DIR 1317 53615
Stiles, Jo LEGIS ASST 1317 53615
Weatherbee, Nicholas CHIEF OF STAFF 1317 53615

DISTRICT OFFICE

ROCHESTER—3120 FED BLDG, 100 STATE ST, ROCHESTER, NY 14614
Benedict, Kaleigh DIR - COMMUNITY AFFAIRS 585-232-4850
Bergin, Robert COUNSEL 585-232-4850
Hart, Sean COMMUNICATIONS DIR 585-232-4850
Jablonski, Jordan DIST STAFF ASST 585-232-4850
Leathersich, Joseph COMMUNICATIONS AIDE 585-232-4850
McCann, Kristin DIST DIR 585-232-4850
Pellito, John COMMUNITY LIAISON/DIST LIAISON 585-232-4850
Vernetti, Dana PRESS SECY 585-232-4850

Representative Seth Moulton

Massachusetts, 6th

1127 LONGWORTH HOB (ZIP: 20515-2106) 225-8020
Biba, Tim COMMUNICATIONS DIR 1127 58020
Farina, Adam SPEECHWRITER 1127 58020
Lainez, Julio LEGIS DIR 1127 58020
MacDonald, Asher SPECIAL ASST 1127 58020
Prieur L'Heureux, Alexis CHIEF OF STAFF 1127 58020
Raymond, Chrissy POLICY ADVISOR 1127 58020
Stolitzka, Anna SCHEDULER 1127 58020
Wagner, Christy SR ADVISOR - FOREIGN POLICY 1127 58020

DISTRICT OFFICE

SALEM—21 FRONT ST, SALEM, MA 01970
Bell, Morgan DIST REP 978-531-1669
Devin, Michael DIST REP 978-531-1669
Hyppolite, Marven CASEWKR 978-531-1669
Jakious, Rick DIST DIR 978-531-1669
Meeker, Anne CASEWKR 978-531-1669
Santos, Lucas DIST REP 978-531-1669
Suarez, Neesha CASEWKR 978-531-1669

Representative Debbie Mucarsel-Powell

Florida, 26th

114 CANNON HOB (ZIP: 20515-0926) 225-2778
Breslin, William STAFF ASST 114 CHOB 52778
Fogwell, Courtney LEGIS DIR/DPTY CHIEF OF STAFF 114 CHOB 52778
Forero, Laura DC SCHEDULER/LEGIS CORRES 114 CHOB 52778
Nystrom, Katy DIGITAL PRESS SECY 114 CHOB 52778
Rebold, Liza LEGIS CORRES 114 CHOB 52778
Rodriguez, Laura CHIEF OF STAFF 114 CHOB 52778
Silva, Sebastian COMMUNICATIONS DIR 114 CHOB 52778
Yim, Daniel LEGIS ASST 114 CHOB 52778

DISTRICT OFFICES

KEY WEST—1100 SIMONTON ST, 1-213, KEY WEST, FL 33040
Moeller, Lea DIR - COMMUNITY OUTREACH 305-292-4485

MIAMI—12851 SW 42ND ST, MIAMI, FL 33175
Bracy, Bobby Joe CONSTIT SVCS ASST 305-222-0160
Brito, Yokasta DIST STAFF ASST 305-222-0160
Chambliss, Kevin DIST OUTREACH REP 305-222-0160
Horton-Diaz, Daniel DIST DIR 305-222-0160
Vanegas, Natalia DPTY DIST DIR 305-222-0160

Representative Markwayne Mullin

Oklahoma, 2d

2421 RAYBURN HOB (ZIP: 20515-3602) **225-2701**
Brownlee, Matthew LEGIS AIDE 2421 ..... **52701**
Hittle, Taylor LEGIS DIR 2421 ..... **52701**
Larkin, Brenna STAFF ASST 2421 ..... **52701**
Lawrence, Amy COMMUNICATIONS DIR 2421 ..... **52701**
Moorman, Miranda SR LEGIS ASST 2421 ..... **52701**
Priehs, Kayla DPTY CHIEF OF STAFF 2421 ..... **52701**
Thames, Madison SCHEDULER 2421 ..... **52701**

DISTRICT OFFICES

CLAREMORE—223 W PATTI PAGE BLVD, CLAREMORE, OK 74017
Dooley, Debbie FIELD REP **918-283-6262**
Greeves, Trina CASEWKR **918-283-6262**

MCALESTER—1 E CHOCTAW AVE, SUITE 175, MCALESTER, OK 74501
Bull, Leasha CASEWKR **918-423-5951**
Dempsey, Eddy FIELD REP **918-423-5951**
Ford, Betty FIELD REP **918-423-5951**

MUSKOGEE—811-A NORTH YORK ST, MUSKOGEE, OK 74403
Barnes, William CASEWKR/FIELD REP **918-687-2533**
Owen, Joshua FIELD REP **918-687-2533**
Self, Jason CASEWKR **918-687-2533**
Stopp, Mike CHIEF OF STAFF **918-687-2533**

Representative Stephanie N. Murphy

Florida, 7th

1710 LONGWORTH HOB (ZIP: 20515-0907) **225-4035**
Carton, Jennifer POLICY ADVISOR 1710 ..... **54035**
Cruz, Gabriel MIL FELLOW 1710 ..... **54035**
Everton, Alli SCHEDULER 1710 ..... **54035**
Heidegger, Ken LEGIS CORRES 1710 ..... **54035**
Howard, Brad CHIEF OF STAFF 1710 ..... **54035**
Kline, Rachel STAFF ASST 1710 ..... **54035**
Laufer, John DPTY CHIEF OF STAFF/LEGIS DIR 1710 ..... **54035**
Nguyen, Dao SR POLICY ADVISOR 1710 ..... **54035**
Rapp, Jeffrey SR LEGIS ASST 1710 ..... **54035**
Uriarte, Jonathan COMMUNICATIONS DIR 1710 ..... **54035**

DISTRICT OFFICES

ORLANDO—225 E ROBINSON RD, SUITE 525, ORLANDO, FL 32801
Allen, Lauren DIST DIR **888-205-5421**
Palacios, Stephanie CONSTIT ADVOCATE **888-205-5421**
Reyes-Palma, Nicole COORD - OUTREACH **888-205-5421**
Thorp, Kyle CONSTIT ADVOCATE **888-205-5421**
Tucker, Mark DIST SCHEDULER **888-205-5421**

SANFORD—110 W FIRST ST, SUITE 210, SANFORD, FL 32771
McKinney, Tamel DIST FIELD REP **888-205-5421**
Steenekamp, Thomas CONSTIT SVCS SPEC **888-205-5421**

Representative Jerrold Nadler

New York, 10th

2132 RAYBURN HOB (ZIP: 20515-3210) **225-5635**
Bonner, Jazmine STAFF ASST 2132 ..... **55635**
Campbell, Brigid SCHEDULER 2132 ..... **55635**
Connolly, Melissa LEGIS DIR 2132 ..... **55635**
Doty, John DIRECTOR 2132 ..... **55635**
Hamedi, Kayla LEGIS ASST/PRESS ASST 2132 ..... **55635**
Heineman, Andrew LEGIS ASST 2132 ..... **55635**
Morton, Lisette POLICY DIR 2132 ..... **55635**
Pinckney, Janna SYS ADMIN 2132 ..... **55635**
Schwarz, Daniel COMMUNICATIONS DIR 2132 ..... **55635**
Siegel, Janice DIR - OPS 2132 ..... **55635**

DISTRICT OFFICES

BROOKLYN—6605 FORT HAMILTON PKWY, BROOKLYN, NY 11219 718-373-3198

MANHATTAN—201 VARICK ST, SUITE 669, NEW YORK, NY 10014
Atterbury, Robert SR ASST **212-367-7350**
Dorfman, Clara OFC ASST **212-367-7350**
Geiser, Lauren CASEWKR **212-367-7350**
Gottheim, Robert DIST DIR **212-367-7350**
Jaffe, Jenna CASEWKR **212-367-7350**
Mizrahi, Celine DIR - COMMUNITY RELATIONS **212-367-7350**
Rutkin, Amy CHIEF OF STAFF **212-367-7350**
Weinerman, Hannah COMMUNITY LIAISON **212-367-7350**

Representative Grace F. Napolitano

California, 32d

1610 LONGWORTH HOB (ZIP: 20515-0532) **225-5256**
Chao, Daniel CHIEF OF STAFF 1610 ..... **55256**
Ciccone, Joseph LEGIS ASST/SCHEDULER 1610 ..... **55256**
Havenner, Sheila SYS ADMIN 1610 ..... **55256**
Leonard, Morgan LEGIS ASST 1610 ..... **55256**
O'Donnell, Jerry DIR - PRESS & COMMUNICATIONS/LEGIS ASST 1610 ..... **55256**
Sheehy, Joe LEGIS DIR 1610 ..... **55256**

DISTRICT OFFICE

EL MONTE—4401 SANTA ANITA AVE, SUITE 201, EL MONTE, CA 91731
Berdin, Leandra DIST SCHEDULER **626-350-0150**
Dickerson, Barbara CONG LIAISON **626-350-0150**
Elizalde, Hector DPTY DIST DIR **626-350-0150**
Hernandez Trumkul, Perla DIST DIR **626-350-0150**
Lam, Carrie CASEWKR **626-350-0150**
Pence, Robert FIELD REP/CASEWKR **626-350-0150**
Robles, Elena CASEWKR/SR FIELD REP **626-350-0150**

Representative Richard E. Neal

Massachusetts, 1st

2309 RAYBURN HOB (ZIP: 20515-2101) **225-5601**
Dupont, Zach LEGIS ASST/LEGIS CORRES 2309 ..... **55601**
Getz, Kara COUN TO THE CHAIRMAN 2309 ..... **55601**
O'Connor, Patrick LEGIS ASST 2309 ..... **55601**
O'Hara, Elizabeth DPTY CHIEF OF STAFF 2309 ..... **55601**
Ranstrom, Tim SCHEDULER/LEGIS ASST 2309 ..... **55601**
Scully, Timothy STAFF ASST 2309 ..... **55601**
Tranghese, William PRESS SECY/CHIEF OF STAFF 2309 ..... **55601**
Tremblay, Robert STAFF ASST 2309 ..... **55601**

DISTRICT OFFICES

PITTSFIELD—78 CENTER ST, PITTSFIELD, MA 01201
Clark, Cynthia AIDE **413-442-0946**
Russett, Matthew DIST AIDE **413-442-0946**

SPRINGFIELD—300 STATE ST, SUITE 200, SPRINGFIELD, MA 01105
Ahern, Jeanne B AIDE **413-785-0325**
Boyle, Margaret AIDE **413-785-0325**
Brown, Michelle DIST AIDE **413-785-0325**
Kibodya, Abdul-Kareem AIDE **413-785-0325**

Panos, Peter AIDE 413-785-0325
Powers, William LEGAL COUNSEL 413-785-0325
Quigley, Elizabeth AIDE 413-785-0325

Representative Joe Neguse

Colorado, 2d

1419 LONGWORTH HOB (ZIP: 20515-0602) 225-2161
Bianco, Lisa CHIEF OF STAFF 1419 52161
Burge, Carissa LEGIS ASST 1419 52161
Callahan, Abbie LEGIS CORRES 1419 52161
Coker, Max STAFF ASST 1419 52161
Douglas, Madeline SCHEDULER 1419 52161
Morris, Bo LEGIS DIR 1419 52161
Patel, Miya LEGIS ASST 1419 52161
Tucker, Sally COMMUNICATIONS DIR 1419 52161
Wallace, Katie LEGIS ASST 1419 52161

DISTRICT OFFICES

BOULDER—2503 WALNUT ST, UNIT 300, BOULDER, CO 80302
Blum, Erika CONSTIT ADVOCATE 303-335-1045
Grano, Jill DIR - COMMUNITY AFFAIRS 303-335-1045
Robb, Priya CONSTIT ADVOCATE 303-335-1045

FORT COLLINS—1220 S COLLEGE AVE, UNIT 100A, FORT COLLINS, CO 80524
Anderson, Sally DPTY CHIEF OF STAFF 970-372-3971
Cubbedge Redd, Kim CONSTIT ADVOCATE 970-372-3971
Harrell, Ewo CONSTIT ADVOCATE 970-372-3971

Representative Dan Newhouse

Washington, 4th

1414 LONGWORTH HOB (ZIP: 20515-4704) 225-5816
Alavez, Johnny STAFF ASST 1414 55816
Boyington, Will COMMUNICATIONS DIR 1414 55816
Heinrich, Stephanie STAFF ASST 1414 55816
Martinez, Travis LEGIS ASST 1414 55816
Meadows, Carrie CHIEF OF STAFF 1414 55816
O'Brien, Sean LEGIS DIR 1414 55816
Pettit, Matthew LEGIS CORRES/LEGIS AIDE 1414 55816
Wallace, Lacey EXEC ASST/SCHEDULER 1414 55816

DISTRICT OFFICES

RICHLAND—3100 GEORGE WASHINGTON WAY, SUITE 135, RICHLAND, WA 99354
Lozano, Josh DPTY DIST DIR 509-713-7374

YAKIMA—402 E YAKIMA AVE, SUITE 445, YAKIMA, WA 98901
Daniels, Jamie DIST DIR 509-452-3243
Flint, Derek DIST REP 509-452-3243
Holleman-Perez, Vicki DIST REP 509-452-3243
McCarthy, Jessica DIST REP 509-452-3243
Navratil, Eileen DIST REP 509-452-3243

Representative Donald Norcross

New Jersey, 1st

2437 RAYBURN HOB (ZIP: 20515-3001) 225-6501
Ally, Kehoe COMMUNICATIONS DIR 2437 56501
Ehly, Ryan LEGIS DIR 2437 56501
Krupnick, Alexander LEGIS ASST 2437 56501
Maitland, Michael CHIEF OF STAFF 2437 56501
Pauls, Michael LEGIS CORRES 2437 56501
Sarubbi, Vincent LEGIS ASST 2437 56501
Stanley, Elizabeth STAFF ASST 2437 56501
Weinstein, Lara DIR - OPS/SCHEDULER 2437 56501

DISTRICT OFFICE

CHERRY HILL—10 MELROSE AVE, SUITE 210, CHERRY HILL, NJ 08003
Cordero, Ginamarie CASEWK DIR 856-427-7000
Cruz, Mary DIST DIR 856-427-7000
El, Olga DIST REP/CASEWKR 856-427-7000
Estevez Perez, Ashley DIST REP 856-427-7000
O'Connor, Shaun CONSTIT OUTREACH REP 856-427-7000
Pittman, Anthony ASST 856-427-7000
Szczesniewski, Linda DIST REP 856-427-7000
Townsend, Digna COORD - OUTREACH 856-427-7000

Representative Ralph Norman

South Carolina, 5th

319 CANNON HOB (ZIP: 20515-4005) 225-5501
Hammond, Kimberly OFFICE MGR/PRESS ASST 319 CHOB 55501
Harti, Kellie FINANCIAL ADMIN 319 CHOB 55501
Hilkin, Jacob LEGIS DIR 319 CHOB 55501
Holland, Meghan LEGIS COUNSEL 319 CHOB 55501
Jønler, Simon PRESS SECY/LEGIS CORRES 319 CHOB 55501
Peoples, Amber SCHEDULER 319 CHOB 55501
Piland, Mark CHIEF OF STAFF 319 CHOB 55501

DISTRICT OFFICE

ROCK HILL—454 S ANDERSON RD, ROCK HILL, SC 29732
Allen, Leslie CASEWKR 803-327-1114
Gross, Charles CONG AIDE 803-327-1114
Hicklin, Cathy Rose CASEWK DIR 803-327-1114
Livingston, Austin COMMUNICATIONS DIR 803-327-1114
Neece, Michael DIST OUTREACH REP 803-327-1114
O'Neal, David DIST DIR 803-327-1114
Palmer, Mark FIELD REP/CASEWKR 803-327-1114
Taylor, Carissa DIST SCHEDULER/DIST OFFICE MGR 803-327-1114

Delegate Eleanor Holmes Norton

District of Columbia, Delegate

2136 RAYBURN HOB (ZIP: 20515-5101) 225-8050
Adelstein, Lillian LEGIS CORRES 2136 58050
Boone, Portia LEGIS ASST 2136 58050
Coburn, Try SCHEDULER/EXEC ASST 2136 58050
Holbrook, Trent LEGIS ASST 2136 58050
Miller, Jack COMMUNICATIONS DIR 2136 58050
Reeder, Raven CHIEF OF STAFF 2136 58050
Truding, Bradley CHIEF COUNSEL/LEGIS DIR 2136 58050
Woods, Marquis STAFF ASST 2136 58050

DISTRICT OFFICES

K STREET—90 K ST NE, NO. 100, WASHINGTON, DC 20001
Berríos-Vázquez, Ana COORD - COMMUNITY OUTREACH/CONSTIT LIAISON 202-408-9041
Brown, Kaitlin CONSTIT LIAISON 202-408-9041
Johnson, Cilicia CONSTIT LIAISON 202-408-9041
McDuffie, Damion CONSTIT LIAISON 202-408-9041
Moore, Cartwright SR CONSTIT LIAISON 202-408-9041
Owens, Karen DIST DIR 202-408-9041
Thomas, Nia STAFF ASST 202-408-9041

SHANNON PLACE—2235 SHANNON PL SE, SUITE 2032, WASHINGTON, DC 20020 202-678-8900

Representative Devin Nunes

California, 22d

1013 LONGWORTH HOB (ZIP: 20515-0522) **225-2523**
Kugler, Rebecca PRESS AIDE 1013 .... **52523**
Langer, Jack COMMUNICATIONS DIR 1013 .... **52523**
Lewis, Katherine LEGIS AIDE 1013 .... **52523**
Morrow, Jennifer OFFICE MGR/SCHEDULER/EXEC ASST 1013 **52523**
Plank, Jilian CHIEF OF STAFF 1013 .... **52523**
Wagner, Mattheus LEGIS AIDE 1013 .... **52523**

DISTRICT OFFICES

CLOVIS—264 CLOVIS AVE, SUITE 206, CLOVIS, CA 93612
Blackney, Mark DIST FIELD REP **559-323-5235**

VISALIA—113 N CHURCH ST, SUITE 208, VISALIA, CA 93291
Fowler, Kendra DIR - CONSTIT SVCS **559-733-3861**
Headrick, Terrie CONSTIT LIAISON **559-733-3861**
Henderson, Clarissa SPECIAL PROJ COORD **559-733-3861**
Ragan, Crystal DIST DIR **559-733-3861**
Semoes, Melissa DIR - CONSTIT SVCS **559-733-3861**

Representative Alexandria Ocasio-Cortez

New York, 14th

229 CANNON HOB (ZIP: 20515-3214) **225-3965**
Abreu, Randy ADVISOR 229 CHOB **53965**
Akhter, Naureen DPTY DIST DIR 229 CHOB **718-662-5970**
Animley, Kingsley ADVISOR 229 CHOB **53965**
Bonthius, Daniel SCHEDULER 229 CHOB **53965**
Chakrabarti, Saikat CHIEF OF STAFF 229 CHOB **51830**
Eckblad, Ariel LEGIS DIR 229 CHOB **53965**
Legrand-Wittich, Anika PRESS ASST 229 CHOB **53965**
Pagon Marchena, Claudia STAFF ASST/LEGIS CORRES 229 CHOB **53965**
Reynoso, Klarissa LEGIS CORRES 229 CHOB **51823**
Riffle, Daniel POLICY ADVISOR - FINANCIAL SVCS 229 CHOB ... **53965**
Trent, Brian COMMUNICATIONS DIR 229 CHOB **53965**

DISTRICT OFFICE

JACKSON HEIGHTS—74-09 37TH AVE, SUITE 305, JACKSON HEIGHTS, NY 11372-6303
Hernandez, Michelle CASEWKR **718-662-5970**
Hernandez Rivera, Maribel DIST DIR **718-662-5970**

Representative Tom O'Halleran

Arizona, 1st

324 CANNON HOB (ZIP: 20515-0301) **225-3361**
Babbitt, Paul SR ADVISOR 324 CHOB **53361**
Burgin, Charlie SCHEDULER 324 CHOB **53361**
Farry, Margaret LEGIS ASST 324 CHOB **53361**
Hooker, Kaitlin DIGITAL DIR 324 CHOB **53361**
Nordquist, Jeremy CHIEF OF STAFF 324 CHOB **53361**
Rivas, Edgar LEGIS ASST 324 CHOB **53361**
Uhing, Cody COMMUNICATIONS DIR 324 CHOB **53361**

DISTRICT OFFICES

CASA GRANDE—211 N FLORENCE ST, SUITE 1, CASA GRANDE, AZ 85122
Jackson, Jack DIST DIR **520-316-0839**
McCarthy, Kyle STAFF ASST **520-316-0839**
Mendoza, Joanna FIELD REP - VETS **520-316-0839**
Varela, Blanca DIST DIR **520-316-0839**

FLAGSTAFF—405 N BEAVER ST, SUITE 6, FLAGSTAFF, AZ 86001
Brekhus, Keith DIST OFFICE MGR **928-286-5338**
Burns-Sulltrop, Judy CASEWK MGR **928-286-5338**
Davis, Chip DIST DIR **928-286-5338**
Lacapa, Rochelle CONSTIT SVCS REP **928-286-5338**
Lee, Luther CONSTIT SVCS REP **928-286-5338**

ORO VALLEY—3037 W INA RD, SUITE 101, TUCSON, AZ 85741
Dell'Oliver, Max CONSTIT SVCS REP **928-304-0131**

Representative Pete Olson

Texas, 22d

2133 RAYBURN HOB (ZIP: 20515-4322) **225-5951**
Ayala, Juan STAFF ASST 2133 .... **55951**
Cullen, Cate COMMUNICATIONS DIR 2133 .... **55951**
England, Richard LEGIS DIR 2133 .... **55951**
Hartley, Kevin LEGIS ASST 2133 .... **55951**
Kelly, Melissa CHIEF OF STAFF 2133 .... **55951**
Naughton, Alex DPTY PRESS SECY 2133 .... **55951**
Richards, Michael SR LEGIS ASST 2133 .... **55951**
Smith, Marissa LEGIS AIDE 2133 .... **55951**
Tenney, Keeley EXEC ASST 2133 .... **55951**

DISTRICT OFFICES

PEARLAND—6117 BROADWAY ST, PEARLAND, TX 77581 .... **281-485-4855**

SUGAR LAND—2277 PLAZA DR, SUITE 195, SUGAR LAND, TX 77479
Anders, John Paul FIELD REP **281-494-2690**
Bionat, Christian DIST DIR **281-494-2690**
Davis, Mary CASEWK DIR **281-494-2690**
MacFarlan, Tori SR FIELD REP **281-494-2690**
Murray, Amber STAFF ASST **281-494-2690**
Ours, Nick CASEWKR **281-494-2690**

Representative Ilhan Omar

Minnesota, 5th

1517 LONGWORTH HOB (ZIP: 20515-2305) **225-4755**
McNutt, Connor CHIEF OF STAFF 1517 .... **54755**
Misselwitz, Kelly LEGIS DIR 1517 .... **54755**
Morgan, Ryan LEGIS ASST 1517 .... **54755**
Proby, Tera OFFICE MGR 1517 .... **54755**
Slevin, Jeremy COMMUNICATIONS DIR 1517 .... **54755**
Sorour, Mahyar SR LEGIS ASST 1517 .... **54755**
Teclu, Yonathan LEGIS CORRES 1517 .... **54755**
Vig, Jasleen STAFF ASST 1517 .... **54755**

DISTRICT OFFICES

BUSHWOOD—PO BOX 67, BUSHWOOD, MD 20618
Allen, Amber FINANCIAL MGR **202-302-5337**

MINNEAPOLIS—404 3RD AVE N, SUITE 203, MINNEAPOLIS, MN 55401
Bussa, Biftu DIST STAFF ASST **612-333-1272**
Gbadamosi, Akolade COMMUNITY REP **612-333-1272**
Glass, Talia COMMUNITY REP **612-333-1272**
Isse, Ali DPTY DIST DIR **612-333-1272**
Leingang, Nicky SR COMMUNITY REP **612-333-1272**
Ogbeifun, Matthew COMMUNITY REP **612-333-1272**
Senseman, Davis DIST DIR **612-333-1272**

Representative Steven M. Palazzo

Mississippi, 4th

2349 RAYBURN HOB (ZIP: 20515-2404) **225-5772**
Kennedy, Colleen PRESS SECY 2349 .... **55772**

Large, Patrick DPTY CHIEF OF STAFF 2349 55772
Lipscomb, Hunter CHIEF OF STAFF 2349 55772
Messer, Lizzie LEGIS CORRES 2349 55772
Schmucker, Lauren STAFF ASST 2349 55772
Snyder, Nathaniel CONG FELLOW 2349 55772
Stevens, Courtney SR LEGIS ASST 2349 55772

DISTRICT OFFICES

GULFPORT—84 48TH ST, GULFPORT, MS 39507
TOLL-FREE NUMBER 1-855-255-8740
Churchwell, Leslie DIST OFFICE MGR 228-864-7670
Gargiulo, Michele DIST DIR 228-864-7670
Putnam, Gabi DIST STAFF ASST 228-864-7670

HATTIESBURG—641 MAIN ST, SUITE 142, HATTIESBURG, MS 39401
Bourn, Anita CASEWK DIR 601-582-3246
Duckworth, Jill COMMUNICATIONS DIR 601-582-3246
Moore, Stephen FIELD DIR 601-582-3246

PASCAGOULA—3118 PASCAGOULA ST, SUITE 181, PASCAGOULA, MS 39567
Hembree, Debra CONSTIT LIAISON 228-202-8104

Representative Frank Pallone, Jr.

New Jersey, 6th

2107 RAYBURN HOB (ZIP: 20515-3006) 225-4671
Ertel, Elizabeth ADMIN - FINANCE & PAYROLL 2107 54671
Fitzsimmons, Liam CHIEF OF STAFF 2107 54671
Freed, Jake STAFF ASST 2107 54671
Gristina, Alexander STAFF ASST/SCHEDULER 2107 54671
Johnson, James LEGIS AIDE 2107 54671
Nixon, Keith ASST FOR TECH SUPPORT 2107 54671
Peterson, Miranda LEGIS ASST 2107 54671
Sada, Roberto LEGIS AIDE 2107 54671

DISTRICT OFFICES

LONG BRANCH—504 BROADWAY, LONG BRANCH, NJ 07740-5950
TOLL-FREE NUMBER 1-888-423-1140
Arnold, Alex DIST REP/STAFF ASST 732-571-1140
Briggs, Laura STAFF ASST/DIST SCHEDULER 732-571-1140
Chulak, Daniel DIST REP/STAFF ASST 732-571-1140
Rebscher, Dawn DIST FIELD REP 732-571-1140

NEW BRUNSWICK—67/69 CHURCH ST, NEW BRUNSWICK, NJ 08901
Davis, Jael DIST FIELD REP 732-249-8892
Ford, Janet STAFF ASST 732-249-8892
Maldonado, Alexandra DIST REP 732-249-8892
Simon, Nicholas DIST REP/STAFF ASST 732-249-8892

Representative Gary J. Palmer

Alabama, 6th

207 CANNON HOB (ZIP: 20515-0106) 225-4921
Bayles, Chris LEGIS ASST 207 CHOB 54921
Earwood, Elizabeth LEGIS CORRES 207 CHOB 54921
Fike, Cari LEGIS DIR 207 CHOB 54921
Hance, Elizabeth PRESS SECY 207 CHOB 54921
Hobart, Hunter LEGIS ASST 207 CHOB 54921
Smith, Camille SCHEDULER 207 CHOB 54921
Smith, William CHIEF OF STAFF 207 CHOB 54921
Yerbey, Lindsey STAFF ASST 207 CHOB 54921

DISTRICT OFFICES

BIRMINGHAM—3535 GRANDVIEW PKWY, SUITE 525, BIRMINGHAM, AL 35243
Amason, Virginia COORD - COMMUNITY OUTREACH 205-968-1290
Melick, Ray DIST DIR 205-968-1290
Vice, Ethan FIELD DIR/DPTY DIST DIR 205-968-1290
Weaver, Denise CASEWKR 205-968-1290

CLANTON—703 2ND AVE N, BOX 502, CLANTON, AL 35045 205-280-6846

Representative Jimmy Panetta

California, 20th

212 CANNON HOB (ZIP: 20515-0520) 225-2861
Andrus, Carly STAFF ASST 212 CHOB 52861
Assini, John LEGIS ASST 212 CHOB 52861
Bailey, Joel CHIEF OF STAFF 212 CHOB 52861
Davey, Sarah PRESS SECY 212 CHOB 52861
Manning, Matt LEGIS DIR 212 CHOB 52861
Moon, Katharine CONG AIDE 212 CHOB 52861
Mulka, Stephanie EXEC ASST/SCHEDULER 212 CHOB 52861
Perepelyuk, Marina CONG AIDE 212 CHOB 52861
Vitale, Austin LEGIS CORRES 212 CHOB 52861

DISTRICT OFFICES

SALINAS—100 W ALISAL ST, SALINAS, CA 93901
Alcott, Brooklyn STAFF ASST 831-424-2229
Chavez, Carina DPTY DIST DIR 831-424-2229
Lee, Kathleen DIST DIR 831-424-2229
Munoz, Bertha CONG AIDE 831-424-2229

SANTA CRUZ—701 OCEAN ST, 318C, SANTA CRUZ, CA 95060
Garcia, Emmanuel CONG AIDE 831-429-1976
Sellers, Joshua CONG AIDE 831-429-1976

Representative Chris Pappas

New Hampshire, 1st

323 CANNON HOB (ZIP: 20515-2901) 225-5456
Carlson, Steven LEGIS DIR 323 CHOB 55456
Cosgrove, Kat SR LEGIS ASST 323 CHOB 55456
Curran, Susan PRESS SECY 323 CHOB 55456
Edelson, Oliver LEGIS CORRES 323 CHOB 55456
Kulig, Liz SCHEDULER 323 CHOB 55456
Lee, Matt CHIEF OF STAFF 323 CHOB 55456
Samuel, Asha FELLOW 323 CHOB 55456

DISTRICT OFFICE

DOVER—660 CENTRAL AVE, SUITE 101, DOVER, NH 03820
Carroll, Patrick DIR - CONSTIT SVCS/OUTREACH DIRECTOR 603-285-4300
Hayes, Molly CONSTIT SVCS REP 603-285-4300
Motta, Ashley SR CONSTIT SVCS REP 603-285-4300
Ronan, Wyatt COMMUNICATIONS DIR 603-285-4300
Seasholtz, Christian CONSTIT SVCS REP 603-285-4300
Thurman, Kari DIST DIR 603-285-4300

Representative Bill Pascrell, Jr.

New Jersey, 9th

2409 RAYBURN HOB (ZIP: 20515-3009) 225-5751
Greenbaum, Mark COMMUNICATIONS DIR 2409 55751
Hadad, Christopher STAFF ASST 2409 55751
Houser, Elaina LEGIS DIR 2409 55751
Rich, Benjamin CHIEF OF STAFF 2409 55751
Sodaro, Dylan SR LEGIS ASST 2409 55751
Swope, Carrie ADVISOR - HEALTH POLICY 2409 55751

DISTRICT OFFICES

ENGLEWOOD—2-10 N VAN BRUNT ST, ENGLEWOOD, NJ 07631 ... 201-935-2248

LYNDHURST—367 VALLEY BROOK AVE, LYNDHURST, NJ 07071

Fuentes, Leonardo CASEWKR/FIELD REP ... 201-935-2248

PASSAIC—330 PASSAIC ST, PASSAIC, NJ 07055

Anderson, Celia FIELD REP ... 973-472-4510

PATERSON—200 FED PLAZA, SUITE 500, PATERSON, NJ 07505

Deloatch-Everett, Nancy CASEWKR ... 973-523-5152
DePadua, Carmen CASEWKR ... 973-523-5152
Godfrey, Ian FIELD REP ... 973-523-5152
Martin, Eric SCHEDULER ... 973-523-5152
Moralez-Diaz, Ritzy DIST DIR ... 973-523-5152
Tighe, Stephen PRESS ASST ... 973-523-5152

Representative Donald M. Payne, Jr.

New Jersey, 10th

103 CANNON HOB (ZIP: 20515-3010) ... 225-3436

Alagood, Kyle COMMUNICATIONS DIR 103 CHOB ... 53436
Alexander, LaVerne CHIEF OF STAFF/CHIEF POLICY ADVISOR 103 CHOB ... 53436
Casey, Shannon SCHEDULER 103 CHOB ... 53436
DeHart, Bridgette LEGIS DIR 103 CHOB ... 53436
Goddard, Ruben LEGIS CORRES 103 CHOB ... 53436
Peters, Jamiyl SR LEGIS ASST 103 CHOB ... 53436
Schultz, Steven LEGIS ASST 103 CHOB ... 53436
Thompson, Cora SYS ADMIN 103 CHOB ... 53436

DISTRICT OFFICES

HILLSIDE—1455 LIBERTY AVE, HILLSIDE, NJ 07205

Johnson, Blake COORD - COMMUNITY OUTREACH ... 862-229-2994

JERSEY CITY—253 MARTIN LUTHER KING DR, JERSEY CITY, NJ 07305

Lorenzo, Elizabeth CONSTIT SVCS ASST ... 201-369-0392

NEWARK—60 NELSON PL, 14TH FLOOR, NEWARK, NJ 07102

Clark-Donald, Onaray STAFF ASST ... 973-645-3213
Cruz, Isabel COORD - CONSTIT SVCS ... 973-645-3213
Gray, Michael DIST DIR ... 973-645-3213
Washington, Samantha STAFF ASST ... 973-645-3213

Representative Nancy Pelosi

California, 12th

1236 LONGWORTH HOB (ZIP: 20515-0512) ... 225-4965

Ambriz, Josue LEGIS AIDE 1236 ... 54965
Beal, Owen STAFF ASST 1236 ... 54965
Edmonson, Robert CHIEF OF STAFF 1236 ... 54965
Fields, McKenzie STAFF ASST 1236 ... 54965
Haynes, Wilfred DIR - INFO TECH 1236 ... 54965
Jackson, Sarah POLICY ASSOC 1236 ... 54965
Lea, Robyn MGR - CORRES 1236 ... 54965
Mangrum, Pearl FINANCIAL ADMIN 1236 ... 54965
Ross, Patricia SR POLICY ADVISOR 1236 ... 54965
Silverman, David MGR - CORRES 1236 ... 54965
Swig, Sarah LEGIS CORRES 1236 ... 54965

DISTRICT OFFICE

SAN FRANCISCO—90 SEVENTH ST, SUITE 2-800, SAN FRANCISCO, CA 94103

Bernal, Dan DIST CHIEF OF STAFF ... 415-556-4862
Guerrero, Miguel Louis FIELD REP/CASEWKR ... 415-556-4862
Hidalgo, Adriana DIST SCHEDULER/EXEC ASST ... 415-556-4862
Latt, Zay CASEWKR - IMMIGRATION ... 415-556-4862
McCoy, Raymond CONG AIDE ... 415-556-4862
Rubio, Tina DIST OFFICE MGR ... 415-556-4862

Representative Greg Pence

Indiana, 6th

222 CANNON HOB (ZIP: 20515-1406) ... 225-3021

Bice, Victoria LEGIS AIDE 222 CHOB ... 53021
Goodman, Ted COMMUNICATIONS DIR 222 CHOB ... 53021
Hart, Meaghan LEGIS CORRES 222 CHOB ... 53021
Herbert, Jacob STAFF ASST 222 CHOB ... 53021
Hill, Katherine EXEC ASST/OFFICE MGR 222 CHOB ... 53021
Lassiter, Hillary LEGIS DIR 222 CHOB ... 53021
Robertson, Kyle CHIEF OF STAFF 222 CHOB ... 53021
Van Buren, Jon SR LEGIS ASST 222 CHOB ... 53021
Weintraub, Josh STAFF ASST 222 CHOB ... 53021

DISTRICT OFFICE

COLUMBUS—555 1ST ST, SUITE B, COLUMBUS, IN 47201

Buwalda, Dale DIST FIELD REP/CONSTIT SVCS ... 812-799-5230
Dees-Hollis, Misty CONSTIT SVCS REP ... 812-799-5230
Dessauer, Liz DPTY DIST DIR ... 812-799-5230
Hall, Jordan FIELD REP ... 812-799-5230
Hatter, John CONSTIT SVCS ... 812-799-5230
Jarmula, Ryan DPTY CHIEF OF STAFF/DIST DIR ... 812-799-5230
Pardieck, Karrie CONSTIT SVCS ... 812-799-5230

Representative Ed Perlmutter

Colorado, 7th

1226 LONGWORTH HOB (ZIP: 20515-0607) ... 225-2645

Anonson, Colin LEGIS ASST 1226 ... 52645
Bogeljic, Tia STAFF ASST 1226 ... 52645
Buhr, Patrick LEGIS CORRES 1226 ... 52645
Harrington, Julia LEGIS ASST 1226 ... 52645
Inderfurth, Alison CHIEF OPERATING OFFICER 1226 ... 52645
Minges, Joe LEGIS ASST 1226 ... 52645
O'Neil, Jeff LEGIS DIR 1226 ... 52645

DISTRICT OFFICE

LAKEWOOD—12600 W COLFAX AVE, SUITE B400, LAKEWOOD, CO 80215

Lukken, Garrett CONSTIT SVCS REP ... 303-274-7944
Mullen, Hannah SPECIAL EVENTS/DIR - CONSTIT SVCS ... 303-274-7944
Radovich Piper, Danielle CHIEF OF STAFF ... 303-274-7944
Rodriguez, Jeremy CONSTIT SVCS REP ... 303-274-7944
Verville, Ashley COMMUNICATIONS DIR/PRESS SECY ... 303-274-7944
Villagomez, Macarena DIST STAFF ASST ... 303-274-7944

Representative Scott Perry

Pennsylvania, 10th

1207 LONGWORTH HOB (ZIP: 20515-3810) ... 225-5836

Brown, Brandy COMMUNICATIONS DIR 1207 ... 55836
Culver, Jared LEGIS DIR 1207 ... 55836
Detter, Laura LEGIS ASST 1207 ... 55836
Fernandez, Chris LEGIS CORRES 1207 ... 55836
Maiale, Mike STAFF ASST 1207 ... 55836
Muglia, Lauren CHIEF OF STAFF 1207 ... 55836
Schilling, Patrick LEGIS ASST 1207 ... 55836

DISTRICT OFFICES

CUMBERLAND COUNTY—730 N FRONT ST, WORMLEYSBURG, PA 17043

Stroud, Ceason STAFF ASST 717-635-9504
Sutphin, Holly FIELD REP 717-635-9504

DAUPHIN COUNTY—800 CORPORATE CIRCLE, SUITE 202, HARRISBURG, PA 17110

Marsico, Jodi CONSTIT SVCS REP 717-603-4980
Ostrich, Jay DIST DIR 717-603-4980
Wallace, Tyra DIR - CONSTIT SVCS 717-603-4980
Wiest, Carol SCHEDULER 717-603-4980

YORK COUNTY—2501 CATHERINE ST, YORK, PA 17408

Austin, Donna CONSTIT SVCS REP 717-635-9504

Representative Scott H. Peters

California, 52d

2338 RAYBURN HOB (ZIP: 20515-0552) 225-0508
Banks, Linda FINANCIAL ADMIN 2338 50508
Borja, Anais SR LEGIS ASST 2338 50508
Brown, Baillee SR LEGIS ASST 2338 50508
Greenfield, George SYS ADMIN 2338 50508
McHale, Sterling LEGIS DIR 2338 50508
Pun, Arlene STAFF ASST/LEGIS AIDE 2338 50508
Spieker, Martha PRESS SECY 2338 50508
Stern, Hannah SCHEDULER/LEGIS AIDE 2338 50508
Sugarman, Elise LEGIS CORRES 2338 50508
Zawitoski, Daniel DC CHIEF OF STAFF 2338 50508

DISTRICT OFFICE

SAN DIEGO—4350 EXECUTIVE DR, SUITE 105, SAN DIEGO, CA 92121

Bercovitch, Jason FIELD REP 858-455-5550
Galloway, Kiera DIR - CONSTIT SVCS 858-455-5550
LaCapra, Quin DIR - DIGITAL MEDIA 858-455-5550
Magee, Erin DIST SCHEDULER/FIELD REP 858-455-5550
Nguyen, Anthony DIST DIR 858-455-5550
Pintar, Maryanne CHIEF OF STAFF 858-455-5550
Solis, Cesar FIELD REP 858-455-5550

Representative Collin C. Peterson

Minnesota, 7th

2204 RAYBURN HOB (ZIP: 20515-2307) 225-2165
Cornett, Chelsea STAFF ASST 2204 52165
Durand, Adam DPTY CHIEF OF STAFF/LEGIS DIR 2204 52165
Hollerich, Cody STAFF ASST 2204 52165
Lee, Richard LEGIS ASST 2204 52165
Martin, Zach LEGIS ASST 2204 52165
Solem, Rebekah SR LEGIS ASST/SCHEDULER 2204 52165

DISTRICT OFFICES

DETROIT LAKES—714 LAKE AVE, SUITE 101, DETROIT LAKES, MN 56501

Dey, Jodi STAFF ASST 218-847-5056
Stock, Allison CHIEF OF STAFF 218-847-5056
Stumpf, LeRoy STAFF ASST 218-847-5056

MARSHALL—1420 E COLLEGE DR, MARSHALL, MN 56258

Louwagie, Meg STAFF ASST 507-537-2299

WILLMAR—1700 TECHNOLOGY DR, SUITE 119, WILLMAR, MN 56201

Anderson, Jacki ECON DEV SPEC/OUTREACH DIR 320-235-1061
Bertram, Mary STAFF ASST 320-235-1061
Herfindahl, Grant ADVISOR 320-235-1061
Ness, Robert STAFF ASST 320-235-1061

Representative Dean Phillips

Minnesota, 3d

1305 LONGWORTH HOB (ZIP: 20515-2303) 225-2871
Augustus, Imani LEGIS DIR 1305 52871
Berman, Mia DIST STAFF ASST 1305 52871
Bertocci, Tim DC CHIEF OF STAFF 1305 52871
Effingham, Damon LEGIS COUNSEL 1305 52871
Houlihan, Ryan LEGIS CORRES 1305 52871
Mirviss, Sophie DC SCHEDULER 1305 52871
Simon, David SPECIAL PROJ DIR 1305 52871
Welch, Brendan COMMUNICATIONS DIR 1305 52871

DISTRICT OFFICE

MINNETONKA—13911 RIDGEDALE DR, SUITE 200, MINNETONKA, MN 55305

Anderson, Sam DIST PRESS SECY 952-656-5176
Grady, Caitlin DIST SCHEDULER 952-656-5176
Montgomery, Meg CASEWKR 952-656-5176
Olson, Rollie DIST STAFF ASST 952-656-5176
Rodvold, Zach DIST CHIEF OF STAFF 952-656-5176
Sawyer, Decontee CASEWKR 952-656-5176
Youngquist, Emma CASEWK SUPERVISOR 952-656-5176

Representative Chellie Pingree

Maine, 1st

2162 RAYBURN HOB (ZIP: 20515-1901) 225-6116
Blazek, Kelliann LEGIS ASST 2162 56116
Colton, Kimber COUNSEL 2162 56116
Johnson, Tucker STAFF ASST/LEGIS ASST 2162 56116
Johnston, Evan LEGIS DIR 2162 56116
Melcher, Eloise LEGIS CORRES 2162 56116
Stein, Todd LEGIS ASST 2162 56116

DISTRICT OFFICES

PORTLAND—2 PORTLAND FISH PIER, SUITE 304, PORTLAND, ME 04101

TOLL-FREE NUMBER 1-888-862-6500
Beausang, Bethany CASEWKR/COUNSEL/CONSTIT OUTREACH REP 207-774-5019
Bonney, Victoria COMMUNICATIONS DIR 207-774-5019
Connolly, Jesse CHIEF OF STAFF 207-774-5019
Frazee, Skeek CASEWKR 207-774-5019
Goodridge, Ann CASEWKR/CASEWK MGR 207-774-5019
Horton, Emily FIELD REP 207-774-5019
Merrill, Leslie CASEWKR 207-774-5019
Sayed, Rona DIST STAFF ASST 207-774-5019
Sudbay, Karen SCHEDULER 207-774-5019

WATERVILLE—1 SILVER ST, WATERVILLE, ME 04902

TOLL-FREE NUMBER 1-888-862-6500
Trinward, Pam DIST OUTREACH REP 207-873-5713

Delegate Stacey E. Plaskett

Virgin Islands, Delegate

2404 RAYBURN HOB (ZIP: 20515-5500) 225-1790
Francois, Conrad STAFF ASST 2404 51790
Jabbar, Angeline LEGIS DIR 2404 51790
McQuerry, Michael COMMUNICATIONS DIR 2404 51790
Myers, Lewis DIR - ADMIN OPS 2404 51790
Nowill, Jeffrey SR COUNSEL 2404 51790
Petersen, Barbara SPECIAL PROJ 2404 51790
Prince, Erik CHIEF 2404 51790
Thomas, Tiana LEGIS ASST 2404 51790

DISTRICT OFFICES

ST. CROIX—60 KING ST, FREDERIKSTED, VI 00840

Joseph, Laverne CASEWKR 340-778-5900

ST. THOMAS—9100 HAVENSIGHT, SUITE 22, PORT OF SALES, ST. THOMAS, VI 00802

Callwood, Kyza STAFF ASST 340-774-4408
Clendinen, Cletis DIST DIR 340-774-4408

Representative Mark Pocan

Wisconsin, 2d

1421 LONGWORTH HOB (ZIP: 20515-4902) 225-2906
Bagby, David DPTY CHIEF OF STAFF 1421 52906
Boehmer, Ron COMMUNICATIONS DIR 1421 52906
Huffman, Kate LEGIS ASST 1421 52906
McCabe, Conor DIGITAL DIR/PRESS SECY 1421 52906
McCone, Kelly OFFICE MGR/SCHEDULER 1421 52906
O'Neill, Andrew LEGIS ASST 1421 52906
Scott, Sydney LEGIS CORRES/STAFF ASST 1421 52906
Wavrunek, Glenn CHIEF OF STAFF 1421 52906
Zelenko, Leslie SR LEGIS ASST 1421 52906

DISTRICT OFFICE

MADISON—10 E DOTY ST, ROOM 405, MADISON, WI 53703

Boldebuck, Calvin FIELD REP 608-258-9800
Cohen, Audra CASEWKR/CASEWK MGR 608-258-9800
Kelly, Mike CASEWKR 608-258-9800
Kostelic, Luanne DIST OFFICE MGR/CASEWKR 608-258-9800
Schlueter, Erik FIELD REP 608-258-9800
Varese, Dane DIST DIR 608-258-9800
Young, Anna STAFF ASST 608-258-9800

Representative Katie Porter

California, 45th

1117 LONGWORTH HOB (ZIP: 20515-0545) 225-5611
Alatorre, Angelica CASEWK DIR 1117 55611
Cohn, Karen SR FIELD REP 1117 55611
Falcone, Anthony CASEWKR 1117 55611
Fischer, Amanda CHIEF OF STAFF 1117 55611
Frank, Florence STAFF ASST 1117 55611
Jones, Kelly DIST DIR 1117 55611
Lee, Daniel FIELD REP 1117 55611
Marticorena, Brieana LEGIS DIR 1117 55611
Murray, Elizabeth DIR - OPS 1117 55611
Narayan, Rishaun DIST STAFF ASST 1117 55611
Niemasik, Kaylee LEGIS COUNSEL 1117 55611
Schulte, Victoria DIST SCHEDULER 1117 55611
Smith, Megan DIR - OUTREACH & MEMB SVCS 1117 55611
Tam, Catalina STAFF ASST 1117 55611
Wong, Jordan COMMUNICATIONS DIR 1117 55611

Representative Bill Posey

Florida, 8th

2150 RAYBURN HOB (ZIP: 20515-0908) 225-3671
Burns, Stuart CHIEF OF STAFF 2150 53671
Cecala, George COMMUNICATIONS DIR/DPTY CHIEF OF STAFF 2150 53671
McCullough, Tom LEGIS CORRES/STAFF ASST 2150 53671
Podliska, Rick SR POLICY ADVISOR 2150 53671
Shelton, John LEGIS ASST/LEGIS CORRES 2150 53671
Stanley, Mathew FELLOW 2150 53671
Valenta, Valentina LEGIS DIR 2150 53671
Vinesett, Molly DC SCHEDULER/EXEC ASST/COORD - INTERN & FELLOW 2150 53671

DISTRICT OFFICES

MELBOURNE—2725 JUDGE FRAN JAMIESON WAY, BLDG C, MELBOURNE, FL 32940

Febro, Patti LIAISON - CONSTIT SVCS 321-632-1776
Gavin, Patrick DIST DIR/DIST SCHEDULER 321-632-1776
Greene, Chelsea CASEWKR 321-632-1776
Medina, Rob DIR - MIL & COMMUNITY RELATIONS 321-632-1776

TITUSVILLE—BREVARD COUNTY GOVT OFFICES, TITUSVILLE, FL 32780

Moore, Cheryl DIR - COMMUNITY RELATIONS 321-383-6090

VERO BEACH—INDIAN RIVER COUNTY ADMIN BLDG A, VERO BEACH, FL 32960

Jackson, David DIR - COMMUNITY RELATIONS 772-226-1701

Representative Ayanna Pressley

Massachusetts, 7th

1108 LONGWORTH HOB (ZIP: 20515-2107) 225-5111
Barrett, Dennis LEGIS CORRES 1108 55111
Canchola, Aissa LEGIS DIR 1108 55111
Douglas, Errin STAFF ASST 1108 55111
Flynn, George PRESS ASST 1108 55111
Francis, Lina COMMUNICATIONS DIR 1108 55111
Groh, Sarah CHIEF OF STAFF 1108 55111
Ibrahim, Aya LEGIS ASST 1108 55111
Wallace, Lynese POLICY ADVISOR 1108 55111
Watts, Lona SCHEDULING DIR 1108 55111

DISTRICT OFFICE

BOSTON—1700 DORCHESTER AVE, BOSTON, MA 02122

Claude, Ronald FIELD REP 617-850-0040
Colombo, Erina CIVIC ENGAGEMENT MANAGER 617-850-0040
Remal, Colin MGR - CONSTIT SVCS 617-850-0040
Villar, Luz DIST EXEC ASST 617-850-0040
White, Eric DIST DIR 617-850-0040

Representative David E. Price

North Carolina, 4th

2108 RAYBURN HOB (ZIP: 20515-3304) 225-1784
Adkins, Elizabeth STAFF ASST/LEGIS CORRES 2108 51784
Blalock, Nora SR LEGIS ASST 2108 51784
Castro, Antonio SYS ADMIN 2108 51784
Lipkowitz, Dan LEGIS ASST 2108 51784
Maxwell, Sean LEGIS DIR 2108 51784
Nlewedim, Gloria PRESS SECY 2108 51784
Schifrin, Samantha NATIONAL SECUR ADVISOR 2108 51784
Wein, Justin DPTY CHIEF OF STAFF 2108 51784
White, Janssen SCHEDULER/EXEC ASST 2108 51784
Whittaker, Leigh LEGIS ASST 2108 51784

DISTRICT OFFICES

CHAPEL HILL-DURHAM—1777 FORDHAM BLVD, SUITE 204, CHAPEL HILL, NC 27514

Lovett, Tracy DIST LIAISON 919-967-7924
Russell, Dave DIST LIAISON 919-967-7924

RALEIGH—436 N HARRINGTON ST, SUITE 100, RALEIGH, NC 27603

Alston, Nadia CASEWKR 919-859-5999

Anderson, Katelynn COMMUNICATIONS DIR 919-859-5999
Barnes, Sonia DIST LIAISON 919-859-5999
Hildebrand, Asher DIST DIR/CHIEF OF STAFF 919-859-5999
Reyes, Arturo DIST STAFF ASST 919-859-5999
Tilghman, Anna SR ADVISOR 919-859-5999
Winneberger, Robyn CASEWK MGR 919-859-5999

Representative Mike Quigley

Illinois, 5th

2458 RAYBURN HOB (ZIP: 20515-1305) 225-4061
Chertow, Elazar STAFF ASST 2458 54061
Frankel, Max SR LEGIS ASST 2458 54061
Hinojosa, Juan CHIEF OF STAFF 2458 54061
Jarus, Allison SR POLICY ADVISOR 2458 54061
Lee, Doug LEGIS DIR/DPTY CHIEF OF STAFF 2458 54061
Mansbach, Hannah LEGIS AIDE 2458 54061
Plasky, Naomi LEGIS FELLOW 2458 54061
Siddiqui, Faisal SYS ADMIN 2458 54061
Spinozzi, Isabella SCHEDULER/DIR - OPS 2458 54061

DISTRICT OFFICES

CHICAGO—4345 N MILWAUKEE AVE, CHICAGO, IL 60641
Herman, Jenny OUTREACH COORD 773-267-5926
Levar, Mary Ann DIST DIR 773-267-5926
Merritt, Jessica CONG AIDE 773-267-5926
Pizer, Jonathan COMMUNITY & OUTREACH LIAISON . 773-267-5926
Solock, Mark LEGAL COUNSEL 773-267-5926
Song, Elli CONG AIDE 773-267-5926

SATELLITE OFFICE—3223 N SHEFFIELD AVE, CHICAGO, IL 60657
Bach, Mitzi DIST SCHEDULER 773-267-5926
Reardon, Erica POLICY ADVISOR 773-267-5926
Winters, Adam DIST STAFF ASST 773-267-5926

Delegate Aumua Amata Coleman Radewagen

American Samoa, Delegate

1339 LONGWORTH HOB (ZIP: 20515-5200) 225-8577
Black, Daniel LEGIS ASST/ASST COMMUNICATIONS DIR 1339 . 58577
Christel, Jared LEGIS ASST/CASEWKR 1339 58577
Dehlinger, Nancy EXEC ASST/EXEC SCHEDULER/OFFICE MGR 1339 58577
Hannahs, Joel COMMUNICATIONS DIR 1339 58577
Roberts, Angie STAFF ASST 1339 58577
Stanton, Rich LEGIS DIR 1339 58577
Yahn, Ina CHIEF OF STAFF 1339 58577

DISTRICT OFFICE

AMERICAN SAMOA—1 FAGATOGO SQUARE LANE, PAGO PAGO, AS 96799
Ae, Pulu DIST DIR 684-633-3601
Aita'oto, Tafito DIST PRESS SECY 684-633-3601
Foster, Ola OFFICE MGR/SCHEDULER/DIST EXEC ASST 684-633-3601
Fuatagavi, Fua COORD - HEALTH POLICY/CASEWKR/CASEWKR - IMMIGRATION 684-633-3601
Howard, Howard FIELD REP/EDUC POLICY ADVISOR/COORD - GRANTS 684-633-3601
Ledoux, Leroy FIELD DIR 684-633-3601
Newton, John WEB ADMIN/INFO TECH MGR 684-633-3601
Pa'au, Ina CASEWKR 684-633-3601
Seva'aetasi, Tago CONSTIT REP/CASEWKR - IMMIGRATION/ CASEWORK - VETS 684-633-3601
Tagoilelagi, Uta SR POLICY ADVISOR 684-633-3601
Tatupu, Jeremiah SR CASEWKR 684-633-3601
Vaiau, Steve DIST FIELD REP 684-633-3601

Representative Jamie Raskin

Maryland, 8th

412 CANNON HOB (ZIP: 20515-2008) 225-5341
Adamson, Diane ASST LEGIS CORRES 412 CHOB 55341
Brown, Samantha DPTY COMMUNICATIONS DIR 412 CHOB 55341
Doney, Lauren COMMUNICATIONS DIR/DPTY CHIEF OF STAFF 412 CHOB 55341
Idelson, Holly CHIEF COUNSEL 412 CHOB 55341
Johnson, Candace SCHEDULER 412 CHOB 55341
Nadherny, Taylor STAFF ASST 412 CHOB 55341
Ombres, Devon SR COUNSEL 412 CHOB 55341
Sanchez, Martha LEGIS ASST 412 CHOB 55341
Shaw, Lucy LEGIS CORRES 412 CHOB 55341
Tagen, Julie CHIEF OF STAFF 412 CHOB 55341

DISTRICT OFFICE

ROCKVILLE—51 MONROE ST, SUITE 503, ROCKVILLE, MD 20850
Burton, Christa OUTREACH DIR 301-354-1000
Connor, Kathleen DIST DIR 301-354-1000
Eyong, Joseph FIELD REP 301-354-1000
Foont, Jennie SR CASEWKR 301-354-1000
Moore, Jarrett CONSTIT SVCS 301-354-1000
Weisbroth, Nina CONSTIT SVCS 301-354-1000

Representative John Ratcliffe

Texas, 4th

223 CANNON HOB (ZIP: 20515-4304) 225-6673
Bailey, Jennifer FINANCIAL ADMIN 223 CHOB 56673
Boogaard, Paige STAFF ASST 223 CHOB 56673
Carmack, Dustin CHIEF OF STAFF 223 CHOB 56673
Davis, Ben LEGIS FELLOW 223 CHOB 56673
Goessler, Maggie LEGIS AIDE 223 CHOB 56673
Johnson, Crystal SCHEDULER 223 CHOB 56673
Pace, Davis LEGIS DIR 223 CHOB 56673
Peters, Robert LEGIS ASST 223 CHOB 56673
Stephens, Rachel PRESS SECY/COMMUNICATIONS DIR 223 CHOB 56673
Yazdani-Zonoz, Ebrahim LEGIS COUNSEL 223 CHOB 56673

DISTRICT OFFICES

ROCKWALL (FLAGSHIP)—6531 HORIZON RD, SUITE A, ROCKWALL, TX 75032
Hannan, Virginia CONSTIT SVCS REP 972-771-0100
Ross, Jason DIST CHIEF OF STAFF 972-771-0100
Zook, Michelle MGR - CONSTIT SVCS 972-771-0100

SHERMAN—100 W HOUSTON ST, 1ST FLOOR, SHERMAN, TX 75090
Baker, James POLICY DIR 903-816-5270

TEXARKANA—2500 N ROBISON RD, SUITE 190, TEXARKANA, TX 75599
Bass, Robbin DPTY DIST DIR 903-823-3173
Jordan, Charles LIAISON - CONSTIT SVCS 903-823-3173

Representative Tom Reed

New York, 23d

2263 RAYBURN HOB (ZIP: 20515-3223) 225-3161
Brown, Samara LEGIS ASST 2263 53161

Daugherty, Abbey COMMUNICATIONS ADVISOR 2263 53161
Hoover, Logan SR LEGIS ASST 2263 53161
Hyland, Thomas STAFF ASST 2263 53161
Murphy, Johannah SCHEDULER 2263 53161
Reinert, Will COMMUNICATIONS DIR 2263 53161
Tollefson, Elise LEGIS DIR 2263 53161
Wayne, Drew CHIEF OF STAFF 2263 53161
Yackel, Rick LEGIS CORRES 2263 53161

DISTRICT OFFICES

CORNING—89 W MARKET ST, CORNING, NY 14830
Hunt, Alison DIST DIR 607-654-7566
Murphy, Sharon EXEC ASST 607-654-7566
Safreed, Molly CASEWKR 607-654-7566
Schmitz, Doc LIAISON - MIL & VET 607-654-7566

GENEVA—433 EXCHANGE ST, GENEVA, NY 14456
Pitifer, Mark CASEWKR 315-759-5229
Windheim, Taryn REGIONAL DIR 315-759-5229

JAMESTOWN—2 E 2ND ST, SUITE 208, JAMESTOWN, NY 14701
Fuller, Katrina CASEWKR 716-708-6369

OLEAN—1 BLUEBIRD SQUARE, OLEAN, NY 14760
James, Lee REGIONAL DIR/CONSTIT SVCS SPEC 716-379-8434

Representative Guy Reschenthaler

Pennsylvania, 14th

531 CANNON HOB (ZIP: 20515-3814) 225-2065
Ackerman, Emily LEGIS DIR/DPTY CHIEF OF STAFF 531 CHOB 52065
Argall, Elise COMMUNICATIONS DIR 531 CHOB 52065
Barton, Liz SCHEDULER 531 CHOB 52065
Bonnaure, Aaron CHIEF OF STAFF 531 CHOB 52065
D'Orazio, Mike LEGIS AIDE 531 CHOB 52065
Healy, Christian SR LEGIS ASST 531 CHOB 52065
Lomis, Alana EXEC ASST 531 CHOB 52065
Wade, Melissa ADMIN - FINANCE & PAYROLL 531 CHOB 52065

DISTRICT OFFICES

WASHINGTON—14 S MAIN ST, WASHINGTON, PA 15301
Reibach, Stacey DIST DIR 724-206-4800
Youngdahl, Sarah CONSTIT SVCS REP 724-206-4800

WESTMORELAND—700 PELLIS RD, GREENSBURG, PA 15601
Yauger, Patricia DIR - CONSTIT SVCS 724-219-4200

Representative Kathleen M. Rice

New York, 4th

2435 RAYBURN HOB (ZIP: 20515-3204) 225-5516
Aciman, Michael COMMUNICATIONS DIR 2435 55516
Amster, Liz LEGIS DIR 2435 55516
Chiucchini, Kate LEGIS COUNSEL 2435 55516
Coyle, Steven LEGIS ASST 2435 55516
Demakos, Michael LEGIS ASST 2435 55516
Mecher, David LEGIS CORRES 2435 55516
Reilly, Nell CHIEF OF STAFF 2435 55516
Shefelman, Will STAFF ASST 2435 55516
Wade, Landy SCHEDULER 2435 55516

DISTRICT OFFICE

GARDEN CITY—229 7TH ST, SUITE 300, GARDEN CITY, NY 11530
Block-Levin, Natalie COMMUNITY REP 516-739-3008
Connelly, Erin DIST STAFF ASST 516-739-3008
Curry, Tom DIR - CONSTIT AFFAIRS 516-739-3008
Fuller, Hannah STAFF ASST 516-739-3008
Komisarjevsky, Stephen COMMUNITY REP 516-739-3008
Mehlman, Beth COMMUNITY LIAISON 516-739-3008
Miller, Keisha CONG LIAISON 516-739-3008
Moye, Imani COMMUNITY REP 516-739-3008
Walsh, Amanda DIST DIR 516-739-3008

Representative Tom Rice

South Carolina, 7th

512 CANNON HOB (ZIP: 20515-4007) 225-9895
Bacher, Chelsea LEGIS ASST 512 CHOB 59895
Clarke, Philipp LEGIS CORRES 512 CHOB 59895
Collins, Elle TAX COUNSEL/LEGIS ASST 512 CHOB 59895
Dunn, McKayla SCHEDULER 512 CHOB 59895
Seid, Sophica PRESS SECY 512 CHOB 59895
Truluck, Walker LEGIS DIR 512 CHOB 59895
Wilson, Jennifer CHIEF OF STAFF 512 CHOB 59895

DISTRICT OFFICES

GRAND STRAND—2411 N OAK ST, SUITE 405, MYRTLE BEACH, SC 29577
Gaillard, Phillip COORD - COMMUNITY OUTREACH 843-445-6459
Hudson, Susan FIELD REP 843-445-6459
Keegan, Tom FIELD REP 843-445-6459
Mims, Andrew DIR - DIST AFFAIRS 843-445-6459
Needham, Chris CONSTIT SVCS REP 843-445-6459

PEE DEE—1831 W EVANS ST, SUITE 300, FLORENCE, SC 29501
Berry, Rodney DIR - ECON DEV 843-679-9781
Ratliffe, Pam DIST STAFF ASST/CONSTIT SVCS REP 843-679-9781
Yarborough, Joe, III FIELD REP 843-679-9781

Representative Cedric L. Richmond

Louisiana, 2d

506 CANNON HOB (ZIP: 20515-1802) 225-6636
Dennis-Morial, Kemah SR ADVISOR 506 CHOB 56636
Etienne, Christopher LEGIS AIDE 506 CHOB 56636
Hunter, Peter LEGIS DIR 506 CHOB 56636
Lustig, Joseph LEGIS ASST 506 CHOB 56636
Melton, Chyna LEGIS AIDE 506 CHOB 56636
Nsiah, Kwabena CHIEF OF STAFF 506 CHOB 56636
Porter, Jalina COMMUNICATIONS DIR 506 CHOB 56636

DISTRICT OFFICES

BATON ROUGE—1520 THOMAS H. DELPIT DR, SUITE 126, BATON ROUGE, LA 70802
Fields, Darlene DPTY DIST DIR 225-636-5600

GRETNA—200 DERBIGNY ST, SUITE 3200, GRETNA, LA 70053
Russell, DeShannon CASEWKR/DPTY DIST DIR 504-365-0390

NEW ORLEANS—2021 LAKESHORE DR, SUITE 309, NEW ORLEANS, LA 70122
Ambrose, Lisa CASEWKR 504-288-3777
Bernhard, James SPECIAL PROJ DIR 504-288-3777
Domino, Karen DPTY DIST DIR 504-288-3777
Simeon, Jessica STAFF ASST 504-288-3777
Smith, Enix DPTY CHIEF OF STAFF 504-288-3777
Wright, Wayne LIAISON - SMALL BUSINESS 504-288-3777

Representative Denver Riggleman

Virginia, 5th

1022 LONGWORTH HOB (ZIP: 20515-4605) 225-4711
Brady, Haley DIR - OPS 1022 54711
Chelak, Joseph COMMUNICATIONS DIR 1022 54711

Eagleburger, Jason SR ADVISOR - FOREIGN POLICY 1022 ...... **54711**
Hoskins, Borden LEGIS DIR 1022 ...... **54711**
Keady, Jimmy SR ADVISOR 1022 ...... **54711**
Klein, Lexi STAFF ASST 1022 ...... **54711**
Mullany, Ben STAFF ASST 1022 ...... **54711**
Natonski, David CHIEF OF STAFF 1022 ...... **54711**
Nentwich, Nicole LEGIS CORRES 1022 ...... **54711**
Woerpel, Eli LEGIS ASST 1022 ...... **54711**

DISTRICT OFFICES

CHARLOTTESVILLE—686 BERKMAR CIRCLE, CHARLOTTESVILLE, VA 22901
Harvey, Stephen OUTREACH DIR **434-973-9631**
Lofquist, Kurt SPECIAL ASST **434-973-9631**
Page, Esther DIR - CONSTIT SVCS **434-973-9631**
Pomeroy, James CONSTIT SVCS REP **434-973-9631**

DANVILLE—308 CRAGHEAD ST, SUITE 102-D, DANVILLE, VA 24541
Becker, Matthew OUTREACH DIR **434-791-2596**
Van Valkenburg, Denise DIST DIR **434-791-2596**

Representative Martha Roby

Alabama, 2d

504 CANNON HOB (ZIP: 20515-0102) 225-2901
Albares, Mike CHIEF OF STAFF 504 CHOB **52901**
Allen, David LEGIS DIR 504 CHOB **52901**
Buyak, Caroline LEGIS ASST 504 CHOB **52901**
Hollis, Kate SCHEDULER 504 CHOB **52901**
Johnson, Emily COMMUNICATIONS DIR 504 CHOB **52901**
Lester, Dean OFFICE ADMIN 504 CHOB **52901**
McKnight, Luke STAFF ASST 504 CHOB **52901**
Smith, Judd SR COUNSEL 504 CHOB **52901**
Stephens, Harper LEGIS CORRES/PRESS ASST 504 CHOB **52901**

DISTRICT OFFICES

ANDALUSIA—505 E THREE NOTCH ST, SUITE 322, ANDALUSIA, AL 36420
McMahon, Amelia CONSTIT SVCS REP **334-428-1129**

DOTHAN—217 GRACELAND DR, SUITE 5, DOTHAN, AL 36305
Light, Barbara CONSTIT SVCS REP **334-794-9680**

MONTGOMERY—401 ADAMS AVE, SUITE 160, MONTGOMERY, AL 36104
Pate, Cynthia FIELD REP **334-262-7718**
Rogers, Casey FIELD REP **334-262-7718**
Ward Williams, Lori DIST DIR **334-262-7718**

Representative Cathy McMorris Rodgers

Washington, 5th

1035 LONGWORTH HOB (ZIP: 20515-4705) 225-2006
Cameron, Michael STAFF ASST 1035 ...... **52006**
Dehnel, Kendall LEGIS CORRES 1035 ...... **52006**
Hnat, Olivia DPTY CHIEF OF STAFF 1035 ...... **52006**
Hodson, Nathan CHIEF OF STAFF 1035 ...... **52006**
King, Emily DIR - OPS 1035 ...... **52006**
Kopec, Rachel DIR - COALITIONS 1035 ...... **52006**
Miller, Kayla STAFF ASST 1035 ...... **52006**
Neighbors, Matt LEGIS COUNSEL 1035 ...... **52006**
Oliver, Brooke ADMIN - FINANCE & PAYROLL 1035 ...... **52006**
Powell, Jared PRESS SECY 1035 ...... **52006**
Roos, Amber ADMIN - FINANCE & PAYROLL 1035 ...... **52006**
Taggart, Michael LEGIS DIR 1035 ...... **52006**
Thorne, Dray DIR - INFO TECH 1035 ...... **52006**

DISTRICT OFFICES

COLVILLE—555 S MAIN ST, SUITE C, COLVILLE, WA 99114
Engell, David Jr REGIONAL REP **509-684-3481**

SPOKANE—10 N POST ST, SUITE 625, SPOKANE, WA 99201
Bell, Patrick DPTY DIST DIR **509-353-2374**
Blackburn, Paige CONSTIT RELATIONS REP **509-353-2374**
Couture, Traci DIST DIR **509-353-2374**
Tracy, Collin DIST SCHEDULER **509-353-2374**

WALLA WALLA—26 E MAIN ST, SUITE 2, WALLA WALLA, WA 99362
Valerio, Victor REGIONAL REP **509-529-9358**

Representative David P. Roe

Tennessee, 1st

102 CANNON HOB (ZIP: 20515-4201) 225-6356
Alexander, Whitley PRESS SECY 102 CHOB **56356**
Bill, Aaron LEGIS DIR 102 CHOB **56356**
Eubanks, Courtney SCHEDULER/OFFICE MGR/EXEC ASST 102 CHOB **56356**
Jacobs, Kyle LEGIS ASST 102 CHOB **56356**
MacDonald, Liam LEGIS CORRES 102 CHOB **56356**
Mackey, Alex LEGIS FELLOW 102 CHOB **56356**
Meyer, Matthew CHIEF OF STAFF 102 CHOB **56356**
Russell, Chance STAFF ASST 102 CHOB **56356**
Witherspoon, John SR LEGIS ASST 102 CHOB **56356**

DISTRICT OFFICES

KINGSPORT—205 REVERE ST, KINGSPORT, TN 37660
Darden, Bill DIST DIR **423-247-8161**
Ferguson, Carolyn CONSTIT SVCS REP **423-247-8161**
Houser, Sheila ADMIN ASST **423-247-8161**
O'Hara, Tracie CONSTIT SVCS REP **423-247-8161**

MORRISTOWN—1609 WALTERS STATE CC DR, SUITE 4, MORRISTOWN, TN 37813
Bennett, Cheryl CONSTIT SVCS REP **423-254-1400**
Brady, Daryl FIELD REP **423-254-1400**
Jarnagin, Angie CONSTIT SVCS REP **423-254-1400**

Representative Harold Rogers

Kentucky, 5th

2406 RAYBURN HOB (ZIP: 20515-1705) 225-4601
Bell, Megan CHIEF OF STAFF 2406 ...... **54601**
Brown, Sarah SCHEDULER 2406 ...... **54601**
Gage, Austin LEGIS ASST 2406 ...... **54601**
Jarrett, Chelsea OFFICE MGR/SYS ADMIN 2406 ...... **54601**
Johnsen, Jakob LEGIS DIR 2406 ...... **54601**
Pinson, Alex LEGIS ASST 2406 ...... **54601**
Smith, Rebekah LEGIS CORRES 2406 ...... **54601**
Tener, William STAFF ASST 2406 ...... **54601**

DISTRICT OFFICES

HAZARD—48 S KY HWY 15, HAZARD, KY 41701
Begley, Andrea FIELD REP **606-439-0794**
Estep, Nana RECEPTIONIST **606-439-0794**

PRESTONSBURG—110 RESOURCE CT, SUITE A, PRESTONSBURG, KY 41653
Owens, Tonya CASEWKR/RECEPTIONIST **606-886-0844**
Rice, Adam FIELD REP **606-886-0844**

SOMERSET—551 CLIFTY ST, SOMERSET, KY 42503
TOLL-FREE NUMBER 1-800-632-8588
Anderson, Gena CASEWKR **606-679-8346**

Cameron, Carlos FIELD REP 606-679-8346
Gragg, Jordan RECEPTIONIST 606-679-8346
Kelly, Karen DIR - DIST AFFAIRS 606-679-8346
Matthews, Stacey CASEWKR 606-679-8346
Smoot, Danielle DIR - PRESS & COMMUNICATIONS ... 606-679-8346
Sumner, Rebecca CASEWKR 606-679-8346

Representative Mike Rogers

Alabama, 3d

2184 RAYBURN HOB (ZIP: 20515-0103) **225-3261**
Barranca, Alexis SCHEDULER 2184 53261
Brinson, Chris CHIEF OF STAFF 2184 53261
Latta, Dave FELLOW 2184 53261
McBride, Debby OFFICE MGR/CASEWKR 2184 53261
Miller, Shea PRESS SECY 2184 53261
Verett, Whitney LEGIS DIR 2184 53261
Wilson, Haley LEGIS ASST 2184 53261

DISTRICT OFFICES

ANNISTON—1129 NOBLE ST, ROOM 104, ANNISTON, AL 36201
Graben, Beverly CASEWKR 256-236-5655
Rollins, Sheri DIST DIR 256-236-5655
Smith-Baker, Margaret ADMIN ASST/CASEWKR 256-236-5655

OPELIKA—701 AVE A, SUITE 300, OPELIKA, AL 36801
Dunbar, Avis CASEWKR 334-745-6221
Lewis, Alvin FIELD REP/SPECIAL PROJ DIR 334-745-6221
Vanoy, Lee CONSTIT SVCS REP 334-745-6221

Representative Francis Rooney

Florida, 19th

120 CANNON HOB (ZIP: 20515-0919) **225-2536**
Bartlett, Joe LEGIS ASST 120 CHOB 52536
Berardi, Chris COMMUNICATIONS DIR 120 CHOB 52536
Brown, Trevor CASEWKR 120 CHOB 52536
Carr, Nick DIR - DIGITAL MEDIA 120 CHOB 52536
Carter, Jessica CHIEF OF STAFF 120 CHOB 52536
Clifford, Ken LEGIS ASST 120 CHOB 52536
Nixon, Andrew LEGIS CORRES 120 CHOB 52536
Nolin, Sarah PRESS AIDE 120 CHOB 52536
Schrodt, Corey LEGIS DIR 120 CHOB 52536
Wick, Chloe SCHEDULER 120 CHOB 52536

DISTRICT OFFICES

COLLIER COUNTY—3299 TAMIAMI TRAIL E, SUITE 105, NAPLES, FL 34112 239-252-6225

LEE COUNTY—1039 SE 9TH AVE, SUITE 308, CAPE CORAL, FL 33990
Goulet, Dana DIR - CONSTIT SVCS 239-599-6033
Griffith, Albert CASEWKR 239-599-6033
Hernandez, Melany DIST REP 239-599-6033
Holliday, Tami DPTY CHIEF OF STAFF 239-599-6033

Representative John W. Rose

Tennessee, 6th

1232 LONGWORTH HOB (ZIP: 20515-4206) **225-4231**
Carney, Conor SR LEGIS ASST 1232 54231
Colona, Zac STAFF ASST 1232 54231
Hilleary, Van CHIEF OF STAFF 1232 54231
Igleheart, Alex LEGIS DIR 1232 54231
Kroitor, Jason LEGIS CORRES 1232 54231
Lee, Rachel COMMUNICATIONS DIR 1232 54231
Stover, Braden SCHEDULER 1232 54231

DISTRICT OFFICES

COOKEVILLE—321 E SPRING ST, SUITE 301, COOKEVILLE, TN 38501
Foster, Rebecca DIST DIR 931-854-9430
Nave, Lou FIELD REP 931-854-9430
Warren, Bonny CASEWKR 931-854-9430

GALLATIN—355 N BELVEDERE DR, SUITE 308, GALLATIN, TN 37066
Mash, Kim CASEWKR 615-206-8204
Render, Ray DPTY DIST DIR 615-206-8204

Representative Max Rose

New York, 11th

1529 LONGWORTH HOB (ZIP: 20515-3211) **225-3371**
Burgess, Amy FINANCIAL ADMIN 1529 53371
Colon, Hector LEGIS ASST 1529 53371
Doty, Brian STAFF ASST 1529 53371
Edwards-Jenks, Jonas COMMUNICATIONS DIR 1529 53371
Meegan, Erin LEGIS DIR 1529 53371
Sokolov, Anne CHIEF OF STAFF 1529 53371
Wacker, Lillian SCHEDULER 1529 53371
Zlotnik, Asher LEGIS ASST 1529 53371

DISTRICT OFFICE

STATEN ISLAND—265 NEW DORP LANE, STATEN ISLAND, NY 10306
Ahmed, Zunera CASEWKR - IMMIGRATION 718-667-3313
Clinton, James CASEWKR 718-667-3313
Elkins, Kevin DIST DIR 718-667-3313
Fall, Yvette CASEWKR 718-667-3313
Mahmood, Saman AREA DIR 718-667-3313
Markman, Clio AREA DIR 718-667-3313
McBeth, Agnes ECON DEV REP 718-667-3313
Procaccino, Gabriel DIST SCHEDULER 718-667-3313

Representative Harley Rouda

California, 48th

2300 RAYBURN HOB (ZIP: 20515-0548) **225-2415**
Bovair, Caroline ADMIN DIR/SCHEDULER 2300 52415
Bress, Matilda STAFF ASST 2300 52415
Commins, Zac SR LEGIS ASST 2300 52415
Crerand, Emily CHIEF OF STAFF 2300 52415
Hammon, Beth LEGIS ASST 2300 52415
Helder, Zach COMMUNICATIONS DIR 2300 52415
Jackson, Matt LEGIS CORRES 2300 52415
Muhammad, Sabir STAFF ASST 2300 52415
Noh, Andrew LEGIS DIR/DPTY CHIEF OF STAFF 2300 52415
Zams, Kelly ADMIN - FINANCE & PAYROLL 2300 52415

DISTRICT OFFICE

NEWPORT BEACH—4000 WESTERLY PL, SUITE 270, NEWPORT BEACH, CA 92660
Barich, Lauren CONSTIT SVCS REP 714-960-6483
Kaushal, Natasha FIELD REP 714-960-6483
Limbach, Shannon CONSTIT SVCS REP 714-960-6483
Napuri, Alyssa FIELD DIR 714-960-6483
Nong, Eric DIST FIELD REP 714-960-6483
Oatman, Laura DIST DIR 714-960-6483

Representative David Rouzer

North Carolina, 7th

2439 RAYBURN HOB (ZIP: 20515-3307) 225-2731
Billy, Kelley EXEC ASST 2439 52731
Chappell, Perry LEGIS ASST 2439 52731
Cooke, Jason LEGIS DIR 2439 52731
Cooke, Marylou STAFF ASST 2439 52731
McBride, Erin LEGIS CORRES 2439 52731
Murphy, Melissa CHIEF OF STAFF 2439 52731
Smotkin, Danielle DIR - PRESS & COMMUNICATIONS 2439 52731
Whitson, Ian LEGIS ASST 2439 52731

DISTRICT OFFICES

BRUNSWICK COUNTY—301 GOVT CENTER DR, UNIT 1, BOLIVIA, NC 28422
Lambeth, Chance DIST DIR 910-253-6111
Neville, Pam DIST OFFICE MGR 910-253-6111

JOHNSTON COUNTY—4001 U.S. HWY 301 S, SUITE 106, FOUR OAKS, NC 27524
Barker, Billy FIELD DIR 919-938-3040
Littler, Lisa DPTY DIST DIR 919-938-3040

NEW HANOVER COUNTY—230 GOVT CENTER DR, SUITE 113, WILMINGTON, NC 28403
Christ, Billy FIELD REP 910-395-0202
Dmeza, Gilbert CASEWORK - VETS 910-395-0202
Young, Anna CASEWORK - VETS 910-395-0202

Representative Chip Roy

Texas, 21st

1319 LONGWORTH HOB (ZIP: 20515-4321) 225-4236
Andzel, Christian STAFF ASST 1319 54236
Butler, Courtney EXEC SCHEDULER 1319 54236
Donachie, Robert COMMUNICATIONS DIR 1319 54236
Fletcher, John LEGIS CORRES 1319 54236
Hancock, Sabrina LEGIS ASST 1319 54236
Harrell, Maggie LEGIS DIR 1319 54236
Miller, Wade CHIEF OF STAFF 1319 54236
Smith, Robby SR LEGIS ASST 1319 54236
Wendt, Jonah STAFF ASST 1319 54236

DISTRICT OFFICES

AUSTIN—5900 SW PKWY, BLDG 2, SUITE 201A, AUSTIN, TX 78735-6204
Cook, Jordan FIELD REP 512-871-5959
McFall, Morgan CONSTIT LIAISON 512-871-5959

KERRVILLE—125 LEHMANN DR, SUITE 201, KERRVILLE, TX 78028-6060
Overby, Anne LIAISON - MIL 830-896-0154
Tirella, Maxie COORD - DIST OUTREACH 830-896-0154

SAN ANTONIO—1100 NE LOOP 410, SUITE 640, SAN ANTONIO, TX 78209-1530
Andrade, Edwina DIR - CONSTIT SVCS 210-821-5024
Casanova, Anna CONSTIT SVCS 210-821-5024
McDaniel, Nathan DIST DIR 210-821-5024

Representative Lucille Roybal-Allard

California, 40th

2083 RAYBURN HOB (ZIP: 20515-0540) 225-1766
Caplan, Josh LEGIS DIR 2083 51766
Castillo, Victor G CHIEF OF STAFF 2083 51766
Jessup, Debbie ADVISOR - HEALTH POLICY 2083 51766
Miranda, Jose LEGIS ASST 2083 51766
Ochoa, Christine EXEC ASST/OFFICE MGR 2083 51766
Randaccio, James STAFF ASST/LEGIS CORRES 2083 51766
Rippeteau, Judy RECEPTIONIST 2083 51766
Rivas, Victoria LEGIS ASST 2083 51766
Soskin, Benjamin COMMUNICATIONS DIR 2083 51766

DISTRICT OFFICE

LOS ANGELES—500 CITADEL DR, SUITE 320, COMMERCE, CA 90040-1572
Avila, Sinnai FIELD DPTY 323-721-8790
Castro, Luz FIELD DPTY 323-721-8790
Figueroa, Ana DIST CHIEF OF STAFF 323-721-8790
Lira, Nancy CASEWK MGR 323-721-8790
Loera-Martinez, Monica EXEC ASST/SCHEDULER 323-721-8790
Martinez, Vanessa DIST OFFICE MGR/SPECIAL ASST 323-721-8790
Tachiki-Chin, Kimberlee SR FIELD REP 323-721-8790

Representative Raul Ruiz

California, 36th

2342 RAYBURN HOB (ZIP: 20515-0536) 225-5330
Del Monico, Tim CHIEF OF STAFF 2342 55330
Doty, Erin LEGIS DIR 2342 55330
Gonzalez, Sergio SYS ADMIN 2342 55330
Heasley, Lauren SCHEDULER 2342 55330
Porroa, Ivelisse LEGIS ASST 2342 55330
Rubin, Isaac LEGIS CORRES/PRESS ASST 2342 55330
Yager, Austin LEGIS ASST 2342 55330

DISTRICT OFFICES

HEMET—445 E FLORIDA AVE, HEMET, CA 92543
Keplinger, Patrick DIST FIELD REP 951-765-2304

PALM DESERT—43875 WASHINGTON ST, SUITE F, PALM DESERT, CA 92211
Carlstrom, Peter FIELD REP 760-424-8888
Lopez, Jacqueline DIST DIR 760-424-8888
Patrida, Deyssi CASEWKR 760-424-8888
Quintas, Hernan PRESS SECY 760-424-8888
Rorick, Lisa DIR - CONSTIT SVCS 760-424-8888
Strizak, Alexander STAFF ASST 760-424-8888

Representative C. A. Dutch Ruppersberger

Maryland, 2d

2206 RAYBURN HOB (ZIP: 20515-2002) 225-3061
Brower, Justin LEGIS ASST - MIL 2206 53061
Gonzales, Walter LEGIS DIR/DPTY CHIEF OF STAFF 2206 53061
Graham, Victoria DIGITAL ASST/STAFF ASST 2206 53061
Heitlinger, David LEGIS ASST 2206 53061
Linnehan Oursler, Tara CHIEF OF STAFF 2206 53061
Phaup, Elliott SCHEDULER/POLICY ADVISOR/EXEC ASST 2206 53061
Strong, Kendall LEGIS CORRES/LEGIS ASST 2206 53061

DISTRICT OFFICE

TIMONIUM—THE ATRIUM, 375 W PADONIA RD, SUITE 200, TIMONIUM, MD 21093
TOLL-FREE NUMBER 1-877-727-6802
Baker, Michael OUTREACH DIR 410-628-2701
Duggins, Cori DIST DIR/CASEWK SUPERVISOR 410-628-2701
Lennon, Jaime COMMUNICATIONS DIR 410-628-2701
Linnehan Oursler, Tara CHIEF OF STAFF 410-628-2701

McGuire, Kevin STAFF ASST 410-628-2701
Meyer, Ashley COORD - BUSINESS & STATE/LOCAL GOVT COALITIONS/DIR - GOVT & BUSINESS RELATIONS 410-628-2701
Pleasant-Jones, P J COMMUNITY AFFAIRS LIAISON . 410-628-2701
Stuart, Jasmine CONSTIT LIAISON 410-628-2701
Yates, Lynn LIAISON - CONSTIT SVCS 410-628-2701

Representative Bobby L. Rush

Illinois, 1st

2188 RAYBURN HOB (ZIP: 20515-1301) 225-4372
Citron, Lauren LEGIS ASST 2188 54372
Gavin-Parks, Ingrid DPTY DIR 2188 54372
Johnson, Ryan COMMUNICATIONS DIR 2188 54372
Marshall, John SR POLICY ADVISOR 2188 54372
Motley, Essence ASST TO THE CONGRESSMAN/STAFF ASST 2188 54372
Myers, Lenette DIR - ADMIN STAFF 2188 54372
Pandya, Nishith LEGIS DIR 2188 54372
Pollas, Yardly SR COUNSEL/CHIEF OF STAFF 2188 54372

DISTRICT OFFICE

CHICAGO—11750 S WESTERN AVE, CHICAGO, IL 60643-4732
Bearden, Lalique OFFICE COORD 773-779-2400
Fountain, Melvin DIST AIDE 773-779-2400
Grange, Robyn DIST DIR 773-779-2400
Hall, Dottie SR CONSTIT SVCS REP 773-779-2400
Hall, Rosemary SECY/EXEC ASST 773-779-2400
McCollum, Sandra RECEPTIONIST 773-779-2400
Sparkman, Walter DIST AIDE 773-779-2400
Teague, James CONSTIT SVCS ASSOC 773-779-2400

Representative John H. Rutherford

Florida, 4th

1711 LONGWORTH HOB (ZIP: 20515-0904) 225-2501
Bird, Jessica LEGIS CORRES 1711 52501
Heffernan, Katie LEGIS ASST 1711 52501
Lanfranconi, Alex PRESS SECY 1711 52501
Nawrocki Bradley, Jenifer LEGIS DIR 1711 52501
Simpson, Kelly CHIEF OF STAFF 1711 52501
Spohn, Carole Anne SCHEDULING DIR 1711 52501
Vance, Nicholas SR LEGIS ASST 1711 52501
Wagner, Zachary STAFF ASST 1711 52501

DISTRICT OFFICE

JACKSONVILLE—4130 SALISBURY RD, SUITE 2500, JACKSONVILLE, FL 32216
Malspeis, Momi DIR - CONSTIT SVCS 904-831-5205
Miller, Chris DIST DIR 904-831-5205
Noland-Dennis, Meleah DIST OFFICE MGR 904-831-5205
Smith, Jackie DIR - DIST PROJ 904-831-5205
Wallace, Amanda CONSTIT SVCS REP 904-831-5205

Representative Tim Ryan

Ohio, 13th

1126 LONGWORTH HOB (ZIP: 20515-3513) 225-5261
Fay, Samantha LEGIS ASST 1126 55261
Grimes, Ron CHIEF OF STAFF 1126 55261
Isenberg, Erin DPTY CHIEF OF STAFF 1126 55261
Jenkins, Rachel LEGIS ASST 1126 55261
Keating, Ryan SR ADVISOR/DPTY CHIEF OF STAFF/LEGIS DIR 1126 55261
Lowe, Sean STAFF ASST 1126 55261
Sibulo, Cody PRESS SECY/DIGITAL DIR 1126 55261
Zetts, Michael COMMUNICATIONS DIR 1126 55261

DISTRICT OFFICES

AKRON—1030 E TALLMADGE AVE, AKRON, OH 44310
Breck, Catey ECON DEV REP 330-630-7311

WARREN—197 W MARKET ST, WARREN, OH 44481
Crockett, Gene LIAISON - CONSTIT SVCS 330-373-0074
Hayes, Debra DIST SCHEDULER/EXEC ASST 330-373-0074
Leonard, Rick DIST DIR 330-373-0074
Peterson, Vincent COMMUNITY AFFAIRS LIAISON 330-373-0074
Vadas, Matt CONSTIT LIAISON 330-373-0074

YOUNGSTOWN—241 FED PLAZA W, YOUNGSTOWN, OH 44503
Wigley, Pearlette COORD - COMMUNITY DEV/CONSTIT ADVOCATE 330-740-0193

Delegate Gregorio Kilili Camacho Sablan

Northern Mariana Islands, Delegate

2411 RAYBURN HOB (ZIP: 20515-5201) 225-2646
TOLL-FREE NO. 1-877-446-3465
Cornibert, Agnes OFFICE MGR/EXEC ASST 2411 52646
Del Rosario, John STAFF ASST 2411 52646
Diaz, Frances SR LEGIS ASST 2411 52646
Maiman, Seth LEGIS DIR 2411 52646
Schwalbach, Bob CHIEF OF STAFF 2411 52646
Tanga, Adam SR ADVISOR 2411 52646
Yamada, Herbert LEGIS ASST 2411 52646

DISTRICT OFFICES

ROTA—P.O. BOX 1361, ROTA, MP 96951
Masga, Harry James STAFF ASST 670-532-2647

SAIPAN—P.O. BOX 504879, SAIPAN, MP 96950
Bermudes-Castro, Paula DIST MGR/SCHEDULER 670-323-2647
Camacho, Antoinette STAFF ASST 670-323-2647
Nogis, Janine STAFF ASST 670-323-2647
Sablan, Tina COORD - OUTREACH 670-323-2647
Tenorio, Peter Michael DIST DIR 670-323-2647

TINIAN—P.O. BOX 520394, TINIAN, MP 96952 670-433-2647

Representative Linda T. Sánchez

California, 38th

2329 RAYBURN HOB (ZIP: 20515-0538) 225-6676
Abbott, Jacob LEGIS CORRES 2329 56676
Kiedrowicz, Melissa LEGIS DIR 2329 56676
McConnell, Meghan LEGIS AIDE 2329 56676
Nguyen, Alexander COMMUNICATIONS DIR 2329 56676
Rangel, Juan LEGIS AIDE 2329 56676
Silverton-Peel, Oliver SCHEDULER 2329 56676
Sulkala, Lea CHIEF OF STAFF 2329 56676
Willming, Cody LEGIS AIDE 2329 56676

DISTRICT OFFICE

NORWALK—12440 E IMPERIAL HWY, SUITE 140, NORWALK, CA 90650
Centeno, Crystal DIST SCHEDULER 562-860-5050
Gorrocino, Irma FIELD REP 562-860-5050
Nagy, Steven FIELD REP 562-860-5050
Ortiz, Griselda FIELD REP 562-860-5050
Rumley, Matthew CASEWK MGR 562-860-5050
Shahinian, Yvette DIST DIR 562-860-5050

Delegate Michael F. Q. San Nicolas

Guam, Delegate

1632 LONGWORTH HOB (ZIP: 20515-5301) 225-1188
TOLL-FREE NO. 1-844-482-6671
Defensor, Sahara COUNSEL/CHIEF POLICY ADVISOR 1632 ..... **51188**
Molina, David LEGIS ASST 1632 .... **51188**
Mori, T'Nelta EXEC ASST/FINANCIAL & ADMIN OFFICER 1632 ... **51188**
Pineiro, Eli EXEC ASST 1632 .... **51188**

DISTRICT OFFICE

HAGATNA—330 HERNAN CORTEZ AVE, SUITE 300, HAGATNA, GU 96910
TOLL-FREE NUMBER.......... 1-844-482-6671
Aien, Nelta T CASEWKR **671-475-6453**
Calvo, Thomas Jerome, Jr EXEC ASST **671-475-6453**
Cariaso, Vanessa Ann Sanchez EXEC ASST **671-475-6453**
Crisostomo, Jose A RECEPTIONIST **671-475-6453**
Janssen, Julian Christopher CASEWKR **671-475-6453**
Kilayko, Michael Manejero EXEC ASST **671-475-6453**
Leon Guerrero, Kenneth W B CASEWKR - MIL/CASEWORK - VETS **671-475-6453**
Perez, Benjie H. EXEC ASST **671-475-6453**
Winn, Jennifer DIST DIR **671-475-6453**

Representative John P. Sarbanes

Maryland, 3d

2370 RAYBURN HOB (ZIP: 20515-2003) 225-4016
Bragdon, Stephanie LEGIS CORRES 2370 .... **54016**
Crisp, Timia LEGIS ASST 2370 .... **54016**
Gelman, Peter LEGIS ASST 2370 .... **54016**
Jacobs, Daniel COMMUNICATIONS DIR 2370 .... **54016**
Lovinger, Dvora CHIEF OF STAFF 2370 .... **54016**
Moura, Kelly SCHEDULER 2370 .... **54016**
O'Mara, Raymond DPTY CHIEF OF STAFF/LEGIS DIR 2370 ...... **54016**
Wolfe, Jordan LEGIS AIDE 2370 .... **54016**

DISTRICT OFFICES

ANNAPOLIS—44 CALVERT ST, SUITE 349, ANNAPOLIS, MD 21401.......... 410-265-1679
TOWSON—600 BALTIMORE AVE, SUITE 300, TOWSON, MD 21204
Garcia, Vikki COMMUNITY OUTREACH SPEC **410-832-8890**
Hassell, Fred DIR - CONSTIT SVCS **410-832-8890**
McCleaf, Colin CONSTIT SVCS REP **410-832-8890**
Simms, Cecilia CONSTIT SVCS REP **410-832-8890**
Smith, Brigid DIR - GOVT, BUSINESS, & COMMUNITY AFFAIRS **410-832-8890**

Representative Steve Scalise

Louisiana, 1st

2049 RAYBURN HOB (ZIP: 20515-1801) 225-3015
Battaglia, Jacqueline SCHEDULER 2049 .... **53015**
Gosnell, Ellen DIR - OPS 2049 .... **53015**
Green, Geoffrey LEGIS DIR 2049 .... **53015**
McCarthy, John FELLOW 2049 .... **53015**
McKeogh, Katie PRESS ASST 2049 .... **53015**
Miller, Megan Bel DC CHIEF OF STAFF 2049 .... **53015**
Shea, Mitch STAFF ASST 2049 .... **53015**
Trokey, Claire LEGIS ASST 2049 .... **53015**
Trowbridge, Fred DIR - PROJ 2049 .... **53015**
Watson, Greg LEGIS ASST 2049 .... **53015**

DISTRICT OFFICES

HAMMOND—1514 MARTENS DR, SUITE 10, HAMMOND, LA 70401.......... 985-340-2185
HOUMA—8026 MAIN ST, SUITE 700, HOUMA, LA 70360.......... 985-879-2300
MANDEVILLE—21454 KOOP DR, SUITE 1-E, MANDEVILLE, LA 70471
Evans Morrison, Danielle FIELD REP **985-893-9064**
METAIRIE—110 VETERANS MEMORIAL BLVD, SUITE 500, METAIRIE, LA 70005
Henry, Charles DIST CHIEF OF STAFF **504-837-1259**
Jewell, Matthew FIELD REP **504-837-1259**
Marphis, Pamela LIAISON - CONSTIT SVCS **504-837-1259**
Williamson, Ramona FIELD REP **504-837-1259**

Representative Mary Gay Scanlon

Pennsylvania, 5th

1535 LONGWORTH HOB (ZIP: 20515-3805) 225-2011
Clancy, Tom LEGIS ASST/RULES ASSOC 1535 .... **52011**
Clement, Mary Kate DPTY CHIEF OF STAFF/SCHEDULER 1535 .... **52011**
Flynn, Roddy CHIEF OF STAFF 1535 .... **52011**
Ischiropoulos, Dean LEGIS CORRES 1535 .... **52011**
Pedramrazi, Armita LEGIS DIR 1535 .... **52011**
Richards, Gabby COMMUNICATIONS DIR 1535 .... **52011**
Rivera, Keanu LEGIS ASST 1535 .... **52011**
Tatarian-Sarkasian, Lisa FINANCIAL ADMIN/OFFICE MGR 1535 .... **52011**
Wilcox, Faith STAFF ASST 1535 .... **52011**

DISTRICT OFFICE

EAST LANSDOWNE—927 E BALTIMORE AVE, EAST LANSDOWNE, PA 19050
Boyd, Heather DIST DIR **610-626-1913**
McDonald, Therese MGR - CONSTIT SVCS **610-626-1913**
Okolosi, Nailah MGR - CONSTIT SVCS **610-626-1913**
Rice, Rose STAFF ASST **610-626-1913**
Yates, Malcolm DIR - CONSTIT SVCS **610-626-1913**

Representative Janice D. Schakowsky

Illinois, 9th

2367 RAYBURN HOB (ZIP: 20515-1309) 225-2111
Ayala, Miguel COMMUNICATIONS DIR 2367 .... **52111**
Durkin, Kate LEGIS ASST 2367 .... **52111**
Lohr, Mitch LEGIS CORRES/STAFF ASST 2367 .... **52111**
Marcus, Robert CHIEF OF STAFF 2367 .... **52111**
Muzeroll, Kim DPTY CHIEF OF STAFF/EXEC ASST 2367 .... **52111**
Okolo, Osaremen LEGIS ASST 2367 .... **52111**
Terry, Syd LEGIS DIR 2367 .... **52111**

DISTRICT OFFICES

CHICAGO—5533 BROADWAY, SUITE 2, CHICAGO, IL 60640
Castano, Paola CONSTIT ADVOCATE **773-506-7100**
Combs, Leslie DIST DIR **773-506-7100**
Rodriguez, Taina CONSTIT ADVOCATE **773-506-7100**
Somani, Zahra STAFF ASST **773-506-7100**
Stein, Maribeth CONSTIT ADVOCATE **773-506-7100**
GLENVIEW—1852 JOHNS DR, GLENVIEW, IL 60025
Eusebio, Abbey CONSTIT ADVOCATE **847-328-3409**
Goczkowski, Andrew COORD - GRANTS/CONSTIT ADVOCATE **847-328-3409**
Limjoco, Marie DIR - COMMUNITY AFFAIRS **847-328-3409**

Representative Adam B. Schiff

California, 28th

2269 RAYBURN HOB (ZIP: 20515-0528) 225-4176
Boland, Patrick COMMUNICATIONS DIR/SR ADVISOR/DPTY CHIEF OF STAFF 2269 .... **54176**
Hoven, Christopher ADMIN ASST 2269 .... **54176**
Jankiewicz, Joe LEGIS DIR 2269 .... **54176**
Lowenstein, Jeffrey CHIEF OF STAFF 2269 .... **54176**
Nicholas, Caroline STAFF ASST 2269 .... **54176**
Simons, Emily COMMUNICATIONS DIR 2269 .... **54176**
Sorenson, Zach LEGIS AIDE 2269 .... **54176**
Theissen, Anthony LEGIS ASST 2269 .... **54176**

DISTRICT OFFICES

BURBANK—245 E OLIVE AVE, SUITE 200, BURBANK, CA 91502
Aguilera, Mike DIST REP **818-450-2900**
DeSousa, Sierra DIST REP **818-450-2900**
Gutierrez, Margarita CASEWKR **818-450-2900**
Hovagimian, Mary DIST REP **818-450-2900**
Marcello, Pamela DIST REP **818-450-2900**
Oinuma, Colleen DPTY DIST DIR **818-450-2900**
Peifer, Ann DIST DIR **818-450-2900**
Simpson, Teresa DIST REP **818-450-2900**
Vuna, Elizabeth DIST REP **818-450-2900**

HOLLYWOOD—5500 HOLLYWOOD BLVD, SUITE 416, LOS ANGELES, CA 90028........ 323-315-5555

Representative Bradley Scott Schneider

Illinois, 10th

1432 LONGWORTH HOB (ZIP: 20515-1310) 225-4835
Bernton, Jessica LEGIS DIR 1432 .... **54835**
Brown, Tommy LEGIS ASST 1432 .... **54835**
Glezer, Claire DIR - OPS 1432 .... **54835**
Goetz, Vic SR POLICY ADVISOR 1432 .... **54835**
Kirsch, Steven COMMUNICATIONS DIR 1432 .... **54835**
Means, Jade STAFF ASST 1432 .... **54835**
O'Shea, Casey CHIEF OF STAFF 1432 .... **54835**
Rice-Davis, Chelsey LEGIS CORRES 1432 .... **54835**

DISTRICT OFFICE

LINCOLNSHIRE—111 BARCLAY BLVD, SUITE 200, LINCOLNSHIRE, IL 60069
Claus, Greg DPTY DIST DIR **847-383-4870**
Davidman, Karyn CASEWK DIR **847-383-4870**
Duby, Sarah CONSTIT SVCS REP **847-383-4870**
Duque, Carolina DIST AIDE **847-383-4870**
Kaplan, Jake DIST AIDE **847-383-4870**
Melara, Alvaro CONSTIT SVCS REP **847-383-4870**
Perez, Robert STAFF ASST **847-383-4870**
Ryan, Magen DIST DIR **847-383-4870**

Representative Kurt Schrader

Oregon, 5th

2431 RAYBURN HOB (ZIP: 20515-3705) 225-5711
Ballinger, Adrian STAFF ASST 2431 .... **55711**
Deshler, Andrew STAFF ASST 2431 .... **55711**
Gage, Paul CHIEF OF STAFF 2431 .... **55711**
Griffeth, Carlee COMMUNICATIONS DIR 2431 .... **55711**
Hackbarth, Andy LEGIS CORRES 2431 .... **55711**
Holland, Stephen LEGIS ASST/COUNSEL 2431 .... **55711**
Huckleberry, Chris LEGIS DIR/DPTY CHIEF 2431 .... **55711**
Parker, Larkin EXEC ASST 2431 .... **55711**
Stafford, Julia LEGIS ASST 2431 .... **55711**
Stokes, Zachary LEGIS ASST 2431 .... **55711**

DISTRICT OFFICES

OREGON CITY—621 HIGH ST, OREGON CITY, OR 97045
Klein, Michael CASEWORK - VETS **503-557-1324**
Kunse, Suzanne DIST DIR **503-557-1324**
Markgraf, Teresa DIST SCHEDULER **503-557-1324**
McKibben, Megan FIELD REP **503-557-1324**
Serra, John DIST FIELD REP **503-557-1324**

SALEM—544 FERRY ST SE, SUITE 2, SALEM, OR 97302
Smith, Mary Ann CASEWKR **503-588-9100**

Representative Kim Schrier

Washington, 8th

1123 LONGWORTH HOB (ZIP: 20515-4708) 225-7761
Bissonnette, Alicia LEGIS CORRES 1123 .... **57761**
Carlson, Libby COMMUNICATIONS DIR 1123 .... **57761**
Cash, Jennifer LEGIS ASST 1123 .... **57761**
Miller, Shanley SCHEDULER 1123 .... **57761**
O'Quinn, Erin CHIEF OF STAFF 1123 .... **57761**
Payne, Alex LEGIS DIR 1123 .... **57761**
Perlmutter, Ari STAFF ASST 1123 .... **57761**

DISTRICT OFFICE

ISSAQUAH—1445 NW MALL ST, SUITE 4, ISSAQUAH, WA 98027
Leininger, Maria DIST DIR **425-657-1001**

Representative David Schweikert

Arizona, 6th

1526 LONGWORTH HOB (ZIP: 20515-0306) 225-2190
Angulo, Tiffany POLICY ADVISOR/SR CAUCUS POLICY ADVISOR 1526 .... **52190**
Dimenstein, Katherina CHIEF OF STAFF 1526 .... **52190**
Duveneck, Katherine LEGIS DIR 1526 .... **52190**
Laven, Zack LEGIS ASST 1526 .... **52190**
Sabol, Samantha LEGIS CORRES 1526 .... **52190**
Sylvester, Ashley OFFICE MGR/SCHEDULER 1526 .... **52190**
White, Grace PRESS SECY 1526 .... **52190**

DISTRICT OFFICE

SCOTTSDALE—14500 N NORTHSIGHT BLVD, SUITE 221, SCOTTSDALE, AZ 85260
Borquez-Smith, Ernestina DIR - CONSTIT AFFAIRS/OFFICE MGR **480-946-2411**
Hodges, Hayley CASEWKR **480-946-2411**
Knight, Kevin DPTY CHIEF OF STAFF/DIST DIR **480-946-2411**
Okula, Victoria STAFF ASST/CASEWKR **480-946-2411**
Wentz, Blaise CASEWKR **480-946-2411**

Representative Austin Scott

Georgia, 8th

2417 RAYBURN HOB (ZIP: 20515-1008) 225-6531
Anderson, Craig LEGIS ASST 2417 .... **56531**
Anfinson, Thomas FINANCE LIAISON 2417 .... **56531**
Goodwin, Amber MIL FELLOW 2417 .... **56531**
Lawrence, Jason CHIEF OF STAFF 2417 .... **56531**
Ledbetter, Rachel PRESS SECY 2417 .... **56531**
Pierson, Crawford SCHEDULER/OFFICE MGR 2417 .... **56531**

Roberts, Zach LEGIS CORRES 2417 56531
Sanders, Mark LEGIS ASST 2417 56531
Tehrani, Michael LEGIS ASST - MIL/LEGIS DIR 2417 56531
Wainright, Abby STAFF ASST 2417 56531

DISTRICT OFFICES

TIFTON—127-B N CENTRAL AVE, TIFTON, GA 31794

Fortson, Rene DIST REP 229-396-5175
Johnson, Alice COORD - DIST OUTREACH 229-396-5175
Paulk, Elaine CONSTIT SVCS REP 229-396-5175
Watson, Jackie DIR - CONSTIT SVCS 229-396-5175

WARNER ROBINS—230 MARGIE DR, SUITE 500, WARNER ROBINS, GA 31088

Carter, Slayten FIELD REP/DIST OFFICE MGR 478-971-1776
Chalkley, Regina CONSTIT SVCS REP 478-971-1776
Pascarella, David CONSTIT SVCS REP 478-971-1776

Representative David Scott

Georgia, 13th

225 CANNON HOB (ZIP: 20515-1013) 225-2939

Egekeze, Ijeoma LEGIS ASST 225 CHOB 52939
Henderson, Gerard OFFICE MGR/SCHEDULER 225 CHOB 52939
Kuerbitz, Catherine LEGIS ASST 225 CHOB 52939
Rodriguez, Leonardo LEGIS CORRES 225 CHOB 52939
Woodward, Gary CHIEF OF STAFF 225 CHOB 52939

DISTRICT OFFICES

JONESBORO—173 N MAIN ST, JONESBORO, GA 30236-3567

Cooke-Cooper, Teresa CONSTIT SVCS REP/FIELD REP 770-210-5073
Harris, Chandra DIST DIR 770-210-5073
Nurse, Dylan CONSTIT SVCS REP 770-210-5073
Smalls, Cherrie CONSTIT SVCS REP 770-210-5073

SMYRNA—888 CONCORD RD, SUITE 100, SMYRNA, GA 30080

Davis, Sheila CONSTIT SVCS REP/FIELD REP 770-432-5405
Dodoo, Isaac DPTY DIST DIR 770-432-5405
Husbands, Patrick CONSTIT SVCS REP 770-432-5405
Matthews-Storey, Angie CONSTIT SVCS/FIELD REP/OFFICE MGR 770-432-5405

Representative Robert C. "Bobby" Scott

Virginia, 3d

1201 LONGWORTH HOB (ZIP: 20515-4603) 225-8351

Barbera, Austin PRESS SECY 1201 58351
Dailey, David CHIEF OF STAFF 1201 58351
Estes-Petty, Randi DPTY CHIEF OF STAFF 1201 58351
Ingram, Christina LEGIS ASST 1201 58351
Jones, Allen STAFF ASST 1201 58351
Patel, Nina LEGIS COUNSEL 1201 58351
Schwartz, Paige SR LEGIS ASST 1201 58351
Valentine, Natalie LEGIS CORRES 1201 58351

DISTRICT OFFICE

NEWPORT NEWS—2600 WASHINGTON AVE, SUITE 1010, NEWPORT NEWS, VA 23607

Alston, Thomas CONSTIT SVCS REP 757-380-1000
Bailey, Benjamin CONSTIT SVCS REP 757-380-1000
Boone, Demontre DIR - CONSTIT SVCS 757-380-1000
George, Scott SR CONSTIT SVCS REP 757-380-1000
George-Winkler, Nkechi SR ADVISOR 757-380-1000
Haro-Perez, Khenia SPECIAL ASST 757-380-1000
Jackson, Ryan CONSTIT SVCS REP 757-380-1000
Russell, Gisele DIST DIR 757-380-1000

Representative F. James Sensenbrenner, Jr.

Wisconsin, 5th

2449 RAYBURN HOB (ZIP: 20515-4905) 225-5101

Bisenius, Matt CHIEF OF STAFF 2449 55101
Bos, Amy LEGIS DIR 2449 55101
Cobb, Nate DC SCHEDULER/OFFICE MGR/SYS ADMIN 2449 55101
Czarnecki, Chris STAFF ASST 2449 55101
Kinney, Erik LEGIS ASST 2449 55101
Krepich, Christopher COMMUNICATIONS DIR 2449 55101
Lawler, Will LEGIS ASST 2449 55101
Steger, Michael LEGIS ASST 2449 55101
Steinhafel, Ben LEGIS ASST/LEGIS CORRES 2449 55101

DISTRICT OFFICE

BROOKFIELD—120 BISHOPS WAY, ROOM 154, BROOKFIELD, WI 53005-6294

Cole, Sally SR CASEWKR 262-784-1111
Hagerup, Loni CHIEF OF STAFF 262-784-1111
Holsen, Matt COORD - DIST OUTREACH 262-784-1111
Leisemann, John STAFF ASST 262-784-1111

Representative José E. Serrano

New York, 15th

2354 RAYBURN HOB (ZIP: 20515-3215) 225-4361

Alpert, Matthew CHIEF OF STAFF 2354 54361
Amador, Paola COMMUNICATIONS DIR 2354 54361
Camara, Hatou COMMUNITY LIAISON 2354 54361
Castillo, Valentin LEGIS ASST/PRESS ASST 2354 54361
Chandler, Danny SYS ADMIN 2354 54361
Dominguez De Marty, Idalia EXEC ADMIN 2354 54361
Garza, Marcus LEGIS ASST 2354 54361
Nigaglioni, Angel LEGIS COUNSEL/LEGIS DIR 2354 54361
Vogel Philbrick, Alexis LEGIS AIDE/SCHEDULER 2354 54361

DISTRICT OFFICE

BRONX—1231 LAFAYETTE AVE, 4TH FLOOR, BRONX, NY 10474

Cabral, Ramon DPTY DIST DIR 718-620-0084
Castro, Evelyn STAFF ASST 718-620-0084
Davila, Kitty HOUSING SPEC/DIR - INTAKE 718-620-0084
Espaillat, Edili CONG ASST 718-620-0084
Jordan, Anthony DIST DIR 718-620-0084
Reyes, Shayra COMMUNITY LIAISON 718-620-0084
Rivera, Awilda SR STAFF ASST 718-620-0084
Wagner-Anderson, Clara SCHEDULER/EXEC SECY . 718-620-0084

Representative Terri A. Sewell

Alabama, 7th

2201 RAYBURN HOB (ZIP: 20515-0107) 225-2665

Beard, Hillary SR POLICY ADVISOR 2201 52665
English, Cachavious CHIEF OF STAFF 2201 52665
Giesemann, Evan ADVISOR - ECON POLICY 2201 52665
Hamilton, Perry SCHEDULER/LEGIS AIDE 2201 52665
Harris, Scott LEGIS CORRES 2201 52665
McGuinness, Jackie COMMUNICATIONS DIR 2201 52665
Nuttall, Robert LEGIS ASST 2201 52665

DISTRICT OFFICES

BIRMINGHAM—TWO 20TH ST N, SUITE 1130, BIRMINGHAM, AL 35203

Davison, Ollie DPTY DIST DIR 205-254-1960

Greene, Kaia COORD - GRANTS/CONSTIT SVCS REP 205-254-1960
Hutchinson, Myeisha COORD - OUTREACH 205-254-1960

MONTGOMERY—101 S LAWRENCE ST, ANNEX 3, MONTGOMERY, AL 36104

King, Shanna CONSTIT SVCS REP 334-262-1919
Williams, Melinda DIST DIR 334-262-1921

SELMA—908 ALABAMA AVE, FED BLDG, SUITE 112, SELMA, AL 36701

Johnson, Dianna CONSTIT SVCS REP 334-877-4414
Stewart, Robert COORD - COMMUNITY OUTREACH 334-877-4414

TUSCALOOSA—2501 7TH ST, SUITE 300, TUSCALOOSA, AL 35401

Love, Reba CASEWK MGR 205-752-5380

Representative Donna E. Shalala

Florida, 27th

1320 LONGWORTH HOB (ZIP: 20515-0927) 225-3931

Boffelli, Claudio STAFF ASST 1320 53931
Horta, Christofer LEGIS ASST 1320 53931
Killin, Jessica CHIEF OF STAFF 1320 53931
Marquez, Nicole DC SCHEDULER 1320 53931
McGarvey, Carla LEGIS DIR 1320 53931
Paulson, Katie LEGIS CORRES 1320 53931
Puente, Joseph COMMUNICATIONS DIR 1320 53931
Talus, Ben SR LEGIS ASST 1320 53931

DISTRICT OFFICE

MIAMI—7700 N KENDALL DR, SUITE 605, MIAMI, FL 33156

Benitez, Reimy CONG AIDE 305-668-2285
Chambliss, Kevin OUTREACH REP 305-668-2285
Condarco-Quesada, Carlos CONG AIDE 305-668-2285
Elias, Christina CONG AIDE 305-668-2285
Martinez, Raul DIST DIR 305-668-2285
Sanchez, Jaclyn STAFF ASST 305-668-2285
Secada, Irene OUTREACH REP 305-668-2285

Representative Brad Sherman

California, 30th

2181 RAYBURN HOB (ZIP: 20515-0530) 225-5911

Ansari, Arya PRESS SECY 2181 55911
MacDonald, Don CHIEF OF STAFF 2181 55911
Nodvin, Leah LEGIS AIDE 2181 55911
Pillis, Maggie SCHEDULING DIR 2181 55911
Propst, Johan LEGIS AIDE 2181 55911
Schein, Michelle STAFF ASSOC 2181 55911
Wolman, Lauren LEGIS DIR/DPTY CHIEF 2181 55911

DISTRICT OFFICE

SHERMAN OAKS—5000 VAN NUYS BLVD, SUITE 420, SHERMAN OAKS, CA 91403-1791

Abrams, Scott DIST DIR 818-501-9200
Alford, John SR FIELD REP 818-501-9200
Brodtke, John FIELD REP 818-501-9200
Chakerian, Mary STAFF ASST 818-501-9200
Krawiec, Carolina DIR - CONSTIT SVCS 818-501-9200
Montano, Lisa CONSTIT SVCS OFFICER 818-501-9200
Sachartoff, Noah STAFF ASST 818-501-9200

Representative Mikie Sherrill

New Jersey, 11th

1208 LONGWORTH HOB (ZIP: 20515-3011) 225-5034

Burns, Jackie COMMUNICATIONS DIR 1208 55034
Gebbia, Jack LEGIS CORRES 1208 55034
Jochem, Julie DC SCHEDULER 1208 55034
Robinson, Hannah LEGIS CORRES 1208 55034
Saxon, Ethan CHIEF OF STAFF 1208 55034
Stewart, Tom LEGIS DIR 1208 55034

DISTRICT OFFICE

PARSIPPANY—8 WOOD HOLLOW RD, PARSIPPANY, NJ 07054

DeGregorio, Nick CASEWKR 973-526-5668
Doucette, Kellie DIST DIR 973-526-5668
Gagliardi, Shala CASEWKR - IMMIGRATION 973-526-5668
Grisafi, Jen DIST SCHEDULER 973-526-5668
Hirsch, Jill DIST DIR 973-526-5668
Tolba, Willy CASEWORK - VETS/CASEWKR - MIL 973-526-5668

Representative John Shimkus

Illinois, 15th

2217 RAYBURN HOB (ZIP: 20515-1315) 225-5271

Acornley, Mark FINANCIAL ADMIN 2217 55271
Boyer, Davis LEGIS CORRES 2217 55271
Clanahan, Chase SR LEGIS ASST 2217 55271
Harris, Molly DIR - OPS/EXEC ASST 2217 55271
Haverly, Jordan COMMUNICATIONS DIR 2217 55271
Kirsh, Ari LEGIS ASST 2217 55271
Looser, Brian LEGIS DIR 2217 55271
Roberts, Craig CHIEF OF STAFF 2217 55271

DISTRICT OFFICES

DANVILLE—201 N VERMILION ST, DANVILLE, IL 61832

Hantz, Chuck DIST AIDE 217-446-0664
Jamison, Reno DIST AIDE 217-446-0664

EFFINGHAM—101 N FOURTH ST, SUITE 303, EFFINGHAM, IL 62401

Hall, Mike REGIONAL DIR 217-347-7947

HARRISBURG—110 E LOCUST ST, ROOM 12, HARRISBURG, IL 62946-1557

Shull, Kristen DIST AIDE 618-252-8271

MARYVILLE—15 PROFESSIONAL PARK PL, MARYVILLE, IL 62062

Bugger, Doug DPTY PRESS SECY 618-288-7190
Fansler, Debra DIST DIR 618-288-7190
Rice, Matt DIST AIDE 618-288-7190
Weber, Amy DIST AIDE 618-288-7190

Representative Michael K. Simpson

Idaho, 2d

2084 RAYBURN HOB (ZIP: 20515-1202) 225-5531

Cannon, Sarah LEGIS DIR 2084 55531
Davis, Melanie SYS ADMIN 2084 55531
Henshaw, Emilee SCHEDULER 2084 55531
Myers, Katherine LEGIS ASST 2084 55531
Neill, James SR LEGIS ASST 2084 55531
Slater, Lindsay CHIEF OF STAFF 2084 55531

DISTRICT OFFICES

BOISE—802 W BANNOCK ST, SUITE 600, BOISE, ID 83702

Linehan, Solara LEGIS ASST 208-334-1953
Quarterman, Craig REGIONAL DIR 208-334-1953
Tensen, Julie SCHEDULER/OFFICE MGR 208-334-1953
Wallace, Nikki COMMUNICATIONS DIR 208-334-1953

IDAHO FALLS—410 MEMORIAL DR, SUITE 203, IDAHO FALLS, ID 83402

Sorensen, Amy DIST FIELD REP 208-523-6701

Sorensen, Joshua FIELD REP 208-523-6701
Summers, Brennan FIELD REP 208-523-6701

TWIN FALLS—1341 FILLMORE ST, SUITE 202, TWIN FALLS, ID 83301

Culver, Linda AREA DIR 208-734-7219

Representative Albio Sires

New Jersey, 8th

2268 RAYBURN HOB (ZIP: 20515-3008) 225-7919

Duval, Jhostyn LEGIS ASST 2268 57919
Flenar, Chelsea LEGIS ASST 2268 57919
Gardner, Ashanee STAFF ASST 2268 57919
Latu, Dan LEGIS CORRES 2268 57919
Martorony, Gene CHIEF OF STAFF 2268 57919
Plassche, Clare LEGIS DIR 2268 57919
Wolford, Judith ADMIN DIR/SCHEDULER 2268 57919

DISTRICT OFFICES

ELIZABETH—800 ANNA ST, ELIZABETH, NJ 07201

Morell, Ada DPTY CHIEF OF STAFF 908-820-0692

JERSEY CITY—257 CORNELISON AVE, SUITE 4408, JERSEY CITY, NJ 07302

Chess, Daarina DIR - CONSTIT SVCS 201-309-0301
Daughtrey, Erica COMMUNICATIONS DIR 201-309-0301
Victorin, Liz CONG AIDE 201-309-0301

WEST NEW YORK—5500 PALISADE AVE, SUITE A, WEST NEW YORK, NJ 07093

Barsa, Richard CONG AIDE 201-558-0800
Reslen, Carmen FIELD REP 201-558-0800
Robles, Martha CONG AIDE 201-558-0800
Turner, Richard DIST DIR 201-558-0800

Representative Elissa Slotkin

Michigan, 8th

1531 LONGWORTH HOB (ZIP: 20515-2208) 225-4872

Birleson, Megan DC SCHEDULER 1531 54872
Brandenburg, Rachel LEGIS ASST - MIL 1531 54872
Caal Skonos, Francesca STAFF ASST 1531 54872
DeGroot, Elliot LEGIS ASST 1531 54872
Girelli, Austin LEGIS CORRES 1531 54872
Kirsch, Isabel LEGIS FELLOW 1531 54872
Lindow, Hannah PRESS SECY 1531 54872
Most, Danielle LEGIS DIR 1531 54872
Norman, Mela Lousie CHIEF OF STAFF 1531 54872

DISTRICT OFFICE

LANSING—1100 W SAGINAW ST, SUITE 3A, LANSING, MI 48915

Brown, Anne FIELD REP 517-993-0510
Capuzzi, Nina DIST SCHEDULER 517-993-0510
Murphy, Laura DIST LIAISON 517-993-0510
Shand, Mona DIST REP 517-993-0510
Shireman, Gina CASEWKR 517-993-0510
Stanard, Alexa DPTY CHIEF OF STAFF 517-993-0510
Szajner, Karsten CASEWKR 517-993-0510
Woll, Samantha DPTY DIST DIR 517-993-0510

Representative Adam Smith

Washington, 9th

2264 RAYBURN HOB (ZIP: 20515-4709) 225-8901

Bryant, Rebecca COMMUNICATIONS DIR 2264 58901
Chandler, Shana CHIEF OF STAFF 2264 68453
Liebenson, Justine LEGIS CORRES 2264 58901
Mariam, Salem SCHEDULING DIR 2264 58901
Pawlow, Jonathan LEGIS DIR/DPTY CHIEF OF STAFF 2264 58901
Purdy, Julian OFFICE MGR/LEGIS ASST 2264 58901
Ruiz, Fernando LEGIS ASST 2264 58901
Stubbs, Connor LEGIS ASST 2264 58901

DISTRICT OFFICE

RENTON—101 EVERGREEN BLDG, 15 S GRADY WAY, RENTON, WA 98057

TOLL-FREE NUMBER 1-888-SMITH-09

Bervar, Lyndall DIST REP 425-793-5180
Carpenter, Glenn DIST REP 425-793-5180
Cole, Caitlyn DIST SCHEDULER/DIST OFFICE MGR 425-793-5180
Eng, Marvin DIST REP 425-793-5180
Moore, Garrett DIST REP 425-793-5180
Servin, Sarah DIST DIR 425-793-5180
Smith, Jayna CASEWKR 425-793-5180
Yang, Jena CASEWKR 425-793-5180

Representative Adrian Smith

Nebraska, 3d

502 CANNON HOB (ZIP: 20515-2703) 225-6435

Didiuk, Monica CHIEF OF STAFF 502 CHOB 56435
Goulding, Matthew COMMUNICATIONS DIR 502 CHOB 56435
Jackson, Joshua LEGIS DIR 502 CHOB 56435
Keralis, Joel LEGIS ASST 502 CHOB 56435
Kuehn, Dillon STAFF ASST 502 CHOB 56435
Salter, Rebecca SCHEDULER 502 CHOB 56435
Stout, Doug LEGIS ASST 502 CHOB 56435

DISTRICT OFFICES

GRAND ISLAND—1811 W SECOND ST, SUITE 275, GRAND ISLAND, NE 68803

Atkins, Sallie LIAISON - AG 308-384-3900
Bogner, Michael CONSTIT SVCS REP 308-384-3900
Hoehne, Jena DIST DIR 308-384-3900
Hofer, Brian DIST STAFF ASST 308-384-3900
Reimers, Jerad COMMUNITY LIAISON 308-384-3900
Spencer, Jacy LIAISON - AG/COMMUNITY LIAISON 308-384-3900
Straatmann, Alex DIR - CONSTIT SVCS 308-384-3900

SCOTTSBLUFF—416 VALLEY VIEW DR, SUITE 600, SCOTTSBLUFF, NE 69361

Brotzman, Lenora OFFICE COORD 308-633-6333

Representative Christopher H. Smith

New Jersey, 4th

2373 RAYBURN HOB (ZIP: 20515-3004) 225-3765

Fellows, Courtney Webb SR LEGIS ASST 2373 53765
Griffin, Kristin FINANCIAL ADMIN 2373 53765
Griswold, Kelsey LEGIS DIR 2373 53765
Hadro, Matthew PRESS SECY 2373 53765
Hansell, Christopher LEGIS CORRES 2373 53765
Henniger, Christian STAFF ASST 2373 53765
Herman, Monica LEGIS ASST 2373 53765
Noonan, Mary McDermott CHIEF OF STAFF 2373 53765
Ryan, Angela EXEC SCHEDULER/OFFICE MGR 2373 53765
Tozzi, Piero COUNSEL 2373 53765

DISTRICT OFFICES

MERCER—4573 S BROAD ST, HAMILTON, NJ 08620-2215

Courtney, Jennifer SR CASEWKR 609-585-7878
Gomez, Nancy STAFF ASST 609-585-7878

Hollendonner, Jeffrey DIST DIR 609-585-7878
Wisniewski, Kathleen STAFF ASST 609-585-7878

MONMOUTH—112 VILLAGE CENTER DR, FREEHOLD, NJ 07728-2510

Morales, Jill SR CASEWKR 732-780-3035
Rohr, Jessica STAFF ASST/CASEWKR 732-780-3035
Schaufler, Lisa STAFF ASST/CASEWKR 732-780-3035
Schloeder, Jo DPTY CHIEF OF STAFF/DIST DIR 732-780-3035

OCEAN--BY APPOINTMENT—405 ROUTE 539, PLUMSTED, NJ 08514-2303

Courtney, Jennifer SR CASEWKR 732-350-2300
Hollendonner, Jeffrey Sagnip DIST DIR 609-585-7878

Representative Jason Smith

Missouri, 8th

2418 RAYBURN HOB (ZIP: 20515-2508) 225-4404

Blaine, Jarilyn DIGITAL DIR 2418 54404
Brown, Joey COMMUNICATIONS DIR 2418 54404
Burke, Sarah DIST DIR/DPTY CHIEF OF STAFF 2418 54404
Chakmak, Kathryn LEGIS ASST 2418 54404
Gradison, Andrew ADVISOR - HEALTH POLICY 2418 54404
Pinegar, Hilary LEGIS ASST 2418 54404
Roman, Mark CHIEF OF STAFF 2418 54404
Stallings, Marshall STAFF ASST 2418 54404

DISTRICT OFFICES

CAPE GIRARDEAU—2502 TANNER DR, SUITE 205, CAPE GIRARDEAU, MO 63703

Griffin, Deborah CONSTIT SVCS SPEC 573-335-0101
Herbst, Leslie CONSTIT SVCS SPEC/OFFICE MGR 573-335-0101
Middleton, John LEGIS CORRES 573-335-0101
Robins, Heath DIST REP 573-335-0101

FARMINGTON—22 E COLUMBIA ST, FARMINGTON, MO 63640

Hickman, Donna DIST OFFICE MGR 573-756-9755
Schoelhamer, Mike DIST FIELD REP 573-756-9755

POPLAR BLUFF—2725 N WESTWOOD BLVD, SUITE 5A, POPLAR BLUFF, MO 63901 573-609-2996

ROLLA—830A S BISHOP AVE, ROLLA, MO 65401

Cook, Bennie FIELD REP 573-364-2455
Riegel, Jenni MGR - CONSTIT SVCS 573-364-2455

WEST PLAINS—35 COURT SQUARE, SUITE 300, WEST PLAINS, MO 65775 417-255-1515

Representative Lloyd Smucker

Pennsylvania, 11th

127 CANNON HOB (ZIP: 20515-3811) 225-2411

Butler, Elizabeth ADMIN DIR 127 CHOB 52411
Eddowes, Chris LEGIS ASST 127 CHOB 52411
Facchiano, Greg CHIEF OF STAFF 127 CHOB 52411
Geiselhart, Mike LEGIS CORRES 127 CHOB 52411
Lloyd, Elizabeth STAFF ASST 127 CHOB 52411
Nielsen, Allison COMMUNICATIONS DIR 127 CHOB 52411
O'Connor, Mary ADMIN - FINANCE & PAYROLL 127 CHOB 52411
Robreno, Andrew LEGIS DIR 127 CHOB 52411
Verhelst, Noelle LEGIS ASST 127 CHOB 52411

DISTRICT OFFICES

HANOVER—118 CARLISLE ST, HANOVER, PA 17331 717-969-6132

LANCASTER—51 S DUKE ST, LANCASTER, PA 17602

Cammauf, Nick CASEWKR 717-393-0667
Fitzpatrick, Mike STAFF ASST 717-393-0667
Horn, Joanne CASEWK DIR 717-393-0667
Peirson, Zach DIST DIR 717-393-0667
Reath, Eric OUTREACH REP 717-393-0667

RED LION—100 REDCO AVE, RED LION, PA 17356

Taylor, Jake FIELD REP 717-969-6133

Representative Darren Soto

Florida, 9th

1507 LONGWORTH HOB (ZIP: 20515-0909) 225-9889

Biron, Christine CHIEF OF STAFF 1507 59889
Guerra, Liana DPTY CHIEF OF STAFF 1507 59889
McLaren, Nicole LEGIS COUNSEL 1507 59889
Nichola, Mike LEGIS DIR 1507 59889
Pina, Oriana COMMUNICATIONS DIR 1507 59889
Rivera, Martin LEGIS ASST 1507 59889
Rockwood, Bill LEGIS ASST 1507 59889

DISTRICT OFFICES

HAINES CITY—620 E MAIN ST, HAINES CITY, FL 33844 202-600-0843

KISSIMMEE—804 BRYAN ST, KISSIMMEE, FL 34741

Brooks, Tracy FIELD REP 407-452-1171
Martinez, Michelle DIST DIR 407-452-1171
Orama, Valerie FIELD REP 407-452-1171
Reyes, Dilenny DIST STAFF ASST 407-452-1171
Rodriguez, Vivian OUTREACH DIR 407-452-1171
Shaffer, Shasta CASEWK DIR 407-452-1171

LAKE WALES—201 W CENTRAL AVE, LAKE WALES, FL 33853

Vierday, Darren FIELD REP 202-600-0843

VETERAN'S AFFAIRS OFFICE—13800 VETERANS WAY, SUITE 1F806, ORLANDO, FL 32827 407-452-1171

WINTER HAVEN—451 3RD ST NW, WINTER HAVEN, FL 33881

West, Leah FIELD REP 202-615-1308

Representative Abigail Davis Spanberger

Virginia, 7th

1239 LONGWORTH HOB (ZIP: 20515-4607) 225-2815

Baker, Cole LEGIS CORRES 1239 52815
Carl, Emma SCHEDULER 1239 52815
Eichmann, Rebecca STAFF ASST 1239 52815
Janani, Maryam LEGIS DIR 1239 52815
Johannes, Sigrid PRESS ASST 1239 52815
Jones, Roscoe CHIEF OF STAFF 1239 52815
Joseph, Connor PRESS SECY 1239 52815
Krenz, Bonnie LEGIS ASST 1239 52815
Weiss, Bettina MGR - OPS 1239 52815

DISTRICT OFFICES

HENRICO—4201 DOMINION BLVD, SUITE 110, GLEN ALLEN, VA 23058-2306

Glenn, Courtney DIST COORD 804-401-4110
Mask, Karen DIST DIR 804-401-4110
Miller, MacKenzie DIST COORD 804-401-4110

SPOTSYLVANIA—9104 COURTHOUSE RD, ROOM 249, SPOTSYLVANIA, VA 22553-1902

Black, Kristi DIST COORD 540-321-6130

Representative Ross Spano

Florida, 15th

224 CANNON HOB (ZIP: 20515-0915) 225-1252

Ashton, Gus LEGIS DIR 224 CHOB 51252
Bedrosian, Scott DPTY CHIEF OF STAFF 224 CHOB 51252

Bucheli, Daniel COMMUNICATIONS DIR 224 CHOB 51252
Dever, Tyler STAFF ASST 224 CHOB 51252
Hilton, Naomi SCHEDULER 224 CHOB 51252
Robinette, Jamie CHIEF OF STAFF 224 CHOB 51252
Wright, Grace LEGIS CORRES 224 CHOB 51252
Wright, Logan GEN COUNSEL/LEGIS ASST 224 CHOB 51252

DISTRICT OFFICE

POLK COUNTY—124 S FLORIDA AVE, SUITE 304, LAKELAND, FL 33801

Gravitt, Blaine DIST DIR 863-644-8215
Jacobs, James CONSTIT RELATIONS 863-644-8215
Sebright, Taunia CONSTIT SVCS 863-644-8215
Surdin, Samantha FIELD REP 863-644-8215

Representative Jackie Speier

California, 14th

2465 RAYBURN HOB (ZIP: 20515-0514) **225-3531**
Boisseau, Anne-Marie LEGIS CORRES 2465 53531
Connolly, Josh CHIEF OF STAFF 2465 53531
Fishman, Molly LEGIS DIR 2465 53531
Galisewski, Ryan LEGIS ASST 2465 53531
Hochberg, Mitchel LEGIS ASST 2465 53531
Manzer, Tracy COMMUNICATIONS DIR 2465 53531
Musser, Alexandria LEGIS ASST 2465 53531
Small, Emily STAFF ASST 2465 53531

DISTRICT OFFICE

SAN MATEO—155 BOVET RD, SUITE 780, SAN MATEO, CA 94402

Nagales, Mark DIR - CONSTIT SVCS 650-342-0300
Perkins, Brian DIR - DIST AFFAIRS 650-342-0300
Rill, Katrina DIST PRESS SECY/DPTY DIST DIR 650-342-0300
Steffen, Richard SR ADVISOR 650-342-0300
Wentworth, Kathleen CASEWKR 650-342-0300

Representative Greg Stanton

Arizona, 9th

128 CANNON HOB (ZIP: 20515-0309) **225-9888**
Diederich, Anna LEGIS ASST 128 CHOB 59888
Ellison, Amber LEGIS CORRES 128 CHOB 59888
Guilbeau, Morgan STAFF ASST 128 CHOB 59888
Munoz Lopez, Laura LEGIS ASST 128 CHOB 59888
Pasteur, Nicole COMMUNICATIONS DIR/POLICY ADVISOR 128 CHOB 59888
Sutton, Tracee LEGIS DIR/DPTY CHIEF OF STAFF 128 CHOB ... 59888
Zafaranlou, Ashley EXEC ASST/MEDIA ASST 128 CHOB 59888

DISTRICT OFFICE

PHOENIX—2944 N 44TH ST, SUITE 150, PHOENIX, AZ 85018

Alvarez, DeAnna SR CASEWKR 602-956-2285
Chalmers, Eric SR DIST REP 602-956-2285
Dominguez, Rebecca STAFF ASST 602-956-2285
Sandigo, Larry POLICY ADVISOR 602-956-2285
Scott, Seth CHIEF OF STAFF/GEN COUNSEL 602-956-2285

Representative Pete Stauber

Minnesota, 8th

126 CANNON HOB (ZIP: 20515-2308) **225-6211**
Acornley, Mark FINANCIAL ADMIN 126 CHOB 56211
Bishop, Jeff LEGIS DIR 126 CHOB 56211
Esau, Allie LEGIS ASST 126 CHOB 56211
Kaardal, Sam STAFF ASST 126 CHOB 56211
Koetzle, Desiree CHIEF OF STAFF 126 CHOB 56211
Melbye, Linnea SCHEDULER 126 CHOB 56211
Mix, Kelsey COMMUNICATIONS DIR 126 CHOB 56211
Morley, Andrew LEGIS ASST 126 CHOB 56211
Tarwid, Caroline LEGIS CORRES 126 CHOB 56211

DISTRICT OFFICES

BRAINERD—501 LAUREL ST, BRAINERD, MN 56401

Crombie, Louis FIELD REP 218-355-0862

CAMBRIDGE—300 3RD AVE NE, CAMBRIDGE, MN 55008

Janssen, Miranda FIELD REP 763-552-3359

CHISHOLM—316 W LAKE ST, ROOM 7, CHISHOLM, MN 55719

Igo, Spencer FIELD REP 218-355-0726

HERMANTOWN—5094 MILLER TRUNK HWY, SUITE 900, HERMANTOWN, MN 55811

Cavanaugh, Margaret DIR - CONSTIT SVCS 218-481-6396
Eloranta, John DIR - GRANTS 218-481-6396
Haglin, Marilyn CASEWKR/OFFICE MGR 218-481-6396
Schultz, Isaac DIST DIR 218-481-6396

Representative Elise M. Stefanik

New York, 21st

318 CANNON HOB (ZIP: 20515-3221) **225-4611**
Anderson, Madison COMMUNICATIONS DIR 318 CHOB 54611
Angelotti, Julia LEGIS DIR 318 CHOB 54611
Cosci, Emily SCHEDULING DIR 318 CHOB 54611
DeGrasse, Alexander DIR - STRATEGIC COMMUNICATIONS 318 CHOB 54611
Hester, Patrick DPTY LEGIS DIR 318 CHOB 54611
Kum, Courtney LEGIS ASST - MIL 318 CHOB 54611
Mautz, James STAFF ASST 318 CHOB 54611
Nyce, Benjamin LEGIS CORRES 318 CHOB 54611
Pileggi, Anthony CHIEF OF STAFF 318 CHOB 54611
Shefchik, Cheryl MIL FELLOW 318 CHOB 54611

DISTRICT OFFICES

GLENS FALLS—5 WARREN ST, SUITE 4, GLENS FALLS, NY 12801

Boucher, Taylor CONSTIT LIAISON 518-743-0964
Ostrander, Michael DIST DIR 518-743-0964

PLATTSBURGH—23 DURKEE ST, SUITE C, PLATTSBURGH, NY 12901

Carman, Jonathan CONSTIT LIAISON 518-561-2324
Wood, Joel REGIONAL DIR 518-561-2324

WATERTOWN—88 PUBLIC SQUARE, SUITE A, WATERTOWN, NY 13601

Richards, Mary Jo REGIONAL DIR 315-782-3150
Shaver, Jacob STAFF ASST 315-782-3150

Representative Bryan Steil

Wisconsin, 1st

1408 LONGWORTH HOB (ZIP: 20515-4901) **225-3031**
Brown, Matthew DIR - OPS & PLANNING 1408 53031
Carney, Ryan CHIEF OF STAFF 1408 53031
Davis, Charlotte LEGIS ASST 1408 53031
Fox, Sally COMMUNICATIONS DIR 1408 53031
Goldfarb, David LEGIS DIR 1408 53031
Langnes, James STAFF ASST 1408 53031
Neitzel, William LEGIS CORRES 1408 53031

DISTRICT OFFICES

JANESVILLE—20 S MAIN ST, JANESVILLE, WI 53545

Cullum, Rebekah CONSTIT SVCS 608-752-4050

Farnsworth, Brandon DIR - OPS & PLANNING 608-752-4050
Iverson, Andrew SPECIAL ASST 608-752-4050
Mora, Teresa DIR - OUTREACH & MEMB SVCS 608-752-4050
Zipperer, Richard CHIEF OF STAFF 608-752-4050

KENOSHA COUNTY—7511 12TH ST, SOMERS, WI 53171 262-654-1901

RACINE—RACINE COUNTY COURTHOUSE, ROOM 101, 730 WISCONSIN AVE, RACINE, WI 53403 262-637-0510

Representative W. Gregory Steube

Florida, 17th

521 CANNON HOB (ZIP: 20515-0917) **225-5792**
Blair, Alex CHIEF OF STAFF 521 CHOB 55792
Cirenza, Gabrielle SCHEDULER 521 CHOB 55792
Clark, Elena LEGIS CORRES 521 CHOB 55792
Darby, Reginald LEGIS DIR 521 CHOB 55792
Kim-Hummel, Justin LEGIS AIDE 521 CHOB 55792
Lester, Dean ADMIN - FINANCE & PAYROLL 521 CHOB 55792
Patel, Twinkle SR LEGIS ASST 521 CHOB 55792
Tamayo, Justin LEGIS COUNSEL 521 CHOB 55792

DISTRICT OFFICES

OKEECHOBEE—304 NW 2ND ST, ROOM 105, OKEECHOBEE, FL 34972 863-402-9082

PUNTA GORDA—226 TAYLOR ST, NO. 200, PUNTA GORDA, FL 33950
Bolles, Libby DPTY DIST DIR 941-575-9101
Gruters, Sydney DIST DIR 941-575-9101
Vient, Darla CASEWKR 941-575-9101

SEBRING—4507 GEORGE BLVD, SEBRING, FL 33875 863-402-9082

Representative Haley M. Stevens

Michigan, 11th

227 CANNON HOB (ZIP: 20515-2211) **225-8171**
Aiken, Hannah LEGIS ASST 227 CHOB 58171
Denoyer, Casey LEGIS ASST 227 CHOB 58171
German, Justin CHIEF OF STAFF 227 CHOB 58171
Greenlee, Brendan STAFF ASST 227 CHOB 58171
Martin, John SCHEDULER 227 CHOB 58171
McCarren, Blake PRESS SECY 227 CHOB 58171
Reddy, Sanjay LEGIS CORRES 227 CHOB 58171
Reingold, Sarah LEGIS DIR 227 CHOB 58171

DISTRICT OFFICE

LIVONIA—37695 PEMBROKE AVE, LIVONIA, MI 48152
Isaguirre, Eli DPTY DIST DIR 734-853-3040
Pobur, Colleen DIST DIR 734-853-3040
Rich, Zach CASEWKR 734-853-3040
Tash, Michael CASEWK MGR 734-853-3040

Representative Chris Stewart

Utah, 2d

2242 RAYBURN HOB (ZIP: 20515-4402) **225-9730**
Coffield, Mark EXEC ASST/SCHEDULER 2242 59730
Griffiths, Luci LEGIS ASST 2242 59730
Madsen, Cam LEGIS DIR 2242 59730
Maloy, Celeste COUNSEL 2242 59730
Parkinson, Rachel CONSTIT SVCS 2242 59730
Shupe, Madi COMMUNICATIONS DIR 2242 59730
White, Clay CHIEF OF STAFF 2242 59730

DISTRICT OFFICES

SALT LAKE CITY—420 E SOUTH TEMPLE ST, NO. 390, SALT LAKE CITY, UT 84111
Hunsaker, Abigail DIR - CONSTIT AFFAIRS 801-364-5550
Perkes, Rhonda FIELD REP 801-364-5550
Webster, Gary DIST DIR 801-364-5550

ST. GEORGE—253 W ST. GEORGE BLVD, SUITE 100, ST. GEORGE, UT 84770
Snow, Adam DPTY DIST DIR 435-627-1500

Representative Steve Stivers

Ohio, 15th

2234 RAYBURN HOB (ZIP: 20515-3515) **225-2015**
Bair, Mimi LEGIS ASST 2234 52015
Bush, Nick LEGIS DIR/DPTY CHIEF OF STAFF 2234 52015
Dodge, Barbara FINANCIAL ADMIN 2234 52015
Gilbride, Mark LEGIS ASST/DPTY LEGIS DIR 2234 52015
Graham, AnnMarie COMMUNICATIONS ASST/PRESS ASST 2234 52015
Hancock, Hannah COMMUNICATIONS ASST 2234 52015
Hatter, Drew LEGIS CORRES/LEGIS AIDE 2234 52015
MacMann, Julie STAFF ASST 2234 52015
Whetstone, Courtney CHIEF OF STAFF 2234 52015

DISTRICT OFFICES

COLUMBUS—3790 MUNICIPAL WAY, HILLIARD, OH 43026
Donlon, Sara SCHEDULER/DIR - OPS 614-771-4968
Slane, Adam SR CASEWKR 614-771-4968

LANCASTER—104 E MAIN ST, LANCASTER, OH 43130
Enochs, Chase STAFF ASST/FIELD REP 740-654-2654
Lloyd, William FIELD REP 740-654-2654
Meyer, Branden LIAISON - MIL 740-654-2654
Stiverson, Brittany CASEWORK - VETS 740-654-2654

WILMINGTON—69 N SOUTH ST, WILMINGTON, OH 45177
Stuckert, Sherry CASEWKR 937-283-7049

Representative Thomas R. Suozzi

New York, 3d

214 CANNON HOB (ZIP: 20515-3203) **225-3335**
Bhargava, Jay PRESS SECY 214 CHOB 53335
Christesen, Michael STAFF ASST 214 CHOB 53335
Ciampa, Deane LEGIS CORRES 214 CHOB 53335
Dakheel, Lina LEGIS ASST/ADVISOR - FOREIGN POLICY 214 CHOB 53335
Hupper, Dani LEGIS AIDE/DC SCHEDULER 214 CHOB 53335
Moore, Shane MGR - PAYROLL & BENEFITS 214 CHOB 53335
Shust, Diane DPTY CHIEF OF STAFF/LEGIS DIR 214 CHOB 53335
Walsh, Conor LEGIS ASST 214 CHOB 53335

DISTRICT OFFICES

HUNTINGTON—478A PARK AVE, HUNTINGTON, NY 11743
Anderson, Emily CASEWKR - IMMIGRATION 631-923-4100
Bhalla, Ratina CASEWK MGR 631-923-4100
Davidson, Betsy PRESS ASST 631-923-4100
DiGnan, Mariah Caitlin DIST SCHEDULER/LEGIS AIDE 631-923-4100
Felt, Nicholas FIELD REP 631-923-4100
Florio, Michael CHIEF OF STAFF 631-923-4100
Geller, Matt CASEWORK - VETS 631-923-4100
Rogers, Cindy DIST DIR 631-923-4100

QUEENS—250-02 NORTHERN BLVD, LITTLE NECK, NY 11362
Connor, Justin FIELD REP/DPTY DIST DIR 718-631-0400

Representative Eric Swalwell

California, 15th

407 CANNON HOB (ZIP: 20515-0515) **225-5065**
Adesina, Adeola LEGIS ASST 407 CHOB **55065**
Elkins, Olivia SCHEDULER 407 CHOB **55065**
Ginsburg, Andrew LEGIS DIR 407 CHOB **55065**
Keosian, Chris ASST LEGIS CORRES 407 CHOB **55065**
McNamee, Cait PRESS SECY 407 CHOB **55065**
Miller, Jonathan LEGIS ASST 407 CHOB **55065**
Motta, Art LEGIS ASST 407 CHOB **55065**
Olivas, Celia STAFF ASST 407 CHOB **55065**
Reed, Michael CHIEF OF STAFF 407 CHOB **55065**

DISTRICT OFFICE

CASTRO VALLEY—3615 CASTRO VALLEY BLVD, CASTRO VALLEY, CA 94546
DeLauro, Mallory DIST DIR/ADVISOR - FOREIGN POLICY **510-370-3322**
Martin, Amanda CONSTIT SVCS REP **510-370-3322**
Miller, Scott CONSTIT SVCS REP **510-370-3322**
Mora, Edward CONSTIT SVCS REP **510-370-3322**
Richman, Josh COMMUNICATIONS DIR **510-370-3322**
Tragni, Lina DIST OFFICE MGR/DIST SCHEDULER **510-370-3322**
Tucker, Phil FIELD REP/CASEWKR **510-370-3322**

Representative Mark Takano

California, 41st

420 CANNON HOB (ZIP: 20515-0541) **225-2305**
Beckelman, Yuri DPTY CHIEF OF STAFF 420 CHOB **52305**
Castro, Adrienne LEGIS ASST 420 CHOB **52305**
Ceja, Matthew LEGIS CORRES 420 CHOB **52305**
Courchene, Brien LEGIS AIDE 420 CHOB **52305**
Maturo, Justin LEGIS DIR 420 CHOB **52305**
McPike, Richard CHIEF OF STAFF 420 CHOB **52305**
O'Neal, Whitley SR LEGIS ASST 420 CHOB **52305**
Ramirez, Dayanara COMMUNICATIONS DIR 420 CHOB **52305**
Wroten, Desiree SCHEDULER/EXEC ASST 420 CHOB **52305**

DISTRICT OFFICE

RIVERSIDE—3403 10TH ST, SUITE 610, RIVERSIDE, CA 92501
Abbasi, Lana PRESS SECY **951-222-0203**
Alvarez, Tiffany FIELD REP **951-222-0203**
Elizalde, Rafael DIST DIR **951-222-0203**
Ling, Melanie CONSTIT SVCS REP **951-222-0203**
Romero, Ignacio CASEWK MGR **951-222-0203**

Representative Van Taylor

Texas, 3d

1404 LONGWORTH HOB (ZIP: 20515-4303) **225-4201**
Blankenship, April FINANCIAL ADMIN 1404 .... **54201**
Dietz, Lonnie CHIEF OF STAFF 1404 .... **54201**
Lyon, Laura SR LEGIS ASST 1404 .... **54201**
Perdichizzi, Gabriela LEGIS ASST 1404 .... **54201**
Pflieger, Charles STAFF ASST 1404 .... **54201**
Stoner, Hunter SCHEDULER 1404 .... **54201**
Thompson, Jett LEGIS DIR 1404 .... **54201**
Vetter, Anna COMMUNICATIONS DIR 1404 .... **54201**

DISTRICT OFFICE

PLANO—5600 TENNYSON PKWY, NO. 275, PLANO, TX 75024
Coleman-Jones, Sable DIST DIR **972-202-4150**
Laman, Denise SR CONSTIT SVCS REP **972-202-4150**
Moore, Cole FIELD REP **972-202-4150**
Pate, Gabriella DIR - COMMUNITY OUTREACH **972-202-4150**
Smith, Maggie SR CONSTIT SVCS REP **972-202-4150**

Representative Bennie G. Thompson

Mississippi, 2d

2466 RAYBURN HOB (ZIP: 20515-2402) **225-5876**
Henderson, Claytrice LEGIS ASST 2466 .... **55876**
James, Ty PRESS SECY/LEGIS ASST 2466 .... **55876**
Lee, Andrea CHIEF OF STAFF/SCHEDULER 2466 .... **55876**
Shoulders, Meco LEGIS CORRES/STAFF ASST 2466 .... **55876**

DISTRICT OFFICES

BOLTON—P.O. BOX 610, 107 W MADISON ST, BOLTON, MS 39041
TOLL-FREE NUMBER **1-800-355-9003**
Booker, Stephanie CASEWKR/FIELD REP **601-866-9003**
Cowan, Tonia EXEC ASST **601-866-9003**
Funches, Brenda CASEWKR/FIELD REP **601-866-9003**
Key-Shinard, Jean DIST SCHEDULER **601-866-9003**
Owen, Nekia EXEC SECY/FINANCIAL ADMIN **601-866-9003**
Ware, Fannie DIST DIR **601-866-9003**

GREENVILLE—910 COURTHOUSE LANE REAR, GREENVILLE, MS 38701
Beale, Ashley CASEWKR/FIELD REP **662-335-9003**
Washington, Timla COORD - COMMUNITY OUTREACH **662-335-9003**

GREENWOOD—509 HWY 82 W, GREENWOOD, MS 38930
Moore, Reginald FIELD REP/CASEWKR **662-455-9003**

JACKSON—3607 MEDGAR EVERS BLVD, JACKSON, MS 39213
Gavin, Stephen SR CASEWKR **601-946-9003**

MARKS—263 E MAIN ST, MARKS, MS 38646
Jamison, Sandra FIELD REP/CASEWKR **662-326-9003**

MOUND BAYOU—MOUND BAYOU CITY HALL, ROOM 134, 106 W GREEN ST, MOUND BAYOU, MS 38762
Watkins, Cedric CASEWKR/FIELD REP **662-741-9003**

Representative Glenn Thompson

Pennsylvania, 15th

400 CANNON HOB (ZIP: 20515-3815) **225-5121**
Brennan, Matthew CHIEF OF STAFF 400 CHOB **55121**
Busovsky, John LEGIS DIR 400 CHOB **55121**
Durst, Jacob STAFF ASST 400 CHOB **55121**
Gamela, Renee COMMUNICATIONS DIR 400 CHOB **55121**
Mulcahey, Chris LEGIS CORRES 400 CHOB **55121**
Nulty, Scott SR LEGIS ASST 400 CHOB **55121**
Rockwell, Nick LEGIS ASST 400 CHOB **55121**
Shaw, Jacqui STAFF ASST 400 CHOB **55121**
Stechschulte, Alissa SCHEDULER/OFFICE MGR 400 CHOB **55121**

DISTRICT OFFICES

BELLEFONTE—3555 BENNER PIKE, SUITE 101, BELLEFONTE, PA 16823
Bickel, Heather CASEWKR **814-353-0215**
Dubbs, Andrea SR CASEWKR/DIST OFFICE MGR **814-353-0215**
Kunes, Cindy DIST SCHEDULER **814-353-0215**

EBENSBURG—107 S CENTER ST, EBENSBURG, PA 15931
Subich, Brian FIELD REP **814-419-8583**
Verobish, Andrea DIST STAFF ASST **814-419-8583**

OIL CITY—217 ELM ST, SUITE B, OIL CITY, PA 16301
Ives, Barbara SR CASEWKR **814-670-0432**

Moore, Brad DIST DIR 814-670-0432
Pontzer, Deborah ECON DEV SPEC 814-670-0432

Representative Mike Thompson

California, 5th

406 CANNON HOB (ZIP: 20515-0505) 225-3311
Bentham, Nate LEGIS ASST 406 CHOB 53311
Connor, Crozer LEGIS ASST 406 CHOB 53311
Dodge, Suzanne FELLOW 406 CHOB 53311
Goedke, Jennifer DPTY CHIEF OF STAFF/LEGIS DIR 406 CHOB 53311
Golding, Ishaan SCHEDULER 406 CHOB 53311
MacFarlane, Alex COMMUNICATIONS DIR 406 CHOB 53311
Ornstein, Nick LEGIS CORRES 406 CHOB 53311
Rhinehart Van Tassell, Melanie CHIEF OF STAFF 406 CHOB 53311
Stevens, Kim FINANCIAL ADMIN 406 CHOB 53311
Wheatley, Miriam SR COUNSEL 406 CHOB 53311
Wysocky, Jess STAFF ASST 406 CHOB 53311
Zirngibl, Wendy FELLOW 406 CHOB 53311

DISTRICT OFFICES

NAPA—2721 NAPA VALLEY CORPORATE DR, NAPA, CA 94558
Ayala, Maira DIST REP 707-226-9898
Chang, Shao CONSTIT SVCS REP 707-226-9898
Onorato, Brad DPTY CHIEF OF STAFF 707-226-9898

SANTA ROSA—2300 COUNTY CENTER DR, SUITE A100, SANTA ROSA, CA 95403
Gale, Stephen DIST REP 707-542-7182
Hermosillo, Rebecca SR FIELD REP 707-542-7182
Plaugher, Joe FIELD REP 707-542-7182

VALLEJO—420 VIRGINIA ST, SUITE 1C, VALLEJO, CA 94590
Orpilla, Mel SR DIST REP 707-645-1888
Roberts, Becca CONSTIT SVCS REP 707-645-1888
Young, Cora DIST FIELD REP/LIAISON - VETS 707-645-1888

Representative Mac Thornberry

Texas, 13th

2208 RAYBURN HOB (ZIP: 20515-4313) 225-3706
Hunter, Jordan COMMUNICATIONS DIR 2208 53706
Link, Adam MIL FELLOW 2208 53706
Martin, Josh CHIEF OF STAFF 2208 53706
Patel, Kamal LEGIS ASST 2208 53706
Seeds, Michael LEGIS DIR/DPTY CHIEF OF STAFF 2208 53706
Stagno, Laura STAFF ASST 2208 53706
Sunday, Jessica EXEC ASST 2208 53706

DISTRICT OFFICES

AMARILLO—620 S TAYLOR ST, SUITE 200, AMARILLO, TX 79101
Barber, Danelle CONSTIT SVCS REP 806-371-8844
Kalka, Melissa CONSTIT SVCS REP 806-371-8844
Pool, Caleb DIST REP 806-371-8844
Simpson, Paul DPTY DIST DIR 806-371-8844

WICHITA FALLS—2525 KELL BLVD, SUITE 406, WICHITA FALLS, TX 76308
Lytle, Michael CONSTIT SVCS REP 940-692-1700
Ross, Sandra DIST DIR 940-692-1700

Representative William R. Timmons IV

South Carolina, 4th

313 CANNON HOB (ZIP: 20515-4004) 225-6030
Brown, Dan LEGIS CORRES 313 CHOB 56030
Goodwin, Joshua COMMUNICATIONS DIR 313 CHOB 56030
McLaren, Moutray CHIEF OF STAFF 313 CHOB 56030
Partin, John LEGIS ASST 313 CHOB 56030
Ranieri, Hilary LEGIS DIR 313 CHOB 56030
Smith, Cameron LEGIS CORRES 313 CHOB 56030
Widenhouse, Olivia SCHEDULER 313 CHOB 56030

DISTRICT OFFICES

GREENVILLE—104 S MAIN ST, SUITE 801, GREENVILLE, SC 29601
Blackley, Hope DIST DIR 864-241-0175
Burns, Mike SR ADVISOR 864-241-0175
Stahl, Mike SR ADVISOR 864-241-0175
Turner, Kam COORD - GRANTS 864-241-0175

SPARTANBURG—101 W ST. JOHN ST, SUITE 303, SPARTANBURG, SC 29306
Blanton, Seth DIR - CONSTIT SVCS 864-583-3264
Gault, Freddie DIR - OUTREACH & MEMB SVCS 864-583-3264

Representative Scott R. Tipton

Colorado, 3d

218 CANNON HOB (ZIP: 20515-0603) 225-4761
Atwood, Matthew PRESS SECY 218 CHOB 54761
Babine, Olivia LEGIS CORRES 218 CHOB 54761
Green, Joshua CHIEF OF STAFF 218 CHOB 54761
Pardal, Agustina SCHEDULER/FINANCIAL ADMIN 218 CHOB 54761
Payne, Liz LEGIS DIR 218 CHOB 54761
Riggs, Ezra STAFF ASST 218 CHOB 54761
Smith, Jackson LEGIS ASST 218 CHOB 54761
Williams, Evan LEGIS ASST 218 CHOB 54761

DISTRICT OFFICES

ALAMOSA—609 MAIN ST, NO. 105, BOX 11, ALAMOSA, CO 81101
Felmlee, Brenda FIELD REP 719-587-5105

DURANGO—835 E SECOND AVE, SUITE 230, DURANGO, CO 81301
Greco, Ashley DIST FIELD REP 970-259-1490

GRAND JUNCTION—225 N 5TH ST, SUITE 702, GRAND JUNCTION, CO 81501
Bainer, Brandon CASEWKR 970-241-2499
Rossman, George FIELD REP 970-241-2499

PUEBLO—503 N MAIN ST, SUITE 658, PUEBLO, CO 81003
Fitzgerald, Doug CASEWKR/DIST FIELD REP/REGIONAL DIR 719-542-1073
McCain, Brian DIST DIR 719-542-1073

Representative Dina Titus

Nevada, 1st

2464 RAYBURN HOB (ZIP: 20515-2801) 225-5965
Chrobak, Catherine LEGIS CORRES 2464 55965
Gerson, Kevin COMMUNICATIONS DIR 2464 55965
Gertsema, Jay CHIEF OF STAFF 2464 55965
Godinez, Christine LEGIS ASST 2464 55965
Hearin, Colleen SCHEDULER/EXEC ASST 2464 55965
Riordan, Erica LEGIS ASST 2464 55965
Rosenbaum, Ben LEGIS DIR/DPTY CHIEF OF STAFF 2464 55965

DISTRICT OFFICE

LAS VEGAS—495 S MAIN ST, 3RD FLOOR, LAS VEGAS, NV 89101
Cain, Hunter DIR - COMMUNITY OUTREACH/DIST REP 702-220-9823
Care, Terry CASEWKR 702-220-9823
Farray, Susy STAFF ASST 702-220-9823
Munoz, Cassandra CASEWKR 702-220-9823
Quintanilla, Ana DIR - CONSTIT AFFAIRS/DIST REP 702-220-9823

Spotleson, Vinny DIST DIR 702-220-9823
Valdez, Craig OUTREACH SPEC/STAFF ASST 702-220-9823

Representative Rashida Tlaib

Michigan, 13th

1628 LONGWORTH HOB (ZIP: 20515-2213) 225-5126
Anderson, Ryan CHIEF OF STAFF 1628 55126
Dubad, Arwa STAFF ASST 1628 55126
Maaiki, Sara SCHEDULER/OFFICE MGR 1628 55126
Murphy, Chastity LEGIS ASST 1628 55126
Salazar, Adrienne PRESS SECY 1628 55126
Warren, Dominique LEGIS DIR 1628 55126

DISTRICT OFFICES

DETROIT CENTRAL—7700 2ND AVE, DETROIT, MI 48202
Arbulu, Oscar CASEWKR 313-463-6220
Goddeeris, Andrew COUNSEL 313-463-6220
Joyce, Annetta CASEWKR 313-463-6220
Kaye, Amanda DIST SCHEDULER 313-463-6220
McCampbell, Denzel COMMUNICATIONS DIR 313-463-6220
Richardson, Larissa DIST DIR 313-463-6220
Tencer, Lisa CASEWKR 313-463-6220

DETROIT EAST—4401 CONNOR ST, DETROIT, MI 48215 313-550-4649

DOWN RIVER—10600 W JEFFERSON, 2ND FLOOR, RIVER ROUGE, MI 48218
Turner, Mary CASEWKR 313-203-7540

Representative Paul Tonko

New York, 20th

2369 RAYBURN HOB (ZIP: 20515-3220) 225-5076
Britt, Clinton CHIEF OF STAFF 2369 55076
Greenberg, Katie LEGIS CORRES 2369 55076
Larkin, Brendan SR POLICY ADVISOR 2369 55076
Laverdiere, Maria EXEC DIR 2369 55076
Mastrangelo, David DIR - OPS 2369 55076
Morgan, Jeff LEGIS DIR 2369 55076
Silverberg, Emily SR LEGIS ASST 2369 55076
Sonneborn, Matt COMMUNICATIONS DIR 2369 55076
Teebi, Noor LEGIS ASST 2369 55076
Whittaker, Larry SYS ADMIN 2369 55076

DISTRICT OFFICES

ALBANY—19 DOVE ST, SUITE 302, ALBANY, NY 12210
Bennett, Diana DIST COORD 518-465-0700
Dunn, Katie FIELD REP 518-465-0700
Prime, Max CONG AIDE 518-465-0700
Smith, Marilyn ECON DEV REP 518-465-0700
Williams, Colleen DIST DIR 518-465-0700

AMSTERDAM—61 CHURCH ST, ROOM 309, AMSTERDAM, NY 12010
Quist-Demars, Kelly CONSTIT REP 518-843-3400

SCHENECTADY—105 JAY ST, ROOM 15, SCHENECTADY, NY 12305
Schroeter, Cora DIR - CONSTIT SVCS/DIST OFFICE MGR 518-374-4547

Representative Norma J. Torres

California, 35th

2444 RAYBURN HOB (ZIP: 20515-0535) 225-6161
Boggs, Clay LEGIS DIR 2444 56161
Bonilla, Veronica PRESS SECY 2444 56161
Carey, Leah DC SCHEDULER/OFFICE MGR 2444 56161
Carray, Mariah LEGIS ASST 2444 56161
Cho, James CHIEF OF STAFF 2444 56161
Murphy, Kelly FINANCIAL ADMIN 2444 56161
Pickney, Janna SHARED EMPLOYEE 2444 56161
Rodriguez, Edgar DPTY PRESS SECY 2444 56161
Vazquez, Maru STAFF ASST 2444 56161
Wellen, Sophie LEGIS CORRES 2444 56161

DISTRICT OFFICE

ONTARIO—3200 INLAND EMPIRE BLVD, SUITE 200B, ONTARIO, CA 91764
Enz, Daniel DIST DIR 909-481-6474
Guerra, Marisol DPTY DIST DIR 909-481-6474
Leyba, Julie FIELD REP 909-481-6474
Marquez, Denise DIST SCHEDULER 909-481-6474
Ramos, Mario FIELD REP/CASEWKR 909-481-6474
Trujillo, Rafael CASE MGR 909-481-6474

Representative Xochitl Torres Small

New Mexico, 2d

430 CANNON HOB (ZIP: 20515-3102) 225-2365
Galvis-Delgado, Felipe LEGIS ASST 430 CHOB 52365
Holdridge, Rachelle LEGIS CORRES 430 CHOB 52365
Jackson, Jake LEGIS ASST 430 CHOB 52365
Lee, Jenn PRESS SECY/DIGITAL DIR 430 CHOB 52365
Munoz, Rene CHIEF OF STAFF 430 CHOB 52365
Sowyrda, Brian DPTY CHIEF/COMMUNICATIONS DIR 430 CHOB 52365
Stuedell, Brooke LEGIS DIR 430 CHOB 52365
Tapia, Edna SCHEDULER 430 CHOB 52365

DISTRICT OFFICES

CARLSBAD—101 N HALAGUENO, CARLSBAD, NM 88220
McCarty, Cody DIST FIELD REP/CASEWKR 575-323-6384

LAS CRUCES—240 S WATER ST, LAS CRUCES, NM 88001
Beyer, Ashley FIELD REP 575-323-6384
Valdez, Nayomi DIST DIR 575-323-6384

ROSWELL—1717 W. SECOND ST., ROSWELL, NM 88201
Luna, Eli CASEWKR 575-323-6384

VALENCIA—719 S MAIN ST, BELEN, NM 87002
Anaya, Libby CASEWKR 575-323-6384
Otero, Simon CASEWKR 575-323-6384

Representative Lori Trahan

Massachusetts, 3d

1616 LONGWORTH HOB (ZIP: 20515-2103) 225-3411
Carlton, Ron LEGIS DIR 1616 53411
Degou, Lisa SCHEDULER 1616 53411
Hamilton, Ryan CASEWKR 1616 53411
Karabatsos, Alex LEGIS CORRES 1616 53411
Lim, Woo LEGIS ASST 1616 53411
McDevitt, Mark COMMUNICATIONS DIR 1616 53411
Molt-West, Alicia CHIEF OF STAFF 1616 53411
Villalvazo, Jose LEGIS ASST 1616 53411

DISTRICT OFFICE

LOWELL—126 JOHN ST, SUITE 12, LOWELL, MA 01852
Bart, Jackie DPTY CHIEF OF STAFF 978-459-0101
Byrne, Emily DIST DIR 978-459-0101
Gallagher, Meaghan DIST STAFF ASST 978-459-0101
Grosky, Gretchen PRESS SECY 978-459-0101

Keene, Sarah REGIONAL DIR 978-459-0101
Khun Leng, Sara DIR - CONSTIT SVCS 978-459-0101
Saldana, Vladimir REGIONAL DIR 978-459-0101
Thibodeau, Joe REGIONAL DIR 978-459-0101

Representative David J. Trone

Maryland, 6th

1213 LONGWORTH HOB (ZIP: 20515-2006) **225-2721**
Flick, Andy CHIEF OF STAFF 1213 .... **52721**
Kosova, Elly STAFF ASST 1213 .... **52721**
Muldavin, Hannah COMMUNICATIONS DIR 1213 .... **52721**
Parker, Sydney STAFF ASST 1213 .... **52721**
Segmen, Cortney LEGIS ASST 1213 .... **52721**
Semachko, Jessica LEGIS ASST 1213 .... **52721**
Sparling, Jeri DIR - OPS 1213 .... **52721**
Tsafoulias, Christina LEGIS DIR 1213 .... **52721**

DISTRICT OFFICES

GAITHERSBURG—9801 WASHINGTONIAN BLVD, SUITE 330, GAITHERSBURG, MD 20878
Ainge, Caitlin FIELD REP **301-926-0300**
Donlon, Andrew FIELD REP **301-926-0300**
Donoghue, Taylor SR FIELD REP **301-926-0300**
Glaser, Megan STAFF ASST **301-926-0300**
Holding, Sonny DIST DIR **301-926-0300**
Riley, Regan FIELD REP **301-926-0300**
Roth, Sarah STAFF ASST **301-926-0300**

HAGERSTOWN—1850 DUAL HWY, UNIT 101, HAGERSTOWN, MD 21740 301-926-0300

Representative Michael R. Turner

Ohio, 10th

2082 RAYBURN HOB (ZIP: 20515-3510) **225-6465**
Calcagni, Michael LEGIS ASST - MIL 2082 .... **56465**
Di Palma, Mason STAFF & PRESS ASST 2082 .... **56465**
Donches, Michelle MGR - BUDGET 2082 .... **56465**
Hare, Dan SR LEGIS ASST 2082 .... **56465**
Holman, Regina DIST REP 2082 .... **56465**
Howard, Adam CHIEF OF STAFF 2082 .... **56465**
Mann, Nikita LEGIS ASST - MIL 2082 .... **56465**
Molina, James LEGIS CORRES 2082 .... **56465**
Pietkiewicz, Kate SCHEDULER 2082 .... **56465**
Rako, Morgan PRESS SECY 2082 .... **56465**
Wilson, Jeffrey LEGIS DIR 2082 .... **56465**

DISTRICT OFFICE

DAYTON—120 W 3RD ST, SUITE 305, DAYTON, OH 45402-1819
DeBrosse, Frank DIST DIR **937-225-2843**
Douglas, Daniel DIST STAFF ASST **937-225-2843**
Harrah, Angie CASEWKR **937-225-2843**
Heide, Marty SPECIAL EVENTS DIR/CONSTIT OUTREACH REP **937-225-2843**
Saunders, Eugene DIST STAFF ASST **937-225-2843**
Vaughn, Bill DIST FIELD REP **937-225-2843**

Representative Lauren Underwood

Illinois, 14th

1118 LONGWORTH HOB (ZIP: 20515-1314) **225-2976**
Clayton, Ashley SCHEDULER/DIST SCHEDULER 1118 .... **52976**
Harris, Andrea CHIEF OF STAFF 1118 .... **52976**
Hartman, Kirsten DPTY CHIEF OF STAFF - COMMUNICATIONS 1118 .... **52976**
Paris-Behr, Caroline SR POLICY ADVISOR 1118 .... **52976**
Renteria, Alejandro LEGIS DIR 1118 .... **52976**
Walker, Quristin STAFF ASST 1118 .... **52976**

DISTRICT OFFICE

WEST CHICAGO—490 E ROOSEVELT RD, SUITE 202, WEST CHICAGO, IL 60185
Girmscheid, Jake DIST STAFF ASST **630-549-2190**
Muhammad, Jacqui DIST MGR **630-549-2190**

Representative Fred Upton

Michigan, 6th

2183 RAYBURN HOB (ZIP: 20515-2206) **225-3761**
Bailey, Don FINANCIAL ADMIN 2183 .... **53761**
DeMarco, Stephanie LEGIS ASST 2183 .... **53761**
Herron, Angela LEGIS CORRES/PRESS ASST 2183 .... **53761**
Hillebrands, Joan CHIEF OF STAFF 2183 .... **53761**
Huyen, Thanh APPLICA SYS ADMIN 2183 .... **53761**
Johnson, Ingrid STAFF ASST/DIST SCHEDULER 2183 .... **53761**
Moffitt, Katherine SR LEGIS ASST 2183 .... **53761**
Paciorek, Josh COMMUNICATIONS DIR 2183 .... **53761**
Ratner, Mark LEGIS DIR/DPTY CHIEF OF STAFF 2183 .... **53761**
Scruggs, Suzanne SCHEDULER 2183 .... **53761**

DISTRICT OFFICES

KALAMAZOO—350 E MICHIGAN AVE, SUITE 130, KALAMAZOO, MI 49007
Dillon, Chad CONSTIT SVCS REP **269-385-0039**
Fitzpatrick, Mitzi CONSTIT SVCS REP **269-385-0039**
Henschel, Nate DIST REP **269-385-0039**
Marquis, Nivia CONSTIT SVCS REP **269-385-0039**

ST. JOSEPH—720 MAIN ST, ST. JOSEPH, MI 49085
Hansen, Corey CONSTIT SVCS REP **269-982-1986**
Ryan, Michael DIST REP **269-982-1986**
Zielke, Janet SR CONSTIT SVCS REP **269-982-1986**

Representative Jefferson Van Drew

New Jersey, 2d

331 CANNON HOB (ZIP: 20515-3002) **225-6572**
Gamboa, Javier LEGIS DIR 331 CHOB **56572**
Kaczmarski, Edward DPTY CHIEF OF STAFF 331 CHOB **56572**
Lucas, Mackenzie COMMUNICATIONS DIR 331 CHOB **56572**
Murphy, Allison CHIEF OF STAFF 331 CHOB **56572**
O'Leary, Justin DPTY CHIEF OF STAFF 331 CHOB **56572**
Wood, Caroline LEGIS ASST 331 CHOB **56572**

DISTRICT OFFICE

MAYS LANDING—5914 MAIN ST, SUITE 103, MAYS LANDING, NJ 08330
Dhyne, Noel EXEC ASST **609-625-5008**
Doherty, CeCe DIR - CONSTIT SVCS **609-625-5008**
Kirk, John DIST DIR **609-625-5008**
Pinkett, Durwood CASEWK DIR **609-625-5008**

Representative Juan Vargas

California, 51st

2244 RAYBURN HOB (ZIP: 20515-0551) **225-8045**
Ceja, Hannah LEGIS CORRES 2244 .... **58045**
Farvour, Beth SCHEDULER 2244 .... **58045**

Goyzueta, Annie PRESS AIDE 2244 58045
Hinkle, Scott LEGIS DIR/DPTY CHIEF OF STAFF 2244 58045
McDonald, Diamond STAFF ASST 2244 58045
Meyer, Eddie LEGIS ASST 2244 58045
Walsh, Tim CHIEF OF STAFF 2244 58045

DISTRICT OFFICES

CHULA VISTA—333 F ST, SUITE A, CHULA VISTA, CA 91910
Allen, Stephanie FIELD REP 619-422-5963
Bryant, Janine DIST DIR 619-422-5963
Guzman, Paola FIELD REP 619-422-5963
Maldonado, Jenn FIELD REP 619-422-5963
Marquez, Angel FIELD REP 619-422-5963
Perez, Stephanie DIST AIDE 619-422-5963

EL CENTRO—380 N 8TH ST, SUITE 14, EL CENTRO, CA 92243
Oliva, Tomas SR FIELD REP 760-312-9900

Representative Marc A. Veasey

Texas, 33d

2348 RAYBURN HOB (ZIP: 20515-4333) 225-9897
Dube, Luke STAFF ASST 2348 59897
Pacilio, Anna COMMUNICATIONS DIR 2348 59897
Phipps, Jane EXEC ASST 2348 59897
Saheb, Zahraa LEGIS ASST 2348 59897
Suruma, Askia CHIEF OF STAFF 2348 59897
Vargas, Jazmin DIGITAL PRESS SECY 2348 59897
Varner, Nicole LEGIS DIR 2348 59897
Woody, Thaddeus SR LEGIS ASST 2348 59897

DISTRICT OFFICES

DALLAS—1881 SYLVAN AVE, SUITE 108, DALLAS, TX 75208
Castro, Daniel FIELD REP 214-741-1387

FORT WORTH—6707 BRENTWOOD STAIR RD, SUITE 200, FORT WORTH, TX 76112
Hagan, Anne DIST DIR 817-920-9086
Schlesinger, Julian COORD - OUTREACH 817-920-9086
Vallejo, Jose FIELD REP 817-920-9086
Ward, Jennifer DIR - CONSTIT SVCS 817-920-9086

Representative Filemon Vela

Texas, 34th

307 CANNON HOB (ZIP: 20515-4334) 225-9901
Beltran, Nate STAFF ASST 307 CHOB 59901
Brody, Perry CHIEF OF STAFF 307 CHOB 59901
De Los Santos, Karen DPTY CHIEF 307 CHOB 59901
Lynch, Liza SCHEDULER/OFFICE MGR 307 CHOB 59901
Merberg, Julie SR POLICY ADVISOR 307 CHOB 59901
Portillo, Deborah SR ADVISOR 307 CHOB 59901
Sheppard, Abigail STAFF ASST 307 CHOB 59901
Theriot, Luke SR ADVISOR - POLICY & OUTREACH 307 CHOB .. 59901

DISTRICT OFFICES

ALICE—500 E MAIN ST, ALICE, TX 78332
Pereida, Jose DIST DIR 361-230-9776

BROWNSVILLE—800 N EXPRESSWAY 77/83, SUITE 9, BROWNSVILLE, TX 78521
Cortez, Marisela DIST DIR 956-544-8352
Jaross, Maria SR CASEWKR 956-544-8352
Rangel, Brenda CASEWKR/PRESS AIDE 956-544-8352

SAN BENITO—1390 W EXPRESSWAY 83, SAN BENITO, TX 78586
Lara, Sally CASEWKR 956-276-4497

WESLACO—301 W RAILROAD ST, WESLACO, TX 78596
Guajardo, Anissa CASEWKR 956-520-8273

Representative Nydia M. Velázquez

New York, 7th

2302 RAYBURN HOB (ZIP: 20515-3207) 225-2361
Alsina, Neysa SR POLICY ADVISOR 2302 52361
Bruno, Richard DC SCHEDULER 2302 52361
Erkel, Richard FINANCIAL SVCS COUNSEL 2302 52361
Garay, Monica STAFF & PRESS ASST 2302 52361
Garcia, Mory OFFICE MGR 2302 52361
Haurek, Alex COMMUNICATIONS DIR 2302 52361
Hochberg, Jacob LEGIS ASST 2302 52361
Martinez, Jonathan SR LEGIS ASST 2302 52361
Minehardt, Adam CHIEF OF STAFF 2302 52361
Pelletier, Justin LEGIS DIR 2302 52361

DISTRICT OFFICES

BROOKLYN—266 BROADWAY, SUITE 201, BROOKLYN, NY 11211
Alves, Mercy CASEWKR 718-599-3658
Cruz, Evelyn DIST DIR 718-599-3658
Del Valle Ortiz, Melissa COMMUNITY & HOUSING COORD 718-599-3658
Febus, Diana CASEWKR 718-599-3658
Morcelo, Lucy EXEC ASST/DIST SCHEDULER 718-599-3658
Ortiz, Sammy CONG AIDE 718-599-3658
Rosario, Maritza STAFF ASST 718-599-3658
Salazar, Julio COMMUNITY LIAISON 718-599-3658
Wiley, Daniel DIST DIR 718-599-3658

LOWER EAST SIDE—500 PEARL ST, SUITE 973, NEW YORK, NY 10007
Hsia, Jacqueline COMMUNITY LIAISON 212-619-2606
Quinones, Iris COMMUNITY LIAISON 212-619-2606

Representative Peter J. Visclosky

Indiana, 1st

2328 RAYBURN HOB (ZIP: 20515-1401) 225-2461
Baack, Korry EXEC ASST/SYS MGR 2328 52461
DeVooght, Joseph DPTY CHIEF OF STAFF 2328 52461
Engdahl, Seth SR LEGIS ASST 2328 52461
Peterson, Michael LEGIS ASST 2328 52461
Salrin, Megan STAFF ASST 2328 52461
Sans, Nate LEGIS ASST 2328 52461
Schaefer, Sonja LEGIS ASST 2328 52461
Spicer, Kevin COMMUNICATIONS DIR 2328 52461

DISTRICT OFFICE

MERRILLVILLE—7895 BROADWAY, SUITE A, MERRILLVILLE, IN 46410-9202
Escalante, Clarissa STAFF ASST 219-795-1844
Gulvas, Greg DIR - CONSTIT SVCS 219-795-1844
Gurnak, Mary CASEWKR 219-795-1844
Johnson, Elizabeth DIR - PROJ 219-795-1844
Kubon, Tom CASEWKR 219-795-1844
Lopez, Mark CHIEF OF STAFF 219-795-1844
Reed, Dawn SCHEDULER/CONSTIT RELATIONS LIAISON 219-795-1844
Reed, Krystie CASEWKR 219-795-1844

Representative Ann Wagner

Missouri, 2d

2350 RAYBURN HOB (ZIP: 20515-2502) 225-1621
Bryant, Arthur COMMUNICATIONS DIR 2350 51621
Burke, Molly LEGIS ASST 2350 51621

Davis, Melanie SYS ADMIN 2350 51621
Gates, Zach SR LEGIS ASST 2350 51621
Keller, Charlie CHIEF OF STAFF 2350 51621
Kerman, Allison STAFF ASST 2350 51621
O'Connor, Mary SHARED EMPLOYEE/FINANCIAL ADMIN 2350 . 51621
Smith, Emily Ann SCHEDULER 2350 51621
Wagley, Rachel LEGIS DIR 2350 51621

DISTRICT OFFICE

BALLWIN—301 SOVEREIGN CT, SUITE 201, BALLWIN, MO 63011
Cook, Kris DIST REP 636-779-5449
Fears, Jordan DIST FIELD REP 636-779-5449
Hollander, Emily CONSTIT SVCS REP 636-779-5449
Stonebraker, Miriam DIST DIR 636-779-5449
Winship, Jacqueline FIELD REP 636-779-5449

Representative Tim Walberg

Michigan, 7th

2266 RAYBURN HOB (ZIP: 20515-2207) 225-6276
Brown, Joanna LEGIS DIR 2266 56276
Kotman, Dan COMMUNICATIONS DIR 2266 56276
Laukitis, R J CHIEF OF STAFF 2266 56276
Rodgers, Kevin LEGIS CORRES 2266 56276
Rorke, Michael STAFF ASST 2266 56276
Stringer, Mary Elizabeth SCHEDULER 2266 56276
Viau, Evan LEGIS ASST 2266 56276

DISTRICT OFFICE

JACKSON—401 W MICHIGAN AVE, JACKSON, MI 49201
Anderson, Wendy FIELD REP 517-780-9075
Bourdon, Sue CONSTIT RELATIONS REP 517-780-9075
Dawson, Billie CONSTIT RELATIONS REP 517-780-9075
Krasny, Dustin DIST DIR/DIR - OPS 517-780-9075
Layton, Elise SR CASEWKR 517-780-9075
Rajzer, Stephen DIST DIR/DIR - ADMIN OPS 517-780-9075
Yamakawa, Leeann OFFICE MGR 517-780-9075

Representative Greg Walden

Oregon, 2d

2185 RAYBURN HOB (ZIP: 20515-3702) 225-6730
Ahern, Nolan LEGIS ASST 2185 56730
Bounds, Lorissa CHIEF OF STAFF 2185 56730
Bushue, Riley LEGIS DIR 2185 56730
Discigil, Justin COMMUNICATIONS DIR 2185 56730
Forrest, Jennifer SCHEDULER 2185 56730
Murphy, Morgan LEGIS CORRES 2185 56730
Ray, Rebecca LEGIS ASST 2185 56730
Rea, Ryan STAFF ASST 2185 56730

DISTRICT OFFICES

BEND—1051 NW BOND ST, SUITE 400, BEND, OR 97701
Anderson, Margie FIELD REP - VETS 541-389-4408
Strader, Nick DIST FIELD REP 541-389-4408

HOOD RIVER—600 E PORT MARINA DR, SUITE C, HOOD RIVER, OR 97031
Wonsyld, Risa DIST FIELD REP 541-308-0300

LA GRANDE—1211 WASHINGTON AVE, LA GRANDE, OR 97850
Billman, Tucker FIELD REP 541-624-2400

MEDFORD—14 N CENTRAL AVE, SUITE 112, MEDFORD, OR 97501
TOLL-FREE NUMBER 1-800-533-3303
James, Wyndess FIELD REP - VETS 541-776-4646
Pay, Katelyn DIST FIELD REP 541-776-4646
Stiles, Melissa DIST FIELD REP 541-776-4646

Representative Mark Walker

North Carolina, 6th

1725 LONGWORTH HOB (ZIP: 20515-3306) 225-3065
Babb, Alison ADMIN - FINANCE & PAYROLL 1725 53065
Cambon, Emily SCHEDULER 1725 53065
Frazier, Janae PRESS SECY 1725 53065
Hilliard, Grace DIR - OPS 1725 53065
Luginbill, Scott CHIEF OF STAFF 1725 53065
McCabe, Sean SR LEGIS ASST 1725 53065
McKay, Kyle STAFF ASST 1725 53065
Prabhu, Sruthi LEGIS ASST 1725 53065
Steelman, Carson LEGIS CORRES 1725 53065
Walker, Ryan LEGIS DIR 1725 53065

DISTRICT OFFICES

ASHEBORO—222 SUNSET AVE, SUITE 101, ASHEBORO, NC 27203
Mitchem, Luke CONSTIT LIAISON 336-626-3060

GRAHAM—P.O. BOX 812, GRAHAM, NC 27253
Emmons, Julie DIST DIR 336-229-0159
Osborne, Janine DIR - CONSTIT SVCS 336-229-0159

GREENSBORO—809 GREEN VALLEY RD, SUITE 104, GREENSBORO, NC 27404
Allen, Amber DIST STAFF ASST 336-333-5005
Malloy, Jerome CONSTIT LIAISON 336-333-5005
Minor, Jack COMMUNICATIONS DIR 336-333-5005
Perkins, Olga CONSTIT LIAISON 336-333-5005
Wynn, Keifer FIELD REP 336-333-5005

Representative Jackie Walorski

Indiana, 2d

419 CANNON HOB (ZIP: 20515-1402) 225-3915
Ammen, Faith SCHEDULER 419 CHOB 53915
Dankler, Mike CHIEF OF STAFF 419 CHOB 53915
Dillon, Joe STAFF ASST 419 CHOB 53915
Fertitta, Ella PRESS ASST 419 CHOB 53915
Morrissey, John COMMUNICATIONS DIR 419 CHOB 53915
Ruhlen, Mary Ellen FINANCIAL ADMIN 419 CHOB 53915
Schultz, Marty LEGIS DIR 419 CHOB 53915
Simonetti, Stephen LEGIS ASST 419 CHOB 53915
Welsh, James LEGIS ASST 419 CHOB 53915

DISTRICT OFFICES

MISHAWAKA—202 LINCOLNWAY E, SUITE 101, MISHAWAKA, IN 46544
Blazey, James DIST FIELD REP 574-204-2645
Christophel, Sharon CONSTIT LIAISON 574-204-2645
Lee, Chris DIST DIR 574-204-2645
Parsons, Ben CONSTIT LIAISON 574-204-2645
Spaulding, Brian DPTY CHIEF OF STAFF 574-204-2645

ROCHESTER—709 MAIN ST, ROCHESTER, IN 46975
Faker, Janet CONSTIT LIAISON 574-223-4373

Representative Michael Waltz

Florida, 6th

216 CANNON HOB (ZIP: 20515-0906) 225-2706
Arguello, Hector LEGIS STAFF 216 CHOB 52706
Barrett, Walker LEGIS DIR/DPTY CHIEF 216 CHOB 52706
Carr, Melissa FINANCIAL MGR 216 CHOB 52706
Haberly, Kelsey CORRES ASST 216 CHOB 52706
Hansen, Deborah OFFICE ADMIN 216 CHOB 52706

Ketchel, Micah CHIEF OF STAFF 216 CHOB 52706
Rafferty, Caitriona LEGIS CORRES 216 CHOB 52706
Rodriguez, Joanna COMMUNICATIONS DIR 216 CHOB 52706
Schuler, Robert STAFF ASST 216 CHOB 52706

DISTRICT OFFICES

DELAND—120 S FLORIDA AVE, SUITE 324, DELAND, FL 32720
Roeder, Debby CONSTIT SVCS 386-279-0707

PALM COAST—31 LUPI CT, SUITE 130, PALM COAST, FL 32137
Christ-Miller, Cynthia CONSTIT SVCS 386-302-0442
Stapleford, Randy MIL FIELD REP 386-302-0442

PORT ORANGE—1000 CITY CENTER CIRCLE, 2ND FLOOR, PORT ORANGE, FL 32129
Audino, Ernest DIST DIR 386-238-9711
Bower, Sue CONSTIT SVCS 386-238-9711
Norman, Sherry CONSTIT SVCS 386-238-9711

Representative Debbie Wasserman Schultz

Florida, 23d

1114 LONGWORTH HOB (ZIP: 20515-0923) 225-7931
Bowles, Maureen FINANCIAL ADMIN 1114 57931
Chandler, Danny SYS ADMIN 1114 57931
Damron, David COMMUNICATIONS DIR 1114 57931
Dolberg, Andrew COORD - DIST OUTREACH 1114 57931
Gerson, Kevin DIGITAL DIR/PRESS SECY 1114 57931
Gonzalez, Leilani STAFF ASST 1114 57931
Harris, Michael LEGIS ASST 1114 57931
Kugler, Sara DIGITAL PRESS SECY 1114 57931
Mylott, Lauren SCHEDULING DIR/SPECIAL ASST 1114 57931
Paikowsky, Steven SR ADVISOR 1114 57931
Pough, Tracie CHIEF OF STAFF 1114 57931
Turbyfill, Brian DIR - APPRO 1114 57931
Viggiano, Michael JR LEGIS ASST 1114 57931
Wang, Jackii LEGIS ASST 1114 57931

DISTRICT OFFICES

AVENTURA—19200 W COUNTRY CLUB DR, 3RD FLOOR, AVENTURA, FL 33180
Flink, Laurie DPTY DIST DIR 305-936-5724

SUNRISE—777 SAWGRASS CORPORATE PKWY, SUNRISE, FL 33325
Gallagher, Bettyanne CASEWK DIR 954-845-1179
Grandwilliams, Harrison DPTY DIST DIR 954-845-1179
Liquerman, Michael COORD - OUTREACH /PRESS ASST 954-845-1179
Piereschi, Vivian SR CONSTIT ADVOCATE 954-845-1179

Representative Maxine Waters

California, 43d

2221 RAYBURN HOB (ZIP: 20515-0543) 225-2201
Bascumbe, Andres LEGIS COUNSEL 2221 52201
Dorsey, Rykia PRESS SECY 2221 52201
Fergusson, Patrick LEGIS DIR 2221 52201
Samuel, Twaun CHIEF OF STAFF 2221 52201
Sengstock, Kathleen LEGIS ASST 2221 52201
Smith, Symonne SCHEDULER 2221 52201

DISTRICT OFFICE

LOS ANGELES—10124 S BROADWAY, SUITE 1, LOS ANGELES, CA 90003
Cloud, Hamilton SPECIAL PROJ DIR 323-757-8900
Jimenez, Blanca DIST DIR 323-757-8900
Nicholson, Terry RECEPTIONIST 323-757-8900
Robinson, Nicole EXEC ASST 323-757-8900
Woodward, Nathaniel AIDE 323-757-8900

Representative Steve Watkins

Kansas, 2d

1205 LONGWORTH HOB (ZIP: 20515-1602) 225-6601
Brainard, Colin CHIEF OF STAFF 1205 56601
Churchill, Tim LEGIS ASST 1205 56601
Herron, Kayla EXEC ASST/SCHEDULER 1205 56601
Joice, Jim COMMUNICATIONS DIR 1205 56601
Jones, Dylan STAFF ASST 1205 56601
Lothian, Lainey SR LEGIS ASST 1205 56601
Reasor, Christiana LEGIS AIDE 1205 56601
Walker, Amanda FINANCIAL ADMIN 1205 56601
York, Adam LEGIS DIR 1205 56601

DISTRICT OFFICES

PITTSBURG—1001 N BROADWAY ST, NO. C, PITTSBURG, KS 66762
Callen, Will CASEWKR 620-231-5966

TOPEKA—3550 SW 5TH ST, TOPEKA, KS 66606
Abraham, Katrina OFFICE MGR/DIST SCHEDULER 785-234-5966
Askew, Allen MIL FIELD REP 785-234-5966
Kovach, Ron CASEWKR 785-234-5966
Roe, Bill DPTY CHIEF OF STAFF 785-234-5966
Tempel, Whitney DIST REP 785-234-5966

Representative Bonnie Watson Coleman

New Jersey, 12th

2442 RAYBURN HOB (ZIP: 20515-3012) 225-5801
Block, Kevin LEGIS DIR 2442 55801
Cochran, Courtney DPTY CHIEF OF STAFF 2442 55801
Gee, James CHIEF OF STAFF 2442 55801
Korten, Bradley LEGIS ASST 2442 55801
Lee, Carianne LEGIS CORRES 2442 55801
Lee, Kaozouapa SR POLICY ADVISOR 2442 55801
Nickson, Michael FINANCIAL ADMIN 2442 55801
Shanahan, Michael PRESS SECY 2442 55801
Simmons, Jermaine SPECIAL ASST 2442 55801

DISTRICT OFFICE

EWING—850 BEAR TAVERN RD, SUITE 201, EWING, NJ 08628
Boztepe, Dilara DIST REP 609-883-0026
Edwards, Jasi SPECIAL ASST 609-883-0026
Gaskins, Petra DIR - COMMUNITY OUTREACH 609-883-0026
Gilmartin, Jaimee SCHEDULER 609-883-0026
Hood, Patricia DIST REP 609-883-0026
Lewis, Jordan DIST REP 609-883-0026
Matos-Moran, Robert CONSTIT SVCS 609-883-0026
Osmond, Kari DPTY CHIEF OF STAFF 609-883-0026

Representative Randy K. Weber, Sr.

Texas, 14th

107 CANNON HOB (ZIP: 20515-4314) 225-2831
Christian, "Bill" LEGIS DIR 107 CHOB 52831
Harvey, Tom LEGIS AIDE 107 CHOB 52831
Lefaive, Erica LEGIS AIDE 107 CHOB 52831
McMichael, Chara CHIEF OF STAFF 107 CHOB 52831
Polefka, Emma COMMUNICATIONS DIR 107 CHOB 52831
Vidor, Kelly EXEC SCHEDULER 107 CHOB 52831

DISTRICT OFFICES

BEAUMONT—350 PINE ST, SUITE 730, BEAUMONT, TX 77701
Brown, Janet CASEWKR 409-835-0108
Hopper, Blake DPTY DIST DIR 409-835-0108

LAKE JACKSON—122 WEST WAY, SUITE 301, LAKE JACKSON, TX 77566
Armstrong, Dodie CONSTIT LIAISON 979-285-0231
Thigpen, Christine CASEWKR - IMMIGRATION 979-285-0231

LEAGUE CITY—174 CALDER RD, SUITE 150, LEAGUE CITY, TX 77573
Burnett, Bradie DIST SCHEDULER 281-316-0231
Webb, Jed DIST DIR 281-316-0231

Representative Daniel Webster

Florida, 11th

1210 LONGWORTH HOB (ZIP: 20515-0911) **225-1002**
Emhof, Jaryn CHIEF OF STAFF/COMMUNICATIONS DIR 1210 ... 51002
Newgaard, Luke LEGIS ASST 1210 51002
Pakledinaz, Adam STAFF ASST 1210 51002
Thompson, Jessica LEGIS CORRES 1210 51002

DISTRICT OFFICES

BROOKSVILLE—15 N MAIN ST, SUITE B, BROOKESVILLE, FL 34601
Pearson, Christa DIST DIR 352-241-9230

INVERNESS—212 W MAIN ST, SUITE 208A, INVERNESS, FL 34450
White, Victoria COMMUNITY RELATIONS ASST 352-241-9204

LEESBURG—318 S 2ND ST, NO. A, LEESBURG, FL 34748
Dobkowski, Natasha DIST STAFF ASST 352-241-9220
Green, Samuel CONSTIT SVCS 352-241-9220
Jones, Pamela COMMUNITY RELATIONS SPEC 352-241-9220
Knight, Natali SCHEDULER 352-241-9220
Shylkofski, Stephen DIR - CONSTIT SVCS 352-241-9220
Warren, Debra CONSTIT SVCS 352-241-9220

THE VILLAGES—8015 E COUNTY RD 466, SUITE B, THE VILLAGES, FL 32162
Brown, Cindy COMMUNITY RELATIONS SPEC 352-383-3552

Representative Peter Welch

Vermont, At Large

2187 RAYBURN HOB (ZIP: 20515-4500) **225-4115**
Cohn, Maya STAFF ASST 2187 54115
Etka, Patrick SCHEDULER/EXEC ASST/OFFICE MGR 2187 54115
Fowler, Mark SR LEGIS ASST 2187 54115
Loeb, Isaac SR LEGIS ASST 2187 54115
Lynn, Hans LEGIS CORRES 2187 54115
Morris, Alexandra LEGIS AIDE 2187 54115
Peek, Lincoln COMMUNICATIONS DIR 2187 54115
Rogan, Bob CHIEF OF STAFF 2187 54115
Satalin, Patrick LEGIS DIR/DPTY CHIEF OF STAFF 2187 54115
Wemple, Douglas PRESS ASST/STAFF ASST 2187 54115

DISTRICT OFFICE

BURLINGTON—128 LAKESIDE AVE, SUITE 235, BURLINGTON, VT 05401
TOLL-FREE NUMBER 1-888-605-7270
Ellis, Rebecca STATE DIR 802-652-2450
Furnari, Shannon DPTY STATE DIR 802-652-2450
Haskell, Elizabeth STAFF ASST 802-652-2450
McLaren, Ryan OUTREACH REP 802-652-2450
Morris, Elizabeth CONSTIT SVCS REP 802-652-2450
Wurzburg, Thea CONSTIT SVCS REP 802-652-2450

Representative Brad R. Wenstrup

Ohio, 2d

2419 RAYBURN HOB (ZIP: 20515-3502) **225-3164**
Brooks, Greg LEGIS DIR/DPTY CHIEF OF STAFF 2419 53164
Dierker, Ryan SR LEGIS ASST 2419 53164
Graeter, Luke LEGIS ASST/LEGIS CORRES 2419 53164
Harley, Derek CHIEF OF STAFF 2419 53164
Moelk, Carter DPTY COMMUNICATIONS DIR 2419 53164
Palmer, Jonathan STAFF ASST/LEGIS CORRES 2419 53164
Prus, Julia LEGIS ASST 2419 53164
Sadler, Hailey COMMUNICATIONS AIDE 2419 53164
Sumbrum, Abbie SCHEDULER/OFFICE MGR 2419 53164
Tumolo, Ann COMMUNICATIONS DIR 2419 53164

DISTRICT OFFICES

CINCINNATI—7954 BEECHMONT AVE, SUITE 200, CINCINNATI, OH 45255
Cummins, Annie CASEWKR 513-474-7777
Heller, Austin FELLOW 513-474-7777
McAfee, Andrew FIELD REP 513-474-7777
Scharfetter, Alex DIST DIR 513-474-7777

PEEBLES—170 N MAIN ST, PEEBLES, OH 45660
Lewis, Teresa REGIONAL DIR 513-605-1380
Shivener, Kellie CASEWKR 513-605-1380

UNION TOWNSHIP—4350 AICHOLTZ RD, CINCINNATI, OH 45245 513-474-7777

Representative Bruce Westerman

Arkansas, 4th

209 CANNON HOB (ZIP: 20515-0404) **225-3772**
Bryant, Madeline SCHEDULER 209 CHOB 53772
Deming, Jefferson LEGIS DIR 209 CHOB 53772
Jorgensen, Rebekah COMMUNICATIONS DIR 209 CHOB 53772
Layden, William LEGIS ASST 209 CHOB 53772
Lisowski, Nick LEGIS AIDE 209 CHOB 53772
Mace, Emily LEGIS COUNSEL 209 CHOB 53772
Moeglein, Vivian CHIEF OF STAFF 209 CHOB 53772
Ruhlen, Mary Ellen ADMIN - FINANCE & PAYROLL 209 CHOB .. 53772

DISTRICT OFFICES

EL DORADO—101 N WASHINGTON ST, SUITE 406, EL DORADO, AR 71730
Boyer, Melinda FIELD REP 870-864-8946

HOT SPRINGS—101 RESERVE ST, SUITE 200, HOT SPRINGS, AR 71901
McGehee, J D DIST DIR 501-609-9796
Sharp, Raegan DIST SCHEDULER/FIELD REP 501-609-9796
Witte, David DPTY DIST DIR/MIL FIELD REP 501-609-9796

OZARK—211 W COMMERCIAL ST, OZARK, AR 72949
Ballinger, Bobby DIST FIELD REP 479-667-0075
Cross, Tracy DIST FIELD REP/CASEWK DIR 479-667-0075

PINE BLUFF—100 E 8TH AVE, ROOM 2521, PINE BLUFF, AR 71601 870-536-8178

Representative Jennifer Wexton

Virginia, 10th

1217 LONGWORTH HOB (ZIP: 20515-4610) **225-5136**
Avin, Amir COMMUNICATIONS DIR 1217 55136
Barnes, Anthony COORD - CONSTIT SVCS 1217 55136
Callejas, Courtney SR POLICY ADVISOR 1217 55136
Carter, Abigail CHIEF OF STAFF 1217 55136
Faraco-Hadlock, Amelia STAFF ASST 1217 55136

Gibson, Chris LEGIS CORRES 1217 .... **55136**
Johnson, Meaghan SCHEDULER 1217 .... **55136**
Leslie, Matt LEGIS ASST 1217 .... **55136**
Lucier, Mike LEGIS DIR 1217 .... **55136**
Vangrow, Ali LEGIS ASST 1217 .... **55136**
Westfall, Lana CONSTIT SVCS REP 1217 .... **55136**

DISTRICT OFFICE

STERLING—21351 GENTRY DR, SUITE 140, STERLING, VA 20166
Bhatti, Saira CONSTIT SVCS REP **703-234-3800**
Constance, Erica DIST DIR **703-234-3800**
Davis, Tami SR OUTREACH DIR **703-234-3800**

Representative Susan Wild

Pennsylvania, 7th

1607 LONGWORTH HOB (ZIP: 20515-3807) **225-6411**
Adekunle, Dorcas DPTY CHIEF OF STAFF/LEGIS DIR 1607 .... **56411**
Cinquegrani, Julia LEGIS ASST 1607 .... **56411**
DeStefano, Gabriella STAFF ASST 1607 .... **56411**
Fowler, Zach SR LEGIS COUNSEL 1607 .... **56411**
Kirkwood, Rebekah SCHEDULER 1607 .... **56411**
Ober, Jed CHIEF OF STAFF 1607 .... **56411**
Schinazi, Yann LEGIS AIDE/SPEECHWRITER 1607 .... **56411**
Stevens, Kim FINANCIAL ADMIN 1607 .... **56411**
Wilson-Meyer, Zoe COMMUNICATIONS DIR 1607 .... **56411**

DISTRICT OFFICES

ALLENTOWN—840 HAMILTON ST, SUITE 303, ALLENTOWN, PA 18101
Beste, Megan DIST DIR **484-781-6000**
Brown, Taylor COMMUNITY & OUTREACH LIAISON **484-781-6000**
Laboy, Elsie CONSTIT ADVOCATE **484-781-6000**
McLaughlin, Sabrina SR CONSTIT ADVOCATE **484-781-6000**
Roopchand, Fern CONSTIT ADVOCATE **484-781-6000**

EASTON—400 NORTHAMPTON ST, SUITE 503, EASTON, PA 18042
Lauritzen, Anne CONSTIT ADVOCATE **610-333-1170**
Winchester, Selina CONSTIT ADVOCATE **610-333-1170**

Representative Roger Williams

Texas, 25th

1708 LONGWORTH HOB (ZIP: 20515-4325) **225-9896**
Arlantico, Pat LEGIS DIR/DPTY CHIEF OF STAFF 1708 .... **59896**
Barth, Zack LEGIS ASST 1708 .... **59896**
Crane, Katie STAFF ASST 1708 .... **59896**
Curry, Cat SCHEDULER 1708 .... **59896**
Johnson, Benjamin LEGIS ASST 1708 .... **59896**
Wright, Monique CONSTIT LIAISON 1708 .... **59896**

DISTRICT OFFICES

AUSTIN—1005 CONGRESS AVE, SUITE 925, AUSTIN, TX 78701
Etue, John CHIEF OF STAFF **512-473-8910**
Helton, Aaron DIST FIELD REP/DPTY DIST DIR **512-473-8910**
Nicholas, Donald DIST FIELD REP/MIL FIELD REP **512-473-8910**

CLEBURNE—115 S MAIN ST, SUITE 206, CLEBURNE, TX 76033
Parker, Robyn DIST DIR **817-774-2575**
Zachary, Ruth CASEWKR/DPTY DIR - CONSTIT SVCS **817-774-2575**

Representative Frederica S. Wilson

Florida, 24th

2445 RAYBURN HOB (ZIP: 20515-0924) **225-4506**
Jones, Joyce COMMUNICATIONS DIR 2445 .... **54506**
Lewis, Chasseny CHIEF OF STAFF 2445 .... **54506**
Range, Cheyenne SPECIAL ASST 2445 .... **54506**
Roseme, Jean DPTY CHIEF OF STAFF 2445 .... **54506**
Simon, David SR LEGIS ASST 2445 .... **54506**
Wolf-Johnson, Maximilian PRESS SECY 2445 .... **54506**

DISTRICT OFFICE

MIAMI GARDENS—18425 NW 2ND AVE, SUITE 355, MIAMI GARDENS, FL 33169
Austin-Shipp, Nikki DIR - COMMUNITY RELATIONS **305-690-5905**
Carter, D'Andrea COMMUNICATIONS AIDE **305-690-5905**
Cohen, Quincy DIR - FIELD OPS **305-690-5905**
Lafleur, Shirlee DIR - FIELD OPS **305-690-5905**
Postell, Joyce DIST DIR **305-690-5905**
Scott, Charles DPTY DIR - OUTREACH/MBR SVCS ADVISOR **305-690-5905**
Sears, Sandra ADVISOR - HEALTH POLICY **305-690-5905**
Sinkfield, Jessica DPTY POLICY DIR **305-690-5905**
Snyder, Alexis DIST CHIEF OF STAFF **305-690-5905**
Thomas, Delvin COORD - OPS **305-690-5905**
Williams, Jakaria CONG AIDE **305-690-5905**

Representative Joe Wilson

South Carolina, 2d

1436 LONGWORTH HOB (ZIP: 20515-4002) **225-2452**
Adaki, Oren LEGIS DIR 1436 .... **52452**
Day, Jonathan CHIEF OF STAFF 1436 .... **52452**
Denny, Leah Grace LEGIS ASST 1436 .... **52452**
Grant, Joshua STAFF ASST/LEGIS CORRES 1436 .... **52452**
Ibarra, Jay DPTY PRESS SECY 1436 .... **52452**
Kennedy, Drew SR LEGIS ASST/LEGIS ASST - MIL 1436 .... **52452**
Pendarvis, Stephanie SCHEDULER/EXEC ASST 1436 .... **52452**
Saleeby, Emily LEGIS ASST/OFFICE MGR 1436 .... **52452**
Williams, Stami COMMUNICATIONS DIR 1436 .... **52452**

DISTRICT OFFICES

AIKEN—1930 UNIVERSITY PKWY, SUITE 1600, P.O. BOX 104, AIKEN, SC 29801
Dragano, Garrett SPECIAL ASST/CASEWKR **803-642-6416**
Ruthven, Martha SPECIAL ASST/CASEWKR **803-642-6416**

MIDLANDS—1700 SUNSET BLVD, SUITE 1, WEST COLUMBIA, SC 29169
Batey, Laura DIR - CONSTIT SVCS **803-939-0041**
Habib, Phillip ADMIN ASST/SPECIAL ASST **803-939-0041**
Morris, Alex CASEWKR - MIL/DPTY DIST DIR **803-939-0041**
Powell, Millie EXEC ASST/DIST OFFICE MGR **803-939-0041**
Thomas, Byron SPECIAL ASST/CASEWKR **803-939-0041**
Wade, Hal SPECIAL ASST/CASEWKR **803-939-0041**
Wallace, Butch DIST DIR **803-939-0041**

Representative Robert J. Wittman

Virginia, 1st

2055 RAYBURN HOB (ZIP: 20515-4601) **225-4261**
Ferrari, Jake MIL FELLOW 2055 .... **54261**
Gayle, Kathleen COMMUNICATIONS DIR/LEGIS ASST 2055 .... **54261**
Huntley, Maxwell LEGIS ASST - MIL 2055 .... **54261**
King, Carolyn CHIEF OF STAFF 2055 .... **54261**
Mazzola, Katherine LEGIS CORRES 2055 .... **54261**
Ragsdale, Chris MIL FELLOW 2055 .... **54261**
Robinson, Brent DPTY CHIEF OF STAFF 2055 .... **54261**
Smolinsky, Curran STAFF ASST 2055 .... **54261**

Taylor, Gloria DPTY PRESS SECY 2055 54261
Walton, Austin SR LEGIS ASST 2055 54261
Wilson, Jordan SCHEDULER/OFFICE MGR 2055 54261

DISTRICT OFFICES

HANOVER—6501 MECHANICSVILLE TURNPIKE, SUITE 102, MECHANICSVILLE, VA 23111

Schumacher, Joe DIST DIR/OUTREACH DIR 804-730-6595
Whitehouse, Christina DIST REP 804-730-6595

STAFFORD—95 DUNN DR, SUITE 201, STAFFORD, VA 22554

Kimball, Cheryl CASEWKR 540-659-2734
Klotz, Karen COORD - OUTREACH 540-659-2734

TAPPAHANNOCK—508 CHURCH LANE, TAPPAHANNOCK, VA 22560

Jones, Chris DIST REP/DPTY DIST DIR 804-443-0668

Representative Steve Womack

Arkansas, 3d

2412 RAYBURN HOB (ZIP: 20515-0403) 225-4301

Deatherage, Zach STAFF ASST 2412 54301
Dieringer, Brett LEGIS CORRES 2412 54301
Hempelmann, Goeff LEGIS DIR 2412 54301
Morley, Katie STAFF ASST 2412 54301
Nash, Madison SCHEDULER 2412 54301
Powell, Jessica LEGIS ASST 2412 54301
Runkel, Nick LEGIS CORRES 2412 54301
Sikora, Alexia COMMUNICATIONS DIR 2412 54301
Walker, Beau CHIEF OF STAFF 2412 54301

DISTRICT OFFICES

FORT SMITH—6101 PHOENIX AVE, SUITE 4, FORT SMITH, AR 72903

Bader, Chris CONSTIT SVCS REP 479-424-1146
Scaggs, Janice FIELD REP 479-424-1146

HARRISON—303 N MAIN ST, SUITE 102, HARRISON, AR 72601

Garrett, Teri FIELD REP 870-741-6900

ROGERS—3333 PINNACLE HILLS PKWY, SUITE 120, ROGERS, AR 72758

Ackerman, Bootsie DIST DIR 479-464-0446
Brandolini, Gillie CONSTIT SVCS REP 479-464-0446
Foster, Janet MGR - CONSTIT SVCS 479-464-0446
Thacker, Jeff FIELD REP 479-464-0446
Weaver, Kyle DIR - PROJ 479-464-0446

Representative Rob Woodall

Georgia, 7th

1724 LONGWORTH HOB (ZIP: 20515-1007) 225-4272

Boileau, Ryan STAFF ASST 1724 54272
Copeland, Laney LEGIS ASST 1724 54272
Kurtz, Kelley ADMIN ASST/SCHEDULER 1724 54272
Naft, Jeff COMMUNICATIONS DIR 1724 54272
Reynolds, Thomas LEGIS ASST 1724 54272
Rossi, Janet LEGIS DIR 1724 54272
Scoufaras, Nicholas LEGIS ASST 1724 54272
Williams, Lauren LEGIS CORRES 1724 54272

DISTRICT OFFICE

GWINNETT—75 LANGLEY DR, LAWRENCEVILLE, GA 30046

Corbett, Derick CHIEF OF STAFF 770-232-3005
Gabrysh, Elena CONSTIT SVCS REP 770-232-3005
Kurspahic, Vesna CONSTIT SVCS REP 770-232-3005
Oh, Paul FIELD REP 770-232-3005
Pillsbury, Naomi CONSTIT SVCS REP 770-232-3005
Poirot, Debra DIST DIR 770-232-3005

Representative Ron Wright

Texas, 6th

428 CANNON HOB (ZIP: 20515-4306) 225-2002

Cavanaugh, Micah DPTY CHIEF OF STAFF 428 CHOB 52002
Hardimon, Madison LEGIS AIDE 428 CHOB 52002
Howard, Mike STAFF ASST 428 CHOB 52002
Rotert, Blair LEGIS DIR 428 CHOB 52002
Thompson, Ryan CHIEF OF STAFF 428 CHOB 52002
Van Sickle, Ben LEGIS CORRES 428 CHOB 52002
Waller, Caroline SCHEDULER 428 CHOB 52002

DISTRICT OFFICES

ARLINGTON—5840 RONALD REAGAN MEMORIAL HWY, ARLINGTON, TX 76017

Hguyen, Andy DIST DIR 817-077-5037
Rollins, Deborah CASEWKR 817-077-5037
Saegesser, Jodi CASEWKR 817-077-5037

WAXAHACHIE—209 E MAIN ST, WAXAHACHIE, TX 75165 202-440-0762

Representative John A. Yarmuth

Kentucky, 3d

402 CANNON HOB (ZIP: 20515-1703) 225-5401

Carr, Julie CHIEF OF STAFF 402 CHOB 55401
Clark, Raymel INFO TECH MGR 402 CHOB 55401
Dicio, Erica LEGIS ASST 402 CHOB 55401
Elliott, Claire EXEC ASST 402 CHOB 55401
Grimes, Benjamin LEGIS CORRES 402 CHOB 55401
Nelson, Jonathan ACCOUNTANT 402 CHOB 55401
Perelmuter, Stuart SPEECHWRITER 402 CHOB 55401
Reyes, Gil LEGIS ASST 402 CHOB 55401
Robinson, Walker LEGIS CORRES 402 CHOB 55401
Rowley, Katy LEGIS DIR 402 CHOB 55401
Schuler, Christopher PRESS SECY 402 CHOB 55401

DISTRICT OFFICES

DOWNTOWN—MAZZOLI FED BLDG, 600 MARTIN LUTHER KING JR PL, SUITE 216, LOUISVILLE, KY 40202

Drake, Seth CONG AIDE 502-582-5129
Look, Judy CONG AIDE 502-582-5129
Moore, Stephon CONG AIDE 502-582-5129
Thompson, Jacqueline CONG AIDE 502-582-5129
Wittebort, Marisa SR LEGIS ASST 502-582-5129
Yates, Nicole DIST DIR 502-582-5129

SOUTH END—7219 DIXIE HWY, LOUISVILLE, KY 40258

Spratt, Shelley SR CONG AIDE 502-933-5863

Representative Ted S. Yoho

Florida, 3d

1730 LONGWORTH HOB (ZIP: 20515-0903) 225-5744

Atwater, Courtney STAFF ASST 1730 55744
Blankenship, April FINANCIAL ADMIN 1730 55744
Calhoun, Larry CHIEF OF STAFF 1730 55744
Cicchella, Jamie LEGIS ASST 1730 55744
Gillespie, Lauren LEGIS CORRES 1730 55744
Kaveney, Brian COMMUNICATIONS DIR 1730 55744
Turk, Allison SCHEDULER 1730 55744
Walsh, James LEGIS DIR 1730 55744
Woodward, Josh LEGIS ASST 1730 55744

DISTRICT OFFICES

GAINESVILLE—5000 NW 27TH CT, SUITE E, GAINESVILLE, FL 32606

Cammack, Kat DPTY CHIEF OF STAFF **352-505-0838**
Dilan, Tess ADMIN ASST **352-505-0838**
Hill, Dave CASEWKR **352-505-0838**
Norfleet, Jessica DIST DIR **352-505-0838**
Parrish, Hannah EXEC ASST **352-505-0838**

OCALA—115 SE 25TH AVE, OCALA, FL 34471

Miller, Patrick CONSTIT ADVOCATE **352-390-6413**

ORANGE PARK—35 KNIGHT BOXX RD, SUITE 1, ORANGE PARK, FL 32065

Richardson, Dorothy CASEWK MGR **904-276-9626**
Silva, Ed CONSTIT ADVOCATE **904-276-9626**

PALATKA—2509 CRILL AVE, SUITE 200, PALATKA, FL 32177 .... **386-326-7221**

Representative Don Young

Alaska, At Large

2314 RAYBURN HOB (ZIP: 20515-0200) 225-5765

Brown, Zack PRESS SECY 2314 .... **55765**
Conru, Paula EXEC ASST/SCHEDULER 2314 .... **55765**
Crosley, Kemorley LEGIS CORRES 2314 .... **55765**
Day, Pamela CHIEF OF STAFF 2314 .... **55765**
Humphrey, Cameron LEGIS ASST 2314 .... **55765**
Newell, Martha LEGIS ASST 2314 .... **55765**
Newman, Bruce SPECIAL ASST 2314 .... **55765**
Ortiz, Alexander LEGIS DIR/DPTY CHIEF OF STAFF 2314 .... **55765**
Reed, Truman LEGIS ASST 2314 .... **55765**
Songer, Michael LEGIS ASST - MIL 2314 .... **55765**
Von Stein, Jesse LEGIS ASST 2314 .... **55765**

DISTRICT OFFICES

ANCHORAGE—471 W 36TH AVE, SUITE 201, ANCHORAGE, AK 99503

TOLL-FREE NUMBER **1-866-990-5979**
George, Daniel STATE DIR **907-271-5978**
Ordaz, Azabel SPECIAL ASST **907-271-5978**
Petty, Catherine DPTY STATE DIR **907-271-5978**
Risinger, Tara SPECIAL ASST **907-271-5978**

FAIRBANKS—100 CUSHMAN ST, SUITE 307, FAIRBANKS, AK 99707

TOLL-FREE NUMBER **1-866-990-5979**
Peterson-Wood, Emily SPECIAL ASST **907-456-0210**

Representative Lee M. Zeldin

New York, 1st

2441 RAYBURN HOB (ZIP: 20515-3201) 225-3826

Dowling, Kevin LEGIS DIR 2441 .... **53826**
Grace, Andrea EXEC ASST/SCHEDULER 2441 .... **53826**
Hrinkevich, Mary LEGIS CORRES/PRESS ASST 2441 .... **53826**
Matar, Sara SR LEGIS AIDE 2441 .... **53826**
McNamee, James STAFF ASST 2441 .... **53826**
Talmage, Sarah LEGIS AIDE 2441 .... **53826**
Vincentz, Kathleen COMMUNICATIONS DIR 2441 .... **53826**

DISTRICT OFFICES

EAST END—30 W MAIN ST, RIVERHEAD, NY 11901

Woolley, Michelle CONG AIDE **631-209-4235**

LONG ISLAND—31 OAK ST, SUITE 20, PATCHOGUE, NY 11772

Amidon, Eric CHIEF OF STAFF **631-289-1097**
Buckley, Christopher SPECIAL ASST **631-289-1097**
Doyle, William DIR - CONSTIT AFFAIRS **631-289-1097**
Erb, Logan PRESS ASST **631-289-1097**
Groneman, Belinda CONG AIDE/CASEWKR - IMMIGRATION/ IMMIGRATION SPEC **631-289-1097**
Johnson, Cleveland CONG AIDE/CASEWORK - VETS/COORD - VETS OUTREACH **631-289-1097**
Malloy, Terri STAFF ASST **631-289-1097**
Monachino, Benedict CONG AIDE/SOCIAL WKR **631-289-1097**
Saccardi, Adam CONG AIDE/FIELD REP **631-289-1097**
Woolley, Mark DIST DIR **631-289-1097**

COMMITTEE MEMBERS AND STAFF

Three-digit room numbers are in the Cannon HOB or the Ford HOB, as indicated. Four-digit room numbers beginning with 1 are in the Longworth HOB; with 2, the Rayburn HOB; and with 3, 4, 5, or 6, the O'Neill HOB. Capitol room numbers begin with SB, ST, HB, HC, and HT or with H or S, followed by three digits. Room numbers beginning with CVC, HVC, or SVC are in the Capitol Visitor Center. Room numbers beginning with SD are in the Dirksen SOB, room numbers beginning with SH are in the Hart SOB, and room numbers beginning with SR are in the Russell SOB.

Calls from outside the Capitol complex can be made by dialing (202) 22 plus the five-digit number listed in this directory.

Democrats in roman; Republicans in *italic*; Resident Commissioner and Delegates in **boldface**.

COMMITTEE ON AGRICULTURE

1301 LONGWORTH HOB (ZIP: 20515-6001)....................225-2171

Collin C. Peterson, MN, Chair

David Scott, GA
Jim Costa, CA
Marcia L. Fudge, OH
James P. McGovern, MA
Filemon Vela, TX
Stacey E. Plaskett, VI
Alma S. Adams, NC, Vice Chair
Abigail Davis Spanberger, VA
Jahana Hayes, CT
Antonio Delgado, NY
TJ Cox, CA
Angie Craig, MN
Anthony Brindisi, NY
Jefferson Van Drew, NJ
Josh Harder, CA
Kim Schrier, WA
Chellie Pingree, ME
Cheri Bustos, IL
Sean Patrick Maloney, NY
Salud O. Carbajal, CA
Al Lawson, Jr., FL
Tom O'Halleran, AZ
Jimmy Panetta, CA
Ann Kirkpatrick, AZ
Cynthia Axne, IA

K. Michael Conaway, TX
Glenn Thompson, PA
Austin Scott, GA
Eric A. "Rick" Crawford, AR
Scott DesJarlais, TN
Vicky Hartzler, MO
Doug LaMalfa, CA
Rodney Davis, IL
Ted S. Yoho, FL
Rick W. Allen, GA
Mike Bost, IL
David Rouzer, NC
Ralph Lee Abraham, LA
Trent Kelly, MS
James Comer, KY
Roger W. Marshall, KS
Don Bacon, NE
Neal P. Dunn, FL
Dusty Johnson, SD
James R. Baird, IN
Jim Hagedorn, MN

MAJORITY

Adesina, Kellie CHIEF COUNSEL 1301.......... 52171
Blum-Evitts, Lyron MEMB RELATIONS COORD 1301.......... 52171
Bridgeforth, Carlton PROF STAFF 1301.......... 52171
Carter, Mickeala COORD - OUTREACH 1301.......... 52171
Cep, Melinda LEGIS POLICY DIR 1301.......... 52171
Delaney, Patrick COMMUNICATIONS DIR 1301.......... 52171
Dickerson, Jasmine SUBCOMM STAFF DIR 1301.......... 52171
German, Emily LEGIS ASST 1301.......... 52171
Hettervig, Ross DIGITAL OUTREACH SPEC 1301.......... 52171
Honeycutt, Brandon SUBCOMM STAFF DIR 1301.......... 52171
Jones, Keith SR PROF STAFF 1301.......... 52171
Konya, John DIR - INFO TECH 1301.......... 52171
MacKenzie, Matthew SR COUNSEL 1301.......... 52171
Martin, Prescott SR COUNSEL 1301.......... 52171
Mattocks, Tom PRESS SECY 1301.......... 52171
Phillips, Troy DPTY STAFF DIR 1301.......... 52171
Sandman, Dana CHIEF CLERK/DIR - SCHEDULING 1301.......... 52171
Shelton, Lisa SR PROF STAFF 1301.......... 52171

Siddiqui, Faisal SYS ADMIN 1301 52171
Simmons, Anne STAFF DIR 1301 52171
Smith, Ashley SUBCOMM STAFF DIR 1301 52171
Stranz, Mike SUBCOMM STAFF DIR 1301 52171
Thomas, Faye ADMIN - COMMITTEE 1301 52171
Titus, Alison LEGIS ASST 1301 52171
Wetherald, Margaret ADMIN DIR 1301 52171
Yezak, Jennifer DPTY CLERK 1301 52171
Zenk, Katie SUBCOMM STAFF DIR/ECONOMIST 1301 52171

MINORITY

Balzano, Paul SR PROF STAFF 1010 50317
Crosswhite, Caleb DPTY CHIEF COUNSEL/PROF STAFF 1010 50317
Fischer, Bart DPTY STAFF DIR/CHIEF ECONOMIST 1010 50317
Johnston, Ashton PROF STAFF 1010 50317
Maxwell, Josh SR PROF STAFF 1010 50317
McAdams, Callie DEPUTY CHIEF ECONOMIST 1010 50317
Millard, Rachel COMMUNICATIONS DIR 1010 50317
Schertz, Matt STAFF DIR 1010 50317
Schroeder, Ricki LEGIS ASST/MBR SVCS COORD 1010 50317
Straughn, Patricia CHIEF COUNSEL 1010 50317
Tiller, Jennifer SR PROF STAFF 1010 50317
White, Trevor PROF STAFF 1010 50317
Witte, Jeremy PROF STAFF 1010 50317

SUBCOMMITTEES OF THE COMMITTEE ON AGRICULTURE

[The chairman and ranking minority member are ex officio members of all subcommittees.]

SUBCOMMITTEE ON NUTRITION, OVERSIGHT, AND DEPARTMENT OPERATIONS

1301 LONGWORTH HOB (ZIP: 20515) 225-2171

Marcia L. Fudge, OH, Chair

James P. McGovern, MA
Alma S. Adams, NC
Jahana Hayes, CT
Kim Schrier, WA
Jefferson Van Drew, NJ
Al Lawson, Jr., FL
Jimmy Panetta, CA

Dusty Johnson, SD
Scott DesJarlais, TN
Rodney Davis, IL
Ted S. Yoho, FL
Don Bacon, NE
Jim Hagedorn, MN

SUBCOMMITTEE ON CONSERVATION AND FORESTRY

1301 LONGWORTH HOB (ZIP: 20515) 225-2171

Abigail Davis Spanberger, VA, Chair

Marcia L. Fudge, OH
Tom O'Halleran, AZ
Chellie Pingree, ME
Cynthia Axne, IA

Doug LaMalfa, CA
Rick W. Allen, GA
Ralph Lee Abraham, LA
Trent Kelly, MS

SUBCOMMITTEE ON GENERAL FARM COMMODITIES AND RISK MANAGEMENT

1301 LONGWORTH HOB (ZIP: 20515) 225-2171

Filemon Vela, TX, Chairman

Angie Craig, MN
David Scott, GA
Al Lawson, Jr., FL
Jefferson Van Drew, NJ
Salud O. Carbajal, CA

Glenn Thompson, PA
Austin Scott, GA
Eric A. "Rick" Crawford, AR
Rick W. Allen, GA
Ralph Lee Abraham, LA

SUBCOMMITTEE ON LIVESTOCK AND FOREIGN AGRICULTURE

1301 LONGWORTH HOB (ZIP: 20515)........225-2171

Jim Costa, CA, Chairman

Anthony Brindisi, NY
Jahana Hayes, CT
TJ Cox, CA
Angie Craig, MN
Josh Harder, CA
Filemon Vela, TX
Stacey E. Plaskett, VI
Salud O. Carbajal, CA
Cheri Bustos, IL
Jimmy Panetta, CA

David Rouzer, NC
Glenn Thompson, PA
Scott DesJarlais, TN
Vicky Hartzler, MO
Trent Kelly, MS
James Comer, KY
Roger W. Marshall, KS
Don Bacon, NE
Jim Hagedorn, MN

SUBCOMMITTEE ON BIOTECHNOLOGY, HORTICULTURE, AND RESEARCH

1301 LONGWORTH HOB (ZIP: 20515)........225-2171

Stacey E. Plaskett, VI, Chair

Antonio Delgado, NY
TJ Cox, CA
Josh Harder, CA
Anthony Brindisi, NY
Jefferson Van Drew, NJ
Kim Schrier, WA
Chellie Pingree, ME
Salud O. Carbajal, CA
Jimmy Panetta, CA
Sean Patrick Maloney, NY
Al Lawson, Jr., FL

Neal P. Dunn, FL
Glenn Thompson, PA
Vicky Hartzler, MO
Doug LaMalfa, CA
Rodney Davis, IL
Ted S. Yoho, FL
Mike Bost, IL
James Comer, KY
James R. Baird, IN

SUBCOMMITTEE ON COMMODITY EXCHANGES, ENERGY, AND CREDIT

1301 LONGWORTH HOB (ZIP: 20515)........225-2171

David Scott, GA, Chairman

Jefferson Van Drew, NJ
Filemon Vela, TX
Stacey E. Plaskett, VI
Abigail Davis Spanberger, VA
Antonio Delgado, NY
Angie Craig, MN
Sean Patrick Maloney, NY
Ann Kirkpatrick, AZ
Cynthia Axne, IA

Austin Scott, GA
Eric A. "Rick" Crawford, AR
Mike Bost, IL
David Rouzer, NC
Roger W. Marshall, KS
Neal P. Dunn, FL
Dusty Johnson, SD
James R. Baird, IN

COMMITTEE ON APPROPRIATIONS

H307 CAPITOL (ZIP: 20515-6015)....................225-2771

Nita M. Lowey, NY, Chair

Marcy Kaptur, OH
Peter J. Visclosky, IN
José E. Serrano, NY
Rosa L. DeLauro, CT
David E. Price, NC
Lucille Roybal-Allard, CA
Sanford D. Bishop, Jr., GA
Barbara Lee, CA
Betty McCollum, MN
Tim Ryan, OH
C. A. Dutch Ruppersberger, MD
Debbie Wasserman Schultz, FL
Henry Cuellar, TX
Chellie Pingree, ME
Mike Quigley, IL
Derek Kilmer, WA
Matt Cartwright, PA
Grace Meng, NY
Mark Pocan, WI
Katherine M. Clark, MA
Pete Aguilar, CA, Vice Chair
Lois Frankel, FL
Cheri Bustos, IL
Bonnie Watson Coleman, NJ
Brenda L. Lawrence, MI
Norma J. Torres, CA
Charlie Crist, FL
Ann Kirkpatrick, AZ
Ed Case, HI

Kay Granger, TX
Harold Rogers, KY
Robert B. Aderholt, AL
Michael K. Simpson, ID
John R. Carter, TX
Ken Calvert, CA
Tom Cole, OK
Mario Diaz-Balart, FL
Tom Graves, GA
Steve Womack, AR
Jeff Fortenberry, NE
Charles J. "Chuck" Fleischmann, TN
Jaime Herrera Beutler, WA
David P. Joyce, OH
Andy Harris, MD
Martha Roby, AL
Mark E. Amodei, NV
Chris Stewart, UT
Steven M. Palazzo, MS
Dan Newhouse, WA
John R. Moolenaar, MI
John H. Rutherford, FL
Will Hurd, TX

MAJORITY STAFF

Adkins, William PROF STAFF MEMB H405.................. **52847**
Allen, Amber FINANCIAL ADMIN H307.................. **52771**
Anderson, Matthew SCOREKEEPER 2005.................. **52718**
Berg, Adam CHIEF COUNSEL H307.................. **52771**
Bigelow, Christopher DPTY STAFF DIR H307.................. **52771**
Burns, Michael DPTY COMMUNICATIONS DIR H307.................. **52771**
Cahill, James EDITOR HB13A.................. **52851**
Edwards, Catherine ADMIN AIDE HB13A.................. **52851**
Gray, Jason PROF STAFF MEMB H307.................. **52771**
Hamlin Bias, Lori SCOREKEEPER 2005.................. **52718**
Hansen, Anna ADMIN ASST H307.................. **52771**
Hollander, Evan COMMUNICATIONS DIR H307.................. **52771**
Jackson, Eric SYS ADMIN 2005.................. **52718**
Johnson, Lonnie SYS ADMIN 2005.................. **52718**
Little, Cathy DIR - INFO TECH 2005.................. **52718**
Mariani, Ian COMMUNICATIONS ASST H307.................. **52771**
Muir, Linda SCOREKEEPER 2005.................. **52718**
Tucker, Tom DIR - OPS H307.................. **52771**
Young, Shalanda STAFF DIR H307.................. **52771**

MINORITY STAFF

Attebery, Alexander DPTY COMMUNICATIONS DIR 1016.................. **53481**
Chotvacs, Anne Marie STAFF DIR 1016.................. **53481**
Davis, Alec PROF STAFF MEMB 1016.................. **53481**
Flaim, Sarah COMMUNICATIONS DIR 1016.................. **53481**
Hinman, Alyssa MBR SVCS ASST 1016.................. **53481**
Kaberle, Jonni DPTY STAFF DIR 1016.................. **53481**
Muscolini, John ADMIN ASST 1016.................. **53481**
Reinshuttle, Michelle MBR SVCS ASST 1016.................. **53481**

INVESTIGATIVE STAFF

Ervin, Dana PROF STAFF MEMB 283 FHOB.................. **53881**
Garcia, Melissa PROF STAFF MEMB 283 FHOB.................. **53881**
Garcia, Natasha PROF STAFF MEMB 283 FHOB.................. **53881**
Goldie, Monica PROF STAFF MEMB 283 FHOB.................. **53881**
Hall, Amy PROF STAFF MEMB 283 FHOB.................. **53881**
Linskey, Kevin DIR - INVESTIGATIONS H307.................. **53881**
McGarry, Daniel PROF STAFF MEMB 283 FHOB.................. **53881**
Rambow, Andrea PROF STAFF MEMB 283 FHOB.................. **53881**
Russell, Tracey ADMIN AIDE 283 FHOB.................. **53881**
Smith, Connor ADMIN ASST 283 FHOB.................. **53881**

SUBCOMMITTEES OF THE COMMITTEE ON APPROPRIATIONS

[The chair and ranking minority member are authorized to sit as members of all subcommittees.]

SUBCOMMITTEE ON AGRICULTURE, RURAL DEVELOPMENT, FOOD AND DRUG ADMINISTRATION, AND RELATED AGENCIES

2362A RAYBURN HOB (ZIP: 20515)..225-2638

Sanford D. Bishop, Jr., GA, Chair

Rosa L. DeLauro, CT, Vice Chair
Chellie Pingree, ME
Mark Pocan, WI
Barbara Lee, CA
Betty McCollum, MN
Henry Cuellar, TX

Jeff Fortenberry, NE
Robert B. Aderholt, AL
Andy Harris, MD
John R. Moolenaar, MI

MAJORITY STAFF

Foley, Martha CLERK 2362A........ **52638**
Jones, Diem-Linh PROF STAFF MEMB 2362A........ **52638**
Layman, Joseph PROF STAFF MEMB 2362A........ **52638**
Masucci, Justin PROF STAFF MEMB 2362A........ **52638**
Staples, Randall ADMIN ASST 2362A........ **52638**
Yates, Perry PROF STAFF MEMB 2362A........ **52638**

MINORITY STAFF

O'Brien, Tom PROF STAFF MEMB 1001........ **53481**

SUBCOMMITTEE ON COMMERCE, JUSTICE, SCIENCE, AND RELATED AGENCIES

H310 CAPITOL (ZIP: 20515)..225-3351

José E. Serrano, NY, Chair

Matt Cartwright, PA, Vice Chair
Grace Meng, NY
Brenda L. Lawrence, MI
Charlie Crist, FL
Ed Case, HI
Marcy Kaptur, OH

Robert B. Aderholt, AL
Martha Roby, AL
Steven M. Palazzo, MS
Tom Graves, GA

MAJORITY STAFF

Ashford, Jeff PROF STAFF MEMB H310........ **53351**
Bonner, Robert CLERK H310........ **53351**
Lowdermilk, T J PROF STAFF MEMB H310........ **53351**
McCully, Shannon PROF STAFF MEMB H310........ **53351**
Smith, Matthew PROF STAFF MEMB H310........ **53351**
Wright, B G PROF STAFF MEMB H310........ **53351**

MINORITY STAFF

Gadbois, Stephanie PROF STAFF MEMB 1001........ **53481**

U.S. HOUSE OF REPRESENTATIVES

SUBCOMMITTEE ON DEFENSE

H405 CAPITOL (ZIP: 20515) 225-2847

Peter J. Visclosky, IN, Chair

Betty McCollum, MN, Vice Chair
Tim Ryan, OH
C. A. Dutch Ruppersberger, MD
Marcy Kaptur, OH
Henry Cuellar, TX
Derek Kilmer, WA
Pete Aguilar, CA
Cheri Bustos, IL
Charlie Crist, FL
Ann Kirkpatrick, AZ

Ken Calvert, CA
Harold Rogers, KY
Tom Cole, OK
Steve Womack, AR
Robert B. Aderholt, AL
John R. Carter, TX
Mario Diaz-Balart, FL

MAJORITY STAFF

Bortnick, David PROF STAFF MEMB H405 **52847**
Bower, Matthew PROF STAFF MEMB H405 **52847**
Boyer, Brooke PROF STAFF MEMB H405 **52847**
Chartrand, Jennifer PROF STAFF MEMB H405 **52847**
Hearne, Walter PROF STAFF MEMB H405 **52847**
Kilbride, Paul PROF STAFF MEMB H405 **52847**
Leggieri, Rebecca CLERK H405 **52847**
Milberg, Hayden PROF STAFF MEMB H405 **52847**
Richter, Shannon PROF STAFF MEMB H405 **52847**
Ripke, Jackie PROF STAFF MEMB H405 **52847**
Sarar, Ariana PROF STAFF MEMB H405 **52847**
Young, Sherry ADMIN AIDE H405 **52847**

MINORITY STAFF

Albright, Leslie PROF STAFF MEMB 1001 **53481**

SUBCOMMITTEE ON ENERGY AND WATER DEVELOPMENT, AND RELATED AGENCIES

2362B RAYBURN HOB (ZIP: 20515) 225-3421

Marcy Kaptur, OH
Chair

Peter J. Visclosky, IN
Vice Chair
Debbie Wasserman Schultz, FL
Ann Kirkpatrick, AZ
Derek Kilmer, WA
Mark Pocan, WI
Lois Frankel, FL

Michael K. Simpson, ID
Ken Calvert, CA
Charles J. "Chuck" Fleischmann, TN
Dan Newhouse, WA

MAJORITY STAFF

Arnone, Mark PROF STAFF MEMB 2362B **53421**
Brain, Michael PROF STAFF MEMB 2362B **53421**
Caldwell, Marcel ADMIN ASST 2362B **53421**
McKee, Scott PROF STAFF MEMB 2362B **53421**
Ophaso, Farouk PROF STAFF MEMB 2362B **53421**
Shimek, Jaime CLERK 2362B **53421**

MINORITY STAFF

Giancarlo, Angie PROF STAFF MEMB 1001 **53481**

SUBCOMMITTEE ON FINANCIAL SERVICES AND GENERAL GOVERNMENT

2000 RAYBURN HOB (ZIP: 20515)........225-7245

Mike Quigley, IL, Chair

José E. Serrano, NY, Vice Chair
Matt Cartwright, PA
Sanford D. Bishop, Jr., GA
Norma J. Torres, CA
Charlie Crist, FL
Ann Kirkpatrick, AZ

Tom Graves, GA
Mark E. Amodei, NV
Chris Stewart, UT
David P. Joyce, OH

MAJORITY STAFF

Cylke, Laura PROF STAFF MEMB 2000........ **57245**
Doomes, Elliot PROF STAFF MEMB 2000........ **57245**
Mehta, Aalok PROF STAFF MEMB 2000........ **57245**
Molyneux, Lisa CLERK 2000........ **57245**
Nassif, Marybeth PROF STAFF MEMB 2000........ **57245**
Van De Water, Parker ADMIN ASST 2000........ **57245**

MINORITY STAFF

Martens, John PROF STAFF MEMB 1016........ **53481**

SUBCOMMITTEE ON HOMELAND SECURITY

2006 RAYBURN HOB (ZIP: 20515)........225-5834

Lucille Roybal-Allard, CA, Chair

Henry Cuellar, TX, Vice Chair
C. A. Dutch Ruppersberger, MD
David E. Price, NC
Debbie Wasserman Schultz, FL
Grace Meng, NY
Pete Aguilar, CA

Charles J. "Chuck" Fleischmann, TN
Steven M. Palazzo, MS
Dan Newhouse, WA
John H. Rutherford, FL

MAJORITY STAFF

Herman, Michael PROF STAFF MEMB 2006........ **55834**
Joachim, Robert PROF STAFF MEMB 2006........ **55834**
Mallard, Kris PROF STAFF MEMB 2006........ **55834**
Newby, Darek CLERK 2006........ **55834**
Richman, Karyn PROF STAFF MEMB 2006........ **55834**
Roth, David ADMIN AIDE 2006........ **55834**

MINORITY STAFF

Baron, Dena PROF STAFF MEMB 1016........ **53481**

SUBCOMMITTEE ON INTERIOR, ENVIRONMENT, AND RELATED AGENCIES

2007 RAYBURN HOB (ZIP: 20515)........225-3081

Betty McCollum, MN, Chair

Chellie Pingree, ME, Vice Chair
Derek Kilmer, WA
José E. Serrano, NY
Mike Quigley, IL
Bonnie Watson Coleman, NJ
Brenda L. Lawrence, MI

David P. Joyce, OH
Michael K. Simpson, ID
Chris Stewart, UT
Mark E. Amodei, NV

MAJORITY STAFF

Coe, Tyler ADMIN ASST 2007........ **53081**
Culp, Rita CLERK 2007........ **53081**
Erickson, Janet PROF STAFF MEMB 2007........ **53081**
Hunn, Jocelyn PROF STAFF MEMB 2007........ **53081**
Kiefhaber, Peter PROF STAFF MEMB 2007........ **53081**
Merchant, Kusai PROF STAFF MEMB 2007........ **53081**
Richmond, Kristin ADMIN AIDE 2007........ **53081**
Shahbaz, Donna PROF STAFF MEMB 2007........ **53081**

MINORITY STAFF

Benjamin, Darren PROF STAFF MEMB 1001 53481

SUBCOMMITTEE ON LABOR, HEALTH AND HUMAN SERVICES, EDUCATION, AND RELATED AGENCIES

2358B RAYBURN HOB (ZIP: 20515) 225-3508

Rosa L. DeLauro, CT, Chair

Lucille Roybal-Allard, CA, Vice Chair
Barbara Lee, CA
Mark Pocan, WI
Katherine M. Clark, MA
Lois Frankel, FL
Cheri Bustos, IL
Bonnie Watson Coleman, NJ

Tom Cole, OK
Andy Harris, MD
Jaime Herrera Beutler, WA
John R. Moolenaar, MI
Tom Graves, GA

MAJORITY STAFF

Allen, Brad ADMIN AIDE 2358B 53508
Bass, Jared PROF STAFF MEMB 2358B 53508
Cama, Jennifer PROF STAFF MEMB 2358B 53508
Juliano, Robin PROF STAFF MEMB 2358B 53508
Kilroy, Jaclyn PROF STAFF MEMB 2358B 53508
Mignone, Laurie PROF STAFF MEMB 2358B 53508
Steigleder, Stephen CLERK 2358B 53508
Tizzani, Philip PROF STAFF MEMB 2358B 53508

MINORITY STAFF

Ross, Susan PROF STAFF MEMB 1016 53481
Salmon, Kathryn PROF STAFF MEMB 1001 53481

SUBCOMMITTEE ON LEGISLATIVE BRANCH

H306 CAPITOL (ZIP: 20515) 226-7252

Tim Ryan, OH, Chair

C. A. Dutch Ruppersberger, MD, Vice Chair
Katherine M. Clark, MA
Ed Case, HI

Jaime Herrera Beutler, WA
Dan Newhouse, WA

MAJORITY STAFF

Cobb, Faye PROF STAFF MEMB H306 67252
Quantius, Sue PROF STAFF MEMB H306 67252
Reich, David CLERK H306 67252

MINORITY STAFF

Panone, Jenny PROF STAFF MEMB 1001 53481

SUBCOMMITTEE ON MILITARY CONSTRUCTION, VETERANS AFFAIRS, AND RELATED AGENCIES

HT2 CAPITOL (ZIP: 20515) 225-3047

Debbie Wasserman Schultz, FL, Chair

Sanford D. Bishop, Jr., GA, Vice Chair
Ed Case, HI
Tim Ryan, OH
Chellie Pingree, ME
Matt Cartwright, PA
Cheri Bustos, IL

John R. Carter, TX
Martha Roby, AL
John H. Rutherford, FL
Will Hurd, TX

MAJORITY STAFF

Cohen, Nicole PROF STAFF MEMB HT2 53047
Hollrah, Jennifer PROF STAFF MEMB HT2 53047

Washington, Matthew CLERK HT2 53047
Young, Sarah PROF STAFF MEMB HT2 53047

MINORITY STAFF

Batmanglidj, Kiyalan PROF STAFF MEMB 1040A 53481
Bina, Betsy PROF STAFF MEMB 1001 53481

SUBCOMMITTEE ON STATE, FOREIGN OPERATIONS, AND RELATED PROGRAMS

HT2 CAPITOL (ZIP: 20515) 225-2041

Nita M. Lowey, NY, Chair

Barbara Lee, CA, Vice Chair
Grace Meng, NY
David E. Price, NC
Lois Frankel, FL
Norma J. Torres, CA

Harold Rogers, KY
Jeff Fortenberry, NE
Martha Roby, AL

MAJORITY STAFF

Alvarado, Clelia ADMIN AIDE HT2 52041
Higgins, Craig PROF STAFF MEMB HT2 52041
Kolodjeski, Erin PROF STAFF MEMB HT2 52041
Koulouris, Dean PROF STAFF MEMB HT2 52041
Kwon, Jean PROF STAFF MEMB HT2 52041
Marchese, Steve CLERK HT2 52041
Stein, Marin PROF STAFF MEMB HT2 52041
Wheelock, Jason PROF STAFF MEMB HT2 52041

MINORITY STAFF

Adams, Susan PROF STAFF MEMB 1016 53481
McCormick, James PROF STAFF MEMB 1040A 53481

SUBCOMMITTEE ON TRANSPORTATION, AND HOUSING AND URBAN DEVELOPMENT, AND RELATED AGENCIES

2358A RAYBURN HOB (ZIP: 20515) 225-2141

David E. Price, NC, Chair

Mike Quigley, IL, Vice Chair
Katherine M. Clark, MA
Bonnie Watson Coleman, NJ
Brenda L. Lawrence, MI
Norma J. Torres, CA
Pete Aguilar, CA

Mario Diaz-Balart, FL
Steve Womack, AR
John H. Rutherford, FL
Will Hurd, TX

MAJORITY STAFF

Barcena, Gladys ADMIN ASST 2358A 52141
Carlile, Joe CLERK 2358A 52141
Chang, Winnie PROF STAFF MEMB 2358A 52141
Eckert, Josephine PROF STAFF MEMB 2358A 52141
Ohm, Angela PROF STAFF MEMB 2358A 52141
Puro, Sarah PROF STAFF MEMB 2358A 52141
Salay, Rebecca PROF STAFF MEMB 2358A 52141

MINORITY STAFF

Disrud, Douglas PROF STAFF MEMB 1001 53481

COMMITTEE ON ARMED SERVICES

2216 RAYBURN HOB (ZIP: 20515-6035)..... 225-4151

Adam Smith, WA, Chair

Susan A. Davis, CA
James R. Langevin, RI
Rick Larsen, WA
Jim Cooper, TN
Joe Courtney, CT
John Garamendi, CA
Jackie Speier, CA
Tulsi Gabbard, HI
Donald Norcross, NJ
Ruben Gallego, AZ
Seth Moulton, MA
Salud O. Carbajal, CA
Anthony G. Brown, MD, Vice Chair
Ro Khanna, CA
William R. Keating, MA
Filemon Vela, TX
Andy Kim, NJ
Kendra S. Horn, OK
Gilbert Ray Cisneros, Jr., CA
Chrissy Houlahan, PA
Jason Crow, CO
Xochitl Torres Small, NM
Elissa Slotkin, MI
Mikie Sherrill, NJ
Katie Hill, CA
Veronica Escobar, TX
Debra A. Haaland, NM
Jared F. Golden, ME
Lori Trahan, MA
Elaine G. Luria, VA

Mac Thornberry, TX
Joe Wilson, SC
Rob Bishop, UT
Michael R. Turner, OH
Mike Rogers, AL
K. Michael Conaway, TX
Doug Lamborn, CO
Robert J. Wittman, VA
Vicky Hartzler, MO
Austin Scott, GA
Mo Brooks, AL
Paul Cook, CA
Bradley Byrne, AL
Sam Graves, MO
Elise M. Stefanik, NY
Scott DesJarlais, TN
Ralph Lee Abraham, LA
Trent Kelly, MS
Mike Gallagher, WI
Matt Gaetz, FL
Don Bacon, NE
Jim Banks, IN
Liz Cheney, WY
Paul Mitchell, MI
Jack Bergman, MI
Michael Waltz, FL

STAFF MEMBERS

Arcangeli, Paul STAFF DIR - MAJ 2117..... **54158**
Blyden, Chidi PROF STAFF 2117..... **67164**
Bope, Heath PROF STAFF 2340..... **53040**
Bush, Douglas DPTY STAFF DIR 2117..... **61645**
Carroll, Jessica PROF STAFF 2340..... **54440**
Chafin, Claude COMMUNICATIONS DIR - MIN 2340..... **63988**
Coleman, Everett PROF STAFF G2L2..... **50883**
Diehl, Glen PROF STAFF MEMB 2340..... **66504**
Dopkeen, Bess PROF STAFF 2340..... **56710**
Drummond, Elizabeth PROF STAFF 2340..... **67171**
Falvey, Sean CLERK 2216..... **54151**
Garrett, Brian PROF STAFF 2340..... **53439**
Giachetti, David PROF STAFF 2340..... **66162**
Goggin, Kelly PROF STAFF 2340..... **63229**
Gray, Betty EXEC ASST 2117..... **54158**
Greene, Craig PROF STAFF 2340..... **55540**
Greer, Brian PROF STAFF 2340..... **68454**
Halcrow, Stephanie PROF STAFF 2340..... **66164**
Handal, Megan CLERK 2340..... **68979**
Harris, Melanie PROF STAFF 2340..... **66120**
Hawley, Tom PROF STAFF MEMB 2340..... **65688**
Hermann, Michael PROF STAFF 2117..... **68971**
Jackson, Jamie DPTY GEN COUNSEL 2117..... **53432**
Johnson, John STAFF ASST 2216..... **54151**
Johnson, Spencer GEN COUNSEL 2117..... **54224**
Johnson, Will PROF STAFF MEMB 2216..... **51977**
Kavanaugh, Lindsay PROF STAFF 2340..... **55416**
Kehrli, Caroline CLERK 2340..... **62843**
Lehn, Kim PROF STAFF MEMB 2340..... **62923**
Lord, Jonathan PROF STAFF 2117..... **66235**
Lynch, Justin CLERK 2117..... **63297**
MacNaughton, John PROF STAFF 2340..... **64532**
Matoush, Monica COMMUNICATIONS DIR 2117..... **65048**
Mineiro, Sarah PROF STAFF MEMB 2340..... **60120**
Morehouse, Mark PROF STAFF 2340..... **52340**
Najieb-Locke, Halimah PROF STAFF 2117..... **61055**
Quinn, Katherine PROF STAFF 2340..... **62167**
Rauch, Laura PROF STAFF MEMB 2119..... **66712**
Rhoades, Matthew PROF STAFF 2117..... **62583**
Ross, Rebecca PROF STAFF 2216..... **54100**
Scheenstra, Hannah EXEC ASST 2340..... **68980**
Schmid, Jason PROF STAFF 2340..... **64952**

Schneider, Grant PROF STAFF 2340 .... **57150**
Sennott, Daniel PROF STAFF MEMB 2340 .... **57192**
Sharma, Sapna PROF STAFF 2117 .... **55050**
Sienicki, David PROF STAFF 2340 .... **54469**
Snelgrove, Eric PROF STAFF 2340 .... **66064**
Steacy, Zachary DIR - LEGIS OPS 2117 .... **68634**
Steitz, Danielle CLERK 2340 .... **57560**
Stewart, Jennifer STAFF DIR - MIN 2340 .... **68980**
Stiefel, Joshua PROF STAFF 2340 .... **66339**
Sutey, William PROF STAFF 2340 .... **62099**
Taylor, Zachary CLERK 2340 .... **51967**
Thompson, Katie DIR - SECUR 2337 .... **55733**
Tolleson, Jesse PROF STAFF 2340 .... **68774**
Tomero, Leonor COUNSEL 2340 .... **52526**
Vastola, Maria PROF STAFF MEMB 2340 .... **54252**
Villano, Peter PROF STAFF 2340 .... **60080**
White, Shenita CLERK 2216 .... **54151**
Womble, Jeanine PROF STAFF 2340 .... **62336**
Yin, Jocelyn GAO DETAILEE 2117 .... **65610**
Youngsmith, Barron PROF STAFF 2117 .... **65662**
Zeppieri, Carla PROF STAFF 2340 .... **56703**

SUBCOMMITTEES OF THE COMMITTEE ON ARMED SERVICES

SUBCOMMITTEE ON INTELLIGENCE AND EMERGING THREATS AND CAPABILITIES

2340 RAYBURN HOB (ZIP: 20515)........ 226-2843

James R. Langevin, RI, Chairman

Rick Larsen, WA
Jim Cooper, TN
Tulsi Gabbard, HI
Anthony G. Brown, MD
Ro Khanna, CA
William R. Keating, MA
Andy Kim, NJ
Chrissy Houlahan, PA
Jason Crow, CO, Vice Chair
Elissa Slotkin, MI
Lori Trahan, MA

Elise M. Stefanik, NY
Sam Graves, MO
Ralph Lee Abraham, LA
K. Michael Conaway, TX
Austin Scott, GA
Scott DesJarlais, TN
Mike Gallagher, WI
Michael Waltz, FL
Don Bacon, NE
Jim Banks, IN

SUBCOMMITTEE ON MILITARY PERSONNEL

2340 RAYBURN HOB (ZIP: 20515)........ 225-7560

Jackie Speier, CA, Chairwoman

Susan A. Davis, CA
Ruben Gallego, AZ
Gilbert Ray Cisneros, Jr., CA, Vice Chair
Veronica Escobar, TX
Debra A. Haaland, NM
Lori Trahan, MA
Elaine G. Luria, VA

Trent Kelly, MS
Ralph Lee Abraham, LA
Liz Cheney, WY
Paul Mitchell, MI
Jack Bergman, MI
Matt Gaetz, FL

U.S. HOUSE OF REPRESENTATIVES

SUBCOMMITTEE ON READINESS

2340 RAYBURN HOB (ZIP: 20515)....................226-8979

John Garamendi, CA, Chairman

Tulsi Gabbard, HI	*Doug Lamborn*, CO
Andy Kim, NJ, Vice Chair	*Austin Scott*, GA
Kendra S. Horn, OK	*Joe Wilson*, SC
Chrissy Houlahan, PA	*Rob Bishop*, UT
Jason Crow, CO	*Mike Rogers*, AL
Xochitl Torres Small, NM	*Mo Brooks*, AL
Elissa Slotkin, MI	*Elise M. Stefanik*, NY
Veronica Escobar, TX	*Jack Bergman*, MI
Debra A. Haaland, NM	

SUBCOMMITTEE ON SEAPOWER AND PROJECTION FORCES

2340 RAYBURN HOB (ZIP: 20515)....................226-2211

Joe Courtney, CT, Chairman

James R. Langevin, RI	*Robert J. Wittman*, VA
Jim Cooper, TN	*K. Michael Conaway*, TX
Donald Norcross, NJ	*Mike Gallagher*, WI
Seth Moulton, MA	*Jack Bergman*, MI
Filemon Vela, TX	*Michael Waltz*, FL
Gilbert Ray Cisneros, Jr., CA	*Vicky Hartzler*, MO
Mikie Sherrill, NJ	*Paul Cook*, CA
Katie Hill, CA	*Bradley Byrne*, AL
Jared F. Golden, ME	*Trent Kelly*, MS
Elaine G. Luria, VA, Vice Chair	

SUBCOMMITTEE ON STRATEGIC FORCES

2340 RAYBURN HOB (ZIP: 20515)....................225-1967

Jim Cooper, TN, Chairman

Susan A. Davis, CA	*Michael R. Turner*, OH
Rick Larsen, WA	*Joe Wilson*, SC
John Garamendi, CA	*Rob Bishop*, UT
Jackie Speier, CA	*Mike Rogers*, AL
Seth Moulton, MA	*Mo Brooks*, AL
Salud O. Carbajal, CA	*Bradley Byrne*, AL
Ro Khanna, CA	*Scott DesJarlais*, TN
William R. Keating, MA	*Liz Cheney*, WY
Kendra S. Horn, OK, Vice Chair	

COMMITTEE MEMBERS AND STAFF

SUBCOMMITTEE ON TACTICAL AIR AND LAND FORCES

2340 RAYBURN HOB (ZIP: 20515)..225-4440

Donald Norcross, NJ, Chairman

James R. Langevin, RI
Joe Courtney, CT
Ruben Gallego, AZ
Salud O. Carbajal, CA
Anthony G. Brown, MD
Filemon Vela, TX
Xochitl Torres Small, NM, Vice Chair
Mikie Sherrill, NJ
Katie Hill, CA
Jared F. Golden, ME

Vicky Hartzler, MO
Paul Cook, CA
Matt Gaetz, FL
Don Bacon, NE
Jim Banks, IN
Paul Mitchell, MI
Michael R. Turner, OH
Doug Lamborn, CO
Robert J. Wittman, VA

U.S. HOUSE OF REPRESENTATIVES

COMMITTEE ON THE BUDGET

204E CANNON HOB (ZIP: 20515-6065)........................ 226-7200

John A. Yarmuth, KY, Chair

Seth Moulton, MA
Hakeem S. Jeffries, NY
Brian Higgins, NY
Brendan F. Boyle, PA
Ro Khanna, CA
Rosa L. DeLauro, CT
Lloyd Doggett, TX
David E. Price, NC
Janice D. Schakowsky, IL
Daniel T. Kildee, MI
Jimmy Panetta, CA
Joseph D. Morelle, NY
Steven Horsford, NV
Robert C. "Bobby" Scott, VA
Sheila Jackson Lee, TX
Barbara Lee, CA
Pramila Jayapal, WA
Ilhan Omar, MN
Albio Sires, NJ
Scott H. Peters, CA
Jim Cooper, TN

Steve Womack, AR
Rob Woodall, GA
Bill Johnson, OH
Jason Smith, MO
Bill Flores, TX
George Holding, NC
Chris Stewart, UT
Ralph Norman, SC
Chip Roy, TX
Daniel Meuser, PA
William R. Timmons IV, SC
Dan Crenshaw, TX
Kevin Hern, OK
Tim Burchett, TN

MAJORITY STAFF

Antista, Jonathan BUDGET ANALYST 204E CHOB........ 67200
Appel, Erika BUDGET ANALYST/COORD - COALITION & MBR SVCS 204E CHOB........ 67200
Balis, Ellen STAFF DIR - MAJ 204E CHOB........ 67200
Baugh, Patrick FINANCIAL ADMIN 204E CHOB........ 67200
Elul, Gabrielle ECONOMIST 204E CHOB........ 67200
Etzkorn, Edward BUDGET ANALYST 204E CHOB........ 67200
Guillen, José SYS ADMIN 204E CHOB........ 67200
Harris, Jocelyn COUNSEL/BUDGET ANALYST 204E CHOB........ 67200
Jeppson, Chelsie DIGITAL DIR 204E CHOB........ 67200
King, Emily BUDGET ANALYST 204E CHOB........ 67200
Lau, Sam COMMUNICATIONS DIR 204E CHOB........ 67200
Lee, Sarah BUDGET ANALYST 204E CHOB........ 67200
McDowell, Sheila OFFICE MGR 204E CHOB........ 67200
Meredith, Diana DPTY STAFF DIR - MAJ STAFF 204E CHOB........ 67200
Overbeek, Kimberly BUDGET ANALYST 204E CHOB........ 67200
Russell, Scott R BUDGET ANALYST 204E CHOB........ 67200
Santos, Laura STAFF ASST 204E CHOB........ 67200
Spencer, Raquel GEN COUNSEL 204E CHOB........ 67200
Weinroth, Alexandra PRESS SECY 204E CHOB........ 67200
Wheelock, Jennifer BUDGET ANALYST 204E CHOB........ 67200
Zegers, Ted BUDGET ANALYST 204E CHOB........ 67200

MINORITY STAFF

Aronson, Lauren Blair COMMUNICATIONS DIR - MIN 507 CHOB........ 67270
Davis, Eric POLICY ADVISOR 507 CHOB........ 67270
Gardenhour, Benjamin EXEC ASST 507 CHOB........ 67270
Gonzalez, Steve POLICY ADVISOR 507 CHOB........ 67270
Haglund, Gary POLICY ADVISOR 507 CHOB........ 67270
Hayes, Colin POLICY ADVISOR 507 CHOB........ 67270
Keniry, Dan STAFF DIR - MIN 507 CHOB........ 67270
Peterson, Sage ADVISOR - MBR SVCS/OUTREACH ADVISOR 507 CHOB........ 67270
Popadiuk, Mary GEN COUNSEL 507 CHOB........ 67270
Relic, Becky DPTY STAFF DIR - MIN STAFF 507 CHOB........ 67270
Spealman, Jennafer POLICY DIR 507 CHOB........ 67270
Steinmetz, Adam POLICY ADVISOR 507 CHOB........ 67270
Stonebraker, Austin M DIGITAL DIR 507 CHOB........ 67270
Watson, Brad SR POLICY ADVISOR 507 CHOB........ 67270

COMMITTEE ON EDUCATION AND LABOR

2176 RAYBURN HOB (ZIP: 20515-6100).......... 225-3725

Robert C. "Bobby" Scott, VA, Chair

Susan A. Davis, CA
Raúl M. Grijalva, AZ
Joe Courtney, CT
Marcia L. Fudge, OH
Gregorio Kilili Camacho Sablan, MP
Frederica S. Wilson, FL
Suzanne Bonamici, OR
Mark Takano, CA
Alma S. Adams, NC
Mark DeSaulnier, CA
Donald Norcross, NJ
Pramila Jayapal, WA
Joseph D. Morelle, NY
Susan Wild, PA
Josh Harder, CA
Lucy McBath, GA
Kim Schrier, WA
Lauren Underwood, IL
Jahana Hayes, CT
Donna E. Shalala, FL
Andy Levin, MI, Vice Chair
Ilhan Omar, MN
David J. Trone, MD
Haley M. Stevens, MI
Susie Lee, NV
Lori Trahan, MA
Joaquin Castro, TX

Virginia Foxx, NC
David P. Roe, TN
Glenn Thompson, PA
Tim Walberg, MI
Brett Guthrie, KY
Bradley Byrne, AL
Glenn Grothman, WI
Elise M. Stefanik, NY
Rick W. Allen, GA
Francis Rooney, FL
Lloyd Smucker, PA
Jim Banks, IN
Mark Walker, NC
James Comer, KY
Ben Cline, VA
Russ Fulcher, ID
Van Taylor, TX
Steve Watkins, KS
Ron Wright, TX
Daniel Meuser, PA
William R. Timmons IV, SC
Dusty Johnson, SD

MAJORITY STAFF

Alli, Tylease CHIEF CLERK 2176.......... **53725**
Barab, Jordan SR LABOR POLICY ADVISOR 230 FHOB.......... **53725**
Berger, Katie PROF STAFF 2257.......... **53725**
Brown, Nekea DPTY CLERK 2176.......... **53725**
Brunner, Ilana GEN COUNSEL 2176.......... **53725**
Chevalier Mosely, Jacque DIR - EDUC POLICY 2257.......... **53725**
Dailey, David COUNSEL TO THE CHAIRMAN/SHARED EMPLOYEE 1201.......... **58351**
DeCant, Kyle COUNSEL - LABOR POLICY 2051C.......... **53725**
Eatman, Emma PRESS AIDE 2176.......... **53725**
Estes-Petty, Randi-Joanne A SPECIAL ASST TO THE CHAIRMAN/SHARED EMPLOYEE 1201.......... **58351**
Foster, Daniel COUNSEL - HEALTH & LABOR 2257.......... **53725**
Freeman, Mishawn STAFF ASST 2176.......... **53725**
Haines, Christian GEN COUNSEL 2257.......... **53725**
Hard, Alison PROF STAFF 2257.......... **53725**
Havenner, Sheila DIR - INFO TECH 2051A.......... **53725**
Hollis, Elizabeth "Liz" DIR - FINANCE & PERSONNEL 2051B.... **53725**
Hovland, Eli STAFF ASST 2051C.......... **53725**
Hughes, Carolyn "Carrie" DIR - HEALTH & HUMAN SVCS 2257.......... **53725**
Ikene, Eunice LABOR POLICY ADVISOR 2051C.......... **53725**
Jona, Ariel STAFF ASST 2257.......... **53725**
Knackstedt, Kimberly DISABILITY POLICY ADVISOR 230 FHOB.......... **53725**
Lalle, Stephanie DPTY COMMUNICATIONS DIR 2176.......... **53725**
Lee, Bertram POLICY COUNSEL 230 FHOB.......... **53725**
Lindsay, Andre STAFF ASST 2257.......... **53725**
Martin, Jaria STAFF ASST 2176.......... **53725**
McClelland, Katherine PROF STAFF 230 FHOB.......... **50868**
McDermott, Kevin SR LABOR POLICY ADVISOR 2051C.......... **53725**
Miller, Richard D DIR - LABOR POLICY 2051C.......... **53725**
Mizutani, Kota STAFF WRITER 2176.......... **53725**
Moore, Max OFFICE AIDE 230 FHOB.......... **53725**
Nelson, Merrick DIGITAL MGR 2176.......... **53725**
Onwubiko, Udochi COUNSEL - LABOR POLICY 2051C.......... **53725**
Pluviose, Veronique STAFF DIR 2176.......... **53725**
Ronis, Carolyn COUNSEL - CIVIL RIGHTS 230 FHOB.......... **53725**
Ruskowsky, Dianna FINANCE & PERSONNEL ADVISOR 2051B.......... **53725**
Sinoff, Benjamin DIR - EDUC OVERSIGHT 230 FHOB.......... **53725**
Steele, Lakeisha PROF STAFF 2257.......... **53725**
Valle, Katherine SR EDUC POLICY ADVISOR 2257.......... **53725**
Vassar, Banyon DPTY DIR - INFO TECH 2051A.......... **53725**
Viall, Claire PROF STAFF 2257.......... **53725**
Walker, Katelyn COUNSEL 2176.......... **53725**
Weisz, Joshua COMMUNICATIONS DIR 2176.......... **53725**
West, Rachel SR ECON & ENERGY POLICY ADVISOR 230 FHOB.......... **50868**

Winnick, Everett SYS ADMIN/SHARED EMPLOYEE 2051A........ **53725**
Yu, Cathy DIR - LABOR OVERSIGHT 230 FHOB........ **53725**

MINORITY STAFF

Artz, Cyrus PARLIAMENTARIAN/SHARED EMPLOYEE 2462........ **52071**
Blankenship, April FINANCIAL ADMIN/SHARED EMPLOYEE 2101........ **54527**
Boughton, Marty PRESS SECY 2178........ **69440**
Butcher, Courtney DIR - COALITIONS & MBR SVCS 6150........ **54527**
Chougule, Akash PROF STAFF MEMB 6150........ **57101**
Green, Robert DIR - WORKFORCE POLICY 6150........ **54527**
Handy, Bridget LEGIS ASST 6140........ **54527**
Johnson, Blake STAFF ASST 2101........ **54527**
Jones, Amy Raaf DIR - EDUC & HUMAN SVCS POLICY 6140........ **54527**
Martin, John COUNSEL - WORKFORCE POLICY 6150........ **57101**
Martin, Sarah PROF STAFF MEMB 6150........ **57101**
Matesic, Hannah DIR - OPS 2101........ **54527**
McNabb, Kelley COMMUNICATIONS DIR 2178........ **69440**
Middlebrooks, Jake PROF STAFF MEMB 6140........ **56558**
Murray, Alexis PROF STAFF MEMB 6150........ **57101**
Pic, Jordan SHARED EMPLOYEE 2462........ **52071**
Renz, Brandon STAFF DIR 2101........ **54527**
Ricci, Alex PROF STAFF MEMB 6140........ **56558**
Ridder, Benjamin LEGIS ASST 6150........ **57101**
Schaumburg, Mandy DPTY DIR - EDUC & HUMAN SVCS POLICY/CHIEF COUNSEL 6140........ **56558**
Schellin, Meredith DPTY PRESS SECY/DIGITAL MGR 2178........ **69440**
Thomas, Brad SR POLICY ADVISOR - EDUC 6140........ **56558**
Wadyka, Heather STAFF ASST 2101........ **54527**
Williams, Lauren PROF STAFF MEMB 6150........ **57101**

SUBCOMMITTEES OF THE COMMITTEE ON EDUCATION AND LABOR

[The chairman and the ranking minority member are ex officio, non-voting members of all subcommittees to which they are not assigned.]

SUBCOMMITTEE ON EARLY CHILDHOOD, ELEMENTARY, AND SECONDARY EDUCATION

2176 RAYBURN HOB (ZIP: 20515)........ 225-3725

Gregorio Kilili Camacho Sablan, MP, Chair

Kim Schrier, WA
Jahana Hayes, CT
Donna E. Shalala, FL
Susan A. Davis, CA
Frederica S. Wilson, FL
Mark DeSaulnier, CA
Joseph D. Morelle, NY

Rick W. Allen, GA
Glenn Thompson, PA
Glenn Grothman, WI
Van Taylor, TX
William R. Timmons IV, SC

SUBCOMMITTEE ON WORKFORCE PROTECTIONS

2176 RAYBURN HOB (ZIP: 20515)........ 225-3725

Alma S. Adams, NC, Chair

Mark DeSaulnier, CA
Mark Takano, CA
Pramila Jayapal, WA
Susan Wild, PA
Lucy McBath, GA
Ilhan Omar, MN
Haley M. Stevens, MI

Bradley Byrne, AL
Francis Rooney, FL
Mark Walker, NC
Ben Cline, VA
Ron Wright, TX

SUBCOMMITTEE ON HIGHER EDUCATION AND WORKFORCE INVESTMENT

2176 RAYBURN HOB (ZIP: 20515)..225-3725

Susan A. Davis, CA, Chair

Joe Courtney, CT
Mark Takano, CA
Pramila Jayapal, WA
Josh Harder, CA
Andy Levin, MI
Ilhan Omar, MN
David J. Trone, MD
Susie Lee, NV
Lori Trahan, MA
Joaquin Castro, TX
Raúl M. Grijalva, AZ
Gregorio Kilili Camacho Sablan, MP
Suzanne Bonamici, OR
Alma S. Adams, NC
Donald Norcross, NJ

Lloyd Smucker, PA
Brett Guthrie, KY
Glenn Grothman, WI
Elise M. Stefanik, NY
Jim Banks, IN
Mark Walker, NC
James Comer, KY
Ben Cline, VA
Russ Fulcher, ID
Steve Watkins, KS
Daniel Meuser, PA
William R. Timmons IV, SC

SUBCOMMITTEE ON CIVIL RIGHTS AND HUMAN SERVICES

2176 RAYBURN HOB (ZIP: 20515)..225-3725

Suzanne Bonamici, OR, Chair

Raúl M. Grijalva, AZ
Marcia L. Fudge, OH
Kim Schrier, WA
Jahana Hayes, CT
David J. Trone, MD
Susie Lee, NV

James Comer, KY
Glenn Thompson, PA
Elise M. Stefanik, NY
Dusty Johnson, SD

SUBCOMMITTEE ON HEALTH, EMPLOYMENT, LABOR, AND PENSIONS

2176 RAYBURN HOB (ZIP: 20515)..225-3725

Frederica S. Wilson, FL, Chair

Donald Norcross, NJ
Joseph D. Morelle, NY
Susan Wild, PA
Lucy McBath, GA
Lauren Underwood, IL
Haley M. Stevens, MI
Joe Courtney, CT
Marcia L. Fudge, OH
Josh Harder, CA
Donna E. Shalala, FL
Andy Levin, MI
Lori Trahan, MA
Robert C. "Bobby" Scott, VA

Tim Walberg, MI
David P. Roe, TN
Rick W. Allen, GA
Francis Rooney, FL
Jim Banks, IN
Russ Fulcher, ID
Van Taylor, TX
Steve Watkins, KS
Ron Wright, TX
Daniel Meuser, PA
Dusty Johnson, SD

COMMITTEE ON ENERGY AND COMMERCE

2125 RAYBURN HOB (ZIP: 20515-6115)........225-2927

Frank Pallone, Jr., NJ, Chair

Bobby L. Rush, IL
Anna G. Eshoo, CA
Eliot L. Engel, NY
Diana DeGette, CO
Michael F. Doyle, PA
Janice D. Schakowsky, IL
G. K. Butterfield, NC
Doris O. Matsui, CA
Kathy Castor, FL
John P. Sarbanes, MD
Jerry McNerney, CA
Peter Welch, VT
Ben Ray Luján, NM
Paul Tonko, NY
Yvette D. Clarke, NY, Vice Chair
David Loebsack, IA
Kurt Schrader, OR
Joseph P. Kennedy III, MA
Tony Cárdenas, CA
Raul Ruiz, CA
Scott H. Peters, CA
Debbie Dingell, MI
Marc A. Veasey, TX
Ann M. Kuster, NH
Robin L. Kelly, IL
Nanette Diaz Barragán, CA
A. Donald McEachin, VA
Lisa Blunt Rochester, DE
Darren Soto, FL
Tom O'Halleran, AZ

Greg Walden, OR
Fred Upton, MI
John Shimkus, IL
Michael C. Burgess, TX
Steve Scalise, LA
Robert E. Latta, OH
Cathy McMorris Rodgers, WA
Brett Guthrie, KY
Pete Olson, TX
David B. McKinley, WV
Adam Kinzinger, IL
H. Morgan Griffith, VA
Gus M. Bilirakis, FL
Bill Johnson, OH
Billy Long, MO
Larry Bucshon, IN
Bill Flores, TX
Susan W. Brooks, IN
Markwayne Mullin, OK
Richard Hudson, NC
Tim Walberg, MI
Earl L. "Buddy" Carter, GA
Jeff Duncan, SC
Greg Gianforte, MT

MAJORITY STAFF

Aslami, Mohammad COUNSEL 2125........52927
Banez, Joe PROF STAFF 2125........52927
Barstow, Kevin CHIEF OVERSIGHT COUNSEL 2125........52927
Benjamin, Billy SYS ADMIN 2125........52927
Bolen, Jacquelyn PROF STAFF 2125........54407
Boyer, Jesseca PROF STAFF 2125........52927
Brown, A J COUNSEL 2125........52927
Carroll, Jeff STAFF DIR 2125........52927
Chasick, Alex COUNSEL 2125........52927
Cohen, Jacqueline CHIEF ENVIRON COUNSEL 2125........54407
Davis, Sharon CHIEF CLERK 2125........52927
Ertel, Elizabeth OFFICE MGR 2125........52927
Fischer, Adam POLICY ANALYST 2125........54407
Fruci, Jean ENERGY & ENVIRON POLICY ADVISOR 2125........54407
Gilbert, Evan DPTY PRESS SECY 2125........52927
Goldman, Lisa SR COUNSEL 2125........52927
Gordon, Waverly DPTY CHIEF COUNSEL 2125........52927
Guarascio, Tiffany DPTY STAFF DIR 2125........52927
Haberman, Caitlin PROF STAFF 2125........54407
Harvey, Judy COUNSEL 2125........52927
Hoehn-Saric, Alex CHIEF COUN COMMUNICATIONS & CONSUMER PROTECTION 2125........52927
Holland, Stephen HEALTH COUNSEL 2125........55056
Kahan, Zach OUTREACH & MBR SVCS COORD 2125........52927
Kessler, Rick SR ADVISOR/STAFF DIR - ENERGY & ENVIRON 2125........54407
Khaterzai, Saha PROF STAFF 2125........55056
Knauer, Chris STAFF DIR FOR OVERSIGHT 2125........52927
Krantz, Josh POLICY ANALYST 2125........52927
Larkin, Brendan POLICY COORD 2125........52927
Lee, Una CHIEF HEALTH COUNSEL 2125........55056
Leverich, Gerald SR COUNSEL 2125........52927
Lewis, Jourdan POLICY ANALYST 2125........52927
Maghamfar, Dustin AIR & CLIMATE COUNSEL 2125........54407
Marshall, John POLICY COORD 2125........52927
McAloon, Kevin PROF STAFF MEMB 2125........52927
McDonough, Aisling POLICY COORD 2125........52927
Miller, Dan POLICY ANALYST 2125........52927
Monger, Jon COUNSEL 2125........52927
Montfort, Elysa PRESS SECY 2125........52927
Mullon, Meghan STAFF ASST 2125........52927

Murphy, Phil POLICY COORD 2125 52927
Orlando, Joe STAFF ASST 2125 52927
Peel, Kaitlyn DIGITAL DIR 2125 52927
Roberts, Alivia PRESS ASST 2125 52927
Robinson, Timothy CHIEF COUNSEL 2125 52927
Rodriquez, Chloe POLICY ANALYST 2125 52927
Roy, Nikki POLICY COORD 2125 52927
Sada, Roberto POLICY COORD 2125 52927
Satchell, Samantha PROF STAFF 2125 54407
Souvall, Andrew COMMUNICATIONS DIR/OUTREACH DIR/DIR - MBR SVCS 2125 52927
Terry, Sydney POLICY COORD 2125 52927
Trzeciak, Kimberlee CHIEF HEALTH ADVISOR 2125 55056
Van Buren, Rick HEALTH COUNSEL 2125 52927
Walker, Edward TECH DIR 2125 52927
Wright, Tuley ENERGY & ENVIRON POLICY ADVISOR 2125 54407
Young, C J PRESS SECY 2125 52927

MINORITY STAFF

Ahern, Nolan POLICY ADVISOR 2322A 53641
Barblan, Jennifer CHIEF COUNSEL 2322A 53641
Bloomquist, Mike STAFF DIR 2322A 53641
Bounds, Lorissa POLICY COORD 2322A 53641
Buckalew, Adam “Buck” DIR - COALITIONS/DPTY CHIEF COUNSEL 2322A 53641
Colwell, Robin CHIEF COUNSEL 2322A 53641
Couri, Jerry DPTY CHIEF COUNSEL 564 FHOB 53641
Davis, Jordan SR ADVISOR 2322A 53641
Fogarty, Margaret Tucker STAFF ASST 2322A 53641
Froelich, Melissa CHIEF COUNSEL 2322A 53641
Gambo, Theresa HR SPEC/OFFICE ADMIN 2322A 53641
Graff, Caleb PROF STAFF MEMB 2322A 53641
Havens, Brittany PROF STAFF MEMB 564 FHOB 53641
Kielty, Peter GEN COUNSEL 2322A 53641
Koohmaraie, Bijan COUNSEL 564 FHOB 53641
Kurth, Tim DPTY CHIEF COUNSEL 564 FHOB 53641
Long, Ryan DPTY STAFF DIR 2322A 53641
Martin, Mary CHIEF COUNSEL 2322A 53641
Matthews, Sarah PRESS SECY 2322A 53641
Mooney, Brandon DPTY CHIEF COUNSEL 564 FHOB 53641
Paluskiewicz, J P CHIEF COUNSEL 2322A 53641
Rains, Brannon STAFF ASST 2322A 53641
Ratner, Mark POLICY COORD 2322A 53641
Roday, Zack COMMUNICATIONS DIR 2322A 53641
Shatynski, Kristen PROF STAFF MEMB 2322A 53641
Slobodin, Alan SR INVESTIGATIVE COUNSEL 564 FHOB 53641
Sohn, Natalie COUNSEL 564 FHOB 53641
Spencer, Peter SR PROF STAFF MBR 564 FHOB 53641
Steele, Danielle COUNSEL 2322A 53641
Winnick, Everett DIR - INFO TECH 2322A 53641

SUBCOMMITTEES OF THE COMMITTEE ON ENERGY AND COMMERCE

[The chairman and ranking minority member are ex officio members, with vote, of all subcommittees.]

SUBCOMMITTEE ON COMMUNICATIONS AND TECHNOLOGY

2125 RAYBURN HOB (ZIP: 20515) 225-2927

Michael F. Doyle, PA, Chairman

Jerry McNerney, CA
Yvette D. Clarke, NY
David Loebsack, IA
Marc A. Veasey, TX
A. Donald McEachin, VA
Darren Soto, FL
Tom O'Halleran, AZ
Anna G. Eshoo, CA
Diana DeGette, CO
G. K. Butterfield, NC
Doris O. Matsui, CA, Vice Chair
Peter Welch, VT
Ben Ray Luján, NM
Kurt Schrader, OR
Tony Cárdenas, CA
Debbie Dingell, MI
Frank Pallone, Jr., NJ (Ex Officio)

Robert E. Latta, OH
John Shimkus, IL
Steve Scalise, LA
Pete Olson, TX
Adam Kinzinger, IL
Gus M. Bilirakis, FL
Bill Johnson, OH
Billy Long, MO
Bill Flores, TX
Susan W. Brooks, IN
Tim Walberg, MI
Greg Gianforte, MT
Greg Walden, OR (Ex Officio)

SUBCOMMITTEE ON CONSUMER PROTECTION AND COMMERCE

2125 RAYBURN HOB (ZIP: 20515)..225-2927

Janice D. Schakowsky, IL, Chairwoman

Kathy Castor, FL
Marc A. Veasey, TX
Robin L. Kelly, IL
Tom O'Halleran, AZ
Ben Ray Luján, NM
Tony Cárdenas, CA, Vice Chair
Lisa Blunt Rochester, DE
Darren Soto, FL
Bobby L. Rush, IL
Doris O. Matsui, CA
Jerry McNerney, CA
Debbie Dingell, MI
Frank Pallone, Jr., NJ (Ex Officio)

Cathy McMorris Rodgers, WA
Fred Upton, MI
Michael C. Burgess, TX
Robert E. Latta, OH
Brett Guthrie, KY
Larry Bucshon, IN
Richard Hudson, NC
Earl L. "Buddy" Carter, GA
Greg Gianforte, MT
Greg Walden, OR (Ex Officio)

SUBCOMMITTEE ON ENERGY

2125 RAYBURN HOB (ZIP: 20515)..225-2927

Bobby L. Rush, IL, Chairman

Scott H. Peters, CA
Michael F. Doyle, PA
John P. Sarbanes, MD
Jerry McNerney, CA, Vice Chair
Paul Tonko, NY
David Loebsack, IA
G. K. Butterfield, NC
Peter Welch, VT
Kurt Schrader, OR
Joseph P. Kennedy III, MA
Marc A. Veasey, TX
Ann M. Kuster, NH
Robin L. Kelly, IL
Nanette Diaz Barragán, CA
A. Donald McEachin, VA
Tom O'Halleran, AZ
Lisa Blunt Rochester, DE
Frank Pallone, Jr., NJ (Ex Officio)

Fred Upton, MI
Robert E. Latta, OH
Cathy McMorris Rodgers, WA
Pete Olson, TX
David B. McKinley, WV
Adam Kinzinger, IL
H. Morgan Griffith, VA
Bill Johnson, OH
Larry Bucshon, IN
Bill Flores, TX
Richard Hudson, NC
Tim Walberg, MI
Jeff Duncan, SC
Greg Walden, OR (Ex Officio)

SUBCOMMITTEE ON ENVIRONMENT AND CLIMATE CHANGE

2125 RAYBURN HOB (ZIP: 20515)..225-2927

Paul Tonko, NY, Chairman

Yvette D. Clarke, NY
Scott H. Peters, CA
Nanette Diaz Barragán, CA
A. Donald McEachin, VA
Lisa Blunt Rochester, DE
Darren Soto, FL
Diana DeGette, CO
Janice D. Schakowsky, IL
Doris O. Matsui, CA
Jerry McNerney, CA
Raul Ruiz, CA, Vice Chair
Debbie Dingell, MI
Frank Pallone, Jr., NJ (Ex Officio)

John Shimkus, IL
Cathy McMorris Rodgers, WA
David B. McKinley, WV
Bill Johnson, OH
Billy Long, MO
Bill Flores, TX
Markwayne Mullin, OK
Earl L. "Buddy" Carter, GA
Jeff Duncan, SC
Greg Walden, OR (Ex Officio)

SUBCOMMITTEE ON HEALTH

2125 RAYBURN HOB (ZIP: 20515)..225-2927

Anna G. Eshoo, CA, Chairwoman

Eliot L. Engel, NY
G. K. Butterfield, NC, Vice Chair
Doris O. Matsui, CA
Kathy Castor, FL
John P. Sarbanes, MD
Ben Ray Luján, NM
Peter Welch, VT
Joseph P. Kennedy III, MA
Tony Cárdenas, CA
Kurt Schrader, OR
Raul Ruiz, CA
Debbie Dingell, MI
Ann M. Kuster, NH
Robin L. Kelly, IL
Nanette Diaz Barragán, CA
Lisa Blunt Rochester, DE
Bobby L. Rush, IL
Frank Pallone, Jr., NJ (Ex Officio)

Michael C. Burgess, TX
Fred Upton, MI
John Shimkus, IL
Brett Guthrie, KY
H. Morgan Griffith, VA
Gus M. Bilirakis, FL
Billy Long, MO
Larry Bucshon, IN
Susan W. Brooks, IN
Markwayne Mullin, OK
Richard Hudson, NC
Earl L. "Buddy" Carter, GA
Greg Gianforte, MT
Greg Walden, OR (Ex Officio)

U.S. HOUSE OF REPRESENTATIVES

SUBCOMMITTEE ON OVERSIGHT AND INVESTIGATIONS

2125 RAYBURN HOB (ZIP: 20515).. 225-2927

Diana DeGette, CO, Chair

Janice D. Schakowsky, IL
Joseph P. Kennedy III, MA, Vice Chair
Raul Ruiz, CA
Ann M. Kuster, NH
Kathy Castor, FL
John P. Sarbanes, MD
Paul Tonko, NY
Yvette D. Clarke, NY
Scott H. Peters, CA
Frank Pallone, Jr., NJ (Ex Officio)

Brett Guthrie, KY
Michael C. Burgess, TX
David B. McKinley, WV
H. Morgan Griffith, VA
Susan W. Brooks, IN
Markwayne Mullin, OK
Jeff Duncan, SC
Greg Walden, OR (Ex Officio)

COMMITTEE ON ETHICS

1015 LONGWORTH HOB (ZIP: 20515-6328) 225-7103

Theodore E. Deutch, FL, Chair

Grace Meng, NY	*Kenny Marchant*, TX
Susan Wild, PA	*John Ratcliffe*, TX
Dean Phillips, MN	*George Holding*, NC
Anthony G. Brown, MD	*Jackie Walorski*, IN
	Michael Guest, MS

STAFF MEMBERS

Arrojo, David COUNSEL TO THE CHAIRMAN 1015 **57103**
Baker, Jessica COUNSEL 1015 **57103**
Barber, Craig SYS ADMIN 1015 **57103**
Barnes, Cheryl STAFF ASST 1015 **57103**
Bethea, Deborah SR FINANCIAL DISCLOSURE MGR 508 FHOB **57103**
Donahue, Kathryn SR COUNSEL 1015 **57103**
Donesa, Chris COUNSEL TO THE RANKING MEMBER 1015 **57103**
Eskridge, Robert COUNSEL 1015 **57103**
Foster, Janet COUNSEL 1015 **57103**
Hamilton, Mark INVESTIGATIVE CLERK 1015 **57103**
Herbert, Donna DIR - ADMIN STAFF 1015 **57103**
Hickenlooper, Audrey CLERK - ADVICE AND EDUC 1015 **57103**
Johnson, Ken COUNSEL 1015 **57103**
Knight, Alissa STAFF ASST 1015 **57103**
Lax, Kelsey STAFF ASST 1015 **57103**
McCarty, Molly INVESTIGATOR 1015 **57103**
Mutschall, Sarah COUNSEL 1015 **57103**
Nedzar, Tamar SR COUNSEL 1015 **57103**
Opachan, Mark COUNSEL 1015 **57103**
Pescatore, Brittney DIR - INVESTIGATIONS 1015 **57103**
Ross, Zeke COUNSEL 1015 **57103**
Rust, Thomas CHIEF COUNSEL/STAFF DIR 1015 **57103**
Sloans, Tonya SR COUNSEL 508 FHOB **57103**
Smith, Tonia DIRECTOR 1015 **57103**
Steiner, Matthew FINANCIAL DISCLOSURE CLERK 1015 **57103**
Szabo, John COUNSEL 1015 **57103**
Wambold, Adam PROF STAFF 1015 **57103**

COMMITTEE ON FINANCIAL SERVICES

2129 RAYBURN HOB (ZIP: 20515-6050)........225-4247

Maxine Waters, CA, Chair

<table>
<tr><td>Carolyn B. Maloney, NY
Nydia M. Velázquez, NY
Brad Sherman, CA
Gregory W. Meeks, NY
Wm. Lacy Clay, MO
David Scott, GA
Al Green, TX
Emanuel Cleaver, MO
Ed Perlmutter, CO
James A. Himes, CT
Bill Foster, IL
Joyce Beatty, OH
Denny Heck, WA
Juan Vargas, CA
Josh Gottheimer, NJ
Vicente Gonzalez, TX
Al Lawson, Jr., FL
Michael F. Q. San Nicolas, GU
Rashida Tlaib, MI
Katie Porter, CA
Cynthia Axne, IA
Sean Casten, IL
Ayanna Pressley, MA
Ben McAdams, UT
Alexandria Ocasio-Cortez, NY
Jennifer Wexton, VA
Stephen F. Lynch, MA
Tulsi Gabbard, HI
Alma S. Adams, NC
Madeleine Dean, PA
Jesús G. "Chuy" García, IL
Sylvia R. Garcia, TX
Dean Phillips, MN</td>
<td>Patrick T. McHenry, NC
Peter T. King, NY
Frank D. Lucas, OK
Bill Posey, FL
Blaine Luetkemeyer, MO
Bill Huizenga, MI
Sean P. Duffy, WI
Steve Stivers, OH
Ann Wagner, MO
Andy Barr, KY
Scott R. Tipton, CO
Roger Williams, TX
J. French Hill, AR
Tom Emmer, MN
Lee M. Zeldin, NY
Barry Loudermilk, GA
Alexander X. Mooney, WV
Warren Davidson, OH
Ted Budd, NC
David Kustoff, TN
Trey Hollingsworth, IN
Anthony Gonzalez, OH
John W. Rose, TN
Bryan Steil, WI
Lance Gooden, TX
Denver Riggleman, VA</td></tr>
</table>

MAJORITY STAFF

Abonyi, Clement COORD - MBR SVCS & OUTREACH 2129....... **57141**
Abramowitz, David PARLIAMENTARIAN 2129........ **54247**
Allison, Terisa EDITOR 2129........ **54247**
Burris, Kevin CHIEF OVERSIGHT COUNSEL 2129........ **54247**
Erickson, Kristofor DPTY STAFF DIR 2129........ **54247**
Fierro, Alia PROF STAFF - MAJ 2129........ **54247**
Forman, Alfred SYS ADMIN 2129........ **54247**
Hahn, Carolyn SR COUNSEL - MAJ 2129........ **54247**
Heinemann, John COUNSEL 2129........ **54247**
Hersey, Eric COMMUNICATIONS DIR 2129........ **54247**
Johnson, Bruce DPTY CHIEF COUNSEL 2129........ **54247**
Kahng, Esther DIR - HOUSING POLICY 2129........ **54247**
Ladet, Janae PROF STAFF - MAJ 2129........ **54247**
Lindholm, Danielle NATIONAL SECUR ADVISOR 2129........ **54247**
Loewe, Erica PRESS SECY 2129........ **54247**
Mallik, Avy SR COUNSEL - MAJ 2129........ **54247**
Manosalvas, Marcos DIGITAL DIR 2129........ **54247**
Marter, Jean CLERK 2129........ **54247**
McGlinchey, Daniel DIR - INTERNATIONAL AFFAIRS 2129........ **54247**
Miles, Erica DIRECTOR 2129........ **54247**
Miles, Yana SR COUNSEL - MAJ 2129........ **54247**
Ng, Lauri COUNSEL - MAJ 2129........ **54247**
Ouertatani, Charla STAFF DIR 2129........ **54247**
Peto, Lisa CHIEF COUNSEL/LEGIS DIR 2129........ **54247**
Read, Jennifer COUNSEL 2129........ **54247**
Roach, Bob INVESTIGATOR 2129........ **54247**
Robinson, Kalvin STAFF ASST 2129........ **54247**
Scott, Denise FINANCIAL & ADMIN OFFICER 2129........ **54247**
Sears, Glen DIR - POLICY 2129........ **54247**
Strohmaier, Kathryn COUNSEL - MAJ 2129........ **54247**
Thomas, Petrina STAFF ASST - MAJ 2129........ **54247**
Whatley, Pierre PROF STAFF MEMB 2129........ **54247**
Williams, Ola SR PROF STAFF MBR 2129........ **54247**

MINORITY STAFF

Baker, Stacy SYS ADMIN 4340	57502
Bennett, McArn LEGIS ASST - MIN 4340	57502
Betz, Kim GEN COUNSEL 4340	57502
Bradley, Katelynn DIRECTOR 3320	60736
Brown, Chris SR PROF STAFF 4340	57502
Castella, Francesco LEGIS ASST - MIN 4340	57502
Chang, Anthony SR PROF STAFF 4340	57502
Cote, Steve STAFF DIR - MIN 4340	57502
Gallagher, Megan STAFF ASST 4340	57502
Haslett, Brighton COUNSEL 4340	57502
Johnson, Tallman SR PROF STAFF 4340	57502
Jones, Clinton SR PROF STAFF 4340	57502
McCune, Collin DIR - MBR SVCS & COALITIONS 4340	57502
Mulder, Matt DPTY STAFF DIR 4340	57502
Peavey, Laura PRESS SECY 4340	57502
Planning, David MBR SVCS & COALITIONS ASST 4340	57502
Poe, Phil POLICY ASST 4340	57502
Schreiber, Charlie COUNSEL 4340	57502
Shackelford, Lindsey DIR - OPS 4340	57502
Simpson, Kyle STAFF ASST - MIN 4340	57502
Skala, Ed SR PROF STAFF 4340	57502
Skladany, Jon CHIEF OVERSIGHT COUNSEL 4340	57502

SUBCOMMITTEES OF THE COMMITTEE ON FINANCIAL SERVICES

SUBCOMMITTEE ON INVESTOR PROTECTION, ENTREPRENEURSHIP, AND CAPITAL MARKETS

2129 RAYBURN HOB (ZIP: 20515)........225-4247

Carolyn B. Maloney, NY, Chair

Brad Sherman, CA
David Scott, GA
James A. Himes, CT
Bill Foster, IL
Gregory W. Meeks, NY
Juan Vargas, CA
Josh Gottheimer, NJ
Vicente Gonzalez, TX
Michael F. Q. San Nicolas, GU
Katie Porter, CA
Cynthia Axne, IA
Sean Casten, IL
Alexandria Ocasio-Cortez, NY

Bill Huizenga, MI
Peter T. King, NY
Sean P. Duffy, WI
Steve Stivers, OH
Ann Wagner, MO
J. French Hill, AR
Tom Emmer, MN
Alexander X. Mooney, WV
Warren Davidson, OH
Trey Hollingsworth, IN

SUBCOMMITTEE ON CONSUMER PROTECTION AND FINANCIAL INSTITUTIONS

2129 RAYBURN HOB (ZIP: 20515)........225-4247

Gregory W. Meeks, NY, Chair

David Scott, GA
Nydia M. Velázquez, NY
Wm. Lacy Clay, MO
Denny Heck, WA
Bill Foster, IL
Al Lawson, Jr., FL
Rashida Tlaib, MI
Katie Porter, CA
Ayanna Pressley, MA
Ben McAdams, UT
Alexandria Ocasio-Cortez, NY
Jennifer Wexton, VA

Blaine Luetkemeyer, MO
Frank D. Lucas, OK
Bill Posey, FL
Andy Barr, KY
Scott R. Tipton, CO
Roger Williams, TX
Barry Loudermilk, GA
Ted Budd, NC
David Kustoff, TN
Denver Riggleman, VA

SUBCOMMITTEE ON HOUSING, COMMUNITY DEVELOPMENT, AND INSURANCE

2129 RAYBURN HOB (ZIP: 20515)........................ 225-4247

Wm. Lacy Clay, MO, Chair

Nydia M. Velázquez, NY	*Sean P. Duffy*, WI
Emanuel Cleaver, MO	*Blaine Luetkemeyer*, MO
Brad Sherman, CA	*Bill Huizenga*, MI
Joyce Beatty, OH	*Scott R. Tipton*, CO
Al Green, TX	*Lee M. Zeldin*, NY
Vicente Gonzalez, TX	*David Kustoff*, TN
Carolyn B. Maloney, NY	*Anthony Gonzalez*, OH
Denny Heck, WA	*John W. Rose*, TN
Juan Vargas, CA	*Bryan Steil*, WI
Al Lawson, Jr., FL	*Lance Gooden*, TX
Rashida Tlaib, MI	
Cynthia Axne, IA	

SUBCOMMITTEE ON NATIONAL SECURITY, INTERNATIONAL DEVELOPMENT, AND MONETARY POLICY

2129 RAYBURN HOB (ZIP: 20515)........................ 225-4247

Emanuel Cleaver, MO, Chair

Ed Perlmutter, CO	*Steve Stivers*, OH
James A. Himes, CT	*Peter T. King*, NY
Denny Heck, WA	*Frank D. Lucas*, OK
Brad Sherman, CA	*Roger Williams*, TX
Juan Vargas, CA	*J. French Hill*, AR
Josh Gottheimer, NJ	*Tom Emmer*, MN
Michael F. Q. San Nicolas, GU	*Anthony Gonzalez*, OH
Ben McAdams, UT	*John W. Rose*, TN
Jennifer Wexton, VA	*Denver Riggleman*, VA
Stephen F. Lynch, MA	
Tulsi Gabbard, HI	
Jesús G. "Chuy" García, IL	

SUBCOMMITTEE ON DIVERSITY AND INCLUSION

2129 RAYBURN HOB (ZIP: 20515)........................ 225-4247

Joyce Beatty, OH, Chairwoman

Wm. Lacy Clay, MO	*Ann Wagner*, MO
Al Green, TX	*Frank D. Lucas*, OK
Josh Gottheimer, NJ	*Alexander X. Mooney*, WV
Vicente Gonzalez, TX	*Ted Budd*, NC
Al Lawson, Jr., FL	*David Kustoff*, TN
Ayanna Pressley, MA	*Trey Hollingsworth*, IN
Tulsi Gabbard, HI	*Anthony Gonzalez*, OH
Alma S. Adams, NC	*Bryan Steil*, WI
Madeleine Dean, PA	*Lance Gooden*, TX
Sylvia R. Garcia, TX	
Dean Phillips, MN	

COMMITTEE MEMBERS AND STAFF

SUBCOMMITTEE ON OVERSIGHT AND INVESTIGATIONS

2129 RAYBURN HOB (ZIP: 20515)..225-4247

Al Green, TX, Chair

Joyce Beatty, OH
Stephen F. Lynch, MA
Nydia M. Velázquez, NY
Ed Perlmutter, CO
Rashida Tlaib, MI
Sean Casten, IL
Madeleine Dean, PA
Sylvia R. Garcia, TX
Dean Phillips, MN

Andy Barr, KY
Bill Posey, FL
Lee M. Zeldin, NY
Barry Loudermilk, GA
Warren Davidson, OH
John W. Rose, TN
Bryan Steil, WI

U.S. HOUSE OF REPRESENTATIVES

COMMITTEE ON FOREIGN AFFAIRS

2170 RAYBURN HOB (ZIP: 20515-6128)........225-5021

Eliot L. Engel, NY, Chair

Brad Sherman, CA
Gregory W. Meeks, NY
Albio Sires, NJ
Gerald E. Connolly, VA
Theodore E. Deutch, FL
Karen Bass, CA
William R. Keating, MA
David N. Cicilline, RI
Ami Bera, CA
Joaquin Castro, TX
Dina Titus, NV
Adriano Espaillat, NY
Ted Lieu, CA
Susan Wild, PA
Dean Phillips, MN
Ilhan Omar, MN
Colin Z. Allred, TX
Andy Levin, MI
Abigail Davis Spanberger, VA
Chrissy Houlahan, PA
Tom Malinowski, NJ
David J. Trone, MD
Jim Costa, CA
Juan Vargas, CA
Vicente Gonzalez, TX

Michael T. McCaul, TX
Christopher H. Smith, NJ
Steve Chabot, OH
Joe Wilson, SC
Scott Perry, PA
Ted S. Yoho, FL
Adam Kinzinger, IL
Lee M. Zeldin, NY
F. James Sensenbrenner, Jr., WI
Ann Wagner, MO
Brian J. Mast, FL
Francis Rooney, FL
Brian K. Fitzpatrick, PA
John R. Curtis, UT
Ken Buck, CO
Ron Wright, TX
Guy Reschenthaler, PA
Tim Burchett, TN
Greg Pence, IN
Steve Watkins, KS
Michael Guest, MS

MAJORITY STAFF

Bellamy, Raven STAFF ASSOC 2171........**55021**
Billerbeck, Peter POLICY ANALYST 2420........**55021**
Bursey, Evan STAFF ASSOC 2170........**55021**
Cahan, Jaclyn COUNSEL 2173........**55021**
Campbell, Doug DPTY STAFF DIR 2152........**55021**
Carey, Laura SR PROF STAFF 2471........**55021**
Cerga, Vlad INFO RESOURCE MGR 2170........**57575**
Colvett, Jacqueline DIGITAL MGR 2152........**55021**
Crosby, Katy SR PROF STAFF MBR 2471........**55201**
Finkel, Matthew STAFF ASSOC 2170........**55021**
Fletcher, Letitia PRINTING MGR 5190........**51045**
Gandhi, Sajit SR PROF STAFF 2064........**55021**
Gleason, John FINANCIAL OFFICER 5190........**54291**
Hendrixson-White, Jennifer SR PROF STAFF 2170........**55021**
Iozzi, Mark DPTY CHIEF COUNSEL 2173........**55021**
Jacobstein, Eric SR POLICY ADVISOR 2170........**55021**
Jones, Sophie STAFF ASSOC 2152........**55021**
Kaguyutan, Janice CHIEF COUNSEL 2173........**55021**
Levitan, Rachel DPTY COMMUNICATIONS DIR/POLICY ADVISOR 2152........**55021**
Lou, Theresa POLICY ANALYST 2064........**55021**
Marca, Danny ASST SYS ADMIN 2170........**66592**
Matlaga, Michael POLICY ANALYST 2420........**55021**
Mulvey, Timothy COMMUNICATIONS DIR - DEM 2170........**55021**
Ramos, Jacqueline SR PROF STAFF 2420........**55021**
Redick, Taylor POLICY ANALYST 2471........**55021**
Resnick, Mira SR PROF STAFF 2170........**55021**
Rice, Edmund B SR PROF STAFF 2170........**55021**
Ritchey, George PROF STAFF/SECUR OFFICER G324........**55021**
Sadler, Alex POLICY ANALYST 2064........**55021**
Skretny, Brian PROF STAFF - MAJ 2426........**52464**
Stanton, Kimberly SR PROF STAFF MBR 5100........**53599**
Steinbaum, Jason STAFF DIR - MAJ 2152........**55021**
Stiles, Samantha DIR - OPS 2171........**55021**
Warner, Lesley PROF STAFF MEMB 2471........**55021**

MINORITY STAFF

Anderson, Doug GEN COUNSEL 2066........**68467**
Brahimi, Samia SR PROF STAFF 4150........**68467**
Burack, Bryan PROF STAFF - MIN 4150........**68467**
Campbell, Caroline PRESS SECY - MIN 2066........**68467**
Curtis, Katherine SPECIAL ASST TO THE STAFF DIR 2066........**68467**
Duval, Claire DIR - MBR SVCS & COALITIONS 2066........**68467**
Figel, Claire STAFF ASSOC 2066........**68467**
Figel, Claire STAFF ASSOC 2066........**68467**
Fullerton, Laura DPTY STAFF DIR - MIN STAFF 2066........**68467**
Gallagher, Meghan PROF STAFF - MIN 2066........**68467**
Gorski, Jennifer DIR - OPS 2066........**68467**
Markley, Sarah STAFF ASSOC 2066........**68467**
Monje, Carlos PROF STAFF 2066........**68467**
Mullins, Grant SR COUNSEL - MIN 2066........**68467**

Rice, Thomas PROF STAFF 2066 68467
Shields, Brendan STAFF DIR - MIN 2066 68467
Silberman, Zachary SR PROF STAFF 4150 68467
Stapleton, John SR PROF STAFF 4150 68467
Steffens, Jessica SR PROF STAFF 4150 68467
Taylor, Andrew SR ECON ADVISOR 4150 68467
Zach, Gabriella SR PROF STAFF 4150 68467

SUBCOMMITTEES OF THE COMMITTEE ON FOREIGN AFFAIRS

[The chairman and ranking minority member may attend the meetings and participate in the activities of all subcommittees except for voting and being counted for a quorum.]

SUBCOMMITTEE ON AFRICA, GLOBAL HEALTH, GLOBAL HUMAN RIGHTS, AND INTERNATIONAL ORGANIZATIONS

2170 RAYBURN HOB (ZIP: 20515) 226-1500

Karen Bass, CA, Chair

Susan Wild, PA
Dean Phillips, MN
Ilhan Omar, MN
Chrissy Houlahan, PA

Christopher H. Smith, NJ
F. James Sensenbrenner, Jr., WI
Ron Wright, TX
Tim Burchett, TN

MAJORITY STAFF

Suggs-Brigety, Naomia STAFF ASSOC 5190 61500
Yarwood, Janette STAFF DIR 5190 61500

SUBCOMMITTEE ON ASIA, THE PACIFIC, AND NONPROLIFERATION

2170 RAYBURN HOB (ZIP: 20515) 226-6434

Brad Sherman, CA, Chair

Dina Titus, NV
Chrissy Houlahan, PA
Gerald E. Connolly, VA
Ami Bera, CA
Andy Levin, MI
Abigail Davis Spanberger, VA

Ted S. Yoho, FL
Scott Perry, PA
Ann Wagner, MO
Brian J. Mast, FL
John R. Curtis, UT

MAJORITY STAFF

Nodvin, Leah STAFF ASSOC 5212 66434

MINORITY STAFF

MacDonald, Don PROF STAFF - MIN 5212 66434

SUBCOMMITTEE ON EUROPE, EURASIA, ENERGY, AND THE ENVIRONMENT

2170 RAYBURN HOB (ZIP: 20515)..225-5021

William R. Keating, MA, Chair

Abigail Davis Spanberger, VA
Gregory W. Meeks, NY
Albio Sires, NJ
Theodore E. Deutch, FL
David N. Cicilline, RI
Joaquin Castro, TX
Dina Titus, NV
Susan Wild, PA
David J. Trone, MD
Jim Costa, CA
Vicente Gonzalez, TX

Adam Kinzinger, IL
Joe Wilson, SC
Ann Wagner, MO
F. James Sensenbrenner, Jr., WI
Francis Rooney, FL
Brian K. Fitzpatrick, PA
Greg Pence, IN
Ron Wright, TX
Michael Guest, MS
Tim Burchett, TN

MAJORITY STAFF

Gould, Gabrielle STAFF DIR 5193.. **53111**
Thomson, Shestin STAFF ASSOC 5193.. **53111**

SUBCOMMITTEE ON MIDDLE EAST, NORTH AFRICA, AND INTERNATIONAL TERRORISM

2170 RAYBURN HOB (ZIP: 20515)..226-7812

Theodore E. Deutch, FL, Chair

Gerald E. Connolly, VA
David N. Cicilline, RI
Ted Lieu, CA
Colin Z. Allred, TX
Tom Malinowski, NJ
David J. Trone, MD
Brad Sherman, CA
William R. Keating, MA
Juan Vargas, CA

Joe Wilson, SC
Steve Chabot, OH
Adam Kinzinger, IL
Lee M. Zeldin, NY
Brian J. Mast, FL
Brian K. Fitzpatrick, PA
Guy Reschenthaler, PA
Steve Watkins, KS

MAJORITY STAFF

Abusch, Aviva STAFF ASSOC 5211.. **67812**
Doherty, Ryan PROF STAFF MEMB 5211.. **67812**
Kustin, Casey STAFF DIR 5211.. **67812**

SUBCOMMITTEE ON OVERSIGHT AND INVESTIGATIONS

2170 RAYBURN HOB (ZIP: 20515)..225-5021

Ami Bera, CA, Chair

Ilhan Omar, MN
Adriano Espaillat, NY
Ted Lieu, CA
Tom Malinowski, NJ
David N. Cicilline, RI

Lee M. Zeldin, NY
Scott Perry, PA
Ken Buck, CO
Guy Reschenthaler, PA

MAJORITY STAFF

Burroughs, Nikole STAFF DIR 5102.. **62754**
Uyehara, Ryan PROF STAFF MEMB 5102.. **55716**

SUBCOMMITTEE ON WESTERN HEMISPHERE, CIVILIAN SECURITY, AND TRADE

2170 RAYBURN HOB (ZIP: 20515)........ 225-3345

Albio Sires, NJ, Chair

Gregory W. Meeks, NY
Joaquin Castro, TX
Adriano Espaillat, NY
Dean Phillips, MN
Andy Levin, MI
Vicente Gonzalez, TX
Juan Vargas, CA

Francis Rooney, FL
Christopher H. Smith, NJ
Ted S. Yoho, FL
John R. Curtis, UT
Ken Buck, CO
Michael Guest, MS

MAJORITY STAFF

Brockwehl, Alexander PROF STAFF MEMB 5220........ **53345**
Cruz Munoz, Mariana STAFF ASSOC 5222........ **53345**
Khan, Sadaf STAFF DIR 5222........ **53345**

COMMITTEE ON HOMELAND SECURITY

176 FORD HOB (ZIP: 20515-6480) 226-2616

Bennie G. Thompson, MS, Chair

Sheila Jackson Lee, TX
James R. Langevin, RI
Cedric L. Richmond, LA
Donald M. Payne, Jr., NJ
Kathleen M. Rice, NY
J. Luis Correa, CA
Xochitl Torres Small, NM
Max Rose, NY
Lauren Underwood, IL
Elissa Slotkin, MI
Emanuel Cleaver, MO
Al Green, TX
Yvette D. Clarke, NY
Dina Titus, NV
Bonnie Watson Coleman, NJ
Nanette Diaz Barragán, CA
Val Butler Demings, FL

Mike Rogers, AL
Peter T. King, NY
Michael T. McCaul, TX
John Katko, NY
John Ratcliffe, TX
Mark Walker, NC
Clay Higgins, LA
Debbie Lesko, AZ
Mark E. Green, TN
Van Taylor, TX
John Joyce, PA
Dan Crenshaw, TX
Michael Guest, MS

MAJORITY STAFF

Bergin, Moira SUBCOMM STAFF DIR - CYBERSECURITY, INFRASTRUCTURE PROTECTION, AND INNOVATION SUBCOMM/COUNSEL - CYBERSECURITY, INFRASTRUCTURE PROTECTION, AND INNOVATION SUBCOMM 176 FHOB **62616**
Canini, Lisa SUBCOMM STAFF DIR - OVERSIGHT, MANAGEMENT, AND ACCOUNTABILITY SUBCOMM 176 FHOB **62616**
Carithers, Charles PROF STAFF 176 FHOB **62616**
Carnes, Alexandra SUBCOMM STAFF DIR - BORDER SECURITY, FACILITATION, AND OPERATIONS SUBCOMM 176 FHOB **62616**
Clerinx, Wendy PROF STAFF 176 FHOB **62616**
Cohen, Rosaline CHIEF COUNSEL 176 FHOB **62616**
Comis, Adam COMMUNICATIONS DIR 176 FHOB **62616**
Dyson, Nzinga COUNSEL 176 FHOB **62616**
Goins, Hope STAFF DIR 176 FHOB **62616**
Hajinazarian, Ike DPTY PRESS SECY 176 FHOB **62616**
Hollowell, Christian EXEC ASST 176 FHOB **62616**
Hopkins, Jenna LEGIS ASST 176 FHOB **62616**
Jazayeri, Naveed PROF STAFF 176 FHOB **62616**
Johnson, Camisha LEGIS ASST 176 FHOB **62616**
Jones, Taylor SUBCOMM CLERK 176 FHOB **62616**
Kupe, Laura COUNSEL 176 FHOB **62616**
Lynch, Brittany PROF STAFF MEMB 176 FHOB **62616**
Marston, Alexander SUBCOMM STAFF DIR - TRANSPORTATION AND MARITIME SECURITY SUBCOMM 176 FHOB **62616**
McClain, Lauren SUBCOMM STAFF DIR - EMERGENCY PREPAREDNESS, RESPONSE, AND RECOVERY SUBCOMM 176 FHOB **62616**
McClelland, Ethan PARLIAMENTARIAN 176 FHOB **62616**
Mims, Amanda OFFICE MGR 176 FHOB **62616**
Nixon, Natalie CHIEF ADMIN OFFICER 176 FHOB **62616**
Northrop, Alison DIR - OVERSIGHT 176 FHOB **62616**
Parnes, Jonathan COUNSEL 176 FHOB **62616**
Prasanna, Sandeep COUNSEL 176 FHOB **62616**
Smith, Alicia COUNSEL 176 FHOB **62616**
Tisdale, Nicole SUBCOMM STAFF DIR - INTELLIGENCE AND COUNTERTERRORISM SUBCOMM/COUNSEL - INTELLIGENCE AND COUNTERTERRORISM SUBCOMM 176 FHOB **62616**
Vega, Emmanuel DIGITAL COORD 176 FHOB **62616**
Walsh, Joel PROF STAFF 176 FHOB **62616**

MINORITY STAFF

Bergwin, Diana SUBCOMM STAFF DIR - EMERGENCY PREPAREDNESS, RESPONSE, AND RECOVERY SUBCOMM 117 FHOB **68417**
Bondi, Emily PRESS ASST/STAFF ASST 117 FHOB **68417**
Bowers, Mandy SUBCOMM STAFF DIR - INTELLIGENCE AND COUNTERTERRORISM SUBCOMM 117 FHOB **68417**
Flynn, Kathleen SUBCOMM STAFF DIR - OVERSIGHT, MANAGEMENT, AND ACCOUNTABILITY SUBCOMM 117 FHOB **68417**
Gosselin, Geoffrey DPTY STAFF DIR 117 FHOB **68417**
Hager, Nicole PRESS SECY 117 FHOB **68417**
Kirlin, Michael DPTY STAFF DIR 117 FHOB **68417**
Klein, Kyle SUBCOMM STAFF DIR - TRANSPORTATION AND MARITIME SECURITY SUBCOMM 117 FHOB **68417**
Loden, Kathleen DPTY STAFF DIR 117 FHOB **68417**
McConnell, Forrest GEN COUNSEL 117 FHOB **68417**
Meehan, Colin RESEARCH ASST 117 FHOB **68417**
Moxley, Sarah SUBCOMM STAFF DIR - CYBERSECURITY, INFRASTRUCTURE PROTECTION, AND INNOVATION SUBCOMM 117 FHOB **68417**
Noyes, Kyle PROF STAFF MEMB 117 FHOB **68417**
Pointer, Katherine DIR - MBR SVCS 117 FHOB **68417**
Ronk, Joshua PROF STAFF MEMB 117 FHOB **68417**
Trapani, Emily SUBCOMM STAFF DIR - BORDER SECURITY, FACILITATION, AND OPERATIONS SUBCOMM 117 FHOB **68417**
Vieson, Christopher STAFF DIR 117 FHOB **68417**

SHARED STAFF

Crowell, Heather GPO DETAILEE 176 FHOB 62616
Johnson, Marc CLERK 176 FHOB 62616
Johnson, Nicholas CLERK 176 FHOB 62616
McFarland, Kyle DIR - SECUR 176 FHOB 62616

SUBCOMMITTEES OF THE COMMITTEE ON HOMELAND SECURITY

[The chairman and ranking minority member are non-voting ex officio members of all subcommittees on which they do not hold a regular assignment.]

SUBCOMMITTEE ON INTELLIGENCE AND COUNTERTERRORISM

176 FORD HOB (ZIP: 20515) 226-2616

Max Rose, NY, Chairman

Sheila Jackson Lee, TX
James R. Langevin, RI
Elissa Slotkin, MI
Bennie G. Thompson, MS (Ex Officio)

Mark Walker, NC
Peter T. King, NY
Mark E. Green, TN
Mike Rogers, AL (Ex Officio)

SUBCOMMITTEE ON OVERSIGHT, MANAGEMENT, AND ACCOUNTABILITY

176 FORD HOB (ZIP: 20515) 226-2616

Xochitl Torres Small, NM, Chairwoman

Dina Titus, NV
Bonnie Watson Coleman, NJ
Nanette Diaz Barragán, CA
Bennie G. Thompson, MS (Ex Officio)

Dan Crenshaw, TX
Clay Higgins, LA
Van Taylor, TX
Mike Rogers, AL (Ex Officio)

SUBCOMMITTEE ON TRANSPORTATION AND MARITIME SECURITY

176 FORD HOB (ZIP: 20515) 226-2616

J. Luis Correa, CA, Chairman

Emanuel Cleaver, MO
Dina Titus, NV
Bonnie Watson Coleman, NJ
Nanette Diaz Barragán, CA
Val Butler Demings, FL
Bennie G. Thompson, MS (Ex Officio)

Debbie Lesko, AZ
John Katko, NY
John Ratcliffe, TX
Mark E. Green, TN
Mike Rogers, AL (Ex Officio)

SUBCOMMITTEE ON BORDER SECURITY, FACILITATION, AND OPERATIONS

176 FORD HOB (ZIP: 20515) 226-2616

Kathleen M. Rice, NY, Chairwoman

Donald M. Payne, Jr., NJ
J. Luis Correa, CA
Xochitl Torres Small, NM
Al Green, TX
Yvette D. Clarke, NY
Bennie G. Thompson, MS (Ex Officio)

Clay Higgins, LA
Debbie Lesko, AZ
John Joyce, PA
Michael Guest, MS
Mike Rogers, AL (Ex Officio)

SUBCOMMITTEE ON CYBERSECURITY, INFRASTRUCTURE PROTECTION, AND INNOVATION

176 FORD HOB (ZIP: 20515)..226-2616

Cedric L. Richmond, LA, Chairman

Sheila Jackson Lee, TX	*John Katko*, NY
James R. Langevin, RI	*John Ratcliffe*, TX
Kathleen M. Rice, NY	*Mark Walker*, NC
Lauren Underwood, IL	*Van Taylor*, TX
Elissa Slotkin, MI	*Mike Rogers*, AL (Ex Officio)
Bennie G. Thompson, MS (Ex Officio)	

SUBCOMMITTEE ON EMERGENCY PREPAREDNESS, RESPONSE, AND RECOVERY

176 FORD HOB (ZIP: 20515)..226-2616

Donald M. Payne, Jr., NJ, Chairman

Cedric L. Richmond, LA	*Peter T. King*, NY
Max Rose, NY	*John Joyce*, PA
Lauren Underwood, IL	*Dan Crenshaw*, TX
Al Green, TX	*Michael Guest*, MS
Yvette D. Clarke, NY	*Mike Rogers*, AL (Ex Officio)
Bennie G. Thompson, MS (Ex Officio)	

COMMITTEE ON HOUSE ADMINISTRATION

1309 LONGWORTH HOB (ZIP: 20515-6157)........ 225-2061

Zoe Lofgren, CA, Chairperson

Jamie Raskin, MD, Vice Chairperson	*Rodney Davis*, IL, Ranking Member
Susan A. Davis, CA	*Mark Walker*, NC
G. K. Butterfield, NC	*Barry Loudermilk*, GA
Marcia L. Fudge, OH	
Pete Aguilar, CA	

MAJORITY STAFF

Abboud, Khalil DPTY STAFF DIR 1309........ **52061**
Allen, Aaron PROF STAFF 1307........ **52061**
Arias, Hector STAFF ASST 1307........ **52061**
Burns, Sydney STAFF ASST 1309........ **52061**
Connor, Meredith PROF STAFF 1309........ **52061**
DeFreitas, Matt DIR - FRANKING COMMISSION 1307........ **52061**
Flaherty, Eddie CHIEF CLERK 1313........ **55172**
Fleet, Jamie STAFF DIR 1309........ **52061**
Haddad, Mannal PRESS SECY 1313........ **52061**
Hendrix, Kemba PROF STAFF 1306A........ **52061**
Henline, Robert DIR - MBR SVCS 1309........ **52061**
Hira, Elizabeth COUNSEL - ELECTIONS 1309........ **52061**
Jones, Sean LEGIS CLERK 1309........ **52061**
LaSure, Aaron PROF STAFF 1309........ **52061**
Malik, Mariam STAFF ASST 1309........ **52061**
Morgan, Teri DPTY STAFF DIR 1309........ **52061**
Nasta, Sarah COUNSEL - ELECTIONS 1309........ **52061**
Sehgal, Tanya SR ELECTIONS COUNSEL 1309........ **52061**
Spaulding, Stephen COUNSEL - ELECTIONS 1309........ **52061**
Taylor, Daniel CHIEF COUNSEL 1309........ **52061**
Tucker, David PARLIAMENTARIAN 1309........ **52061**
Whippy, Peter COMMUNICATIONS DIR 1313........ **52061**
Wright, Gina PROF STAFF 1309........ **52061**

MINORITY STAFF

Blanford, Thomas STAFF ASST - MIN 1216........ **58281**
Crocker, Nicholas PROF STAFF - MIN 1216........ **58281**
Daulby, Jennifer STAFF DIR - MIN 1316........ **58281**
Englund, Mary Sue DIR - ADMIN OPS 1216........ **58281**
Felder, Cole GEN COUNSEL 1216........ **58281**
Lee, Joy COUNSEL - MIN 1216........ **58281**
Monahan, Timothy DIR - OVERSIGHT 1216........ **58281**
Parella, Courtney COMMUNICATIONS DIR - MIN 1216........ **58281**
Randall, Brittany DIR - MEMB SVCS 1316........ **58281**
Roberts, Jesse COUNSEL - MIN 1216........ **58281**
Schwalb, Janet PROF STAFF - MIN 1216........ **58281**
Sullivan, Timothy DIR - FRANKING COMMISSION 1216........ **58281**

SUBCOMMITTEES OF THE COMMITTEE ON HOUSE ADMINISTRATION

SUBCOMMITTEE ON ELECTIONS

1309 LONGWORTH HOB (ZIP: 20515)........ 225-2061

Marcia L. Fudge, OH, Chairperson

G. K. Butterfield, NC	*Rodney Davis*, IL, Ranking Member
Pete Aguilar, CA	

COMMITTEE ON THE JUDICIARY

2138 RAYBURN HOB (ZIP: 20515-6216)........................225-3951

Jerrold Nadler, NY, Chair

Zoe Lofgren, CA
Sheila Jackson Lee, TX
Steve Cohen, TN
Henry C. "Hank" Johnson, Jr., GA
Theodore E. Deutch, FL
Karen Bass, CA
Cedric L. Richmond, LA
Hakeem S. Jeffries, NY
David N. Cicilline, RI
Eric Swalwell, CA
Ted Lieu, CA
Jamie Raskin, MD
Pramila Jayapal, WA
Val Butler Demings, FL
J. Luis Correa, CA
Mary Gay Scanlon, PA
Sylvia R. Garcia, TX
Joe Neguse, CO
Lucy McBath, GA
Greg Stanton, AZ
Madeleine Dean, PA
Debbie Mucarsel-Powell, FL
Veronica Escobar, TX

Doug Collins, GA
F. James Sensenbrenner, Jr., WI
Steve Chabot, OH
Louie Gohmert, TX
Jim Jordan, OH
Ken Buck, CO
John Ratcliffe, TX
Martha Roby, AL
Matt Gaetz, FL
Mike Johnson, LA
Andy Biggs, AZ
Tom McClintock, CA
Debbie Lesko, AZ
Guy Reschenthaler, PA
Ben Cline, VA
Kelly Armstrong, ND
W. Gregory Steube, FL

MAJORITY STAFF

Animley, Kingsley DIR - ADMIN OPS 2035........ **53951**
Apelbaum, Perry CHIEF COUNSEL/STAFF DIR 2138........ **53951**
Baugh, Patrick FINANCIAL ADMIN 2138........ **53951**
Dashow, Jordan PROF STAFF 2138........ **53951**
Doty, John SR ADVISOR 2138........ **53951**
Gayle, Charles COUNSEL - OVERSIGHT 2035........ **53951**
Gerson, Julian STAFF ASST 2138........ **53951**
Greengrass, David SR COUNSEL 2138........ **53951**
Hariharan, Arya COUNSEL - OVERSIGHT 2138........ **53951**
Hiller, Aaron DPTY CHIEF COUNSEL - OVERSIGHT 2138........ **53951**
Istel, Sarah COUNSEL - OVERSIGHT 2035........ **53951**
Jensen, Susan SR COUNSEL/PARLIAMENTARIAN 2138........ **53951**
Keller, Keenan SR COUNSEL 2138........ **53951**
Morton, Lisette POLICY DIR/DIR - MBR SVCS 2138........ **53951**
Pearson, Tim PUBLICATIONS CLERK 367 FHOB........ **53951**
Pinckney, Janna DIR - INFO TECH 2451........ **53951**
Presley, Jessica DIR - DIGITAL COMMUNICATIONS 2035........ **53951**
Reddick-Smith, Shadawn COMMUNICATIONS DIR 2138........ **53951**
Rutkin, Amy CHIEF OF STAFF 2138........ **53951**
Schwarz, Daniel DIR - STRATEGIC COMMUNICATIONS 2138... **53951**
Sharma, Moh ADVISOR - MBR SVCS/OUTREACH ADVISOR 2035........ **53951**
Siddiqui, Faisal DPTY DIR - INFO TECH 2451........ **53951**
Strasser, Madeline CHIEF CLERK 2138........ **53951**

MINORITY STAFF

Andrews, Jessica COMMUNICATIONS DIR 2226........ **56906**
Ashworth, Daniel COUNSEL 1504........ **56906**
Baker, Stacy DIR - INFO TECH 1504........ **56906**
Barker, Erica CHIEF LEGIS CLERK 1504........ **56906**
Belair, Brendan STAFF DIR - MIN 2142........ **56906**
Callen, Ashley SR ADVISOR/COUNSEL 189 FHOB........ **56906**
Davis, Carlton CHIEF OVERSIGHT COUNSEL 2226........ **56906**
Ferro, Jonathan PARLIAMENTARIAN/COUNSEL 2142........ **56906**
Greenberg, Jake COUNSEL - OVERSIGHT 2226........ **56906**
Hasenberg, Amy PRESS SECY 2226........ **56906**
Johnson, Daniel INVESTIGATIVE COUNSEL 189 FHOB........ **56906**
Larson, Sally POLICY ADVISOR 1504........ **56906**
Parmiter, Robert DPTY STAFF DIR - MIN STAFF 2142........ **56906**
Richardson, Anne DIGITAL DIR 2226........ **56906**
Yates, Ella DIR - MBR SVCS & COALITIONS 2142........ **56906**

SUBCOMMITTEES OF THE COMMITTEE ON THE JUDICIARY

SUBCOMMITTEE ON THE CONSTITUTION, CIVIL RIGHTS, AND CIVIL LIBERTIES

2138 RAYBURN HOB (ZIP: 20515)........225-3951

Steve Cohen, TN, Chair

Jamie Raskin, MD
Eric Swalwell, CA
Mary Gay Scanlon, PA
Madeleine Dean, PA
Sylvia R. Garcia, TX
Veronica Escobar, TX
Sheila Jackson Lee, TX

Mike Johnson, LA
Louie Gohmert, TX
Jim Jordan, OH
Guy Reschenthaler, PA
Ben Cline, VA
Kelly Armstrong, ND

MAJORITY STAFF

Brill, Sophia COUNSEL 2035........ **53951**
Emmons, William PROF STAFF 2035........ **53951**
McElvein, Elizabeth PROF STAFF MEMB 2138........ **53951**
Morgan, Matthew COUNSEL 2138........ **53951**
Park, James CHIEF COUNSEL 2138........ **53951**

MINORITY STAFF

Taylor, Paul CHIEF COUNSEL 362 FHOB........ **56906**

SUBCOMMITTEE ON COURTS, INTELLECTUAL PROPERTY, AND THE INTERNET

6310 O'NEILL HOB (ZIP: 20515)........225-5741

Henry C. "Hank" Johnson, Jr., GA, Chair

Theodore E. Deutch, FL
Cedric L. Richmond, LA
Hakeem S. Jeffries, NY
Ted Lieu, CA
Greg Stanton, AZ
Zoe Lofgren, CA
Steve Cohen, TN
Karen Bass, CA
Eric Swalwell, CA
J. Luis Correa, CA

Martha Roby, AL
Steve Chabot, OH
Jim Jordan, OH
John Ratcliffe, TX
Matt Gaetz, FL
Mike Johnson, LA
Andy Biggs, AZ
Guy Reschenthaler, PA
Ben Cline, VA

MAJORITY STAFF

Jackson, Rosalind PROF STAFF 6310........ **55741**
Simpson, Jamie CHIEF COUNSEL 6310........ **55741**

MINORITY STAFF

Stoll, Thomas COUNSEL 189 FHOB........ **56906**
Woodard, Andrea CLERK 189 FHOB........ **56906**

SUBCOMMITTEE ON CRIME, TERRORISM AND HOMELAND SECURITY

6340 O'NEILL HOB (ZIP: 20515)..225-5727

Karen Bass, CA, Chair

Sheila Jackson Lee, TX
Val Butler Demings, FL
Lucy McBath, GA
Theodore E. Deutch, FL
Cedric L. Richmond, LA
Hakeem S. Jeffries, NY
David N. Cicilline, RI
Ted Lieu, CA
Madeleine Dean, PA
Debbie Mucarsel-Powell, FL
Steve Cohen, TN

John Ratcliffe, TX
F. James Sensenbrenner, Jr., WI
Steve Chabot, OH
Louie Gohmert, TX
Tom McClintock, CA
Debbie Lesko, AZ
Guy Reschenthaler, PA
Ben Cline, VA
W. Gregory Steube, FL

MAJORITY STAFF

Dugue, Monalisa DPTY CHIEF COUNSEL 6340........................ **55727**
Eligan, Veronica PROF STAFF 6340........................ **55727**
Graupensperger, Joe CHIEF COUNSEL 6340........................ **55727**
Hernandez-Stern, Benjamin COUNSEL 6340........................ **55727**
Rossi, Rachel COUNSEL 6340........................ **55727**

MINORITY STAFF

Breitenbach, Ryan CHIEF COUNSEL 362 FHOB........................ **56906**
Cervenak, Jason CHIEF COUNSEL - MIN 362 FHOB........................ **56906**

SUBCOMMITTEE ON IMMIGRATION AND CITIZENSHIP

6320 O'NEILL HOB (ZIP: 20515)..225-3926

Zoe Lofgren, CA, Chair

Pramila Jayapal, WA
J. Luis Correa, CA
Sylvia R. Garcia, TX
Joe Neguse, CO
Debbie Mucarsel-Powell, FL
Veronica Escobar, TX
Sheila Jackson Lee, TX
Mary Gay Scanlon, PA

Ken Buck, CO
Andy Biggs, AZ
Tom McClintock, CA
Debbie Lesko, AZ
Kelly Armstrong, ND
W. Gregory Steube, FL

MAJORITY STAFF

Breisblatt, Joshua COUNSEL 6320........................ **53926**
Calanni, Rachel PROF STAFF 6320........................ **53926**
Lawrence, Betsy COUNSEL 6320........................ **53926**
Reynolds, Sarnata COUNSEL 6320........................ **53926**
Shahoulian, David CHIEF COUNSEL 6320........................ **53926**

MINORITY STAFF

Loving, Andrea CHIEF COUNSEL 189 FHOB........................ **56906**

SUBCOMMITTEE ON ANTITRUST, COMMERCIAL, AND ADMINISTRATIVE LAW

6240 O'NEILL HOB (ZIP: 20515)........226-7680

David N. Cicilline, RI, Chair

Henry C. "Hank" Johnson, Jr., GA
Jamie Raskin, MD
Pramila Jayapal, WA
Val Butler Demings, FL
Mary Gay Scanlon, PA
Joe Neguse, CO
Lucy McBath, GA

F. James Sensenbrenner, Jr., WI
Matt Gaetz, FL
Ken Buck, CO
Kelly Armstrong, ND
W. Gregory Steube, FL

MAJORITY STAFF

Bond, Slade CHIEF COUNSEL 6240........ **67680**
Ehrenkrantz, Joseph PROF STAFF 6240........ **67680**
Khan, Lina COUNSEL 6240........ **67680**
Van Wye, Joseph PROF STAFF 6240........ **67680**

MINORITY STAFF

Flores, Daniel CHIEF COUNSEL 189 FHOB........ **56906**

COMMITTEE ON NATURAL RESOURCES

1324 LONGWORTH HOB (ZIP: 20515-6201)........ 225-6065

Raúl M. Grijalva, AZ, Chair

Grace F. Napolitano, CA
Jim Costa, CA
Gregorio Kilili Camacho Sablan, MP
Jared Huffman, CA
Alan S. Lowenthal, CA
Ruben Gallego, AZ
TJ Cox, CA
Joe Neguse, CO
Mike Levin, CA
Debra A. Haaland, NM
Jefferson Van Drew, NJ
Joe Cunningham, SC
Nydia M. Velázquez, NY
Diana DeGette, CO
Wm. Lacy Clay, MO
Debbie Dingell, MI
Anthony G. Brown, MD
A. Donald McEachin, VA
Darren Soto, FL
Ed Case, HI
Steven Horsford, NV
Michael F. Q. San Nicolas, GU
Matt Cartwright, PA
Paul Tonko, NY
(Vacancy)

Rob Bishop, UT
Don Young, AK
Louie Gohmert, TX
Doug Lamborn, CO
Robert J. Wittman, VA
Tom McClintock, CA
Paul A. Gosar, AZ
Paul Cook, CA
Bruce Westerman, AR
Garret Graves, LA
Jody B. Hice, GA
Aumua Amata Coleman Radewagen, AS
Daniel Webster, FL
Liz Cheney, WY
Mike Johnson, LA
Jenniffer González-Colón, PR
John R. Curtis, UT
Kevin Hern, OK
Russ Fulcher, ID

MAJORITY STAFF

Clauson, Ilene DIR - OPS 1327A........ **56065**
Coleman, Joycelyn CALENDAR CLERK 1324........ **56065**
DeMarco, David DIR - INFO TECH 1322........ **56065**
Espinosa, Christopher DIR - COMMUNITY RELATIONS 1324... **56065**
Garza, Johnathan COORD - OUTREACH 186 FHOB........ **56065**
Le Grant, Carlyn STAFF ASST 1324........ **56065**
Lim, Sarah CHIEF COUNSEL 1324........ **56065**
Locke, Nancy CHIEF CLERK 1324........ **56065**
Miller, Glenn SR POLICY ADVISOR 1511........ **56065**
Modeste, Brian SUBCOMM STAFF DIR 186 FHOB........ **56065**
Sanchez, Monica DPTY PRESS SECY 1334........ **56065**
Sarvana, Adam COMMUNICATIONS DIR 1334........ **56065**
Schafer, Katie PRESS ASST 1324........ **56065**
Shen, David CONTENT & MULTIMEDIA PRODUCER 1334........ **56065**
Urbina, Luis DPTY COUNSEL 1324........ **56065**
Varela Rosa, Margarita OUTREACH COORD 186 FHOB........ **56065**
Villa, Cristina SCHEDULER 1511........ **56065**
Watkins, David STAFF DIR FOR NAT RESCS CMTE 1324........ **56065**
Winnick, Everett DPTY DIR - INFO TECH 1322........ **56065**
Zahran, Tariq COORD - MBR SVCS & OUTREACH 186 FHOB.... **56065**

MINORITY STAFF

Baum, Kristina COMMUNICATIONS DIR 1329........ **52761**
Braden, Parish STAFF DIR 1329........ **52761**
Hacker, Austin DPTY PRESS SECY 1329........ **52761**
Hanson, Tanner SR ADVISOR 4170........ **52761**
Miller, Annick PROF STAFF - MIN 4120........ **52761**
Pittman, Lisa CHIEF COUNSEL 1329........ **52761**
Stookey, Megan CLERK 1329........ **52761**

SUBCOMMITTEES OF THE COMMITTEE ON NATURAL RESOURCES

[The chairman and ranking minority member are non-voting ex officio members of all subcommittees on which they do not hold a regular assignment.]

SUBCOMMITTEE ON ENERGY AND MINERAL RESOURCES

1522 LONGWORTH HOB (ZIP: 20515)........225-6065

Alan S. Lowenthal, CA, Chair

Mike Levin, CA	*Paul A. Gosar*, AZ
Joe Cunningham, SC	*Doug Lamborn*, CO
A. Donald McEachin, VA	*Bruce Westerman*, AR
Diana DeGette, CO	*Garret Graves*, LA
Anthony G. Brown, MD	*Liz Cheney*, WY
Jared Huffman, CA	*Kevin Hern*, OK
Matt Cartwright, PA	*Rob Bishop*, UT (Ex Officio)
Raúl M. Grijalva, AZ (Ex Officio)	

MAJORITY STAFF

Cairns, Becky PROF STAFF - MAJ 1522........ **56065**
Feldgus, Steve DPTY STAFF DIR - MAJ STAFF/SUBCOMM STAFF DIR 1522........ **56065**
Gallagher, Peter PROF STAFF - MAJ 1522........ **56065**
Weiss, Sarina SUBCOMM CLERK 1522........ **56065**

MINORITY STAFF

Konolige, Rebecca PROF STAFF 4120........ **52761**
Nichols, Ashley PROF STAFF 4120........ **52761**

SUBCOMMITTEE ON NATIONAL PARKS, FORESTS, AND PUBLIC LANDS

1328 LONGWORTH HOB (ZIP: 20515)........225-6065

Debra A. Haaland, NM, Chair

Joe Neguse, CO	*Don Young*, AK
Diana DeGette, CO	*Louie Gohmert*, TX
Debbie Dingell, MI	*Tom McClintock*, CA
Steven Horsford, NV	*Paul Cook*, CA
Jared Huffman, CA	*Bruce Westerman*, AR
Ruben Gallego, AZ	*Jody B. Hice*, GA
Alan S. Lowenthal, CA	*Daniel Webster*, FL
Ed Case, HI	*John R. Curtis*, UT
Paul Tonko, NY	*Russ Fulcher*, ID
(Vacancy)	*Rob Bishop*, UT (Ex Officio)
Raúl M. Grijalva, AZ (Ex Officio)	

MAJORITY STAFF

Bragato, Brandon SUBCOMM STAFF DIR 1328........ **56065**
Wang, Lily CLERK 1328........ **56065**
Wykowski, Henry PROF STAFF - MAJ 1328........ **56065**

MINORITY STAFF

Camp, Terry PROF STAFF 4170........ **52761**
Miller, Brandon PROF STAFF 4170........ **52761**
Petersen, Steven SUBCOMM STAFF DIR 4120........ **52761**

SUBCOMMITTEE ON OVERSIGHT AND INVESTIGATIONS

186 FORD HOB (ZIP: 20515)........225-6065

TJ Cox, CA, Chair

Debbie Dingell, MI
A. Donald McEachin, VA
Michael F. Q. San Nicolas, GU
Raúl M. Grijalva, AZ

Louie Gohmert, TX
Paul A. Gosar, AZ
Mike Johnson, LA
Jenniffer González-Colón, PR
Rob Bishop, UT (Ex Officio)

MAJORITY STAFF

Bell, Auburn SUBCOMM CLERK 186 FHOB........ **56065**
Edgerton, Vic SUBCOMM STAFF DIR 186 FHOB........ **56065**
Gressard, Lindsay PROF STAFF 186 FHOB........ **56065**

MINORITY STAFF

Strom, John SR COUNSEL 4170........ **52761**
Yi, Sang SUBCOMM STAFF DIR 4170........ **52761**

SUBCOMMITTEE FOR INDIGENOUS PEOPLES OF THE UNITED STATES

1331 LONGWORTH HOB (ZIP: 20515)........225-6065

Ruben Gallego, AZ, Chair

Darren Soto, FL
Michael F. Q. San Nicolas, GU
Debra A. Haaland, NM
Ed Case, HI
Matt Cartwright, PA
(Vacancy)
(Vacancy)
Raúl M. Grijalva, AZ (Ex Officio)

Paul Cook, CA
Don Young, AK
Aumua Amata Coleman Radewagen, AS
John R. Curtis, UT
Kevin Hern, OK
(Vacancy)
Rob Bishop, UT (Ex Officio)

MAJORITY STAFF

Kaumo, Christopher SUBCOMM STAFF DIR/DPTY STAFF DIR 1413A........ **56065**
Miguel, Naomi PROF STAFF - MAJ 1331........ **56065**

MINORITY STAFF

Degenfelder, Ken PROF STAFF 4450........ **52761**
Fluhr, Chris SUBCOMM STAFF DIR/PROF STAFF - MIN 4450........ **52761**

SUBCOMMITTEE ON WATER, OCEANS, AND WILDLIFE

1332 LONGWORTH HOB (ZIP: 20515)........225-6065

Jared Huffman, CA, Chair

Grace F. Napolitano, CA
Jim Costa, CA
Gregorio Kilili Camacho Sablan, MP
Jefferson Van Drew, NJ
Nydia M. Velázquez, NY
Anthony G. Brown, MD
Ed Case, HI
Alan S. Lowenthal, CA
TJ Cox, CA
Joe Neguse, CO
Mike Levin, CA
Joe Cunningham, SC
Raúl M. Grijalva, AZ (Ex Officio)

Tom McClintock, CA
Doug Lamborn, CO
Robert J. Wittman, VA
Garret Graves, LA
Jody B. Hice, GA
Aumua Amata Coleman Radewagen, AS
Daniel Webster, FL
Mike Johnson, LA
Jenniffer González-Colón, PR
Russ Fulcher, ID
Rob Bishop, UT (Ex Officio)

MAJORITY STAFF

Brown, Carlee PROF STAFF - MAJ 1332 **56065**
Gentile, Rachel PROF STAFF - MAJ 1332 **56065**
Kremer, Marnie PROF STAFF - MAJ 1332 **56065**
MacLean, Casey SUBCOMM CLERK 1332 **56065**
Muirragui, Matthew SUBCOMM STAFF DIR 1333 **56065**
Snyder, Lora SUBCOMM STAFF DIR 1332 **56065**
Vernon, Lauren SUBCOMM CLERK 1332 **56065**

MINORITY STAFF

Alberts, Marc PROF STAFF 4120 **52761**
Ball, Bill SUBCOMM STAFF DIR 4120 **52761**
Youpel, Mary PROF STAFF 4120 **52761**

COMMITTEE ON OVERSIGHT AND REFORM

2157 RAYBURN HOB (ZIP: 20515-6143)........225-5051

Elijah E. Cummings, MD, Chair

Carolyn B. Maloney, NY
Eleanor Holmes Norton, DC
Wm. Lacy Clay, MO
Stephen F. Lynch, MA
Jim Cooper, TN
Gerald E. Connolly, VA
Raja Krishnamoorthi, IL
Jamie Raskin, MD
Harley Rouda, CA
Katie Hill, CA
Debbie Wasserman Schultz, FL
John P. Sarbanes, MD
Peter Welch, VT
Jackie Speier, CA
Robin L. Kelly, IL
Mark DeSaulnier, CA
Brenda L. Lawrence, MI
Stacey E. Plaskett, VI
Ro Khanna, CA
Jimmy Gomez, CA
Alexandria Ocasio-Cortez, NY
Ayanna Pressley, MA
Rashida Tlaib, MI

Jim Jordan, OH
Justin Amash, MI
Paul A. Gosar, AZ
Virginia Foxx, NC
Thomas Massie, KY
Mark Meadows, NC
Jody B. Hice, GA
Glenn Grothman, WI
James Comer, KY
Michael Cloud, TX
Bob Gibbs, OH
Clay Higgins, LA
Ralph Norman, SC
Chip Roy, TX
Carol D. Miller, WV
Mark E. Green, TN
Kelly Armstrong, ND
W. Gregory Steube, FL

MAJORITY STAFF

Anderson, Tori COUNSEL 2157........ **55051**
Anello, Russell CHIEF OVERSIGHT COUNSEL 2157........ **55051**
Badu-Nimako, Yvette LEGIS DIR 2157........ **55051**
Benjamin, William SYS ADMIN 2157........ **55051**
Blacksberg, Aaron COUNSEL 2157........ **55051**
Blumenthal, Jordan COUNSEL/POLICY ADVISOR 2157........ **55051**
Bourke, Jaron ADMIN DIR 2157........ **55051**
Bowden, Jamitress PRESS SECY 2157........ **55051**
Boyd, Krista GEN COUNSEL 2157........ **55051**
Bradford, Aryele COMMUNICATIONS DIR 2157........ **55051**
Broady, Marc POLICY ADVISOR 2157........ **55051**
Butler, Robin FINANCIAL ADMIN 2157........ **55051**
Castagnola, Michael PROF STAFF MEMB 2157........ **55051**
Chalhoub, Theresa COUNSEL 2157........ **55051**
Chang, Lena SR COUNSEL 2157........ **55051**
Chukwu, Chioma SR EXEC COUNSELOR 2157........ **55051**
Cooper, Kadeem COUNSEL 2157........ **55051**
Dulaney, Emmalynn DPTY PRESS SECY 2157........ **55051**
Eichar, Andrew PRESS SECY 2157........ **55051**
Fields, Cassandra COUNSEL 2157........ **55051**
Foster, Olivia EXEC ASST 2157........ **55051**
French, Courtney SR COUNSEL 2157........ **55051**
Gao, Greta COUNSEL 2157........ **55051**
Gaspar, Jennifer COUNSEL 2157........ **55051**
Golden, Alexandra CHIEF HEALTH COUNSEL 2157........ **55051**
Goss, Trinity STAFF ASST 2157........ **55051**
Grooms, Susanne DPTY STAFF DIR/CHIEF COUNSEL 2157........ **55051**
Heller, Jessica COUNSEL 2157........ **55051**
Jacobs, Brandon STAFF ASST 2157........ **55051**
Kenny, Peter CHIEF INVESTIGATIVE COUNSEL 2157........ **55051**
Kiles, Keith COUNSEL 2157........ **55051**
Kim, Gina COUNSEL 2157........ **55051**
Kim, Janet CHIEF COUNSEL - INVESTIGATIONS 2157........ **55051**
LaNier, Elisa DIR - OPS/CHIEF CLERK 2157........ **55051**
Larkin, Kellie PARLIAMENTARIAN/SR COUNSEL 2157........ **55051**
Lessley, Lucinda POLICY DIR 2157........ **55051**
Lichtman, Miles PROF STAFF MEMB 2157........ **55051**
Powell, Jason DPTY GEN COUNSEL 2157........ **55051**
Rapallo, David STAFF DIR 2157........ **55051**
Rios, Brandon Ricardo COUNSEL 2157........ **55051**
Rush, Laura DPTY CHIEF CLERK/SECUR OFFICER 2157........ **55051**
Shah, Amish COUNSEL 2157........ **55051**
Smith, Carissa DIGITAL PRESS SECY 2157........ **55051**
Stephenson, Mark LEGIS DIR 2157........ **55051**
Stratton, Amy CLERK 2157........ **55051**
Truding, Bradley COUNSEL 2157........ **55051**
Walker, Edward TECH DIR 2157........ **55051**
Waters, Laura COUNSEL 2157........ **55051**
Zucker, Joshua ASST CLERK 2157........ **55051**

MINORITY STAFF

Baker, Stacy DIR - INFO TECH 2105........ **55074**
Benzine, Mitchell COUNSEL 2105........ **55074**
Bidelman, Kiley CLERK 2105........ **55074**
Brebbia, Sean SR COUNSEL 2105........ **55074**
Brewer, David DPTY STAFF DIR 2105........ **55074**
Buddharaju, Deep COUNSEL 2105........ **55074**

Castor, Stephen GEN COUNSEL 2105 .... **55074**
Dye, Russell COMMUNICATIONS COUNSEL 2105 .... **55074**
Feeney, Sarah STAFF ASST 2105 .... **55074**
Ferguson, Betsy COUNSEL 2105 .... **55074**
Grimm, Tyler CHIEF ADVISOR FOR POLICY, STRATEGY & COMMUNICATIONS 2105 .... **55074**
Hixon, Christopher STAFF DIR 2105 .... **55074**
Huddleston, Charli PRESS SECY 2105 .... **55074**
Johnson, Ellen SR PROF STAFF MBR 2105 .... **55074**
Koren, Michael PROF STAFF MEMB 2105 .... **55074**
Lesinski, James COUNSEL 2105 .... **55074**
Marin, Mark DIR - OVERSIGHT 2105 .... **55074**
Nabity, Caroline COUNSEL 2105 .... **55074**
Rother, Katy POLICY DIR 2105 .... **55074**
Sanderson, Tyler COUNSEL 2105 .... **55074**
Scala, David PROF STAFF MEMB 2105 .... **55074**
Smithwick, Kyle COUNSEL 2105 .... **55074**
Vance, Sarah SR PROF STAFF MBR/OUTREACH DIR 2105 .... **55074**

SUBCOMMITTEES OF THE COMMITTEE ON OVERSIGHT AND REFORM

[The chairman and ranking minority member are ex officio members of all subcommittees.]

SUBCOMMITTEE ON CIVIL RIGHTS AND CIVIL LIBERTIES

6440 O'NEILL HOB (ZIP: 20515) 225-5051

Jamie Raskin, MD, Chairman

Carolyn B. Maloney, NY
Wm. Lacy Clay, MO
Debbie Wasserman Schultz, FL
Robin L. Kelly, IL
Jimmy Gomez, CA
Alexandria Ocasio-Cortez, NY
Ayanna Pressley, MA
Eleanor Holmes Norton, DC

Chip Roy, TX
Justin Amash, MI
Thomas Massie, KY
Mark Meadows, NC
Jody B. Hice, GA
Michael Cloud, TX
Carol D. Miller, WV

MAJORITY STAFF

Phoenix, Candyce SUBCOMM STAFF DIR 6440 .... **55051**
Shen, Valerie CHIEF COUNSEL/SR POLICY ADVISOR 6440 .... **55051**

SUBCOMMITTEE ON ECONOMIC AND CONSUMER POLICY

6430 O'NEILL HOB (ZIP: 20515) 225-5051

Raja Krishnamoorthi, IL, Chairman

Mark DeSaulnier, CA
Katie Hill, CA
Ro Khanna, CA
Ayanna Pressley, MA
Rashida Tlaib, MI
Gerald E. Connolly, VA

Michael Cloud, TX
Glenn Grothman, WI
James Comer, KY
Chip Roy, TX
Carol D. Miller, WV

MAJORITY STAFF

Cunningham, William COUNSEL/SR POLICY ADVISOR 6430 .... **55051**
Trumka, Richard SUBCOMM STAFF DIR 6430 .... **55051**

SUBCOMMITTEE ON ENVIRONMENT

6440 O'NEILL HOB (ZIP: 20515)........225-5051

Harley Rouda, CA, Chairman

Katie Hill, CA	*James Comer*, KY
Rashida Tlaib, MI	*Paul A. Gosar*, AZ
Raja Krishnamoorthi, IL	*Bob Gibbs*, OH
Jackie Speier, CA	*Clay Higgins*, LA
Jimmy Gomez, CA	*Kelly Armstrong*, ND
Alexandria Ocasio-Cortez, NY	

MAJORITY STAFF

Hammon, Beth PROF STAFF MEMB 6440........ **55051**
Jenkins, Britteny SUBCOMM STAFF DIR 6440........ **55051**

SUBCOMMITTEE ON GOVERNMENT OPERATIONS

6460 O'NEILL HOB (ZIP: 20515)........225-5051

Gerald E. Connolly, VA, Chairman

Eleanor Holmes Norton, DC	*Mark Meadows*, NC
John P. Sarbanes, MD	*Thomas Massie*, KY
Jackie Speier, CA	*Jody B. Hice*, GA
Brenda L. Lawrence, MI	*Glenn Grothman*, WI
Stacey E. Plaskett, VI	*James Comer*, KY
Ro Khanna, CA	*Ralph Norman*, SC
Stephen F. Lynch, MA	*W. Gregory Steube*, FL
Jamie Raskin, MD	

MAJORITY STAFF

Ginsberg, Wendy SUBCOMM STAFF DIR 6460........ **55051**
Lam, Kristine DPTY STAFF DIR 6460........ **55051**

SUBCOMMITTEE ON NATIONAL SECURITY

6470 O'NEILL HOB (ZIP: 20515)........225-5051

Stephen F. Lynch, MA, Chairman

Jim Cooper, TN	*Jody B. Hice*, GA
Peter Welch, VT	*Justin Amash*, MI
Harley Rouda, CA	*Paul A. Gosar*, AZ
Debbie Wasserman Schultz, FL	*Virginia Foxx*, NC
Robin L. Kelly, IL	*Mark Meadows*, NC
Mark DeSaulnier, CA	*Michael Cloud*, TX
Stacey E. Plaskett, VI	*Mark E. Green*, TN
Brenda L. Lawrence, MI	

MAJORITY STAFF

Fernandez, Bruce PROF STAFF MEMB 6470........ **55051**
Rebnord, Daniel SUBCOMM STAFF DIR 6470........ **55051**

COMMITTEE ON RULES

H312 CAPITOL (ZIP: 20515-6269)......225-9091

James P. McGovern, MA, Chair

Alcee L. Hastings, FL
Norma J. Torres, CA
Ed Perlmutter, CO
Jamie Raskin, MD
Mary Gay Scanlon, PA
Joseph D. Morelle, NY
Donna E. Shalala, FL
Mark DeSaulnier, CA

Tom Cole, OK, Ranking Member
Rob Woodall, GA
Michael C. Burgess, TX
Debbie Lesko, AZ

MAJORITY STAFF

Corbin, Kim SR HEALTH POLICY ADVISOR H312...... **59091**
Delaney, Eric PROF STAFF - MAJ H312...... **59091**
Gohringer, Jeff COMMUNICATIONS DIR H312...... **59091**
Hodgkins, Caitlin POLICY DIR H312...... **59091**
Ismail, Lori PROF STAFF - MAJ H312...... **59091**
Laughlin, Rose PROF STAFF - MAJ H312...... **59091**
Martinez, Ana STAFF ASST H312...... **59091**
Mueller, Lauren PRESS ASST H312...... **59091**
Pardue, Liz DPTY STAFF DIR H312...... **59091**
Perkins, Nate DIR - LEGIS OPS H312...... **59091**
Price, Matt PROF STAFF - MAJ H312...... **59091**
Russell, Sam STAFF ASST H312...... **59091**
Sisson, Donald STAFF DIR H312...... **59091**
Suh, Jessica DPTY CLERK H312...... **59091**

MINORITY STAFF

Corley, Sarah COMMUNICATIONS DIR 1116...... **59191**
Diller, Matthew POLICY DIR 1116...... **59191**
Dixon, Kelly STAFF DIR H152...... **59191**
Erb, Chris DIR - INFO TECH/DIR - ADMIN OPS 1116...... **59191**
Fitzella, James SR PROF STAFF H152...... **59191**
Gill, Hannah PROF STAFF 1116...... **59191**
Lackey, Jennifer SR PROF STAFF H152...... **59191**
Roberts, Drew RESEARCH ASST 1116...... **59191**
Shepard, Eric PROF STAFF 1116...... **59191**
Waskiewicz, Steve SR PROF STAFF H152...... **59191**

SUBCOMMITTEES OF THE COMMITTEE ON RULES

SUBCOMMITTEE ON EXPEDITED PROCEDURES

H312 CAPITOL (ZIP: 20515)......225-9091

Jamie Raskin, MD, Chair

Donna E. Shalala, FL, Vice Chair
Norma J. Torres, CA
Mark DeSaulnier, CA
James P. McGovern, MA

Michael C. Burgess, TX, Ranking Member
Debbie Lesko, AZ

SUBCOMMITTEE ON LEGISLATIVE AND BUDGET PROCESS

H312 CAPITOL (ZIP: 20515)......225-9091

Alcee L. Hastings, FL, Chair

Joseph D. Morelle, NY, Vice Chair
Mary Gay Scanlon, PA
Donna E. Shalala, FL
James P. McGovern, MA

Rob Woodall, GA, Ranking Member
Michael C. Burgess, TX

U.S. HOUSE OF REPRESENTATIVES

SUBCOMMITTEE ON RULES AND ORGANIZATION OF THE HOUSE

H312 CAPITOL (ZIP: 20515)..225-9091

Norma J. Torres, CA, Chair

Ed Perlmutter, CO, Vice Chair
Mary Gay Scanlon, PA
Joseph D. Morelle, NY
James P. McGovern, MA

Debbie Lesko, AZ, Ranking Member
Rob Woodall, GA

COMMITTEE ON SCIENCE, SPACE, AND TECHNOLOGY

2321 RAYBURN HOB (ZIP: 20515-6301)........225-6375

Eddie Bernice Johnson, TX, Chair

Zoe Lofgren, CA
Daniel Lipinski, IL
Suzanne Bonamici, OR
Ami Bera, CA, Vice Chair
Conor Lamb, PA
Lizzie Fletcher, TX
Haley M. Stevens, MI
Kendra S. Horn, OK
Mikie Sherrill, NJ
Brad Sherman, CA
Steve Cohen, TN
Jerry McNerney, CA
Ed Perlmutter, CO
Paul Tonko, NY
Bill Foster, IL
Donald S. Beyer, Jr., VA
Charlie Crist, FL
Sean Casten, IL
Katie Hill, CA
Ben McAdams, UT
Jennifer Wexton, VA

Frank D. Lucas, OK, Ranking Member
Mo Brooks, AL
Bill Posey, FL
Randy K. Weber, Sr., TX
Brian Babin, TX
Andy Biggs, AZ
Roger W. Marshall, KS
Ralph Norman, SC
Michael Cloud, TX
Troy Balderson, OH
Pete Olson, TX
Anthony Gonzalez, OH
Michael Waltz, FL
James R. Baird, IN
Jaime Herrera Beutler, WA
Jenniffer González-Colón, PR
(Vacancy)

MAJORITY STAFF

Anderson, Cassie PRESS ASST - MAJ 2321........ **56375**
Eskandani, Rebekah COMMUNICATIONS DIR 2321........ **56375**
Johnson, Stanton DPTY CHIEF COUNSEL 2321........ **56375**
Kopshever, Kristin ADMIN DIR/DIR OF MBR SVCS – MAJ 2321........ **56375**
McAuliffe, Emily STAFF ASST - MAJ 2321........ **56375**
Obermann, Richard CHIEF OF STAFF - MAJ 2321........ **56375**
Piazza, John CHIEF COUNSEL - MAJ 2321........ **56375**
Whittaker, Larry SYS ADMIN 2321........ **56375**
Wood, Kendra CLERK 2321........ **56375**

MINORITY STAFF

Blevins, Brent SR POLICY ADVISOR - REPUB 394 FHOB........ **56371**
Connally, Tom COUNSEL 394 FHOB........ **56371**
Domenech, Emily SR POLICY ADVISOR - REPUB 394 FHOB.... **56371**
Dziadon, Daniel PROF STAFF MBR - REPUB 394 FHOB........ **56371**
Ferrara, Anna STAFF ASST - REPUB 394 FHOB........ **56371**
Hammond, Tom SR POLICY ADVISOR - REPUB 394 FHOB...... **56371**
Johnson, Cate PROF STAFF MBR - REPUB 394 FHOB........ **56371**
Mathis, Josh STAFF DIR 394 FHOB........ **56371**
O'Brien, Hillary PROF STAFF MBR - REPUB 394 FHOB........ **56371**
Traynham, Benjamin COUNSEL/SR POLICY ADVISOR - REPUB 394 FHOB........ **56371**
Vaughan, Heather COMMUNICATIONS DIR - REPUB 394 FHOB........ **56371**
Wickre, Jenn SR POLICY ADVISOR - REPUB 394 FHOB........ **56371**

SUBCOMMITTEES OF THE COMMITTEE ON SCIENCE, SPACE, AND TECHNOLOGY

[The chairman and ranking minority member are ex officio members of all subcommittees.]

SUBCOMMITTEE ON ENERGY

2321 RAYBURN HOB (ZIP: 20515)..225-6375

Conor Lamb, PA, Chairman

Daniel Lipinski, IL
Lizzie Fletcher, TX
Haley M. Stevens, MI
Kendra S. Horn, OK
Jerry McNerney, CA
Bill Foster, IL
Sean Casten, IL
Eddie Bernice Johnson, TX (Ex Officio)

Randy K. Weber, Sr., TX, Ranking Member
Andy Biggs, AZ
Ralph Norman, SC
Michael Cloud, TX
(Vacancy)
Frank D. Lucas, OK (Ex Officio)

MAJORITY STAFF

Das, Tanya PROF STAFF - MAJ 2321.. **56375**
Rosenberg, Adam STAFF DIR - MAJ 2321.. **56375**
Wright, Sangina RESEARCH ASST - MAJ 2321.. **56375**

SUBCOMMITTEE ON ENVIRONMENT

2321 RAYBURN HOB (ZIP: 20515)..225-6375

Lizzie Fletcher, TX, Chairwoman

Suzanne Bonamici, OR
Conor Lamb, PA
Paul Tonko, NY
Charlie Crist, FL
Sean Casten, IL
Ben McAdams, UT
Donald S. Beyer, Jr., VA
Eddie Bernice Johnson, TX (Ex Officio)

Roger W. Marshall, KS, Ranking Member
Brian Babin, TX
Anthony Gonzalez, OH
James R. Baird, IN
Jenniffer González-Colón, PR
Frank D. Lucas, OK (Ex Officio)

MAJORITY STAFF

Hooghan, Priyanka STAFF DIR - MAJ 2321.. **56375**
Kovalovich, Aria RESEARCH ASST - MAJ 2321.. **56375**
Linsmayer, Lauren PROF STAFF - MAJ 2321.. **56375**

SUBCOMMITTEE ON INVESTIGATIONS AND OVERSIGHT

2321 RAYBURN HOB (ZIP: 20515)..225-6375

Mikie Sherrill, NJ, Chairwoman

Suzanne Bonamici, OR
Steve Cohen, TN
Donald S. Beyer, Jr., VA
Jennifer Wexton, VA
Eddie Bernice Johnson, TX (Ex Officio)

Ralph Norman, SC, Ranking Member
Andy Biggs, AZ
Michael Waltz, FL
Frank D. Lucas, OK (Ex Officio)

MAJORITY STAFF

Palasits, Sara PROF STAFF - MAJ 2321.. **56375**
Schneider, Joshua PROF STAFF - MAJ 2321.. **56375**

SUBCOMMITTEE ON RESEARCH AND TECHNOLOGY

2321 RAYBURN HOB (ZIP: 20515)........225-6375

Haley M. Stevens, MI, Chairwoman

Daniel Lipinski, IL
Mikie Sherrill, NJ
Brad Sherman, CA
Paul Tonko, NY
Ben McAdams, UT
Steve Cohen, TN
Bill Foster, IL
Eddie Bernice Johnson, TX (Ex Officio)

James R. Baird, IN, Ranking Member
Roger W. Marshall, KS
Troy Balderson, OH
Anthony Gonzalez, OH
Jaime Herrera Beutler, WA
Frank D. Lucas, OK (Ex Officio)

MAJORITY STAFF

Barber, Sara PROF STAFF - MAJ 2321........ **56375**
Berger, Benjamin RESEARCH ASST - MAJ 2321........ **56375**
English, Brystol PROF STAFF - MAJ 2321........ **56375**
Sokolov, Dahlia STAFF DIR - MAJ 2321........ **56375**

SUBCOMMITTEE ON SPACE AND AERONAUTICS

2321 RAYBURN HOB (ZIP: 20515)........225-6375

Kendra S. Horn, OK, Chairwoman

Zoe Lofgren, CA
Ami Bera, CA
Ed Perlmutter, CO
Donald S. Beyer, Jr., VA
Charlie Crist, FL
Katie Hill, CA
Jennifer Wexton, VA
Eddie Bernice Johnson, TX (Ex Officio)

Brian Babin, TX, Ranking Member
Mo Brooks, AL
Bill Posey, FL
Pete Olson, TX
Michael Waltz, FL
Frank D. Lucas, OK (Ex Officio)

MAJORITY STAFF

Reinecke, Griffin RESEARCH ASST - MAJ 2321........ **56375**
Whitney, Pam STAFF DIR - MAJ 2321........ **56375**

COMMITTEE ON SMALL BUSINESS

2361 RAYBURN HOB (ZIP: 20515-6315)........................225-4038

Nydia M. Velázquez, NY, Chair

Abby Finkenauer, IA
Jared F. Golden, ME
Andy Kim, NJ
Jason Crow, CO
Sharice Davids, KS
Judy Chu, CA
Marc A. Veasey, TX
Dwight Evans, PA
Bradley Scott Schneider, IL
Adriano Espaillat, NY
Antonio Delgado, NY
Chrissy Houlahan, PA
Angie Craig, MN

Steve Chabot, OH
Aumua Amata Coleman Radewagen, AS
Trent Kelly, MS
Troy Balderson, OH
Kevin Hern, OK
Jim Hagedorn, MN
Pete Stauber, MN
Tim Burchett, TN
Ross Spano, FL
John Joyce, PA

MAJORITY STAFF

Bonilla, Gerardo SR ECON ADVISOR 2361........ **54038**
Bruno, Richard DC SCHEDULER 2361........ **54038**
Ennesser, Tracy STAFF ASST 2361........ **54038**
Finks, Lauren CLERK 2361........ **54038**
Garcia, Mory OFFICE MGR 2361........ **54038**
Gomez, Matthew COUNSEL 2361........ **54038**
Harrington, Ellen SR PROF STAFF MBR 2361........ **54038**
Haurek, Alex SR ADVISOR 2361........ **54038**
Jung, Melissa DPTY STAFF DIR/CHIEF COUNSEL 2361........ **54038**
McGinnis, Michael DPTY PRESS SECY/DIGITAL STRATEGIST 2361........ **54038**
Minehardt, Adam STAFF DIR 2361........ **54038**
Parmar, Naveen POLICY DIR/GEN COUNSEL 2361........ **54038**
Pelletier, Justin SR ADVISOR 2361........ **54038**
Quartz, Evelyn PRESS SECY 2361........ **54038**
Rivera, Irene PROCUREMENT COUN 2361........ **54038**
Sunn, Meagan PROF STAFF MEMB 2361........ **54038**

MINORITY STAFF

Barr, Delia PROF STAFF 2069........ **55821**
Fitzpatrick, Kevin STAFF DIR 2069........ **55821**
Hartz, Joe POLICY DIR 2069........ **55821**
Ling, Vivian COUNSEL 2069........ **55821**
Oliver, Jan CHIEF COUNSEL/DPTY STAFF DIR 2069........ **55821**
Schmidt, Hannah PROF STAFF 2069........ **55821**
Yavor, Robert SR PROF STAFF 2069........ **55821**

SUBCOMMITTEES OF THE COMMITTEE ON SMALL BUSINESS

SUBCOMMITTEE ON RURAL DEVELOPMENT, AGRICULTURE, TRADE AND ENTREPRENEURSHIP

2361 RAYBURN HOB (ZIP: 20515)........................225-4038

Abby Finkenauer, IA, Chairwoman

Jared F. Golden, ME
Jason Crow, CO
Angie Craig, MN
(Vacancy)
(Vacancy)

John Joyce, PA
Aumua Amata Coleman Radewagen, AS
Trent Kelly, MS
Jim Hagedorn, MN

SUBCOMMITTEE ON CONTRACTING AND INFRASTRUCTURE

2361 RAYBURN HOB (ZIP: 20515)........................225-4038

Jared F. Golden, ME, Chairman

Marc A. Veasey, TX	*Pete Stauber*, MN
Judy Chu, CA	*Jim Hagedorn*, MN
(Vacancy)	*Troy Balderson*, OH
(Vacancy)	(Vacancy)
(Vacancy)	

SUBCOMMITTEE ON ECONOMIC GROWTH, TAX AND CAPITAL ACCESS

2361 RAYBURN HOB (ZIP: 20515)........................225-4038

Andy Kim, NJ, Chairman

Sharice Davids, KS	*Kevin Hern*, OK
Bradley Scott Schneider, IL	*Ross Spano*, FL
Adriano Espaillat, NY	***Aumua Amata Coleman Radewagen***, AS
Antonio Delgado, NY	*Pete Stauber*, MN
Jason Crow, CO	

SUBCOMMITTEE ON INNOVATION AND WORKFORCE DEVELOPMENT

2361 RAYBURN HOB (ZIP: 20515)........................225-4038

Jason Crow, CO, Chairman

Marc A. Veasey, TX	*Troy Balderson*, OH
Chrissy Houlahan, PA	*Tim Burchett*, TN
Abby Finkenauer, IA	*Kevin Hern*, OK
Andy Kim, NJ	*John Joyce*, PA
Sharice Davids, KS	

SUBCOMMITTEE ON INVESTIGATIONS, OVERSIGHT AND REGULATIONS

2361 RAYBURN HOB (ZIP: 20515)........................225-4038

Judy Chu, CA, Chairwoman

Dwight Evans, PA	*Ross Spano*, FL
Angie Craig, MN	*Trent Kelly*, MS
(Vacancy)	*Tim Burchett*, TN
(Vacancy)	(Vacancy)
(Vacancy)	

COMMITTEE ON TRANSPORTATION AND INFRASTRUCTURE

2165 RAYBURN HOB (ZIP: 20515-6256)........ 225-4472

Peter A. DeFazio, OR, Chair

Eleanor Holmes Norton, DC
Eddie Bernice Johnson, TX
Elijah E. Cummings, MD
Rick Larsen, WA
Grace F. Napolitano, CA
Daniel Lipinski, IL
Steve Cohen, TN
Albio Sires, NJ
John Garamendi, CA
Henry C. "Hank" Johnson, Jr., GA
André Carson, IN
Dina Titus, NV
Sean Patrick Maloney, NY
Jared Huffman, CA
Julia Brownley, CA
Frederica S. Wilson, FL
Donald M. Payne, Jr., NJ
Alan S. Lowenthal, CA
Mark DeSaulnier, CA
Stacey E. Plaskett, VI
Stephen F. Lynch, MA
Salud O. Carbajal, CA, Vice Chair
Anthony G. Brown, MD
Adriano Espaillat, NY
Tom Malinowski, NJ
Greg Stanton, AZ
Debbie Mucarsel-Powell, FL
Lizzie Fletcher, TX
Colin Z. Allred, TX
Sharice Davids, KS
Abby Finkenauer, IA
Jesús G. "Chuy" García, IL
Antonio Delgado, NY
Chris Pappas, NH
Angie Craig, MN
Harley Rouda, CA

Sam Graves, MO
Don Young, AK
Eric A. "Rick" Crawford, AR
Bob Gibbs, OH
Daniel Webster, FL
Thomas Massie, KY
Mark Meadows, NC
Scott Perry, PA
Rodney Davis, IL
Rob Woodall, GA
John Katko, NY
Brian Babin, TX
Garret Graves, LA
David Rouzer, NC
Mike Bost, IL
Randy K. Weber, Sr., TX
Doug LaMalfa, CA
Bruce Westerman, AR
Lloyd Smucker, PA
Paul Mitchell, MI
Brian J. Mast, FL
Mike Gallagher, WI
Gary J. Palmer, AL
Brian K. Fitzpatrick, PA
Jenniffer González-Colón, PR
Troy Balderson, OH
Ross Spano, FL
Pete Stauber, MN
Carol D. Miller, WV
Greg Pence, IN

MAJORITY STAFF

Bell, Chris LEGIS ASST 2165........ **54472**
Blankenship, April ADMIN - FINANCE & PAYROLL 2165........ **54472**
Dedrick, Katherine W STAFF DIR 2165........ **54472**
Dudley, Lauren COUNSEL - INVESTIGATIONS & OVERSIGHT 2165........ **54472**
Frias, Marcus DIGITAL DIR 2029........ **54472**
Harrell, James ADMIN 2165........ **54472**
Harrelson, Jill BUDGET DIR - MAJ/DPTY COUNSEL 2165........ **54472**
Legg, Mike DIR - TRAVEL, SECUR, & FACILITIES 2165........ **54472**
McGlone, Edward PROF STAFF 2165........ **54472**
O'Brien, Kristine DIR - OUTREACH & MEMB SVCS 2165........ **54472**
Old Crow, Alexa LEGIS ASST 2165........ **54472**
Pasternak, Douglas DIR - INVESTIGATIONS 587 FHOB........ **54472**
Putz, Scott ASST SYS ADMIN 2253........ **54472**
Sandy, Bayley DPTY COMMUNICATIONS DIR 2029........ **54472**
Syed, Mohsin GEN COUNSEL 2165........ **54472**
Twinchek, Michael CLERK 588 FHOB........ **55082**
Whittaker, Larry SYS ADMIN 2253........ **54472**

MINORITY STAFF

Camp, Abigail DIR - COALITIONS 2164........ **59446**
Christensen, Nick DIR - COALITIONS & MBR SVCS 2164........ **59446**
Como, Peter STAFF ASST 2164........ **59446**
Cooke, Corey DPTY GEN COUNSEL 2164........ **59446**
Harclerode, Justin COMMUNICATIONS DIR 2164........ **59446**
Miller, Fred GEN COUNSEL 2164........ **59446**
Ruddy, Jack DPTY STAFF DIR 2164........ **59446**
Sarmiento, Victor RESEARCH ASST 2164........ **59446**

Sass, Paul STAFF DIR 2164 59446
Youngblood, Suzanne DPTY COMMUNICATIONS DIR 2164 59446

SUBCOMMITTEES OF THE COMMITTEE ON TRANSPORTATION AND INFRASTRUCTURE

[The chairman and ranking minority member are ex officio members, with vote, of all subcommittees.]

SUBCOMMITTEE ON AVIATION

2165 RAYBURN HOB (ZIP: 20515) 225-4472

Rick Larsen, WA, Chair

André Carson, IN
Stacey E. Plaskett, VI
Stephen F. Lynch, MA
Eleanor Holmes Norton, DC
Daniel Lipinski, IL
Steve Cohen, TN
Henry C. "Hank" Johnson, Jr., GA
Dina Titus, NV
Julia Brownley, CA
Anthony G. Brown, MD
Greg Stanton, AZ
Colin Z. Allred, TX
Jesús G. "Chuy" García, IL
Eddie Bernice Johnson, TX
Sean Patrick Maloney, NY
Donald M. Payne, Jr., NJ
Sharice Davids, KS
Angie Craig, MN
Grace F. Napolitano, CA
Salud O. Carbajal, CA
Peter A. DeFazio, OR, Ex Officio

Garret Graves, LA
Don Young, AK
Daniel Webster, FL
Thomas Massie, KY
Scott Perry, PA
Rob Woodall, GA
John Katko, NY
David Rouzer, NC
Lloyd Smucker, PA
Paul Mitchell, MI
Brian J. Mast, FL
Mike Gallagher, WI
Brian K. Fitzpatrick, PA
Troy Balderson, OH
Ross Spano, FL
Pete Stauber, MN
Sam Graves, MO, Ex Officio

MAJORITY STAFF

Devine, Rachel STAFF DIR/SR COUNSEL 2251 54472
Tien, Michael SR COUNSEL 2251 54472

MINORITY STAFF

Lyons, Holly Woodruff STAFF DIR/SR COUNSEL 592 FHOB 54472
Presti, Hunter PROF STAFF 592 FHOB 54472

SUBCOMMITTEE ON COAST GUARD AND MARITIME TRANSPORTATION

2165 RAYBURN HOB (ZIP: 20515) 225-4472

Sean Patrick Maloney, NY, Chair

Elijah E. Cummings, MD
Rick Larsen, WA
Stacey E. Plaskett, VI
John Garamendi, CA
Alan S. Lowenthal, CA
Anthony G. Brown, MD
Chris Pappas, NH
Peter A. DeFazio, OR, Ex Officio

Bob Gibbs, OH
Don Young, AK
Randy K. Weber, Sr., TX
Brian J. Mast, FL
Mike Gallagher, WI
Carol D. Miller, WV
Sam Graves, MO, Ex Officio

MAJORITY STAFF

Dwyer, Matthew PROF STAFF 2165 .... **54472**

Jansen, Dave STAFF DIR 507 FHOB **54472**

MINORITY STAFF

Rayfield, John STAFF DIR 505 FHOB **54472**

SUBCOMMITTEE ON ECONOMIC DEVELOPMENT, PUBLIC BUILDINGS, AND EMERGENCY MANAGEMENT

2165 RAYBURN HOB (ZIP: 20515) 225-4472

Dina Titus, NV, Chair

Debbie Mucarsel-Powell, FL
Sharice Davids, KS
Eleanor Holmes Norton, DC
Henry C. "Hank" Johnson, Jr., GA
John Garamendi, CA
Anthony G. Brown, MD
Lizzie Fletcher, TX
Peter A. DeFazio, OR, Ex Officio

Mark Meadows, NC
Gary J. Palmer, AL
Jenniffer González-Colón, PR
Carol D. Miller, WV
Greg Pence, IN
Sam Graves, MO, Ex Officio

MAJORITY STAFF

Davis, Aaron STAFF DIR 2165 .... **54472**

MINORITY STAFF

Hardy, Johanna STAFF DIR 505 FHOB **54472**

COMMITTEE MEMBERS AND STAFF

SUBCOMMITTEE ON HIGHWAYS AND TRANSIT

2165 RAYBURN HOB (ZIP: 20515)..225-4472

Eleanor Holmes Norton, DC, Chair

Eddie Bernice Johnson, TX
Steve Cohen, TN
John Garamendi, CA
Henry C. "Hank" Johnson, Jr., GA
Jared Huffman, CA
Julia Brownley, CA
Frederica S. Wilson, FL
Alan S. Lowenthal, CA
Mark DeSaulnier, CA
Salud O. Carbajal, CA
Anthony G. Brown, MD
Adriano Espaillat, NY
Tom Malinowski, NJ
Greg Stanton, AZ
Colin Z. Allred, TX
Sharice Davids, KS
Abby Finkenauer, IA
Jesús G. "Chuy" García, IL
Antonio Delgado, NY
Chris Pappas, NH
Angie Craig, MN
Harley Rouda, CA
Grace F. Napolitano, CA
Albio Sires, NJ
Sean Patrick Maloney, NY
Donald M. Payne, Jr., NJ
Daniel Lipinski, IL
Dina Titus, NV
Stacey E. Plaskett, VI
Peter A. DeFazio, OR, Ex Officio

Rodney Davis, IL
Don Young, AK
Eric A. "Rick" Crawford, AR
Bob Gibbs, OH
Daniel Webster, FL
Thomas Massie, KY
Mark Meadows, NC
Rob Woodall, GA
John Katko, NY
Brian Babin, TX
David Rouzer, NC
Mike Bost, IL
Doug LaMalfa, CA
Bruce Westerman, AR
Lloyd Smucker, PA
Paul Mitchell, MI
Mike Gallagher, WI
Gary J. Palmer, AL
Brian K. Fitzpatrick, PA
Troy Balderson, OH
Ross Spano, FL
Pete Stauber, MN
Carol D. Miller, WV
Greg Pence, IN
Sam Graves, MO, Ex Officio

MAJORITY STAFF

Bell, Brian COUNSEL 2165.. **54472**
Lundberg, Brittany POLICY ANALYST 2251........................ **54472**
Mahar-Piersma, Auke PROF STAFF 2251........................ **54472**
Napoliello, David SR POLICY ADVISOR 2251........................ **54472**
Zyblikewycz, Helena SUBCOMM STAFF DIR 2251........................ **54472**

MINORITY STAFF

Barrett, Murphie STAFF DIR 593 FHOB........................ **54472**
Tucker, Cheryle SR PROF STAFF 2165........................ **54472**

SUBCOMMITTEE ON RAILROADS, PIPELINES, AND HAZARDOUS MATERIALS

2165 RAYBURN HOB (ZIP: 20515)........ 225-4472

Daniel Lipinski, IL, Chair

Albio Sires, NJ
Donald M. Payne, Jr., NJ
Lizzie Fletcher, TX
Elijah E. Cummings, MD
André Carson, IN
Frederica S. Wilson, FL
Mark DeSaulnier, CA
Stephen F. Lynch, MA
Tom Malinowski, NJ
Grace F. Napolitano, CA
Steve Cohen, TN
Jesús G. "Chuy" García, IL
Eleanor Holmes Norton, DC
Eddie Bernice Johnson, TX
Alan S. Lowenthal, CA
Colin Z. Allred, TX
Angie Craig, MN
Peter A. DeFazio, OR, Ex Officio

Eric A. "Rick" Crawford, AR
Scott Perry, PA
Rodney Davis, IL
Brian Babin, TX
Mike Bost, IL
Randy K. Weber, Sr., TX
Doug LaMalfa, CA
Lloyd Smucker, PA
Paul Mitchell, MI
Brian K. Fitzpatrick, PA
Troy Balderson, OH
Ross Spano, FL
Pete Stauber, MN
Greg Pence, IN
Sam Graves, MO, Ex Officio

MAJORITY STAFF

Hill, Elizabeth STAFF DIR 2251........ **54472**
Wohleber, Andrea PROF STAFF 2251........ **54472**

MINORITY STAFF

Falencki, Michael STAFF DIR 2165........ **54472**

SUBCOMMITTEE ON WATER RESOURCES AND ENVIRONMENT

2165 RAYBURN HOB (ZIP: 20515)........ 225-4472

Grace F. Napolitano, CA, Chair

Debbie Mucarsel-Powell, FL
Eddie Bernice Johnson, TX
John Garamendi, CA
Jared Huffman, CA
Alan S. Lowenthal, CA
Salud O. Carbajal, CA
Adriano Espaillat, NY
Lizzie Fletcher, TX
Abby Finkenauer, IA
Antonio Delgado, NY
Chris Pappas, NH
Angie Craig, MN
Harley Rouda, CA
Frederica S. Wilson, FL
Stephen F. Lynch, MA
Tom Malinowski, NJ
Peter A. DeFazio, OR, Ex Officio

Bruce Westerman, AR
Daniel Webster, FL
Thomas Massie, KY
Rob Woodall, GA
Brian Babin, TX
Garret Graves, LA
David Rouzer, NC
Mike Bost, IL
Randy K. Weber, Sr., TX
Doug LaMalfa, CA
Brian J. Mast, FL
Gary J. Palmer, AL
Jenniffer González-Colón, PR
Sam Graves, MO, Ex Officio

MAJORITY STAFF

Bermudez, Navis PROF STAFF 2165........ **54472**
Seiger, Ryan STAFF DIR/SR COUNSEL 505 FHOB........ **54472**
Touton, Camille PROF STAFF 585 FHOB........ **54472**

MINORITY STAFF

Bennitt, Ian STAFF DIR 585 FHOB **54472**

Pawlow, Jonathan SR COUNSEL 585 FHOB **54472**

COMMITTEE ON VETERANS' AFFAIRS

B234 LONGWORTH HOB (ZIP: 20515-6335)......225-9756

Mark Takano, CA, Chair

Julia Brownley, CA
Kathleen M. Rice, NY
Conor Lamb, PA
Mike Levin, CA
Anthony Brindisi, NY
Max Rose, NY
Chris Pappas, NH
Elaine G. Luria, VA
Susie Lee, NV
Joe Cunningham, SC
Gilbert Ray Cisneros, Jr., CA
Collin C. Peterson, MN
Gregorio Kilili Camacho Sablan, MP
Colin Z. Allred, TX
Lauren Underwood, IL

David P. Roe, TN, Ranking Member
Gus M. Bilirakis, FL
Aumua Amata Coleman Radewagen, AS
Mike Bost, IL
Neal P. Dunn, FL
Jack Bergman, MI
Jim Banks, IN
Andy Barr, KY
Daniel Meuser, PA
Steve Watkins, KS
Chip Roy, TX
W. Gregory Steube, FL

MAJORITY STAFF

Austin-Mackenzie, Elizabeth SUBCOMM STAFF DIR - HEALTH SUBCOMM 3470...... **59756**
Beckelman, Yuri SR ADVISOR B234 LHOB...... **59756**
Bennett, Christopher PROF STAFF MEMB - ECONOMIC OPPORTUNITY SUBCOMM 3470...... **59756**
Berstell, Daria STAFF ASST B234 LHOB...... **59756**
Bland, Megan PROF STAFF MEMB - HEALTH SUBCOMM 3470. **59756**
Blaydes, Carolyn SUBCOMM STAFF DIR - DISABILITY ASSISTANCE AND MEMORIAL AFFAIRS SUBCOMM B234 LHOB...... **59756**
Dean, Sarah PROF STAFF MEMB - HEALTH SUBCOMM 3470... **59756**
Dotson, Bernadine FINANCIAL ADMIN/OFFICE MGR 3470...... **59756**
Franco, Sam PROF STAFF MEMB - DISABILITY ASSISTANCE AND MEMORIAL AFFAIRS SUBCOMM B234 LHOB...... **59756**
Garcia, Sarah SUBCOMM STAFF DIR - TECHNOLOGY MODERNIZATION SUBCOMM B234 LHOB...... **59756**
Geurink, Jenni PRESS ASST B234 LHOB...... **59756**
Goldstein, Andrea POLICY ADVISOR - HEALTH SUBCOMM 3470...... **59756**
Harry, John PROF STAFF MEMB - TECHNOLOGY MODERNIZATION SUBCOMM B234 LHOB...... **59756**
Hasan, Rasheedah CHIEF CLERK - COMMITTEES B234 LHOB...... **59756**
Kelley, Raymond STAFF DIR - MAJ B234 LHOB...... **59756**
Murray, Carol OFFICE MGR B234 LHOB...... **59756**
Reel, Matt DPTY STAFF DIR 3470...... **59756**
Rodden, Grace GEN COUNSEL B234 LHOB...... **59756**
Salazar, Miguel COMMUNICATIONS DIR B234 LHOB...... **59756**
Turner, Julie COUNSEL - DISABILITY ASSISTANCE AND MEMORIAL AFFAIRS SUBCOMM B234 LHOB...... **59756**

MINORITY STAFF

Chapman, Parker LEGIS AIDE 3460...... **53527**
Clark, Jon SUBCOMM STAFF DIR - ECONOMIC OPPORTUNITY SUBCOMM 3460...... **65491**
Gonzalez, Samantha SR PROF STAFF - HEALTH SUBCOMM 3460...... **59154**
Hill, Christine SUBCOMM STAFF DIR - HEALTH SUBCOMM 3460...... **59154**
Jenkins, Molly PRESS SECY 3460...... **53527**
Large, Alex PROF STAFF MEMB 3460...... **53527**
Mallison, Bill SUBCOMM STAFF DIR - TECHNOLOGY MODERNIZATION SUBCOMM 3460...... **51900**
McNamee, Christopher DPTY STAFF DIR - MIN STAFF/ SUBCOMM STAFF DIR/GEN COUNSEL 3460...... **53569**
Meyer, Matt MBR - SVCS ASSOC 3460...... **53527**
Smith, Katherine LEGIS AIDE - DISABILITY ASSISTANCE AND MEMORIAL AFFAIRS SUBCOMM 3460...... **53527**
Towers, Jon STAFF DIR - MIN 3460...... **53527**
Tripplaar, Maria SUBCOMM STAFF DIR - DISABILITY ASSISTANCE AND MEMORIAL AFFAIRS SUBCOMM 3460...... **59164**
Westmoreland, Grayson LEGIS ASST 3460...... **53527**

SUBCOMMITTEES OF THE COMMITTEE ON VETERANS' AFFAIRS

SUBCOMMITTEE ON DISABILITY ASSISTANCE AND MEMORIAL AFFAIRS

B234 LONGWORTH HOB (ZIP: 20515)....................225-9756

Elaine G. Luria, VA, Chairwoman

Gilbert Ray Cisneros, Jr., CA
Gregorio Kilili Camacho Sablan, MP
Colin Z. Allred, TX
Lauren Underwood, IL

Mike Bost, IL, Ranking Member
Gus M. Bilirakis, FL
Steve Watkins, KS
W. Gregory Steube, FL

SUBCOMMITTEE ON ECONOMIC OPPORTUNITY

B234 LONGWORTH HOB (ZIP: 20515)....................225-9756

Mike Levin, CA, Chairman

Kathleen M. Rice, NY
Anthony Brindisi, NY
Chris Pappas, NH
Elaine G. Luria, VA
Susie Lee, NV
Joe Cunningham, SC

Gus M. Bilirakis, FL, Ranking Member
Jack Bergman, MI
Jim Banks, IN
Andy Barr, KY
Daniel Meuser, PA

SUBCOMMITTEE ON HEALTH

B234 LONGWORTH HOB (ZIP: 20515)....................225-9756

Julia Brownley, CA, Chairwoman

Conor Lamb, PA
Mike Levin, CA
Anthony Brindisi, NY
Max Rose, NY
Gilbert Ray Cisneros, Jr., CA
Collin C. Peterson, MN

Neal P. Dunn, FL, Ranking Member
Aumua Amata Coleman Radewagen, AS
Andy Barr, KY
Daniel Meuser, PA
W. Gregory Steube, FL

SUBCOMMITTEE ON OVERSIGHT AND INVESTIGATIONS

B234 LONGWORTH HOB (ZIP: 20515)....................225-9756

Chris Pappas, NH, Chairman

Kathleen M. Rice, NY
Max Rose, NY
Gilbert Ray Cisneros, Jr., CA
Collin C. Peterson, MN

Jack Bergman, MI, Ranking Member
Aumua Amata Coleman Radewagen, AS
Mike Bost, IL
Chip Roy, TX

U.S. HOUSE OF REPRESENTATIVES

SUBCOMMITTEE ON TECHNOLOGY MODERNIZATION

B234 LONGWORTH HOB (ZIP: 20515)......225-9756

Susie Lee, NV, Chairwoman

Julia Brownley, CA	*Jim Banks*, IN, Ranking Member
Conor Lamb, PA	*Steve Watkins*, KS
Joe Cunningham, SC	*Chip Roy*, TX

COMMITTEE ON WAYS AND MEANS

1102 LONGWORTH HOB (ZIP: 20515-6348) 225-3625

Richard E. Neal, MA, Chair

John Lewis, GA
Lloyd Doggett, TX
Mike Thompson, CA
John B. Larson, CT
Earl Blumenauer, OR
Ron Kind, WI
Bill Pascrell, Jr., NJ
Danny K. Davis, IL
Linda T. Sánchez, CA
Brian Higgins, NY
Terri A. Sewell, AL
Suzan K. DelBene, WA
Judy Chu, CA
Gwen Moore, WI
Daniel T. Kildee, MI
Brendan F. Boyle, PA
Donald S. Beyer, Jr., VA
Dwight Evans, PA
Bradley Scott Schneider, IL
Thomas R. Suozzi, NY
Jimmy Panetta, CA
Stephanie N. Murphy, FL
Jimmy Gomez, CA
Steven Horsford, NV

Kevin Brady, TX
Devin Nunes, CA
Vern Buchanan, FL
Adrian Smith, NE
Kenny Marchant, TX
Tom Reed, NY
Mike Kelly, PA
George Holding, NC
Jason Smith, MO
Tom Rice, SC
David Schweikert, AZ
Jackie Walorski, IN
Darin LaHood, IL
Brad R. Wenstrup, OH
Jodey C. Arrington, TX
A. Drew Ferguson IV, GA
Ron Estes, KS

MAJORITY STAFF

Breidenbach, Carrie CLERK 1102 **53625**
Brown, Danielle GEN COUNSEL/PARLIAMENTARIAN 1102 **53625**
Casey, Brandon STAFF DIR - DEM 1102 **53625**
Cruz-De Jesus, Victoria STAFF ASST 1102 **53625**
Getz, Kara COUN TO THE CHAIRMAN 1102 **53625**
Hatch, Erin PRESS SECY - DEM 1102 **53625**
Koontz, Cara DIGITAL DIR 1102 **53625**
Larochelle, Scott STAFF ASST 1102 **53625**
O'Connor, Jennifer ADMIN - COMMITTEE 1102 **53625**
O'Hara, Lizzy DPTY STAFF DIR 1102 **53625**
Perkins, Wuan SYS ADMIN 1102 **53625**
Poitevien, Erika ASST TO THE STAFF DIR 1102 **53625**
Rubin, Dan COMMUNICATIONS DIR - DEM 1102 **53625**
Slater, Lee DIR - OUTREACH & MEMB SVCS 1102 **53625**
Walker, Antoine TECH DIR 1102 **53625**

MINORITY STAFF

Andres, Gary STAFF DIR - MIN 1139 **54021**
Blankenship, April FINANCIAL ADMIN 1139 **54021**
Carr, Machalagh PARLIAMENTARIAN/GEN COUNSEL 1139 **54021**
Damschen, Robert COMMUNICATIONS DIR 1139 **54021**
Decker, Paige DIR - COALITIONS & MBR SVCS 1139 **54021**
Fromm, Molly PARLIAMENTARIAN/GEN COUNSEL 1139 **54021**
Gingrich, Amy STAFF DIR 1139 **54021**
Jones, Caroline CLERK 1139 **54021**
Reese, Kristi DIGITAL DIR 1139 **54021**
Rosenfeld, Jan SYS ADMIN 1139 **54021**
Solis, Jesse PRESS SECY 1139 **54021**
Walker, Jacob STAFF ASST 1139 **54021**
Warren, Gregory ASST CLERK 1139 **54021**

SUBCOMMITTEES OF THE COMMITTEE ON WAYS AND MEANS

SUBCOMMITTEE ON HEALTH

1104 LONGWORTH HOB (ZIP: 20515)....................225-3943

Lloyd Doggett, TX, Chairman

Mike Thompson, CA
Ron Kind, WI
Earl Blumenauer, OR
Brian Higgins, NY
Terri A. Sewell, AL
Judy Chu, CA
Dwight Evans, PA
Bradley Scott Schneider, IL
Jimmy Gomez, CA
Steven Horsford, NV

Devin Nunes, CA
Vern Buchanan, FL
Adrian Smith, NE
Kenny Marchant, TX
Tom Reed, NY
Mike Kelly, PA
George Holding, NC

MAJORITY STAFF

Dolin, Rachel PROF STAFF 1104.................... **53943**
Egorin, Melanie DPTY STAFF DIR - SUBCOMM 1104.................... **53943**
Hall, Amy SUBCOMM STAFF DIR 1104.................... **53943**
Levin, Sarah PROF STAFF 1104.................... **53943**
Patil, Neil SUBCOMM CLERK/LEGIS ASST 1104.................... **53943**
Zhu, Jen PROF STAFF 1104.................... **53943**

MINORITY STAFF

Diblasio, Carla HEALTH COUNSEL 1139.................... **54021**
Gerzof, Devin PROF STAFF - MIN 1139.................... **54021**
Mlinar, Alyene PROF STAFF 1139.................... **54021**
Parks, Stephanie SUBCOMM STAFF DIR 1139.................... **54021**

SUBCOMMITTEE ON OVERSIGHT

2018 RAYBURN HOB (ZIP: 20515)....................225-3625

John Lewis, GA, Chairman

Suzan K. DelBene, WA
Linda T. Sánchez, CA
Thomas R. Suozzi, NY
Judy Chu, CA
Gwen Moore, WI
Brendan F. Boyle, PA

Mike Kelly, PA
Jackie Walorski, IN
Darin LaHood, IL
Brad R. Wenstrup, OH

MAJORITY STAFF

Athy, Susan TAX COUNSEL 1129.................... **53625**
Baron, Zachary COUNSEL - OVERSIGHT 1129.................... **53625**
McAfee, Karen STAFF DIR FOR OVERSIGHT 1129.................... **51025**
McCoy, Moyer CLERK/LEGIS ASST 1129.................... **51025**
More, Isabella COUNSEL - OVERSIGHT 1129.................... **51025**

MINORITY STAFF

Kaldahl, Rachel SUBCOMM STAFF DIR 1139.................... **54021**
Navin, Liz LEGIS ASST 1139.................... **54021**
Steward, Lindsay PROF STAFF 1139.................... **54021**

SUBCOMMITTEE ON SELECT REVENUE MEASURES

1136 LONGWORTH HOB (ZIP: 20515)........225-5522

Mike Thompson, CA, Chairman

Lloyd Doggett, TX
John B. Larson, CT
Linda T. Sánchez, CA
Suzan K. DelBene, WA
Gwen Moore, WI
Brendan F. Boyle, PA
Donald S. Beyer, Jr., VA
Thomas R. Suozzi, NY

Adrian Smith, NE
Tom Rice, SC
David Schweikert, AZ
Darin LaHood, IL
Jodey C. Arrington, TX
A. Drew Ferguson IV, GA

MAJORITY STAFF

Bell, Beth TAX COUNSEL 1136........ **53625**
Grossman, Andrew CHIEF TAX COUNSEL 1136........ **55522**
Kalyanam, Aruna SUBCOMM STAFF DIR/DPTY CHIEF COUNSEL 1136........ **55522**
Lin, Alice POLICY ADVISOR 1136........ **55522**
McGlinch, Peg SR COUNSEL 1136........ **55522**
Prichard, Ji TAX COUNSEL 1136........ **55522**
Winnick, Daniel TAX COUNSEL 1136........ **55522**

MINORITY STAFF

Friedman, Aharon TAX COUNSEL 1139........ **54021**
Gartin, Randy CHIEF TAX COUNSEL 1139........ **54021**
Hope, Karin TAX COUNSEL 1139........ **54021**

SUBCOMMITTEE ON SOCIAL SECURITY

2018 RAYBURN HOB (ZIP: 20515)........225-9263

John B. Larson, CT, Chairman

Bill Pascrell, Jr., NJ
Linda T. Sánchez, CA
Daniel T. Kildee, MI
Brendan F. Boyle, PA
Bradley Scott Schneider, IL
Brian Higgins, NY

Tom Reed, NY
Jodey C. Arrington, TX
A. Drew Ferguson IV, GA
Ron Estes, KS

MAJORITY STAFF

Olson, Kathryn SUBCOMM STAFF DIR 2018........ **59263**
Seddighi, Andrew SUBCOMM CLERK 2018........ **59263**
Sutcliffe, T J PROF STAFF 2018........ **59263**
Walker, Elisa PROF STAFF 2018........ **59263**

MINORITY STAFF

Rosner, Lara PROF STAFF 1139........ **54021**
Shuart, Amy SUBCOMM STAFF DIR 1139........ **54021**

U.S. HOUSE OF REPRESENTATIVES

SUBCOMMITTEE ON TRADE

1103 LONGWORTH HOB (ZIP: 20515)........225-6649

Earl Blumenauer, OR, Chairman

Bill Pascrell, Jr., NJ
Ron Kind, WI
Danny K. Davis, IL
Brian Higgins, NY
Daniel T. Kildee, MI
Jimmy Panetta, CA
Stephanie N. Murphy, FL
Terri A. Sewell, AL
Suzan K. DelBene, WA
Donald S. Beyer, Jr., VA

Vern Buchanan, FL
Devin Nunes, CA
George Holding, NC
Tom Rice, SC
Kenny Marchant, TX
Jason Smith, MO
David Schweikert, AZ

MAJORITY STAFF

Catalfamo, John CLERK/LEGIS ASST 1103........ **53625**
Friedman, Julia COUNSEL 1103........ **56649**
Mull, Keigan TRADE COUNSEL 1103........ **56649**
Tai, Katherine CHIEF COUNSEL - TRADE 1103........ **56649**
White, Katie TRADE COUNSEL 1103........ **56649**
Whittaker, Alexandra TRADE COUNSEL 1103........ **56649**

MINORITY STAFF

Ellard, Angela CHIEF COUNSEL - TRADE/STAFF DIR - MIN 1139........ **54021**
Giordano, David PROF STAFF 1139........ **54021**
Harden, Blake TRADE COUNSEL 1139........ **54021**
Snead, Josh COUNSEL 1139........ **54021**

SUBCOMMITTEE ON WORKER AND FAMILY SUPPORT

1129 LONGWORTH HOB (ZIP: 20515)........225-9263

Danny K. Davis, IL, Chairman

Terri A. Sewell, AL
Judy Chu, CA
Gwen Moore, WI
Dwight Evans, PA
Stephanie N. Murphy, FL
Jimmy Gomez, CA

Jackie Walorski, IN
Brad R. Wenstrup, OH
Ron Estes, KS
Tom Reed, NY

MAJORITY STAFF

Downs, Taylor SUBCOMM CLERK/LEGIS ASST 2018........ **59263**
Kanter, Jason PROF STAFF 2018........ **59263**
Meinert, Kimberly PROF STAFF 2018........ **59263**
Miller, Morna SUBCOMM STAFF DIR 2018........ **59263**

MINORITY STAFF

DeCesaro, Anne SUBCOMM STAFF DIR 1139........ **54021**

PERMANENT SELECT COMMITTEE ON INTELLIGENCE

HVC304 CAPITOL (ZIP: 20515-6415)........225-7690

Adam B. Schiff, CA, Chairman

James A. Himes, CT
Terri A. Sewell, AL
André Carson, IN
Jackie Speier, CA
Mike Quigley, IL
Eric Swalwell, CA
Joaquin Castro, TX
Denny Heck, WA
Peter Welch, VT
Sean Patrick Maloney, NY
Val Butler Demings, FL
Raja Krishnamoorthi, IL

Devin Nunes, CA
K. Michael Conaway, TX
Michael R. Turner, OH
Brad R. Wenstrup, OH
Chris Stewart, UT
Eric A. "Rick" Crawford, AR
Elise M. Stefanik, NY
Will Hurd, TX
John Ratcliffe, TX

STAFF

Bennett, Wells DPTY GEN COUNSEL HVC304........ **57690**
Bergreen, Timothy STAFF DIR HVC304........ **57690**
Bitar, Maher GEN COUNSEL HVC304........ **57690**
Blake, Carly DPTY STAFF DIR HVC304........ **57690**
Boland, Patrick COMMUNICATIONS DIR HVC304........ **57690**
Breaux, Kris SUBCOMM STAFF DIR HVC304........ **57690**
Ciarlante, Nick REPUB BUDGET DIR & INVESTIGATION COORD HVC304........ **54121**
Cohen, Linda PROF STAFF - MAJ HVC304........ **57690**
Eager, Thomas PROF STAFF - MAJ HVC304........ **57690**
Evans, William COUNSEL - OVERSIGHT HVC304........ **57690**
Flanigan, Bill PROF STAFF - MIN HVC304........ **54121**
Goldman, Daniel SR ADVISOR & DIR OF INVESTIGATIONS HVC304........ **57690**
Grace, Abigail PROF STAFF - MAJ HVC304........ **57690**
Green, Meghan COUNSEL HVC304........ **54121**
Green, Shannon SR COUNSEL FOR INVESTIGATIONS HVC304........ **57690**
Harvey, Derek SR ADVISOR FOR ANALYSIS HVC304........ **54121**
House, Andrew PROF STAFF - MIN HVC304........ **54121**
Hull, Cordell GEN COUNSEL HVC304........ **54121**
Hulme, Betsy STAFF ASST HVC304........ **54121**
Jepson, Kristin DIR - SECUR HVC304........ **57690**
Keith, Steve PROF STAFF - MIN HVC304........ **54121**
Kerr, Kim DIR - INFORMATION MANAGEMENT HVC304........ **57690**
Langer, Jack COMMUNICATIONS DIR - MIN HVC304........ **54121**
Major, Lisa PROF STAFF - MIN HVC304........ **54121**
Miller, Scott CONG FELLOW HVC304........ **57690**
Mitchell, Nicolas INVESTIGATIVE COUNSEL HVC304........ **57690**
Noble, Daniel SR COUNSEL FOR INVESTIGATIONS HVC304........ **57690**
Pappas, George SR ADVISOR - MBR SVCS HVC304........ **54121**
Pilipenko, Diana PROF STAFF - MAJ HVC304........ **57690**
Reardon, Brian CONG FELLOW HVC304........ **57690**
Rogers Thorpe, Amanda PROF STAFF - MAJ HVC304........ **57690**
Sikorskyj, Lucian SUBCOMM STAFF DIR HVC304........ **57690**
Skaggs, Marissa PROF STAFF - MIN HVC304........ **54121**
Smith, Brandon DIR - OPS HVC304........ **57690**
Souza, Allen STAFF DIR - MIN HVC304........ **54121**
Stosz, Conrad RESEARCH ASST HVC304........ **57690**
Suber, Kathy SUBCOMM STAFF DIR HVC304........ **57690**
Thompson, Scott TREASURY DETAILEE HVC304........ **57690**
Thurman, Aaron SUBCOMM STAFF DIR HVC304........ **57690**
Wakeman, Raffaela PROF STAFF - MAJ/COUNSEL HVC304........ **57690**
Wirkkala, Rheanne PROF STAFF HVC304........ **57690**
Wu, William BUDGET DIR - MAJ HVC304........ **57690**

SUBCOMMITTEES OF THE PERMANENT SELECT COMMITTEE ON INTELLIGENCE

SUBCOMMITTEE ON COUNTERTERRORISM, COUNTERINTELLIGENCE, AND COUNTERPROLIFERATION

HVC304 CAPITOL (ZIP: 20515)........225-7690

André Carson, IN, Chair

Jackie Speier, CA
Mike Quigley, IL
Joaquin Castro, TX
Peter Welch, VT
Sean Patrick Maloney, NY

Eric A. "Rick" Crawford, AR
K. Michael Conaway, TX
Brad R. Wenstrup, OH
Chris Stewart, UT

SUBCOMMITTEE ON DEFENSE INTELLIGENCE AND WARFIGHTER SUPPORT

HVC304 CAPITOL (ZIP: 20515)........225-7690

Terri A. Sewell, AL, Chair

James A. Himes, CT
Denny Heck, WA
Peter Welch, VT
Sean Patrick Maloney, NY
Val Butler Demings, FL

Brad R. Wenstrup, OH
Michael R. Turner, OH
K. Michael Conaway, TX
Will Hurd, TX

SUBCOMMITTEE ON INTELLIGENCE MODERNIZATION AND READINESS

HVC304 CAPITOL (ZIP: 20515)........225-7690

Eric Swalwell, CA, Chair

Terri A. Sewell, AL
Jackie Speier, CA
Joaquin Castro, TX
Val Butler Demings, FL
Raja Krishnamoorthi, IL

Will Hurd, TX
K. Michael Conaway, TX
Elise M. Stefanik, NY
John Ratcliffe, TX

SUBCOMMITTEE ON STRATEGIC TECHNOLOGIES AND ADVANCED RESEARCH

HVC304 CAPITOL (ZIP: 20515)........225-7690

James A. Himes, CT, Chair

André Carson, IN
Mike Quigley, IL
Denny Heck, WA
Eric Swalwell, CA
Raja Krishnamoorthi, IL

Chris Stewart, UT
Elise M. Stefanik, NY
John Ratcliffe, TX
Michael R. Turner, OH

SELECT COMMITTEE ON THE CLIMATE CRISIS

359 FORD HOB (ZIP: 20515)........225-1106

Kathy Castor, FL, Chair

Ben Ray Luján, NM
Suzanne Bonamici, OR
Julia Brownley, CA
Jared Huffman, CA
A. Donald McEachin, VA
Mike Levin, CA
Sean Casten, IL
Joe Neguse, CO

Garret Graves, LA
H. Morgan Griffith, VA
Gary J. Palmer, AL
Earl L. "Buddy" Carter, GA
Carol D. Miller, WV
Kelly Armstrong, ND

STAFF

Ahmad, Fatima SR COUNSEL 359 FHOB........ **51106**
Ayrea, Maggie PROF STAFF MBR - REPUB 361 FHOB........ **51107**
Banks, George David CHIEF STRATEGIST - REPUB 361 FHOB........ **51107**
Borne, Adele STAFF ASST - REPUB 361 FHOB........ **51107**
Cassady, Alison DPTY STAFF DIR - DEM 359 FHOB........ **51106**
Davidson, Dustin PROF STAFF MBR - REPUB 361 FHOB........ **51107**
Gansman, Dana CLERK 359 FHOB........ **51106**
Hall, Marty STAFF DIR – REPUB 361 FHOB........ **51107**
Huertas, Aaron COMMUNICATIONS DIR - DEM 359 FHOB........ **51106**
Landa, Mackenzie COUNSEL 359 FHOB........ **51106**
Unruh Cohen, Ana STAFF DIR - DEM 359 FHOB........ **51106**

SELECT COMMITTEE ON THE MODERNIZATION OF CONGRESS

226 CANNON HOB (ZIP: 20515)..225-1530

Derek Kilmer, WA, Chair

Emanuel Cleaver, MO
Suzan K. DelBene, WA
Zoe Lofgren, CA
Mark Pocan, WI
Mary Gay Scanlon, PA

Tom Graves, GA, Vice Chair
Rob Woodall, GA
Susan W. Brooks, IN
Rodney Davis, IL
Dan Newhouse, WA
William R. Timmons IV, SC

JOINT COMMITTEE MEMBERS AND STAFF

JOINT ECONOMIC COMMITTEE

SD-G01 DIRKSEN SOB (ZIP: 20510-6432)........................ 224-5171

Mike Lee, Senator from UT—Chair
Carolyn B. Maloney, Representative from NY—Vice Chair

SENATE	HOUSE
Tom Cotton, AR	Donald S. Beyer, Jr., VA
Ben Sasse, NE	Denny Heck, WA
Rob Portman, OH	David J. Trone, MD
Bill Cassidy, LA	Joyce Beatty, OH
Ted Cruz, TX	Lois Frankel, FL
Martin Heinrich, NM	*David Schweikert*, AZ
Amy Klobuchar, MN	*Darin LaHood*, IL
Gary C. Peters, MI	*Kenny Marchant*, TX
Maggie Hassan, NH	*Jaime Herrera Beutler*, WA

STAFF

Ackerman, Melanie RESEARCH ANALYST - DEM SH-804.. **228-0189**
Brody, Rachel SOCIAL MEDIA MGR - DEM SH-804...... **224-0379**
Burns, Daniel DPTY DIR - REPUB SD-G01.................... **224-0647**
Calder, Vanessa Brown SR POLICY ADVISOR - REPUB SD-G01.. **224-3922**
Dexter, Barry SYS ADMIN SD-G01.................................. **224-0374**
Espinoza, Sol SR POLICY ANALYST - DEM SH-804..... **228-0188**
Evans, Rodney POLICY ADVISOR - REPUB SD-G01... **228-1195**
Gandhi, Ricky ECONOMIST - DEM 244 FHOB............... **225-6024**
George, Natalie POLICY ANALYST - DEM SH-804....... **228-1377**
Gural, Harry STAFF DIR - DEM SH-804.......................... **224-5171**
Haaga, Owen SR ECONOMIST - DEM 244 FHOB......... **225-2223**
Healy, Colleen FINANCIAL DIR SD-G01......................... **224-0370**
King, Christina SR ECONOMIST - REPUB SD-G01....... **224-0367**
King, Wells POLICY ADVISOR - REPUB SD-G01........... **224-5426**
Leboeuf, Beila SR ECONOMIST - REPUB SD-G01....... **224-7578**
Marlin, John Tepper SR ECONOMIST - DEM 368 FHOB.. **226-3228**
Menon, Vijay POLICY ADVISOR - REPUB SD-G01....... **224-0377**
Pearson, Michael RESEARCH ASST - DEM SH-804.... **224-0364**
Sheffield, Rachel SR POLICY ADVISOR - REPUB SD-G01.. **224-5171**
Sheils, Hope RESEARCH ASST - DEM SH-804............ **228-1341**
Treasure, Kyle DIGITAL MEDIA DIR - REPUB SD-G01. **224-6419**
Wheeler, Jillian COMMUNICATIONS DIR - REPUB SD-G01.. **224-3616**
Whitney, Jim SR POLICY ADVISOR - DEM 246 FHOB.. **225-3923**
Winship, Scott EXEC DIR SD-G01.................................. **224-5171**
Woods, Randy COMMUNICATIONS DIR - DEM SD-G01.. **224-2599**

JOINT COMMITTEE ON THE LIBRARY

SR-305 RUSSELL SOB (ZIP: 20515-6157)..........224-6352

Roy Blunt, Senator from MO—Chair
Zoe Lofgren, Representative from CA—Vice Chairperson

SENATE	HOUSE
Pat Roberts, KS	Tim Ryan, OH
Richard C. Shelby, AL	G. K. Butterfield, NC
Amy Klobuchar, MN	*Rodney Davis*, IL
Patrick Leahy, VT	*Barry Loudermilk*, GA

STAFF

Abboud, Khalil DPTY STAFF DIR 1309..........	**225-2061**	Monahan, Tim DIR - OVERSIGHT 1216..........	**225-8281**
Kotschwar, Nichole PROF STAFF SR-305..........	**224-6352**	Talvitie, Travis DPTY STAFF DIR - DEM SR-481..........	**224-6352**

JOINT COMMITTEE ON PRINTING

1309 LONGWORTH HOB (ZIP: 20515-6446)........ 225-2061

Zoe Lofgren, Representative from CA—Chairperson
Roy Blunt, Senator from MO—Vice Chair

HOUSE	SENATE
Jamie Raskin, MD	Pat Roberts, KS
Susan A. Davis, CA	Roger F. Wicker, MS
Rodney Davis, IL	*Amy Klobuchar*, MN
Barry Loudermilk, GA	*Tom Udall*, NM

STAFF

Abboud, Khalil DPTY STAFF DIR 1309........ **225-2061**
Kotschwar, Nichole PROF STAFF SR-305........ **224-6352**
Monahan, Tim DIR - OVERSIGHT 1216........ **225-8281**
Talvitie, Travis DPTY STAFF DIR - DEM SR-481........ **224-6352**

U.S. HOUSE OF REPRESENTATIVES

JOINT COMMITTEE ON TAXATION

502 FORD HOB (ZIP: 20515-6453).. 225-3621

Richard E. Neal, Representative from MA—Chairman
Chuck Grassley, Senator from IA—Vice Chairman

HOUSE	SENATE
John Lewis, GA	Mike Crapo, ID
Lloyd Doggett, TX	Michael B. Enzi, WY
Kevin Brady, TX	*Ron Wyden*, OR
Devin Nunes, CA	*Debbie Stabenow*, MI

STAFF

Arbeit, Jeffrey LEGIS COUNSEL 502 FHOB................ **225-3621**
Asher, Nita LEGIS COUNSEL 502 FHOB........................ **225-3621**
Barthold, Thomas A CHIEF OF STAFF 502 FHOB...... **225-3621**
Brand, Norman SR COUNSEL IRS-3565........................ **317-4463**
Bull, Nick SR ECONOMIST 595 FHOB............................ **226-7575**
Butler, Tanya T STATISTICAL ANALYST 595 FHOB.... **226-7575**
Chandrasekhar, Vivek LEGIS COUNSEL 502 FHOB.. **225-3621**
Cilke, James M SR ECONOMIST 595 FHOB................ **225-7575**
Clay, Gordon M SR LEGIS COUNSEL SD-G18............ **224-5561**
Derby, Elena ANALYST 595 FHOB................................ **226-7575**
Dowd, Timothy A SR ECONOMIST 595 FHOB............ **226-7575**
Gibson, Chase COUNSEL IRS-3565.............................. **317-4463**
Giosa, Chris SR ECONOMIST 595 FHOB...................... **226-7575**
Gotwald, Robert COUNSEL IRS-3565.......................... **317-4463**
Gropper, Adam LEGIS COUNSEL SD-G18.................. **224-5561**
Gunn, Sylvester STAFF ASST 502 FHOB.................... **225-3621**
Habib, Sameh ECONOMIST 595 FHOB......................... **226-7575**
Harman, Heather LEGIS TAX ACCOUNTANT 502 FHOB.. **225-3621**
Harvey, Robert P DPTY CHIEF OF STAFF 595 FHOB. **226-7575**
High, Mark R INFO TECH SYS ANALYST 595 FHOB.... **226-7575**
Hirsch, Harold E SR LEGIS COUNSEL 502 FHOB........ **225-3621**
Holtmann, Thomas P SR ECONOMIST 595 FHOB..... **226-7575**
Houser, Melani CHIEF STATISTICAL ANALYST 595 FHOB.. **226-7575**
James, Deirdre A SR LEGIS COUNSEL 502 FHOB...... **225-3621**
Jedlicka, Damion DIR - INFO TECH 595 FHOB........... **226-7575**
Kwak, Sally ECONOMIST SD-G18................................ **224-5561**
Landefeld, Paul ECONOMIST 595 FHOB...................... **226-7575**
LeCates, Joseph ECONOMIST 595 FHOB.................... **226-7575**
Leonard, Shelley LEGIS COUNSEL 502 FHOB............ **225-3621**
Lue, Bert ECONOMIST 502 FHOB.................................. **225-3621**
Mackie, Kathleen T SR ECONOMIST 595 FHOB......... **226-7575**
McGuire, James C ECONOMIST 595 FHOB................ **226-7575**
McLaughlin, Paul LEGIS COUNSEL 502 FHOB........... **225-3621**
McMullen, Debra SR STAFF ASST 502 FHOB............. **225-3621**
Means, Kristine M EXEC ASST 502 FHOB.................. **225-3621**
Migdail, Rhonda LEGIS COUNSEL 502 FHOB............. **225-3621**
Moomau, Pamela H SR ECONOMIST 595 FHOB........ **226-7575**
Moore, Rachel ECONOMIST 595 FHOB......................... **226-7575**
Munday, J DIR - SECUR 595 FHOB................................ **226-7575**
Murthy, Veena LEGIS COUNSEL 502 FHOB................ **225-3621**
Newton, Jonathan INFO TECH SYS ANALYST 595 FHOB.. **226-7575**
Northern, Jayne E EXEC ASST SD-G18...................... **224-5561**
O'Brien, Melissa A TAX RESOURCE SPEC SD-462.... **224-0494**
Ortega, Dennis HELP DESK TECH 595 FHOB............. **226-7575**
Overend, Christopher J SR ECONOMIST 595 FHOB. **226-7575**
Pavlak, Michael RESEARCH ASST 595 FHOB.............. **226-7575**
Pecoraro, Brandon ECONOMIST 595 FHOB............... **226-7575**
Richards, Zachary ECONOMIST 595 FHOB................. **226-7575**
Rock, Cecily W SR LEGIS COUNSEL 502 FHOB.......... **225-3621**
Rogers, Lucia J EXEC ASST 502 FHOB....................... **225-3621**
Roth, Kristine SR LEGIS COUNSEL SD-G18................. **224-5561**
Schramm, Heidi ECONOMIST 595 FHOB...................... **226-7575**
Shima, Frank J ADMIN SPEC 502 FHOB....................... **225-3621**
Simmons, Chris DOCU PROD SPEC 502 FHOB.......... **225-3621**
Splinter, David ECONOMIST 595 FHOB........................ **226-7575**
Trigg, H Brenton SR ECONOMIST 595 FHOB.............. **226-7575**
Tucker, Natalie LEGIS TAX ACCOUNTANT 502 FHOB **225-3621**
Way, Kashi M SR LEGIS COUNSEL SD-G18................. **224-5561**
Williams, Pamela OFFICE ADMIN 502 FHOB.............. **225-3621**
Xu, Lin ECONOMIST 595 FHOB....................................... **226-7575**

LEADERSHIP OFFICES AND STAFF

OFFICE OF THE SPEAKER

The Honorable Nancy Pelosi (California)

H232 CAPITOL (ZIP: 20515) 225-0100

Androff, Blake EXEC DIR - DEM POLICY & COMMUNICATIONS CMTE H232 .... **50100**
Beltran, Elizabeth STAFF ASST H232 .... **50100**
Berret, Emily DIR - OPS H232 .... **50100**
Capron, Margaret SR POLICY ADVISOR - POLICY & COMMUNICATIONS H232 .... **50100**
Cherry, Stephanie DIR - MEDIA AFFAIRS H232 .... **50100**
Connelly, Henry DPTY COMMUNICATIONS DIR H232 .... **50100**
DeGraff, Kenneth SR POLICY ADVISOR H232 .... **50100**
Dewhirst, Diane DPTY CHIEF OF STAFF H232 .... **50100**
Edmonson, Robert POLICY ADVISOR H232 .... **50100**
Ehrenberg, Mia PRESS ASST H232 .... **50100**
Etienne, Ashley COMMUNICATIONS DIR/SR ADVISOR H232 .... **50100**
Gibson, Dylan DIGITAL DIR H232 .... **50100**
Greener, April RESEARCH DIR H232 .... **50100**
Griffin, Taylor PRESS SECY H232 .... **50100**
Hammill, Andrew DPTY CHIEF OF STAFF H232 .... **50100**
Haynes, Wilfred DIR - INFO TECH H232 .... **50100**
Hidalgo, Adriana SCHEDULER H232 .... **50100**
Holmes, Nathaniel DPTY DIR - SCHEDULING & ADVANCE H232 .... **50100**
Hurwitz, Ross DPTY DIR - SPEECHWRITING H232 .... **50100**
Iacobellis, Samuel MBR SVCS STAFF ASST H232 .... **50100**
Jeter, Kristina DPTY DIR/SPECIAL EVENTS/PROTOCOL H232 .... **50100**
Kaplan, Emma FLOOR ASST H232 .... **50100**
Keita, Kamilah DPTY DIR/INFO TECH MGR H232 .... **50100**
Knudson, Kate DIRECTOR/SPECIAL EVENTS H232 .... **50100**
Kuhn, Elena PRESS/ADVISOR H232 .... **50100**
Kundanis, George DPTY CHIEF OF STAFF H232 .... **50100**
La, Alisa SPECIAL ASST TO THE SPEAKER H232 .... **50100**
Lee, Seryeung DPTY PRESS SECY H232 .... **50100**
Lizarraga, Jaime SR ADVISOR H232 .... **50100**
Long, Michael SR ADVISOR/DIR - MEMB SVCS H232 .... **50100**
Mangrum, Pearl FINANCIAL DIR H232 .... **50100**
Mansbach, Shana DIR - SPEECHWRITING H232 .... **50100**
McCullough, Mary CHIEF OF STAFF H232 .... **50100**
Meltzer, Richard POLICY DIR H232 .... **50100**
Monge, Katherine SR COUNSEL H232 .... **50100**
Obscura, Julio CREATIVE DIR H232 .... **50100**
Pampati, Shivani STAFF ASST H232 .... **50100**
Parker, Wyndee NATIONAL SECUR ADVISOR H232 .... **50100**
Polzin, Savannah DPTY DIR - SCHEDULING H232 .... **50100**
Powell, Latrice DPTY FLOOR DIR H232 .... **50100**
Price, Reva OUTREACH DIRECTOR/SR ADVISOR H232 .... **50100**
Primus, Wendell SR HEALTH & BUDGET POLICY ADVISOR H232 .... **50100**
Ramirez, Matthew OUTREACH ADVISOR H232 .... **50100**
Ross, Patricia SR POLICY ADVISOR H232 .... **50100**
Smith, Kelsey DIR - SCHEDULER & ADVANCE H232 .... **50100**
Smith, Shane SCHEDULE & ADVANCE COORD H232 .... **50100**
Stern, Keith DIR - FLOOR OPS H232 .... **50100**
Tecklenburg, Michael COUNSEL H232 .... **50100**
Welch, Haydn STAFF ASST H232 .... **50100**
West, Julius SR ADVISOR H232 .... **50100**
Wilkes, Christina SR PRESS ASST H232 .... **50100**
Wong, Stephanie SPECIAL ASST TO THE EXEC OFFICE H232 .... **50100**
York, Jemma DPTY DIR H232 .... **50100**

OFFICE OF THE MAJORITY LEADER

The Honorable Steny H. Hoyer (Maryland)

H107 CAPITOL (ZIP: 20515) 225-3130

Abouchar, Keith SR POLICY ADVISOR H107 .... **53130**
Bauserman, Trent SR POLICY ADVISOR H107 .... **53130**
Bayer, Jake EXEC ASST/OFFICE MGR H107 .... **53130**
Brennan, Bridget DIR - SCHEDULING H107 .... **53130**
Covey-Brandt, Alexis CHIEF OF STAFF H107 .... **53130**
Dwyer, Steve SR POLICY ADVISOR/DIGITAL DIR H107 .... **53130**
Fry, Courtney DPTY DIR - OUTREACH/MBR SVCS ADVISOR H107 .... **53130**
Goff, Shuwanza DIR - FLOOR H107 .... **53130**
Grant, Katie COMMUNICATIONS DIR H107 .... **53130**
Leuschen, James SR POLICY ADVISOR H107 .... **53130**
Mahr, Tom POLICY DIR H107 .... **53130**
Merz, Julie SR ADVISOR H107 .... **53130**
Mulkerrin, Margaret DPTY PRESS SECY H107 .... **53130**
Romick, Brian DPTY CHIEF OF STAFF H107 .... **53130**
Rowe, Deborah FLOOR ASST H107 .... **53130**
Saez, Mariel DPTY COMMUNICATIONS DIR H107 .... **53130**
Salazar, Ray DPTY FLOOR DIR H107 .... **53130**
Silverberg, Daniel SR POLICY ADVISOR H107 .... **53130**
Spak, Michael STAFF ASST H107 .... **53130**
Trauberman, Jacob SPECIAL ASST H107 .... **53130**
Urrabazo, Claudia OUTREACH ADVISOR H107 .... **53130**
Weissmann, Adam SPEECHWRITER H107 .... **53130**

U.S. HOUSE OF REPRESENTATIVES

OFFICE OF THE MAJORITY WHIP

The Honorable James E. Clyburn (South Carolina)

H329 CAPITOL (ZIP: 20515) 226-3210

Brumfield, Renard FLOOR ASST H329........ **63210**
Butler, Morgan DIGITAL DIR H329........ **63210**
Daniels, Ryan DPTY COMMUNICATIONS DIR H329........ **63210**
Derrick, Hope COMMUNICATIONS DIR H329........ **63210**
Edari, Nialah STAFF ASST H329........ **63210**
Ellison, Matthew DPTY POLICY DIR H329........ **63210**
Garrett, Emerald SR STAFF ASST H329........ **63210**
Green, Courtney PRESS ASST H329........ **63210**
Hacker, Michael SR ADVISOR H329........ **63210**
Julien, Robert STAFF ASST H329........ **63210**
Kelly, Lindy SR ADVISOR H329........ **63210**
Link, Craig DPTY FLOOR DIR H329........ **63210**
Mason, Tamika TECH DIR H329........ **63210**
Palmer, Ashli DIR - FLOOR H329........ **63210**
Ubezonu, Nd FLOOR ASST H329........ **63210**
Vallejo, Jessica FLOOR ASST H329........ **63210**
Watkins, Yelberton CHIEF OF STAFF H329........ **63210**
Whitehouse, Lin ADVISOR - MBR SVCS H329........ **63210**
Woldemariam, Wintta POLICY DIR H329........ **63210**

OFFICE OF THE ASSISTANT SPEAKER

The Honorable Ben Ray Luján (California)

H132 CAPITOL (ZIP: 20515) 225-2020

Goff, Hans DIR - MEMB SVCS H132........ **52020**
Jones, Ashley SR ADVISOR H132........ **52020**
Ramirez, Angela CHIEF H132........ **52020**
Sanchez, Carlos SR ADVISOR H132........ **52020**
Soenksen, Amy OUTREACH DIR H132........ **52020**

OFFICE OF THE SENIOR CHIEF DEPUTY MAJORITY WHIP

The Honorable John Lewis (Georgia)

300 CANNON HOB (ZIP: 20515) 225-3801

Collins, Michael CHIEF OF STAFF 343 CHOB........ **53801**

OFFICE OF THE SENIOR CHIEF DEPUTY MAJORITY WHIP

The Honorable Janice D. Schakowsky (Illinois)

2367 RAYBURN HOB (ZIP: 20515) 225-2111

Terry, Syd LEGIS DIR 2367........ **52111**

OFFICE OF THE MINORITY LEADER

The Honorable Kevin McCarthy (California)

H204 CAPITOL (ZIP: 20515) 225-4000

Bien, Christopher DPTY FLOOR DIR H204........ **54000**
Bogorowski, Hanna COMMUNICATIONS AIDE H204........ **54000**
Bonner, Lee DPTY SCHEDULER H204........ **54000**
Buchanan, Natalie DIR - MEMB SVCS H204........ **54000**
Burke, Robby STAFF ASST H204........ **54000**
Cameron, Christina DPTY PRESS SECY H204........ **54000**
Carr, Machalagh GEN COUNSEL H204........ **54000**
Correll, Charles SPEECHWRITER H204........ **54000**
Coyle, Sarah ASST MGR - CLOAKRM H204........ **54000**
Dunham, Will POLICY DIR H204........ **54000**
Engling, Maximilian DPTY DIR - OUTREACH/MBR SVCS ADVISOR H204........ **54000**
Florio, Drew DIR - STRATEGIC COMMUNICATIONS H204........ **54000**
Gillespie, James ASST MGR - CLOAKRM H204........ **54000**
Gourdikian, Alexandra SCHEDULING DIR H204........ **54000**
Hill, Preston POLICY ADVISOR H204........ **54000**
Hochschild, Keenan COORD - DIGITAL MEDIA H204........ **54000**
Humes, Alexandra COORD - MBR SVCS & OUTREACH H204.. **54000**
Karr, Elizabeth CHIEF OF STAFF H204........ **54000**
Leganski, John DIR - FLOOR OPS H204........ **54000**
Lombardi, Kyle LEGIS DIR H204........ **54000**
Loraine, Jennifer SR POLICY ADVISOR H204........ **54000**
Martinez, Brittany DPTY PRESS SECY H204........ **54000**
Meyer, Katherine SR POLICY ADVISOR H204........ **54000**

LEADERSHIP OFFICES AND STAFF

Min, James DPTY CHIEF OF STAFF H204 ..... **54000**
Murphy, Braden LEGIS ASST H204 ..... **54000**
Murphy, Cullen AIDE H204 ..... **54000**
Murry, Luke NATIONAL SECUR ADVISOR H204 ..... **54000**
O'Toole, Ryan CLOAKROOM DIR H204 ..... **54000**
Rindels, Emma LEGIS ASST H204 ..... **54000**
Rosemond, John SPECIAL ASST H204 ..... **54000**
Smith, Caleb DIR - DIGITAL COMMUNICATIONS H204 ..... **54000**
Smith, Trevor SR LEGIS ASST H204 ..... **54000**
Sparks, Matthew COMMUNICATIONS DIR H204 ..... **54000**
Specht, Brittan SR POLICY ADVISOR H204 ..... **54000**

OFFICE OF THE MINORITY WHIP

The Honorable Steve Scalise (Louisiana)

H148 CAPITOL (ZIP: 20515) 225-0197

Battaglia, Jacqueline SCHEDULER H148 ..... **50197**
Clarke, John SPECIAL ASST H148 ..... **50197**
Comer, Michael DIGITAL STRATEGIST H148 ..... **50197**
Fine, Lauren COMMUNICATIONS DIR H148 ..... **50197**
Gosnell, Ellen DIR - OPS H148 ..... **50197**
Horton, Brett CHIEF OF STAFF/COUNSEL H148 ..... **50197**
Hughes, William POLICY DIR H148 ..... **50197**
Krieger, Robyn STAFF ASST H148 ..... **50197**
McKeogh, Katherine PRESS ASST H148 ..... **50197**
Minkler, Ann DPTY FLOOR DIR H148 ..... **50197**
Nalls, Dennis FLOOR ASST H148 ..... **50197**
Napier, Benjamin DIR - FLOOR OPS H148 ..... **50197**
Reiser, Martin DPTY POLICY DIR H148 ..... **50197**
Reising, John DIR - OPS & MBR SVCS H148 ..... **50197**
Sadlosky, Daniel POLICY ADVISOR H148 ..... **50197**
Satterthwaite, Sean SPEECHWRITER H148 ..... **50197**
Walker, Steven SR STAFF ASST H148 ..... **50197**
Wieand, Jeffrey COUNSEL H148 ..... **50197**

DEMOCRATIC CLOAKROOM

H222 CAPITOL (ZIP: 20515) 225-7330

Fischer, Robert, Jr ASST FLOOR CHIEF H222 ..... **57330**
Jackson, Audra ASST MGR - CLOAKRM H222 ..... **57330**
Keating, Rosemary ASST FLOOR MGR H222 ..... **57330**

REPUBLICAN CLOAKROOM

H223 CAPITOL (ZIP: 20515) 225-7350

O'Toole, Ryan CLOAKROOM DIR H223 ..... **57350**

HOUSE OFFICERS/OFFICIALS AND STAFF

OFFICE OF THE CLERK

The Honorable Cheryl L. Johnson

H154 CAPITOL (ZIP: 20515-6601) 225-7000

Bias, Gregory MGR - OPS H154.......... **57000**
Harris, Clifford A, Jr OPS ASST H154.......... **57000**
Horwich, Lloyd LEGAL COUNSEL H154.......... **57000**
Jones, Davita EXEC ADMIN H154.......... **57000**
Lett, Gloria J DPTY CLERK H154.......... **57000**
Muller, Cheryl PERSONNEL DIR H154.......... **57000**
Murphy, Victoria F SPECIAL ASST TO THE CLERK H154.......... **57000**
Myhill, Don SPECIAL ASST TO THE CLERK H154.......... **57000**
Owens, Kibwe ADMIN ASST H154.......... **57000**
Plaster, Will ASST TO THE CLERK H154.......... **57000**
Reeves, Robert DPTY CLERK H154.......... **57000**
Stringfield, Joyce ADMIN - BUDGET & PROJ H154.......... **57000**
Thompson, Teneisha ADMIN - CONTRACTS H154.......... **57000**

OFFICE OF ART AND ARCHIVES

JEFFERSON BUILDING, ATTIC (ZIP: 20515) 226-1300

Bates, Alicia ARCHIVAL ASST JEFFERSON BUILDING, ATTIC... **61300**
Bourk, Heather MGR - ARCHIVES JEFFERSON BUILDING, ATTIC.......... **61300**
Elliott, Farar P CHIEF JEFFERSON BUILDING, ATTIC.......... **61300**
Good, Mackenzie L COLLECTIONS SPEC JEFFERSON BUILDING, ATTIC.......... **61300**
Haskins, Selena ADMIN ASST JEFFERSON BUILDING, ATTIC.. **61300**
McKinstry, Karen DPTY CHIEF JEFFERSON BUILDING, ATTIC. **61300**
Russell, Morgan CURATORIAL RESEARCH ASST JEFFERSON BUILDING, ATTIC.......... **61300**
Strizever, Michelle H PHOTOGRAPHY & DIGITAL CONTENT SPECIALIST JEFFERSON BUILDING, ATTIC.......... **61300**
Trulock, Alison ASSOC ARCHIVIST JEFFERSON BUILDING, ATTIC.......... **61300**
Wivchar, Felicia ASSOC CURATOR JEFFERSON BUILDING, ATTIC.......... **61300**

CAPITOL SERVICE GROUPS

H154 CAPITOL (ZIP: 20515-6601) 225-7000

Alstork, Kim M COORD - MBR & FAM RM H324.......... **50622**
Marroquin, Dixie HOUSE FLOOR OPS CLERK H222.......... **57330**
McCaffrey, Barbara COORD - CONGRESSWOMN STE H235... **54196**
McCall, Ronda CLOAKRM FOOD MGR - MAJ H222.......... **61154**
Meyer, Andrew HOUSE FLOOR OPS CLERK H223.......... **57350**
Rogers, Doris ASST CLOAKRM FOOD MGR - MIN H223.......... **63637**
Smith, Patricia CLOAKRM FOOD MGR - MIN H223.......... **63637**
Terry, Ella ASST CLOAKRM FOOD MGR - MAJ H222.......... **61154**

OFFICE OF COMMUNICATIONS

293 CANNON HOB (ZIP: 20515) 225-1908

Christensen, Eric SR CONTENT DEVELOPER 293 CHOB.......... **51908**
Cooke, Catherine CHIEF 293 CHOB.......... **51908**
Doan, Phoebe GRAPHIC DESIGNER 293 CHOB.......... **51908**
Haynes, Yutiva Michelle ADMIN ASST 293 CHOB.......... **51908**
Laubon, Ashlee SR GRAPHIC DESIGNER 293 CHOB.......... **51908**
Layman-Wood, January DPTY CHIEF 293 CHOB.......... **51908**
Salas, Damien MULTIMEDIA DEVELOPER 293 CHOB.......... **51908**
Wyszynski, Whitney CONTENT DEVELOPER 293 CHOB.......... **51908**

OFFICE OF HOUSE EMPLOYMENT COUNSEL

4300 O'NEILL HOB (ZIP: 20515) 225-7075

Borovsky, Joel ASSOC COUNSEL 4300.......... **57075**
Gore, Russell SR ASSOC COUNSEL 4300.......... **57075**
Hayes, Mark SR ASSOC COUNSEL 4300.......... **57075**
Jolly, Lisa V SR SECY 4300.......... **57075**
Rogers, Ann COUNSEL 4300.......... **57075**
Terrell, Myra J SR SECY 4300.......... **57075**
Williams, Kimberly Carey SR ASSOC COUNSEL 4300.......... **57075**

LEGISLATIVE COMPUTER SYSTEMS

2401 RAYBURN HOB (ZIP: 20515-6618) 225-1182

Help Desk 225-8484

Afeefy, Yomna INFO TECH TESTING ANALYST 2401 .... **51182**
Amick, Eric SOFTWARE ENGINEER 2401 .... **51182**
Beran, Lynn SR IT SECUR ANALYST 2401 .... **51182**
Brace, Gordon S SR HARDWARE ENGINEER 2401 .... **51182**
Bruner, Charles AUDIO TECH 2401 .... **51182**
Carter, Cephas SR AUDIO TECH 2401 .... **51182**
Chhem, Steven SOFTWARE ENGINEER 2401 .... **51182**
Cho, Wonjun APPLICA SUPPORT ANALYST 2401 .... **51182**
Conaghan, Sean P SOFTWARE ENGINEER 2401 .... **51182**
Corbet, Drew HELP DESK TECH 2401 .... **51182**
Donahue, Kyle F DIR - APPLICA DEVELOPMENT 2401 .... **51182**
Fitzmaurice, Paul A HELP DESK TECH 2401 .... **51182**
Gold, Jeffrey E DIR - SYS AND OPS 2401 .... **51182**
Gullickson, Kirsten PRINCIPAL LEGIS ANALYST 2401 .... **51182**
Ingram, Kara SOFTWARE ENGINEER 2401 .... **51182**
Katikanani, Shivajyothi DEVELOPER/SR ANALYST 2401 .... **51182**
Khau, Dennis SR SOFTWARE ENGINEER 2401 .... **51182**
Kim, Scott CHIEF 2401 .... **51182**
Lambert, Jimmy SR SOFTWARE ENGINEER 2401 .... **51182**
Lauron, Antonio SR SOFTWARE ENGINEER 2401 .... **51182**
Law, Marianne OPS ASST 2401 .... **51182**
Leach, Cindy S DIR - SYS ANALYSIS AND QA 2401 .... **51182**
Lucero, Kimberly DPTY CHIEF 2401 .... **51182**
Mills, Michael SR SOFTWARE ENGINEER 2401 .... **51182**
Multani, Dalvinder DIR - PROJ 2401 .... **51182**
Mun, Andrey V SR SOFTWARE ENGINEER 2401 .... **51182**
Okhlopkov, Sergei SYS ENGINEER 2401 .... **51182**
Owusu-Mensah, Kwasi NETWK ADMIN 2401 .... **51182**
Rueff, Glenn SR SOFTWARE ENGINEER 2401 .... **51182**
Scott, Hugh Jay AUDIO TECH 2401 .... **51182**
Smith, Veneice G INFO TECH SYS ANALYST 2401 .... **51182**
Varandani, Rajinder SR NETWORK ADMIN 2401 .... **51182**

OFFICE OF LEGISLATIVE OPERATIONS

HT13 CAPITOL (ZIP: 20515-6602) 225-7925

Alexin, Aaron ASST TALLY CLERK HT13 .... **57347**
Austin, Teresa L TALLY CLERK HT13 .... **57347**
Benson, Carla M ASST ENROLLING CLERK HT13 .... **53153**
Brady, Kevin ADMIN ASST HT13 .... **57925**
Chiappardi, Frances CHIEF HT13 .... **57925**
Cole, Susan READING CLERK HT13 .... **57925**
Coufal, Teresa BILL CLERK HT13 .... **57598**
Fields, Peggy ASST BILL CLERK HT13 .... **57598**
Frappoli, Amelia ASST TALLY CLERK HT13 .... **57925**
Holmes, Adam ASST ENROLLING CLERK HT13 .... **53153**
McCumber, Kevin DPTY CHIEF HT13 .... **51454**
McLaughlin, Lawrence P JOURNAL CLERK HT13 .... **55558**
Novotny, Josef READING CLERK HT13 .... **57584**
Pulis, Jenelle ASST JOURNAL CLERK HT13 .... **55558**
Rager, Jessica CLERK - CMTE DIGEST HT13 .... **57925**
Regan, Timothy ASST TALLY CLERK HT13 .... **57347**
Rota, Robert V, Jr ENROLLING CLERK HT13 .... **53153**
Rupnow, Colton ASST BILL CLERK HT13 .... **57925**
Shuman, Nichole ASST JOURNAL CLERK HT13 .... **52868**
Strodel, Allison ASST JOURNAL CLERK HT13 .... **57925**
Webb, Glennis DAILY DIGEST CLERK HT13 .... **51501**
Yahner, Kelly ASST BILL CLERK HT13 .... **57598**

LEGISLATIVE RESOURCE CENTER

B81 CANNON HOB (ZIP: 20515-6612) 226-5200

292 CANNON HOB House Library 225-9000

Bacskocky, Argus T MGR - DOCU & REQUISITIONS B81 CHOB **65200**
Benavides, Sophia SR EXEC COMMUNICATIONS CLERK B81 CHOB **65200**
Best, Rae Ellen MGR - LIBRARY SVCS B81 CHOB **65200**
Branch, Ora SR REFERENCE LIBRARIAN B81 CHOB **65200**
Carreiro, David DOCU CLERK B81 CHOB **65200**
Caskey, Aurora ASST REGISTRATION & COMPLIANCE CLERK B81 CHOB **65200**
Cathcart, Kenna CATALOG LIBRARIAN B81 CHOB **65200**
Cho, Austin OPS ASST B81 CHOB **65200**
Clemonts-James, Corliss DPTY CHIEF B81 CHOB **65200**
Cobb, Brittany ASST REGISTRATION & COMPLIANCE CLERK B81 CHOB **65200**
Cole, Susan INTEGRATED RESOURCES LIBRARIAN B81 CHOB **65200**
Evans, Kyle PUBLIC INFO SPEC B81 CHOB **65200**
Farel, James M DOCU PROD CLERK B81 CHOB **65200**
Gerbo, George PUBLIC INFO SPEC B81 CHOB **65200**
Glosson, Janice L REGISTRATION & COMPLIANCE CLERK B81 CHOB **65200**
Gonzalez, Elizabeth PUBLIC INFO SPEC B81 CHOB **65200**
Granger, Karen MGR - PUBLIC INFO B81 CHOB **65200**
Gunn, Robert EXEC COMMUNICATIONS CLERK B81 CHOB **65200**
Hanger, Lillian REGISTRATION & COMPLIANCE CLERK B81 CHOB **65200**
Hayes, Renaldo LIBRARY ASST B81 CHOB **65200**
James, Capre ASST RECORDS MGMT SPEC B81 CHOB **65200**
Kanakis, Marcie EDITOR B81 CHOB **65200**
Maddatu, Patricia OUTREACH LIBRARIAN B81 CHOB **65200**
McDuffie, Bennetta ADMIN ASST B81 CHOB **65200**
McGee, Mike SR REQUISITIONS & PRINTING CLERK B81 CHOB **65200**
Pingeton, Stephen E MGR - RECORDS & REGISTRATION B81 CHOB **65200**
Queen, Michael DIGITAL LIBRARIAN B81 CHOB **65200**
Russell, David PUBLIC INFO SPEC B81 CHOB **65200**
Safo, Edward ASST REGISTRATION & COMPLIANCE CLERK B81 CHOB **65200**
Shumate, Nicholas REFERENCE ASST B81 CHOB **65200**
Sivak, Amanda EXEC COMMUNICATIONS CLERK B81 CHOB **65200**
Smith, Matthew PUBLIC INFO SPEC B81 CHOB **65200**

HOUSE OFFICERS/OFFICIALS AND STAFF

St. Dennis, Monica REFERENCE LIBRARIAN B81 CHOB.......... 65200
Tew, Sophia ASST EDITOR B81 CHOB.......... 65200
Thomas, Ronald CHIEF B81 CHOB.......... 65200
Villagomez, Candy G RECORDS MGMT SPEC B81 CHOB.......... 65200
Villagomez, Walter F DOCU PROD CLERK B81 CHOB.......... 65200
Washington, Velmon C ASST REQUISITIONS & PRINTING CLERK B81 CHOB.......... 65200
White, Frankie PUBLIC INFO SPEC B81 CHOB.......... 65200
Wood, Zachary PUBLIC INFO SPEC B81 CHOB.......... 65200

OFFICIAL REPORTERS

1718 LONGWORTH HOB (ZIP: 20515-6615) 225-2627

Alldridge, Susan OFFICIAL REPORTER 1718.......... 52627
Bingham, Elizabeth S OFFICIAL REPORTER HT59.......... 55621
Branch, Roderick V PROD ASST 193 CHOB.......... 57187
Bryant, Sherry OFFICIAL REPORTER 1718.......... 52627
Cartagena, George ASST CHIEF CLERK - DEBATES HT59.......... 55621
Coverton, Antoinette SR LEGIS DATA ANALYST HT59.......... 55621
Cox, William M ADMIN AND TECH SUPPORT SPEC 1718.......... 52627
Crystal, Howard EDITOR - COMMITTEES 1718.......... 52627
Dean, Penny M OFFICIAL REPORTER 1718.......... 52627
Dotzler, Doreen SR OFFICIAL REPORTER HT59.......... 55621
Foradori, Lisa OFFICIAL REPORTER 1718.......... 52627
Hall, Daniel CHIEF CLERK - COMMITTEES 1718.......... 52627
Hofstad, Elizabeth EDITOR - COMMITTEES 1718.......... 52627
Humiston, Kellie OFFICIAL REPORTER HT59.......... 55621
Humke, Diane EDITOR - COMMITTEES 1718.......... 52627
Italiano, Christopher EDITOR HT59.......... 55621
Jackson, Damien C DPTY CHIEF 1718.......... 52627
Johnson, Keith OFFICIAL REPORTER 1718.......... 52627
Kean, Chandra OFFICIAL REPORTER HT59.......... 55621
LaCava, Julia OFFICIAL REPORTER HT59.......... 55621
Line, Nelson M SYS ANALYST HT59.......... 55621
Martin, Gail EDITOR HT59.......... 55621
McConnell, Karen OFFICIAL REPORTER HT59.......... 55621
Merchant, Elaine A OFFICIAL REPORTER HT59.......... 55621
Mertens, Traci OFFICIAL REPORTER 1718.......... 52627
Molnar, Wendy OFFICIAL REPORTER 1718.......... 52627
Morris, Susan ASST CHIEF CLERK - DEBATES HT59.......... 55621
Pedone, Jeanette ASST CHIEF CLERK - DEBATES HT59.......... 55621
Pump, Barry CHIEF CLERK - DEBATES HT59.......... 55621
Rosen, Kenneth EDITOR - COMMITTEES 1718.......... 52627
Seal, Matt PROD ASST 193 CHOB.......... 57187
Seckman, Cristina L EDITOR - COMMITTEES 1718.......... 52627
Smith, Christina A OFFICIAL REPORTER HT59.......... 55621
Taft, Tammy E OFFICE AND PROD ASST 1718.......... 52627
Tell, Regina OFFICIAL REPORTER 1718.......... 52627
Thomas, Vincent PROD ASST 193 CHOB.......... 57187
Vetrano, Mary Lynn EDITOR - COMMITTEES HT59.......... 55621
Walker, Melinda CHIEF HT59.......... 52627
Zamora, Katy OFFICIAL REPORTER 1718.......... 52627
Zamora, Raquel EDITOR - COMMITTEES 1718.......... 52627

OFFICE OF THE SERGEANT AT ARMS

The Honorable Paul D. Irving

H124 CAPITOL (ZIP: 20515-6634) 225-2456

Blodgett, Tim DPTY SGT AT ARMS H124.......... 52456
Commodore, Lakeisha EXEC ASST H124.......... 52456
Dohr, Bob CHIEF OPERATING OFFICER H124.......... 52456
Foreman, Lorraine SPECIAL ASST H124.......... 52456
Joyce, Kathleen ASST SGT AT ARMS H124.......... 52456
Kellaher, Don SR ADVISOR TO THE SGT AT ARMS H124.......... 52456
Moffitt, Melissa TACTICAL COMMUNICATIONS SPEC H124.......... 52456
Riley, Carmelitta ADMIN SPEC H124.......... 52456
Sensenbrenner, Bob COUNSEL H124.......... 52456
Strickland, Kelle CHIEF OF STAFF H124.......... 52456

APPOINTMENTS DESK

HB6 CAPITOL (ZIP: 20515) 225-2551

Belt, Camelia ASST - APPTS DESK CAPITOL.......... 52551
Cobb, Everett ASST - APPTS DESK CANNON.......... 52551
Coleman, Cheryl ASST - APPTS DESK CVC.......... 52551
Combs, Bobbie ASST - APPTS DESK RAYBURN.......... 52551
Dixon-Tymus, Vivian ASST - APPTS DESK RAYBURN.......... 52551
Gutrick, Patrice ASST - APPTS DESK CANNON.......... 52551
Johnson, Teresa MGR – APPTS DESK HB6.......... 50067
Legrand, Nadine ASST - APPTS DESK CAPITOL.......... 52551
Miles, Steven ASST - APPTS DESK CVC.......... 52551
Miller, Deborah ASST - APPTS DESK CAPITOL.......... 52551
Moran, Yanira ASST - APPTS DESK HVC.......... 52551
Myers, Mike ASST - APPTS DESK CVC.......... 52551
Reyes, Elsy ASST - APPTS DESK CANNON.......... 52551
Robertson, James ASST - APPTS DESK CVC.......... 52551
Robinson, Taesha ASST - APPTS DESK CVC.......... 52551
Topping, Brandon ASST - APPTS DESK CAPITOL.......... 52551

EMERGENCY MANAGEMENT

192 FORD HOB (ZIP: 20515) 226-0950

Beckerle, Hana PROGRAM MGR 192 FHOB.......... 60950
Brennan, Kevin DPTY ASST SGT AT ARMS – EMERGENCY MGMT 192 FHOB.......... 60950
Higgins, Haydn EMERGENCY MGMT SPEC 192 FHOB.......... 60950
Janis, Evan PROGRAM MGR 192 FHOB.......... 60950
LeNard, Dennis EMERGENCY MGMT SPEC 192 FHOB.......... 60950
Lowry, Joe DIR - PREPAREDNESS 192 FHOB.......... 60950
McBride, Lauren EMERGENCY MGMT SPEC 192 FHOB.......... 60950
McEvoy, Daniel EMERGENCY MGMT SPEC 192 FHOB.......... 60950
McNamara, Ellen EXEC ASST 192 FHOB.......... 60950

HOUSE OFFICERS/OFFICIALS AND STAFF

Scanlon, Emily DIR - CONTINUITY PLANS & OPS 192 FHOB **60950**
Speranza, Erik ASST SGT AT ARMS - EMERGENCY MGMT 192 FHOB **60950**
Taylor, Anita EMERGENCY MGMT SPEC 192 FHOB **60950**
Walvort, Bradley EMERGENCY MGMT SPEC 192 FHOB **60950**
Wengloski, Laura PROGRAM MGR 192 FHOB **60950**

HOUSE GARAGES AND PARKING SECURITY

G2-28 RAYBURN HOB (ZIP: 20515) 225-6749

Abbott, Jim DIRECTOR G2-28 ..... **56749**
Brown, Christopher SUPERVISOR G2-28 ..... **56749**
Coleman, Emanuel ASST SUPERVISOR G2-28 ..... **56749**
Meadows, Sonya ADMIN SPEC G2-28 ..... **56749**
Rodriguez, Diana SPECIAL PROJ ASST G2-28 ..... **56749**
Seales, Donnell ASST DIR G2-28 ..... **56749**

HOUSE SECURITY

HVC301 CAPITOL (ZIP: 20515) 226-2044

Fitzpatrick, Caitlin STAFF ASST HVC301 ..... **62044**
Foster, Michael SECUR OFFICER HVC301 ..... **62044**
Grajeda, Claudio SYS ADMIN HVC301 ..... **62044**
Leech, Katie STAFF ASST HVC301 ..... **62044**
McFarland, William DIRECTOR HVC301 ..... **62044**
Ravas, Joslyn SECUR OFFICER HVC301 ..... **62044**
Wilson, Ricky ASST DIR HVC301 ..... **62044**

ID SERVICES

321 CANNON HOB (ZIP: 20515) 225-3820

Hughes, Tanya ASST/ID SVCS 321 CHOB **53820**
Lonergan, Vincent ASST/ID SVCS 321 CHOB **53820**
Looney, Jack DIRECTOR/ID SVCS 321 CHOB **53820**
Lowe, Susan G ASST/ID SVCS 321 CHOB **53820**
Milton, Ashton ASST/ID SVCS 116 FHOB **53820**
Pegues, Robin ASST/ID SVCS 321 CHOB **53820**
Thomas-Wright, Patricia ASST/ID SVCS 321 CHOB **53820**
Titus, Tony ASST/ID SVCS 321 CHOB **53820**

INFORMATION SERVICES

H124 CAPITOL (ZIP: 20515) 225-2456

Hill, Bernard, Jr SYS ADMIN H124 ..... **52456**
Kaelin, Jim CHIEF INFO OFFICER H124 ..... **52456**
Stevenson, Marisa SYS ADMIN H124 ..... **52456**

POLICE SERVICES

HT8 CAPITOL (ZIP: 20515) 225-1000

Alexander, Purvis LAW ENFORCEMENT COMMUNICATIONS LIAISON COMMAND **49859**
Bieret, Stefan SR ASST HT8 ..... **51000**
Comer, Jonathan DIST SECUR SPECIALIST 173 FHOB **53380**
Fitzpatrick, Robert DPTY ASST SGT AT ARMS - POLICE SVCS/LAW ENFORCEMENT HT8 ..... **51000**
Franger, Melissa LEC PROGRAM ADMIN 173 FHOB **53380**
Grubbs, Kevin DPTY ASST SGT AT ARMS - POLICE SVCS/ LAW ENFORCEMENT HT8 ..... **51000**
Keating, Sean SR ASST FOR POLICE SVCS/LAW ENFORCEMENT HT8 ..... **51000**
Lundmark, Joseph DIST SECUR SPECIALIST 173 FHOB **53380**
Quattrone, John ASST SGT AT ARMS - POLICE SVCS/LAW ENFORCEMENT HT8 ..... **51000**
Spriggs, Brandon ASST FOR TECH SUPPORT 173 FHOB **53380**
Susalla, Michael LAW ENFORCEMENT COMMUNICATIONS LIAISON COMMAND **49859**
Wojciechowski, Ed SR LAW ENFORCEMENT LIAISON HT8 ..... **51000**

PROTOCOL AND CHAMBER OPERATIONS

HB6 CAPITOL (ZIP: 20515) 225-0067

Burns, Andrew MGR - CHAMBER SUPPORT SVCS HB6 ..... **50067**
Daniel, Ted ASST SGT AT ARMS HB6 ..... **50067**
Hamlett, Joyce ASST TO THE SGT AT ARMS - FLOOR SECUR HB6 ..... **50067**
Huddleston, Catherine ASST SPECIAL EVENTS/PROTOCOL HB6 ..... **50067**
Villa, Rick ASST TO THE SGT AT ARMS - FLOOR SECUR HB6 ..... **50067**

OFFICE OF THE CHIEF ADMINISTRATIVE OFFICER

The Honorable Philip G. Kiko

HB28 CAPITOL (ZIP: 20515) 225-5555

Awan, Omar DIR - STRATEGY B227 LHOB **58000**
Bath, George SR ADVISOR 217 FHOB **64315**

HOUSE OFFICERS/OFFICIALS AND STAFF

Binsted, Anne CHIEF OF STAFF HB28 .... **55555**
Clocker, John DEPUTY CAO HB28 .... **55555**
Emery, Micelle ADMIN SPEC HB28 .... **55555**
Fine, Sarah ANALYST B227 LHOB **58000**
Hemphill, Maurice MGR HB28 .... **55555**
Mahfood, Maggie EXEC ASST HB28 .... **55555**
Morris, Nicole DIRECTOR 217 FHOB **61045**
Ryan, Katie DIRECTOR B227 LHOB **65174**

ACCOUNTING

3110 O'NEILL HOB (ZIP: 20515) 226-4740

Angeles, Anna Katrina ACCNT TECH 3110 .... **54539**
Carcamo, Alicia STAFF ACCOUNTANT 3110 .... **61792**
Chaletzky, Ana MGR 3110 .... **54539**
Colom, Belane ACCNT TECH 3110 .... **60432**
Cooper, Richard STAFF ACCOUNTANT 3110 .... **56525**
Hamner, Philip DIRECTOR 3110 .... **56551**
Lee, Nga STAFF ACCOUNTANT 3110 .... **54538**
Lim, Chau SR ACCOUNTANT 3110 .... **61019**
Marsh, Steve MGR 3110 .... **62292**
Nelson, Juan STAFF ACCOUNTANT 3110 .... **61573**
Oulahyane, Melissia ACCNT TECH 3110 .... **65063**
Parker, Kevina ACCNT TECH 3110 .... **59909**
Phillips, Lisa STAFF ACCOUNTANT 3110 .... **69350**
Robertson, Deborah SR ACCOUNTANT 3110 .... **55028**
Springfield, Clyde SR ACCOUNTANT 3110 .... **61540**
Stanley, Angel STAFF ACCOUNTANT 3110 .... **59902**
Thompson, Adam STAFF ACCOUNTANT 3110 .... **57922**

OFFICE OF ACQUISITIONS MANAGEMENT

5110 O'NEILL HOB (ZIP: 20515) 225-2921

Bridgeforth, Toinetta SR CONTRACTS SPEC 5110 .... **52921**
Buckler, Troy PURCHASING AGENT 5110 .... **61080**
Clayton-Bullock, Latoya SR PROCUREMENT SPEC 5110 .... **52921**
Dobbins, Mark PURCHASING MGR 5110 .... **52921**
Grant, Lisa CHIEF 5110 .... **52921**
Green, Mitchell CONTRACT SUPPORT ADMIN 5110 .... **52921**
Ilog, Angela RESOURCE MGR 5110 .... **52921**
Masheter, Frederick PURCHASING AGENT 5112 .... **61080**
Moran, Ryan SR CONTRACTS SPEC 5110 .... **52921**
Morris, Kevin ADMIN - CONTRACTS 5110 .... **52921**
Sadler, Brooke PURCHASING AGENT 5110 .... **61080**
Sims, Carolyn PURCHASING AGENT 5110 .... **61080**
Stewart, Christine DIRECTOR 5110 .... **52921**
Suydam, Marcus ADMIN - CONTRACTS 5110 .... **52921**
Tiani, James SR CONTRACTS SPEC 5110 .... **52921**

ADMINISTRATIVE COUNSEL

217 FORD HOB (ZIP: 20515) 225-6969

Boldig, Christopher ASSOC COUNSEL 217 FHOB **56969**
Brewster, Christopher ADMIN COUNSEL 217 FHOB **56969**
Daly, Cecilia ADMIN COUNSEL 217 FHOB **56969**
Jenkins, Jenelle PARALEGAL 217 FHOB **56969**

ASSET MANAGEMENT

6110 O'NEILL HOB (ZIP: 20515) 225-6792

Best, Charlene MGR 6110 .... **50090**
Boger, Kelly SUPERVISOR 6110 .... **50090**
Bowlding, Sonia REC & WAREHOUSE SPEC 161 FHOB **60538**
Carney, Michael MGR 6110 .... **50090**
Clarke, John SUPERVISOR WA23 RHOB **58214**
Cuffee, Danielle ACCNT MGMT COUNSELOR 6110 .... **50090**
Cuffey, Lawrence SR REC & WAREHOUSE SPEC WA23 RHOB **58214**
Denegri, Andre FINANCIAL ANALYST 6110 .... **50090**
Dozier, Brian SR REC & WAREHOUSE SPEC 161 FHOB **60538**
Ewing, John ACCNT MGMT COUNSELOR 6110 .... **56792**
Gepert, Darla SPECIAL ASST 6110 .... **50090**
Haney, Winston ACCNT MGMT COUNSELOR 6110 .... **50090**
Herbert, Gregory REC & WAREHOUSE SPEC WA23 RHOB **58214**
Hughes, Jamal ACCNT MGMT COUNSELOR 6110 .... **56792**
Hunter, Steve ACCNT MGMT COUNSELOR 6110 .... **56792**
Johann, Derek SUPERVISOR WA23 RHOB **58214**
Joy, Adam ACCNT MGMT COUNSELOR 6110 .... **56792**
Kimosh, Michael ANALYST 6110 .... **50090**
Marable, Eugene ACCNT MGMT COUNSELOR 6110 .... **56792**
Shorter, Quincy MGR 6110 .... **56792**
Soults, Daniel REC & WAREHOUSE SPEC WA23 RHOB **58214**
Thompson, Stephen REC & WAREHOUSE SPEC WA23 RHOB **50090**
Wright, Richard SR REC & WAREHOUSE SPEC WA23 RHOB **58214**

BUDGET POLICY AND PLANNING

3240 O'NEILL HOB (ZIP: 20515) 225-6792

Asata, Heather BUDGET ANALYST 3240 .... **61454**
Eleftherion, Anthony BUDGET ANALYST 3240 .... **61457**
Jackson, Sarah DIRECTOR 3240 .... **56792**
McFadden, Miranda FINANCIAL ANALYST 3240 .... **61474**

CAPITOL SERVICE CENTER

HT3 CAPITOL (ZIP: 20515) 225-8000

Cicale, Michael SR CAPITOL SVC REP HT3 .... **58000**
Johnson, Robert CAPITOL SVC REP HT3 .... **58000**

HOUSE OFFICERS/OFFICIALS AND STAFF

Judge, Nancy CAPITOL SVC REP HT3 .... **58000**
Long, John DIR - CAPITOL SVC CENTER HT3 .... **58000**

OFFICE OF THE CHIEF FINANCIAL OFFICER

3140 O'NEILL HOB (ZIP: 20515) 226-4616

Ahmad, Viquar DPTY CHIEF 3140 .... **64650**
Cade, Sanya DPTY CHIEF 3140 .... **64650**
Peterson, Carol FINANCE LIAISON 3140 .... **50665**
Puzzuoli, Len CHIEF 3140 .... **64616**
Stricklen, Elizabeth OFFICE MGR 3140 .... **54391**

OFFICE OF THE CHIEF HUMAN RESOURCES OFFICER

102 FORD HOB (ZIP: 20515) 225-2926

Abbott, Jessica ANALYST 102 FHOB **65987**
Carter, Tiffany ADMIN SPEC 102 FHOB **52926**
Cunningham, Candace GENERALIST 102 FHOB **61426**
Gillis, Daniel ADA AIDE 102 FHOB **52926**
Holman, Ella COMMUNICATIONS STRATEGIST 102 FHOB **61403**
Jecko, Brittany MGR 102 FHOB **67472**
Kraly, Elizabeth DPTY CHIEF 102 FHOB **66138**
Lee, Darnell DPTY CHIEF 102 FHOB **66451**
Lesnewsky, Erik ADA AIDE 102 FHOB **52926**
Lueken, Paige GENERALIST 102 FHOB **60247**
McCrea-Wood, Artrice HUMAN RESOURCES COORD 102 FHOB **60266**
McLean, Mikkyla GENERALIST 102 FHOB **60274**
Meister, Darlene DIRECTOR 102 FHOB **52926**
Oliver, Ebbony HUMAN RESOURCES COORD 102 FHOB **60272**
Penharlow, Kevin SAFETY & OCCUPATIONAL HEALTH SPEC 643A FHOB **60295**
Salamone, John CHIEF 102 FHOB **50012**
Sarnowski, Angelisa MGR 102 FHOB **67472**
Space, Melissa DIRECTOR 102 FHOB **64078**
Tuck, Emily DIR - PRIVACY 102 FHOB **50668**
Wood, Salley SPECIAL PROJ DIR 217 FHOB **65116**

OFFICE OF THE CHIEF INFORMATION OFFICER (HIR)

631 FORD HOB (ZIP: 20515) 226-9789

Black, Justin CHIEF TECH OFFICER 630A FHOB **66011**
Jordan, Christopher CHIEF OPS OFFICER 631 FHOB **62082**
Szpindor, Catherine CIO 631 FHOB **69788**
Vickers, Randal CHIEF INFO SECUR OFFICER 630A FHOB **66205**

OFFICE OF THE CHIEF LOGISTICS OFFICER

WA35 RAYBURN HOB (ZIP: 20515) 225-8000

Coyne, Thomas CHIEF LOGISTICS OFFICER WA35 RHOB **51896**
Daniel, George ASST CLO WA29 RHOB **66645**
Gaines, Julia SPECIAL ASST WB2 RHOB **61985**
Shah, Kirat RESOURCE MGR WA26 RHOB **54057**

CHILD CARE CENTER

147 FORD HOB (ZIP: 20515) 226-9320

Barnabae, Monica ADMIN DIR 147 FHOB **69320**
Beatty, Paige DIRECTOR 1100 .... **69321**
Detweiler, Bethany ADMIN SPEC 147 FHOB **69320**

CONGRESSIONAL STAFF ACADEMY

B241 LONGWORTH HOB (ZIP: 20515) 226-3800

Bautista, Yamilette PROGRAM MGR B241 LHOB **63800**
Bunn, Ashley SR INSTRUCTIONAL DESIGNER B241 LHOB **63800**
Maddux, David DIRECTOR B241 LHOB **63800**
Miller, Shawn OPS ASST B241 LHOB **63800**

CUSTOMER EXPERIENCE CENTER

B227 LONGWORTH HOB (ZIP: 20004) 225-8000

Ames, Kenneth CUSTOMER ADVOCATE B227 LHOB **58000**
Armstrong, Janciera DPTY CHIEF B227 LHOB **58000**
Cappetto, Richard CHIEF B227 LHOB **66769**
Cincotta, Sam ANALYST B227 LHOB **58000**
Gerarden, Paul CUSTOMER ADVOCATE B227 LHOB **58000**
Jarrell, Dan COORD - OPS B227 LHOB **58000**
Johnston, Glen DIRECTOR B227 LHOB **58000**
Leiby, Frederick SR CONTRACT ADMIN B227 LHOB **58000**
Lyman, April CUSTOMER ADVOCATE B227 LHOB **58000**
O'Boyle, David MGR - COMMUNICATIONS 217 FHOB **66660**
Pany, Christopher CONTRACT SUPPORT ADMIN B227 LHOB **58000**
Phillips, Ashleigh CUSTOMER ADVOCATE B227 LHOB **58000**
Pritschau, Mary CUSTOMER ADVOCATE B227 LHOB **58000**
Quintanilla, Iliana GRAPHIC DESIGNER 217 FHOB **58000**
Seidel, Aly COMMUNICATIONS ANALYST 217 FHOB **58000**
Sims, Aislan EXEC ASST B227 LHOB **58000**
Weiser, Daniel COMMUNICATIONS DIR 217 FHOB **61091**

HOUSE OFFICERS/OFFICIALS AND STAFF

OFFICE OF EMPLOYEE ADVOCACY

301 FORD HOB (ZIP: 20515) 225-8800

Dadlani, Priya ASSOC COUNSEL 301 FHOB **58800**
Givand, Diana ASSOC COUNSEL 301 FHOB **58800**
Lopez-Campillo, Juan SR ASSOC COUNSEL 301 FHOB **58800**
Skolky, Ashley PARALEGAL 301 FHOB **58800**
Wilhite, L DIRECTOR 301 FHOB **58800**

EMPLOYEE ASSISTANCE

140 FORD HOB (ZIP: 20515-6619) 225-2400

Anderson, Tiara EMPLOYEE ASST COUNSELOR 140 FHOB **52400**
Becker, Breanna EMPLOYEE ASST COUNSELOR 140 FHOB **52400**
Hawkins-Green, Margot EMPLOYEE ASSISTANCE SPEC 140 FHOB **52400**
McBride-Chambers, Liz DIRECTOR 140 FHOB **52400**
Swartz, Emily COORD 140 FHOB **66312**
Tewksbury, Paul SR EMPLOYEE ASSISTANCE COUNSELOR 140 FHOB **52400**
Weiss, Bryan PROGRAM MGR 140 FHOB **61997**

FINANCIAL COUNSELING

B215 LONGWORTH HOB (ZIP: 20515) 225-7474

Alvey, Lisa COUNSELOR B215 LHOB **63548**
Anderson, Dontrell FINANCIAL COUNSELOR B215 LHOB **60903**
Bowman, Shelia COUNSELOR B215 LHOB **62819**
Ewers, Gretchen MGR B215 LHOB **52220**
Farley, Joann FINANCIAL COUNSELOR B215 LHOB **50189**
Gates, Trena COUNSELOR B215 LHOB **62088**
Gilmore, Joan ANALYST B215 LHOB **61174**
Greco, Jackie COUNSELOR B215 LHOB **60537**
Gugliotta, Norman COUNSELOR B215 LHOB **63549**
Harrington, Keith COUNSELOR B215 LHOB **61538**
Hughes, Michael FINANCIAL COUNSELOR B215 LHOB **703-490-8578**
Jennings, Araceli FINANCIAL ASST B215 LHOB **63560**
Jones, Deborah FINANCIAL COUNSELOR B215 LHOB **50160**
Lorenzo, Vanessa FINANCIAL COUNSELOR B215 LHOB **61197**
Mauldin, Evan MGR B215 LHOB **61186**
McCauley, Erica FINANCIAL COUNSELOR B215 LHOB **65082**
Minor, Leslie COUNSELOR B215 LHOB **61194**
Moore, Edwarda FINANCIAL COUNSELOR B215 LHOB **50137**
Reimers, Jackson MGR B215 LHOB **61531**
Sessoms, Shawn FINANCIAL COUNSELOR B215 LHOB **68967**
Shoemaker, Airlie FINANCIAL COUNSELOR B215 LHOB **50180**
Turek, Stanley FINANCIAL COUNSELOR B215 LHOB **69451**
Warfield, Tazmyah FINANCIAL COUNSELOR B215 LHOB **60913**
Washington, Jason FINANCIAL COUNSELOR B215 LHOB **61582**
Wells, Royale FINANCIAL COUNSELOR B215 LHOB **60901**
White, Byron FINANCIAL COUNSELOR B215 LHOB **61133**
Wilson, Kellie FINANCIAL COUNSELOR B215 LHOB **60245**

FIRST CALL

B227 LONGWORTH HOB (ZIP: 20515) 225-8000

Brown, Pamela CUSTOMER SOLUTIONS REP B227 LHOB **58000**
Forgione, John SR CUSTOMER SOLUTIONS REP B227 LHOB **58000**
Gonzalez, Rosario SR CUSTOMER SOLUTIONS REP B227 LHOB **58000**
Hayes, Kathleen CUSTOMER SOLUTIONS REP B227 LHOB **58000**
Kelley, Kevin CUSTOMER SOLUTIONS REP B227 LHOB **58000**
Murphy, Larrisa CUSTOMER SOLUTIONS REP B227 LHOB **58000**
Naughton, Christopher PROGRAM MGR B227 LHOB **58000**
Orrick, Michael CUSTOMER SOLUTIONS REP B227 LHOB **58000**
Thiessen, Gary MGR B227 LHOB **58000**

FURNISHINGS

WA29 RAYBURN HOB (ZIP: 20515) 225-8000

Allen, Keith JOURNEYMAN CABINET MAKER WA25 RHOB **58000**
Brady, John APPRENTICE UPHOLSTERER WA33 RHOB **58000**
Brown, Keith APPRENTICE CABINET MAKER WA39 RHOB **58000**
Dahlstrom, Darren MGR WA25 RHOB **58000**
Dean, Joseph LEAD UPHOLSTERER WA33 RHOB **58000**
Delisle, Kaldon JOURNEYMAN - FURN SPEC WA22 RHOB **58000**
Dent, Richard MASTER CARPET MECHANIC WA32 RHOB **58000**
Egerson, Troy MASTER UPHOLSTERER WA33 RHOB **58000**
English, Josh MASTER CABINET MAKER WA25 RHOB **58000**
Fry, Lance DIRECTOR WA29A RHOB **66886**
Garcia, John MASTER FINISHER WA22 RHOB **58000**
Gates, Corey MASTER UPHOLSTERER WA33 RHOB **58000**
Harris, Kevin MASTER FINISHER WA22 RHOB **58000**
Magruder, Timothy MASTER FINISHER WA22 RHOB **58000**
Martin, Christopher MASTER CABINET MAKER WA25 RHOB **58000**
McGarry, Thomas LEAD CABINET MAKER WA25 RHOB **58000**
Morgan, Cody MASTER CARPET MECHANIC WA32 RHOB **58000**
Morrison, Samuel JOURNEYMAN - TEXT SPEC WA33 RHOB **58000**
Nora, Myrtle MASTER DRAPERY MANUFACTURER WA32 RHOB **58000**
Overby, Frank MASTER CARPET MECHANIC WA32 RHOB **58000**
Pastran, Rafael JOURNEYMAN - FURN SPEC WA22 RHOB **58000**
Perkins, Tommy APPRENTICE UPHOLSTERER WA33 RHOB **58000**
Perry, John MASTER CABINET MAKER WA25 RHOB **58000**
Plowden, Vincent LEAD FINISHER WA22 RHOB **58000**
Rogers, Justin DRAPERY INSTALLER WA32 RHOB **58000**
Rogerson, Randy APPRENTICE CABINET MAKER WA25 RHOB **58000**
Rossiter, Paul JOURNEYMAN LOCKSMITH WA15 RHOB **64185**
Russell, George JOURNEYMAN - TEXT SPEC WA33 RHOB **58000**
Solorzano, Willis APPRENTICE CABINET MAKER WA25 RHOB **58000**

Stein, Christopher JOURNEYMAN CABINET MAKER WA25 RHOB.......... **58000**
Swan, Carol MGR - FURNISHINGS WA32 RHOB.......... **58000**
Trombetta, Joseph MASTER CARPET MECHANIC WA32 RHOB.......... **58000**
Tylee, Dustin MASTER CARPET MECHANIC WA32 RHOB.......... **58000**
Vallandingham, George LEAD CARPET MECHANIC WA32 RHOB.......... **58000**
Vaughan, Alan MGR - FURNISHINGS WA32 RHOB.......... **58000**
Wiese, Karl JOURNEYMAN CABINET MAKER WA25 RHOB.......... **58000**
Wilbourn, Jeffrey MASTER FINISHER WA22 RHOB.......... **58000**
Williams, Bradley JOURNEYMAN CABINET MAKER WA25 RHOB.......... **58000**
Wimberly, DeShun JOURNEYMAN - FURN SPEC WA25 RHOB **58000**
Wood, Kevin MASTER CARPET MECHANIC WA32 RHOB.......... **58000**

HIR - CYBERSECURITY

630A FORD HOB (ZIP: 20515) 225-6002

Adeniji, Addie DIR - INFO ASSURANCE 628A FHOB **61599**
Afram, Amanda SR INFO SYS SECUR ANALYST 650 FHOB **66574**
Appiah-Kubi, Felix SR INFO TECH ENGINEER SITE... **571-921-3117**
Bessaha, Nabil SR INFO SYS SECUR ANALYST 650 FHOB **63868**
Blackerby, Bruce INFO SYS SECUR ANALYST 613 FHOB **68769**
Crotts, Jamie MGR - OUTREACH & COMMUNICATIONS 642A FHOB **66207**
Eaglin, Hope SR INFO SYS SECUR ANALYST 650 FHOB **61586**
Elliott, Ronald SR INFO SYS SECUR ANALYST 612 FHOB **65575**
Evans, Tom INFO SYS SECUR ANALYST 612 FHOB **62231**
Gallagher, Renee SR INFO SYS SECUR ANALYST 612 FHOB.. **67296**
Gizara, Michael OPS TEAM LEAD 612 FHOB **66577**
Goodlow, Lisa SR COMMUNICATIONS SECUR ANALYST 602 FHOB **64551**
Hargadon, Laural MGR - INFO ASSURANCE 650 FHOB **63807**
Lau, David ENTERPRISE COMPLIANCE LEAD 650 FHOB **63826**
Lea, Sam SR SYS SECUR ENGINEER 612 FHOB **64151**
McSwain, Jennifer SPECIAL ASST 630A FHOB **61116**
Minturn, John ACTING DIR - INFO SECUR 612A FHOB **64554**
Moxley, Steven SR INFO SYS SECUR ANALYST 612 FHOB **65562**
Norris, Matthew ACTING MGR - INFO SECUR 612 FHOB **65561**
Pinson, Stephen SR INFO SYS SECUR ANALYST 612 FHOB.... **66579**
Schmidt, Derrick FORENSIC LEAD 613 FHOB **68773**
Shankar, Murthy SYS SECUR ENGINEER 650 FHOB **66252**
Teasley, Richard SYS SECUR ENGINEER 612 FHOB **64111**
Vemuri, Kumar SR SYS ENGINEER 612 FHOB **61254**

HIR - ENTERPRISE APPLICATIONS

B73 FORD HOB (ZIP: 20515) 226-6223

Ahmed, Muneer APPLICA SYS ADMIN B65 FHOB **66234**
Akula, Mallik SR SOFTWARE SPEC B71 FHOB **63365**
Barrett, Robert DIRECTOR B70B FHOB **66223**
Bilinski, John SR BUSINESS PROCESS APPLICA SPEC B77 FHOB **66280**
Bouchot, Enrique SR BUSINESS PROCESS APPLICA SPEC B73 FHOB **66208**
Boyle, Kevin SR BUSINESS PROCESS APPLICA SPEC B70 FHOB **64223**
Buckler, Ricky BUSINESS PROCESS APPLICA SPEC B70 FHOB **53230**
Burch, Kenneth BUSINESS PROCESS APPLICA SPEC B75 FHOB **51513**
Carrico, Ron SR BUSINESS PROCESS APPLICA SPEC B77 FHOB **64601**
Carter, Delisa SR SOFTWARE SPEC B75 FHOB **51832**
Chiu, Jimmy HRIS - APPLICA SYS ANALYST B73 FHOB **62189**
Ciango, Jacob APPLICA SYS ADMIN B75 FHOB **62230**
Cox, Bridget SR SYS ANALYST B77 FHOB **66041**
Dieffenderfer, Gary APPLICA DATABASE SPEC/SR BUSINESS PROCESS APPLICA SPEC 638 FHOB **66246**
Dooley, Geneva SR SOFTWARE ENGINEER B70 FHOB **51835**
Gould, Michael MGR B74 FHOB **60811**
Gronski, Robert SR BUSINESS PROCESS APPLICA SPEC B73 FHOB **51411**
Haq, Rabia BUSINESS PROCESS APPLICA SPEC B70 FHOB.... **63838**
Heeb, John SR BUSINESS PROCESS APPLICA SPEC B69 FHOB **62187**
Hornburg, Richard BUSINESS PROCESS APPLICA SPEC B75 FHOB **66233**
Jonnala, Jay SR BUSINESS PROCESS APPLICA SPEC B70 FHOB **60892**
Knell, Katherine MGR B73 FHOB **68496**
Kuppuri, Manjula SR BUSINESS PROCESS APPLICA SPEC B70 FHOB **59915**
Langley, William BUSINESS PROCESS APPLICA SPEC B77 FHOB **66061**
Leck, Kelsey BUSINESS PROCESS APPLICA SPEC B77 FHOB. **66043**
Lev, Mark SR BUSINESS PROCESS APPLICA SPEC B77 FHOB. **51420**
Loving, Anthony APPLICA DATABASE SPEC 638 FHOB **66214**
McDonald, Bradley MGR B70A FHOB **66437**
McKittrick, David SR BUSINESS PROCESS APPLICA SPEC B69 FHOB **61053**
Nghiem, Hieu SR BUSINESS PROCESS APPLICA SPEC B73 FHOB **61153**
Nowak, Jason SR SOFTWARE SPEC B75 FHOB **69414**
Ohlis, Carla SR INTERNET SYS ENGINEER B69 FHOB **66273**
Pugh, Kim SR BUSINESS PROCESS APPLICA SPEC B73 FHOB **66294**
Reeves, Octavian RESOURCE ANALYST 630A FHOB **66539**
Rice, Lawrence SR BUSINESS PROCESS APPLICA SPEC B70 FHOB **59925**
Riddle, Donald SR BUSINESS PROCESS APPLICA SPEC B73 FHOB **66236**
Roche, Kevin APPLICA DATABASE SPEC 638 FHOB **66136**
Samuels, Michael MGR - SUPPORT SYS B74B FHOB **62186**
Sanusi-Hopes, Zainab SR BUSINESS PROCESS APPLICA SPEC B70 FHOB **60172**
Schellhaas, Melissa BUSINESS PROCESS APPLICA SPEC B69 FHOB **66717**
Shabbeer, Mohammed LEAD SYS ADMIN B75 FHOB **66231**
Solomon, William BUSINESS PROCESS APPLICA SPEC B62 FHOB **66263**
Vo, Quoc-An BUSINESS PROCESS APPLICA SPEC B77 FHOB. **69830**
Watkins, Sarah SR BUSINESS PROCESS APPLICA SPEC B70 FHOB **62346**
Williams, Jerome SVC MGR B62 FHOB **66029**
Wright, Lawrence BUSINESS PROCESS APPLICA SPEC B77 FHOB **53285**

HIR - ENTERPRISE ARCHITECTURE

630A FORD HOB (ZIP: 20515) 225-6002

Dyson, Laura SR ENTERPRISE ARCHITECT 645 FHOB **60592**

HIR - ENTERPRISE INFRASTRUCTURE

686 FORD HOB (ZIP: 20515) **226-9785**

Acuesta, July SR SYS ENGINEER 619 FHOB........ **571-921-3116**
Andrews, Thomas MGR 687A FHOB........ **61350**
Carr, Josh SR SYS ENGINEER 619 FHOB........ **571-921-3121**
Coakley, Kristen TELEPHONE SYS CONSULT 692 FHOB........ **56002**
Cornejo, Luis SR SYS ENGINEER 617 FHOB........ **66522**
Deluca, Alan MGR - OPS 679 FHOB........ **66452**
Erving, James COMMUNICATIONS SPEC 677 FHOB........ **571-921-3333**
Fritz, Eric OPS TEAM LEAD 618 FHOB........ **63840**
Fyock, Bradley MGR SITE........ **571-921-3105**
Gates, Thomas SR SYS ENGINEER 617 FHOB........ **66167**
Guduru, Pratap OPS TEAM LEAD 639 FHOB........ **62048**
Hair, Robert DIRECTOR 686B FHOB........ **62359**
Hall, Morgan FACILITIES MGMT SPEC SITE........ **571-921-3125**
Harris, Rafael OPS TEAM LEAD 618 FHOB........ **61243**
Hokhold, Mark SYS ENGINEER 617 FHOB........ **571-921-3109**
Houghton, Joseph MGR 686 FHOB........ **61607**
Kahler, Kent SYS ENGINEER 622 FHOB........ **61259**
Kannan, Valadi SR SYS ENGINEER 639 FHOB........ **66181**
Kelley, Tara COMMUNICATIONS SPEC 01GG48........ **61356**
Kuper, Karen MGR - OPS/SPECIAL ASST 677 FHOB........ **571-921-3321**
Leatherbury, Michelle COMMUNICATIONS SPEC 687 FHOB........ **60200**
Linville, Ray SR SYS ENGINEER 622 FHOB........ **59276**
May-Gillespie, Sarita SR TELECOMMUNICATIONS ADMIN 680 FHOB........ **56677**
Michalek, William ADMIN - BILLING 686 FHOB........ **69785**
Mitchell, Maggie ADMIN - BILLING 678A FHOB........ **66415**
Nusinzon, Igor SR SYS ENGINEER 622 FHOB........ **63720**
Patel, Dhaval MGR SITE........ **571-921-3307**
Santa, Leidy SYS ENGINEER 620 FHOB........ **66024**
Schubert, Jason SR SYS ENGINEER 619 FHOB........ **571-921-3434**
Shepperson, Baxter SR SYS ENGINEER 619 FHOB........ **571-921-3108**
Smith, Cynthia ADMIN SPEC 686 FHOB........ **69785**
Snyder, Les SR SYS ENGINEER SITE........ **571-921-3325**
Souvandara, Sinthasone ADMIN 620 FHOB........ **66270**
Tammadge, James SR SYS ENGINEER 617 FHOB........ **69826**
Taylor, Ronald, Sr SYS ENGINEER 641 FHOB........ **66333**
Thompson, Mark MGR 620C FHOB........ **66264**
Tobias, Teona SR TELECOMMUNICATIONS ADMIN 692 FHOB. **56002**
Velasquez, Melvin SYS ENGINEER SITE........ **571-921-3157**
Wenzel, Kenneth OPS TEAM LEAD 618 FHOB........ **60124**
White, Daniel SR SYS ENGINEER SITE........ **571-921-3198**
Wilder, Donald OPS TEAM LEAD SITE........ **571-921-3123**
Wray, Sherrye SYS ENGINEER 639 FHOB........ **63794**

HIR - ENTERPRISE MESSAGING AND MOBILITY

619 FORD HOB (ZIP: 20515) **225-6002**

Anderson, Denine SPECIAL ASST 619C FHOB........ **66245**
Blakney, Harold SR SYS ENGINEER 622 FHOB........ **66181**
Fontneau, Bruce SR SYS ENGINEER 624 FHOB........ **61522**
Gaskins, James TEAM LEAD 616 FHOB........ **66259**
Jacobson, Bradley BRANCH MGR 619 FHOB........ **63841**
Jefferson, Kenyatta TECH SOLUTIONS ENGINEER 621 FHOB. **66057**
Jones, Stephen TEAM LEAD 621 FHOB........ **69919**
Jordan, Chelsa SYS ENGINEER 624 FHOB........ **66529**
Marlow, Joel SR SYS ENGINEER 623 FHOB........ **64040**
Moya, David SYS ENGINEER 619 FHOB........ **571-921-3255**
Phillips, Jamali SR SYS ENGINEER 621 FHOB........ **60010**
Remke, Matthew SR SYS ENGINEER 623 FHOB........ **56153**
Roach, Kevin TEAM LEAD 624 FHOB........ **66229**
Thompson, Phillip SR SYS ENGINEER 623 FHOB........ **68483**
Underwood, Ricardo SR TECH SUPPORT REP 621 FHOB........ **67112**
Youmans, Donald SR SYS ENGINEER 624 FHOB........ **66361**

HIR - ESCALATIONS AND OPERATIONS

631 FORD HOB (ZIP: 20515) **225-6002**

Bell, Frank MGR 608B FHOB........ **66199**
Duenas, Joseph SR SYS SUPPORT ENGINEER 604 FHOB........ **69470**
Ellis, Franklin SR SYS SUPPORT ENGINEER 601 FHOB........ **62723**
Gallagher, Tom MGR 608C FHOB........ **66172**
Green, Caroline TECH SUPPORT REP 601 FHOB........ **63001**
Little, Andreal ASST PROJ MGR 607 FHOB........ **69896**
Mullen, Kelly SR SYS SUPPORT ENGINEER 601 FHOB........ **67090**
Vargas, Jose NETWK TECH 601 FHOB........ **66430**
Woodrow, Jean PROJ MGR 601 FHOB........ **66256**

HIR - HOUSE WEB SERVICES

627 FORD HOB (ZIP: 20515) **226-2140**

Ahuja, Kalpana DIRECTOR 636 FHOB........ **61488**
Caraballo, Madeline INTERNET SYS SPEC 636 FHOB........ **61633**
Carnnia, Casey INTERNET SYS ENGINEER 636 FHOB........ **63846**
Cuff, Loren INTERNET SYS SPEC 627 FHOB........ **58035**
Freeney, Malcolm PROJ MGR 637 FHOB........ **66197**
Gould, Melissa PROD ANALYST 646 FHOB........ **66196**
Jefferson, Shawn INTERNET SYS SPEC 644C FHOB........ **66165**
Maas, Jennifer MGR 645A FHOB........ **66156**
Miller, Michael MGR 626 FHOB........ **66279**
Moll, Andrew SR INTERNET SYS SPEC 640 FHOB........ **66054**
Nguyen, Van SR SOFTWARE ENGINEER 644B FHOB........ **65685**
Rakhimov, Mukhsimjon SR INTERNET SYS ENGINEER 627 FHOB........ **62140**
Rawat, Vinod INTERNET SYS SPEC 646 FHOB........ **66283**
Richards, John INTERNET SYS SPEC 626 FHOB........ **60581**
Singh, Gagan MGR 636 FHOB........ **67128**
Tonizzo, David SR INTERNET SYS SPEC 642A FHOB **571-921-3205**
Venable, Tommy MGR 644C FHOB........ **63362**
Wallace, Sharon INTERNET SYS SPEC 627 FHOB........ **63809**

HIR - IDENTITY GOVERNANCE AND ADMINISTRATION

631 FORD HOB (ZIP: 20515) **225-6002**

Frech, Jason SR SYS ENGINEER 01W60ACF **64455**
Johnson, Robert SR SYS ENGINEER 615 FHOB **51329**
Murphy, Robert DIRECTOR 620B FHOB **61709**
Nguyen, Nho SR SYS ENGINEER 615 FHOB **63094**
Wang, Gary SR ADVISOR 647 FHOB **60574**
Young, James TEAM LEAD 616 FHOB **571-921-3114**

HIR - IT CUSTOMER SOLUTIONS

607B FORD HOB (ZIP: 20515) **225-6002**

Abel, Timothy SR TECH SUPPORT REP 604 FHOB **61143**
Adelakun, Deen SR TECH SOLUTIONS ENGINEER 694 FHOB **56002**
Alexander, Gordon TECH SOLUTIONS ENGINEER 694 FHOB **56002**
Alston, Mark TECH SOLUTIONS ENGINEER 694 FHOB **56002**
Archie, Tyreis TECH SUPPORT REP 100 CHOB **69313**
Bailey, Dave SR TECH SUPPORT REP 100 CHOB **66242**
Barton, Tisha SPECIAL ASST 608 FHOB **66155**
Basilio, Tyrone TECH SUPPORT REP 2067 .... **65761**
Bickham, Andrew ANALYST 608C FHOB **66288**
Boone, Russell TECH SUPPORT REP 2067 .... **66345**
Dunklin, Kelda SR TECH SUPPORT REP 604 FHOB **66179**
Emamali, Nicole SR TECH SUPPORT REP 608B FHOB **66411**
Fisher, Jerome SR TECH SOLUTIONS ENGINEER 694 FHOB **56002**
Ford, Darin SR TECH SUPPORT REP 2067 .... **64043**
Fountain, Anika TECH SOLUTIONS TECH 694 FHOB **56002**
Fravel, Don TECH SOLUTIONS TECH 694 FHOB **56002**
Goldsborough-Lee, Angel DIR - IT CUSTOMER SOLUTIONS 607A FHOB **65108**
Harvey, Jamie SR TELECOMMUNICATIONS ADMIN 692 FHOB. **56002**
Jackson, Reggie SR TECH SUPPORT REP 606 FHOB **66979**
Jackson, Wanda MGR 678 FHOB **60416**
Jones, Rodney SR TECH SUPPORT REP 2067 .... **66419**
Jordan, Yong SR TECH SOLUTIONS ENGINEER 694 FHOB **56002**
Kimball, Mark SR TECH SUPPORT REP 605 FHOB **64437**
Little, Harold SR TECH SOLUTIONS ENGINEER 694 FHOB **56002**
Malloy, Deon SUPERVISOR 2067 .... **64796**
Nurse, Courtney SR TECH SUPPORT REP 100 CHOB **61849**
Perkins, Janet TECH SOLUTIONS ENGINEER 694 FHOB **56002**
Powerz, Darius SR TECH SUPPORT REP 100 CHOB **62299**
Rhodes, Mashell SR TELECOMMUNICATIONS ADMIN 692 FHOB **56002**
Richter, Robin TELEPHONE SYS CONSULT 692 FHOB **56002**
Seal, Robert SR TELECOMMUNICATIONS ADMIN 692 FHOB **56002**
Sierra, David TECH SUPPORT REP 100 CHOB **66274**
Strott, Carol TECH SUPPORT REP 2067 .... **64044**
Turney, Bob SR TECH SUPPORT REP 100 CHOB **66099**
Tyree-Edwards, Cynthia TECH SUPPORT REP 2067 .... **60550**
Vaughns, Thomas SR TELECOMMUNICATIONS ADMIN 692 FHOB **56002**
Weadon, Andrea BRANCH MGR 608B FHOB **66352**
Wesley, Shanel SR TELECOMMUNICATIONS ADMIN 677 FHOB **56002**
Whitaker, Laura TECH SUPPORT REP 2067 .... **62208**
White, Gregg SR TECH SUPPORT REP 100 CHOB **66077**
Whitmyer, John SR TECH SUPPORT REP 694 FHOB **56002**
Wilson, Diane SUPERVISOR 694 FHOB **56002**
Wilson, James TECH SOLUTIONS ENGINEER 694 FHOB **56002**

HIR - NETWORKING ENGINEERING AND OPERATIONS

686 FORD HOB (ZIP: 20515) **226-6430**

Baker, Darrell SR NETWK COMMUNICATIONS SPEC 663 FHOB **64244**
Barbee, Glenn NETWK TECH 652C FHOB **64101**
Billard, Michael COMMUNICATIONS SPEC 681 FHOB **64215**
Billups, Brian NETWK TECH 681 FHOB **66357**
Cook, Eric NETWK TECH 680 FHOB **64435**
Ellin, James NETWK SYS ENGINEER 664 FHOB **62833**
French, Charles SR NETWK TECH 652C FHOB **66430**
Goggins, James NETWK COMMUNICATIONS SPEC 685 FHOB **64214**
Graeub, Andrew MGR 663 FHOB **66291**
Harrell, Vickie SR NETWK COMMUNICATIONS SPEC 685 FHOB **60260**
Harris, Donald SUPERVISOR 663A FHOB **63854**
Hibbs, Cynthia NETWK COORD 679 FHOB **66410**
Hunt, Daniel SR NETWK COMMUNICATIONS SPEC 685 FHOB **61829**
Johnson, Andre SR NETWK TECH 652C FHOB **66430**
Jones, Charles SR NETWK COMMUNICATIONS SPEC 685 FHOB **63521**
Jones, Clarence SR NETWK TECH 652C FHOB **66430**
Kilson, Franklin NETWK TECH 652C FHOB **66430**
Martins, Richard MGR 687 FHOB **66268**
Mason, Tron SR NETWK COMMUNICATIONS SPEC 663 FHOB. **60482**
Mathis, Marc NETWK TECH 652C FHOB **66430**
Milasi, Francesco SR NETWK TECH 652C FHOB **66430**
Milbut, Anthony SR NETWK COMMUNICATIONS SPEC 687 FHOB **571-921-3167**
Moore, Gary SR NETWK TECH 652C FHOB **66430**
Moretti, Scott NETWK TECH 652C FHOB **66430**
Muncy, James SR NETWK TECH 680 FHOB **66034**
Myers, Anthony NETWK COMMUNICATIONS SPEC 685 FHOB. **66412**
Pearson, Stephen SR NETWK SYS ENGINEER 664 FHOB **63544**
Phan, Dean SUPERVISOR 663A FHOB **66307**
Romano, Karli SPECIAL ASST SITE **63983**
Schooler, Sherri NETWK COMMUNICATIONS SPEC 677 FHOB **571-921-3303**
Slifko, Brian NETWK TECH 680 FHOB **62831**
Sumner, Nancy SR NETWK TECH 652C FHOB **66430**
Suplee, Andrew SR NETWK SYS ENGINEER 664 FHOB **61827**
Tabarzadi, Shahla SR NETWK COMMUNICATIONS SPEC 688 FHOB **66266**
Truong, Mike SR NETWK COMMUNICATIONS SPEC 680 FHOB **765-9238**
Ventre, James SR NETWK SYS ENGINEER SITE **571-921-3113**
Whitaker, Jason NETWK SYS ENGINEER 681 FHOB **61669**
Williams, James SR NETWK COMMUNICATIONS SPEC 685A FHOB **69339**
Williams, Louis, Jr NETWK SYS ENGINEER 664 FHOB **66267**
Williams, Waverly SR NETWK COMMUNICATIONS SPEC 688 FHOB **66498**

HIR - OPERATIONS AND CONTINUITY

629 FORD HOB (ZIP: 20515) 226-7742

Allen, Pat DIRECTOR 629 FHOB........ **67742**
Barrineau, Sara MGR 634 FHOB........ **67202**
English, Joseph COMMUNICATIONS SPEC 648 FHOB........ **60069**
Escubio, John TECH SUPPORT REP 648 FHOB........ **66141**
Gonzalez, Pablo COMMUNICATIONS SPEC 632A FHOB........ **571-921-3339**
Kreitzer, Tom MGR - OPS 632A FHOB........ **60302**
McSwain, Jennifer SPECIAL ASST 630A FHOB........ **61116**
Scales, Bret COMMUNICATIONS SPEC 633 FHOB........ **63020**
Stacey, Royal INFO TECH MGR 634A FHOB........ **63360**
Starkey, Charles MGR 634 FHOB........ **66131**
Toney, Fred SR SYS ENGINEER 634A FHOB........ **64573**
Wright, Timothy SR COMMUNICATIONS SPEC 632A FHOB........ **60195**

HIR - TECHNOLOGY GOVERNANCE AND COMPLIANCE

643 FORD HOB (ZIP: 20515) 226-6418

Arjev, Michael PROGRAM MGR 647 FHOB........ **66425**
Hayes, Michelle SR SYS ENGINEER 647 FHOB........ **66108**
Nash, Michael MGR 643 FHOB........ **66418**
Von Harders, Kimberly SVC MGR 644A FHOB........ **66048**

HIR - VENDOR MANAGEMENT

643A FORD HOB (ZIP: 20515) 226-4232

Kimbrough, Jhamene SYS ANALYST 643C FHOB........ **63734**
Modica, Michael MGR 642 FHOB........ **64232**
Shalhoub, Fadlou SR SYS ANALYST 643C FHOB........ **60477**

HOUSE CREATIVE SERVICES

2002 RAYBURN HOB (ZIP: 20515) 225-2700

Banks, David SR MULTIMEDIA DEVELOPER 2002........ **52700**
Barciniak, Dana OFFICE MGR 2002........ **52700**
Blakley, Jeff DIRECTOR 2002........ **52700**
Boyd, Kristie PHOTOGRAPHER 2002........ **52700**
Bradley, Nathaniel DIR - SVC DESK & QUALITY ASSURANCE 607B FHOB........ **66107**
Brown, Demetrice SR TECH SUPPORT REP 605 FHOB........ **66149**
Clark, Marion SR TELECOMMUNICATIONS ADMIN 692 FHOB... **52700**
Cuprill, Carlos SUPERVISOR 100 CHOB........ **69314**
Derrick, Scott GRAPHIC DESIGNER 2002........ **52700**
Faison, Shawna GRAPHIC DESIGNER 2002........ **52700**
Freeman, Antoinette ADMIN SPEC 2002........ **52840**
Herman, Leah PHOTOGRAPHER 2002........ **52700**
Metzler, Franmarie PHOTOGRAPHER 2002........ **52700**
Nguyen, Phi PHOTOGRAPHER 2002........ **52700**
Rowe, Teresa DIRECTOR 2002........ **52700**
Schemm, Cari GRAPHIC DESIGNER 2002........ **52700**

HOUSE DAILY PRESS GALLERY

H315 CAPITOL (ZIP: 20515) 225-3945

Andersen, Frederic ASST DIR H315........ **53945**
Kachinske, Edward ASST DIR H315........ **53945**
Michalson, Kristine ASST DIR H315........ **53945**
Supon, Justin DPTY DIR H315........ **53945**
Tin, Yadana DIRECTOR H315........ **53945**

HOUSE PERIODICAL PRESS GALLERY

H304 CAPITOL (ZIP: 20515) 225-2941

Hamel, Ryan THIRD ASST H304........ **52941**
Rupert, Gerald FIRST ASST H304........ **52941**
Walters, Jennifer SECOND ASST H304........ **52941**
Zatkowski, Robert DIRECTOR H304........ **52941**

HOUSE RADIO AND TELEVISION GALLERY

H320 CAPITOL (ZIP: 20515) 225-5214

Carpenter, Christopher COORD - DIGITAL MEDIA H320........ **55214**
Dahl, Ryan MEDIA LOGISTICS COORD H320........ **55214**
Elias, Andrew DPTY DIR H320........ **55214**
Harvey, Kinsey MEDIA LOGISTICS COORD H320........ **55214**
Kellaher, Anthony MEDIA LOGISTICS COORD H320........ **55214**
Oates, Kimberly SR MEDIA LOGISTICS COORD H320........ **55214**
Ramirez Kornacki, Olga DIRECTOR H320........ **55214**

HOUSE RECORDING STUDIO

2010 RAYBURN HOB (ZIP: 20515) 225-3941

Anthony, Tony BROADCAST ENGINEER/PROD SPEC 2010........ **53941**
Atchison, Darryl CHIEF ENGINEER 2010........ **53941**

HOUSE OFFICERS/OFFICIALS AND STAFF

Baham, Todd BROADCAST PROD TECH 2010 53941
Banfield, Kelli BROADCAST ENGINEER/PROD SPEC 2010 53941
Barbour, June BROADCAST PROD TECH 2010 53941
Barefoot, Jeffrey BROADCAST ENGINEER/PROD SPEC 2010 53941
Bates, Deborah PROD/ENGINEERING SPEC 2010 53941
Benn, Phillip ELECTRONICS TECH 2010 53941
Berger, Donald W TECH DIR 2010 53941
Brackens, Robert BROADCAST PROD TECH 2010 53941
Brown, Jason TECH DIR 2010 53941
Brown, Lawrence BROADCAST ENGINEER/PROD SPEC 2010 53941
Callaway, Robert SR BROADCAST ENGINEER 2010 53941
Chargualaf, Jesse BROADCAST ENGINEER/PROD SPEC 2010 53941
Colbert, Ray SR BROADCAST ENGINEER/PROD SPEC 2010 53941
Collins, John BROADCAST PROD TECH 2010 53941
Davis, John J BROADCAST PROD TECH 2010 53941
Dickie, James MGR - ENGINEERING OPS 2010 53941
Duran, Rolando ELECTRONICS TECH 2010 53941
Evans, William R, Jr ELECTRONICS TECH 2010 53941
Garay, German BROADCAST PROD TECH 2010 53941
Hirsch, Patrick DIR - HOUSE RECORDING STUDIO 2010 53941
Holt, Clinton BROADCAST ENGINEER/PROD SPEC 2010 53941
Koztoski, Douglas BROADCAST PROD TECH 2010 53941
Lane, Carey AUDIO SPEC 2010 53941
Marcus, Ralph TECH DIR 2010 53941
Massengale, Doug CHIEF ENGINEER 2010 53941
Miller-Lamill, Eloise BROADCAST PROD TECH 2010 53941
Mosley, Joseph TECH DIR 2010 53941
Nasr, Haitham SR BROADCAST ENGINEER/PROD SPEC 2010 53941
Owens, Michael BROADCAST PROD TECH 2010 53941
Pilkerton, Sandra OFFICE MGR 2010 53941
Rampey, Dominick PROD SPEC/SR BROADCAST ENGINEER 2010 53941
Reid, Edward BROADCAST PROD TECH 2010 53941
Rouse, Patricia AUDIO SPEC 2010 53941
Scherling, Grant PRINCIPAL ENGINEER 2010 53941
Schmitt, Regina MGR - PROD OPS 2010 53941
Smith, William BROADCAST PROD TECH 2010 53941
Steinmuller, April ADMIN SPEC 2010 53941
Stepney, Eric AUDIO SPEC 2010 53941
Swartzendruber, Douglas BROADCAST ENGINEER/PROD SPEC 2010 53941
Tilson, Daniel BROADCAST PROD TECH 2010 53941
Urman, John BROADCAST PROD TECH 2010 53941
Vaughan, Nicole ADMIN SPEC 2010 53941

HOUSE WELLNESS CENTER

140 FORD HOB (ZIP: 20515) 225-0800

Swartz, Emily PROGRAM COORD 140 FHOB 52400
Weiss, Bryan PROGRAM MGR 140 FHOB 61997

LOGISTICS

WA27 RAYBURN HOB (ZIP: 20515) 225-9474

Allison, Kevin LOGISTICS & DIST SPEC HT19 59474
Barr, Paul SUPERVISOR RSBC4 55057
Braxton, Brandon REC & WAREHOUSE SPEC RSBC4 55057
Brewster, James LOGISTICS & DIST SPEC WA16 RHOB 59474
Briscoe, Kevin LOGISTICS & DIST SPEC WA16 RHOB 59474
Edward, Ryley REC & WAREHOUSE SPEC RSBC4 55057
Hargrove, Brian BLDG SUPERVISOR WA16 RHOB 59474
Holland, Gregory LOGISTICS & DIST SPEC HT19 59474
Holley, Steven LOGISTICS & DIST SPEC WA16 RHOB 59474
Jefferson, Lynwood LOGISTICS & DIST SPEC WA16 RHOB 59474
Jenkins, James PROGRAM MGR WA26 RHOB 66643
Johnson, Kwasi LOGISTICS & DIST SPEC WA16 RHOB 59474
Jordan, James LOGISTICS & DIST SPEC HT19 59474
Labrake, Andre REC & WAREHOUSE SPEC RSBC4 55057
Maiden, Lewis LOGISTICS & DIST SPEC B23 FHOB 59474
Mallon, Michael MGR - LOGISTICS WA23 RHOB 51637
Meredith, Dwaine LOGISTICS & DIST SPEC WA16 RHOB 59474
Pratt, Michael LOGISTICS & DIST SPEC HT19 59474
Rhones, Sherman LOGISTICS & DIST SPEC WA16 RHOB 59474
Ridgell, William LOGISTICS & DIST SPEC WA16 RHOB 59474
Rivers, Marlian BLDG SUPERVISOR B23 FHOB 59474
Rose, Thomas SUPERVISOR - LOGISTICS & DIST WA16 RHOB 59474
Simmons, Ronald SUPERVISOR - LOGISTICS & DIST WA16 RHOB 59474
Simpkins, Damon LOGISTICS & DIST SPEC B23 FHOB 59474
Small, Bobby MGR - LOGISTICS WA16 RHOB 59474
Summers, Damon REC & WAREHOUSE SPEC RSBC4 59474
Thomas, Denise REC & WAREHOUSE SPEC RSBC4 55057
Thomas, Jason LOGISTICS & DIST SPEC WA16 RHOB 59474
Wallace, Alfonzo BLDG SUPERVISOR WA16 RHOB 59474
Ware, Calvin LOGISTICS & DIST SPEC WA33A RHOB 59474
Washington, Terrence LOGISTICS & DIST SPEC RAYBURN 59474
Woodburn, Charles DIR - LOGISTICS WA27 RHOB 59474
Yerge, James REC & WAREHOUSE SPEC RSBC4 55057

MEMBERS' SERVICES

B235 LONGWORTH HOB (ZIP: 20515-9970) 225-3644

Burnham, Elizabeth MBR SVCS COORD B235 LHOB 53644
Ellis-Jones, Deborah PAYROLL ADMIN B235 LHOB 53644

OFFICE DESIGN AND MOVE SERVICES

B216 LONGWORTH HOB (ZIP: 20515) 226-4742

Daniel, Jada MGR B216 LHOB 64742
Davis, Stachia DIRECTOR B216 LHOB 64742
Johnson, Margaret SR PROJ SPECIALIST B216 LHOB 64742
Jordan, Ashley ADMIN SPEC B216 LHOB 64742
Partridge, Willard SR PROJ SPECIALIST B216 LHOB 64742
Smith, Charles PROJ SPEC B216 LHOB 64742

OFFICE SUPPLY/GIFT SHOP

B217 LONGWORTH HOB (ZIP: 20515) 225-3321

Banks, Bianca MGR B217 LHOB.......... **53321**
Barbee, Donell RETAIL INVENTORY SPEC B217 LHOB.......... **53321**
Bogan, David SUPERVISOR B217 LHOB.......... **53321**
Booker, Carlos SALES SPEC B217 LHOB.......... **53321**
Bounds, Jazmine SALES SPEC B217 LHOB.......... **53321**
Boyd, Petrina SALES SPEC B217 LHOB.......... **53321**
Carson, Lawrence SALES SPEC B217 LHOB.......... **53321**
Hodges, John DIRECTOR B217 LHOB.......... **53321**
Johnson, Dwayne RETAIL INVENTORY SPEC B217 LHOB.......... **53321**
Miller, Louis, III RETAIL INVENTORY SPEC B217 LHOB.......... **53321**
O'Brien, Mary SALES SPEC B217 LHOB.......... **53321**
Reid, Karen SUPPLY ACCNT SPEC B217 LHOB.......... **53321**

PAYROLL AND BENEFITS

B215 LONGWORTH HOB (ZIP: 20515-6604) 225-1435

Appiah, Joyce COUNSELOR B215 LHOB.......... **50116**
Armour, Tiana COUNSELOR B215 LHOB.......... **67870**
Batson, Denise COUNSELOR B215 LHOB.......... **56454**
Bowling-Stokes, Chaunette MGMT ANALYST B215 LHOB.......... **64518**
Butler, James DIRECTOR B215 LHOB.......... **54599**
Chace, Karen COUNSELOR B215 LHOB.......... **57119**
Davis, Scott GENERALIST B215 LHOB.......... **54550**
Ellis-Gregg, Sharon ASST B215 LHOB.......... **55089**
Etchison, Cheryl MGR - PAYROLL & BENEFITS B215 LHOB.......... **64611**
Foster, Charles ASST B215 LHOB.......... **54579**
Haigler, Monique COUNSELOR B215 LHOB.......... **60073**
Jones, Yolanda GENERALIST B215 LHOB.......... **50674**
Kremkau, Rebecca SYS ANALYST B215 LHOB.......... **61473**
McFadden, Saint Juan SR GENERALIST B215 LHOB.......... **56456**
Mendoza, Lydia COUNSELOR B215 LHOB.......... **58051**
Miller, Rose SR COUNSELOR B215 LHOB.......... **54578**
Murphy, Lori COUNSELOR B215 LHOB.......... **69377**
Oldham, Lindsay FINANCIAL ANALYST B215 LHOB.......... **53793**
Piazza, Richard MGMT ANALYST B215 LHOB.......... **52562**
Randall, Robin GENERALIST B215 LHOB.......... **52275**
Sollers, Danielle COUNSELOR B215 LHOB.......... **60048**
Thompson, Una GENERALIST B215 LHOB.......... **54595**
Tillman, Arrica MGR B215 LHOB.......... **54581**
Ward, Cheraisse GENERALIST B215 LHOB.......... **50667**
Williams, Shenette COUNSELOR B215 LHOB.......... **61495**
Williams, Tommy COUNSELOR B215 LHOB.......... **60036**
Zubkoff, Jordana MGMT ANALYST B215 LHOB.......... **60788**

OFFICE OF RISK MANAGEMENT

217 FORD HOB (ZIP: 20515) 226-6766

Simpson, Susan CHIEF 217 FHOB.......... **66766**
Ward, James SR ANALYST 217 FHOB.......... **67257**

WORKFLOW MANAGEMENT

WA35 RAYBURN HOB (ZIP: 20515) 226-5888

Hawkins, Johanna COORD WA35 RHOB.......... **65888**
Johnson, Eric COORD WA35 RHOB.......... **65888**
Keane, Michael MGR WA35 RHOB.......... **65888**
Sneden, Susan COORD WA35 RHOB.......... **65888**

WOUNDED WARRIOR

354 FORD HOB (ZIP: 20515) 226-1965

Jennings, Solomon PROGRAM MGR 354 FHOB.......... **61944**
Lieteau, Karim PROJ SPEC 354 FHOB.......... **61954**
Tolar, Mac DIRECTOR 355 FHOB.......... **61915**

OFFICE OF THE CHAPLAIN

The Honorable Patrick J. Conroy

HB25 CAPITOL (ZIP: 20515-6655) 225-2509

Bronson, Karen A MBR OFFICE LIAISON & PROGRAM COORD HC2.......... **64835**

HOUSE OFFICERS/OFFICIALS AND STAFF

OFFICE OF THE PARLIAMENTARIAN

Thomas J. Wickham, Jr.

H209 CAPITOL (ZIP: 20515-6731) **225-7373**

Cook, Julia ASST PARLIAMENTARIAN H209.......... **57373**
Donahue, Kristen ASST CLERK TO THE PARLIAMENTARIAN H209.......... **57373**
Feldblum, Bryan INFO TECH MGR HT52.......... **51122**
Gooch, Anne ASST PARLIAMENTARIAN H209.......... **57373**
Jenkins, Lloyd CLERK TO THE PARLIAMENTARIAN H209.......... **57373**
Jones, Kyle ASST PARLIAMENTARIAN H209.......... **57373**
Kowalewski, Matthew ASST CLERK TO THE PARLIAMENTARIAN H209.......... **57373**
Moran, Catherine PRECEDENT DIGITAL EDITOR 4470.......... **51122**
Neal, Andrew PRECEDENT EDITOR 4470.......... **51122**
Osheroff, Benjamin ASST PARLIAMENTARIAN H209.......... **57373**
Smith, Jason DPTY PARLIAMENTARIAN H209.......... **57373**
Spitzer, Max PRECEDENT EDITOR 4470.......... **51122**

OFFICE OF INTERPARLIAMENTARY AFFAIRS

HC4 CAPITOL (ZIP: 20515) **226-1766**

Jeter, Kristina DPTY DIR/SPECIAL EVENTS/PROTOCOL HC4.......... **64576**
Keita, Kamilah DPTY DIR - INFO TECH HC4.......... **61766**
Knudson, Kate DIRECTOR HC4.......... **61437**
Mangrum, Pearl FINANCIAL ADMIN HC4.......... **61766**

OFFICE OF THE LAW REVISION COUNSEL

Ralph V. Seep

308 FORD HOB (ZIP: 20515-6711) **226-2411**

Belcher, Robert E PRINTING EDITOR 308 FHOB.......... **62411**
Cohen, Joseph ASST COUNSEL 308 FHOB.......... **62411**
Evans, Michelle ASST COUNSEL 308 FHOB.......... **62411**
Hall, Katrina ASST COUNSEL 308 FHOB.......... **62411**
Lane, Katherine ASST COUNSEL 308 FHOB.......... **62411**
Letz, Deborah ASST COUNSEL 308 FHOB.......... **62411**
Lindsey, Brian SR COUNSEL 308 FHOB.......... **62411**
Loach, Eric M SR SYS ENGINEER 308 FHOB.......... **62411**
Mulligan, Edward T ASST COUNSEL 308 FHOB.......... **62411**
Paretzky, Kenneth I SR COUNSEL 308 FHOB.......... **62411**
Skarvelis, Michele ASST COUNSEL 308 FHOB.......... **62411**
Skouras, Lindsey ASST COUNSEL 308 FHOB.......... **62411**
Sukol, Robert M DPTY COUNSEL 308 FHOB.......... **62411**
Tahirkheli, Sylvia STAFF ASST 308 FHOB.......... **62411**
Thomas, Kenneth SYS ADMIN 308 FHOB.......... **62411**
Thompson, Monica STAFF ASST 308 FHOB.......... **62411**
Wagner, John F, Jr SR COUNSEL 308 FHOB.......... **62411**

OFFICE OF THE LEGISLATIVE COUNSEL

Wade Ballou

337 FORD HOB (ZIP: 20515-6721) **225-6060**

Ambinder, Michael ASST COUNSEL 337 FHOB.......... **56060**
Anderson, Ashley W OFC MANAGERIAL ASST 337 FHOB.......... **56060**
Anderson, Karen COUNSEL 337 FHOB.......... **56060**
Anderson, Lauren STAFF ASST/PARALEGAL 337 FHOB.......... **56060**
Barksdale, Marshall W COUNSEL 337 FHOB.......... **56060**
Bernstein, Eric ASST COUNSEL 337 FHOB.......... **56060**
Birch, Debby ASST OFC ADMIN 337 FHOB.......... **56060**
Birch, Joseph STAFF ASST 337 FHOB.......... **56060**
Blount, Willie INFO SYS ANALYST 337 FHOB.......... **56060**
Brazelton, Hallet COUNSEL 337 FHOB.......... **56060**
Brown, Ebony ASST COUNSEL 337 FHOB.......... **56060**
Burke, Warren COUNSEL 337 FHOB.......... **56060**
Callen, Paul SR COUNSEL 337 FHOB.......... **56060**
Cassidy, Thomas COUNSEL 337 FHOB.......... **56060**
Castillo, Lisa ASST COUNSEL 337 FHOB.......... **56060**
Casturo, Robert ASST COUNSEL 337 FHOB.......... **56060**
Chasnoff, Megan L COUNSEL 337 FHOB.......... **56060**
Christrup, Henry COUNSEL 337 FHOB.......... **56060**
Cox, Ken ASST COUNSEL 337 FHOB.......... **56060**
Crotty, Mairead STAFF ASST/PARALEGAL 337 FHOB.......... **56060**
Daly, Lisa SR COUNSEL 337 FHOB.......... **56060**
Davis, Rachel STAFF ASST 337 FHOB.......... **56060**
Dillon, Thomas HUMAN RESOURCES ADMIN 337 FHOB.......... **56060**
Ducksworth, Monique STAFF ASST 337 FHOB.......... **56060**
Ebner, Casey ASST COUNSEL 337 FHOB.......... **56060**
Eckstein, Mathew SR COUNSEL 337 FHOB.......... **56060**
Fleishman, Susan SR COUNSEL 337 FHOB.......... **56060**
Gallagher, Brendan J ASST COUNSEL 337 FHOB.......... **56060**
Gilley, Allison ASST COUNSEL 337 FHOB.......... **56060**
Gross, Justin COUNSEL 337 FHOB.......... **56060**
Grossman, James D SR COUNSEL 337 FHOB.......... **56060**
Hagenbuch, Stephen ASST COUNSEL 337 FHOB.......... **56060**
Hagnauer, Karl ASST COUNSEL 337 FHOB.......... **56060**
Harmann, Jean SR COUNSEL 337 FHOB.......... **56060**
Hartwich, Alison COUNSEL 337 FHOB.......... **56060**
Hauff, Kevin STAFF ASST/PARALEGAL 337 FHOB.......... **56060**

HOUSE OFFICERS/OFFICIALS AND STAFF

Hawkins, Megan ASST COUNSEL 337 FHOB **56060**
Heckscher, Fiona ASST COUNSEL 337 FHOB **56060**
Joyner, Miekl STAFF ASST 337 FHOB **56060**
Kubicki, Paul ASST COUNSEL 337 FHOB **56060**
Lin, Kakuti COUNSEL 337 FHOB **56060**
Loggie, Matthew STAFF ASST 337 FHOB **56060**
McNeillie, Nancy OFFICE ADMIN 337 FHOB **56060**
Meryweather, Kelly STAFF ASST/PARALEGAL 337 FHOB **56060**
Meryweather, Tom STAFF ASST/PARALEGAL 337 FHOB **56060**
Molina, Amanda ASST COUNSEL 337 FHOB **56060**
Osborne, Christopher COUNSEL 337 FHOB **56060**
Parthasarathy, Kalyani ASST COUNSEL 337 FHOB **56060**
Plater, Angelina STAFF ASST 337 FHOB **56060**
Probst, Scott COUNSEL 337 FHOB **56060**
Rens, Sarah ASST COUNSEL 337 FHOB **56060**
Rich, Elonda STAFF ASST/PARALEGAL 337 FHOB **56060**
Ross, Hadley SR COUNSEL 337 FHOB **56060**
Schilt, Adam ASST COUNSEL 337 FHOB **56060**
Sciascia, Anthony COUNSEL 337 FHOB **56060**
Shapiro, Jessica COUNSEL 337 FHOB **56060**
Shpak, Anna COUNSEL 337 FHOB **56060**
Srinivasa, Veena COUNSEL 337 FHOB **56060**
Sterkx, Craig COORD - PUBLICATIONS 337 FHOB **56060**
Swindle, Alex LEGIS RESEARCH ANALYST 337 FHOB **56060**
Swiss, Kathryn ASST COUNSEL 337 FHOB **56060**
Synnes, Mark SR COUNSEL 337 FHOB **56060**
Szwec, Peter SR SYS ANALYST 337 FHOB **56060**
Topper, David ASST SYS ADMIN 337 FHOB **56060**
Vanek, Michelle COUNSEL 337 FHOB **56060**
Walker, Sally COUNSEL 337 FHOB **56060**
Weinhagen, Robert F, Jr SR COUNSEL 337 FHOB **56060**
Wofsy, Noah DPTY LEGIS COUNSEL 337 FHOB **56060**
Young, Brady SR COUNSEL 337 FHOB **56060**

OFFICE OF GENERAL COUNSEL

Douglas N. Letter

219 CANNON HOB (ZIP: 20515-6532) 225-9700

Barbero, Megan ASSOC COUNSEL 219 CHOB **59700**
Clouse, Sarah "Sally" ATTORNEY 219 CHOB **59700**
Coogle, Christine LAW CLERK 219 CHOB **59700**
Friedman, Sarah LAW CLERK 219 CHOB **59700**
Hamm, Kimberly ASSOC COUNSEL 219 CHOB **59700**
Hanner, Brooks ASST COUNSEL 219 CHOB **59700**
Hsu, Lily LAW CLERK 219 CHOB **59700**
James, Melissa ADMIN DIR 219 CHOB **59700**
Shapiro, Kristin ASST COUNSEL 219 CHOB **59700**
Tatelman, Todd DPTY COUNSEL 219 CHOB **59700**

OFFICE OF INSPECTOR GENERAL

Michael Ptasienski

386 FORD HOB (ZIP: 20515-9990) 226-1250

Akowuah, Emmanuel AUDITOR - INFO SYS AUDITS 386 FHOB **61250**
Cornell, Kevin MGMT ANALYST 386 FHOB **61250**
DeMarco, David MGMT ANALYST 386 FHOB **61250**
Howard, Michael ASST DIR - INFO SYS AUDITS 386 FHOB **61250**
Johnson, Steven L ASST DIR 386 FHOB **61250**
Jones, Deborah E ADMIN ASST 386 FHOB **61250**
Kozubski, Susan ASST DIR 386 FHOB **61250**
Leahy, Terry MGMT ANALYST 386 FHOB **61250**
Loutsenhizer, Nicole AUDITOR 386 FHOB **61250**
Patel, Saad DIR - INFO SYS 386 FHOB **61250**
Persaud, Clifton ASST DIR - INFO SYS AUDITS 386 FHOB **61250**
Picolla, Joseph DPTY INSPECTOR GENERAL 386 FHOB **61250**
Poole, Julie ASST DIR 386 FHOB **61250**
Price, Larry DIRECTOR 386 FHOB **61250**
Stevenson, Christen Janell ASST DIR 386 FHOB **61250**
Sullenberger, Keith A ASST DIR 386 FHOB **61250**
Torres, Rosario AUDITOR 386 FHOB **61250**
Upshur, R Terry ADMIN DIR 386 FHOB **61250**
Wolfgang, Donna K ASST DIR 386 FHOB **61250**

OFFICE OF THE HOUSE HISTORIAN

Matthew A. Wasniewski

JEFFERSON BUILDING, ATTIC (ZIP: 20515) 226-1300

Ethier, Virginia RESEARCH ASST JEFFERSON BUILDING, ATTIC........ **61300**
Hromada, Erin DIR - HISTORIAN STAFF JEFFERSON BUILDING, ATTIC........ **61300**
Johnson, Kathleen M MGR - ORAL HISTORY JEFFERSON BUILDING, ATTIC........ **61300**
Kato, Ken ASSOC HISTORIAN JEFFERSON BUILDING, ATTIC... **61300**
Kowalewski, Albin HISTORICAL PUBLICATIONS SPEC JEFFERSON BUILDING, ATTIC........ **61300**
Litten, Josh SR RESEARCH ASST JEFFERSON BUILDING, ATTIC........ **61300**
Murphy, Michael HISTORICAL PUBLICATIONS SPEC JEFFERSON BUILDING, ATTIC........ **61300**
O'Hara, Laura T SR HISTORICAL WEB EDITOR JEFFERSON BUILDING, ATTIC........ **61300**
Rucker, Terrance HISTORICAL PUBLICATIONS SPEC JEFFERSON BUILDING, ATTIC........ **61300**
Winter, Samuel RESEARCH ASST JEFFERSON BUILDING, ATTIC........ **61300**

GENERAL SUPPORT SERVICES

Three-digit room numbers are in the Cannon HOB or the Ford HOB, as indicated. Four-digit room numbers beginning with 1 are in the Longworth HOB; with 2, the Rayburn HOB; and with 4, 5, or 6, the O'Neill HOB. Capitol room numbers begin with SB, ST, HB, HC, and HT or with H or S, followed by three digits. Room numbers beginning with CVC, HVC, or SVC are in the Capitol Visitor Center.

Calls from outside the Capitol complex can be made by dialing (202) 22 plus the five-digit number listed in this directory.

Acquisitions and Contract Management 5110 OHOB........ **52921**

Air Conditioning

Capitol........ **88800**
House Office Buildings........ **54141**

Airline Ticket Office, Combined (CATO)

Reservations........ **703-522-2286**
Conner, Misty OFFICE MGR B222 LHOB........ **56692**

Amtrak

Toll-free........ **1-800-872-7245**

Appointments Desk

Sergeant at Arms South Door of Capitol........ **52551**
(Limited-access areas of House side of Capitol)

Architect of the Capitol

Bailey, Teresa CHIEF HUMAN CAPITAL OFFICER 295 FHOB........ **61285**
Baltimore, Jason GEN COUNSEL 271 FHOB........ **51210**
Bittner, Mamie DIR - COMMUNICA & CONG RELATIONS SB16........ **81793**
Carroll, Tom ASST TO THE ACTING ARCHITECT SB16........ **81793**
Chapotin, Saharah Moon EXEC DIR - U.S. BOTANIC GARDEN........ **56670**
Cohen, Michele CURATOR HT5........ **81222**
Condeluci, Laura COMMUNICA OFFICER SB16........ **81793**
Dentamaro, Andrew CONG LIAISON SB16........ **86680**
Failla, Chris INSPECTOR GEN 518 FAIRCHILD........ **593-0260**
Hutcherson, Tony CHIEF - ACQUISITION AND MATERIAL MGMT 263 FHOB........ **62557**
Kraft, Jonathan CHIEF FINANCIAL OFFICER 5174 FHOB **50038**
Merdon, Christine A ACTING ARCHITECT SB16........ **81793**
Mueller, Peter DIR - PLANNING & PROJ MGMT 537A FHOB........ **55900**
O'Keefe, James ACTING CHIEF ADMIN OFFICER 290 FHOB........ **61222**
Pajak, M J SR ADVISOR TO THE COO SB16........ **81793**
Plemmons, Beth CEO - CVC VISITOR SVCS SVC101 **593-1746**
Reed, Mark CAPITOL BUILDING SUPT HB29........ **88800**
Wiegmann, Jay CHIEF INFO OFFICER 209 FHOB........ **54321**
Williams, Patricia DIR - SAFETY, FIRE & ENVIRON PROGRAM 571 FHOB........ **60630**

Art and Archives, Office of LJ-Attic........ **61300**

Attending Physician

Monahan, Brian ATTENDING PHYSICIAN H166........ **55421**
Pray, Keith CHIEF OF STAFF H166........ **55421**

Audio Visual B227 LHOB
(screens, projectors and TVs)........ **58000**

Automobile Services

Car Pooling Information........ **1-800-745-RIDE**
Member License Tags H124........ **52456**
Parking (see Parking Permits & Security)
Reciprocity Stickers, Information G2-28 RHOB........ **56749**

Banking Facilities

Credit Union........ **63100**

Bells

(clocks, hearing rooms, cable TV network)
Office of the Architect of the Capitol........ **49827**

Benefits

(see Payroll and Benefits)

Bill Status B81 CHOB........ **65200**
(see Legislative Resource Center)

Bills and Sponsors/Cosponsors Forms HT13........ **57598**
(see Legislative Operations, Office of)

Botanic Garden

Chapotin, Saharah Moon EXEC DIR........ **56670**

Conservatory **60672**

Building Superintendents (Maintenance)

Capitol **88800**
House Office Buildings 2046 RHOB **54141**

Calendar, House Legislative HT13 .... **57925**
(see Legislative Operations, Office of)

Capitol Visitor Center **68000**

Reservations, Visitor Services, and General Tour Questions **593-1762**
Special Events and Room Booking **593-1775**
Communications and Media Inquiries **593-0099**
Executive Office **593-1816**
Plemmons, Beth CEO - VISITOR SVCS SVC101 .... **593-1746**
Apostolides, Nik DPTY CEO SVC101 .... **593-1809**
Brackett, Lee Ann CONG LIAISON SVC101 .... **593-0048**
Casey, Tom DIR - MARKETING & COMMUNICATIONS SVC101 .... **593-0099**
Larkin, David WEBMASTER CVC230 .... **593-2211**
McConnell, Melanie STF ASST TO THE CEO SVC101 .... **593-1842**
Pearson, Tina DIR - VISITOR SVCS HVC101 .... **593-1752**
Trivers, Laura MGR - COMMUNICATIONS SVC101 .... **593-1829**
Ward, Beverly CONG LIAISON SVC101 .... **593-1782**

Carpenter Shop

Capitol Building **88800**
House Office Buildings **54141**

Chaplain

Conroy, Rev. Patrick J CHAPLAIN HB25 .... **52509**
Bronson, Karen A MBR OFFICE LIAISON/PROGRAM COORD HC2 .... **64835**

Chief Administrative Officer

Kiko, Philip G CAO HB28 .... **55555**
Frequently Called Services
  Financial Counseling **57474**
  First Call **58000**
  House Information Resources **56002**
  Payroll and Benefits **51435**

Child Care Center 147 FHOB **69320**

Clerk of the House

Johnson, Cheryl L CLERK OF THE HOUSE H154 .... **57000**

Cloakrooms

Democratic
  Fischer, Robert, Jr ASST FLOOR CHIEF H222 .... **57330**
Floor Information (recording) **57400**
Republican
  O'Toole, Ryan CLOAKROOM DIR H223 .... **57350**

Clocks

(wall and vote-keyed clocks)
Office of the Architect of the Capitol **49827**

Communications, Office of (Clerk) 293 CHOB **51908**

Congressional Accessibility Services, Office of S156 .... **44048**

TTY **44049**
Hauck, David DIR S156 .... **44048**

Congressional Budget Office 402 FHOB **62600**

  Human Resources 410 FHOB **62628**
Angres, Leigh ASSOC DIR - LEGIS AFFAIRS 406B FHOB **62701**
Banthin, Jessica DPTY ASST DIR - HEALTH & HUMAN RESOURCES 419A FHOB **62669**
Edelberg, Wendy ASSOC DIR - ECONOMIC ANALYSIS 404A FHOB **62784**
Evans, Joseph, Jr CHIEF ADMIN OFFICER 405 FHOB **62600**
Gay, Sebastien ASST DIR - FINANCIAL ANALYSIS 470A FHOB **62770**
Gullo, Theresa ASST DIR - BUDGET ANALYSIS 430 FHOB **62800**
Hadley, Mark DEPUTY DIR 402 FHOB **62633**
Hall, Keith DIR 402 FHOB **62700**
Hutchinson, Brianne EXEC ASST - DIR OFC 402 FHOB **62700**
Kile, Joseph ASST DIR - MICROECONOMIC STUDIES 493E FHOB **62940**
Kilroe, Deborah ASSOC DIR - OFC OF COMMUNICATIONS 404 FHOB **62602**
Kling, Jeffrey ASSOC DIR - ECONOMIC ANALYSIS 404B FHOB **60210**
Kowalewski, Kim SR ADVISOR - MACROECONOMIC ANALYSIS 458 FHOB **62750**
Lex, Leo DPTY ASST DIR - BUDGET ANALYSIS 430 FHOB **62800**
McClelland, John ASST DIR - TAX ANALYSIS 498E FHOB **62689**
Mosher, David ASST DIR - NATIONAL SECURITY 462 FHOB **62900**
Ruiz, Stephanie DPTY ASST DIR - MGMT, BUSINESS, & INFO SVCS/HUMAN RESOURCES DIR 410 FHOB **62600**
Shirley, Chad DPTY ASST DIR - MICROECONOMIC STUDIES 493 FHOB **62940**
Sunshine, Robert A SR ADVISOR 402 FHOB **62194**
Weaver, David ASST DIR - HEALTH & HUMAN RESOURCES 419 FHOB **62666**
Werling, Jeffrey ASST DIR - MACROECONOMIC ANALYSIS 456D FHOB **62750**

Congressional Ethics, Office of **59739**

  425 3rd St SW, Washington, DC 20024
  Mailing Address: 895 FHOB, Washington, DC 20515

Ashmawy, Omar STAFF DIR/CHIEF COUNSEL 59739
Barnes, Michael D BOARD MBR 59739
Brown, Jeffrey INVESTIGATIVE COUNSEL 59739
Cable, Bill SR COUNSEL 59739
Cho, Annie ANALYST 59739
Eagen, Jay BOARD MBR 59739
Eisner, Helen INVESTIGATIVE COUNSEL 59739
English, Karan BOARD MBR 59739
Flanagan, Mary K ADMIN DIR 59739
Hayward, Allison R CO-CHAIR 59739
Pinckney, Belinda BG (R) BOARD MBR 59739
Skaggs, David E CHAIR 59739
Solis, Paul DPTY CHIEF COUNSEL 59739
Vinovich, Paul BOARD MBR 59739
Westmoreland, Lynn BOARD MBR 59739

Congressional Record

Official Reporters HT59 55621
Record Index Office (GPO) 512-0275
Reprints
Congressional Publishing Services (GPO) 512-0224

Congressional Research Service 75700

To order CRS products by number 75700
To fax a request to CRS 76745
To place a research request 75700
Director 75775
Deputy Director 75775
Office of Finance and Administration 75700
Office of Congressional Information and Publishing 78636
Office of the Counselor to the Director 75775
Office of Workforce Development 78841
American Law Division 76006
Domestic Social Policy Division 76228
Foreign Affairs, Defense, and Trade Division 75050
Government and Finance Division 75821
Knowledge Services Group 78900
Resources, Science, and Industry Division 76044

Congressional Staff Academy B241 LHOB 63800

Congressional Workplace Rights, Office of LA200 724-9250

Altema, Kimberly CASE ADMINISTRATOR LA200 724-9250
Barber, Crystal OCCUPATIONAL SAFETY & HEALTH SPECIALIST LA200 724-9250
Benson, Hillary ASSOC GEN COUNSEL LA200 724-9250
Cech, Laura COMMUNICA DIR LA200 724-9250
Clark, Julie DPTY GEN COUNSEL LA200 724-9250
Crane, Martin DPTY EXEC DIR - SENATE LA200 724-9250
Glover, Shaina ADR SPECIALIST LA200 724-9250
Gogola, Heather ASSOC GEN COUNSEL LA200 724-9250
Grundmann, Susan EXEC DIR LA200 724-9250
James, Teresa DPTY EXEC DIR - HOUSE LA200 724-9250
Jenkins, Simone STAFF ATTORNEY LA200 724-9250
McCuiston, Jennifer ADMIN OFFICER LA200 724-9250
Medicherla, Ravi IT MGR LA200 724-9250
Mizelle, Tiara CHIEF FINANCIAL OFFICER LA200 724-9250
Nester, Mark OCCUPATIONAL SAFETY & HEALTH SPECIALIST LA200 724-9250
Perkins, Shonda OSH INSPECTION COORD LA200 724-9250
Peterson, Jim OCCUPATIONAL SAFETY & HEALTH SPECIALIST LA200 724-9250
Robinson, Christopher SR OCCUPATIONAL SAFETY & HEALTH SPECIALIST LA200 724-9250
Ruvinsky, Alexander CHIEF PERFORMANCE IMPROVEMENT OFFICER LA200 724-9250
Smith, Ganella EDUC & TRAINING PROJ MGR LA200 724-9250
Turbitt, Daniel DIR - ADR PROGRAM LA200 724-9250
Uelmen, John GEN COUNSEL LA200 724-9250

Credit Union

Personal Financial Services 63100

Customer Service Center B227 LHOB 58000

Daily Digest

Floor 51501
Committees 52868

Discharge Petitions HT13 55558
(see Legislative Operations, Office of)

Doctor
(see Attending Physician)

Documents (Bills/Resolutions) B81 CHOB 65200
(see Legislative Resource Center)

Dry Cleaning B239 LHOB 68698

EFT Help Line (Reimbursement Direct Deposit) 62277

Electrician

Capitol 88800
House Office Buildings 54141

Elevators

Capitol 88800
House Office Buildings 54141

Emergency Management, Office of

Speranza, Erik ASST SGT AT ARMS - EMERGENCY MGMT 192 FHOB 60950

Employee Assistance, Office of 140 FHOB **52400**

Enrolling of House Bills HT13 .... **57925**
(see Legislative Operations, Office of)

Envelopes, Public Document
Congressional Publishing Services (GPO) **512-0224**

Equipment **58000**

Executive Communications B81 CHOB **65200**
(see Legislative Resource Center)

Financial Counseling B215 LHOB **57474**

Financial Disclosure Reports B81 CHOB **65200**
(see Legislative Resource Center)

Financial Systems Access and Password Resets for Document Direct, FFS, PD, and Finmart **65800**

First Call B227 LHOB **58000**
Furniture, notary, passports, special events **58000**

Fitness
Gold's Gym **554-4653**
House Staff Fitness Center G2-24 RHOB **51500**
Sport and Health **703-486-3380**

Flags
Flag Office **84239**
Purchase of B217 LHOB **53321**

Food Services
First Call Room Reservations and Special Event Assistance B227 LHOB **58000**
Sodexo **64358**
Cafeterias
- Capitol Market **53919**
- Ford Cafe **63979**
- Longworth Cafe **64359**
- Rayburn Cafe **64358**

Carryout Food Services
- Au Bon Pain 192 CHOB **64358**
- Dunkin' Donuts/Baskin-Robbins B219 LHOB **64359**
- Ford Convenience Store 126 FHOB **52238**
- Longworth Convenience Store B224B LHOB **64359**
- &pizza 2073 RHOB **64358**
- Subway 2025 RHOB **56768**

Catering
- Capitol Host **51403**

Restaurants
- Capitol Visitor Center **593-1785**
- Members' Dining Room Reservations **56300**

Vending **64358**

Franked Mail Expenses (Mass Mailings)
Regulations (Commission on Congressional Mailing Standards) **59337**

Furniture and Furnishings **58000**
(carpet, drapes, file cabinets, lamps, safes, and refrigerators)

Gallery Passes
Sergeant at Arms H124 .... **52456**

Garages (see Parking Permits & Security)

General Counsel
Letter, Douglas N GENERAL COUNSEL CHOB 219 .... **59700**

Gift Shops
Capitol Visitor Center Gift Shop HVC103 .... **593-1903**
Gift Shop B218 LHOB **65362**

Government Publishing Office
Publications Ordering Desk
- Congressional Publications **512-1808**
- Departmental Publications **512-1808**

Office of Congressional Publishing Services **512-0224**
Congressional Record Mail List Information **512-0224**
Public Document Envelopes **512-0224**
Receiving and Shipping Clerks
- Wilson, Randy T SUPERVISOR **51565**

Gym
(see Fitness)

Health Units
CHOB
- Nurse 110 .... **53470**

CVC
- Nurse HVC 100 .... **55442**

FHOB
- Nurse 145 .... **52442**

LHOB
- Nurse 1204 .... **52500**

OHOB
- Nurse 4160 .... **60800**

RHOB
- Nurse 2050 .... **57131**
- Medical Surveillance G2-050 .... **50611**

Capitol (House)
- OAP, Nurse H166 .... **55421**

GENERAL SUPPORT SERVICES

Capitol (Senate)
Capitol Health Unit S153 ..... **64830**

House Creative Services 2002 ..... **52700**

House Employment Counsel, Office of 4300 OHOB **57075**

House Historian, Office of
Wasniewski, Matthew A HOUSE HISTORIAN LJ - ATTIC **61300**

House Information Resources
Information Technology Support Call Center **56002**

House Library 292 CHOB **59000**

House Vacancy Announcement and Placement Service (HVAPS) 102 FHOB **52926**

Human Resources (CAO) 102 FHOB **52926**
Office of Administration 102 FHOB **52926**

Identification Cards
Members
Office of the Clerk H154 ..... **57000**
Officers, employees, Members' spouses, interns, liaison personnel
Sergeant at Arms 321 CHOB **53820**
For Press:
House Daily Press Gallery H319 ..... **53945**
House Periodical Press Gallery H304 ..... **52941**
House Radio and Television Gallery H320 ..... **55214**

Information Technology Support
(see House Information Resources)

Inspector General, Office of
Ptasienski, Michael INSPECTOR GENERAL 386 FHOB ... **61250**

Interparliamentary Affairs, Office of
Knudson, Kate DIR HC4 ..... **61766**

Job Line **64504**

Journal, House HT13 ..... **55558**
(see Legislative Operations, Office of)

Laborers' Room
Capitol **88800**

House Office Buildings (Superintendent's Office) **54141**

Ladies' Reading Room
Lindy Claiborne Boggs Congressional Women's Reading Room H235 ..... **54196**

Law Library
(see Library of Congress)

Law Revision Counsel
Seep, Ralph V LAW REVISION COUNSEL 308 FHOB **62411**

Legal Counsel
(see General Counsel)

Legislative Computer Systems 2401 ..... **51182**

Legislative Counsel
Ballou, Wade LEGISLATIVE COUNSEL 337 FHOB **56060**

Legislative Operations, Office of HT13 ..... **57925**

Legislative Resource Center B81 CHOB **65200**

Library of Congress
Loan Division:
To fax a request **75986**
To order books **75445**
To return books **75717**
Questions about accounts **75441**
Congressional Relations Office **76577**
Law Library LM-240 ..... **75065**
Law Library Reading Room LM-242 ..... **75080**
Visitor Services Office LJ-G59 ..... **79779**
Congressional Tours **74683**

Library Services 292 CHOB **59000**
(see Legislative Resource Center)

Lobbying Registrations/Reports B81 CHOB **65200**
(see Legislative Resource Center)

Locksmith (desks, file cabinets, and safes) **58000**

Machine Shop (sheet metal for Capitol only) **88800**

Mail Collection
(see Postal Services Call Center)

Mail List Processing B227 LHOB **54355**

Mass Mailings
Payments (see Financial Counseling)
Approval (CHA Franking)
Mail List Processing **54355**
NCOA (National Change of Address) **54355**

Members and Family Committee Room H324 .... **50622**

Office Supply Service B217 LHOB **53321**

Official Reporters
Committees 1718 .... **52627**
Floor HT59 .... **55621**

Operators
(see Telephone Exchange)

Painters
Capitol **88800**
House Office Buildings **54141**

Parking Permits & Security
Abbott, Jim DIR - HOUSE GARAGES & PARKING SECURITY
G2-28 RHOB **56749**
Fax **61950**
CHOB **55090**
RHOB
First St G2-28 .... **56750**
C St G3-22 .... **54310**
Underground Garage
East, B Level **57565**
West, B Level **57600**
Parking Lot 1st & C St SE **65457**

Parliamentarian
Wickham, Thomas J, Jr PARLIAMENTARIAN H209 .... **57373**

Payroll and Benefits
Members **53644**
Staff **51435**

Periodical Press Gallery
Zatkowski, Robert DIR H304 .... **52941**

Plumber
Capitol **88800**
House Office Buildings **54141**

Police (Capitol)
Fire **911**
Medical Emergency **911**
Emergency **911**
TTY **80911**
Chief of Police USCP HQ **49806**
Capitol Division Police Office CVC315 .... **42985**
Capitol Police Office of Professional Responsibility **512-2170**
Chief Administrative Officer USCP HQ **593-3500**
Chief of Operations USCP HQ **49806**
Command Center USCP HQ **40908**
Communications **45152**
General Counsel USCP HQ **593-3619**
Headquarters 119 D St NE **45151**
House Division Police Office B220 LHOB **50400**
Investigations Division USCP HQ (Criminal) **40928**
Lost and Found B220 LHOB **50400**
Patrol Division Police Office USCP HQ **593-3720**
Protective Services Bureau USCP HQ **228-3100**
Public Information Office USCP HQ **41677**
Senate Division Police Office USCP HQ **44841**
Special Events Section USCP HQ **48891**
Threat Assessment Section USCP HQ **41495**
Uniformed Services Bureau USCP HQ **49810**

Post Office (U.S. Postal Service)
Ford 121 .... **65413**
Longworth B202 .... **65425**

Postal Services Call Center **56000**

Power Plant
Potter, Chris DIR 25 E ST SE **63864**

Press Gallery
Tin, Annie DIR H315 .... **53945**

Public Document Envelopes
Congressional Publishing Services (GPO) **512-0224**

Publication Services B81 CHOB **65200**

Radio and Television Gallery
Ramirez Kornacki, Olga DIR H320 .... **55214**

Reading Clerks HT13 .... **57925**
(see Legislative Operations, Office of)

Recording Studio 2010 .... **53941**

Recycling
Capitol HT42 .... **88800**
House Office Buildings 2042 .... **54141**

Restaurants
(see Food Services)

Resume Referral Service
(see House Vacancy Announcement and Placement Service)

Salon Services
Barber Shop 2023 .... **57024**

Sergeant at Arms
Irving, Paul D SERGEANT AT ARMS H124 .... **52456**

Sheet Metal Shop
Capitol **88800**
House Office Buildings **54141**

Shoe Shine
Ford HOB 3rd St Entrance **62236**
Barber Shop 2023 .... **57024**

Social Security
Liaison Office G1 RHOB, Lobby 3 .... **53133**

Speaker of the House
Speaker's Office
Nancy Pelosi, Speaker H232 .... **50100**
Speaker's Floor Office H209 .... **53400**
Speaker's Congressional Office 1236 .... **54965**

State Department
Liaison Office 2028 .... **64642**

Stationery Store
(see Office Supply Service)

Superintendent of Buildings
(see Building Superintendents)

Superintendent's Office
Capitol **88800**
House Office Buildings **54141**

Telephone Exchange **43121**

Telephone Repair **56002**

Voting Records HT13 .... **57925**
(see Legislative Operations, Office of)

HOUSE COMMISSIONS

COMMISSION ON CONGRESSIONAL MAILING STANDARDS

1307 LONGWORTH HOB 59337

Members not yet named

MAJORITY STAFF

Allen, Aaron PROF STAFF 1307 59337
Arias, Hector STAFF ASST 1307 59337
DeFreitas, Matt STAFF DIR 1307 59337
Wright, Gina PROF STAFF 1307 59337

MINORITY STAFF

Sullivan, Tim STAFF DIR - MIN 1216 60647

COMMISSION ON SECURITY AND COOPERATION IN EUROPE

234 FORD HOB 51901

Hon. Alcee L. Hastings, FL, Chairman
Hon. Roger F. Wicker, MS, Co-Chairman
Hon. Benjamin L. Cardin, MD, Ranking Member
Hon. Christopher H. Smith, NJ, Ranking Member
Hon. Robert B. Aderholt, AL
Hon. John Boozman, AR
Hon. Michael C. Burgess, TX
Hon. Steve Cohen, TN
Hon. Richard Hudson, NC
Hon. Sheila Jackson Lee, TX
Hon. Gwen Moore, WI
Hon. Marco Rubio, FL
Hon. Jeanne Shaheen, NH
Hon. Thom Tillis, NC
Hon. Tom Udall, NM
Hon. Sheldon Whitehouse, RI

EXECUTIVE BRANCH COMMISSIONERS

Department of State VACANT
Department of Commerce VACANT
Department of Defense VACANT

COMMISSION STAFF

Bauman, Rachel POLICY ADVISOR 234 FHOB 51901
Hand, Robert POLICY ADVISOR 234 FHOB 51901
Helwig, Janice POLICY ADVISOR 234 FHOB 51901
Hollabaugh, Allison COUNSEL 234 FHOB 51901
Hope, Stacy COMMUNICATIONS DIR 234 FHOB 51901
Hurd, Nathaniel POLICY ADVISOR 234 FHOB 51901
Johnson, Alex CHIEF OF STAFF 234 FHOB 51901
Massaro, A Paul, III POLICY ADVISOR 234 FHOB 51901
Parker, Allison COUNSEL 234 FHOB 51901
Parker, Kyle SR SENATE STAFF REP 234 FHOB 51901
Price, Everett POLICY ADVISOR 234 FHOB 51901
Schlager, Erika COUNSEL 234 FHOB 51901
Thompson, Mischa POLICY ADVISOR 234 FHOB 51901
Tiersky, Alex POLICY ADVISOR 234 FHOB 51901
Toner, Mark SR ADVISOR 234 FHOB 51901
Warlick, Jordan OFFICE DIR 234 FHOB 51901

CONGRESSIONAL-EXECUTIVE COMMISSION ON THE PEOPLE'S REPUBLIC OF CHINA

243 FORD HOB 63766

Hon. James P. McGovern, MA, Chairman
Hon. Marco Rubio, FL, Co-Chairman
Hon. Marcy Kaptur, OH
Hon. Thomas R. Suozzi, NY
Hon. Tom Malinowski, NJ
Hon. Ben McAdams, UT
Hon. Christopher H. Smith, NJ
Hon. Brian J. Mast, FL
Hon. James Lankford, OK
Hon. Tom Cotton, AR
Hon. Steve Daines, MT
Hon. Todd Young, IN

COMMISSION STAFF

Adams, Luke RESEARCH ASSOC 243 FHOB 63766
Andrews, Steve COUNSEL 243 FHOB 63832
Chen, Mingzhi RESEARCH ASSOC 243 FHOB 63795
Flipse, Scott COMMUNICATIONS DIR 243 FHOB 63777
Fluker, Megan RESEARCH ASSOC 243 FHOB 63831
Jin, Sophie RESEARCH ASSOC 243 FHOB 63778
Lindblom, John RESEARCH ASSOC 243 FHOB 63766
Petrick, David RESEARCH ASSOC 243 FHOB 63766
Reger, Amy RESEARCH ASSOC 243 FHOB 63769
Salen, Jen SR RESEARCH ASSOC 243 FHOB 63766
Stivers, Jon STAFF DIR 243 FHOB 63766
Tsai, Sabrina RESEARCH ASSOC 243 FHOB 63833
Wong, Andy COUNSEL 243 FHOB 63791
Wright, Judy ADMIN DIR 243 FHOB 63767

TOM LANTOS HUMAN RIGHTS COMMISSION

5100 O'NEILL HOB 53599

Hon. James P. McGovern, MA, Co-Chairman
Hon. Christopher H. Smith, NJ, Co-Chairman

HOUSE COMMISSIONS

COMMISSION STAFF

Berman, Rosie STAFF ASSOC 5100 .... **65285**
Stanton, Kimberly SR PROF STAFF 5100 .... **58097**
Tozzi, Piero SR PROF STAFF 5100 .... **53765**

PARTY ORGANIZATIONS

Three-digit room numbers are in the Cannon HOB or the Ford HOB, as indicated. Four-digit room numbers beginning with 1 are in the Longworth HOB, and four-digit room numbers beginning with 2 are in the Rayburn HOB.

Capitol room numbers begin with SB, ST, HB and HT or with H or S, followed by three digits.

Calls from outside the Capitol complex can be made by dialing (202) 22 plus the five-digit number listed in this directory.

HOUSE DEMOCRATIC CAUCUS

B245 LONGWORTH HOB (ZIP: 20515) 225-1400

Hon. Hakeem S. Jeffries, CHAIRMAN
Hon. Katherine M. Clark, VICE CHAIR

Alcala, Sandra DIR - MEMB SVCS.......... **51400**
Araya, Meseret POLICY ADVISOR.......... **51400**
Bragin, Gideon EXEC DIR.......... **51400**
Byon, Fiona DIGITAL ASST.......... **51400**
Carrillo, Manuel Joe DIR - OPS.......... **51400**
Dawson, Earnestine DIGITAL DIR.......... **51400**
Foster Stickney, Lakecia POLICY DIR.......... **51400**
Hardaway, Michael COMMUNICATIONS DIR/SR ADVISOR.......... **51400**
Leibell, Zach DPTY PRESS SECY.......... **51400**
Miller, Rikki PRESS ASST.......... **51400**
Nelson, Jacob POLICY ASSOC.......... **51400**
Rudd, Diana VICE CHAIR COUN/VICE CHAIR DIR - MEMB SVCS.. **51400**
Ruiz, Xenia VICE CHAIR DIR - OUTREACH.......... **51400**
Sachse, Andrew DPTY DIR - MBR SVCS.......... **51400**
Scheuer, Alex CAUCUS ASST.......... **51400**
Stephenson, Christiana PRESS SECY.......... **51400**

HOUSE DEMOCRATIC CONGRESSIONAL CAMPAIGN COMMITTEE

430 S CAPITOL ST SE, 2ND FLOOR (ZIP: 20003) 863-1500

Hon. Cheri Bustos, CHAIR

Benton, Charles DIR - MBR SVCS.......... **863-1500**
Boysen, Dan NATIONAL FINANCE DIR.......... **863-1500**
Forte-Mackay, Jackie CHIEF FINANCIAL OFFICER.......... **863-1500**
Jaslow, Allison EXEC DIR.......... **863-1500**
Kazin, Danny DPTY EXEC DIR/DIR - CAMPAIGNS.......... **863-1500**
Kozloski, Kory NATIONAL POLITICAL DIR - FRONTLINE.......... **863-1500**
Marron, Brenna DIR - MBR ENGAGEMENT & POLITICAL STRATEGY.......... **863-1500**
Newman, Jacqui CHIEF OPERATING OFFICER.......... **863-1500**
Pancrazio, Nick DPTY EXEC DIR - ADMINISTRATION & PLANNING.......... **863-1500**
Ritner, Molly NATIONAL POLITICAL DIR - CAMPAIGNS & RECRUITMENT.......... **863-1500**
Smith, Jared COMMUNICATIONS DIR.......... **863-1500**
Smith, Mike DPTY EXEC DIR - FINANCE & MBR ENGAGEMENT.......... **863-1500**
Thompson, Ryan CHIEF DIGITAL OFFICER.......... **863-1500**

HOUSE DEMOCRATIC POLICY AND COMMUNICATIONS COMMITTEE

HB18 CAPITOL (ZIP: 20515) 226-8468

Hon. David N. Cicilline, CHAIRMAN
Hon. Matt Cartwright, CO-CHAIR
Hon. Debbie Dingell, CO-CHAIR
Hon. Ted Lieu, CO-CHAIR

Androff, Blake EXEC DIR.......... **68468**
LaRosa, Michael COMMUNICATIONS DIR.......... **67204**
York, Jemma DPTY DIR.......... **50251**

HOUSE DEMOCRATIC STEERING AND POLICY COMMITTEE

H232 CAPITOL (ZIP: 20515) 225-0100

Hon. Nancy Pelosi, CHAIR
Hon. Rosa L. DeLauro, CO-CHAIR
Hon. Barbara Lee, CO-CHAIR
Hon. Eric Swalwell, CO-CHAIR
Hon. Donald Norcross, PARLIAMENTARIAN

HOUSE REPUBLICAN CONFERENCE

1420 LONGWORTH HOB (ZIP: 20515) 225-5107

Hon. Liz Cheney, CHAIR
Hon. Mark Walker, VICE CHAIR
Hon. Jason Smith, SECRETARY

Adler, Jeremy COMMUNICATIONS DIR.......... **55107**
Ahern, Kara CHIEF OF STAFF.......... **55107**
Anderson, Morgan DIGITAL DIR.......... **55107**
Boothe, Caroline DIR - MBR SVCS.......... **55107**
Drzewicki, John POLICY DIR.......... **55107**
Guaglianone, Paul DIR - COALITIONS.......... **55107**
Henderson, William SPECIAL ASST TO THE CHAIR.......... **55107**
Hofmann, Ryan LEGIS ASST.......... **55107**
Johnson, Natalie DPTY PRESS SECY.......... **55107**
Lifhits, Jenna DPTY POLICY DIR.......... **55107**
Martin, Christopher DIR - RAPID RESPONSE.......... **55107**
Pardo, Ali NATIONAL PRESS SECY.......... **55107**
Plaut, Brian DIR - OPS.......... **55107**
Porter, Megan MBR SVCS ASST.......... **55107**
Sullivan, Michael POLICY COORD.......... **55107**
Sun, Kevin STAFF ASST.......... **55107**
Thorne, Dray DIR - INFO TECH.......... **55107**

HOUSE REPUBLICAN POLICY COMMITTEE

207 CANNON HOB (ZIP: 20515) **225-4921**

Hon. Gary J. Palmer, CHAIRMAN

Smith, Cameron EXEC DIR.......... **54921**
Wall, Kelsey SR POLICY ADVISOR.......... **54921**

HOUSE REPUBLICAN STUDY COMMITTEE

418 CANNON HOB (ZIP: 20515) **225-2777**

Hon. Mike Johnson, CHAIRMAN

Bonifacio, Noelani POLICY STAFF.......... **52777**
Dickerson, Matt POLICY DIR.......... **52777**
Fields, Jay POLICY STAFF.......... **52777**
Holyfield, Ainsley COMMUNICATIONS DIR.......... **52777**
Lincoln, Amanda POLICY STAFF.......... **52777**
Proffitt, Gavin POLICY STAFF.......... **52777**
Rodman, Nicholas POLICY STAFF.......... **52777**
Schutte, Corinna DIGITAL ASST.......... **52777**
Stern, Richard POLICY STAFF.......... **52777**
Walker, Alexa DIR - OUTREACH & COALITIONS.......... **52777**
Weinhart, Jennifer POLICY STAFF.......... **52777**
Woltornist, Alexei COMMUNICATIONS DIR.......... **52777**
Ziegler, Daniel EXEC DIR.......... **52777**

NATIONAL REPUBLICAN CONGRESSIONAL COMMITTEE

320 1ST ST SE (ZIP: 20003) **479-7000**

Hon. Tom Emmer, CHAIRMAN

Hoffnagle, Nick DIR - DATA.......... **479-7000**
Klein, Dana DIR - FINANCE.......... **479-7000**
Munschauer, Lyman DIGITAL DIR.......... **479-7000**
Pack, Chris COMMUNICATIONS DIR.......... **479-7000**
Poling, Parker EXEC DIR.......... **479-7000**
Richards, Justin POLITICAL DIR.......... **479-7000**
Wall, Matt RESEARCH DIR.......... **479-7000**
Winkelman, Chris GEN COUNSEL.......... **479-7000**
Wissmann, Yvette POLICY DIR.......... **479-7000**

CONGRESSIONAL MEMBER ORGANIZATIONS

The inclusion of organizations on this list is subject to the approval of the Committee on House Administration.

The most recent version of this list is available at http://cha.house.gov/

Access to Legal Aid Caucus

Rep. Susan W. Brooks
Rep. Debbie Dingell
Rep. Joseph P. Kennedy III
Rep. Fred Upton

Rob Hicks 52276
Natalie Martinez 54071
Eric Fins 55931
Katherine Moffitt 53761

Addiction, Treatment and Recovery Caucus

Rep. David P. Joyce
Rep. Tim Ryan
Rep. F. James Sensenbrenner, Jr.
Rep. Paul Tonko

Catherine Wilson 55731
Lauren Harris 55261
Amy Bos 55101
Jeff Morgan 55076

Adult Literacy Caucus

Rep. David P. Roe
Rep. John A. Yarmuth

Alex Mackey 55714
Erica DiCio 55401

Agriculture Research Caucus

Rep. Rodney Davis
Rep. Jimmy Panetta

Janie Costa 52371
Brandon Honeycutt 52861

Air Force Caucus

Rep. Kathy Castor
Rep. John Garamendi
Rep. Adam Kinzinger
Rep. Michael R. Turner

Elizabeth Brown 53376
Betsy Thompson 51880
Sebastian DeLuca 53635
Courtney Kum 56465

Airborne ISR Caucus

Rep. Don Bacon
Rep. John Garamendi

Patrick Flood 54155
Betsy Thompson 51880

Algae Caucus

Rep. Andy Biggs
Rep. Derek Kilmer
Rep. Darin LaHood
Rep. Scott H. Peters

Cesar Ybarra 52635
Katie Allen 55916
Ashley Antoskiewicz 56201
Andis Borja 50508

Aluminum Caucus

Rep. Larry Bucshon
Rep. Suzan K. DelBene
Rep. Bill Johnson
Rep. David Loebsack

Susey Davis 44636
Shantanu Tata 56311
David Rardin 57505
Will Collier 56576

Alzheimer's Caucus

Rep. Christopher H. Smith
Rep. Maxine Waters

Kelsey Griswold 53765
Kathleen Sengstock 52201

Animal Protection Caucus

Rep. Earl Blumenauer
Rep. Larry Bucshon

Kevin Stockert 54811
Christian Spencer 55015

Anti-Terrorism & Proliferation Financing Caucus

Rep. Peter T. King
Rep. Stephen F. Lynch

Tim Ursprung 57896
Kevin Ryan 58273

Appalachian National Scenic Trail Caucus

Rep. Donald S. Beyer, Jr.
Rep. David P. Roe

Kate Schisler 54376
Kyle Jacobs 56356

CONGRESSIONAL MEMBER ORGANIZATIONS

The inclusion of organizations on this list is subject to the approval of the Committee on House Administration.

The most recent version of this list is available at http://cha.house.gov

Apprenticeship Caucus

Rep. Susan A. Davis
Rep. Brett Guthrie

Brandon Mendoza 52040
Elaina Murphy 53501

Arctic Working Group Caucus

Rep. Rick Larsen
Rep. Don Young

J Z Golden 52605
Cameron Humphrey 55765

Army Caucus

Rep. John R. Carter
Rep. C. A. Dutch Ruppersberger

Karl Yurik 53864
Justin Brower 53061

Army Corps of Engineers Reform Caucus

Rep. Doug Collins

William Smith 59893

Artificial Intelligence Caucus

Rep. Jerry McNerney
Rep. Pete Olson

Svetlana Matt 51947
Michael Richards 55951

Arts Caucus

Rep. Chellie Pingree
Rep. Elise M. Stefanik

Evan Johnston 56116
Patrick Hester 54611

ASEAN Caucus

Rep. Joaquin Castro
Rep. Ann Wagner

Danielle Moon 53236
Rachel Wagley 51621

Autism Research and Education Caucus

Rep. Michael F. Doyle
Rep. Christopher H. Smith

Kate Werley 52135
Kelsey Griswold 53765

Auto Care Caucus

Rep. Brendan F. Boyle
Rep. Scott Perry

Helena Mastrogianis 56111
Patrick Schilling 55836

Automotive Caucus

Rep. Marcy Kaptur
Rep. Mike Kelly

Jenny Perrino 54146
Brendan Fulmer 55406

Automotive Performance and Motorsports Caucus

Rep. Sanford D. Bishop, Jr.
Rep. Bill Posey

Jonathan Black 53631
Rick Podliska 53671

Azerbaijan Caucus

Rep. Steve Chabot
Rep. Steve Cohen

Mark Erste 52216
Betsy Dudley 53265

Beef Caucus

Rep. Henry Cuellar
Rep. Roger W. Marshall

Zack Linick 51640
Dalton Henry 52715

Biofuels Caucus

Rep. Rodney Davis
Rep. David Loebsack
Rep. Roger W. Marshall
Rep. Collin C. Peterson

Jimmy Ballard 52371
Will Collier 56576
Dalton Henry 52715
Zach Martin 52165

CONGRESSIONAL MEMBER ORGANIZATIONS

The inclusion of organizations on this list is subject to the approval of the Committee on House Administration.

The most recent version of this list is available at http://cha.house.gov/

Biomedical Research Caucus

Rep. Steve Cohen
Rep. John R. Curtis
Rep. Jackie Speier
Rep. Steve Stivers

Lauren Citron 53265
Liz Whitlock 57751
Molly Fishman 53531
Drew Hatter 52015

Bipartisan Congressional Refugee Caucus

Rep. Mario Diaz-Balart
Rep. Zoe Lofgren
Rep. Joe Neguse
Rep. Christopher H. Smith

Cesar Gonzalez 54211
Sarnata Reynolds 60614
Miya Patel 61125
Courtney Fellows 53765

Bipartisan Task Force for Combating Anti-Semitism

Rep. Theodore E. Deutch
Rep. Eliot L. Engel
Rep. Brian K. Fitzpatrick
Rep. Kay Granger
Rep. Nita M. Lowey
Rep. Christopher H. Smith
Rep. Marc A. Veasey
Rep. Randy K. Weber Sr.

Jason Attermann 53001
Rachel Levitan 68467
Joseph Knowles 54276
Suzi Plasencia 55021
Liz Leibowitz 56505
Nathaniel Hurd 54051
Thaddeus Woody 59897
Chara McMichael 52831

Black Maternal Health Caucus

Rep. Alma S. Adams
Rep. Lauren Underwood

Kichelle Webster 51510
Andrea Harris 52976

Black Men and Boys Caucus

Rep. Danny K. Davis
Rep. Eleanor Holmes Norton

Lavell Brown 55006
Hazle Crawford 58050

Black Women and Girls Caucus

Rep. Yvette D. Clarke
Rep. Robin L. Kelly
Rep. Bonnie Watson Coleman

Kwamme Anderson 56231
Mia Keeys 50773
Courtney Cochran 55801

Blue Collar Caucus

Rep. Brendan F. Boyle
Rep. Marc A. Veasey

Helena Schwarz 56111
Thaddeus Woody 59897

Boating Caucus

Rep. Lois Frankel
Rep. Jackie Walorski

Bradley Solyan 59890
Mike Dankler 53915

Border Security Caucus

Rep. Brian Babin
Rep. Andy Biggs

Lauren Ziegler 51555
Kate LaBorde 52635

Bosnia Caucus

Rep. Eddie Bernice Johnson
Rep. Christopher H. Smith

Nawaid Ladak 58885
Kelsey Griswold 53765

Bourbon Caucus

Rep. Andy Barr
Rep. John A. Yarmuth

Claire Osborn 54706
Katy Rowley 55401

Brazil Caucus

Rep. Darin LaHood
Rep. Gregory W. Meeks

Ashley Antoskiewicz 56201
Florence Akinyemi 53461
Sophia Lafargue 53461

CONGRESSIONAL MEMBER ORGANIZATIONS

The inclusion of organizations on this list is subject to the approval of the Committee on House Administration.

The most recent version of this list is available at http://cha.house.gov

Building Trades Caucus

Rep. David B. McKinley
Rep. Donald Norcross

Mike Hamilton 54172
Vincent Sarubbi 56501

Burn Pits Caucus

Rep. Raul Ruiz
Rep. Brad R. Wenstrup

Ivelisse Porroa 55330
Greg Brooks 53164

Bus Caucus

Rep. Darin LaHood
Rep. Rick Larsen

Samantha Dybas 56201
Alexandra Menardy 52605

Buy American Caucus

Rep. David P. Joyce
Rep. Daniel Lipinski

Catherine Wilson 55731
Sofya Leonova 55701

California Aerospace Caucus

Rep. Ken Calvert
Rep. Ted Lieu

Rebecca Keightley 51986
Corey Jacobson 53976

California Democratic Congressional Delegation

Rep. Zoe Lofgren

Matt Weiner 53072

Cambodia Caucus

Rep. Steve Chabot
Rep. Alan S. Lowenthal

Mark Erste 52216
Ngoc Nguyen 57924

Candy Caucus

Rep. Ann M. Kuster
Rep. Jackie Walorski

Travis Krogman 55206
Martin Schultz 53915

Cannabis Caucus

Rep. Earl Blumenauer
Rep. David P. Joyce
Rep. Barbara Lee
Rep. Don Young

Laura Thrif 54811
Kendall Kalagher 55731
Diala Jadallah-Redding 52661
Jesse von Stein 55765

Career and Technical Education Caucus

Rep. James R. Langevin
Rep. Glenn Thompson

Kerry McKittrick 52735
Nick Rockwell 55121

Chemistry Caucus

Rep. Daniel Lipinski
Rep. John R. Moolenaar

Joel Creswell 55701
Eva Cline 53561

Chesapeake Bay Watershed Task Force

Rep. Andy Harris
Rep. John P. Sarbanes
Rep. Robert C. "Bobby" Scott
Rep. Robert J. Wittman

Tim Daniels 55311
Timia Crisp 54016
Natalie Valentine 58351
Brent Robinson 54261

Chicken Caucus

Rep. Jim Costa
Rep. Steve Womack

Ben Goldeen 53341
Nick Runkel 54301

Childhood Cancer Caucus

Rep. G. K. Butterfield
Rep. Mike Kelly
Rep. Michael T. McCaul
Rep. Jackie Speier

Dennis Sills 53101
Brendan Fulmer 55406
Thomas Rice 52401
Molly Fishman 53531

CONGRESSIONAL MEMBER ORGANIZATIONS

The inclusion of organizations on this list is subject to the approval of the Committee on House Administration.

The most recent version of this list is available at http://cha.house.gov/

Chronic Obstructive Pulmonary Disease (COPD) Caucus

Rep. John Lewis
Rep. Chris Stewart

Thomas Dorney 53801
Luci Arveseth 59730

Civility & Respect Caucus

Rep. Joyce Beatty
Rep. Steve Stivers

Nicholas Semanko 54324
Nick Bush 52015

Coal Caucus

Rep. David B. McKinley

Brian Garand 54172

Colombia Caucus

Rep. Mario Diaz-Balart
Rep. Gregory W. Meeks
Rep. Francis Rooney

Gisselle Reynolds 54211
Florence Akinyemi 53461
Corey Schrodt 52536

Colorado River Caucus

Rep. Paul A. Gosar

Rory Burke 52315

Community Health Centers Caucus

Rep. Danny K. Davis
Rep. Kay Granger
Rep. Elise M. Stefanik

Caleb Gilchrist 55006
Suzi Plasencia 55071
Julia Angelotti 54611

Congenital Heart Caucus

Rep. Gus M. Bilirakis
Rep. Adam B. Schiff

Shayne Woods 55755
Anthony Theissen 54176

Copper Caucus

Rep. Brian Higgins
Rep. Robert E. Latta

Kayla Williams 53306
Mike Davin 56405

Corrosion Prevention Caucus

Rep. Daniel T. Kildee
Rep. Pete Olson

Jordan Dickinson 53611
Michael Richards 55951

Cure Blood Cancers and Other Blood Disorders

Rep. Gus M. Bilirakis
Rep. Doris O. Matsui

Shayne Woods 55755
Kristen Donheffner 57163

Cut Flower Caucus

Rep. Salud O. Carbajal

Erin Sandlin 53601

Cybersecurity Caucus

Rep. James R. Langevin
Rep. Michael T. McCaul

Nick Leiserson 52735
Thomas Rice 52401

Czech Caucus

Rep. Debbie Dingell
Rep. Janice D. Schakowsky
Rep. Ron Wright

Timothy Huebner 54071
Robert Marcus 66890
Blair Rotert 52002

Dairy Farmer Caucus

Rep. Joe Courtney
Rep. Suzan K. DelBene
Rep. Sean P. Duffy
Rep. Tom Reed
Rep. Michael K. Simpson
Rep. Peter Welch

Alexa Combelic 52076
Shantanu Tata 56311
Ryan McCormack 53365
Samara Brown 53161
James Neill 55531
Mark Fowler 54115

CONGRESSIONAL MEMBER ORGANIZATIONS

The inclusion of organizations on this list is subject to the approval of the Committee on House Administration.
The most recent version of this list is available at http://cha.house.gov

Diabetes Caucus

Rep. Diana DeGette
Rep. Tom Reed

Sahil Chaudhary 54431
Logan Hoover 53161

Dietary Supplement Caucus

Rep. Tony Cárdenas
Rep. John R. Curtis
Rep. Andy Harris

Jose Villalvazo 56131
Liz Whitlock 57751
John Dutton 55311

Digital Trade Caucus

Rep. Suzan K. DelBene
Rep. Darin LaHood

Shantanu Tata 56311
Ashley Antoskiewicz 56201

Direct Selling Caucus

Rep. Richard Hudson
Rep. Marc A. Veasey

Dyslexia Caucus

Rep. Julia Brownley
Rep. Bruce Westerman

Gavin Ross 55811
Emily Mace 53772

E-Commerce Caucus

Rep. Pete Aguilar
Rep. Brett Guthrie

Chelsea Glynn 53201
Katherine Fleming 53501

Effective Foreign Assistance Caucus

Rep. Adam Smith
Rep. Ted S. Yoho

Connor Stubbs 58901
Lauren Gillespie 55744

Elder Justice Caucus

Rep. Suzanne Bonamici
Rep. Peter T. King

Allison Smith 50855
Deena Tauster 57896

Electromagnetic Pulse Caucus

Rep. Yvette D. Clarke
Rep. Doug Lamborn

Charlyn Stanberry 56231
Andrew Braun 54422

Electronic Warfare Working Group

Rep. Don Bacon
Rep. James R. Langevin
Rep. Rick Larsen
Rep. Austin Scott

Patrick Flood 54155
Leigh Maiden 52735
J Z Golden 52605
Michael Tehrani 56531

End Sexual Violence Task Force

Rep. David P. Joyce
Rep. John Katko
Rep. Ann M. Kuster
Rep. Jackie Speier

Kendall Kalagher 55731
Tristan Southard 53701
Sam Cooper-Wall 55206
Molly Fishman 53531

Energy Caucus

Rep. Sheila Jackson Lee
Rep. Bobby L. Rush

Lillie Coney 53816
John Marshall 54372

Energy Savings Performance Caucus

Rep. Richard Hudson
Rep. Adam Kinzinger
Rep. Seth Moulton
Rep. Peter Welch

Elliott Guffin 53715
Michael Mansour 53635
Charlotte Mooney 58020
Mark Fowler 54115

CONGRESSIONAL MEMBER ORGANIZATIONS

The inclusion of organizations on this list is subject to the approval of the Committee on House Administration.

The most recent version of this list is available at http://cha.house.gov/

Estuary Caucus

Rep. Suzanne Bonamici
Rep. Rick Larsen
Rep. Brian J. Mast
Rep. Bill Posey

Maxine Sugarman 50855
Alexandra Menardy 52605
Barry Smith 53026
Valentina Valenta 53671

Ethiopian-American Caucus

Rep. John Garamendi
Rep. Joe Wilson

Betsy Thompson 51880
Oren Adaki 55931

Ethnic and Religious Freedom in Sri Lanka

Rep. Danny K. Davis
Rep. Bill Johnson

Caleb Gilchrist 55006
Laura Wilson 55705

EU Caucus

Rep. Gregory W. Meeks
Rep. Joe Wilson

Florence Akinyemi 53461
Oren Adaki 52452

Everglades Caucus

Rep. Mario Diaz-Balart
Rep. Alcee L. Hastings

Chris Sweet 54211
Lindsey Garber 51313

Explosive Ordnance Disposal Caucus

Rep. Eric A. "Rick" Crawford
Rep. Susan A. Davis
Rep. Brian J. Mast
Rep. Jimmy Panetta

Abbi Burgess 54076
Ian Staples 52040
Barry Smith 53026
Matt Manning 52861

Financial and Economic Literacy Caucus

Rep. Joyce Beatty
Rep. Steve Stivers

Scott Farnin 54324
Mark Gilbride 52015

Fintech and Payments Caucus

Rep. Barry Loudermilk
Rep. David Scott

Colin Carr 52931
Catherine Kuerbitz 52939

Flat Tax Caucus

Rep. Michael C. Burgess

Rachel Huggins 57772

Foster Youth Caucus

Rep. Don Bacon
Rep. Karen Bass
Rep. James R. Langevin
Rep. Brenda L. Lawrence
Rep. Paul Mitchell

Rachel Pearce 54155
Nina DeJonghe 57084
Kerry McKittrick 52735
Alex Huang 55802
Sarah Feldpausch 52106

Fourth Amendment Caucus

Rep. Justin Amash
Rep. Zoe Lofgren

Carolyn Iodice 53831
Z J Hull 53072

Fragrance Caucus

Rep. Barry Loudermilk
Rep. Bonnie Watson Coleman

Eric Johnson 68726
Kevin Block 67303

Freshman Working Group on Addiction

Rep. David J. Trone

Christina Tsafoulias 52721

Friends of a Free, Stable, and Democratic Syria Caucuses

Rep. Brendan F. Boyle
Rep. Adam Kinzinger

Carly Frame 56111
Sebastian DeLuca 53635

CONGRESSIONAL MEMBER ORGANIZATIONS

The inclusion of organizations on this list is subject to the approval of the Committee on House Administration.

The most recent version of this list is available at http://cha.house.gov

Friends of Australia Caucus

Rep. Joe Courtney
Rep. Mike Gallagher

Claire Wardius 52076
Charles Morrison 55665

Friends of Denmark Caucus

Rep. Tom Cole
Rep. Steny H. Hoyer

Maria Bowie 56165
Daniel Silverberg 56631

Friends of Egypt Caucus

Rep. Jeff Fortenberry
Rep. C. A. Dutch Ruppersberger

Mena Hanna 54808
Walter Gonzales 53061

Friends of Finland Caucus

Rep. Vern Buchanan
Rep. Debbie Dingell
Rep. Sean P. Duffy
Rep. Ann M. Kuster

Lewis Plush 60828
Kevin Rambosk 54071
Dylan Chandler 53365
Travis Krogman 55206

Friends of Ireland Caucus

Rep. Peter T. King
Rep. Richard E. Neal

Kevin Fogarty 57896
William Tranghese 55601

Friends of Liechtenstein Caucus

Rep. Donald S. Beyer, Jr.
Rep. Larry Bucshon
Rep. Daniel T. Kildee
Rep. F. James Sensenbrenner, Jr.

Zach Cafritz 54376
Susey Davis 44636
Troy Nienberg 53611
Erik Kinney 55101

Friends of New Zealand Caucus

Rep. Kevin Brady
Rep. Rick Larsen

John Porter 54901
Terra Sabag 52605

Friends of Norway Caucus

Rep. Kelly Armstrong
Rep. Rick Larsen
Rep. Betty McCollum
Rep. F. James Sensenbrenner, Jr.

Casey Fitzpatrick 52611
Terra Sabag 52605
Libby Foley 56631
Erik Kinney 55101

Friends of Sweden Caucus

Rep. Jack Bergman
Rep. Donald S. Beyer, Jr.

Michelle Jelnicky 54735
Zach Cafritz 54376

Friends of Wales Caucus

Rep. H. Morgan Griffith

Kevin Baird 53861

Future Forum Caucus

Rep. Stephanie N. Murphy

Dao Nguyen 54035

Future of Work Caucus

Rep. Lisa Blunt Rochester

Gabriella Vesay 54165

General Aviation Caucus

Rep. Sam Graves
Rep. Marc A. Veasey

Nick Grimes 57041
Luke Dube 59897

Georgia Caucus

Rep. Gerald E. Connolly
Rep. Adam Kinzinger

Molly Cole 51492
Sebastian DeLuca 53635

German-American Caucus

Rep. William R. Keating
Rep. Glenn Thompson

Gabrielle Gould 53111
Scott Nulty 55121

CONGRESSIONAL MEMBER ORGANIZATIONS

The inclusion of organizations on this list is subject to the approval of the Committee on House Administration.

The most recent version of this list is available at http://cha.house.gov/

Global Investment in America Caucus

Rep. Andy Barr
Rep. James A. Himes
Rep. George Holding
Rep. Gregory W. Meeks

David Simons 54706
Nicholas Larsen 55541
Matt Stross 53032
Ernie Jolly 53461

Global Road Safety Caucus

Rep. Alcee L. Hastings

Evan Polisar 51313

GOP Doctors Caucus

Rep. Andy Harris
Rep. David P. Roe

Bryan Shuy 55311
Aaron Bill 56356

Government Efficiency Caucus

Rep. Gerald E. Connolly
Rep. Jackie Walorski

Kristine Lam 51492
James Welsh 53635

Grid Innovation Caucus

Rep. Robert E. Latta
Rep. Jerry McNerney

Madeline Vey 56405
Rishi Sahgal 51947

Gulf War Veterans Caucus

Rep. Paul A. Gosar

Rory Burke 52315

Health and Wellness Caucus

Rep. Judy Chu
Rep. Jackie Walorski

Ellen Hamilton 55464
Martin Schultz 53915

Health Care Caucus

Rep. Michael C. Burgess

Elizabeth Allen 57772

Hearing Health Caucus

Rep. David B. McKinley
Rep. Mike Thompson

Christopher Buki 54172
Casey Badmington 53311

Heart and Stroke Coalition

Rep. Joyce Beatty
Rep. Christopher H. Smith

Chonya Davis Johnson 54324
Kelsey Griswold 53765

Hellenic Caucus

Rep. Gus M. Bilirakis
Rep. Carolyn B. Maloney

Shayne Woods 55755
Max Whitcomb 57944

High Performance Building Caucus

Rep. David B. McKinley
Rep. Peter Welch

Brian Garand 54172
Mark Fowler 54115

High Speed Rail Caucus

Rep. J. Luis Correa
Rep. Jim Costa
Rep. Zoe Lofgren

Laurie Sarof 52965
Alexa Fox 53341
Arlet Abrahamian 53072

Hispanic Caucus

Rep. Joaquin Castro

Alma Acosta 53236

Hispanic Conference Caucus

Rep. Mario Diaz-Balart
Rep. Jenniffer González-Colón

Laura Hernandez 54211
Janille Rodríguez-Beamud 52651

Historically Black Colleges and Universities (HBCU) Caucus

Rep. Alma S. Adams
Rep. Bradley Byrne

John Christie 51510
Miriam Fry 54931

CONGRESSIONAL MEMBER ORGANIZATIONS

The inclusion of organizations on this list is subject to the approval of the Committee on House Administration.

The most recent version of this list is available at http://cha.house.gov

Hockey Caucus

Rep. Tom Emmer
Rep. Brian Higgins
Rep. John Katko
Rep. Mike Quigley

Nicholas Lunneborg 52331
Nick Montalbano 53306
William Bensur 53701
Juan Hinojosa 54061

Home Protection Caucus

Rep. Garret Graves
Rep. Steven M. Palazzo
Rep. Bill Pascrell, Jr.
Rep. Cedric L. Richmond

Jennifer Bollinger 53901
Colleen Kennedy 55772
Dylan Sodaro 55751
Peter Hunter 56636

Homelessness Caucus

Rep. Alcee L. Hastings
Rep. Eddie Bernice Johnson

Evan Polisar 51313
Murat Gokcigdem 58885

Honor and Civility Caucus

Rep. Emanuel Cleaver
Rep. Charlie Crist
Rep. Mike Johnson

Herline Mathieu 54535
Erin Moffet 55961
Ruth Ward 52777

Hospitality Caucus

Rep. Sean P. Duffy
Rep. Derek Kilmer

Dylan Chandler 53365
Clayton Swope 55916

House Liberty Caucus

Rep. Justin Amash

Carolyn Iodice 53831

House Manufacturing Caucus

Rep. Tom Reed
Rep. Tim Ryan

K C Morris 53161
Zachary Prager 55261

House Military Depot and Industrial Facilities Caucus

Rep. David Loebsack

Erin Schnell 56576

House National Guard and Reserve Caucus

Rep. Steven M. Palazzo
Rep. Tim Ryan

Patrick Large 55772
Zachary Prager 55261

House Nursing Caucus

Rep. Suzanne Bonamici
Rep. Rodney Davis
Rep. Tulsi Gabbard
Rep. David P. Joyce

Jack Arriaga 50855
Jimmy Ballard 52371
Patrick Koetzle 54906
Catherine Wilson 55731

House Oceans Caucus

Rep. Suzanne Bonamici
Rep. Don Young

Maxine Sugarman 50855
Martha Newell 55765

House Outdoor Recreation Caucus

Rep. Michael K. Simpson
Rep. Peter Welch

Jamie Neill 55531
Mark Fowler 54115

House Public Service Loan Forgiveness Caucus

Rep. Brendan F. Boyle
Rep. David P. Joyce

Helena Schwarz 56111
Catherine Wilson 55731

House Quiet Skies Caucus

Rep. Eleanor Holmes Norton
Rep. Stephen F. Lynch

Portia Boone 58050
Natasha Silva 58273

CONGRESSIONAL MEMBER ORGANIZATIONS

The inclusion of organizations on this list is subject to the approval of the Committee on House Administration.

The most recent version of this list is available at http://cha.house.gov/

House Trails Caucus

Rep. Earl Blumenauer
Rep. Jeff Fortenberry

Kevin Stockert 54811
Alan Feyerherm 54806

Human Trafficking Caucus

Rep. Kay Granger
Rep. Carolyn B. Maloney
Rep. Robert C. "Bobby" Scott
Rep. Christopher H. Smith

Suzie Plasencia 55071
Kelly Hennessy 57944
Natalie Valentine 58351
Allison Hollabaugh 68664

Humane Bond Caucus

Rep. Gus M. Bilirakis
Rep. Henry Cuellar

Chris Jones 55755
Zack Linick 51640

Hungarian Caucus

Rep. Debbie Dingell
Rep. Andy Harris
Rep. Marcy Kaptur
Rep. Christopher H. Smith

Timothy Huebner 54071
Tim Daniels 55311
Nick Kazvini-Gore 54146
Kelsey Griswold 53765

I-14 Caucus

Rep. Ralph Lee Abraham
Rep. Brian Babin

Allen Cambon 58490
Ben Taylor 51555

Independent Colleges Caucus

Rep. Derek Kilmer
Rep. Martha Roby

Michele Viterise 55196
Caroline Buyak 52901

India and Indian Americans Caucus

Rep. George Holding
Rep. Brad Sherman

Curtis Rhyne 53032
Maggie Pillis 55911

International Conservation Caucus

Rep. Henry Cuellar
Rep. Jeff Fortenberry
Rep. David P. Joyce
Rep. Betty McCollum

Zack Linick 51640
Alan Feyerherm 54806
Kendall Kalagher 55731
Rebecca Taylor 56631

Interstate 11 Caucus

Rep. Paul A. Gosar
Rep. Dina Titus

Rory Burke 52315
Ben Rosenbaum 55965

Invasive Species Caucus

Rep. Elise M. Stefanik
Rep. Mike Thompson

Patrick Hester 54611
Crozer Connor 53311

Iraq Caucus

Rep. Adam Kinzinger
Rep. Seth Moulton

Sebastian DeLuca 53635
Peter Billerbeck 58020

Joint Strike Fighter Caucus

Rep. John B. Larson
Rep. Martha Roby
Rep. Michael R. Turner
Rep. Marc A. Veasey

Srdan Banjac 52265
David Allen 52901
Courtney Kum 56465
Nicole Varner 59897

Kingdom of Netherlands Caucus

Rep. Bill Huizenga
Rep. Derek Kilmer

Trevor TenBrink 54401
Clayton Swope 55916

CONGRESSIONAL MEMBER ORGANIZATIONS

The inclusion of organizations on this list is subject to the approval of the Committee on House Administration.

The most recent version of this list is available at http://cha.house.gov

Korea Caucus

Rep. Ami Bera
Rep. Gerald E. Connolly
Rep. Mike Kelly
Rep. Joe Wilson

Ryan Uyehara 55716
Molly Cole 51492
Brendan Fulmer 55406
Oren Adaki 52452

Kyrgyzstan Caucus

Rep. Bill Flores
Rep. Dina Titus

Judith Crews 56105
Erica Riordan 55965

Labor and Working Families Caucus

Rep. Stephen F. Lynch
Rep. Linda T. Sánchez

Natasha Silva 58273
Juan Rangel 56676

Law Enforcement Caucus

Rep. Bill Pascrell, Jr.
Rep. John H. Rutherford

Dylan Sodaro 55751
Katie Heffernan 52501

LGBT Equality Caucus

Rep. David N. Cicilline
Rep. Sean Patrick Maloney
Rep. Mark Pocan
Rep. Mark Takano

Aliya Bean 54911

Library of Congress Caucus

Rep. Robert B. Aderholt
Rep. Earl Blumenauer

Megan Medley 54876
Jon Bosworth 54811

Long-Range Strike Caucus

Rep. Susan A. Davis
Rep. Vicky Hartzler

Ian Staples 52040
Chrissi Lee 52876

Lung Cancer Caucus

Rep. Brendan F. Boyle
Rep. John H. Rutherford

Kim Soffen 56111
Katie Hefferman 52501

Lyme Disease Caucus

Rep. Collin C. Peterson
Rep. Christopher H. Smith

Tamir Elnabarawy 52165
Monica Herman 53765

Macedonia and Macedonian-American Caucus

Rep. Brendan F. Boyle
Rep. Debbie Dingell
Rep. Paul Mitchell
Rep. Steve Stivers

Carly Frame 56111
Timothy Huebner 54071
Derek Judd 52106
Mimi Bair 52015

Malaria and Tropical Disease Caucus

Rep. Gregory W. Meeks
Rep. Christopher H. Smith

Andrei Vasilescu 53461
Piero Tozzi 53765

Maternity Care Caucus

Rep. Jaime Herrera Beutler
Rep. Lucille Roybal-Allard

Anna Breen 53536
Debbie Jessup 42766

Media Diversity Congressional Brain Trust

Rep. Val Butler Demings

Wendy Anderson 52176

Mental Health Caucus

Rep. John Katko
Rep. Grace F. Napolitano

Jennifer Wood 53701
Joseph Ciccone 55256

CONGRESSIONAL MEMBER ORGANIZATIONS

The inclusion of organizations on this list is subject to the approval of the Committee on House Administration.

The most recent version of this list is available at http://cha.house.gov/

Men's Health Caucus

Rep. Markwayne Mullin
Rep. Donald M. Payne, Jr.

Taylor Hittle 52701
Steven Schultz 53436

Middle Class Jobs Caucus

Rep. Mike Gallagher
Rep. Raja Krishnamoorthi

Mike Jacobs 55665
Rachel Sorensen 53647

Military Family Caucus

Rep. Sanford D. Bishop, Jr.
Rep. Cathy McMorris Rodgers

LeVar Armstrong 53631
Matt Neighbors 52006

Military Sexual Assault Prevention Caucus

Rep. Susan A. Davis
Rep. Michael R. Turner

Ian Staples 52040
Courtney Kum 56465

Missile Defense Caucus

Rep. Doug Lamborn

Andrew Braun 54422

Mississippi River Caucus

Rep. Eric A. "Rick" Crawford
Rep. Ron Kind
Rep. Betty McCollum
Rep. Jason Smith

Ashley Shelton 54076
Olivia Kirchberg 55506
Patrick Maillet 56631
Hillary Pinegar 54404

Mobility Air Forces Caucus

Rep. John Garamendi
Rep. Cathy McMorris Rodgers

Betsy Thompson 51880
Matt Neighbors 52006

Modeling and Simulation Caucus

Rep. Stephanie N. Murphy
Rep. Martha Roby
Rep. John H. Rutherford
Rep. Robert C. "Bobby" Scott

John Laufer 54035
David Allen 52901
Nicholas Vance 52501
Christina Ingram 58351

Moldova Caucus

Rep. Pete Olson
Rep. David E. Price

Richard England 55951
Samantha Schifrin 51784

Mongolia Caucus

Rep. Dina Titus
Rep. Don Young

Erica Riordan 55965
Jesse von Stein 55765

Montenegro Caucus

Rep. Doug Lamborn
Rep. Chellie Pingree

Andrew Braun 54422
Todd Stein 56116

Morocco Caucus

Rep. Gerald E. Connolly
Rep. Bennie G. Thompson
Rep. Joe Wilson
Rep. Ted S. Yoho

Molly Cole 51492
Claytrice Henderson 55876
Oren Adaki 52452
James Walsh 55744

Motorcycle Caucus

Rep. Michael C. Burgess
Rep. Tim Walberg

Rachel Huggins 57772
Mac McKinney 56276

Motorsports Caucus

Rep. Bill Posey
Rep. Mike Thompson

Rick Podliska 53671
Casey Badmington 53311

CONGRESSIONAL MEMBER ORGANIZATIONS

The inclusion of organizations on this list is subject to the approval of the Committee on House Administration.

The most recent version of this list is available at http://cha.house.gov

Multicultural Media Caucus

Rep. Tony Cárdenas
Rep. Judy Chu
Rep. Yvette D. Clarke

Tejasi Thatte 56131
Linda Shim 55464
Charlyn Stanberry 56231

Municipal Finance Caucus

Rep. C. A. Dutch Ruppersberger
Rep. Steve Stivers

David Heitlinger 53061
Mark Gilbride 52015

National Heritage Area Caucus

Rep. David B. McKinley
Rep. Paul Tonko

Bryce Mongeon 56411
Emily Duhovny 55076
Sydney Pettit 54172
Emily Silverberg 55076

National Labs Caucus

Rep. Charles J. "Chuck" Fleischmann
Rep. Bill Foster
Rep. Ben Ray Luján
Rep. Lee M. Zeldin

Minsu Crowder-Han 53271
Samantha Warren 53515
Graham Mason 56190
Sara Mattar 53826

National Service Caucus

Rep. Doris O. Matsui
Rep. David E. Price

Robert Clark 57163
Leigh Whittaker 51784

Native American Caucus

Rep. Tom Cole
Rep. Debra A. Haaland

Joshua Jackson 56165
Heidi Todacheene 56631

Navy and Marine Corps Caucus

Rep. Susan A. Davis
Rep. Robert J. Wittman

Ian Staples 52040
Patrick Thompson 54261

Neuroscience Caucus

Rep. Earl Blumenauer
Rep. Cathy McMorris Rodgers

Martha Cramer 54811
Matt Neighbors 52006

Nigeria Caucus

Rep. Steve Chabot
Rep. Sheila Jackson Lee

Mark Erste 59893
Isabela Belchior 53816

Northwest Energy Caucus

Rep. Peter A. DeFazio
Rep. Cathy McMorris Rodgers

Kris Pratt 56416
Matt Neighbors 52006

Nuclear Cleanup Caucus

Rep. Charles J. "Chuck" Fleischmann
Rep. Ben Ray Luján

Minsu Crowder-Han 280-8837
Levi Patterson 56190

Nuclear Security Working Group

Rep. Charles J. "Chuck" Fleischmann
Rep. Jeff Fortenberry
Rep. Bill Foster
Rep. Ben Ray Luján

Minsu Crowder-Han 53271
Reyn Archer 54806
Gary Timmins 53515
Graham Mason 56190

Ohio River Basin Caucus

Rep. Bill Johnson
Rep. John A. Yarmuth

David Rardin 55705
Katy Rowley 55401

Oil & Gas Caucus

Rep. Vicente Gonzalez

Louise Bentsen 52531

CONGRESSIONAL MEMBER ORGANIZATIONS

The inclusion of organizations on this list is subject to the approval of the Committee on House Administration.
The most recent version of this list is available at http://cha.house.gov/

Parkinson's Disease Caucus

Rep. Gus M. Bilirakis
Rep. Henry C. "Hank" Johnson, Jr.
Rep. Peter T. King
Rep. Carolyn B. Maloney

Shayne Woods 55755
Chelsea Grey 51605
Deena Tauster 57896
Christina Parisi 57944

Peace Corps Caucus

Rep. John Garamendi
Rep. Garret Graves
Rep. Joseph P. Kennedy III

Betsy Thompson 51880
Alex Erwin 53901
Qais Roshan 55931

Peru Caucus

Rep. Gregory W. Meeks
Rep. Chris Stewart

Florence Akinyemi 53461
Luci Arveseth 59730

Pilots Caucus

Rep. Sam Graves
Rep. Collin C. Peterson

Nick Grimes 57041
Tamir Elnabarawy 52165

Planetary Science Caucus

Rep. Derek Kilmer
Rep. Steven M. Palazzo

Clayton Swope 55516
Laura Lee Burkett 55772

Poland Caucus

Rep. Marcy Kaptur
Rep. Daniel Lipinski
Rep. Christopher H. Smith
Rep. Jackie Walorski

Nick Kazvini-Gore 54146
Joel Creswell 55701
Piero Tozzi 53765
James Welsh 53915

Pollinator Protection Caucus

Rep. Rodney Davis
Rep. Alcee L. Hastings

Janie Costa 54540

Polyfluoroalkyl Substances (PFAS) Task Force

Rep. Brian K. Fitzpatrick
Rep. Daniel T. Kildee

Ports, Opportunity, Renewal, Trade, and Security (PORTS) Caucus

Rep. Alan S. Lowenthal
Rep. Randy K. Weber Sr.

Chris Gorud 57924
William Christian 52831

Prayer Caucus

Rep. Mark Walker

Grace Hilliard 53065

Problems Solvers Caucus

Rep. Josh Gottheimer
Rep. Tom Reed

Ashley Lantz 54465
Drew Wayne 53161

Progressive Caucus

Rep. Pramila Jayapal
Rep. Mark Pocan

Michael Darner 53106
Keane Bhatt 66725

Propane Caucus

Rep. Robert E. Latta
Rep. David Loebsack

Madeline Vey 56405
Will Collier 56576

Puget Sound Recovery Caucus

Rep. Denny Heck
Rep. Derek Kilmer

David Marten 59740
Katie Allen 55916

CONGRESSIONAL MEMBER ORGANIZATIONS

The inclusion of organizations on this list is subject to the approval of the Committee on House Administration.

The most recent version of this list is available at http://cha.house.gov

Purple Heart Caucus

Rep. Paul Cook
Rep. Mike Thompson

Jon Cochran 55861
Jen Almendarez 53311

Range and Testing Center Caucus

Rep. Julia Brownley
Rep. Scott DesJarlais

Sharon Wagener 55811
Richard Wilkins 56831

Recreational Vehicle Caucus

Rep. Dina Titus
Rep. Jackie Walorski

Ben Rosenbaum 55965
Stephen Simonetti 53915

Republican Israel Caucus

Rep. Doug Lamborn
Rep. Joe Wilson
Rep. Lee M. Zeldin

Lindsay Schneider 54422
Oren Adaki 52452
Sara Matar 53826

Rice Caucus

Rep. Eric A. "Rick" Crawford
Rep. Bennie G. Thompson

Allison Crittenden 54076
Claytrice Henderson 55876

Road Safety Caucus

Emily Ackerman 56511
Matthew Colvin 54476

Rock Caucus

Sen. Marsha Blackburn
Rep. Marcia L. Fudge
Rep. David P. Joyce
Rep. Collin C. Peterson
Rep. David P. Roe
Rep. Bennie G. Thompson

Jessica Vu 85827
Felix Muniz 57032
Chris Cooper 55731
Zach Martin 52165
Kyle Jacobs 56356
Claytrice Henderson 52876

Romania Caucus

Rep. Daniel Lipinski
Rep. Michael R. Turner

Joel Creswell 55701
Courtney Kum 56465

Rural Broadband Caucus

Rep. Adam Kinzinger
Rep. Robert E. Latta
Rep. David Loebsack
Rep. Mark Pocan
Rep. Peter Welch
Rep. Robert J. Wittman

Michael Mansour 53635
Rachel Rathore 56405
Scott Stockwell 56576
Sydney Scott 52906
Patrick Satalin 54115
Austin Walton 54261

Rural Caucus

Rep. Terri A. Sewell
Rep. Adrian Smith

Rob Nuttall 52665
Doug Stout 56435

Safe Climate Caucus

Rep. Donald S. Beyer, Jr.
Rep. Alan S. Lowenthal

Kate Schisler 54376
Emily Strombom 57924

School Safety Caucus

Rep. Susan W. Brooks
Rep. Rick Larsen

Rob Hicks 52276
Katy Nazaretova 52605

Scouting Caucus

Rep. Jim Cooper
Rep. Glenn Thompson

Jimmy Balser 54311
Jacob Durst 55121

Services Caucus

Rep. Kenny Marchant
Rep. Gregory W. Meeks

John Deoudes 56605
Florence Akinyemi 53461

CONGRESSIONAL MEMBER ORGANIZATIONS

The inclusion of organizations on this list is subject to the approval of the Committee on House Administration.
The most recent version of this list is available at http://cha.house.gov/

Shellfish Caucus

Rep. John B. Larson
Rep. Steve Scalise
Rep. Mike Thompson
Rep. Robert J. Wittman

Alicia Garten 52265
Geoffrey Green 53015
Crozer Connor 52265
Brent Robinson 54261

Shipbuilding Caucus

Rep. Joe Courtney
Rep. Robert J. Wittman

Claire Wardius 52076
Chris Ragsdale 54261

Singapore Caucus

Rep. Bradley Byrne
Rep. Denny Heck

Miriam Fry 54931
Jami Burgess 59740

Skilled American Workforce Caucus

Rep. J. French Hill
Rep. Brenda L. Lawrence

Lesley Hill 52506
Alex Huang 55802

Small Brewers Caucus

Rep. Peter A. DeFazio

Kris Pratt 56416

Smart Cities Caucus

Rep. Susan W. Brooks
Rep. Yvette D. Clarke

Mimi Strobel 52276
Charlyn Stanberry 56231

Soccer Caucus

Rep. Don Bacon
Rep. Kathy Castor
Rep. Darin LaHood
Rep. Rick Larsen

Jeff Kratz 54155
Didier Barjon 53376
Mary Ellen Richardson 56201
Terra Sabag 52605

Social Work Caucus

Rep. Barbara Lee

Emma Mehrabi 52661

Solar Caucus

Rep. Raja Krishnamoorthi
Rep. Ralph Norman

Hillary Caron 53788
Meghan Holland 55501

Space Power Caucus

Rep. Doug Lamborn

Andrew Braun 54422

Special Operations Forces Caucus

Rep. Kathy Castor
Rep. Scott H. Peters

Elizabeth Brown 53376
Sterling McHale 50508

Sportmen's Caucus

Rep. Debbie Dingell
Rep. Richard Hudson
Rep. Austin Scott
Rep. Marc A. Veasey

Kevin Rambosk 54071
Shaun Taylor 53715
Mark Sanders 56531
Thaddeus Woody 59897

Sri Lanka Caucus

Rep. Robert B. Aderholt
Rep. Dina Titus

Megan Medley 54876
Erica Riordan 55965

STARBASE Caucus

Rep. Tom Emmer
Rep. Alan S. Lowenthal

Catherine Lenz 52331
Andrew Bower 57924

STEAM Caucus

Rep. Suzanne Bonamici
Rep. Elise M. Stefanik

Allison Smith 50855
Patrick Hester 54611

CONGRESSIONAL MEMBER ORGANIZATIONS

The inclusion of organizations on this list is subject to the approval of the Committee on House Administration.

The most recent version of this list is available at http://cha.house.gov

Steel Caucus

Rep. Mike Bost
Rep. Eric A. "Rick" Crawford
Rep. Conor Lamb

Mark Ratto 55661
Ashley Shelton 54076
Chris Bowman 52301

Suburban Caucus

Rep. Ann Wagner

Rachel Wagley 51621

Sugar Caucus

Rep. Alcee L. Hastings
Rep. Michael K. Simpson

Lindsey Garber 51313
James Neill 55531

Taiwan Caucus

Rep. Steve Chabot
Rep. Gerald E. Connolly
Rep. Mario Diaz-Balart
Rep. Albio Sires

Mark Erste 52216
Molly Cole 51492
Gisselle Reynolds 54211
Clare Plassche 57919

Telehealth Caucus

Rep. Bill Johnson
Rep. David Schweikert
Rep. Mike Thompson
Rep. Peter Welch

Kelli Ripp 55705
Camille Lepire 52190
Casey Badmington 53311
Issac Loeb 54115

Term Limits Caucus

Rep. Jodey C. Arrington
Rep. Ro Khanna

Timothy Cummings 54005
Chris Schloesser 52631

Tourette Syndrome Caucus

Rep. Steve Cohen
Rep. Peter T. King

Lauren Citron 53265
Deena Tauster 57896

Trademark Caucus

Rep. Theodore E. Deutch
Rep. Martha Roby

Ellen McLaren 53001
Judd Smith 52901

Trauma Informed Care Caucus

Rep. Danny K. Davis
Rep. Mike Gallagher

Jill Hunter-Williams 55006
Maggie Woodin 55665

Travel and Tourism Caucus

Rep. Gus M. Bilirakis
Rep. Dina Titus

Chris Jones 55755
Ben Rosenbaum 55965

Tuesday Group Caucus

Rep. Susan W. Brooks
Rep. John Katko

Rob Hicks 52276
Jennifer Wood 53701

Tunisia Caucus

Rep. Alcee L. Hastings
Rep. David Schweikert

Tom Carnes 51313
Katherina Dimenstein 52190

UK Caucus

Rep. George Holding
Rep. Derek Kilmer
Rep. Ron Kind
Rep. Joe Wilson

Curtis Rhyne 53032
Clayton Swope 55916
Ben Hutterer 55506
Oren Adaki 52452

Ukraine Caucus

Rep. Brian K. Fitzpatrick
Rep. Andy Harris
Rep. Marcy Kaptur
Rep. Mike Quigley

Joseph Knowles 59211
Tim Daniels 55311
Nick Kazvini-Gore 54146
Allison Jarus 54061

CONGRESSIONAL MEMBER ORGANIZATIONS

The inclusion of organizations on this list is subject to the approval of the Committee on House Administration.

The most recent version of this list is available at http://cha.house.gov/

Unexploded Ordnance (UXO)/Demining Caucus

Rep. Bill Johnson
Rep. Jackie Speier

Laura Wilson 55705
Heather Melancon 53531

U.S. Expatriate (Expat) Caucus

Rep. Steven M. Palazzo

Patrick Large 55772

US-China Working Group

Rep. Darin LaHood
Rep. Rick Larsen

Ashely Antoskiewicz 56201
Terra Sabag 52605

U.S.-Japan Caucus

Rep. Joaquin Castro
Rep. Adrian Smith

Danielle Moon 53236
Joel Keralis 56435

U.S.-Lebanon Friendship Caucus

Rep. Charlie Crist
Rep. Darin LaHood

Ryan McGuire 55961
Mary Ellen Richardson 56201

U.S.-Turkey Relations and Turkish American

Rep. Steve Chabot
Rep. Steve Cohen
Rep. Gerald E. Connolly
Rep. Joe Wilson

Mark Erste 52216
Betsy Dudley 53265
Molly Cole 51492
Oren Adaki 52454

Uzbekistan Caucus

Rep. Vicente Gonzalez
Rep. Trent Kelly

Louise Bentsen 52531
Anne Hall Brashier 59527

Values Action Team

Rep. Robert B. Aderholt
Rep. Vicky Hartzler
Rep. Jody B. Hice
Rep. Doug Lamborn

Megan Medley 54876
Katie Doherty 52876
Nicholas Brown 54101
Jamie Dangers 54422

Veterinary Medicine Caucus

Rep. Kurt Schrader
Rep. Ted S. Yoho

Julia Stafford 68045
Joshua Woodward 63405

Voting Rights Caucus

Rep. Robert C. "Bobby" Scott
Rep. Terri A. Sewell
Rep. Marc A. Veasey

Paige Schwartz 58351
Perry Hamilton 52665
Zahraa Saheb 59897

Warrior Caucus

Rep. Trent Kelly
Rep. Seth Moulton

Anne Hall Brashier 54306
Julio Lainez 58020

Wild Salmon Caucus

Rep. Jared Huffman
Rep. Don Young

Christine Sur 55161
Martha Newell 55765

Wildlife Refuge Caucus

Rep. David P. Joyce
Rep. Ron Kind
Rep. Mike Thompson
Rep. Robert J. Wittman

Zach Moses 55731
Ben Hutterer 55506
Crozer Connor 53311
Austin Walton 54261

Wine Caucus

Rep. Dan Newhouse
Rep. Mike Thompson

CONGRESSIONAL MEMBER ORGANIZATIONS

The inclusion of organizations on this list is subject to the approval of the Committee on House Administration.

The most recent version of this list is available at http://cha.house.gov

Wire and Wire Products Caucus

Rep. Jim Cooper
Rep. Sam Graves

Bess McWherter 54311
Nick Grimes 57041

Working Forests Caucus

Rep. Sanford D. Bishop, Jr.
Rep. Jaime Herrera Beutler
Rep. Collin C. Peterson
Rep. Bruce Westerman

Jonathan Black 53631
Jordan Evich 53536
Zach Martin 52165
Will Layden 53772

Wrestling Caucus

Rep. Markwayne Mullin

Miranda Moorman 52701

Writers Caucus

Rep. Mark Takano

Brien Courchene 52305

Youth Challenge Caucus

Rep. Salud O. Carbajal
Rep. David B. McKinley
Rep. Grace F. Napolitano

Annie Yea 53601
Christopher Buki 54172
Joseph Ciccone 55256

Youth Development Caucus

Rep. Tony Cárdenas

Meghann Galloway 56131

Youth Mentoring Caucus

Rep. Susan A. Davis

Brandon Mendoza 52040

Youth Sports Caucus

Rep. Rodney Davis
Rep. Ron Kind
Rep. Marc A. Veasey

David Ross 52371
Alex Eveland 55506
Zahraa Saheb 59897

Zoo and Aquarium Caucus

Rep. Jeff Fortenberry
Rep. Daniel Lipinski

Alan Feyerherm 54806
Joel Creswell 55701

CONGRESSIONAL STAFF ORGANIZATIONS

The inclusion of organizations on this list is subject to the approval of the Committee on House Administration.

The most recent version of this list is available at http://cha.house.gov

Clean Energy and Technology Staff Association

Sponsor: Rep. Joaquin Castro
Officers:

Danielle Moon 67531

Congressional Black Associates

Sponsor: Rep. Yvette D. Clarke
Officers:

Audra Jackson 56231

Congressional Catholic Staff Association

Sponsors: Rep. Jeff Fortenberry and Rep. Daniel Lipinski
Officers:

Katie Ryan 65174

Congressional Hispanic Staff Association

Sponsors: Rep. Veronica Escobar and Rep. Jenniffer González-Colón
Officers:

Valeria Sandoval 42023
Christine Godinez 55965

Democratic Digital Communications Staff Association

Sponsor: Rep. Mark Takano
Officers:

Yuri Beckelman 52305

Dreamers Congressional Staff Organization

Sponsor: Rep. Pete Aguilar
Officers:

Xenia Ruiz 60679

Friends of Hungary

Sponsor: Rep. Andy Harris
Officers:

Tim Daniels 55311

Korean American Staff Association

Sponsor: Rep. Mike Kelly
Officers:

Diana Shin 61506

Latter-day Saint (LDS) Staff Organization

Sponsor: Rep. Rob Bishop
Officers:

Ryan Martin 44515

Lesbian, Gay, Bisexual and Transgender (LGBT) Congressional Staff Association

Sponsors: Rep. Angie Craig; Rep. Sharice Davids; Rep. Katie Hill; Rep. Chris Pappas; Rep. Mark Pocan; and Rep. Mark Takano
Officers:

Chris Cunningham 53011

Luso American Staff Association

Sponsors: Rep. Jim Costa and Rep. Stephen F. Lynch
Officers:

Natasha Silva 60525

South Asian-American Staff Association

Sponsors: Rep. Ami Bera; Rep. Pramila Jayapal; Rep. Ro Khanna; and Rep. Raja Krishnamoorthi
Officers:

Nishith Pandya 54372

Space Advocates

Sponsor: Rep. Bill Posey
Officers:

John Shelton 53671

Women's Congressional Staff Association

Sponsor: Rep. Lois Frankel
Officers:

Emily Richardson 59890

UNITED STATES SENATE

SENATE LEADERSHIP

Title	Name	Phone	Room and Bldg.
Majority (Republican) Leader	Mitch McConnell	**224-3135**	**S230 Capitol**
Majority (Republican) Whip	John Cornyn	**224-2708**	**S208 Capitol**
Minority (Democratic) Leader	Charles E. Schumer	**224-2158**	**S221 Capitol**
Minority (Democratic) Whip	Richard J. Durbin	**224-9447**	**S321 Capitol**
Assistant Minority (Democratic) Leader	Patty Murray	**224-2621**	**S205 Capitol**

OFFICERS OF THE SENATE

Title	Name	Phone	Room and Bldg.
President of the Senate	Michael R. Pence	**224-2424**	
President pro tempore	Chuck Grassley	**224-9400**	**S125 Capitol**
Secretary of the Senate	Julie E. Adams	**224-3622**	**S312 Capitol**
Sergeant at Arms	Michael C. Stenger	**224-2341**	**S151 Capitol**
Secretary for the Majority (Republicans)	Laura Dove	**224-3837**	**S337 Capitol**
Secretary for the Minority (Democrats)	Gary Myrick	**224-3735**	**S309 Capitol**
Parliamentarian	Elizabeth MacDonough	**224-6128**	**S133 Capitol**
Chaplain	Barry C. Black	**224-2510**	**S332 Capitol**

SENATORS

Room numbers beginning with SD are in the Dirksen Bldg., SH are in the Hart Bldg., and SR are in the Russell Bldg.

Republicans in roman; Democrats in *italic*; Independents in SMALL CAPS.

Name and State	Phone	Room
Vice Pres., Pence, Michael R.	**42424**	
Alexander, Lamar (TN)	**44944**	**SD-455**
Baldwin, Tammy (WI)	**45653**	**SH-709**
Barrasso, John (WY)	**46441**	**SD-307**
Bennet, Michael F. (CO)	**45852**	**SR-261**
Blackburn, Marsha (TN)	**43344**	**SD-357**
Blumenthal, Richard (CT)	**42823**	**SH-706**
Blunt, Roy (MO)	**45721**	**SR-260**
Booker, Cory A. (NJ)	**43224**	**SH-717**
Boozman, John (AR)	**44843**	**SH-141**
Braun, Mike (IN)	**44814**	**SR-374**
Brown, Sherrod (OH)	**42315**	**SH-503**
Burr, Richard (NC)	**43154**	**SR-217**
Cantwell, Maria (WA)	**43441**	**SH-511**
Capito, Shelley Moore (WV)	**46472**	**SR-172**
Cardin, Benjamin L. (MD)	**44524**	**SH-509**
Carper, Thomas R. (DE)	**42441**	**SH-513**
Casey, Robert P., Jr. (PA)	**46324**	**SR-393**
Cassidy, Bill (LA)	**45824**	**SH-520**
Collins, Susan M. (ME)	**42523**	**SD-413**
Coons, Christopher A. (DE)	**45042**	**SR-218**
Cornyn, John (TX)	**42934**	**SH-517**
Cortez Masto, Catherine (NV)	**43542**	**SH-516**
Cotton, Tom (AR)	**42353**	**SR-326**
Cramer, Kevin (ND)	**42043**	**SR-400**
Crapo, Mike (ID)	**46142**	**SD-239**
Cruz, Ted (TX)	**45922**	**SR-404**
Daines, Steve (MT)	**42651**	**SH-320**
Duckworth, Tammy (IL)	**42854**	**SH-524**
Durbin, Richard J. (IL)	**42152**	**SH-711**
Enzi, Michael B. (WY)	**43424**	**SR-379A**
Ernst, Joni (IA)	**43254**	**SH-730**
Feinstein, Dianne (CA)	**43841**	**SH-331**
Fischer, Deb (NE)	**46551**	**SR-454**
Gardner, Cory (CO)	**45941**	**SR-354**
Gillibrand, Kirsten E. (NY)	**44451**	**SR-478**
Graham, Lindsey (SC)	**45972**	**SR-290**
Grassley, Chuck (IA)	**43744**	**SH-135**
Harris, Kamala D. (CA)	**43553**	**SH-112**
Hassan, Maggie (NH)	**43324**	**SH-324**
Hawley, Josh (MO)	**46154**	**SR-212**
Heinrich, Martin (NM)	**45521**	**SH-303**
Hirono, Mazie K. (HI)	**46361**	**SH-713**
Hoeven, John (ND)	**42551**	**SR-338**
Hyde-Smith, Cindy (MS)	**45054**	**SH-702**
Inhofe, James M. (OK)	**44721**	**SR-205**
Isakson, Johnny (GA)	**43643**	**SR-131**
Johnson, Ron (WI)	**45323**	**SH-328**
Jones, Doug (AL)	**44124**	**SH-330**
Kaine, Tim (VA)	**44024**	**SR-231**
Kennedy, John (LA)	**44623**	**SR-416**
KING, ANGUS S., JR. (ME)	**45344**	**SH-133**
Klobuchar, Amy (MN)	**43244**	**SD-425**
Lankford, James (OK)	**45754**	**SH-316**
Leahy, Patrick (VT)	**44242**	**SR-437**
Lee, Mike (UT)	**45444**	**SR-361A**
Manchin, Joe, III (WV)	**43954**	**SH-306**
Markey, Edward J. (MA)	**42742**	**SD-255**
McConnell, Mitch (KY)	**42541**	**SR-317**
McSally, Martha (AZ)	**42235**	**SR-404**
Menendez, Robert (NJ)	**44744**	**SH-528**
Merkley, Jeff (OR)	**43753**	**SH-313**
Moran, Jerry (KS)	**46521**	**SD-521**
Murkowski, Lisa (AK)	**46665**	**SH-522**
Murphy, Christopher (CT)	**44041**	**SH-136**
Murray, Patty (WA)	**42621**	**SR-154**
Paul, Rand (KY)	**44343**	**SR-167**
Perdue, David (GA)	**43521**	**SR-455**
Peters, Gary C. (MI)	**46221**	**SH-724**
Portman, Rob (OH)	**43353**	**SR-448**
Reed, Jack (RI)	**44642**	**SH-728**
Risch, James E. (ID)	**42752**	**SR-483**
Roberts, Pat (KS)	**44774**	**SH-109**
Romney, Mitt (UT)	**45251**	**SR-124**
Rosen, Jacky (NV)	**46244**	**SR-144**
Rounds, Mike (SD)	**45842**	**SH-502**
Rubio, Marco (FL)	**43041**	**SR-284**
SANDERS, BERNARD (VT)	**45141**	**SD-332**
Sasse, Ben (NE)	**44224**	**SR-107**
Schatz, Brian (HI)	**43934**	**SH-722**
Schumer, Charles E. (NY)	**46542**	**SH-322**
Scott, Rick (FL)	**45274**	**SH-716**
Scott, Tim (SC)	**46121**	**SH-104**
Shaheen, Jeanne (NH)	**42841**	**SH-506**
Shelby, Richard C. (AL)	**45744**	**SR-304**
Sinema, Kyrsten (AZ)	**44521**	**SH-317**
Smith, Tina (MN)	**45641**	**SH-720**
Stabenow, Debbie (MI)	**44822**	**SH-731**
Sullivan, Dan (AK)	**43004**	**SH-302**
Tester, Jon (MT)	**42644**	**SH-311**

Name and State	Phone	Room
Thune, John (SD)	**42321**	**SD-511**
Tillis, Thom (NC)	**46342**	**SD-113**
Toomey, Patrick J. (PA)	**44254**	**SR-248**
Udall, Tom (NM)	**46621**	**SH-531**
Van Hollen, Chris (MD)	**44654**	**SH-110**
Warner, Mark R. (VA)	**42023**	**SH-703**
Warren, Elizabeth (MA)	**44543**	**SH-309**
Whitehouse, Sheldon (RI)	**42921**	**SH-530**
Wicker, Roger F. (MS)	**46253**	**SD-555**
Wyden, Ron (OR)	**45244**	**SD-221**
Young, Todd (IN)	**45623**	**SD-185**

SENATE COMMITTEES

	Phone	Room
Agriculture, Nutrition and Forestry Chairman—Pat Roberts (KS)	**224-2035**	**SR-328A**
Commodities, Risk Management, and Trade Chairman—John Boozman (AR)	**224-2035**	**SR-328A**
Rural Development and Energy Chairman—Joni Ernst (IA)	**224-2035**	**SR-328A**
Conservation, Forestry and Natural Resources Chairman—Mike Braun (IN)	**224-2035**	**SR-328A**
Nutrition, Agricultural Research, and Specialty Crops Chairman—Deb Fischer (NE)	**224-2035**	**SR-328A**
Livestock, Marketing and Agriculture Security Chairman—Cindy Hyde-Smith (MS)	**224-2035**	**SR-328A**
Appropriations Chairman—Richard C. Shelby (AL)	**224-7257**	**S-128**
Agriculture, Rural Development, Food and Drug Administration, and Related Agencies Chairman—John Hoeven (ND)	**224-7257**	**S-128**
Commerce, Justice, Science, and Related Agencies Chairman—Jerry Moran (KS)	**224-7257**	**S-128**
Defense Chairman—Richard C. Shelby (AL)	**224-7257**	**S-128**
Energy and Water Development Chairman—Lamar Alexander (TN)	**224-7257**	**S-128**
Financial Services and General Government Chairman—John Kennedy (LA)	**224-7257**	**S-128**
Homeland Security Chairman—Shelley Moore Capito (WV)	**224-7257**	**S-128**
Interior, Environment, and Related Agencies Chairman—Lisa Murkowski (AK)	**224-7257**	**S-128**
Labor, Health and Human Services, Education, and Related Agencies Chairman—Roy Blunt (MO)	**224-7257**	**S-128**
Legislative Branch Chairman—Cindy Hyde-Smith (MS)	**224-7257**	**S-128**
Military Construction, Veterans Affairs, and Related Agencies Chairman—John Boozman (AR)	**224-7257**	**S-128**
State, Foreign Operations, and Related Programs Chairman—Lindsey Graham (SC)	**224-7257**	**S-128**
Transportation, Housing and Urban Development, and Related Agencies Chairman—Susan M. Collins (ME)	**224-7257**	**S-128**

SENATE COMMITTEES

Committee	Phone	Room
Armed Services Chairman—James Inhofe (OK)	**224-3871**	**SR-228**
Airland Chairman—Tom Cotton (AR)	**224-3871**	**SR-228**
Cybersecurity Chairman—Mike Rounds (SD)	**224-3871**	**SR-228**
Emerging Threats and Capabilities Chairman—Joni Ernst (IA)	**224-3871**	**SR-228**
Personnel Chairman—Thom Tillis (NC)	**224-3871**	**SR-228**
Readiness and Management Support Chairman—Dan Sullivan (AK)	**224-3871**	**SR-228**
Seapower Chairman—David Perdue (GA)	**224-3871**	**SR-228**
Strategic Forces Chairman—Deb Fischer (NE)	**224-3871**	**SR-228**
Banking, Housing and Urban Affairs Chairman—Mike Crapo (ID)	**224-7391**	**SD-534**
Economic Policy Chairman—Tom Cotton (AR)	**224-7391**	**SD-534**
Housing, Transportation, and Community Development Chairman—David Perdue (GA)	**224-7391**	**SD-534**
Financial Institutions and Consumer Protection Chairman—Tim Scott (SC)	**224-7391**	**SD-534**
National Security and International Trade and Finance Chairman—Ben Sasse (NE)	**224-7391**	**SD-534**
Securities, Insurance, and Investment Chairman—Patrick J. Toomey (PA)	**224-7391**	**SD-534**
Budget Chairman—Michael B. Enzi (WY)	**224-0642**	**SD-624**
Commerce, Science, and Transportation Chairman—Roger F. Wicker (MS)	**224-1251**	**SD-512**
Aviation and Space Chairman—Ted Cruz (TX)	**224-1251**	**SD-512**
Communications, Technology, Innovation and the Internet Chairman—John Thune (SD)	**224-1251**	**SD-512**
Manufacturing, Trade, and Consumer Protection Chairman—Jerry Moran (KS)	**224-1251**	**SD-512**
Science, Oceans, Fisheries, and Weather Chairman—Cory Gardner (CO)	**224-1251**	**SD-512**
Transportation and Safety Chairman—Deb Fischer (NE)	**224-1251**	**SD-512**
Security Chairman—Dan Sullivan (AK)	**224-1251**	**SD-512**
Energy and Natural Resources Chairman—Lisa Murkowski (AK)	**224-4971**	**SD-304**

	Phone	Room
Energy Chairman—Bill Cassidy (LA)	**224-4971**	**SD-304**
National Parks Chairman—Steve Daines (MT)	**224-4971**	**SD-304**
Public Lands, Forests, and Mining Chairman—Mike Lee (UT)	**224-4971**	**SD-304**
Water and Power Chairman—Martha McSally (AZ)	**224-4971**	**SD-304**
Environment and Public Works Chairman—John Barrasso (WY)	**224-6176**	**SD-410**
Clean Air and Nuclear Safety Chairman—Mike Braun (IN)	**224-6176**	**SD-410**
Fisheries, Water, and Wildlife Chairman—Kevin Cramer (ND)	**224-6176**	**SD-410**
Superfund, Waste Management, and Regulatory Oversight Chairman—Mike Rounds (SD)	**224-6176**	**SD-410**
Transportation and Infrastructure Chairman—Shelley Moore Capito (WV)	**224-6176**	**SD-410**
Finance Chairman—Chuck Grassley (IA)	**224-4515**	**SD-219**
Energy, Natural Resources, and Infrastructure Chairman—Tim Scott (SC)	**224-4515**	**SD-219**
Fiscal Responsibility and Economic Growth Chairman—Bill Cassidy (LA)	**224-4515**	**SD-219**
Health Care Chairman—Patrick J. Toomey (PA)	**224-4515**	**SD-219**
International Trade, Customs, and Global Competitiveness Chairman—John Cornyn (TX)	**224-4515**	**SD-219**
Social Security, Pensions, and Family Policy Chairman—Rob Portman (OH)	**224-4515**	**SD-219**
Taxation and IRS Oversight Chairman—John Thune (SD)	**224-4515**	**SD-219**
Foreign Relations Chairman—James E. Risch (ID)	**224-4651**	**SD-423**
Africa and Global Health Policy Chairman—Lindsey Graham (SC)	**224-4651**	**SD-423**
East Asia, the Pacific, and International Cybersecurity Policy Chairman—Cory Gardner (CO)	**224-4651**	**SD-423**
Europe and Regional Security Cooperation Chairman—Ron Johnson (WI)	**224-4651**	**SD-423**
State Department and USAID Management, International Operations, and Bilateral International Development Chairman—Johnny Isakson (GA)	**224-4651**	**SD-423**
Multilateral International Development, Multilateral Institutions, and International Economic, Energy, and Environmental Policy Chairman—Todd Young (IN)	**224-4651**	**SD-423**

	Phone	Room
Near East, South Asia, Central Asia, and Counterterrorism Chairman—Mitt Romney (UT)	**224-4651**	**SD-423**
Western Hemisphere, Transnational Crime, Civilian Security, Democracy, Human Rights, and Global Women's Issues Chairman—Marco Rubio (FL)	**224-4651**	**SD-423**
Health, Education, Labor, and Pensions Chairman—Lamar Alexander (TN)	**224-5375**	**SD-428**
Children and Families Chairman—Rand Paul (KY)	**224-0121**	**SH-404**
Employment and Workplace Safety Chairman—Johnny Isakson (GA)	**224-5800**	**SH-828**
Primary Health and Retirement Security Chairman—Michael B. Enzi (WY)	**224-5406**	**SH-828**
Homeland Security and Governmental Affairs Chairman—Ron Johnson (WI)	**224-4751**	**SD-340**
Permanent Subcommittee on Investigations Chairman—Rob Portman (OH)	**224-3721**	**SR-199**
Federal Spending Oversight and Emergency Management Chairman—Rand Paul (KY)	**224-7155**	**SH-439**
Regulatory Affairs and Federal Management Chairman—James Lankford (OK)	**224-4551**	**SH-601**
Indian Affairs Chairman—John Hoeven (ND)	**224-2251**	**SH-838**
Judiciary Chairman—Lindsey Graham (SC)	**224-5225**	**SD-224**
Antitrust, Competition Policy and Consumer Rights Chairman—Mike Lee (UT)	**224-5444**	**SH-305**
Border Security and Immigration Chairman—John Cornyn (TX)	**224-7840**	**SD-141**
The Constitution Chairman—Ted Cruz (TX)	**224-5922**	**SH-807**
Crime and Terrorism Chairman—Josh Hawley (MO)	**224-6342**	**SD-157**
Oversight, Agency Action, Federal Rights and Federal Courts Chairman—Ben Sasse (NE)	**224-4224**	**SD-153**
Intellectual Property Chairman—Thom Tillis (NC)	**224-6342**	**SD-155**
Rules and Administration Chairman—Roy Blunt (MO)	**224-6352**	**SR-305**
Small Business and Entrepreneurship Chairman—Marco Rubio (FL)	**224-5175**	**SR-428A**
Veterans' Affairs Chairman—Johnny Isakson (GA)	**224-9126**	**SR-412**
Select—Ethics Chairman—Johnny Isakson (GA)	**224-2981**	**SH-220**

	Phone	Room
Select—Intelligence	**224-1700**	**SH-211**
Chairman—Richard Burr (NC)		
Special—Aging	**224-5364**	**SD-G31**
Chairman—Susan M. Collins (ME)		

EXECUTIVE BRANCH

The President

Donald J. Trump	**456-1414**
Office of Legislative Affairs—Shahira Knight	**456-7878**
House Liaison—Ben Howard	**456-2756**
Senate Liaison—Amy Swonger	**456-2756**

The Vice President

Michael R. Pence	**224-2424**
Assistant to the Vice President and Director of Legislative Affairs—Jonathan Hiler	**224-2424**

Cabinet Members

Secretary of State	Hon. Mike Pompeo	**647-9572**
Asst Secy for Legis Affairs	Mary Elizabeth Taylor	**647-8802**
Secretary of the Treasury	Hon. Steven T. Mnuchin	**622-1100**
Asst Secy for Legis Affairs	Vacant	**622-1900**
Secretary of Defense (Acting)	Hon. Patrick M. Shanahan	**703-692-7100**
Asst Secy for Legis Affairs	Robert R. Hood	**703-697-6210**
Attorney General	Hon. William P. Barr	**514-2141**
Asst Atty Gen for Legis Affairs	Stephen E. Boyd	**514-2141**
Secretary of the Interior	Hon. David Bernhardt	**208-7351**
Cong and Legis Affairs Dir	John Tanner	**208-7693**
Secretary of Agriculture	Hon. Sonny Perdue	**720-3631**
Cong Relations Dir	Abbey Fretz	**720-7095**
Secretary of Commerce	Hon. Wilbur L. Ross, Jr.	**482-2112**
Asst Secy for Legis & Intergovt Affairs	Mike Platt	**482-3663**
Secretary of Labor	Hon. R. Alexander Acosta	**693-6000**
Asst Secy for Cong & Intergovt Affairs	Vacant	**693-4601**
Secretary of Health and Human Services	Hon. Alex Azar	**690-7000**
Dpty Asst Secy for Cong Affairs	Sara Morse	**690-6786**
Secretary of Education	Hon. Elisabeth Prince DeVos	**401-3000**
Asst Secy for Legis Affairs	Peter Oppenheim	**401-1028**
Secretary of Housing and Urban Dev	Hon. Benjamin S. Carson, Sr.	**708-0417**
Asst Secy for Cong & Intergovt Relations	Len Wolfson	**708-0005**

Secretary of Transportation	Hon. Elaine L. Chao	**366-1111**
Dpty Asst Secy for Govt Affairs	Adam Sullivan	**366-4573**
Secretary of Energy	Hon. James Richard Perry	**586-6210**
Asst Secy for Cong & Intergovt Affairs	Melissa Burnison	**586-5450**
Secretary of Veterans Affairs	Hon. Robert Wilkie	**461-4809**
Asst Secy for Cong & Legis Affairs	Brooks Tucker	**461-6462**
Secretary of Homeland Security (Acting)	Hon. Kevin McAlneenan	**282-8000**
Asst Secy for Legis Affairs	Christine Ciccone	**447-5890**

House Liaison Offices

Air Force, Room 2021, RHOB	**225-6656**
Army, Room 2024, RHOB	**225-3853**
Coast Guard, Room 2019, RHOB	**225-4775**
Marine Corps, Room 2022, RHOB	**225-7124**
Navy, Room 2022, RHOB	**225-7126**
Personnel Management, Office of, Room 2030, RHOB	**225-4955**
Social Security, Room RG1C2, G1, Lobby 3, RHOB	**225-3133**
State Department, Room 2028, RHOB	**226-4642**
Veterans Affairs, Room 2026, RHOB	**225-2280**

CONGRESSIONAL LIAISON OFFICES OF GOVERNMENT AGENCIES

All telephone numbers carry Washington, D.C., area code 202 unless otherwise indicated. Area codes 301, 410, and 240 are for Maryland, and area code 703 is for Virginia.

A

Agency	Phone
African Development Foundation	**233-8800**
Agriculture Research Service	**260-9494**
American Battle Monuments Commission	**703-696-6323**
Amtrak	**906-3918**
Appalachian Regional Commission	**884-7674**
Archives (see National Archives and Records Administration)	
Army Corps of Engineers (see U.S. Army Corps of Engineers)	

B

Agency	Phone
Beltsville Agricultural Research Center	**301-504-6591**
Bonneville Power Administration	**586-5640**
Broadcasting Board of Governors (Voice of America)	**203-4545**
Bureau of Alcohol, Tobacco, Firearms and Explosives	**648-8510**
Bureau of Indian Affairs	**208-5706**
Bureau of Labor Statistics	**691-7800**
Bureau of Land Management	**912-7429**
Bureau of Ocean Energy Management	**208-3502**
Bureau of Prisons	**514-9663**
Bureau of Reclamation	**513-0565**

C

Agency	Phone
Census Bureau (see U.S. Census Bureau)	
Center for Medicaid and Medicare Services	**690-8220**
Centers for Disease Control and Prevention	**245-0600**
Central Intelligence Agency (CIA)	**703-482-4151**
Coast Guard (see U.S. Coast Guard)	
Commission of Fine Arts	**504-2200**
Commission on Civil Rights	**376-8371**
Commodity Futures Trading Commission	**418-5075**
Comptroller of the Currency	**649-6440**
Congressional Budget Office	**226-2837**
Consumer Product Safety Commission	**301-504-7853**
Corporation for National and Community Service	**606-6707**
Council of Economic Advisers	**395-5084**
Council on Environmental Quality	**395-5750**
Court of Appeals for the Federal Circuit	**275-8000**
Customs Service (see U.S. Customs and Border Protection)	

D

Agency	Phone
Defense Intelligence Agency	**231-0800**
Defense Logistics Agency	**703-767-5264**
Department of Agriculture	**720-7095**
Department of the Air Force	**703-695-7364**
House offices	**225-6656**
Senate offices	**224-2481**
Department of the Army	**703-697-8381**
House offices	**225-3853**
Senate offices	**224-2881**
Department of Commerce	**482-3663**
Department of Defense	**703-697-6210**
Department of Education	**401-0020**
Department of Energy	**586-5450**
Department of Health and Human Services	**690-7627**
Department of Homeland Security, Office of Legislative Affairs	**447-5890**
Department of Housing and Urban Development (HUD)	**708-0005**
Department of the Interior	**208-7693**
Department of Justice	**514-2141**
Department of Labor	**693-4600**
Department of the Navy	**703-614-3710**
House offices	**225-7126**
Senate offices	**685-6003**
Department of State	**647-1050**
House Liaison Office	**226-4642**
Senate Liaison Office	**228-1602**
Department of Transportation	**366-4573**
Department of the Treasury	**622-1900**
Department of Veterans Affairs	**461-6490**
House offices	**225-2280**
Senate offices	**224-5351**
Disability and Employment Policy	**693-4600**
District of Columbia (Office of the Senior Advisor)	**724-7173**
Drug Enforcement Administration	**307-7423**

E

Agency	Phone
Economic Development Administration	**482-2900**
Environmental Protection Agency	**564-5200**
Equal Employment Opportunity Commission	**663-4191**
Export-Import Bank of the United States	**565-3230**

	Phone
F	
Farm Credit Administration	**703-883-4056**
Federal Aviation Administration (FAA)	**267-3277**
Federal Bureau of Investigation (FBI)	**324-5051**
Federal Communications Commission	**418-1900**
Federal Deposit Insurance Corporation (FDIC)	**898-7055**
Federal Election Commission	**694-1006**
Federal Emergency Management Agency (FEMA)	**646-4500**
Federal Energy Regulatory Commission	**502-8004**
Federal Highway Administration	**366-2205**
Federal Labor Relations Authority	**218-7927**
Federal Maritime Commission	**523-0334**
Federal Mediation and Conciliation Services	**606-8090**
Federal Reserve System	**452-3456**
Federal Trade Commission	**326-2195**
Fish and Wildlife Service	**703-358-2240**
Food and Drug Administration	**301-796-8900**
Forest Service	**205-1637**
G	
General Services Administration	**501-0563**
Government Accountability Office (GAO)	**512-4400**
Government Publishing Office (GPO)	**512-0224**
Congressional publications	**512-0224**
Sales program order desk	**512-1800**
Superintendent of documents	**512-1800**
I	
Internal Revenue Service (IRS)	**317-6985**
International Monetary Fund	**623-7000**
International Trade Administration	**482-3015**
J	
Joint Chiefs of Staff	**703-614-1777**
L	
Legal Services Corporation	**295-1614**
M	
Marine Corps (see U.S. Marine Corps)	
Marshals Service (see U.S. Marshals Service)	
Merit Systems Protection Board	**254-4485**
Mine Safety and Health Administration	**693-4600**
Minority Business Development Agency	**482-6272**
N	
National Academy of Sciences	**334-1601**
National Aeronautics and Space Administration (NASA)	**358-1055**
National Archives and Records Administration (NARA)	**357-5100**
National Capital Planning Commission	**482-7200**
National Council on Disability	**272-0104**
National Credit Union Administration	**703-518-6330**
National Endowment for the Arts	**682-5477**
National Endowment for the Humanities	**606-8273**
National Highway Traffic Safety Administration	**366-1836**
National Institute of Standards and Technology	**301-975-3080**
National Institutes of Health	**301-496-3471**
National Labor Relations Board	**273-1991**
National Library of Medicine	**301-496-6308**
National Mediation Board	**692-5040**
National Oceanic and Atmospheric Administration (NOAA)	**482-4981**
National Park Service	**208-7331**
National Research Council	**334-1601**
National Science Foundation	**703-292-8070**
National Security Agency/Central Security Service	**301-688-7246**
National Security Council	**456-9174**
National Telecommunications and Information Administration	**482-1830**
National Transportation Safety Board	**314-6007**
Nuclear Regulatory Commission	**301-415-1776**
O	
Occupational Safety and Health Administration	**693-4600**
Occupational Safety and Health Review Commission	**606-5370**
Office of Disability Employment Policy	**693-7880**
Office of Federal and Regional Affairs	**727-0096**
Office of Justice Programs	**307-0703**
Office of Management and Budget (OMB)	**395-4790**
Office of National Drug Control Policy	**395-6602**
Office of Personnel Management	**606-1300**
House Liaison Office	**225-4955**
Office of Science and Technology Policy	**456-7116**
Office of Surface Mining Reclamation and Enforcement	**208-2838**
Office of the U.S. Trade Representative	**395-6951**
Overseas Private Investment Corporation (OPIC)	**336-8400**
P	
Passport Office	**877-487-2778**
Patent and Trademark Office	**571-272-7300**
Peace Corps	**692-2330**
Pension Benefit Guaranty Corporation	**326-4223**
Postal Regulatory Commission	**789-6803**
Postal Service (see U.S. Postal Service)	
President's Council on Fitness, Sports and Nutrition	**240-276-9567**
S	
Securities and Exchange Commission	**551-2010**
Securities Investor Protection Corporation	**371-8300**

CONGRESSIONAL LIAISON OFFICES OF GOVERNMENT AGENCIES

	Phone
Selective Service System	**703-605-4103**
Small Business Administration	**205-6700**
House Liaison Office	**205-6806**
Senate Liaison Office	**205-6635**
Smithsonian Institution	**633-5125**
Social Security Administration	**358-6030**
House Liaison Office	**225-3133**
Substance Abuse and Mental Health Services Administration	**240-276-2009**
Supreme Court (see U.S. Supreme Court)	
Surface Transportation Board	**245-0245**

T

Tax Court (see U.S. Tax Court)	
Tennessee Valley Authority	**898-2999**

U

U.S. Access Board	**272-0010**
U.S. Agency for International Development (USAID)	**712-4300**
U.S. Army Corps of Engineers	**761-1944**
U.S. Census Bureau	**301-763-6100**
U.S. Citizenship and Immigration Services (USCIS)	**272-1940**
U.S. Coast Guard	**245-0520**
House offices	**225-4775**
Senate offices	**224-2913**
U.S. Court of Federal Claims	**357-6400**
U.S. Customs and Border Protection	**344-1760**
U.S. Geological Survey	**703-648-4455**
U.S. International Trade Commission	**205-3151**
U.S. Marine Corps	**703-614-1686**
House Liaison Office	**225-7124**
Senate Liaison Office	**685-6009**
U.S. Marshals Service	**703-740-1603**
U.S. Postal Service	**268-2506**
U.S. Railroad Retirement Board	**272-7742**
U.S. Supreme Court	**479-3000**
U.S. Tax Court	**521-0700**
U.S. Trade and Development Agency	**703-875-4357**

W

World Bank	**473-1000**

TELEPHONE USER GUIDE

https://housenet.house.gov/office-support/telephones

PLACING A CALL

- Lift handset.
- Listen for dial tone.

To reach a House, Senate, Library of Congress, or GAO number:

- Dial the five-digit extension.

To place a local call:

- For calls elsewhere in Washington, D.C., dial 9 plus the number.
- For local numbers in Maryland, dial 9 + 1 + 301, followed by the number.
- For local numbers in Virginia, dial 9 + 1 + 703, followed by the number.

To place a long-distance call:

- Dial 9 + 1, followed by the area code and number.

To place an international call:

- Dial 9 + 011, followed by the country code, city code, and number.

To obtain operator assistance:

- For Congressional, dial 0.
- For outside, dial 9 + 0.

CONFERENCE CALLS

To add another party to a call (for a total of up to six parties):

- From an existing call, press CONFERENCE.
- Dial number of the second party, and wait for answer.
- Press CONFERENCE again.
- Repeat above steps, and add up to three more parties.
- Press DROP to disconnect the last party added.

To conference more than six parties:

- Contact the CAO Telecommunications to obtain your authorization code.
- Dial 9-1-800-475-4700 for WorldCom conferencing. You will be asked for your authorization code. Listen for dial tone.

HOLD

- Press HOLD.
- To return to the call, press the flashing line.

TRANSFER

- Press TRANSFER.
- Listen for dial tone.
- Place second call, listen for ring, and press TRANSFER; OR wait for an answer, announce call, and press TRANSFER.

LAST NUMBER DIALED

- Lift handset; press REDIAL or #99.

CALL FORWARD/BUSY DON'T ANSWER (CFBD)

To temporarily redirect calls to another extension if your line is busy or the calls are unanswered after three rings:

- Press CFBD button OR dial *74, followed by the five-digit number to which the calls are to be forwarded.
- Listen for confirmation tone.

To cancel:

- Press CFBD; OR dial *73.
- Listen for confirmation tone.

CALL PARK

To park a call at your extension for retrieval at another extension:

- Press TRANSFER.
- Press CALL PARK; OR dial *22.
- Press TRANSFER again.
- Hang up.

To retrieve a parked call from another extension:

- Press UNPARK; OR dial #22.
- Dial extension where call is parked.

SEND ALL CALLS (SAC)

To send all calls immediately from your line to a coverage point such as AUDIX:

- Press SAC button; OR dial *30.

To cancel:

- Press SAC button; OR dial #30.

CALL FORWARD ALL CALLS

To temporarily redirect all calls to another extension:

- Press CALL FORWARD or dial *72; then dial the five-digit number to which calls are to be forwarded.
- Listen for confirmation tone.
- If you have AUDIX and the recipient line is busy or goes unanswered, your call will be redirected to your voice mailbox.

To cancel:

- Press CALL FORWARD, or dial *73.
- Listen for confirmation tone.

ON-HOOK DIALING

- Press SPEAKER.
- Dial the number.
- Use speaker phone, or lift handset to talk.

ABBREVIATED DIALING (AD)

To program a single number on your AD button:

- Press SPEAKER; OR lift handset and dial *80.
- Press AD button to be programmed.
- Dial the number you wish to program, adding 9 or 9 + 1 for outside or long-distance calls.
- Press the AD button again.
- Listen for confirmation tone.

To dial:

- Press SPEAKER; OR, lift handset.
- Press AD button.

INTERCOM/GROUP LIST

Intercom is a function of a group speed dial list configured individually for each office. To call:

- Lift handset; OR press SPEAKER.
- Press INTERCOM button and dial the two-digit code for the person you are calling.
- The call will ring on that person's private number.

You may also transfer within your office via the Intercom/Group list button:

- After receiving a call, press TRANSFER, press INTERCOM, and dial the two-digit code; then listen for ring OR wait for an answer and announce the call, and press TRANSFER.

SELECT RING

To select a personalized ring:

- Press SHIFT, and HOLD (current ring pattern plays).
- Continue to press HOLD to cycle through all eight-ring patterns. When you hear your desired ring pattern, press SHIFT again.

System Map

ata.com
omer Information Service: 202-637-7000
Phone: 202-962-2033
o Transit Police: 202-962-2121

Legend

- RD Red Line • Glenmont / Shady Grove
- OR Orange Line • New Carrollton / Vienna
- BL Blue Line • Franconia-Springfield / Largo Town Center
- GR Green Line • Branch Ave / Greenbelt
- YL Yellow Line • Huntington / Mt Vernon Sq / Fort Totten
- SV Silver Line • Wiehle-Reston East / Largo Town Center

Station Features

- Bus to Airport
- P Parking
- H Hospital
- Airport

Connecting Rail Systems

AMTRAK VRE MARC

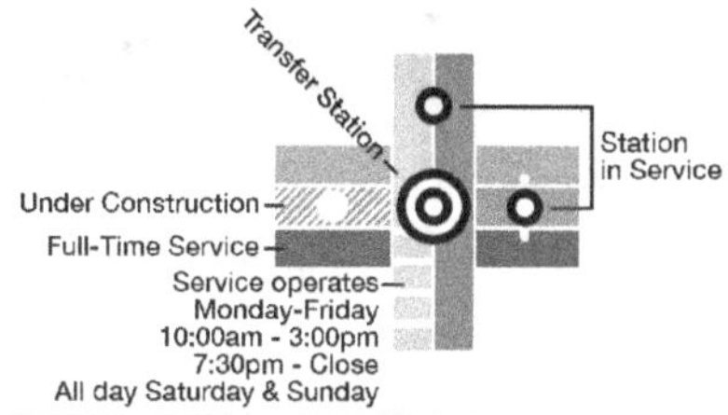

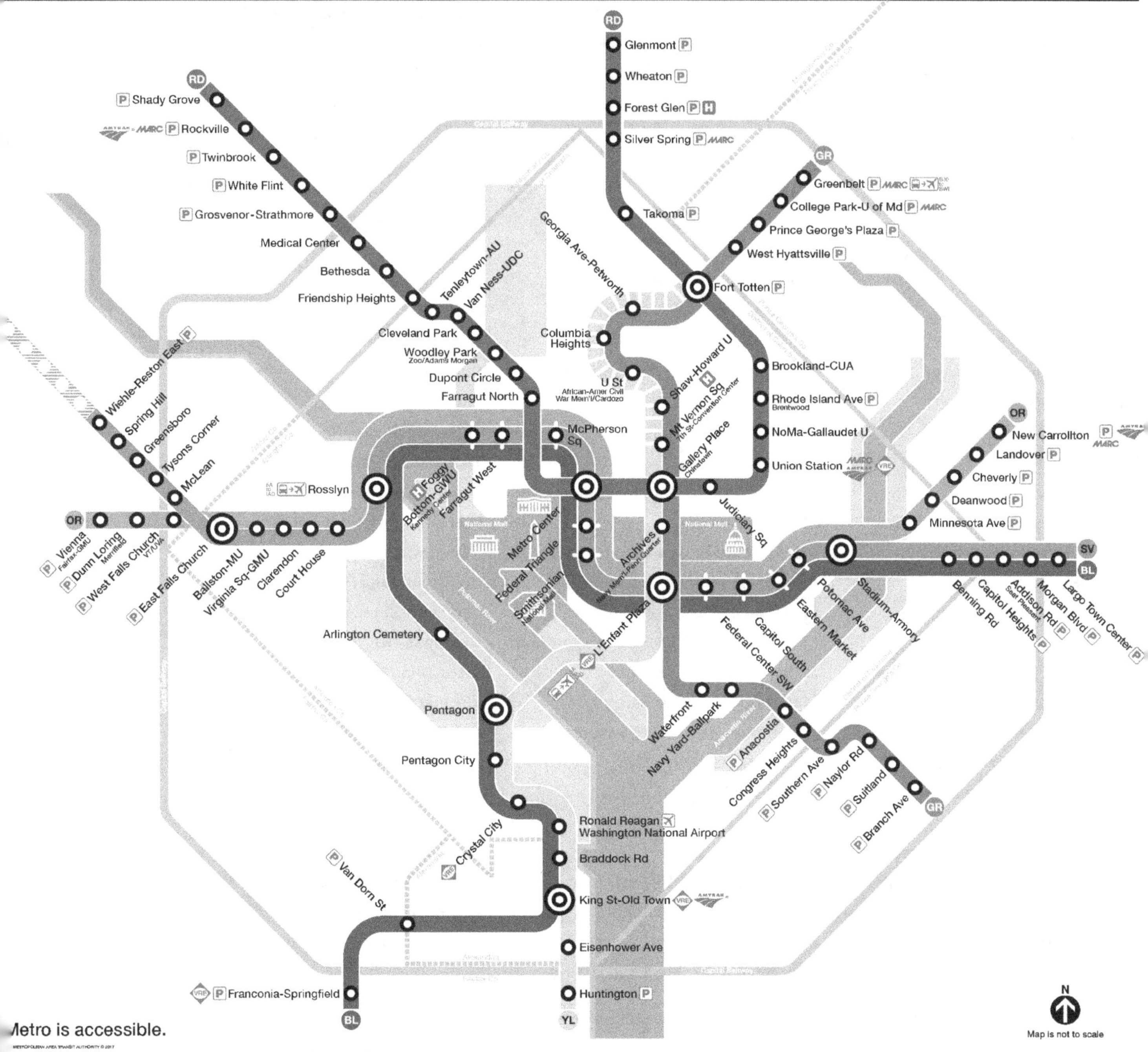

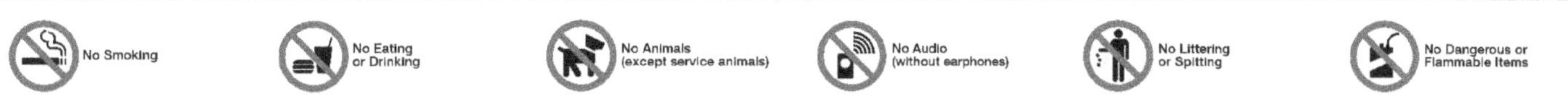

METRORAIL STATION NAMES

metro

*Alphabetical listing – Station names are in **bold**, corresponding line names follow.*

Addison Road-Seat Pleasant | Silver/Blue
Anacostia | Green
Archives-Navy Mem'l Penn Qtr| Yellow/Green
Arlington Cemetery | Blue
Ballston-MU | Orange/Silver
Benning Road | Silver/Blue
Bethesda | Red
Braddock Road | Blue/Yellow
Branch Ave | Green
Brookland-CUA | Red
Capitol Heights | Silver/Blue
Capitol South | Blue/Silver/Orange
Cheverly | Orange
Clarendon | Orange/Silver
Cleveland Park | Red
College Park- U of MD | Green
Columbia Heights | Green/Yellow
Congress Heights | Green
Court House | Orange/Silver
Crystal City | Blue/Yellow
Deanwood | Orange
Dunn Loring-Merrifield | Orange
Dupont Circle | Red
East Falls Church | Orange/Silver
Eastern Market | Blue/Orange/Silver
Eisenhower Ave | Yellow
Farragut North | Red
Farragut West | Blue/Orange/Silver
Federal Center SW | Blue/Orange/Silver
Federal Triangle | Blue/Orange/Silver
Foggy Bottom-GWU | Blue/Orange/Silver
Forest Glen | Red
Fort Totten | Red/Green/Yellow
Franconia-Springfield | Blue
Friendship Heights | Red
Gallery Pl-Chinatown | Red/Green/Yellow
Georgia Ave-Petworth | Green/Yellow
Glenmont | Red
Greenbelt | Green
Greensboro | Silver
Grosvenor-Strathmore | Red
Huntington | Yellow
Judiciary Square | Red
King St-Old Town | Blue/Yellow
L'Enfant Plaza | Green/Yellow/Blue/Orange/Silver
Landover | Orange
Largo Town Center | Blue/Silver
McLean | Silver
McPherson Square | Blue/Orange/Silver
Medical Center | Red
Metro Center | Red/Blue/Orange/Silver
Minnesota Ave | Orange
Morgan Blvd | Blue/Silver
Mt Vernon Sq/7th St Convention Center | Green/Yellow
Navy Yard-Ballpark | Green
Naylor Road | Green
New Carrollton | Orange
NoMa-Gallaudet U | Red
Pentagon | Blue/Yellow
Pentagon City | Blue/Yellow
Potomac Ave | Blue/Orange/Silver
Prince George's Plaza | Green
Rhode Island Ave-Brentwood | Red
Rockville | Red
Ronald Reagan Washington National Airport | Blue/Yellow
Rosslyn | Blue/Orange/Silver
Shady Grove | Red
Shaw-Howard U | Green/Yellow
Silver Spring | Red
Smithsonian | Blue/Orange/Silver
Southern Ave | Green
Spring Hill | Silver
Stadium-Armory | Blue/Orange/Silver
Suitland | Green
Takoma | Red
Tenleytown-AU | Red
Twinbrook | Red
Tysons Corner | Silver
U St/African-Amer Civil War Memorial/Cardozo | Green/Yellow
Union Station | Red
Van Dorn St | Blue
Van Ness-UDC | Red
Vienna/Fairfax-GMU | Orange
Virginia Square-GMU | Orange/Silver
Waterfront | Green
West Falls Church-VT/UVA | Orange
West Hyattsville | Green
Wheaton | Red
White Flint | Red
Wiehle-Reston East | Silver
Woodley Park-Zoo/Adams Morgan | Red

Metro map and station information provided courtesy of the Washington Metro Area Transit Authority.

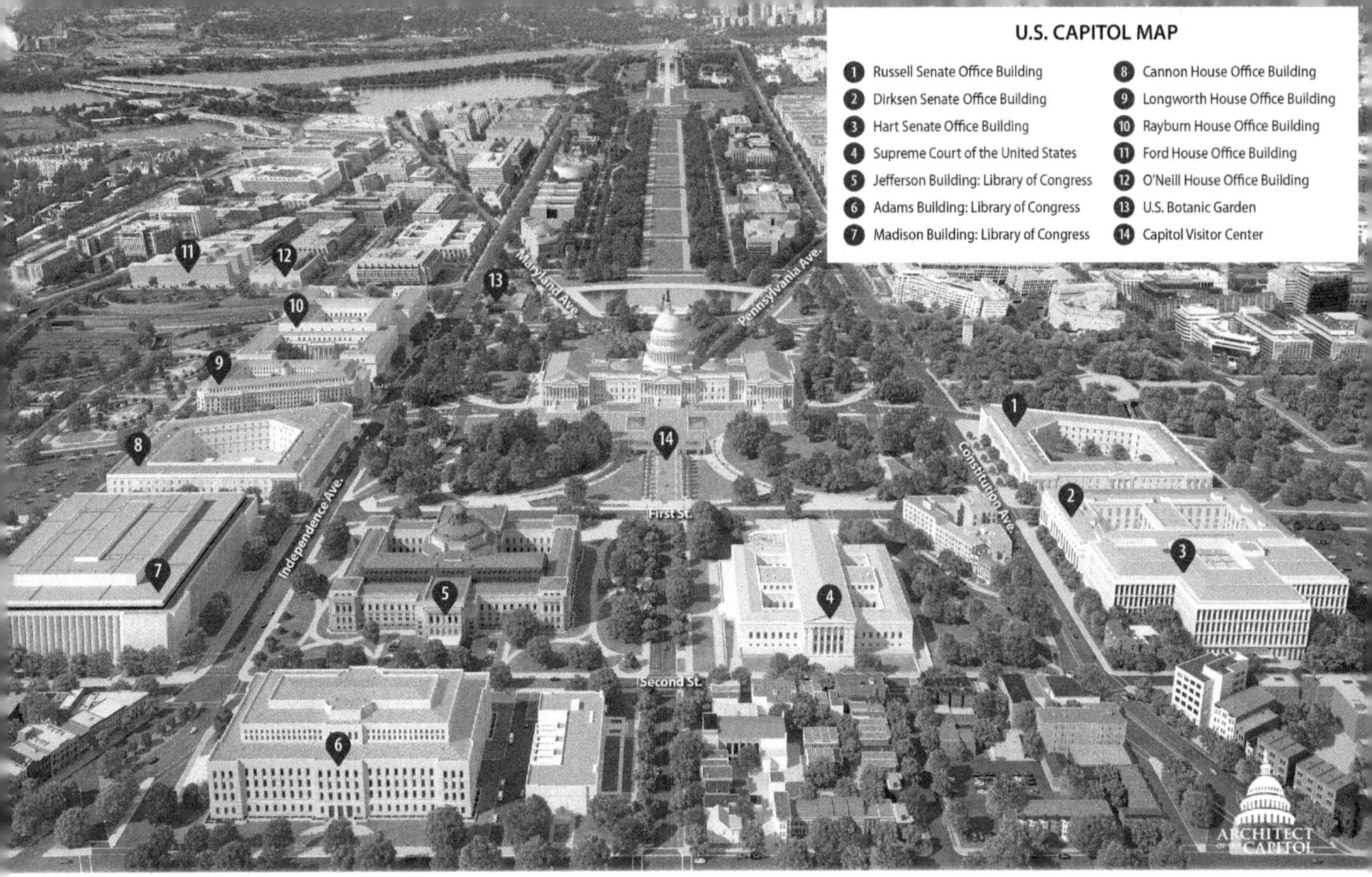
U.S. CAPITOL MAP
1 Russell Senate Office Building
2 Dirksen Senate Office Building
3 Hart Senate Office Building
4 Supreme Court of the United States
5 Jefferson Building: Library of Congress
6 Adams Building: Library of Congress
7 Madison Building: Library of Congress
8 Cannon House Office Building
9 Longworth House Office Building
10 Rayburn House Office Building
11 Ford House Office Building
12 O'Neill House Office Building
13 U.S. Botanic Garden
14 Capitol Visitor Center
Maryland Ave.
Pennsylvania Ave.
Constitution Ave.
Independence Ave.
First St.
Second St.
ARCHITECT OF THE CAPITOL

www.ingramcontent.com/pod-product-compliance
Lightning Source LLC
La Vergne TN
LVHW080528210926
848481LV00022B/3656
9780160950131